THE GREAT ENCYCLOPEDIA OF 19TH-CENTURY MAJOR LEAGUE BASEBALL

THE GREAT ENCYCLOPEDIA OF 19TH-CENTURY MAJOR LEAGUE BASEBALL

DAVID NEMEC

DONALD I. FINE BOOKS
New York

DONALD I. FINE BOOKS
Published by the Penguin Group
Penguin Books USA Inc., 375 Hudson Street,
New York, New York 10014, U.S.A.
Penguin Books Ltd, 27 Wrights Lane,
London W8 5TZ, England
Penguin Books Australia Ltd, Ringwood,
Victoria, Australia
Penguin Books Canada Ltd, 10 Alcorn Avenue,
Toronto, Ontario, Canada M4V 3B2
Penguin Books (N.Z.) Ltd, 182–190 Wairau Road,
Auckland 10, New Zealand

Penguin Books Ltd, Registered Offices:
Harmondsworth, Middlesex, England

First published by Donald I. Fine Books, an imprint of
Penguin Books USA Inc.

First Printing, March, 1997
10 9 8 7 6 5 4 3 2 1

Library of Congress Cataloging-in-Publication Data

Nemec, David.
    The great encyclopedia of 19th-century major league baseball /
David Nemec.
      p.   cm.
    Includes bibliographical references
    ISBN 1-55611-500-8
    1. Baseball—United States—History—19th century.   2. Baseball—
United States—Encyclopedias.   3. Baseball players—United States—
Registers.   I. Title.
GV863.A1N47   1996
796.357'0973'09034—dc20   96-34167
                                                   CIP

Printed in the United States of America
Set in Times Roman
Designed by Irving Perkins Associates

CONTENTS

ACKNOWLEDGMENTS

Many baseball historians, researchers, editors and publishers furnished me with information and guidance that I am pleased to acknowledge. To all of them I extend my deepest appreciation.

I thank Ken Samelson, editor of the Macmillan *Baseball Encyclopedia*, and Pete Palmer, coeditor of *Total Baseball*, for providing me with much of the nineteenth-century statistical data used by their respective publications as well as for patiently responding to my many questions regarding disputed individual and team pitching, batting and fielding totals. I also thank Morris Eckhouse, the executive director of the Society for American Baseball Research (SABR), and the National Association Box Score Project for the Nineteenth-Century Research Committee of SABR for generously allowing me to use the amended 1871–75 National Association statistics the project generated.

A number of other SABR committee chairpersons and members rendered their assistance during the preparation of this book, notably Bill Carle, chairperson of the Biographical Committee, Frederick Ivor-Campbell, chairperson of the Nineteenth-Century Committee, Lyle Spatz, chairperson of the Records Committee, and Carlos Bauer, chairperson of the Minor League Committee. To the many members of their respective committees who helped to run to earth the information utilized in their invaluable committee newsletters I extend a special note of gratitude.

Grateful acknowledgment is also made to the following researchers and historians for their expert assistance and guidance. Bob Tiemann, Ray Nemec and Bob Hoie drew upon their exhaustive research to compile the 1900 data for the American League, and Ray also contributed other minor-league data that was used in this book. Frank Williams painstakingly shared the findings of his groundbreaking work on pitching records to help steer me to plausible solutions for virtually all of the multitude of disputed nineteenth-century individual season and career pitching totals, and Joe Wayman, Bill Deane and Walt Wilson also availed me of the fruits of their extensive research work in this area. Scot Mondore of the

National Baseball Hall of Fame Library was always prepared whenever I needed information about a particular game or player.

I am profoundly indebted to Dick Thompson for furnishing me with a wealth of information on nineteenth-century players, especially from the New England area. Owing to Dick's generous contributions, I am also indebted to the late Tom Shea, who left his own priceless research efforts in Dick's charge.

I would once again like to thank Bob Tiemann for calling upon his matchless expertise to serve as the fact checker for *The Great Encyclopedia of Nineteenth-Century Major League Baseball.* Bob, in addition, helped mightily in pinning down ballpark names and accurate home and road statistics.

Mark Rucker of Transcendental Graphics provided most of the pictures in *The Great Encyclopedia of Nineteenth-Century Major League Baseball.* Having worked with Mark before, I knew he would produce a bounty of rare and exciting images, and once again he exceeded expectations. Many of the pictures from Mark's collection are new to me and, I would expect, to most readers as well. I also happily thank Joseph Santry, Tom Hill and Phillip Von Borries for allowing me to use numerous pictorial treasures from their private collections.

I am particularly grateful to Tom Burke, my editor at Donald I. Fine, for his expert assistance.

On a personal note, I thank Scott Flatow for his steadfast interest and enthusiasm. Pamela Strong, Tony Salin, Dorothy McMurray and Carol Stack also offered support and encouragement when it was needed.

The Great Encyclopedia of Nineteenth-Century Major League Baseball bears no formal dedication because so many people were its source of inspiration. It is to men like Lee Allen, Tom Shea, Ernest Lanigan, Charles Mears and John Tattersall that the greatest debt is owed. This book, then, is a testimony to the many baseball historians whose countless hours of research and unflagging attention to detail opened the way for it.

INTRODUCTION

In the brief twenty-year span between the early 1840s and the Civil War, baseball evolved from a game with many variants that was played almost exclusively by children to an organized sport with standardized rules. By the end of the 1860s baseball had matured so much that it was no longer merely a sport but, for many men, a profession. Though amateurism was still the order of the day, it was often a sham. Star players were either paid under the table or given lucrative jobs that demanded little or no work for employers who also had a financial interest in the local ball club.

The first team to abandon all pretense of amateurism was the Cincinnati Red Stockings. Organized by Harry Wright with financial help from Aaron Champion, Cincinnati openly acknowledged in 1869 that all of its team members were paid a regular salary strictly to play baseball. When the Red Stockings went undefeated for the entire 1869 season, they transformed the approach to the game taken by virtually every team that played them with aspirations of winning. Less than two years after Cincinnati's juggernaut demonstrated that amateur clubs could no longer hope to compete with professionals, the National Association of Professional Base Ball Players, the first professional sports league in our nation's history, was born.

Many excellent books have told the story of baseball's evolution from a simple game in the 1840s to its swiftly escalated status less than two decades later as our national pastime. The intention here is narrower and at the same time unique. In *The Great Encyclopedia of Nineteenth-Century Major League Baseball* our aim is to serve as the first comprehensive reference work devoted solely to the 30-year period between 1871 and 1900 that began with the appearance of the first professional league, the National Association, and ended with the last year of the century and, by happy coincidence, the final season that the game had only one recognized major league—the National League. To meet that objective we offer five features that have never before appeared in book form, let alone in a single volume:

1. Complete player and manager rosters for every major league team between 1871 and 1900, accompanied by individual batting and pitching statistics and the name of the park where the team played most of its home games.
2. Complete position workups for every major league team between 1871 and 1900, showing how many games each team member played at a given position.
3. A complete alphabetical register of every player who appeared in a major league game in the nineteenth century, with players organized in subregisters according to the primary positions they played and their vital statistics provided, when known, along with their central career batting and pitching statistics.
4. A complete alphabetical register of every major league manager in the nineteenth century.
5. A complete alphabetical register of every regular major league umpire in the nineteenth century, organized by leagues.

To add to the mix of flavors, *The Great Encyclopedia of Nineteenth-Century Major League Baseball* is designed as if it had been compiled at the turn of the twentieth century. Consequently the career statistics in player, manager and umpire registers are complete only

Woodcut team portraits and collages were popular in the last century. This one of the 1869 Cincinnati Red Stockings, the first all-professional baseball team, originally appeared in Frank Leslie's Weekly Newspaper. *Clockwise, from top: George Wright, Andy Leonard, Charlie Gould, Cal McVey, Doug Allison, Asa Brainard, Fred Waterman, Will Hurley, Charlie Swezsy. Center: Harry Wright.*

through the 1900 season. At that juncture Cy Young already had nearly 300 wins and Ed Delahanty had over 2,000 hits. But while their career totals by 1900 certified that they would surely take their places among the game's greatest players, men such as Nap Lajoie and Honus Wagner still possessed relatively modest totals that offered only a hint of their eventual towering achievements, and Christy Mathewson, for another, had yet to earn his first major league win.

Only in the annual reports and the sidebar items does the future intrude. Yet, while we might on occasion break the fantasy that the world was poised on the brink of the twentieth century when this book was put together, our goal remains to capture the look and the feel of the way baseball was played in the late 1800s.

In any event, we want you to have a good time and to make some exciting discoveries as you look through *The Great Encyclopedia of Nineteenth-Century Major League Baseball.* Even if you already know a fair amount about the first thirty years of major league play, you are still guaranteed plenty of new information. Above all else, you now have, all in one volume, nineteenth-century team rosters and player registers together with a bounty of charts, lists, photographs and stories that appear here for the first time anywhere. We hope that you have as much fun with this book as we had putting it together.

THE ANNUAL RECORD

In June 1953 I took a chunk of money I'd saved from my *Cleveland Plain Dealer* paper route and bought a copy of Hy Turkin and S.C. Thompson's *The Official Encyclopedia of Baseball*. I knew it for the treasure it was almost the moment I began digging into it, but by the end of that summer I'd also begun to feel a slight sense of dissatisfaction.

It wasn't so much that each player's season and career statistics were confined to his position, his batting average and the number of games he had played, although that certainly left me wishing for more. What really gnawed away at me was that I could get almost no picture from Turkin and Thompson's book of the great teams throughout baseball history and, specifically, who played for them. Oh, I knew the starting nine for the 1927 New York Yankees, and of course I knew my champion 1948 Cleveland Indians down to the most obscure substitute, but I yearned for an encyclopedia that would assemble for me in their entirety the 1884 Providence Grays, the 1906 Chicago Cubs and the 1940 Cincinnati Reds—to say nothing of all the Federal League and National Association teams with great names like the Brooklyn Tip Tops and the Elizabeth Resolutes.

It took me until the winter of 1954 to recognize that if I wanted those team rosters, I was going to have to create them myself. And as long as I was at it, I decided to go the whole nine yards and draw up a complete roster for every major league team from 1871 through 1950, where Turkin and Thompson left off in their encyclopedia's first edition. So I hunkered down in my bedroom with a stack of three-by-five-inch cards and got to work. Using the alphabetical register of players in the encyclopedia, I started with the first name, Abadie, John and headed the top card in my pile "1875 Centennial," Abadie's initial major league team.

Right away I realized that I'd undertaken one mammoth project, and there were many days when I was on the verge of quitting. But somehow I kept pushing ahead. My grades in school hit bottom that winter and my social life was zero, but it was worth it. By blowing every spare moment I had, I managed to plow through the whole encyclopedia by March,

1955, and finally one evening I arrived at Zwilling, Edward Harrison and the end of my long, long road.

I still have those hundreds of three-by-five cards. I dug them out of the cigar box where they were stored in the fall of 1969, when Macmillan unveiled the first edition of *The Baseball Encyclopedia* with its yearly rosters of all the regular position players and pitchers for each major league team, and I dug them out again in 1974 when Neft and Cohen went a step further than Macmillan and produced complete yearly rosters for each team since 1901 in their first edition of *The Sports Encyclopedia: Baseball.* My stack of cards looked meager in comparison to what Macmillan contained and even skimpier up against Neft and Cohen. And yet I had in those cards something that neither of those magnificent encyclopedias could boast and that no other book ever has either. I had complete rosters—or as complete, anyway, as I could make them at that time—for every nineteenth-century major league team as well.

In the forty-odd years since 1955 my nineteenth-century team cards have undergone hordes of changes and refinements, thanks not only to my own efforts but also to the research incorporated in the Macmillan encyclopedia and *Total Baseball* and Bill Carle's monthly SABR Biographical Committee newsletters. My team cards are still not 100 percent complete, though gaps may simply be inevitable, for a book like this in a sense is eternally a work in progress.

As you may have already guessed, teams and their composition have long been my foremost passion and the subjects to which I've devoted most of my research hours, and I'm happy to share the contents of the cigar box that I kept for so many years in hopes of the day when a book like this at last could happen.

The teams are organized by season and by league. A team nickname or the name of a manager will differ in some instances in *The Great Encyclopedia of Nineteenth-Century Major League Baseball* from the team nickname or manager's name listed in other encyclopedias because my research strongly indicates that the nickname or manager at issue is something other than what previous works believe it or him to have been. For a good 90 percent of the information in this book, though, I'm indebted to Macmillan and *Total Baseball*—except in situations when they themselves are at loggerheads. Pitchers' season and career won-lost totals especially seem to breed conflict between these two otherwise impeccably reliable sources, so much so that on several occasions in the *The Great Encyclopedia of Nineteenth-Century Major League Baseball* I've had to go with my own instincts as to what the won-lost totals were in a particular year for Kid Nichols or John Clarkson or Mickey Welch. But, as I've said, absolute accuracy in a book of this sort is constantly sought but is ever elusive.

THE SEASONAL RECORD AND REPORT

The Seasonal Record is a chronological listing of the team standings, league leaders and complete team rosters for every major league team from 1871 through 1900. This section also provides each team's manager, the name of its home park and the nickname by which the team was most commonly known. The statistical history of each season is preceded by a Report of the pennant race and other significant events, including changes in the playing rules.

All information, codes and abbreviations that may be unfamiliar are explained in the two sample formats presented below. Both are from the 1871 season.

Official Standings*

	G	W	L	PCT	H	R	GB
Philadelphia Athletics	29	22	7	.759	11–3	8–4	—
Boston Red Stockings	33	22	10	.688	11–4	8–5	1.5
Chicago White Stockings	29	20	9	.690	13–3	6–5	2
New York Mutuals	35	17	18	.486	12–7	4–10	8
Washington Olympics	33	16	15	.516	7–4	5–9	7
Troy Unions	31	15	15	.500	7–9	5–6	7.5
Cleveland Forest Citys	29	10	19	.345	3–8	7–8	12
Fort Wayne Kekiongas	28	7	21	.250	5–4	2–7	14.5
Rockford Forest Citys	27	6	21	.222	2–4	1–17	15.5

*Games played at neutral sites omitted from Home and Road records.

Official Standings Column Headings Information

G	Total games played including ties and forfeits
W	Wins
L	Losses
PCT	Winning percentage
H	Home record
R	Road record
GB	Number of games finished behind the league leader

The second sample format is the complete roster of the Philadelphia Athletics. They finished first in 1871, and all team rosters are presented in the order of final standings.

PHILADELPHIA **Dick McBride** **Athletic Park**

Pos	Player	G	AB	H	R	2B	3B	HR	RBI	BB	BA	SA
LF	Ned Cuthbert	27	150	37	47	7	5	3	30	10	.247	.420
1B	Wes Fisler	26	147	41	43	8	2	0	16	3	.279	.361
SS	John Radcliff	28	145	44	47	7	5	0	22	6	.303	.421
C	Fergie Malone	27	134	46	33	7	1	1	33	9	.343	.433
2B	Al Reach	26	133	47	43	7	6	0	34	5	.353	.496
P	Dick McBride	25	132	31	36	3	0	0	17	7	.235	.295
3B	Levi Meyerle	26	130	64	45	9	3	**4**	40	2	**.492**	**.700**
CF	Count Sensenderfer	25	127	41	38	5	2	0	23	0	.329	.394
UT	George Bechtel	20	94	33	24	9	1	1	21	2	.351	.500
RF	George Heubel	16	75	23	18	4	2	0	13	2	.307	.413
Sub	Tom Pratt	1	6	2	2	0	0	0	1	0	.333	.333
Sub	Tom Berry	1	4	1	0	0	0	0	0	0	.250	.250
Sub	Nate Berkenstock	1	4	0	0	0	0	0	0	0	.000	.000
		28	1281	410	376	66	27	9	250	46	**.320**	**.435**

1B   Fisler 26, Pratt 1, Heubel 1
2B   Reach 26, Fisler 2
SS   Radcliff 28
3B   Meyerle 26, Bechtel 3
OF   Cuthbert 27, Sensenderfer 25, Heubel 16, Bechtel 15, Berkenstock 1, Berry 1
C   Malone 27, Cuthbert 1
P   McBride 25, Bechtel 3, Meyerle 1

	G	IP	GS	CG	W	L	K	BB	SH	SV	ERA
Dick McBride	25	222	25	25	18	5	15	40	0	0	4.58
George Bechtel	3	26	3	2	1	2	1	11	0	0	7.96
Levi Meyerle	1	1	0	0	0	0	0	2	0	0	9.00
—3 forfeit Wins: 2 vs Rockford; 1 vs Kekionga—											
		249	28	27	19	7	16	53	0	0	4.95

Roster Column Headings Information

Batters
POS Primary Fielding Position
G   Games Played
AB   At Bats
H   Hits
R   Runs
2B   Doubles
3B   Triples
HR   Home Runs
RBI Runs Batted In (when available)
BB   Bases on Balls
SB   Stolen Bases (when available)
BA   Batting Average
SA   Slugging Average

Fielders
1B   First Basemen
2B   Second Basemen
SS   Shortstops
3B   Third Basemen
LF   Left Fielders
CF   Center Fielders
RF   Right Fielders
C   Catchers
P   Pitchers
Sub Substitutes
UT   Utilitymen

Pitchers
G   Games Pitched
IP   Innings Pitched
GS   Games Started
CG   Completed Games
W   Wins
L   Losses
K   Strikeouts
BB   Bases on Balls
SH   Shutouts
SV   Saves
ERA Earned Run Average

Other Information Explanation

Players—Players are listed by surname and most commonly used first name or nickname.

Roster order—Team batting rosters are arranged in order of at bats; fielding rosters are arranged in order of games played at each position; and pitching rosters are arranged in order of innings pitched. When two or more players have the same number of at bats or innings pitched, they appear in order of base hits or pitching decisions.

Bold Facing—indicates league leading total.

*—after a figure in bold indicates that a player led his league in that department while playing for more than one team.

Forfeits—forfeit wins and losses listed only for games in which no pitchers were credited with decisions.

THE NATIONAL ASSOCIATION ERA (1871-75)

Alexander Cartwright, and the compatriots who helped him draft the first codified set of baseball rules and stage matches between New York social clubs, originally viewed the game as a vehicle for unifying and perpetuating their clubs. By the Civil War, however, this notion of what baseball ought to be was obsolete. The men from Cartwright's Knickerbocker club, who carried on the game in his stead after he moved west, played baseball to heighten their social stature and recognition. But professional players were now receiving all the recognition, and the clubs that would not deign to hire professionals could no longer hold their own. The game had become stratified, with professional players at the top and those who wanted baseball to remain a leisure activity for gentlemen far beneath them.

Pioneer baseball writer and rulesmaker Henry Chadwick decried what he saw happening to the game and campaigned vigorously for several years in his New York *Clipper* columns for a separation between professional and amateur interests. Chadwick's efforts finally bore fruit on St. Patrick's Day in 1871 when representatives of ten baseball clubs met at Collier's Rooms, a drinking establishment at the corner of Broadway and Thirteenth Street in New York. As recounted in Turkin and Thompson's *The Official Encyclopedia of Baseball*: "There, in a smoky gaslit hallroom adjoining the Cafe (saloon), pro baseball suffered its first real birth pangs, for that meeting established the National Association of Professional Base-Ball Players."

The ten delegates elected James W. Kerns of Philadelphia president of the NAPBBP (soon shortened to NA), J.S. Evans of Cleveland vice president, Nick Young of Washington Olympics secretary, J.W. Schofield of Troy treasurer, and then set to work drawing up a set of championship rules. Although no fixed schedule was adopted, it was agreed that every club would play each of its fellow clubs a best three-out-of-five series, making for a potential 45 championship games per club. The team with the most victories at the end of the season would be entitled to parade the championship banner, called the "whip pennant," at its ballground the following year.

The association's entry fee was a mere $10, but the delegate from Brooklyn's Eckford club decided that even this meager sum was too steep and declined to enroll his team in the fledgling organization. The nine remaining clubs were the Athletics* of Philadelphia, the Mutuals of New York, the White Stockings of Chicago, the Haymakers of Troy, the Olympics of Washington, the Forest Citys of Cleveland, the Kekiongas of Fort Wayne, the Red Stockings of Boston and the Forest Citys of Rockford, Illinois. Apart from the hope of financial profit, all the clubs had one other thing in common: Local politicians occupied most of the positions of power on their boards of directors. Their economic structures otherwise varied widely, owing to the vast differences in the class composition of each club's backers. The clubs ranged in financial stability from the Chicago club, which was owned by a stock company headed by Windy City treasurer David Gage, who had at his disposal some $250,000, which he'd embezzled from his office, to the Kekionga club controlled by clerks and salesmen who ran their club on a shoestring and lured players to Fort Wayne by promising them a share of the gate receipts rather than a fixed salary.

Yet from its inception the National Association was an enterprise run largely by its playing personnel. The loop president selected in 1872 was third baseman Bob Ferguson of the Brooklyn Atlantics. During the two seasons Ferguson served in the office, NA business was conducted in irregular meetings arranged by him for the club managers, most of whom, like himself, were players as well.

Financially, the first professional league was a disaster. Very few teams made any money for their backers, and much of the reason so many clubs sank in a sea of red ink was because the NA was an even bigger failure as a spectator sport. Only in its first season did the NA stage anything approaching an exciting pennant race. Every other year the Boston entry was a runaway victor, making for a very uneven desire to win among the other teams and a strong temptation to look elsewhere for motivation. Chadwick's baseball columns in the *Clipper* became increasingly peppered with stern warnings against the growing dangers of "fraudulent play" or "Hippodroming," as throwing games was then called. By 1875, Boston's seemingly endless monopoly on the pennant and the infestation of gamblers had all but destroyed the NA and made the professional game ripe for a cabal that would take control away from the players.

---

*Many club nicknames in the early years of baseball were singular—i.e. Athletic, Mutual, Forest City, etc. In this book, to avoid confusion, they are pluralized throughout because the clubs themselves soon began to pluralize them.

1871
FORFEITS AND FIRE

In his history of the National Association, William Ryczek writes, "If America was different in 1871, the game of baseball was also a far cry from that which is played on the Astroturf saucers of the 1990s . . . Even the name was different. The words 'base' and 'ball' were not merged until the twentieth century. During the nineteenth it was known as 'Base Ball.'"

To ease the reader's task, in this book baseball is one word and much of its nineteenth-century terminology has similarly been modernized. But there is no way to soften the fact that the game in 1871 was truly a far cry from baseball today.

Home plate, for example, was a 12-inch square made of marble or stone and set in the ground so that one corner pointed toward the pitcher and the other toward the catcher: these two positions were therefore called "the points." The bases were located half in fair and half in foul territory (unlike today when the entire base is in fair ground), and it was for the umpire to judge whether a hot shot down the line crossed the fair or foul part of the bag.

The pitcher delivered the ball from a flat six-foot square-shaped box situated 45 feet from the plate. His delivery had to be executed with a straight arm swinging perpendicular to the ground, meaning that essentially he threw underhand. Facing him was a batter who stood astride a three-foot line drawn through the center of the plate. The batter was allowed to request either "high" pitches (between his waist and shoulders) or "low" pitches (between his waist and knees). As now, a batter was given just three strikes, but in 1871 an umpire could not call the first pitch a batter saw a strike, regardless of its location, unless it was swung at and missed. *Missed* we need emphasize, for in 1871, as was true throughout the nineteenth century, a foul ball, even with fewer than two strikes, was not counted as a strike.

In the first National Association season, a batter was awarded first base after three called balls. However, before deeming a pitch a ball an umpire was obliged to warn a pitcher an unspecified number of times for not delivering "fair" pitches or for delaying the game.

Hence, a batter had to receive many more than three pitches outside his chosen strike zone before he was given his base. And if an errant pitch should happen to smack him in the ribs, it was simply his hard luck. A hit batsman was not given his base until the mid-1880s. He might not even be awarded a ball if the pitcher had not as yet been warned for failing to deliver fair pitches.

The dual between batter and fielder was also quite different in 1871. Since a hit was deemed fair or foul depending on where it first struck earth, many batters thrived on accumulating fair-foul hits by chopping sharply down on the ball to give it "English" so that it would hit the front half of the marble plate, which was in fair territory, and then instantly spin off into foul ground. To guard against hitters who had mastered this maneuver, either the first or third baseman—and at times both—would hug the line and sometimes even station himself in foul territory.

The visiting team was required to furnish one new game ball although, in the event the clubs played a series of games at the same grounds, the visiting and the home team took turns providing the contest's centerpiece. The ball was expected to last the entire game, but replacement balls were kept on hand by the home club in case the original ball was lost or damaged so severely it could no longer be kept in play. In 1871 the teams tossed a coin to see which would bat first or last, and the winner often chose the former so that its hitters would get first crack at the new game ball.

Substitutions were rare, usually occurring only when a player was injured or ill. An injured player could have a substitute run the bases for him, though, and still remain in the game provided the opposing captain agreed to it. The substitute would start from behind home plate and begin running as soon as the batter for whom he was a surrogate struck the ball.

Barring injury, a pitcher was expected to hurl the full nine innings no matter how badly he was being mauled. When a pitcher was replaced, it was almost always by a player already in the game with whom he would simply swap positions.

In 1871 catchers did not yet wear masks, chest protectors or shin guards (let alone gloves), and consequently stayed well behind the batter to prevent being struck by foul tips. In fact, in 1871 no fielders—not even first basemen—wore gloves. Nor did baserunners wear sliding pads.

For the sake of economy and simplicity, a single umpire worked each game. He was stationed behind the catcher and seldom ventured into the playing field. In 1875 it was even made a rule that an umpire could not set foot in fair territory while the ball was in play. In time that rule, and many of the other regulations that seem odd beyond belief today, would be rescinded, but when the first major league season commenced on May 4, 1871, they were all an integral part of the fabric of the game. The unlikely site of the historic inaugural was Fort Wayne, Indiana, where the Cleveland Forest Citys opposed the local Kekiongas, largely because Boston and the Olympics, the two blue-ribbon clubs that had been slated to break the ice for the new league, were rained out in their opener in Washington.

The Fort Wayners won 2–0 in an extraordinarily well-played game, especially for so early in the season, and seized first place. They were swiftly deposed, however, by Chicago,

The 1871 Washington Olympics with Harry Berthrong, one of the finest all-around athletes of the post–Civil War era. Even though four Olympics—Andy Leonard, Fred Waterman, Charlie Sweasy and Asa Brainard—were on the 1869 Cincinnati Red Stockings juggernaut, Washington was barely a .500 team, a clue of how much the game had sharpened in just two years. Clockwise, from top left: Andy Leonard, George Hall, Harry Berthrong, Everett Mills, Asa Brainard, John Glenn, Doug Allison, Henry Burroughs, Davy Force and Fred Waterman. Center is team captain Charlie Sweasy.

which won its first seven games. Still unbeaten, Chicago met the New York Mutuals in Brooklyn on June 5. Mutuals owner William Cammeyer's stiff 50-cent admission fee kept many away, but around 6,000 paid their way into the Union Grounds and another 4,000 or so watched from rooftops or by standing on pushcarts outside the fences. New York won 8–5 and took over first place; but then, perhaps deliberately, started losing at an alarming rate. Charges of dumping games were constantly leveled at the Mutuals during the NA's tenure. Upon hearing that Boss Tweed had invested $7,500 in the club, one wag said, "He probably got it all back again." The inference was that Tweed bet against his own team.

Tweed was at the zenith of his power in 1871, but a year later he would be in jail. The Troy team was also under dubious auspices. Its founder was Jim Morrisey, an ex-congressman who ran a national election-betting cartel in 1876 but canceled all bets when he got wind that the Democrats aimed to sell the Tilden presidency to the Republicans in return for a promise to end Reconstruction in the South. The Philadelphia Athletics had among their directors several billiard parlor operators and liquor store owners, all of them staunch Republicans eager to take advantage of the "open Sunday" period in what was the nation's second largest city in the early 1870s. The Athletics' business manager, Hicks Hayhurst, was a city councilman who had close ties to the lucrative business of tax collecting.

But if the Mutuals and Troy and Philadelphia had the strongest political and financial clout, Boston, on paper at least, had the best team. Manager-centerfielder Harry Wright had

THE HASTINGS CASE

Born in 1848 during the Mexican War, Scott Hastings was named after its most heroic figure, Winfield Scott. In 1870 Hastings played with Al Spalding and Ross Barnes on a strong Rockford team but then went south that winter to earn extra money playing for the Lone Star club in New Orleans. Hastings was still with the Lone Stars on April 16 when they met Chicago in an exhibition game prior to the opening of the first NA season. It was his last game for the New Orleans club. His next appearance came with Rockford on May 6 in its opening loss to Cleveland.

Hastings's presence on the Rockfords was protested by every rival club because of a rule the NA devised to prevent its teams from raiding one another during the season by offering a coveted player more money. Fearing that players would otherwise jump teams or "revolve" at will, the NA stipulated that no player under contract could play with another club for a period of 60 days from his last game with his old club. Since Hastings had been under contract to the Lone Stars and last played with them on April 16, he was not eligible to play for Rockford until June 16. Upon a motion made by F.H. Mason of Cleveland at the league meeting on November 3, 1871, the four games Rockford won before June 16 were erased and given instead to their opponents. One should suppose that Philadelphia, which stood to gain two of those disputed games, prodded Mason more than gently to put up his hand.

corralled the cream of the unbeaten 1869 Cincinnati Red Stockings—including himself, his brother George, first baseman Charlie Gould and all-purpose star Cal McVey. To round out the roster he snagged pitcher Al Spalding, second sacker Ross Barnes and outfielder Fred Cone, the collective heart of the Rockford team in 1870. Injuries to George Wright and other key regulars cost Boston a number of games, but no club was more beset by ill luck in the early going than the Kekiongas. By mid-August the co-op club, whose players had to rely on a share of the gate receipts in lieu of regular salaries, was forced to fold after Bobby Mathews and Tom Carey defected and more followed when the club treasury grew so depleted that compensation was no longer even a dream. The Eckford club of Brooklyn, after declining to join the NA, replaced the Kekiongas on August 29, with the agreement that their games would not count in the standings and that all unplayed games by the Kekiongas necessary to complete a season series were declared forfeit.

Nine such games were at stake, and fortunately the top three contenders, Chicago, Boston and Philadelphia, profited equally. Each received one bonus forfeit win due to the Kekiongas' precipitous departure—but it was the lone issue in the 1871 pennant race upon which the three would agree.

All of the brouhaha might have been averted but for the infamous mishap in Mrs. O'Leary's barn. Whether that kerosene lamp was kicked over by a clumsy cow or by a certain Louis Cohn who got overexcited in the midst of a craps game, the Rockford team, ar-

A collage of the 1871 Chicago White Stockings, the only major league team that, literally, almost caught fire. Clockwise, from top: Joe Simmons, Ed Pinkham, Bub McAtee, Mart King, Tom Foley, Ed Atwater, Charlie Hodes, Ed Duffy and Fred Treacey. Center: Jimmy Wood with George Zettlein below him.

Many still aren't convinced that these 1871 Philadelphia Athletics won the first major league pennant. Clockwise, from top: Ned Cuthbert, George Heubel, Wes Fisler, Fergy Malone, George Bechtel, Al Reach, John Radcliff, Levi Meyerle and Count Sensenderfer. Center: Dick McBride.

ONE-GAMER I

The first man to make his major league debut after celebrating his 40th birthday was Nate Berkenstock. In the game between Chicago and Philadelphia on October 30, 1871, which ultimately decided the initial NA pennant, Berkenstock patrolled right field for the Athletics. It was his lone big league appearance. Berkenstock's opportunity came when Count Sensenderfer hurt his knee, forcing the Athletics to move George Bechtel to center from his customary post in right. In the 1860s, Berkenstock had played for the Athletics but was considered too old to hold his spot on the team when the NA formed. The judgment seemed right. After being brought out of moth balls and dusted off, Berkenstock fanned three times in four plate appearances. The Athletics won nevertheless, 4–1, to stake claim to the championship flag.

---

riving in Chicago on the morning of October 8 for an afternoon game, was repelled by a gargantuan blaze. The great Chicago fire destroyed not only the Chicago team's ballpark but also decimated the homes of many players as well the banks holding their money. Broke and bereft of equipment and uniforms, the demoralized White Stockings finished the season on the road, garnering three straight losses.

The final defeat came on October 30 at Brooklyn's Union Grounds with Chicago acting as "home team" against the Athletics in a game that was billed as being for the pennant. But even after Philadelphia won 4–1, the race was far from settled. Still unresolved were four early-season games that Rockford had won with an allegedly ineligible player, Scott Hastings, behind the bat. Worse yet, the Championship Committee had never definitely decided whether the pennant belonged to the team with the most total wins or the team that had won the most season series. Nor was the committee clear on whether games should count after a team had already clinched a best-of-five series. Thoroughly befuddled, different newspapers printed different standings on different days. Often the same paper would print standings one week that were at odds with the standings it had run the previous week.

On November 3, in Philadelphia, loop president James W. Kerns called a meeting to sort out the confusion and find a way to name a champion by November 15. Harry Wright could not have felt easy when he realized that Kerns and the Athletics, in their role as hosts of the meeting, meant to provide refreshments—namely champagne. In the convivial atmosphere it was perhaps inevitable that the committee, after waffling all season, resolved enough of the contested issues in the Athletics' favor to crown them the first major league champions. The most crucial decision was the committee's vote to revoke the Rockford club's four wins prior to June 16 in which Hastings had taken part. Once two of the wins, which had come at the Athletics' expense, were changed to Philadelphia victories, the Athletics had one more win than Boston in games actually played and a better winning percentage even after unplayed forfeits were added to the mix.

THE FIRST MAJOR LEAGUE GAME

FOREST CITY (Cleveland) at KEKIONGAS (Fort Wayne)
May 4, 1871

CLEVELAND	AB	R	H	O	A	FORT WAYNE	AB	R	H	O	A
J. White, c	4	0	3	9	0	Selman, rf	4	0	0	4	0
Kimball, 2b	4	0	0	3	4	Mathews, p	4	0	0	1	0
Pabor, cf	4	0	0	0	0	Foran, 3b	4	0	1	2	0
Allison, rf	4	0	1	2	0	Goldsmith, 2b	4	0	0	3	1
E. White, lf	3	0	0	1	0	Lennon, c	4	1	1	9	1
Pratt, p	3	0	0	1	2	Carey, ss	3	0	0	3	1
Sutton, 3b	3	0	1	0	0	Mincher, lf	3	0	0	2	0
Carleton, 1b	3	0	0	9	0	McDermott, cf	3	0	1	0	1
Bass, ss	3	0	0	2	4	Kellly, 1b	3	1	1	3	0
Totals	31	0	5	24	10	Totals	32	2	4	27	4
Cleveland	000	000	000	—	0	Fort Wayne	010	010	000	—	2

First base by errors—Cleveland 4, Fort Wayne 0. Two base hits—J. White, Lennon. Double play—Carey (unassisted). Walks, by—Mathews 1, Pratt 1. Strikeouts, by—Mathews 6. Passed balls—J. White 2, Lennon 1. Umpire—J. L. Boake. Time—2 hours.

Bobby Mathews, winner of the first game in major league history. Not only did Mathews also gain the honor of throwing the first shutout but his 2–0 lid-lifter proved to be the lowest-scoring game of the entire 1871 NA season. Mathews fell only three wins short of becoming the first pitcher to collect 300 victories.

Here is the box score of the National Association's inaugural game together with the story of it that a long-forgotten reporter dispatched to the New York *Herald*. The play-by-play account has been edited for the sake of clarity, but nothing will ever change how crisp a game it was, or the remarkably prominent role that both catchers played.

"The finest game of base ball ever witnessed in this country was played on the grounds of the Kekiongas of this city this afternoon, the playing throughout being without precedent in the annals of base ball, and the members of both clubs establishing beyond doubt their reputation as among the most perfect ball players in the United States. Not an error was made by Cleveland, and only three by Fort Wayne. The batting was not as heavy as some, though the pitching was superior. Especially was that of Mathews, of Fort Wayne, commented upon. The umpiring was fair, impartial, and entirely satisfactory to both clubs. Owing to the threatening indications of the weather, not over five hundred persons were on the ground. The enthusiasm ran high among the spectators, and we doubt if a game in this country was ever witnessed with closer attention.

"The Kekiongas won the toss and sent the Forest Citys to the bat. The following is the game by innings:"

FIRST INNING

CLEVELAND—J. White doubled. Kimball lined out to Carey, who made an unassisted double play when White strayed off second thinking the ball would go through. Pabor fouled out to Lennon.

FORT WAYNE—Selman fouled out to J. White. Mathews was retired when J. White took his foul fly on one bounce. Foran singled. Goldsmith fouled out to J. White.

SECOND INNING

CLEVELAND—Allison struck out but reached first when Lennon mishandled the third strike. E. White struck out, but Allison moved to second after escaping a run-down involving Carey and Kelley. Pratt fouled out to Foran. Mincher made a fine running catch of Sutton's drive to retire the side and strand Allison at second.

FORT WAYNE—Lennon doubled to left. Allison snagged Carey's fly with one hand after a long run. Mincher flied to Kimball. McDermott singled to score Lennon from second. Kelley fouled out to J. White. One run.

THIRD INNING

CLEVELAND—Carleton fanned. Bass flied to Mincher. J. White fouled out to Lennon.

FORT WAYNE—J. White put out Selman by grabbing his foul fly on one bounce and then retired Mathews with a fine catch of his foul tip. (Note: A batter was out in 1871 if a catcher caught a foul tip on either the fly or the first bounce.) Foran flied out to E. White.

FOURTH INNING

CLEVELAND—Kimball and Pabor both flied to Selman. Allison fouled out to Lennon.

FORT WAYNE—Goldsmith drew a base on balls. Lennon fouled out to J. White. Carey reached first after forcing Goldsmith at second. Mincher popped to Pratt.

FIFTH INNING

CLEVELAND—E. White struck out. Pratt walked. Sutton singled, sending Pratt to third, but was caught off first when he rounded the bag too far. Carleton flied to Mincher.

FORT WAYNE—McDermott grounded out. Kelley singled, moved to third on two passed balls and then scored when Selman grounded out. J. White caught Mathews's foul fly on one bounce. One run.

SIXTH INNING

CLEVELAND—Bass flied to Mincher. J. White reached first on Goldsmith's error and went to second on a passed ball. Kimball flied to Foran. Pabor popped to Mathews.

FORT WAYNE—Foran flied to Kimball. Goldsmith's foul tip was caught by J. White. Lennon flied to Bass.

SEVENTH INNING

CLEVELAND—Allison reached first on Goldsmith's error. Lennon nailed Allison when he tried to steal to second as E. White struck out. Pratt popped to Carey.

FORT WAYNE—Carey, Mincher and McDermott all grounded out.

EIGHTH INNING

CLEVELAND—Sutton fouled out to Lennon. Carleton grounded out. Bass popped to Goldsmith.

FORT WAYNE—Kelley flied to Allison. Selman flied to Kimball. Mathews grounded out.

NINTH INNING

CLEVELAND—J. White singled to center but was caught at second by McDermott when he tried to stretch it. Kimball flied to Selman. Pabor reached first when McDermott muffed his fly. Allison fanned.

FORT WAYNE—Since the rules in 1871 required that a full game be played even if the team up last was ahead going into the bottom of the ninth, the Kekiongas took their last raps. Foran and Goldsmith both grounded to Pratt. Moments after Lennon grounded to Bass, rain, which had threatened all day, began coming down in sheets.

THE SEASONAL RECORD

Official Standings*

	G	W	L	PCT	H	R	GB
Philadelphia Athletics	29	22	7	.759	11–3	8–4	—
Boston Red Stockings	33	22	10	.688	11–4	8–5	1.5
Chicago White Stockings	29	20	9	.690	13–3	6–5	2
New York Mutuals	35	17	18	.486	12–7	4–10	8
Washington Olympics	33	16	15	.516	7–4	5–9	7
Troy Unions	31	15	15	.500	7–9	5–6	7.5
Cleveland Forest Citys	29	10	19	.345	3–8	7–8	12
Fort Wayne Kekiongas	28	7	21	.250	5–4	2–7	14.5
Rockford Forest Citys	27	6	21	.222	2–4	1–17	15.5

*Games played at neutral sites omitted from Home and Road records.

STANDINGS (including only games actually played)

	G	W	L	PCT	GB
Athletics	28	21	7	.750	—
Boston	31	20	10	.667	2
Chicago	28	19	9	.679	2
New York	33	16	17	.485	7.5
Washington	32	15	15	.500	7
Troy	29	13	15	.464	8
Cleveland	29	10	19	.345	11.5
Kekiongas	19	7	12	.368	9.5
Rockford	25	4	21	.160	15.5

STANDINGS (restoring Rockford wins later declared forfeits)

	G	W	L	PCT	GB
Boston	31	20	10	.667	—
Chicago	28	19	9	.679	—
Athletics	28	19	9	.679	—
New York	33	16	17	.485	5.5
Washington	32	14	16	.467	6
Troy	29	13	15	.464	6
Cleveland	29	10	19	.345	9.5
Rockford	25	8	17	.320	9.5
Kekiongas	19	6	13	.316	8.5

	Ath	Bos	Chi	NY	Was	Tro	Cle	Kek	Roc	
Athletics	—	1	3	3	3	3	3	3	3	22
Boston	3	—	1	3	3	3	3	3	3	22
Chicago	2	3	—	3	3	1	2	3	3	19
New York	2	2	1	—	3	1	2	3	3	17
Washington	0	1	2	1	—	3	3	3	3	16
Troy	0	2	1	3	2	—	2	3	2	15
Cleveland	0	1	1	3	0	2	—	0	3	10
Kekiongas	0	0	0	1	1	1	3	—	1	7
Rockford	0	0	0	1	0	1	1	3	—	6
	7	10	9	18	15	15	19	21	21	135

SEASON LEADERS

Batting Average

1.	Meyerle, Athletics	.492
2.	McVey, Boston	.431
3.	Wright, Boston	.412
4.	Barnes, Boston	.401
5.	King, Troy	.396

On-Base Percentage

1.	Meyerle, Athletics	.500
2.	G. Wright, Boston	.453
3.	Barnes, Boston	.447
4.	McVey, Boston	.435
5.	Wood, Chicago	.425

Home Runs

1.	Pike, Troy	4
	Treacey, Chicago	4
	Meyerle, Athletics	4
4.	Bass, Cleveland	3
	Cuthbert, Athletics	3
	Sutton, Cleveland	3

Runs

1.	Barnes, Boston	66
2.	Birdsall, Boston	51
3.	Radcliff, Athletics	47
	Cuthbert, Athletics	47
5.	Waterman, Washington	46

Bases on Balls

1.	Pinkham, Chicago	18
2.	H. Wright, Boston	13
	Barnes, Boston	13
4.	Wood, Chicago	11
5.	Cuthbert, Athletics	10
	Waterman, Washington	10
	Wolters, New York	10

Slugging Average

1.	Meyerle, Athletics	.700
2.	Pike, Troy	.654
3.	Bass, Cleveland	.640
4.	G. Wright, Boston	.625
5.	Barnes, Boston	.580

Total Bases

1.	Meyerle, Athletics	91
	Barnes, Boston	91
3.	Pike, Troy	85
	McVey, Boston	85
5.	King, Troy	79

RBI

1.	Wolters, New York	44
2.	McVey, Boston	43
3.	Meyerle, Athletics	40
4.	Pike, Troy	39
5.	S. King, Troy	34
	Reach, Athletics	34
	Start, New York	34
	Barnes, Boston	34

Hits

1.	McVey, Boston	66
2.	Meyerle, Athletics	64
3.	Barnes, Boston	63
4.	Start, New York	58
5.	S. King, Troy	57

Stolen Bases (Data incomplete)

1.	McGeary, Troy	20
2.	Wood, Chicago	16
	Cuthbert, Athletics	16
4.	Leonard, Washington	14
	Eggler, New York	14

PITCHING

Wins

1.	Spalding, Boston	19
2.	McBride, Athletics	18
	Zettlein, Chicago	18
4.	Wolters, New York	16
5.	McMullin, Troy	12
	Brainard, Washington	12

Losses

1.	Pratt, Cleveland	17
2.	Wolters, New York	16
	Fisher, Rockford	16
4.	McMullin, Troy	15
	Brainard, Washington	15

Innings

1.	Wolters, New York	283
2.	Brainard, Washington	264
3.	Spalding, Boston	257.1
4.	McMullin, Troy	249
5.	Zettlein, Chicago	240.2

Strikeouts

1.	Pratt, Cleveland	34
2.	Spalding, Boston	23
3.	Zettlein, Chicago	22
	Wolters, New York	22
5.	Mathews, Kekionga	17

ERA (100 innings)

1.	Zettlein, Chicago	2.73
2.	Spalding, Boston	3.36
3.	Wolters, New York	3.43
4.	Pratt, Cleveland	3.77
5.	Fisher, Rockford	4.35

Complete Games

1.	Wolters, New York	31
2.	Brainard, Washington	30
3.	McMullin, Troy	28
4.	Zettlein, Chicago	25
	McBride, Athletics	25

Winning Percentage (10 decisions)

1.	McBridge, Athletics	.783
2.	Zettlein, Chicago	.667
3.	Spalding, Boston	.655
4.	Wolters, New York	.500

Lowest On-Base Percentage

1.	Zettlein, Chicago	.283
2.	Wolters, New York	.285
3.	Spalding, Chicago	.290
4.	Fisher, Rockford	.302
5.	McBride, Athletics	.307

FIELDING

Total Chances

1B	Gould, Boston	382
2B	Wood, Chicago	212
3B	Schafer, Boston	187
SS	Force, Washington	243
OF	Hall, Washington	104
C	J. White, Cleveland	190
P	Fisher, Rockford	82

Fielding Average

Fisler, Athletics	.972
Wood, Chicago	.886
Sutton, Athletics	.795
Force, Washington	.844
Treacy, Chicago	.918
McGeary, Troy	.897
Fisher, Rockford	.927

PHILADELPHIA   **Dick McBride**   **Athletic Park**

Pos	Player	G	AB	H	R	2B	3B	HR	RBI	BB	BA	SA
LF	Ned Cuthbert	27	150	37	47	7	5	3	30	10	.247	.420
1B	Wes Fisler	26	147	41	43	8	2	0	16	3	.279	.361
SS	John Radcliff	28	145	44	47	7	5	0	22	6	.303	.421
C	Fergie Malone	27	134	46	33	7	1	1	33	9	.343	.433
2B	Al Reach	26	133	47	43	7	6	0	34	5	.353	.496
P	Dick McBride	25	132	31	36	3	0	0	17	7	.235	.295
3B	Levi Meyerle	26	130	64	45	9	3	**4**	40	2	**.492**	**.700**
CF	Count Sensenderfer	25	127	41	38	5	2	0	23	0	.329	.394
UT	George Bechtel	20	94	33	24	9	1	1	21	2	.351	.500
RF	George Heubel	16	75	23	18	4	2	0	13	2	.307	.413
Sub	Tom Pratt	1	6	2	2	0	0	0	1	0	.333	.333
Sub	Tom Berry	1	4	1	0	0	0	0	0	0	.250	.250
Sub	Nate Berkenstock	1	4	0	0	0	0	0	0	0	.000	.000
		28	1281	410	376	66	27	9	250	46	**.320**	**.435**

1B	Fisler 26, Pratt 1, Heubel 1
2B	Reach 26, Fisler 2
SS	Radcliff 28
3B	Meyerle 26, Bechtel 3
OF	Cuthbert 27, Sensenderfer 25, Heubel 16, Bechtel 15, Berkenstock 1, Berry 1
C	Malone 27, Cuthbert 1
P	McBride 25, Bechtel 3, Meyerle 1

		G	IP	GS	CG	W	L	K	BB	SH	SV	ERA
	Dick McBride	25	222	25	25	18	5	15	40	0	0	4.58
	George Bechtel	3	26	3	2	1	2	1	11	0	0	7.96
	Levi Meyerle	1	1	0	0	0	0	0	2	0	0	9.00

—3 forfeit Ws: 2 vs Rockford; 1 vs Kekionga—

			249	28	27	19	7	16	53	0	0	4.95

BOSTON   Harry Wright   South End Grounds

		G	AB	H	R	2B	3B	HR	RBI	BB	BA	SA
2B	Ross Barnes	31	157	63	**66**	10	9	0	34	13	.401	.580
C	Cal McVey	29	153	**66**	43	9	5	0	43	1	.431	.556
RF	Dave Birdsall	29	152	46	51	3	3	0	24	4	.303	.362
1B	Charlie Gould	31	151	43	38	9	2	2	32	3	.285	.411
3B	Harry Schafer	31	149	42	38	7	5	0	28	3	.282	.396
CF	Harry Wright	31	147	44	42	5	2	0	26	13	.299	.361
P	Al Spalding	31	144	39	43	10	1	1	31	8	.271	.375
Sub	Frank Barrows	18	86	13	13	2	1	0	11	0	.151	.198
SS	George Wright	16	80	33	33	7	5	0	11	6	.412	.625
LF	Fred Cone	19	77	20	17	3	1	0	16	8	.260	.325
Sub	Sam Jackson	16	76	17	17	5	3	0	11	1	.224	.368
		31	1372	**426**	**401**	**70**	37	3	267	**60**	.310	.422

1B Gould 30, G. Wright 1
2B Barnes 16, Jackson 14, Barrows 1, Schafer 1
SS G. Wright 15, Barnes 15, H. Wright 1, Jackson 1
3B Schafer 31, McVey 1
OF H. Wright 30, Birdsall 27, Cone 19, Barrows 17, Spalding 9, McVey 5, Jackson 1, Gould 1
C   McVey 29, Birdsall 7
P   Spalding 31, H. Wright 9

	G	IP	GS	CG	W	L	K	BB	SH	SV	ERA
Al Spalding	31	257.1	31	22	19	10	23	38	1	0	3.36
Harry Wright	9	18.2	0	0	1	0	0	4	0	3	6.27

—2 forfeit Ws: 1 vs Kekiongas; 1 vs Mutuals on October 16—

	276	31	22	20	10	23	42	1	3	3.55

CHICAGO   Jimmy Wood   Lake Park

		G	AB	H	R	2B	3B	HR	RBI	BB	BA	SA
2B	Jimmy Wood	28	135	51	45	10	6	1	29	11	.378	.563
1B	Bub McAtee	26	135	37	34	8	2	0	10	5	.274	.363
C	Charlie Hodes	28	130	36	32	4	1	2	25	7	.277	.369
RF	Joe Simmons	27	129	28	29	6	1	0	17	1	.217	.279
P	George Zettlein	28	128	32	23	3	0	0	18	2	.250	.273
LF	Fred Treacey	25	124	42	39	7	5	**4**	33	2	.339	.573
SS	Ed Duffy	26	121	28	30	5	0	0	15	3	.231	.273
CF	Mart King	20	101	21	23	1	0	2	16	8	.208	.277
3B	Ed Pinkham	24	95	25	27	5	5	1	17	**18**	.263	.453
Sub	Tom Foley	18	84	22	18	3	1	0	13	3	.262	.321
Sub	Mike Brannock	3	14	1	2	0	0	0	0	0	.071	.071
		28	1196	323	302	52	21	**10**	193	**60**	.270	.374

1B McAtee 26, Simmons 2
2B Wood 28
SS Duffy 26, King 3, Hodes 1
3B Pinkham 18, Hodes 10, Brannock 3, Duffy 1, Foley 1, King 1
OF Treacey 25, Simmons 25, Foley 16, King 11, Pinkham 8, Hodes 4, Zettlein 3
C   Hodes 20, King 9, Foley 4
P   Zettlein 28, Pinkham 3

	G	IP	GS	CG	W	L	K	BB	SH	SV	ERA
George Zettlein	28	240.2	28	25	18	9	22	25	0	0	2.73
Ed Pinkham	3	10.1	0	0	1	0	0	3	0	1	3.48
—1 forfeit W vs Kekionga—											
	251		28	25	19	9	22	**28**	0	1	**2.76**

NEW YORK   Bob Ferguson   Union Grounds (Brooklyn)

		G	AB	H	R	2B	3B	HR	RBI	BB	BA	SA
LF	John Hatfield	33	168	43	41	3	2	0	22	4	.256	.298
SS	Dickey Pearce	33	163	44	31	5	0	0	20	4	.270	.301
1B	Joe Start	33	161	58	35	5	1	1	34	3	.360	.422
3B	Bob Ferguson	33	158	38	30	6	1	0	25	3	.241	.291
RF	Dan Patterson	32	151	31	31	2	0	0	13	1	.205	.219
CF	Dave Eggler	33	147	47	37	7	3	0	18	4	.320	.408
C	Charlie Mills	32	146	36	27	4	3	0	22	1	.247	.315
P	Rynie Wolters	32	138	51	33	6	9	0	**44**	10	.370	.413
2B	Dick Higham	21	94	34	21	3	1	0	9	2	.362	.415
Sub	Charley Smith	14	72	19	15	2	1	0	5	1	.264	.319
Sub	Frank Fleet	1	6	2	1	0	0	0	1	0	.333	.333
		33	1404	403	302	43	21	1	213	33	.287	.350

1B	Start 33
2B	Higham 12, Ferguson 11, Hatfield 7, Smith 3, Patterson 2, Mills 1
SS	Pearce 33
3B	Ferguson 20, Smith 12, Hatfield 2, Mills 1, Wolters 1
OF	Eggler 33, Patterson 31, Hatfield 24, Higham 8, Mills 4
C	Mills 29, Ferguson 5, Higham 1
P	Wolters 32, Fleet 1, Ferguson 1

	G	IP	GS	CG	W	L	K	BB	SH	SV	ERA
Rynie Wolters	32	283	32	31	16	16	22	39	1	0	3.43
Frank Fleet	1	9	1	1	0	1	0	3	0	0	10.00
Bob Ferguson	1	1	0	0	0	0	0	0	0	0	27.00
—1 forfeit W vs Kekiongas; 1 forfeit L vs Boston on Oct. 16—											
	293		33	**32**	16	17	22	42	**1**	0	3.72

WASHINGTON   Nick Young   Olympic Grounds

		G	AB	H	R	2B	3B	HR	RBI	BB	BA	SA
SS	Davy Force	32	162	45	45	9	4	0	29	4	.278	.383
3B	Fred Waterman	32	158	50	46	7	4	0	17	10	.316	.411
1B	Everett Mills	32	157	43	38	6	4	1	24	3	.274	.382
2B	Andy Leonard	31	148	43	33	8	3	0	30	3	.291	.385
CF	George Hall	32	136	40	31	3	3	2	17	8	.294	.404
P	Asa Brainard	30	134	30	24	4	0	0	21	7	.224	.254
C	Doug Allison	27	133	44	28	10	2	2	27	0	.331	.481
RF	John Glenn	26	120	37	25	3	2	0	21	3	.308	.367
LF	Harry Berthrong	17	73	17	17	1	1	0	8	4	.233	.274
Sub	Henry Burroughs	12	63	15	11	2	3	1	14	1	.238	.413
Sub	Tommy Beals	10	36	7	6	0	0	0	1	2	.194	.194
Sub	Charlie Sweasy	5	19	4	5	1	0	0	4	1	.211	.263
P	Bill Stearns	2	9	0	1	0	0	0	1	2	.000	.000
Sub	Warren White	1	4	0	0	0	0	0	0	0	.000	.000
Sub	Frank Norton	1	1	0	0	0	0	0	0	0	.000	.000
		32	1353	375	310	54	26	6	214	48	.277	.369

1B	Mills 32
2B	Leonard 19, Sweasy 5, Berthrong 5, Beals 2, White 1, Burroughs 1
3B	Waterman 28, Burroughs 5, Force 1, Norton 1
SS	Force 31, Leonard 1
OF	Hall 32, Glenn 26, Berthrong 12, Leonard 11, Beals 8, Burroughs 8, Norton 1
C	Allison 27, Waterman 6, Berthrong 1
P	Brainard 30, Stearns 2

	G	IP	GS	CG	W	L	K	BB	SH	SV	ERA
Asa Brainard	30	264	30	30	12	15	13	37	0	0	4.50
Bill Stearns	2	18	2	2	2	0	0	8	0	0	2.50
		—2 forfeit Ws: 1 vs Kekiongas; 1 vs Rockford—									
		282	32	**32**	14	15	13	45	0	0	4.37

TROY   Lip Pike (1–3)   Bill Craver (12–12)   Rensselaer Park

		G	AB	H	R	2B	3B	HR	RBI	BB	BA	SA
C	Mike McGeary	29	148	39	42	4	0	0	12	6	.264	.291
CF	Tom York	29	145	37	36	5	7	2	23	9	.255	.428
LF	Steve King	29	144	57	45	10	6	0	34	1	.396	.549
1B	Clipper Flynn	29	142	48	43	6	1	0	27	4	.338	.394
P	John McMullin	29	136	38	38	0	5	0	32	8	.279	.353
RF	Lip Pike	28	130	49	43	10	7	**4**	39	5	.377	.654
3B	Steve Bellan	29	128	32	26	3	3	0	23	9	.250	.320
2B	Bill Craver	27	118	38	26	8	1	0	26	3	.322	.407
SS	Dickie Flowers	21	105	33	39	5	4	0	18	4	.314	.438
Sub	Ned Connors	7	33	7	6	0	0	0	2	0	.212	.212
Sub	E.P. Beavens	3	15	6	7	0	0	0	5	0	.400	.400
Sub	Dave Abercrombie	1	4	0	0	0	0	0	0	0	.000	.000
		29	1248	384	351	51	34	6	241	49	.308	.417

1B	Flynn 19, Connors 4, Pike 4, Craver 2
2B	Craver 18, Pike 7, Beavens 3, Connors 1, Flowers 1, Flynn 1
SS	Flowers 20, Craver 4, McGeary 3, Bellan 1, Abercrombie 1, McMullin 1
3B	Bellan 28, Flynn 1
OF	King 29, York 29, Pike 18, Flynn 8, Connors 3, Craver 1
C	McGeary 26, Craver 3
P	McMullin 29, Flowers 1

	G	IP	GS	CG	W	L	K	BB	SH	SV	ERA
John McMullin	29	249	29	28	12	15	12	75	0	0	5.53
Dick Flowers	1	1	0	0	0	0	0	0	0	0	0.00
		—3 forfeit Ws vs Kekiongas—									
		250	29	28	12	15	12	75	0	0	5.51

CLEVELAND Charlie Pabor **National Association Grounds**

		G	AB	H	R	2B	3B	HR	RBI	BB	BA	SA
C	Deacon White	29	146	47	40	6	5	1	21	4	.322	.452
LF	Charlie Pabor	29	142	42	24	2	4	0	18	1	.296	.368
CF	Art Allison	29	137	40	28	4	5	0	19	2	.292	.394
2B	Gene Kimball	29	131	25	18	1	0	0	9	3	.191	.198
P	Al Pratt	29	130	34	31	6	8	0	20	1	.262	.408
3B	Ezra Sutton	29	128	45	35	3	7	3	23	1	.352	.555
1B	Jim Carleton	29	127	32	31	8	1	0	18	8	.252	.331
SS	John Bass	22	89	27	18	1	**10**	3	18	3	.303	.640
RF	Elmer White	15	70	18	13	2	0	0	9	1	.257	.286
Sub	Caleb Johnson	16	67	15	10	1	0	0	7	0	.224	.239
Sub	Joe Quest	3	13	3	1	1	0	0	2	1	.231	.308
Sub	Joe Battin	1	3	0	0	0	0	0	0	1	.000	.000
Sub	George Ewell	1	3	0	0	0	0	0	0	0	.000	.000
		29	1186	328	249	35	**40**	7	164	26	.277	.391

1B Carleton 29
2B Kimball 17, Johnson 10, Quest 2, Allison 2, D. White 1
SS Bass 22, Kimball 6, D. White 2, Quest 1
3B Sutton 29, Kimball 2, D. White 1
OF Allison 29, Pabor 28, E. White 15, Kimball 9, Johnson 6, Pratt 6, Sutton 2, Battin 1, Ewell 1, D. White 1
C D. White 29, E. White 3, Bass 1, Sutton 1
P Pratt 28, Pabor 7

	G	IP	GS	CG	W	L	K	BB	SH	SV	ERA
Al Pratt	28	224.2	28	22	10	17	**34**	47	0	0	3.77
Charlie Pabor	7	29.1	1	1	0	2	0	6	0	0	6.75
	254		29	23	10	19	**34**	53	0	0	4.11

FORT WAYNE Bill Lennon (5–9) Harry Deane (2–3) **The Grand Duchess**

		G	AB	H	R	2B	3B	HR	RBI	BB	BA	SA
1B	Jim Foran	19	89	31	21	1	3	1	18	2	.348	.461
P	Bobby Mathews	19	89	24	15	3	1	0	10	2	.270	.326
SS	Wally Goldsmith	19	88	18	8	1	0	0	12	4	.205	.216
2B	Tom Carey	19	87	20	16	2	0	0	10	2	.230	.253
RF	Bill Kelley	18	67	15	16	1	1	0	7	6	.224	.284
3B	Frank Selman	14	65	15	14	3	0	1	10	4	.231	.323
CF	Sam Armstrong	12	49	11	9	2	1	0	5	0	.224	.306
C	Bill Lennon	12	48	11	5	3	0	0	5	1	.229	.292
LF	Ed Mincher	9	36	8	4	0	0	0	5	0	.222	.222
Sub	Pete Donnelly	9	34	7	7	1	1	0	3	1	.206	.294
Sub	Jimmy Hallinan	5	25	5	7	0	0	0	2	2	.200	.200
Sub	Harry Deane	5	22	4	3	0	1	0	2	2	.182	.273
Sub	Joe Quinn	5	17	4	8	0	0	0	2	4	.235	.235
Sub	Harry Kohler	3	12	2	0	1	0	0	1	0	.167	.333
Sub	Joe McDermott	2	8	2	3	0	0	0	1	1	.250	.250
Sub	Bill Barrett	1	5	1	1	1	0	0	1	0	.200	.400
Sub	Nealy Phelps	1	3	0	0	0	0	0	0	1	.000	.000
Sub	Charlie Bearman	1	2	0	0	0	0	0	0	1	.000	.000
		19	746	178	137	19	8	2	94	33	.239	.294

1B Foran 16, Kohler 2, Phelps 1, Bearman 1
2B Carey 19
SS Goldsmith 14, Hallinan 5, Lennon 2, Selman 2, Carey 1

3B   Selman 14, Goldsmith 8, Donnelly 2, Kohler 1, Barrett 1
OF   Kelley 18, Armstrong 12, Donnelly 9, Mincher 9, Deane 5, Foran 4, McDermott 2,
     Lennon 1
C   Lennon 12, Quinn 5, Selman 5, Goldsmith 2, Kohler 2, Barrett 1
P   Mathews 19

	G	IP	GS	CG	W	L	K	BB	SH	SV	ERA
Bobby Mathews	19	169	19	19	6	11	17	21	**1**	0	5.17

—1 forfeit W vs Rockford and 9 forfeit Ls: 3 to Troy, 2 to Rockford, 1 to New York, 1 to
Washington, 1 to Chicago, 1 to Boston and 1 to Athletics—

ROCKFORD   **Scott Hastings**   **Fairgrounds Park**

		G	AB	H	R	2B	3B	HR	RBI	BB	BA	SA
P	Cherokee Fisher	25	123	28	24	3	3	1	22	3	.228	.325
1B	Denny Mack	25	122	30	34	7	1	0	17	8	.246	.320
3B	Cap Anson	25	120	39	29	**11**	3	0	16	2	.325	.467
2B	Bob Addy	25	118	32	30	6	0	0	13	4	.271	.322
C	Scott Hastings	25	118	30	27	6	4	0	20	2	.254	.373
LF	Ralph Ham	25	113	28	25	4	0	0	12	1	.248	.283
RF	Gat Stires	25	110	30	23	4	6	2	24	7	.271	.473
CF	George Bird	25	106	28	19	2	5	0	13	3	.264	.377
SS	Chick Fulmer	16	63	17	11	1	3	0	3	5	.270	.381
Sub	Pony Sager	4	39	11	9	0	0	0	5	2	.282	.282
Sub	Al Barker	1	4	1	0	0	0	0	2	1	.250	.250
		25	1036	274	231	**44**	25	3	147	38	.264	.364

1B   Mack 24, Fisher 2, Fulmer 1, Anson 1, Hastings 1
2B   Addy 22, Anson 2, Hastings 2, Fisher 1
SS   Fulmer 16, Sager 5, Addy 3, Ham 2, Fisher 1, Mack 1
3B   Anson 20, Ham 7
OF   Stires 25, Bird 25, Ham 19, Sager 4, Hastings 2, Barker 1, Anson 1, Mack 1
C   Hastings 23, Anson 5
P   Fisher 24, Mack 3

	G	IP	GS	CG	W	L	K	BB	SH	SV	ERA
Cherokee Fisher	24	213	24	22	4	16	15	31	1	0	4.35
Denny Mack	3	13	1	1	0	1	1	3	0	0	3.46

—4 forfeit Ls owing to the use of ineligible player: 2 to Athletics, 1 to Washington
and 1 to Kekiongas

	226	25	23	4	17	16	34	1	0	4.30

1872

HARRY WRIGHT BRINGS BOSTON
ITS FIRST CHAMPIONSHIP

The 1872 season featured the first rule pertaining to base coaches. To prevent their interference with fielders they were prohibited from coming within 15 feet of the foul lines while coaching runners. Coaches were still permitted to interfere with runners, however, even if it meant tackling them to detain them from making a foolhardy dash to the next base.

An even wider-reaching rule change in 1872 forever altered the duel between pitcher and batter. That season it became legal for a pitcher to jerk his arm, snap his wrist or bend his elbow when he delivered the ball as long as he kept his hand below his hip at the point of release. This revision licensed sidearm pitching and opened the door for teams to employ curveball artisans. The first club to avail itself of the privilege was New York. William Cammeyer's Mutuals jettisoned Rynie Wolters, letting him slip off to Cleveland, and handed his pitching slot to rookie Candy Cummings, who had caught the New Yorkers' fancy when he drubbed them 14–3 in an exhibition game the previous year while a member of the unaffiliated Brooklyn Stars. At the time the Mutuals had howled that Cummings, considered by some historians to have invented the curveball, was throwing "unfair" sidearm pitches, but now that his delivery was legal he was their man.

Other pitchers who reportedly had the curveball in their arsenal in 1872 were Troy newcomer Phoney Martin and Bobby Mathews, late of the Kekiongas, who had returned to his hometown of Baltimore when Nick Young left the Washington Olympics to organize a new team in that city and decked them out in yellow hose, causing them to be called the Canaries. Mathews was followed to Maryland by a Kekionga teammate, second baseman Tom Carey; the combination gave Young a solid nucleus upon which to build. By the time he completed his roster, Baltimore had an NA veteran at every position. From his former Washington club, Young skimmed first baseman Everett Mills and center fielder George Hall. Catcher Bill Craver, right fielder Lip Pike, left fielder Tom York and handyman Cherokee Fisher were robbed from Troy. Dick Higham, the Canaries' top hitter at .343, came from the Mutuals, and shortstop John Radcliff left the pennant-winning Athletics after losing his job to Mike McGeary.

Candy Cummings, the NA's top rookie pitcher in 1872. He compensated for his frail physique—he weighed only 120 pounds—by throwing the best curveball of his day. Whether it was also the first curveball will always be food for debate.

MYSTERIOUS McCARTON

The Middletown Mansfields began the 1872 season with a crew of raw rookies. Nary a member of the Mansfields' opening day lineup on April 26 had played in so much as a single NA game in 1871. Though the Mansfields folded little more than three months later, four of their opening day starters—Eddie Booth, John Clapp, Jim Tipper and Tim Murnane—hooked on with other teams and eventually had major league careers of some substance. A fifth team member, Jim O'Rourke (though he might not have been the Mansfields' most talented player), would have a career so substantial that he made the Hall of Fame.

In center field for the Mansfields on opening day was Frank McCarton, a Middletown native. The 1996 Macmillan lists a birthdate for McCarton that would have made him just 14 on April 26, 1871; the 1995 edition of *Total Baseball* contends that he was 17. In either event McCarton was the youngest player in the NA's second season. He was also among the most promising. Though again the records are in conflict, McCarton apparently batted at least .329 in the 19 games he played; he may have hit as high as .373. The latter figure, if correct, would have led the Mansfields, and even at .329 McCarton was second only to Murnane's .359. McCarton took part in 19 of the Mansfields' 24 games, but was not on the field in the team's last contest on August 9. He never again appeared in a big league uniform.

"Orator" Jim O'Rourke began playing amateur ball at 14. He was in his fifth season with Middletown when the club went major league in 1872. O'Rourke would only agree to join the Mansfields in making baseball a full-time profession after the club found a worker to take his place on the family farm. He proceeded to play longer in the majors than any other 19th-century performer except Cap Anson.

With the Reserve Clause not yet in force to bind a player to a team for longer than the length of his contract (usually one year), the movement even among the established teams was dizzying. The champion Athletics garnered four new regulars—Cap Anson, Denny Mack, Fred Treacey and Mike McGeary. The first two had belonged to the defunct Rockford team, and Treacey and McGeary had committed to Chicago for 1872 before the great fire knocked the Windy City entry out of business. Along with Cummings, New York picked up half a dozen new faces—but only after losing captain-third baseman Bob Ferguson to the Brooklyn Atlantics. Disturbed by the heavy gambling aroma surrounding the New York club, Ferguson chose to cast his fate with one of the five new entries in 1872.

In addition to Baltimore and the Atlantics was a second Brooklyn-based team, the Eckfords, which had informally joined the NA the previous August. The Nationals, a Washington rival to the Olympics, and the Mansfield club from Middletown, Connecticut, also threw in their caps. Named for Union general Joseph Mansfield, who was slain at Antietam, the Mansfields billed themselves as the Connecticut champions and mailed their $10 entry fee to NA headquarters. Since in 1872 there was no screening committee to judge the worth of applicants, the fee was accepted—though much to the dismay of Henry Chadwick, who viewed the team as unqualified for the professional arena.

In actuality, if the final standings are an accurate indicator, the Mansfields were third among the new entries, ranking ahead of the Eckfords and Nationals as well as the incumbent Olympics. If the 1871 NA season was the epitome of confusion, the 1872 campaign was the height of instability. Though 12 teams began the chase in May, only six played enough games to qualify for the championship. The Olympics were the first to expire, doing so on May 24. Scarcely a month later the Nationals stripped Washington of its other big league representative when they threw in the towel on June 26 after being trounced 9–1 by Baltimore. Troy quit on July 23. The Mansfields survived until August 9; Cleveland breathed its last on August 19. Though the Eckfords finished out the season, they played only 29 games, little more than half the number Baltimore and New York totaled.

Amidst all the turmoil, Harry Wright's Boston Red Stockings stood almost unchanged from the 1871 club that had come within a hair of winning the flag. Wright obtained Andy Leonard from the Olympics to man left field and gave Boston's right field post to rookie Fraley Rogers but otherwise retained the same cast. With himself in center field, his brother George at shortstop, batting champ Ross Barnes at second base, Al Spalding in the box, Charlie Gould at the first sack, Harry Schafer holding down third base and Cal McVey behind the plate, Wright had need for only one substitute all season—Dave Birdsall, the club's regular right fielder in 1871.

The Athletics, in contrast, began shifting players from position to position after playing a sct lineup for most of the 1871 season. By juggling his personnel, pitcher-manager Dick

The Baltimore Canaries formed in 1872 by raiding veteran clubs. Each of these Canaries played with another NA team in 1871. From left, top and bottom: Everett Mills/Lip Pike; George Hall/Tom York; John Radcliff/Dick Higham; Bobby Mathews/Cherokee Fisher; Tom Carey/Bill Craver.

The Rockford Forest Citys were Al Spalding's first pro team. Here he and Ross Barnes are with the Rockfords in 1870, two years before the pair sparked the first of five straight pennant-winning teams. Also here is team captain Scott Hastings, whose eligibility violation bore heavily on the 1871 pennant race.

THE EXECRABLE ECKFORDS

While pennant-winning Boston played just 10 men in 49 games in 1872, the Brooklyn Eckfords needed 26 players to get through their 29 championship games. Only three Eckfords—shortstop Jim Snyder, third baseman Jim Clinton and first baseman Andy Allison—played in as many as two-thirds of the team's frays, and none of them was in the lineup in both the Eckfords' opening game on May 7 and the team's finale on September 22. The previous year the Eckfords had been a strong independent team, but personnel changes and a general lack of continuity made them such an unattractive draw in 1872 that not even their Brooklyn cohabitor, the Atlantics, wanted to play them. The two clubs from the City of Churches avoided a confrontation on the playing field until August 19. Over the next two months the pair consented to play each other just three more times. When their series ended in a two-all draw, it was a moral victory for the Eckfords. Against the other nine NA clubs, the Brooklyn entry that had believed the NA too flimsy to join the previous year was a miserable 1–26.

McBride won his first six games of the season before losing on June 1 to New York. The defeat pushed Boston into the lead with a 9–1 record to Philadelphia's 6–1. Once they grabbed the top rung, the Red Stockings were never caught. The pennant race was in effect over on September 4, when Boston saddled McBride with his worst loss of the season, 16–4.

Hoping to pep up sagging gate receipts in every NA city, Boston, New York and Philadelphia staged several late-season round-robin tournaments, ostensibly for the league championship. Unfortunately, all such attempts failed to perk fan interest. It was too obvious that the Boston team was far superior. The final standings only partly reflect the Red Stockings' dominance. Of the 24 championship games with their three closest pursuers, Wright's team was triumphant in 18. Excluding the eight games with Philadelphia, which were split 4–4, Boston posted a 35–4 record.

McBRIDE OR HAYHURST?

Early editions of Macmillan list Hicks Hayhurst as the manager of the Philadelphia Athletics from 1871 through 1873 and Al Reach as the manager for the 1874 and 1875 seasons. All current baseball encyclopedias agree that pitcher Dick McBride managed the Athletics every year the team was part of the National Association. No papers were recently unearthed proving that McBride secretly held the job. He is credited with the position now because the manager has come to be regarded as the man who actually ran the club on the field.

In the early days many teams labeled the man who handled their business affairs the manager even if he had little or nothing to do with field operations. Hayhurst was the Athletics' secretary, responsible for scheduling games, keeping count of the gate receipts and such; if he ever sat on the team bench, it was only to observe. Reach, though a part-time player in 1874 and 1875, was mainly a club official. When the umpire shouted "Play Ball!" it was directed to McBride and whomever the other team's captain was. The captains were then in charge, and so are now considered to have been the field managers of their teams.

Some glitches still exist, though. At one time Macmillan listed Joe Gerhardt as Louisville's manager for part of the 1883 season and the first half of the 1884 season. Now both Macmillan and *Total Baseball* credit Gerhardt with managing Louisville during all of the 1883 season, but say Mike Walsh ran the club in 1884. That would be news to Pete Browning, Guy Hecker and everyone else from those days still keeping up on the game. Gerhardt ran the team on the field in 1884 until August, when he was replaced as captain. The local papers all made a big to-do of his being canned. Perhaps Walsh, a club official and ex-umpire, was the one who decided to axe Gerhardt and take on the job himself, but until it was a *fait accompli* the team was under Gerhardt's wing. Macmillan had it right originally. Gerhardt ran the show in the Falls City for most of the year that Hecker won 52.

THE SEASONAL RECORD

	G	W	L	PCT	H	R	GB
Boston Red Stockings	48	39	8	.830	20–1	19–7	—
Baltimore Canaries	58	35	19	.648	20–7	12–12	7.5
New York Mutuals	56	34	20	.630	23–8	10–11	8.5
Philadelphia Athletics	47	30	14	.682	22–4	7–10	7.5
Troy Haymakers	25	15	10	.600	5–3	8–4	13
Brooklyn Atlantics	37	9	28	.243	6–13	3–15	25
Cleveland Forest Citys	22	6	16	.273	2–3	4–11	20.5
Middletown Mansfields	24	5	19	.208	4–6	1–12	22.5
Brooklyn Eckfords	29	3	26	.103	2–13	0–13	27.5
Washington Olympics	9	2	7	.222	1–6	1–1	18
Washington Nationals	11	0	11	.000	0–7	0–4	21

* Games played at neutral sites omitted from Home and Road records.

	Bos	Bal	NY	Ath	Tro	Atl	Cle	Man	Eck	Oly	Nat	
Boston	—	7	7	4	2	7	4	3	3	1	1	39
Baltimore	0	—	5	4	3	4	4	4	4	2	3	35
New York	2	4	—	6	3	6	2	4	5	1	1	34
Athletics	4	5	3	—	2	4	3	2	5	1	1	30
Troy	1	0	2	0	—	2	1	4	3	1	1	15
Atlantics	1	1	2	0	0	—	1	2	2	*	*	9
Cleveland	0	1	1	0	0	1	—	0	1	1	1	6
Mansfield	0	0	0	0	0	1	1	—	2	*	1	5
Eckford	0	1	0	0	0	2	0	0	—	*	*	3
Olympics	0	0	0	0	0	*	0	*	*	—	2	2
Nationals	0	0	0	0	0	*	0	0	*	0	—	0
	8	19	20	14	10	28	16	19	26	7	11	178

* Teams did not play one another

SEASON LEADERS

Batting Average (100 ABs)

1.	Barnes, Boston	.432
2.	Force, Troy–Baltimore	.418
3.	Anson, Athletics	.417
4.	Hastings, Cleve–Baltimore	.362
5.	McGeary, Athletics	.360

On–Base Percentage

1.	Anson, Athletics	.455
2.	Barnes, Boston	.444
3.	Force, Troy–Baltimore	.411
4.	Hastings, Cleve–Baltimore	.374
5.	White, Cleveland	.366

Home Runs

1.	Pike, Baltimore	6
2.	Gedney, Troy–Eckford	3
3.	Six with 2	

Slugging Average

1.	Barnes, Boston	.585
2.	Anson, Athletics	.525
3.	Wood, Troy–Eckford	.503
4.	Force, Troy–Baltimore	.493
5.	Meyerle, Athletics	.486

Total Bases

1.	Barnes, Boston	134
2.	Pike, Baltimore	127
3.	G. Wright, Boston	120
4.	Eggler, New York	118
5.	Hall, Baltimore	116

RBI

1.	Pike, Baltimore	60
2.	Anson, Athletics	50
	Start, New York	50
4.	Fisler, Athletics	48
5.	Spalding, Boston	47
	Cuthbert, Athletics	47

Hits

1. Barnes, Boston	99
2. Eggler, New York	98
3. Force, Troy–Baltimore	94
4. Hatfield, New York	92
5. Anson, Athletics	90

Bases on Balls

1. Mack, Athletics	23
2. Anson, Athletics	16
3. McMullin, New York	11
4. Barnes, Boston	9
H. Wright, Boston	9
Hatfield, New York	9

Runs

1. Eggler, New York	94
2. G. Wright, Boston	87
3. Cuthbert, Athletics	83
4. Barnes, Boston	81
5. Hatfield, New York	76

Stolen Bases (Data incomplete)

1. Eggler, New York	18
2. Cuthbert, Athletics	14
G. Wright, Boston	14
4. McGeary, Athletics	13
5. Barnes, Boston	12
Hatfield, New York	12

PITCHING

Wins

1. Spalding, Boston	38
2. Cummings, New York	33
3. McBride, Athletics	29
4. Mathews, Baltimore	25
5. Zettlein, Troy–Eckford	15

Innings

1. Cummings, New York	497
2. McBride, Athletics	419.
3. Mathews, New York	406
4. Spalding, Boston	404..
5. Britt, Atlantics	336

Strikeouts

1. Mathews, Baltimore	55
2. McBride, Athletics	44
3. Cummings, New York	43
4. Spalding, Boston	27
5. Zettlein, Troy–Eckfords	25

ERA (60 innings)

1. Fisher, Baltimore	1.80
2. Spalding, Boston	1.85
3. Zettlein, Troy–Eck	2.33
4. Britt, Atlantics	2.58
5. McBride, Athletics	2.85

Losses

1. Britt, Atlantics	28
2. Cummings, New York	20
3. Mathews, Baltimore	18
4. Bentley, Mansfield	15
Zettlein, Troy–Eckford	15

Complete Games

1. Cummings, New York	53
2. McBride, Athletics	47
3. Spalding, Boston	41
4. Mathews, New York	39
5. Britt, Atlantics	37

Winning Percentage (10 decisions)

1. Fisher, Baltimore	.909
2. Spalding, Boston	.826
3. McBride, Athletics	.682
4. Cummings, New York	.623
5. Mathews, Baltimore	.581

Lowest On–Base Percentage

1. Fisher, Baltimore	.207
2. Spalding, Boston	.252
3. Zettlein, Troy–Eck	.273
4. Mathews, Baltimore	.277
5. McBride, Athletics	.278

FIELDING

Total Chances

1B	Gould, Boston	556
2B	Hatfield, New York	380
3B	Ferguson, Atlantics	324
SS	G. Wright, Boston	334
OF	Eggler, New York	180
C	Hicks, New York	375
P	Spalding, Boston	143

Fielding Average

Start, New York		.955
Barnes, Boston		.901
Force, Troy–Balt		.857
Pearce, New York		.839
Eggler, New York		.922
Hicks, New York		.875
Spalding, Boston		.902

BOSTON   Harry Wright   South End Grounds

		G	AB	H	R	2B	3B	HR	RBI	BB	BA	SA
SS	George Wright	48	255	86	87	16	6	2	32	3	.337	.471
LF	Andy Leonard	46	240	84	57	7	1	2	43	0	.350	.413
P	Al Spalding	48	237	84	60	11	5	0	47	3	.354	.443
C	Cal McVey	46	237	76	56	10	2	0	41	1	.321	.380
2B	Ross Barnes	45	229	**99**	81	**28**	2	1	44	9	**.432**	**.585**
3B	Harry Schafer	48	225	65	51	10	4	1	37	0	.289	.382
1B	Charlie Gould	45	211	54	50	9	**8**	0	33	2	.256	.374
CF	Harry Wright	48	208	52	39	5	1	0	23	9	.250	.284
RF	Fraley Rogers	45	204	56	39	7	1	1	28	1	.275	.333
Sub	Dave Birdsall	16	76	16	11	3	0	0	15	1	.211	.250
		48	2122	672	521	**106**	**30**	7	343	29	.317	**.405**

1B	Gould 44, Rogers 6
2B	Barnes 45, Leonard 4
SS	G. Wright 48, Leonard 1
3B	Schafer 43, Leonard 6, McVey 1
OF	H. Wright 48, Rogers 41, Leonard 38, McVey 11, Birdsall 8, Spalding 7, Schafer 5, Gould 2
C	McVey 40, Birdsall 12, Schafer 2
P	Spalding 48, H. Wright 7

	G	IP	GS	CG	W	L	K	BB	SH	SV	ERA
Al Spalding	48	404.2	48	41	38	8	27	27	**3**	0	1.85
Harry Wright	7	25.2	0	0	1	0	1	0	*	4	1.75
	—One combined shutout—Wright 5 innings, Spalding 4 innings—										
	430.1	48	41	39	8	28	27	4	4	**1.84**	

BALTIMORE   Bill Craver (27–13)   Everett Mills (8–6)   Newington Park

		G	AB	H	R	2B	3B	HR	RBI	BB	BA	SA
SS	John Radcliff	56	**297**	86	71	13	4	1	44	0	.290	.370
UT	Lipman Pike	56	288	84	67	15	5	**6**	**60**	3	.292	.441
1B	Everett Mills	55	266	79	55	14	2	0	34	3	.297	.365
CF	George Hall	53	250	84	69	17	6	1	37	3	.336	.464
LF	Tom York	51	248	66	66	10	4	1	41	4	.266	.351
RF	Dick Higham	50	245	84	72	10	1	2	38	2	.343	.416
UT	Cherokee Fisher	46	225	52	39	10	3	1	36	2	.231	.316
P	Bobby Mathews	50	223	50	36	1	0	0	21	3	.224	.229
2B	Tom Carey	42	198	57	42	7	0	2	27	0	.288	.354
C	Bill Craver	35	179	50	55	3	2	0	23	5	.279	.318
3B	Davy Force	19	95	41	29	2	2	0	13	1	.432	.495
Sub	Scott Hastings	13	62	19	16	3	1	0	4	1	.311	.387
		58	2576	752	**617**	105	**30**	**14**	378	27	.292	.372

1B   Mills 55, Carey 1, Higham 1, Hall 1
2B   Carey 29, Pike 24, Higham 5, Craver 4, Hastings 2, Radcliff 1
SS   Radcliff 50, Carey 9
3B   Force 19, Fisher 18, Pike 9, Radcliff 6, Higham 2, Craver 2, Mathews 3, Carey 3, Hastings 1
OF   Hall 52, York 51, Pike 25, Higham 24, Fisher 19, Mathews 8, Craver 4, Carey 3, Hastings 1
C   Craver 27, Higham 25, Hastings 12
P   Mathews 49, Fisher 19

	G	IP	GS	CG	W	L	K	BB	SH	SV	ERA
Bobby Mathews	49	406	47	39	25	18	55	52	0	0	3.19
Cherokee Fisher	19	110	11	9	10	1	20	11	1	1	1.80
		516	58	48	35	19	75	63	1	1	2.90

NEW YORK   Dickey Pearce (10–6)   John Hatfield (24–14)   Union Grounds (Brooklyn)

		G	AB	H	R	2B	3B	HR	RBI	BB	BA	SA
CF	Dave Eggler	56	290	98	**94**	20	0	0	20	8	.338	.393
2B	John Hatfield	56	288	92	76	15	1	1	45	9	.319	.389
1B	Joe Start	55	282	76	61	4	0	0	50	0	.270	.284
C	Nat Hicks	56	268	82	55	12	2	0	33	5	.306	.366
P	Candy Cummings	55	250	52	36	9	3	0	27	4	.200	.268
RF	George Bechtel	51	248	74	60	11	2	0	41	6	.298	.359
LF	John McMullin	54	237	61	48	6	1	0	25	11	.257	.291
SS	Dickey Pearce	44	206	40	33	1	1	1	23	4	.194	.223
Sub	Chick Fulmer	36	166	51	28	1	1	1	14	2	.307	.343
3B	Bill Boyd	35	165	44	26	6	1	1	32	6	.267	.333
Sub	Charlie Mills	6	31	4	6	0	0	0	2	0	.129	.129
		56	2431	674	523	85	12	4	312	55	.277	.327

1B   Start 55, Bechtel 1
2B   Hatfield 56
SS   Pearce 42, Fulmer 14
3B   Boyd 34, Fulmer 22
OF   Eggler 56, McMullin 53, Bechtel 50, Mills 4, Hicks 3, Pearce 2, Cummings 2, Boyd 1
C   Hicks 54, Mills 3
P   Cummings 55, McMullin 3

	G	IP	GS	CG	W	L	K	BB	SH	SV	ERA
Candy Cummings	**55**	**497**	**55**	**53**	33	20	43	30	**3**	0	2.97
John McMullin	3	15	1	1	1	0	1	2	0	1	3.60
		512	56	**54**	34	20	44	32	3	1	2.99

PHILADELPHIA   Dick McBride   Athletic Park

		G	AB	H	R	2B	3B	HR	RBI	BB	BA	SA
LF	Ned Cuthbert	47	260	88	83	10	0	1	47	6	.338	.388
P	Dick McBride	47	258	74	57	6	1	0	39	3	.287	.318
2B	Wes Fisler	47	243	85	49	10	3	0	48	4	.350	.416
CF	Fred Treacey	47	236	65	53	7	3	2	29	5	.275	.356
SS	Mike McGeary	47	225	81	68	9	2	0	35	3	.360	.418
3B	Cap Anson	46	217	90	60	10	7	0	50	16	.417	.525
C	Fergie Malone	41	213	60	46	5	3	0	39	4	.282	.333
1B	Denny Mack	47	205	59	68	9	1	0	34	**23**	.288	.341
RF	Levi Meyerle	27	146	48	31	10	5	1	31	0	.329	.486
Sub	Al Reach	24	118	23	21	0	0	0	11	4	.195	.195
Sub	Dickie Flowers	3	15	4	1	0	0	0	4	2	.267	.267
Sub	Count Sensenderfer	1	5	2	2	0	0	0	1	0	.400	.400
		47	2141	679	539	79	25	4	366	**69**	**.317**	.383

1B	Mack 26, Malone 17, Reach 4
2B	Fisler 47
SS	Mack 21, McGeary 23, Flowers 3
3B	Anson 46, Meyerle 1
OF	Treacey 47, Cuthbert 47, Meyerle 26, Reach 20, Sensenderfer 1, McGeary 1
C	McGeary 23, Malone 24
P	McBride 47

	G	IP	GS	CG	W	L	K	BB	SH	SV	ERA
Dick McBride	47	419.1	47	47	29	14	44	26	1	0	2.85

—1 forfeit W vs Eckfords on Aug. 31—

TROY   Jimmy Wood   Rensselaer Park

		G	AB	H	R	2B	3B	HR	RBI	BB	BA	SA
3B	Davy Force	25	130	53	40	11	0	0	16	1	.408	.492
1B	Bub McAtee	25	129	28	30	3	1	0	15	1	.217	.256
LF	Steve King	25	128	39	33	8	0	0	21	1	.305	.367
RF	Phoney Martin	25	117	36	27	2	1	0	14	0	.308	.342
C	Doug Allison	23	115	35	23	4	2	0	20	1	.304	.374
SS	Steve Bellan	23	114	30	22	4	0	0	16	0	.263	.298
2B	Jimmy Wood	25	113	38	40	11	4	2	27	2	.336	.558
P	George Zettlein	25	113	29	25	9	0	0	21	0	.257	.336
Sub	Charlie Hodes	13	61	15	17	3	0	0	12	1	.246	.295
CF	Count Gedney	9	47	20	14	3	0	3	18	0	.426	.681
Sub	Candy Nelson	4	20	7	2	0	0	0	4	0	.350	.350
Sub	Mart King	3	11	0	0	0	0	0	1	0	.000	.000
		25	1098	330	273	58	8	5	185	7	.301	.382

1B	McAtee 25
2B	Wood 25
SS	Bellan 9, Force 9, Hodes 5, Allison 1, Nelson 1
3B	Force 16, Bellan 8, Hodes 1
OF	S. King 25, Martin 25, Gedney 9, Bellan 6, Hodes 4, M. King 3, Nelson 3, Zettlein 8
C	Allison 22, Hodes 3
P	Zettlein 25, Martin 8

	G	IP	GS	CG	W	L	K	BB	SH	SV	ERA
George Zettlein	25	187.2	22	17	14	8	17	8	2	1	2.16
Phoney Martin	8	37.1	3	0	1	2	1	2	0	0	4.82
	225	25	17	15	10	18	10	2	1		2.60

BROOKLYN ATLANTICS   Bob Ferguson   Capitoline Grounds

		G	AB	H	R	2B	3B	HR	RBI	BB	BA	SA
SS	Jack Burdock	37	174	46	26	3	0	0	15	3	.264	.282
C	Tom Barlow	37	171	53	34	1	0	0	10	1	.310	.316
3B	Bob Ferguson	37	165	46	33	5	0	0	19	3	.279	.339
1B	Dutch Dehlman	37	165	36	30	3	1	0	14	3	.218	.248
CF	Jack Remsen	37	164	40	25	4	5	0	13	5	.244	.329
P	Jim Britt	37	156	40	26	7	0	0	10	2	.256	.301
LF	Al Thake	18	78	23	14	2	2	0	15	0	.295	.372
Sub	Eddie Booth	15	62	19	11	4	0	0	8	0	.306	.371
RF	Jack McDonald	15	62	16	9	3	1	0	4	0	.258	.339
2B	Jim Hall	13	57	18	9	0	1	0	6	1	.316	.351
Sub	E.P. Beavans	10	43	9	6	2	0	0	2	1	.209	.256
Sub	? Barrett	8	34	7	7	1	1	0	2	0	.206	.294
Sub	Charlie Lowe	7	31	5	1	0	0	0	3	0	.161	.161

		G	AB	H	R	2B	3B	HR	RBI	BB	BA	SA
Sub	Herm Doscher	6	25	9	4	0	0	0	5	0	.360	.360
Sub	John Kenney	5	19	0	0	0	0	0	1	0	.000	.000
Sub	Oliver Brown	4	15	2	0	0	0	0	0	0	.133	.133
Sub	Sam Jackson	4	12	2	0	0	0	0	0	0	.167	.167
Sub	John Bass	2	7	1	0	1	0	0	1	0	.143	.286
Sub	Denny Clare	2	7	1	1	0	0	0	0	0	.143	.143
Sub	Herb Worth	1	5	1	1	1	0	0	1	0	.200	.400
Sub	John Galvin	1	4	0	0	0	0	0	0	0	.000	.000
Sub	? Higby	1	4	0	0	0	0	0	0	0	.000	.000
		37	1460	374	237	37	10	0	129	19	.256	.295

1B Dehlman 37
2B Hall 13, Beavans 10, Lowe 7, Kenney 3, Clare 2, Burdock 2, Galvin 1, Thake 1, Booth 1, Jackson 1
SS Burdock 36, Barlow 4, Beavans 1, Clare 1
3B Ferguson 37, Barlow 1, Jackson 1
OF Remsen 37, Thake 18, McDonald 15, Booth 14, Barrett 8, Doscher 6, Brown 4, Jackson 3, Kenney 2, Bass 2, Worth 1, Higby 1, Beavens 1
C   Barlow 36, Burdock 4, Ferguson 1
P   Britt 37

	G	IP	GS	CG	W	L	K	BB	SH	SV	ERA
Jim Britt	37	336	37	37	9	28	13	19	0	0	2.58

CLEVELAND   **Scott Hastings (6–14)**   **Deacon White (0–2)**   **Association Grounds**

		G	AB	H	R	2B	3B	HR	RBI	BB	BA	SA
UT	Scott Hastings	22	115	45	34	4	0	0	16	3	.391	.426
SS	Jim Holdsworth	22	110	33	19	0	0	0	5	1	.300	.300
C	Deacon White	22	109	37	21	2	2	0	22	4	.339	.394
3B	Ezra Sutton	22	107	30	30	6	1	0	10	1	.280	.355
LF	Charlie Pabor	22	92	19	12	0	0	0	7	0	.207	.207
1B	Joe Simmons	18	90	23	11	5	1	0	9	1	.256	.333
CF	Art Allison	19	87	23	13	4	0	0	8	0	.264	.310
RF	Rynie Wolters	16	69	16	7	1	0	0	11	4	.232	.246
P	Al Pratt	16	65	18	10	0	1	0	12	0	.277	.308
2B	Charlie Sweasy	12	57	16	8	0	0	0	6	2	.281	.281
1B	Jim Carlton	7	38	12	8	1	0	0	4	1	.316	.342
Sub	?Mullen	1	4	0	1	0	0	0	0	0	.000	.000
		22	943	272	174	28	5	0	116	17	.288	.329

1B Simmons 15, Carleton 7
2B Sweasy 11, White 7, Hastings 6
SS Holdsworth 22
3B Sutton 22
OF Pabor 20, Allison 19, Wolters 11, Pratt 6, Hastings 5, White 5, Simmons 3, Mullen 1, Sweasy 1
C   White 14, Hastings 12
P   Pratt 15, Wolters 12, Pabor 2

	G	IP	GS	CG	W	L	K	BB	SH	SV	ERA
Al Pratt	15	105.2	12	8	2	9	7	14	0	0	5.79
Rynie Wolters	12	75.1	8	5	3	6	4	7	0	0	6.09
Charlie Pabor	2	18	2	2	1	1	0	3	0	0	4.00
		199	22	15	6	16	11	24	0	0	5.74

MIDDLETOWN   John Clapp   Fort Hill Grounds

		G	AB	H	R	2B	3B	HR	RBI	BB	BA	SA
1B	Tim Murnane	24	117	42	30	1	0	0	13	0	.359	.368
2B	Eddie Booth	24	117	38	25	4	2	0	12	0	.325	.393
P	Cy Bentley	23	115	27	25	1	2	0	10	0	.235	.287
LF	Jim Tipper	24	112	31	23	5	1	0	15	0	.277	.339
SS	Jim O'Rourke	23	101	31	25	4	1	0	12	2	.307	.366
C	John Clapp	19	97	28	28	6	1	1	10	1	.289	.402
RF	Frank Buttery	18	93	24	19	0	0	0	8	0	.258	.258
3B	George Fields	18	87	21	16	3	1	0	9	0	.241	.299
CF	Frank McCarton	19	85	28	17	4	1	0	10	1	.329	.400
OF	Ham Allen	16	66	18	8	1	0	0	7	0	.273	.288
Sub	Asa Brainard	6	25	5	2	0	0	0	0	1	.200	.200
Sub	Billy Arnold	2	7	1	2	0	0	0	0	0	.143	.143
		24	1002	294	220	29	9	1	106	5	.288	.345

1B   Murnane 24
2B   Booth 20, Brainard 4
SS   O'Rourke 16, Allen 8, Clapp 2, Fields 1
3B   Fields 12, Buttery 5, Tipper 5, O'Rourke 2
OF   McCarton 19, Tipper 19, Allen 9, Buttery 8, Bentley 8, Fields 5, Booth 4, Arnold 2, Clapp 1, Brainard 1
C   Clapp 19, O'Rourke 8
P   Bentley 18, Buttery 7, Brainard 2

	G	IP	GS	CG	W	L	K	BB	SH	SV	ERA
Cy Bentley	18	149	17	15	2	15	5	12	0	0	6.10
Frank Buttery	7	54	5	5	3	2	0	2	0	0	4.50
Asa Brainard	2	8	2	1	0	2	0	0	0	0	5.62
		211	24	21	5	19	5	14	0	0	5.67

BROOKLYN ECKFORDS   Andy Allison (0–11)   Jimmy Wood (2–7)   Phoney Martin (1–8)
Union Grounds

		G	AB	H	R	2B	3B	HR	RBI	BB	BA	SA
SS	Jim Snyder	26	107	28	16	2	2	0	11	0	.262	.318
3B	Jim Clinton	25	97	25	13	3	1	0	6	0	.258	.309
1B	Andy Allison	22	93	15	11	3	0	0	9	0	.161	.194
C	Doug Allison	18	79	27	18	2	1	0	5	1	.342	.392
P	Phonney Martin	18	78	12	13	0	0	0	9	1	.154	.154
2B	Candy Nelson	18	76	19	12	2	0	0	8	2	.250	.276
LF	Count Gedney	18	71	13	4	1	0	0	7	2	.183	.197
Sub	Marty Swandell	14	55	11	7	0	0	0	4	2	.200	.200
Sub	Frank Fleet	13	53	13	10	1	0	0	5	0	.245	.264
RF	Dick Hunt	11	48	15	11	1	1	0	5	1	.312	.375
CF	Dan Patterson	12	47	9	5	2	0	0	4	0	.191	.234
Sub	Josh Snyder	9	37	6	2	2	0	0	1	1	.162	.216
P	George Zettlein	10	34	3	1	0	0	0	0	0	.088	.088
P	Joe McDermott	7	32	9	3	3	0	0	3	1	.281	.375
Sub	Jimmy Wood	7	30	6	10	1	1	0	0	4	.200	.333
Sub	? Kavanaugh	5	23	6	3	1	0	0	2	0	.261	.304
Sub	Bill Allison	5	19	5	3	0	0	0	1	0	.158	.158
Sub	Al Martin	4	18	5	2	0	0	0	2	0	.278	.278
P	Martin Malone	5	16	5	2	0	0	0	1	1	.312	.312
Sub	? Bestick	4	14	4	0	0	0	0	1	0	.286	.286
Sub	? Leutz	4	12	2	1	0	0	0	0	0	.083	.083
Sub	George Fletcher	2	8	3	1	0	0	0	0	0	.375	.375

	G	AB	H	R	2B	3B	HR	RBI	BB	BA	SA
Sub Nat Jewett	2	8	1	1	0	0	0	0	0	.125	.125
Sub Jim Holdsworth	2	7	2	1	0	0	0	0	0	.286	.286
Sub ? McDonald	1	4	0	0	0	0	0	0	0	.000	.000
Sub ? O'Rourke	1	4	0	0	0	0	0	0	0	.000	.000
	29	1070	241	152	24	6	0	85	14	.225	.259

1B A. Allison 22, Kavanaugh 4, B. Allison 2, Patterson 1, Swandell 1
2B Nelson 9, Wood 7, A. Martin 4, Hunt 3, Clinton 3, Fleet 2, B. Allison 1, Swandell 1
SS Jim Snyder 25, Clinton 2, Holdsworth 2, McDonald 1
3B Fleet 10, Clinton 10, Swandell 8, Nelson 3
OF Gedney 18, Patterson 11, Clinton 11, Josh Snyder 9, P. Martin 9, Nelson 8, Hunt 8, Swandell 4, Jim Snyder 1, Fletcher 2, B. Allison 2, Kavanaugh 2, Malone 2, Fleet 2, A. Allison 1, Zettlein 1
C D. Allison 18, Bestick 4, Leutz 4, Jewett 2, Clinton 2, Jim Snyder 1
P P. Martin 10, Zettlein 9, McDermott 7, Malone 3, O'Rourke 1

	G	IP	GS	CG	W	L	K	BB	SH	SV	ERA
Phonney Martin	10	85	9	9	2	7	2	4	0	0	4.24
George Zettlein	9	75.1	9	8	1	7	8	6	0	0	2.75
Joe McDermott	7	63	7	7	0	7	1	12	0	0	8.14
Martin Malone	3	27	3	3	0	3	0	0	0	0	10.33
? O'Rourke	1	9	1	1	0	1	0	2	0	0	8.00
—1 forfeit L vs Athletics on Aug. 31—											
	259.1	29	28	3	25	11	24	0	0	5.52	

WASHINGTON OLYMPICS   Fred Waterman   Olympic Grounds

		G	AB	H	R	2B	3B	HR	RBI	BB	BA	SA
3B	Fred Waterman	9	45	17	13	1	2	0	6	0	.378	.444
P	Asa Brainard	9	43	16	8	3	0	0	6	0	.372	.442
C	Frank Selman	9	42	10	3	2	0	0	1	0	.238	.286
SS	Wally Goldsmith	9	41	10	4	2	0	0	5	0	.244	.293
1B	Clipper Flynn	9	40	9	4	1	0	0	2	0	.225	.250
LF	John Glenn	9	39	6	6	0	0	0	3	1	.154	.154
2B	Tommy Beals	9	36	11	6	1	1	0	5	1	.306	.389
RF	Val Robinson	7	30	6	6	0	0	0	4	1	.200	.200
CF	George Heubel	5	23	3	2	0	0	0	1	0	.130	.130
Sub	Bob Reach	2	8	2	1	0	0	0	0	0	.250	.250
Sub	Henry Burroughs	2	7	1	1	0	0	0	0	1	.143	.143
Sub	Dick Hurley	2	7	0	0	0	0	0	0	0	.000	.000
Sub	Bill Barrett	1	4	0	0	0	0	0	0	0	.000	.000
		9	365	91	54	10	3	0	33	4	.249	.293

1B Flynn 9
2B Beals 5, Goldsmith 4
SS Goldsmith 5, Beals 2, Reach 2
3B Waterman 7, Selman 2
OF Glenn 9, Robinson 7, Heubel 5, Burroughs 2, Hurley 2, Beals 2
C Selman 7, Waterman 2, Barrett 1
P Brainard 9

	G	IP	GS	CG	W	L	K	BB	SH	SV	ERA
Asa Brainard	9	79	9	9	2	7	1	5	0	0	6.38

WASHINGTON NATIONALS   **Warren White**   **National Grounds**

		G	AB	H	R	2B	3B	HR	RBI	BB	BA	SA
C	Bill Lennon	11	54	12	11	1	0	0	6	0	.222	.241
LF	Ed Mincher	11	53	6	5	0	0	0	4	0	.113	.113
1B	Paul Hines	11	49	12	9	1	0	0	5	0	.245	.265
RF	Oscar Bielaski	10	46	9	13	0	0	0	0	0	.196	.196
3B	Warren White	10	45	13	7	0	0	0	4	0	.289	.289
P	Bill Stearns	11	45	12	8	1	0	0	4	0	.267	.289
2B	Holly Hollingshead	9	44	15	12	1	1	0	6	1	.341	.409
SS	Joe Doyle	9	41	12	6	1	0	0	9	0	.293	.317
Sub	Dennis Coughlin	8	37	13	7	1	0	0	1	0	.351	.378
CF	Seem Studley	5	21	2	3	0	0	0	2	0	.095	.095
Sub	John Glenn	1	4	2	0	0	0	0	0	0	.500	.500
Sub	Joe Miller	1	4	1	0	0	0	0	0	0	.250	.250
Sub	? Spencer	1	4	0	1	0	0	0	0	0	.000	.000
Sub	Bill Yeatman	1	4	0	0	0	0	0	0	0	.000	.000
		11	451	109	80	6	1	0	50	1	.242	.259

1B	Hines 9, Miller 1, Coughlin 1, Lennon 1
2B	Hollingshead 9, Coughlin 1, Doyle 1
SS	Doyle 8, Coughlin 1, Spencer 1, White 1
3B	White 9, Hines 2
OF	Mincher 11, Bielaski 10, Studley 5, Coughlin 5, Yeatman 1, Glenn 1
C	Lennon 11, Hines 1
P	Stearns 11

	G	IP	GS	CG	W	L	K	BB	SH	SV	ERA
Bill Stearns	11	99	11	11	0	11	2	3	0	0	6.18

1873
ROSS BARNES EMERGES AS THE NA'S FIRST GREAT STAR

Despite winning the second National Association pennant, the Boston franchise was in deep financial trouble. Harry Wright's team ended the 1872 season some $5,000 in the hole, and many Red Stockings went home for the winter without their final paychecks. Compounding the team's plight, an October fire left much of Boston in ruins.

Fast talking by Wright enabled him to keep most of his nine in the fold, but first baseman Charlie Gould elected to sit out the 1873 season and catcher Cal McVey fled to Baltimore when he was offered the Canaries' captaincy and a sizeable pay hike. To fill the void McVey left, Wright garnered Deacon White, set loose when Cleveland folded in 1872; Gould's spot went to Jack Manning, up from Boston's junior team. When Fraley Rogers threatened to quit the game, Wright assigned his right field station to Jim O'Rourke of the defunct Mansfields.

The other NA entries had to do considerable retooling as well. Nick Young, ever restless, organized his third new team in three years. Based in Washington, it featured mostly the same cast that had been with the Nationals in 1872 but was known as the Blue Legs owing to Young's choice of hosiery. Meanwhile, Young's old team, the Canaries, faced competition in Baltimore from a second new NA entry, the Marylands. Comprised of local amateurs and a sprinkling of players from the 1871 Kekiongas, the Marylands formed as a co-op team, as did a third newcomer, the Elizabeth Resolutes. Completing the field were the Philadelphia White Stockings. Thus in 1873 the NA had a decidedly provincial flavor, with two of its nine teams in Philadelphia, three in the Baltimore-Washington area and two, the Mutuals and the Atlantics, in Brooklyn.

On the field, at least, the game promised to have a veneer of stability in 1873. The only major rule changes addressed spectator and fielder interference. In the former case, it was stipulated that if a person not part of the game came in contact with a batted or thrown ball a runner could no longer be put out until the ball had first been returned to the pitcher while he was inside the pitcher's box. Likewise, beginning in 1873, each baserunner was awarded one base if a fielder stopped or caught a batted or thrown ball with his cap.

39

The 1873 Brooklyn Atlantics. The following year Tom Barlow made a rare career move when he converted from catcher to shortstop. In September he was injured in a game against Chicago. Given morphine to kill the pain, Barlow soon became a hopeless addict and vanished into the nation's netherworld, never to be heard from again.

BOSTON'S HITS PER GAME AVERAGES

In 1873 the notion of ranking hitters according to their batting averages was not as yet universally accepted. Some analysts preferred to rank players by the number of hits they made per game. Regardless of which method was used, however, mathematical errors were common. Typical is the following chart showing the hits per game averages for Boston's players in 1873 listed in the 1874 edition of *Dime Base-Ball Player,* as opposed to their currently accepted hits per game averages.

	Dime Base-Ball	Current
Ross Barnes	2.31	2.08
George Wright	2.18	2.14
Deacon White	2.06	2.02
Bob Addy	1.83	1.74
Al Spalding	1.80	1.77
Jim O'Rourke	1.80	1.72
Andy Leonard	1.72	1.64
Jack Manning	1.35	1.34
Harry Schafer	1.41	1.32
Harry Wright	1.24	1.16

Others: 1.00 (6 hits in 6 games) Current: 1.00 (5 hits in 5 games)

The Marylands lasted just six games—the shortest life-span of any entry in major league history—before quitting with a .156 team batting average and a runs-for-and-against ratio of 26 to 152. The Resolutes survived until early August, and the reorganized Washington club, although it finished the season, won only eight games and just two of 20 with the top three teams. But the Philadelphia White Stockings proved to be the most formidable new entry in NA history. No sooner had the White Stockings posted their $10 league fee and arranged to share Jefferson Street Grounds with the Athletics than they mercilessly raided their co-tenants. Levi Meyerle, Fred Treacey, Fergy Malone, Ned Cuthbert and Denny Mack all abandoned the old-line Philadelphia team for White Stockings garb. The upstart club then gambled on George Bechtel, an ex-New York Mutual long suspected of dumping games. George Zettlein arrived from the disbanded Brooklyn Eckfords to handle the pitching chores, and a few weeks later Zettlein's Eckfords teammate, Jimmy Wood, came out of a brief retirement to play second base after Bob Addy was released.

BOSTON BASE 1873 BALL CLUB.

The 1873 NA champion Boston Red Stockings. Clockwise from top left: George Wright, Ross Barnes, Al Spalding, Jim O'Rourke, Deacon White, Charlie Sweasy, Dave Birdsall, Jack Manning and Andy Leonard. Center from top: Harry Wright and Harry Schafer. Boston stood nearly alone in a league that Bob Carroll said "had a reputation that would embarrass the town harlot. Hard-drinking players were loaded on the field more often than the bases, gamblers knew tomorrow's standings this morning, and the whole mess was about as disciplined as the theater crowd when the Bijou burned down."

Ross Barnes, the NA's first great star. His 1873 season was arguably the best all-around performance during the loop's five-year existence.

By mid-July, Zettlein sported a glittering 27–3 record and the White Stockings sat atop the NA by eight and a half games. Confident of the pennant, the new Philadelphia entry then took three weeks off from baseball to vacation at Cape May, New Jersey. During the heat of summer the Athletics also closed up shop. Boston, meanwhile, began to rally. Following a shocking 11–2 loss to Hugh Campbell of the lowly Resolutes on Independence Day morning, Harry Wright was thankful he had had the foresight to schedule two games at South End Grounds that day. By lambasting the Resolutes 32–3 in the afternoon contest, the Red Stockings quickly regained their equilibrium and set off in pursuit of the seemingly uncatchable White Stockings.

MAJOR RECORDS HELD BY ROSS BARNES

National League:	Highest Batting Average (1876–92 era): .429 in 1876
	Highest Slugging Average (1876–92 era): .590 in 1876
	Highest Fielding Average, Second Baseman: .910 in 1876 (broken in 1878)
National Association:	Most Hits, Season: 143 in 1875
	Most Runs, Season: 125 in 1873
	Most Total Bases, Season: 188 in 1873
All-time:	Most Runs per at bat, Career (Minimum 2,000 at bats): .292 (699 runs in 2,392 at bats)
	Most Runs per at bat, Season (Minimum 100 runs): .388 (125 runs in 322 at bats, 1873)
Nineteenth century:	Highest career batting average, second baseman: .359

Wright, wisely, had put off scheduling most of his team's games with Washington until late in the season, when he judged the Blue Legs would be too far off the pace to put up more than token resistance. After the Red Stockings ripped Washington six straight times in September and October, they were suddenly within striking distance of first place. Al Spalding's 7–5 victory over the White Stockings on September 15 at Jefferson Street Grounds moved Boston past Baltimore and into second place, just four games out of first. Under such relentless pressure the White Stockings wilted. Following its Cape May retreat, the Philadelphia club won just nine of its last 23 games of the season. By the time Boston returned to Jefferson Street Grounds on October 2, mere percentage points separated the two clubs, and an easy 18–7 win gave the Red Stockings a lead they would only increase.

When the season closed the Red Stockings had seven more wins than the White Stockings, but the pennant was not quite theirs yet. Still to be settled was the White Stockings' protest that Boston had used an ineligible player, none other than Bob Addy, down the stretch. Upon being released by the White Stockings, Addy had set out for Rockford, where he'd played in 1871, and hung around town long enough to get into a game there on July 4. Several days later Addy was signed by Boston when Harry Wright decided to move Jim O'Rourke from right field to first base, where rookie Jack Manning had struggled. The White Stockings argued that Addy's participation in the July 4 Rockford game came under the 60-day rule; therefore, all the games he played for Boston prior to September 4 should be forfeited. As always, the Championship Committee vacillated interminably. Not until January 20, 1874, did it decide that the Rockford game was a pickup affair not subject to the 60-day rule. Boston was awarded the 1873 pennant.

The Baltimore Canaries were 13–0 against the NA's three weak sisters in 1873 but only 5–13 against its top two clubs, explaining their third-place finish. Top: Lip Pike, Tom York, Candy Cummings, Davy Force and Cal McVey. Bottom: George Hall, John Radcliff, Scott Hastings and Everett Mills.

Addy's performance in Boston livery no doubt grieved the White Stockings. He hit .355 in the last half of the season as the Red Stockings won 23 of their last 27 games. But the real catalyst for Boston's extraordinary comeback was Ross Barnes. Following up on his batting title in 1872 with his second straight batting championship, the Boston second baseman also paced the NA in hits, runs, total bases, slugging average and on-base percentage. Boston, as a unit, hit .338 and scored 12.3 runs per game. Minus Barnes's output, Boston's batting average would have been reduced by 12 points and 17 percent of its runs would have been lost.

FAMOUS FIRSTS I

The Elizabeth Resolutes not only were the first major league team from the state of New Jersey, but are New Jersey's only major league entry to date with the sole exception of the 1915 Newark Federal League club. The Resolutes actually played their home games not in Elizabeth but in nearby Waverly, no longer an existing town. Their ballground was at the current site of Weequahic City Park and the B'Nai Jeshuron Cemetery on the Elizabeth/Newark border. The Resolutes' first home game was on April 28, 1873, their last on July 23. Little more than a month after their stunning win over Boston on Independence Day at South End Grounds, the Resolutes disbanded following a 20–3 loss to the New York Mutuals.

New Jersey's first major league team also achieved another distinguished first. The Resolutes were the first club to have two pairs of brothers: the Campbells, Hugh and Mike; and the Allisons, Doug and Art.

THE SEASON RECORD

	G	W	L	PCT	H	R	GB
Boston Red Stockings	60	43	16	.729	21–7	19–8	—
Philadelphia White Stockings	53	36	17	.679	23–6	12–10	4
Baltimore Canaries	57	34	22	.607	19–7	15–15	7.5
New York Mutuals	53	29	24	.547	22–11	7–13	11
Philadelphia Athletics	52	28	23	.549	21–13	7–9	11
Brooklyn Atlantics	55	17	37	.315	14–21	3–16	23.5
Washington Blue Legs	39	8	31	.205	6–12	2–19	25
Elizabeth Resolutes	23	2	21	.087	0–7	2–13	23
Maryland	6	0	6	.000	0–5	0–1	16.5

* Games played at neutral sites omitted from Home and Road records

	Bos	WS	Bal	NY	Ath	Bro	Was	Eli	Mar	
Boston	—	5	7	6	4	8	9	4	*	43
White Stockings	4	—	6	4	8	7	3	4	*	36
Baltimore	2	3	—	6	3	7	6	3	4	34
New York	3	4	3	—	4	7	4	4	*	29
Athletics	5	1	4	5	—	5	6	2	*	28
Brooklyn	1	2	2	2	4	—	3	3	*	17
Washington	0	2	0	1	0	2	—	1	2	8
Elizabeth	1	0	0	0	1	0	0	—	*	2
Maryland	*	*	0	*	*	*	0	*	*	0
	16	17	22	24	23	37	31	21	6	197

* Teams did not play one another

SEASON LEADERS

Batting Average (160 ABs)

1.	Barnes, Boston	.425
2.	Anson, Athletics	.398
3.	White, Boston	.390
4.	G. Wright, Boston	.388
5.	McVey, Baltimore	.380

On–Base Percentage

1.	Barnes, Boston	.456
2.	Anson, Athletics	.409
3.	G. Wright, Boston	.402
4.	Force, Baltimore	.391
5.	White, Boston	.390

Home Runs

1.	Pike, Baltimore	4
2.	G. Wright, Boston	3
	Meyerle, White Stockings	3
4.	Eight with	2

Slugging Average

1.	Barnes, Boston	.584
2.	G. Wright, Boston	.523
3.	McVey, Baltimore	.484
4.	Meyerle, White Stockings	.479
5.	White, Boston	.477

Total Bases

1.	Barnes, Boston	188
2.	G. Wright, Boston	170
3.	White, Boston	148
4.	Pike, Baltimore	132
5.	Spalding, Boston	131

RBI

1.	White, Boston	66
2.	Barnes, Boston	62
3.	Leonard, Boston	61
4.	Spalding, Boston	60
5.	Meyerle, White Stockings	58

Hits

1.	Barnes, Boston	137
2.	G. Wright, Boston	126
3.	White, Boston	121
4.	Spalding, Boston	106
5.	Anson, Athletics	101

Runs

1.	Barnes, Boston	125
2.	G. Wright, Boston	99
3.	Spalding, Boston	83
4.	Eggler, New York	82
5.	Leonard, Boston	81

Bases on Balls

1.	Barnes, Boston	18
2.	Mack, White Stockings	15
3.	O'Rourke, Boston	14
	Malone, White Stockings	14
5.	Mathews, New York	10
	H. Wright, Boston	10

Stolen Bases (Data incomplete)

1.	Cuthbert, White Stockings	13
	Barnes, Boston	13
3.	McMullin, Athletics	9
4.	Wood, White Stockings	8
	Pike, Baltimore	8

PITCHING

Wins

1.	Spalding, Boston	41
2.	Zettlein, White Stockings	36
3.	Mathews, New York	29
4.	Cummings, Baltimore	28
5.	McBride, Athletics	24

Losses

1.	Britt, Atlantics	36
2.	Stearns, Washington	25
3.	Mathews, New York	23
4.	McBride, Athletics	19
5.	Campbell, Elizabeth	16

Innings

1.	Spalding, Boston	497.2
2.	Britt, Atlantics	480.2
3.	Zettlein, White Stockings	460
4.	Mathews, New York	443
5.	McBride, Athletics	382.2

Complete Games

1.	Britt, Atlantics	51
2.	Zettlein, White Stockings	49
3.	Spalding, Boston	47
	Mathews, New York	47
5.	Cummings, Baltimore	42

Strikeouts

1.	Mathews, New York	75
2.	Cummings, Baltimore	34
3.	Spalding, Boston	31
4.	Zettlein, White Stockings	28
5.	McBride, Athletics	25

Winning Percentage (25 decisions)

1.	Spalding, Boston	.745
2.	Zettlein, White Stockings	.706
3.	Cummings, Baltimore	.667
4.	McBride, Athletic	.558
	Mathews, New York	.558

ERA (60 innings)

1.	Fisher, Athletics	1.81
2.	Spalding, Boston	2.46
3.	Mathews, New York	2.56
4.	Cummings, Baltimore	2.66
5.	Zettlein, White Stockings	2.70

Lowest On–Base Percentage

1.	Fisher, Athletics	.246
2.	Mathews, New York	.274
3.	McBride, Athletics	.282
4.	Cummings, Baltimore	.287
5.	Spalding, Boston	.292

FIELDING

Total Chances

1B	Dehlman, Atlantics	742
2B	Burdock, Atlantics	412
3B	Ferguson, Atlantics	424
SS	G. Wright, Boston	412
OF	Gedney, New York	225
C	White, Boston	323
P	Spalding, Boston	200

Fielding Average

Mills, Baltimore	.949
Barnes, Boston	.857
Force, Baltimore	.820
G. Wright, Boston	.808
York, Baltimore	.870
Clapp, Athletics	.908
Spalding, Boston	.855

BOSTON Harry Wright South End Grounds

		G	AB	H	R	2B	3B	HR	RBI	BB	BA	SA
SS	George Wright	59	**325**	126	99	19	8	3	50	8	.388	.523
2B	Ross Barnes	60	322	**137**	**125**	**29**	8	2	62	**18**	**.425**	**.584**
P	Al Spalding	60	322	106	83	18	2	1	60	3	.329	.407
C	Deacon White	60	310	121	79	15	6	0	**66**	0	.390	.477
LF	Andy Leonard	58	302	95	85	12	7	0	61	4	.315	.401
3B	Harry Schafer	60	295	79	65	12	3	2	46	3	.268	.349
1B	Jim O'Rourke	57	280	98	79	19	3	1	48	14	.350	.450
CF	Harry Wright	58	266	67	57	10	4	2	35	10	.252	.342
Sub	Jack Manning	32	159	43	29	6	1	0	22	1	.270	.321
RF	Bob Addy	31	152	54	37	5	2	1	36	1	.355	.434
Sub	Dave Birdsall	3	12	1	4	0	0	0	1	0	.083	.083
Sub	Fraley Rogers	1	6	2	1	1	0	0	2	0	.333	.500
Sub	Charlie Sweasy	1	4	1	0	0	0	0	0	0	.250	.250
		60	2755	**930**	**739**	**146**	**44**	**12**	489	62	.338	.436

```
1B   O'Rourke 32, Manning 29, Leonard 2, Rogers 1
2B   Barnes 47, Leonard 12, Sweasy 1
SS   G. Wright 59, Leonard 1
3B   Schafer 47, Barnes 13
OF   H. Wright 55, Leonard 45, Addy 31, O'Rourke 20, Schafer 13, Manning 5, White 5 Spalding 3, Birdsall 3
C    White 55, O'Rourke 5
P    Spalding 60, H. Wright 13
```

	G	IP	GS	CG	W	L	K	BB	SH	SV	ERA
Al Spalding	60	**497.2**	55	47	**41**	14	31	28	1	2	2.46
Harry Wright	13	38.1	5	0	2	2	0	7	0	**4**	4.26
		536	60	47	43	16	31	**35**	1	**6**	**2.59**

PHILADELPHIA WHITE STOCKINGS Fergie Malone Athletic Park

		G	AB	H	R	2B	3B	HR	RBI	BB	BA	SA
LF	Ned Cuthbert	51	278	77	78	5	3	2	33	2	.277	.338
C	Fergy Malone	53	259	75	59	11	2	0	43	14	.290	.347
RF	George Bechtel	53	258	63	53	12	1	1	40	9	.244	.310
CF	Fred Treacey	51	243	62	49	7	2	1	32	5	.255	.313
P	George Zettlein	51	241	50	39	2	0	0	22	1	.207	.216
3B	Levi Meyerle	49	238	83	53	14	4	3	58	2	.349	.479
SS	Chick Fulmer	49	236	66	42	11	3	1	38	2	.280	.364
2B	Jimmy Wood	42	209	67	67	11	1	0	27	8	.321	.383
1B	Denny Mack	48	205	60	55	5	0	0	20	15	.293	.317
UT	Jim Devlin	23	99	24	18	4	4	0	10	2	.242	.364
Sub	Bob Addy	10	51	16	12	1	0	0	10	2	.314	.333
Sub	Johnny Ryan	2	8	2	1	0	0	0	1	0	.250	.250
		53	2325	645	526	83	20	8	334	62	.277	.341

```
1B   Mack 42, Devlin 12, Ryan 1, Fulmer 1, Zettlein 1
2B   Wood 42, Addy 10, Mack 1
SS   Fulmer 49, Devlin 5, Mack 3, Malone 1, Meyerle 1
3B   Meyerle 48, Devlin 6
OF   Bechtel 52, Treacey 51, Cuthbert 51, Mack 4, Devlin 1, Ryan 1
C    Malone 53, Fulmer 1
P    Zettlein 51, Bechtel 3, Fulmer 2
```

	G	IP	GS	CG	W	L	K	BB	SH	SV	ERA
George Zettlein	51	460	51	49	36	15	28	41	0	0	2.70
George Bechtel	3	16	2	1	0	2	0	2	0	0	4.50
Chick Fulmer	2	5	0	0	0	0	0	1	0	0	2.57
		481	53	50	36	17	28	44	0	0	2.77

BALTIMORE   Cal McVey (20–13)   Tom Carey (14–9)   Newington Park

		G	AB	H	R	2B	3B	HR	RBI	BB	BA	SA
2B	Tom Carey	56	290	97	76	19	3	1	55	1	.344	.431
RF	Lip Pike	56	286	90	71	14	8	4	50	7	.315	.462
LF	Tom York	57	277	84	70	10	7	2	49	3	.303	.412
1B	Everett Mills	54	263	87	64	19	9	0	57	2	.331	.471
SS	John Radcliff	45	245	70	59	7	0	0	33	3	.286	.314
3B	Davy Force	49	234	86	77	8	1	0	31	2	.368	.410
C	Bill Craver	41	196	57	45	9	2	0	28	2	.291	.357
UT	Cal McVey	38	192	73	49	4	5	2	34	3	.380	.484
P	Candy Cummings	42	192	48	30	5	0	0	35	5	.250	.276
CF	George Hall	35	168	58	44	6	3	0	30	2	.345	.417
C	Scott Hastings	30	146	41	41	4	0	0	15	4	.281	.308
P	Asa Brainard	16	69	18	18	1	0	0	8	0	.261	.275
Sub	Bill Barrett	2	4	1	0	0	0	0	0	0	.250	.250
		57	2562	810	644	106	38	9	425	41	.316	.398

1B   Mills 53, McVey 3, Craver 3
2B   Carey 54, McVey 4, Pike 2, Hastings 1, Radcliff 1, Brainard 1
SS   Radcliff 23, Force 17, Craver·15, McVey 5, Carey 3, Barrett 1
3B   Force 34, Radcliff 24, Carey 4, McVey 2
OF   York 57, Pike 56, Hall 35, Hastings 12, Craver 7, McVey 6, Brainard 2, Barrett 1, Mills 1
C   McVey 25, Craver 22, Hastings 19
P   Cummings 42, Brainard 14, Force 3

	G	IP	GS	CG	W	L	K	BB	SH	SV	ERA
Candy Cummings	42	382	42	42	28	14	34	33	1	0	2.66
Asa Brainard	14	108.2	14	12	5	7	3	9	0	0	4.14
Davy Force	3	18	1	1	1	1	0	0	0	0	3.50
		508.2	57	55	34	32	37	42	1	0	3.01

NEW YORK   John Hatfield (11–17)   Joe Start (18–7)   Union Grounds (Brooklyn)

		G	AB	H	R	2B	3B	HR	RBI	BB	BA	SA
CF	Dave Eggler	53	268	90	82	13	4	0	34	5	.336	.414
3B	John Hatfield	52	255	78	54	5	6	2	45	3	.306	.396
1B	Joe Start	53	251	67	42	8	3	1	28	4	.267	.335
UT	Dick Higham	49	245	77	57	5	4	0	34	2	.314	.367
SS	Jim Holdsworth	53	233	75	46	4	8	0	28	0	.322	.408
LF	Count Gedney	53	224	60	41	5	5	1	25	7	.268	.348
P	Bobby Mathews	52	223	43	40	3	3	0	13	10	.193	.233
2B	Candy Nelson	36	168	55	28	4	1	0	22	1	.327	.363
RF	Phoney Martin	31	140	31	12	1	0	0	14	0	.221	.229
C	Nat Hicks	28	121	29	12	1	2	1	14	7	.240	.306
C	Doug Allison	12	48	10	6	0	0	0	3	2	.208	.208
Sub	Steve Bellan	7	32	7	4	2	0	0	3	1	.219	.281
Sub	Nealy Phelps	2	6	0	0	0	0	0	0	0	.000	.000
		53	2214	622	424	51	36	5	263	42	.281	.343

1B   Start 53, Nelson 1, Phelps 1
2B   Nelson 27, Higham 18, Hatfield 11, Bellan 3
SS   Holdsworth 53

3B   Hatfield 45, Bellan 7, Nelson 5, Eggler 1
OF   Eggler 53, Gedney 53, Martin 30, Higham 18, Nelson 6, Mathews 5, Start 2, Phelps 1,Hatfield 1, Allison 1
C   Hicks 28, Higham 17, Allison 11, Nelson 1
P   Mathews 52, Martin 6

	G	P	GS	CG	W	L	K	BB	SH	SV	ERA
Bobby Mathews	52	443	52	47	29	23	75	62	2	0	2.56
Phoney Martin	6	34	1	1	0	1	1	7	0	0	3.44
		477	53	48	29	24	76	69	2	0	2.62

PHILADELPHIA ATHLETICS   Dick McBride   Athletic Park

		G	AB	H	R	2B	3B	HR	RBI	BB	BA	SA
SS	Mike McGeary	52	275	83	63	8	1	0	31	1	.302	.338
1B	Cap Anson	52	254	101	53	9	2	0	36	5	.398	.449
P	Dick McBride	49	253	71	41	6	0	0	41	2	.281	.304
RF	Cherokee Fisher	51	253	66	50	4	3	1	35	4	.261	.312
3B	Ezra Sutton	51	242	81	51	7	6	0	33	2	.335	.413
LF	John McMullin	52	227	62	54	7	1	0	29	8	.273	.313
2B	Wes Fisler	44	218	75	44	11	4	1	42	2	.344	.445
C	John Clapp	45	204	62	36	10	2	1	28	2	.304	.387
CF	Tim Murnane	41	176	39	53	3	0	1	10	8	.222	.256
Sub	Count Sensenderfer	20	86	24	12	1	0	0	8	0	.279	.291
Sub	Al Reach	16	73	16	13	5	1	0	9	0	.219	.315
Sub	Joe Battin	1	5	3	4	0	0	0	2	1	.600	.600
		52	2266	683	474	71	20	4	304	35	.301	.356

1B   Anson 36, Murnane 10, Fisler 10, Fisher 1, Sensenderfer 1
2B   Fisler 36, Murnane 6, Reach 9, Anson 3, Fisher 3, Sutton 2, Clapp 1
SS   McGeary 44, Sutton 8, Clapp 6
3B   Sutton 43, Anson 11, McGeary 1
OF   McMullin 51, Fisher 45, Murnane 29, Sensenderfer 19, McBride 11, Reach 7, Anson 3, Battin 1, Clapp 1
C   Clapp 43, McGeary 13, Anson 3
P   McBride 46, Fisher 13, McMullin 1

	G	IP	GS	CG	W	L	K	BB	SH	SV	ERA
Dick McBride	46	382.2	46	38	24	19	25	47	**3**	0	3.32
Cherokee Fisher	13	84.1	5	5	3	4	14	10	0	2	**1.81**
John McMullin	1	8	1	1	1	0	2	1	0	0	2.25
		475	52	44	28	23	41	58	3	2	3.03

BROOKLYN   Bob Ferguson   Union Grounds

		G	AB	H	R	2B	3B	HR	RBI	BB	BA	SA
C	Tom Barlow	55	271	74	48	0	2	1	14	4	.273	.299
SS	Dickey Pearce	55	262	72	42	5	0	1	26	8	.275	.305
2B	Jack Burdock	55	245	62	56	7	1	2	36	7	.253	.314
P	Jim Britt	54	240	47	29	3	0	0	14	8	.196	.208
LF	Charlie Pabor	55	228	82	36	8	3	0	42	6	.360	.421
3B	Bob Ferguson	51	228	59	36	3	5	0	25	4	.259	.316
RF	Bill Boyd	48	227	63	31	5	4	1	31	3	.278	.348
1B	Dutch Dehlman	54	221	52	50	4	1	0	17	9	.235	.262
CF	Jack Remsen	50	207	61	29	4	6	1	29	2	.295	.386
Sub	Eddie Booth	16	70	14	8	3	1	0	8	2	.200	.271
Sub	Herm Doscher	1	6	1	1	0	0	0	1	0	.167	.167
Sub	Harry Kessler	1	5	1	0	0	0	0	1	0	.200	.200
		55	2210	588	366	42	23	6	244	53	.266	.314

1B	Dehlman 54, Kessler 1, Pearce 1
2B	Burdock 55, Pearce 1, Barlow 1
SS	Pearce 55, Dehlman 1, Barlow 1
3B	Ferguson 50, Boyd 8
OF	Pabor 55, Remsen 50, Boyd 43, Booth 16, Britt 3, Doscher 1
C	Barlow 55, Burdock 2
P	Britt 54, Ferguson 4

	G	IP	GS	CG	W	L	K	BB	SH	SV	ERA
Jim Britt	54	480.2	54	**51**	17	**36**	15	40	1	0	3.89
Bob Ferguson	4	19.1	1	1	0	1	0	2	0	0	6.05
		500	55	52	17	37	15	42	1	0	3.98

WASHINGTON   Nick Young   Olympic Grounds

		G	AB	H	R	2B	3B	HR	RBI	BB	BA	SA
1B	John Glenn	39	185	49	39	8	2	1	21	3	.265	.346
LF	Paul Hines	39	181	60	33	6	3	1	29	1	.331	.414
RF	Oscar Bielaski	38	173	49	35	3	2	0	23	4	.283	.323
2B	Tommy Beals	37	169	46	35	9	5	0	24	1	.272	.385
3B	Warren White	39	160	43	29	3	4	0	21	1	.269	.338
SS	Pete Donnelly	30	137	35	15	1	0	0	20	1	.255	.263
CF	Holly Hollingshead	30	136	35	25	2	2	0	22	0	.257	.301
P	Bill Stearns	32	133	24	22	0	0	0	8	4	.180	.180
C	Pop Snyder	28	108	21	16	2	0	0	4	3	.194	.213
Sub	Fred Waterman	15	80	28	20	1	1	0	12	1	.350	.388
Sub	Joe Gerhardt	13	56	12	6	3	0	0	7	0	.214	.268
P	? Greason	7	28	4	4	0	0	0	1	1	.143	.143
Sub	Ed Atkinson	2	8	0	2	0	0	0	0	0	.000	.000
Sub	Bob Reach	1	5	1	1	0	0	0	0	0	.200	.200
Sub	Howard Wall	1	4	1	1	0	0	0	0	0	.250	.250
		39	1563	408	283	38	19	2	192	19	.261	.313

1B	Glenn 39
2B	Beals 26, Donnelly 12, Hines 2, Hollingshead 2
SS	Donnelly 13, Gerhardt 13, Waterman 9, White 3, Reach 1, Wall 1
3B	White 37, Waterman 2, Donnelly 1
OF	Bielaski 38, Hines 36, Hollingshead 30, Donnelly 6, Waterman 4, Snyder 3, Atkinson 2, Beals 1
C	Snyder 28, Beals 13, Hines 1
P	Stearns 32, Greason 7

	G	IP	GS	CG	W	L	K	BB	SH	SV	ERA
Bill Stearns	32	283	32	32	7	25	4	15	0	0	4.55
? Greason	7	63	7	7	1	6	3	7	0	0	5.43
		346	39	39	8	31	7	22	0	0	4.71

ELIZABETH   Doug Allison   Waverly Fair Grounds

		G	AB	H	R	2B	3B	HR	RBI	BB	BA	SA
RF	Henry Austin	23	101	25	10	3	3	0	11	0	.248	.337
CF	Art Allison	23	99	32	12	2	0	0	11	0	.323	.343
2B	Frank Fleet	22	90	23	11	2	0	0	10	1	.256	.278
P	Hugh Campbell	22	87	13	9	0	1	0	6	1	.149	.172
C	Doug Allison	19	83	24	11	5	0	0	8	1	.289	.349
1B	Mike Campbell	21	83	12	9	0	0	0	3	2	.145	.145
LF	Eddie Booth	18	72	21	11	3	2	0	4	0	.292	.389
3B	? Nevins	13	53	11	7	1	2	0	2	1	.208	.302
Sub	Ben Laughlin	12	50	12	3	0	0	0	6	0	.240	.240
Sub	John Farrow	12	48	8	2	1	0	0	3	0	.167	.188
SS	Favel Wordsworth	12	42	10	5	0	0	0	3	2	.238	.238

		G	AB	H	R	2B	3B	HR	RBI	BB	BA	SA
Sub	Jim Clinton	9	38	9	5	1	0	0	4	0	.237	.263
Sub	Marty Swandell	2	9	1	1	0	0	0	1	0	.111	.111
P	Len Lovett	1	5	2	1	0	0	0	1	0	.400	.400
Sub	Fred Crane	1	4	1	0	0	0	0	1	0	.250	.250
P	Rynie Wolters	1	4	0	1	0	0	0	0	0	.000	.000
		23	868	204	98	18	8	0	74	8	.235	.274

1B   M. Campbell 18, A. Allison 3, Swandell 2, Fleet 1, Farrow 1
2B   Laughlin 12, Fleet 9, H. Campbell 1, Crane 1, Booth 1
SS   Wordsworth 11, Fleet 9, M. Campbell 3, Farrow 1, H. Campbell 1
3B   Nevins 12, Clinton 9, Fleet 2
OF   Austin 23, A. Allison 21, Booth 17, Farrow 3, D. Allison 2, Nevins 1, M. Campbell 1, H. Campbell 1, Wordsworth 1
C   D. Allison 18, Farrow 9, A. Allison 1
P   H. Campbell 19, Fleet 3. Wolters 1, Lovett 1

	G	IP	GS	CG	W	L	K	BB	SH	SV	ERA
Hugh Campbell	19	165	18	18	2	16	5	7	0	0	2.85
Frank Fleet	3	24	3	2	0	3	1	0	0	0	5.62
Rynie Wolters	1	9	1	1	0	1	1	1	0	0	0.00
Len Lovett	1	9	0	0	0	1	1	1	0	0	7.00
		207	**23**	**22**	2	21	8	9	0	0	3.22

MARYLAND   **Bill Smith**   **Madison Avenue Grounds**

		G	AB	H	R	2B	3B	HR	RBI	BB	BA	SA
3B	Harry Kohler	6	25	3	1	0	0	0	0	0	.120	.120
UT	John Smith	5	23	4	2	1	0	0	1	0	.174	.217
1B	Bill Lennon	5	19	4	2	0	0	0	2	0	.211	.211
CF	Bill Smith	6	19	2	2	0	0	0	1	0	.105	.105
UT	Bill French	6	18	4	3	0	0	0	1	0	.222	.222
P	Ed Stratton	4	16	2	2	0	0	0	0	0	.125	.125
2B	Marty Simpson	4	15	2	4	0	0	0	2	0	.133	.133
Sub	Mike Hooper	3	14	3	3	1	0	0	2	0	.214	.286
SS	Lew Say	3	12	2	1	0	0	0	2	0	.167	.167
Sub	John Sheppard	3	11	0	1	0	0	0	0	0	.000	.000
Sub	Joe Kernan	2	8	3	1	0	0	0	1	0	.375	.375
Sub	Red Woodhead	1	5	0	1	0	0	0	0	0	.000	.000
Sub	? Jones	1	4	3	0	0	0	0	1	0	.750	.750
P	? McDoolan	1	4	0	1	0	0	0	0	0	.000	.000
Sub	Wally Goldsmith	1	4	0	0	0	0	0	0	0	.000	.000
Sub	Tom Johns	1	4	0	0	0	0	0	0	0	.000	.000
Sub	George Popplein	1	4	0	0	0	0	0	0	0	.000	.000
P	Frank Selman	1	3	1	1	0	0	0	0	0	.333	.333
Sub	? Eland	1	3	0	0	0	0	0	0	0	.000	.000
		6	211	33	26	1	0	0	14	0	.156	.161

1B   Lennon 4, French 2, Kohler 1
2B   Simpson 3, Kernan 1, Goldsmith 1, B. Smith 1
SS   J. Smith 3, Say 2, Woodhead 1, Popplein 1
3B   Kohler 6, Lennon 1, French 1
OF   B. Smith 3, J. Smith 2, French 2, Sheppard 2, Hooper 2, Johns 1, Kernan 1, Say 1, Stratton 1, Popplein 1, Eland 1, Jones 1, Kohler 1
C   B. Smith 2, Sheppard 1, Hooper 1, Simpson 1, Kohler 1, Lennon 1
P   Stratton 3, Selman 1, McDoolan 1, French 1

	G	P	GS	CG	W	L	K	BB	SH	SV	ERA
Ed Stratton	3	27	3	3	0	3	0	1	0	0	8.33
Frank Selman	1	9	1	1	0	1	0	0	0	0	8.00
Bill French	1	9	1	1	0	1	0	0	0	0	12.00
? McDoolan	1	9	1	1	0	1	0	0	0	0	3.00
		54	6	6	0	6	0	1	0	0	8.00

1874
THE MUTUALS CHALLENGE
BOSTON'S REIGN

Prior to the 1874 season National Association officials reluctantly acknowledged that the reputation of their product had been tainted by constant charges of "Hippodroming" or dumping games. As a result, they passed a rule prohibiting players, umpires and official scorers from betting on the outcome of an NA game in which they participated. Any violation could result in permanent expulsion. Unfortunately, this rule lacked teeth.

An even more revolutionary rule change was proposed by Henry Chadwick in 1874. Chadwick wanted baseball to become a 10-man, 10-inning game and was vexed when his notion was rejected. However, the NA did endorse several more moderate revisions of the playing rules. As of 1874, a batter was required to stand within a space six feet long and three feet wide rather than astride a line through home plate. This represented the first use of the current batter's box, but in other ways the game was still very much in an experimental stage. Also in 1874, the rulebook defined two separate kinds of unfair pitches: Balls and Wide Balls. A Ball was a pitch that crossed the plate but was not within the batter's chosen high or low strike zone; a Wide Ball was a pitch that missed the plate. A batter needed to receive either three Wide Balls or nine Balls before being given his base. Since neither the first Ball nor the first Wide Ball was called by an umpire, a batter might look at as many as 13 unfair deliveries before he finally earned a base on balls.

Yet, while the rulebook remained in flux, the Boston Red Stockings continued to seem immutable. In 1874, Harry Wright added only two new ingredients to his two-time pennant winner. Tommy Beals left Washington to fill the substitute's slot and George Hall came from Baltimore to replace Wright's own aging legs in center field. In addition, Cal McVey returned from a year's exile in Baltimore to take over Bob Addy's right field post.

Boston's chief rivals in 1873, the Philadelphia White Stockings, were not so lucky. Chicago, returning to the big-league arena for the first time since the great fire in 1871, looted the White Stockings of six regulars: Jimmy Wood, Levi Meyerle, George Zettlein, Jim Devlin, Fergy Malone and Ned Cuthbert. An infection that forced the amputation of his right leg abruptly ended Wood's playing career, but the other five combined with three veteran acquisitions—Davy Force, John Glenn and Paul Hines—and rookie shortstop John Peters to make the revived Chicago club the preseason choice of many to dethrone Boston.

Hartford fielded the NA's only other new entry in 1874. Following Chicago's example, the Connecticut franchise gathered experienced NA players to fill its ranks. But whereas Chicago skimmed off the cream, Hartford emerged with only one bonafide star: Lip Pike. The NA's top slugger in its early years, Pike joined the mass exodus of the financially strapped Baltimore team's ensemble, leaving the Canaries without a single returning regular from 1873's third-place finisher. The Philadelphia White Stockings, similarly besieged by rival clubs, changed their nickname to the Pearls (corresponding with a change in hosiery), and attracted enough new talent to remain competitive in 1874. But Baltimore had no such recourse. By any name, the Maryland club was dead before the season began.

In 1874 action started slowly in every NA locality due to poor weather. The many postponements in the early going kept the better NA teams from demonstrating their class, but nothing could hide Baltimore's weakness. At one point in May the Canaries lost nine straight games in which they were outscored 160 to 39. By mid-July, with the weather improved, Boston sat atop the NA standings, as expected, with a 30–8 mark. The Philadelphia Athletics were second at 23–10.

The two leaders then did something unprecedented in professional sports history. They took an eight-week sabbatical and journeyed to England, where they played a string of exhibition games to promote baseball among the British. The tour was neither an esthetic nor a financial success. Furthermore, it severely impaired Boston's chances for a third straight pennant. During the stretch from July 16 to September 9, while Boston and the Athletics were abroad, the New York Mutuals shot into contention by wreaking havoc on the NA's lesser lights. In the process the Mutuals managed to squelch accusations that they had thrown a game to Chicago on August 5.

The Philadelphia Pearls, similarly charged, were less successful. On September 8, after heated debate, the Pearls' stockholders voted to expel shortstop John Radcliff for

Jack Manning, the lone bright light for Baltimore in 1874. He led the last-place Canaries in runs, BA, winning percentage and ERA.

A GOLD BOND PERFORMANCE

As late as 1874, a professional audience had yet to see a no-hit game. On October 19, less than two weeks before the season ended, some 500 fans at Brooklyn's Union Grounds nearly witnessed the first such masterpiece in major league history when Tommy Bond of the Atlantics stifled the bats of the New York Mutuals through

the first eight innings of play. The eighteen-year-old rookie began the ninth frame by easily retiring Dick Higham and Doug Allison. With only one more out between him and immortality, Bond faced Joe Start. The lefty-hitting Mutuals' first sacker took Bond the opposite way, slapping a pitch to left field that fell in for a double. His no-hit bid ended, Bond then nearly lost his shutout, surrendering a single that moved Start to third before he got the last out on a deep fly to Jack Chapman in right field.

Bond's 5–0 blanking of the Mutuals was but one of 22 wins in his rookie season, making him the youngest 20-game winner in major league history to that point. Two years later, in the National League's maiden season, Bond notched 31 wins at age 20 to become the youngest 30-game winner ever. He went on to collect 221 wins before he reached his twenty-fifth birthday, but had only 13 more victories after that.

Tommy Bond.

betting $350 against his own team in a game with Chicago. According to the NA's new antigambling rule, Radcliff's expulsion ought to have been permanent. In fact, it lasted only the balance of the 1874 season; by the following spring Radcliff was back in uniform with Philadelphia's newest NA entry, the Centennials.

On September 24, following an 8–5 win over Boston, the Mutuals had 34 victories to the Red Stockings' 32 and owned first place. By October 9 the Red Stockings had knotted the race again at 39 wins apiece but held a substantial edge since they had played five fewer games than the Mutuals. Henry Chadwick continued to hold to his prediction of a few days earlier, saying: "If [the Mutuals] keep playing like they have in September, and Boston shows no improvement, the Mutuals will succeed."

The 1874 Philadelphia Athletics. Top: Count Gedney, Mike McGeary, Tim Murnane, Cap Anson and Joe Battin. Middle: Wes Fisler, Count Sensenderfer, Dick McBride, John Clapp and John McMullin. Front: Ezra Sutton and Al Reach.

DENNY MACK

At first base for the Philadelphia Pearls in 56 of their 58 1874 championship games was Denny Mack. After three years of alternating between the first sack and several other positions, Mack finally seemed to have found his niche as a gateway guardian, only to lose it when he hit just .206.

Mack returned to the majors two years later in the National League's inaugural season—but as a shortstop. Many men have gravitated to first base after launching their careers as middle infielders, but Mack and Jackie Robinson are the only two men in major league history to have become regulars at one of the two middle infield positions after debuting as first sackers.

Cal McVey, the NA pacesetter in hits and runs in 1874. An outstanding batsmen, he was also amazingly versatile, capable of playing every position.

But Boston suddenly did show dramatic improvement. In the final three weeks of the season, the Red Stockings went 13–3 while the Mutuals were winning just two of their last six games. When the curtain finally closed on November 1, Boston had 10 more victories than the Mutuals. A tight race had once again been broken wide open in the final lap, this time by Wright's best team yet. Even with star second baseman Ross Barnes hampered by a broken hand for much of the season, Boston still dominated the batting leaders charts. Led by Cal McVey, the Red Stockings had the top five run-makers in the NA. Among them was Al Spalding, who also notched all 52 of Boston's wins and finished high among the leaders in every central pitching department as well.

THE SEASONAL RECORD

	G	W	L	PCT	H*	R	GB
Boston Red Stockings	71	52	18	.743	26–8	26–10	—
New York Mutuals	65	42	23	.646	30–10	12–23	7.5
Philadelphia Athletics	55	33	22	.600	25–9	8–13	11.5
Philadelphia Pearls	58	29	29	.500	16 14	13–15	17
Chicago White Stockings	59	28	31	.475	18–10	10–21	18.5
Brooklyn Atlantics	56	22	33	.400	15–13	7–20	22.5
Hartford Dark Blues	53	16	37	.302	13–17	3–20	27.5
Baltimore Canaries	47	9	38	.191	7–13	2–25	31.5

*Beginning in 1874, Home-Road records are calculated according to which team was the home team regardless of where the game was played.

	Bos	NY	Ath	Phi	Chi	Atl	Har	Bal	
Boston	—	5	8	8	7	6	9	9	52
New York	5	—	4	1	9	7	8	8	42
Athletics	2	6	—	9	3	6	5	2	33
Pearls	2	5	1	—	7	6	4	4	29
Chicago	3	1	4	3	—	4	4	9	28
Brooklyn	4	3	1	3	3	—	5	3	22
Hartford	1	2	2	4	1	3	—	3	16
Baltimore	1	1	2	1	1	1	2	—	9
	18	23	22	29	31	33	37	38	231

SEASON LEADERS

Batting Average (160 ABs)

1.	Meyerle, Chicago	.394
2.	McVey, Boston	.359
3.	Pike, Hartford	.355
4.	Manning, Balt–Hartford	.346
	McMullin, Athletics	.346

On–Base Percentage

1.	Meyerle, Chicago	.401
2.	Pike, Hartford	.368
3.	McMullin, Athletics	.366
4.	McVey, Boston	.360
	Barnes, Boston	.360

Home Runs

1.	O'Rourke, Boston	5
2.	McVey, Boston	3
	D. White, Boston	3
	Clapp, Athletics	3
5.	Six tied with 2	

HITS

1.	McVey, Boston	123
2.	Spalding, Boston	119
3.	Leonard, Boston	108
4.	D. White, Boston	106
5.	O'Rourke, Boston	104

Bases on Balls

1.	Nelson, New York	9
2.	Barnes, Boston	8
	McMullin, Athletics	8
4.	Four tied with 7	

Slugging Average

1.	Pike, Hartford	.504
2.	Craver, Pearls	.498
3.	Meyerle, Chicago	.488
4.	McVey, Boston	.481
5.	G. Wright, Boston	.476

Total Bases

1.	McVey, Boston	165
2.	O'Rourke, Boston	150
3.	G. Wright, Boston	149
4.	D. White, Boston	134
	Leonard, Boston	134
	Spalding, Boston	134

RBI

1.	McVey, Boston	71
	O'Rourke, Boston	71
3.	Craver, Pearls	56
4.	Spalding, Boston	54
5.	D. White, Boston	52

RUNS

1.	McVey, Boston	91
2.	O'Rourke, Boston	82
3.	Spalding, Boston	80
4.	G. Wright, Boston	76
5.	D. White, Boston	75

Stolen Bases (Data Incomplete)

1.	Craver, Pearls	11
	O'Rourke, Boston	11
	Leonard, Boston	11
4.	McGeary, Athletics	10
5.	Barlow, Hartford	9

PITCHING

Wins

1.	Spalding, Boston	52
2.	Mathews, New York	42
3.	McBride, Athletics	33
4.	Cummings, Pearls	28
5.	Zettlein, Chicago	27

Losses

1.	Bond, Brooklyn	32
2.	Zettlein, Chicago	30
3.	Cummings, Pearls	26
4.	Fisher, Hartford	23
5.	McBride, Athletics	22
	Mathews, New York	22
	Brainard, Baltimore	22

Innings

1.	Spalding, Boston	617.1
2.	Mathews, New York	578
3.	Zettlein, Chicago	515.2
4.	Bond, Brooklyn	497
5.	McBride, Athletics	487

Strikeouts

1.	Mathews, New York	100
2.	Cummings, Pearls	61
3.	Bond, Brooklyn	39
4.	McBride, Athletics	36

ERA (60 innings)

1.	McBride, Athletics	1.64
2.	Mathews, New York	1.88
3.	Spalding, Boston	1.92
4.	Cummings, Pearls	1.96
5.	Bond, Brooklyn	2.03

Complete Games

1.	Spalding, Boston	65
2.	Mathews, New York	62
3.	Zettlein, Chicago	57
4.	McBride, Athletics	55
	Bond, Brooklyn	55

Winning Percentage (25 decisions)

1.	Spalding, Boston	.765
2.	Mathews, New York	.656
3.	McBride, Athletics	.600
4.	Cummings, Pearls	.519
5.	Others all below	.500

Lowest On–Base Percentage

1.	McBride, Athletics	.251
2.	Bond, Brooklyn	.268
3.	Mathews, New York	.273
4.	Manning, Baltimore	.276
5.	Spalding, Boston	.278

FIELDING

Total Chances

1B	O'Rourke, Boston	813
2B	Craver, Pearls	388
3B	Schafer, Boston	396
SS	G. Wright, Boston	358
OF	Ryan, Baltimore	210
C	Hicks, Pearls	389
P	Spalding, Boston	212

Fielding Average

Start, New York	.961
Barnes, Boston	.856
Burdock, New York	.820
Pearce, Brooklyn	.845
Eggler, Pearls	.906
McGeary, Athletics	.837
Spalding, Boston	.854

BOSTON **Harry Wright** **South End Grounds**

		G	AB	H	R	2B	3B	HR	RBI	BB	BA	SA
P	Al Spalding	71	**362**	119	80	15	1	0	54	3	.329	.370
C	Deacon White	70	353	106	75	5	7	3	52	4	.300	.380
RF	Cal McVey	70	343	**123**	**91**	21	6	3	71	1	.359	.481
LF	Andy Leonard	71	339	108	68	18	4	0	51	2	.319	.395
1B	Jim O'Rourke	70	331	104	82	15	7	5	61	4	.314	.453
3B	Harry Schafer	71	327	87	69	10	2	1	45	1	.266	.318
SS	George Wright	60	313	103	76	10	**15**	2	44	5	.329	.476
2B	Ross Barnes	51	259	88	72	12	4	0	41	8	.340	.417
UT	George Hall	47	222	64	58	10	8	1	32	1	.288	.419
CF	Harry Wright	40	184	58	44	4	2	2	27	4	.315	.391
Sub	Tommy Beals	19	97	19	20	3	4	0	17	0	.196	.309
		71	3130	**979**	**735**	**121**	**61**	**17**	**495**	33	**.313**	**.407**

1B	O'Rourke 70, White 1
2B	Barnes 51, Beals 12, Leonard 11, White 1
SS	G. Wright 60, Leonard 11, Schafer 1
3B	Schafer 71, G. Wright 1
OF	McVey 57, Leonard 51, Hall 47, H. Wright 40, White 21, Beals 9, Spalding 6, Barnes 1
C	White 58, McVey 23
P	Spalding 71, H. Wright 6

	G	IP	GS	CG	W	L	K	BB	SH	SV	ERA
Al Spalding	**71**	617.1	**69**	**65**	**52**	16	30	19	**4**	0	1.92
Harry Wright	6	16.2	2	0	0	2	0	4	0	**3**	2.16
		634	71	**65**	52	18	30	23	**4**	**3**	1.93

NEW YORK   Tom Carey (13–12) Dick Higham (29–11)   Union Grounds (Brooklyn)

		G	AB	H	R	2B	3B	HR	RBI	BB	BA	SA
C	Dick Higham	65	331	87	58	14	3	1	37	4	.261	.332
RF	Doug Allison	65	318	90	68	7	5	0	28	6	.283	.336
1B	Joe Start	63	306	96	67	13	3	2	45	4	.314	.395
P	Bobby Mathews	65	298	72	46	6	1	0	30	3	.242	.268
2B	Candy Nelson	65	297	73	55	7	5	0	32	9	.246	.303
LF	John Hatfield	63	292	66	47	12	1	0	30	7	.226	.274
SS	Tom Carey	64	286	82	56	10	3	1	39	2	.287	.353
CF	Jack Remsen	64	284	65	52	9	3	2	37	0	.229	.303
3B	Jack Burdock	61	273	75	45	11	4	1	27	1	.275	.355
Sub	Nealy Phelps	6	24	5	3	0	0	0	2	0	.125	.125
Sub	Billy Geer	2	8	2	0	0	0	0	1	0	.250	.250
Sub	Dan Patterson	1	5	2	1	0	0	0	2	0	.400	.400
Sub	Orator Shaffer	1	5	1	1	0	0	0	0	0	.200	.200
		65	2729	714	501	89	28	7	310	**36**	.262	.322

1B Start 63, Remsen 1, Hatfield 1, Patterson 1
2B Nelson 51, Carey 13, Higham 1, Allison 1
SS Carey 51, Nelson 14, Hatfield 1
3B Burdock 60, Hatfield 7, Mathews 1
OF Remsen 63, Hatfield 58, Allison 47 Higham 33, Phelps 6, Burdock 3, Geer 2, Start 2, Patterson 1, Shaffer 1, Mathews 1, Nelson 1
C   Higham 48, Allison 34
P   Mathews 65, Hatfield 3

	G	IP	GS	CG	W	L	K	BB	SH	SV	ERA
Bobby Mathews	65	578	65	62	42	22	**100**	41	4	0	1.88
John Hatfield	3	8	0	0	0	1	0	0	0	0	2.25
		586	65	62	42	23	**100**	41	4	0	1.89

PHILADELPHIA ATHLETICS   Dick McBride   Athletic Park

		G	AB	H	R	2B	3B	HR	RBI	BB	BA	SA
SS	Mike McGeary	54	271	87	61	10	2	0	22	1	.321	.373
P	Dick McBride	55	263	57	30	7	1	0	34	1	.217	.251
CF	John McMullin	55	260	90	61	10	2	2	32	8	.346	.423
1B	Cap Anson	55	259	87	51	8	3	0	37	4	.336	.390
3B	Ezra Sutton	55	243	71	54	10	3	0	28	0	.292	.358
2B	Joe Battin	51	226	52	40	11	1	0	27	1	.230	.288
LF	Count Gedney	54	222	61	49	4	1	1	34	7	.275	.315
1B	Wes Fisler	37	180	59	26	12	1	0	22	0	.328	.406
C	John Clapp	39	165	48	46	7	4	3	20	1	.291	.436
RF	Tim Murnane	21	81	17	11	2	0	0	11	1	.207	.231
Sub	Al Reach	14	55	7	8	2	0	0	2	0	.127	.164
Sub	Tom Miller	4	16	8	1	0	0	0	5	0	.500	.500
Sub	Count Sensenderfer	5	16	3	3	0	0	0	2	0	.188	.188
		55	2258	647	441	83	18	6	276	24	.287	.347

1B Fisler 28, Anson 24, Gedney 4, Murnane 3
2B Battin 41, Fisler 9, Murnane 6
SS McGeary 26, Sutton 20, Anson 6, Battin 5, Clapp 1
3B Sutton 36, Anson 20
OF McMullin 55, Gedney 51, Clapp 15, Reach 14, Murnane 14, Anson 8, Battin 7, Sensenderfer 5, McGeary 4, Fisler 1, Miller 1
C McGeary 28, Clapp 27, Miller 4, Anson 1
P McBride 55

	G	IP	GS	CG	W	L	K	BB	SH	SV	ERA
Dick McBride	55	487	55	55	33	22	36	32	0	0	1.64

PHILADELPHIA PEARLS   Nat Hicks   Athletic Park

		G	AB	H	R	2B	3B	HR	RBI	BB	BA	SA
CF	Dave Eggler	58	299	95	70	13	8	0	31	5	.318	.415
3B	Jim Holdsworth	57	285	97	60	8	9	0	37	1	.340	.432
2B	Bill Craver	55	265	91	68	19	11	0	56	4	.343	.498
C	Nat Hicks	58	266	73	51	8	1	0	30	5	.274	.312
SS	Chic Fulmer	57	258	72	49	3	2	0	37	2	.279	.306
1B	Denny Mack	56	246	51	48	8	4	0	22	2	.207	.272
P	Candy Cummings	54	231	52	32	4	2	0	19	0	.225	.260
LF	Tom York	50	224	56	36	4	7	0	37	5	.250	.330
RF	George Bechtel	32	151	42	29	4	5	1	34	2	.278	.391
Sub	John Radcliff	23	103	25	20	7	0	1	14	2	.243	.340
Sub	Charlie Pabor	17	77	17	11	0	1	0	1	0	.221	.247
Sub	John Donnelly	6	22	5	2	0	0	0	2	0	.227	.227
Sub	? Quinlan	1	4	1	0	0	0	0	1	0	.250	.250
Sub	Ed McKenna	1	4	0	0	0	0	0	0	0	.000	.000
		58	2435	677	476	78	50	2	321	28	.278	.354

1B Mack 56, Radcliff 2, McKenna 1, Craver 1, Holdsworth 1
2B Craver 54, Radcliff 4, Eggler 2, Holdsworth 2, Donnelly 1, Hicks 1
SS Fulmer 32, Holdsworth 21, Radcliff 3, Donnelly 2, Quinlan 1
3B Holdsworth 31, Fulmer 25, Radcliff 3
OF Eggler 56, York 50, Bechtel 28, Pabor 17, Radcliff 15, Holdsworth 6, Hicks 4, Donnelly 3, Cummings 1
C Hicks 57, Craver 5
P Cummings 54, Bechtel 6

	G	IP	GS	CG	W	L	K	BB	SH	SV	ERA
Candy Cummings	54	483	54	52	28	26	61	18	3	0	1.96
George Bechtel	6	39	4	4	1	3	0	1	0	0	1.63
		522	58	56	29	29	61	19	3	0	1.93

CHICAGO   Fergie Malone (18–18)   Jimmy Wood (10–13)   23rd Street Grounds

		G	AB	H	R	2B	3B	HR	RBI	BB	BA	SA
3B	Davy Force	59	294	92	61	9	0	0	26	3	.313	.344
LF	Ned Cuthbert	58	295	79	65	6	1	2	22	5	.268	.315
CF	Paul Hines	59	271	80	47	10	2	0	34	4	.295	.347
2B	Levi Meyerle	53	254	100	65	19	1	1	47	3	**.394**	.488
P	George Zettlein	57	244	47	26	7	0	0	18	1	.193	.221
SS	John Peters	55	239	69	39	10	0	1	25	2	.289	.343
1B	John Glenn	55	237	67	33	9	0	0	33	5	.283	.321
C	Fergy Malone	47	223	56	33	5	0	0	29	4	.251	.274
1B	Jim Devlin	45	203	58	26	5	0	0	27	2	.286	.310
RF	Fred Treacey	35	148	28	18	5	0	0	12	2	.189	.230
Sub	? Gilroy	8	38	8	4	1	0	0	7	1	.211	.237
P	Dan Collins	3	12	1	1	1	0	0	0	0	.083	.167
Sub	Terry Connell	1	4	0	0	0	0	0	0	0	.000	.000
		59	2462	685	418	87	4	4	280	32	.278	.322

1B   Glenn 37, Devlin 24
2B   Meyerle 31, Peters 19, Hines 11
SS   Peters 36, Force 18, Meyerle 5, Hines 2, Collins 1
3B   Force 42, Meyerle 14, Devlin 5
OF   Cuthbert 55, Hines 50, Treacey 35, Glenn 19, Devlin 17, Meyerle 5, Collins 2, Force 1
C   Malone 47, Gilroy 8, Cuthbert 4, Connell 1
P   Zettlein 57, Collins 2, Force 1

	G	IP	GS	CG	W	L	K	BB	SH	SV	ERA
George Zettlein	57	515.2	57	57	27	30	26	43	3	0	2.42
Dan Collins	2	11	2	1	1	1	0	2	0	0	4.91
Davy Force	1	7	0	0	0	0	0	0	0	0	15.43
		533.2	59	58	28	31	26	45	3	0	2.65

BROOKLYN ATLANTICS   Bob Ferguson   Union Grounds

		G	AB	H	R	2B	3B	HR	RBI	BB	BA	SA
SS	Dickey Pearce	56	255	75	48	1	0	0	25	76	.294	.298
3B	Bob Ferguson	56	245	64	34	4	0	0	18	2	.261	.278
P	Tommy Bond	55	245	54	25	10	1	0	20	1	.220	.269
RF	Jack Chapman	53	242	64	32	10	2	0	25	4	.264	.322
1B	Dutch Dehlman	53	216	49	40	3	1	0	18	7	.225	.248
LF	Eddie Booth	44	187	47	24	4	3	1	16	3	.254	.324
CF	Bobby Clack	33	135	23	22	1	0	0	13	4	.170	.178
C	John Farrow	27	122	26	16	3	0	0	10	1	.213	.238
C	Frank Fleet	22	97	22	18	0	0	0	10	1	.227	.227
C	Jake Knowdell	24	86	12	8	1	1	0	3	1	.140	.175
Sub	Charlie Hodes	21	81	12	8	3	0	0	7	0	.148	.185
Sub	Pat McGee	16	65	11	4	1	0	0	6	0	.169	.185
Sub	Henry Kessler	14	56	17	8	1	0	0	4	0	.304	.321
Sub	Charlie Sweasy	10	44	5	4	1	0	0	3	0	.114	.136
2B	Billy West	9	35	8	4	1	0	0	2	1	.229	.257
Sub	Al Martin	7	29	4	1	0	0	0	1	0	.138	.138
Sub	Jim Clinton	2	11	2	3	1	0	0	2	0	.182	.273
Sub	Jim Hall	2	9	1	0	0	0	0	0	0	.111	.111
Sub	Mike Ledwith	1	4	1	1	0	0	0	1	0	.250	.250
Sub	? Gavern	1	4	0	1	0	0	0	0	0	.000	.000
Sub	Charlie Snow	1	1	1	0	0	0	0	0	0	1.000	1.000
		56	2169	498	301	45	8	1	184	31	.230	.259

1B   Dehlman 53, Clack 2, Chapman 1, Hodes 1
2B   Farrow 12, Fleet 11, Sweasy 10, West 9, Martin 6, Kessler 4, Hodes 3, Hall 2, McGee 1, Clinton 1, Gavern 1, Booth 1, Pearce 1
SS   Pearce 56, McGee 2, West 1
3B   Ferguson 55, Pearce 2, Kessler 1
OF   Chapman 53, Booth 44, Clack 31, Hodes 19, McGee 15, Knowdell 4, Kessler 4, Farrow 3, Martin 1, Clinton 1, Fleet 1, Hall 1, Snow 1
C   Knowdell 21, Farrow 16, Fleet 13, Kessler 9, Hodes 3, Ferguson 2, Ledwith 1
P   Bond 55, Ferguson 1

	G	IP	GS	CG	W	L	K	BB	SH	SV	ERA
Tommy Bond	55	497	55	55	22	32	39	8	1	0	2.03
Bob Ferguson	1	9	1	1	0	1	0	3	0	0	4.00
		506	56	56	22	33	39	**11**	1	0	2.06

HARTFORD   Lip Pike   Hartford Baseball Grounds

		G	AB	H	R	2B	3B	HR	RBI	BB	BA	SA
C	Scott Hastings	52	246	80	60	11	2	0	29	5	.325	.386
P	Cherokee Fisher	52	241	54	28	7	0	0	28	2	.224	.253
1B	Everett Mills	53	243	69	39	6	1	0	17	4	.284	.317
CF	Lip Pike	52	234	83	58	**22**	5	1	51	5	.355	**.504**
2B	Bob Addy	50	213	51	25	9	2	0	23	1	.239	.300
LF	Jim Tipper	45	197	60	36	8	0	0	20	1	.305	.345
RF	Billy Barnie	45	190	35	21	4	2	0	19	1	.184	.226
SS	Tom Barlow	32	156	46	37	4	1	0	10	0	.295	.333
P	Bill Stearns	33	132	21	16	1	0	0	9	7	.159	.167
3B	Bill Boyd	26	117	41	22	8	4	0	20	1	.350	.487
3B	Steve Brady	27	118	37	19	5	1	0	14	2	.314	.373
Sub	Orator Shaffer	9	35	8	6	0	0	1	3	0	.229	.314
Sub	Jack Farrell	3	13	5	3	0	0	0	0	1	.385	.385
Sub	Jack Manning	1	5	1	1	0	0	0	0	0	.200	.200
Sub	Fancy O'Neal	1	3	0	0	0	0	0	0	0	.000	.000
		53	2143	591	371	85	18	2	243	30	.276	.335

1B   Mills 53
2B   Addy 45, Pike 7, Hastings 1
SS   Barlow 32, Pike 20, Fisher 2, Barnie 1, Addy 1, Brady 1, Hastings 1
3B   Boyd 25, Brady 16, Fisher 7, Addy 5, Manning 1, Pike 1
OF   Tipper 45, Barnie 29, Pike 27, Hastings 26, Stearns 19, Fisher 14, Brady 11, Shaffer 9, Farrell 3, O'Neal 1, Boyd 1
C   Hastings 39, Barnie 29
P   Fisher 39, Stearns 22

	G	IP	GS	CG	W	L	K	BB	SH	SV	ERA
Cherokee Fisher	39	322.1	35	31	13	23	20	13	0	0	2.26
Bill Stearns	22	158.2	18	14	3	14	14	14	0	1	3.01
		481	53	45	16	37	34	27	0	1	2.51

BALTIMORE   **Warren White**   **Newington Park**

		G	AB	H	R	2B	3B	HR	RBI	BB	BA	SA
3B	Warren White	45	212	57	21	1	0	0	18	1	.269	.274
CF	Harry Deane	47	203	50	29	8	1	0	13	5	.246	.296
P	Asa Brainard	47	196	47	19	3	0	0	8	2	.240	.255
RF	Oscar Bielaski	43	187	45	24	0	0	0	8	2	.241	.241
LF	Johnny Ryan	47	182	35	29	8	1	0	19	5	.192	.247
2B	Jack Manning	42	174	61	32	8	2	0	18	2	.351	.420
C	Pop Snyder	39	151	33	24	4	0	1	17	1	.219	.265
1B	Charlie Gould	33	143	32	20	6	0	0	14	2	.224	.266
SS	Lew Say	18	66	14	4	3	0	0	5	0	.212	.258
SS	Joe Gerhardt	14	61	19	10	0	1	0	6	0	.311	.344
Sub	Frank Selman	12	54	16	9	3	2	0	5	0	.296	.426
1B	Zach Taylor	13	48	12	3	0	0	0	3	0	.250	.250
Sub	Charlie Sweasy	8	33	8	2	0	0	0	4	2	.242	.242
Sub	John Smith	6	21	4	1	1	0	0	1	0	.190	.238
Sub	? Brown	2	9	0	0	0	0	0	0	0	.000	.000
Sub	L. Jones	2	7	1	0	0	0	0	1	0	.143	.143
Sub	Bill Smiley	2	7	0	0	0	0	0	0	0	.000	.000
Sub	? Wood	1	5	0	0	0	0	0	0	0	.000	.000
Sub	Henry Kohler	2	4	0	0	0	0	0	0	0	.000	.000
Sub	Hugh Reed	1	4	0	0	0	0	0	0	0	.000	.000
Sub	Henry Reville	1	4	0	0	0	0	0	0	0	.000	.000
Sub	Fred Boardman	1	4	1	0	0	0	0	0	0	.250	.250
Sub	Lew Carl	1	3	0	0	0	0	0	0	0	.000	.000
		47	1778	435	227	45	7	1	140	22	.245	.280

1B	Gould 32, Taylor 13, Kohler 2, Bielaski 1, Manning 1
2B	Manning 21, Brainard 20, Sweasy 8, Selman 2, Deane 2, Wood 1, Bielaski 1
SS	Say 18, Gerhardt 14, Selman 6, Smith 6, Manning 4, Brown 2, Deane 1, Kohler 1
3B	White 45, Smiley 2, Selman 1, Manning 1
OF	Ryan 47, Deane 46, Bielaski 42, Brainard 2, Smith 1, Reed 1, Reville 1, Boardman 1, Selman 1, Sweasy 1, Jones 1, Manning 1
C	Snyder 39, Selman 6, White 2, Carl 1, Gould 1, Jones 1
P	Brainard 30, Manning 22, Ryan 1

	G	IP	GS	CG	W	L	K	BB	SH	SV	ERA
Asa Brainard	30	240	27	25	5	22	8	27	0	0	3.68
Jack Manning	22	176.2	20	18	4	16	11	11	0	0	2.04
Johnny Ryan	1	3.1	0	0	0	0	0	0	0	0	16.20
		420	47	43	9	38	19	38	0	0	3.09

1875

BOSTON ROLLS TO A FOURTH
STRAIGHT FLAG

In the spring of 1875 groundskeepers in National Association ballparks had a choice. They could either dig up home plate and relocate it, or, they could redesign the foul lines. For a new rule that season required home plate to be situated entirely in foul territory. This rule change, which bade an umpire call a ball foul that first struck the plate regardless of where it went from there, was devised in the hope of reducing the number of fair-foul hits but failed in its intent.

The many umpires and players who had only just begun to digest the difference between a Ball and a Wide Ball were unnerved when the 1874 rule change pertaining to unfair pitches was abandoned and a batter was once again awarded first base after three called Balls (really nine unfair pitches), but their distress was mild compared to what sportswriters like Henry Chadwick felt in the spring of 1875. After a season in which only eight teams vied for the NA pennant, and all but Baltimore (which folded on October 16) were still in the chase at the finish, Chadwick foresaw disaster when six new teams ponied up the necessary $10 to join the NA. The half dozen newcomers swelled the NA's membership to 13, both an unwieldy and an unlucky number, as events would prove.

The interlopers were evenly divided between the east and the west. Comprising the eastern contingent were the Washington Nationals, back for a third try to make a go of it in the NA, and two parvenus, the New Haven Elm Citys and the Philadelphia Centennials. From the western sector came the first two major league entries from the nation's largest city west of Chicago—the St. Louis Brown Stockings and the St. Louis Red Stockings (shortened to Reds to distinguish them from the Boston Red Stockings)—and the first, and last, major league entry from the state of Iowa, the Keokuk Westerns. The Keokuk club was the sort of entry that Chadwick most abhorred: short of proven talent, located way out west, and based in a small population center. Yet the Chicago White Stockings welcomed Keokuk if only because its presence swelled the number of western clubs to four.

Nevertheless, the White Stockings found themselves short of allies when they went to the mat with the Philadelphia Athletics over possession of Davy Force, one of the game's

Lip Pike, sprawled far right, with the 1871 Troy Unions. In 1875, Pike, a lifelong Easterner, went west to star for the St. Louis Brown Stockings. Other Unions: Steve King, Bill Craver, Dickie Flowers, Steve Bellan, Mike McGeary, John McMullin, Clipper Flynn, Tom York and Pike.

THE AWFUL ATLANTICS

In 1874 the Brooklyn Atlantics were on the upswing, winning 23 games in 55 outings and finishing just four and a half games out of the NA's first division. The following season the bottom fell out after manager/third-baseman Bob Ferguson absconded to Hartford, accompanied by rookie pitching phenom Tommy Bond. In 1875 the Atlantics collected their first win early in the campaign, beating New Haven 3–2 on April 26, but their second victory did not come until exactly one month later when they decked the still winless Elm Citys again. The Atlantics' 14–4 verdict over New Haven on May 26 put them at 2–11 for a .154 winning percentage. Alas, it was to be their high point. Over the next five months the Atlantics lost 31 straight games to finish with an .042 winning percentage, the poorest full-season showing ever by a major league team.

In a frantic effort to end his team's losing skein, Atlantics business manager Benjamin Van Delft tried virtually every man who came to the team's Union Grounds park and claimed to be a player. As a result, the Atlantics employed an NA record 35 different players, many of them for only a single day. A wealth of the Atlantics' cameo performers are known by their last names only, and in some cases not even that much is a certainty. There were, however, some bit players who possessed a fair amount of talent, even if it was not apparent to Van Delft. Among the more notable performers who debuted with the 1875 Atlantics were Barney Gilligan and Doc Bushong, later to become two of the better catchers of the 1880s.

The 1875 Hartford Dark Blues. Top: Doug Allison, Tom York, Candy Cummings, Tommy Bond and Bill Harbidge. Bottom: Jack Burdock, Everett Mills, Captain Bob Ferguson, Jack Remsen and Tom Carey.

finest middle infielders. Although Chicago seemed to establish that it had signed Force for the 1875 season, the NA Judiciary Committee awarded him to the Athletics. For the White Stockings and major stock holder, William Hulbert, the lesson was twofold. Hulbert inwardly vowed that the power in professional baseball would soon be shifted from the east to the west and from players such as Force—who for the moment could revolve almost totally unrestrained from team to team—to men like himself who handled the pursestrings.

Initially, Hulbert had one sympathizer among the eastern bloc of teams. Harry Wright proclaimed that his Boston Red Stockings would refuse to play the Athletics as long as Force remained in Philadelphia livery. When it was pointed out to Wright that if Boston did not play the Athletics the requisite number of games in 1875 to constitute a season series (now six) both teams would be disqualified from pennant consideration, he soon recanted. The season began with Force acceptable to all as a member of the Athletics.

Al Spalding commenced Boston's bid for a fourth successive NA championship by blanking the fledgling Elm Citys 6–0 at Boston on April 19, the Centennial Anniversary of Lexington and Concord. Ten days later the Red Stockings participated in the first major league game south of the Mason-Dixon line, beating Washington in Richmond. On May 15,

Boston was in first place at 14–0; Hartford was in second at 10–0. The St. Louis Brown Stockings, at 5–0, also had a perfect record; New Haven (0–8) and Washington (0–11) were still winless. The difference between the haves and the have-nots only increased in the last and, in many ways, the most uneven of the NA's five seasons. The Philadelphia Centennials, despite a veteran crew, were saddled with too many disruptive personalities (such as John Radcliff and Bill Craver) and disbanded on May 24, winners of just two of their 14 games. Keokuk's Westerns toppled on June 15 after a rain-abbreviated 1–0 loss to New York which typified the team's performance: good pitching and defense but anemic hitting. Washington lasted just a couple of weeks longer before adjourning. St. Louis's crimson-hosed entry never officially quit the hunt but, for all practical purposes, retired from it when the Reds refused to make any road trips after July 4 and could no longer entice any of their NA rivals to play them in St. Louis. New Haven, although winless in its first 15 games, survived the season, its cause helped by adding players from defunct teams. But the Elm Citys won just seven times in 47 outings. Of the six new entries, only the St. Louis Brown Stockings offered a competitive product in 1875. By finishing a solid fourth, the Brown Stockings not only far outstripped their fellow newcomers, winning nearly as many games as the other five combined, but also beat out four veteran teams: the Philadelphia Pearls, the New York Mutuals, the Chicago White Stockings and the Brooklyn Atlantics.

Yet no NA team, veteran or newcomer, provided much of a test for Boston. On May 18

THE FIRST GREAT FIREMAN

Harry Wright died in 1895, unaware that 20 years earlier one of his Boston Red Stockings pitchers had set a nineteenth-century season record for saves. Wright had never even heard of a pitching save at the time of his death (nor, in fact, had any one else as yet; the term did not come into popular usage until the 1960s). Wright was well aware, though, of the value that a so-called "change" pitcher could have to a team. Early in the 1870s Wright used himself in the role, swapping places with Al Spalding by moving to the box from his center field post while Spalding took a spot elsewhere on the diamond. Wright featured an exasperating variety of junk pitches which confounded enemy hitters because they contrasted with Spalding's speedballs. When Wright became almost solely a bench manager in 1875, he made Jack Manning his new change pitcher, and utilized Manning much as he had once utilized himself. Since Manning had enough stamina to serve also as a starter, Wright received an added bonus. He was able to rest Spalding on some days by putting him in Manning's spot in the outfield and leaving him there unless Manning got in trouble. Wright cared only that his strategic use of Manning and Spalding got the desired result—the last outs in a close game. Historians, after applying today's standards for a save to yesterday's box scores, have noted that in 1875 Spalding notched a nineteenth-century record nine saves, and Manning had six.

both Boston and Hartford were still undefeated when they met for the first time in 1875. With their 10–5 win, Boston set the tone for the season. The Red Stockings ran their streak to 26–0 before losing for the first time to the St. Louis Browns on June 5, 5–4; meanwhile Hartford, already far back at 19–5, would not win a game over the defending champions until October 29.

FAMOUS FIRSTS II

Joe Borden's major league career lasted only some 14 months, but he packed an astounding number of significant "firsts" into his brief period in the limelight.

In July, 1875, the Philadelphia Pearls cut pitcher Cherokee Fisher for drunkenness and general misbehavior and replaced him with a 21-year-old hurler from a local amateur team. To prevent his father from learning that he was playing ball for a living, the newcomer asked Pearls manager Mike McGeary to list him on the lineup card as Joe Josephs. Four days after making his big league debut on July 24, "Josephs" took the box against Chicago. Nine innings later the rookie put the final touches on a 4–0 victory in which he had held the White Stockings hitless, the first such achievement in professional baseball history.

By the beginning of the 1876 season Joe Josephs had acknowledged that his real name was Borden, and it was as Joe Borden that he won the first National League game ever played on April 22. A month later Borden nearly achieved yet a third remarkable first when he beat Cincinnati. Some 75 years afterward, baseball historian Lee Allen determined that the two hits charged against Borden in his win over Cincinnati were really walks—walks called hits by Opie Caylor, the lone official scorer in the National League, who customarily counted walks as hits. Allen also tracked down Caylor's explanation for doing so, which made considerable sense under the scoring rules that year. Allen's discovery seemed to make Borden, rather than George Bradley, the author of the first no-hitter in National League history, as well as of the first in professional history the previous year. Since then enough doubt has been cast on Borden's effort against Cincinnati to erase his honor of tossing the first National League no-hitter, but the other two famous firsts will always and indisputably belong to him.

These 1875 Boston Red Stockings are tailored to look like what they were—a team headed for its fourth straight pennant. Al Spalding, Andy Leonard, Cal McVey, Ross Barnes, Deacon White, Harry Schafer, Tommy Beals, Jim O'Rourke, Jack Manning and George Wright.

In July, after Hulbert clandestinely signed Spalding, Ross Barnes, Cal McVey and Deacon White to play with Chicago in 1876, White inadvertently let the cat out of the bag to Harry Wright. So brazen was Hulbert's theft that the deserters were labeled the "Big Four." But rather than unraveling as expected after the quartet's treason was revealed, Boston only grew stronger. When the book closed on the final NA campaign, the Red Stockings had just eight losses in 79 decisions for an all-time major league record .899 winning percentage. Even more impressive, during the five years of the NA's existence Boston won at a .788 clip overall, with 226 victories and 60 defeats. This sort of competitive imbalance ultimately destroyed the NA, but the manner in which Wright assembled and maintained his dynasty is a model as valid today as it was in the early 1870s.

ONE-GAMER II

The New Haven Elm Citys were 6–35 when Charlie Pabor replaced Juice Latham as captain near the end of the season. Their lone win for Pabor came on September 28 when he put one George Knight, a former Yale college star from Lakeville, Connecticut, in the box. After that day, Knight never again appeared in big league livery, preferring a medical career to baseball; by 1885 he had succeeded his father, also a doctor, as the superintendent of the Connecticut school for imbeciles at Lakeville. Knight is the lone NA performer to achieve a complete-game win in his one and only appearance as a pitcher.

THE SEASONAL RECORD

	G	W	L	PCT	H	R	GB
Boston Red Stockings	82	71	8	.899	37–0	34–8	—
Hartford Dark Blues	86	54	28	.659	26–11	28–17	18.5
Philadelphia Athletics	77	53	20	.726	29–9	24–11	15
St. Louis Browns	70	39	29	.574	21–12	18–17	26.5
Philadelphia Pearls	70	37	31	.544	16–21	21–10	28.5
Chicago White Stockings	69	30	37	.448	16–16	14–21	35
New York Mutuals	71	30	38	.441	13–21	17–17	35.5
New Haven Elm Citys	47	7	40	.149	3–24	4–16	48
Washington	28	5	23	.179	2–10	3–13	40.5
St. Louis Reds	19	4	15	.211	3–11	1–4	37
Philadelphia Centennials	14	2	12	.143	0–7	2–5	36.5
Brooklyn Atlantics	44	2	42	.045	1–30	1–12	51.5
Keokuk Westerns	13	1	12	.077	1–7	0–5	37

	Bos	Har	Ath	BS	Phi	Chi	NY	NH	Was	Red	Cen	Bro	Keo	
Boston	—	9	8	7	6	8	10	5	6	1	4	6	1	71
Hartford	1	—	4	5	4	6	8	8	4	3	1	10	*	54
Athletics	2	3	—	6	8	7	6	7	5	*	2	7	*	53
Brown Stockings	2	5	1	—	5	5	8	2	3	2	*	2	4	39
Pearls	0	4	2	5	—	7	2	4	2	1	3	7	*	37
Chicago	2	4	1	5	3	—	3	2	*	4	*	2	4	30
New York	0	2	3	0	5	3	—	5	*	2	2	7	1	30
New Haven	1	1	0	1	0	1	1	—	1	*	0	1	*	7
Washington	0	0	0	0	0	*	*	4	—	1	*	*	*	5
Reds	0	0	*	0	0	0	0	*	2	—	*	*	2	4
Centennials	0	0	1	*	0	*	0	1	*	*	—	*	*	2
Brooklyn	0	0	0	0	0	0	0	2	0	*	*	—	*	2
Keokuk	0	*	*	0	*	0	0	*	*	1	*	*	—	1
	8	28	20	29	31	37	38	40	23	15	12	42	12	335

*Teams did not play one another.

SEASON LEADERS

Batting Average (200 ABs)

1.	White, Boston	.367
2.	Barnes, Boston	.364
3.	McVey, Boston	.355
4.	Pike, St. Louis	.346
5.	G. Wright, Boston	.333

Slugging Average

1.	McVey, Boston	.517
2.	Pike, St. Louis	.494
3.	Craver, Cent–Athletics	.455
4.	White, Boston	.453
5.	Barnes, Boston	.443

On–Base Percentage

1.	Barnes, Boston	.375
2.	White, Boston	.373
3.	McVey, Boston	.356
4.	Pike, St. Louis	.352
5.	G. Wright, Boston	.337

Total Bases

1.	McVey, Boston	201
2.	G. Wright, Boston	176
3.	Barnes, Boston	174
4.	White, Boston	168
5.	Leonard, Boston	156

Home Runs

1.	O'Rourke, Boston	6
2.	Hall, Athletics	4
	Start, New York	4
4.	Hallinan, Western–NY	3
	McVey, Boston	3

Bases on Balls

1.	Dehlman, St. Louis	11
2.	Harbridge, Hartford	9
	Hastings, Chicago	9
	O'Rourke, Boston	9
	Nelson, New York	9

Hits

1.	Barnes, Boston	143
2.	McVey, Boston	138
3.	White, Boston	136
	G. Wright, Boston	136
5.	Leonard, Boston	127

RBI

1.	McVey, Boston	87
2.	Leonard, Boston	74
3.	O'Rourke, Boston	72
4.	Hall, Athletics	62
5.	G. Wright, Boston	61

Runs

1.	Barnes, Boston	115
2.	G. Wright, Boston	106
3.	O'Rourke, Boston	97
4.	McVey, Boston	89
5.	Leonard, Boston	87

Stolen Bases (Data Incomplete)

1.	Murnane, Pearls	30
2.	Barnes, Boston	29
3.	Pike, Brown Stockings	25
4.	Dehlman, Brown Stockings	23
5.	Burdock, Hartford	20

PITCHING

Wins

1.	Spalding, Boston	54
2.	McBride, Athletics	44
3.	Cummings, Hartford	35
4.	Bradley, St. Louis	33
5.	Mathews, New York	29
	Zettlein, Chic–Pearls	29

Innings

1.	Mathews, New York	625.2
2.	Spalding, Boston	570.2
3.	McBride, Athletics	538
4.	Bradley, St. Louis	535.2
5.	Zettlein, Chic–Pearls	463.1

Strikeouts

1.	Cummings, Hartford	82
2.	Spalding, Boston	75
	Mathews, New York	75
4.	Bond, Hartford	70
5.	Bradley, Brown Stockings	60

ERA (75 innings)

1.	Bond, Hartford	1.41
2.	Spalding, Boston	1.59
	Zettlein, Chic–Pearls	1.59
4.	Cummings, Hartford	1.60
5.	Golden, Keokuk–Chic	1.86

Losses

1.	Mathews, New York	38
2.	Nichols, New Haven	29
3.	Bradley, Brown Stockings	26
4.	Zettlein, Chic–Pearls	22
5.	Cassidy, Brooklyn	21

Complete Games

1.	Mathews, New York	69
2.	McBride, Athletics	59
3.	Bradley, Brown Stockings	57
4.	Spalding, Boston	52
5.	Zettlein, Chic–Pearls	49

Winning Percentage (15 decisions)

1.	Spalding, Boston	.915
2.	Manning, Boston	.889
3.	McBride, Athletics	.759
4.	Cummings, Hartford	.745
5.	Zettlein, Chic–Pearls	.569

Lowest On–Base Percentage

1.	Bond, Hartford	.219
2.	Fisher, Athletics	.233
3.	Cummings, Hartford	.236
4.	Spalding, Boston	.247
5.	Zettlein, Chic–Pearls	.250

FIELDING

Total Chances

1B	Dehlman, Brown Stockings	902
2B	Barnes, Boston	576
3B	Ferguson, Hartford	399
SS	Force, Athletics	423
OF	Gedney, New York	248
C	White, Boston	502
P	Spalding, Boston	203

Fielding Average

Fisler, Athletics	.958
Burdock, Hartford	.895
Ferguson, Hartford	.827
Force, Athletics	.887
Eggler, Athletics	.921
Allison, Hartford	.896
McBride, Athletics	.955

BOSTON   Harry Wright   South End Grounds

		G	AB	H	R	2B	3B	HR	RBI	BB	SB	BA	SA
SS	George Wright	79	**408**	136	106	20	7	2	61	2	13	.333	.431
LF	Andy Leonard	80	396	127	87	14	6	1	74	2	14	.321	.394
2B	Ross Barnes	78	393	**143**	**115**	20	4	1	58	7	29	.364	.443
1B	Cal McVey	82	389	138	89	**36**	9	3	87	1	7	.355	**.517**
C	Deacon White	80	371	136	76	23	3	1	60	3	2	**.367**	.453
CF	Jim O'Rourke	75	358	106	97	13	7	**6**	72	9	17	.296	.422
P	Al Spalding	74	343	107	68	15	3	0	56	3	2	.312	.373
RF	Jack Manning	77	348	94	71	11	3	1	46	2	5	.270	.328
3B	Harry Schafer	52	222	64	49	9	0	0	17	1	3	.288	.329
OF	Tommy Beals	35	155	41	38	2	6	0	16	3	1	.265	.355
Sub	Juice Latham	16	78	21	23	4	0	0	13	0	0	.269	.321
Sub	Frank Heifer	11	50	14	11	0	3	0	5	0	0	.280	.400
Sub	Harry Wright	1	4	1	1	0	0	0	0	0	0	.250	.250
		82	3515	**1128**	**831**	167	51	**15**	565	33	93	**.321**	**.410**

1B McVey 55, Latham 16, Heifer 9, O'Rourke 6, Spalding 4, Manning 3, Leonard 2, White 1
2B Barnes 76, Beals 8, Leonard 2
SS G. Wright 79, Leonard 3, Barnes 2
3B Schafer 51, O'Rourke 27, Leonard 3, Manning 1
OF Leonard 73, Manning 65, O'Rourke 45, Beals 30, McVey 23, White 14, Spalding 18, Heifer 6, Barnes 3, H. Wright 1, Schafer 1
C   White 75, McVey 16, O'Rourke 1
P   Spalding 72, Manning 27, McVey 3, Heifer 2, G. Wright 2

	G	IP	GS	CG	W	L	K	BB	SH	SV	ERA
Al Spalding	72	570.2	62	52	**54**	5	75	18	**7**	**9**	1.59
Jack Manning	27	139.2	18	8	16	2	34	14	1	0	2.38
Cal McVey	3	11	2	0	1	0	1	1	0	1	4.91
Frank Heifer	2	2.1	0	0	0	0	0	0	0	1	15.43
George Wright	2	4	0	0	0	1	0	0	0	0	6.75
		732	82	60	71	8	110	33	10	**17**	1.87

HARTFORD   Bob Ferguson   Hartford Baseball Grounds

		G	AB	H	R	2B	3B	HR	RBI	BB	SB	BA	SA
SS	Tom Carey	86	382	101	63	6	2	0	38	1	13	.264	.291
LF	Tom York	86	375	111	68	14	7	0	37	3	7	.296	.371
3B	Bob Ferguson	85	366	88	65	10	4	0	43	3	2	.240	.290
CF	Jack Remsen	86	358	96	70	10	4	0	34	5	6	.268	.318
2B	Jack Burdock	74	350	103	72	12	5	0	35	3	20	.294	.357
1B	Everett Mills	80	342	89	59	8	4	1	48	0	6	.260	.316
P	Tommy Bond	72	289	77	32	11	3	0	33	0	5	.266	.325
C	Doug Allison	61	269	67	38	7	0	0	21	6	2	.249	.275
P	Candy Cummings	53	221	44	30	7	2	0	15	3	1	.199	.249
C	Bill Harbidge	53	208	50	32	3	3	0	26	9	2	.240	.284
RF	Art Allison	40	175	42	26	4	1	1	19	0	1	.240	.291
Sub	Paddy Quinn	5	13	3	1	0	0	0	1	1	0	.231	.231
Sub	Charley Jones	1	4	0	1	0	0	0	0	0	0	.000	.000
Sub	Steve Brady	1	4	0	0	0	0	0	0	0	0	.000	.000
		86	3356	871	557	92	35	2	350	34	65	.260	.310

1B Mills 80, Bond 4, Harbidge 3, D. Allison 2, A. Allison 1
2B Burdock 73, Harbidge 11, Bond 3, A. Allison 2, Carey 1
SS Carey 86, Harbridge 1
3B Ferguson 85, Burdock 2

OF   York 86, Remsen 86, A. Allison 37, Bond 29, Harbidge 13, Cummings 5, Quinn 3, D. Allison 2, Brady 1, Jones 1
C   D. Allison 59, Harbidge 31, Quinn 3, Burdock 1, A. Allison 1
P   Cummings 49, Bond 40, Ferguson 1

	G	IP	GS	CG	W	L	K	BB	SH	SV	ERA
Candy Cummings	48	416	47	46	35	12	82	4	**7**	0	1.60
Tommy Bond	40	352	39	37	19	16	70	7	6	0	1.41
Bob Ferguson	1	2	0	0	0	0	0	0	0	0	22.50
		770	86	**83**	54	28	**152**	**11**	**13**	0	1.57

PHILADELPHIA ATHLETICS   Dick McBride (49–18)   Cap Anson (4–2)   Athletic Park

		G	AB	H	R	2B	3B	HR	RBI	BB	SB	BA	SA
SS	Davy Force	77	386	120	78	22	5	0	49	7	6	.311	.394
LF	George Hall	77	358	107	71	10	**12**	4	62	3	8	.299	.427
3B	Ezra Sutton	75	358	116	83	11	7	1	59	1	13	.324	.402
UT	Cap Anson	69	326	106	84	15	3	0	58	4	11	.325	.390
CF	Dave Eggler	66	295	89	66	13	7	0	33	1	6	.302	.393
C	John Clapp	60	292	77	65	8	7	0	39	7	9	.264	.339
P	Dick McBride	60	270	73	42	9	0	0	45	4	2	.270	.304
1B	Wes Fisler	58	268	74	54	13	3	0	31	4	1	.276	.347
2B	Bill Craver	54	260	83	71	11	**11**	2	40	4	8	.319	.469
RF	George Bechtel	35	164	46	33	6	2	0	20	1	2	.280	.341
Sub	John Richmond	29	125	25	29	2	0	0	12	1	1	.200	.216
Sub	Adam Rocap	16	69	12	13	1	0	0	4	1	3	.174	.188
P	Lon Knight	13	47	6	5	2	0	0	2	0	2	.128	.170
Sub	Al Reach	3	14	4	4	1	0	0	1	0	2	.286	.357
Sub	William Coon	4	12	2	1	0	0	0	1	0	1	.167	.167
Sub	? Gilroy	2	6	1	0	0	0	0	0	0	0	.167	.167
		77	3250	941	699	124	**57**	7	456	**38**	75	.290	.369

1B   Fisler 44, Anson 32, Sutton 2, Hall 1
2B   Craver 53, Richmond 17, Fisler 5, Rocap 4, Reach 1
SS   Force 77, Knight 1, Sutton 1
3B   Sutton 73, Anson 5, Force 2, Craver 1
OF   Hall 77, Eggler 66, Bechtel 31, Anson 25, Rocap 12, Richmond 11, Fisler 10, Reach 2, Sutton 1, Gilroy 1, Coon 1, McBride 1
C   Clapp 60, Anson 13, Coon 4, Richmond 3, Craver 2, Gilroy 1
P   McBride 60, Knight 13, Bechtel 4, Sutton 2

	G	IP	GS	CG	W	L	K	BB	SH	SV	ERA
Dick McBride	60	538	60	59	44	14	27	**24**	6	0	2.33
Lon Knight	13	107	13	12	6	5	15	12	0	0	2.27
George Bechtel	4	36	4	4	3	1	3	3	0	0	.250
Ezra Sutton	2	6	0	0	0	0	0	0	0	0	10.50
		687	77	75	53	20	45	39	6	0	2.40

ST. LOUIS BROWN STOCKINGS   Dickey Pearce   Grand Avenue Park

		G	AB	H	R	2B	3B	HR	RBI	BB	SB	BA	SA
LF	Ned Cuthbert	68	319	78	68	9	2	0	17	3	18	.245	.285
CF	Lip Pike	70	312	108	61	22	**12**	0	44	3	25	.346	.494
SS	Dickey Pearce	70	311	77	51	6	3	0	29	7	8	.248	.286
2B	Joe Battin	67	284	71	31	6	3	0	33	0	15	.250	.292
3B	Bill Hague	62	260	57	24	2	0	0	22	2	3	.219	.227
P	George Bradley	60	254	62	28	7	3	0	24	1	3	.244	.295

		G	AB	H	R	2B	3B	HR	RBI	BB	SB	BA	SA
1B	Dutch Dehlman	67	254	57	42	12	2	0	14	**11**	23	.224	.287
C	Tom Miller	55	214	35	18	2	0	0	12	1	2	.164	.173
RF	Jack Chapman	43	195	44	28	5	3	0	30	1	4	.226	.282
Sub	Charlie Waitt	30	113	23	14	10	0	0	12	2	3	.204	.292
Sub	George Seward	25	96	24	12	2	0	0	8	1	1	.250	.271
P	Pud Galvin	13	46	6	8	2	1	0	2	0	3	.130	.217
P	Frank Fleet	4	16	1	1	0	0	0	1	0	0	.063	.063
		70	2674	643	386	85	29	0	248	32	108	.240	.294

1B Dehlman 67, Waitt 4, Hague 1, Chapman 1
2B Battin 62, Pike 10, Seward 2, Bradley 1, Cuthbert 1
SS Pearce 70, Bradley 2, Pike 1
3B Hague 62, Battin 6, Miller 2, Pike 2, Bradley 1, Fleet 1
OF Cuthbert 67, Pike 64, Chapman 43, Waitt 30, Seward 7, Galvin 6, Dehlman 2, Bradley 1,
    Battin 1, Fleet 1, Hague 1, Miller 1
C   Miller 53, Seward 18, Cuthbert 3, Battin 2
P   Bradley 60, Galvin 8, Fleet 3, Pearce 2

	G	IP	GS	CG	W	L	K	BB	SH	SV	ERA
George Bradley	60	535.2	60	57	33	26	60	17	5	0	2.13
Pud Galvin	8	62	7	7	4	2	8	1	0	1	1.16
Frank Fleet	3	27	3	3	2	1	3	3	0	0	3.33
Dickey Pearce	2	5.1	0	0	0	0	0	0	0	0	3.38
		630	70	67	39	29	71	21	5	0	2.10

PHILADELPHIA PEARLS   **Mike McGeary (34–27) Bob Addy (3–4)**   **Athletic Park**

		G	AB	H	R	2B	3B	HR	RBI	BB	SB	BA	SA
1B	Tim Murnane	69	313	85	71	5	0	1	30	7	30	.272	.297
RF	Bob Addy	69	310	80	60	8	4	0	43	0	16	.258	.310
3B	Mike McGeary	68	310	90	71	6	2	0	37	1	19	.290	.323
2B	Levi Meyerle	68	301	95	55	14	8	1	54	0	7	.316	.425
SS	Chick Fulmer	69	295	65	50	6	1	0	24	0	10	.220	.247
C	Pop Snyder	66	263	64	38	8	2	1	25	4	3	.243	.300
CF	John McMullin	54	222	57	33	9	4	2	19	5	6	.257	.360
LF	Fred Treacey	43	179	38	23	3	3	0	15	1	6	.212	.263
P	Cherokee Fisher	41	177	41	26	3	1	0	11	1	4	.232	.260
Sub	Fergy Malone	29	123	28	15	2	1	0	10	1	1	.228	.260
P	George Zettlein	21	83	15	10	0	0	0	6	0	1	.181	181
Sub	Orator Shaffer	19	70	17	10	2	1	0	6	0	2	.243	.300
Sub	Bill Crowley	9	37	3	4	0	0	0	3	1	1	.081	081
P	Joe Borden	7	28	3	3	0	0	0	1	0	0	.107	.107
P	Bill Parks	2	6	1	0	0	0	0	0	0	0	.167	167
P	Sam Weaver	1	4	1	1	1	0	0	1	0	0	.250	.500
		70	2721	683	470	67	27	5	285	21	105	.251	.301

1B Murnane 31, Malone 22, Meyerle 16, Shaffer 2, Crowley 1, Snyder 1
2B Meyerle 36, McGeary 23, Murnane 15, Addy 2
SS Fulmer 53, McGeary 18
3B McGeary 27, Meyerle 20, Fulmer 17, Shaffer 5, Crowley 4
OF Addy 68, McMullin 54, Treacey 43, Murnane 26, Shaffer 12, Fisher 5, Crowley 4, McGeary 3, Malone 2,
    Parks 2, Snyder 1
C   Snyder 66, Malone 6
P   Fisher 41, Zettlein 21, Borden 7, McMullin 4, Parks 2, Weaver 1

	G	IP	GS	CG	W	L	K	BB	SH	SV	ERA
Cherokee Fisher	41	358	41	36	22	19	18	9	2	0	1.99
George Zettlein	21	181.1	21	20	12	8	13	10	**1***	0	2.08
Joe Borden #	7	66	7	7	2	4	9	7	2	0	1.50
John McMullin	4	11.1	0	0	0	0	0	1	0	0	7.94
Sam Weaver	1	6	1	1	1	0	2	2	0	0	1.50
Bill Parks	2	5.1	0	0	0	0	0	1	0	0	8.44
		628	70	64	37	31	42	30	5	0	2.12

No-hit game 4–0 vs Chicago, July 28

CHICAGO   Jimmy Wood   23rd Street Grounds

		G	AB	H	R	2B	3B	HR	RBI	BB	SB	BA	SA
1B	Jim Devlin	69	318	92	60	17	6	0	40	4	6	.289	.381
2B/CF	Paul Hines	68	308	101	45	14	4	0	36	1	6	.328	.399
LF	John Glenn	69	308	75	46	8	0	0	27	3	10	.244	.269
SS	John Peters	69	297	85	40	16	2	0	34	0	12	.286	.354
3B	Warren White	69	287	71	37	9	0	0	23	0	5	.247	.279
UT	Scott Hastings	65	287	73	43	9	0	0	30	9	13	.254	.286
C	Dick Higham	42	208	49	44	5	3	0	12	0	6	.236	.288
RF	Oscar Bielaski	51	201	48	21	1	0	0	11	2	5	.239	.244
P	Mike Golden	39	155	40	16	3	0	0	14	2	3	.258	.277
P	George Zettlein	32	133	29	7	0	0	0	9	0	0	.218	.218
Sub	Paddy Quinn	17	61	14	12	0	0	0	1	0	0	.230	.230
Sub	Joe Miller	15	54	8	1	0	0	0	1	0	0	.148	.148
Sub	George Keerl	6	23	3	2	0	0	0	3	0	0	.130	.130
Sub	Fred Waterman	5	20	6	2	0	0	0	3	0	0	.300	.300
Sub	Will Foley	3	12	3	0	1	0	0	1	0	0	.250	.333
Sub	Mike Brannock	2	9	1	2	0	0	0	0	0	0	.111	.111
Sub	? Brady	1	4	1	1	0	1	0	0	0	0	.250	.750
		69	2685	699	379	83	16	0	245	21	69	.260	.303

1B   Devlin 42, Glenn 29, Zettlein 3, Golden 1
2B   Hines 30, Miller 14, Higham 13, Keerl 6, Peters 6, Hastings 3, White 2
SS   Peters 65, White 5, Hines 1
3B   White 59, Waterman 5, Foley 3, Brannock 2
OF   Bielaski 51, Glenn 44, Hines 39, Hastings 29, Golden 27, Higham 14, Quinn 10, White 5, Devlin 4, Miller 1, Brady 1
C   Hastings 46, Higham 24, Quinn 11, Hines 1
P   Zettlein 31, Devlin 28, Golden 14

	G	IP	GS	CG	W	L	K	BB	SH	SV	ERA
George Zettlein	31	282	31	29	17	14	18	6	**6***	0	1.28
Jim Devlin	28	224	24	24	7	16	23	12	0	0	1.93
Mike Golden	14	119	14	12	6	7	14	8	1	0	1.89
		625	69	65	30	37	55	26	7	0	1.63

NEW YORK   Nat Hicks   Union Grounds (Brooklyn)

		G	AB	H	R	2B	3B	HR	RBI	BB	SB	BA	SA
CF	Jim Holdsworth	71	324	92	45	12	1	0	23	1	3	.284	.327
1B	Joe Start	69	314	90	58	10	5	4	30	3	1	.287	.389
RF	Eddie Booth	68	281	56	33	3	4	0	18	0	4	.199	.238
2B	Candy Nelson	70	276	55	28	7	1	0	23	9	4	.199	.232
C	Nat Hicks	62	269	67	32	10	0	0	22	2	1	.249	.286

		G	AB	H	R	2B	3B	HR	RBI	BB	SB	BA	SA
P	Bobby Mathews	70	264	48	23	6	2	0	15	2	1	.182	.220
LF	Count Gedney	68	267	55	30	12	2	0	17	0	2	.206	.266
3B	Joe Gerhardt	58	252	54	29	7	3	0	20	0	0	.214	.266
SS	Jimmy Hallinan	44	203	58	29	6	3	3	21	1	2	.286	.389
Sub	Pat McGee	25	95	17	4	2	0	0	9	0	0	.179	.200
Sub	Dick Higham	15	64	25	12	5	0	0	10	0	0	.391	.469
Sub	Billy Barnie	9	34	5	1	0	0	0	1	1	0	.147	.147
Sub	Al Metcalf	8	32	7	2	0	0	0	1	0	2	.219	.219
Sub	Nealy Phelps	2	6	2	1	1	0	0	0	0	0	.333	.500
Sub	John Hatfield	1	4	2	1	1	0	0	1	0	0	.500	.750
		71	2685	633	328	82	21	7	211	19	20	.236	.290

1B Start 69, Higham 2
2B Nelson 49, Gerhardt 13, Booth 8, Higham 6
SS Hallinan 43, Holdsworth 26, Nelson 2, Gerhardt 1, Metcalf 1
3B Gerhardt 47, Nelson 23, Metcalf 5, Hallinan 1
OF Gedney 67, Booth 63, Holdsworth 45, McGee 25, Hicks 5, Barnie 3, Higham 3, Metcalf 2, Phelps 2, Hatfield 1, Nelson 1, Gerhardt 1, Hallinan 1, Mathews 1
C   Hicks 60, Higham 8, Barnie 6
P   Mathews 70, Gedney 2

	G	IP	GS	CG	W	L	K	BB	SH	SV	ERA
Bobby Mathews	70	625.2	70	69	29	38	75	20	3	0	2.49
Count Gedney	2	11	1	1	1	0	2	1	0	0	0.82
		636.2	71	70	30	38	77	21	3	0	2.46

NEW HAVEN   Charlie Gould (2–21)   Juice Latham (4–14)   Charlie Pabor (1–5)
Howard Avenue Grounds

		G	AB	H	R	2B	3B	HR	RBI	BB	SB	BA	SA
RF	John McKelvey	43	188	43	26	3	1	0	10	5	3	.229	.255
3B	Henry Luff	38	166	45	15	10	3	2	18	0	3	.271	.404
UT	Billy Geer	37	164	40	20	4	1	0	9	1	2	.244	.280
CF	Jim Tipper	41	159	25	10	1	0	0	4	1	1	.157	.164
LF	Johnny Ryan	37	146	23	17	2	2	0	8	3	10	.158	.199
2B	Ed Somerville	33	136	29	14	5	0	0	7	1	1	.213	.250
C	Tim McGinley	32	131	36	13	3	1	0	10	0	1	.275	.313
SS	Sam Wright	33	127	24	10	4	0	0	5	1	1	.189	.220
P	Tricky Nichols	34	119	23	12	0	2	0	5	0	5	.193	.227
1B	Charlie Gould	27	109	29	9	4	1	0	8	1	0	.266	.321
Sub	Juice Latham	20	76	15	6	1	0	0	5	0	6	.197	.211
C	Stud Bancker	19	72	11	3	0	0	0	2	0	1	.153	.153
Sub	George Trenwith	6	25	6	1	2	0	0	3	0	0	.240	.320
Sub	Charlie Pabor	6	23	8	4	0	2	0	2	0	0	.348	.522
Sub	John Cassidy	6	22	3	3	1	0	0	1	0	0	.136	.182
Sub	Jim Keenan	3	13	1	1	0	0	0	0	0	0	.077	.077
Sub	? Sullivan	2	8	3	3	0	0	0	2	0	1	.375	.375
Sub	Tom Barlow	1	5	1	1	0	0	0	0	0	0	.200	.200
Sub	? Evans	1	4	2	1	0	0	0	1	0	0	.500	.500
Sub	Lester Dole	1	4	2	1	0	0	0	0	0	0	.500	.500
Sub	Fred Goldsmith	1	4	2	0	0	0	0	1	0	0	.500	.500
Sub	Rit Harrison	1	4	2	0	1	0	0	0	0	0	.500	.750
P	George Knight	1	4	0	0	0	0	0	0	0	0	.000	.000
Sub	John Smith	1	3	0	0	0	0	0	0	1	0	.000	.000
Sub	? Booth	1	2	0	0	0	0	0	0	0	0	.000	.000
		47	1714	373	170	41	13	2	102	14	35	.218	.260

1B   Gould 26, Latham 14, Cassidy 6, Somerville 1, Geer 1, Bancker 1
2B   Somerville 29, Geer 13, Bancker 4, Goldsmith 1
SS   Wright 33, Geer 6, Latham 4, Somerville 1, Bancker 1, Smith 1, Barlow 1, Ryan 1, Booth 1, Harrison 1, Luff 1
3B   Luff 30, Trenwith 6, McKelvey 5, Latham 3, Bancker 3, Keenan 2, McGinley 2, Somerville 2, Geer 1, Ryan 1
OF   Tipper 41, McKelvey 39, Ryan 30, Geer 17, Pabor 6, Luff 4, Nichols 3, Sullivan 2, Dole 1, Evans 1, Gould 1, Bancker 1, Keenan 1
C   McGinley 32, Bancker 14, Ryan 4, Keenan 3, Harrison 1, Gould 1
P   Nichols 34, Luff 10, Ryan 10, Knight 1

	G	IP	GS	CG	W	L	K	BB	SH	SV	ERA
Tricky Nichols	34	288	33	30	4	29	48	9	0	0	2.38
Henry Luff	10	68.2	7	5	1	6	5	3	0	0	3.28
Johnny Ryan	10	59.1	6	4	1	5	1	9	0	0	3.19
George Knight	1	9	1	1	1	0	0	0	0	0	3.00
		425	47	40	7	40	54	21	0	0	2.65

WASHINGTON   **Holly Hollingshead (4–16)**   **Bill Parks (0–7)**   **Olympic Grounds**

		G	AB	H	R	2B	3B	HR	RBI	BB	SB	BA	SA
LF	Bill Parks	27	111	20	13	0	0	0	6	1	1	.180	.180
1B	Art Allison	26	112	24	18	3	1	0	3	1	6	.214	.259
RF	Larry Ressler	27	108	21	17	1	0	0	5	0	4	.194	.204
SS	John Dailey	27	110	20	16	5	4	0	13	0	3	.182	.300
2B	Steve Brady	21	91	13	7	0	0	0	3	0	5	.143	.143
CF	Holly Hollingshead	19	81	20	8	1	1	0	5	1	2	.247	.284
3B	Herman Doscher	22	81	15	5	4	0	0	5	0	1	.185	.235
P	Bill Stearns	21	78	20	9	0	0	0	7	1	0	.256	.256
C	Andrew Thompson	11	41	4	3	0	1	0	3	0	0	.098	.146
C	? McCloskey	11	40	7	1	0	0	0	4	1	0	.175	.175
Sub	Lew Say	11	38	10	4	0	0	0	2	0	0	.263	.263
Sub	Charlie Mason	8	33	3	2	0	0	0	1	0	0	.091	.091
Sub	? Terry	6	22	4	0	0	1	0	2	0	0	.182	.273
Sub	John Lowry	6	22	3	2	0	0	0	0	1	0	.136	.136
Sub	Sam Field	5	16	5	0	0	0	0	1	0	1	.313	.313
Sub	Jim Gilmore	3	12	3	2	0	0	0	0	0	0	.250	.250
Sub	Bob Stevens	1	4	1	0	0	0	0	0	0	0	.250	.250
Sub	Frank Selman	1	3	1	0	0	0	0	0	0	0	.333	.333
P	? Witherow	1	1	0	0	0	0	0	0	0	0	.000	.000
		28	1004	194	107	14	8	0	60	6	23	.193	.223

1B   Allison 23, Terry 4, Brady 1, Selman 1
2B   Brady 18, Ressler 7, Dailey 2, Say 2
SS   Dailey 20, Say 8, Doscher 2
3B   Doscher 22, Dailey 5, Gilmore 1
OF   Ressler 20, Hollingshead 19, Parks 17, Mason 8, Stearns 7, Lowry 6, Terry 4, Allison 3, Brady 2, Say 1, Thompson 1, Gilmore 1, Field 1, Stevens 1
C   McCloskey 11, Thompson 11, Field 4, Gilmore 2, Allison 1, Brady 1
P   Stearns 17, Parks 14, Witherow 1, Mason 1

	G	IP	GS	CG	W	L	K	BB	SH	SV	ERA
Bill Stearns	17	141	16	14	1	14	3	4	0	0	4.02
Bill Parks	14	106.2	11	9	4	8	3	5	0	0	3.29
? Witherow	1	1	1	0	0	1	0	0	0	0	18.00
Charlie Mason	1	2	0	0	0	0	0	1	0	0	4.50
		250.2	28	23	5	23	6	10	0	0	3.77

ST. LOUIS REDS   **Charlie Sweasy**   **Red Stocking Park**

		G	AB	H	R	2B	3B	HR	RBI	BB	SB	BA	SA
1B	Charlie Hautz	19	83	25	5	3	0	0	4	0	5	.301	.337
SS	Billy Redmond	19	82	16	12	2	0	0	1	2	3	.195	.220
RF	Tom Oran	19	81	15	7	3	1	0	10	1	3	.185	.247
2B	Charlie Sweasy	19	76	13	7	1	0	0	4	3	2	.171	.184
LF	Art Croft	19	75	15	5	3	0	0	2	0	5	.200	.240
CF	Bill Morgan	19	69	18	11	4	0	0	1	5	2	.261	.319
P	Joe Blong	16	68	10	3	2	0	0	5	0	1	.147	.176
C	Silver Flint	17	61	5	4	0	0	0	1	1	2	.082	.082
3B	Trick McSorley	15	52	11	4	0	0	0	2	0	3	.212	.212
Sub	Joe Ellick	7	27	6	1	1	0	0	1	0	1	.222	.259
Sub	Packy Dillon	3	13	3	1	1	0	0	0	0	0	.231	.308
Sub	John Dillon	1	1	0	0	0	0	0	0	0	0	.000	.000
		19	688	137	60	20	1	0	32	12	27	.199	.231

1B	Hautz 19
2B	Sweasy 19
SS	Redmond 19, J. Dillon 1, Oran 1
3B	McSorley 9, Morgan 7, Ellick 5, Flint 1
OF	Croft 19, Oran 19, Morgan 10, McSorley 7, Blong 4, Ellick 2, Flint 2
C	Flint 16, P. Dillon 3, Redmond 2
P	Blong 15, Morgan 7

	G	IP	GS	CG	W	L	K	BB	SH	SV	ERA
Joe Blong	15	129	15	12	3	12	14	2	1	0	3.07
Bill Morgan	7	42	4	4	1	3	7	1	1	0	1.29
		171	19	16	4	15	21	3	2	0	2.62

PHILADELPHIA CENTENNIALS   **Bill Craver**   **Centennial Grounds**

		G	AB	H	R	2B	3B	HR	RBI	BB	SB	BA	SA
SS	Bill Craver	14	65	18	8	4	2*	0	5	2	1	.277	.400
P	George Bechtel	14	61	17	12	5	0	0	7	1	0	.279	.361
CF	Fred Warner	14	57	14	11	4	0	0	2	1	0	.246	.316
2B	Ed Somerville	14	57	13	6	3	0	0	6	2	1	.228	.281
C	Tim McGinley	13	52	12	5	0	1	0	5	0	0	.231	.269
RF	Charlie Mason	12	47	11	5	0	0	0	3	0	0	.234	.234
LF	Fred Treacey	11	46	12	9	3	0	0	2	2	1	.261	.326
1B	John Abadie	11	45	10	3	0	0	0	4	0	1	.222	.222
3B	George Trenwith	10	45	8	5	2	0	0	4	1	0	.178	.222
Sub	John Radcliff	5	23	4	2	0	0	0	0	1	0	.174	.174
Sub	Len Lovett	6	21	5	2	1	0	0	2	1	0	.238	.286
Sub	Sam Field	3	11	1	2	0	0	0	0	0	0	.091	.091
		14	530	125	70	22	3	0	40	10	4	.236	.289

1B	Abadie 11, Mason 2, Craver 1
2B	Somerville 14, Craver 1
SS	Craver 9, Radcliff 5, Somerville 1
3B	Trenwith 10, Craver 4
OF	Warner 14, Treacey 11, Mason 10. Lovett 6, McGinley 1, Field 1
C	McGinley 12, Field 2, Mason 1
P	Bechtel 14

	G	IP	GS	CG	W	L	K	BB	SH	SV	ERA
George Bechtel	14	126	14	14	2	12	6	5	0	0	2.71

BROOKLYN ATLANTICS **Charlie Pabor (2–40)** **Bill Boyd (0–2)** **Union Grounds**

		G	AB	H	R	2B	3B	HR	RBI	BB	SB	BA	SA
P	John Cassidy	41	166	29	14	3	2	1	6	0	0	.175	.235
C	Jake Knowdell	43	163	32	17	2	0	0	9	1	0	.196	.209
LF	Charlie Pabor	42	153	36	14	2	2	0	11	1	0	.235	.275
2B/RF	Bill Boyd	36	151	44	14	11	0	1	10	1	0	.291	.384
3B	Al Nichols	32	131	20	4	2	0	0	9	0	0	.153	.168
UT	Frank Fleet	26	111	25	13	2	0	0	9	1	0	.225	.243
SS	Harry Kessler	25	105	26	17	2	0	0	7	1	0	.248	.267
Sub	Molly Moore	21	86	19	5	4	0	0	5	0	0	.221	.267
P	Jim Clinton	22	81	10	3	0	0	0	0	0	0	.123	.123
1B	Fred Crane	21	81	17	7	1	0	0	4	0	0	.210	.222
Sub	Pat McGee	18	65	10	3	3	1	0	5	1	0	.154	.231
CF	Bobby Clack	17	59	6	1	0	0	0	1	0	0	.102	.102
Sub	Dan Patterson	12	45	9	4	0	0	0	4	0	1	.200	.200
P	J. O'Neill	7	26	2	3	0	0	0	1	1	0	.077	.077
Sub	Al Martin	6	26	3	1	0	0	0	1	0	0	.115	.115
Sub	Tom Smith	3	13	1	0	0	0	0	1	0	0	.077	.077
Sub	Oliver Brown	3	10	0	0	0	0	0	0	0	0	.000	.000
Sub	? Stoddard	2	9	1	1	1	0	0	0	0	0	.111	.222
Sub	Barney Gilligan	2	8	2	2	0	0	0	0	0	0	.250	.250
Sub	John Dailey	2	8	1	3	0	0	0	0	0	0	.125	.125
Sub	Paddy Quinn	2	8	1	2	0	0	0	0	0	0	.125	.125
Sub	Doc Bushong	1	5	3	0	0	1	0	0	0	0	.600	1.000
Sub	Frank Thompson	1	5	2	1	0	0	0	1	0	0	.400	.400
Sub	? Edwards	1	5	1	1	0	0	0	0	0	0	.200	.200
Sub	Washington Fulmer	1	4	2	1	0	0	0	1	0	0	.500	.500
Sub	John Abadie	1	4	1	1	0	0	0	1	0	0	.250	.250
Sub	? Hellings	1	4	1	0	0	0	0	0	0	0	.250	.250
Sub	Bill Rexter	1	4	0	0	0	0	0	0	0	0	.000	.000
P	Harry Arundel	1	4	0	0	0	0	0	0	0	0	.000	.000
Sub	Tom Barlow	1	4	0	0	0	0	0	0	0	0	.000	.000
Sub	? Boland	1	4	0	0	0	0	0	0	0	0	.000	.000
Sub	Horatio Munn	1	4	0	0	0	0	0	0	0	0	.000	.000
Sub	? Shaffer	1	4	0	0	0	0	0	0	0	0	.000	.000
Sub	? Sheridan	1	4	0	0	0	0	0	0	0	0	.000	.000
Sub	Oscar Walker	1	2	0	0	0	0	0	0	1	0	.000	.000
		44	1562	304	132	33	6	2	86	8	1	.195	.227

1B   Crane 20, Cassidy 10, Moore 8, Clinton 5, Brown 2, Boyd 2, Dailey 1, Abadie 1, Clack 1, Kessler 1, O'Neill 1, Walker 1

2B   Boyd 15, Fleet 10, Patterson 7, McGee 6, Smith 3, Cassidy 2, Munn 1, Barlow 1, Hellings 1, Clinton 1, Kessler 1, Clinton 1, Knowdell 1, Moore 1

SS   Kessler 18, Moore 14, Knowdell 11, Fleet 9, Boyd 1, Crane 1, Dailey 1, Quinn 1

3B   Nichols 32, Boyd 9, Moore 1, Boland 1, Fleet 1, McGee 1

OF   Pabor 42, Clack 17, McGee 13, Boyd 12, Cassidy 12, Clinton 7, Patterson 7, Kessler 7, Martin 6, Knowdell 4, O'Neill 3, Moore 2, Quinn 2, Dailey 2, Stoddard 2, Brown 2, Walker 1, Thompson 1, Sheridan 1, Shaffer 1, Rexter 1, Gilligan 1, Edwards 1, Crane 1, Arundel 1, Fulmer 1

C   Knowdell 33, Fleet 11, Kessler 3, Bushong 1, Gilligan 1, Moore 1

P   Cassidy 30, Clinton 17, O'Neill 5, Fleet 2, Edwards 1, Arundel 1, Pabor 1, Boyd 1

	G	IP	GS	CG	W	L	K	BB	SH	SV	ERA
John Cassidy	30	213.2	22	18	1	21	9	11	0	0	3.03
Jim Clinton	17	123	14	9	1	13	7	5	0	0	2.41
J. O'Neill	5	34	4	3	0	4	0	0	0	0	5.03
Frank Fleet	2	15.1	1	1	0	1	0	0	0	0	4.70
Charlie Pabor	1	4	1	0	0	1	0	1	0	0	9.00
? Edwards	1	2	1	0	0	1	0	0	0	0	4.50
Harry Arundel	1	2.1	1	0	0	1	0	0	0	0	7.71
Bill Boyd	1	1.2	0	0	0	0	0	0	0	0	0.00
		394.1	44	31	2	42	16	17	0	0	3.16

KEOKUK WESTERNS   **Joe Simmons**   **Perry Park**

		G	AB	H	R	2B	3B	HR	RBI	BB	SB	BA	SA
CF	Joe Simmons	13	53	9	5	1	0	0	4	0	1	.170	.189
SS	Jimmy Hallinan	13	51	14	12	2	1	0	3	0	2	.275	.333
3B	Wally Goldsmith	13	51	6	3	0	0	0	1	0	0	.118	.118
2B	Joe Miller	13	50	6	4	1	0	0	0	0	0	.120	.140
LF	Charley Jones	12	47	13	4	2	4	0	10	0	1	.277	.489
P	Mike Golden	13	46	6	6	0	0	0	1	0	0	.130	.130
C	Paddy Quinn	11	43	14	4	1	0	0	5	0	0	.326	.349
1B	Jack Carbine	10	36	3	0	0	0	0	2	0	0	.083	.083
C	Billy Barnie	10	36	4	3	1	0	0	2	0	0	.111	.139
RF	Billy Riley	8	33	5	4	1	0	0	1	1	0	.152	.182
Sub	Jim Hall	1	3	1	0	0	1	0	1	0	0	.333	1.000
		13	449	81	45	9	6	0	30	1	4	.180	.227

1B	Carbine 10, Simmons 3
2B	Miller 13
SS	Hallinan 13
3B	Goldsmith 13
OF	Jones 12, Simmons 10, Riley 8, Barnie 5, Quinn 4, Hall 1
C	Quinn 10, Barnie 3
P	Golden 13

	G	IP	GS	CG	W	L	K	BB	SH	SV	ERA
Mike Golden	13	112	13	13	1	12	20	12	0	0	1.83

THE HULBERT ERA
(1876–81)

On February 2, 1876, representatives from several professional baseball clubs met in a locked room at the Grand Central Hotel on lower Broadway in New York. Members of the press and the sporting public who knew of the meeting had been led to believe its purpose was to address reforms pertaining to three thorny problems that were undermining the professional sport: the absence of sanctions for players caught fixing games, the unstable financial organization of many professional clubs, and a need for sweeping changes in the playing rules. But the announced reason for the meeting was a ruse; its real objective was known to only a few of the men who suddenly found themselves the captive audience of the self-designated chairman of the proceeding—William Hulbert, the president of the Chicago White Stockings.

Holding the only key to the room in his pocket, Hulbert revealed to his guests that he had ensconced them there to join with him in forming the National League, a new professional federation having as its cornerstone the elimination of players from any position of authority in club or league financial affairs. Hulbert went on to outline reforms that he would implement to curb inept leadership, player drunkenness and the infiltration of gamblers, but his motives were never so much altruistic as self-serving. Midway through the 1875 season Hulbert had raided Harry Wright's four-time National Association champion Boston Red Stockings and induced a quartet of Wright's stars—Al Spalding, Cal McVey, Deacon White and Ross Barnes—to sign contracts with his Chicago club for the following year. Soon thereafter he had enticed young Philadelphia Athletics star Adrian Anson to come west. Recognizing that other NA chieftains would endeavor to expel Chicago for his skullduggery, Hulbert cut them off at the pass with his Grand Central Hotel *coup d'etat*. Spalding later related in his memoirs that Hulbert had told him when he signed with Chicago: "I have a scheme. Let us anticipate the eastern cusses and organize a new association before the March meeting, and then see who will do the expelling."

Hulbert was successful in his plan not only because he was able to argue persuasively that his new league would produce larger profits for team owners and a greater respect for

83

William Hulbert, the National League's founder and by far its most influential executive in its formative years. Unaccountably he was not enshrined in the Hall of Fame until 1995, long after many lesser contributors.

the national game stemming from the elimination of the gambling influence. Far more important, in the long view, was that Hulbert's National League accomplished three things that had eluded NA leaders. First and foremost, it built a network of baseball clubs run on business principles, enabling the men at the top of the corporate hierarchy to rake in the bulk of the profits. Second, by keeping the players out of the business end of the game, the National League ensured that they would get a much smaller percentage of the gate receipts. Finally, Hulbert's fierce monitions for honest play disguised a wish to present his new league as a bastion of Victorian propriety and to eliminate the riffraff from the grandstands of his ballparks in order to gain the confidence of the right-minded and the well-heeled who were willing and able to pay double the previous standard admission price—fifty cents instead of a quarter. To this end, Hulbert imposed what were almost Draconian measures for a coalition trying to attract a sporting crowd: no beer or whiskey allowed in the ballpark, no Sunday games, no cursing on the field or public drunkenness by its players.

Of the three rebel leagues that did battle with the National League between 1876 and 1900 over its claim to a monopoly on major league status, only the Players League quarreled with Hulbert's first and second innovations. Ironically, however, the player-controlled Players League accepted without reservation in his third innovation. In contrast, both the American Association and the Union Association, the National League's two other rivals for supremacy, flaunted Victorian standards of propriety by allowing the sale of intoxicants at their games, playing on Sundays in cities where permitted and holding the standard admission price to a quarter so that their product was more accessible to workingmen and ethnics whose trade the National League eschewed.

1876

AL SPALDING LANDS ON HIS
FIFTH STRAIGHT FLAG WINNER

National League chieftains strove to fulfill their pledge to help reform the game by legislating many new rules before launching their inaugural season in 1876. Among the more significant changes were those requiring the home team to furnish all game balls and awarding a baserunner one base if a fielder obstructed him.

Another major innovation required a batter to remain inside the batter's box while swinging at a pitch or risk being declared out. But the new league was still as loath as its predecessor to make a batter suffer the ignominy of being called out on strikes. Indeed, in 1876 a batter could not receive a called third strike until he had first been warned for not swinging at a "good ball." This meant that in some instances a batter got the equivalent of four strikes. As might be expected, strikeout totals throughout the 1870s were absurdly low. In 1876 the entire Philadelphia pitching staff compiled only 22 K's in 60 games.

The new league was similarly laggard in addressing the scheduling problems that had plagued the National Association. In 1876 it was still left to teams and their secretaries to arrange their own games with each other.

The honor of hosting the first game in National League history fell to Philadelphia. On Saturday, April 22, 1876, with Billy McLean officiating and some 3,000 on hand at Jefferson Street Grounds, Lon Knight of the local Athletics lost to Boston's Joe Borden, 6–5. Jim O'Rourke of Boston, the third batter in the top of the first inning, stroked the first hit in National League history, and O'Rourke's teammate, Tim McGinley, scored the first run the following inning. But as in most games of that time, defense was the deciding element. Philadelphia made 11 errors behind Knight, leading to five unearned Boston runs, while the Hub team committed just seven bobbles.

Riding a string of four straight pennants in the National Association, the Boston entry, formerly the Red Stockings, was now called the Red Caps or Reds. By any nickname, Borden's Opening Day win gave them undisputed possession of first place in the new league. But their lead was short-lived. Two days later Philadelphia blasted Boston, 20–3, in

George Hall, the NL's first home-run king. After Philadelphia was expelled from the NL, in 1877 he went to Louisville, where he was enmeshed in the game's biggest scandal prior to the 1919 World Series fixing.

the season's second contest, and the following afternoon three other clubs—New York, Louisville and Cincinnati—staged their home openers. Of the three host teams only Cincinnati won, edging St. Louis's George Bradley 2–1. On April 27 Cincinnati was again victorious, 5–2, over the St. Louis ace, boosting the Queen City into a first-place tie with Chicago, which had blanked Louisville in each of its first two outings.

Yet to be scored upon, pitcher-manager Al Spalding led his White Stockings to Cincinnati on April 29. With first place at stake, Chicago burst the Queen City club's bubble, 11–5, then triumphed again three days later in the second game of the series. By the time the Windy City crew left Cincinnati the two teams were on courses that would take them in very opposite directions. After starting with four straight wins, Chicago sustained its first loss on May 5 at St. Louis, falling 1–0 to Bradley. But after Spalding beat Bradley in the next game, the White Stockings did not

THE "CHICAGO" KING

In 1876 a shutout was still a rarity and was called a "Chicago" dating from a humiliating 9–0 loss suffered by the original Chicago White Stockings in 1870. Chicago's Al Spalding began the 1876 season with two straight shutouts against Louisville, but the "Chicago" king that year turned out not to be Spalding. Though he logged eight shutouts to break a major league record he and two other hurlers—George Zettlein and Candy Cummings—had set a year earlier in the final NA season, his total was exactly doubled by George Bradley of St. Louis. Bradley's 16 shutouts in 1876 are still a major league record, though the mark has since been tied by Pete Alexander. Oddly, Bradley's first "Chicago" victim of the season was none other than Chicago, which succumbed 1–0 on May 6. His 16th and final shutout came in his 53rd start of the season, against the New York Mutuals on September 5 at Brooklyn's Union Grounds.

In this woodcut is every man who played for the NL's first champion in 1876, including Oscar Bielaski, the game's first Polish player, and outfield sub Fred Andrus, who returned to Chicago eight years later for one game as a pitcher. Top left (clockwise): Anson, Glenn, A.G. Spalding, Barnes, Bielaski, Peters, Hines, McVey, Jas. White, Andrus, Addy,

lose again until May 19 when St. Louis made its first appearance of the season in Chicago. Another Bradley low-hit gem put the Brown Stockings in striking distance of first place, but they soon fell back. Hartford then mounted a charge, coming within one game of the top in early July before Cal McVey stopped the Dark Blues, 9–3, to start Chicago on an 11-game winning streak.

Spalding's sterling arm, which amassed 47 wins, and second baseman Ross Barnes's deft bat, which averaged over two hits a game, were much of the reason the White Stockings never lost more than two games in a row in 1876. But there was considerably more. First baseman Cal McVey (.347), third baseman Cap Anson (.356) and shortstop John Peters (.351) teamed with Barnes (.429) to give Chicago the finest hitting infield quartet in major league history. In addition, Barnes and Peters paced all fielders at their respective positions, and center fielder Paul Hines led all gardeners in fielding average.

Cincinnati, meanwhile, dropped 11 straight contests in May to plummet deep into the basement. When New York and Philadelphia also lagged far off the pace, in mid-September both eastern clubs elected not to make their final western road trips, believing that the League needed them far more than they needed the League. But they underestimated William Hulbert. Their failure to honor their schedule commitments was a crime—one for which Hulbert mustered the vote to dismiss them from the League at a loop meeting on December 7, 1876, at Cleveland's Kennard House hotel.

The departure of Philadelphia and New York sheared the League of the two largest cities in the country and pared it to just six teams entering its second season. This prospect up-staged another event at the League meeting that would soon have an even greater impact on

Louisville's first major league team—the 1876 Grays. Note that the players are posed behind a generic team mural with holes cut out for them to poke their heads through. This was a common trick when photography was in its infancy and it was nearly impossible to keep a group of people frozen long enough for the camera to capture them. Top: Scott Hastings, Jim Devlin and Pop Snyder. Middle: John Carbine, Bill Hague, Chick Fulmer, player-manager Jack Chapman, Joe Gerhardt and Art Allison. Front: George Bechtel and Johnny Ryan.

WHICH TEAM FINISHED SECOND?

St. Louis appeared to sew up second place when George Bradley beat the Hartford Dark Blues 6–4 on September 16 in Hartford's last home game of the season. But the Connecticut team then took to the road with a vengeance. Hartford ended the season in a furious rush with nine straight wins, the first one in St. Louis, to vault past the Brown Stockings. Though most encyclopedias today list St. Louis in second place with a .703 winning percentage, Hartford was acclaimed the second-place team in 1876 with 47 wins, as compared to St. Louis's 45. Prior to 1882, total wins, not winning percentage, determined a team's spot in the standings.

WHEN WALKS WERE EXPENSIVE

In 1876, National League official scorers were required to count a base on balls as a hitless turn at bat and reduce a player's batting average accordingly. Ironically, the player most affected by this rule was the league's leading hitter, Ross Barnes, who also topped the loop in walks with 20. For nearly a century Barnes was charged with 342 at bats in 1876, and his batting average was calculated to be .404. Not until the first edition of the Macmillan *Encyclopedia* were Barnes's walks deducted, shaving his total at bats to 322 and hoisting his batting average to its presently accepted .429 mark. If one buys the argument that today's rules should be applied to all past achievements, then Barnes's .429 figure in 1876 stands as the National League's highest batting average prior to the adoption of the 60'6" pitching distance. The same is true of his .590 slugging average that year. In 1876, Barnes also led the National League in both doubles and triples, tending to belie the view of many historians that he was no more than a slap hitter who took ruthless advantage prior to 1877 of the fair-foul rule.

the struggling organization's future. Pitcher Jim Devlin traveled to the meeting at his own expense to beg for his release from Louisville, claiming the team had failed to fulfill the conditions of his contract. The Grays' vice president, Charles Chase, presented his side of the dispute, and the other three directors—Hartford player-manager Bob Ferguson, Boston president Nicholas Appolonio and St. Louis club secretary Charles Fowle—sided with Chase against Devlin, compelling the disgruntled pitcher to remain in Louisville at least for the 1877 season.

For all of Hulbert's careful planning, his brainchild was less than a resounding success in 1876. Though it pleased him that his Chicago club won 79 percent of its championship games, he could only blame himself for the fact that the one-sided race prevented any of the other teams from turning a profit. That five of them were willing to undertake another season was due in large part to Hulbert's grudgingly given approval for his member clubs to schedule exhibition games with nonmember teams. According to Henry Chadwick's calculations, League clubs lost 37 of those exhibition games in 1876. Presumably they won more than that number, since many of their exhibition contests came against weak opponents; but Chadwick, demonstrating his prejudice against the League's claims of superiority, never tabulated their wins.

And at the close of the 1876 season Chadwick could mount a strong argument. For all its monetary blandishments, the League had still left a bounty of outstanding players spread among the more than 50 professional teams not under its umbrella. Many of those players preferred less compensation to leaving their hometown clubs for the larger League cities. Moreover, it was only Hulbert and his minions who maintained that theirs was the lone true "major" operation. As a result, there was as yet no stigma attached to being a big frog in a small pond. A player who hit .429 or won 47 games in 1876 was feted nearly equally whether he did it for a League team in Chicago or an independent club in Dubuque.

MEET DORY DEAN

The nineteenth century was rife with pitchers who compiled huge loss totals in their one and only major league seasons, but none achieved as much negative distinction as Dory Dean. Even though the 1876 season was nearly two months old before he made his big league debut, Dean led last-place Cincinnati in losses. Moreover, his .133 winning percentage is the worst ever by a one-year pitcher involved in a minimum of 20 decisions. Later in life, however, Dean founded a prosperous electrotype business and became an outstanding tennis player, good enough to continue winning tournaments in the 1930s after his 80th birthday. A list of nineteenth-century players who lost 14 or more games in their only seasons as pitchers:

	Year	Team	W	L	PCT
George Cobb	1892	Bal-LA	10	37	.213
Fleury Sullivan	1884	Pit-AA	16	35	.314
Doc Landis	1882	Phi/Bal-AA	12	28	.300
Parke Swartzel	1889	KC-AA	19	27	.413
Dory Dean	1876	Cin-NL	4	26	.133
John Keefe	1890	Syr-AA	17	24	.415
Charlie McCullough	1890	Bro/Syr-A	5	23	.179
Charlie Knepper	1899	Cle-NL	4	22	.154
Alex Voss	1884	Was/KC-UA	5	20	.200
John Hamill	1884	Was-AA	2	17	.105
Hugh Campbell	1872	Eliz-NA	2	16	.111
Cy Bentley	1872	Mans-NA	2	15	.118
Ed Green	1890	Phi-AA	7	15	.318
Ed Dugan	1884	Vir-AA	5	14	.263
Ezra Lincoln	1890	Cle-N/Syr-AA	3	14	.176

THE SEASONAL RECORD

	G	W	L	PCT	H	R	GB
1. Chicago White Stockings	66	52	14	.788	25–6	27–8	—
2. Hartford Dark Blues	69	47	21	.691	23–9	24–12	6
3. St. Louis Brown Stockings	64	45	19	.703	24–6	21–13	6
4. Boston Red Caps	70	39	31	.557	19–17	20–14	15
5. Louisville Grays	69	30	36	.455	15–16	15–20	22
6. New York Mutuals	57	21	35	.375	13–20	8–15	22
7. Philadelphia Athletics	60	14	45	.237	10–24	4–21	34.5
8. Cincinnati Red Stockings	65	9	56	.138	6–24	3–32	42.5

	Chi	Har	StL	Bos	Lou	NY	Phi	Cin	
Chicago	—	6	4	9	9	7	7	10	52
Hartford	4	—	4	8	9	4	9	9	47
St. Louis	6	6	—	6	6	6	8	7	45
Boston	1	2	4	—	5	8	9	10	39
Louisville	1	1	4	5	—	5	6	8	30
New York	1	4	1	2	3	—	3	7	21
Philadelphia	1	1	0	1	2	4	—	5	14
Cincinnati	0	1	2	0	2	1	3	—	9
	14	21	19	31	36	35	45	56	257

SEASON LEADERS

Batting Average (150 ABs)

1.	Barnes, Chicago	.429
2.	Hall, Philadelphia	.366
3.	Anson, Chicago	.356
4.	Peters, Chicago	.351
5.	McVey, Chicago	.347

On–Base Percentage

1.	Barnes, Chicago	.462
2.	Hall, Philadelphia	.384
3.	Anson, Chicago	.380
4.	White, Chicago	.358
	O'Rourke, Boston	.358

Home Runs

1.	Hall, Philadelphia	5
2.	C. Jones, Cincinnati	4
3.	Seven with	2

Hits

1.	Barnes, Chicago	138
2.	Peters, Chicago	111
3.	Anson, Chicago	110
4.	McVey, Chicago	107
5.	White, Chicago	104

Bases on Balls

1.	Barnes, Chicago	20
2.	J. O'Rourke, Boston	15
3.	Burdock, Hartford	13
4.	Glenn, Chicago	12
	Anson. Chicago	12

Slugging Average

1.	Barnes, Chicago	.590
2.	Hall, Philadelphia	.545
3.	Pike, St. Louis	.472
4.	Anson, Chicago	.450
5.	Meyerle, Philadelphia	.449

Total Bases

1.	Barnes, Chicago	190
2.	Hall, Philadelphia	146
3.	Anson, Chicago	136
4.	Hines, Chicago	134
5.	Pike, St. Louis	133

RBI

1.	White, Chicago	60
2.	Hines, Chicago	59
	Anson, Chicago	59
	Barnes, Chicago	59
5.	McVey, Chicago	53

Runs

1.	Barnes, Chicago	126
2.	G. Wright, Boston	72
3.	Peters, Chicago	70
4.	White, Chicago	66
	Burdock, Hartford	66

Strikeouts

1.	Ryan, Louisville	23
2.	L. Brown, Boston	22
3.	R. Snyder, Cincinnati	19
4.	O'Rourke, Boston	17
	C. Jones, Cincinnati	17

PITCHING

Wins

1.	Spalding, Chicago	47
2.	G. Bradley, St. Louis	45
3.	Bond, Hartford	31
4.	Devlin, Louisville	30
5.	Mathews, New York	21

Innings

1.	Devlin, Louisville	622
2.	G. Bradley, St. Louis	573
3.	Spalding, Chicago	529
4.	Mathews, New York	516
5.	Bond, Hartford	408

Losses

1.	Devlin, Louisville	35
2.	Mathews, New York	34
3.	Dean, Cincinnati	26
4.	Knight, Philadelphia	22
5.	Zettlein, Philadelphia	20
	Fisher, Cincinnati	20

Complete Games

1.	Devlin, Louisville	66
2.	G. Bradley, St. Louis	63
3.	Mathews, New York	55
4.	Spalding, Chicago	53
5.	Bond, Hartford	45

Strikeouts

1.	Devlin, Louisville	122
2.	G. Bradley, St. Louis	103
3.	Bond, Hartford	88
4.	Spalding, Chicago	39
5.	Mathews, New York	37

ERA (70 innings)

1.	G. Bradley, St. Louis	1.23
2.	Devlin, Louisville	1.56
3.	Cummings, Hartford	1.67
4.	Bond, Hartford	1.68
5.	Spalding, Chicago	1.75

Winning Percentage (20 decisions)

1.	Spalding, Chicago	.783
	Manning, Boston	.783
3.	Bond, Hartford	.705
4.	G. Bradley, St. Louis	.703
5.	Cummings, Hartford	.667

Lowest On–Base Percentage

1.	G. Bradley, St. Louis	.224
2.	Bond, Hartford	.227
3.	Devlin, Louisville	.235
4.	Cummings, Hartford	.251
5.	Spalding, Chicago	.256

FIELDING

Total Chances

1B	Dehlman, St. Louis	791
2B	Somerville, Louisville	530
3B	Anson, Chicago	332
SS	Force, Phila–New York	397
OF	Treacy, New York	250
C	Clapp, St. Louis	445
P	Devlin, Louisville	153

Fielding Average

Start, New York	.964
Barnes, Chicago	.910
Battin, St. Louis	.867
Peters, Chicago	.932
Hines, Chicago	.923
D. Allison, Hartford	.881
Spalding, Boston	.951

CHICAGO   **Al Spalding**   **23rd Street Grounds**

		G	AB	H	R	2B	3B	HR	RBI	BB	BA	SA
2B	Ross Barnes	66	322	**138**	**126**	**21**	**14**	1	59	20	**.429**	**.590**
SS	John Peters	66	316	111	70	14	2	1	47	3	.351	.418
3B	Cap Anson	66	309	110	63	9	7	2	59	12	.356	.440
1B	Cal McVey	63	308	107	62	15	0	1	53	2	.347	.406
CF	Paul Hines	64	305	101	62	**21**	3	2	59	1	.331	.439
C	Deacon White	66	303	104	66	18	1	1	**60**	7	.343	.419
P	Al Spalding	66	292	91	54	14	2	0	44	6	.312	.373
LF	John Glenn	66	276	84	55	9	2	0	32	12	.304	.351
RF	Bob Addy	32	142	40	36	4	1	0	16	5	.282	.324
Sub	Oscar Bielaski	32	139	29	24	3	0	0	10	2	.209	.230
Sub	Fred Andrus	8	36	11	6	3	0	0	2	0	.306	.389
		66	2748	**926**	**624**	**131**	32	8	**441**	70	**.337**	**.416**

1B	McVey 55, Glenn 15, Spalding 3, White 3
2B	Barnes 66, Hines 1
SS	Peters 66, Spalding 1
3B	Anson 66, McVey 1, White 1
OF	Hines 64, Glenn 56, Addy 32, Bielaski 32, Spalding 10, Andrus 8, White 3, McVey 1
C	White 63, McVey 6, Anson 2
P	Spalding 61, McVey 11, Peters 1, Barnes 1, White 1

	G	IP	GS	CG	W	L	K	BB	SH	SV	ERA
Al Spalding	61	528.2	60	53	**47**	12	39	26	9	0	1.75
Cal McVey	11	59.1	6	5	5	2	9	2	0	2	1.52
Deacon White	1	2	0	0	0	0	3	0	0	1	0.00
Ross Barnes	1	1.1	0	0	0	0	0	0	0	0	20.25
John Peters	1	1	0	0	0	0	0	1	0	1	0.00
		592.1	66	58	52	14	51	29	9	4	1.76

ST. LOUIS   Mase Graffen (39–17)   George McManus (6–2)   Grand Avenue Park

		G	AB	H	R	2B	3B	HR	RBI	BB	BA	SA
C	John Clapp	64	298	91	60	4	2	0	29	8	.305	.332
3B	Joe Battin	64	283	85	34	11	4	0	46	6	.300	.367
LF	Ned Cuthbert	63	283	70	46	10	1	0	25	7	.247	.290
CF	Lip Pike	63	282	91	55	19	10	1	50	8	.323	.472
2B	Mike McGeary	61	276	72	48	3	0	0	30	2	.261	.272
P	George Bradley	64	265	66	29	7	6	0	28	3	.249	.321
RF	Joe Blong	62	264	62	30	7	4	0	30	2	.235	.292
1B	Dutch Dehlman	64	245	45	40	6	0	0	9	9	.184	.208
SS	Denny Mack	48	180	39	32	5	0	1	7	11	.217	.261
Sub	Dickey Pearce	25	102	21	12	1	0	0	10	3	.206	.216
		64	2478	642	386	73	27	2	264	59	.259	.313

- 1B Dehlman 64
- 2B McGeary 56, Mack 5, Pike 2, Pearce 1, Clapp 1, Battin 1
- SS Mack 41, Pearce 23
- 3B Battin 63, McGeary 1
- OF Cuthbert 63, Blong 62, Pike 62, Clapp 4, Mack 2, Pearce 1, McGeary 1
- C   Clapp 61, McGeary 5
- P   Bradley 64, Blong 1

	G	IP	GS	CG	W	L	K	BB	SH	SV	ERA
George Bradley#	64	573	64	63	45	19	103	38	**16**	0	**1.23**
Joe Blong	1	4	0	0	0	0	0	1	0	0	0.00
		577	64	63	45	19	103	39	**16**	0	**1.22**

#No hit game 2–0 vs Hartford, July 15

HARTFORD   Bob Ferguson   Hartford Baseball Grounds

		G	AB	H	R	2B	3B	HR	RBI	BB	BA	SA
CF	Jack Remsen	69	**324**	89	62	12	5	1	30	1	.275	.352
RF	Dick Higham	67	312	102	59	**21**	2	0	35	2	.327	.407
3B	Bob Ferguson	69	310	82	48	8	5	0	32	2	.265	.323
2B	Jack Burdock	69	309	80	66	9	1	0	23	13	.259	.294
SS	Tom Carey	68	289	78	51	7	0	0	26	3	.270	.294
LF	Tom York	67	263	68	47	12	7	1	39	10	.259	.369
1B	Everett Mills	63	254	66	28	8	1	0	23	1	.260	.299
P	Tommy Bond	45	182	50	18	8	0	0	21	0	.275	.319
C	Doug Allison	44	163	43	19	4	0	0	15	3	.264	.288
C	Bill Harbidge	30	106	23	11	2	1	0	6	3	.217	.255
P	Candy Cummings	24	105	17	14	3	0	0	7	0	.162	.190
Sub	John Cassidy	12	47	13	6	2	0	0	8	1	.277	.319
		69	2664	711	429	96	22	2	265	39	.267	.322

1B   Mills 63, Cassidy 4, Harbidge 2
2B   Burdock 69, Higham 1
SS   Carey 68, Higham 1
3B   Ferguson 69, Burdock 1
OF   Remsen 69, York 67, Higham 59, Cassidy 8, Harbidge 6, Allison 6
C   Allison 40, Harbidge 24, Higham 13
P   Bond 45, Cummings 24

	G	IP	GS	CG	W	L	K	BB	SH	SV	ERA
Tommy Bond	45	408	45	45	31	13	88	13	6	0	1.68
Candy Cummings	24	216	24	24	16	8	26	14	5	0	1.67
	624	69	**69**	47	21	114	27	11	0	1.67

BOSTON   **Harry Wright**   **South End Grounds (I)**

		G	AB	H	R	2B	3B	HR	RBI	BB	BA	SA
SS	George Wright	70	**335**	100	72	18	6	1	34	8	.299	.397
CF	Jim O'Rourke	70	312	102	61	17	3	2	43	15	.327	.420
1B	Tim Murnane	69	308	87	60	4	3	2	34	8	.282	.334
LF	Andy Leonard	64	303	85	53	10	2	0	27	4	.281	.327
RF	Jack Manning	70	288	76	52	13	0	2	25	7	.264	.330
3B	Harry Schafer	70	286	72	47	11	0	0	35	4	.252	.290
2B	John Morrill	66	278	73	38	5	2	0	26	3	.263	.295
C	Lew Brown	46	195	41	23	6	6	2	21	3	.210	.333
OF	Frank Whitney	34	139	33	27	7	1	0	15	1	.237	.302
P	Joe Borden	32	121	25	19	3	0	0	7	3	.207	.231
P	Foghorn Bradley	22	82	19	12	2	1	0	8	2	.232	.280
Sub	Tim McGinley	9	40	6	5	0	0	0	2	0	.150	.150
P	Dick McBride	4	16	3	2	0	0	0	4	0	.188	.188
Sub	Sam Wright	2	8	1	0	0	0	0	0	0	.125	.125
P	Tricky Nichols	1	4	0	0	0	0	0	0	0	.000	.000
Sub	Bill Parks	1	4	0	0	0	0	0	0	0	.000	.000
Sub	Harry Wright	1	3	0	0	0	0	0	0	1	.000	.000
		70	2722	723	471	96	24	**9**	281	58	.266	.328

1B   Murnane 65, Morrill 3, O'Rourke 2
2B   Morrill 37, Leonard 30, G. Wright 2, Manning 1, Murnane 1, Whitney 1
SS   G. Wright 68, S. Wright 2, Manning 1
3B   Schafer 70
OF   O'Rourke 68, Manning 56, Leonard 35, Whitney 34, Borden 16, McGinley 6, Morrill 5,
     Bradley 4, Murnane 3, McBride 1, Parks 1, H. Wright 1, Brown 1
C   Brown 45, Morrill 23, McGinley 3, O'Rourke 1
P   Manning 34, Borden 29, Bradley 22, McBride 4, Nichols 1, G. Wright 1

	G	IP	GS	CG	W	L	K	BB	K	SV	ERA
Joe Borden	29	218.1	24	16	11	12	34	**51**	2	1	2.89
Jack Manning	34	197.1	20	13	18	5	24	32	0	5	2.14
Foghorn Bradley	22	173.1	21	16	9	10	16	16	1	1	2.49
Dick McBride	4	33	4	3	0	4	2	5	0	0	2.73
Tricky Nichols	1	9	1	1	1	0	0	0	0	0	1.00
George Wright	1	1	0	0	0	0	1	0	0	0	0.00
	632	70	49	39	31	77	104	3	**7**	2.51

LOUISVILLE   Jack Chapman   Louisville Baseball Park

		G	AB	H	R	2B	3B	HR	RBI	BB	BA	SA
P	Jim Devlin	68	298	94	38	14	1	0	28	1	.315	.369
3B	Bill Hague	67	294	78	31	8	0	1	22	2	.265	.303
1B	Joe Gerhardt	66	292	76	33	10	3	2	18	3	.260	.336
CF	Scott Hastings	67	283	73	36	6	1	0	21	5	.258	.286
SS	Chick Fulmer	66	267	73	28	9	5	1	29	1	.273	.356
2B	Ed Somerville	64	256	48	29	5	1	0	14	1	.188	.215
LF	Johnny Ryan	64	241	61	32	5	1	1	18	6	.253	.295
C	Pop Snyder	56	224	44	21	4	1	1	9	2	.196	.237
RF	Art Allison	31	130	27	9	2	1	0	10	2	.208	.238
Sub	Jack Chapman	17	67	16	4	1	0	0	5	1	.239	.254
Sub	Jim Clinton	16	65	22	8	2	0	0	0	0	.338	.369
Sub	George Bechtel	14	55	10	2	1	0	0	2	0	.182	.200
C	Bill Holbert	12	43	11	3	0	0	0	5	0	.256	.256
Sub	Dan Collins	7	28	4	3	1	0	0	9	0	.143	.179
Sub	Jack Carbine	7	25	4	3	0	0	0	1	0	.160	.160
P	Frank Pearce	1	2	0	0	0	0	0	0	0	.000	.000
		69	2570	641	280	68	14	6	191	24	.249	.294

1B   Gerhardt 54, Allison 8, Carbine 6, Devlin 1, Clinton 1
2B   Somerville 64, Gerhardt 5
SS   Fulmer 66, Gerhardt 3, Hague 1
3B   Hague 67, Gerhardt 2, Chapman 1
OF   Hastings 64, Ryan 64, Allison 23, Chapman 17, Clinton 14, Bechtel 14, Collins 7, Snyder 4, Gerhardt 2, Carbine 1
C   Snyder 55, Holbert 12, Hastings 5
P   Devlin 68, Pearce 1, Clinton 1, Ryan 1

	G	IP	GS	CG	W	L	K	BB	SH	SV	ERA
Jim Devlin	68	622	68	66	30	35	122	37	5	0	1.56
Jim Clinton	1	9	1	1	0	1	1	0	0	0	6.00
Johnny Ryan	1	8	0	0	0	0	1	0	0	0	5.63
Frank Pearce	1	4	0	0	0	0	1	1	0	0	4.50
		643	69	67	30	36	125	38	5	0	1.69

NEW YORK   Nat Hicks   Union Grounds (Brooklyn)

		G	AB	H	R	2B	3B	HR	RBI	BB	BA	SA
1B	Joe Start	56	264	73	40	6	0	0	21	1	.277	.299
LF	Fred Treacey	57	256	54	47	5	1	0	18	1	.211	.238
2B	Bill Craver	56	246	55	24	4	0	0	22	2	.224	.240
CF	Jim Holdsworth	52	241	64	23	3	2	0	19	1	.266	.295
SS	Jimmy Hallinan	54	240	67	45	7	6	2	36	2	.279	.383
RF	Eddie Booth	57	228	49	17	2	1	0	7	2	.215	.232
P	Bobby Mathews	56	218	40	19	4	1	0	9	3	.183	.211
3B	Al Nichols	57	212	38	20	4	0	0	9	2	.179	.198
C	Nat Hicks	45	188	44	20	4	1	0	15	3	.234	.266
Sub	Mike Hayes	5	21	3	1	0	2	0	2	0	.143	.333
Sub	George Bechtel	2	10	3	2	0	0	0	0	0	.300	.300
Sub	Jim Shandley	2	8	1	0	0	0	0	0	0	.125	.125
Sub	John Maloney	2	7	2	1	0	1	0	2	0	.286	.571
Sub	Pete Treacey	2	5	0	1	0	0	0	0	1	.000	.000
Sub	John Hatfield	1	4	1	0	0	0	0	1	0	.250	.250
Sub	John McGuinness	1	4	0	0	0	0	0	0	0	.000	.000
Sub	George Fair	1	4	0	0	0	0	0	0	0	.000	.000
P	Terry Larkin	1	4	0	0	0	0	0	0	0	.000	.000

		G	AB	H	R	2B	3B	HR	RBI	BB	BA	SA
Sub	Billy West	1	4	0	0	0	0	0	0	0	.000	.000
Sub	George Heubel	1	4	0	0	0	0	0	0	0	.000	.000
Sub	Davy Force	1	3	0	0	0	0	0	0	0	.000	.000
Sub	George Seward	1	3	0	0	0	0	0	0	0	.000	.000
Sub	Nealy Phelps	1	3	0	0	0	0	0	0	0	.000	.000
Sub	Bob Valentine	1	3	0	0	0	0	0	0	0	.000	.000
		57	2180	494	260	39	15	2	161	18	.227	.261

1B   Start 56, Heubel 1
2B   Craver 42, Booth 5, Hallinan 4, Holdsworth 3, Fair 1, McGuinness 1, Seward 1, West 1, Hatfield 1
SS   Hallinan 50, Craver 6, P. Treacey 2, Force 1
3B   Nichols 57
OF   F. Treacey 57, Booth 53, Holdsworth 49, Hayes 5, Bechtel 2, Shandley 2, Maloney 2, Hallinan 2, Phelps 1, Mathews 1
C   Hicks 45, Craver 11, McGuinness 1, Valentine 1
P   Mathews 56, Larkin 1, Booth 1

	G	IP	GS	CG	W	L	K	BB	SH	SV	ERA
Bobby Mathews	56	516	56	55	21	34	37	24	2	0	2.86
Terry Larkin	1	9	1	1	0	1	0	0	0	0	3.00
Eddie Booth	1	5	1	0	0	0	0	0	0	0	9.31
		530	58	56	21	35	37	**24**	2	0	2.94

PHILADELPHIA   **Al Wright**   **Jefferson Street Grounds**

		G	AB	H	R	2B	3B	HR	RBI	BB	BA	SA
SS	Davy Force	60	284	66	48	6	0	0	17	5	.232	.254
2B	Wes Fisler	59	278	80	42	15	1	1	30	2	.288	.360
LF	George Hall	60	268	98	51	7	13	5	45	8	.366	.545
3B	Levi Meyerle	55	256	87	46	12	8	0	34	3	.340	.449
P	Lon Knight	55	240	60	32	9	3	0	24	2	.250	.313
1B	Ezra Sutton	54	236	70	45	12	7	1	31	3	.297	.419
RF	William Coon	54	220	50	30	5	5	1	0	22	2	.227	.259
CF	Dave Eggler	39	174	52	28	4	0	0	19	2	.299	.322
P	George Zettlein	32	128	27	11	2	1	0	11	0	.211	.242
C	Fergy Malone	22	96	22	14	2	0	0	6	0	.229	.250
Sub	Bill Fouser	21	89	12	11	0	1	0	2	0	.135	.157
Sub	Whitey Ritterson	16	52	13	8	3	0	0	4	0	.250	.308
Sub	Doc Bushong	5	21	1	4	0	0	0	1	0	.048	.048
Sub	Pete Curren	3	12	4	5	1	0	0	2	0	.333	.417
Sub	Lou Paul	3	12	2	2	1	0	0	0	0	.167	.250
Sub	Jim Ward	1	4	2	1	0	0	0	1	0	.500	.500
Sub	John Bergh	1	4	0	0	0	0	0	0	0	.000	.000
Sub	Nealy Phelps	1	4	0	0	0	0	0	0	0	.000	.000
P	Flip Lafferty	1	3	0	0	0	0	0	0	0	.000	.000
Sub	Fred Warner	1	3	0	0	0	0	0	0	0	.000	.000
Sub	John Mullen	1	3	0	0	0	0	0	0	0	.000	.000
		60	2387	646	378	79	**35**	7	249	27	.271	.342

1B   Sutton 29, Fisler 14, Knight 13, Zettlein 7, Fouser 1
2B   Fisler 21, Sutton 15, Fouser 14, Knight 6, Coon 4, Meyerle 3, Zettlein 1
SS   Force 60, Malone 1, Fisler 1
3B   Meyerle 49, Sutton 8, Coon 4, Force 2, Ritterson 1

OF   Hall 60, Eggler 39, Coon 29, Fisler 24, Knight 9, Fouser 7, Ritterson 4, Sutton 4, Malone 3, Meyerle 3, Warner 1, Zettlein 1, Bergh 1, Curren 1
C   Malone 20, Coon 18, Ritterson 14, Bushong 5, Paul 3, Curren 2, Ward 1, Phelps 1, Bergh 1, Mullen 1
P   Knight 34, Zettlein 28, Coon 2, Meyerle 2, Lafferty 1

	G	IP	GS	CG	W	L	K	BB	SH	SV	ERA
Lon Knight	34	282	32	27	10	22	12	34	0	0	2.62
George Zettlein	28	234	25	23	4	20	10	6	1	2	3.88
Levi Meyerle	2	18	2	2	0	2	0	1	0	0	5.00
Flip Lafferty	1	9	1	1	0	1	0	0	0	0	0.00
William Coon	2	7	0	0	0	0	0	0	0	0	5.14
		550	60	53	14	45	22	41	1	2	3.22

CINCINNATI   Charlie Gould   Avenue Grounds

		G	AB	H	R	2B	3B	HR	RBI	BB	BA	SA
CF	Charley Jones	64	276	79	40	17	4	4	38	7	.286	.420
C	Amos Booth	63	272	71	31	3	0	0	14	9	.261	.272
1B	Charlie Gould	61	258	65	27	7	0	0	11	6	.252	.279
SS	Harry Kessler	59	248	64	26	5	0	0	11	7	.258	.278
RF	Dave Pierson	57	233	55	33	4	1	0	13	1	.236	.262
2B	Charlie Sweasy	56	225	46	18	5	2	0	10	2	.204	.244
3B	Will Foley	58	221	50	19	3	2	0	9	0	.226	.258
LF	Redleg Snyder	55	205	31	10	3	1	0	12	1	.151	.176
P	Dory Dean	34	138	36	9	3	1	0	4	2	.261	.297
P	Cherokee Fisher	35	129	32	12	1	0	0	4	0	.248	.256
Sub	Bobby Clack	32	118	19	10	0	1	0	5	5	.161	.178
P	Dale Williams	9	35	7	1	0	0	0	1	0	.200	.200
Sub	Sam Field	4	14	0	2	0	0	0	0	1	.000	.000
		65	2372	555	238	51	12	4	132	41	.234	.271

1B   Gould 61, Clack 5, Fisher 1
2B   Sweasy 55, Clack 8, Field 2, Pierson 1
SS   Kessler 46, Booth 22, Dean 2, Pierson 1, Fisher 1
3B   Foley 46, Booth 24, Clack 3, Pierson 1
OF   Jones 64, Snyder 55, Pierson 30, Clack 17, Kessler 16, Fisher 11, Dean 5, Booth 3, Sweasy 1
C   Pierson 31, Booth 24, Foley 20, Field 3
P   Dean 30, Fisher 28, Williams 9, Booth 3, Gould 2, Clack 1, Pierson 1

	G	IP	GS	CG	W	L	K	BB	SH	SV	ERA
Dory Dean	30	262.2	30	26	4	26	22	24	0	0	3.73
Cherokee Fisher	28	229.1	24	22	4	20	29	6	0	0	3.02
Dale Williams	9	83	9	9	1	8	9	4	0	0	4.23
Amos Booth	3	9.2	1	0	0	1	0	0	0	0	9.31
Charlie Gould	2	4.1	0	0	0	0	0	0	0	0	0.00
Bobby Clack	1	2	0	0	0	0	0	0	0	0	4.50
Dave Pierson	1	—	1	0	0	1	0	0	0	0	—
		591	65	57	9	56	60	34	0	0	3.62

1877
SCANDAL IN
LOUISVILLE

Many baseball historians feel that 1877 produced the most pivotal season in the last century. Not only did it feature the only pennant race in major league history that was unequivocally proven to have been rigged, but it was also the first year that the National League schedule was done by loop officials rather than by individual teams. It was also the first year that home plate was placed entirely in fair territory, where it has remained ever since, as well as the first year that a forerunner of the present rule was introduced declaring a baserunner out if he is struck by a batted ball. But far and away the most important revision in 1877 was the abolition of the "fair-foul" hit. That season the rulebook was amended so that a batted ball striking first in foul territory and then moving into fair ground is fair, whereas a batted ball striking first in fair territory and then moving into foul ground before it passes either first or third base is foul. This rule change altered the game dramatically and might even be said to have "modernized" it.

Forced to function as a six-team circuit after expelling the New York and Philadelphia franchises the previous fall, League moguls in 1877 reduced the schedule from 70 to 60 games but required teams to play each opponent 12 times rather than 10, as in 1876. Clubs averaged three championship contests per week, usually on Tuesday, Thursday and Saturday, but had few off days as such, choosing instead to pad their coffers between championship games by playing each other in exhibition games that did not count or by playing exhibitions against nonleague opponents. Tickets at all League parks still sold for fifty cents but were reduced to a dime by the fourth inning.

The League's second season opened on April 30 with an unsatisfying 1–1 tie between Boston and a team that officially represented Hartford but was listed by most newspapers as Brooklyn in the League standings for the simple reason that it played its home games at Brooklyn's Union Grounds. But not even using the heavily populated Brooklyn as its home base could spare the Connecticut-owned team from financial ruin. As in 1876, Chicago was the only League team to turn a profit. One newspaper estimated the losses of the other five clubs at $17,300, and Cincinnati had such dire cash-flow problems that it folded briefly in

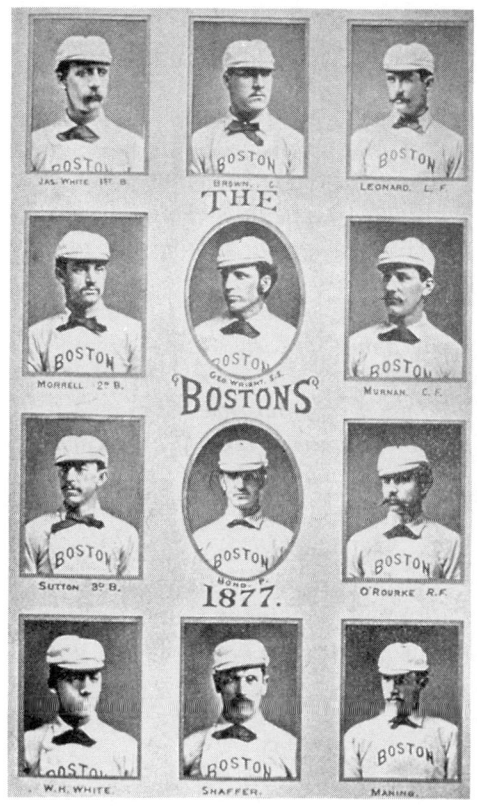

Though pictured with the 1877 NL champions, Jack Manning was actually on loan to Cincinnati that year. Seen here is every other man who played on the Hub's first NL titlist except manager Harry Wright, who got into just one game.

June and its games were thrown out of the standings (they were later restored and then thrown out again). In the few days Cincinnati was out of business, William Hulbert pilfered three of its players—Charley Jones, Jimmy Hallinan and Harry Smith—for his Chicago White Stockings. The outcry from the other league cities against this piracy forced Hulbert to remember that he was also loop president. He returned Jones, the best of the three, but kept the other two even after the Chicago *Tribune* vowed to stop running the scores of the White Stockings' games on its sports page.

Hulbert's poaching notwithstanding, Chicago was never a factor in the 1877 race. Despite retaining all of the stars from his 1876 champion with the sole exception of Deacon White, manager Al Spalding saw his team sink to next-to-last place. In fact, much of the White Stockings' shocking crash was attributable to Spalding himself. The game's top pitcher in 1876, he was no more than a mediocre first baseman when he opted to station himself there after relinquishing his pitching duties to George Bradley. In the offseason Spalding had urged Hulbert to sign Bradley, sensing that St. Louis's 1876 ace would only improve whereas his own best days in the box were behind him. Spalding guessed wrong on Bradley as well as on his own ability to fill the hole at first base created by White's departure to Boston. But an even larger reason for Chicago's sharp tumble toward the basement in 1877 was Ross Barnes's swift demise as an offensive force, owing to illness and the elimination of the fair-foul rule.

Once it grew clear that the White Stockings would not repeat, attention fell on Boston and Louisville. The Red Caps still had several members from their four-time National Association championship team, most prominently shortstop George Wright and outfielders Andy Leonard and Jim O'Rourke. Deacon White's return after a year in Chicago brought Boston the 1877 loop batting and RBI leader, and the team's 1876 pitching woes, after losing Spalding to Chicago, were remedied when manager Harry Wright coaxed Hartford ace Tommy Bond to come north for the 1877 season.

CHICAGO'S ORIGINAL HITLESS WONDERS

Cap Anson, nearly 20 years down the road from 1877 when he was a member of the homerless Chicago White Stockings. Rather incredibly, Anson, overwhelmingly the 19th-century total-base and extra-base hit leader, was blanked in the home-run department in nine of his 27 seasons. From top: (standing) Reiley, Friend, Griffith, Parker, Ryan, McBride, Flynn. (Seated) Truby, Briggs, Decker, Lange, Anson, Donahue, Everett, Terry, McFarland. (Front) Dahlen, Kittridge.

The Chicago White Stockings, first by a wide margin in both batting and slugging the previous year, set an unwanted record in 1877 when they went homerless for the entire season. No other major league team since, with the exception of two teams that were members of the Union Association for just a few games in 1884, has failed to hit at least one four-bagger.

Still, Boston could not shake Louisville. As stellar as Bond was in the box, no team had a more yeoman tosser in 1877 than Jim Devlin of the Grays. With Devlin hurling every game and ranking among the team's best hitters as well, Louisville shot to a commanding lead in early August. After the Grays won a pair of games in Chicago on August 11 and 13, Eastern sportswriters eagerly awaited their last trip east to Boston and Hartford (Brooklyn). Wrote one: "Never before has the glorious uncertainty of the national game been so conspicuously displayed as it has in the professional arena this year. A series of surprises have followed each other in rapid succession . . . This year no one has known where the little joker has been hid and in consequence a spicy interest has been added to the betting business on base ball matches." The same reporter then observed with unintentional irony: "Thus far the season has been an exceptional one in the integrity of play exhibited by all the contesting teams in the League arena, and it is to be hoped that nothing will occur to mar the record in this important respect."

The reporter's hope was brutally dashed when Louisville suffered four straight losses in Boston and three losses and a tie in its final four games in Brooklyn. The unexpected string of defeats dropped the Grays behind Boston by the time they left the east, and they never recovered. When Devlin lost 4–0 to Laurie Reis in Chicago on October 6, the final day of the season, the Grays finished seven full games behind Boston after holding a seemingly insurmountable lead on their previous visit to Chicago just eight weeks earlier.

Louisville's inexplicable collapse left so rank an aroma that club officials were compelled to investigate rumors that Devlin and other team members had thrown the pennant to Boston. When the rumors were borne out and Hulbert acted quickly and decisively, expelling four Louisville players for life, the decimated Falls City team dropped out of the

BENEATH THE LOUISVILLE SCANDAL

The transgression that enabled Boston to win the 1877 pennant was unearthed after John Haldeman used his influence as both a sportswriter on the Louisville *Courier-Journal* and the son of Grays president Walter Haldeman to prod Grays vice president Charles Chase to look into the team's late-season collapse. A former college player at Washington and Lee, Haldeman got into one game with Louisville in 1877; his push for an investigation was perhaps motivated partly by his resentment that manager Jack Chapman hadn't given him more of a chance. Chase grew alarmed by the huge number of wires substitute Al Nichols received and asked to inspect them. When Nichols refused, Chase announced that it was the act of a guilty man. Nichols then reluctantly allowed the wires to be examined.

The evidence was damning. Eastern gamblers telegraphed the code word "sash" for any game they wanted the Grays to dump. Center fielder George Hall and pitcher Jim Devlin confessed, implicating Nichols and third baseman Bill Craver. Craver, long under suspicion of dumping games, proclaimed his innocence and in-

voked his constitutional right to deny permission to have his mail examined; this was taken as evidence of guilt and he too was barred. For years Devlin hounded League president William Hulbert, begging to be reinstated. His pleas always fell on deaf ears, though Hulbert sometimes slipped him money for his family. Devlin was working as a beat cop in Philadelphia when he died in 1883.

Bill Craver was a rough piece of work. Many were glad to see him banished after the 1877 season, but the evidence of his guilt in the Louisville pennant-dumping scandal is less than compelling.

league, as did St. Louis, which had secretly arranged to sign two of the miscreants for the 1878 season. Hartford, too, quit when the club drew no better in Brooklyn than it had in Connecticut. This latest exodus meant that after only two seasons of operation, the League would begin its third year with just three of its original eight members still in place.

THE FIRST "MINOR" LEAGUE

The 1877 Indianapolis Blues, members of the League Alliance, a fledging minor league, included several key performers on the 1878 Indianapolis NL entry. Front: Charlie Hautz, Trick McSorley, Adam Rocap, Mike Golden and Joe Quest. Rear: Fred Warner, The Only Nolan, Denny Mack, Frank Flint and Pigtail Billy Riley. Golden was shopped when Indy garnered Jim McCormick from the Columbus Buckeyes to pair with Nolan in the pitcher's box. McCormick and King Kelly, both New Jersey natives, formed the famed "Jersey battery" for Columbus in 1877.

The battle for the public baseball dollar spread in February 1877 when representatives of 18 teams assembled in Pittsburgh, home of the independent Allegheny club, to form a new organization which would replace the old National Association the League had killed. Candy Cummings, who had pitched for the Hartford League entry in 1876, was elected president of the rival loop, which called itself the International Association of Professional Baseball Players. Upon the close of the 1876 season, Cummings had joined the Live Oak club of Lynn, Massachusetts, preferring to return to a player-controlled atmosphere. Other League performers who believed that craftsmen should have a voice in how their workshop is run also jumped ship after the League's inaugural season to sign with IA teams.

Though the IA is now considered to have been the first minor league, in no sense did its organizers view themselves as "minor" operators in 1877, and the events of that season support their contention that their circuit was in most respects the National League's equal. In 1877, League clubs lost no fewer than 72 games to outside clubs. Though its tickets were higher-priced and its player salaries correspondingly greater, the League had no monopoly on talent in 1877. Collectively, the players on the top six IA clubs that year accrued more past or future seasons of major league ball than the players on the six National League clubs.

THE SEASONAL RECORD

	W	L	PCT	H	R	GB
1. Boston Red Caps	42	18	.700	27–5	15–13	—
2. Louisville Grays	35	25	.583	21–9	14–16	7
3. Hartford Dark Blues	31	27	.534	19–8	12–19	10
4. St. Louis Brown Stockings	28	32	.467	20–10	8–22	14
5. Chicago White Stockings	26	33	.441	17–12	19–21	15.5
6. Cincinnati Red Stockings	15	42	.263	12–17	3–25	25.5

	Bos	Lou	Har	StL	Chi	Cin	
Boston	—	8	7	6	10	11	42
Louisville	4	—	6	10	8	7	35
Hartford	5	6	—	5	8	7	31
St. Louis	6	2	4	—	4	12	28
Chicago	2	4	7	8	—	5	26
Cincinnati	1	5	3	3	3	—	15
	18	25	27	32	33	42	177

SEASON LEADERS

Batting Average (200 ABs)

1.	D. White, Boston	.387
2.	Cassidy, Hartford	.378
3.	McVey, Chicago	.368
4.	O'Rourke, Boston	.362
5.	Anson, Chicago	.337

On–Base Percentage

1.	O'Rourke, Boston	.407
2.	D. White Boston	.405
3.	McVey, Chicago	.387
4.	Cassidy, Hartford	.386
5.	Anson, Chicago	.360

Home Runs

1.	Pike, Cincinnati	4
2.	Shaffer, Louisville	3
3.	Jones, Cin–Chi–Cin	2
	D. White, Boston	2
	Snyder, Louisville	2

Hits

1.	D. White, Boston	103
2.	McVey, Chicago	98
3.	O'Rourke, Boston	96
4.	Cassidy, Hartford	95
5.	Start, Hartford	90

Slugging Average

1.	D. White, Boston	.545
2.	C. Jones, Cin–Chi–Cin	.471
3.	Cassidy, Hartford	.458
4.	McVey, Chicago	.455
5.	O'Rourke, Boston	.445

Total Bases

1.	D. White, Boston	145
2.	McVey, Chicago	121
3.	O'Rourke, Boston	118
	Hall, Louisville	118
5.	Cassidy, Hartford	115

RBI

1.	D. White, Boston	49
2.	Peters, Chicago	41
3.	Sutton, Boston	39
4.	Jones, Cin–Chi–Cin	38
5.	York, Hartford	37

Runs

1.	O'Rourke, Boston	68
2.	G. Wright, Boston	58
	McVey, Chicago	58
4.	Start, Hartford	55
5.	Hall, Louisville	53

Bases on Balls

1.	J. O'Rourke, Boston	20
2.	Jones, Cin–Chi–Cin	15
3.	Hall, Louisville	12
	Booth, Cincinnati	12
5.	Force, St. Louis	11

Strikeouts

1.	L. Brown, Boston	33
2.	Devlin, Louisville	27
3.	C. Jones, Cin–Chi–Cin	25
4.	Larkin, Hartford	23
5.	Blong, St. Louis	22

PITCHING

Wins

1.	Bond, Boston	40
2.	Devlin, Louisville	35
3.	Larkin, Hartford	29
4.	Nichols, St. Louis	18
	G. Bradley, Chicago	18

Losses

1.	Devlin, Louisville	25
	Larkin, Hartford	25
3.	Nichols, St. Louis	23
	G. Bradley, Chicago	23
5.	Bond, Boston	17

Innings

1.	Devlin, Louisville	559
2.	Bond, Boston	521
3.	Larkin, Hartford	501
4.	G. Bradley, Chicago	394
5.	Nichols, St. Louis	350

Complete Games

1.	Devlin, Louisville	61
2.	Bond, Boston	58
3.	Larkin, Hartford	55
4.	Nichols. St. Louis	35
	G. Bradley, Chicago	35

Strikeouts

1.	Bond, Boston	170
2.	Devlin, Louisville	141
3.	Larkin, Hartford	96
4.	Nichols, St. Louis	80
5.	G. Bradley, Chicago	59

Winning Percentage (15 decisions)

1.	Bond, Boston	.702
2.	Devlin, Louisville	.583
3.	Larkin, Hartford	.537
4.	Blong, St. Louis	.526
5.	Others all below	.500

ERA (60 innings)

1.	Bond, Boston	2.11
2.	Larkin, Hartford	2.14
3.	Devlin, Louisville	2.25
4.	Nichols, St. Louis	2.60
5.	Blong, St. Louis	2.74

Lowest On–Base Percentage

1.	Bond, Boston	.261
2.	Larkin, Hartford	.264
3.	Devlin, Louisville	.283
4.	G. Bradley, Chicago	.286
5.	Nichols, St. Louis	.289

FIELDING

Total Chances

1B	Start, Hartford	741
2B	Gerhardt, Louisville	463
3B	Ferguson, Hartford	314
SS	Peters, Chicago	384
OF	C. Jones, Cin–Chi	181
C	Brown, Boston	476
P	Devlin, Louisville	150

Fielding Average

Start, Hartford	.964
Burdock, Hartford	.903
Anson, Chicago	.883
Force, St. Louis	.914
Glenn, Chicago	.944
Snyder, Louisville	.910
Bradley, Chicago	.950

BOSTON **Harry Wright** **South End Grounds (I)**

		G	AB	H	R	2B	3B	HR	RBI	BB	BA	SA
2B	George Wright	61	**290**	80	58	15	1	0	35	9	.276	.334
LF	Andy Leonard	58	272	78	46	5	0	0	27	5	.287	.305
1B	Deacon White	59	266	**103**	51	14	**11**	2	**49**	8	**.387**	**.545**
CF	Jim O'Rourke	61	265	96	**68**	14	4	0	23	20	.362	.445
P	Tommy Bond	61	259	59	32	4	3	0	30	1	.228	.266
SS	Ezra Sutton	58	253	74	43	10	6	0	39	4	.292	.379
3B	John Morrill	61	242	73	47	5	1	0	28	6	.302	.331
C	Lew Brown	58	221	56	27	12	8	1	31	6	.253	.394
RF	Harry Schafer	33	141	39	20	5	2	0	13	0	.277	.340
Sub	Tim Murnane	35	140	39	23	7	1	1	15	6	.279	.364
P	Will White	3	15	3	4	0	0	0	1	0	.200	.200
Sub	**Harry Wright**	1	4	0	0	0	0	0	0	0	.000	.000
		61	2368	**700**	**419**	**91**	**37**	4	**291**	65	**.296**	**.370**

1B D. White 35, Morrill 18, Murnane 5, Brown 4, O'Rourke 1
2B G. Wright 58, Morrill 3
SS Sutton 36, Leonard 21, G. Wright 3, Schafer 1
3B Morrill 30, Sutton 22, Schafer 9
OF O'Rourke 60, Leonard 37, Murnane 30, Schafer 23, D. White 19, Morrill 11, Bond 3, H. Wright 1
C Brown 55, D. White 7
P Bond 58, W. White 3

	G	IP	GS	CG	W	L	K	BB	SH	SV	ERA
Tommy Bond	58	521	58	58	**40**	17	**170**	36	**6**	0	**2.11**
Will White	3	27	3	3	2	1	7	2	1	0	3.00
	61	548	61	**61**	42	18	**177**	**38**	**7**	0	**2.15**

LOUISVILLE **Jack Chapman** **Louisville Baseball Park**

		G	AB	H	R	2B	3B	HR	RBI	BB	BA	SA
1B	Juice Latham	59	278	81	42	10	6	0	22	5	.291	.371
LF	George Hall	61	269	87	53	15	8	0	26	12	.323	.439
P	Jim Devlin	61	268	72	38	6	3	1	27	7	.269	.325
3B	Bill Hague	59	263	70	38	7	1	1	24	7	.266	.312
RF	Orator Shaffer	61	260	74	38	9	5	3	34	9	.285	.392
2B	Joe Gerhardt	59	250	76	41	6	5	1	35	5	.304	.380
C	Pop Snyder	61	248	64	23	7	2	2	28	3	.258	.327
CF	Bill Crowley	61	238	67	30	9	3	1	23	4	.282	.357
SS	Bill Craver	57	238	63	33	5	2	0	29	5	.265	.303
Sub	Al Nichols	6	19	4	1	0	1	0	0	0	.211	.316
Sub	Flip Lafferty	4	17	1	2	1	0	0	0	0	.059	.118
Sub	John Haldeman	1	4	0	0	0	0	0	0	0	.000	.000
Sub	Harry Little	1	3	0	0	0	0	0	0	1	.000	.000
		61	2355	659	339	75	36	**9**	248	58	.280	.354

1B Latham 59, Nichols 1, Gerhardt 1, Shaffer 1
2B Gerhardt 57, Nichols 3, Little 1, Haldeman 1, Crowley 1
3B Hague 59, Crowley 1, Nichols 1
SS Craver 57, Crowley 2, Nichols 1, Gerhardt 1, Snyder 1
OF Hall 61, Shaffer 60, Crowley 58, Lafferty 4, Snyder 1, Gerhardt 1
C Snyder 61, Crowley 2
P Devlin 61

	G	IP	GS	CG	W	L	K	BB	SH	SV	ERA
Jim Devlin	**61**	**559**	**61**	**61**	35	**25**	141	41	4	0	2.25

HARTFORD   **Bob Ferguson**   **Union Grounds (Brooklyn)**

		G	AB	H	R	2B	3B	HR	RBI	BB	BA	SA
2B	Jack Burdock	58	277	72	35	6	0	0	9	2	.260	.282
SS	Tom Carey	60	274	70	38	3	2	1	20	0	.255	.292
1B	Joe Start	60	271	90	55	3	6	1	21	6	.332	.399
CF	Jim Holdsworth	55	260	66	26	5	2	0	20	2	.254	.288
3B	Bob Ferguson	58	254	65	40	7	2	0	35	3	.256	.299
RF	John Cassidy	60	251	95	43	10	5	0	27	3	.378	.458
LF	Tom York	56	237	67	43	16	7	1	37	3	.283	.422
P	Terry Larkin	58	228	52	28	6	5	1	18	5	.228	.311
C	Bill Harbidge	41	167	37	18	5	2	0	8	3	.222	.275
C	Doug Allison	29	115	17	14	2	0	0	6	3	.148	.165
Sub	Oak Taylor	2	8	3	0	0	0	0	0	0	.375	.375
Sub	Jay Pike	1	4	1	1	0	0	0	0	0	.250	.250
Sub	John Bass	1	4	1	1	0	0	0	0	0	.250	.250
Sub	John Maloney	1	4	1	0	0	0	0	0	0	.250	.250
Sub	Josh Bunce	1	4	0	0	0	0	0	0	0	.000	.000
		60	2358	637	341	63	31	4	201	30	.270	.328

1B Start 60
2B Burdock 55, Harbidge 4, Larkin 1
SS Carey 60
3B Ferguson 56, Burdock 3, Larkin 2, Harbidge 1
OF Cassidy 58, York 56, Holdsworth 55, Harbidge 5, Taylor 2, Maloney 1, Bass 1, Bunce 1, Pike 1
C Harbidge 32, Allison 29
P Larkin 56, Ferguson 3, Cassidy 2

	G	IP	GS	CG	W	L	K	BB	SH	SV	ERA
Terry Larkin	56	501	56	55	29	**25**	96	**53**	4	0	2.14
Bob Ferguson	3	25	2	2	1	1	1	2	0	0	3.96
John Cassidy	2	18	2	2	1	1	2	1	0	0	5.00
	60	544	60	59	31	27	99	56	4	0	2.32

ST. LOUIS   **George McManus**   **Grand Avenue Park**

		G	AB	H	R	2B	3B	HR	RBI	BB	BA	SA
LF	Mike Dorgan	60	266	82	45	9	7	0	23	9	.308	.395
2B	Mike McGeary	57	258	65	35	3	2	0	20	2	.252	.279
C	John Clapp	60	255	81	47	6	6	0	34	8	.318	.388
3B	Joe Battin	57	226	45	28	3	7	1	22	6	.199	.288
SS	Davy Force	58	225	59	24	5	3	0	22	11	.262	.311
UT	Art Croft	54	220	51	23	5	2	0	27	1	.232	.273
RF	Joe Blong	58	218	47	17	8	3	0	13	4	.216	.280
P	Tricky Nichols	51	186	31	22	4	2	0	9	3	.167	.210
CF	Jack Remsen	33	123	32	14	3	4	0	13	4	.260	.350
1B	Dutch Dehlman	32	119	22	24	4	0	0	11	7	.185	.218
Sub	Dickey Pearce	8	29	5	1	0	0	0	4	1	.172	.172
Sub	Leonidas Lee	4	18	5	0	1	0	0	0	0	.278	.333
Sub	Harry Little	3	12	2	2	0	0	0	0	1	.167	.167
Sub	Tom Loftus	3	11	2	2	0	0	0	0	0	.182	.182
Sub	Ed McKenna	1	5	1	0	0	0	0	0	0	.200	.200
Sub	**Jack Gleason**	1	4	1	0	0	0	0	0	9	.250	.250
Sub	**T. E. Newell**	1	3	0	0	0	0	0	0	0	.000	.000
		60	2178	531	284	51	36	1	198	57	.244	.302

1B Dehlman 31, Croft 28, Clapp 1
2B McGeary 39, Battin 21, Croft 1, Dorgan 1

SS Force 50, Pearce 8, Newell 1, Lee 1, Dorgan 1
3B Battin 32, McGeary 19, Force 8, Dorgan 2
OF Dorgan 50, Blong 40, Remsen 33, Croft 25, Nichols 16, Clapp 10, Battin 5, Lee 4, Little 3, Loftus 3, McKenna 1, Gleason 1, Dehlman 1
C   Clapp 53, Dorgan 12
P   Nichols 42, Blong 25, Battin 1

	G	IP	GS	CG	W	L	K	BB	SH	SV	ERA
Tricky Nichols	42	350	39	35	18	23	80	53	1	0	2.60
Joe Blong	25	187.1	21	17	10	9	51	38	0	0	2.74
Joe Battin	1	3.2	0	0	0	0	1	1	0	0	4.91
	60	541	60	52	28	32	132	92	1	0	2.66

CHICAGO   Al Spalding   23rd Street Grounds

		G	AB	H	R	2B	3B	HR	RBI	BB	BA	SA
C	Cal McVey	60	266	98	58	9	7	0	36	8	.368	.455
SS	John Peters	60	265	84	45	10	3	0	41	1	.317	.377
RF	Paul Hines	60	261	73	44	11	7	0	23	1	.280	.375
3B	Cap Anson	59	255	86	52	19	1	0	32	9	.337	.420
1B	Al Spalding	60	254	65	29	7	6	0	35	3	.256	.331
P	George Bradley	55	214	52	31	7	3	0	12	6	.243	.304
LF	John Glenn	50	202	46	31	6	1	0	20	8	.228	.267
CF	Dave Eggler	33	136	36	20	3	0	0	20	1	.265	.287
Sub	Harry Smith	24	94	19	7	1	0	0	3	4	.202	.213
2B	Ross Barnes	22	92	25	16	1	0	0	5	7	.272	.283
Sub	Jimmy Hallinan	19	89	25	17	4	1	0	11	4	.281	.348
Sub	Charlie Eden	15	55	12	9	0	1	0	5	3	.218	.255
Sub	Charlie Waitt	10	41	4	2	0	0	0	2	0	.098	.098
P	Laurie Reis	4	16	2	3	0	0	0	1	0	.125	.125
Sub	Joe Quinn	4	14	1	1	0	0	0	0	1	.071	.071
Sub	Charley Jones	2	8	3	1	1	0	0	2	1	.375	.500
Sub	Dave Rowe	2	7	2	0	0	0	0	0	0	.286	.286
Sub	Cherokee Fisher	1	4	0	0	0	0	0	0	0	.000	.000
		60	2273	633	366	79	30	0	248	57	.278	.340

1B Spalding 45, Glenn 14, Bradley 3, McVey 1
2B Barnes 22, Smith 14, Spalding 13, Hines 11, McVey 1
SS Peters 60
3B Anson 40, McVey 17, Bradley 16, Spalding 2, Fisher 1
OF Hines 49, Glenn 36, Eggler 33, Hallinan 19, Eden 15, Waitt 10, Smith 10, Quinn 4, Rowe 2, Jones 2, Bradley 1
C   McVey 40, Anson 31
P   Bradley 50, McVey 17, Reis 4, Spalding 4, Rowe 1

	G	IP	GS	CG	W	L	K	BB	SH	SV	ERA
George Bradley	50	394	44	35	18	23	59	39	2	0	3.31
Cal McVey	17	92	10	6	4	8	20	11	0	2	4.50
Laurie Reis	4	36	4	4	3	1	11	6	1	0	0.75
Al Spalding	4	11	1	0	1	0	2	0	0	1	3.27
Dave Rowe	1	1	1	0	0	1	0	2	0	0	18.00
	60	534	60	45	26	33	92	58	3	3	3.37

CINCINNATI **Lip Pike (3–11)** **Bob Addy (5–19)** **Jack Manning (9–12)** **Avenue Grounds**

		G	AB	H	R	2B	3B	HR	RBI	BB	BA	SA
CF	Lip Pike	58	262	78	45	12	4	4	23	9	.298	.420
SS	Jack Manning	57	252	80	47	16	7	0	36	5	.317	.437
RF	Bob Addy	57	245	68	27	2	3	0	31	6	.278	.310
LF	Charley Jones	55	232	72	52	11	10	2	36	14	.310	.470
3B	Will Foley	56	216	41	23	5	1	0	18	4	.190	.222
UT	Amos Booth	44	157	27	16	2	1	0	13	12	.172	.197
Sub	Levi Meyerle	27	107	35	11	7	2	0	15	0	.327	.430
1B	Charlie Gould	24	91	25	5	2	1	0	13	5	.275	.319
2B	Jimmy Hallinan	16	73	27	18	1	1	0	7	1	.370	.411
C	Scott Hastings	20	71	10	7	1	0	0	3	3	.141	.155
P	Candy Cummings	19	70	14	6	1	2	0	4	4	.200	.271
P	Bobby Mathews	15	59	10	5	0	0	0	0	1	.169	.169
Sub	Ned Cuthbert	12	56	10	6	5	0	0	2	1	.179	.268
P	Bobby Mitchell	13	49	10	5	3	0	0	5	1	.204	.265
Sub	George Miller	11	37	6	4	1	0	0	3	5	.162	.189
Sub	Harry Smith	10	36	9	4	2	1	0	3	1	.250	.361
Sub	Chubb Sullivan	8	32	8	4	0	0	0	4	1	.250	.250
C	Nat Hicks	8	32	6	3	0	0	0	3	1	.188	.188
Sub	Johnny Ryan	6	26	4	2	0	1	0	2	1	.154	.231
C	Harry Kessler	6	20	2	0	0	0	0	0	2	.100	.100
Sub	Billy Redmond	3	12	3	1	1	0	0	3	1	.250	.333
		58	2135	545	291	72	34	6	224	78	.255	.329

1B Gould 24, Manning 17, Jones 10, Sullivan 8, Kessler 1
2B Pike 22, Hallinan 16, Meyerle 12, Booth 10, Smith 3, Manning 2
SS Manning 26, Meyerle 18, Booth 13, Redmond 3, Pike 2, Mathews 1
3B Foley 56, Booth 3
OF Addy 57, Jones 46, Pike 38, Cuthbert 12, Manning 12, Ryan 6, Cummings 3, Smith 3, Mitchell 2, Gould 1, Booth 1, Mathews 1, Hastings 1, Meyerle 1
C Hastings 20, Booth 12, Miller 11, Smith 8, Hicks 8, Kessler 5
P Cummings 19, Mathews 15, Booth 12, Mitchell 12, Manning 10

	G	IP	GS	CG	W	L	K	BB	SH	SV	ERA
Candy Cummings	19	155.2	19	16	5	14	11	13	0	0	4.34
Bobby Mathews	15	129.1	15	13	3	12	9	17	0	0	4.04
Bobby Mitchell	12	100	12	11	6	5	41	11	1	0	3.51
Amos Booth	12	86	8	6	1	7	18	13	0	0	3.56
Jack Manning	10	44	4	2	0	4	6	7	0	1	6.95
	58	515	58	48	15	42	85	61	1	1	4.19

1878

THE NINE "IRON MEN" GIVE HARRY WRIGHT ONE LAST FLAG

Shorn of St. Louis, the second largest city in the West, together with Louisville and Hartford, both first-division teams in 1877, loop president William Hulbert had to scramble in the early months of 1878 to restore the National League to six entries. His solution was to spirit Providence away from the International Association and cajole teams from Milwaukee and Indianapolis to become partners in his tottering enterprise. Once the League's future was assured for at least one more season, Hulbert launched a ruthless campaign to cut off the blood supply of the smalltown clubs that comprised most of the IA's membership. Since the League had parks with much greater gate-receipt potential than did his rival, Hulbert decreed that League clubs could no longer allow outside teams to play in their parks. This proscription meant that while Boston, for example, could still play neighboring Lowell in Lowell's tiny park with a capacity of around 2,000, Lowell was denied the monetary windfall from playing in Boston's South End Grounds, capable of holding some 10,000. Though almost every League club relied on games against outside teams for much of its revenue, all reluctantly complied with Hulbert's mandate.

Money issues weighed heavily on the League in 1878. Beginning that season, the umpire fee of five dollars was paid by the visiting club. Balancing that expense for visitors was a new system for dividing gate receipts, made possible by the invention the previous year of the self-registering turnstile. As a result, visitors now received 15 cents for each spectator admitted to the home club's park through the turnstile, which recorded the count each time an entering body turned its mechanism. The visiting club's secretary was given the keys to the turnstile before each game; he opened it, checked its count and then affixed a seal to it after the last customer entered.

On the field, the changes were few but meaningful. An 1877 rule requiring the home team to bat first gave way to a new statute allowing the two captains to determine which side took first raps, usually by flipping a coin, with the home team accorded the right to call the toss. A second rule modification eliminated the use of a substitute runner until a batter actually reached base safely.

Paul Hines, the true 1878 NL batting champ. That season Hines, Tom York and Dick Higham formed the first all-.300-hitting outfield in NL history for Providence, but meanwhile the Grays had no infielders who hit above .239.

The new-fangled self-registering turnstiles revolved all too seldom in several League parks in 1878. By the end of the season Indianapolis owner William Perritt owed so much money that he was forced to flee Indiana to avoid his many creditors. The bulk of Perritt's debt was incurred before the season even began, when he raided the Maple Leaf team of Guelph, Ontario, for talent. Perritt had taste if insufficient capital. In 1878, despite finishing next to last, Indianapolis introduced three future League stars: Ned Williamson, Silver Flint and Jim McCormick. Cellar-dwelling Milwaukee likewise unveiled a trio of impact rookies: catcher Charlie Bennett, disputed batting king Abner Dalrymple and the luckless Sam Weaver. Though he surrendered less than two earned runs a start in 1878, Weaver lost 31 of his 43 decisions as his mates averaged over six errors per game behind him.

The erratic play of the two western newcomers and Chicago's continued perplexing lack of cohesion, for all its talent, helped the Cincinnati Red Stockings rise all the way to second place after two straight basement finishes. An even greater boost to the Queen City club's fortunes came from its entry into the "free-agent" market. After fielding a team of dregs in the first two league seasons, in 1878 the Red Stockings outbid all rivals to procure two of the game's biggest stars, Cal McVey and Deacon White. McVey ran the team and anchored the infield at third base, and White returned to catching, his original position, in order to work with his brother Will. The Whites gave Cincinnati the first sibling battery in big league history, and the bespectacled Will was the leading winner among an outstanding crop of rookie pitchers. But another yearling, right fielder King Kelly, would turn out to be the Red Stockings' and the 1878 season's greatest find.

Only defending champion Boston uncovered no standout rookies in 1878. Given the losses of 1877 batting king Deacon White to Cincinnati and catcher Lew Brown to Providence, Boston manager Harry Wright seemingly needed a new star. But he made do without one. For the 1878 season Wright shifted handyman John Morrill from third base to first, replacing White; moved Ezra Sutton from shortstop to third base; and put his brother

WRIGHT'S MAGIC DESERTS HIM

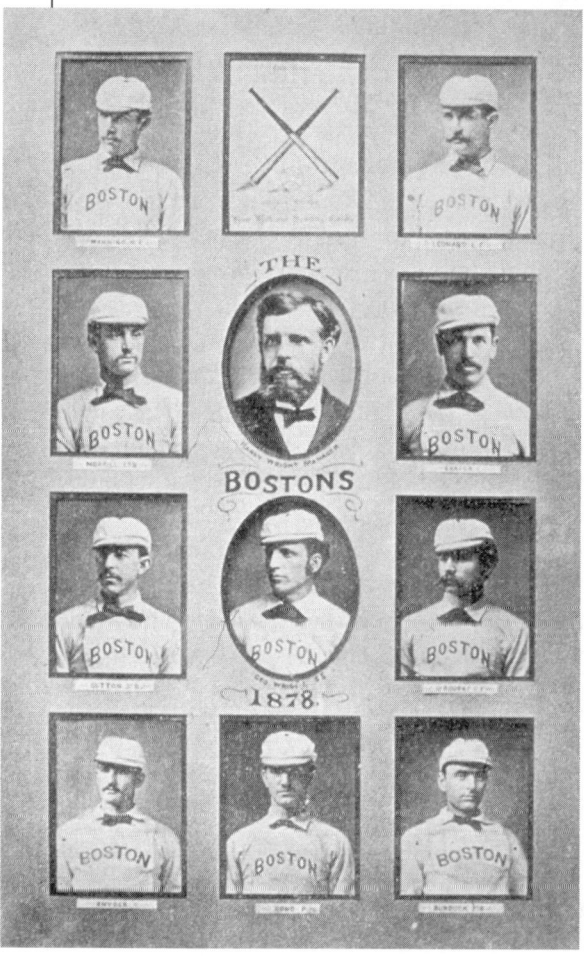

Harry Wright became strictly a bench manager in 1878, seldom even wearing a uniform. Harry Schafer seldom needed one either; the Red Caps lone sub in 1878 got into just two games when each of the nine regulars played virtually every inning of every game.

In the 10 seasons between 1869 and 1878 Harry Wright managed an undefeated national champion—the 1869 Cincinnati Red Stockings—and six major league pennant winners. Though he remained a pilot for 15 more years after 1878, he never won another pennant. It was not that the game passed him by, as it did other long-term managers such as Connie Mack. Wright's undoing was the fact that, once he left Boston following the 1881 season, he never again had the horses. An unparalleled expert at assembling a team prior to the 1880 adoption of the Reserve Clause, Wright was less successful when he had to rely on more modern methods to acquire talent.

Wright's managerial skills were also best suited to the kind of game Henry Chadwick adored: tightly contested with little scoring. It was no coincidence that his best teams in the latter portion of his career—the 1885–88 Philadelphia Phillies—had the same strengths, pitching and defense, as his 1877–78 Boston champs, as well as the same flaw: the weakest hitting of any winning team during the era. Wright's last season as a pilot, in 1893, was laden with irony. By then his Philadelphia club had the top batting attack in the majors and one of the worst pitching staffs. Even if his health had not betrayed him, the paradox might have been more than he cared to endure.

George, mostly a second baseman in 1877, back at short. As his new second baseman, Wright signed Jack Burdock of the defunct Hartford team. The defunct Louisville team furnished Wright's catching replacement, Pop Snyder. Wright's final personnel move was to reacquire Jack Manning from Cincinnati to play right field, a trouble spot in 1877. Manning's return to Boston banished incumbent right fielder Harry Schafer to the bench, where he was destined to rot. After seven years as a starter, Schafer got into just two games in 1878. Those were the only two games all year in which Boston had need for a substitute, as seven of the Red Stockings' nine regulars played every inning of every game and the other two, George Wright and pitcher Tommy Bond, missed only one contest each.

Boston's amazing "iron man" performance, unequaled in that era or any other, was only one reason that Harry Wright bagged his sixth pennant in seven years. Defense, in large capital letters, was a much larger ingredient in Wright's formula for success. In 1878 his nine iron men owned the second-worst team batting average in the League and could put no one among the loop's top ten in batting, on-base percentage or total bases. Bond, moreover, had the fifth-best ERA among pitchers in 100 or more innings, no great achievement since there were only eight of them. But Burdock and George Wright were the best keystone pair in the League, and the Boston team as a whole combined to set a new fielding average record of .914 and become the first club ever to average fewer than four errors per game.

A typical Red Caps' contest was their 10-inning battle at Indianapolis on September 11, deemed the best League game of the year by *Dime Base-Ball Player.* After being blanked by Indy's Jim McCormick for nine innings on just five scattered singles, Boston broke the longest scoreless deadlock in the 1878 league season by pushing across two runs in the top of the tenth on a pair of singles, a sacrifice, a steal and an error. The Red Caps then held the Blues runless in the bottom half to win 2–0.

THE NINETEENTH CENTURY'S BEST YEAR FOR ROOKIE PITCHERS

Of the nine National League pitchers who logged 100 or more innings in 1877, only two—Tommy Bond and Terry Larkin—reached triple digits again in 1878. Jim Devlin would surely have been a third had he not been banished in the Louisville scandal, but the other six were little missed. In 1878, even though it had just six teams, three of which used what was essentially a one-man pitching rotation, the National League ushered in three rookie pitchers who combined for 659 wins in the majors. Two others, the Only Nolan and Sam Weaver, might have been standouts had they not toiled for miserable teams.

Two of the trio who clicked for 659 wins, Will White and Monte Ward, ranked second and fourth, respectively, in victories in 1878. The third, Jim McCormick, looked at one point in his career as if he would surely be the first major league pitcher to win 300 games. The five rookies accounted for nearly half of the pitching wins in 1878 (82 of 180), easily the highest percentage ever by frosh hurlers.

THE FIERY FERGUSON

The 1878 Chicago White Stockings were a disappointment despite leading the NL in runs and batting. Field captain Bob Ferguson, himself a .351 hitter in 1878, got the blame for the club's failure to get more mileage out of all its lumber.

As baffling to casual observers as Harry Wright's success in 1878 with the light-hitting Boston Red Caps was Bob Ferguson's inability to lift the heavy-hitting Chicago White Stockings out of the second division. In 1878 the White Stockings topped the National League in both batting and runs by a wide margin, had a staff ERA that was just .05 runs higher than first-place Boston's and committed fewer errors than third-place Providence. Hiring Ferguson to play third base and pilot the White Stockings was Al Spalding's idea. Spalding had admiringly watched Ferguson's firebrand style of leadership spur mediocre Hartford teams to first-division finishes in both 1876 and 1877. Yet in his memoirs, Spalding would call Ferguson "tactless" and hopelessly lacking any knowledge "of the subtle science of handling men by strategy rather than by force."

Before he came to Chicago, Ferguson's reputation rested as much on his impeccable honesty and haste to flatten any gambler foolish enough to approach him as on the performance of teams he ran. Prior to 1878 he generally had his pick of jobs. When the stern example of the Louisville scandal lessened the need for paragons of integrity and Ferguson's impatient, irascible personality helped sink what Spalding felt ought to have been a dominant Chicago team, he began a long downward course to near obscurity. No man was more knowledgeable about the game, or more versatile in what he could do to earn a living at it, than Ferguson. He had moments of brilliance as a player, a manager and an umpire and might have made a lasting mark at any or all of the three venues. Yet when he is remembered now it is chiefly by trivia buffs who know him as the game's first switchhitter.

THE TEAM THAT HAD THE BEST RECORD
BUT FINISHED SECOND

A nifty carte of Buffalo, the 1878 International Association champion. Top: Tom Dolan, Jack Allen, Bill McGunnigle and Pud Galvin. Middle: Bill Crowley, Dave Eggler, Steve Libby, Chick Fulmer and Denny Mack. Bottom: Captain Davy Force and Trick McSorley. Most of these men were on the 1879 Buffaloes, which finished third in their initial NL season, evidence that the two loops were very close in quality.

Never in major league history has a team that possessed the best winning percentage at the end of a season finished anywhere but first. The rules prior to 1882 made such an occurrence possible, however, and it happened on at least one occasion in a professional league. At the close of the 1878 season the final International Association standings showed the Syracuse Stars with 27 wins and 10 losses for a .729 winning percentage. Buffalo, meanwhile, finished 32–12 with a .727 winning rate. Many reference books nowadays consider Syracuse the pennant winner, but in 1878 the Buffaloes were crowned the IA champs because they compiled the most wins. Since Buffalo won then, who are we to say otherwise?

The 1878 IA standings:

	W	L	PCT	GB
Buffalo	32	12	.727	—
Syracuse	27	10	.729	1.5
London (Tecumseh)	27	15	.643	4
Utica	26	13	.667	3.5
Rochester	23	20	.535	8.5
Hornellsville	21	16	.567	7.5
Manchester	20	18	.526	9
Lowell	18	21	.461	11.5
Binghamton	14	16	.467	11
Lynn/Worcester	13	27	.325	17
Springfield	11	25	.306	17
Pittsburgh	2	24	.077	21
New Haven/Hartford	1	18	.053	18.5

THE SEASONAL RECORD

	W	L	PCT	H	R	GB
1. Boston Red Caps	41	19	.683	23–7	18–12	—
2. Cincinnati Reds	37	23	.617	25–8	12–15	4
3. Providence Grays	33	27	.550	17–13	16–14	8
4. Chicago White Stockings	30	30	.500	17–18	13–12	11
5. Indianapolis Blues	24	36	.400	10–17	14–19	17
6. Milwaukee Grays	15	45	.250	7–18	8–27	26

	Bos	Cin	Pro	Chi	Ind	Mil	
Boston	—	6	6	8	10	11	41
Cincinnati	6	—	9	10	4	8	37
Providence	6	3	—	6	10	8	33
Chicago	4	2	6	—	8	10	30
Indianapolis	2	8	2	4	—	8	24
Milwaukee	1	4	4	2	4	—	15
	19	23	27	30	36	45	180

SEASON LEADERS

Batting Average

1. Hines, Providence	.358
2. Dalrymple, Milwaukee	.354
3. Ferguson, Chicago	.351
Start, Chicago	.351
5. Anson, Chicago	.341

On–Base Percentage

1. Ferguson, Chicago	.375
2. Anson, Chicago	.372
3. Shaffer, Indianapolis	.369
4. Dalrymple, Milwaukee	.368
5. Hines, Providence	.363

Home Runs

1. Hines, Providence	4
2. Jones, Cincinnati	3
3. McVey, Cincinnati	2
4. McKelvy, Indianapolis	2
5. Many with 1	

Hits

1. Start, Chicago	100
2. Dalrymple, Milwaukee	96
3. Hines, Providence	92
4. Ferguson, Chicago	91
5. Higham, Providence	90
Shaffer, Indianapolis	90

Slugging Average

1. Hines, Providence	.486
2. York, Providence	.465
3. Shaffer, Indianapolis	.455
4. L. Brown, Providence	.453
5. Jones, Cincinnati	.441

Total Bases

1. York, Providence	125
Start, Chicago	125
Hines, Providence	125
4. Shaffer, Indianapolis	121
5. Higham, Providence	117

RBI

1. Hines, Providence	50
2. L. Brown, Providence	43
3. Anson, Chicago	40
4. Jones, Cincinnati	39
Ferguson, Chicago	39

Runs

1. Higham, Providence	60
2. Start, Chicago	58
3. York, Providence	56
4. Anson, Chicago	55
5. Dalrymple, Milwaukee	52

Bases on Balls

1.	Remsen, Chicago	17
	Larkin, Chicago	17
3.	Shaffer, Indianapolis	13
	Clapp, Indianapolis	13
	Anson, Chicago	13

Strikeouts

1.	W. White, Cincinnati	41
2.	McKelvy, Indianapolis	38
3	L. Brown, Providence	37
4.	Hankinson, Chicago	36
5.	Golden, Milwaukee	35

PITCHING

Wins

1.	Bond, Boston	40
2.	W. White, Cincinnati	30
3.	Larkin, Chicago	29
4.	Ward, Providence	22
5.	Nolan, Indianapolis	13

Losses

1.	Weaver, Milwaukee	31
2.	Larkin, Chicago	26
3.	Nolan, Indianapolis	22
4.	W. White, Cincinnati	21
5.	Bond, Boston	19

Innings

1.	Bond, Boston	532.2
2.	Larkin, Chicago	506
3.	W. White, Cincinnati	468
4.	Weaver, Milwaukee	383
5.	Nolan, Indianapolis	347

Complete Games

1.	Bond, Boston	57
2.	Larkin, Chicago	56
3.	W. White, Cincinnati	52
4.	Weaver, Milwaukee	39
5.	Ward, Providence	37

Strikeouts

1.	Bond, Boston	182
2.	W. White, Cincinnati	169
3.	Larkin, Chicago	163
4.	Nolan, Indianapolis	125
5.	Ward, Providence	116

Winning Percentage (15 decisions)

1.	Bond, Boston	.678
2.	Ward, Providence	.629
3.	W. White, Cincinnati	.588
4.	Larkin, Chicago	.527
5.	All others below .500	

ERA (60 innings)

1.	Ward, Providence	1.51
2.	McCormick, Indianapolis	1.69
3.	W. White, Cincinnati	1.79
4.	Weaver, Milwaukee	1.95
5.	Bond, Boston	2.06

Lowest On–Base Percentage

1.	Weaver, Milwaukee	.247
2.	Ward, Providence	.251
3.	Larkin, Chicago	.257
4.	Mitchell, Cincinnati	.265
5.	W. White, Cincinnati	.269

FIELDING

Total Chances

1B	Start, Chicago	765
2B	Burdock, Boston	498
3B	Hague, Providence	279
SS	Ferguson, Chicago	337
OF	Dalrymple, Milwaukee	167
C	Snyder, Boston	478
P	Bond, Boston	153

Fielding Average

Sullivan, Cincinnati	.975
Burdock, Boston	.918
Hague, Providence	.925
G. Wright, Boston	.947
Remsen, Chicago	.944
Snyder, Boston	.912
Bond, Boston	.941

BOSTON   **Harry Wright**   **South End Grounds (I)**

		G	AB	H	R	2B	3B	HR	RBI	BB	BA	SA
SS	George Wright	59	267	60	35	5	1	0	12	6	.225	.251
LF	Andy Leonard	60	262	68	41	8	5	0	16	3	.260	.328
CF	Jim O'Rourke	60	255	71	44	17	7	1	29	5	.278	.412
RF	Jack Manning	60	248	63	41	10	1	0	23	10	.254	.302
2B	Jack Burdock	60	246	64	37	12	6	0	25	3	.260	.358
3B	Ezra Sutton	60	239	54	31	9	3	1	29	2	.226	.301
P	Tommy Bond	59	236	50	22	4	1	0	23	0	.212	.237
1B	John Morrill	60	233	56	26	5	1	0	23	5	.240	.270
C	Pop Snyder	60	226	48	21	5	0	0	14	1	.212	.235
Sub	Harry Schafer	2	8	1	0	0	0	0	0	0	.125	.125
		60	2220	535	298	75	25	2	194	35	.241	.300

1B   Morrill 59, O'Rourke 2
2B   Burdock 60
SS   Wright 59, Sutton 1
3B   Sutton 59, Morrill 1
OF   Leonard 60, Manning 59, O'Rourke 57, Snyder 2, Schafer 2, Bond 2, Morrill 1
C   Snyder 58, O'Rourke 2
P   Bond 59, Manning 3

	G	IP	GS	CG	W	L	K	BB	SH	SV	ERA
Tommy Bond	59	532.2	59	57	40	19	182	33	9	0	2.06
Jack Manning	3	11.1	1	1	1	0	2	5	0	0	14.29
		544	60	58	41	19	184	38	9	0	2.32

CINCINNATI   **Cal McVey**   **Avenue Grounds**

		G	AB	H	R	2B	3B	HR	RBI	BB	BA	SA
3B	Cal McVey	61	271	83	43	10	4	2	28	5	.306	.395
LF	Charley Jones	61	261	81	50	11	7	3	39	4	.310	.441
2B	Joe Gerhardt	60	259	77	46	7	2	0	28	7	.297	.340
C	Deacon White	61	258	81	41	4	1	0	29	10	.314	.337
1B	Chub Sullivan	61	244	63	29	4	2	0	20	2	.258	.291
RF	King Kelly	60	237	67	29	7	1	0	27	7	.283	.321
SS	Billy Geer	61	237	52	31	13	2	0	20	10	.219	.291
P	Will White	52	197	28	15	1	0	0	9	8	.142	.157
CF	Lip Pike	31	145	47	28	5	1	0	11	4	.324	.372
Sub	Buttercup Dickerson	29	123	38	17	5	1	0	9	0	.309	.366
P	Bobby Mitchell	12	49	12	4	0	0	0	8	1	.245	.245
		61	2281	629	333	67	22	5	228	58	.276	.331

1B   Sullivan 61
2B   Gerhardt 60, Geer 2
SS   Geer 60, Mitchell 2
3B   McVey 61, Kelly 2, D. White 1
OF   Jones 61, Kelly 47, Pike 31, Dickerson 29, D. White 16, Mitchell 1
C   D. White 48, Kelly 17, McVey 3
P   W. White 52, Mitchell 9

	G	IP	GS	CG	W	L	K	BB	SH	SV	ERA
Will White	52	468	52	52	30	21	169	45	5	0	1.79
Bobby Mitchell	9	80	9	9	7	2	51	18	1	0	2.14
		548	61	61	37	23	220	63	6	0	**1.84**

PROVIDENCE   **Tom York**   **Messer Street Park**

		G	AB	H	R	2B	3B	HR	RBI	BB	BA	SA
RF	Dick Higham	62	281	90	**60**	**22**	1	1	29	5	.320	.416
LF	Tom York	62	269	83	56	19	**10**	1	26	8	.309	.465
CF	Paul Hines	62	257	92	42	13	4	**4**	50	2	**.358**	**.486**
SS	Tom Carey	61	253	60	33	10	3	0	24	0	.237	.300
3B	Bill Hague	62	250	51	21	3	0	0	25	5	.204	.216
C	Lew Brown	58	243	74	44	21	6	1	43	7	.305	.453
2B	Charlie Sweasy	55	212	37	23	3	0	0	8	7	.175	.189
1B	Tim Murnane	49	188	45	35	6	1	0	14	8	.239	.282
P	Monte Ward	37	138	27	14	5	4	1	15	2	.196	.312
C	Doug Allison	19	76	22	9	2	0	0	7	1	.289	.316
P	Tricky Nichols	11	49	9	2	2	0	0	2	2	.184	.224
P	Harry Wheeler	7	27	4	7	0	0	0	1	2	.148	.148
Sub	Lip Pike	5	22	5	4	0	1	0	4	1	.227	.318
Sub	Fred Corey	7	21	3	3	0	0	0	1	0	.143	.143
P	Tom Healey	3	9	2	0	1	0	0	2	0	.222	.333
P	Cherokee Fisher	1	3	0	0	0	0	0	0	0	.000	.000
		62	2298	604	353	**107**	**30**	8	251	50	.263	.346

1B   Murnane 48, Brown 15, Corey 1
2B   Sweasy 55, Pike 5, Corey 2
SS   Carey 61, Hines 1
3B   Hague 62
OF   York 62, Higham 62, Hines 61, Brown 1, Murnane 1
C   Brown 45, Allison 19, Higham 1
P   Ward 37, Nichols 11, Wheeler 7, Corey 5, Healey 3, Fisher 1, Allison 1, Brown 1

	G	IP	GS	CG	W	L	K	BB	SH	SV	ERA
Monte Ward	37	334	37	37	22	13	116	34	6	0	**1.51**
Tricky Nichols	11	98	10	10	4	7	21	8	0	0	4.22
Harry Wheeler	7	62	6	6	6	1	25	25	0	0	3.48
Tom Healey	3	24	3	3	0	3	2	7	0	0	3.00
Fred Corey	5	23	5	2	1	2	7	7	0	0	2.35
Cherokee Fisher	9	1	1	1	0	1	2	0	0	0	4.00
Doug Allison	1	5	0	0	0	0	0	1	0	0	1.80
Lew Brown	1	1	0	0	0	0	0	4	0	0	18.00
		556	62	59	33	27	173	86	6	0	2.38

CHICAGO   **Bob Ferguson**   **Lake Front Park (I)**

		G	AB	H	R	2B	3B	HR	RBI	BB	BA	SA
1B	Joe Start	61	**285**	**100**	58	12	5	1	27	2	.351	.439
LF	Cap Anson	60	261	89	55	12	2	0	40	13	.341	.402
SS	Bob Ferguson	62	259	91	44	10	2	0	39	10	.351	.405
RF	John Cassidy	61	256	68	33	7	1	0	29	9	.266	.301
C	Bill Harbidge	54	240	71	32	12	0	0	37	6	.296	.346
3B	Frank Hankinson	58	240	64	38	8	3	1	27	5	.267	.338
P	Terry Larkin	58	226	65	33	9	4	0	32	17	.288	.363
CF	Jack Remsen	56	224	52	32	11	1	1	19	17	.232	.304
2B	Bill McClellan	48	205	46	26	6	1	0	29	2	.224	.263
Sub	Jim Hallinan	16	67	19	14	3	0	0	2	5	.284	.328
Sub	Phil Powers	8	31	5	2	1	1	0	2	1	.161	.258
P	Laurie Reis	5	20	3	2	0	0	0	0	1	.150	.150
Sub	Bill Traffley	2	9	1	1	0	0	0	1	0	.111	.111
Sub	Bill Sullivan	2	6	1	1	0	0	0	0	0	.167	.167
Sub	Al Spalding	1	4	2	0	0	0	0	0	0	.500	.500
		61	2333	**677**	**371**	91	20	3	**284**	88	**.290**	.350

1B   Start 61
2B   McClellan 42, Anson 9, Hallinan 5, Ferguson 4, Spalding 1
SS   Ferguson 57, McClellan 5
3B   Hankinson 57, Anson 3, Larkin 1
OF   Cassidy 60, Remsen 56, Anson 48, Harbidge 8, Hallinan 11, Sullivan 2, Reis 1, Larkin 1, McClellan 1
C   Harbidge 50, Powers 8, Anson 3, Traffley 2, Cassidy 1, Ferguson 1
P   Larkin 56, Reis 4, Hankinson 1

	G	IP	GS	CG	W	L	K	BB	SH	SV	ERA
Terry Larkin	56	506	56	56	29	26	163	31	1	0	2.24
Laurie Reis	4	36	4	4	1	3	8	4	0	0	3.25
Frank Hankinson	1	9	1	1	0	1	4	0	0	0	6.00
		551	61	**61**	30	30	175	**35**	1	0	2.37

INDIANAPOLIS   John Clapp   South Street Park

		G	AB	H	R	2B	3B	HR	RBI	BB	BA	SA
2B	Joe Quest	62	278	57	45	3	2	0	13	12	.205	.230
RF	Orator Shaffer	63	266	90	48	19	6	0	30	13	.338	.455
LF	John Clapp	63	263	80	42	10	2	0	29	13	.304	.357
C	Silver Flint	62	254	57	23	7	0	0	18	2	.224	.252
CF	Russ McKelvy	63	253	57	33	4	3	2	36	5	.225	.289
3B	Ned Williamson	63	250	58	31	10	2	1	19	5	.232	.300
1B	Art Croft	60	222	35	22	6	0	0	16	5	.158	.185
SS	Fred Warner	43	165	41	19	4	0	0	10	2	.248	.273
P	The Only Nolan	38	152	37	11	8	0	0	16	2	.243	.296
Sub	Candy Nelson	19	84	11	12	1	0	0	5	5	.131	.143
P	Jim McCormick	15	56	8	5	1	0	0	0	0	.143	.161
P	Tom Healey	12	45	8	2	1	0	0	4	0	.178	.200
Sub	Jim Hallinan	3	12	3	0	2	0	0	1	0	.250	.417
		63	2300	542	293	76	15	3	197	64	.236	.286

1B   Croft 51, Clapp 12
2B   Quest 62, Clapp 1
SS   Warner 41, Nelson 19, Clapp 3
3B   Williamson 63 , Creamer 6
OF   Shaffer 63, McKelvy 62, Clapp 44, Flint 9, Croft 9, Hallinan 3, Healey 3, McCormick 3, Warner 2, Nolan 1
C   Flint 59, Clapp 9, Ellick 2
P   Nolan 38, McCormick 14, Healey 11, McKelvy 4

	G	IP	GS	CG	W	L	K	BB	SH	SV	ERA
The Only Nolan	38	347	38	37	13	22	125	**56**	1	0	2.57
Jim McCormick	14	117	14	12	5	8	36	15	1	0	1.69
Tom Healey	11	89	10	9	6	4	18	13	0	**1**	2.22
Russ McKelvy	4	25	1	1	0	2	3	3	0	0	2.16
		578	63	59	24	36	182	87	2	**1**	2.32

MILWAUKEE   **Jack Chapman**   **Milwaukee Baseball Grounds**

		G	AB	H	R	2B	3B	HR	RBI	BB	BA	SA
LF	Abner Dalrymple	61	271	96	52	10	4	0	15	6	.354	.421
1B	Jake Goodman	60	252	62	28	4	3	1	27	7	.246	.298
2B	John Peters	55	246	76	33	6	1	0	22	5	.309	.341
3B	Will Foley	56	229	62	33	8	5	0	22	7	.271	.349
CF	Mike Golden	55	214	44	16	6	3	0	20	3	.206	.262
UT	George Creamer	50	193	41	30	7	3	0	15	5	.212	.280
SS	Billy Redmond	48	187	43	16	8	0	0	21	8	.230	.273
C	Charlie Bennett	49	184	45	16	9	0	1	12	10	.245	.310
RF	Bill Holbert	45	173	32	10	2	0	0	12	3	.185	.197
P	Sam Weaver	48	170	34	15	4	1	0	3	11	.200	.235
Sub	Bill Morgan	14	56	11	2	0	0	0	5	3	.196	.196
Sub	Jake Knowdell	4	14	3	2	1	0	0	2	0	.214	.286
Sub	Joe Ellick	3	13	2	2	0	0	0	1	0	.154	.154
Sub	Frank Bliss	2	8	1	1	0	0	0	0	0	.125	.125
Sub	Alamazoo Jennings	1	2	0	0	0	0	0	0	1	.000	.000
		61	2212	552	256	65	20	2	177	69	.250	.300

1B	Goodman 60, Golden 1
2B	Peters 34, Creamer 28, Morgan 1
SS	Redmond 39, Peters 22, Knowdell 1
3B	Foley 53, Creamer 3, Redmond 3, Morgan 3, Ellick 1, Bliss 1
OF	Dalrymple 61. Golden 39, Holbert 30, Bennett 20, Creamer 17, Morgan 13, Weaver 9, Redmond 7, Knowdell 1
C	Bennett 35, Holbert 21, Foley 7, Knowdell 2, Bliss 1, Jennings 1, Redmond 1
P	Weaver 45, Golden 22, Ellick 1

	G	IP	GS	CG	W	L	K	BB	SH	SV	ERA
Sam Weaver	45	383	43	39	12	**31**	95	21	1	0	1.95
Mike Golden	22	161	18	15	3	13	52	33	0	0	4.14
Joe Ellick	1	3	0	0	0	1	0	1	0	0	3.00
		547	61	54	15	45	147	55	1	0	2.60

1879
THE PLAYERS' LAST YEAR
OF FREEDOM

William Hulbert was a realist. Much as he desired the National League to have a strong western flavor, he came to accept that few western cities were ready as yet to support major league ball. For the 1879 season Hulbert decided to dump the Indianapolis and Milwaukee franchises and expand eastward, taking on Buffalo and Syracuse, the 1878 International Association champion and runner-up, respectively. Also incorporated was Troy, the top club in the New York State Association. A new team from Cleveland was also added, giving the League eight entries for the first time since its maiden season.

Particularly since it robbed the IA, the League's chief rival, of its best two teams, the expansion enabled Hulbert to field his most impressive array of pennant aspirants to date. Furthermore, it allowed the League to increase its schedule to 84 games, thereby reducing the need for its teams to play games with outside opponents to augment gate receipts. Finally, Hulbert's expansion cut the opportunities for talented players on IA teams and independent clubs to match their skills on the playing field against their League counterparts. The consequence was that in 1879, for the first time, playing in the League became a status symbol. When the League took in Worcester the following season and became a stable eight-team circuit, it effectively killed the IA as a worthy rival.

As Hulbert continued to search for the right blend of teams, so did rulesmakers continue to tinker with the game itself. In 1879 the width of the pitcher's box was reduced from six feet to four, and pitchers were now assessed a ball for every unfair pitch rather than for every third unfair pitch. A batter still had to collect nine unfair balls before he earned a walk, however.

Beginning in 1879, a batter could no longer be retired on a foul ball unless it was caught on the fly, and umpires were authorized to fine a pitcher from $10 to $50 if they judged the boxman to have deliberately hit a batter with a pitch. But in 1880 the rule allowing a batter to be retired on a foul ball caught on one bounce was restored, and meanwhile few umpires had the courage to fine a head-hunting pitcher when their jobs depended on their relationship with the team for which the pitcher played.

George Wright properly occupies center stage in this pic of the 1879 NL champions. The game's first "King of Short Stops" is still the lone man to win a pennant in his one and only year as a big league manager.

Still, there were several rule changes in 1879 that hit the mark. One stipulated that the batter was automatically out after a swinging or called third strike if the catcher caught the ball before it hit the ground. This rule encouraged catchers to play up closer to the plate, particularly when a batter had two strikes. Another change in 1879, at Al Spalding's behest, was the replacement of the Mahn ball by the "Spalding League Ball," made by Spalding's sporting goods firm, as the league's official ball.

Spalding, who by 1879 also owned a piece of the Chicago White Stockings, then jubilantly watched his club roar out of the starting gate by sweeping successive three-game series at home from Syracuse and Troy. Alone in first place at 6–0, Chicago next entertained the Providence Grays. A 14–5 loss to the Grays seemed only a momentary detour, for the White Stockings were completely refurbished in 1879 and looked to be loaded. The sole returning regulars from the disappointing 1878 entry were pitcher Terry Larkin and Cap Anson. Anson, after bouncing from one position to another for eight years, was finally under the wing of a manager—himself—who knew his proper place on the diamond and planted him at the White Stockings' vacant first-base post, where he would remain for 19 years.

The vacancy at first base was there because Joe Start, Chicago's former gateway guardian, had skipped to Providence. For the 1879 campaign the Grays also replaced second baseman

PAUL WHO?

The 1879 Cleveland Blues. Top: Jack Glasscock, Bill Phillips, Jim McCormick and George Strief. Center: Charlie Eden, Tom Carey, business manager Joe Mack, Doc Kennedy and Pigtail Billy Riley. Front: Fred Warner and Bobby Mitchell, the first southpaw to win a game in the NL. Execrable hitting by out-fielders Strief (.174) and Riley (.145) killed the Blues in 1879. The following year the club beefed up its outfield by picking up rookie star Al Hall from Troy, only to have Hall break his leg in an early-season game at Cincinnati. The Queen City club held a benefit for Hall, which Cleveland owner J. Ford Evans refused to attend, saying, "I have to go to a champagne breakfast." Evans then gave Hall his release and abandoned him in a Cincinnati hospital, never to play again.

Spalding's Official Base Ball Guide for 1879 crowned Milwaukee's Abner Dalrymple the 1878 National League batting champ with a .356 mark. The 1880 Guide awarded the 1879 batting title to Cap Anson, claiming Anson had compiled 90 hits in 221 at bats for a .407 average. For years, Dalrymple was considered to have been the first rookie to win a major league batting title, and *Total Baseball* still deems Anson the 1879 titlist because major league baseball officials obdurately continue to regard him as such. In actuality, any casual student of the game with the time to comb through two seasons-worth of old box scores can confirm what has long since been discovered: that in 1878, even if Dalrymple had hit .356 instead of his real figure of .354, it wouldn't have been good enough; and that Anson, rather than hitting at a .407 clip in 1879 with 90 hits in 221 at bats, had just 72 hits in 227 at bats to finish at .317.

So what happened back there? In 1878 hits made in tie games were thrown out but have since been restored, and the following year the scorekeeper for the Chicago team apparently either failed first-grade math or got a lot of his dinner checks picked up by a certain first baseman. In any case, the player punished on both occasions was Providence center fielder Paul Hines. After hitting .358 in 1878, Hines was told he had in fact hit .351 and would have to look up at Dalrymple for the rest of his life. The following year the Spalding *Guide* did Hines right, in a sense, when it fixed him at .357. But instead of hitting 50 points less than Anson's .407, Hines, we now know, was 40 points better than the Chicagoan's .317.

We also now know that in 1878 Hines was the first Triple Crown winner in major league history. When he was 68 years old, Hines was arrested in Washington, where he worked for the Department of Agriculture post office, for pickpocketing. Nobody knew that they had a two-time batting champ and the first Triple Crown winner in custody; all of these discoveries were still down the road. Yet another discovery waiting to be made was that Hines, from his Providence center field post, snared a short fly ball behind shortstop Tom Carey in the third game of the 1878 season. Then, according to the scoring rules at that time, he engineered the first unassisted triple play ever seen on a baseball diamond by sprinting to third base ahead of two Boston baserunners who had proceeded home, gambling that the ball would fall safely.

Charlie Sweasy (.175 in 1878) with Mike McGeary and invited shortstop George Wright to leave Boston, where he had played on six championship teams, and see if his winning habit could transfer to Rhode Island. Wright accepted the challenge, bringing Jim O'Rourke with him. The pair's move was just enough to tip the balance of power in the East.

Still, the Grays started slowly under their new manager-shortstop, hovering around the .500 mark until they took a tense 10–9 battle from Cincinnati on May 22. For the next three months Providence chased Chicago, which had sped to an early lead, while Boston even without O'Rourke in center field and George Wright at short, hung just off the pace. Minus his brother, Harry Wright had to reshuffle his infield again in 1879, leaving only Jack Burdock intact at second base. Used to writing J. O'Rourke in center field on his lineup card, Wright found a way to continue doing so. He hired O'Rourke's brother, John. When the younger O'Rourke and Charley Jones, snatched from Cincinnati during the offseason, combined for more home runs and RBI than any other two players in the League, traditionally weak-hitting Boston showed unaccustomed punch.

Chicago held a comfortable lead into August, but when a liver ailment idled Anson for the rest of the season, the White Stockings collapsed, leaving the race to the two Eastern powers. The schedulemaker took a bow for having arranged for Boston and Providence to meet in the final six games of the season. When the second-place Red Caps hosted the first-place Grays at South End Grounds on September 23, they were three lengths behind, needing to win five of their last six games to claim their third straight flag. Jim Tyng gave the Hub faithful a flicker of hope by winning the Series opener, 7–3, but it quickly died when Providence belted Tyng 15–4 on September 25 and then took a hard-fought 7–6 thriller the following afternoon at Providence to clinch the pennant.

On October 1, the night after the season ended, George Wright was given a floral bat and ball at a reception held for the champion Grays, and as each member of the Grays received a gold medal from the Providence mayor, his name blazed out in colored fire from a halo-shaped iron frame near the podium. The extravagance was intended to encourage the small-market team to hold together and defend its championship, but it was unnecessary. Most of the Grays' top players could no longer go elsewhere anyway. Two days earlier, at a league meeting in Buffalo, the Reserve Clause had been voted into existence, granting every team the right to designate up to five players as "reserved" by it for the following year. Concocted by Arthur Soden, one of Boston's ruling triumvirate, it was adopted to save struggling team owners from having to watch helplessly as star players were lost to a higher bidder. The very day the Reserve Clause was born, September 29, 1879, the International Association collapsed. The league's only serious obstacle to a virtual monopoly on the professional game was gone.

Three months later, with the arrival of a new year, came the dawn of a new era in baseball history.

The Providence Grays (left) and the Boston Red Caps (right) prior to an 1879 game at Providence's Messer Park. Note the grandstand screen; Messer Park was the first to install this sort of protective device to save spectators in the "Slaughter Pens" behind home plate from being skulled by foul balls.

LEE WHO?

On September 27, 1879, at Boston, Red Caps manager Harry Wright started a slender ex-Brown University star in the box against Providence. His name was Lee Richmond, and he hurled the most exceptional game to that point in history by a lefthander when he fanned 11 Grays in his victorious debut.

Richmond's 11 strikeouts remained the record for the most by a pitcher in his inaugural major league game until May 1, 1884, when Ed Morris of Columbus in the American Association fanned 13 Cincinnati Reds. But another feat Richmond accomplished the following year went unequaled for nearly 80 years. When Boston did not include Richmond among the players it reserved for the 1880 season, he signed with Worcester. On June 12 of that year the Massachusetts team hosted the Cleveland Blues, with Richmond in the box against Jim McCormick. Worcester pushed across a run in the bottom of the fifth when shortstop Arthur Irwin scored after singling earlier in the inning. Irwin's hit was one of only three McCormick surrendered. Richmond, meanwhile, did not allow a single Cleveland player to reach base safely. His perfect game was not only a major league first—albeit by a margin of just five days—but it was the only perfecto of nine or more innings by a southpaw prior to 1958.

How perfect, really, was Richmond that afternoon? We know that a Cleveland player hit a drive to right field that ordinarily would have been at least a single if Lon Knight, assumedly playing shallow, had not picked it up on the hop and fired to first baseman Chub Sullivan in time to get the out. We can only wonder if perhaps Jack Glasscock, up with one out in the ninth, swung at a 7-and-2 pitch and made out. A count like that was entirely possible then, with eight balls needed for a walk. So is it conceivable that, with two outs in the ninth, Cleveland's last batter, left fielder Ned Hanlon, was driven off the plate time and again by pitches nicking his legs until finally he gave up and made an out just to leave the field in one piece. In 1880 the hit-batsman rule was still some seven years away from adoption by the National League.

By the same token, though, Richmond might have fired an inside pitch that ticked Hanlon's bat as he ducked away and dribbled back to the box for what should have been an easy final out. But umpire Foghorn Bradley would properly have ruled it "No Pitch" and told Hanlon to bat again—for it was also a rule then that a batter could not make out on a pitch his bat struck unintentionally.

All of these things—or none of them—might have happened on June 12, 1880. We will never know.

Lee Richmond, the first southpaw pitcher of note, was also the first hurler to collect as many as 10 strikeouts in his big league debut, the first man to throw a perfect game and the first to win 20 games for a last-place team. With all that, Richmond won only 75 games in the majors.

THE SEASONAL RECORD

	W	L	PCT	H	R	GB
1. Providence Grays	59	25	.702	34–8	25–17	—
2. Boston Red Caps	54	30	.643	29–13	25–17	5
3. Buffalo Bisons	46	32	.590	23–16	23–16	10
4. Chicago White Stockings	46	33	.582	29–13	17–20	10.5
5. Cincinnati Reds	43	37	.538	21–16	22–21	14
6. Cleveland Blues	27	55	.329	15–27	12–28	31
7. Syracuse Stars	22	48	.314	11–22	11–26	30
8. Troy Trojans	19	56	.253	12–27	7–29	35.5

	Pro	Bos	Buf	Chi	Cin	Cle	Syr	Tro	
Providence	—	8	6	7	10	8	10	10	59
Boston	4	—	9	4	7	10	9	11	54
Buffalo	6	3	—	6	7	8	5	11	46
Chicago	5	8	6	—	3	8	8	8	46
Cincinnati	2	5	3	8	—	8	8	9	43
Cleveland	4	2	4	4	4	—	4	5	27
Syracuse	2	3	3	1	4	7	—	2	22
Troy	2	1	1	3	2	6	4	—	19
	25	30	32	33	37	55	48	19	316

SEASON LEADERS

Batting Average

1.	Hines, Providence	.357
2.	Jim O'Rourke, Providence	.348
	Kelly, Cincinnati	.348
4.	John O'Rourke, Boston	.341
5.	D. White, Cincinnati	.330

On–Base Percentage

1.	Jim O'Rourke, Providence	.371
2.	Hines, Providence	.369
3.	Jones, Boston	.367
4.	Kelly, Cincinnati	.363
5.	John O'Rourke, Boston	.357

Home Runs

1.	Jones, Boston	9
2.	John O'Rourke, Boston	6
3.	Brouthers, Troy	4
4.	Eden, Cleveland	3
5.	Eight with	2

Hits

1.	Hines, Providence	146
2.	Jim O'Rourke, Providence	126
3.	Kelly, Cincinnati	120
4.	Jones, Boston	112
5.	D. White, Cincinnati	110

Slugging Average

1.	John O'Rourke, Boston	.521
2.	C. Jones, Boston	.510
3.	Kelly, Cincinnati	.493
4.	Hines, Providence	.482
5.	Jim O'Rourke, Providence	.459

Total Bases

1.	Hines, Providence	197
2.	Jones, Boston	181
3.	Kelly, Cincinnati	170
4.	Jim O'Rourke, Providence	166
5.	John O'Rourke, Boston	165

RBI

1.	John O'Rourke, Boston	62
	Jones, Boston	62
3.	Dickerson, Cincinnati	57
4.	McVey, Cincinnati	55
5.	Hines, Providence	52

Runs

1.	Jones, Boston	85
2.	Hines, Providence	81
3.	Wright, Providence	79
4.	Kelly, Cincinnati	78
5.	Dickerson, Cincinnati	73

Bases on Balls

1.	Jones, Boston	29
2.	Williamson, Chicago	24
3.	York, Providence	19
4.	Barnes, Cincinnati	16
	Richardson, Buffalo	16

Strikeouts

1.	Galvin, Buffalo	56
	W. White, Cincinnati	56
3.	M. Mansell, Syracuse	45
4.	Flint, Chicago	44
5.	Eggler, Buffalo	41

PITCHING

Wins

1.	Ward, Providence	47
2.	W. White, Cincinnati	43
	Bond, Boston	43
4.	Galvin, Buffalo	37
5.	Larkin, Chicago	31

Losses

1.	G. Bradley, Troy	40
	J. McCormick, Cleveland	40
3.	H. McCormick, Syracuse	33
4.	W. White, Cincinnati	31
5.	Galvin, Buffalo	27

Innings

1.	W. White, Cincinnati	680
2.	Galvin, Buffalo	593
3.	Ward, Providence	587
4.	Bond, Boston	555.1
5.	J. McCormick, Cleveland	546.1

Complete Games

1.	W. White, Cincinnati	75
2.	Galvin, Buffalo	65
3.	J. McCormick, Cleveland	59
4.	Ward, Providence	58
5.	Galvin, Buffalo	.578

Strikeouts

1.	Ward, Providence	239
2.	W. White, Cincinnati	232
3.	J. McCormick, Cleveland	197
4.	Bond, Boston	155
5.	Larkin, Chicago	142

Winning Percentage (20 decisions)

1.	Ward, Providence	.712
2.	Bond, Boston	.694
3.	Hankinson, Chicago	.600
4.	W. White, Cincinnati	.581
5.	Galvin, Buffalo	.578

ERA (90 innings)

1.	Bond, Boston	1.96
2.	W. White, Cincinnati	1.99
3.	Ward, Providence	2.15
4.	Salisbury, Troy	2.22
5.	Galvin, Buffalo	2.28

Lowest On–Base Percentage

1.	Larkin, Chicago	.250
	Ward, Providence	.250
3.	Galvin, Buffalo	.253
4.	W. White, Cincinnati	.256
5.	Bond, Boston	.259

FIELDING

Total Chances

1B	Walker, Buffalo	907
2B	Burdock, Boston	662
3B	Williamson, Chicago	318
SS	G. Wright, Boston	449
OF	M. Mansell, Syracuse	244
C	Snyder, Boston	584
P	Galvin, Buffalo	202

Fielding Average

Anson, Chicago	.975
Quest, Chicago	.925
Morrill, Boston	.878
Force, Buffalo	.929
C. Jones, Boston	.933
Snyder, Boston	.925
Bond, Boston	.957

PROVIDENCE   **George Wright**   **Messer Street Grounds**

		G	AB	H	R	2B	3B	HR	RBI	BB	BA	SA
CF	Paul Hines	85	**409**	**146**	81	25	10	2	52	8	**.357**	.482
SS	George Wright	85	388	107	79	15	10	1	42	13	.276	.374
2B	Mike McGeary	85	374	103	62	7	2	0	35	5	.275	.305
P	Monte Ward	83	364	104	71	9	4	2	41	7	.286	.349
RF	Jim O'Rourke	81	362	126	69	19	9	1	46	13	.348	.459
LF	Tom York	81	342	106	69	25	5	1	50	19	.310	.421
1B	Joe Start	66	317	101	70	11	5	2	37	7	.319	.404
C	Lew Brown	53	229	59	23	13	4	2	38	4	.258	.376
3B	Bill Hague	51	209	47	20	3	1	0	21	3	.225	.249
P	Bobby Mathews	43	173	35	25	2	0	1	10	7	.202	.231
C	Emil Gross	30	132	46	31	9	5	0	24	4	.348	.492
Sub	Jack Farrell	12	51	13	5	2	0	0	5	1	.255	.294
Sub	Denny Sullivan	5	19	5	5	2	0	0	2	1	.263	.368
Sub	Dan O'Leary	2	7	3	1	0	0	0	2	0	.429	.429
Sub	Rudy Kemmler	2	7	1	0	0	0	0	0	0	.143	.143
Sub	Doug Allison	1	5	0	0	0	0	0	0	0	.000	.000
Sub	Bill White	1	4	1	1	0	0	0	0	0	.250	.250
		85	3392	**1003**	**612**	142	**55**	12	**405**	92	**.296**	**.381**

1B   Start 65, O'Rourke 20, White 1
2B   McGeary 73, Farrell 12
SS   Wright 85
3B   Hague 51, Ward 16, McGeary 12, Mathews 5, Sullivan 4, O'Rourke 3
OF   Hines 85, York 81, O'Rourke 56, Mathews 21, Ward 8, Brown 6, O'Leary 2, Sullivan 1, Start 1
C   Brown 48, Gross 30, O'Rourke 5, Kemmler 2, Allison 1
P   Ward 70, Mathews 27

	G	IP	GS	CG	W	L	K	BB	SH	SV	ERA
Monte Ward	70	587	60	58	**47**	19	**239**	36	2	**1**	2.15
Bobby Mathews	27	189	25	15	12	6	90	26	1	**1**	2.29
		776	85	73	59	25	**329**	62	3	**2**	**2.18**

BOSTON   **Harry Wright**   **South End Grounds (I)**

		G	AB	H	R	2B	3B	HR	RBI	BB	BA	SA
2B	Jack Burdock	84	359	86	64	10	3	0	36	9	.240	.284
RF	Sadie Houck	80	356	95	69	24	9	2	49	4	.267	.402
LF	Charley Jones	83	355	112	**85**	22	10	**9**	**62**	29	.315	.510
3B	John Morrill	84	348	98	56	18	5	0	49	14	.282	.362
SS	Ezra Sutton	84	339	84	54	13	4	0	34	2	.248	.310
C	Pop Snyder	81	329	78	42	16	3	2	35	5	.237	.322
CF	John O'Rourke	71	317	108	69	17	11	6	**62**	8	.341	**.521**
P	Tommy Bond	65	257	62	35	3	1	0	21	6	.241	.261
1B	Ed Cogswell	49	236	76	51	8	1	1	18	8	.322	.377
Sub	Bill Hawes	38	155	31	19	3	3	0	9	2	.200	.258
P	Curry Foley	35	146	46	16	3	1	0	17	3	.315	.349
P	Jim Tyng	3	14	5	2	1	0	0	0	0	.357	.429
P	Lee Richmond	1	6	2	0	0	0	0	1	0	.333	.333
		84	3217	883	562	138	51	**20**	393	90	.274	.368

1B   Cogswell 49, Morrill 33, Foley 2, Bond 1
2B   Burdock 84
SS   Sutton 51, Houck 33
3B   Morrill 51, Sutton 33
OF   Jones 83, O'Rourke 71, Houck 47, Hawes 34, Foley 17, Bond 5, Snyder 2
C   Snyder 80, Hawes 5
P   Bond 64, Foley 21, Tyng 3, Richmond 1

	G	IP	GS	CG	W	L	K	BB	SH	SV	ERA
Tommy Bond	64	555.1	64	59	43	19	155	24	11	0	**1.96**
Curry Foley	21	161.2	16	16	9	9	57	15	1	1	2.51
Jim Tyng	3	27	3	3	1	2	7	6	0	0	5.00
Lee Richmond	1	9	1	1	1	0	11	1	0	0	2.00
	*One combined shutout on Aug. 21: Bond 8 innings, Foley 1 inning										
	753	84	79	54	30	230	**46**	**13**	1	2.19	

BUFFALO   John Clapp   Riverside Park

		G	AB	H	R	2B	3B	HR	RBI	BB	BA	SA
3B	Hardy Richardson	79	336	95	54	18	10	0	37	16	.283	.396
LF	Joe Hornung	78	319	85	46	18	7	0	38	2	.266	.367
CF	Dave Eggler	78	317	66	41	5	7	0	27	11	.208	.268
SS	Davy Force	79	316	66	36	5	2	0	8	13	.209	.237
2B	Chick Fulmer	76	306	82	30	11	5	0	28	11	.268	.337
C	John Clapp	70	292	77	47	12	5	1	36	5	.264	.349
1B	Oscar Walker	72	287	79	35	15	6	1	35	8	.275	.380
P	Pud Galvin	67	265	66	34	11	6	0	27	1	.249	.336
RF	Bill Crowley	60	261	75	41	9	5	0	30	6	.287	.360
P	Bill McGunnigle	47	171	30	22	0	1	0	5	0	.175	.187
Sub	Jack Rowe	8	34	12	8	1	0	0	8	5	.353	.382
Sub	Steve Libby	1	2	0	0	0	0	0	0	0	.000	.000
		79	2906	733	394	105	54	2	279	78	.252	.328

```
1B   Walker 72, Crowley 7, Libby 1, Hornung 1
2B   Fulmer 76, Crowley 3
SS   Force 78, Galvin 1
3B   Richardson 78, Force 1
OF   Eggler 78, Hornung 77, Crowley 43, McGunnigle 34, Clapp 7, Rowe 2
C    Clapp 63, Crowley 10, Rowe 6, Richardson 1
P    Galvin 66, McGunnigle 14
```

	G	IP	GS	CG	W	L	K	BB	SH	SV	ERA
Pud Galvin	66	593	66	65	37	27	136	31	6	0	2.28
Bill McGunnigle	14	120	13	13	9	5	62	16	2	0	2.63
	713	79	78	46	32	198	47	8	0	2.34	

CHICAGO   Cap Anson (41–21)   Silver Flint (5–12)   Lake Front Park (I)

		G	AB	H	R	2B	3B	HR	RBI	BB	BA	SA
SS	John Peters	83	379	93	45	13	2	1	31	1	.245	.298
2B	Joe Quest	83	334	69	38	16	1	0	22	9	.207	.260
LF	Abner Dalrymple	71	333	97	47	25	1	0	23	4	.291	.372
C	Silver Flint	79	324	92	46	22	6	1	41	6	.284	.398
3B	Ned Williamson	80	320	94	66	20	13	1	36	24	.294	.447
RF	Orator Shaffer	73	316	96	53	13	0	0	35	6	.304	.345
CF	George Gore	63	266	70	43	17	4	0	32	8	.263	.357
P	Terry Larkin	60	228	50	26	12	2	0	18	8	.219	.289
1B	Cap Anson	51	227	72	40	20	1	0	34	2	.317	.414
P	Frank Hankinson	44	171	31	14	4	0	0	8	2	.181	.205
Sub	Jack Remsen	42	152	33	14	4	2	0	8	2	.217	.270
Sub	Lew Brown	6	21	6	2	1	0	0	3	1	.286	.333
Sub	Bill Harbidge	4	18	2	2	0	0	0	1	0	.111	.111
Sub	John Stedronsky	4	12	1	0	0	0	0	0	0	.083	.083
Sub	Herm Doscher	3	11	2	1	0	0	0	1	0	.182	.182
Sub	Tom Dolan	1	4	0	0	0	0	0	0	0	.000	.000
		83	3116	808	437	**167**	32	3	293	73	.259	.336

1B Anson 51, Remsen 11, Gore 9, Williamson 6, Brown 6
2B Quest 83
SS Peters 83
3B Williamson 70, Hankinson 5, Stedronsky 4, Doscher 3, Shaffer 1
OF Shaffer 72, Dalrymple 71, Gore 54, Remsen 31, Hankinson 14, Harbidge 4, Larkin 3, Flint 1
C   Flint 78, Williamson 4, Dolan 1
P   Larkin 58, Hankinson 26

	G	IP	GS	CG	W	L	K	BB	SH	SV	ERA
Terry Larkin	58	513.1	58	57	31	23	142	30	4	0	2.44
Frank Hankinson	26	230.2	25	25	15	10	69	27	2	0	2.50
	744	83	**82**	46	33	211	57	6	0	2.46	

CINCINNATI Deacon White (9–9) Cal McVey (34–28) Avenue Grounds

		G	AB	H	R	2B	3B	HR	RBI	BB	BA	SA
CF	Pete Hotaling	81	369	103	64	20	9	1	27	12	.279	.390
1B	Cal McVey	81	354	105	64	18	6	0	55	8	.297	.381
LF	Buttercup Dickerson	81	350	102	73	18	**14**	2	57	3	.291	.440
3B	King Kelly	77	345	120	78	20	12	2	47	8	.348	.493
C	Deacon White	78	333	110	55	16	6	1	52	6	.330	.423
SS	Ross Barnes	77	323	86	55	9	2	1	30	16	.266	.316
2B	Joe Gerhardt	79	313	62	22	12	3	1	39	3	.198	.265
P	Will White	76	294	40	28	6	0	0	17	6	.136	.156
RF	Will Foley	56	218	46	22	5	1	0	25	2	.211	.243
Sub	Mike Burke	28	117	26	13	3	0	0	8	2	.222	.248
Sub	Blondie Purcell	12	50	11	10	0	0	0	4	1	.220	.220
P	Jack Neagle	3	12	2	1	0	0	0	2	0	.167	.167
Sub	John Magner	1	4	0	0	0	0	0	1	0	.000	.000
P	Harry Wheeler	1	3	0	0	0	0	0	0	0	.000	.000
		81	3085	813	485	127	53	8	364	67	.264	.347

1B McVey 72, Gerhardt 8, D. White 2
2B Gerhardt 55, Barnes 16, Hotaling 6, Foley 3, Kelly 1
SS Barnes 61, Burke 19, Gerhardt 1
3B Kelly 33, Foley 29, Gerhardt 16, Burke 5, Hotaling 3, McVey 1
OF Dickerson 81, Hotaling 69, Kelly 29, Foley 25, D. White 21, Purcell 10, McVey 7, Burke 5, Neagle 2, Magner 1, Wheeler 1
C   D. White 59, Kelly 21, Hotaling 8, McVey 1
P   W. White 76, McVey 3, Purcell 2, Neagle 2, Wheeler 1

	G	IP	GS	CG	W	L	K	BB	SH	SV	ERA
Will White	**76**	**680**	75	75	43	21	232	68	4	0	1.99
Blondie Purcell	2	18	2	2	0	2	3	2	0	0	4.00
Cal McVey	3	14	1	1	0	2	7	2	0	0	8.36
Jack Neagle	2	13	2	1	0	1	4	5	0	0	3.46
Harry Wheeler	1	1	1	0	0	1	0	4	0	0	81.00
	726	81	79	43	37	246	81	4	0	2.29	

CLEVELAND   Jim McCormick   Kennard Street Park

		G	AB	H	R	2B	3B	HR	RBI	BB	BA	SA
1B	Bill Phillips	81	365	99	58	15	4	0	29	2	.271	.334
RF	Charlie Eden	81	353	96	40	**31**	7	3	34	6	.272	.425
SS	Tom Carey	80	335	80	30	14	1	0	32	5	.239	.287
2B	Jack Glasscock	80	325	68	31	9	3	0	29	6	.209	.255
3B	Fred Warner	76	316	77	32	11	4	0	22	2	.244	.304
P	Jim McCormick	75	282	62	35	10	2	0	20	1	.220	.270
CF	George Strief	71	264	46	24	7	1	0	15	10	.174	.208
C	Barney Gilligan	52	205	35	20	6	2	0	11	0	.171	.220
C	Doc Kennedy	49	193	56	19	8	2	1	18	2	.290	.368
LF	Billy Riley	44	165	24	14	2	0	0	9	2	.145	.158
P	Bobby Mitchell	30	109	16	11	2	2	0	6	0	.147	.202
Sub	Jack Allen	16	60	7	7	1	1	0	4	1	.117	.167
Sub	Len Stockwell	2	6	0	0	0	0	0	0	0	.000	.000
Sub	Hickey Hoffman	2	6	0	0	0	0	0	0	0	.000	.000
Sub	Fred Gunkle	1	3	0	1	0	0	0	0	0	.000	.000
		82	2987	666	322	116	29	4	226	37	.223	.285

1B   Phillips 75, McCormick 4, Kennedy 4, Eden 3, Warner 1, Riley 1
2B   Glasscock 66, Strief 16
SS   Carey 80, Gilligan 2
3B   Warner 54, Glasscock 14, Allen 14
OF   Eden 80, Strief 55, Riley 43, Gilligan 23, Warner 21, McCormick 13, Mitchell 9, Allen 2, Phillips 2, Stockwell 2, Hoffman 1, Gunkle 1
C   Kennedy 46, Gilligan 27, Phillips 11, Hoffman 2, Riley 1, Eden 1, Gunkle 1
P   McCormick 62, Mitchell 23

	G	IP	GS	CG	W	L	K	BB	SH	SV	ERA
Jim McCormick	62	546.1	60	59	20	**40**	197	**74**	3	0	2.42
Bobby Mitchell	23	194.2	22	20	7	15	90	42	0	0	3.28
	741		82	79	27	55	287	116	3	0	2.65

SYRACUSE   Mike Dorgan (17–26)   Bill Holbert (0–1)   Jimmy Macullar (5–21)   Newell Park

		G	AB	H	R	2B	3B	HR	RBI	BB	BA	SA
RF	Blondie Purcell	63	277	72	32	6	3	0	25	2	.260	.303
UT	Mike Dorgan	59	270	72	38	11	5	1	17	4	.267	.356
1B	Hick Carpenter	65	261	53	30	6	0	0	20	2	.203	.226
CF	John Richmond	62	254	54	31	8	4	1	23	4	.213	.287
SS	Jimmy Macullar	64	246	52	24	9	0	0	13	3	.211	.248
LF	Mike Mansell	67	242	52	24	4	2	1	13	5	.215	.260
2B	Jack Farrell	54	241	73	40	6	2	1	21	2	.303	.357
P	Harry McCormick	57	230	51	21	4	1	1	21	0	.222	.261
C	Bill Holbert	59	229	46	11	0	0	0	21	1	.201	.201
3B	Red Woodhead	34	131	21	4	1	0	0	2	0	.160	.168
Sub	George Creamer	15	60	13	3	2	0	0	3	1	.217	.250
Sub	John McGuinness	12	51	15	7	1	1	0	4	0	.294	.353
Sub	Jack Allen	11	48	9	7	2	1	0	3	1	.188	.271
Sub	Honest John Kelly	10	36	4	4	1	0	0	2	0	.111	.139
Sub	George Adams	4	13	3	0	0	0	0	0	1	.231	.231
Sub	Frank Decker	3	10	1	0	0	0	0	0	0	.100	.100
Sub	Charlie Osterhout	2	8	0	0	0	0	0	0	0	.000	.000
Sub	Tom Mansell	1	4	1	0	0	0	0	0	0	.250	.250
		71	2611	592	276	61	19	5	188	26	.227	.270

1B Carpenter 34, Dorgan 21, McGuinness 12, Adams 2, Kelly 2, Decker 1
2B Farrell 54, Creamer 10, Macullar 4, Carpenter 3, Dorgan 1
SS Macullar 37, Richmond 28, Creamer 3, Dorgan 6
3B Woodhead 34, Carpenter 18, Dorgan 11, Allen 8, Macullar 1
OF M. Mansell 67, Purcell 47, Richmond 35, Macullar 26, Dorgan 16, Carpenter 11, McCormick 7, Holbert 4, Allen 3, Creamer 2, Adams 2, Decker 1, T. Mansell 1, Osterhout 1
C Holbert 56, Kelly 8, Dorgan 4, Decker 2, Richmond 2, Purcell 1, Osterhout 1
P McCormick 54, Purcell 22, Dorgan 2

	G	IP	GS	CG	W	L	K	BB	SH	SV	ERA
Harry McCormick	54	457.1	54	49	11	33	96	31	5	0	2.99
Blondie Purcell	22	179.2	17	15	4	15	28	19	0	0	3.76
Mike Dorgan	2	12	0	0	0	0	8	2	0	0	2.25
		649	71	64	22	48	132	52	5	0	3.19

TROY   Horace Phillips (12–34)   Bob Ferguson (7–22)   Putnam Grounds

		G	AB	H	R	2B	3B	HR	RBI	BB	BA	SA
CF	Al Hall	67	306	79	30	7	3	0	14	3	.258	.301
SS	Ed Caskin	70	304	78	32	13	2	0	21	2	.257	.313
RF	Jake Evans	72	280	65	30	9	5	0	17	5	.232	.300
P	George Bradley	63	251	62	36	9	5	0	23	1	.247	.323
2B	Thorny Hawkes	64	250	52	24	6	1	0	20	4	.208	.240
C	Charlie Reilley	62	236	54	17	5	1	0	19	1	.229	.258
3B	Herm Doscher	47	191	42	16	8	0	0	18	2	.220	.262
LF	Tom Mansell	40	177	43	29	6	0	0	11	3	.243	.277
1B	Dan Brouthers	39	168	46	17	12	1	4	17	1	.274	.429
Sub	Aaron Clapp	36	146	39	24	9	3	0	18	6	.267	.370
Sub	Bob Ferguson	30	123	31	10	5	2	0	4	4	.252	.325
Sub	Candy Nelson	28	106	28	17	7	1	0	10	8	.264	.349
Sub	Sandy Taylor	24	97	21	10	4	0	0	8	1	.216	.258
Sub	John Shoupe	11	44	4	5	0	0	0	1	0	.091	.091
P	Fred Goldsmith	9	38	9	6	1	0	0	2	1	.237	.263
Sub	John Cassidy	9	37	7	4	1	0	0	1	1	.189	.216
P	Harry Salisbury	10	36	2	3	0	0	0	0	1	.056	.056
Sub	Honest John Kelly	6	22	5	1	0	0	0	0	0	.227	.227
Sub	Bill Holbert	4	15	4	1	0	0	0	2	0	.267	.267
P	Pat McManus	2	8	1	0	0	0	0	0	0	.125	.125
P	Gid Gardner	2	6	1	1	0	0	0	0	0	.167	.167
		77	2841	673	321	102	24	4	206	45	.237	.294

1B Brouthers 37, Clapp 25, Reilly 11, Bradley 3, Cassidy 2, Goldsmith 1
2B Hawkes 64, Caskin 6, Ferguson 6, Shoupe 1
SS Caskin 42, Nelson 24, Shoupe 10, Bradley 1
3B Doscher 47, Ferguson 24, Bradley 5, Kelly 1
OF Evans 72, Hall 67, Mansell 40, Taylor 24, Clapp 11, Cassidy 8, Nelson 4, Goldsmith 2, Kelly 2, Reilly 2, Salisbury 1, Bradley 1
C Reilly 49, Caskin 22, Holbert 4, Kelly 3
P Bradley 54, Salisbury 10, Goldsmith 8, Brouthers 3, McManus 2, Gardner 2

	G	IP	GS	CG	W	L	K	BB	SH	SV	ERA
George Bradley	54	487	54	53	13	**40**	133	26	3	0	2.85
Harry Salisbury	10	89	10	9	4	6	31	11	0	0	2.22
Fred Goldsmith	8	63	7	7	2	4	31	1	0	0	1.57
Dan Brouthers	3	21	2	2	0	2	6	8	0	0	5.57
Pat McManus	2	21	2	2	0	2	6	1	0	0	3.00
Gid Gardner	2	14	2	2	0	2	3	0	0	0	5.79
		695	77	75	19	56	210	47	3	0	2.80

1880
ANSON ASCENDS
AND CINCINNATI SECEDES

The 1880 season brought the first standard player contracts that contained a Reserve Clause. Until 1883 each team could reserve a maximum of five players for the following season; beginning in 1883, the number was hiked to 11 and soon the reserve rule embraced a team's entire roster. While the limit was still five, teams generally reserved their best pitcher and catcher, together with three other regulars chosen for a wide variety of reasons, ranging from whether the owner's daughter liked them to how much they were coveted by other teams. At least initially, being reserved was viewed by most players as a mark of status rather than servitude. Since roster sizes in the early 1880s ran around 11, about half the players on a team were given "status," leaving the others to shop for a better deal.

A natural outgrowth of the Reserve Clause was a sharp drop in player salaries. The Boston Red Caps were particularly quick to seize upon the new device as a tool for imprisoning players and slashing their pay for any offense the front office deemed punishable. In 1880, once Boston was out of the running, owner Arthur Soden, the creator of the Reserve Clause, suspended Charley Jones. Drunkenness and insubordination were the reasons alleged for the suspension, but in fact the high-paid Jones had had the temerity to refuse to wait for his paycheck, as was customary, until the club returned home from a road trip. Jones, the League's slugging leader in 1879, was subsequently blacklisted by Soden, with the support of Soden's fellow moguls. He never played in the League again.

On the field, the game underwent only minor revisions in 1880. The number of unfair pitches a batter needed to draw a walk was pared from nine to eight. Several other changes, regarding when and how a baserunner could be retired on a caught fly or a caught foul fly, brought the rulebook ever closer to the modern version. In most respects, though, with the exception of the Reserve Clause, the 1880 season broke little new ground. The schedule remained stationary after being expanded to 84 games in 1879 when the League grew to eight teams, and, as had been true since 1877, teams still met each other 12 times.

Charley Jones, the NL's premier slugger until he was blackballed in 1880. At one time he was believed to have been killed by lightning in 1910. Lee Allen, who found Jones's disappearance "the most absorbing baseball story" he'd ever encountered, proved the lightning tale was apocryphal. Jones's death date and place are still a mystery.

John Day, the Manhattan tobacconist and later president of the Metropolitan Exhibition Company, owners of both the New York Giants and the New York Metropolitans. In 1880, together with Jim Mutrie, Day founded the Mets as an independent pro team. On September 29, 1880, the Mets staged the first pro game ever in New York City—every club that had previously represented New York played in Brooklyn, a separate city until 1898.

Action began on May 1 with Boston at Providence, Chicago at Cincinnati, Buffalo at Cleveland and Worcester at Troy. Worcester was a newcomer, replacing Syracuse, but the other three matchups were between teams that had previously established natural geographic rivalries. In Providence some 2,750, including about 400 Boston fans who'd bought a special one-dollar round-trip railway ticket, watched the defending-champion Grays march to the flagpole, hoist the 1879 pennant, and blank the Red Caps, their closest pursuer

---

ONE-GAMER III

On September 30, at Chicago, in the White Stockings' final game of the 1880 season, Cap Anson gave the ball to Charlie Guth on something of a whim. The 24-year-old Guth had a local reputation as a speedballer, and lived up to expectations by fanning seven Buffalo Bisons while surrendering just one walk. Guth was tapped for 12 hits, however, leading to eight runs (albeit only five of them were earned). When the White Stockings plated 10 tallies, Guth staggered a 10–8 win. It was to be his lone major league appearance. A complete list of pitchers who hurled complete game wins in their only major league appearances between 1876, the National League's inaugural season, and 1881, when the pitching distance was lengthened by five feet, begins and ends with Charlie Guth.

---

in 1879, 8–0. The Opening Day victory put the Grays in a four-way tie for first place at 1–0 with Chicago, Buffalo and Worcester. But exactly a week later, following a 10–8 loss at Worcester, Providence ceded its share of the top rung, never to regain it in 1880.

Providence's sag was directly attributable to the Reserve Clause. The Grays reserved George Wright for the 1880 season, only to lose their shortstop-manager's services when he elected to retire so he could attend to his burgeoning sporting goods firm in Boston. Wright had hoped to return to the Red Caps in 1880 together with Jim O'Rourke, who was not one of the five members of its 1879 championship squad Providence chose to reserve. Missing Wright's leadership as much as his shortstopping, the Grays stumbled to a 26–20 record under, first, Mike McGeary and then pitcher Monte Ward. When Mike Dorgan assumed the reins in August, the Grays suddenly came alive, winning 26 of their last 38 games. But it was too little too late.

By August the Chicago White Stockings had long since taken command of the 1880 race. In Cap Anson's second season at the helm, the White Stockings revamped by garnering King Kelly, whom Cincinnati had neglected to reserve, to man right field; rookie shortstop Tom Burns; and two new pitchers, freshman Larry Corcoran and Fred Goldsmith, an 1879 yearling with Troy whom Chicago pilfered after a contract snafu. Burns led all League middle infielders with a .309 batting average, and between them, Corcoran and Goldsmith logged 64 victories while incurring just 17 losses. To support his new pitching tandem, Anson had his own heavy bat, which had produced a loop-high 74 RBI, plus batting titlist George Gore (.360) and left fielder Abner Dalrymple (.330). Beginning on June 2 at Boston, Chicago set a nineteenth-century League record by reeling off 21 straight wins, marred only by a 1–1 tie with Providence. During their skein the White Stockings won six games from Providence, six each from Troy and Worcester, and three from Boston, omitting only Buffalo and Cincinnati, the League's two weakest clubs in 1880, and third-place Cleveland, the loop's most surprising team. On July 10, Cleveland's rookie sensation Fred Dunlap ended Chicago's streak when he cracked a two-run homer in the bottom of the ninth to give teammate Jim McCormick a hard-earned 2–0 verdict.

TOUGH TWOSOME

LARRY CORCORAN, Pitcher.

Larry Corcoran. His 43 wins in 1880 are considered the all-time rookie record by many authorities.

In 1880 the Chicago White Stockings became the first major league team to own two 20-game winners when Fred Goldsmith bagged 21 wins and his rookie teammate Larry Corcoran 43. Goldsmith also set the all-time record for the fewest pitching appearances (24) by a 20-game winner, and until 1951 his .875 winning percentage in 1880 was the highest ever by a pitcher who achieved 20 or more victories. Corcoran meanwhile notched a no-hitter in 1880, the first of three during his brief career.

Corcoran and Goldsmith were both often in the lineup even on days when they didn't pitch. Each was a good fielder, and not only as a pitcher. Corcoran especially was talented enough to fill in just about anywhere, even at shortstop, and might have converted to another position when his arm started to fail had he been a better hitter.

Between 1880 and 1884, the Corcoran-Goldsmith combo gave Chicago 277 wins, by far the most of any pitching tandem during a comparable period before 1887 when the schedule in both major leagues was increased to 140 games. Both hurlers complained that Cap Anson was ruining their arms by overusing them, and though no one listened at the time—Corcoran was labeled a sniveling whiner for even raising the subject—the fact remains that the 277 wins for which they combined between 1880 and 1884 were all but 12 of their 289 aggregate total career wins.

McCormick beat the White Stockings four times in 1880 while no other team, let alone individual pitcher, registered more than three wins that year against Anson's powerhouse. Playing an 84-game schedule, Chicago romped home first by 15 full games and finished 42 and 44 games ahead of seventh-place Buffalo and last-place Cincinnati, respectively.

Cincinnati, nearly the equal of Chicago's 1879 team (43–37 to the White Stockings' 46–33), was the first casualty of the Reserve Clause. The Reds had hoped to keep Cal

GORE THE GREAT

Harry Stovey, the NL home-run leader as a Worcester rookie in 1880. Ten years later Stovey became the first man ever to compile 100 career circuit clouts in major league play. Worcester's other hard-hitting out-fielder in 1880, Buttercup Dickerson, was blacklisted after this exchange with manager Freeman Brown. Brown, upon hearing Dickerson had pledged to stop drinking: "When does the good work start?"
Dickerson: "As soon as they shut down the distilleries."

The primary goal in baseball is to score runs. In that respect there was no better performer in the pre-1893 era than George Gore. Of all the men who accumulated a minimum of 1,000 runs in one of the five major leagues in operation between 1871 and 1892, Gore ranks first in runs scored per 1,000 at bats. In 1880, though he led the National League in batting, Gore tallied just 70 runs in 77 games. It would be the last time until 1887 that he averaged less than a run a game. During the six intervening seasons Gore scored 659 runs in 579 games, culminating in 1886 when he crossed the plate 150 times in just 118 contests.

After two injury-marred seasons in the late 1880s, Gore rebounded to tally 132 runs in 120 games in 1889. He then enjoyed what was perhaps his finest season in 1890 with New York of the Players League. Though held by injuries to just 93 games, Gore accounted for 132 runs. He finished his career in 1892 as one of only three players—Billy Hamilton and Harry Stovey are the others—to participate in 1,000 or more major league games and to average better than one run in each.

BEST RUNS PER AT BATS CAREER RATIO 1871–92 (MINIMUM 1000 RUNS)

	At Bats	Runs	Per 1000 ABS
George Gore	5357	1327	.248
Harry Stovey	5937	1445	.243
King Kelly	5827	1348	.231
Dan Brouthers	5561	1272	.229
Arlie Latham	5264	1150	.218

McVey and Deacon White, but McVey stunned the Queen City club by quitting the game, and White sat out the first half of the season in a bitter holdout battle. Unable to compete either on the field or at the box office, Cincinnati flaunted two of League founder William Hulbert's strictest prohibitions in an attempt to keep afloat. It rented its Bank Street park to local semipro teams and permitted them to sell beer at their games and to play on Sundays.

At a special postseason meeting in Rochester on October 4, 1880, representatives of all eight League clubs but Cincinnati pledged to vote at the upcoming annual loop meeting for an amendment to the League Constitution "that will, under penalty of forfeiture of membership in the League, prohibit the sale of every description of malt, spiritous or vinous liquors upon its grounds, nor in any building owned or occupied by it." Two days later, when Cincinnati refused to bow to the new legislation regarding the sale of liquor, the other seven clubs voted unanimously to expel the Red Stockings from the League. On December 8, at the annual League meeting in New York, Detroit was accepted in Cincinnati's place, setting into motion a string of vengeful egos and clandestine events that would result, some ten months later, in the birth of the League's most formidable nineteenth-century challenger.

THE SEASONAL RECORD

	W	L	PCT	H	R	GB
1. Chicago White Stockings	67	17	.798	37–5	30–12	—
2. Providence Grays	52	32	.619	31–12	21–20	15
3. Cleveland Blues	47	37	.560	23–19	24–18	20
4. Troy Trojans	41	42	.494	20–21	21–21	25.5
5. Worcester Ruby Legs	40	43	.482	24–17	16–26	26.5
6. Boston Red Caps	40	44	.476	25–17	15–27	27
7. Buffalo Bisons	24	58	.293	13–29	11–29	42
8. Cincinnati Reds	21	59	.263	14–25	7–34	44

	Chi	Pro	Cle	Tro	Wor	Bos	Buf	Cin	
Chicago	—	9	8	10	10	9	11	10	67
Providence	3	—	9	7	6	7	10	10	52
Cleveland	4	3	—	9	6	7	9	9	47
Troy	2	5	3	—	5	5	11	10	41
Worcester	2	6	6	7	—	8	3	8	40
Boston	3	5	5	7	4	—	9	7	40
Buffalo	1	2	3	1	9	3	—	5	24
Cincinnati	2	2	3	1	3	5	5	—	21
	17	32	37	42	43	44	58	59	332

SEASON LEADERS

Batting Average (200 ABs)

1.	Gore, Chicago	.360
2.	Anson, Chicago	.337
3.	Connor, Troy	.332
4.	Dalrymple, Chicago	.330
5.	Burns, Chicago	.309

On–Base Percentage

1.	Gore, Chicago	.399
2.	Anson, Chicago	.362
3.	Connor, Troy	.357
4.	Dalrymple, Chicago	.355
5.	Cogswell, Troy	.336

Home Runs

1.	Stovey, Worcester	6
	Jim O'Rourke, Boston	6
3.	Jones, Boston	5
4.	Dunlap, Cleveland	4
5.	Hines, Providence	3
	Connor, Troy	3
	John O'Rourke, Boston	3
	Farrell, Providence	3

Hits

1.	Dalrymple, Chicago	126
2.	Anson, Chicago	120
3.	Gore, Chicago	116
4.	Hines, Providence	115
5.	Connor, Troy	113

Bases on Balls

1.	Ferguson, Troy	24
2.	Gore, Chicago	21
	Clapp, Cincinnati	21
	Jim O'Rourke, Boston	21
5.	Crowley, Buffalo	19

Slugging Average

1.	Gore, Chicago	.463
2.	Connor, Troy	.459
3.	Dalrymple, Chicago	.458
4.	Stovey, Troy	.454
5.	Jim O'Rourke, Boston	.441

Total Bases

1.	Dalrymple, Chicago	175
2.	Stovey, Worcester	161
3.	Jim O'Rourke, Boston	160
	Dunlap, Cleveland	160
5.	Connor, Troy	156

RBI

1.	Anson, Chicago	74
2.	Kelly, Chicago	60
3.	Gore, Chicago	47
	Connor, Troy	47
5.	Jim O'Rourke, Boston	45

Runs

1.	Dalrymple, Chicago	91
2.	Stovey, Worcester	76
3.	Kelly, Chicago	72
4.	Jim O'Rourke, Boston	71
5.	Gore, Chicago	70

Strikeouts

1.	Galvin, Buffalo	57
2.	Stovey, Worcester	46
3.	Bradley, Providence	38
4.	Wood, Worcester	37
	Morrill, Boston	37

PITCHING

Wins

1.	McCormick, Cleveland	45
2.	Corcoran, Chicago	43
3.	Ward, Providence	39
4.	Welch, Troy	34
5.	Richmond, Worcester	32

Innings

1.	McCormick, Cleveland	657.2
2.	Ward, Providence	595
3.	Richmond, Worcester	590.2
4.	Welch, Troy	574
5.	Corcoran, Chicago	536.1

Losses

1.	W. White, Cincinnati	42
2.	Galvin, Buffalo	35
3.	Richmond, Worcester	32
4.	Welch, Troy	30
5.	Bond, Boston	29

Complete Games

1.	McCormick, Cleveland	72
2.	Welch, Troy	64
3.	Ward, Providence	59
4.	W. White, Cincinnati	58
5.	Richmond, Worcester	50

Strikeouts

1.	Corcoran, Chicago	268
2.	McCormick, Cleveland	260
3.	Richmond, Worcester	243
4.	Ward, Providence	230
5.	W. White, Cincinnati	161

ERA (96 innings)

1.	Keefe, Troy	0.86
2.	Bradley, Providence	1.38
3.	Ward, Providence	1.74
4.	Goldsmith, Chicago	1.75
5.	McCormick, Cleveland	1.85

Winning Percentage (20 decisions)

1.	Goldsmith, Chicago	.875
2.	Corcoran, Chicago	.754
3.	Ward, Providence	.619
4.	McCormick, Cleveland	.616
5.	Bradley, Providence	.571

Lowest On–Base Percentage

1.	Bradley, Providence	.217
2.	Keefe, Troy	.222
3.	Ward, Providence	.232
4.	Corcoran, Chicago	.236
5.	Corey, Worcester	.239

FIELDING

Total Chances

1B	Start, Providence	993
2B	Burdock, Boston	653
3B	Connor, Troy	335
SS	Irwin, Worcester	485
OF	Gillespie, Troy	220
C	Gross, Providence	641
P	Bond, Boston	228

Fielding Average

Anson, Chicago	.977
Force, Buffalo	.939
Williamson, Chicago	.893
Peters, Providence	.900
York, Providence	.934
Flint, Chicago	.932
Ward, Providence	.983

CHICAGO   Cap Anson   Lake Front Park (I)

		G	AB	H	R	2B	3B	HR	RBI	BB	BA	SA
LF	Abner Dalrymple	86	**382**	**126**	**91**	25	12	0	36	3	.330	.458
1B	Cap Anson	86	356	120	54	24	1	1	**74**	14	.337	.419
RF	King Kelly	84	344	100	72	17	9	1	60	12	.291	.401
SS	Tom Burns	85	333	103	47	17	3	0	43	12	.309	.378
CF	George Gore	77	322	116	70	23	2	2	47	21	**.360**	**.463**
3B	Ned Williamson	75	311	78	65	20	2	0	31	15	.251	.328
2B	Joe Quest	82	300	71	37	12	1	0	27	8	.237	.283
P	Larry Corcoran	72	286	66	41	11	1	0	25	10	.231	.276
C	Silver Flint	74	284	46	30	10	4	0	17	5	.162	.225
P	Fred Goldsmith	35	142	37	24	4	2	0	15	2	.261	.317
Sub	Tommy Beals	13	46	7	4	0	0	0	3	1	.152	.152
Sub	Tom Poorman	7	25	5	3	1	2	0	0	0	.200	.400
P	Charlie Guth	1	4	1	0	0	0	0	0	1	.250	.250
		86	3135	**876**	**538**	164	39	4	**378**	104	**.279**	**.360**

1B	Anson 81, Gore 7, Goldsmith 4
2B	Quest 80, Williamson 3, Beals 3, Kelly 1, Anson 1
SS	Burns 79, Corcoran 8, Quest 2, Anson 1, Kelly 1
3B	Williamson 63, Kelly 14, Anson 9, Burns 9, Quest 1
OF	Dalrymple 86, Gore 74, Kelly 64, Flint 13, Beals 10, Goldsmith 10, Corcoran 8, Poorman 7
C	Flint 67, Kelly 17, Williamson 11, Burns 2
P	Corcoran 63, Goldsmith 26, Poorman 2, Kelly 1, Burns 1, Guth 1

	G	IP	GS	CG	W	L	K	BB	SH	SV	ERA
Larry Corcoran#	63	536.1	60	57	43	14	**268**	**99**	4	2	1.95
Fred Goldsmith	26	210.1	24	22	21	3	90	18	4	1	1.75
Tom Poorman	2	15	1	0	2	0	0	8	0	0	2.40
Charlie Guth	1	9	1	1	1	0	7	1	0	0	5.00
King Kelly	1	3	0	0	0	0	1	1	0	0	0.00
Tom Burns	1	1.1	0	0	0	0	1	2	0	0	0.00
		775	86	80	67	17	**367**	129	8	3	1.93

#No hit game 5–0 vs Worcester, September 20

PROVIDENCE   Mike McGeary (8–7)   Monte Ward (18–13)   Mike Dorgan (26–12)
Messer Street Grounds

		G	AB	H	R	2B	3B	HR	RBI	BB	BA	SA
CF	Paul Hines	85	374	115	64	20	2	3	35	13	.307	.396
SS	John Peters	86	359	82	30	5	0	0	24	5	.228	.242
P	Monte Ward	86	356	81	53	12	2	0	27	6	.228	.272
C	Emil Gross	87	347	90	43	18	3	1	34	16	.259	.337
1B	Joe Start	82	345	96	53	14	6	0	27	13	.278	.354
2B	Jack Farrell	80	339	92	46	12	5	3	36	10	.271	.363
RF	Mike Dorgan	79	321	79	45	10	1	0	31	10	.246	.283
3B	George Bradley	82	309	70	32	7	6	0	23	5	.227	.288
LF	Tom York	53	203	43	21	9	2	0	18	8	.212	.276
Sub	Sadie Houck	49	184	37	27	7	7	1	22	6	.201	.332
Sub	Mike McGeary	18	59	8	5	0	0	0	1	6	.136	.136
		87	3196	793	419	114	34	8	278	89	.248	.313

1B	Start 82, Hines 4, Bradley 2
2B	Farrell 80, Hines 6, McGeary 2
SS	Peters 86, McGeary 1
3B	Bradley 57, Ward 25, McGeary 17, Dorgan 2
OF	Dorgan 77, Hines 75, York 53, Houck 49, Bradley 7, Ward 2
C	Gross 87
P	Ward 70, Bradley 28, Dorgan 1

	G	IP	GS	CG	W	L	K	BB	SH	SV	ERA
Monte Ward #	70	595	67	59	39	24	230	45	**8**	1	1.74
George Bradley	28	196	20	16	13	8	54	6	4	1	1.38
Mike Dorgan	1	8	0	0	0	0	2	0	0	0	1.13
*One combined shutout on Sept. 23: Ward 4 innings, Bradley 5 innings											
		799	87	75	52	32	286	**51**	**13**	2	**1.64**

Perfect game 5–0 vs Buffalo, June 17

CLEVELAND   Jim McCormick   Kennard Street Park

		G	AB	H	R	2B	3B	HR	RBI	BB	BA	SA
2B	Fred Dunlap	85	373	103	61	**27**	9	4	30	7	.276	.429
RF	Orator Shaffer	83	338	90	62	14	9	0	21	17	.266	.361
1B	Bill Phillips	85	334	85	41	14	10	1	36	6	.254	.365
CF	Pete Hotaling	78	325	78	40	17	8	0	41	10	.240	.342
SS	Jack Glasscock	77	296	72	37	13	3	0	27	2	.243	.307
P	Jim McCormick	78	289	71	34	11	0	0	26	5	.246	.284
LF	Ned Hanlon	73	280	69	30	10	3	0	32	11	.246	.304
3B	Frank Hankinson	69	263	55	32	7	4	1	19	1	.209	.278
C	Doc Kennedy	66	250	50	26	10	1	0	18	5	.200	.248
Sub	Mike McGeary	31	111	28	14	2	1	0	6	4	.252	.288
C	Barney Gilligan	30	99	17	9	4	3	1	13	6	.172	.303

		G	AB	H	R	2B	3B	HR	RBI	BB	BA	SA
P	Gid Gardner	10	32	6	0	1	1	0	4	2	.188	.281
Sub	Al Hall	3	8	1	1	0	0	0	0	0	.125	.125
Sub	Harry Wheeler	1	4	1	0	0	0	0	0	0	.250	.250
		85	3002	726	387	130	**52**	7	273	76	.242	.327

1B Phillips 85
2B Dunlap 85
SS Glasscock 77, Hanlon 4, Gilligan 4
3B Hankinson 56, McGeary 29
OF Shaffer 83, Hotaling 78, Hanlon 69, Hankinson 12, McCormick 5, Gilligan 4, Hall 3, Kennedy 2, McGeary 2, Wheeler 1, Gardner 1
C Kennedy 65, Gilligan 23, Hotaling 2
P McCormick 74, Gardner 9, Hankinson 4

	G	IP	GS	CG	W	L	K	BB	SH	SV	ERA
Jim McCormick	**74**	**657.2**	**74**	**72**	**45**	28	260	75	7	0	1.85
Gid Gardner	9	77	9	9	1	8	21	20	0	0	2.57
Frank Hankinson	4	25	2	2	1	1	8	3	0	1	1.08
		759.2	85	**83**	47	37	289	98	7	1	1.90

TROY Bob Ferguson Haymakers' Grounds

		G	AB	H	R	2B	3B	HR	RBI	BB	BA	SA
CF	John Cassidy	83	352	89	40	14	8	0	29	12	.253	.338
LF	Pete Gillespie	82	346	84	50	20	5	2	24	17	.243	.347
3B	Roger Connor	83	340	113	53	18	8	3	47	13	.332	.459
SS	Ed Caskin	82	333	75	36	5	4	0	28	7	.225	.264
2B	Bob Ferguson	82	332	87	55	9	0	0	22	**24**	.262	.289
P	Mickey Welch	66	251	72	25	20	3	0	27	5	.287	.390
C	Bill Holbert	61	212	40	18	5	1	0	8	9	.189	.222
1B	Ed Cogswell	47	209	63	41	7	3	0	13	11	.301	.364
RF	Jake Evans	47	180	46	31	8	1	0	22	7	.256	.311
Sub	Bill Tobin	33	136	22	14	1	1	0	8	4	.162	.184
OF	Buttercup Dickerson	30	119	23	15	2	2	0	10	2	.193	.244
Sub	Buck Ewing	13	45	8	1	1	0	0	5	1	.178	.200
P	Tim Keefe	12	43	10	4	3	0	0	3	1	.233	.302
Sub	Bill Harbidge	9	27	10	3	0	1	0	2	0	.370	.444
P	Terry Larkin	6	20	3	1	1	0	0	1	3	.150	.200
Sub	Joe Straub	3	12	3	1	0	0	0	3	1	.250	.250
Sub	Dan Brouthers	3	12	2	0	0	0	0	1	1	.167	.167
P	Frank Mountain	2	9	2	1	0	0	0	0	0	.222	.222
Sub	Mike Lawlor	4	9	1	1	0	0	0	0	1	.111	.111
Sub	Fred Haley	2	7	0	0	0	0	0	0	1	.000	.000
Sub	Dick Higham	1	5	1	1	0	0	0	0	0	.200	.200
Sub	Charlie Ahearn	1	4	1	1	0	0	0	0	0	.250	.250
Sub	Fatty Briody	1	4	0	0	0	0	0	0	0	.000	.000
		83	3007	755	392	114	37	5	253	**120**	.251	.319

1B Cogswell 47, Tobin 33, Brouthers 3
2B Ferguson 82, Cassidy 1
SS Caskin 82, Dickerson 1, Larkin 1
3B Connor 83
OF Gillespie 82, Cassidy 82, Evans 47, Dickerson 30, Ewing 4, Holbert 3, Welch 2, Larkin 2, Higham 1, Harbidge 1
C Holbert 58, Ewing 10, Harbidge 9, Lawlor 4, Straub 3, Haley 2, Caskin 2, Higham 1, Briody 1, Ahearn 1
P Welch 65, Keefe 12, Larkin 5, Mountain 2, Evans 1

	G	IP	GS	CG	W	L	K	BB	SH	SV	ERA
Mickey Welch	65	574	64	64	34	30	123	80	4	0	2.54
Tim Keefe	12	105	12	12	6	6	43	17	0	0	**0.86**
Terry Larkin	5	38	5	3	0	5	5	10	0	0	8.76
Frank Mountain	2	17	2	2	1	1	2	6	0	0	5.29
Jake Evans	1	4	0	0	0	0	0	0	0	0	13.50
	738		83	81	41	42	173	113	4	0	2.74

WORCESTER   **Frank Bancroft**   **Worcester Driving Park Grounds**

		G	AB	H	R	2B	3B	HR	RBI	BB	BA	SA
CF	Harry Stovey	83	355	94	76	21	**14**	**6**	28	12	.265	.454
SS	Arthur Irwin	85	352	91	53	19	4	1	35	11	.259	.344
LF	George Wood	81	327	80	37	16	5	0	28	10	.245	.324
P	Lee Richmond	77	309	70	44	8	4	0	34	9	.227	.278
2B	George Creamer	85	306	61	40	6	3	0	27	4	.199	.239
3B	Art Whitney	76	302	67	38	13	5	1	36	9	.222	.308
RF	Lon Knight	49	201	48	31	11	3	0	21	5	.239	.323
C	Charlie Bennett	51	193	44	20	9	3	0	18	10	.228	.306
1B	Chubb Sullivan	43	166	43	22	6	3	0	0	4	.259	.331
C	Doc Bushong	41	146	25	13	3	0	0	19	1	.171	.192
P	Fred Corey	41	138	24	11	8	1	0	6	4	.174	.246
OF	Buttercup Dickerson	31	133	39	22	8	6	0	20	1	.293	.444
Sub	Jerry Dorgan	10	35	7	2	1	0	0	1	0	.200	.229
Sub	Joe Ellick	5	18	1	1	0	0	0	0	1	.056	.056
Sub	Bill Tobin	5	16	2	1	0	0	0	3	0	.125	.125
Sub	Steve Dignan	3	10	3	1	0	1	0	2	0	.300	.500
P	Tricky Nichols	2	7	0	0	0	0	0	0	0	.000	.000
Sub	Billy Geer	2	6	0	0	0	0	0	0	0	.000	.000
Sub	Bill McGunnigle	1	4	0	0	0	0	0	0	0	.000	.000
		85	3024	699	412	129	**52**	8	278	81	.231	.316

1B   Sullivan 43, Stovey 37, Tobin 5, Corey 1, Wood 1
2B   Creamer 85
SS   Irwin 82, Corey 3, Geer 1
3B   Whitney 76, Ellick 5, Irwin 3, Wood 2, Corey 1, Bushong 1
OF   Wood 80, Knight 49, Stovey 46, Dickerson 31, Corey 29, Richmond 20, Dorgan 9, Bennett 6, Dignan 3, Geer 1, Bushong 1, McGunnigle 1
C   Bennett 46, Bushong 40, Dorgan 1, Irwin 1
P   Richmond 74, Corey 25, Nichols 2, Stovey 2

	G	IP	GS	CG	W	L	K	BB	SH	SV	ERA
Lee Richmond#	**74**	590.2	66	57	32	32	243	74	5	**3**	2.15
Fred Corey	25	148.1	17	9	8	9	47	16	2	2	2.43
Tricky Nichols	2	17.2	2	2	0	2	4	4	0	0	4.08
Harry Stovey	2	6	0	0	0	0	3	3	0	0	4.50
		762.2	85	68	40	43	297	97	7	**5**	2.27

#Perfect game 1–0 vs Cleveland, June 12

BOSTON   **Harry Wright**   **South End Grounds (I)**

		G	AB	H	R	2B	3B	HR	RBI	BB	BA	SA
UT	Jim O'Rourke	86	363	100	71	20	11	6	45	21	.275	.441
2B	Jack Burdock	86	356	90	58	17	4	2	35	8	.253	.340
1B	John Morrill	86	342	81	51	16	8	2	44	11	.237	.348
RF	Curry Foley	80	332	97	44	13	2	2	31	8	.292	.361
CF	John O'Rourke	81	313	86	30	22	8	3	36	18	.275	.425
3B	Ezra Sutton	76	288	72	41	9	2	0	25	7	.250	.295
P	Tommy Bond	76	282	62	27	4	1	0	24	8	.220	.241
LF	Charley Jones	66	280	84	44	15	3	5	37	11	.300	.429
SS	John Richmond	32	129	32	12	3	1	0	9	2	.248	.287
C	Phil Powers	37	126	18	11	5	0	0	10	5	.143	.183
C	Sam Trott	39	125	26	14	4	1	0	9	3	.208	.256
Sub	Sadie Houck	12	47	7	2	0	0	0	2	0	.149	.149
Sub	John Bergh	11	40	8	2	3	0	0	0	2	.200	.275
Sub	Steve Dignan	8	34	11	4	1	0	0	4	0	.324	.353
Sub	Dan O'Leary	3	12	3	1	2	0	0	1	0	.250	.417
Sub	George Wright	1	4	1	2	0	0	0	0	0	.250	.250
Sub	Denny Sullivan	1	4	1	1	0	0	0	1	0	.250	.250
P	Jack Leary	1	3	0	1	0	0	0	0	1	.000	.000
		86	3080	779	416	134	41	20	314	105	.253	.343

1B   Morrill 46, Foley 25, Jm. O'Rourke 19, Bond 1
2B   Burdock 86
SS   Sutton 39, Richmond 31, Jm. O'Rourke 17, Wright 1
3B   Morrill 40, Sutton 37, Jm. O'Rourke 10, Bond 1
OF   Jn. O'Rourke 81, Jones 66, Jm. O'Rourke 37, Foley 35, Bond 26, Houck 12, Dignan 8, Trott 4, O'Leary 3, Powers 2, Richmond 1, Leary 1
C   Powers 37, Trott 36, Bergh 11, Jm. O'Rourke 9, Sullivan 1
P   Bond 63, Foley 36, Morrill 3, Leary 1

	G	IP	GS	CG	W	L	K	BB	SH	SV	ERA
Tommy Bond	63	493	57	49	26	29	118	45	3	0	2.67
Curry Foley	36	238	28	21	14	14	68	40	1	0	3.89
John Morrill	3	10.2	0	0	0	0	0	1	0	0	0.84
Jack Leary	1	3	1	0	0	1	1	0	0	0	15.00
		744.2	86	70	40	44	187	86	4	0	3.08

BUFFALO   **Sam Crane**   **Riverside Park**

		G	AB	H	R	2B	3B	HR	RBI	BB	BA	SA
CF	Bill Crowley	85	354	95	57	16	4	0	20	19	.268	.336
3B	Hardy Richardson	83	343	89	48	18	8	0	17	14	.259	.359
LF	Joe Hornung	85	342	91	47	8	11	1	42	8	.266	.363
C	Jack Rowe	79	326	82	43	10	6	1	36	6	.252	.328
2B	Davy Force	81	290	49	22	10	0	0	17	10	.169	.203
1B	Dude Esterbrook	64	253	61	20	12	1	0	35	0	.241	.296
P	Pud Galvin	66	241	51	25	9	2	0	12	5	.212	.266
Sub	Oscar Walker	34	126	29	12	4	2	1	15	6	.230	.317
RF	Dan Stearns	28	104	19	8	6	1	0	13	3	.183	.260
SS	Mike Moynahan	27	100	33	12	5	1	0	14	6	.330	.400
Sub	Arlie Latham	22	79	10	9	3	1	0	3	1	.127	.190
P	Stump Weidman	23	78	8	8	1	0	0	3	2	.103	.115
P	Tom Poorman	19	70	11	5	1	0	0	1	0	.157	.171
P	Denny Driscoll	18	65	10	1	1	0	0	4	1	.154	.169
Sub	Denny Mack	17	59	12	5	0	0	0	3	5	.203	.203
Sub	Chick Fulmer	11	44	7	3	0	0	0	1	2	.159	.159

		G	AB	H	R	2B	3B	HR	RBI	BB	BA	SA
Sub	Sam Crane	10	31	4	4	0	0	0	2	1	.129	.129
Sub	Bill McGunnigle	7	22	4	0	0	0	0	1	0	.182	.182
Sub	Hoss Radbourn	6	21	3	1	0	0	0	1	0	.143	.143
Sub	Jim Keenan	2	7	1	1	0	0	0	0	1	.143	.143
Sub	Tom Kearns	2	7	0	0	0	0	0	0	0	.000	.000
		85	2962	669	331	104	37	3	240	90	.226	.289

1B   Esterbrook 47, Walker 24, Hornung 18
2B   Force 53, Fulmer 11, Crane 10, Esterbrook 6, Hornung 5, Radbourn 3, Mack 1
SS   Force 30, Moynahan 27, Mack 16, Latham 12, Stearns 1, Esterbrook 1
3B   Richardson 81, Stearns 5, Rowe 3
OF   Crowley 74, Hornung 67, Rowe 25, Stearns 20, Galvin 19, Esterbrook 15, Driscoll 14, Weidman 13, Walker 11, Poorman 10, Latham 10, McGunnigle 3, Radbourn 3, Crane 1
C   Rowe 60, Crowley 22, Stearns 8, Richardson 5, Keenan 2, Kearns 2, Latham 1, Esterbrook 1
P   Galvin 58, Weidman 17, Poorman 11, Driscoll 6, McGunnigle 5, Hornung 1

	G	IP	GS	CG	W	L	K	BB	SH	SV	ERA
Pud Galvin#	58	458.2	54	46	20	35	128	32	5	0	2.71
Stump Weidman	17	113.2	13	9	0	9	25	9	0	0	3.40
Tom Poorman	11	85	9	9	1	8	13	19	0	1	4.13
Denny Driscoll	6	41.2	4	4	1	3	17	9	0	0	3.89
Bill McGunnigle	5	37	5	4	2	3	3	8	1	0	3.41
Joe Hornung	1	3	0	0	0	0	0	1	0	0	6.00
	739	85	72	24	58	186	78	6	1	3.09	

#No hit game 1–0 vs Worcester, August 20

CINCINNATI   John Clapp   Bank Street Grounds

		G	AB	H	R	2B	3B	HR	RBI	BB	BA	SA
2B	Pop Smith	83	334	69	35	10	9	0	27	6	.207	.290
CF	Blondie Purcell	77	325	95	48	13	6	1	24	5	.292	.378
C	John Clapp	80	323	91	33	16	4	1	20	21	.282	.365
3B	Hick Carpenter	77	300	72	32	6	4	0	23	2	.240	.287
1B	Long John Reilly	73	272	56	21	8	4	0	16	3	.206	.265
P	Will White	62	207	35	16	7	1	0	14	6	.169	.213
SS	Lew Say	48	191	38	14	8	1	0	15	4	.199	.251
RF	Jack Manning	48	190	41	20	6	3	2	17	7	.216	.311
LF	Mike Mansell	53	187	36	22	6	2	2	12	4	.193	.278
Sub	Deacon White	35	142	42	21	4	2	0	7	9	.298	.355
Sub	Andy Leonard	33	133	28	15	3	0	1	17	8	.211	.256
Sub	Charlie Reilley	30	103	21	8	1	0	0	9	0	.204	.214
Sub	Joe Sommer	24	88	16	10	1	0	0	6	0	.182	.193
Sub	Harry Wheeler	17	65	6	1	2	0	0	2	0	.092	.123
Sub	Sam Wright	9	34	3	0	0	0	0	0	0	.088	.088
Sub	Amos Booth	1	2	0	0	0	0	0	0	0	.000	.000
		83	2895	649	296	91	36	7	209	75	.224	.288

1B   Reilly 72, Carpenter 9, D. White 3, Manning 1
2B   Smith 83, D. White 1
SS   Say 48, Leonard 23, Wright 9, Sommer 1, Purcell 1, Carpenter 1
3B   Carpenter 67, Leonard 10, Reilley 4, Sommer 1, Booth 1
OF   Purcell 55, Mansell 53, Manning 47, D. White 33, Sommer 22, Wheeler 17, Reilley 16, Clapp 10, Reilly 3, W. White 3
C   Clapp 73, Reilley 13, Sommer 1
P   W. White 62, Purcell 25

	G	IP	GS	CG	W	L	K	BB	SH	SV	ERA
Will White	62	517.1	62	58	18	**42**	161	56	3	0	2.14
Blondie Purcell	25	196	21	21	3	17	47	32	0	0	3.20
		713.1	83	79	21	59	208	88	3	0	2.44

1881

THE YEAR THE NATIONAL LEAGUE ENJOYED ITS GREATEST PARITY

After ousting the Cincinnati franchise the previous fall for selling liquor in its park and conniving to play home games on Sunday. National League president William Hulbert must have felt the irony when he realized that May 1, the League's traditional opening date, would fall on a Sunday in 1881. To dodge the conflict, Chicago and Worcester advanced their home openers to Saturday, April 30, while Detroit and Providence staged their lidlifters two afternoons later on Monday.

The opening games viewed by fans in those four League cities were markedly different from any seen before. A batter in 1881 could now draw a walk after only seven unfair deliveries or balls rather than eight, but balancing that was a new rule removing the batter's luxury of receiving a "good ball" warning on the first third strike he failed to swing at before being called out on strikes. The substitution rule was also tightened, as was the rule regarding forfeits. These rule revisions would exert considerable impact on the game in the years ahead, but the most influential change moved the front line of the pitcher's box five feet farther from home plate. Increasing the pitching distance to fifty feet and reducing by one the number of balls needed for a walk combined to add fifteen points to the league batting average in 1881 and hike walk totals by 40 percent.

For all the changes, the Chicago White Stockings continued to rule the roost. The advent of the Reserve Clause and continuing financial success enabled Chicago to retain the entire starting nine from its 1880 championship team and add only one new face, rookie outfielder Hugh Nicol, for bench strength. With Larry Corcoran and Fred Goldsmith again operating as a tandem and collecting 55 wins between them, split almost evenly, Cap Anson's club started fast and was never headed. At the end of the season's first month Chicago had a 13–6 record and led second-place Worcester by just a game and a half. But in June the White Stockings went 12–4 to increase their lead to four and a half games over Buffalo, which had taken over the runner-up spot.

Silver Flint, the NL's leading catcher in 1881. His .310 BA followed on the heels of a .162 mark in 1880 that was more representative. Injuries and hard-living helped to saddle Flint with a .239 career BA and the record for the fewest walks (53) of any nonpitcher who played 10 or more seasons in the majors.

A woodcut portrait of the 1882 Bostons with Jim Whitney, who led all NL pitchers in both wins and losses in 1881. In 1882–83, Whitney and fellow pitcher Charlie Buffinton also platooned in center field. Here too is Sam Wise, the first documented major leaguer to strike out as many as 100 times in a season. Top: Joe Hornung, Ezra Sutton, Sam Wise, Jack Burdock. Bottom: Charlie Buffinton, Paul Radford, Jim Whitney, John Morrill, Mike Hines, Mert Hackitt, Pop Smith.

Though Chicago eventually won easily, triumphing by nine games, the other seven league teams were so tightly bunched that only 14 games separated second-place Providence and cellar-dwelling Worcester. The surprise teams in this, the season the league enjoyed its greatest parity during the last century, were the new Detroit entry, which claimed a first-division spot by finishing fourth (a remarkable achievement for a novice franchise), and the Buffalo Bisons. After a dismal seventh-place finish in 1880, Buffalo snared Deacon White from the defunct Cincinnati club and Jim O'Rourke when Boston left him off its reserve list. The pair joined with Dan Brouthers, an earlier flop with Troy, and emerging star Hardy Richardson to vault the Bisons upward to third place with an 82 percent improvement in winning percentage, from .298 to .542.

Abysmal offensive output from its two middle infielders, Davy Force (.180) and John Peters (.214), prevented Buffalo from advancing even higher in the standings. Providence was similarly hampered when its new shortstop, Bill McClellan, hit just .166, but no team was hurt more by a weak attack than Troy. The previous year the Trojans had snuck into the first division after unearthing four rookies—Mickey Welch, Tim Keefe, Roger Connor and Buck Ewing—who were destined to make the Hall of Fame. But although the quartet of future greats continued to blossom in 1881, Troy slipped a notch to fifth place despite setting a new team fielding average record of .917. A lackluster outfield and Frank Hankinson's .193 bat at third base were the Trojans' undoing. Nevertheless, Troy got home half a length ahead of Boston, saddling Harry Wright with his second straight sixth-place finish.

RICHMOND AGAIN

In 1881, Lee Richmond of Worcester became the first pitcher in major league history to win 20 or more games for a last-place team. The National League's unprecedented parity that year was much of the reason. Worcester won 32 games, the most by far of any cellar-dweller to that point. A list of 20-game winners in the nineteenth century with last-place teams:

	Team	League	Year	Record
Lee Richmond	Worcester	NL	1881	25–26
Hardie Henderson	Baltimore	AA	1885	25–35
Matt Kilroy	Baltimore	AA	1886	29–34
Mark Baldwin	Pittsburgh	NL	1891	22–28
Sadie McMahon	Baltimore	LA	1892	20–25*

*Disputed: Early encyclopedias credited McMahon with 20 wins; both *Total Baseball* and Macmillan now give him only 19 in 1892.

Boston's continued downward spiral drove Wright to leave the Hub team at the conclusion of the 1881 season after 11 years at its helm. But if things in Beantown seemed chaotic, the other seven League cities could not have been more stable. When all eight League clubs announced they would return in 1882, it marked the first time that Hulbert's loop would field the same crew of teams two years in a row.

But while Hulbert felt only satisfaction with himself, his team and his federation in the waning days of 1881, it could not last. By the spring of 1882, the National League's founder lay dying of heart failure, and his brainchild faced the first serious challenge to its self-proclaimed monopoly on major league status.

THE RIGHT GEORGE

Baseball record books continue to consider George Bradley the record holder for the most shutouts by a rookie with 16 in 1876. Since Bradley won 33 games the previous year for St. Louis in the National Association, it makes about as much sense to call him the rookie record holder for shutouts as it does to assign the rookie record for wins to Al Spalding because he landed 47 victories in the National League's inaugural season. Granted, Spalding had five NA seasons under his belt to Bradley's one, but either the NA is deemed a major league or it isn't. If it is, whether Bradley pitched in it for one year or five he was simply not a rookie in 1876. If it is not, Spalding then was also a rookie, which wipes out his first 157 wins and five seasons of professional work but makes him the holder of virtually every significant all-time rookie pitching record that doesn't belong to Bradley.

The problem stems from major league baseball's refusal to call the National Association a major league. This stubborn stance creates all sorts of foolishness, like having to think that 33-year-old Joe Start, who had about 15 years of top-level ball under his belt, was a rookie in 1876 and that Harry Wright, after winning four NA flags plus a national championship, was nevertheless still a yearling manager. The argument stops here. *The Great Encyclopedia of Nineteenth-Century Major League Baseball* says the right George—George Derby—is the all-time record holder for the most shutouts by a rookie. In 1881 Detroit's pitching staff led the National League with 10 shutouts. Nine of them belonged to Derby, who also set a new frosh strikeout mark that year with 212. His strikeout record fell three years later, but no other rookie hurler has ever compiled more than eight shutouts. Derby is our man.

THE TRAIL EAST FROM CALIFORNIA

Northern California by the early 1880s had become a rich source of young baseball talent. The main problem major league teams, or for that matter, minor league teams, had was convincing these talented players to come East. Major league baseball at that time was still basically an "Eastern" concept. Players in California didn't automatically jump when someone said he was from Chicago or Boston, let alone Providence or Buffalo. True, they knew who the White Stockings were, but they were skeptical that those Chicagoans were really any better than they, or that the Easterners played against competition that was substantially better than what they faced themselves. Moreover, many young California players were reluctant to leave their home areas for the alien East. It was a long trek from the Pacific Coast, travel by train could be harrowing, and not all cared to brave the unknown and leave behind a baseball arena where they were accepted and even revered.

Some help came from early major leaguers who later lived or worked in California, most notably Cal McVey and Len Stockwell, a Cleveland substitute in 1879. McVey and Stockwell could bear witness to what the Eastern game and the Eastern cities were like. No doubt they—and McVey in particular—helped convince Andy Piercy, a native of the San Jose area, to give it a try. Piercy played briefly with Chicago in 1881 and so became the first California-born player to make the majors. But the first California-groomed player to make a significant impact on the Eastern game was Jerry Denny, who joined Providence in 1881. Denny was a rough sort who had grown up in an orphanage after losing both his parents soon after moving from New York to the San Francisco Bay Area. He was a crack third baseman, though, and was probably recruited by Monte Ward, then Providence's pitching ace, who came out to San Francisco in the winter of 1880 to play ball. In those days, players themselves often acted as scouts for their teams. In any event, when Harry Wright became Providence's manager in 1882 he relied heavily on Ward's judgment—which had certainly been right the previous year about Denny—and took on catcher Sandy Nava, sometimes thought to be the first San Franciscan to reach the majors. Soon afterward Wright hired another San Franciscan, Charlie Sweeney. Nava couldn't hit a lick and was never more than a backup catcher, but Sweeney proved to be an outstanding pitcher—at least for a time. The two of them, together with Denny, constituted Providence's California contingent for the moment and made the Grays the first major league team to have a definite "Pacific" flavor.

However, Wright moved to Philadelphia in 1884 to take on a fresh challenge: trying to rescue the newly created Phillies, which had been a disaster in their inaugural major league season. One of Wright's first ventures was to tap the California lode for new talent. Since he no longer had Ward to rely on, he turned to Bob Blakiston, who had joined the American Association Philadelphia Athletics in 1882.

It's unclear what Blakiston's link was to Wright, beyond the fact that he had longstanding ties to the Philadelphia baseball scene. Blakiston was also born in San Francisco, and his real name was Blackstone, making him a descendent of the famous magician. He actually debuted in the majors with the Association Athletics on May 2, 1882, three days before Nava played his first game with Providence—a fact that is at odds with the claim that Nava was the first San Franciscan to play major league ball, although it leaves intact, for the moment, the possibility that the latter was the first to play in the National League.

With Blakiston's help, Wright bagged San Franciscan Jim Fogarty, soon to become perhaps the best defensive outfielder in the National League in the 1880s; Mike DePanger, a young catcher; and—potentially the biggest prize of all—John Patrick Cahill, known as Patsy. Then only 19, Cahill was a San Francisco–born short, stocky type with a quick bat and a rare ability to play every diamond position. He had spent the winter of 1883–84 in Texas, playing for the K.O.M. team against the Galveston Gulf Citys, which boasted such players as Len Stockwell, Charlie Ingraham, who had played a bit with Baltimore in 1883, and George Crawford, also a Californian, who was regarded at the time as the "best all-around player in Texas." Though Crawford seems to have disappeared (there was a George Crawford who played a couple of games with the Philadelphia Athletics at the tag end of their embarrassingly dreadful 1890 season, but it probably wasn't the same man), Harry Wright got wind of Cahill and Ingraham and brought them to the Phillies' training camp in the spring of 1884 to join Fogarty and DePanger. Like Wright's previous team, Providence, the Phillies now had a strong San Francisco Bay Area flavor.

Those were the two main Northern California–National League arteries in the early 1880s, but there were two others that led to rival major leagues. One involved Henry Moore, the Union Association star who holds virtually every important batting record by a one-year major leaguer and about whom not a single firm biographical fact is known—but we'll leave Moore and his bizarre Washington Unions for the moment to talk about the Columbus Buckeyes, one of the most illuminating nineteenth-century team studies. The Buckeyes were formed from scratch in 1883, the American Association's second season. Unlike almost every other major league team started from scratch, however, they didn't finish last, but sixth—ahead of Pittsburgh and Baltimore, two veteran American Association teams—in their first year.

Hoping to improve even on that remarkable start, for the 1884 season the Buckeyes dumped Hustling Horace Phillips, one of their prime organizers, and brought in Gus Schmelz, a popular local promoter, to manage the club. Even more important, Columbus garnered a new battery composed of hard-hitting catcher Fred Carroll and Ed Morris, arguably the best lefthanded pitcher in the last century. Carroll was from Sacramento and had first played professionally, with Morris, the previous year, for the Reading Active in the Inter-State League. The two of them had come east together in the spring of 1883 to join the Reading club after playing as sandlotters in the San Francisco Bay Area, and at the close of the season had returned to San Francisco to do battle in a strangely designed three-team winter league. The league included Denny's Combination, which had as its centerpiece Jerry Denny and which also numbered Charlie Sweeney, Mike DePanger, Andy Piercy and another soon-to-be major leaguer named Marty Creegan; the Haverlys, which featured Jim Fogarty and future major leaguers Pete Meegan, Jim McDonald and most especially Charlie

Geggus; and the Occidentals, which boasted a battery of Carroll and Morris and also numbered Bob Blakiston and the man who most historians of the California game now believe was the first native-born San Franciscan to play in the majors—first baseman John Smith.

Smith had been with Troy and Worcester in 1882; he debuted in the majors exactly one day before Blakiston and four days before Sandy Nava. Ever after that 1882 season, Smith had offers from big league teams to return east. Sometimes he went so far as to sign a contract for the coming season, as he did with Louisville in 1886, but at the last moment he would always recant and stay on the west coast. In 1884, Smith declined to accompany Morris and Carroll back to Columbus after the winter league season ended. The culmination was a pair of games, played on February 21 and 22, 1884, between two all-star teams, one representing the California League and the other, major leaguers who'd wintered in the Bay Area. On February 21 the big leaguers won 10–2; the following day they pummeled the locals 22–1 behind Charlie Sweeney's pitching and two long home runs by Ed Morris. The two contests probably went a long way toward convincing young local players that the major leagues were the place to be if they really wanted to test themselves against the best. But Morris and Carroll still couldn't entice John Smith to go with them. They did, however, link up with Patsy Cahill, who was back in California by this time and played with their team as a prospective member now of the Phillies.

Somehow Cahill didn't make it with the Phillies in the spring of 1884—again, it's unclear why. It is known, though, that that spring the Columbus Buckeyes released Harry Wheeler, their 1883 left fielder, and began the 1884 season without a bonafide replacement. This forced Schmelz to use his change pitcher—whether it be Morris or Frank Mountain or a third boxman, Dummy Dundon—out in left. Morris was the best fielder of the three—he'd played a lot of center field the previous year for the Reading team—and Mountain was the most dangerous hitter. Dundon was the oddest. The first graduate of the Ohio School for the Deaf to play in the majors, preceding Dummy Hoy by some five years, Dundon was the only home-grown member of an ambitious Columbus team that by mid-May was beginning to look like a surprise contender for the American Association pennant despite lacking a worthy left fielder.

So convinced was Schmelz that his team had a real chance that he listened when Morris and Fred Carroll told him they knew someone, a fine all-around player the Phillies had left at liberty, who they thought would be perfect. On their recommendation Schmelz signed Patsy Cahill. Cahill arrived in Baltimore on May 31 and debuted with the Buckeyes that very day—making Columbus the first team in major league history with three Northern Californian products serving as regulars.

But Cahill had arrived at a juncture when Schmelz needed a pitcher even more than a left fielder because Mountain had just hurt his knee and Morris was exhausted by a hard stretch of games on the Memorial Day weekend. So Schmelz put Cahill in the box for his big league debut, and the newest Buckeye went two-for-five and staggered through nine innings to beat Orioles ace Hardie Henderson, 15–12. Cahill didn't start another game in the majors until 1887, but in the meantime he

The 1884 Columbus Buckeyes, the first team with three starters—Ed Morris, Fred Carroll and Patsy Cahill—from California. Top: Cahill, Ed Dundon, Carroll, Rudy Kemmler, Jim Fields and Willie Kuehne. Middle: Fred Mann, Tom Brown, manager Gus Schmelz, Pop Smith and John Richmond. Morris sits front right beside Frank Mountain, the team's other pitching stalwart.

gave the Buckeyes a solid third outfielder and helped lift them into pennant contention. Columbus hung tough against the eventual champion New York Mets until late August when Cahill broke his ankle sliding in a game against Cincinnati. Without Cahill, who was shelved for the season, the Buckeyes eventually had to settle for second place, but they will always have the distinction of being the first team to have three Bay Area performers in feature roles.

Next and last, the fourth artery from the Bay Area to the majors in the mid-1880s—the Washington Unions. Though around for only one year, the Unions are worth a chapter in their own right. For one, prior to 1915 they held the major league record for using the most players in a season. The foremost Washington Unions performer was certainly Henry Moore, who, interestingly enough, had played with Morris and Fred Carroll for none other than the Reading Active in 1883 (until mid-August, that is, when he was suspended for not running out a ground ball). Moore was a piece of work—an independent spirit, always in hot water with every manager he played under—making it all the more remarkable that he has so completely eluded all efforts to track down what eventually became of him.

At any event, upon discovering that Moore played with Morris and Carroll in 1883, one might expect that he too went out to San Francisco to play in the winter of 1883–84 and was then instrumental in bringing several members of that asymmetrical three-team winter league to Washington with him. But this doesn't seem to be the case. There is no evidence that Moore was in San Francisco in the winter of 1883–84.

So it looks as though the Haverlys' battery of Charlie Geggus and Jim McDonald, plus Marty Creegan of Denny's Combination, wound up in Washington some other way. Probably it's useful to know that Geggus too was with the Reading Active, replacing Morris in 1884 as the team's ace pitcher. (This Active team almost undoubtedly will prove to be particularly fertile for anyone interested in looking more closely into what drew so many young California players to come east in the early 1880s.) Geggus stayed with the Active until early August, when Washington owner-manager Mike Scanlon bought him for the last two months of the Union Association season. In that short stretch Geggus won 10 games, averaged nearly eight strikeouts a start and played a good outfield on the days when he wasn't pitching, but thereafter he never again appeared in the majors. It's another mystery. There is no question that Geggus was good; he'd more than held his own in winter league duels against both Sweeney and Morris. Jim McDonald, Geggus's Haverlys batterymate who joined him on the Washingtons for a brief spell, did play again for a couple of weeks the following year, with Buffalo in the National League, but then returned to the Bay Area, as did Geggus. Eventually Moore joined them there and played several seasons in the California League.

All this makes the Washington contingent the only one of the four arteries that never really came to fruition in the majors. In contrast, the Providence, Philadelphia and Columbus arteries all involved players who were important contributors for many years, and who helped draw more and more young Northern Californians to the East. By the end of the 1880s there was a steady flow from the Pacific Coast of players such as George Van Haltren, Phil Knell and Willard Brown, followed by Bill Lange, Joe Corbett, Mike Donlin and many more like them. It would become a torrent of talent soon after the century turned.

THE SEASONAL RECORD

	W	L	PCT	H	R	GB
1. Chicago White Stockings	56	28	.667	32–10	24–18	—
2. Providence Grays	47	37	.560	23–20	24–17	9
3. Buffalo Bisons	45	38	.542	25–16	20–22	10.5
4. Detroit Wolverines	41	43	.488	23–19	18–24	15
5. Troy Trojans	39	45	.464	24–18	15–27	17
6. Boston Red Caps	38	45	.458	19–22	19–23	17.5
7. Cleveland Blues	36	48	.429	20–22	16–26	20
8. Worcester Ruby Legs	32	50	.390	19–22	13–28	23

	Chi	Pro	Buf	Det	Tro	Bos	Cle	Wor	
Chicago	—	9	7	7	8	10	6	9	56
Providence	3	—	5	8	6	7	9	9	47
Buffalo	5	7	—	9	3	8	7	6	45
Detroit	5	4	3	—	7	8	7	7	41
Troy	4	6	9	5	—	5	6	4	39
Boston	2	5	4	4	7	—	8	8	38
Cleveland	6	3	5	5	6	4	—	7	36
Worcester	3	3	5	5	8	3	5	—	32
	28	37	38	43	45	45	48	50	334

SEASON LEADERS

Batting Average (200 ABs)

1.	Anson, Chicago	.399
2.	Powell, Detroit	.338
3.	Rowe, Buffalo	.333
4.	Start, Providence	.328
5.	Dunlap, Cleveland	.325

Slugging Average

1.	Brouthers, Buffalo	.541
2.	Anson, Chicago	.510
3.	Rowe, Buffalo	.480
4.	Bennett, Detroit	.478
5.	Dunlap, Cleveland	.444

On–Base Percentage

1.	Anson, Chicago	.442
2.	Powell, Detroit	.380
3.	York, Providence	.362
4.	Brouthers, Buffalo	.361
5.	Dunlap, Cleveland	.358

Home Runs

1.	Brouthers, Buffalo	8
2.	Bennett, Detroit	7
3.	Farrell, Providence	5
4.	Burns, Chicago	4
5.	L. Brown, Detroit	3
	Dunlap, Cleveland	3

Hits

1.	Anson, Chicago	137
2.	Dalrymple, Chicago	117
3.	Dickerson, Worcester	116
4.	Dunlap, Cleveland	114
	Kelly, Chicago	114
	Start, Providence	114

Bases on Balls

1.	Clapp, Cleveland	31
2.	York, Providence	29
	Ferguson, Troy	29
	Farrell, Providence	29
5.	Gore, Chicago	27
	O'Rourke, Buffalo	27

Total Bases

1.	Anson, Chicago	175
2.	Dunlap, Cleveland	156
3.	Kelly, Chicago	153
4.	Dalrymple, Chicago	150
5.	Dickerson, Worcester	149

RBI

1.	Anson, Chicago	82
2.	Bennett, Detroit	64
3.	Kelly, Chicago	55
4.	Richardson, Buffalo	53
	D. White, Buffalo	53
	Ward, Providence	53

Runs

1.	Gore, Chicago	86
2.	Kelly, Chicago	84
3.	Dalrymple, Chicago	72
4.	Jim O'Rourke, Buffalo	71
5.	Farrell, Providence	69

Strikeouts

1.	Galvin, Buffalo	70
2.	Denny, Providence	44
3.	Hankinson, Troy	41
4.	Flint, Chicago	39
5.	Bennett, Detroit	37

PITCHING

Wins

1.	Whitney, Boston	31
	Corcoran, Chicago	31
3.	Derby, Detroit	29
4.	Galvin, Buffalo	28
5.	McCormick, Cleveland	26

Innings

1.	Whitney, Boston	552.1
2.	McCormick, Cleveland	526
3.	Derby, Detroit	494.2
4.	Galvin, Buffalo	474
5.	Richmond, Worcester	462.1

Strikeouts

1.	Derby, Detroit	212
2.	McCormick, Cleveland	178
3.	Whitney, Boston	162
4.	Richmond, Worcester	156
5.	Corcoran, Chicago	150

Losses

1	Whitney, Boston	33
2.	McCormick, Cleveland	30
3.	Keefe, Troy	27
4.	Richmond, Worcester	26
	Derby, Detroit	26

Complete Games

1.	Whitney, Boston	57
	McCormick, Cleveland	57
3.	Derby, Detroit	55
4.	Richmond, Worcester	50
5.	Galvin, Buffalo	48

Winning Percentage (20 decisions)

1.	Radbourn, Providence	.694
2.	Corcoran, Chicago	.689
3.	Goldsmith, Chicago	.649
4.	Welch, Troy	.538
	Galvin, Buffalo	.538

ERA (84 innings)

1.	Weidman, Detroit	1.80
2.	Ward, Providence	2.13
3.	Derby, Detroit	2.20
4.	Corcoran, Chicago	2.31
5.	Galvin, Buffalo	2.37

Lowest On–Base Percentage

1.	Weidman, Detroit	.258
2.	McCormick, Cleveland	.265
3.	Radbourn, Providence	.270
4.	Goldsmith, Chicago	.271
	Ward, Providence	.271

FIELDING

Total Chances

1B	Anson, Chicago	959
2B	Ferguson, Troy	572
3B	Denny, Providence	387
SS	Glasscock, Cleveland	416
OF	Richardson, Buffalo	245
C	Bushong, Worcester	536
P	Galvin, Buffalo	178

Fielding Average

Anson, Chicago	.975
Force, Buffalo	.937
Williamson, Chicago	.909
Glasscock, Cleveland	.911
Hornung, Boston	.948
Bennett, Detroit	.962
Richmond, Worcester	.937

CHICAGO **Cap Anson** **Lake Front Park (I)**

		G	AB	H	R	2B	3B	HR	RBI	BB	BA	SA
LF	Abner Dalrymple	82	362	117	72	22	4	1	37	15	.323	.414
RF	King Kelly	82	353	114	84	**27**	3	2	55	16	.323	.433
1B	Cap Anson	84	343	**137**	67	21	7	1	**82**	26	**.399**	.510
3B	Ned Williamson	82	343	92	56	12	6	1	48	19	.268	.347
SS	Tom Burns	84	342	95	41	20	3	4	42	14	.278	.389
CF	George Gore	73	309	92	**86**	18	9	1	44	27	.298	.424
C	Silver Flint	80	306	95	46	18	0	1	34	6	.310	.379
2B	Joe Quest	77	293	72	35	6	0	1	26	2	.246	.276
P	Larry Corcoran	47	189	42	25	8	0	0	9	5	.222	.265
P	Fred Goldsmith	39	158	38	24	3	4	0	16	6	.241	.310
OF	Hugh Nicol	26	106	22	13	2	0	0	7	4	.204	.222
Sub	Andy Piercy	1	8	2	1	0	0	0	0	0	.250	.250
		84	3114	**918**	**550**	**157**	36	12	**400**	140	**.295**	**.380**

1B	Anson 84, Flint 1, Gore 1
2B	Quest 77, Williamson 4, Burns 3, Piercy 1
SS	Burns 80, Corcoran 2, Williamson 2, Nicol 1, Anson 1, Quest 1
3B	Williamson 76, Kelly 8, Burns 3, Piercy 1, Gore 1
OF	Dalrymple 82, Kelly 72, Gore 72, Nicol 26, Flint 8, Goldsmith 3, Corcoran 1
C	Flint 80, Kelly 11, Anson 2, Williamson 1
P	Corcoran 45, Goldsmith 39, Williamson 3

	G	IP	GS	CG	W	L	K	BB	SH	SV	ERA
Larry Corcoran	45	396.2	44	43	**31**	14	150	78	4	0	2.31
Fred Goldsmith	39	330	39	37	24	13	76	44	5	0	2.59
Ned Williamson	3	18	1	1	1	1	2	0	0	0	2.00
		744.2	84	81	56	28	228	122	9	0	2.43

PROVIDENCE   Jack Farrell (24–27)   Tom York (23–10)   **Messer Street Grounds**

		G	AB	H	R	2B	3B	HR	RBI	BB	BA	SA
CF	Paul Hines	80	361	103	65	**27**	5	2	31	13	.285	.404
RF	Monte Ward	82	357	87	56	18	6	0	53	5	.244	.328
1B	Joe Start	79	348	114	56	12	6	0	29	9	.328	.397
2B	Jack Farrell	84	345	82	69	16	5	5	36	29	.238	.357
3B	Jerry Denny	85	320	77	38	16	2	1	24	5	.241	.313
LF	Tom York	85	316	96	57	23	5	2	47	29	.304	.427
P	Hoss Radbourn	72	270	59	27	9	0	0	28	10	.219	.252
SS	Bill McClellan	68	259	43	30	3	1	0	16	15	.166	.185
C	Barney Gilligan	46	183	40	19	7	2	0	20	9	.219	.279
C	Emil Gross	51	182	50	15	9	4	1	24	13	.275	.385
Sub	Lew Brown	18	75	18	9	3	1	0	10	4	.240	.307
P	Bobby Mathews	16	57	11	6	1	0	0	4	5	.193	.211
Sub	Henry Myers	1	4	0	0	0	0	0	0	0	.000	.000
		85	3077	780	447	144	37	11	322	**146**	.253	.335

1B   Start 79, Brown 5, Hines 1
2B   Farrell 82, Hines 4, McClellan 1
SS   McClellan 50, Ward 13, Radbourn 13, Gilligan 10, Myers 1
3B   Denny 85
OF   York 85, Hines 78, Ward 40, Radbourn 25, McClellan 17, Brown 13, Mathews 5, Farrell 3, Gross 1, Gilligan 1
C   Gross 50, Gilligan 36,
P   Radbourn 41, Ward 39, Mathews 14

	G	IP	GS	CG	W	L	K	BB	SH	SV	ERA
Monte Ward	39	330	35	32	18	18	119	53	3	0	2.13
Hoss Radbourn	41	325.1	36	34	25	11	117	64	3	0	2.43
Bobby Mathews	14	102.1	14	10	4	8	28	21	1	**0***	3.17
		757.2	85	76	47	37	264	138	7	0	**2.40**

BUFFALO   Jim O'Rourke   **Riverside Park**

		G	AB	H	R	2B	3B	HR	RBI	BB	BA	SA
RF	Curry Foley	83	**375**	96	58	20	2	1	25	7	.256	.328
3B	Jim O'Rourke	83	348	105	71	21	7	0	30	27	.302	.402
CF	Hardy Richardson	83	344	100	62	18	9	2	53	12	.291	.413
LF	Deacon White	78	319	99	58	24	4	0	53	9	.310	.411
2B	Davy Force	75	278	50	21	9	1	0	15	11	.180	.219
1B	Dan Brouthers	65	270	86	60	18	9	**8**	45	18	.319	**.541**
C	Jack Rowe	64	246	82	30	11	**11**	1	43	1	.333	.480
P	Pud Galvin	62	236	50	19	12	4	0	21	3	.212	.297
SS	John Peters	54	229	49	21	8	1	0	25	3	.214	.258
C	Sleeper Sullivan	35	121	23	13	4	0	0	15	1	.190	.223
Sub	Blondie Purcell	34	113	33	15	7	2	0	17	8	.292	.389
P	Jack Lynch	23	78	13	6	3	0	0	3	4	.167	.205
Sub	John Morrissey	12	47	10	3	2	0	0	3	0	.213	.255
Sub	Pop Smith	3	11	0	3	0	0	0	1	3	.000	.000
Sub	Ed Swartwood	1	3	1	0	0	0	0	0	1	.333	.333
Sub	Jack Manning	1	1	0	0	0	0	0	0	0	.000	.000
		83	3019	797	440	**157**	50	12	349	108	.264	.361

1B   Brouthers 30, Foley 27, White 26, O'Rourke 1
2B   Force 51, White 25, Richardson 5, Smith 3
SS   Peters 53, Force 21, Rowe 7, O'Rourke 3, Galvin 1, Richardson 1
3B   O'Rourke 56, Morrissey 12, Rowe 7, White 7, Force 1, Richardson 1

OF   Richardson 79, Foley 55, Brouthers 35, Purcell 25, O'Rourke 18, White 17, Galvin 14, Lynch 6, Rowe 5, Sullivan 5, Force 3, Swartwood 1, Manning 1, Peters 1
C   Rowe 46, Sullivan 31, O'Rourke 8, White 4
P   Galvin 56, Lynch 20, Foley 10, Purcell 9

	G	IP	GS	CG	W	L	K	BB	SH	SV	ERA
Pud Galvin	56	474	53	48	28	24	136	46	5	0	2.37
Jack Lynch	20	165.2	19	17	10	9	32	29	0	0	3.59
Blondie Purcell	9	61.2	5	5	4	1	15	9	0	0	2.77
Curry Foley	10	41	6	2	3	4	2	5	0	0	5.27
		742.1	83	72	45	38	185	**89**	5	0	2.84

DETROIT   Frank Bancroft   Recreation Park

		G	AB	H	R	2B	3B	HR	RBI	BB	BA	SA
RF	Lon Knight	83	340	92	67	16	3	1	52	23	.271	.344
LF	George Wood	80	337	100	54	18	9	2	32	19	.297	.421
SS	Sadie Houck	75	308	86	43	16	6	1	36	6	.279	.380
CF	Ned Hanlon	76	305	85	63	14	8	2	28	22	.279	.397
C	Charlie Bennett	76	299	90	44	18	7	7	64	18	.301	.478
2B	Joe Gerhardt	79	297	72	35	13	6	0	36	7	.242	.327
P	George Derby	59	236	44	17	3	1	0	12	4	.186	.208
1B	Martin Powell	55	219	74	47	9	4	1	38	15	.338	.429
3B	Art Whitney	58	214	39	23	7	5	0	9	7	.182	.262
Sub	Lew Brown	27	108	26	16	3	1	3	14	3	.241	.370
Sub	Charlie Reilley	19	70	12	8	2	0	0	3	0	.171	.200
P	Stump Weidman	13	47	12	8	1	0	0	5	2	.255	.277
Sub	Dasher Troy	11	44	15	2	3	0	0	4	3	.341	.409
Sub	Mike Dorgan	8	34	8	5	1	0	0	5	1	.235	.265
Sub	Sam Trott	6	25	5	3	2	1	0	2	1	.200	.360
P	Frank Mountain	7	25	4	0	1	1	0	4	2	.160	.280
P	Tony Mullane	5	19	5	0	0	0	0	1	0	.263	.263
Sub	Will Foley	5	15	2	0	0	0	0	1	2	.133	.133
P	Jack Leary	3	11	3	2	1	1	0	4	1	.273	.545
Sub	Dan Stearns	3	11	1	1	1	0	0	0	0	.091	.182
Sub	Dan O'Leary	2	8	0	0	0	0	0	0	0	.000	.000
P	Will White	2	7	0	0	0	0	0	0	0	.000	.000
Sub	Billy Taylor	1	4	2	0	2	0	0	1	0	.500	1.000
Sub	Sam Wise	1	4	2	0	0	0	0	0	0	.500	.500
Sub	Mike Moynahan	1	4	1	1	0	0	0	0	0	.250	.250
Sub	George Bradley	1	4	0	0	0	0	0	0	0	.000	.000
		84	2995	780	439	131	**53**	**17**	351	136	.260	.357

1B   Powell 55, Brown 27, Reilley 1, Dorgan 1, Knight 1
2B   Gerhardt 79, Troy 4, Knight 1
SS   Houck 75, Stearns 3, Reilley 3, Hanlon 2, Bradley 1
3B   Whitney 58, Troy 7, Foley 5, Bennett 5, Reilley 3, Dorgan 2, Wise 1, Moynahan 1, Taylor 1, Gerhardt 1
OF   Knight 82, Wood 80, Hanlon 74, Dorgan 5, Derby 4, Reilley 4, Bennett 3, O'Leary 2, Leary 2
C   Bennett 70, Reilley 10, Trott 6, Powell 1
P   Derby 56, Weidman 13, Mountain 7, Mullane 5, White 2, Leary 2

	G	IP	GS	CG	W	L	K	BB	SH	SV	ERA
George Derby	56	494.2	55	55	29	26	**212**	86	**9**	0	2.20
Stump Weidman	13	115	13	13	8	5	26	12	1	0	**1.80**
Frank Mountain	7	60	7	7	3	4	13	18	0	0	5.25
Tony Mullane	5	44	5	5	1	4	7	17	0	0	4.91
Will White	2	18	2	2	0	2	5	2	0	0	5.00
Jack Leary	2	13	2	1	0	2	2	2	0	0	4.15
		744.2	84	83	41	43	**265**	137	**10**	0	2.65

TROY   **Bob Ferguson**   **Haymakers' Grounds**

		G	AB	H	R	2B	3B	HR	RBI	BB	BA	SA
CF	John Cassidy	84	370	82	57	13	3	1	11	18	.222	.281
1B	Roger Connor	85	367	107	55	17	6	2	31	15	.292	.387
LF	Pete Gillespie	84	348	96	43	14	3	0	41	9	.276	.333
2B	Bob Ferguson	85	339	96	56	13	5	1	35	29	.283	.360
3B	Frank Hankinson	84	321	62	34	15	0	1	19	10	.193	.249
RF	Jake Evans	83	315	76	35	11	5	0	28	14	.241	.308
C	Buck Ewing	67	272	68	40	14	7	0	25	7	.250	.353
SS	Ed Caskin	63	234	53	33	7	1	0	21	13	.226	.265
C	Bill Holbert	43	180	49	16	3	0	0	14	3	.272	.289
P	Tim Keefe	46	152	35	18	7	1	0	19	21	.230	.289
P	Mickey Welch	40	148	30	12	10	0	0	11	1	.203	.270
		85	3046	754	399	124	31	5	255	140	.248	.314

1B	Connor 85
2B	Ferguson 85
SS	Caskin 63, Ewing 22, Hankinson 1, Cassidy 1
3B	Hankinson 84, Ewing 1
OF	Gillespie 84, Cassidy 84, Evans 83, Holbert 3, Ewing 2, Keefe 1
C	Ewing 44, Holbert 43
P	Keefe 45, Welch 40

	G	IP	GS	CG	W	L	K	BB	SH	SV	ERA
Tim Keefe	45	402	45	45	18	27	103	81	4	0	3.25
Mickey Welch	40	368	40	40	21	18	104	78	4	0	2.67
	85	770	85	**85**	39	45	207	159	8	0	2.97

BOSTON   **Harry Wright**   **South End Grounds (I)**

		G	AB	H	R	2B	3B	HR	RBI	BB	BA	SA
3B	Ezra Sutton	83	333	97	43	12	4	0	31	13	.291	.351
RF	Joe Hornung	83	324	78	40	12	8	2	25	5	.241	.346
1B	John Morrill	81	311	90	47	19	3	1	39	12	.289	.379
SS	Ross Barnes	69	295	80	42	14	1	0	17	16	.271	.325
P	Jim Whitney	75	282	72	37	17	3	0	32	19	.255	.337
2B	Jack Burdock	72	282	67	36	12	4	1	24	7	.238	.319
CF	Bill Crowley	72	279	71	33	12	0	0	31	14	.254	.297
C	Pop Snyder	62	219	50	14	8	0	0	16	3	.228	.265
Sub	Pat Deasley	43	147	35	13	5	2	0	8	5	.238	.299
P	John Fox	30	118	21	8	0	0	0	4	0	.178	.178
RF	Fred Lewis	27	114	25	17	6	0	0	9	7	.219	.272
Sub	John Richmond	27	98	27	13	2	2	1	12	6	.276	.367
Sub	Bobby Mathews	19	71	12	2	2	0	0	4	0	.169	.197
Sub	George Wright	7	25	5	4	0	0	0	0	3	.200	.200
P	Tommy Bond	3	10	2	0	0	0	0	0	0	.000	.000
Sub	Sam Wright	1	4	1	0	0	0	0	0	0	.250	.250
Sub	Paddy Quinn	1	4	0	0	0	0	0	0	0	.000	.000
		83	2916	733	349	121	27	5	252	110	.251	.317

1B	Morrill 74, Fox 6, Deasley 2, Whitney 2, Quinn 1
2B	Burdock 72, Barnes 7, Morrill 4, Snyder 1
SS	Barnes 63, Deasley 7, G. Wright 7, Richmond 2, Sutton 2, S. Wright 1, Snyder 1, Burdick 1
3B	Sutton 81, Morrill 2
OF	Hornung 83, Crowley 72, Lewis 27, Richmond 25, Mathews 18, Whitney 15, Fox 12, Deasley 7, Snyder 1
C	Snyder 60, Deasley 28
P	Whitney 66, Fox 17, Mathews 5, Bond 3, Morrill 3

	G	IP	GS	CG	W	L	K	BB	SH	SV	ERA
Jim Whitney	66	552.1	63	57	31	33	162	90	6	0	2.48
John Fox	17	124.1	16	12	6	8	30	39	0	0	3.33
Tommy Bond	3	25.1	3	2	0	3	2	2	0	0	4.26
Bobby Mathews	5	23	1	1	1	0	5	11	0	2*	3.17
John Morrill	3	5.2	0	0	0	1	0	1	0	1	6.35
		730.2	83	72	38	45	199	143	6	3	2.71

CLEVELAND   **Mike McGeary (4–7)**   **John Clapp (32–41)**   **Kennard Street Park**

		G	AB	H	R	2B	3B	HR	RBI	BB	BA	SA
1B	Bill Phillips	85	357	97	51	18	10	1	44	5	.272	.387
2B	Fred Dunlap	80	351	114	60	25	4	3	24	18	.325	.444
RF	Orator Shaffer	85	343	88	48	13	6	1	34	23	.257	.338
SS	Jack Glasscock	85	335	86	49	9	5	0	33	15	.257	.313
P	Jim McCormick	70	309	79	45	9	4	0	26	5	.256	.311
C	John Clapp	68	261	66	47	12	2	0	25	35	.253	.314
3B	George Bradley	60	241	60	21	10	1	2	18	4	.249	.324
CF	Jack Remsen	48	172	30	14	4	3	0	13	9	.174	.233
P	The Only Nolan	41	168	41	12	5	1	0	18	4	.244	.286
C	Doc Kennedy	39	150	47	19	7	1	0	15	5	.313	.373
LF	Mike Moynahan	33	135	31	12	5	1	0	8	3	.230	.281
Sub	Billy Taylor	24	103	25	6	1	0	0	12	0	.243	.252
Sub	Blondie Purcell	20	80	14	3	2	1	0	4	6	.175	.225
Sub	Mike McGeary	11	41	9	1	0	0	0	5	0	.220	.220
Sub	Pop Smith	10	34	4	1	0	0	0	3	0	.118	.118
Sub	Herm Doscher	5	19	4	2	0	0	0	0	0	.211	.211

Sub	Phil Powers	5	15	1	1	0	0	0	0	1	.067	.067
Sub	Rudy Kemmler	1	3	0	0	0	0	0	0	0	.000	.000
		85	3117	796	392	120	39	7	282	133	.255	.326

1B Phillips 85
2B Dunlap 79, Glasscock 6, McCormick 1
SS Glasscock 79, Bradley 6
3B Bradley 48, McGeary 11, Smith 10, Nolan 6, Doscher 5, Dunlap 1, Moynahan 1, Taylor 1, McCormick 1, Kennedy 1, Powers 1
OF Shaffer 85, Remsen 48, Moynahan 32, Taylor 23, Clapp 21, Purcell 20, Nolan 14, McCormick 10, Kennedy 3, Bradley 1
C   Clapp 48, Kennedy 35, Powers 4, Kemmler 1
P   McCormick 59, Nolan 22, Bradley 6, Taylor 1

	G	IP	GS	CG	W	L	K	BB	SH	SV	ERA
Jim McCormick	59	526	58	**57**	26	30	178	84	2	0	2.45
The Only Nolan	22	180	21	20	8	14	54	38	0	0	3.05
George Bradley	6	51	6	5	2	4	6	3	0	0	3.88
Billy Taylor	1	3	0	0	0	0	2	1	0	0	0.00
	760	85	82	36	48	240	126	2	0	2.68

WORCESTER   Mike Dorgan (24–32)   Harry Stovey (8–18)   Worcester Driving Park Grounds

		G	AB	H	R	2B	3B	HR	RBI	BB	BA	SA
LF	Buttercup Dickerson	80	367	116	48	18	6	1	31	8	.316	.406
3B	Hick Carpenter	83	347	75	40	12	2	2	31	19	.216	.280
1B	Harry Stovey	75	341	92	57	25	7	2	30	12	.270	.402
CF	Pete Hotaling	77	317	98	51	15	3	1	35	18	.309	.385
2B	George Creamer	80	309	64	42	9	2	0	25	11	.207	.249
C	Doc Bushong	76	275	64	35	7	4	0	21	21	.233	.287
P	Lee Richmond	61	252	63	31	5	1	0	28	10	.250	.278
UT	Mike Dorgan	51	220	61	36	5	0	0	18	8	.277	.300
SS	Art Irwin	50	206	55	27	8	2	0	24	7	.267	.325
RF	Fred Corey	51	203	45	22	8	4	0	10	5	.222	.300
Sub	Candy Nelson	24	103	29	13	1	0	1	15	5	.282	.320
P	Harry McCormick	12	45	6	1	0	0	0	3	5	.133	.133
Sub	Pop Smith	11	41	3	1	0	0	0	2	3	.073	.073
Sub	Billy Taylor	6	28	3	3	1	0	0	2	0	.107	.143
Sub	Lip Pike	5	18	2	1	0	0	0	0	4	.111	.111
Sub	Charlie Reilley	2	8	3	2	0	0	0	1	0	.375	.375
Sub	Paddy Quinn	2	7	1	0	0	0	0	1	1	.143	.143
Sub	Asa Stratton	1	4	1	0	0	0	0	0	0	.250	.250
Sub	Marty Flaherty	1	2	0	0	0	0	0	0	0	.000	.000
		83	3093	781	410	114	31	7	277	121	.253	.316

1B Stovey 57, Dorgan 26
2B Creamer 80, Smith 3
SS Irwin 50, Nelson 24, Corey 7, Dorgan 2, Stratton 1
3B Carpenter 83
OF Dickerson 80, Hotaling 74, Corey 25, Dorgan 23, Stovey 18, Richmond 11, Smith 8, Taylor 5, Pike 5, Flaherty 1
C   Bushong 76, Hotaling 3, Quinn 2, Reilley 2
P   Richmond 53, Corey 23, McCormick 9, Taylor 1

	G	IP	GS	CG	W	L	K	BB	SH	SV	ERA
Lee Richmond	53	462.1	52	50	25	26	156	68	3	0	3.39
Fred Corey	23	188.2	21	20	6	15	33	31	1	0	3.72
Harry McCormick	9	78.1	9	9	1	8	7	15	1	0	3.56
Billy Taylor	1	8	1	0	0	1	0	6	0	0	7.88
		737.1	83	80	32	50	196	120	5	0	3.54

THE REBEL LEAGUES ERA (1882-91)

Between 1869 and the close of the nineteenth century nearly 900 professional baseball franchises were launched; more than three-quarters of them went belly up in two years or less and only 50 lasted as long as six years. Six of the 50 teams that had a significant life span were the six original American Association entrants in 1882—Cincinnati, St. Louis, Philadelphia, Baltimore, Louisville and Pittsburgh. Actually, all but Philadelphia survived at least until 1899. They were joined in 1884 by Brooklyn, giving the rebel Association seven long-lived franchises while only four of the eight National League franchises that same season were still extant by the end of the 1880s, let alone the 1890s.

Considering the multitude of failures even on the major league level, professional baseball's appeal to investors in the last century was remarkable. The most fertile period for attracting entrepreneurs came during the ten years between 1882 and 1891 when the upstart Association fought the National League to the death for the right to coexist as a major league. Largely due to the Association's contributions, the ten seasons it was alive are known as baseball's "Golden Age." The professional game exploded from one eight-team league at the start of the 1880s to 17 leagues just seven years later. The decade also introduced much of the flavor that the game still carries today. Inaugurated were the first postseason "World's Series" between two rival major leagues, the notion that preseason training might best be conducted in the sunny South, and inning-by-inning reports from the Western Union telegraph company enabling fans in all parks to follow the progress of other games of interest on rudimentary scoreboards, known then as "bulletin" boards. Even the term "fan" was first coined in 1883 by St. Louis Browns manager Ted Sullivan when owner Chris Von der Ahe persisted in calling his team's rabid supporters or "kranks" fanatics. Meanwhile, the standard equipment for the average fan at a Browns' game became a stein of beer, a sausage in a roll and a scorecard with his favorite Browns player pictured on the cover. Though National League teams offered their customers some of these same enticements, their games by and large were not as much fun, and it was this distinction that gave the American Association its staying power.

Conflicts over the control of baseball pitting the entrenched National League against one challenger after another would mark the course of the national pastime from 1877 until 1901 and the climactic showdown with the American League. The first war came with the player-run International Association. After the players lost this three-year battle in 1879 when the Reserve Clause was devised, some five years would pass before a new champion of the rank and file appeared. In 1884 the Union Association surfaced as a major league expressly—or so its promoters said—to crusade against the Reserve Clause. Though the Union leaders were called "Onions" and otherwise treated pejoratively by the media, they shook the establishment to its roots with their player raids. The Union Association's demise in January 1885 after only one season was largely traceable to the same two failings that had undermined the International Association—glaring competitive imbalance and too many teams in small-market areas.

Still hoping to escape the tyranny of the Reserve Clause, the players formed their own trade union or "Brotherhood" that same year, and in 1890 they struck by forming the Players League and engineering "Baseball's Great Rebellion." Using the lessons learned from the abortive International Association and Union Association experiments, Players League founders installed franchises only in large population centers and took care to organize them as stock companies, with players and investors alike being equal shareholders. Notwithstanding its seemingly solid base, the Players League went the way of the International Association and the Union Association, lasting only one season before agreeing to an almost unconditional surrender.

The American Association survived ten times longer than either of the other two rebel federations during its lifetime not because it was sounder financially or because its progenitors had greater business acumen. It endured, if anything, *in spite of* the shaky financial underpinnings and inept business practices of many of its teams. It endured because it offered accouterments that National League teams either could not or would not give their patrons. In the fullness of time, the American Association would leave an irrevocable stamp on the game by introducing affordable ticket prices for the workingman, a carousel atmosphere at its ballparks, and Sunday games. It would also bring about revolutionary umpiring and rule reforms and—for a brief while anyway—would be the only major league from 1871 on, until the arrival in 1947 of Jackie Robinson, to employ African-American players.

While the founder of every other major league is known beyond all doubt, exactly who sired the American Association will probably always remain a mystery. The most credible tale is that "Hustling" Horace Phillips, the original manager of the Troy club in the National League, and Opie Caylor, a Cincinnati lawyer and newspaperman, put their heads together in a Philadelphia hotel room one September night in 1881. Phillips was living in the City of Brotherly Love at the time and running the Philadelphia baseball club, and Caylor had helped put together a semipro team in Cincinnati. Both found it intolerable that their respective cities were without major league teams at the moment, and they realized, as the night wore on, that they were of a similar mind in their thirst for remedying that.

The following morning they embarked on a telegram scheme that lured more than a dozen baseball-minded men to a preliminary meeting in Pittsburgh on October 10, 1881. Some three weeks later, on November 2, at Cincinnati's Gibson House Hotel, the American Association was officially born. Since there was beer or liquor money behind all six of its founding teams, National League adherents dubbed the rebel group "The Beer and Whisky League." The elder loop also took great solace in the fact that the Association club directors were cut from decidedly rough cloth. The Philadelphia entry, after freezing out Phillips, was run by a trio that included Bill Sharsig, Charlie Mason, an ex-player and the owner of a saloon and bookie joint, and Lew Simmons, a minstrel show producer and performer. Von der Ahe, a Prussian immigrant, operated a brewery in St. Louis; and Louisville, Baltimore, Cincinnati and the Allegheny club from the Pittsburgh area also were run by coalitions of retail merchants, saloonists and brewers.

But if National League owners viewed their American Association counterparts as *déclasse,* they could not dismiss the Association's performance once its teams actually started play. In 1882 the Association became the first professional league, major or minor, to boast of having played a full schedule in its initial season without any franchise transfers or casualties. Even more to the mark, the Association was a sparkling success at the box office as all six of its teams made money and in the process had a higher combined attendance than the National League's eight teams. Uniformly arrogant and militant just a few months earlier, several League owners now were ready to capitulate to the Association. Others simply wanted peaceful coexistence. Sager heads, like Chicago's Al Spalding, counseled that the long view dictated the League offer the Association an olive branch in one hand while keeping the other behind its back.

1882
CINCINNATI REDUX

In setting up shop as a rival major league the American Association elected to adopt a different rule book than the National League. The two circuits would remain at variance until 1887. Among the more significant differences in 1882 were that the Association condoned the sale of liquor in its member parks and played on Sunday in cities where permitted by law. The Association also allowed its member clubs to set their own minimum and maximum admission prices and espoused a different ball. For its first official ball the American Association chose the Mahn ball, the same brand the National League had used prior to adopting the Spalding ball in 1879.

The Association later decided the Mahn ball was lacking and changed to a ball made by Al Reach, an early-day player turned sporting goods magnate who was also given the task of issuing the Association's annual guide, but while the Mahn ball at least survived the 1882 season several of the Association's departures from tradition were scrapped before they barely got off the launching pad. One such was to respond to threats from League moguls by reneging on a November 1881 pledge to reinstate players such as Charley Jones and Joe Gerhardt whom the league had blacklisted. A second Association deviation that suffered a quick death was choosing to adorn each of its six teams in identical multihued silk uniforms, with each player's shirt color corresponding to his position. The National League, fearing that this innovation, crazy as it seemed, might fly, voted to adopt color-coded uniforms too during its annual meeting in Chicago on December 9, 1881, the last session over which William Hulbert presided before his death on April 10, 1882.

The uniform experiment ended soon after enough confusing on-field incidents made it apparent that fans and players alike could not tell who was friend and who was foe. Having been burned once, League moguls reverted to a wait-and-see policy in early July when the Association broke with the tradition of allowing the home team to pick the umpire for each game and selected three men who had no affiliations with any particular team to serve as full-time salaried umpires for the rest of the season. Upon realizing this was a notion whose time had come, the league soon copied its junior, and within a few years all professional leagues had followed suit.

In the quality of play its teams exhibited the Association was not nearly so precocious in its first season. The Cincinnati Red Stockings, piloted by catcher Pop Snyder, the lone established player to ditch the League and sign with a rebel Association team, featured three regulars from the 1880 Cincinnati team that had been expelled by the League, and eight of the club's other performers, including Snyder, had previous major league experience. As a result, Cincinnati, following a dispiriting run of preseason injuries and thrashings by League teams in exhibition games, swiftly got untracked once the opening bell rang. By the end of June the Red Stockings had slipped past the Philadelphia Athletics and grabbed first place at 20–10. Cincinnati then went on a tear, playing .700 ball over the remaining 50 games, to win the first Association pennant by a whopping 11½ lengths.

The League race, in sharp contrast, was a dogfight until the last week. No fewer than six of the eight senior loop teams finished above .500, and Troy, in seventh place, had a respectable .422 winning percentage despite undergoing a 16-game losing streak. Only last-place Worcester destroyed the benchmark parity the league had brandished the previous

Harry Wright and his 1882 Providence Grays in his first season at their helm. After piloting Boston for 11 years, Wright lasted just two seasons in the Rhode Island capital before scooting to Philadelphia, where he finished his managerial career in 1893. Top: Paul Hines, Jerry Denny, Hoss Radbourn, Jack Farrell. Center: Tom York, Joe Start, Harry Wright, George Wright, Monte Ward. Bottom: Charlie Reilly, Sandy Nava, Barney Gilligan.

year. When free-wheeling Buttercup Dickerson, Worcester's best hitter in 1881, was black-listed and Doc Bushong batted .158, awful even for a catcher, the Ruby Legs got off to a 9–32 start under Freeman Brown, formerly the club's secretary-treasurer, and never recovered. Worcester's .214 winning percentage was the poorest of any major league team's since 1876.

At the other end of the ladder, Chicago and Providence gradually drew away from the pack. Seeking their third straight flag, the White Stockings made only one change in the batting order that had produced 23 percent more runs than any other team in 1881. Joe Quest went to the bench, and Tom Burns vacated shortstop to take Quest's spot at second base, with King Kelly coming in from right field to play short and 1881 sub Hugh Nicol taking over in right. Then, trailing Providence by three games with just 16 to play, Anson benched Nicol and reinstalled Quest. The improved defense resulted in a 15–1 tear and another pennant. For the third season in a row Fred Goldsmith and Larry Corcoran split the pitching load, working all but three of the innings Chicago played. In 1882 the burden was so evenly shared that Goldsmith collared 28 wins and Corcoran 27, but Chicago was no longer alone in realizing the game had changed to a point where a team now needed two front-line pitchers. Both Providence and Boston very narrowly missed also having a pair of 20-game winners, and only Cleveland and Worcester still relied almost entirely on one pitcher.

Providence's ace was now Hoss Radbourn, whose 33 wins in 1882 were second in the league only to the 36 Jim McCormick racked up for Cleveland. But as in 1881, negligible offensive contributions from their shortstop doomed the Grays. Still, even with George

THE AMERICAN ASSOCIATION'S PLAYER COMPOSITION

The six teams that answered the gong for the American Association's first season were as disparate in their composition as they were in their performance. Although the champion Cincinnati Red Stockings had the highest percentage of players with previous major league experience—11 of 15—they did not have the most former major leaguers. Of the 20 players who wore a Pittsburgh uniform at one time or another during the 1882 season, 15 had seen earlier major league action. As should be expected, last-place Baltimore had 17 players completely new to the majors among its cast of 23, but Louisville, which finished third, also had 17 raw rookies. The difference was that many of Louisville's recruits had played together on the Eclipse team for several years before it joined the association. The complete breakdown:

	Players in 1882	ML Experience	Percentage
Cincinnati	15	11	.73
Pittsburgh	20	15	.67
St. Louis	22	9	.41
Philadelphia	24	9	.38
Baltimore	23	6	.26
Louisville	21	4	.19

A collage of the 1882 Buffalo Bisons. Clockwise from top: Hardy Richardson, Davy Force, Pud Galvin, Deacon White, Blondie Purcell, Tom Dolan, Jack Rowe and Curry Foley. Center, clockwise from top: Jim O'Rourke, Dan Brouthers and Hugh "One Arm" Daily. Richardson, White, Rowe and Brouthers gained renown as the second "Big Four" three years later when they were packaged and sold to Detroit after the Buffalo franchise slid into bankruptcy.

Wright hitting .162 after coming out of retirement in mid-June, Providence finished just three games behind Chicago and might have won out but for a crucial late-season loss to the White Stockings on Wright's two-run throwing error. The Grays insisted, though, that what really sank them was a controversial schedule change that switched the final three games of the season between Buffalo and Chicago from the Bisons' home park to the Windy City. Succumbing to the howls of protest from the Rhode Island capital, Al Spalding, who had assumed the White Stockings presidency upon Hulbert's death, agreed to play the Grays a best-of-nine postseason series with the winner declared the undisputed 1882 League champion.

First, though, Chicago stopped off in Cincinnati for two games with the association champion Red Stockings. The pair of clashes were the first in history between pennant winners from rival major leagues and resulted in an inconclusive 1–1 split. Cap Anson, perhaps overconfident, left Kelly behind in New York and put Corcoran at short in the opener. After losing 4–0 to Will White, Anson sent Corcoran to the box the following afternoon and got a measure of revenge when Corcoran, given a pair of unearned first-inning runs, blanked White 2–0. Contrary to the popular tale that Association president Denny McKnight halted the interleague affair by threatening to expel Cincinnati if it continued, the truth is there probably never was a plan to play more than two games. Newspaper accounts, in any event, bewailed the impossibility of playing a rubber game because both teams had other commitments.

IRON MAN WHITING

In 1882 Ed Whiting was behind the plate in 72 of Baltimore's 74 games and played the outfield in the Orioles' other two contests. Impressive as his "iron man" catching performance was, it was not without precedent. Just three years earlier, on June 25, 1879, John Clapp of Buffalo had ended a record-setting skein of 212 consecutive games played, most of them behind the bat. The following season Emil Gross caught every inning of every game for Providence and was also the only Gray to play in all of his team's 87 championship contests.

While Whiting's performance in 1882 was not as sustained as Clapp's or Gross's, he accomplished something that was done only once thereafter in the nineteenth century. In the American Association's inaugural season, Whiting became the next-to-last catcher in the 1800s to lead his team in at bats. Previously it had been done a fair number of times, and there were even instances in the National Association's early years when a pitcher led his team in at bats. In 1883, however, the schedule in both major leagues was expanded to 98 games, and by 1887 teams in both circuits were playing 140 games. For the remainder of the 1800s, with a couple of notable exceptions, catchers seldom worked more than two-thirds of the time, and that remained true until the second decade of the twentieth century. In fact, not until 1944 did a twentieth-century catcher, Frankie Hayes, manage to lead his team in at bats.

A list of nineteenth-century catchers and pitchers who led their teams in at bats:

	Po	Team	League	Year	G	AB	BA
Mike McGeary	C	Troy	NA	1871	29	148	.264
Deacon White	C	Cleveland	NA	1871	29	146	.322
Cherokee Fisher	P	Kekiongas	NA	1871	25	123	.228
Bill Lennon	C	Nationals	NA	1872	11	54	.222
Tom Barlow	C	Atlantics	NA	1873	55	271	.273
Al Spalding	P	Boston	NA	1874	71	359	.379
Dick Higham	C*	New York	NA	1874	65	331	.335
Scott Hastings	C*	Hartford	NA	1874	52	248	.343
John Cassidy	P*	Atlantics	NA	1875	41	165	.176
John Clapp	C	St. Louis	NL	1876	64	298	.305
Jim Devlin	P	Louisville	NL	1876	68	298	.315
Cal McVey	C*	Chicago	NL	1877	60	266	.368
Ed Whiting	C	Baltimore	AA	1882	74	308	.260
Deacon McGuire	C	Washington	LA	1895	132	533	.336

*Also played a sizable number of games at other positions

Note: In 1884, Kid Baldwin led the UA Kansas City Cowboys in ABs, but the team was in existence for only part of the season. In 1897 St. Louis's regular catcher Klondike Douglass tied for the team lead in ABs with 516 but more than half the games he played were at other positions.

The White Stockings, seemingly, would have been strictly concerned with the upcoming series with Providence, but their first three games with the Grays aroused suspicion. When Anson persisted in playing several of his regulars out of position and Chicago fell behind 3–0 in the series, many observers accused the White Stockings of trying to prolong the affair in order to maximize gate receipts. After Chicago evened the match at 4-all, the results seemed to support the suspicious. A 19–7 slaughter of the Grays in the ninth and deciding game on October 24, at Fort Wayne, Indiana, brought the series to a merciful if unsavory end and made the White Stockings the first team to claim three straight League championships. The previous day, October 23, at its season-ending meeting, the Association voted to expand to eight teams for the 1883 season by enlisting Columbus and the New York Metropolitans. Now that Hulbert was dead, the League was no longer bound by his prejudices against the nation's two largest cities, New York and Philadelphia, dating back to their expulsion in 1876. Anticipating the Association's move, acting president Arthur Soden fought to put new franchises in New York and Philadelphia near the close of the 1882 season by jettisoning seventh-place Troy and last-place Worcester. Though the League's two smallest cities violently protested their ouster, they drew only around 40,000 combined in 1882, including "crowds" of six and 18, respectively, in their final two games of their League tenure against one another at Worcester.

This drawing of the 1882 NL pennant winner appeared in Frank Leslie's Illustrated Newspaper *on October 14, 1882, while the White Stockings were in the midst of their ill-conceived postseason series with Providence. Top: Ned Williamson, King Kelly, Silver Flint, Fred Goldsmith. Center: Joe Quest, Tom Burns, Cap Anson, Abner Dalrymple, George Gore. Front: Hugh Nicol and Larry Corcoran.*

FAMOUS FIRSTS III

An "autographed" picture of Pete Browning, the AA's first batting king as well as the first rookie to win a hitting crown. A near illiterate, Browning wasn't helped when Juice Latham joined Louisville in 1883. Latham habitually kept a bottle of whiskey on the bench, hidden in his bat bag. One day a teammate found it and laced the whiskey with turpentine. Latham's only comment was that it had "more body than usual." In 1884, Latham's major league coda, his BA was little more than half of Browning's—.169 to .336.

Browning Can Write.

A statement has been going the rounds to the effect that Pete Browning could not write. This caught the eye of the tall center-fielder, and in refutation he has sent the following autograph, with his compliments to the base-ball editor:

From 1882 until the close of the 1886 season players in the American Association operated under a different set of rules than their National League elders. A fascinating and far-reaching application of one of the rule differences occurred in the Association's first no-hit game on September 11, 1882. With Cincinnati on the verge of clinching the first Association pennant and 1,922 expectant Queen City fans on hand, Tony Mullane of Louisville put up a momentary roadblock by holding the Red Stockings hitless while blanking them 2–0.

Uneventful as the box score makes Mullane's no-hitter look, it was nearly lost at the last turn. After Mullane retired the first two Cincinnati hitters in the ninth, most of the crowd started toward the exits when Pop Snyder lifted an easy fly to John Reccius in center field. Reccius returned everyone to his place, however, by muffing the ball. Perched on first base, Snyder then tried to rattle Mullane, as he had done the entire game, by complaining to umpire Mike Walsh that Mullane was bringing his arm above his shoulder illegally as he delivered the ball to the plate. Walsh would have none of it, though, nor would Mullane. Keeping his cool, the Louisville ace preserved his no-hitter by inducing Dan Stearns to hit a bouncer that forced Snyder at second base.

Among the Eclipse players who clustered around Mullane to congratulate him on the first Association no-hitter was Pete Browning, himself the perpetrator just minutes earlier of an Association first that would, in the full scheme of things, have wider implications than Mullane's. In the eighth inning Browning had become the first, and quite probably the only, Association player to reach base safely after singling and yet not be credited with a hit because he was ruled out for being an illegal baserunner. Losing that hit would cost Browning dearly, as we will learn, but here, first, is how it happened:

In 1882, although the National League had eliminated substitute runners for injured players, the American Association still allowed them if both captains consented to it. Prior to Mullane's no-hit game, Snyder, Cincinnati's captain and catcher, had agreed to Louisville captain Denny Mack's plea to let Guy Hecker run for Browning, who had a pulled leg muscle. As a result, each time Browning came to bat Hecker stood behind him and behind home plate, prepared to run as soon as the ball was struck. Until the eighth inning Will White held Browning hitless, but then in his final at bat the Association's top hitter in 1882 lined sharply to right field. Forgetting the situation in his excitement, Browning bolted out of the batter's box and Hecker, perplexed, stopped running.

After Browning reached base safely and the ball was returned to the pitcher's box, Snyder told White to throw it to first baseman Stearns. Stearns no sooner tagged the bag than Walsh called Browning out, ruling that Hecker was the proper baserunner and had failed to run. The lost hit had no bearing on the 1882 batting race. Browning won by 36 points with a .378 average (109 for 288) instead of the .382 he ought to have hit. That lost hit was costly, though, in another, arguably more important respect. Browning's career batting average is .34149. Restoring that lost hit would hike it to .34170, which rounds off to .342 and would tie Browning with Dan Brouthers for the highest career batting average among players active primarily before 1893 when the pitching distance was lengthened. If Browning had a share now of that distinction, would it matter to enough of the people who have control of which players get into the Hall of Fame? Doubtlessly not. Actually Browning's 1882 average was carried for years as .382 (110 for 288), and in early Macmillans he and Brouthers both had .343 career marks. Being tied with Brouthers didn't help him make the Hall of Fame then and it wouldn't now, but that lost hit matters nonetheless. Every lost hit matters. Check with Jerry Goff, the Astros catcher who lost a hit to an equally bizarre umpire's interpretation of a quirk in the rules on July 6, 1995. With the score tied, the bases full and one out in the bottom of the 12th, Goff lined a hit to center field, winning the game. However, when San Diego center fielder Steve Finley fired the ball to second base, the umpire there signaled a force out even though the winning run had already crossed the plate and the out meant nothing. Surely Goff too will say that on September 11, 1882, Pete Browning got a single in the eighth inning, end of argument.

THE SEASONAL RECORD

NATIONAL LEAGUE

	W	L	PCT	HOME	ROAD	GB
1. Chicago White Stockings	55	29	.655	35–10	20–19	—
2. Providence Grays	52	32	.619	30–12	22–20	3
3. Boston Red Caps	45	39	.536	27–15	18–24	10
Buffalo Bisons	45	39	.536	26–13	19–26	10
5. Cleveland Blues	42	40	.512	21–19	21–21	12
6. Detroit Wolverines	42	41	.506	24–18	18–23	12.5
7. Troy Trojans	35	48	.422	22–20	13–28	19.5
8. Worcester Ruby Legs	18	66	.214	12–30	6–36	37

	Chi	Pro	Bos	Buf	Cle	Det	Tro	Wor	
Chicago	—	8	6	6	9	8	9	9	55
Providence	4	—	6	6	8	9	9	10	52
Boston	6	6	—	7	7	8	4	7	45
Buffalo	6	6	5	—	6	5	6	11	45
Cleveland	3	4	5	6	—	4	9	11	42
Detroit	4	3	4	7	7	—	8	9	42
Troy	3	3	8	6	2	4	—	9	35
Worcester	3	2	5	1	1	3	3	—	18
	29	32	39	39	40	41	48	66	334

SEASON LEADERS

Batting Average (200 ABs)

1. Brouthers, Buffalo — .368
2. Anson, Chicago — .362
3. Connor, Troy — .330
4. Start, Providence — .329
5. Whitney, Boston — .323

On–Base Percentage

1. Brouthers, Buffalo — .403
2. Anson, Chicago — .397
3. Whitney, Boston — .382
4. Gore, Chicago — .369
5. Connor, Troy — .354

Home Runs

1. Wood, Detroit — 7
2. Muldoon, Cleveland — 6
   Brouthers, Buffalo — 6
4. Whitney, Boston — 5
   Hanlon, Detroit — 5
   Bennett, Detroit — 5
   Stovey, Worcester — 5

Slugging Average

1. Brouthers, Buffalo — .547
2. Connor, Troy — .530
3. Whitney, Boston — .510
4. Anson, Chicago — .500
5. Hines, Providence — .467

Total Bases

1. Brouthers, Buffalo — 192
2. Connor, Troy — 185
3. Hines, Providence — 177
4. Anson, Chicago — 174
5. Dalrymple, Chicago — 167

RBI

1. Anson, Chicago — 83
2. Brouthers, Buffalo — 63
3. Williamson, Chicago — 60
4. Richardson, Buffalo — 57
5. Kelly, Chicago — 55

Hits

1.	Brouthers, Buffalo	129
2.	Anson, Chicago	126
3.	Dalrymple, Chicago	117
	Gore, Chicago	117
	Hines, Providence	117
	Start, Providence	117
	Hornung, Boston	117

Runs

1.	Gore, Chicago	99
2.	Dalrymple, Chicago	96
3.	Stovey, Worcester	90
4.	Kelly, Chicago	81
5.	Purcell, Buffalo	79

Bases on Balls

1.	Gore, Chicago	29
2.	Williamson, Chicago	27
	Shaffer, Cleveland	27
4.	Hanlon, Detroit	26
5.	Sutton, Boston	24
	Whitney, Boston	24

Strikeouts

1.	Flint, Chicago	50
2.	Galvin, Buffalo	49
3.	Denny, Providence	46
	Keefe, Troy	46
5.	Wise, Boston	45

PITCHING

Wins

1.	McCormick, Cleveland	36
2.	Radbourn, Providence	33
3.	Goldsmith, Buffalo	28
	Galvin, Buffalo	28
5.	Corcoran, Chicago	27

Losses

1.	Richmond, Worcester	33
2.	McCormick, Cleveland	29
3.	Keefe, Troy	26
4.	Galvin, Buffalo	23
5.	Whitney, Boston	21

Innings

1.	McCormick, Cleveland	595.2
2.	Radbourn, Providence	574
3.	Galvin, Buffalo	445.1
4.	Whitney, Boston	420
5.	Weidman, Detroit	411
	Richmond, Worcester	411

Complete Games

1.	McCormick, Cleveland	65
2.	Radbourn, Providence	51
3.	Galvin, Buffalo	48
4.	Whitney, Boston	46
5.	Goldsmith, Chicago	45

Strikeouts

1.	Radbourn, Providence	201
2.	McCormick, Cleveland	200
3.	Derby, Detroit	182
4.	Whitney, Boston	180
5.	Corcoran, Chicago	170

Winning Percentage (20 decisions)

1	Corcoran, Chicago	.692
2.	Radbourn, Providence	.623
3.	Goldsmith, Chicago	.622
4.	Ward, Providence	.613
5.	Mathews, Boston	.559

ERA (84 innings)

1.	Corcoran, Chicago	1.95
2.	Radbourn, Providence	2.09
3.	McCormick, Cleveland	2.37
4.	Goldsmith, Chicago	2.42
5.	Keefe, Troy	2.50

Lowest On-Base Percentage

1.	Corcoran, Chicago	.234
2.	Mathews, Boston	.246
	Radbourn, Providence	.246
4.	Weidman, Detroit	.253
5.	Goldsmith, Chicago	.254

FIELDING

Total Chances

1B	Start, Providence	951
2B	Dunlap, Cleveland	628
3B	Denny, Providence	397
SS	Pfeffer, Troy	510
OF	Hanlon, Detroit	240
C	Flint, Chicago	568
P	McCormick, Cleveland	156

Fielding Average

Brouthers, Buffalo	.974
Burdock, Boston	.932
Williamson, Chicago	.881
Force, Buffalo	.908
Hornung, Boston	.932
Deasley, Boston	.958
Derby, Detroit	.957

CHICAGO Cap Anson Lake Front Park (I)

		G	AB	H	R	2B	3B	HR	RBI	BB	BA	SA
LF	Abner Dalrymple	84	**397**	117	96	25	11	1	36	14	.295	.421
SS	King Kelly	84	377	115	81	**37**	4	1	55	10	.305	.432
CF	George Gore	84	367	117	**99**	15	7	3	51	**29**	.319	.422
2B	Tom Burns	84	355	88	55	23	6	0	48	15	.248	.346
1B	Cap Anson	82	348	126	69	29	8	1	**83**	20	.362	.500
3B	Ned Williamson	83	348	98	66	27	4	3	60	27	.282	.408
C	Silver Flint	81	331	83	48	18	8	4	44	2	.251	.390
RF	Hugh Nicol	47	186	37	19	9	1	1	16	7	.199	.274
P	Fred Goldsmith	45	183	42	23	11	1	0	19	4	.230	.301
P	Larry Corcoran	39	169	35	23	10	2	1	24	6	.207	.308
Sub	Joe Quest	42	159	32	24	5	2	0	15	8	.201	.258
Sub	Milt Scott	1	5	2	1	0	0	0	0	0	.400	.400
		84	3225	**892**	**604**	**209**	54	15	**451**	**142**	**.277**	**.389**

1B	Anson 82, Scott 1, Goldsmith 1, Kelly 1
2B	Burns 43, Quest 41
SS	Kelly 42, Burns 41, Nicol 8, Quest 1
3B	Williamson 83, Kelly 3, Corcoran 1
OF	Gore 84, Dalrymple 84, Nicol 47, Kelly 38, Flint 10
C	Flint 81, Kelly 12, Anson 1
P	Goldsmith 45, Corcoran 39, Williamson 1

	G	IP	GS	CG	W	L	K	BB	SH	SV	ERA
Fred Goldsmith	45	405	45	45	28	17	109	38	4	0	2.42
Larry Corcoran #	39	355.2	39	38	27	12	170	63	3	0	**1.95**
Ned Williamson	1	3	0	0	0	0	0	1	0	0	6.00
		763.2	84	**83**	55	29	279	102	7	0	**2.22**

No hit game 5–0 vs Worcester, September 20

PROVIDENCE Harry Wright Messer Street Grounds

		G	AB	H	R	2B	3B	HR	RBI	BB	BA	SA
CF	Paul Hines	84	379	117	73	28	10	4	34	10	.309	.467
2B	Jack Farrell	84	366	93	67	21	6	2	31	16	.254	.361

		G	AB	H	R	2B	3B	HR	RBI	BB	BA	SA
1B	Joe Start	82	356	117	58	8	10	0	48	11	.329	.407
RF	Monte Ward	83	355	87	58	10	3	1	39	13	.245	.299
3B	Jerry Denny	84	329	81	54	10	9	2	42	4	.246	.350
P	Hoss Radbourn	83	326	78	30	11	0	1	32	12	.239	.282
LF	Tom York	81	321	86	48	23	7	1	40	19	.268	.393
C	Barney Gilligan	56	201	45	32	7	6	0	26	4	.224	.318
SS	George Wright	46	185	30	14	1	2	0	9	4	.162	.189
C	Sandy Nava	28	97	20	15	2	0	0	7	1	.206	.227
Sub	Tim Manning	21	76	8	7	0	0	0	8	5	.105	.105
Sub	Cliff Carroll	10	41	5	4	0	0	0	2	0	.122	.122
Sub	Art Whitney	11	40	3	2	0	0	0	1	2	.075	.075
Sub	Dasher Troy	4	17	4	1	0	0	0	1	0	.235	.235
Sub	Charlie Reilley	3	11	2	0	0	0	0	2	1	.182	.182
Sub	Charlie Sweeney	1	4	0	0	0	0	0	0	0	.000	.000
		84	3104	776	463	72	37	5	227	76	.250	.334

1B   Start 82, Hines 2
2B   Farrell 84
SS   Wright 46, Manning 17, Whitney 11, Ward 4, Troy 4, Gilligan 2, Radbourn 1
3B   Denny 84
OF   Hines 82, York 81, Ward 50, Radbourn 31, Carroll 10, Nava 1, Sweeney 1
C   Gilligan 54, Nava 27, Manning 4, Reilley 3
P   Radbourn 55, Ward 33

	G	IP	GS	CG	W	L	K	BB	SH	SV	ERA
Hoss Radbourn	55	474	52	51	33	20	**201**	51	**6**	0	2.09
Monte Ward	33	278	32	29	19	12	72	36	4	1	2.59
		752	84	80	52	32	273	87	**10**	1	2.27

BOSTON   John Morrill   South End Grounds (I)

		G	AB	H	R	2B	3B	HR	RBI	BB	BA	SA
LF	Joe Hornung	85	388	117	67	14	11	1	50	2	.302	.402
CF	Pete Hotaling	84	378	98	64	16	5	0	28	16	.259	.328
1B	John Morrill	83	349	101	73	19	11	2	54	18	.289	.424
RF	Ed Rowen	84	327	81	36	7	4	1	43	19	.248	.303
3B	Ezra Sutton	81	319	80	44	8	1	2	38	24	.251	.301
2B	Jack Burdock	83	319	76	36	6	7	0	27	9	.238	.301
SS	Sam Wise	78	298	66	44	11	4	4	34	5	.221	.326
C	Pat Deasley	67	264	70	36	8	0	0	29	7	.265	.295
P	Jim Whitney	61	251	81	49	18	7	5	48	24	.323	.510
P	Bobby Mathews	45	169	38	17	6	0	0	13	8	.225	.260
UT	Charlie Buffinton	15	50	13	5	1	0	0	4	2	.260	.280
Sub	Hal McClure	2	6	2	1	0	0	0	0	0	.333	.333
		85	3118	823	472	114	50	15	368	134	.264	.347

1B   Morrill 76, Whitney 6, Buffinton 5, Hornung 1
2B   Burdock 83, Morrill 2
SS   Wise 72, Rowen 6, Sutton 4, Morrill 3, Mathews 1, Deasley 1
3B   Sutton 77, Wise 6, Rowen 1, Morrill 1
OF   Hotaling 84, Hornung 84, Rowen 48, Deasley 14, Mathews 13, Whitney 9, Buffinton 7, McClure 2, Morrill 1
C   Deasley 56, Rowen 34
P   Whitney 49, Mathews 34, Buffinton 5, Morrill 1

	G	IP	GS	CG	W	L	K	BB	SH	SV	ERA
Jim Whitney	49	420	48	46	24	21	180	41	3	0	2.64
Bobby Mathews	34	285	32	31	19	15	153	22	0	0	2.87
Charlie Buffinton	5	42	5	4	2	3	17	14	1	0	4.07
John Morrill	1	2	0	0	0	0	2	0	0	0	0.00
		749	85	81	45	39	352	**77**	4	0	2.80

BUFFALO   Jim O'Rourke   Riverside Park

		G	AB	H	R	2B	3B	HR	RBI	BB	BA	SA
LF	Blondie Purcell	84	380	105	79	18	6	2	40	14	.276	.371
CF	Jim O'Rourke	84	370	104	62	15	6	2	37	13	.281	.370
2B	Hardy Richardson	83	354	96	61	20	8	2	57	11	.271	.390
1B	Dan Brouthers	84	351	**129**	71	23	11	6	63	21	**.368**	**.547**
RF	Curry Foley	84	341	104	51	16	4	3	49	12	.305	.402
3B	Deacon White	83	337	95	51	17	0	1	33	15	.282	.341
C	Jack Rowe	75	308	82	43	14	5	1	42	12	.266	.354
SS	Davy Force	73	278	67	39	10	1	1	28	12	.241	.295
P	Pud Galvin	54	206	44	21	7	4	0	17	2	.214	.286
P	One Arm Daily	29	110	18	10	6	1	0	9	2	.164	.236
C	Tom Dolan	22	89	14	12	0	1	0	8	2	.157	.180
P	James Burke	1	4	0	0	0	0	0	0	0	.000	.000
		84	3128	858	500	146	47	18	383	116	.274	.368

1B	Brouthers 84
2B	Richardson 83, Force 1
SS	Force 61, Rowe 22, O'Rourke 2
3B	White 63, Force 11, Rowe 7, Dolan 2, O'Rourke 1
OF	Foley 84, Purcell 82, O'Rourke 81, Galvin 6, Dolan 4, Rowe 1, Burke 1
C	Rowe 46, White 20, Dolan 18, O'Rourke 2
P	Galvin 52, Daily 29, Purcell 6, Burke 1, Foley 1

	G	IP	GS	CG	W	L	K	BB	SH	SV	ERA
Pud Galvin	52	445.1	51	48	28	23	162	40	3	0	3.17
One Arm Daily	29	255.2	29	29	15	14	116	70	0	0	2.99
Blondie Purcell	6	31	3	2	2	1	9	4	0	0	4.94
James Burke	1	4	1	0	0	1	0	0	0	0	11.25
Curry Foley	1	1	0	0	0	0	0	0	0	0	18.00
		737	84	79	45	39	287	114	3	0	3.25

CLEVELAND   Jim McCormick (0–4)   Fred Dunlap (42–36)   Kennard Street Park

		G	AB	H	R	2B	3B	HR	RBI	BB	BA	SA
2B	Fred Dunlap	84	364	102	68	19	4	0	28	23	.280	.354
SS	Jack Glasscock	84	358	104	66	27	9	4	46	13	.291	.450
3B	Mike Muldoon	84	341	84	50	17	5	6	45	10	.246	.378
1B	Bill Phillips	78	335	87	40	17	7	4	47	7	.260	.388
RF	Orator Shaffer	84	313	67	37	14	2	3	28	27	.214	.300
P	Jim McCormick	70	262	57	35	7	3	2	15	2	.218	.290
C	Fatty Briody	53	194	50	30	13	0	0	13	9	.258	.325
LF	Dude Esterbrook	45	179	44	13	4	3	0	19	5	.246	.302
CF	John Richmond	41	140	24	12	6	2	0	11	11	.171	.243
P	George Bradley	30	115	21	16	5	0	0	6	4	.183	.226
Sub	Herm Doscher	25	104	25	7	2	0	0	10	0	.240	.260
C	Kick Kelly	30	104	14	6	2	0	0	5	1	.135	.154
Sub	Dave Rowe	23	97	25	13	4	3	1	17	4	.258	.392
Sub	John Tilley	15	56	5	2	1	1	0	4	2	.089	.143

		G	AB	H	R	2B	3B	HR	RBI	BB	BA	SA
Sub	Julius Willigrod	9	36	5	5	1	1	0	2	3	.139	.222
Sub	Bill McGunnigle	1	5	1	2	0	0	0	0	0	.200	.200
Sub	Doc Kennedy	1	3	1	0	0	0	0	0	1	.333	.333
Sub	John Dwyer	1	3	0	0	0	0	0	1	0	.000	.000
		84	3009	716	402	139	40	**20**	297	122	.238	.331

1B Phillips 78, Bradley 6, Esterbrook 1
2B Dunlap 84
SS Glasscock 83, Doscher 1
3B Muldoon 61, Doscher 22, Glasscock 1
OF Shaffer 84, Esterbrook 45, Richmond 41, Muldoon 23, Rowe 23, Tilley 15, Bradley 9, Willigrod 9, McCormick 4, Doscher 2, McGunnigle 1, Dwyer 1
C Briody 53, Kelly 30, Dwyer 1, Kennedy 1, Phillips 1
P McCormick 68, Bradley 18, Rowe 1

	G	IP	GS	CG	W	L	K	BB	SH	SV	ERA
Jim McCormick	**68**	**595.2**	**67**	**65**	**36**	30	200	**103**	4	0	2.37
George Bradley	18	147	16	15	6	9	32	22	0	0	3.73
Dave Rowe	1	9	1	1	0	1	0	7	0	0	12.00
		751.2	84	81	42	40	232	132	4	0	2.75

DETROIT   **Frank Bancroft**   **Recreation Park**

		G	AB	H	R	2B	3B	HR	RBI	BB	BA	SA
LF	George Wood	84	375	101	69	12	12	**7**	29	14	.269	.421
CF	Ned Hanlon	83	347	80	68	18	6	5	38	26	.231	.360
RF	Lon Knight	86	347	72	39	12	6	0	24	16	.207	.277
C	Charlie Bennett	84	342	103	43	16	10	5	51	20	.301	.450
1B	Martin Powell	80	338	81	44	13	0	0	29	19	.240	.278
3B	Joe Farrell	69	283	70	34	12	2	1	24	4	.247	.314
P	Stump Weidman	50	193	42	20	7	1	0	20	2	.218	.264
2B	Dasher Troy	40	152	37	22	7	2	0	14	5	.243	.235
P	George Derby	40	149	29	13	2	1	0	8	7	.195	.221
SS	Mike McGeary	34	133	19	14	4	1	0	2	2	.143	.188
Sub	Sam Trott	32	129	31	11	7	1	0	12	0	.240	.310
Sub	Art Whitney	31	115	21	10	0	0	0	4	1	.183	.183
2B	Tom Forster	21	76	7	5	0	0	0	2	5	.092	.092
SS	Walt Kinzie	13	53	5	5	0	1	0	2	0	.094	.132
Sub	Bob Casey	9	39	9	5	2	1	1	7	0	.231	.410
Sub	Yank Robinson	11	39	7	1	1	0	0	2	1	.179	.205
Sub	Tom Kearns	4	13	4	2	2	0	0	1	0	.308	.462
Sub	Henry Luff	3	11	3	1	2	0	0	1	0	.273	.455
Sub	John Morrissey	2	7	2	1	0	0	0	0	0	.286	.286
Sub	Julius Willigrod	1	3	1	0	0	0	0	1	0	.333	.333
		86	3144	724	407	117	44	19	271	122	.230	.314

1B Powell 80, Trott 3, Knight 2, Bennett 1
2B Troy 31, Forster 21, Farrell 18, Bennett 7, Kearns 4, Luff 3, McGeary 3, Trott 3, Hanlon 1, Casey 1
SS McGeary 33, Kinzie 13, Troy 11, Robinson 10, Farrell 9, Whitney 8, Trott 3, Willigrod 1, Weidman 1, Bennett 1
3B Farrell 42, Whitney 22, Bennett 11, Casey 8, Morrissey 2, Trott 1
OF Wood 84, Knight 84, Hanlon 82, Weidman 6, Trott 2, Derby 2, Robinson 1, Luff 1
C Bennett 65, Trott 23
P Weidman 46, Derby 40, Whitney 3, Robinson 1

	G	IP	GS	CG	W	L	K	BB	SH	SV	ERA
Stump Weidman	46	411	45	43	25	20	161	39	4	0	2.63
George Derby	40	362	39	38	17	20	182	81	3	0	3.26
Art Whitney	3	18	2	1	0	1	11	8	0	0	6.00
Yank Robinson	1	2	0	0	0	0	0	1	0	0	0.00
		793	86	82	42	41	**354**	129	7	0	2.98

TROY   Bob Ferguson   Troy Ball Club Grounds

		G	AB	H	R	2B	3B	HR	RBI	BB	BA	SA
CF	Roger Connor	81	349	115	65	22	**18**	4	42	13	.330	.530
RF	Chief Roseman	82	331	78	41	21	6	1	29	3	.236	.344
SS	Fred Pfeffer	85	330	72	26	7	4	1	43	1	.218	.273
3B	Buck Ewing	74	328	89	67	16	11	2	29	10	.271	.405
2B	Bob Ferguson	81	319	82	44	15	2	0	32	23	.257	.317
LF	Pete Gillespie	74	298	82	46	5	4	2	33	9	.275	.339
C	Bill Holbert	73	251	46	24	5	0	0	23	11	.183	.203
P	Tim Keefe	53	189	43	24	8	7	1	19	17	.228	.360
P	Mickey Welch	38	151	37	26	6	0	1	17	5	.245	.305
1B	John Smith	35	149	36	27	4	3	0	14	3	.242	.309
Sub	Bill Harbidge	32	123	23	11	1	1	0	13	10	.187	.211
Sub	John Cassidy	29	121	21	14	3	1	0	9	3	.174	.215
UT	Jim Egan	30	115	23	15	3	2	0	10	1	.200	.261
Sub	Jim Holdsworth	1	3	0	0	0	0	0	0	0	.000	.000
		85	3057	747	430	116	**59**	12	313	109	.244	.333

1B   Connor 43, Smith 35, Harbidge 6, Ewing 1
2B   Ferguson 79, Pfeffer 2, Ewing 2
SS   Pfeffer 83, Ferguson 2
3B   Ewing 44, Connor 14, Cassidy 13, Holbert 12, Ewing 4, Keefe 3
OF   Roseman 82, Gillespie 74, Connor 24, Harbidge 23, Egan 18, Cassidy 16, Welch 8, Keefe 8, Holbert 3, Holdsworth 1, Ewing 1
C   Holbert 58, Ewing 25, Harbidge 3, Egan 2
P   Keefe 43, Welch 33, Egan 12, Ewing 1

	G	IP	GS	CG	W	L	K	BB	SH	SV	ERA
Tim Keefe	43	375	42	41	17	26	116	81	1	0	2.50
Mickey Welch	33	281	33	30	14	16	53	62	5	0	3.46
Jim Egan	12	100	10	10	4	6	20	24	0	0	4.14
Buck Ewing	1	1	0	0	0	0	0	1	0	0	9.00
		757	85	81	35	48	189	168	6	0	3.08

WORCESTER   Freeman Brown (9–32)   Tommy Bond (2–4)   Jack Chapman (7–30)
Worcester Driving Park Grounds

		G	AB	H	R	2B	3B	HR	RBI	BB	BA	SA
1B	Harry Stovey	84	360	104	90	13	10	5	26	22	.289	.422
RF	Jake Evans	80	334	71	33	10	4	0	25	7	.213	.266
3B	Arthur Irwin	84	333	73	30	12	4	0	30	14	.219	.279
CF	Jackie Hayes	78	326	88	27	22	4	4	54	6	.270	.399
2B	George Creamer	81	282	65	27	16	6	1	29	14	.227	.336
SS	Fred Corey	64	255	63	33	7	12	0	29	5	.247	.369
C	Doc Bushong	69	253	40	20	4	1	1	15	5	.158	.194
P	Lee Richmond	55	228	64	50	8	9	2	28	9	.281	.421
LF	Jim Clinton	26	98	16	9	2	0	0	3	7	.163	.184
Sub	Tom O'Brien	22	89	18	9	1	1	0	7	1	.202	.236
P	Frank Mountain	25	86	20	9	2	2	2	6	3	.233	.372
Sub	Fred Mann	19	77	18	12	5	0	0	7	2	.234	.299

		G	AB	H	R	2B	3B	HR	RBI	BB	BA	SA
1B	John Smith	19	70	17	10	3	2	0	5	5	.243	.343
Sub	Frank McLaughlin	15	55	12	7	0	2	1	4	0	.218	.345
Sub	Ed Cogswell	13	51	7	10	1	0	0	1	6	.137	.157
Sub	Tommy Bond	8	30	4	1	0	0	0	2	2	.133	.133
Sub	Dan O'Leary	6	22	4	2	1	0	0	2	5	.182	.227
P	John Clarkson	3	11	4	0	2	0	0	2	0	.364	.545
Sub	Ed Merrill	2	8	1	0	0	0	0	4	0	.125	.125
Sub	Jim Halpin	2	8	0	0	0	0	0	0	0	.000	.000
Sub	John Irwin	1	4	0	0	0	0	0	0	0	.000	.000
		84	2984	689	379	109	57	16	279	113	.231	.322

1B Stovey 43, Smith 19, Cogswell 13, Corey 5, Mountain 2, Clarkson 1, Mann 1, J. Irwin 1
2B Creamer 81, O'Brien 2, Evans 1
3B A. Irwin 51, Mann 18, Corey 6, Hayes 5, Merrill 2, Halpin 2, O'Brien 1, Evans 1
SS A. Irwin 33, Corey 26, McLaughlin 14, Evans 11, Mountain 1, Hayes 1
OF Evans 68, Hayes 58, Stovey 41, Clinton 26, O'Brien 20, Corey 15, Richmond 11, Bond 8, Mountain 6,
    O'Leary 6, McLaughlin 1
C   Bushong 69, Hayes 15
P   Richmond 48, Corey 21, Mountain 18, Clarkson 3, Bond 2, Evans 1

	G	IP	GS	CG	W	L	K	BB	SH	SV	ERA
Lee Richmond	40	411	46	44	14	**33**	123	88	0	0	3.74
Frank Mountain	18	144	18	16	2	16	29	35	0	0	3.69
Fred Corey	21	139	14	12	1	13	36	19	0	0	3.56
John Clarkson	3	24	3	2	1	2	3	2	0	0	4.50
Tommy Bond	2	12.1	2	0	0	1	2	7	0	0	4.38
Jake Evans	1	8	1	1	0	1	2	0	0	0	5.63
		738.1	84	75	18	66	195	151	0	0	3.75

AMERICAN ASSOCIATION

	W	L	PCT	HOME	ROAD	GB
1. Cincinnati Red Stockings	55	25	.688	31–11	24–14	—
2. Philadelphia Athletics	41	34	.547	21–18	20–16	11.5
3. Louisville Eclipse	42	37	.532	26–13	16–24	13
4. Pittsburgh Alleghenys	39	39	.500	17–18	22–21	15
5. St. Louis Browns	36	43	.456	23–20	13–23	18
6. Baltimore Orioles	19	54	.260	9–25	10–29	32.5

	Cin	Phi	Lou	Pit	StL	Bal	
Cincinnati	—	10	11	10	10	14	55
Philadelphia	6	—	11	6	11	7	41
Louisville	5	5	—	10	9	13	42
Pittsburgh	6	10	6	—	10	7	39
St. Louis	6	5	6	6	—	13	36
Baltimore	2	4	3	7	3	—	19
	25	34	37	39	43	54	233

SEASON LEADERS*

Batting Average (200 ABs)

1.	Browning, Louisville	.378
2.	Carpenter, Cincinnati	.342
3.	Swartwood, Pittsburgh	.329
4.	O'Brien, Philadelphia	.303
5.	Wolf, Louisville	.299

On-Base Percentage

1.	Browning, Louisville	.430
2.	Swartwood, Pittsburgh	.370
3.	Carpenter, Cincinnati	.360
4.	O'Brien, Philadelphia	.339
5.	Sommer, Cincinnati	.333

Home Runs

1.	Walker, St. Louis	7
2.	Browning, Louisville	5
3.	Swartwood, Pittsburgh	4
4.	Taylor, Pittsburgh	3
	Lane, Pittsburgh	3
	O'Brien, Philadelphia	3
	Hecker, Louisville	3

Hits

1.	Carpenter, Cincinnati	120
2.	Browning, Louisville	109
3.	Swartwood, Pittsburgh	107
4.	Sommer, Cincinnati	102
5.	B. Gleason, St. Louis	100

*RBI leaders unavailable

Slugging Average

l.	Browning, Louisville	.510
2.	Swartwood, Pittsburgh	.498
3.	Taylor, Pittsburgh	.455
4.	Mansell, Pittsburgh	.438
5.	Carpenter, Cincinnati	.422

Total Bases

1.	Swartwood, Pittsburgh	162
2.	M. Mansell, Pittsburgh	152
3.	Carpenter, Cincinnati	148
4.	Browning, Louisville	147
5.	Taylor, Pittsburgh	136

Runs

1.	Swartwood, Pittsburgh	86
2.	Sommer, Cincinnati	82
3.	Carpenter, Cincinnati	78
4.	Browning, Louisville	67
5.	Birchall, Philadelphia	65

Bases on Balls

1.	J. Gleason, St. Louis	27
2.	Browning, Louisville	26
3.	Sommer, Cincinnati	24
4.	J. Reccius, Louisville	23
5.	Swartwood, Pittsburgh	21

PITCHING

Wins

1.	White, Cincinnati	40
2.	Mullane, Louisville	30
3.	Weaver, Philadelphia	26
4.	McGinnis, St. Louis	25
5.	Salisbury, Pittsburgh	20

Innings Pitched

1.	White, Cincinnati	480
2.	Mullane, Louisville	460.1
3.	McGinnis, St. Louis	388.1
4.	Weaver, Philadelphia	371
5.	Landis, Phil–Balt	358

Strikeouts

1.	Mullane, Louisville	170
2.	Salisbury, Pittsburgh	135
3.	McGinnis, St. Louis	134
4.	White, Cincinnati	122
5.	Weaver, Philadelphia	104

Losses

1.	Landis, Phil–Balt	28
2.	Mullane, Louisville	24
3.	Salisbury, Pittsburgh	18
4.	McGinnis, St. Louis	17
5.	Weaver, Philadelphia	15

Complete Games

1.	White, Cincinnati	52
2.	Mullane, Louisville	51
3.	McGinnis, St. Louis	43
4.	Weaver, Philadelphia	41
5.	Salisbury, Pittsburgh	38

Winning Percentage (20 decisions)

1.	White, Cincinnati	.769
2.	Weaver, Philadelphia	.634
3.	Driscoll, Pittsburgh	.591
4.	McGinnis, St. Louis	.581
5.	McCormick, Cincinnati	.560

ERA (80 innings)

1.	Driscoll, Pittsburgh	1.21
2.	Hecker, Louisville	1.30
3.	McCormick, Cincinnati	1.52
4.	White, Cincinnati	1.54
5.	Mullane, Louisville	1.88

Lowest On-Base Percentage

1.	Hecker, Louisville	.199
2.	Driscoll, Pittsburgh	.218
3.	H. McCormick, Cincinnati	.243
4.	White, Cincinnati	.244
5.	Salisbury, Pittsburgh	.253

FIELDING

Total Chances

1B	Comiskey, St. Louis	904
2B	Stricker, Philadelphia	542
3B	Carpenter, Cincinnati	364
SS	B. Gleason, St. Louis	510
OF	Sommer, Cincinnati	213
C	Snyder, Cincinnati	491
P	White, Cincinnati	257

Fielding Average

J. Latham, Philadelphia	.972
McPhee, Cincinnati	.920
Carpenter, Cincinnati	.835
Mack, Louisville	.898
Sommer, Cincinnati	.925
J. O'Brien, Philadelphia	.925
White, Cincinnati	.957

CINCINNATI   Pop Snyder   Bank Street Grounds

		G	AB	H	R	2B	3B	HR	RBI	BB	BA	SA
LF	Joe Sommer	80	**354**	102	82	12	6	1	—	24	.288	.364
3B	Hick Carpenter	80	351	**120**	78	15	5	1	—	10	.342	.422
RF	Harry Wheeler	76	344	86	59	11	11	1	—	7	.250	.355
SS	Chick Fulmer	79	324	91	54	13	4	0	—	10	.281	.346
2B	Bid McPhee	78	311	71	43	8	7	1	31	11	.228	.309
C	Pop Snyder	72	309	90	49	12	2	1	—	9	.291	.353
CF	Jimmy Macullar	79	299	70	44	6	6	0	—	14	.234	.294
1B	Dan Stearns	49	214	55	28	10	2	0	—	6	.257	.322
P	Will White	54	207	55	28	4	0	0	—	5	.266	.285
1B	Henry Luff	28	120	28	16	2	2	0	—	2	.233	.283
P	Harry McCormick	26	93	12	3	0	1	0	—	1	.129	.151
Sub	Phil Powers	16	60	13	4	1	1	0	—	3	.217	.267
Sub	Rudy Kemmler	3	11	1	0	1	0	0	—	0	.091	.182
Sub	Tug Thompson	1	5	1	0	0	0	0	—	0	.000	.000
Sub	Bill Tierney	1	5	0	1	0	0	0	—	0	.000	.000
		80	3007	**795**	**489**	95	47	5	—	102	**.264**	.332

1B   Stearns 35, Luff 27, Wheeler 12, Powers 5, Snyder 2, Tierney 1
2B   McPhee 78, Stearns 2
SS   Fulmer 79, Stearns 1
3B   Carpenter 80
OF   Sommer 80, Macullar 79, Wheeler 64, Stearns 12, McCormick 2, White 2, Luff 1, Thompson 1, Kemmler 1, Powers 1, Snyder 1
C   Snyder 70, Powers 10, Kemmler 3
P   White 54, McCormick 25, Wheeler 4

	G	IP	GS	CG	W	L	K	BB	SH	SV	ERA
Will White	54	**480**	54	**52**	**40**	12	122	71	**8**	0	1.54
Harry McCormick	25	219.2	25	24	14	11	33	42	3	0	1.52
Harry Wheeler	4	21.2	1	1	1	2	10	12	0	0	5.40
		721.1	80	**77**	55	25	165	125	**11**	0	**1.67**

PHILADELPHIA Juice Latham   Oakdale Park

		G	AB	H	R	2B	3B	HR	RBI	BB	BA	SA
LF	Jud Birchall	75	338	89	65	12	1	0	—	8	.263	.305
1B	Juice Latham	74	323	92	47	10	2	0	—	10	.285	.328
RF	Bob Blakiston	72	281	64	40	4	1	0	—	9	.228	.249
2B	Cub Stricker	72	272	59	34	6	1	0	—	15	.217	.246
C	Jack O'Brien	62	241	73	44	13	3	3	—	13	.303	.419
SS	Lew Say	49	199	45	35	4	3	1	—	8	.226	.291
Sub	Jerry Dorgan	44	181	51	25	9	1	0	—	4	.282	.343
P	Sam Weaver	43	155	36	19	3	0	0	—	12	.232	.252
CF	John Mansell	31	126	30	17	3	1	0	—	4	.238	.278
3B	Fred Mann	29	121	28	13	7	4	0	—	4	.231	.355
P	Bill Sweeney	23	88	14	8	4	0	0	—	4	.159	.205
SS	Jimmy Say	22	82	17	12	2	0	1	—	1	.207	.268
Sub	John Richmond	18	65	12	8	2	2	0	—	11	.185	.277
Sub	Pop Smith	20	65	6	10	0	0	0	—	12	.092	.092
P	Frank Mountain	9	36	12	5	3	0	0	—	2	.333	.417
Sub	Bill Kienzle	9	33	11	8	3	2	0	—	5	.333	.545
Sub	Joe Straub	8	32	6	2	2	0	0	—	1	.188	.250
Sub	Bill Greenwood	7	30	9	8	1	0	0	—	1	.300	.333
P	Doc Landis	3	12	2	1	0	0	0	—	0	.167	.167
P	Charlie Reynolds	2	8	1	1	0	0	0	—	0	.125	.125
Sub	Bill Farrell	2	7	2	2	1	0	0	—	1	.286	.429
Sub	Tug Arundel	1	5	0	0	0	0	0	—	0	.000	.000
P	Ed Halbriter	1	4	0	0	0	0	0	—	0	.000	.000
P	George Snyder	1	3	1	2	0	0	0	—	0	.333	.333
		75	2707	660	406	89	21	5	—	125	.244	.298

1B   Latham 74, O'Brien 1
2B   Stricker 72, Smith 2, Greenwood 2, Blakiston 1, Birchall 1
SS   L. Say 49, J. Say 22, Smith 4
3B   Blakiston 34, Mann 29, Smith 11, Dorgan 1, O'Brien 1
OF   Birchall 74, Blakiston 38, Mansell 31, Dorgan 22, Richmond 18, O'Brien 18, Kienzle 9, Greenwood 7, Sweeney 5, Smith 3, Weaver 2, Farrell 1, Straub 1, Reynolds 1, Landis 1, Mountain 1, Stricker 1
C   O'Brien 45, Dorgan 25, Straub 7, Arundel 1, Farrell 1
P   Weaver 42, Sweeney 20, Mountain 8, Landis 2, Stricker 2, Reynolds 2, Snyder 1, Halbriter 1, Wolf 1

	G	IP	GS	CG	W	L	K	BB	SH	SV	ERA
Sam Weaver	42	371	41	41	26	15	104	35	2	0	2.74
Bill Sweeney	20	170	20	18	9	11	48	42	0	0	2.91
Frank Mountain	8	69	8	8	2	5	15	11	0	0	3.91
Doc Landis	2	17	2	2	1	**1***	13	1	0	0	3.18
Charlie Reynolds	2	12	2	1	1	1	4	3	0	0	5.25
George Snyder	1	9	1	1	1	0	0	2	0	0	0.00
Ed Halbriter	1	8	1	1	0	1	4	4	0	0	7.88
Cub Stricker	2	7	0	0	1	0	2	1	0	0	1.29
		663	75	72	41	34	190	99	2	0	2.99

LOUISVILLE   Denny Mack   Eclipse Park (I)

		G	AB	H	R	2B	3B	HR	RBI	BB	BA	SA
1B	Guy Hecker	78	340	94	62	14	4	3	—	5	.276	.368
RF	Chicken Wolf	78	318	95	46	11	8	0	—	9	.299	.384
P	Tony Mullane	77	303	78	46	13	1	0	—	13	.257	.307
2B	Pete Browning	69	288	109	67	17	3	5	—	26	**.378**	**.510**
LF	Leech Maskrey	76	288	65	30	14	2	0	—	9	.226	.288
C	Dan Sullivan	67	286	78	44	8	2	0	—	9	.273	.315
CF	John Reccius	74	266	63	46	12	3	1	—	23	.237	.316
SS	Denny Mack	72	264	48	41	3	1	0	—	16	.182	.201
3B	Bill Schenck	60	231	60	37	11	3	0	—	8	.260	.333
Sub	John Strick	32	110	18	17	6	1	0	—	9	.164	.236
Sub	Gracie Pierce	9	33	10	3	1	0	0	—	1	.303	.333
Sub	Joe Crotty	5	20	2	1	0	0	0	—	0	.100	.100
Sub	Phil Reccius	4	15	2	0	0	0	0	—	0	.133	.133
Sub	Charlie Bohn	4	13	2	0	0	0	0	—	0	.154	.154
Sub	Pop Smith	3	11	2	1	0	0	0	—	0	.182	.182
Sub	Harry McCaffrey	1	4	1	1	0	0	0	—	0	.250	.250
Sub	Jimmy Say	1	4	1	1	0	0	0	—	0	.250	.250
Sub	Amos Booth	1	4	0	0	0	0	0	—	0	.000	.000
Sub	John Dyler	1	4	0	0	0	0	0	—	0	.000	.000
Sub	Harry Maskrey	1	4	0	0	0	0	0	—	0	.000	.000
Sub	Ed Merrill	1	0	0	0	0	0	0	—	0	—	—
		79	2806	728	443	**110**	28	9	—	**128**	.259	.328

1B   Hecker 66, Mullane 13, Strick 1, Wolf 1
2B   Browning 42, Mack 24, Pierce 9, Strick 6, Mullane 2, McCaffrey 1, Booth 1, L. Maskrey 1
SS   Mack 49, Browning 18, Wolf 9, Smith 3, Schenck 2, Sullivan 1, Strick 1
3B   Schenck 58, Browning 13, Sullivan 10, Say 1
OF   L. Maskrey 76, Wolf 70, J.Reccius 65, Mullane 12, Strick 6, Mack 5, Sullivan 4, P. Reccius 4, Hecker 2, Bohn 2, H. Maskrey 1, Dyler 1, Merrill 1
C   Sullivan 54, Strick 21, Crotty 5
P   Mullane 55, Hecker 13, Reccius 13, Schenck 2, Bohn 2, Wolf 1

	G	IP	GS	CG	W	L	K	BB	SH	SV	ERA
Tony Mullane #	**55**	460.1	**55**	51	30	24	**170**	78	5	0	1.88
Guy Hecker ##	13	104	11	10	6	6	33	5	0	0	1.30
John Reccius	13	95	10	9	4	6	31	22	1	0	3.03
Charlie Bohn	2	18	2	2	1	1	1	3	0	0	3.00
Bill Schenck	2	10	1	1	1	0	4	1	0	0	0.90
Chicken Wolf	1	6	0	0	0	0	1	3	0	0	9.00
		693.1	79	73	42	37	240	112	6	0	2.03

\# No-hit game 2 0 vs Cincinnati, September 11
\#\# No-hit game 3–1 vs Pittsburgh, September 19

PITTSBURGH Al Pratt Exposition Park (I)

		G	AB	H	R	2B	3B	HR	RBI	BB	BA	SA
LF	Mike Mansell	79	347	96	59	18	**16**	2	—	7	.277	.438
SS	John Peters	78	333	96	46	10	1	0	—	4	.288	.324
RF	Ed Swartwood	76	325	107	**86**	18	11	4	—	21	.329	.489
UT	Billy Taylor	70	299	84	40	16	13	3	—	7	.281	.452
2B	George Strief	79	297	58	45	9	6	2	—	13	.195	.286
CF	Jack Leary	60	257	75	32	7	3	1	—	5	.292	.354
1B	Chappy Lane	57	214	38	26	8	2	3	—	5	.178	.276
3B	Joe Battin	34	133	28	13	5	1	1	—	3	.211	.286
P	Harry Salisbury	39	145	22	17	2	0	0	—	4	.152	.166
OF	Charlie Morton	25	103	29	12	0	3	0	—	5	.282	.340
C	Rudy Kemmler	24	99	25	7	4	0	0	—	1	.253	.293
C	Jim Keenan	25	96	21	10	7	0	1	—	1	.219	.323
P	Denny Driscoll	23	80	11	12	2	0	1	—	3	.138	.200
Sub	Bill Morgan	17	66	17	10	2	1	0	—	4	.258	.318
P	Harry Arundel	14	53	10	8	0	0	0	—	5	.189	.189
Sub	Jake Goodman	10	41	13	5	2	2	0	—	2	.317	.463
P	Morrie Critchley	1	5	0	0	0	0	0	—	0	.000	.000
P	Jake Seymour	1	4	0	0	0	0	0	—	0	.000	.000
Sub	Russ McKelvey	1	4	0	0	0	0	0	—	0	.000	.000
Sub	Ren Wylie	1	3	0	0	0	0	0	—	0	.000	.000
		79	2904	730	428	**110**	**59**	**18**	—	90	.251	**.348**

1B   Lane 43, Taylor 23, Goodman 10, Swartwood 4, Leary 1
2B   Strief 78, Leary 1, Peters 1
SS   Peters 77, Keenan 1, Morton 1, Arundel 1, Strief 1
3B   Battin 34, Leary 33, Taylor 14, Morton 3
OF   Mansell 79, Swartwood 73, Leary 27, Morton 25, Lane 13, Morgan 11, Taylor 8, Keenan 3, Wylie 1, McKelvy 1, Kemmler 1, Salisbury 1
C   Taylor 27, Kemmler 23, Keenan 22, Morgan 7, Lane 2
P   Salisbury 38, Driscoll 23, Arundel 14, Leary 3, Critchley 1, Seymour 1, Taylor 1

	G	IP	GS	CG	W	L	K	BB	SH	SV	ERA
Harry Salisbury	38	335	38	38	20	18	135	37	1	0	2.63
Denny Driscoll	23	201	23	23	13	9	59	12	0	0	**1.21**
Harry Arundel	14	120	14	13	4	10	47	23	0	0	4.65
Jack Leary	3	18.2	2	1	1	0	5	3	0	0	6.27
Morrie Critchley	1	9	1	1	1	0	3	1	1	0	0.00
Jake Seymour	1	8	1	1	0	1	2	2	0	0	7.88
Billy Taylor	1	5	0	0	0	1	1	4	0	0	16.20
		696.2	79	77	39	39	**252**	**82**	2	0	2.79

ST. LOUIS Ned Cuthbert Sportsman's Park (I)

		G	AB	H	R	2B	3B	HR	RBI	BB	BA	SA
SS	Bill Gleason	79	347	100	63	11	6	1	—	6	.288	.363
3B	Jack Gleason	78	331	84	53	10	1	2	—	**27**	.254	.308
1B	Charlie Comiskey	78	329	80	58	9	5	1	45	4	.243	.310
CF	Oscar Walker	76	318	76	48	15	7	**7**	—	10	.239	.396
2B	Bill Smiley	59	240	51	30	4	2	0	—	6	.213	.246
LF	Ned Cuthbert	60	233	52	28	16	5	0	—	17	.223	.325
P	Jumbo McGinnis	51	203	44	17	6	4	0	—	3	.217	.286
C	Sleeper Sullivan	51	188	34	24	3	3	0	—	3	.181	.229
Sub	Harry McCaffrey	38	153	42	23	8	6	0	—	3	.275	.405
RF	George Seward	38	144	31	23	1	1	0	—	12	.215	.236

		G	AB	H	R	2B	3B	HR	RBI	BB	BA	SA
Sub	Ed Fusselbach	35	136	31	13	2	0	0	—	5	.228	.243
Sub	Ed Brown	17	60	11	4	0	0	0	—	4	.183	.183
P	Jack Schappert	15	50	9	7	1	0	0	—	7	.180	.200
Sub	Charlie Morton	9	32	2	2	0	1	0	—	2	.063	.125
Sub	Joe Crotty	8	28	4	2	1	0	0	—	3	.143	.179
P	Bert Dorr	8	26	4	2	0	0	0	—	0	.154	.154
P	Morrie Critchley	4	14	3	0	0	0	0	—	0	.214	.214
P	John Doyle	3	11	2	0	0	0	0	—	0	.182	.182
Sub	Frank Decker	2	8	2	0	0	0	0	—	0	.250	.250
Sub	John Shoupe	2	7	0	1	0	0	0	—	0	.000	.000
P	Bobby Mitchell	1	4	0	0	0	0	0	—	0	.000	.000
P	Eddie Hogan	1	3	1	1	0	0	0	—	0	.333	.333
		79	2865	663	399	87	41	11	—	112	.231	.302

1B   Comiskey 77, McCaffrey 1, Schappert 1. Walker 1
2B   Smiley 57, McCaffrey 8, Morton 7, Brown 2, Decker 2, Shoupe 2, McGinnis 1, J. Gleason 1, Walker 1
SS   B. Gleason 79
3B   J. Gleason 73, McCaffrey 8
OF   Walker 75, Cuthbert 60, Seward 35, McCaffrey 23, Fusselbach 15, Brown 15, McGinnis 6, J. Gleason 6, Morton 3, Smiley 2, Crotty 1, Mitchell 1, Schappert 1
C   Sullivan 50, Fusselbach 19, Crotty 7, Seward 5, McGinnis 1
P   McGinnis 45, Schappert 15, Dorr 8, Critchley 4, Fusselbach 4, Doyle 3, Comiskey 2, Hogan 1, Brown 1, Mitchell 1

	G	IP	GS	CG	W	L	K	BB	SH	SV	ERA
Jumbo McGinnis	45	388.1	45	43	25	18	134	53	3	0	2.60
Jack Schappert	15	128	14	13	8	7	38	32	0	0	3.52
Bert Dorr	8	66	8	8	2	6	34	1	0	0	2.59
Morrie Critchley	4	34	4	4	0	4	2	7	0	0	4.24
John Doyle	3	24	3	3	0	3	5	3	0	0	2.63
Ed Fusselbach	4	23	2	2	1	2	3	2	0	1	4.70
Charlie Comiskey	2	8	1	1	0	1	2	3	0	0	0.00
Eddie Hogan	1	8	1	1	0	1	4	0	0	0	1.13
Bobby Mitchell	1	7	1	0	0	1	2	2	0	0	7.71
Ed Brown	1	2	0	0	0	0	1	0	0	0	0.00
		688.1	79	75	36	43	225	103	3	1	2.92

BALTIMORE   **Henry Myers**   **Newington Park**

		G	AB	H	R	2B	3B	HR	RBI	BB	BA	SA
C	Ed Whiting	74	308	80	43	14	5	0	—	7	.260	.338
1B	Charlie Householder	74	307	78	42	10	7	1	—	4	.254	.342
SS	Henry Myers	69	294	53	43	3	0	0	—	12	.180	.190
3B	Jimmy Shetzline	73	282	62	23	8	3	0	—	5	.220	.270
LF	Charlie Waitt	72	250	39	19	4	0	0	—	13	.156	.172
RF	Tom Brown	45	181	55	30	5	2	1	23	6	.304	.370
P	Doc Landis	50	175	29	9	1	0	0	—	3	.166	.171
CF	Monk Cline	44	172	38	18	6	2	0	—	3	.221	.279
2B	Gracie Pierce	41	151	30	8	2	1	0	—	3	.199	.225
Sub	Harry Jacoby	31	121	21	17	1	1	1	—	7	.174	.223
P	Tricky Nichols	26	95	15	4	1	0	0	—	7	.158	.168
Sub	Bill Smiley	16	61	9	3	0	0	0	—	0	.148	.148
P	Emil Geis	13	41	6	2	0	1	0	—	1	.146	.195
Sub	Nick Scharf	10	39	8	4	1	1	1	—	0	.205	.359
Sub	Frank Burt	10	36	4	2	2	1	0	—	1	.111	.222
P	Bill Wise	5	20	2	2	1	0	0	—	0	.100	.150
P	Jack Leary	4	18	4	3	1	0	0	—	0	.222	.278
Sub	Bill Jones	4	15	1	1	0	0	0	—	0	.067	.067
Sub	Tom Evers	1	4	0	0	0	0	0	—	0	.000	.000
Sub	Harry East	1	4	0	0	0	0	0	—	0	.000	.000
P	John Russ	1	3	1	0	0	0	0	—	0	.333	.333
Sub	L. Smith	1	3	0	0	0	0	0	—	0	.000	.000
Sub	Amos Booth	1	3	0	0	0	0	0	—	0	.000	.000
		74	2583	535	273	60	24	4	—	72	.207	.254

1B	Householder 74, Whiting 3
2B	Pierce 38, Shetzline 20, Smiley 16, Cline 2, Evers 1, Scharf 1
SS	Myers 68, Cline 8, Smiley 2, Shetzline 1, Pierce 1
3B	Shetzline 52, Jacoby 19, Booth 1, East 1, Cline 1
OF	Waitt 72, Brown 45, Cline 39, Landis 15, Nichols 14, Jacoby 13, Burt 10, Scharf 9, Geiss 4, Pierce 3, Jones 2, Whiting 2, Wise 2, Smith 1, Leary 1, Russ 1, Shetzline 1
C	Whiting 72, Householder 3, Jones 2
P	Landis 42, Nichols 16, Geiss 13, Myers 6, Wise 3, Leary 3, Brown 2, Russ 1

	G	IP	GS	CG	W	L	K	BB	SH	SV	ERA
Doc Landis	42	341	39	35	11	**27***	62	46	0	0	3.33
Tricky Nichols	16	118.1	13	12	1	12	21	17	0	0	5.02
Emil Geis	13	95.2	13	10	4	9	10	22	1	0	4.80
Henry Myers	6	26	2	1	0	2	7	4	0	0	6.58
Bill Wise	3	26	3	3	1	2	9	4	0	0	2.77
Jack Leary	3	26	3	3	2	1	2	8	0	0	1.38
Tom Brown	2	8.1	0	0	0	0	2	6	0	0	1.08
John Russ	1	5	1	0	0	1	0	1	0	0	7.20
		646.1	74	64	19	54	113	108	1	0	3.88

1883
PEACE COMES
IN PARLOR 9

On Saturday, February 17, 1883, at the Fifth Avenue Hotel in New York, three National League and three American Association delegates met face to face for the first time in an attempt to thrash out their differences. Newly elected president Abraham Mills was the league's chief spokesman while Opie Caylor, Cincinnati's club secretary and one of the Association's founders, grabbed the floor most often for the upstart loop. Out of that confabulation between the two wary solons came a temporary agreement to raise the reserve rule to 11 men per team and to honor each other's contracts and blacklists.

But while the peace overture caused Association president Denny McKnight to lift his ban against playing interleague exhibition games, the two warriors remained at odds as to the rules under which such games should be played. The League in 1883 resurrected its 1880 rule that a foul ball had to be caught on the fly before a batter could be retired; the Association continued the archaic one-bounce out rule. Beginning in 1883, the League cut another link to the past by allowing its umpires to call for a new ball at any time; the Association still required an umpire to wait until the close of a complete inning before replacing a ball that was damaged or water-logged. There were other smaller differences too, and it remained to be seen which set of rules would prevail when the two rivals met on the playing field.

Action commenced in earnest in both circuits on May 1. Cincinnati again appeared to be the team to beat in the Association after shoring up weaknesses at center field and first base by enlisting Pop Corkhill and Long John Reilly. St. Louis also looked much improved for having pilfered the multitalented Tony Mullane from Louisville to join teenage workhorse Jumbo McGinnis in the box, and the Philadelphia Athletics were the Association's most altered team after cornering such veteran League performers as Harry Stovey, Lon Knight, George Bradley and Bobby Mathews.

In contrast, the Chicago White Stockings were the least changed nine in the majors. Seeing no reason to stir the mix that had brought him three straight League pennants, Cap Anson kept all but one of his 1882 regular cast. Banjo-hitting Hugh Nicol (.199) was told

FAMOUS FIRSTS IV

In the Philadelphia Athletics' final game of the 1883 season at Columbus on September 13, newcomer Al West filled in for the A's regular shortstop, Mike Moynahan. After Philadelphia won, West divulged that he was really Al Hubbard, a member of Yale's intercollegiate championship team that spring. Two days later, under his real name, Hubbard went behind the bat in Cincinnati to handle his former Yale teammate, Jack Jones. Hubbard and Jones thereupon became the first college battery to perform together in a major league game. It was a less than auspicious initiation for the two Elis as Cincinnati handed Jones his first defeat as an Athletic, an 11–0 drubbing that was the A's worst loss of the season. Hubbard never played again in the majors, but some two weeks later Jones beat Louisville ace Guy Hecker to clinch the 1883 American Association pennant for the A's. it proved to be his final major league outing. Following the 1883 season, Jones quit baseball to follow in the family footsteps by going to dental school. Both of Jones's parents were dentists. In fact, his mother Emeline was the first woman in the United States to open her own dental office. Later Jones also went to medical school. In 1916 he gave up his dental practice to teach voice training and maintained teaching studios at opera houses in New York City, New Haven and Bridgeport, Connecticut. He died in 1936, leaving no surviving relatives.

A childhood illness left Ed Dundon deaf but didn't stop him from pitching for Columbus's first major league entry in 1883. Dundon forced umpires to develop signals whether a pitch was a ball or a strike so he could be kept abreast of the count.

Buck Ewing, the National League's 1883 home run king as he looked 14 years later at the helm of the 1897 Cincinnati Reds. In 1883, Ewing, a Queen City native, promised to play with Cincinnati and then reneged when the NL put a team in New York. Another dozen years would pass before Ewing would come home to play. Standing: Dummy Hoy, Stub Brown, Claude Ritchey, Bug Holliday, Billy Rhines, Jake Beckley, Dusty Miller, Heinie Peitz, Farmer Vaughn, Pop Schriver. Seated: Frank Dwyer, Bid McPhee, Tommy Corcoran, Ewing, Charlie Irwin, Ted Breiten, Red Ehret. Front: Eddie Burke, Mascot (George), Bill Damman.

FAMOUS FIRSTS V

As a Boston rookie in 1881, Jim Whitney became the first pitcher ever to lead a major league in both wins and losses in the same season. Whitney's feat has been matched since—albeit just once—but his work in 1882 has never been matched. That season Whitney became the lone player ever to lead a major league team in wins, home runs, batting and slugging. In 1883, Whitney was content simply to lead Boston in wins, although he also platooned in the outfield with fellow pitcher Charlie Buffinton. Between them, the pair not only accounted for all but one of Boston's 63 wins but also concealed the fact that Boston lacked a center fielder. Edgar Smith, expected to man the post, played only 30 games in the outfield, while Whitney and Buffinton patroled center in the majority of the club's 98 championship contests to become the first and, to date, the only duo ever to serve as both pitching and centerfield tandem for a club.

HOSS RADBOURN'S EASIEST WIN

In their inaugural game in the National League on May 1, 1883, the Philadelphia Quakers gave the Providence Grays fits before finally bowing 4–3. Not until nearly two weeks later, though, did the Quakers first taste victory, beating Chicago. By midsummer the Quakers were so deep in the cellar that the league grudgingly gave them permission to reduce their ticket prices to a quarter so they could compete for fans with the American Association entry in Philadelphia. In search of perks he could use on the road for drawing power, Quakers manager Bob Ferguson gave the ball to Art Hagan, the pride of the mill town of Lonsdale, Rhode Island, when Philadelphia played at Providence on August 21.

Hagan was coming off several rough outings on the Quakers' recent western road swing, but Ferguson figured that Hagan's local reputation would outweigh news of them. He was right. Providence's Messer Park was thronged with a delegation from neighboring Lonsdale as well as several other nearby mill towns. They saw a memorable game if not one they cared to remember. William Perrin wrote: "Hagan started for the Grays and the Grays finished Hagan. He was given the most tremendous punishment ever administered to a pitcher in the major leagues." Normally one would allow for Perrin's bias as the Grays' foremost historian, but in this case not. Hagan gave up 11 runs in four innings, and it got worse. Perrin thought "Ferguson, perhaps in the kindness of heart and good wishes for the large delegation from Lonsdale and way stations, kept Hagan at his task," but others thought Ferguson was a sadist. On August 21, 1883, Hagan was at the wrong end of the most one-sided shutout in major league history. In his 28–0 loss the Quakers made 20 errors behind him. At the right end of the lopsided score was Grays ace Hoss Radbourn, headed for 48 wins in 1883 to set a new major league record that would last only until the following year when he established the current mark of 60.

to seek employment elsewhere, and King Kelly was returned to right field and Tom Burns to shortstop, making way for second sacker Fred Pfeffer. But Chicago got off to a rocky start, losing four of its first six games in back-to-back series with Detroit, while Providence was sweeping successive series with Philadelphia and New York, the league's two new entries.

At 6–0, the Grays were the only team in the majors with a perfect record before suffering their initial loss of the season on May 10 to the Cleveland Blues. The first leg of the League race then boiled down to a two-team tussle between the Grays and the Blues. On July 7, Providence held the top rung at 33–16 with Cleveland a mere three wins behind at 30–15 and Boston and Chicago completing the first division. Six weeks later, on August 20, Cleveland occupied first at 45–27 with Providence right behind, but when the Blues fin-

John Morrill did duty in Boston for over ten years at all four infield positions and also pitched and caught on occasion. He is the only man to play in a Boston uniform under Harry Wright and King Kelly, two managers about as diverse as imaginable in their approach to the game.

ished the month with two losses to Chicago and Providence dropped two at Boston, it became a four-team chase.

The Red Caps went to the fore by winning six straight games, but the Grays broke the streak with back-to-back wins at Providence on September 6 and 7 and came swiftly back into the race. The following day, in Boston, Jim Whitney opposed Hoss Radbourn of the Grays in the pivotal game of the season. A 2–2 tie at the end of regulation length seemed decided when Providence scored a run in the top of the 11th inning, but Joe Hornung tripled in the tying tally in the bottom half and sped home moments later on Jack Burdock's game-winning hit. The tense 4–3 victory was the spark Boston needed. The Red Caps won 13 of their next 14 games to break open what to that point had been a tight race. To John Morrill belonged the distinction of being the first manager ever to win a pennant after taking over a team in midstream. Not until the season was past the halfway mark had Morrill replaced Burdock as Boston's field general. Under the veteran first sacker's guidance the Red Caps played at a torrid .750 clip, winning 33 of their last 44 games.

Boston's overall .643 winning percentage was more than matched by the St. Louis Browns, which played at a .663 pace in 1883, but .663 ball was not sufficient to land the American Association flag. To owner Chris Von der Ahe's chagrin, his Browns trailed the Philadelphia Athletics by two and a half games on the morning of the next-to-last Sunday of the season. George Bradley's 9–2 win for the Athletics that afternoon before a packed house in St. Louis's Sportsman's Park appeared to wrap up the Association title. But the Athletics then proceeded to drop two games at Louisville in their season-closing series while St. Louis was belting Pittsburgh. Still needing one more win to clinch, Philadelphia nailed it on September 28 when Jack Jones topped Guy Hecker 7–6 in 10 innings. A loss two afternoons later on Sunday, the last day of the season, while St. Louis again beat

The boozing, brawling, bad-ass 1883 Alleghenys. Top: Henry Oberbeck, Ed Swartwood, Billy Taylor, Joe Battin and George Creamer. Middle: Jackie Hayes, Buttercup Dickerson, manager Al Pratt, Mike Mansell, and The Only Nolan. Bottom: Denny Driscoll, John Peters and Frank McLaughlin. Hayes was last spotted in the San Francisco area in 1913 when Bill Lange wrote to Cincinnati owner Garry Herrmann begging help for the old catcher who was "stone deaf and . . . cannot walk or get anywhere without assistance." Herrmann sent Hayes $20, but after that he disappeared. His final resting place is still unknown. Taylor's wife was a female ball player. The two married in November 1883 against everyone's advice, and soon thereafter Taylor was collared for robbing an ex-beau of his new wife's.

Pittsburgh shrank the Athletics' final victory margin to one game, the narrowest in history to that point.

Returning to Philadelphia, the Athletics played several exhibition games against the crosstown Quakers that were viewed as a tune-up for a postseason series with League champion Boston. When the lowly Quakers, winners of just 17.3 percent of their games during the regular League season, dealt the Association titlists a string of embarrassing defeats, Athletics officials hastily revised their plans to settle loop supremacy on the field by meeting Boston.

On October 27, the rival leagues again met off the field, however at the Fifth Avenue Hotel in New York. As in February, Mills led the proceeding on the League's behalf and Caylor was the Association's main voice. In Parlor 9 the two, with help from five of their confreres, crafted a permanent peace settlement in the form of a 10-amendment constitution that would be known thereafter as "The National Agreement." Strong and enduring as that agreement felt when the seven League and Association officials adjourned from Parlor 9 that evening, within a week another group of baseball men would embark on a series of meetings designed to undermine it.

THE SEASONAL RECORD

NATIONAL LEAGUE

	W	L	PCT	HOME	ROAD	GB
1. Boston Beaneaters	63	35	.643	41–8	22–27	—
2. Chicago White Stockings	59	39	.602	36–13	23–26	4
3. Providence Grays	58	40	.592	34–15	24–25	5
4. Cleveland Blues	55	42	.567	31–18	24–24	7.5
5. Buffalo Bisons	52	45	.536	36–13	16–32	10.5
6. New York Gothams	46	50	.479	28–19	18–31	16
7. Detroit Wolverines	40	58	.408	23–26	17–32	23
8. Philadelphia Quakers	17	81	.173	9–40	8–41	46

	Bos	Chi	Pro	Cle	Buf	NY	Det	Phi	
Boston	—	7	8	10	7	7	10	14	63
Chicago	7	—	7	6	9	9	9	12	59
Providence	6	7	—	6	7	9	12	11	58
Cleveland	4	8	8	—	7	7	9	12	55
Buffalo	7	5	7	7	—	8	9	9	52
New York	7	5	5	6	5	—	6	12	46
Detroit	4	5	2	5	5	8	—	11	40
Philadelphia	0	2	3	2	5	2	3	—	17
	35	39	40	42	45	50	58	81	390

SEASON LEADERS

Batting Average (225 ABs)
1. Brouthers, Buffalo .374
2. Connor, New York .357
3. Gore, Chicago .334
4. Burdock, Boston .330
5. O'Rourke, Buffalo .328

On–Base Percentage
1. Brouthers, Buffalo .397
2. Connor, New York .394
3. Gore, Chicago .377
4. Dunlap, Cleveland .371
5. Burdock, Boston .353

Slugging Average
1. Brouthers, Buffalo .572
2. Morrill, Boston .525
3. Connor, New York .506
4. Gross, Philadelphia .489
5. Sutton, Boston .486

Total Bases
1. Brouthers, Buffalo 243
2. Morrill, Boston 212
3. Connor, New York 207
4. Sutton, Boston 201
5. Hornung, Boston 199

Home Runs

1.	Ewing, New York	10
2.	Hornung, Boston	8
	Denny, Providence	8
4.	Ward, New York	7
5.	Morrill, Boston	6

Hits

1.	Brouthers, Buffalo	159
2.	Connor, New York	156
3.	O'Rourke, Buffalo	143
4.	Sutton, Boston	134
5.	Wood, Detroit	133

Bases on Balls

1.	York, Cleveland	37
2.	Hanlon, Detroit	34
3.	Powell, Detroit	28
4.	Gore, Chicago	27
	Shaffer, Buffalo	27

RBI

1.	Brouthers, Buffalo	97
2.	Burdock, Boston	88
3.	Sutton, Boston	73
4.	Morrill, Boston	68
	Anson, Chicago	68

Runs

1.	Hornung, Boston	107
2.	Gore, Chicago	105
3.	O'Rourke, Buffalo	102
4.	Sutton, Boston	101
5.	Hines, Providence	94

Strikeouts

1.	Galvin, Buffalo	79
2.	Wise, Boston	74
3.	Flint, Chicago	69
4.	Morrill, Boston	68
5.	Corcoran, Chicago	62

PITCHING

Wins

1.	Radbourn, Providence	48
2.	Galvin, Buffalo	46
3.	Whitney, Boston	37
4.	Corcoran, Chicago	34
5.	McCormick, Cleveland	28

Innings

1.	Galvin, Buffalo	656.1
2.	Radbourn, Providence	632.1
3.	Coleman, Philadelphia	538.1
4.	Whitney, Boston	514
5.	Corcoran, Chicago	473.2

Strikeouts

1.	Whitney, Boston	345
2.	Radbourn, Providence	315
3.	Galvin, Buffalo	279
4.	Corcoran, Chicago	216
5.	Buffinton, Boston	188

ERA (98 innings)

1.	McCormick, Cleveland	1.84
2.	Radbourn, Providence	2.05
3.	Whitney, Boston	2.24
4.	Sawyer, Cleveland	2.36
5.	Daily, Cleveland	2.42

Losses

1.	Coleman, Philadelphia	48
2.	Galvin, Buffalo	29
3.	Radbourn, Providence	25
4.	Weidman, Detroit	24
5.	Welch, New York	23

Complete Games

1.	Galvin, Buffalo	72
2.	Radbourn, Providence	66
3.	Coleman, Philadelphia	59
4.	Whitney, Boston	54
5.	Corcoran, Chicago	51

Winning Percentage (25 decisions)

1.	McCormick, Cleveland	.700
2.	Radbourn, Providence	.648
3.	Buffinton, Boston	.641
4.	Whitney, Boston	.638
5.	Corcoran, Chicago	.630

Lowest On–Base Percentage

1.	Radbourn, Providence	.244
2.	Whitney, Boston	.251
3.	Galvin, Buffalo	.265
4.	Ward, New York	.267
5.	McCormick, Cleveland	.268

FIELDING

Total Chances

1B	Brouthers, Buffalo	1119
2B	Farrell, Providence	674
3B	Williamson, Chicago	450
SS	Houck, Detroit	575
OF	Wood, Detroit	275
C	M. Hines, Boston	547
P	Radbourn, Providence	187

Fielding Average

Morrill, Boston	.974
Farrell, Providence	.924
Denny, Providence	.876
Glasscock, Cleveland	.922
Hornung, Boston	.936
Bennett, Detroit	.944
Daily, Cleveland	.939

BOSTON   Jack Burdock (30–24)   John Morrill (33–11)   South End Grounds (I)

		G	AB	H	R	2B	3B	HR	RBI	BB	BA	SA
LF	Joe Hornung	98	**446**	124	**107**	25	13	8	66	8	.278	.446
3B	Ezra Sutton	94	414	134	101	28	15	3	73	17	.324	.486
P	Jim Whitney	96	409	115	78	27	10	5	57	25	.281	.433
SS	Sam Wise	96	406	110	73	25	7	4	58	13	.271	.397
1B	John Morrill	97	404	129	83	33	16	6	68	15	.319	.525
2B	Jack Burdock	96	400	132	80	27	8	5	88	14	.330	.475
P	Charlie Buffinton	86	341	81	28	8	3	1	26	6	.238	.287
RF	Paul Radford	72	258	53	46	6	3	0	14	9	.205	.252
C	Mike Hines	63	231	52	38	13	1	0	16	7	.225	.290
C	Mert Hackett	46	179	42	20	8	6	2	24	1	.235	.380
CF	Edgar Smith	30	115	25	10	5	3	0	16	5	.217	.313
Sub	Lew Brown	14	54	13	5	4	1	0	9	3	.241	.352
		98	3657	1010	669	209	**86**	**34**	515	123	.276	**.408**

1B	Morrill 81, Brown 14, Buffinton 2, Whitney 2
2B	Burdock 96, Morrill 2
SS	Wise 96, Morrill 2, Sutton 1
3B	Sutton 93, Morrill 6, Hornung 1
OF	Hornung 98, Radford 72, Buffinton 51, Whitney 40, Smith 30, Morrill 7, Hines 7, Hackett 4, Sutton 1
C	Hines 59, Hackett 44, Smith 1
P	Whitney 62, Buffinton 43, Morrill 2

	G	IP	GS	CG	W	L	K	BB	SH	SV	ERA
Jim Whitney	62	514	56	54	37	21	**345**	35	1	**2**	2.24
Charlie Buffinton	43	333	41	34	25	14	188	51	4	1	3.03
John Morrill	2	13	1	1	1	0	5	4	0	0	2.77
*One combined shutout on Sept. 1; Buffinton 5 innings, Whitney 4 innings											
	860	98	89	63	35	**538**	**90**	6	**3**	2.55

CHICAGO   Cap Anson   Lake Front Park (II)

		G	AB	H	R	2B	3B	HR	RBI	BB	BA	SA
RF	King Kelly	98	428	109	92	28	10	3	61	16	.255	.388
1B	Cap Anson	98	413	127	70	36	5	0	68	18	.308	.419
SS	Tom Burns	97	405	119	69	37	7	2	67	13	.294	.435
3B	Ned Williamson	98	402	111	83	**49**	5	2	59	22	.276	.438
CF	George Gore	92	392	131	105	30	9	2	52	27	.334	.472
2B	Fred Pfeffer	96	371	87	41	22	7	1	45	8	.235	.340
LF	Abner Dalrymple	80	363	108	78	24	4	2	37	11	.298	.402
C	Silver Flint	85	332	88	57	23	4	0	32	3	.265	.358
P	Larry Corcoran	68	263	55	40	12	7	0	25	6	.209	.308
P	Fred Goldsmith	60	235	52	38	12	3	1	16	4	.221	.311
Sub	Billy Sunday	14	54	13	6	4	0	0	5	1	.241	.315
		98	3658	1000	**679**	**277**	61	13	**467**	129	.273	.393

1B   Anson 98, Goldsmith 2, Pfeffer 1
2B   Pfeffer 79, Burns 19, Kelly 3, Corcoran 1
SS   Burns 79, Pfeffer 18, Corcoran 3
3B   Williamson 97, Kelly 2, Pfeffer 1
OF   Gore 92, Kelly 82, Dalrymple 80, Flint 23, Goldsmith 16, Sunday 14, Corcoran 13, Burns 1, Anson 1
C   Flint 83, Kelly 38, Williamson 3, Anson 1
P   Corcoran 56, Goldsmith 46, Anson 2, Williamson 1, Kelly 1

	G	IP	GS	CG	W	L	K	BB	SH	SV	ERA
Larry Corcoran	56	473.2	53	51	34	20	216	82	3	0	2.49
Fred Goldsmith	46	383.1	45	40	25	19	82	39	2	0	3.15
Cap Anson	2	3	0	0	0	0	0	1	0	1	0.00
Ned Williamson	1	1	0	0	0	0	1	1	0	0	9.00
King Kelly	1	1	0	0	0	0	0	0	0	0	0.00
	862	98	91	59	39	299	123	5	1	2.78

PROVIDENCE   Harry Wright   Messer Street Grounds

		G	AB	H	R	2B	3B	HR	RBI	BB	BA	SA
CF	Paul Hines	97	442	132	94	32	4	4	45	18	.299	.416
2B	Jack Farrell	95	420	128	92	24	11	3	61	15	.305	.436
SS	Arthur Irwin	98	406	116	67	22	7	0	44	12	.286	.374
3B	Jerry Denny	98	393	108	73	26	8	8	55	9	.275	.443
P	Hoss Radbourn	89	381	108	59	11	3	3	48	14	.283	.352
1B	Joe Start	87	370	105	63	16	7	1	57	22	.284	.373
RF	John Cassidy	89	366	87	46	16	5	0	42	9	.238	.309
C	Barney Gilligan	74	263	52	34	13	3	0	24	26	.198	.270
LF	Cliff Carroll	58	238	63	37	12	3	1	20	4	.265	.353
P	Lee Richmond	49	194	55	41	8	6	1	19	15	.284	.402
C	Sandy Nava	29	100	24	18	4	2	0	16	3	.240	.320
P	Charlie Sweeney	22	87	19	9	3	0	0	15	2	.218	.253
Sub	Joe Mulvey	4	16	2	1	1	0	0	2	0	.125	.188
Sub	Edgar Smith	2	9	2	2	1	0	0	1	0	.222	.333
		98	3685	1001	636	189	59	21	449	149	.272	.372

1B   Start 87, Hines 9, Smith 2, Radbourn 2, Cassidy 1
2B   Farrell 95, Irwin 4, Cassidy 1
SS   Irwin 94, Mulvey 4
3B   Denny 98
OF   Hines 89, Cassidy 88, Carroll 58, Richmond 41, Radbourn 20, Sweeney 7, Smith 2, Nava 2
C   Gilligan 74, Nava 27
P   Radbourn 76, Sweeney 20, Richmond 12

	G	IP	GS	CG	W	L	K	BB	SH	SV	ERA
Hoss Radbourn #	**76**	632.1	68	66	**48**	25	315	56	4	1	2.05
Charlie Sweeney	20	146.2	18	14	7	7	48	28	0	0	3.13
Lee Richmond	12	92	12	8	3	7	13	27	0	0	3.33
—1 forfeit L vs Philadelphia on July 4 AM—											
	871		98	88	58	39	376	111	4	1	2.37

No-hit game 8–0 vs Cleveland, July 25

CLEVELAND   Frank Bancroft   Kennard Street Park

		G	AB	H	R	2B	3B	HR	RBI	BB	BA	SA
CF	Pete Hotaling	100	417	108	54	20	8	0	30	12	.259	.345
2B	Fred Dunlap	93	396	129	81	34	2	4	37	22	.326	.452
SS	Jack Glasscock	96	383	110	67	19	6	0	46	13	.287	.368
1B	Bill Phillips	97	382	94	42	29	8	2	40	8	.246	.380
LF	Tom York	100	381	99	56	29	5	2	46	**37**	.260	.378
3B	Mike Muldoon	98	378	86	54	22	3	0	29	10	.228	.302
RF	Jake Evans	90	332	79	36	13	2	0	31	8	.238	.289
C	Doc Bushong	63	215	37	15	5	0	0	9	7	.172	.195
P	Jim McCormick	43	157	37	21	2	2	0	13	2	.236	.274
C	Fatty Briody	40	145	34	23	5	1	0	10	3	.234	.283
P	One Arm Daily	45	142	18	18	1	0	0	5	10	.127	.134
P	Will Sawyer	17	47	1	3	0	0	0	0	3	.021	.021
Sub	Bill Crowley	11	41	12	3	5	0	0	5	1	.293	.415
Sub	George Bradley	4	16	5	0	0	1	0	1	0	.313	.438
P	Charlie Cady	3	11	0	0	0	0	0	0	1	.000	.000
Sub	Cal Broughton	4	10	2	2	0	0	0	1	2	.200	.200
Sub	Lem Hunter	1	4	1	1	0	0	0	0	0	.250	.250
		100	3457	852	476	184	38	8	303	139	.246	.329

1B   Phillips 97, Briody 2, McCormick 1
2B   Dunlap 93, Briody 4, Glasscock 3, Evans 1
SS   Glasscock 93, Bradley 4, Evans 3
3B   Muldoon 98, Evans 3, Briody 1
OF   Hotaling 100, York 100, Evans 86, Crowley 11, Muldoon 2, Cady 2, McCormick 1, Daily 1, Dunlap 1, Hunter 1
C   Bushong 63, Briody 33, Broughton 4
P   Daily 45, McCormick 43, Sawyer 17, Cady 1, Evans 1, Hunter 1

	G	IP	GS	CG	W	L	K	BB	SH	SV	ERA
One Arm Daily #	43	378.2	43	40	23	19	171	**99**	4	1	2.42
Jim McCormick	43	342	41	36	28	12	145	65	1	1	**1.84**
Will Sawyer	17	141	15	15	4	10	76	47	0	0	2.36
Charlie Cady	1	8	1	1	0	1	5	4	0	0	7.88
Lem Hunter	1	6.1	0	0	0	0	4	2	0	0	1.42
Jake Evans	1	3	0	0	0	0	1	0	0	0	0.00
	879		100	**92**	55	42	402	217	5	2	**2.22**

No–hit game 1–0 vs Philadelphia, September 13

BUFFALO   **Jim O'Rourke**   **Riverside Park**

		G	AB	H	R	2B	3B	HR	RBI	BB	BA	SA
LF	Jim O'Rourke	94	436	143	102	29	8	1	38	15	.328	.438
1B	Dan Brouthers	98	425	**159**	85	41	**17**	3	**97**	16	**.374**	**.572**
RF	Orator Shaffer	95	401	117	67	11	3	0	41	27	.292	.334
2B	Hardy Richardson	92	399	124	73	34	7	1	56	22	.311	.439
3B	Deacon White	94	391	114	62	14	5	0	47	23	.292	.353
SS	Davy Force	96	378	82	40	11	3	0	35	12	.217	.262
C	Jack Rowe	87	374	104	65	18	7	1	38	15	.278	.372
P	Pud Galvin	80	322	71	41	11	2	1	19	3	.220	.276
LF	Jim Lillie	50	201	47	25	7	3	1	29	1	.234	.313
CF	Dave Eggler	38	153	38	13	2	1	0	13	2	.248	.275
Sub	Curry Foley	23	111	30	23	5	3	0	6	4	.270	.369
P	George Derby	16	59	14	10	1	0	0	3	0	.237	.254
P	Ed Cushman	7	23	5	3	0	0	0	1	2	.217	.217
Sub	Doc Kennedy	5	19	6	3	0	0	0	2	2	.316	.316
Sub	Del Darling	6	18	3	1	0	0	0	1	2	.167	.167
Sub	Tony Suck	2	7	0	1	0	0	0	0	1	.000	.000
P	Art Hagan	2	7	0	0	0	0	0	0	0	.000	.000
P	James Burke	1	5	1	0	0	0	0	1	0	.200	.200
		98	3729	**1058**	614	184	59	8	427	147	**.284**	.371

1B   Brouthers 97, Kennedy 1
2B   Richardson 92, Force 7, Lillie 1
SS   Force 78, Rowe 18, O'Rourke 3, Lillie 1
3B   White 77, Force 13, O'Rourke 8, Rowe 3, Lillie 1, Brouthers 1
OF   Shaffer 95, O'Rourke 61, Lillie 47, Eggler 38, Rowe 28, Foley 23, Galvin 8, Kennedy 4, Derby 3, Suck 1, Burke 1, Cushman 1, Hagan 1
C   Rowe 49, O'Rourke 33, White 22, Darling 6, Lillie 2, Suck 1
P   Galvin 76, Derby 14, Cushman 7, Lillie 3, Hagan 2, O'Rourke 2, Burke 1, Foley 1, Brouthers 1

	G	IP	GS	CG	W	L	K	BB	SH	SV	ERA
Pud Galvin	**76**	656.1	75	72	46	29	279	50	**5**	0	2.72
George Derby	14	107.2	13	12	2	10	34	15	0	1	5.85
Ed Cushman	7	17	7	5	3	3	34	17	0	0	3.93
Art Hagan	2	15	2	1	0	2	7	6	0	0	3.60
Jim Lillie	3	12	0	0	0	1	4	2	0	0	3.00
James Burke	1	8	1	0	0	0	1	3	0	0	5.63
Jim O'Rourke	2	7	0	0	0	0	1	1	0	1	6.43
Dan Brouthers	1	2	0	0	0	0	2	3	0	0	31.50
Curry Foley	1	1	0	0	1	0	0	4	0	0	0.00
		859.1	98	90	52	45	362	101	5	2	3.32

NEW YORK   **John Clapp**   **Polo Grounds (I)**

		G	AB	H	R	2B	3B	HR	RBI	BB	BA	SA
LF	Pete Gillespie	98	411	129	64	23	12	1	62	9	.314	.436
1B	Roger Connor	98	409	146	80	28	15	1	50	25	.357	.506
SS	Ed Caskin	85	383	91	47	11	2	1	40	14	.238	.285
CF	Monte Ward	88	380	97	76	18	7	7	54	8	.255	.395
C	Buck Ewing	88	376	114	90	11	13	**10**	41	20	.303	.481
3B	Frank Hankinson	94	337	74	40	13	6	2	30	19	.220	.312
P	Mickey Welch	84	320	75	42	13	5	2	30	10	.234	.331
2B	Dasher Troy	85	316	68	37	7	5	0	20	9	.215	.269
RF	Mike Dorgan	64	261	61	32	11	3	0	27	2	.234	.299
Sub	John Humphries	29	107	12	5	1	0	0	4	1	.112	.121
P	Tip O'Neill	23	76	15	8	3	0	0	5	3	.197	.237

		G	AB	H	R	2B	3B	HR	RBI	BB	BA	SA
Sub	John Clapp	20	73	13	6	0	0	0	5	5	.178	.178
Sub	Gracie Pierce	18	62	5	3	0	1	0	2	1	.081	.113
Sub	Dick Cramer	2	6	0	0	0	0	0	0	1	.000	.000
P	Myron Allen	1	4	0	0	0	0	0	1	0	.000	.000
Sub	Dave Orr	1	3	0	0	0	0	0	0	0	.000	.000
		98	3524	900	530	139	69	24	371	127	.255	.354

1B Connor 98
2B Troy 73, Caskin 13, Ewing 11, Pierce 1, Ward 1
SS Caskin 81, Troy 12, Ewing 4, Ward 2
3B Hankinson 93, Ward 5, Ewing 1
OF Gillespie 98, Dorgan 59, Ward 56, Welch 38, Pierce 18, Ewing 14, Humphries 12, O'Neill 7, Clapp 5, Cramer 2, Orr 1, Hankinson 1
C   Ewing 63, Humphries 20, Clapp 16, Dorgan 6, Caskin 1
P   Welch 54, Ward 33, O'Neill 19, Allen 1, Dorgan 1

	G	IP	GS	CG	W	L	K	BB	SH	SV	ERA
Mickey Welch	55	426	52	46	25	23	144	66	4	0	2.73
Monte Ward	33	277	25	24	16	13	121	31	1	0	2.70
Tip O'Neill	19	148	19	15	5	12	55	64	0	0	4.07
Myron Allen	1	8	1	1	0	1	0	3	0	0	1.13
Mike Dorgan	1	7	1	1	0	1	3	6	0	0	3.86
		866	98	87	46	50	323	170	5	0	2.49

DETROIT   **Jack Chapman**   **Recreation Park**

		G	AB	H	R	2B	3B	HR	RBI	BB	BA	SA
3B	Joe Farrell	101	444	108	58	13	5	0	36	5	.243	.295
LF	George Wood	99	441	133	81	26	11	5	47	25	.302	.444
1B	Martin Powell	101	421	115	76	17	5	1	48	28	.273	.344
SS	Sadie Houck	101	416	105	52	18	12	0	40	9	.252	.353
CF	Ned Hanlon	100	413	100	65	13	2	1	40	34	.242	.291
C	Charlie Bennett	92	371	113	56	34	7	5	55	26	.305	.474
P	Stump Weidman	79	313	58	34	6	1	1	24	4	.185	.220
UT	Sam Trott	75	295	72	27	14	1	0	29	10	.244	.298
P	Dupee Shaw	38	141	29	13	3	0	0	5	3	.206	.227
P	Dick Burns	37	140	26	11	7	1	0	5	2	.186	.250
2B	Joe Quest	37	137	32	22	8	2	0	25	10	.234	.321
RF	Tom Mansell	34	131	29	22	4	1	0	10	8	.221	.267
P	Jack Jones	12	42	8	3	1	0	0	3	1	.190	.214
P	George Radbourn	3	12	2	2	0	0	0	0	0	.167	.167
Sub	Ben Guiney	1	5	1	1	0	0	0	0	0	.200	.200
P	Frank McIntyre	1	4	0	1	0	0	0	0	1	.000	.000
		101	3726	931	524	164	48	13	367	**166**	.250	.330

1B Powell 101, Trott 1
2B Trott 42, Quest 37, Bennett 15, Hanlon 11, Weidman 4, Guiney 1
SS Houck 101
3B Farrell 101
OF Wood 99, Hanlon 90, Weidman 35, Mansell 34, Burns 24, Shaw 15, Bennett 12, Trott 6, Jones 3, Guiney 1, Radbourne 1
C   Bennett 72, Trott 34
P   Weidman 52, Shaw 26, Burns 17, Jones 12, Radbourn 3, McIntyre 1, Wood 1, Mansell 1

	G	IP	GS	CG	W	L	K	BB	SH	SV	ERA
Stump Weidman	52	402.1	47	41	20	24	183	72	3	2	3.53
Dupee Shaw	26	227	25	23	10	15	73	44	1	0	2.50
Dick Burns	17	127.2	13	13	2	12	30	33	0	0	4.51
Jack Jones	12	92.2	12	9	6	5	33	19	1	0	3.50
George Radbourn	3	22	3	1	1	2	2	7	0	0	6.55
Frank McIntyre	1	11	1	1	1	0	0	1	0	0	0.82
Tom Mansell	1	6.2	0	0	0	0	3	5	0	0	16.20
George Wood	1	5	0	0	0	0	0	3	0	0	7.20
		894.1	101	89	40	58	324	184	5	2	3.56

PHILADELPHIA		**Bob Ferguson (4–13)**		**Blondie Purcell (13–68)**			**Recreation Park**				
		G	AB	H	R	2B	3B	HR	RBI	BB	BA	SA
LF	Blondie Purcell	97	425	114	70	20	5	1	32	13	.268	.346
RF	Jack Manning	98	420	112	60	31	5	0	37	20	.267	.364
1B	Sid Farrar	99	377	88	41	19	8	0	29	4	.233	.329
P	John Coleman	90	354	83	33	12	8	0	32	15	.234	.314
2B	Bob Ferguson	86	329	85	39	9	2	0	27	18	.258	.298
SS	Bill McClellan	80	326	75	42	21	4	1	33	19	.230	.328
CF	Bill Harbidge	73	280	62	32	12	3	0	21	24	.221	.286
C	Emil Gross	57	231	71	39	25	7	1	25	12	.307	.489
Sub	Frank Ringo	60	221	42	24	10	1	0	12	6	.190	.244
Sub	Fred Lewis	38	160	40	21	7	0	0	18	4	.250	.294
3B	Fred Warner	39	141	32	13	6	1	0	13	5	.227	.284
Sub	Jack Neagle	18	73	12	6	1	0	0	4	1	.164	.178
Sub	Conny Doyle	16	68	15	3	3	2	0	3	0	.221	.324
P	Art Hagan	17	59	6	3	1	1	0	3	0	.102	.153
Sub	Jim Pirie	5	19	3	1	0	0	0	0	0	.158	.158
Sub	Art Benedict	3	15	4	3	1	0	0	4	0	.267	.333
Sub	Joe Mulvey	3	12	6	2	1	0	0	3	0	.500	.583
Sub	Abe Wolstenholme	3	11	1	1	0	0	0	0	0	.091	.182
P	Charlie Hilsey	3	10	1	0	0	0	0	1	0	.100	.100
P	Hardie Henderson	2	8	2	1	1	0	0	1	0	.250	.375
Sub	Bill Gallagher	2	8	0	1	0	0	0	0	0	.000	.000
Sub	Charlie Kelly	2	7	1	1	0	1	0	0	0	.143	.429
Sub	Piggy Ward	1	5	0	0	0	0	0	0	0	.000	.000
P	Edgar Smith	1	4	3	1	0	0	0	1	0	.750	.750
Sub	Buck Gladman	1	4	0	1	0	0	0	0	0	.000	.000
Sub	Kick Kelly	1	3	0	0	0	0	0	0	0	.000	.000
Sub	Charlie Waitt	1	3	1	0	0	0	0	0	0	.333	.333
P	Alonzo Breitenstein	1	2	0	0	0	0	0	0	0	.000	.000
Sub	C.B. White	1	1	0	0	0	0	0	0	0	.000	.000
		99	3576	859	437	181	48	3	299	141	.240	.320

1B	Farrar 99
2B	Ferguson 86, Harbidge 9, Benedict 3, Ringo 2, Coleman 1
SS	McClellan 78, Harbidge 11, Ringo 6, Pirie 5, White 1
3B	Purcell 46, Warner 38, Ringo 5, Harbidge 5, Mulvey 3, Kelly 2, Ward 1, White 1, Gladman 1, McClellan 1
OF	Manning 98, Purcell 44, Harbidge 44, Lewis 38, Coleman 31, Doyle 16, Neagle 12, Ringo 11, Gross 2, Gallagher 2, McClellan 2, Warner 1, Waitt 1, Wolstenholme 1, Kelly 1
C	Gross 55, Ringo 39, Harbidge 7, Wolstenholme 2
P	Coleman 65, Hagan 17, Purcell 11, Neagle 8, Hilsey 3, Henderson 1, Breitenstein 1, Smith 1, Ferguson 1

	G	IP	GS	CG	W	L	K	BB	SH	SV	ERA
John Coleman	65	538.1	68	59	12	**48**	159	48	3	0	4.87
Art Hagan	17	137	16	15	1	14	39	33	0	0	5.45
Blondie Purcell	11	80	9	7	2	6	30	12	0	0	4.39
Jack Neagle	8	61.1	7	6	1	7	13	21	0	0	6.90
Charlie Hilsey	3	26	3	3	0	3	8	4	0	0	5.54
Hardie Henderson	1	9	1	1	0	1	2	2	0	0	19.00
Edgar Smith	1	7	1	0	0	1	2	3	0	0	15.43
Alonzo Breitenstein	1	5	1	0	0	1	0	2	0	0	9.00
Bob Ferguson	1	1	0	0	0	0	0	0	0	0	9.00
		—1 forfeit W vs Providence on July 4 AM—									
		864.2	99	91	16	81	253	125	3	0	5.34

AMERICAN ASSOCIATION

	W	L	PCT	HOME	ROAD	GB
1. Philadelphia Athletics	66	32	.673	37–14	29–18	—
2. St. Louis Browns	65	33	.663	35–14	30–19	1
3. Cincinnati Red Stockings	61	37	.622	37–13	24–24	5
4. New York Metropolitans	54	42	.563	29–17	25–25	11
5. Louisville Eclipse	52	45	.536	29–19	23–26	13.5
6. Columbus Buckeyes	32	65	.330	18–29	14–36	33.5
7. Pittsburgh Alleghenys	31	67	.316	18–31	13–36	35
8. Baltimore Orioles	28	68	.292	18–31	10–37	37

	Phi	StL	Cin	NY	Lou	Col	Pit	Bal	
Philadelphia	—	9	5	9	7	13	12	11	66
St. Louis	5	—	6	11	8	11	12	12	65
Cincinnati	9	8	—	4	10	11	8	11	61
New York	5	3	10	—	6	11	9	10	54
Louisville	7	6	4	7	—	9	11	8	52
Columbus	1	3	3	3	5	—	10	7	32
Pittsburgh	2	2	6	5	3	4	—	9	31
Baltimore	3	2	3	3	6	6	5	—	28
	32	33	37	42	45	65	67	68	389

SEASON LEADERS*

Batting Average (225 ABs)

1.	Swartwood, Pittsburgh	.356
2.	Browning, Louisville	.338
3.	Rowe, Baltimore	.313
	Clinton, Baltimore	.313
5.	Reilly, Cincinnati	.311

Slugging Average

1.	Stovey, Philadelphia	.506
2.	Reilly, Cincinnati	.485
3.	Swartwood, Pittsburgh	.476
4.	C. Jones, Cincinnati	.471
5.	Browning, Louisville	.464

On–Base Percentage

1.	Swartwood, Pittsburgh	.394
2.	Browning, Louisville	.378
3.	Moynahan, Philadelphia	.360
4.	Clinton, Baltimore	.357
5.	Nelson, New York	.353

Home Runs

1.	Stovey, Philadelphia	14
2.	C. Jones, Cincinnati	10
3.	Reilly, Cincinnati	9
4.	Fulmer, Cincinnati	5
	T. Brown, Columbus	5

*RBI leaders unavailable

Hits

1.	Swartwood, Pittsburgh	147
2.	Reilly, Cincinnati	136
3.	Carpenter, Cincinnati	130
4.	Stovey, Philadelphia	128
5.	Nelson, New York	127

Total Bases

1.	Stovey, Philadelphia	213
2.	Reilly, Cincinnati	212
3.	Swartwood, Pittsburgh	196
4.	C. Jones, Cincinnati	184
5.	B. Gleason, St. Louis	167

Runs

1.	Stovey, Philadelphia	110
2.	Reilly, Cincinnati	103
3.	Carpenter, Cincinnati	99
4.	Knight, Philadelphia	98
5.	Birchall, Philadelphia	95
	Browning, Louisville	95

Bases on Balls

1.	Stearns, Baltimore	34
2.	Nelson, New York	31
	Moynahan, Philadelphia	31
4.	J. Gleason, St L-Lou	29
5.	Clinton, Baltimore	27

PITCHING

Wins

1.	White, Cincinnati	43
2.	Keefe, New York	41
3.	Mullane, St. Louis	35
4.	Mathews, Philadelphia	30
5.	McGinnis, St. Louis	28

Innings Pitched

1.	Keefe, New York	619
2.	White, Cincinnati	577
3.	Mountain, Columbus	503
4.	Mullane, St. Louis	460.2
5.	Hecker, Louisville	451

Strikeouts

1.	Keefe, New York	359
2.	Mathews, Philadelphia	203
3.	Mullane, St. Louis	191
4.	Mountain, Columbus	159
5.	Hecker, Louisville	153

Losses

1.	Mountain, Columbus	33
2.	Henderson, Baltimore	32
3.	Keefe, New York	27
4.	Hecker, Louisville	23
5.	White, Cincinnati	22

Complete Games

1.	Keefe, New York	68
2.	White, Cincinnati	64
3.	Mountain, Columbus	57
4.	Hecker, Louisville	49
	Mullane, St. Louis	49

Winning Percentage (20 decisions)

1.	Mullane, St. Louis	.700
2.	Mathews, Philadelphia	.698
3.	Bradley, Philadelphia	.696
4.	White, Cincinnati	.662
5.	McGinnis, St. Louis	.636

ERA (98 innings)

1.	White, Cincinnati	2.09
2.	Mullane, St. Louis	2.19
3.	Deagle, Cincinnati	2.31
4.	McGinnis, St. Louis	2.33
5.	Keefe, New York	2.41

Lowest On–Base Percentage

1.	Keefe, New York	.237
2.	Mullane, St. Louis	.238
3.	White, Cincinnati	.244
4.	McGinnis, St. Louis	.249
5.	Bradley, Philadelphia	.263

FIELDING

Total Chances

1B	Comiskey, St. Louis	1148
2B	McPhee, Cincinnati	637
3B	Battin, Pittsburgh	459
SS	J. Richmond, Columbus	486
OF	Birchall, Philadelphia	235
C	Holbert, New York	723
P	Keefe, New York	238

Fielding Average

Stovey, Philadelphia	.965
McPhee, Cincinnati	.928
Battin, Pittsburgh	.891
J. Richmond, Columbus	.877
Corkhill, Cincinnati	.930
Deasley, St. Louis	.930
Weaver, Louisville	.944

PHILADELPHIA   Lon Knight   **Jefferson Street Grounds**

		G	AB	H	R	2B	3B	HR	RBI	BB	BA	SA
LF	Judd Birchall	96	**448**	108	95	10	1	1	—	20	.241	.275
RF	Lon Knight	97	429	108	98	23	9	1	—	21	.252	.354
1B	Harry Stovey	94	421	128	**110**	**31**	6	**14**	66	27	.304	**.506**
SS	Mike Moynahan	95	400	124	90	18	10	1	—	31	.308	.410
C	Jack O'Brien	94	390	113	74	14	10	0	—	25	.290	.377
2B	Cub Stricker	88	330	90	67	8	0	1	—	19	.273	.306
3B	George Bradley	76	312	73	47	8	5	1	—	8	.234	.301
UT	Fred Corey	71	298	77	45	16	2	1	—	12	.258	.336
C	Ed Rowen	49	196	43	28	10	1	0	—	11	.219	.281
CF	Bob Blakiston	44	167	41	26	3	3	0	—	9	.246	.299
P	Bobby Mathews	45	167	31	15	2	0	0	—	4	.186	.198
Sub	Bill Crowley	23	96	24	16	4	3	0	—	3	.250	.354
P	Jersey Blakely	8	26	5	4	1	0	0	—	6	.192	.231
P	Jack Jones	7	25	6	3	1	0	0	—	1	.240	.280
Sub	Al Hubbard	2	6	2	2	0	0	0	—	1	.333	.333
Sub	Charlie Mason	1	2	1	0	0	0	0	—	0	.500	.500
		98	3713	974	720	149	50	20	—	198	.262	.346

1B	Stovey 93, Blakiston 6, Bradley 2, Crowley 1, O'Brien 1
2B	Stricker 88, Corey 9, Knight 2, Rowen 1
SS	Moynahan 95, Hubbard 1, Corey 1, O'Brien 1
3B	Bradley 44, Corey 34, O'Brien 19, Blakiston 5, Knight 3, Rowen 1
OF	Birchall 96, Knight 93, Blakiston 37, O'Brien 25, Crowley 22, Corey 14, Bradley 11, Rowen 8, Mathews 3, Stovey 3, Mason 1, Bakely 1
C	O'Brien 58, Rowen 44, Stricker 2, Corey 1, Hubbard 1
P	Mathews 44, Bradley 26, Corey 18, Bakely 8, Jones 7, Stovey 1

	G	IP	GS	CG	W	L	K	BB	SH	SV	ERA
Bobby Mathews	44	381	44	41	30	13	203	31	1	0	2.46
George Bradley	26	214.1	23	22	16	7	56	22	0	0	3.15
Fred Corey	18	148.1	16	15	10	7	42	24	0	0	3.40
Jack Jones	7	65	7	7	5	2	28	6	0	0	2.63
Jersey Bakely	8	61.1	8	7	5	3	14	12	0	0	3.23
Harry Stovey	1	3	0	0	0	0	4	0	0	0	4.50
		873	98	92	66	32	347	**95**	1	0	2.88

ST. LOUIS   Ted Sullivan (53–26)   Charlie Comiskey (12–7)   Sportsman's Park (I)

		G	AB	H	R	2B	3B	HR	RBI	BB	BA	SA
SS	Bill Gleason	98	425	122	81	21	9	2	—	15	.287	.393
3B	Arlie Latham	98	406	96	86	12	7	0	—	18	.236	.300
1B	Charlie Comiskey	96	401	118	87	17	9	2	64	11	.294	.397
RF	Hugh Nicol	94	368	105	73	13	3	0	—	18	.285	.337
P	Tony Mullane	83	307	69	38	11	6	0	—	13	.225	.300
2B	George Strief	82	302	68	22	9	0	1	—	12	.225	.265
LF	Tom Dolan	81	295	63	32	9	2	1	—	9	.214	.268
CF	Fred Lewis	49	209	63	37	8	4	1	—	1	.301	.392
C	Pat Deasley	58	206	53	27	2	1	0	—	6	.257	.277
P	Jumbo McGinnis	45	180	36	20	4	2	0	—	0	.200	.244
Sub	Tom Mansell	28	112	45	23	8	1	0	—	7	.402	.491
Sub	Joe Quest	19	78	20	12	3	1	0	—	1	.256	.321
Sub	Ned Cuthbert	21	71	12	3	1	0	0	—	4	.169	.183
Sub	Jack Gleason	9	34	8	2	0	0	0	—	4	.235	.235
Sub	Sleeper Sullivan	8	27	6	2	0	1	0	—	0	.222	.296
Sub	Tom Loftus	6	22	4	1	0	0	0	—	2	.182	.182
Sub	Harry McCaffrey	5	18	1	0	0	0	0	—	1	.056	.056
Sub	Henry Oberbeck	4	14	0	0	0	0	0	—	0	.000	.000
P	Charlie Hodnett	4	11	2	3	0	0	0	—	2	.182	.182
Sub	John Ewing	1	5	0	0	0	0	0	—	0	.000	.000
Sub	Jack Gorman	1	4	0	0	0	0	0	—	0	.000	.000
		98	3495	891	549	118	46	7	—	124	.255	.321

1B   Comiskey 96, Mullane 2, Cuthbert 1
2B   Strief 67, Quest 19, Nicol 11, Mullane 3
SS   B. Gleason 98
3B   Latham 98, J. Gleason 1
OF   Nicol 84, Lewis 49, Dolan 40, Mullane 30, Mansell 28, Cuthbert 20, Strief 15, J. Gleason 9, Loftus 6, McCaffrey 5, Oberbeck 4, McGinnis 4, Sullivan 2, Deasley 2, Comiskey 1, Hodnett 1, Gorman 1, Ewing 1
C   Deasley 56, Dolan 42, Sullivan 6, Latham 1
P   Mullane 53, McGinnis 45, Hodnett 4, Dolan 1

	G	IP	GS	CG	W	L	K	BB	SH	SV	ERA
Tony Mullane	53	460.2	49	49	35	15	191	74	3	1	2.19
Jumbo McGinnis	45	382.2	45	41	28	16	128	69	6	0	2.33
Charlie Hodnett	4	32	4	3	2	2	6	7	0	0	1.41
Tom Dolan	1	4	0	0	0	0	0	0	0	0	4.50
		879.1	98	93	65	33	325	150	9	1	2.23

CINCINNATI   Pop Snyder   Bank Street Grounds

		G	AB	H	R	2B	3B	HR	RBI	BB	BA	SA
1B	Long John Reilly	98	437	136	103	21	14	9	79	9	.311	.485
3B	Hick Carpenter	95	436	130	99	18	4	3	—	19	.299	.379
LF	Joe Sommer	97	413	115	79	5	7	3	—	20	.278	.346
CF	Charley Jones	90	391	115	84	15	12	10	80	20	.294	.471
RF	Pop Corkhill	88	375	81	53	10	8	2	—	3	216	.301
2B	Bid McPhee	96	367	90	61	10	10	2	42	18	.245	.343
SS	Chick Fulmer	92	362	92	52	13	5	5	—	12	.254	.359
C	Pop Snyder	58	250	64	38	14	6	0	—	8	.256	.360
P	Will White	65	240	54	38	4	3	0	—	16	.225	.267
Sub	Phil Powers	30	114	28	16	1	4	0	—	3	.246	.325
C	Bill Traffley	30	105	21	17	5	0	0	—	4	.200	.248
P	Ren Deagle	19	70	9	9	2	0	0	—	1	.129	.157
P	Harry McCormick	15	55	17	8	2	1	0	—	2	.309	.382

	G	AB	H	R	2B	3B	HR	RBI	BB	BA	SA
Sub Jimmy Macullar	14	48	8	4	2	0	0	—	4	.167	.208
Sub Podgie Weihe	1	4	1	1	0	0	0	—	0	.250	.250
P Billy Mountjoy	1	3	0	0	0	0	0	—	0	.000	.000
	98	3669	961	662	122	74	**34**	—	139	.262	**.363**

1B   Reilly 98, Corkhill 2
2B   McPhee 96, Corkhill 2
SS   Fulmer 92, Snyder 2, Corkhill 2, Traffley 2, Deagle 1, Macullar 1
3B   Carpenter 95, Sommer 3,
OF   Sommer 94, Jones 90, Corkhill 85, Macullar 14, Powers 13, Weihe 1, Deagle 1, Reilly 1
C   Snyder 57, Traffley 29, Powers 17
P   White 65, Deagle 18, McCormick 15, Sommer 1, Mountjoy 1

	G	IP	GS	CG	W	L	K	BB	SH	SV	ERA
Will White	65	577	64	64	**43**	22	141	104	**6**	0	**2.09**
Ren Deagle	18	148	18	17	10	8	48	34	1	0	2.31
Harry McCormick	15	128.2	15	14	8	6	21	27	1	0	2.87
Billy Mountjoy	1	8	1	1	0	1	3	2	0	0	2.25
Joe Sommer	1	5	0	0	0	0	2	1	0	0	5.40
		866.2	98	96	61	37	215	168	8	0	2.26

NEW YORK   **Jim Mutrie**   **Polo Grounds (I) West Diamond (14 games) East Diamond (33 games)**

		G	AB	H	R	2B	3B	HR	RBI	BB	BA	SA
1B	Steve Brady	97	432	117	69	12	6	0	—	11	.271	.326
SS	Candy Nelson	97	417	127	75	19	6	0	—	31	.305	.379
3B	Dude Esterbrook	97	407	103	55	9	7	0	—	15	.253	.310
RF	Chief Roseman	93	398	100	48	13	6	0	—	11	.251	.314
LF	Eddie Kennedy	94	356	78	57	6	7	2	—	17	.219	.292
2B	Sam Crane	96	349	82	57	8	5	0	—	13	.235	.287
CF	John O'Rourke	77	315	85	49	19	5	2	—	21	.270	.381
C	Bill Holbert	73	299	71	26	9	1	0	—	1	.237	.274
P	Tim Keefe	70	259	57	39	6	9	0	—	14	.220	.313
Sub	Charlie Reipschlager	37	145	27	8	4	2	0	—	4	.186	.241
P	Jack Lynch	29	107	20	9	2	1	0	—	4	.187	.224
Sub	Dave Orr	13	50	16	6	4	3	2	11	0	.320	.640
		97	3534	883	498	111	58	6		142	.250	.319

1B   Brady 81, Orr 13, Roseman 2, O'Rourke 1
2B   Crane 96, Holbert 1, Keefe 1
SS   Nelson 97
3B   Esterbrook 97
OF   Kennedy 94, Roseman 91, O'Rourke 76, Brady 16, Reipschlager 8, Holbert 5, Keefe 1, Crane 1
C   Holbert 68, Reipschlager 29
P   Keefe 68, Lynch 29

	G	IP	GS	CG	W	L	K	BB	SH	SV	ERA
Tim Keefe	**68**	**619**	**68**	**68**	41	27	**359**	98	5	0	2.41
Jack Lynch	29	255	29	29	13	15	119	25	1	0	4.09
		874	97	**97**	54	42	**478**	123	6	0	2.90

LOUISVILLE   Joe Gerhardt   Eclipse Park (I)

		G	AB	H	R	2B	3B	HR	RBI	BB	BA	SA
RF	Chicken Wolf	98	389	102	59	17	9	1	—	5	.262	.360
1B	Juice Latham	88	368	92	60	7	6	0	—	12	.250	.302
CF	Leech Maskrey	96	361	73	50	13	8	1	—	10	.202	.291
LF	Pete Browning	84	358	121	95	15	9	4	—	23	.338	.464
3B	Jack Gleason	84	355	106	69	11	4	2	–	25	.299	.369
P	Guy Hecker	79	322	88	56	6	6	1	—	10	.273	.339
2B	Joe Gerhardt	78	319	84	56	11	9	0	—	14	.263	.354
C	Ed Whiting	58	240	70	35	16	4	2	—	9	.292	.417
P	Sam Weaver	55	203	39	22	6	1	0	—	12	.192	.232
SS	Jack Leary	40	165	31	16	1	3	3	—	2	.188	.285
C	Dan Sullivan	37	147	31	8	5	2	0	—	3	.211	.272
Sub	Tommy McLaughlin	42	146	28	16	1	2	0	—	5	.192	.226
Sub	John Reccius	18	63	9	10	2	0	0	—	7	.143	.175
Sub	Lew Brown	14	60	11	6	2	1	0	—	1	.183	.250
Sub	Henry Luff	6	23	4	1	0	0	0	—	0	.174	.174
Sub	George Winkelman	4	13	0	2	0	0	0	—	1	.000	.000
Sub	Walter Prince	4	11	2	1	0	0	0	—	0	.182	.182
Sub	Jack Jones	2	7	0	1	0	0	0	—	0	.000	.000
Sub	Phil Reccius	1	3	1	1	1	0	0	—	0	.333	.667
		98	3553	892	564	114	64	14	—	139	.251	.331

1B	Latham 67, Brown 14, Hecker 10, McLaughlin 5, Luff 4, Prince 2, Weaver 1, Whiting 1, Browning 1
2B	Gerhardt 78, Latham 14, Browning 3, McLaughlin 2, Whiting 2, Wolf 1
SS	Leary 40, Browning 26, McLaughlin 19, Latham 9, Wolf 5, Jones 1, Prince 1, Sullivan 1, Maskrey 1, Gleason 1
3B	Gleason 83, Browning 10, McLaughlin 2, Sullivan 2, Whiting 1
OF	Maskrey 96, Wolf 78, Browning 48, Hecker 23, J. Reccius 18, McLaughlin 17, Whiting 6, Weaver 6, Winkelman 4, Luff 2, Jones 2, Prince 2, Sullivan 2, P. Reccius 1
C	Whiting 50, Sullivan 32, Wolf 20, Brown 1
P	Hecker 51, Weaver 48, J. Reccius 1

	G	IP	GS	CG	W	L	K	BB	SH	SV	ERA
Guy Hecker	51	451	50	49	26	23	153	72	3	0	3.33
Sam Weaver	48	418.2	48	47	26	22	116	38	4	0	3.70
John Reccius	1	4	0	0	0	0	0	0	0	0	2.25
		873.2	98	96	52	45	269	110	7	0	3.50

COLUMBUS   Horace Phillips   Recreation Park (I)

		G	AB	H	R	2B	3B	HR	RBI	BB	BA	SA
RF	Tom Brown	97	420	115	69	12	7	5	32	20	.274	.371
2B	Pop Smith	97	405	106	82	14	17	4	—	22	.262	.410
CF	Fred Mann	96	394	98	61	18	13	1	—	18	.249	.368
SS	John Richmond	92	385	109	63	7	8	0	—	25	.283	.343
3B	Willie Kuehne	95	374	85	38	8	14	1	—	2	.227	.332
LF	Harry Wheeler	82	371	84	42	6	7	0	—	6	.226	.280
C	Rudy Kemmler	84	318	66	27	6	2	0	—	13	.208	.239
1B	Jim Field	76	295	75	31	10	6	1	—	7	.254	.339
P	Frank Mountain	70	276	60	36	14	5	3	—	9	.217	.337
Sub	Joe Straub	27	100	13	4	0	0	0	—	4	.130	.130
P	Dummy Dundon	26	93	15	8	1	0	0	—	3	.161	.172
P	John Valentine	16	60	17	9	4	0	0	—	2	.283	.350
Sub	Gracie Pierce	11	41	7	5	0	0	0	—	0	.171	.171
P	Pete Fries	3	10	3	1	1	0	0	—	1	.300	.400
P	Frank McIntyre	2	7	0	0	0	0	0	—	2	.000	.000
Sub	Pop Schwartz	2	4	1	0	0	0	0	—	0	.250	.250
		97	3553	854	476	101	79	15	—	134	.240	.326

1B   Field 76, Straub 12, Mann 9, Schwartz 1
2B   Smith 73, Kuehne 18, Pierce 6, Wheeler 1, Dundon 1
SS   Richmond 91, Kuehne 7, Mann 1
3B   Kuehne 69, Smith 24, Mann 6
OF   Brown 96, Mann 82, Wheeler 82, Mountain 12, Dundon 9, Pierce 5, Valentine 4, Kuehne 3, Richmond 2, Kemmler 2, Straub 1
C   Kemmler 82, Straub 14, Schwartz 1
P   Mountain 59, Dundon 20, Valentine 13, Smith 3, Brown 3, Fries 3, McIntyre 2, Wheeler 1

	G	IP	GS	CG	W	L	K	BB	SH	SV	ERA
Frank Mountain	59	503	59	57	26	**33**	159	**123**	4	0	3.60
Ed Dundon	20	166.2	19	16	3	16	31	38	0	0	4.48
John Valentine	13	102	12	11	2	10	13	17	0	0	3.53
Pete Fries	3	25	3	3	0	3	7	14	0	0	6.48
Frank McIntyre	2	19	2	2	1	1	6	7	0	0	5.21
Tom Brown	3	14	1	1	0	1	6	10	0	0	5.79
Pop Smith	3	5.2	0	0	0	0	0	0	0	0	6.35
Harry Wheeler	1	5	1	0	0	1	0	2	0	0	7.20
		840.1	97	90	32	65	222	211	4	0	3.96

PITTSBURGH   Al Pratt (12–20)   Ormond Butler (17–36)   Joe Battin (2–11)
Exposition Park (I)

		G	AB	H	R	2B	3B	HR	RBI	BB	BA	SA
1B	Ed Swartwood	94	412	**147**	86	24	8	3	—	25	**.357**	.476
LF	Mike Mansell	96	412	106	90	12	13	3	—	25	.257	.371
3B	Joe Battin	98	388	83	42	9	6	1	—	11	.214	.276
CF	Billy Taylor	83	369	96	43	13	7	2	—	9	.260	.350
2B	George Creamer	91	369	94	54	7	9	0	—	20	.255	.322
RF	Buttercup Dickerson	85	354	88	62	15	1	0	—	18	.249	.297
C	Jackie Hayes	85	351	92	41	23	5	3	—	15	.262	.382
SS	Denny Mack	60	224	44	26	5	3	0	—	13	.196	.246
P	Denny Driscoll	41	148	27	19	2	1	0	—	4	.182	.209
P	Bob Barr	37	142	35	12	4	3	0	—	5	.246	.317
Sub	Frank McLaughlin	29	114	25	15	2	0	1	—	6	.219	.263
Sub	Bill Morgan	32	114	18	12	2	1	0	—	7	.158	.193
P	Jack Neagle	27	101	19	14	0	1	0	—	5	.188	.208
Sub	Wes Blogg	9	34	5	0	0	0	0	—	0	.147	.147
Sub	John Peters	8	28	3	3	0	0	0	—	0	.107	.107
P	The Only Nolan	7	26	8	4	1	0	0	—	1	.308	.346
P	Norman Baker	4	12	0	1	0	0	0	—	0	.000	.000
Sub	Henry Oberbeck	2	9	2	1	1	0	0	—	0	.222	.333
		98	3607	892	525	120	58	13	—	164	.247	.324

1B   Swartwood 60, Mack 25, Taylor 9, Hayes 5, Barr 4, Oberbeck 2
2B   Creamer 91, McLaughlin 2, Dickerson 2, Morgan 2, Mack 1, Hayes 1
SS   Mack 38, McLaughlin 25, Morgan 21, Peters 8, Dickerson 8, Hayes 5
3B   Battin 98, Barr 1, Driscoll 1
OF   Mansell 96, Dickerson 78, Swartwood 37, Taylor 37, Hayes 18, Neagle 15, Barr 14, Morgan 6, Driscoll 4, McLaughlin 4, Blogg 3, Baker 2, Nolan 1
C   Hayes 62, Taylor 33, Blogg 6, Morgan 5, Swartwood 3
P   Driscoll 41, Barr 26, Taylor 19, Neagle 16, Nolan 7, Baker 3, Battin 2, McLaughlin 2

	G	IP	GS	CG	W	L	K	BB	SH	SV	ERA
Denny Driscoll	41	336.1	40	35	18	21	79	39	1	0	3.99
Bob Barr	26	203.1	23	19	6	18	81	28	0	1	4.38
Billy Taylor	19	127	9	8	4	7	41	34	0	0	5.39
Jack Neagle	16	114	16	12	3	12	41	25	0	0	5.84
The Only Nolan	7	55	7	6	0	7	23	10	0	0	4.25
Norman Baker	3	19	3	2	0	2	5	11	0	0	3.32
Frank McLaughlin	2	9	0	0	0	0	1	3	0	0	13.00
Joe Battin	2	4	0	0	0	0	0	1	0	0	2.25
		867.2	98	82	31	67	271	151	1	1	4.62

BALTIMORE   Billy Barnie   Oriole Park (1)

		G	AB	H	R	2B	3B	HR	RBI	BB	BA	SA
LF	Jim Clinton	94	399	125	69	16	8	0	—	27	.313	.393
3B	Jerry McCormick	93	389	102	40	16	6	0	—	2	.262	.334
1B	Dan Stearns	93	382	94	54	10	9	1	—	34	.246	.327
SS	Lew Say	74	324	83	52	13	2	1	—	10	.256	.318
RF	Dave Rowe	59	256	80	40	11	6	0	—	2	.313	.402
C	Kick Kelly	48	202	46	18	9	2	0	—	3	.228	.292
CF	Dave Eggler	53	202	38	15	2	0	0	—	1	.188	.198
P	Hardie Henderson	51	191	31	13	5	1	1	—	10	.162	.215
Sub	Gid Gardner	42	161	44	28	10	3	1	—	18	.273	.391
Sub	Tom O'Brien	33	138	37	16	6	4	0	—	5	.268	.370
Sub	Phil Baker	28	121	33	22	2	1	1	—	8	.273	.331
2B	Tim Manning	35	121	26	23	5	0	0	—	14	.215	.256
C	Rooney Sweeney	25	101	21	13	5	2	0	—	4	.208	.297
Sub	Billy Reid	24	97	27	14	3	0	0	—	4	.278	.309
P	Bob Emslie	27	97	16	14	1	2	0	—	6	.165	.216
P	John Fox	23	92	14	12	3	0	0	—	4	.152	.185
Sub	Bill Gallagher	16	61	10	9	3	1	0	—	3	.164	.246
Sub	Billy Barnie	17	55	11	7	0	0	0	—	2	.200	.200
P	Jack Neagle	10	35	10	3	4	0	0	—	2	.286	.400
Sub	Cal Broughton	9	32	6	1	0	0	0	—	1	.188	.188
Sub	George Baker	7	22	5	0	0	0	0	—	0	.227	.227
Sub	Nick Scharf	3	13	2	1	1	0	0	—	0	.154	.231
Sub	Jack Leary	3	11	2	1	0	2	0	—	0	.182	.545
P	Jim Devine	2	9	2	4	0	0	0	—	0	.222	.222
Sub	Bill Farrell	2	7	0	0	0	0	0	—	1	.000	.000
Sub	Bill Loughlin	1	5	2	0	0	0	0	—	0	.400	.400
Sub	Charlie Ingraham	1	4	1	0	0	0	0	—	0	.250	.250
Sub	Dave Oldfield	1	4	0	0	0	0	0	—	0	.000	.000
Sub	Doug Allison	1	3	2	2	0	0	0	—	0	.667	.667
		96	3534	870	471	125	49	5	—	162	.246	.314

1B	Stearns 92, Rowe 3, Fox 1
2B	Manning 35, O'Brien 29, Reid 23, Gardner 4, Leary 3, Clinton 2
SS	Say 74, Rowe 7, Gallagher 4, G. Baker 4, Scharf 3, Henderson 2, Farrell 2, P. Baker 1, Reid 1, Barnie 1
3B	McCormick 93, Gardner 3, Henderson 1
OF	Clinton 92, Eggler 53, Rowe 50, Gardner 35, P. Baker 14, Kelly 13, Henderson 10, Gallagher 9, Barnie 6, Neagle 5, Emslie 5, O'Brien 4, Fox 4, Sweeney 3, Loughlin 1, G. Baker 1, Allison 1, Broughton 1, Devine 1, Stearns 1
C	Kelly 38, Sweeney 23, P. Baker 19, Barnie 13, Broughton 8, G. Baker 3, Ingraham 1, Oldfield 1, Allison 1
P	Henderson 45, Emslie 24, Fox 20, Gallagher 7, Neagle 6, Gardner 2, Devine 2, Rowe 1

	G	IP	GS	CG	W	L	K	BB	SH	SV	ERA
Hardie Henderson	45	358.1	42	38	10	32	145	87	0	0	4.02
Bob Emslie	24	201.1	23	21	9	13	62	41	1	0	3.17
John Fox	20	165.1	19	18	6	13	49	32	0	0	4.03
Bill Gallagher	7	51.2	5	4	0	5	19	6	0	0	5.40
Jack Neagle	6	46	5	4	1	4	9	20	0	0	4.89
Jim Devine	2	11	2	1	1	1	3	1	0	0	7.36
Gid Gardner	2	7	0	0	1	0	2	1	0	0	5.14
Dave Rowe	1	4	0	0	0	0	1	2	0	0	20.25
		844.2	96	86	28	68	290	190	1	0	4.09

1884
THREE MAJOR LEAGUES
AND 34 TEAMS

In November 1883, even while National League and American Association leaders were crafting a peace treaty that would govern major league baseball, Henry Lucas, the 26-year-old scion of a wealthy St. Louis lawyer and banker, was throwing the game into a state of war again. Lucas's grievance ostensibly was with the Reserve Clause. He claimed he found it intolerable that players were bound for life to teams like chattels and formed yet a third major league, the Union Association, that omitted the Reserve Clause from its player contracts. Events would soon demonstrate, though, that Lucas probably was motivated more by ego. He craved recognition as an organizational genius, and no sooner was he given enough of it to assuage him than his Union Association was history.

In 1884, during the one season the Union Association was alive, a record 34 teams performed at one time or another in the three-ring circus the major league game had become. The National League went with the same eight clubs that had played under its banner in 1883 but persuaded the American Association to expand to 12 teams so it could protect its interest in cities that the Union Association might otherwise usurp. Association president Denny McKnight thereupon took aboard teams representing Brooklyn, Indianapolis, Toledo and Washington. Brooklyn, Toledo and Indianapolis were already intact. Toledo had won the 1883 Northwestern League pennant and Brooklyn was not only the 1883 Inter-State League champion but was backed by Charlie Byrne and Ferd Abell, two casino owners with plenty of capital. The Washington club, in contrast, had to be formed from scratch, always a bad sign.

To combat the two established federations, Lucas put teams in six established major league cities—St. Louis, Chicago, Cincinnati, Baltimore, Boston and Philadelphia—and granted a seventh franchise to co-conspirator Mike Scanlon, a Washington pool-hall owner who owned the Nationals, a veteran semipro outfit in the nation's capital. Stuck for an eighth team, Lucas finally settled on Altoona and then drew up a schedule that called for the tiny Pennsylvania city to meet his own St. Louis Maroons in eight of its first 11 games. Helped by Lucas's chicanery, the Maroons set an all-time record by winning their first 20

This picture of the 1884 Philadelphia Quakers starting nine is treasured for the sweeping view it affords of the interior of the Quakers' ballyard. In 1884 the Quakers played at Recreation Park, located between 23rd and 25th Streets and bounded by Columbia Avenue and Ridge Pike. Prior to the season the seats in the "reserved" section were numbered and the aisles were carpeted—some thought it presumptuous of a team that played .173 ball in 1883.

games of the season. With all pretense of a pennant race gone by the end of May, Lucas's club then proceeded to run up 94 victories and an .832 winning percentage. Poor Altoona meanwhile got off to an 0–11 start and disappeared forever from the major league arena after just six weeks. Two other Union clubs, Chicago and Philadelphia, also soon ran aground, setting off a chain reaction of franchise shifts that eventually confounded the schedule-maker. By the end of the Union season the final standings were in such disarray that St. Louis collected 113 decisions even though the original schedule called for only 112 games while St. Paul figured in a mere eight decisions and never got to play a home game.

The American Association had its share of problems too, resulting in its Washington franchise being surrendered to Richmond, Virginia, on August 5. But unlike the Unions, the association could at least savor a genuine pennant race as no fewer than five of its teams made a serious bid for the flag. The New York Metropolitans ultimately won out over Columbus after the other three contenders—St. Louis, Louisville and Cincinnati—faltered down the stretch. Among the five pitching was the difference. Twin workhorses Tim Keefe and Jack Lynch pitched all but one of the Mets' 112 games in 1884 and made Jim Mutrie the first manager to have two 30-game winners. Columbus, under new skipper Gus Schmelz, also had stronger pitching in 1884 and rose from sixth place to second when rookie Ed "Cannonball" Morris combined with 1883 ace Frank Mountain for 57 wins, but the Union

---

59 OR 60?

Macmillan credits Hoss Radbourn with 60 wins in 1884, as do most current sources. *Total Baseball* insists, though, that he won only 59 and is backed by baseball historian Frederick Ivor-Campbell's carefully reasoned argument. Ivor-Campbell's case for reducing Radbourn's win total in 1884 to 59 is too lengthy to explore here. Suffice it to say that the victory in question came in relief of Cyclone Miller on July 28, 1884, and the conflict is over which rule should prevail, a 1950 rule or a pre-1950 rule. According to the 1950 rule for determining credit for a pitching win, the victory should go to Miller. Under the guidelines used before 1950 to decide credit for a pitching win, a scorer was within his rights to give Radbourn the victory. Since the game occurred in 1884, it would seem the pre-1950 rule should govern. When the first Macmillan edition was being prepared in the late 1960s, however, a Special Baseball Records Committee decreed that the 1950 rule should be applied to all seasons in "the period before 1920, a time that was somewhat chaotic in baseball for record-keeping procedures."

Since then scholars have undertaken to amend the pitching won-lost totals for every pitcher prior to 1920, in keeping with the Special Baseball Records Committee's decree. The work is not yet complete, and even when it is, conflicts will still no doubt exist. Meanwhile the season and career won-lost totals for many pitchers, including Radbourn, remain at issue. For the moment, *The Great Encyclopedia of Nineteenth-Century Major League Baseball* considers Radbourn to have won 60 games in 1884, if only because Radbourn was credited with that disputed relief win by every source until 1983 and it seems highly arbitrary, in any case, to adopt one set of rules after the fact for the period between 1921 and 1949 and another for the rest of baseball history. *The Great Encyclopedia of Nineteenth-Century Major League Baseball* does not always side with Macmillan, however, on individual pitching or hitting stats. There are many seasons when Macmillan and *Total Baseball* are in conflict on how many games a certain pitcher won or lost, and in a few instances neither of them provides a total that enables the pitcher's team won-lost totals to balance. In such cases *The Great Encyclopedia of Nineteenth-Century Major League Baseball* furnishes the total that seems the most logical while reserving the right to change it at a future date and again reminding the reader that a book like this is eternally a work in progress.

Association threat and several major rule changes crippled the other three challengers in the box. Louisville lost 24-game winner Sam Weaver to the Unions; St. Louis's 35-game winner, Tony Mullane, ended up in Toledo as a compromise solution after he'd first jumped to the Unions; and Cincinnati ace Will White, the Association's biggest winner in 1883, was robbed of one of his chief weapons, the ability to intimidate batters by hitting them without penalty, when the Association in 1884 became the first league to give a batter his base if he was struck by a pitch.

Though the National League continued to disdain the hit-batsman rule, it made two changes in its own 1884 rulebook that affected pitchers. The first, reducing to six the number of called balls needed before a batter was granted a walk, might have hampered its hurlers if the second revision had not benefited them so greatly. In 1884 the League lifted all restrictions on pitching deliveries, thereby opening the floodgates to overhand pitching. The result was a mammoth increase in strikeout totals and a corresponding reduction in batting averages that was felt in the League and elsewhere. Even though the Association and the Unions continued to restrict pitchers to deliveries below shoulder level and held the number of called balls needed for a walk to seven, their run production dipped sharply as well. For reasons not totally explicable, the 1884 season was unique. Expansion traditionally favors hitters, but in 1884, although the number of major league roster spots to be filled nearly doubled, pitchers thrived. Guy Hecker won an Association-record 52 games for

The toast of Providence—the 1884 "World's Series" champion Grays. Top: Hoss Radbourn, Charlie Sweeney, Miah Murray, Jerry Denny, Paul Hines, manager Frank Bancroft, Joe Start, Charlie Bassett, John Cattanach, Cliff Carroll, Arthur Irwin and Jack Farrell. Bottom: Barney Gilligan, Paul Radford and Sandy Nava.

THE TAINTED 27

Ned Williamson, the pre-Babe Ruth major league record holder for the most home runs in a season. His 27 four-baggers in the whacky 1884 campaign were nearly half his career total.

Should a record be considered a record regardless of when or under what circumstances it's established? If the answer is yes, then Ned Williamson's 27 home runs for Chicago in 1884 were the major league season home run record prior to 1919. The stumbling block is that the chart below makes Williamson's barrage look pretty fishy. How else could all but two of his home runs come at his home park?

Knowing about that park only makes those 27 dingers seem all the more tainted. The outfield fences were so close to the plate—less than 200 feet in right field—that prior to 1884 balls hit over them were groundruled doubles. Furthermore, Buffalo's park, where Williamson's two road home runs occurred, was the second smallest in the National League. But to give Williamson his due, he hit at least one four-bagger against every first-rate pitcher he faced, including three 300-game winners. On the other hand, three of his teammates also clubbed more than 20 homers in 1884 and one of the trio, Fred Pfeffer, failed to tie Williamson's record mark only because, while he matched Williamson's 25 homers at home, he failed to hit any on the road. Withal, Chicago hammered 149 home runs in just 112 games, easily the most by any team prior to the 1927 New York Yankees.

It's impossible now to determine how many of Williamson's 27 round-trippers were legitimate, but the following season, playing in a different home park, he collected just four home runs. So it seems safe to believe that most of those 27 four-baggers in 1884 were on the cheap side. At the same time, though, it should be noted that Williamson might still have set a record in 1884 if the fences had been farther or the groundrules different. For in 1883, under the old ground rules, he slammed 49 doubles, the most by any National League player in the pre-1893 era.

NO.	DATE	OPPONENT	PITCHER	PARK
1	May 30	Detroit	Stump Weidman	Chicago*
2	May 30	Detroit	Frank Meinke	Chicago
3	May 30	Detroit	Frank Meinke	Chicago
4	June 7	Cleveland	John Harkins	Chicago
5	June 17	Buffalo	Billy Serad	Buffalo
6	June 23	Boston	Charlie Buffinton	Chicago
7	June 24	Boston	Jim Whitney	Chicago
8	June 24	Boston	Jim Whitney	Chicago
9	June 26	Providence	Hoss Radbourn	Chicago
10	July 1	Philadelphia	Charlie Ferguson	Chicago
11	July 3	Philadelphia	John Coleman	Chicago
12	July 4	Philadelphia	John Coleman	Chicago
13	July 7	New York	Ed Begley	Chicago
14	July 8	New York	Mickey Welch	Chicago
15	July 9	New York	Ed Begley	Chicago
16	July 19	Buffalo	Pud Galvin	Buffalo
17	July 28	Detroit	Jim Brill	Chicago
18	July 31	Detroit	Frank Meinke	Chicago
19	August 5	Cleveland	Jim McCormick	Chicago
20	August 9	Buffalo	Billy Serad	Chicago
21	August 11	Buffalo	Pud Galvin	Chicago
22	August 13	Buffalo	Pud Galvin	Chicago
23	September 20	Boston	Charlie Buffinton	Chicago**
24	October 4	New York	Mickey Welch	Chicago
25	October 4	New York	Mickey Welch	Chicago
26	October 10	Philadelphia	Charlie Ferguson	Chicago
27	October 11	Philadelphia	Charlie Ferguson	Chicago

*The season opened on May 1, but the White Stockings played on the road until May 29 because their home park was unavailable while team officials grappled with the city over the right to play there.

**The long dry spell following No. 22 occurred mostly because the White Stockings took to the road on August 16 and did not return home until September 16.

Louisville, and One Arm Daily set a new season strikeout mark when he fanned 483 Union Association hitters, including 19 in a single game, but even their extraordinary accomplishments were dwarfed by Hoss Radbourn of the Providence Grays.

The Grays began the 1884 season under a new manager, Frank Bancroft, who had learned from Harry Wright's mistake in giving the ball too often to Radbourn the previous year. Bancroft vowed that Radbourn would share the pitching load in 1884 with Charlie Sweeney. When Radbourn rebelled at the prospect and performed lackadaisically, he was suspended. Bancroft then found himself in a bind when Sweeney manipulated to have himself suspended too so he could jump to the Union Association. To salvage the season, Bancroft reinstated Radbourn but first had to accept the hard bargain Radbourn drove. Radbourn pledged to pitch every game for the rest of the season if the Grays would agree not to reserve him for the following year.

Radbourn did not actually pitch every game down the stretch—several other Grays took a turn in the box now and then too—but he toiled far more often than necessary, consider-

THE WALKER BROTHERS

On display with his first professional team—the 1883 Northwestern League champion Toledo Blue Stockings—is Moses Walker, who the following year became the first African-American player in major league history. Top: Joe Miller, Jumping Jack Jones, Walker, Chappy Lane and John Tilley. Middle: Sam Moffett, Sam Barkley, Captain Charlie Morton, Curt Welch and Hank O'Day. Front: Tom Poorman and Milo Lockwood.

The 1884 season introduced a welter of rule changes and innovations that forever changed the character of baseball. Unfortunately, though, the innovation that potentially could have been the most influential of all was not permanent. In 1884 the Toledo club brought with it to the American Association the catcher from its 1883 Northwestern League champion. His name was Moses Walker, and when he appeared in Toledo's opening game of the 1884 season at Louisville on May 1, he became the first African-American performer in major league history. Later in the season Walker was joined on the Toledos by his brother Welday for a brief while. Welday was only marginally talented and would probably have been gone from the majors anyway when the Union Association collapsed after the 1884 season, cutting jobs by one-third, but Moses was good enough, especially defensively, to keep playing in top company. Instead, after being the only major league prior to 1947 to allow black players, in 1885 the American Association entered into a secret unwritten compact with the National League to bar them. The League buckled under to threats from several of its stars, led by Cap Anson, to boycott the majors if they were not kept lily-white. In joining the League in its perfidious bargain, the Association lost not only a large talent pool of players but a vital piece of its autonomy, as well as an opportunity to alter baseball history in a way that would have indebted the game to it forever.

ing that the Grays won the pennant by ten and a half games, and eventually it took its toll on his arm. In 1884, though, Radbourn worked 679 innings, just one short of Will White's all-time record of 680 (set in 1879), en route to compiling the most wins ever. Whether it be 60 or just 59, as some sources contend, Radbourn was still not done. At the close of the season Providence officials accepted Mutrie's challenge to a three-game postseason match with his Association champion Mets. Each team put up $1,000 to go to the winner with the purse held by the New York *Clipper*, which billed the event as the first "World's Series." Since the games took place at the Polo Grounds in New York, the Mets' home park, at Mutrie's insistence they were played under Association rules and forbade overhand pitching. This was no handicap for Radbourn, who threw sidearm anyway, but to Mutrie's consternation, Keefe, his starting pitcher in the opening game, hit the first two Providence batters, Paul Hines and Cliff Carroll, giving each a base he would not have received under League rules. When Hines and Carroll both subsequently scored, Radbourn cruised to a 6–0 win. Two more victories by him in the following two days crowned Providence the first World's Series champion.

THE SEASONAL RECORD

NATIONAL LEAGUE

	W	L	PCT	HOME	ROAD	GB
1. Providence Grays	84	28	.750	45–11	39–17	—
2. Boston Beaneaters	73	38	.658	40–16	33–22	10.5
3. Buffalo Bisons	64	47	.577	37–18	27–29	19.5
4. New York Gothams	62	50	.554	34–22	28–28	22
Chicago White Stockings	62	50	.554	39–17	23–33	22
6. Philadelphia Quakers	39	73	.348	19–37	20–36	45
7. Cleveland Blues	35	77	.313	22–34	13–43	49
8. Detroit Wolverines	28	84	.250	18–38	10–46	56

	Pro	Bos	Buf	NY	Chi	Phi	Cle	Det	
Providence	—	9	10	13	11	13	13	15	84
Boston	7	—	9	8	10	13	14	12	73
Buffalo	6	6	—	5	10	11	14	12	64
New York	3	8	11	—	4	11	11	14	62
Chicago	5	6	6	12	—	14	8	11	62
Philadelphia	3	3	5	5	2	—	10	11	39
Cleveland	3	2	2	5	8	6	—	9	35
Detroit	1	4	4	2	5	5	7	—	28
	28	38	47	50	50	73	77	84	447

SEASON LEADERS

Batting Average (350 ABs)

1. Kelly, Chicago .354
2. O'Rourke, Buffalo .347
3. Sutton, Boston .346
4. Anson, Chicago .335
5. Brouthers, Buffalo .327

Slugging Average

1. Brouthers, Buffalo .563
2. Williamson, Chicago .554
3. Anson, Chicago .543
4. Kelly, Chicago .524
5. Pfeffer, Chicago .514

On–Base Percentage

1.	Kelly, Chicago	.414
2.	Gore, Chicago	.404
3.	O'Rourke, Buffalo	.392
4.	Sutton, Boston	.384
5.	Brouthers, Buffalo	.378

Home Runs

1.	Williamson, Chicago	27
2.	Pfeffer, Chicago	25
3.	Dalrymple, Chicago	22
4.	Anson, Chicago	21
5.	Brouthers, Buffalo	14

Hits

1.	O'Rourke, Buffalo	162
	Sutton, Boston	162
3.	Dalrymple, Chicago	161
4.	Kelly, Chicago	160
5.	Anson, Chicago	159

Bases on Balls

1.	Gore, Chicago	61
2.	Kelly, Chicago	46
3.	Hines, Providence	44
4.	Williamson, Chicago	42
5.	Jack Manning, Phila	40
	Hanlon, Detroit	40

Total Bases

1.	Dalrymple, Chicago	263
2.	Anson, Chicago	258
3.	Pfeffer, Chicago	240
4.	Kelly, Chicago	237
5.	Williamson, Chicago	231

RBI

1.	Anson, Chicago	102
2.	Pfeffer, Chicago	101
3.	Kelly, Chicago	95
4.	Williamson, Chicago	84
5.	Connor, New York	82

Runs

1.	Kelly, Chicago	120
2.	O'Rourke, Buffalo	119
	Hornung, Boston	119
4.	Dalrymple, Chicago	111
5.	Anson, Chicago	108

Strikeouts

1.	Wise, Boston	104
2.	Meinke, Detroit	89
3.	Morrill, Boston	87
4.	Galvin, Buffalo	80
	Hornung, Boston	80
	Phillips, Cleveland	80

PITCHING

Wins

1.	Radbourn, Providence	60
2.	Buffinton, Boston	48
3.	Galvin, Buffalo	46
4.	Welch, New York	39
5.	Corcoran, Chicago	35

Innings

1.	Radbourn, Providence	678.2
2.	Galvin, Buffalo	636.1
3.	Buffinton, Boston	587
4.	Welch, New York	557.1
5.	Corcoran, Chicago	516.2

Strikeouts

1.	Radbourn, Providence	441
2.	Buffinton, Boston	417
3.	Galvin, Buffalo	369
4.	Welch, New York	345
5.	Corcoran, Chicago	272

Losses

1.	Harkins, Cleveland	32
2.	Ferguson, Philadelphia	25
3.	Corcoran, Chicage	23
	Meinke, Detroit	23
5.	McCormick, Cleveland	22

Complete Games

1.	Radbourn, Providence	73
2.	Galvin, Buffalo	71
3.	Buffinton, Boston	63
4.	Welch, New York	62
5.	Corcoran, Chicago	57

Winning Percentage (25 decisions)

1.	Radbourn, Providence	.833
2.	Buffinton, Boston	.750
3.	Sweeney, Providence	.680
4.	Galvin, Buffalo	.676
5.	Welch, New York	.650

ERA (112 innings)

1.	Radbourn, Providence	1.38
2.	Sweeney, Providence	1.55
3.	Getzein, Detroit	1.95
4.	Galvin, Buffalo	1.99
5.	Whitney, Boston	2.09

Lowest On–Base Percentage

1.	Sweeney, Providence	.215
2.	Whitney, Boston	.223
3.	Radbourn, Providence	.234
4.	Getzein, Detroit	.237
5.	Buffinton, Boston	.244

FIELDING

Total Chances

1B	Anson, Chicago	1309
2B	Pfeffer, Chicago	905
3B	Mulvey, Philadelphia	440
SS	McClellan, Philadelphia	561
OF	Hanlon, Detroit	310
C	Gilligan, Providence	753
P	Corcoran, Chicago	203

Fielding Average

Start, Providence	.980
Burdock, Boston	.922
Sutton, Boston	.908
Force, Buffalo	.898
Hotaling, Cleveland	.917
J. Rowe, Buffalo	.943
McCormick, Cleveland	1.000

PROVIDENCE   Frank Bancroft   Messer Street Grounds

		G	AB	H	R	2B	3B	HR	RBI	BB	BA	SA
CF	Paul Hines	114	490	148	94	36	10	3	41	44	.302	.435
2B	Jack Farrell	111	469	102	70	13	6	1	37	35	.217	.277
LF	Cliff Carroll	113	452	118	90	16	4	3	54	29	.261	.334
3B	Jerry Denny	110	439	109	57	22	9	6	59	14	.248	.380
SS	Arthur Irwin	192	404	97	73	14	3	2	44	28	.240	.304
1B	Joe Start	93	381	105	80	10	5	2	32	35	.276	.344
P	Hoss Radbourn	87	361	83	48	7	1	1	37	26	.230	.263
RF	Paul Radford	97	355	70	56	11	2	1	29	25	.197	.248
C	Barney Gilligan	82	294	72	47	13	2	1	38	35	.245	.313
P	Charlie Sweeney	41	168	50	24	9	0	1	19	11	.298	.369
Sub	Sandy Nava	34	116	11	10	0	0	0	6	11	.095	.095
Sub	Charlie Bassett	27	79	11	10	2	1	0	6	4	.139	.190
P	Ed Conley	8	28	4	0	0	0	0	0	0	.143	.143
Sub	Miah Murray	8	27	5	1	0	0	0	1	1	.185	.185
P	Cyclone Miller	6	23	1	3	0	0	0	0	1	.043	.043
P	John Cattanach	1	4	0	0	0	0	0	0	0	.000	.000
P	Harry Arundel	1	3	1	2	0	0	0	1	1	.333	.333
		114	4093	987	665	153	43	21	404	300	.241	.315

1B Start 93, Denny 9, Hines 7, Radbourn 5, Sweeney 1, Gilligan 1, Murray 1
2B Farrell 109, Denny 3, Radbourn 1, Bassett 1, Nava 1
SS Irwin 102, Bassett 7, Nava 6, Radbourn 2
3B Denny 99, Bassett 13, Farrell 3, Gilligan 1
OF Carroll 113, Hines 108, Radford 96, Sweeney 17, Radbourn 7, Miller 4, Bassett 2, Murray 1, Cattanach 1
C   Gilligan 81, Nava 27, Murray 7, Denny 1
P   Radbourn 75, Sweeney 27, Conely 8, Miller 6, Radford 2, Cattanach 1, Arundel 1, Irwin 1, Hines 1

	G	IP	GS	CG	W	L	K	BB	SH	SV	ERA
Hoss Radbourn	**75**	**678.2**	**73**	**73**	**60**	12	**441**	98	11	1	**1.38**
Charlie Sweeney	27	221	24	22	17	8	145	29	4	1	1.55
Ed Conley	8	71	8	8	4	4	33	22	1	0	2.15
Cyclone Miller	6	34.2	5	2	2	2	12	11	0	0	2.08
Paul Radford	2	13	2	1	0	2	2	3	0	0	7.62
Harry Arundel	1	9	1	1	1	0	4	4	0	0	1.00
John Cattanach	1	5	1	0	0	0	2	4	0	0	9.00
Arthur Irwin	1	3	0	0	0	0	0	1	0	0	3.00
Paul Hines	1	1	0	0	0	0	0	0	0	0	0.00
		1036.1	114	107	84	28	639	172	**16**	**2**	**1.59**

BOSTON **John Morrill** **South End Grounds (I)**

		G	AB	H	R	2B	3B	HR	RBI	BB	BA	SA
LF	Joe Hornung	115	518	139	119	27	10	7	51	17	.268	.400
3B	Ezra Sutton	110	468	**162**	102	28	7	3	61	29	.346	.455
1B	John Morrill	111	438	114	80	19	7	3	61	30	.260	.356
SS	Sam Wise	114	426	91	60	15	9	4	41	25	.214	.319
RF	Bill Crowley	108	407	110	50	14	6	6	61	33	.270	.378
2B	Jack Burdock	87	361	97	65	14	4	6	49	15	.269	.380
P	Charlie Buffinton	87	352	94	48	18	3	1	39	16	.267	.344
CF	Jim Manning	89	345	83	52	8	6	2	35	19	.241	.316
P	Jim Whitney	66	270	70	41	17	5	3	40	16	.259	.393
C	Mert Hackett	72	268	55	28	13	2	1	20	2	.205	.280
C	Mike Hines	35	132	23	16	3	0	0	3	3	.174	.197
Sub	Bill Annis	27	96	17	17	2	0	0	3	0	.177	.198
Sub	Tom Gunning	12	45	5	4	1	1	0	2	1	.111	.178
P	John Connor	7	25	2	1	0	0	0	1	1	.080	.080
Sub	Gene Moriarty	4	16	1	1	0	0	0	0	0	.063	.063
P	Daisy Davis	4	16	0	0	0	0	0	0	0	.000	.000
Sub	Marty Barrett	3	6	0	0	0	0	0	0	0	.000	.000
		116	4189	1063	684	**179**	60	36	467	207	.254	.351

1B	Morrill 91, Whitney 15, Buffinton 11, Hornung 6
2B	Burdock 87, Morrill 17, Manning 9, Wise 7
SS	Wise 107, Manning 9
3B	Sutton 110, Manning 3, Morrill 2, Whitney 1, Hackett 1, Burdock 1
OF	Hornung 110, Crowley 108, Manning 73, Annis 27, Whitney 15, Buffinton 13, Moriarty 4, Davis 1, Morrill 1
C	Hackett 71, Hines 35, Gunning 12, Barrett 3
P	Buffinton 67, Whitney 41, Morrill 7, Connor 7, Davis 4

	G	IP	GS	CG	W	L	K	BB	SH	SV	ERA
Charlie Buffinton	67	587	67	63	48	16	417	76	8	0	2.15
Jim Whitney	38	336	37	35	23	14	270	27	6	0	2.09
John Connor	7	60	7	7	1	4	29	18	0	0	3.15
Daisy Davis	4	31	4	3	1	3	13	8	0	0	7.84
John Morrill	7	23	1	1	0	1	13	6	0	**2**	7.43
		1037	119	109	73	38	**742**	**135**	14	**2**	2.47

BUFFALO   Jim O'Rourke   Olympic Park (I)

		G	AB	H	R	2B	3B	HR	RBI	BB	BA	SA
RF	Jim Lillie	114	471	105	68	12	5	3	53	5	.223	.289
LF	Jim O'Rourke	108	467	**162**	119	33	7	5	63	35	.347	.480
3B	Deacon White	110	452	147	82	16	11	5	74	32	.325	.442
2B	Hardy Richardson	102	439	132	85	27	9	6	60	22	.301	.444
SS	Davy Force	106	403	83	47	13	3	0	36	27	.206	.253
C	Jack Rowe	93	400	126	85	14	14	4	61	23	.315	.450
1B	Dan Brouthers	93	398	130	82	22	15	14	79	33	.327	**.563**
UT	George Myers	78	325	59	34	9	2	2	32	13	.182	.240
P	Pud Galvin	72	274	49	34	6	1	0	24	2	.179	.208
CF	Dave Eggler	63	241	47	25	3	1	0	20	6	.195	.216
Sub	Chub Collins	45	169	30	24	6	0	0	20	14	.178	.213
P	Billy Serad	37	137	24	12	2	1	0	9	3	.175	.204
P	Art Hagan	3	13	4	3	0	0	0	1	0	.308	.308
P	Ed Coughlin	1	4	1	0	0	0	0	1	0	.250	.250
P	Bones Ely	1	4	0	0	0	0	0	0	0	.000	.000
		115	4197	1099	700	163	**69**	39	533	215	.262	.361

1B   Brouthers 93, O'Rourke 18, Richardson 3
2B   Richardson 71, Collins 42, Force 1
SS   Force 105, Rowe 6, Collins 3
3B   White 108, Richardson 5, Brouthers 1, O'Rourke 1
OF   Lillie 114, O'Rourke 86, Eggler 63, Myers 34, Rowe 30, Richardson 24, Serad 3, Galvin 1, Ely 1, Coughlin 1
C   Rowe 65, Myers 49, O'Rourke 10, White 3
P   Galvin 72, Serad 37, O'Rourke 4, Hagan 3, Lillie 2, Ely 1, Coughlin 1

	G	IP	GS	CG	W	L	K	BB	SH	SV	ERA
Pud Galvin #	72	636.1	72	71	46	22	369	63	**12**	0	1.99
Billy Serad	37	308	37	34	16	20	150	111	2	0	4.27
Art Hagan	3	26	3	3	1	2	4	4	0	0	5.88
Jim Lillie	2	13	1	0	0	1	4	5	0	0	6.23
Jim O'Rourke	4	12.2	0	0	0	1	3	1	0	1	2.84
Bones Ely	1	5	1	0	0	1	4	5	0	0	14.40
Ed Coughlin	1	0	0	0	0	0	0	0	0	0	—
			—1 forfeit W vs Chicago on August 11—								
	1001	114	108	63	47	534	189	14	1	2.95

\# No-hit game 18–0 vs Detroit, August 4

NEW YORK   Jim Price (56–42)   Monte Ward (6–8)   Polo Grounds (I)

		G	AB	H	R	2B	3B	HR	RBI	BB	BA	SA
CF	Monte Ward	113	482	122	98	11	8	2	51	28	.253	.322
2B	Roger Connor	116	477	151	98	28	4	4	82	38	.317	.417
1B	Alex McKinnon	116	470	128	66	21	12	4	73	8	.272	.394
LF	Pete Gillespie	101	413	109	75	7	4	2	44	19	.264	.315
3B	Frank Hankinson	105	389	90	44	16	7	2	43	23	.231	.324
C	Buck Ewing	94	382	106	90	15	**20**	3	41	28	.277	.445
SS	Ed Caskin	100	351	81	49	11	1	1	40	34	.231	.276
RF	Mike Dorgan	83	341	94	61	11	6	1	48	13	.276	.352
Sub	Danny Richardson	74	277	70	36	8	1	1	27	16	.253	.300
P	Mickey Welch	71	249	60	47	14	3	3	29	16	.241	.357
P	Ed Begley	33	121	22	12	4	0	0	8	8	.182	.215
Sub	John Humphries	20	64	6	6	0	0	0	2	9	.094	.094
Sub	Sandy Griffin	16	62	11	7	2	0	0	6	1	.177	.210

		G	AB	H	R	2B	3B	HR	RBI	BB	BA	SA
Sub	? Loughran	9	29	3	4	1	1	0	3	7	.103	.207
Sub	Charlie Manlove	3	10	0	0	0	0	0	0	0	.000	.000
Sub	Henry Oxley	3	4	0	0	0	0	0	0	1	.000	.000
P	Jim Brown	1	3	0	0	0	0	0	0	0	.000	.000
		116	4124	1053	693	149	67	23	497	249	.255	.341

1B McKinnon 116
2B Connor 67, Ward 47, Dorgan 3
SS Caskin 96, Richardson 19, Ewing 3
3B Hankinson 105, Connor 12, Ewing 1
OF Gillespie 101, Dorgan 64, Ward 59, Richardson 55, Connor 37, Griffin 16, Ewing 12, Welch 7, Begley 2, Manlove 1, Hankinson 1, Loughran 1
C   Ewing 80, Humphries 20, Loughran 9, Dorgan 6, Caskin 6, Manlove 3, Oxley 2
P   Welch 65, Begley 31, Dorgan 14, Ward 9, Ewing 1, Brown 1

	G	IP	GS	CG	W	L	K	BB	SH	SV	ERA
Mickey Welch	65	557.1	65	62	39	21	345	**146**	4	0	2.50
Ed Begley	31	266	30	30	12	18	104	99	0	0	4.16
Mike Dorgan	14	113	14	12	8	6	90	51	0	0	3.50
Monte Ward	9	60.2	5	5	3	3	23	18	0	0	3.41
Jim Brown	1	9	1	1	0	1	2	8	0	0	5.00
Buck Ewing	1	8	1	1	0	1	3	4	0	0	1.13
	1014	116	**111**	62	50	567	326	4	0	3.12

CHICAGO   **Cap Anson**   **Lake Front Park (II)**

		G	AB	H	R	2B	3B	HR	RBI	BB	BA	SA
LF	Abner Dalrymple	111	**521**	161	111	18	9	22	69	14	.309	.505
1B	Cap Anson	112	475	159	108	30	3	21	**102**	29	.335	.543
2B	Fred Pfeffer	112	467	135	105	10	10	25	101	25	.289	.514
RF	King Kelly	108	452	160	**120**	28	5	13	95	46	**.354**	.524
CF	George Gore	103	422	134	104	18	4	5	34	**61**	.318	.415
3B	Ned Williamson	107	417	116	84	18	8	**27**	84	42	.278	.554
SS	Tom Burns	83	343	84	54	14	2	7	44	13	.245	.359
C	Silver Flint	73	279	57	35	5	2	9	45	7	.204	.333
P	Larry Corcoran	64	251	61	43	3	4	1	19	10	.243	.299
Sub	Billy Sunday	43	176	39	25	4	1	4	28	4	.222	.324
P	John Clarkson	21	84	22	16	6	2	3	17	2	.262	.488
Sub	Walt Kinzie	19	82	13	4	3	0	2	8	0	.159	.268
P	Fred Goldsmith	22	81	11	11	2	0	2	6	7	.136	.235
P	Joe Brown	15	61	13	6	1	0	0	3	0	.213	.230
P	Tom Lee	6	24	3	0	1	0	0	1	0	.125	.167
Sub	Sy Sutcliffe	4	15	3	4	1	0	0	2	2	.200	.267
P	George Crosby	3	13	4	1	0	0	1	1	0	.308	.538
P	John Hibbard	2	7	0	0	0	0	0	0	0	.000	.000
P	Fred Andrus	1	5	1	3	0	0	0	0	1	.200	.200
P	Tom Lynch	1	4	0	0	0	0	0	0	0	.000	.000
P	Mike Corcoran	1	3	0	0	0	0	0	0	1	.000	.000
		113	4182	**1176**	**834**	162	50	**142**	659	264	**.281**	**.446**

1B Anson 112, Kelly 2, Clarkson 1, Brown 1, Lynch 1
2B Pfeffer 112, Kelly 1
SS Burns 80, Kinzie 17, Kelly 12, Corcoran 2, Anson 1, Lee 1
3B Williamson 99, Kelly 10, Burns 3, Clarkson 2, Kinzie 2

OF Dalrymple 111, Gore 103, Kelly 63, Sunday 43, Brown 9, Clarkson 8, Corcoran 4, Goldsmith 2
C Flint 73, Kelly 28, Williamson 10, Sutcliffe 4, Anson 3, Brown 1
P L. Corcoran 60, Goldsmith 21, Clarkson 14, Brown 7, Lee 5, Crosby 3, Hibbard 2, Kelly 2, Williamson 2, Andrus 1, Anson 1, Pfeffer 1, M. Corcoran 1, Lynch 1

	G	IP	GS	CG	W	L	K	BB	SH	SV	ERA
Larry Corcoran #	60	516.2	59	57	35	23	272	116	7	0	2.40
Fred Goldsmith	21	188	21	20	9	11	34	29	1	0	4.26
John Clarkson	14	118	13	12	10	3	102	25	0	0	2.14
Joe Brown	7	50	6	5	4	2	27	7	0	0	4.68
Tom Lee	5	45.1	5	5	1	4	14	15	0	0	3.77
George Crosby	3	28	3	3	1	2	11	12	0	0	3.54
John Hibbard	2	17	2	2	1	1	4	9	1	0	2.65
Mike Corcoran	1	9	1	1	0	1	2	7	0	0	4.00
Fred Andrus	1	9	1	1	1	0	2	2	0	0	2.00
Tom Lynch	1	7	1	0	0	0	2	3	0	0	2.57
King Kelly	2	5.1	0	0	0	1	1	2	0	0	8.44
Ned Williamson	2	2	0	0	0	0	0	2	0	0	18.00
Cap Anson	1	1	0	0	0	1	1	1	0	0	18.00
Fred Pfeffer	1	1	0	0	0	0	0	1	0	0	9.00
		—1 forfeit L vs Buffalo on August 11—									
		997.1	112	106	62	49	472	231	9	0	3.03

No-hit game 6–0 vs Providence, June 27

PHILADELPHIA		Harry Wright		Recreation Park								
		G	AB	H	R	2B	3B	HR	RBI	BB	BA	SA
SS	Bill McClellan	111	450	110	71	13	2	3	33	28	.258	.316
LF	Blondie Purcell	103	428	108	67	11	7	1	31	29	.252	.318
1B	Sid Farrar	111	428	105	62	16	6	1	45	9	.245	.318
RF	Jack Manning	104	424	115	71	29	4	5	52	40	.271	.394
2B	Ed Andrews	109	420	93	74	21	2	0	23	9	.221	.281
3B	Joe Mulvey	100	401	92	47	11	2	2	32	4	.229	.282
CF	Jim Fogarty	97	378	80	42	12	6	1	37	20	.212	.283
P	Charlie Ferguson	52	203	50	26	6	3	0	20	19	.246	.305
P	John Coleman	43	171	42	16	7	2	0	22	8	.246	.310
C	John Crowley	48	168	41	26	7	3	0	19	15	.244	.321
C	Frank Ringo	26	91	12	4	2	0	0	6	3	.132	.154
P	Bill Vinton	21	78	9	9	1	0	0	4	3	.115	.128
Sub	Tom Lynch	13	48	15	7	4	2	0	3	4	.313	.479
P	Jim McElroy	14	48	7	3	0	0	0	3	1	.146	.146
Sub	Jack Remsen	12	43	9	9	2	0	0	3	6	.209	.256
Sub	Buster Hoover	10	42	8	6	1	0	1	4	4	.190	.286
Sub	Jack Clements	9	30	7	3	0	0	0	0	4	.233	.233
Sub	Tony Cusick	9	29	4	2	0	0	0	1	0	.138	.138
P	Joe Knight	6	24	6	2	3	0	0	2	0	.250	.375
Sub	Joe Kappel	4	15	1	1	0	0	0	0	0	.067	.067
Sub	Gene Vadeboncouer	4	14	3	1	0	0	0	3	1	.214	.214
Sub	Paul Cook	3	12	1	0	0	0	0	0	0	.083	.083
Sub	Mike Depangher	4	10	2	0	0	0	0	0	1	.200	.200
P	Con Murphy	3	10	0	0	0	0	0	0	1	.000	.000
P	Sparrow Morton	2	8	3	0	1	0	0	0	0	.375	.500
Sub	Lew Hardie	3	8	3	0	2	0	0	0	0	.375	.625
P	Shadow Pyle	1	4	0	0	0	0	0	0	0	.000	.000
P	Cyclone Miller	1	4	0	0	0	0	0	0	0	.000	.000
Sub	Bill Conway	1	4	0	0	0	0	0	0	0	.000	.000
Sub	Hezekiah Allen	1	3	2	0	0	0	0	0	0	.667	.667
Sub	Ed Sixsmith	1	2	0	0	0	0	0	0	0	.000	.000
		113	3998	934	549	149	39	14	343	209	.234	.301

1B   Farrar 111, Coleman 2
2B   Andrews 109, Fogarty 4
SS   McClellan 111, Fogarty 4
3B   Mulvey 100, Fogarty 14
OF   Manning 104, Purcell 103, Fogarty 78, Coleman 27, Remsen 12, Hoover 10, Lynch 7, Ferguson 5, McElroy 1, Vinton 1, McClellan 1
C   Crowley 48, Ringo 26, Cusick 9, Clements 9, Lynch 7, Kappel 4, Vadeboncouer 4, Depangher 4, Hardie 3, Cook 3, Conway 1, Allen 1, Sixsmith 1
P   Ferguson 50, Vinton 21, Coleman 21, McElroy 13, Knight 6, Murphy 3, Morton 2, Pyle 1, Miller 1, Fogarty 1, Purcell 1

	G	IP	GS	CG	W	L	K	BB	SH	SV	ERA
Charlie Ferguson	50	416.2	47	46	21	25	194	93	2	1	3.54
Bill Vinton	21	182	21	20	10	10	105	35	0	0	2.23
John Coleman	21	154.1	19	14	5	15	37	22	1	0	4.90
Jim McElroy	13	111	13	13	1	12	45	54	0	0	4.86
Joe Knight	6	51	6	6	2	4	8	21	0	0	5.47
Con Murphy	3	26	3	3	0	3	10	6	0	0	6.58
Sparrow Morton	2	17	2	2	0	2	5	11	0	0	5.29
Shadow Pyle	1	9	1	1	0	1	4	6	0	0	4.00
Cyclone Miller	1	9	1	1	0	1	1	6	0	0	10.00
Blondie Purcell	1	4	0	0	0	0	1	0	0	0	2.25
Jim Fogarty	1	1	0	0	0	0	1	0	0	0	0.00
		981	113	106	39	73	411	254	3	1	3.93

CLEVELAND   **Charlie Hackett**   **Kennard Street Park**

		G	AB	H	R	2B	3B	HR	RBI	BB	BA	SA
1B	Bill Phillips	111	464	128	58	25	12	3	46	18	.276	.401
3B	Mike Muldoon	110	422	101	46	16	6	2	38	18	.239	.320
CF	Pete Hotaling	102	408	99	69	16	6	3	27	28	.243	.333
RF	Jake Evans	80	313	81	32	18	3	1	38	15	.259	.345
2B	Germany Smith	72	291	74	31	14	4	4	26	2	.254	.371
SS	Jack Glasscock	72	281	70	45	4	4	1	22	25	.249	.302
P	Sam Moffett	67	256	47	26	12	2	0	14	8	.184	.246
P	John Harkins	61	229	47	24	4	2	0	20	7	.205	.240
C	Doc Bushong	62	203	48	24	6	1	0	10	17	.236	.276
P	Jim McCormick	42	190	50	15	5	4	0	23	1	.263	.332
LF	Willie Murphy	42	168	38	18	3	3	1	9	1	.226	.298
C	Fatty Briody	42	148	25	17	6	0	1	12	6	.169	.230
Sub	George Pinkney	36	144	45	18	9	0	0	16	10	.313	.375
Sub	Ernie Burch	32	124	26	9	4	0	0	7	5	.210	.242
Sub	Joe Ardner	25	92	16	6	1	1	0	4	1	.174	.207
Sub	Mike Moynahan	12	45	13	9	2	1	0	6	7	.289	.378
Sub	Gurdon Whitely	8	34	5	4	0	0	0	0	1	.147	.147
Sub	Jerrie Moore	9	30	6	1	0	0	0	10	0	.200	.200
Sub	George Strief	8	29	7	2	2	0	0	0	0	.241	.310
P	John Henry	9	26	4	2	0	0	0	0	0	.154	.154
Sub	George Fisher	6	24	3	2	0	0	0	0	0	.125	.125
Sub	Pit Gilman	2	10	1	0	0	0	0	0	0	.100	.100
Sub	Bill Smith	1	3	0	0	0	0	0	0	0	.000	.000
		113	3934	934	458	147	49	16	329	170	.237	.312

1B   Phillips 111, Moffett 2
2B   Smith 42, Ardner 25, Pinkney 25, Fisher 6, Moynahan 6, Evans 4, Glasscock 3, Moffett 1, Hotaling 1, Muldoon 1
SS   Glasscock 69, Smith 30, Pinkney 11, Moynahan 3, Evans 2, Harkins 1
3B   Muldoon 109, Strief 2, Arnder 1, Moffett 1, Harkins 1

OF   Hotaling 102, Evans 76, Murphy 42, Moffett 42, Burch 32, Harkins 17, Whitely 8, McCormick 8, Strief 6, Henry 4, Moynahan 3, Gilman 2, B. Smith 1, Briody 1, Bushong 1, Muldoon 1

C   Bushong 62, Briody 42, Moore 9, Fisher 1

P   Harkins 46, McCormick 42, Moffett 24, Henry 5, Glasscock 2

	G	IP	GS	CG	W	L	K	BB	SH	SV	ERA
John Harkins	46	391	45	42	12	**32**	192	108	3	0	3.68
Jim McCormick	42	359	41	39	19	22	182	75	3	0	2.86
Sam Moffett	24	197.2	22	21	3	19	84	58	0	0	3.87
John Henry	5	42	5	5	1	4	23	26	1	0	3.64
Jack Glasscock	2	5	0	0	0	0	1	2	0	0	5.40
		994.2	113	107	35	77	482	269	7	0	3.43

DETROIT   Jack Chapman   Recreation Park

		G	AB	H	R	2B	3B	HR	RBI	BB	BA	SA
LF	George Wood	114	473	119	79	16	10	8	29	39	.252	.378
3B	Joe Farrell	110	461	104	59	10	5	3	41	14	.226	.289
CF	Ned Hanlon	114	450	119	86	18	6	5	39	40	.264	.364
1B	Milt Scott	110	438	108	29	17	5	3	50	9	.247	.329
C	Charlie Bennett	92	341	90	37	18	6	3	40	36	.264	.380
SS/P	Frank Meinke	92	341	56	28	5	7	6	24	6	.164	.273
RF	Stump Weidman	81	300	49	24	6	0	0	26	13	.163	.183
2B	Bill Geiss	75	283	50	22	11	4	2	16	6	.177	.265
P	Dupee Shaw	36	136	26	16	4	1	1	8	4	.191	.257
Sub	Henry Jones	34	127	28	24	3	1	0	3	16	.220	.260
Sub	Harry Buker	30	111	15	5	1	0	0	3	4	.135	.144
Sub	Frank Cox	27	102	13	6	3	1	0	4	2	.127	.176
Sub	Ed Gastfield	23	82	6	6	1	0	0	2	2	.073	.085
Sub	Tom Kearns	21	79	16	9	0	1	0	7	2	.203	.228
P	Charlie Getzein	17	55	6	4	0	0	0	1	5	.109	.109
P	Frank Brill	13	44	6	5	0	0	0	2	1	.136	.136
Sub	Fred Wood	12	42	2	4	0	0	0	1	3	.048	.048
Sub	Chief Zimmer	8	29	2	0	1	0	0	0	1	.069	.069
Sub	Ed Santry	6	22	4	1	0	0	0	0	1	.182	.182
Sub	Walter Prince	7	21	3	0	0	0	0	1	3	.143	.143
Sub	Frank Jones	2	8	1	0	0	0	0	0	0	.125	.125
Sub	Joe Weber	2	8	0	0	0	0	0	0	0	.000	.000
Sub	Ben Guiney	2	7	0	0	0	0	0	0	0	.000	.000
Sub	Walt Walker	1	4	1	1	0	0	0	0	0	.250	.250
Sub	Dickie Lowe	1	3	1	0	0	0	0	0	0	.333	.333
Sub	Dave Beatle	1	3	0	0	0	0	0	0	0	.000	.000
		114	3970	824	445	114	47	31	297	207	.208	.284

1B   Scott 110, Gastfield 2, Bennett 1, Geiss 1

2B   Geiss 73, Kearns 21, H. Jones 16, Meinke 3, Santry 1, Bennett 1, Weidman 1

SS   Meinke 51, Cox 27, Buker 19, H. Jones 8, Santry 5, Bennett 4, F. Jones 1, F. Wood 1, Weidman 1

3B   Farrell 110, Meinke 3, Bennett 1, G. Wood 1

OF   Hanlon 114, G. Wood 114, Weidman 53, H. Jones 12, Buker 11, Shaw 10, Prince 7, F. Wood 6, Bennett 5, Meinke 4, Gastfield 2, Zimmer 2, Weber 2, F. Jones 1, Beatle 1, Brill 1, Farrell 1, Geiss 1

C   Bennett 79, Gastfield 19, F. Wood 7, Zimmer 6, Guiney 2, Lowe 1, Beatle 1, Walker 1

P   Meinke 35, Shaw 28, Weidman 26, Getzein 17, Brill 12, Geiss 1

	G	IP	GS	CG	W	L	K	BB	SH	SV	ERA
Frank Meinke	35	289	31	31	8	23	124	63	1	0	3.18
Dupee Shaw	28	227.2	28	25	9	18	142	72	0	0	3.04
Stump Weidman	26	212.2	26	24	4	21	96	57	0	0	3.72
Charlie Getzein	17	147.1	17	17	5	12	107	25	1	0	1.95
Frank Brill	12	103	12	12	2	10	18	26	1	0	5.50
Bill Geiss	1	5	0	0	0	0	1	2	0	0	14.40
		984.2	114	109	28	84	488	245	3	0	3.38

WORLD'S SERIES

Providence (NL) defeated New York (AA) 3 games to 0

Game 1 at Polo Grounds (NY), Oct. 23: Pro (Radbourn) 6, NY (Keefe) 0
Game 2 at Polo Grounds (NY), Oct. 24: Pro (Radbourn) 3, NY (Keefe) 1
Game 3 at Polo Grounds (NY), Oct. 24: Pro (Radbourn) 12, NY (Becannon) 2

PROVIDENCE

		G	AB	H	R	2B	3B	HR	RBI	BB	BA	SA
LF	Cliff Carroll	3	10	1	2	0	0	0	1	1	.100	.100
P	Hoss Radbourn	3	10	1	1	0	0	0	2	1	.100	.100
1B	Joe Start	3	10	1	0	0	0	0	1	0	.100	.100
3B	Jerry Denny	3	9	4	3	0	1	1	2	0	**.444**	**1.000**
2B	Jack Farrell	3	9	4	3	2	0	0	0	0	**.444**	.667
C	Barney Gilligan	3	9	4	3	2	0	0	2	0	**.444**	.667
SS	Arthur Irwin	3	9	2	2	0	1	0	2	0	.222	.444
CF	Paul Hines	3	8	2	5	0	0	0	1	3	.250	.250
RF	Paul Radford	3	7	0	1	0	0	0	1	0	.000	.000
		3	81	19	20	4	2	1	12	5	.235	.370

	G	IP	GS	CG	W	L	K	BB	SH	SV	ERA
Hoss Radbourn	3	22	3	3	3	0	16	0	1	0	0.00

NEW YORK

		G	AB	H	R	2B	3B	HR	RBI	BB	BA	SA
3B	Dude Esterbrook	3	10	3	0	1	0	0	0	0	.300	.400
SS	Candy Nelson	3	10	1	0	0	0	0	0	0	.100	.100
LF	Steve Brady	3	10	0	1	0	0	0	0	0	.000	.000
CF	Chief Roseman	3	9	3	1	0	0	0	1	0	.300	.300
1B	Dave Orr	3	9	1	0	0	0	0	0	0	.100	.100
RF	Eddie Kennedy	3	7	0	0	0	0	0	0	0	.000	.000
2B	Dasher Troy	2	5	1	0	0	0	0	1	0	.200	.200
C	Charlie Reipschlager	2	5	0	1	0	0	0	0	0	.000	.000
P	Tim Keefe	2	5	1	0	0	0	0	0	0	.200	.200
2B	Tom Forster	1	3	0	0	0	0	0	0	0	.000	.000
P	Buck Becannon	1	2	1	0	0	0	0	0	0	.500	.500
C	Bill Holbert	1	2	0	0	0	0	0	0	0	.000	.000
		3	77	11	3	1	0	0	2	0	.143	.156

	G	IP	GS	CG	W	L	K	BB	SH	SV	ERA
Tim Keefe	2	15	2	2	0	2	12	3	0	0	3.60
Buck Becannon	1	6	1	1	0	1	1	2	0	0	10.50
		21	3	3	0	3	13	5	0	0	5.57

AMERICAN ASSOCIATION

	W	L	PCT	HOME	ROAD	GB
1. New York Metropolitans	75	32	.701	42–9	33–23	—
2. Columbus Buckeyes	69	39	.639	38–16	31–23	6.5
3. Louisville Eclipse	68	40	.630	41–14	27–26	7.5
4. St. Louis Browns	67	40	.626	38–16	29–24	8
5. Cincinnati Reds	68	41	.624	40–16	28–25	8
6. Baltimore Orioles	63	43	.594	42–13	21–30	11.5
7. Philadelphia Athletics	61	46	.570	38–16	23–30	14
8. Toledo Blue Stockings	46	58	.442	28–25	18–33	27.5
9. Brooklyn Grays	40	64	.385	23–26	17–38	33.5
10. Virginia	12	30	.286	5–15	7–15	30
11. Pittsburgh Alleghenys	30	78	.278	18–37	12–41	45.5
12. Indianapolis Hoosiers	29	78	.271	15–39	12–39	46
13. Washington Statesmen	12	51	.190	10–20	2–31	41

	NY	Co	Lo	SL	Ci	Ba	Ph	To	Bro	Vi	Pi	In	Wa	
New York	—	5	7	5	6	5	8	5	9	2	9	8	6	75
Columbus	4	—	5	5	7	4	5	8	7	2	9	8	5	69
Louisville	3	5	—	5	5	4	6	9	6	4	8	9	4	68
St. Louis	4	5	5	—	6	5	7	5	7	3	9	6	5	67
Cincinnati	4	3	5	4	—	6	4	7	8	4	8	9	6	68
Baltimore	5	6	6	5	4	—	3	5	5	4	9	9	2	63
Philadelphia	2	5	3	3	6	7	—	6	6	2	8	6	7	61
Toledo	4	1	1	5	3	5	3	—	4	4	5	6	5	46
Brooklyn	1	3	3	2	2	5	3	4	—	3	4	7	3	40
Virginia	0	2	1	1	0	0	0	0	2	—	4	2	*	12
Pittsburgh	1	1	2	1	1	0	2	5	6	1	—	6	4	30
Indianapolis	2	2	1	3	1	1	4	3	3	1	4	—	4	29
Washington	2	1	1	1	0	1	1	1	1	*	1	2	—	12
	32	39	40	40	41	43	46	58	64	30	78	78	51	640

*Teams did not play one another.

SEASON LEADERS*

Batting Average (300 ABs)

1.	Orr, New York	.354
2.	Reilly, Cincinnati	.339
3.	Browning, Louisville	.336
4.	Stovey, Philadelphia	.326
5.	Lewis, St. Louis	.323

On–Base Percentage

1.	C. Jones, Cincinnati	.376
2.	Nelson, New York	.375
3.	Stovey, Philadelphia	.368
4.	Fennelly, Wash–Cinc	.367
5.	Reilly, Cincinnati	.366

Slugging Average

1.	Reilly, Cincinnati	.551
2.	Stovey, Philadelphia	.545
3.	Orr, New York	.539
4.	Fennelly, Wash–Cinci	.480
5.	Browning, Louisville	.472

Total Bases

1.	Reilly, Cincinnati	247
	Orr, New York	247
3.	Stovey, Philadelphia	244
4.	C. Jones, Cincinnati	222
5.	Browning, Louisville	211

Home Runs

1.	Reilly, Cincinnati	11
2.	Stovey, Philadelphia	10
3.	Orr, New York	9
4.	Mann, Columbus	7
	C. Jones, Cincinnati	7

Hits

1.	Orr, New York	162
2.	Reilly, Cincinnati	152
3.	Browning, Louisville	150
	Esterbrook, New York	150
5.	Jones, Cincinnati	148

* RBI leaders unavailable

Bases on Balls

1.	Nelson, New York	74
2.	Geer, Brooklyn	38
3.	Jones, Cincinnati	37
4.	Macullar, Baltimore	36
5.	Richmond, Columbus	35

Runs

1.	Stovey, Philadelphia	124
2.	C. Jones, Cincinnati	117
3.	A. Latham, St. Louis	115
4.	Nelson, New York	114
	Reilly, Cincinnati	114

PITCHING

Wins

1.	Hecker, Louisville	52
2.	Lynch, New York	37
	Keefe, New York	37
4.	Mullane, Toledo	36
5.	Morris, Columbus	34
	White, Cincinnati	34

Innings

1.	Hecker, Louisville	670.2
2.	Mullane, Toledo	567
3.	McKeon, Indianapolis	512
4.	Lynch, New York	496
5.	Keefe, New York	482.2

Strikeouts

1.	Hecker, Louisville	385
2.	Henderson, Baltimore	346
3.	Mullane, Toledo	325
4.	Keefe, New York	317
5.	McKeon, Indianapolis	308

ERA (110 innings)

1.	Hecker, Lcuisville	1.80
2.	Foutz, St. Louis	2.18
	Morris, Columbus	2.18
4.	Keefe, New York	2.26
5.	Mountain, Columbus	2.45

Losses

1.	McKeon, Indianapolis	41
2.	Sullivan, Pittsburgh	35
	Terry, Brooklyn	35
4.	Barr, Wash–Ind	34
5.	O'Day, Toledo	28

Complete games

1.	Hecker, Louisville	72
2.	Mullane, Toledo	64
3.	McKeon, Indianapolis	59
4.	Keefe, New York	56
5.	Terry, Brooklyn	55

Winning Percentage (25 decisions)

1.	Morris, Columbus	.723
2.	Hecker, Louisville	.722
3.	Foutz, St. Louis	.714
4.	Lynch, New York	.712
5.	Keefe, New York	.685

Lowest On–Base Percentage

1.	Hecker, Louisville	.226
2.	Morris, Columbus	.234
3.	Lynch, New York	.236
4.	Keefe, New York	.240
5.	Foutz, St. Louis	.255

FIELDING

Total Chances

1B	Comiskey, St. Louis	1311
2B	McPhee, Cincinnati	844
3B	A. Latham, St. Louis	514
SS	Geer, Brooklyn	617
OF	C. Jones, Cincinnati	247
C	Trott, Baltimore	621
P	Hecker, Louisville	205

Fielding Average

Kerins, Indianapolis	.972
Creamer, Pittsburgh	.937
Corey, Philadelphia	.887
Houck, Philadelphia	.893
Corkhill, Cincinnati	.934
Milligan, Philadelphia	.939
Hecker, Louisville	.951

NEW YORK   Jim Mutrie   Metropolitan Park (33 games) (Polo Grounds (I) (22 games)

		G	AB	H	R	2B	3B	HR	RBI	BB	BA	SA
RF	Steve Brady	112	485	122	102	11	3	1	—	21	.252	.293
3B	Dude Esterbrook	112	477	150	110	29	11	1	—	12	.314	.428
1B	Dave Orr	110	458	**162**	82	32	13	9	112	5	**.354**	.539
CF	Chief Roseman	107	436	130	97	16	11	4	—	21	.298	.413
SS	Candy Nelson	111	432	110	114	15	3	1	—	**74**	.255	.310
2B	Dasher Troy	107	421	111	80	22	10	2	—	19	.264	.378
LF	Eddie Kennedy	103	378	72	49	6	2	1	—	16	.190	.225
C	Bill Holbert	65	255	53	28	5	0	0	—	7	.208	.227
C	Charlie Reipschlager	59	233	56	21	13	2	0	—	1	.240	.313
P	Tim Keefe	63	213	50	27	3	6	3	—	18	.235	.347
P	Jack Lynch	54	195	30	21	2	3	0	—	9	.154	.195
Sub	Gracie Pierce	5	20	5	2	1	0	0	—	0	.250	.300
Sub	Tony Murphy	1	3	1	1	0	0	0	—	0	.333	.333
Sub	Henry Oxley	1	3	0	0	0	0	0	—	0	.000	.000
P	Buck Becannon	1	3	0	0	0	0	0	—	0	.000	.000
		112	4012	1052	734	155	64	22	—	203	.262	.349

1B Orr 110, Brady 5
2B Troy 107, Pierce 3, Nelson 1, Brady 1, Kennedy 1
SS Nelson 110, Kennedy 1, Holbert 1
3B Esterbrook 112
OF Brady 110, Roseman 107, Kennedy 100, Reipschlager 8, Holbert 5, Keefe 5, Orr 3, Pierce 3
C   Holbert 59, Reipschlager 51, Oxley 1, Murphy 1, Kennedy 1
P   Keefe 57, Lynch 55, Becannon 1

	G	IP	GS	CG	W	L	K	BB	SH	SV	ERA
Jack Lynch	55	496	54	54	37	15	292	42	5	0	2.64
Tim Keefe	57	482.2	57	56	37	17	317	75	4	0	2.29
Buck Becannon	1	6	1	1	1	0	2	2	0	0	1.50
		984.2	112	**111**	75	32	611	119	9	0	2.46

COLUMBUS   **Gus Schmelz**   **Recreation Park (I)**

		G	AB	H	R	2B	3B	HR	RBI	BB	BA	SA
RF	Tom Brown	107	451	123	93	9	11	5	32	24	.273	.375
2B	Pop Smith	108	445	106	78	18	10	6	—	20	.238	.364
1B	Jim Field	105	417	97	74	9	7	4	—	23	.233	.317
3B	Willie Kuehne	110	415	98	48	13	16	5	—	9	.236	.381
SS	John Richmond	105	398	100	57	13	7	3	—	35	.251	.342
CF	Fred Mann	99	366	101	70	12	18	7	—	25	.276	.464
C	Fred Carroll	69	252	70	46	13	5	6	—	13	.278	.440
C	Rudy Kemmler	61	211	42	28	3	3	0	—	15	.199	.242
P	Frank Mountain	58	210	50	26	7	3	4	—	9	.238	.357
LF	Patsy Cahill	59	210	46	28	3	3	0	—	6	.219	.262
P	Ed Morris	57	199	37	19	4	8	0	—	5	.186	.286
P	Dummy Dundon	26	86	12	6	2	2	0	—	5	.140	.209
OF	Tom Mansell	23	77	15	9	1	3	0	—	6	.195	.286
P	Al Bauers	3	11	3	2	0	0	0	—	0	.273	.273
P	Tom Sullivan	2	11	1	1	0	0	0	—	1	.091	.091
		110	3759	901	585	107	96	**40**	—	196	.240	.351

1B   Field 105, Dundon 3, Kemmler 2
2B   Smith 108, Mann 2
SS   Richmond 105, Cahill 5
3B   Kuehne 109, Mansell 1
OF   Brown 107, Mann 97, Cahill 54, Mansell 22, Mountain 17, Dundon 16, Carroll 15, Morris 10, Kuehne 1, Kemmler 1
C   Kemmler 58, Carroll 54
P   Morris 52, Mountain 42, Dundon 11, Brown 4, Sullivan 4, Bauers 3, Cahill 2

	G	IP	GS	CG	W	L	K	BB	SH	SV	ERA
Ed Morris #	52	429.2	52	47	34	13	302	51	3	0	2.18
Frank Mountain ##	42	360.2	41	40	23	17	156	78	5	**1**	2.45
Ed Dundon	11	81	9	7	6	4	37	15	0	0	3.78
Tom Sullivan	4	31	4	4	2	2	12	3	0	0	4.06
Al Bauers	3	25	3	3	1	2	13	14	0	0	4.68
Tom Brown	4	19	0	0	2	1	5	7	0	0	7.11
Patsy Cahill	2	16	1	1	1	0	1	4	0	0	5.06
		962.1	110	102	69	39	526	172	8	**1**	2.68

No hit game 5–0 vs Pittsburgh, May 29
No hit game 12–0 vs Washington, June 5

LOUISVILLE   **Joe Gerhardt (39–18)**   **Mike Walsh (28–22)**   **Eclipse Park (I)**

		G	AB	H	R	2B	3B	HR	RBI	BB	BA	SA
RF	Chicken Wolf	110	**486**	146	79	24	11	3	73	4	.300	.414
3B	Pete Browning	103	447	150	101	33	8	4	47	13	.336	.472
LF	Leech Maskrey	105	412	103	48	13	4	0	—	17	.250	.301
2B	Joe Gerhardt	106	404	89	39	7	8	0	—	13	.220	.277
CF	Monk Cline	94	396	115	91	16	7	2	—	27	.290	.381
SS	Tom McLaughlin	98	335	67	41	11	6	0	—	22	.200	.269
P	Guy Hecker	78	316	94	53	14	8	4	—	10	.297	.430
1B	Juice Latham	77	308	52	31	3	3	0	—	8	.169	.198
P	Phil Reccius	73	263	63	23	9	2	3	—	5	.240	.323
C	Dan Sullivan	63	247	59	27	8	6	0	—	9	.239	.320
C	Ed Whiting	42	157	35	16	7	3	0	—	9	.223	.306
Sub	Wally Andrews	14	49	10	10	5	1	0	—	4	.204	.347
P	Denny Driscoll	13	48	9	5	1	0	0	—	2	.188	.208

		G	AB	H	R	2B	3B	HR	RBI	BB	BA	SA
P	Ren Deagle	12	45	6	2	1	0	0	—	0	.133	.156
Sub	Buttercup Dickerson	8	28	4	6	0	2	1	—	3	.143	.393
Sub	Len Stockwell	2	9	1	0	0	0	0	—	0	.111	.111
Sub	Bill Hunter	2	7	1	1	0	0	0	—	0	.143	.143
		110	3957	1004	573	152	69	17	—	146	.254	.340

1B   Latham 76, Browning 23, Andrews 9, Whiting 2, Wolf 1
2B   Gerhardt 105, Browning 4, McLaughlin 2
SS   McLaughlin 93, Reccius 10, Cline 6, Andrews 1, Maskrey 1, Wolf 1, Gerhardt 1
3B   Browning 52, Reccius 51, McLaughlin 4, Andrews 3, Maskrey 3, Wolf 1, Latham 1
OF   Maskrey 103, Wolf 101, Cline 90, Browning 24, Dickerson 8, Hecker 5, Deagle 3, Whiting 2, Driscoll 2, Stockwell 2, Andrews 1, Sullivan 1
C   Sullivan 63, Whiting 40, Wolf 11, Hunter 2, Stockwell 1
P   Hecker 76, Reccius 18, Driscoll 13, Deagle 12, Browning 1

	G	IP	GS	CG	W	L	K	BB	SH	SV	ERA
Guy Hecker	**76**	**670.2**	**73**	**72**	**52**	20	**385**	56	6	0	**1.80**
Phil Reccius	18	129.1	11	11	6	7	46	19	0	0	2.71
Denny Driscoll	13	102	13	10	6	6	16	7	0	0	3.44
Ren Deagle	12	87.1	12	8	4	6	23	13	0	0	2.58
Pete Browning	1	0.1	1	0	0	1	0	2	0	0	54.00
		989.2	110	101	68	40	470	**97**	6	0	**2.17**

ST. LOUIS   Jimmy Williams (51–33)   Charlie Comiskey (18–7)   Sportsman's Park (I)

		G	AB	H	R	2B	3B	HR	RBI	BB	BA	SA
3B	Arlie Latham	110	474	130	115	17	12	1	—	19	.274	.367
SS	Bill Gleason	110	472	127	97	21	7	1	—	28	.269	.350
1B	Charlie Comiskey	108	460	110	76	17	6	2	84	5	.239	.315
RF	Hugh Nicol	110	442	115	79	14	5	0	—	22	.260	.314
2B	Joe Quest	81	310	64	46	9	5	0	—	19	.206	.268
CF	Fred Lewis	73	300	97	59	25	3	0	—	16	.323	.427
LF	Tip O'Neill	78	297	82	49	13	11	3	54	12	.276	.424
C	Pat Deasley	75	254	52	27	5	4	0	—	7	.205	.256
Sub	George Strief	43	184	37	22	5	2	2	—	13	.201	.283
P	Jumbo McGinnis	40	146	34	16	9	1	0	—	4	.233	.308
C	Tom Dolan	35	137	36	19	6	2	0	—	6	.263	.336
P	Dave Foutz	33	119	27	17	4	0	0	—	8	.227	.261
P	Daisy Davis	25	87	15	5	0	1	0	—	5	.172	.195
P	Bob Caruthers	23	82	21	15	2	0	2	—	4	.256	.354
Sub	Charlie Krehmeyer	21	70	16	3	0	1	0	—	2	.229	.257
Sub	Johnny Lavin	16	52	11	9	2	0	0	—	3	.212	.250
Sub	Walt Goldsby	5	20	4	2	0	0	0	—	0	.200	.200
Sub	Harry Wheeler	5	19	5	0	2	0	0	—	1	.263	.368
Sub	Walt Kinzie	2	9	1	0	0	0	0	—	0	.111	.111
Sub	Al Struve	1	7	2	2	0	0	0	—	0	.286	.286
Sub	Chick Fulmer	1	5	0	0	0	0	0	—	0	.000	.000
Sub	Nin Alexander	1	4	0	0	0	0	0	—	0	.000	.000
Sub	Jim McCauley	1	2	0	0	0	0	0	—	0	.000	.000
		110	3952	986	658	151	60	11	—	174	.249	.326

1B   Comiskey 108, Strief 1, Krehmeyer 1, Deasley 1, O'Neill 1
2B   Quest 80, Nicol 23, Strief 4, Kinzie 2, Fulmer 1, Comiskey 1
SS   Gleason 110, Nicol 1
3B   Latham 110, Nicol 1, Gleason 1

OF   Nicol 87, Lewis 73, O'Neill 64, Strief 43, Lavin 16, Caruthers 16, Krehmeyer 15, Foutz 14, Goldsby 5, Wheeler 5, Davis 4, Dolan 2, Deasley 2, Alexander 1, Struve 1, Quest 1
C   Deasley 75, Dolan 34, Krehmeyer 7, McCauley 1, Alexander 1, Struve 1, Latham 1
P   McGinnis 40, Foutz 25, Davis 25, O'Neill 17, Caruthers 13, Comiskey 1

	G	IP	GS	CG	W	L	K	BB	SH	SV	ERA
Jumbo McGinnis	40	354.1	40	39	24	16	141	35	5	0	2.84
Dave Foutz	25	206.2	25	19	15	6	95	36	2	0	2.18
Daisy Davis	25	198.1	24	20	10	12	143	35	1	0	2.90
Tip O'Neill	17	141	14	14	11	4	36	51	0	0	2.68
Bob Caruthers	13	82.2	7	7	7	2	58	15	0	0	2.61
Charlie Comiskey	1	4	0	0	0	0	4	0	0	0	2.25
		987	110	99	67	40	477	172	8	0	2.67

CINCINNATI   **Will White (44–27)**   **Pop Snyder (24–14)**   **American Park**

		G	AB	H	R	2B	3B	HR	RBI	BB	BA	SA
3B	Hick Carpenter	108	474	121	80	16	2	4	—	6	.255	.323
LF	Charley Jones	113	472	148	117	19	17	7	71	37	.314	.470
RF	Pop Corkhill	110	452	124	85	13	11	4	—	6	.274	.378
2B	Bid McPhee	112	450	125	107	8	7	5	64	27	.278	.369
1B	Long John Reilly	105	448	152	114	24	19	**11**	91	5	.339	**.551**
C	Pop Snyder	67	268	69	32	9	9	0	—	7	.257	.338
SS	Jimmy Peoples	69	267	45	28	2	2	1	—	6	.169	.202
CF	Tom Mansell	65	266	66	49	4	6	0	—	15	.248	.308
P	Will White	52	184	35	28	1	2	1	—	10	.190	.234
Sub	Buck West	33	131	32	20	2	8	1	—	2	.244	.405
C	Phil Powers	34	130	18	10	1	0	0	—	5	.138	.146
Sub	Frank Fennelly	28	122	43	42	5	8	2	—	11	.352	.574
P	Billy Mountjoy	34	119	18	13	2	1	0	—	9	.151	.185
Sub	Chick Fulmer	31	114	20	13	2	1	0	—	1	.175	.211
P	Gus Shallix	23	84	3	3	0	0	0	—	4	.036	.036
Sub	Jimmy Woulfe	8	34	5	3	0	1	0	—	1	.147	.206
Sub	Frank Berkelbach	6	25	6	3	0	1	0	—	0	.240	.320
Sub	George Miller	6	20	5	6	1	1	0	—	1	.250	.400
Sub	Icicle Reeder	3	14	2	0	0	0	0	—	0	.143	.143
P	Ren Deagle	4	13	0	1	0	0	0	—	1	.000	.000
Sub	John Parsons	1	3	0	0	0	0	0	—	0	.000	.000
		112	4090	1037	**754**	109	96	36	—	154	.254	.354

1B   Reilly 103, Corkhill 6, Powers 2, Snyder 2, Peoples 1
2B   McPhee 112
SS   Peoples 47, Fulmer 29, Fennelly 28, Corkhill 11, Reilly 1
3B   Carpenter 108, Corkhill 3, Fulmer 1, Woulfe 1, Peoples 1
OF   Jones 113, Corkhill 92, Mansell 65, West 33, Peoples 10, Woulfe 7, Berkelbach 6, Reeder 3, Reilly 3, Powers 2, Fulmer 2, Mountjoy 2, Snyder 1, Parsons 1, Carpenter 1
C   Snyder 65, Powers 31, Peoples 14, Miller 6
P   White 52, Mountjoy 33, Shallix 23, Deagle 4, Corkhill 1

	G	IP	GS	CG	W	L	K	BB	SH	SV	ERA
Will White	52	456	52	52	34	18	118	74	7	0	3.32
Billy Mountjoy	33	289	33	32	19	12	96	43	3	0	2.93
Gus Shallix	23	199.2	23	23	11	10	78	53	0	0	3.70
Ren Deagle	4	34	4	4	3	1	12	9	1	0	5.03
Pop Corkhill	1	5	0	0	1	0	4	2	0	0	1.80
		983.2	112	**111**	68	41	308	181	**11**	0	3.33

BALTIMORE   Billy Barnie   Oriole Park (I)

		G	AB	H	R	2B	3B	HR	RBI	BB	BA	SA
3B	Joe Sommer	107	479	129	96	11	10	4	—	8	.269	.379
CF	Jim Clinton	103	437	118	82	12	6	4	—	29	.270	.352
1B	Dan Stearns	100	396	94	61	12	3	3	—	28	.237	.306
SS	Jimmy Macullar	107	360	73	73	16	6	4	—	36	.203	.314
2B	Tim Manning	91	341	70	49	14	5	2	—	26	.205	.293
LF	Tom York	83	314	70	64	14	7	1	—	34	.223	.322
C	Sam Trott	71	284	73	36	17	9	3	—	4	.257	.412
C	Bill Traffley	53	210	37	25	4	6	0	—	3	.176	.252
P	Hardie Henderson	53	203	46	24	7	7	0	—	5	.227	.330
P	Bob Emslie	51	195	37	21	6	3	0	—	2	.190	.251
RF	Gid Gardner	41	173	37	32	6	8	2	—	14	.214	.376
Sub	Dennis Casey	37	149	37	20	7	4	3	—	5	.248	.409
Sub	Oyster Burns	35	131	39	34	2	6	6	23	7	.298	.542
Sub	Buttercup Dickerson	13	56	12	9	2	1	0	—	4	.214	.286
Sub	John Ake	13	52	10	1	0	1	0	—	0	.192	.231
Sub	Pat Burns	6	25	5	3	2	1	0	—	3	.200	.360
P	Jim McLaughlin	5	22	5	3	1	1	0	—	0	.227	.364
P	Fred Goldsmith	4	14	2	2	0	0	0	—	2	.143	.143
Sub	Jim Roxburgh	1	4	2	1	0	0	0	—	1	.500	.500
		108	3845	896	636	133	84	32	—	**211**	.233	.336

1B   Stearns 100, P. Burns 6, Gardner 2, Goldsmith 1, Traffley 1
2B   Manning 91, O. Burns 10, Trott 6, Clinton 1, Sommer 1, Stearns 1
SS   Macullar 107, Ake 1
3B   Sommer 97, Ake 9, Dickerson 1, O. Burns 1
OF   Clinton 103, York 83, Gardner 40, Casey 37, O. Burns 24, Dickerson 12, Sommer 9, Traffley 6, Trott 5, Ake 3, McLaughlin 3, Henderson 3, Emslie 1
C   Trot 60, Traffley 47, Roxburgh 2
P   Henderson 52, Emslie 50, Goldsmith 4, McLaughlin 3, O. Burns 2

	G	IP	GS	CG	W	L	K	BB	SH	SV	ERA
Bob Emslie	50	451.1	50	50	32	17	264	88	4	0	2.75
Hardie Henderson	52	439.1	52	50	27	23	346	116	4	0	2.62
Fred Goldsmith	4	30	4	3	3	1	11	2	0	0	2.70
Jim McLaughlin	3	22	2	2	1	2	8	11	0	0	3.68
Oyster Burns	2	9	0	0	0	0	6	2	0	1	3.00
		955.2	108	105	63	43	**635**	219	8	**1**	2.71

PHILADELPHIA   Lon Knight   Jefferson Street Grounds

		G	AB	H	R	2B	3B	HR	RBI	BB	BA	SA
RF	Lon Knight	108	484	131	94	18	12	1	—	10	.271	.364
SS	Sadie Houck	108	472	140	93	19	14	0	—	7	.297	.396
1B	Harry Stovey	104	448	146	**124**	22	**23**	10	83	26	.326	.545
3B	Fred Corey	104	439	121	64	17	16	5	—	17	.276	.421
2B	Cub Stricker	107	399	92	59	16	11	1	—	19	.231	.333
CF	Henry Larkin	85	326	90	59	21	9	3	37	15	.276	.423
C	Jocko Milligan	66	268	77	39	20	3	3	—	8	.287	.418
LF	Judd Birchall	54	221	57	36	2	2	0	—	4	.258	.285
P	Bobby Mathews	49	184	34	26	5	1	0	—	7	.185	.223
C	Jack O'Brien	36	138	39	25	6	1	1	—	9	.283	.362
Sub	Bob Blakiston	32	128	33	21	6	0	0	—	11	.258	.305
P	Billy Taylor	30	111	28	8	6	2	0	—	2	.252	.342
Sub	John Coleman	28	107	22	16	2	3	2	—	5	.206	.336
P	Al Atkinson	22	83	16	13	3	1	0	—	4	.193	.253

		G	AB	H	R	2B	3B	HR	RBI	BB	BA	SA
Sub	Mike Mansell	20	70	14	6	1	1	0	—	5	.200	.243
P	Charlie Hilsey	6	24	5	5	1	1	0	—	0	.208	.333
Sub	Frank Siffel	7	17	3	3	1	0	0	—	0	.176	.235
Sub	Ed Rowen	4	15	6	4	1	0	0	—	1	.400	.467
Sub	Elmer Foster	5	11	2	4	0	0	0	—	3	.182	.182
Sub	Frank Ringo	2	6	0	0	0	0	0	—	0	.000	.000
P	Phenomenal Smith	1	4	1	1	0	0	0	—	0	.250	.250
Sub	Mike Moynahan	1	4	0	0	0	0	0	—	0	.000	.000
		108	3959	**1057**	700	**167**	**100**	26	—	153	**.267**	**.379**

1B   Stovey 104, Knight 2, Blakiston 1, Coleman 2, O'Brien 1
2B   Stricker 107, Larkin 2, Blakiston 1, Houck 1
SS   Houck 108, Blakiston 1
3B   Corey 104, Blakiston 2, Birchall 2
OF   Knight 108, Larkin 85, Birchall 52, Coleman 24, Blakiston 28, Mansell 20, O'Brien 5, Hilsey 3, Atkinson 2, Foster 1, Moynahan 1, Mathews 1, Milligan 1, Stricker 1
C   Milligan 65, O'Brien 30, Siffel 7, Rowen 4, Foster 4, Ringo 2, Stricker 1
P   Mathews 49, Taylor 30, Atkinson 22, Hilsey 3, Coleman 3, Smith 1, Knight 1, Stricker 1

	G	IP	GS	CG	W	L	K	BB	SH	SV	ERA
Bobby Mathews	49	430.2	49	48	30	18	286	49	3	0	3.31
Billy Taylor	30	260	30	30	18	12	130	44	1	0	2.53
Al Atkinson #	22	184	22	20	11	11	93	21	1	0	4.21
Charlie Hilsey	3	27	3	3	2	1	10	5	0	0	4.67
John Coleman	3	21	2	2	0	2	5	2	0	0	3.43
Lon Knight	2	14	1	1	0	1	2	4	0	0	9.00
Phenomenal Smith	1	9	1	1	0	1	3	1	0	0	4.00
Cub Stricker	1	3	0	0	0	0	1	1	0	0	6.00
		948.2	108	105	61	46	530	127	5	0	3.41

No-hit game 10–1 vs Pittsburgh, May 25

TOLEDO   **Charlie Morton**   **League Park**

		G	AB	H	R	2B	3B	HR	RBI	BB	BA	SA
2B	Sam Barkley	104	435	133	71	**39**	9	1	—	22	.306	.444
CF	Curt Welch	109	425	95	61	24	5	0	—	10	.224	.304
SS	Joe Miller	105	423	101	46	12	8	1	—	26	.239	.312
RF	Tom Poorman	94	382	89	56	8	7	0	—	10	.233	.291
P	Tony Mullane	95	352	97	49	19	3	3	—	33	.276	.372
P	Hank O'Day	64	242	51	23	9	1	0	—	10	.211	.256
1B	Chappy Lane	57	215	49	26	9	5	1	—	2	.228	.330
Sub	Joe Moffett	56	204	41	17	5	3	0	—	2	.201	.255
3B	Ed Brown	42	153	27	13	3	0	0	—	2	.176	.196
C	Moses Walker	42	152	40	23	2	3	0	—	8	.263	.316
C	Deacon McGuire	45	151	28	12	7	0	1	—	5	.185	.252
Sub	George Meister	34	119	23	9	6	0	0	—	3	.193	.244
Sub	Charlie Morton	32	111	18	11	6	2	0	—	7	.162	.252
LF	Frank Olin	26	86	22	16	0	1	1	—	5	.256	.314
Sub	Trick McSorley	21	68	17	12	1	0	0	—	3	.250	.265
Sub	John Tilley	17	56	10	5	2	0	0	—	4	.179	.214
Sub	Tug Arundel	15	47	4	6	0	0	0	—	3	.085	.085
Sub	Sim Bullas	13	45	4	4	0	1	0	—	1	.089	.133
Sub	Ed Miller	8	24	6	2	0	0	0	—	1	.250	.250
Sub	Welday Walker	5	18	4	1	1	0	0	—	0	.222	.278
P	Ed Kent	1	4	0	0	0	0	0	—	0	.000	.000
		110	3712	859	463	153	48	8	—	157	.231	.305

1B	Lane 46, Moffett 38, McSorley 16, Mullane 7, O'Day 3, Welch 1
2B	Barkley 103, Moffett 3, Welch 2, Morton 1, Mullane 1, Brown 1
SS	Miller 105, McGuire 3, Mullane 1
3B	Brown 39, Meister 34, Morton 16, Moffett 12, Mullane 6, O'Day 3, Lane 2, McSorley 1
OF	Welch 106, Poorman 93, Olin 26, O'Day 24, Mullane 18, Tilley 17, Morton 15, Lane 9, Miller 8, W. Walker 5, McSorley 5, McGuire 4, Moffett 3, Bullas 2, Brown 2, M. Walker 1
C	M. Walker 41, McGuire 41, Arundel 15, Bullas 12, Barkley 2, Welch 2, Brown 1, Lane 1
P	Mullane 67, O'Day 41, Morton 3, Poorman 1, McSorley 1, Kent 1, Brown 1

	G	IP	GS	CG	W	L	K	BB	SH	SV	ERA
Tony Mullane	67	567	65	64	36	26	325	89	**7**	0	2.52
Hank O'Day	41	326.2	40	35	9	28	163	66	2	**1**	3.75
Charlie Morton	3	23.1	1	1	0	1	7	5	0	0	3.09
Ed Kent	1	9	1	1	0	1	4	3	0	0	6.00
Tom Poorman	1	9	1	1	0	1	0	2	0	0	3.00
Ed Brown	1	9	1	1	0	1	1	4	0	0	9.00
Trick McSorley	1	2	0	0	0	0	1	0	0	0	4.50
—1 forfeit W vs Virginia on September 24—											
	946	109	103	45	58	501	169	9	**1**		3.06

BROOKLYN **George Taylor** **Washington Park (I)**

		G	AB	H	R	2B	3B	HR	RBI	BB	BA	SA
RF	John Cassidy	106	433	109	57	11	6	2	—	19	.252	.319
SS	Billy Geer	107	391	82	68	15	7	0	—	38	.210	.284
2B	Bill Greenwood	92	385	83	52	8	3	3	—	10	.216	.275
LF	Oscar Walker	95	382	103	59	12	8	2	—	9	.270	.359
3B	Fred Warner	84	352	78	40	4	0	1	—	17	.222	.241
CF	Jack Remsen	81	301	67	45	6	6	3	—	23	.223	.312
1B	Charlie Householder	76	273	66	28	15	3	3	—	12	.242	.352
P	Adonis Terry	68	240	56	16	10	3	0	—	8	.233	.300
OF	Ike Benners	49	189	38	25	11	5	1	—	7	.201	.328
C	Jack Corcoran	52	185	39	17	4	3	0	—	8	.211	.265
Sub	Jim Knowles	41	153	36	19	5	1	1	—	3	.235	.301
P	Sam Kimber	40	138	20	13	1	2	0	—	9	.145	.181
Sub	Charlie Jones	25	90	16	10	1	0	0	—	5	.178	.189
Sub	Hickie Wilson	24	82	19	13	4	0	0	—	5	.232	.280
Sub	John Farrow	16	58	11	7	2	0	0	—	3	.190	.224
Sub	Jackie Hayes	16	51	12	4	3	0	0	—	3	.235	.294
P	Jim Conway	14	47	6	1	0	0	0	—	0	.128	.128
Sub	Jerry Dorgan	4	13	4	2	0	0	0	—	0	.308	.308
		109	3763	845	476	112	47	16	—	179	.225	.292

1B	Householder 40, Walker 36, Knowles 29, Wilson 3, Geer 1, Benners 1
2B	Greenwood 92, Jones 13, Corcoran 4, Geer 2, Wilson 1, Householder 1
SS	Geer 106, Corcoran 2, Conway 2, Knowles 1, Cassidy 1, Greenwood 1
3B	Warner 83, Jones 11, Knowles 11, Cassidy 5
OF	Cassidy 100, Remsen 81, Walker 59, Benners 48, Kimber 13, Terry 13, Wilson 12, Corcoran 9, Householder 6, Jones 2, Conway 2, Hayes 2, Warner 1
C	Corcoran 38, Householder 31, Farrow 16, Hayes 14, Wilson 10, Dorgan 4
P	Terry 57, Kimber 40, Conway 13, Geer 2, Corcoran 1

	G	IP	GS	CG	W	L	K	BB	SH	SV	ERA
Adonis Terry	57	485	56	55	20	35	233	75	3	0	3.49
Sam Kimber #	40	352.1	40	40	17	20	119	69	3	0	3.91
Jim Conway	13	105.1	13	10	3	9	25	15	0	0	4.44
Billy Geer	2	5	0	0	0	0	1	3	0	0	12.60
John Corcoran	1	1	0	0	0	0	0	1	0	0	0.00
		948.2	109	105	40	64	378	163	6	0	3.79

No-hit game 0–0 vs Toledo, October 4 (11 innings, game called by darkness)

VIRGINIA   Felix Moses   Allen Pasture

		G	AB	H	R	2B	3B	HR	RBI	BB	BA	SA
LF	Ed Glenn	43	175	43	26	2	4	1	—	5	.246	.320
3B	Billy Nash	45	166	33	31	8	8	1	—	12	.199	.361
1B	Jim Powell	41	151	37	23	8	4	0	—	7	.245	.351
SS	Bill Schenck	42	151	31	14	4	0	3	—	1	.205	.291
CF	Dick Johnston	39	146	41	23	5	5	2	—	2	.281	.425
2B	Terry Larkin	40	139	28	17	1	4	0	—	9	.201	.266
RF	Mike Mansell	29	113	34	21	2	5	0	—	8	.301	.407
Sub	Marshall Quinton	26	94	22	12	5	0	0	—	0	.234	.287
P	Pete Meegan	22	75	12	6	1	2	0	—	1	.160	.227
P	Ed Dugan	22	70	8	4	0	0	0	—	5	.114	.114
C	John Hanna	22	67	13	6	2	1	0	—	0	.194	.254
Sub	Walt Goldsby	11	40	9	4	1	0	0	—	1	.225	.250
C	Bill Dugan	9	28	2	4	1	0	0	—	0	.071	.107
Sub	Bill Morgan	6	20	2	0	0	0	0	—	2	.100	.100
Sub	Andy Swan	3	10	5	2	0	0	0	—	0	.500	.500
Sub	Wash Williams	2	8	2	0	0	0	0	—	0	.250	.250
P	Wes Curry	2	8	2	1	0	0	0	—	0	.250	.250
Sub	Ed Ford	2	5	0	0	0	0	0	—	0	.000	.000
P	Ted Firth	1	3	1	0	0	0	0	—	0	.333	.333
		46	1469	325	194	40	33	7	—	53	.221	.308

1B	Powell 41, Swan 3, Ford 1
2B	Larkin 40, E. Dugan 2, Schenck 2, Morgan 1
SS	Schenck 40, Quinton 2, Johnston 2, Ford 1, Hanna 1
3B	Nash 45
OF	Glenn 43, Johnston 37, Mansell 29, Goldsby 11, Quinton 10, Williams 2, Morgan 2, Meegan 1
C	Hanna 21, Quinton 14, B. Dugan 9, Morgan 3
P	Meegan 22, E. Dugan 20, Curry 2, Firth 1

	G	IP	GS	CG	W	L	K	BB	SH	SV	ERA
Pete Meegan	22	179	22	22	7	12	106	29	1	0	4.32
Ed Dugan	20	166.1	20	20	5	14	60	15	0	0	4.49
Wes Curry	2	16	2	2	0	2	1	3	0	0	5.06
Ted Firth	1	9	1	1	0	1	0	5	0	0	8.00
		—1 forfeit L vs Toledo on September 24—									
		402	45	45	12	29	167	52	1	0	4.52

PITTSBURGH   **Denny McKnight (4–8)**   **Bob Ferguson (11–31)**   **Joe Battin (6–7)**
George Creamer (0–8)   **Horace Phillips (9–24)**   **Recreation Park**

		G	AB	H	R	2B	3B	HR	RBI	BB	BA	SA
RF	Ed Swartwood	102	399	115	74	19	6	0	—	33	.288	.366
LF	Doggie Miller	89	347	78	46	10	2	0	—	13	.225	.265
2B	George Creamer	98	339	62	38	8	5	0	—	16	.183	.236
SS	Bill White	74	291	66	25	7	10	0	—	13	.227	.320
P	Fleury Sullivan	54	189	29	14	2	1	0	—	5	.153	.175
1B	Jimmy Knowles	46	182	42	19	5	7	0	—	5	.231	.335
C	Bill Colgan	48	161	25	10	4	1	0	—	3	.155	.193
3B	Joe Battin	43	158	28	10	1	2	0	—	3	.177	.209
CF	George Taylor	41	152	32	22	4	1	0	—	6	.211	.250
P	Jack Neagle	43	148	22	13	6	0	0	—	6	.149	.189
Sub	Jim McDonald	38	145	23	11	3	0	0	—	2	.159	.179
Sub	Tom Forster	35	.26	28	10	5	0	0	—	7	.222	.262
C	Jackie Hayes	33	124	28	11	6	1	0	—	4	.226	.290
Sub	Charlie Eden	32	122	33	12	7	4	1	—	7	.270	.418
Sub	Jay Faatz	29	112	27	18	2	3	0	—	1	.241	.313
Sub	Mike Mansell	27	100	14	15	0	3	1	—	7	.140	.230
Sub	Art Whitney	23	94	28	10	4	0	0	—	1	.298	.340
Sub	Billy Reid	19	70	17	11	2	0	0	—	4	.243	.271
Sub	Conny Doyle	15	58	17	8	3	2	0	—	2	.293	.314
Sub	Jimmy Woulfe	15	53	6	7	1	0	0	—	0	.113	.132
Sub	Chuck Lauer	13	44	5	5	0	0	0	—	0	.114	.114
Sub	Joe Quest	12	43	9	2	3	0	0	—	0	.209	.279
Sub	Bob Ferguson	10	41	6	2	0	0	0	—	0	.146	.146
Sub	Jim Dee	12	40	5	0	0	0	0	—	1	.125	.125
Sub	Frank Smith	10	36	9	3	0	1	0	—	0	.250	.306
Sub	Jack Gorman	8	27	4	3	0	1	0	—	1	.148	.222
P	John Fox	8	25	6	4	2	0	0	—	0	.240	.320
Sub	Charlie Hautz	7	24	5	0	0	0	0	—	3	.208	.208
P	Frank Beck	3	12	4	1	1	0	0	—	0	.333	.417
P	Bill Nelson	3	12	2	1	0	0	0	—	0	.167	.167
Sub	Gus Alberts	2	5	1	1	0	0	0		0	.200	.200
Sub	John Peters	1	4	0	0	0	0	0	—	0	.000	.000
P	Phenomenal Smith	1	4	0	0	0	0	0	—	0	.000	.000
Sub	Jim Gray	1	2	1	0	0	0	0	—	0	.500	.500
		110	3689	777	406	105	50	2	—	143	.211	.268

1B   Knowles 46, Faatz 29, Swartwood 22, Hayes 5, Hautz 5, Ferguson 3, Reid 1, Lauer 1, Mansell 1
2B   Creamer 98, Quest 7, Reid 1, Hayes 1, Forster 1, McDonald 1, Miller 1
SS   White 60, Forster 28, Dee 12, Quest 5, Alberts 2, Whitney 1, Doyle 1, Peters 1, Fox 1
3B   Battin 43, McDonald 22, Whitney 21, White 10, Forster 6, Miller 3, Gorman 2, Ferguson 1, Reid 1, Swartwood 1, Gray 1
OF   Swartwood 79, Miller 49, Taylor 41, Eden 31, Mansell 27, Reid 17, Woulfe 15, McDonald 15, Doyle 14, Lauer 10, Neagle 6, Ferguson 6, Colgan 4, White 4, Gorman 3, Hayes 3, F. Smith 3, Sullivan 3, Hautz 2, Whitney 1, Quest 1
C   Colgan 44, Miller 36, Hayes 24, F. Smith 7
P   Sullivan 51, Neagle 38, Fox 7, Beck 3, Gorman 3, Nelson 3, Lauer 3, Eden 2, P. Smith 1, Swartwood 1

	G	IP	GS	CG	W	L	K	BB	SH	SV	ERA
Fleury Sullivan	51	441	51	51	16	35	189	96	2	0	4.20
Jack Neagle	38	326	38	37	11	26	85	70	2	0	3.73
John Fox	7	59	7	7	1	6	22	16	0	0	5.64
Bill Nelson	3	26	3	3	1	2	6	8	0	0	4.50
Frank Beck	3	25	3	3	0	3	11	6	0	0	6.12
Jack Gorman	3	25	3	3	1	2	10	5	0	0	4.68
Chuck Lauer	2	19	3	2	0	2	8	9	0	0	7.58
Charlie Eden	2	12	1	1	0	1	3	3	0	0	6.00
Phenomenal Smith	1	8	1	1	0	1	4	2	0	0	9.00
Ed Swartwood	1	2.1	0	0	0	0	0	1	0	0	11.57
		943.1	110	108	30	78	338	216	4	0	4.35

INDIANAPOLIS — Jim Gifford (25–60)   Bill Watkins (4–18)   Seventh Street Park

		G	AB	H	R	2B	3B	HR	RBI	BB	BA	SA
SS	Marr Phillips	97	413	111	41	18	8	0	—	5	.269	.351
LF	John Peltz	106	393	86	40	13	17	3	—	7	.219	.361
1B	John Kerins	93	364	78	58	10	3	6	—	6	.214	.308
3B	Pat Callahan	61	258	67	38	8	5	2	—	8	.260	.353
RF	Podgie Weihe	62	256	65	29	13	2	4	—	9	.254	.367
C	Jim Keenan	68	249	73	36	14	4	3	—	16	.293	.418
P	Larry McKeon	69	247	53	29	8	1	0	—	1	.215	.255
2B	Ed Merrill	55	196	35	14	3	1	0	—	6	.179	.204
CF	Jon Morrison	44	182	48	26	6	8	1	—	7	.264	.401
Sub	Jerry Dorgan	34	141	42	22	6	1	0	—	2	.298	.355
Sub	Chub Collins	38	138	31	18	3	1	0	—	9	.225	.261
Sub	Jim Donnelly	40	134	34	22	2	2	0	—	5	.254	.299
Sub	Bill Watkins	34	127	26	16	4	0	0	—	5	.205	.236
Sub	John Sneed	27	102	22	14	4	0	1	—	6	.216	.284
Sub	Tug Thompson	24	97	20	10	3	0	0	—	2	.206	.237
Sub	Charlie Robinson	20	80	23	11	2	0	0	—	3	.288	.313
P	Bob Barr	18	65	12	6	3	2	0	—	3	.185	.292
P	Al McCauley	17	53	10	7	0	1	0	—	12	.189	.226
P	Jake Aydelott	13	44	5	1	1	0	0	—	2	.114	.136
Sub	Gene Moriarty	10	37	8	4	0	2	0	—	0	.216	.324
Sub	Bill Butler	9	31	7	7	3	2	0	—	1	.226	.452
Sub	Marshall Locke	7	29	7	5	0	1	0	—	0	.241	.310
P	Tommy Bond	7	23	3	0	1	1	0	—	0	.130	.261
Sub	Jim Tray	6	21	6	2	0	0	0	—	2	.286	.286
P	Mac MacArthur	6	21	2	1	0	0	0	—	1	.095	.095
Sub	Bob Blakiston	6	18	4	0	1	0	0	—	1	.222	.278
Sub	Jim Holdsworth	5	18	2	1	0	0	0	—	2	.111	.111
Sub	Harry Decker	4	15	4	1	1	0	0	—	1	.267	.333
Sub	Marty Barrett	5	13	1	1	1	0	0	—	1	.077	.154
Sub	Charlie Levis	3	10	2	0	0	0	0	—	0	.200	.200
Sub	George Mundinger	3	8	2	1	0	0	0	—	0	.250	.250
Sub	Charlie Reising	2	8	0	0	0	0	0	—	1	.000	.000
Sub	Frank Monroe	2	8	0	1	0	0	0	—	0	.000	.000
Sub	Harry Weber	3	8	0	0	0	0	0	—	0	.000	.000
Sub	Pete Fries	1	3	1	0	1	0	0	—	1	.333	.667
		110	3810	890	462	129	62	20	—	125	.233	.315

1B   Kerins 87, Keenan 6, McCauley 5, McKeon 5, Blakiston 5, Weihe 3, Levis 3, Tray 2, Barr 2, Fries 1
2B   Merrill 55, Collins 38, Watkins 9, Weihe 4, McKeon 3, Donnelly 2
SS   Phillips 97, Donnelly 8, Robinson 3, Watkins 2, Keenan 1
3B   Callahan 61, Donnelly 24, Watkins 23, Kerins 1, Moriarty 1

OF   Peltz 106, Weihe 58, Morrison 44, Dorgan 29, Sneed 27, Thompson 12, Butler 9, Locke 7, Moriarty 7, Donnelly 6, Holdsworth 5, Kerins 4, McCauley 3, Reisling 2, Bond 2, Barr 2, Keenan 2, Barrett 1, Monroe 1, Aydelott 1, McKeon 1, Fries 1, Robinson 1, Blakiston 1

C   Keenan 59, Robinson 17, Thompson 12, Kerins 5, Dorgan 5, Tray 4, Decker 4, Barrett 4, Weber 3, Mundinger 3, Monroe 1

P   McKeon 61, Barr 16, Aydelott 12, McCauley 10, MacArthur 6, Bond 5, Moriarty 2, Keenan 1

	G	IP	GS	CG	W	L	K	BB	SH	SV	ERA
Larry McKeon	61	512	60	59	18	**41**	308	94	2	0	3.50
Bob Barr	16	132	16	15	3	11	69	19	0	0	4.98
Jake Aydelott	12	106	12	11	5	7	30	29	0	0	4.92
Al McCauley	10	76	9	9	2	7	34	25	0	0	5.09
Mac MacArthur	6	52	6	6	1	5	19	21	0	0	5.02
Tommy Bond	5	43	5	5	0	5	15	4	0	0	5.65
Gene Moriarty	2	13.2	2	2	0	2	4	7	0	0	5.27
Jim Keenan	1	3	0	0	0	0	0	0	0	0	3.00
		937.2	110	107	29	78	479	199	2	0	4.20

WASHINGTON   Holly Hollingshead (12–50)   ? Bickerson (0–1)   Athletic Park

		G	AB	H	R	2B	3B	HR	RBI	BB	BA	SA
SS	Frank Fennelly	62	257	75	52	17	7	2	—	20	.292	.436
3B	Buck Gladman	56	224	35	17	5	3	1	—	3	.156	.219
C	John Humphries	49	193	34	23	2	0	0	—	9	.176	.187
1B	Walter Prince	43	166	36	22	3	2	1	—	13	.217	.277
RF	Bill Morgan	45	162	28	8	1	1	0	—	8	.173	.191
2B	Thorny Hawkes	38	151	42	16	4	2	0	—	4	.278	.331
P	Bob Barr	39	135	20	15	3	1	2	—	5	.148	.230
CF	Henry Mullin	34	120	17	13	3	1	0	—	8	.142	.183
Sub	Ed Yewell	27	93	23	14	3	1	0	—	1	.247	.301
UT	Ed Trumbull	25	86	10	5	2	0	0	—	2	.116	.140
Sub	Frank Olin	21	83	32	12	4	1	0	—	8	.386	.458
Sub	John Hanna	23	76	5	8	0	0	0	—	6	.066	.066
P	John Hamill	21	71	7	5	0	2	0	—	6	.099	.155
Sub	Edgar Smith	14	57	5	5	0	1	0	—	1	.088	.123
Sub	John Kiley	14	56	12	9	2	2	0	—	3	.214	.321
LF	Tom Farley	14	52	11	5	4	0	0	—	1	.212	.288
Sub	Sam King	12	45	8	3	2	0	0	—	1	.178	.222
Sub	Jack Beach	8	31	3	3	2	0	0	—	0	.097	.161
Sub	Walt Goldsby	6	24	9	4	0	0	0	—	1	.375	.375
Sub	Willie Murphy	5	21	10	3	0	0	0	—	1	.476	.476
Sub	Andy Swan	5	21	3	3	1	0	0	—	0	.143	.190
Sub	? Jones	4	17	5	2	0	0	0	—	1	.294	.294
Sub	? Wills	4	15	2	1	2	0	0	—	0	.133	.267
Sub	Lyman Drake	2	7	2	0	1	0	0	—	0	.286	.429
Sub	Alex Gardner	1	3	0	0	0	0	0	—	0	.000	.000
Sub	? Joyce	1	0	0	0	0	0	0	—	0	—	—
		63	2166	434	248	61	24	6	—	102	.200	.259

1B   Prince 43, King 12, Humphries 4, Swan 3, Barr 2

2B   Hawkes 38, Olin 12, Yewell 11, Fennelly 4

SS   Fennelly 60, Yewell 2, Morgan 2, Gladman 1

3B   Gladman 53, Yewell 7, Morgan 2, Swan 2, Murphy 1, Mullin 1

OF   Mullin 34, Morgan 31, Trumbull 15, Farley 14, Kiley 14, Humphries 12, Smith 12, Olin 11, Yewell 8, Beach 8, Goldsby 6, Hanna 6, Barr 5, Murphy 4, Wills 4, Jones 4, Hamill 3, Hawkes 2, Drake 2, Gladman 2, Joyce 1

C   Humphries 35, Hanna 18, Morgan 12, Gardner 1

P   Barr 32, Hamill 19, Trumbull 10, Smith 3

	G	IP	GS	CG	W	L	K	BB	SH	SV	ERA
Bob Barr	32	281	32	32	9	23	138	31	2	0	3.46
John Hamill	19	156.2	19	18	2	17	50	43	1	0	4.48
Ed Trumbull	15	84	10	10	1	9	43	31	0	0	4.71
Edgar Smith	3	22	2	2	0	2	4	5	0	0	4.91
		543.2	63	62	12	51	235	110	3	0	4.01

UNION ASSOCIATION

	W	L	PCT	HOME	ROAD	GB
1. St. Louis Maroons	94	19	.832	50–6	44–13	—
2. Milwaukee Brewers	8	4	.667	8–4	0–0	35.5
3. Cincinnati Outlaw Reds	69	36	.657	35–17	34–19	21
4. Baltimore	58	47	.552	29–21	29–26	32
5. Boston Reds	58	51	.532	34–23	24–28	34
6. Chicago–Pittsburgh	41	50	.451	21–18	20–32	42
7. Washington Nationals	47	65	.420	36–27	11–38	46.5
8. Philadelphia Keystones	21	46	.313	13–21	8–25	50
9. St. Paul Apostles	2	6	.250	0–0	2–6	39.5
10. Altoona Mountain Citys	6	19	.240	6–12	0–7	44
11. Kansas City Cowboys	16	63	.203	11–23	5–40	61
12. Wilmington Quicksteps	2	16	.111	1–6	1–10	44.5

	SL	Mi	Ci	Ba	Bo	CP	Wa	Ph	SP	Al	KC	Wm	
St. Louis	—	*	(14)	13	8	(14)	13	8	2	8	10	4	94
Milwaukee	*	—	*	3	2	*	3	*	*	*	*	*	8
Cincinnati	2	*	—	11	11	8	10	8	3	3	10	2	68
Baltimore	2	(1)	3	—	10	6	12	10	*	3	10	1	58
Boston	8	2	5	6	—	4	12	8	*	1	8	4	58
Chi–Pitt	(2)	*	(7)	(5)	8	—	4	3	*	*	12	*	41
Washington	3	1	6	4	4	8	—	8	*	1	8	4	47
Philadelphia	0	*	0	2	3	(6)	(3)	—	*	3	4	*	21
St. Paul	1	*	0	*	*	*	*	*	—	*	1	*	2
Altoona	0	*	0	1	1	*	3	1	*	—	*	*	6
Kansas City	(1)	*	0	2	4	(4)	4	*	1	*	—	*	16
Wilmington	0	*	1	0	0	*	1	*	*	*	*	—	2
	19	4	36	47	51	50	65	46	6	19	63	15	422

NOTE: Figures in parentheses are open to debate.
* Teams did not play one another.

SEASON LEADERS*

Batting Average (250 ABs)

1. Dunlap, St. Louis	.412
2. Hoover, Philadelphia	.364
3. Shaffer, St. Louis	.360
4. Moore, Washington	.336
5. J. Gleason, St. Louis	.324

Slugging Average

1. Dunlap, St. Louis	.621
2. Shaffer, St. Louis	.501
3. Hoover, Philadelphia	.495
4. Burns, Cincinnati	.457
5. Crane, Boston	.451

On–Base Percentage

1.	Dunlap, St. Louis	.448
2.	Shaffer, St. Louis	.398
3.	Hoover, Philadelphia	.390
4.	Moore, Washington	.363
5.	J. Gleason, St. Louis	.361

Home Runs

1.	Dunlap, St. Louis	13
2.	Crane, Boston	12
3.	Levis, Balt–Wash	6
4.	Flynn, Phil–Boston	4
	Boyle, St. Louis	4
	O'Brien, Boston	4
	Hawes, Cincinnati	4
	Burns, Cincinnati	4

Hits

1.	Dunlap, St. Louis	185
2.	Shaffer, St. Louis	168
3.	Moore, Washington	155
4.	Seery, Balt–KC	146
5.	Rowe, St. Louis	142

Total Bases

1.	Dunlap, St. Louis	279
2.	Shaffer, St. Louis	234
3.	Rowe, St. Louis	208
4.	Crane, Boston	193
5.	Seery, Balt–KC	192

Bases on Balls

1.	Robinson, Baltimore	37
2.	G. Shaffer, St.Louis	30
3.	Dunlap, St. Louis	29
4.	Harbidge, Cincinnati	25
5.	Gleason, St. Louis	23

Runs

1.	Dunlap, St. Louis	160
2.	G. Shaffer, St. Louis	130
3.	Seery, Balt–KC	115
4.	Robinson, Baltimore	101
5.	Rowe, St. Louis	95

* Stolen base and RBI leaders unavailable.

PITCHING

Wins

1.	B. Sweeney, Baltimore	40
2.	H. Daily, CP–Wash	28
3.	Taylor, St. Louis	25
	Bradley, Cincinnati	25
5.	C. Sweeney, St. Louis	24

Innings

1.	B. Sweeney, Baltimore	538
2.	Daily, CP–Wash	500.2
3.	Bakely, Phil–Wm–KC	394.2
4.	Wise, Washington	364.1
5.	Bradley, Cincinnati	342

Strikeouts

1.	Daily, CP–Wash	483
2.	B. Sweeney, Baltimore	374
3.	Shaw, Boston	309
4.	Wise, Washington	268
5.	Burke, Boston	255

ERA (100 Innings)

1.	McCormick, Cincinnati	1.54
2.	Taylor, St. Louis	1.68
3.	Boyle, St. Louis	1.74
4.	Shaw, Boston	1.77
5.	C. Sweeney, St. Louis	1.83

Losses

1.	Bakely, Phi–Wm–KC	30
2.	Daily, CP–Wash	28
3.	B. Sweeney, Baltimore	21
4.	Voss, Wash–KC	20
5.	Wise, Washington	18

Complete games

1.	B. Sweeney, Baltimore	58
2.	Daily, CP–Wash	56
3.	Bakely, Phil–Wm–KC	43
4.	Bradley, Cincinnati	36
5.	Shaw, Boston	35

Winning Percentage (20 decisions)

1.	McCormick, Cincinnati	.875
2.	Taylor, St. Louis	.862
3.	C. Sweeney, St. Louis	.774
4.	B. Sweeney, Baltimore	.656
5.	Bradley, Cincinnati	.625

Lowest On–Base Percentage

1.	McCormick, Cincinnati	.202
2.	C. Sweeney, St. Louis	.207
3.	Shaw, Boston	.212
4.	Boyle, St. Louis	.215
5.	Werden, St. Louis	.235

FIELDING

Total Chances

1B	Schoeneck, CP–Balt	1134
2B	Dunlap, St. Louis	692
3B	J. Irwin, Boston	395
SS	L. Say, Balt–KC	531
OF	Seery, Balt–KC	221
C	G. Baker, St. Louis	511
P	B. Sweeney, Baltimore	192

Fielding Average

Schoeneck, CP–Balt	.957
Dunlap, St. Louis	.926
Y. Robinson, Baltimore	.831
W. Hackett, Boston	.855
D. Rowe, St. Louis	.947
G. Baker, St. Louis	.897
C. Sweeney, St. Louis	.943

ST. LOUIS   Ted Sullivan (28–3)   Fred Dunlap (66–16)   Union Park

		G	AB	H	R	2B	3B	HR	RBI	BB	BA	SA
CF	Dave Rowe	109	**485**	142	95	32	11	4	—	10	.293	.429
RF	Orator Shaffer	106	467	168	130	**40**	10	2	—	30	.360	.501
2B	Fred Dunlap	101	449	**185**	160	39	8	13	—	29	**.412**	**.621**
1B	Joe Quinn	103	429	116	74	21	1	0	—	9	.270	.324
3B	Jack Gleason	92	395	128	90	30	2	4	—	23	.324	.441
SS	Milt Whitehead	99	393	83	61	15	1	1	—	8	.211	.262
C	George Baker	80	317	52	39	6	0	0	—	5	.164	.183
UT	Henry Boyle	65	262	68	41	10	3	4	—	9	.260	.366
C	Jim Brennan	56	231	50	38	6	1	0	—	12	.216	.251
LF	Buttercup Dickerson	46	211	77	49	15	1	0	—	8	.365	.445
P	Billy Taylor	43	186	68	44	23	1	3	—	7	.366	.548
P	Charlie Sweeney	45	171	54	31	14	12	1	—	10	.316	.439
P	Perry Werden	18	76	18	7	2	0	0	—	2	.237	.263
Sub	Tom Dolan	19	69	13	9	3	0	0	—	4	.188	.232
P	Charlie Hodnett	18	58	12	9	1	0	0	—	10	.207	.224
Sub	Fred Lewis	8	30	9	6	1	0	0	—	3	.300	.333
Sub	Tom Ryder	8	28	7	4	1	0	0	—	2	.250	.286
Sub	Sleeper Sullivan	2	9	1	0	0	0	0	—	0	.111	.111
P	John Cattanach	2	7	0	0	0	0	0	—	0	.000	.000
Sub	Dan Cronin	1	5	0	0	0	0	0	—	0	.000	.000
P	C.V. Matterson	1	4	0	0	0	0	0	—	0	.000	.000
Sub	Ed Callahan	1	3	0	0	0	0	0	—	0	.000	.000
		114	4285	**1251**	**887**	**259**	41	**32**	—	181	.292	.394

1B   Quinn 100, Taylor 10, Rowe 2, Boyle 1, Sweeney 1, Shaffer 1
2B   Dunlap 100, Shaffer 7, Baker 4, Rowe 2, Whitehead 1, Boyle 1
SS   Whitehead 94, Rowe 14, Baker 2, Boyle 1, Brennan 1, Quinn 1
3B   Gleason 92, Brennan 7, Boyle 4, Dickerson 4, Dolan 3, Baker 3, Whitehead 1
OF   Shaffer 100, Rowe 92, Boyle 43, Dickerson 42, Brennan 16, Sweeney 13, Ryder 8, Lewis 8, Werden 6, Hodnett 6, Baker 5, Taylor 4, Quinn 3, Dolan 2, Whitehead 2, Callahan 1, Cronin 1, Sullivan 1, Matterson 1, Dunlap 1
C   Baker 68, Brennan 33, Dolan 14, Sullivan 1
P   Taylor 33, Sweeney 33, Boyle 19, Werden 16, Hodnett 14, Cattanach 2, Matterson 1, Sullivan 1, Rowe 1, Whitehead 1, Dunlap 1

	G	IP	GS	CG	W	L	K	BB	SH	SV	ERA
Charlie Sweeney	33	271	32	31	24	7	192	13	2	0	1.83
Billy Taylor	33	263	29	29	25	4	154	40	2	**4**	1.68
Henry Boyle	19	150	16	16	15	3	88	10	2	1	1.74
Perry Werden	16	141.1	16	12	12	1	51	22	1	0	1.97
Charlie Hodnett	14	121	14	12	12	2	41	16	1	0	2.01
John Cattanach	2	17	2	2	1	1	13	4	0	0	2.12
Dave Rowe	1	9	1	1	1	0	2	0	0	0	2.00
Milt Whitehead	1	8	1	1	0	1	2	2	0	0	9.00
C. V. Matterson	1	6	1	0	1	0	3	3	0	0	9.00
Sleeper Sullivan	1	6	1	0	1	0	3	0	0	0	4.50
Fred Dunlap	1	0.2	0	0	0	0	1	0	0	1	13.50
—2 forfeit Ws: vs Kansas City on Aug. 22 and vs Washington on October 11—											
	993	113	**104**	92	19	550	110	8	**6**	1.96	

MILWAUKEE   Tom Loftus   **Wright Street Grounds**

		G	AB	H	R	2B	3B	HR	RBI	BB	BA	SA
SS	Tom Sexton	12	47	11	9	2	0	0	—	4	.234	.277
3B	Tom Morrissey	12	47	8	3	2	0	0	—	0	.170	.213
2B	Al Myers	12	46	15	6	6	0	0	—	0	.326	.457
1B	Tom Griffin	11	41	9	5	2	0	0	—	3	.220	.268
P	Henry Porter	11	40	11	4	4	0	0	—	0	.275	.375
C	Cal Broughton	11	39	12	5	5	0	0	—	0	.308	.436
RF	Eddie Hogan	11	37	3	6	1	0	0	—	7	.081	.108
LF	Steve Behel	9	33	8	5	1	0	0	—	3	.242	.273
CF	Lady Baldwin	7	27	6	6	3	0	0	—	0	.222	.333
P	Anton Falch	5	18	2	0	0	0	0	—	0	.111	.111
P	Ed Cushman	4	11	1	1	0	0	0	—	2	.091	.091
Sub	George Bignell	4	9	2	4	0	0	0	—	1	.222	.222
		12	395	88	54	26	0	0	—	20	.223	.286

1B	Griffin 11, Porter 1
2B	Myers 12
SS	Sexton 12
3B	Morrissey 12
OF	Hogan 11, Behel 9, Broughton 5, Baldwin 5, Porter 4, Falch 3
C	Broughton 7, Bignell 4. Falch 2
P	Porter 6, Cushman 4, Baldwin 2

	G	IP	GS	CG	W	L	K	BB	K	SV	ERA
Henry Porter	6	51	6	6	3	3	71	9	1	0	3.00
Ed Cushman #	4	36	4	4	4	0	47	3	2	0	1.00
Lady Baldwin	2	17	2	2	1	1	21	1	0	0	2.65
	104	12	12	8	4	139	13	3	0	2.25	

No-hit game 5–0 vs Washington, September 28

CINCINNATI   Dan O'Leary (20–15)   **Sam Crane (49–21)**   **Bank Street Grounds**

		G	AB	H	R	2B	3B	HR	RBI	BB	BA	SA
UT	Dick Burns	79	350	107	84	17	**12**	4	—	5	.306	.457
RF	Bill Hawes	79	349	97	80	7	4	4	—	5	.278	.355
CF	Bill Harbidge	82	341	95	59	12	5	2	—	25	.279	.361
LF	Lew Sylvester	82	333	89	67	13	8	2	—	18	.267	.372
2B	Sam Crane	80	309	72	56	9	3	1	—	11	.233	.291
SS	Jack Jones	69	272	71	36	5	1	2	—	12	.261	.309
P	George Bradley	58	226	43	31	4	7	0	—	7	.190	.270
3B	Charlie Barber	55	204	41	38	1	4	0	—	11	.201	.245
1B	Martin Powell	43	185	59	46	4	2	1	—	13	.319	.378
SS	Jack Glasscock	38	172	72	48	9	5	2	—	8	.419	.564
C	Kick Kelly	38	142	40	23	5	1	1	—	6	.282	.352
1B	Mox McQuery	35	132	37	31	5	0	2	—	8	.280	.364
Sub	Dan O'Leary	32	132	34	14	0	2	1	—	5	.258	.311
3B	Elmer Cleveland	29	115	37	24	9	2	0	—	4	.322	.435
P	Jim McCormick	27	110	27	12	3	1	0	—	0	.245	.291
C	Pop Schwartz	29	106	25	14	4	0	1	—	3	.236	.302
C	Fatty Briody	22	89	30	11	2	2	0	—	1	.337	.404
Sub	Joe Crotty	21	84	22	11	4	2	1	—	1	.262	.393
SS	Frank McLaughlin	16	67	16	10	4	1	2	—	2	.239	.418
Sub	Ed Kennedy	13	48	10	6	1	1	0	—	1	.208	.271
Sub	Fred Robinson	3	13	3	1	0	0	0	—	0	.231	.231
Sub	John Ewing	1	4	0	0	0	0	0	—	0	.000	.000
Sub	Lew Meyers	2	3	0	1	0	0	0	—	1	.000	.000
		105	3786	1027	703	118	**63**	26	—	147	.271	.356

1B Powell 43, McQuery 35, Hawes 21, Bradley 2, Harbidge 2
2B Crane 80, Jones 19, Robinson 3, Glasscock 2
SS Jones 41, Glasscock 36, McLaughlin 16, Bradley 5, Kennedy 4, Harbidge 3, Burns 2, Sylvester 2
3B Barber 55, Cleveland 29, Jones 10, Kennedy 8, Robinson 3, Schwartz 1
OF Sylvester 81, Harbidge 80, Hawes 58, Burns 44, O'Leary 32, Bradley 16, Schwartz 3, McCormick 3, Kelly 2, Meyers 1, Ewing 1, Kennedy 1
C Kelly 37, Schwartz 25, Briody 22, Crotty 21, Meyers 2
P Bradley 41, Burns 40, McCormick 26, Sylvester 6

	G	IP	GS	CG	W	L	K	BB	SH	SV	ERA
George Bradley	41	342	38	36	25	15	168	23	3	0	2.71
Dick Burns #	40	329.2	40	34	23	15	167	47	1	0	2.46
Jim McCormick	24	210	24	24	21	3	161	14	7	0	**1.54**
Lew Sylvester	6	32.2	1	1	0	1	7	6	0	1	3.58
	—2 forfeit Ls: vs Baltimore on July 5 and vs Boston on October 11—										
	914.1	103	95	69	34	503	**90**	**11**	1	2.38

No-hit game 3–1 vs Kansas City, August 26

BALTIMORE Charlie Levis (53–35) Bill Henderson (5–12) Monumental Park

		G	AB	H	R	2B	3B	HR	RBI	BB	BA	SA
LF	Emmett Seery	105	463	144	113	25	7	2	—	20	.311	.408
3B	Yank Robinson	102	415	111	101	24	4	2	—	**37**	.267	.359
2B	Dick Phelan	101	402	99	63	13	3	3	—	12	.246	.316
1B	Charlie Levis	87	373	85	59	11	4	6	—	3	.228	.327
SS	Lew Say	78	339	81	65	14	2	2	—	11	.239	.310
C	Ed Fusselbach	68	303	86	60	16	3	1	—	3	.284	.366
P	Bill Sweeney	74	296	71	35	7	0	0	—	9	.240	.264
C	Rooney Sweeney	48	186	42	37	7	1	0	—	15	.226	.274
CF	Ned Cuthbert	44	168	34	29	5	0	0	—	10	.202	.232
RF	Bernie Graham	41	167	45	21	11	0	0	—	2	.269	.335
Sub	Henry Oberbeck	33	125	23	19	4	0	0	—	3	.184	.216
P	Tom Lee	21	82	23	11	1	0	0	—	5	.280	.293
Sub	John O'Brien	18	77	19	7	1	1	0	—	2	.247	.286
Sub	Harry Wheeler	17	69	18	3	2	0	0	—	0	.261	.290
Sub	Jumbo Schoeneck	16	60	15	5	2	0	0	—	0	.250	.283
Sub	Joe Battin	17	59	6	3	1	0	0	—	0	.102	.119
Sub	? Scott	13	53	12	10	1	1	1	—	2	.226	.340
P	Phenomenal Smith	10	35	6	2	0	0	0	—	2	.171	.171
P	Al Atkinson	8	29	4	3	1	0	0	—	1	.138	.172
Sub	Joe Ellick	7	27	4	2	0	0	0	—	2	.148	.148
P	John Ryan	8	25	2	2	0	0	0	—	2	.080	.080
Sub	Joe Stanley	6	21	5	3	1	0	0	—	0	.238	.286
P	Frank Beck	5	20	2	1	1	0	0	—	0	.100	.150
P	Chris McFarland	3	14	3	2	1	0	0	—	0	.214	.286
Sub	John Cuff	3	11	1	1	1	0	0	—	1	.091	.182
Sub	Frank Shaffer	3	13	1	1	0	0	0	—	0	.077	.077
Sub	Tony Suck	3	10	3	2	0	0	0	—	0	.300	.300
Sub	Bill Morgan	2	9	2	1	0	0	0	—	1	.222	.222
Sub	Frank Bahret	2	8	0	0	0	0	0	—	0	.000	.000
Sub	Pat Burns	1	4	2	0	0	0	0	—	0	.500	.500
Sub	Gid Gardner	1	4	1	0	0	0	0	—	0	.250	.250
P	? Smith	1	4	1	1	0	0	0	—	0	.250	.250
Sub	Alexander Skinner	1	3	1	0	0	0	0	—	0	.333	.333
Sub	Bill Tierney	1	3	1	0	0	0	0	—	1	.333	.333
P	Jerry Dorsey	1	3	0	0	0	0	0	—	0	.000	.000
P	E. Morris	1	3	0	0	0	0	0	—	0	.000	.000
		106	3883	952	662	150	26	17	—	144	.245	.310

1B Levis 87, Schoeneck 15, Burns 1, B. Sweeney 1, Graham 1

2B Phelan 100, B. Sweeney 6, Robinson 3, Lee 2, Morgan 1

SS Say 78, Robinson 14, Ellick 6, Fusselbach 5, Gardner 1, Lee 1, Schoeneck 1, B. Sweeney 1

3B Robinson 71, Battin 17, Oberbeck 8, Fusselbach 6, Phelan 5, Lee 3, Seery 2, Scott 1, R. Sweeney 1

OF Seery 104, Cuthbert 44, Graham 40, Oberbeck 28, O'Brien 18, Wheeler 17, R. Sweeney 16, Scott 13, B. Sweeney 11, Stanley 6, P. Smith 5, Lee 6, Beck 4, Fusselbach 4, McFarland 3, Shaffer 3, Ryan 2, Bahret 2, Skinner 1, Morgan 1, Tierney 1, Ellick 1, Dorsey 1, Morris 1, Phelan 1

C Fusselbach 54, R. Sweeney 33, Robinson 11, Cuff 3, Seery 3, Suck 3, Morgan 1

P B. Sweeney 62, Lee 15, Robinson 11, P. Smith 9, Atkinson 8, Ryan 6, Beck 2, Oberbeck 2, ? Smith 1, Morris 1, Dorsey 1, McFarland 1

	G	IP	GS	CG	W	L	K	BB	SH	SV	ERA
Bill Sweeney	**62**	**538**	**60**	**58**	**40**	21	374	74	4	0	2.59
Tom Lee	15	122	14	12	5	8	81	29	0	0	3.39
Yank Robinson	11	75	3	3	3	3	61	18	0	0	3.48
Al Atkinson	8	69.2	8	8	3	5	50	12	0	0	2.33
Phenomenal Smith	9	62	8	5	3	4	13	17	0	0	3.48
John Ryan	6	51	6	5	3	2	33	16	0	0	3.35
Frank Beck	2	9	2	1	0	2	7	4	0	0	8.00
Henry Oberbeck	2	6	1	0	0	0	1	2	0	0	3.00
? Smith	1	6	1	0	0	0	2	2	0	0	9.00
Jerry Dorsey	1	4	1	0	0	1	3	0	0	0	9.00
Chris McFarland	1	3	1	0	0	1	3	1	0	0	15.00
E. Morris	1	1	0	0	0	0	0	2	0	0	9.00
		—1 forfeit W vs Cincinnati on July 5—									
		946.2	105	92	57	47	628	177	4	0	3.01

BOSTON   **Tim Murnane**   **Dartmouth Grounds**

		G	AB	H	R	2B	3B	HR	RBI	BB	BA	SA
2B	Tom O'Brien	103	449	118	80	31	8	4	—	12	.263	.394
3B	John Irwin	105	432	101	81	22	6	1	—	15	.234	.319
RF	Cannonball Crane	101	428	122	83	23	6	12	—	14	.285	.451
SS	Walter Hackett	103	415	101	71	19	0	1	—	7	.243	.296
CF	Mike Slattery	106	413	86	60	6	2	0	—	4	.208	.232
C	Lew Brown	85	325	75	50	18	3	1	—	13	.231	.314
1B	Tim Murnane	76	311	73	55	5	2	0	—	22	.235	.264
LF	Kid Butler	71	255	43	36	15	0	0	—	12	.169	.227
Sub	Tommy McCarthy	53	209	45	37	2	2	0	—	6	.215	.244
P	James Burke	47	184	41	21	8	3	0	—	6	.223	.299
P	Tommy Bond	37	162	48	21	8	0	0	—	4	.296	.346
P	Dupee Shaw	44	153	37	13	8	0	0	—	5	.242	.294
Sub	Jim McKeever	18	66	9	13	0	0	0	—	0	.136	.136
Sub	Joe Flynn	9	31	7	4	2	0	0	—	2	.226	.290
Sub	Pat Scanlon	6	24	7	2	1	0	0	—	0	.292	.333
P	Fred Tenney	4	17	2	1	0	0	0	—	0	.118	.118
Sub	Ed Callahan	4	13	5	2	0	0	0	—	1	.385	.385
P	Charlie Daniels	3	11	3	1	0	0	0	—	2	.273	.273
Sub	Charlie Reilley	3	11	0	1	0	0	0	—	0	.000	.000
Sub	Henry Mullin	2	8	0	1	0	0	0	—	0	.000	.000
Sub	Art Sladen	2	7	0	0	0	0	0	—	0	.000	.000
Sub	Clarence Dow	1	6	2	1	0	0	0	—	0	.333	.333
Sub	John Rudderham	1	4	1	0	0	0	0	—	0	.250	.250
Sub	Elias Peak	1	3	2	2	0	0	0	—	1	.667	.667
Sub	? Murphy	1	3	0	0	0	0	0	—	1	.000	.000
		111	3940	928	636	168	32	19	—	128	.236	.309

1B   Murnane 63, Brown 33, Slattery 11, Crane 5, O'Brien 2, Flynn 1
2B   O'Brien 99, Butler 12
SS   Hackett 103, Butler 6
3B   Irwin 105, Butler 2, Reilley 1, Bond 1
OF   Slattery 96, Crane 57, Butler 53, McCarthy 48, Bond 17, Murnane 16, Burke 13, Shaw 9, Scanlan 6, McKeever 4, Flynn 4, Callahan 4, O'Brien 3, Mullin 2, Reilley 2, Sladen 2, Brown 2, Peak 1, Murphy 1, Rudderham 1, Dow 1, Daniels 1
C   Brown 54, Crane 42, McKeever 12, Flynn 7, Murphy 1, O'Brien 1
P   Shaw 39, Burke 38, Bond 23, McCarthy 7, Crane 4, Tenney 4, Daniels 2, Brown 1

	G	IP	GS	CG	W	L	K	BB	SH	SV	ERA
Dupee Shaw	39	315.2	38	35	21	15	309	37	5	0	1.77
James Burke	38	322	36	34	19	15	255	31	0	0	2.85
Tommy Bond	23	189	21	19	13	9	128	14	0	0	3.00
Tommy McCarthy	7	56	6	5	0	7	18	14	0	0	4.82
Fred Tenney	4	35	4	4	3	1	18	5	0	0	2.31
Cannonball Crane	2	18	2	1	0	2	13	6	0	0	4.00
Charlie Daniels	2	16	2	2	0	2	12	2	0	0	4.32
Lew Brown	1	1	0	0	0	0	0	1	0	1	36.00
—2 forfeit Ws: vs Wilmington on August 25; vs Cincinnati on October 11—
	953.1	109	100	56	51	**753**	110	5	1	2.70

CHICAGO/PITTSBURGH   (CHICAGO) Ed Hengle   (PITTSBURGH) Joe Battin (1–5)   Joe Ellick (6–6)
(CHICAGO) South Side Park (I)   (PITTSBURGH) Exposition Park (I)

		G	AB	H	R	2B	3B	HR	RBI	BB	BA	SA
RF	Joe Ellick	92	394	93	71	11	0	0	—	16	.236	.264
1B	Jumbo Schoeneck	90	366	116	66	22	2	2	—	12	.317	.404
LF	Charlie Householder	81	310	74	32	12	5	1	—	8	.239	.319
C	Bill Krieg	71	279	69	35	15	4	0	—	11	.247	.330
P	One Arm Daily	58	196	43	21	6	1	0	—	8	.219	.264
Sub	Tony Suck	53	188	28	18	2	0	0	—	13	.149	.160
CF	Charlie Briggs	49	182	31	29	8	2	1	—	11	.170	.253
Sub	Harry Wheeler	37	158	36	29	5	3	1	—	4	.228	.316
Sub	Gid Gardner	38	149	38	22	10	2	0	—	10	.255	.349
SS	Steve Matthias	37	142	39	24	7	1	0	—	5	.275	.338
C	Emil Gross	23	95	34	13	6	2	4	—	6	.358	.589
2B	Moxie Hengle	19	74	15	9	2	1	0	—	3	.203	.257
3B	Will Foley	19	71	20	15	1	1	0	—	5	.282	.324
Sub	Chippy McGarr	19	70	11	10	2	0	0	—	0	.157	.186
Sub	Joe Battin	18	69	13	8	2	0	0	—	0	.188	.217
P	Al Atkinson	19	68	14	4	0	0	0	—	0	.206	.265
P	John Horan	20	68	6	3	0	0	0	—	1	.088	.088
Sub	Frank McLaughlin	15	67	16	11	4	1	0	—	1	.239	.328
Sub	Charlie Baker	15	57	8	5	2	0	1	—	0	.140	.228
Sub	George Strief	15	53	11	6	5	0	0	—	3	.208	.302
P	Jack Leary	10	40	7	0	1	0	0	—	0	.175	.200
Sub	Charlie Berry	7	27	3	4	2	0	0	—	0	.111	.185
P	Charlie Cady	6	20	2	4	1	1	0	—	1	.100	.250
Sub	Frank Bishop	4	16	3	1	1	0	0	—	0	.188	.250
P	Frank Foreman	3	11	1	0	0	0	0	—	0	.091	.091
Sub	Frank Wyman	2	8	3	1	0	0	0	—	0	.375	.375
Sub	Phillip Corridan	2	7	1	1	0	0	0	—	0	.143	.143
Sub	Bernie Graham	1	5	1	2	0	0	0	—	0	.200	.200
P	Cyclone Miller	1	4	1	1	0	0	0	—	0	.250	.250
Sub	Dan Cronin	1	4	1	1	0	0	0	—	0	.250	.250
Sub	? Richardson	1	4	0	0	0	0	0	—	0	.000	.000
Sub	Charlie Fisher	1	3	2	1	0	0	0	—	1	.667	.667
Sub	Alexander Skinner	1	3	1	1	0	0	0	—	0	.333	.333
Sub	Harry Koons	1	3	0	0	0	0	0	—	0	.000	.000
Sub	Kid Baldwin	1	1	1	0	0	0	0	—	0	1.000	1.000
		93	3212	742	438	127	26	10	—	119	.231	.258

1B   Schoeneck 90, Wyman 2, Cronin 1, Krieg 1
2B   Hengle 19, Strief 15, McLaughlin 14, McGarr 13, Briggs 12, Berry 7, Ellick 4, Leary 4, Corridan 2, Baker 1, Gardner 1, Daily 1, Richardson 1, Cronin 1

SS   Matthias 36, Ellick 33, Suck 15, Gardner 8, McLaughlin 1, Householder 3, Briggs 3, Baker 3, Bishop 1, Daily 1, Krieg 1

3B   Householder 41, Foley 19, Battin 18, Gardner 8, Bishop 3, Leary 3, Koons 1, Fisher 1, Suck 1

OF   Ellick 57, Householder 40, Briggs 37, Wheeler 37, Gardner 29, Krieg 20, Suck 12, Baker 11, Horan 10, Gross 9, McGarr 6, Atkinson 3, Leary 3, Matthias 2, Foreman 2, Daily 2, Cady 2, McLaughlin 1, Graham 1, Skinner 1, Corridan 1

C   Krieg 52, Suck 28, Gross 15, Baldwin 1

P   Daily 56, Atkinson 16, Horan 13, Cady 4, Foreman 3, Leary 2, Householder 2, Miller 1, Gardner 1

	G	IP	GS	CG	W	L	K	BB	SH	SV	ERA
One Arm Daily	56	484.2	56	54	27	27	469*	71	5	0	2.43
Al Atkinson	16	140	16	16	6	10	104	21	1	0	2.33
John Horan	13	98	10	9	3	6	55	24	0	0	3.40
Charlie Cady	4	35	4	4	3	1	15	13	0	0	2.83
Frank Foreman	3	18	3	1	1	2	10	2	0	0	4.00
Jack Leary	2	10	1	1	0	2	6	5	0	0	5.40
Cyclone Miller	1	9	1	1	1	0	13	0	0	0	1.00
Gid Gardner	1	6	1	0	0	1	4	1	0	0	6.00
Charlie Householder	2	3	0	0	0	0	3	0	0	0	3.00
—1 forfeit L vs Washington on September 8—											
		803.2	92	86	41	49	679	137	6		

WASHINGTON   **Mike Scanlon**   **Capitol Grounds**

		G	AB	H	R	2B	3B	HR	RBI	BB	BA	SA
LF	Henry Moore	111	461	155	77	23	5	1	—	19	.336	.414
2B	Tom Evers	109	427	99	54	6	1	0	—	7	.232	.251
1B	Phil Baker	86	371	107	75	12	5	1	—	11	.288	.356
RF	Bill Wise	85	339	79	51	17	1	2	—	12	.233	.307
P	Alex Voss	63	245	47	33	9	0	0	—	5	.192	.229
CF	Abner Powell	48	191	54	36	10	5	0	—	3	.283	.387
C	Chris Fulmer	48	181	50	39	9	0	0	—	11	.276	.326
SS	Jim Halpin	46	168	31	24	3	0	0	—	2	.185	.202
C	Joe Gunson	45	166	23	15	2	0	0	—	3	.139	.151
3B	Jerry McCormick	42	157	34	23	8	2	0	—	1	.217	.293
P	Charlie Geggus	44	154	38	14	7	1	0	—	4	.247	.305
Sub	John Deasley	31	134	29	20	1	1	0	—	3	.216	.239
Sub	Pop Joy	36	130	28	12	0	0	0	—	2	.215	.215
Sub	Fred Tenney	32	119	28	17	3	1	0	—	6	.235	.277
Sub	Ed McKenna	32	117	22	19	1	0	0	—	4	.188	.197
Sub	Terry Larkin	17	70	17	11	0	0	0	—	4	.243	.243
P	Milo Lockwood	20	67	14	9	1	0	0	—	8	.209	.224
Sub	Dave Drew	13	53	16	8	1	2	0	—	1	.302	.396
Sub	Bill Hughes	14	49	6	5	0	0	0	—	2	.122	.122
Sub	Jim McLaughlin	10	37	7	3	3	0	0	—	0	.189	.270
Sub	Jim Green	10	36	5	4	1	0	0	—	0	.139	.167
Sub	Marty Creegan	9	33	5	4	0	0	0	—	1	.152	.152
Sub	John Ryan	7	28	4	2	0	1	0	—	1	.143	.214
Sub	Warren White	4	18	1	2	0	0	0	—	0	.056	.056
Sub	Frank McKee	4	17	3	2	0	0	0	—	1	.176	.176
Sub	Chick Carroll	4	16	4	1	0	0	0	—	0	.250	.250
Sub	Gus Alberts	4	16	4	4	0	0	0	—	4	.250	.250
Sub	Kick Kelly	4	14	5	1	1	0	0	—	0	.357	.429
Sub	Mike Lehane	3	12	4	1	2	0	0	—	0	.333	.500
Sub	Icicle Reeder	3	12	2	0	0	0	0	—	0	.167	.167
Sub	Maury Pierce	2	7	1	0	0	0	0	—	0	.143	.143
Sub	Mike Lawlor	2	7	0	0	0	0	0	—	0	.000	.000
Sub	Jim McDonald	2	6	1	0	0	0	0	—	0	.167	.167

		G	AB	H	R	2B	3B	HR	RBI	BB	BA	SA
Sub	John Ewing	1	5	1	1	0	1	0	—	0	.200	.600
Sub	Charlie Kalbfus	1	5	1	1	0	0	0	—	0	.200	.200
P	One Arm Daily	2	5	0	0	0	0	0	—	1	.000	.000
Sub	John Shoupe	1	4	3	1	0	0	0	—	0	.750	.750
Sub	? Mulligan	1	4	1	2	0	0	0	—	0	.250	.250
Sub	John Ward	1	4	1	0	0	0	0	—	0	.250	.250
Sub	Walter Prince	1	4	1	0	0	0	0	—	0	.250	.250
Sub	Ed Yewell	1	4	0	0	0	0	0	—	0	.000	.000
Sub	Frank Olin	1	4	0	0	0	0	0	—	0	.000	.000
Sub	? Wiley	1	4	0	0	0	0	0	—	0	.000	.000
Sub	Emory Nusz	1	4	0	1	0	0	0	—	0	.000	.000
Sub	Al Bradley	1	3	0	0	0	0	0	—	2	.000	.000
Sub	? Rollinson	1	3	0	0	0	0	0	—	0	.000	.000
Sub	? McRemer	1	3	0	0	0	0	0	—	0	.000	.000
Sub	? Franklin	1	3	0	0	0	0	0	—	0	.000	.000
Sub	P. Morris	1	3	0	0	0	0	0	—	0	.000	.000
P	Art Thompson	1	3	0	0	0	0	0	—	0	.000	.000
Sub	Charlie Levis	1	3	0	0	0	0	0	—	0	.000	.000
		114	3926	931	572	120	26	4	—	118	.237	.284

1B Baker 39, Joy 36, Voss 15, Hughes 9, Tenney 6, Drew 5, Fulmer 5, Wise 1, Levis 1, Creegan 1, Prince 1

2B Evers 109, Powell 2, Geggus 1, White 1

SS Halpin 39, Deasley 31, McLaughlin 9, Moore 8, Drew 8, McCormick 4, Alberts 4, Geggus 3, Lehane 3, Wise 2, Powell 1, Voss 1, White 1, Morris 1

3B McCormick 38, Larkin 17, Voss 16, Green 9, Wise 8, McKenna 7, Halpin 7, Lockwood 3, McKee 2, Creegan 2, White 2, Powell 2, Pierce 2, Lehane 1, Yewell 1, McLaughlin 1, Mulligan 1, Ryan 1, Wiley 1

OF Moore 105, Wise 43, Baker 32, Powell 30, Tenney 27, Geggus 21, Gunson 18, Fulmer 16, Voss 13, Lockwood 11, McKenna 10, Ryan 7, Hughes 6, Creegan 6, Carroll 4, McKee 3, Reeder 3, Franklin 1, Kelly 1, Lehane 1, Kalbfus 1, Bradley 1, Green 1, Drew 1, Nusz 1, Olin 1, McDonald 1, McRemer 1, Shoupe 1, Ward 1, Ewing 1

C Fulmer 34, Gunson 33, Baker 27, McKenna 23, Creegan 3, Kelly 3, Lawlor 2, McKee 1, McDonald 1, Rollinson 1

P Wise 50, Voss 27, Geggus 23, Powell 18, Lockwood 11, Daily 2, Thompson 1

	G	IP	GS	CG	W	L	K	BB	SH	SV	ERA
Bill Wise	50	364.1	41	34	23	18	268	60	4	0	3.04
Alex Voss	27	186.1	20	18	5	14	112	32	0	0	3.57
Charlie Geggus	23	177.1	21	19	10	9	156	38	0	0	2.54
Abner Powell	18	134	17	14	6	12	78	19	1	0	3.43
Milo Lockwood	11	67.2	10	6	1	9	48	15	0	0	7.32
One Arm Daily	2	16	2	2	1	1	**14***	1	0	0	2.25
Art Thompson	1	8	1	1	0	1	8	3	0	0	6.75
—1 forfeit W vs Pittsburgh on September 8; 1 forfeit L vs St. Louis on October 11—											
	953.2	112	94	46	64	684	168	5	0	3.44	

PHILADELPHIA Fergie Malone   **Keystone Park**

		G	AB	H	R	2B	3B	HR	RBI	BB	BA	SA
CF	Bill Kienzle	67	299	76	76	13	8	0	—	21	.254	.351
3B	Jerry McCormick	67	295	84	41	12	2	0	—	4	.285	.339
LF	Buster Hoover	63	275	100	76	20	8	0	—	12	.364	.495
1B	John McGuinness	53	220	52	25	8	1	0	—	5	.236	.282
2B	Elias Peak	54	215	42	35	6	4	0	—	7	.195	.260
RF	Joe Flynn	52	209	52	38	9	4	4	—	11	.249	.388
UT	Jack Clements	41	177	50	37	13	2	3	—	9	.282	.429
P	Jersey Bakely	45	167	22	21	4	2	0	—	11	.132	.180
C	Tom Gillen	29	116	18	5	2	0	0	—	1	.155	.172
SS	Henry Easterday	28	115	28	12	5	0	0	—	5	.243	.287
Sub	Henry Luff	26	111	30	9	4	2	0	—	4	.270	.342
P	Sam Weaver	20	84	18	11	2	0	0	—	2	.214	.238
Sub	Billy Geer	9	36	9	7	2	1	0	—	4	.250	.361
P	? Fisher	10	36	8	7	2	0	0	—	3	.222	.278
Sub	John Siegel	8	31	7	4	2	0	0	—	1	.226	.290
Sub	Chris Rickley	6	25	5	5	2	0	0	—	2	.200	.280
Sub	Pat Carroll	5	19	3	1	1	0	0	—	0	.158	.211
Sub	Bill Jones	4	14	2	2	0	0	0	—	1	.143	.143
P	Bill Gallagher	3	11	1	1	0	0	0	—	0	.091	.091
Sub	Levi Meyerle	3	11	1	0	1	0	0	—	0	.091	.182
Sub	Dave Drew	2	9	4	1	0	0	0	—	0	.444	.444
Sub	Clarence Cross	2	9	2	0	0	0	0	—	0	.222	.222
Sub	Con Daily	2	8	0	0	0	0	0	—	0	.000	.000
Sub	George Pattison	2	7	1	0	0	0	0	—	0	.143	.143
Sub	? O'Donnell	1	4	1	0	0	0	0	—	0	.250	.250
Sub	Fergy Malone	1	4	1	0	0	0	0	—	0	.250	.250
P	Al Maul	1	4	0	0	0	0	0	—	0	.000	.000
Sub	Bill Johnson	1	4	0	0	0	0	0	—	0	.000	.000
Sub	Elmer Foster	1	3	1	0	0	1	0	—	0	.333	1.000
		67	2518	618	414	108	35	7	—	103	.245	.324

1B   McGuinness 48, Hoover 6, Luff 6, Bakely 3, Meyerle 2, Fisher 2, Flynn 1
2B   Peak 47, Hoover 6, McGuinness 5, McCormick 5, Luff 3, Drew 1
SS   Easterday 28, Hoover 15, Geer 9, Rickley 6, McCormick 3, Peak 2, Cross 2, Flynn 1, Clements 1, Bakely 1, Drew 1, McGuinness 1
3B   McCormick 54, Siegel 8, Luff 5, Hoover 1
OF   Kienzle 67, Flynn 43, Hoover 37, Clements 22, Flynn 13, Luff 12, Weaver 6, Peak 5, McCormick 5, Gillen 3, Bakely 3, Pattison 2, Johnson 1, Jones 1, Meyerle 1
C   Gillen 27, Clements 20, Flynn 10, Carroll 5, Jones 4, Daily 2, Malone 1, Foster 1, O'Donnell 1
P   Bakely 39, Weaver 17, Fisher 8, Gallagher 3, Maul 1, McCormick 1, Drew 1

	G	IP	GS	CG	W	L	K	BB	SH	SV	ERA
Jersey Bakely	39	344.2	38	38	14	**25***	204	**76***	1	0	4.47
Sam Weaver	17	136	17	14	5	10	40	11	0	0	5.76
George Fisher	8	70.2	8	8	1	7	42	13	0	0	3.57
Bill Gallagher	3	25	3	3	1	2	12	4	0	0	3.24
Al Maul	1	8	1	1	0	1	7	1	0	0	4.50
Dave Drew	1	7	0	0	0	1	2	0	0	0	3.86
Jerry McCormick	1	2	0	0	0	0	3	0	0	0	9.00
		593.1	67	64	21	46	310	105	1	0	4.63

ST. PAUL   Andrew Thompson   None: Never played a home game

		G	AB	H	R	2B	3B	HR	RBI	BB	BA	SA
2B	Moxie Hengle	9	33	5	2	1	1	0	—	0	.152	.242
1B	Steve Dunn	9	32	8	2	2	0	0	—	0	.250	.313
RF	Scrappy Carroll	9	31	3	3	1	0	0	—	2	.097	.129
3B	Billy O'Brien	8	30	7	1	3	0	0	—	0	.233	.333
CF	Bill Barnes	8	30	6	2	1	0	0	—	0	.200	.233
SS	Joe Werrick	9	27	2	3	0	0	0	—	1	.074	.074
LF	John Tilley	9	26	4	2	1	0	0	—	3	.154	.192
C	Charlie Ganzel	7	23	5	2	0	0	0	—	0	.217	.217
P	Jim Brown	6	16	5	5	4	0	0	—	1	.313	.563
C	Pat Dealey	5	15	2	2	0	0	0	—	0	.133	.133
P	Lou Galvin	3	9	2	0	0	0	0	—	0	.222	.222
		9	272	49	24	13	1	0	—	7	.180	.235

1B   Dunn 9, Brown 1
2B   Hengle 9
SS   Werrick 9
3B   O'Brien 8, Carroll 2, Dunn 1
OF   Tilley 9, Carroll 8, Barnes 8, Brown 1, Ganzel 1, Dealey 1
C   Ganzel 6, Dealey 4
P   Brown 6, Galvin 3, O'Brien 2

	G	IP	GS	CG	W	L	K	BB	SH	SV	ERA
Jim Brown	6	36	6	4	1	4	20	14	1	0	3.75
Lou Galvin	3	25	3	3	0	2	17	10	0	0	2.88
Billy O'Brien	2	10	0	0	1	0	7	3	0	0	1.80
	71	9	7	2	6	44	27	1	0	3.17	

ALTOONA   Ed Curtis   Columbia Park

		G	AB	H	R	2B	3B	HR	RBI	BB	BA	SA
SS	Germany Smith	25	108	34	9	8	1	0	—	1	.315	.407
1B	Frank Harris	24	95	25	10	2	1	0	—	3	.263	.305
CF	John Murphy	24	94	14	10	1	0	0	—	4	.149	.160
RF	Jim Brown	21	88	22	12	2	2	1	—	1	.250	.352
2B	Charlie Dougherty	23	85	22	6	5	0	0	—	2	.259	.318
C	Jerrie Moore	20	80	25	10	3	1	1	—	0	.313	.413
3B	Harry Koons	21	78	18	8	2	1	0	—	2	.231	.282
LF	Frank Shaffer	19	74	21	11	2	0	0	—	3	.284	.311
C	Pat Carroll	11	49	13	4	1	0	0	—	1	.265	.286
Sub	John Grady	9	36	11	5	3	0	0	—	2	.306	.389
UT	Jack Leary	8	33	3	1	0	0	0	—	1	.091	.091
Sub	Charlie Berry	7	25	6	2	0	0	0	—	0	.240	.240
Sub	George Noftsker	7	25	1	0	0	0	0	—	0	.040	.040
P	Joe Connors	3	11	1	0	0	0	0	—	0	.091	.091
Sub	Clarence Cross	2	7	4	1	1	0	0	—	2	.571	.714
Sub	Charlie Manlove	2	7	3	1	0	0	0	—	0	.429	.429
Sub	George Daisey	1	4	0	0	0	0	0	—	0	.000	.000
		25	899	223	90	30	6	2	—	22	.248	.301

1B   Harris 17, Grady 8
2B   Dougherty 16, Berry 7, Murphy 4
SS   Smith 25, Dougherty 1
3B   Koons 21, Cross 2, Leary 1, Connors 1, Shaffer 1
OF   Shaffer 17, Brown 14, Murphy 10, Moore 9, Dougherty 8, Harris 8, Leary 6, Noftsker 5,
     Carroll 3, Manlove 1, Daisey 1, Grady 1, Connors 1
C   Moore 12, Carroll 8, Noftsker 3, Shaffer 2, Manlove 1, Koons 1
P   Murphy 14, Brown 11, Leary 3, Connors 1, Smith 1

	G	IP	GS	CG	W	L	K	BB	SH	SV	ERA
John Murphy	14	111.2	10	10	5	6	46	9	0	0	3.87
Jim Brown	11	74	11	7	1	9	39	36	0	0	5.35
Jack Leary	3	24	3	2	0	3	7	2	0	0	5.25
Joe Connors	1	9	1	1	0	1	0	5	0	0	7.00
Germany Smith	1	1	0	0	0	0	1	0	0	0	9.00
		219.2	25	20	6	19	93	52	0	0	4.63

KANSAS CITY   Harry Wheeler (0–4)   Matt Porter (3–13)   Ted Sullivan (13–46)   Athletic Park

		G	AB	H	R	2B	3B	HR	RBI	BB	BA	SA
C	Kid Baldwin	50	191	37	19	6	3	0	—	4	.194	.257
RF	Frank Shaffer	44	164	28	18	3	2	0	—	15	.171	.213
LF	Barney McLaughlin	42	162	37	15	7	3	0	—	9	.228	.309
P	Bob Black	38	146	36	25	14	2	1	—	10	.247	.390
Sub	Jack Gorman	33	137	38	25	5	2	0	—	4	.277	.343
1B	Jerry Sweeney	31	129	34	16	3	0	0	—	4	.264	.287
CF	Frank Wyman	30	124	27	16	4	0	0	—	3	.218	.250
Sub	Frank McLaughlin	32	123	28	17	11	0	1	—	9	.228	.341
2B	Charlie Berry	29	118	29	15	6	1	1	—	1	.246	.339
Sub	Jim Cudworth	32	116	17	7	3	1	0	—	2	.147	.190
3B	Pat Sullivan	31	114	22	15	3	1	0	—	4	.193	.237
SS	Clarence Cross	25	93	20	13	1	0	0	—	6	.215	.226
Sub	Henry Oberbeck	27	90	17	7	3	0	0	—	7	.189	.222
P	Peekaboo Veach	27	82	11	9	1	0	1	—	9	.134	.183
Sub	Harry Decker	23	75	10	8	2	0	0	—	5	.133	.160
P	Ernie Hickman	19	72	12	4	1	0	0	—	1	.167	.181
Sub	Lew Say	17	70	14	6	2	0	1	—	2	.200	.271
Sub	Nin Alexander	19	65	9	2	0	0	0	—	1	.138	.138
Sub	Harry Wheeler	14	62	16	11	1	0	0	—	3	.258	.274
Sub	Joe Strauss	16	60	12	4	3	0	0	—	1	.200	.250
Sub	George Strief	15	56	6	5	5	0	0	—	4	.107	.196
Sub	Jerry Turbidy	13	49	11	5	4	0	0	—	3	.224	.306
Sub	Charlie Bastian	11	46	9	6	3	0	1	—	4	.196	.326
P	Alex Voss	14	45	4	1	0	0	0	—	0	.089	.089
Sub	Ward Dwight	12	43	10	8	2	0	0	—	2	.233	.279
Sub	Charlie Fisher	10	40	8	3	2	0	0	—	0	.200	.250
Sub	John Deasley	13	40	7	3	2	0	0	—	2	.175	.225
Sub	Jumbo Davis	7	29	6	3	0	0	0	—	0	.207	.207
Sub	Jim Donnelly	6	23	3	2	1	0	0	—	1	.130	.174
Sub	Milt Whitehead	5	22	3	2	0	0	0	—	0	.136	.136
Sub	? Wills	5	21	3	2	1	0	0	—	0	.143	.190
P	Jersey Bakely	6	20	3	3	1	0	0	—	1	.150	.200
Sub	Henry Luff	5	19	1	0	0	0	0	—	1	.053	.053
Sub	Billy O'Brien	4	17	4	2	0	0	0	—	0	.235	.235
P	Dick Blaisdell	4	16	5	1	1	0	0	—	0	.313	.375
P	Doug Crothers	4	15	2	2	0	0	0	—	0	.133	.133
P	Jim Chatterton	4	15	2	4	1	0	0	—	2	.133	.200
Sub	Matt Porter	3	12	1	1	1	0	0	—	0	.083	.167
Sub	Ed Callahan	3	11	4	0	0	0	0	—	0	.364	.364
P	Joe Connors	3	11	1	2	0	0	0	—	1	.091	.091
Sub	Ted Sullivan	3	9	3	0	0	0	0	—	1	.333	.333
P	Bill Hutchison	2	8	2	1	0	0	0	—	0	.250	.250
Sub	Jimmy Say	2	8	2	0	0	0	0	—	0	.250	.250
Sub	Joe Ellick	2	8	0	0	0	0	0	—	0	.000	.000
P	John Kirby	3	7	1	1	0	0	0	—	0	.143	.143
Sub	Bill Dugan	3	6	0	0	0	0	0	—	0	.000	.000

		G	AB	H	R	2B	3B	HR	RBI	BB	BA	SA
Sub	Emmett Seery	1	4	2	2	1	0	0	—	1	.500	.750
P	? Krieger	1	3	0	0	0	0	0	—	0	.000	.000
Sub	Charlie Cady	2	3	0	0	0	0	0	—	0	.000	.000
P	Frank Foreman	1	3	0	0	0	0	0	—	0	.000	.000
		82	2802	557	311	104	15	6	—	123	.199	.253

1B Sweeney 31, Gorman 24, Cudworth 19, Wyman 3, Oberbeck 3, Chatterton 2, Veach 1, O'Brien 1, Dwight 1
2B Berry 22, Strief 15, B. McLaughlin 12, Bastian 11, F. McLaughlin 10, Black 6, Whitehead 3, Strauss 2, Shaffer 1, Baldwin 1, Veach 1, L. Say 1, Cady 1, Ellick 1, Dwight 1
SS Cross 24, L. Say 16, Turbidy 13, Deasley 13, F. McLaughlin 5, Callahan 3, Alexander 2, B. McLaughlin 2, Shaffer 1, Black 1, Whitehead 1, T. Sullivan 1, Fisher 1
3B P. Sullivan 21, Oberbeck 15, Fisher 9, F. McLaughlin 9, Davis 7, Donnelly 5, Gorman 4, Luff 4, Wyman 3, O'Brien 3, J. Say 2, Berry 1, Shaffer 1, Baldwin 1, Hickman 1, Cross 1, Strauss 1, Whitehead 1
OF Shaffer 41, Wyman 25, B. McLaughlin 24, Black 19, Decker 16, Veach 14, Wheeler 13, Cudworth 12, Strauss 10, Baldwin 10, F. McLaughlin 10, P. Sullivan 9, Berry 8, Voss 8, Oberbeck 7, Wills 5, Gorman 5, Luff 4, Hickman 3, Dugan 3, Porter 3, Bakely 3, Chatterton 2, Connors 2, Alexander 2, T. Sullivan 2, Crothers 1, Kirby 1, Krieger 1, Blaisdell 1, Seery 1, Dwight 1, Ellick 1
C Baldwin 44, Alexander 17, Decker 11, Dwight 10, Strauss 3, Shaffer 2, P. Sullivan 1, Cady 1, Whitehead 1, Donnelly 1
P Hickman 17, Black 16, Veach 12, Voss 7, B. McLaughlin 7, Oberbeck 6, Bakely 5, Wyman 3, Crothers 3, Blaisdell 3, Connors 2, Hutchison 2, F. McLaughlin 2, Kirby 2, Cudworth 2, P. Sullivan 1, Krieger 1, Foreman 1, Chatterton 1, Wheeler 1

	G	IP	GS	CG	W	L	K	BB	SH	SV	ERA
Ernie Hickman	17	137.1	17	15	4	13	68	36	0	0	4.52
Bob Black	16	123	15	13	4	9	93	17	0	0	3.22
Peekaboo Veach	12	104	12	12	3	9	62	10	0	0	2.42
Alex Voss	7	53	6	6	0	6	17	7	0	0	4.25
Barney McLaughlin	7	48.2	4	4	1	3	14	15	0	0	5.36
Jersey Bakely	5	33	5	3	2	3*	13	4*	0	0	2.45
Henry Oberbeck	6	29.2	4	3	0	5	6	3	0	0	5.76
Dick Blaisdell	3	26	3	3	0	3	8	4	0	0	8.65
Doug Crothers	3	25	3	3	1	2	11	6	0	0	1.80
Frank Wyman	3	21	1	1	0	1	9	3	0	0	6.86
Bill Hutchison	2	17	2	2	1	1	5	1	0	0	2.65
Jim Cudworth	2	17	1	1	0	0	6	3	0	0	4.24
Joe Connors	2	12	1	1	0	1	1	0	0	0	4.50
John Kirby	2	11	2	1	0	1	1	2	0	0	4.09
Frank McLaughlin	2	10	1	0	0	0	3	2	0	0	5.40
Frank Foreman	1	8	1	1	0	1	5	2	0	0	5.63
Harry Wheeler	1	8	1	1	0	1	6	0	0	0	1.13
? Krieger	1	7	1	0	0	1	3	5	0	0	0.00
Pat Sullivan	1	7	1	0	0	1	1	5	0	0	11.57
Jim Chatterton	1	5	1	0	0	1	2	2	0	0	3.60
—1 forfeit L vs St. Louis on August 22—											
		702.2	82	70	16	62	334	127	0	0	4.06

WILMINGTON   Joe Simmons   Union Street Park

		G	AB	H	R	2B	3B	HR	RBI	BB	BA	SA
2B	Charlie Bastian	17	60	12	6	1	3	2	—	3	.200	.417
3B	Jimmy Say	16	59	13	3	1	2	0	—	1	.220	.305
LF	Tom Lynch	16	58	16	6	3	1	0	—	5	.276	.362
1B	Redleg Snyder	17	52	10	4	0	0	0	—	1	.192	.192
C	Tony Cusick	11	34	5	0	0	0	0	—	1	.147	.147
P	The Only Nolan	9	33	9	5	2	1	0	—	2	.273	.394
Sub	John Cullen	9	31	6	2	0	0	0	—	1	.194	.194
P	John Murphy	10	31	2	4	0	0	0	—	3	.065	.065
Sub	Bill McCloskey	9	30	3	0	0	0	0	—	0	.100	.100
CF	George Fisher	8	29	2	0	0	0	0	—	0	.069	.069
SS	Henry Myers	6	24	3	3	0	0	0	—	0	.125	.125
Sub	Ike Benners	6	22	1	0	0	0	0	—	1	.045	.045
RF	John Munce	7	21	4	1	0	0	0	—	1	.190	.190
Sub	Dennis Casey	2	8	2	1	1	0	0	—	0	.250	.375
Sub	Oyster Burns	2	7	1	0	0	1	0	—	1	.143	.429
Sub	John Ryan	2	6	1	0	0	0	0	—	1	.167	.167
P	Dan Casey	2	6	1	0	0	0	0	—	0	.167	.167
P	Jersey Bakely	2	5	0	0	0	0	0	—	1	.000	.000
P	Fred Tenney	1	3	0	0	0	0	0	—	0	.000	.000
P	Jim McElroy	1	2	0	0	0	0	0	—	0	.000	.000
		18	521	91	35	8	8	2	—	22	.175	.232

1B	Snyder 16, Lynch 1
2B	Bastian 16, Myers 1, Cusick 1
SS	Myers 5, Cusick 3, Cullen 3, Burns 2, Murphy 2, Fisher 2, Bastian 1
3B	Say 16, Murphy 1, Cusick 1
OF	Lynch 8, Munce 7, Fisher 6, Cullen 6, Benners 6, McCloskey 5, Nolan 4, Cusick 3, Den. Casey 2, Ryan 2, Murphy 2, McElroy 2, Snyder 1
C	Lynch 8, Cusick 6, McCloskey 5
P	Murphy 7, Nolan 5, Dan Casey 2, Bakely 2, Tenney 1, McElroy 1, Bastian 1

	G	IP	GS	CG	W	L	K	W	SH	SV	ERA
John Murphy	7	48	6	5	0	6	27	2	0	0	3.00
The Only Nolan	5	40	5	5	1	4	52	7	0	0	2.93
Jersey Bakely	2	17	2	2	0	2*	9	1*	0	0	4.24
Dan Casey	2	18	2	2	1	1	10	4	0	0	1.00
Jim McElroy	1	5	1	0	0	1	3	0	0	0	10.80
Fred Tenney	1	8	1	1	0	1	10	4	0	0	1.13
Charlie Bastian	1	6	0	0	0	0	2	0	0	0	3.00
			—1 forfeit L vs Boston on August 25—							
		142	18	15	2	15	113	18	0	0	3.04

1885

THE DISPUTED CHAMPIONSHIP

The Union Association went to its grave in early January 1885 when the National League formally admitted Henry Lucas and his St. Louis Maroons to replace Cleveland. Deprived of Lucas's financial backing and leadership, the other Union teams either folded entirely or reverted to minor league status.

Once the Union threat was erased, the American Association cut back from 12 to eight teams. Three of the newcomers in 1884—Virginia, Toledo and Indianapolis—were natural choices to go, but Brooklyn, the fourth newborn, was retained when the Columbus franchise closed up shop and merged with Pittsburgh. The fusion included player transfers, bringing the Pennsylvania club Ed Morris, Fred Carroll and enough other new talent to transform it from a tailender into a contender. Brooklyn beefed up considerably too by purchasing the dying Cleveland club in order to gain control of its players, and the St. Louis Browns, after voting to dismiss Toledo from the Association, rifled Toledo's two top players, Curt Welch and Sam Barkley, and then tried to recover Tony Mullane, their former pitching ace who had been assigned to Toledo in 1884 to keep him out of Union Association hands.

The League accepted these quasi-legal transactions largely in the hope of wooing the association into accepting some of its even more questionable machinations. Over the winter John Day, the president of the Metropolitan Exhibition Company, which owned both the New York Mets of the Association and the League's New York Gothams, shifted manager Jim Mutrie from the Mets to the Gothams' helm. Believing that not even a championship Association team in New York that collected 25 cents a head could be as profitable as a League team that got 50 cents, Day then moved pitcher Tim Keefe and third baseman Dude Esterbrook from the Mets to the Gothams after first going through the motions of releasing them and then waiting the required 10 days before signing them to League contracts. Angered by the cavalier manner in which Day had decimated their 1884 pennant winner, Association moguls grew all the more enraged on Browns owner Chris Von Der Ahe's be-

Pittsburgh, a miserable team the previous year, became instantly competitive in 1885 after merging with the Columbus Buckeyes. Many of these faces also appear in the 1884 Columbus team photo, but one of them, that of manager "Hustling" Horace Phillips, appears nowhere else. Top: Art Whitney, Jones (first name unknown), Fred Carroll, Rudy Kemmler, Tom Brown and Milt Scott. Middle: Charlie Eden, Willie Kuehne, Doggie Miller, Phillips, Pop Smith and Fred Mann. Bottom: Pete Meegan and 39-game winner Ed Morris.

half when they learned the League meant to violate the National Agreement by installing a competing team in St. Louis. Eventually Von Der Ahe was placated when Lucas gave him a cash settlement for sharing the Browns' territory and the League assured him that the Maroons would be forbidden his three main perks: beer and baseball on Sunday, all for only a quarter. Von Der Ahe was further placated when Mullane was suspended for the entire 1885 season following yet another round of contract jumping. In one last order of business, the League persuaded the Association to agree to reinstate all of the players who had been blacklisted for jumping to the Union Association.

Lucas's Maroons were the chief beneficiary of the lifting of the ban on the Union jumpers. It freed Lucas to play all the stars from his 1884 championship team on Opening Day against Chicago, plus Jack Glasscock and Fatty Briody, two former Cleveland stalwarts the Maroons acquired when the Cincinnati Union team dissolved. Led by second baseman Fred Dunlap and Charlie Sweeney's pitching, the Maroons celebrated their League debut by beating Chicago, but that Opening Day win would prove to be both their high point and the White Stockings' nadir.

THE BROWNING CASE

In 1885 Pete Browning won his second of three career batting titles. For a while *Total Baseball* gave him a fourth batting crown in 1886 but has since made Dave Orr the winner because major league baseball proclaims he was even though Browning outhit him .340 to .338. In any event, Browning won at least three batting titles, and he is one of only three men who captured hitting crowns in two different major leagues. The other two, Dan Brouthers and Ed Delahanty, have long been in the Hall of Fame. So why not Pete "The Gladiator" Browning?

The rap on Browning has always been that he was not much good at any other phase of the game except hitting and was particularly atrocious as a fielder. How true any of that is will never be simple to determine. For a fact, Browning had some high error totals and awful fielding averages, but in the 1880s there were a bundle of awful fielding averages. What's more, early in his career Browning had seasons as a regular at both second and third base, hardly places where you put a man who's error-prone, and when he was moved to the outfield, most of the time he played center. True, he led American Association outfielders in errors in 1886 and again in 1887, but in the latter year he was third in outfield chances only to Curt Welch and Pop Corkhill, perhaps the two best defensive outfielders active that season. Louisville in those years was first-division material most of the time too, so there goes the argument that it didn't matter to the team where Browning played. On the contrary, it mattered a great deal, and no matter where Browning was put, he did the job decently. Later in his career, when he was on a string of rotten teams, he played left field mostly and not with a whole lot of zest, and by then it was also true that he wasn't much for bunting or hitting behind the runner or taking an extra base or doing anything else that might harm his batting average. But that was only toward the end. In 1887 "The Gladiator" stole 103 bases, and even though the rules were different then with regard to what constituted a stolen base, that was still a Louisville club record any way it's sliced.

So we have a man who won three batting titles and was once deemed by *Total Baseball* to have won a fourth, a man who was a regular at both second and third bases and also in the outfield, a man who could send the feathers flying when necessary on the bases, a man who played most of his career for a team on the Ohio River, a man who didn't make the Hall of Fame as much as anything because he drank and got in the wrong league. Anyone else in baseball history quite like Pete Browning? You bet, almost identical in every way except that he gambled and got under the wrong commissioner. His name was Pete too.

THE GERHARDT CASE

In 1885, Joe Gerhardt played every inning of every game at second base for the New York Gothams, not an easy achievement for a man who hit just .155 and compiled only 78 total bases. Both figures are all-time season lows for an infielder or out-fielder in 100 or more games. Gerhardt kept his job in 1885 because he was a great fielder, perhaps even as good as Fred Dunlap, considered by most authorities to have been the top defensive second baseman in the 1880s. It grew harder and harder, though, to carry Gerhardt's bat once overhand pitching was legalized. A fair hitter, albeit with little power, early in his career, Gerhardt was badly overmatched in his last few seasons. He followed his 1885 debacle by hitting .190 in 1886 and then dropped down to the minors when his offensive decline continued in 1887. When the Players League war in 1890 opened a crack for Gerhardt to return to the majors, he hit a woeful .217 in nearly 500 at bats but showed he had lost none of his defensive skills by leading all American Association second baseman in fielding average and total chances. The following list demonstrates that Gerhardt's place among the poorest hitters in history is assured.

19TH CENTURY PLAYERS BELOW .200 IN 100 OR MORE GAMES

	Year	Team	Pos	G	AB	H	R	TB	BA
Joe Gerhardt	1885	NY-NL	2B	112	399	62	43	78	.155
Jim Canavan	1892	Chi-LA	2B	118	439	73	48	105	.166
Charlie Bastian	1885	Phi-NL	SS	103	389	65	63	98	.167
Ben Conroy	1890	Phi-AA	SS	117	404	69	45	84	.171
Jim Lillie	1886	KC-NL	OF	114	416	73	37	82	.175
Jack Boyle	1892	NY-LA	C	120	436	80	52	104	.183
Milt Scott	1886	Bal-AA	1B	137	484	92	48	117	.190
Joe Gerhardt	1886	NY-NL	2B	123	426	81	44	106	.190
Henry Easterday	1888	KC-AA	SS	115	401	76	42	101	.190
Ed Kennedy	1884	NY-AA	OF	103	378	72	49	85	.190
Germany Smith	1890	Bro-NL	SS	129	481	92	76	111	.191
Bill Greenwood	1888	Bal-AA	2B	115	409	78	69	93	.191
Harry Lyons	1888	StL-AA	OF	123	499	97	66	129	.194
John Morrill	1888	Bos-NL	1B	135	486	96	60	140	.198
Patsy Cahill	1886	StL-NL	OF	125	463	92	43	124	.199
Mike Muldoon	1886	Bal-AA	2B	101	381	76	57	105	.199

Following a 1–0 start, the Maroons soon settled into the league basement while Chicago won 32 of its next 37 games after opening 0–1. A pitching staff rebuilt around John Clarkson, a 53-game winner in his first full major league season, more than compensated for a rule change that cut the White Stockings' power production to 54 four-baggers from a nineteenth-century record 142 home runs the previous year. In 1884, playing in a park with short fences, no fewer than four White Stockings had compiled more than 20 home runs, forcing a rule to be drafted reducing a fairly hit ball from a home run to a groundruled double if it passed over a fence less than 210 feet from home plate.

But despite this revision and a much larger new park, Chicago again led the majors in home runs by a wide margin, powering 24 four-base hits more than the Philadelphia Athletics, the Association's heaviest hitting club in 1885. The Athletics were virtually the only junior circuit team to be spared the sharp offensive decline that accompanied the Association's decision at a special meeting on June 7, 1885, to unite with the League in legalizing overhand pitching. At the same meeting the Association adopted the League rule that a foul ball must be caught on the fly for a batter to be retired and created a new rule giving the home team captain the option to bat either first or last. Earlier, to curtail injuries to runners as they slid across home plate, the Association had fostered another rule change by requiring the plate to be made of rubber rather than stone, but the League would continue to use stone plates until 1887.

By legalizing overhand pitching the American Association put a premium on defense and daring base running, and the Browns quickly adapted under the generalship of first baseman Charlie Comiskey. Never a high-average hitter himself, Comiskey assembled a team that had no batting title qualifiers who hit above .271 and scored nearly 100 fewer runs than the Athletics but nevertheless won the pennant by 16 games while the Philadelphians self-destructed on defense, committing the most errors in the Association, and finished a distant fourth.

The National League team most closely parallel to the Browns was New York. Like the Browns, Mutrie's Gothams topped their loop in fielding average and earned run average. More than that, the Gothams also led in batting average and thus won the team Triple Crown. In 1885, however, the Gothams became the only team Triple Crown winner in the nineteenth century to fail to capture a pennant, though the fault was hardly theirs. Indeed, the Gothams won 85 of 112 games for an astounding .759 success rate. But all their prowess earned them was a new nickname—the Giants—and the best record ever by a second-place team as Chicago won 87 of 112 verdicts. The difference between the two clubs was Clarkson, the majors' most valuable player in 1885, and second base where Chicago's Fred Pfeffer, even at .241, outhit Joe Gerhardt, his New York counterpart, by 86 points and tallied 47 more runs.

Even though they won 77.7 percent of their games, the Chicagos were pushed to the limit before they copped the 1885 NL pennant. Billy Sunday, although the only clean-shaven one, was actually among the team's leading rabble-rousers until he got the calling and quit the game after the 1890 season to become the country's foremost evangelist.

So close together were the two League titans entering the final days of the season that the Giants came into Chicago for an all-critical four-game showdown series between the pair trailing by just two games with eight left on the slate. New York had previously taken nine of the first 12 contests between the pair, but suddenly the tables were turned. On September 29, Jim McCormick beat Mickey Welch, 7–4, to extend Chicago's lead to three games. The following day John Clarkson added a length to it by edging Tim Keefe, 2–1. When McCormick won a rematch with Welch, 8–3, on October 1, it made Keefe's come-from-behind 10–8 triumph two days later necessary just to keep the Giants from being mathematically eliminated. As it was, New York left the Windy City four games back with just four to go, a nearly impossible deficit to overcome.

The White Stockings unquestionably had a more exhausting road to the pennant than the Browns, and in due time the difference showed when the two teams met in the second interleague World's Series. The best-of-seven battle commenced in Chicago on October 14 with a 5–5 tie. The next afternoon in St. Louis, Comiskey pulled his Browns off the field in the sixth inning and refused to play on when umpire Dave Sullivan would not change his

THE MULLANE CASE

Tony Mullane, the only player forced to sit out an entire year for contract-jumping. Notwithstanding his suspension, Mullane's 202 wins in the AA make him the only pitcher to win 200 in a major league other than the NL or the AL.

The Hall of Fame at Cooperstown does not have a single member who was selected solely for his playing accomplishments after spending most of his major league career in the American Association. Indeed, only two enshrinees, Tim Keefe and Tommy McCarthy, spent as many as two seasons in the Association. Tony Mullane might have forced the issue if he had not been suspended for all of the 1885 season. The suspension was meant as both a punishment for Mullane and an example to other players that his constant contract jumping would no longer be tolerated even in an era when each season brought a new interleague war and the Reserve Clause was still embryonic. Mullane was one of the most colorful and versatile players of his time, capable of pitching with both arms and such a natural drawing card with his flamboyant good looks that Cincinnati owner Aaron Stern, never one to miss a trick, designated every weekday afternoon when he was scheduled to pitch as a special "Ladies' Day." Whether or not Mullane's punishment served any worthwhile purpose is questionable, but it deprived him of a full year from the prime of his career. Mullane was 26 in 1885 and coming off a season in which he won 36 games for a second division team. Since he won 33 games upon returning to the game in 1886, even the most conservative estimate would grant him between 25 and 30 victories if he had played in 1885. Mullane finished his career just 16 wins short of 300. Another 25 or 30 wins would have put him well over the 300 pinnacle that has thus far guaranteed eventual enshrinement for every pitcher who attained it. Would reaching 300 wins have done as much for Mullane and perhaps opened the door for other Association stars as well? We will never know.

call on a base hit that Comiskey thought should be ruled a foul ball. From the safety of his hotel room, Sullivan later forfeited the game to Chicago. He was rewarded by never being given another umpiring assignment in the majors.

The Series continued with Harry McCaffrey, a former Browns substitute, doing the officiating. After splitting the next four games, the two combatants then agreed to count the forfeited game as a tie and consider the Series even at two-all so they could play one last game for all the marbles. When the Browns won 13–4 over a weary Chicago team, Von Der Ahe claimed the $1,000 winner-take-all purse but never received it. Weeks later, *Sporting Life*, the game's leading organ and most impartial arbiter, proclaimed all bets off "while the championship of the United States for 1885 remains in abeyance." So it remains to this day.

THE SEASONAL RECORD

NATIONAL LEAGUE

	W	L	PCT	HOME	ROAD	GB
1. Chicago White Stockings	87	25	.777	44–14	43–11	—
2. New York Giants	85	27	.759	51–10	34–17	2
3. Philadelphia Phillies	56	54	.509	29–26	27–28	30
4. Providence Grays	53	57	.482	31–19	22–38	33
5. Boston Beaneaters	46	66	.411	24–34	22–32	41
6. Detroit Wolverines	41	67	.380	29–23	12–44	44
7. Buffalo Bisons	38	74	.339	19–33	19–41	49
8. St. Louis Maroons	36	72	.333	23–33	13–39	49

	Chi	NY	Phi	Pro	Bos	Det	Buf	StL	
Chicago	—	6	11	11	14	15	16	14	87
New York	10	—	11	12	13	12	15	12	85
Philadelphia	5	5	—	8	9	9	11	9	56
Providence	5	4	7	—	7	9	13	8	53
Boston	2	3	7	9	—	7	10	8	46
Detroit	1	4	7	6	9	—	5	9	41
Buffalo	0	1	5	3	6	11	—	12	38
St. Louis	2	4	6	8	8	4	4	—	36
	25	27	54	57	66	67	74	72	442

SEASON LEADERS

Batting Average (350 ABs)

1.	Connor, New York	.371
2.	Brouthers, Buffalo	.359
3.	Dorgan, New York	.326
4.	Richardson, Buffalo	.319
5.	Gore, Chicago	.313
	Sutton, Boston	.313

Slugging Average

1.	Brouthers, Buffalo	.543
2.	Connor, New York	.495
3.	Ewing, New York	.471
4.	Anson, Chicago	.461
5.	Richardson, Buffalo	.458

On–Base Percentage

1.	Connor, New York	.435
2.	Brouthers, Buffalo	.408
3.	Gore, Chicago	.405
4.	Hanlon, Detroit	.372
5.	Anson, Chicago	.357
	Williamson, Chicago	.357

Total Bases

1.	Connor, Buffalo	225
2.	Brouthers, Buffalo	221
3.	Dalrymple, Chicago	219
4.	Anson, Chicago	214
5.	O'Rourke, New York	211

Home Runs

1.	Dalrymple, Chicago	11
2.	Kelly, Chicago	9
3.	Thompson, Detroit	7
	Brouthers, Detroit	7
	Burns, Chicago	7
	Anson, Chicago	7

RBI

1.	Anson, Chicago	108
2.	Kelly, Chicago	75
3.	Pfeffer, Chicago	73
4.	Burns, Chicago	71
5.	Connor, New York	65
	Williamson, Chicago	65

Hits

1.	Connor, New York	169
2.	Brouthers, Buffalo	146
3.	Anson, Chicago	144
4.	Sutton, Boston	143
	O'Rourke, New York	143

Runs

1.	Kelly, Chicago	124
2.	O'Rourke, New York	119
3.	Gore, Chicago	115
4.	Dalrymple, Chicago	109
5.	Connor, New York	102

Bases on Balls

1.	Williamson, Chicago	75
2.	Gore, Chicago	68
3.	Morrill, Boston	64
4.	Connor, New York	51
5.	Hanlon, Detroit	47

Strikeouts

1.	Bastian, Philadelphia	82
2.	Morrill, Boston	78
3.	Wise, Boston	61
4.	Bassett, Providence	60
	Williamson, Chicago	60

PITCHING

Wins

1.	Clarkson, Chicago	53
2.	Welch, New York	44
3.	Keefe, New York	32
4.	Radbourn, Providence	28
5.	Ferguson, Philadelphia	26
	E. Daily, Philadelphia	26

Losses

1.	Whitney, Boston	32
2.	Buffinton, Boston	27
3.	Shaw, Providence	26
4.	Getzein, Detroit	25
5.	Boyle, St. Louis	24
	Weidman, Detroit	24

Innings

1.	Clarkson, Chicago	623
2.	Welch, New York	492
3.	Radbourn, Providence	445.2
4.	Whitney, Boston	441.1
5.	E. Daily, Philadelphia	440

Strikeouts

1.	Clarkson, Chicago	308
2.	Welch, New York	258
3.	Buffinton, Boston	242
4.	Keefe, New York	227
5.	Whitney, Boston	200

ERA (112 innings)

1.	Keefe, New York	1.58
2.	Welch, New York	1.66
3.	Clarkson, Chicago	1.85
4.	Baldwin, Detroit	1.86
5.	Radbourn, Providence	2.20

Complete Games

1.	Clarkson, Chicago	68
2.	Welch, New York	55
3.	Whitney, Boston	50
4.	Buffinton, Boston	49
	E. Daily, Philadelphia	49
	Radbourn, Providence	49

Winning Percentage (25 decisions)

1.	Welch, New York	.800
2.	Clarkson, Chicago	.768
3.	McCormick, Prov–Chic	.750
4.	Keefe, New York	.711
5.	Radbourn, Providence	.571

Lowest On–Base Percentage

1.	Baldwin, Detroit	.228
2.	Clarkson, Chicago	.239
3.	Shaw, Providence	.254
4.	Keefe, New York	.255
5.	E. Daily, Philadelphia	.256
	Welch, New York	.256

FIELDING

Total Chances

1B	Anson, Chicago	1349
2B	Pfeffer, Chicago	802
3B	Williamson, Chicago	416
SS	Glasscock, St. Louis	603
OF	Fogarty, Philadelphia	269
C	Flint, Chicago	492
P	Clarkson, Chicago	220

Fielding Average

McKinnon, St. Louis	.978
Dunlap, St. Louis	.934
Williamson, Chicago	.892
Glasscock, St. Louis	.917
Gillespie, New York	.942
Flint, Chicago	.927
McCormick, Prov–Chicago	.951

CHICAGO   **Cap Anson**   **West Side Park (I)**

		G	AB	H	R	2B	3B	HR	RBI	BB	BA	SA
LF	Abner Dalrymple	113	**492**	135	109	27	12	**11**	61	46	.274	.445
2B	Fred Pfeffer	112	469	113	90	12	7	5	73	26	.241	.328
1B	Cap Anson	112	464	144	100	**35**	7	7	**108**	34	.310	.461
SS	Tom Burns	111	445	121	82	23	9	7	71	16	.272	.411
CF	George Gore	109	441	138	115	21	13	5	57	68	.313	.454
RF	King Kelly	107	438	126	**124**	24	7	9	75	46	.288	.436
3B	Ned Williamson	113	407	97	87	16	5	3	65	**75**	.238	.324
P	John Clarkson	72	283	61	34	11	5	4	32	3	.216	.332
C	Silver Flint	68	249	52	27	8	2	1	17	2	.209	.269
Sub	Billy Sunday	46	172	44	36	3	3	2	20	12	.256	.343
P	Jim McCormick	25	103	23	13	1	4	0	16	1	.223	.311
Sub	Sy Sutcliffe	11	43	8	5	1	1	0	4	2	.186	.256
P	Ted Kennedy	10	36	3	3	0	0	0	0	0	.083	.083
P	Larry Corcoran	8	22	6	6	1	0	0	4	6	.273	.318
Sub	Jimmy Ryan	3	13	6	2	1	0	0	2	1	.462	.538
Sub	Jim McCauley	3	6	1	1	0	0	0	0	2	.167	.167

		G	AB	H	R	2B	3B	HR	RBI	BB	BA	SA
Sub	Wash Williams	1	4	1	0	0	0	0	0	0	.250	.250
Sub	Bill Krieg	1	3	0	0	0	0	0	0	0	.000	.000
Sub	Ed Gastfield	1	3	0	0	0	0	0	0	0	.000	.000
		113	4093	1079	**834**	**184**	**75**	**54**	606	340	.264	**.385**

1B Anson 112, Kelly 2
2B Pfeffer 109, Kelly 6, Burns 1
SS Burns 111, Ryan 2, Corcoran 1
3B Williamson 113, Kelly 2, Kennedy 1, Clarkson 1
OF Dalrymple 113, Gore 109, Kelly 69, Sunday 46, Clarkson 3, McCauley 2, Williams 1, Krieg 1, Sutcliffe 1, McCormick 1, Flint 1, Pfeffer 1, Ryan 1
C Flint 68, Kelly 37, Sutcliffe 10, McCauley 2, Gastfield 1, Williamson 1, Anson 1
P Clarkson 70, McCormick 24, Kennedy 9, Corcoran 7, Pfeffer 5, Williamson 2, Williams 1

	G	IP	GS	CG	W	L	K	BB	SH	SV	ERA
John Clarkson #	**70**	623	70	68	53	16	**308**	97	**10**	0	1.85
Jim McCormick	24	215	24	24	20	4	88	40	3	0	2.43
Ted Kennedy	9	78.2	9	8	7	2	36	28	0	0	3.43
Larry Corcoran	7	59.1	7	6	5	2	10	24	1	0	3.64
Fred Pfeffer	5	31.2	2	2	2	1	13	8	0	2	2.56
Ned Williamson	2	6	0	0	0	0	3	0	0	2	0.00
Wash Williams	1	2	1	0	0	0	0	5	0	0	13.50
		1015.2	113	108	87	25	458	202	14	**4**	2.23

No-hit game 4–0 vs Providence, July 27

NEW YORK   **Jim Mutrie**   **Polo Grounds (I)**

		G	AB	H	R	2B	3B	HR	RBI	BB	BA	SA
CF	Jim O'Rourke	112	477	143	119	21	**16**	5	42	40	.300	.442
1B	Roger Connor	110	455	**169**	102	23	15	1	65	51	**.371**	.495
SS	Monte Ward	111	446	101	72	8	9	0	37	17	.226	.285
LF	Pete Gillespie	102	420	123	67	17	6	0	52	15	.293	.362
2B	Joe Gerhardt	112	399	62	43	12	2	0	33	24	.155	.195
3B	Dude Esterbrook	88	359	92	48	14	5	2	44	4	.256	.340
RF	Mike Dorgan	89	347	113	60	17	8	0	46	11	.326	.421
C	Buck Ewing	81	342	104	81	15	12	6	63	13	.394	.471
C	Pat Deasley	54	207	53	22	5	1	0	24	9	.256	.290
P	Mickey Welch	56	199	41	28	8	0	2	19	14	.206	.276
Sub	Danny Richardson	49	198	52	26	9	3	0	25	10	.263	.338
P	Tim Keefe	47	166	27	20	1	5	0	12	13	.163	.229
P	Larry Corcoran	3	14	5	3	0	0	0	2	0	.357	.357
		112	4029	**1085**	691	150	**82**	16	464	221	**.269**	.359

1B Connor 110, Ewing 1, Dorgan 1
2B Gerhardt 112
SS Ward 111, Ewing 1, Deasley 1
3B Esterbrook 84, Richardson 21, Ewing 8
OF O'Rourke 112, Gillespie 102, Dorgan 88, Richardson 22, Ewing 14, Esterbrook 4, Deasley 2, Keefe 2
C Ewing 63, Deasley 54, O'Rourke 8
P Welch 56, Keefe 46, Richardson 9, Corcoran 3, Ewing 1

	G	IP	GS	CG	W	L	K	BB	SH	SV	ERA
Mickey Welch	56	492	55	55	44	11	258	**131**	7	1	1.66
Tim Keefe	46	400	46	45	32	13	227	102	7	0	1.58
Danny Richardson	9	75	8	7	7	1	21	18	1	0	2.40
Larry Corcoran	3	25	3	2	2	1	10	11	0	0	2.88
Buck Ewing	1	2	0	0	0	1	0	3	0	0	4.50
—One combined shutout on May 25: Keefe 2 innings, Richardson 7 innings—											
	994	112	111	85	27		516	265	**16**	1	**1.72**

PHILADELPHIA   **Harry Wright**   **Recreation Park**

		G	AB	H	R	2B	3B	HR	RBI	BB	BA	SA
RF	Jack Manning	107	445	114	61	24	4	3	40	37	.256	.348
3B	Joe Mulvey	107	443	119	74	25	6	6	64	3	.269	.393
CF	Jim Fogarty	111	427	99	49	13	3	0	39	30	.232	.276
LF	Ed Andrews	103	421	112	77	15	3	0	23	32	.266	.316
1B	Sid Farrar	111	420	103	49	20	3	3	36	28	.245	.329
SS	Charlie Bastian	103	389	65	63	11	5	4	29	35	.167	.252
2B	Al Myers	93	357	73	25	13	2	1	28	11	.204	.261
P	Charlie Ferguson	61	235	72	42	8	3	1	27	23	.306	.379
C	Jack Clements	52	188	36	14	11	3	1	14	2	.191	.298
P	Ed Daily	50	184	38	22	8	2	1	13	0	.207	.288
C	Tony Cusick	39	141	25	12	1	0	0	5	1	.177	.184
C	Charlie Ganzel	34	125	21	15	3	1	0	6	4	.168	.208
Sub	Tom Lynch	13	53	10	7	3	0	0	1	10	.189	.245
P	Bill Vinton	10	30	2	2	0	0	0	1	1	.067	.067
P	The Only Nolan	8	26	2	1	1	0	0	1	3	.077	.115
Sub	John Hiland	3	9	0	0	0	0	0	0	0	.000	.000
		111	3893	891	513	156	35	20	327	220	.229	.302

1B	Farrar 111
2B	Myers 93, Fogarty 10, Andrews 5, Hiland 3
SS	Bastian 103, Fogarty 8
3B	Mulvey 107, Fogarty 5
OF	Manning 107, Andrews 99, Fogarty 88, Ferguson 15, Lynch 13, Clements 11, Nolan 1, Ganzel 1, Cusick 1, Mulvey 1, Vinton 1
C	Clements 41, Cusick 38, Ganzel 33
P	Daily 50, Ferguson 48, Vinton 9, Nolan 7

	G	IP	GS	CG	W	L	K	BB	SH	SV	ERA
Ed Daily	50	440	50	49	26	23	140	90	4	0	2.21
Charlie Ferguson #	48	405	45	45	26	20	197	81	5	0	2.22
Bill Vinton	9	77	9	8	3	6	21	23	0	0	3.04
The Only Nolan	7	54	7	6	1	5	20	24	0	0	4.17
*One combined shutout on July 1: Daily 7 innings, Ferguson 3 innings											
	976	111	108	56	54		378	218	10	0	2.39

No-hit game 1–0 vs Providence, August 29

PROVIDENCE **Frank Bancroft** **Messer Street Park**

		G	AB	H	R	2B	3B	HR	RBI	BB	BA	SA
LF	Cliff Carroll	104	426	99	62	12	3	1	40	29	.232	.282
CF	Paul Hines	98	411	111	63	20	4	1	35	19	.270	.345
1B	Joe Start	101	374	103	47	11	4	0	41	39	.275	.326
RF	Paul Radford	105	371	90	55	12	5	0	32	33	.243	.302
3B	Jerry Denny	83	318	71	40	14	4	3	24	12	.223	.321
UT	Charlie Bassett	82	285	41	21	8	2	0	16	19	.144	.186
2B	Jack Farrell	68	257	53	27	7	1	1	19	10	.206	.253
C	Barney Gilligan	71	252	54	23	7	3	0	12	23	.214	.266
P	Hoss Radbourn	66	249	58	34	9	2	0	22	36	.233	.285
C	Con Daily	60	223	58	20	6	1	0	19	12	.260	.296
SS	Arthur Irwin	59	218	39	16	2	1	0	14	14	.179	.197
P	Dupee Shaw	49	165	22	17	2	0	0	9	4	.133	.145
Sub	Lon Knight	25	81	13	8	1	0	0	8	11	.160	.173
Sub	Tim Manning	10	35	2	3	1	0	0	0	1	.057	.086
Sub	Denny Lyons	4	16	2	3	1	0	0	1	0	.125	.188
P	Jim McCormick	4	14	3	2	1	0	0	0	1	.214	.286
P	Edgar Smith	1	4	1	0	0	0	0	0	0	.250	.250
P	Charlie Hallstrom	1	4	0	1	0	0	0	0	0	.000	.000
Sub	Wiman Andrus	1	4	0	0	0	0	0	0	0	.000	.000
P	Bill Stellberger	1	4	0	0	0	0	0	0	0	.000	.000
P	John Ward	1	3	0	0	0	0	0	0	0	.000	.000
P	Sam Kimber	1	3	0	0	0	0	0	0	0	.000	.000
P	Ed Seward	1	3	0	0	0	0	0	0	0	.000	.000
Sub	Mike Hines	1	3	0	0	0	0	0	0	0	.000	.000
P	John Foley	1	2	0	0	0	0	0	0	1	.000	.000
Sub	Cannonball Crane	1	2	0	0	0	0	0	0	1	.000	.000
		110	3727	820	442	114	30	6	292	265	.220	.272

1B   Start 101, Daily 7, P. Hines 4
2B   Farrell 68, Bassett 39, Radbourn 2, Gilligan 1, P. Hines 1, Radford 1, Irwin 1
SS   Irwin 58, Bassett 23, Radford 16, Manning 10, Gilligan 5, P. Hines 1
3B   Denny 83, Bassett 20, Lyons 4, P. Hines 1, Irwin 1, Andrus 1
OF   Carroll 104, P. Hines 92, Radford 88, Knight 25, Radbourn 16, Daily 6, Shaw 2, Crane 1, Gilligan 1
C   Gilligan 65, Daily 48, M. Hines 1, Bassett 1
P   Radbourn 49, Shaw 49, McCormick 4, Radford 3, Ward 1, Stellberger 1, Foley 1, Hallstrom 1, Kimber 1, Knight 1, Smith 1, Seward 1

	G	IP	GS	CG	W	L	K	BB	SH	SV	ERA
Hoss Radbourn	49	445.2	49	49	28	21	154	83	2	0	2.20
Dupee Shaw	49	399.2	49	47	23	26	194	99	6	0	2.57
Jim McCormick	4	37	4	4	1	3	8	20	0	0	2.43
Paul Radford	3	18.1	2	2	0	2	3	8	0	0	7.85
Charlie Hallstrom	1	9	1	1	0	1	0	6	0	0	11.00
Edgar Smith	1	9	1	1	1	0	1	0	0	0	1.00
John Ward	1	8	1	1	0	1	3	1	0	0	4.50
Bill Stellberger	1	8	1	1	0	1	0	4	0	0	7.88
Sam Kimber	1	8	1	1	0	1	4	5	0	0	11.25
John Foley	1	8	1	1	0	1	2	5	0	0	4.50
Ed Seward	1	6	0	0	0	0	1	0	0	0	0.00
Lon Knight	1	4	0	0	0	1	1	4	0	0	6.75
		960.2	110	108	53	57	371	235	8	0	2.71

BOSTON **John Morrill** **South End Grounds (I)**

		G	AB	H	R	2B	3B	HR	RBI	BB	BA	SA
3B	Ezra Sutton	110	457	143	78	23	8	4	47	17	.313	.425
SS	Sam Wise	107	424	120	71	20	10	4	46	25	.283	.406
1B	John Morrill	111	394	89	74	20	7	4	44	64	.226	.343
P	Charlie Buffinton	82	338	81	26	12	3	1	33	3	.240	.302
CF	Jim Manning	84	306	63	34	8	9	2	27	19	.206	.310
P	Jim Whitney	72	290	68	35	8	4	0	36	17	.234	.290
RF	Tom Poorman	56	227	54	44	5	3	3	25	7	.238	.326
C	Tom Gunning	48	174	32	17	3	0	0	15	5	.184	.201
2B	Jack Burdock	45	169	24	18	5	0	0	7	8	.142	.172
LF	Tommy McCarthy	40	148	27	16	2	0	0	11	5	.182	.196
Sub	Gurdon Whitely	33	135	25	14	2	2	1	7	1	.185	.252
C	Pat Dealey	35	130	29	18	4	1	1	9	2	.223	.292
Sub	Walter Hackett	35	125	23	8	3	0	0	9	3	.184	.208
C	Mert Hackett	34	115	21	9	7	1	0	4	2	.183	.261
Sub	Dick Johnston	26	111	26	17	6	3	1	23	0	.234	.369
Sub	Joe Hornung	25	109	22	14	4	1	1	7	1	.202	.284
Sub	Billy Nash	26	94	24	9	4	0	0	11	2	.255	.298
Sub	Blondie Purcell	21	87	19	9	1	1	0	3	3	.218	.253
Sub	Mike Hines	14	56	13	11	4	0	0	4	4	.232	.304
P	Daisy Davis	11	37	7	4	2	0	0	3	1	.189	.243
Sub	Pop Tate	4	13	2	1	0	0	0	2	1	.154	.154
P	Bill Stemmeyer	2	7	3	1	1	0	0	2	0	.429	.571
Sub	Bill Collver	1	4	0	0	0	0	0	0	0	.000	.000
		113	3950	915	528	144	53	22	375	190	.232	.312

1B	Morrill 92, Buffinton 15, Whitney 5, Dealey 1, Sutton 1
2B	Burdock 45, Wise 22, W. Hackett 20, Morrill 17, Nash 8, Sutton 2
SS	Wise 79, Sutton 16, W. Hackett 15, Dealey 2, Manning 1
3B	Sutton 91, Nash 19, Dealey 3, Morrill 2
OF	Manning 83, Poorman 56, McCarthy 40, Whitely 32, Johnston 26, Hornung 25, Purcell 21, Buffinton 18, Whitney 17, Hines 14, Wise 6, Dealey 2, Collver 1
C	Gunning 48, M. Hackett 34, Dealey 29, Tate 4, Whitely 1
P	Whitney 51, Buffinton 51, Davis 11, Stemmeyer 2

	G	IP	GS	CG	W	L	K	BB	SH	SV	ERA
Jim Whitney	51	441.1	50	50	18	**32**	200	37	2	0	2.98
Charlie Buffinton	51	434.1	50	49	22	27	242	112	6	0	2.88
Daisy Davis	11	94.1	11	10	5	6	30	28	1	0	4.29
Bill Stemmeyer	2	11	2	2	1	1	8	11	1	0	0.00
		981	113	**111**	46	66	480	**188**	10	0	3.03

DETROIT **Charlie Morton (7–31)** **Bill Watkins (34–36)** **Recreation Park**

		G	AB	H	R	2B	3B	HR	RBI	BB	BA	SA
CF	Ned Hanlon	105	424	128	93	18	8	1	29	47	.302	.389
LF	George Wood	82	362	105	62	19	8	5	28	13	.290	.428
C	Charlie Bennett	91	349	94	49	24	13	5	60	47	.269	.456
1B	Mox McQuery	70	278	76	34	15	4	3	30	8	.273	.388
RF	Sam Thompson	63	254	77	58	11	9	7	44	16	.303	.500
2B	Sam Crane	68	245	47	23	4	6	1	20	13	.192	.269
3B	Jim Donnelly	56	211	49	24	4	3	1	22	10	.232	.294
Sub	Joe Quest	55	200	39	24	8	2	0	21	14	.195	.255
Sub	Jerry Dorgan	39	161	46	23	6	2	0	24	8	.286	.348
P	Stump Weidman	44	153	24	7	2	1	1	14	8	.157	.203

		G	AB	H	R	2B	3B	HR	RBI	BB	BA	SA
Sub	Milt Scott	38	148	39	14	7	0	0	12	4	.264	.311
SS	Marr Phillips	33	139	29	13	5	0	0	17	0	.209	.245
P	Charlie Getzein	40	137	29	9	3	0	0	16	4	.212	.234
P	Lady Baldwin	31	124	30	12	6	3	0	18	6	.242	.339
C	Deacon McGuire	34	121	23	11	4	2	0	9	5	.190	.256
Sub	Charlie Morton	22	79	14	9	1	2	0	3	5	.177	.241
Sub	Jim Manning	20	78	21	15	4	0	1	9	4	.269	.359
Sub	Frank Ringo	17	65	16	12	3	0	0	2	0	.246	.292
Sub	Chub Collins	14	55	10	8	0	2	0	6	0	.182	.255
Sub	Jim Halpin	15	54	7	3	2	0	0	1	1	.130	.167
P	Dan Casey	12	43	5	3	0	1	0	1	1	.116	.163
Sub	Gene Moriarty	11	39	1	1	1	0	0	0	0	.026	.051
Sub	Jerrie Moore	6	23	4	2	1	0	0	0	1	.174	.217
Sub	Nat Kellogg	5	17	2	4	1	0	0	0	1	.118	.176
Sub	Frank Olin	1	4	2	1	0	0	0	0	0	.500	.500
Sub	George Bryant	1	4	0	0	0	0	0	1	0	.000	.000
P	Frank Meinke	1	3	0	0	0	0	0	0	0	.000	.000
Sub	Ed Gastfield	1	3	0	0	0	0	0	0	0	.000	.000
		108	3773	917	514	149	65	26	387	216	.243	.337

1B McQuery 69, Scott 38, Donnelly 1
2B Crane 68, Quest 39, Weidman 1, Bryant 1
SS Phillips 33, Manning 20, Halpin 15, Quest 15, Collins 14, Kellogg 5, Morton 4, Wood 1, Moriarty 1
3B Donnelly 55, Morton 16, Wood 12, Bennett 10, Ringo 8, Moriarty 4, Thompson 1, Olin 1
OF Hanlon 105, Wood 70, Thompson 62, Dorgan 39, Bennett 19, Baldwin 12, Moriarty 6, Weidman 6, McGuire 3, Getzein 2, McQuery 1, Meinke 1, Ringo 1, Quest 1
C Bennett 62, McGuire 31, Ringo 8, Moore 6, Gastfield 1
P Weidman 38, Getzein 37, Baldwin 21, Casey 12, Meinke 1, Wood 1, Moriarty 1

	G	IP	GS	CG	W	L	K	BB	SH	SV	ERA
Stump Weidman	38	330	38	37	14	24	149	63	3	0	3.14
Charlie Getzein	37	330	37	37	12	25	110	92	1	0	3.03
Lady Baldwin	21	179.1	20	19	11	9	135	28	1	0	1.86
Dan Casey	12	104	12	12	4	8	79	35	1	0	3.29
Frank Meinke	1	5	1	0	0	1	0	4	0	0	3.60
George Wood	1	4	0	0	0	0	1	1	0	0	0.00
Gene Moriarty	1	2	0	0	0	0	1	1	0	0	9.00
		954.1	108	105	41	67	475	224	6	0	2.88

BUFFALO   **Pud Galvin (7–17)**   **Jack Chapman (31–57)**   **Olympic Park (I)**

		G	AB	H	R	2B	3B	HR	RBI	BB	BA	SA
RF	Jim Lillie	112	430	107	49	13	3	2	30	6	.249	.307
CF	Hardy Richardson	96	426	136	90	19	11	6	44	20	.319	.458
SS	Jack Rowe	98	421	122	62	28	8	2	51	13	.290	.409
1B	Dan Brouthers	98	407	146	87	32	11	7	59	34	.359	**.543**
3B	Deacon White	98	404	118	54	6	6	0	57	12	.292	.337
LF	Bill Crowley	92	344	83	29	14	1	1	36	21	.241	.297
C	George Myers	89	326	67	40	7	2	0	19	23	.206	.239
2B	Davy Force	71	253	57	20	6	1	0	15	13	.225	.257
P	Pud Galvin	34	122	23	14	4	2	1	10	1	.189	.279
Sub	Dan Stearns	30	105	21	7	6	1	0	9	8	.200	.276
P	Pete Wood	28	104	23	10	3	1	0	5	0	.221	.269
P	Billy Serad	30	104	16	8	3	0	0	3	1	.154	.183
P	Pete Conway	29	90	10	7	5	0	1	7	5	.111	.200
Sub	Jim McCauley	24	84	15	4	2	1	0	7	11	.179	.226

		G	AB	H	R	2B	3B	HR	RBI	BB	BA	SA
Sub	Cannonball Crane	13	51	14	5	0	1	2	9	3	.275	.431
Sub	Scrappy Carroll	13	40	3	1	0	0	0	1	2	.075	.075
Sub	Gil Hatfield	11	30	4	1	0	1	0	0	0	.133	.200
Sub	Moxie Hengle	7	26	4	2	0	0	0	0	1	.154	.154
Sub	Dave Eggler	6	24	2	0	0	0	0	0	2	.083	.083
Sub	Joe Staples	7	22	1	0	0	0	0	0	0	.045	.045
Sub	Buttercup Dickerson	5	21	1	1	1	0	0	0	1	.048	.095
Sub	Denny Driscoll	7	19	3	2	0	0	0	0	2	.158	.158
Sub	Dick Phelan	4	16	2	2	0	0	1	3	0	.125	.313
Sub	Jim McDonald	5	14	0	0	0	0	0	0	0	.000	.000
Sub	Charles Ritter	2	6	1	0	0	0	0	0	0	.167	.167
Sub	Fred Wood	1	4	1	0	0	0	0	0	0	.250	.250
P	? Fisher	1	4	0	0	0	0	0	0	0	.000	.000
P	John Connor	1	3	0	0	0	0	0	0	0	.000	.000
		112	3900	980	495	149	50	23	365	179	.251	.333

1B	Brouthers 98, Stearns 12, P. Wood 2, Lillie 1, Conway 1
2B	Richardson 50, Force 42, Driscoll 7, Hengle 5, Phelan 4, Hatfield 3, Ritter 2, Staples 1
SS	Rowe 65, Force 24, Stearns 19, McDonald 4, Lillie 3, Richardson 1, Conway 1
3B	White 98, Hatfield 8, Force 6
OF	Lillie 112, Crowley 92, Richardson 48, Myers 23, Carroll 13, Crane 13, Rowe 12, Eggler 6, Staples 6, Dickerson 5, McCauley 4, Wood 4, Hengle 3, Conway 2, Galvin 1, McDonald 1
C	Myers 69, Rowe 23, McCauley 21, Stearns 2, F. Wood 1
P	Galvin 33, Serad 30, Conway 27, Wood 24, Richardson 1, Fisher 1, Connor 1

	G	IP	GS	CG	W	L	K	BB	SH	SV	ERA
Pud Galvin	33	284	32	31	13	19	93	37	3	1	4.09
Billy Serad	30	241.1	29	27	7	21	90	80	0	0	4.10
Pete Conway	27	210	27	26	10	17	94	44	0	0	4.67
Pete Wood	24	198.2	22	21	8	15	38	66	0	0	4.44
? Fisher	1	9	1	1	0	1	4	2	0	0	5.00
John Connor	1	9	1	1	0	1	0	2	0	0	4.00
Hardy Richardson	1	4	0	0	0	0	1	3	0	0	2.25
	956		112	107	38	74	320	234	3	1	4.29

ST. LOUIS   **Fred Dunlap (30–40)**   **Alex McKinnon (6–32)**   **Union Park**

		G	AB	H	R	2B	3B	HR	RBI	BB	BA	SA
SS	Jack Glasscock	111	446	125	66	18	3	1	40	29	.280	.341
2B	Fred Dunlap	106	423	114	70	11	5	2	25	41	.270	.333
1B	Alex McKinnon	100	411	121	42	21	6	1	44	8	.294	.382
CF	Joe Quinn	97	343	73	27	8	2	0	15	9	.213	.248
P	Charlie Sweeney	71	267	55	27	7	1	0	24	12	.206	.240
3B	Ed Caskin	71	262	47	31	3	0	0	12	12	.179	.191
P	Henry Boyle	72	258	52	24	9	1	1	21	13	.202	.256
RF	Orator Shaffer	69	257	50	30	11	2	0	18	19	.195	.253
LF	Emmett Seery	59	216	35	20	7	0	1	14	16	.162	.208
C	Fatty Briody	62	215	42	14	9	0	1	17	12	.195	.251
Sub	Fred Lewis	45	181	53	12	9	0	1	27	9	.293	.359
C	George Baker	38	131	16	5	0	0	0	5	9	.122	.122
Sub	Dave Rowe	16	62	10	8	3	0	0	3	5	.161	.210
Sub	Dick Burns	14	54	12	2	2	1	0	4	3	.222	.296
P	John Kirby	14	50	3	2	0	0	0	0	1	.060	.060
Sub	Sy Sutcliffe	16	49	6	2	1	0	0	4	5	.122	.143
P	One Arm Daily	11	35	3	1	0	0	0	1	2	.086	.086

		G	AB	H	R	2B	3B	HR	RBI	BB	BA	SA
P	Egyptian Healy	8	24	1	0	0	0	0	0	0	.042	.042
Sub	Rooney Sweeney	3	11	1	1	0	0	0	0	0	.091	.091
P	? Palmer	4	11	1	1	0	0	0	1	3	.091	.091
Sub	Jim Brennan	3	10	1	0	0	0	0	1	1	.100	.100
Sub	Tom Dolan	3	9	2	1	0	0	0	0	2	.222	.222
Sub	Joe Fogarty	2	8	1	1	0	0	0	0	0	.125	.125
Sub	Jack Gleason	2	7	1	0	0	0	0	0	0	.143	.143
Sub	Trick McSorley	2	6	3	2	1	0	0	1	2	.500	.667
Sub	Billy Alvord	2	5	0	0	0	0	0	0	1	.000	.000
Sub	Dick Phelan	1	4	1	1	1	0	0	1	0	.250	.500
Sub	Charlie Krehmeyer	1	3	0	0	0	0	0	0	0	.000	.000
		111	3758	829	390	121	21	8	278	214	.221	.270

1B McKinnon 100, Quinn 11
2B Dunlap 106, Boyle 2, Glasscock 1, Briody 1, Baker 1
SS Glasscock 110, Caskin 1
3B Caskin 69, Quinn 31, Baker 3, Alvord 2, McSorley 2, Gleason 2, Briody 1, Seery 1, Brennan 1, Phelan 1
OF Shaffer 69, Seery 59, Quinn 57, Lewis 45, C. Sweeney 39, Boyle 31, Rowe 16, Burns 14, Baker 2, Sutcliffe 2, Fogarty 2, R. Sweeney 2, Brennan 2, Briody 1
C   Briody 60, Baker 32, Sutcliffe 15, Dolan 3, Caskin 2, R. Sweeney 1, Krehmeyer 1
P   Boyle 42, C. Sweeney 35, Kirby 14, Daily 11, Healy 8, Palmer 4, Burns 1

	G	IP	GS	CG	W	L	K	BB	SH	SV	ERA
Henry Boyle	42	366.2	39	39	16	24	133	100	1	0	2.75
Charlie Sweeney	35	275	35	32	11	21	84	50	2	0	3.93
John Kirby	14	129.1	14	14	5	8	46	44	0	0	3.55
One Arm Daily	11	91.1	11	10	3	8	31	44	1	0	3.94
Egyptian Healy	8	66	8	8	1	7	32	20	0	0	3.00
? Palmer	4	34	4	4	0	4	9	20	0	0	3.44
Dick Burns	1	3	0	0	0	0	2	0	0	0	9.00
		965.1	111	107	36	72	337	278	4	0	3.37

WORLD'S SERIES

St. Louis (AA) tied Chicago (NL) 3 games to 3 with 1 tie game
Game 1 at West Side Park (Chi), Oct. 14: StL (Caruthers) 5, Chi (Clarkson) 5
Game 2 at Sportsman's Park (StL), Oct. 15: Chi (McCormick) 5, StL (Foutz) 4 (forfeit)
Game 3 at Sportsman's Park (StL), Oct. 16: StL (Caruthers) 7, Chi (Clarkson) 4
Game 4 at Sportsman's Park (StL), Oct. 17: StL (Foutz) 3, Chi (McCormick) 2
Game 5 at Recreation Park (Pit), Oct. 22: Chi (Clarkson) 9, StL (Foutz) 2
Game 6 at American Park (Cin), Oct. 23: Chi (McCormick) 9, StL (Caruthers) 2
Game 7 at American Park (Cin), Oct. 24: StL (Foutz) 13, Chi (McCormick) 4

ST. LOUIS

		G	AB	H	R	2B	3B	HR	RBI	BB	BA	SA
CF	Curt Welch	7	27	4	5	1	1	0	—	1	.146	.259
SS	Bill Gleason	7	26	6	5	2	0	0	—	1	.231	.308
1B	Charlie Comiskey	7	24	7	6	0	0	0	—	0	.292	.292
LF	Tip O'Neill	7	24	5	4	0	0	0	—	0	.208	.208
RF/C	Yank Robinson	7	23	4	5	0	1	0	—	0	.174	.304
2B	Sam Barkley	7	23	2	3	0	0	0	—	2	.087	.087
3B	Arlie Latham	7	22	7	5	3	0	0	—	2	.318	.455
P/RF	Bob Caruthers	5	15	3	1	0	1	0	—	1	.200	.333
C	Doc Bushong	4	13	2	1	0	0	0	—	0	.154	.154
P	Dave Foutz	4	12	2	1	0	0	0	—	0	.167	.167
RF	Hugh Nicol	1	2	0	0	0	0	0	—	0	.000	.000
		7	211	42	36	6	3	0	—	7	.199	.256

	G	IP	GS	CG	W	L	K	BB	SH	SV	ERA
Dave Foutz	4	29.1	4	4	2	2	14	9	0	0	0.61
Bob Caruthers	3	26	3	3	1	1	16	4	0	0	2.42
		55.1	7	7	3	3	30	13	0	0	1.46

CHICAGO

		G	AB	H	R	2B	3B	HR	RBI	BB	BA	SA
2B	Fred Pfeffer	7	27	11	5	2	0	1	—	0	.407	**.593**
1B	Cap Anson	7	26	11	8	1	1	0	—	2	**.423**	.538
LF	Abner Dalrymple	7	26	7	4	2	0	1	—	2	.269	.462
RF/C	King Kelly	7	26	9	9	3	1	0	—	2	.346	.538
SS/3B	Tom Burns	7	25	2	3	0	1	0	—	0	.080	.120
3B/SS	Ned Williamson	7	23	2	1	0	0	0	—	4	.087	.087
CF	Billy Sunday	6	22	6	5	2	0	0	—	2	.273	.364
P	Jim McCormick	5	17	3	1	0	0	0	—	0	.176	.176
C	Silver Flint	4	14	2	0	0	0	0	—	0	.143	.143
P/RF	John Clarkson	4	13	2	1	1	0	0	—	0	.154	.231
RF	Bug Holliday	1	4	0	0	0	0	0	—	0	.000	.000
CF	George Gore	1	3	0	1	0	0	0	—	1	.000	.000
		7	226	55	38	11	3	2	—	13	.243	.345

	G	IP	GS	CG	W	L	K	BB	SH	SV	ERA
Jim McCormick	5	36	5	5	3	2	19	6	0	0	2.00
John Clarkson	2	16	2	2	0	1	15	1	0	0	1.13
		52	7	7	3	3	34	7	0	0	1.73

AMERICAN ASSOCIATION

	W	L	PCT	HOME	ROAD	GB
1. St. Louis Browns	79	33	.705	44–11	35–22	—
2. Cincinnati Reds	63	49	.563	36–21	27–28	16
3. Pittsburgh Alleghenys	56	55	.505	37–20	19–35	22.5
4. Philadelphia Athletics	55	57	.491	33–22	22–33	24
5. Brooklyn Grays	53	59	.473	36–22	17–37	26
5. Louisville Colonels	53	59	.473	37–19	16–40	26
7. New York Metropolitans	44	64	.407	28–24	16–40	33
8. Baltimore Orioles	41	68	.376	29–26	12–42	36

	StL	Cin	Pit	Phi	Bro	Lou	NY	Bal	
St. Louis	—	10	10	12	12	9	12	14	79
Cincinnati	6	—	9	9	11	8	10	10	63
Pittsburgh	6	7	—	6	10	10	7	10	56
Philadelphia	4	7	10	—	5	8	11	10	55
Brooklyn	4	5	6	11	—	10	8	9	53
Louisville	7	8	6	8	6	—	9	9	53
New York	4	6	8	5	8	7	—	6	44
Baltimore	2	6	6	6	7	7	7	—	41
	33	49	55	57	59	59	64	68	444

SEASON LEADERS

Batting Average

1.	Browning, Louisville	.362
2.	Orr, New York	.342
3.	Larkin, Philadelphia	.329
4.	C. Jones, Cincinnati	.322
5.	Stovey, Philadelphia	.315

On–Base Percentage

1.	Browning, Louisville	.393
2.	Larkin, Philadelphia	.372
3.	Stovey, Philadelphia	.371
4.	T. Brown, Pittsburgh	.366
5.	Phillips, Brooklyn	.364

Home Runs

1.	Stovey, Philadelphia	13
2.	Fennelly, Cincinnati	10
3.	Browning, Louisville	9
4.	Larkin, Philadelphia	8
5.	Orr, New York	6

Hits

1.	Browning, Louisville	174
2.	C. Jones, Cincinnati	157
3.	Stovey, Philadelphia	153
4.	Orr, New York	152
5.	Larkin, Philadelphia	149

Slugging Average

1.	Orr, New York	.543
2.	Browning, Louisville	.530
3.	Larkin, Philadelphia	.525
4.	Stovey, Philadelphia	.488
5.	C. Jones, Cincinnati	.462

Total Bases

1.	Browning, Louisville	255
2.	Orr, New York	241
3.	Larkin, Philadelphia	238
4.	Stovey, Philadelphia	237
5.	C. Jones, Cincinnati	225

Bases on Balls

1.	Nelson, New York	61
2.	Macullar, Baltimore	49
	Hotaling, Brooklyn	49
4.	Stovey, Philadelphia	39
5.	Fennelly, Cincinnati	38
	Stearns, Baltimore	38

Runs

1.	Stovey, Philadelphia	130
2.	Larkin, Philadelphia	114
3.	C. Jones, Cincinnati	108
4.	Nelson, New York	98
	Browning, Louisville	98

RBI

1.	Fennelly, Cincinatti	89
2.	Larkin, Philadelphia	88
3.	Orr, New York	77
4.	Stovey, Philadelphia	75
5.	Browning, Louisville	73

PITCHING

Wins

1.	Caruthers, St. Louis	40
2.	Morris, Pittsburgh	39
3.	Foutz, St. Louis	33
4.	Porter, Brooklyn	33
5.	Mathews, Philadelphia	30
	Hecker, Louisville	30

Innings

1.	Morris, Pittsburgh	581
2.	Henderson, Baltimore	539.1
3.	Caruthers, St. Louis	482.1
4.	Porter, Brooklyn	481.2
5.	Hecker, Louisville	480

Strikeouts

1.	Morris, Pittsburgh	298
2.	Mathews, Philadelphia	286
3.	Henderson, Baltimore	263
4.	Hecker, Louisville	209
5.	Porter, Brooklyn	197

ERA (112 Innings)

1.	Caruthers, St. Louis	2.07
2.	Hecker, Louisville	2.18
3.	Morris, Pittsburgh	2.35
4.	Mathews, Philadelphia	2.43
5.	Foutz, St. Louis	2.63

Losses

1.	Henderson, Baltimore	35
2.	Morris, Pittsburgh	24
3.	Hecker, Louisville	23
4.	Porter, Brooklyn	21
	Lynch, New York	21
	Cushman, Phila–NY	21

Complete games

1.	Morris, Pittsburgh	63
2.	Henderson, Baltimore	59
3.	Porter, Brooklyn	53
	Caruthers, St. Louis	53
5.	Hecker, Louisville	51

Winning Percentage (25 decisions)

1.	Caruthers, St. Louis	.755
2.	Foutz, St. Louis	.702
3.	Mathews, Philadelphia	.638
4.	Morris, Pittsburgh	.619
5.	Porter, Brooklyn	.611

Lowest On–Base Percentage

1.	Morris, Pittsburgh	.247
2.	Caruthers, St. Louis	.260
3.	Hecker, Louisville	.265
4.	Cushman, Phil-NY	.266
5.	Mathews, Philadelphia	.267

FIELDING

Total Chances

1B	Phillips, Brooklyn	1165
2B	P. Smith, Pittsburgh	820
3B	Carpenter, Cincinnati	300
SS	G. Smith, Brooklyn	697
OF	Welch, St. Louis	276
C	Bushong, St. Louis	591
P	Hecker, Louisville	145

Fielding Average

Phillips, Brooklyn	.973
McPhee, Cincinnati	.936
Hankinson, New York	.906
Whitney, Pittsburgh	.918
Welch, St. Louis	.946
Traffley, Baltimore	.943
McKeon, Cincinnati	.983

ST. LOUIS   Charlie Comiskey   Sportsman's Park (I)

		G	AB	H	R	2B	3B	HR	RBI	BB	BA	SA
3B	Arlie Latham	110	485	100	84	15	3	1	34	18	.206	.256
SS	Bill Gleason	112	472	119	79	9	5	3	53	29	.252	.311
CF	Curt Welch	112	432	117	84	18	8	3	69	23	.271	.370
RF	Hugh Nicol	112	425	88	59	11	1	0	45	34	.207	.238
2B	Sam Barkley	106	418	112	67	18	10	3	53	25	.268	.380
1B	Charlie Comiskey	83	340	87	68	15	7	2	44	14	.256	.359
C	Doc Bushong	85	300	80	42	13	5	0	21	11	.267	.343
UT	Yank Robinson	78	287	75	63	8	8	0	35	29	.261	.345
P	Dave Foutz	65	238	59	42	6	4	0	34	11	.248	.307
P	Bob Caruthers	60	222	50	37	10	2	1	12	20	.225	.302
LF	Tip O'Neill	52	206	72	44	7	4	3	38	13	.350	.466
Sub	Dan Sullivan	17	60	7	4	2	0	0	3	6	.117	.150
P	Jumbo McGinnis	13	50	11	3	0	0	1	7	1	.220	.220
Sub	Mike Drissel	6	20	1	0	0	0	0	0	0	.050	.050
Sub	Cal Broughton	4	17	1	1	0	0	0	1	0	.059	.059
		112	3972	979	677	132	57	17	449	234	.246	.321

1B	Comiskey 83, Foutz 15, Barkley 11, Sullivan 4, Robinson 1
2B	Barkley 96, Robinson 19
SS	Gleason 112
3B	Latham 109, Robinson 2, Nicol 1, Bushong 1
OF	Welch 112, Nicol 111, O'Neill 52, Robinson 52, Caruthers 7, Foutz 4, McGinnis 1
C	Bushong 85, Sullivan 13, Drissel 6, Robinson 5, Broughton 4, Latham 2
P	Caruthers 53, Foutz 47, McGinnis 13

	G	IP	GS	CG	W	L	K	BB	SH	SV	ERA
Bob Caruthers	53	482.1	53	53	**40**	13	190	57	6	0	**2.07**
Dave Foutz	47	407.2	46	46	33	14	147	92	2	0	2.63
Jumbo McGinnis	13	112	13	12	6	6	41	19	3	0	3.38
		1002	112	**111**	79	33	378	**168**	**11**	0	**2.44**

CINCINNATI   Opie Caylor   American Park

		G	AB	H	R	2B	3B	HR	RBI	BB	BA	SA
LF	Charley Jones	112	**487**	157	108	19	17	5	35	21	.322	.462
1B	Long John Reilly	111	482	143	92	18	11	5	60	11	.297	.411
3B	Hick Carpenter	112	473	131	89	12	8	2	61	9	.277	.349
SS	Frank Fennelly	112	454	124	82	14	17	10	**89**	38	.273	.445
RF	Pop Corkhill	112	440	111	64	10	8	1	53	7	.252	.318
2B	Bid McPhee	110	431	114	78	12	4	0	46	19	.265	.311
CF	Jim Clinton	105	408	97	48	5	5	0	34	15	.238	.275
C	Pop Snyder	39	152	36	13	4	3	1	19	6	.237	.322
C	Jim Keenan	36	132	35	16	2	2	1	15	8	.265	.333
C	Kid Baldwin	34	126	17	9	1	0	1	8	3	.135	.167
P	Larry McKeon	33	121	20	14	3	1	0	8	0	.165	.207
P	Will White	34	118	20	9	5	0	0	10	4	.169	.212
Sub	Phil Powers	15	60	16	6	2	0	0	7	0	.267	.300
P	Billy Mountjoy	17	60	10	7	0	0	0	2	8	.167	.167
P	George Pechiney	11	40	6	3	1	1	0	1	0	.150	.225
P	Gus Shallix	13	39	5	3	0	0	0	2	3	.128	.128
Sub	Jimmy Peoples	7	22	4	1	0	0	0	1	1	.182	.182
P	Harry McCaffrey	1	5	0	0	0	0	0	0	0	.000	.000
		112	4050	1046	642	108	77	26	451	153	.258	.342

1B   Reilly 107, Keenan 4, Corkhill 3, Snyder 1
2B   McPhee 110, Baldwin 2
SS   Fennelly 112
3B   Carpenter 112, Baldwin 1
OF   Jones 112, Corkhill 110, Clinton 105, Reilly 7, Baldwin 6, Shallix 3, McKeon 1, Peoples 1
C   Snyder 38, Keenan 33, Baldwin 25, Powers 15, Peoples 5
P   White 34, McKeon 33, Mountjoy 17, Shallix 13, Pechiney 11, Corkhill 8, Peoples 2, Baldwin 2, McCaffrey 1, Keenan 1

	G	IP	GS	CG	W	L	K	BB	SH	SV	ERA
Will White	34	293.1	34	33	18	15	80	64	2	0	3.53
Larry McKeon	33	290	33	32	20	13	117	50	2	0	2.86
Billy Mountjoy	17	153.2	17	17	10	7	50	52	1	0	3.16
George Pechiney	11	98	11	11	7	4	49	30	1	0	2.02
Gus Shallix	13	91.1	12	7	6	4	15	33	0	0	3.25
Pop Corkhill	8	37	1	0	1	4	12	10	0	1	3.65
Jimmy Peoples	2	15	2	1	0	2	4	2	0	0	12.00
Harry McCaffrey	1	9	1	1	1	0	2	2	0	0	6.00
Jim Keenan	1	8	0	0	0	0	0	1	0	0	1.13
Kid Baldwin	2	4	1	0	0	0	1	6	0	0	9.00
*One combined shutout on May 9: White 3 innings, Shallix 6 innings											
	999.2	112	102	63	49	330	250	6	1	3.26

PITTSBURGH   **Horace Phillips**   **Recreation Park**

		G	AB	H	R	2B	3B	HR	RBI	BB	BA	SA
2B	Pop Smith	106	453	113	85	11	13	0	35	25	.249	.331
RF	Tom Brown	108	437	134	81	16	12	4	68	34	.307	.426
3B	Willie Kuehne	104	411	93	54	9	19	0	43	15	.226	.341
LF	Charlie Eden	98	405	103	57	18	6	0	38	17	.254	.328
CF	Fred Mann	99	391	99	60	17	6	0	41	31	.253	.327
SS	Art Whitney	90	373	87	53	10	4	0	28	16	.233	.282
C	Fred Carroll	71	280	75	45	13	8	0	30	7	.268	.371
P	Ed Morris	64	237	44	19	3	3	0	14	5	.186	.224
1B	Milt Scott	55	210	52	15	7	1	0	18	5	.248	.290
1B	Jim Field	56	209	50	28	9	1	1	15	13	.239	.306
Sub	Doggie Miller	42	166	27	19	3	1	0	13	4	.163	.193
Sub	John Richmond	34	131	27	14	2	2	0	12	8	.206	.252
P	Pete Meegan	19	67	13	3	1	0	0	3	3	.194	.209
Sub	Rudy Kemmler	18	64	13	2	2	1	0	5	2	.203	.266
P	Hank O'Day	13	49	12	7	2	1	0	3	1	.245	.327
P	Pud Galvin	11	38	4	2	0	0	0	2	0	.105	.105
P	Frank Mountain	5	20	2	1	0	1	0	1	1	.100	.200
Sub	Marr Phillips	4	15	4	1	0	0	0	2	2	.267	.267
Sub	Frank Ringo	3	11	2	0	0	0	0	0	0	.182	.182
P	John Hofford	3	8	1	1	0	0	0	0	0	.125	.125
		111	3975	955	547	123	79	5	371	189	.240	.315

1B   Field 56, Scott 55
2B   Smith 106, Whitney 4, Meegan 1
SS   Whitney 75, Richmond 23, Kuehne 7, Phillips 4, Miller 2
3B   Kuehne 97, Whitney 8, Mann 3, Eden 2, Miller 2
OF   Brown 108, Mann 97, Eden 96, Carroll 12, Richmond 11, Miller 6, O'Day 3, Meegan 3, Whitney 3, Morris 1, Galvin 1
C   Carroll 60, Miller 33, Kemmler 18, Ringo 3
P   Morris 63, Meegan 18, O'Day 12, Galvin 11, Mountain 5, Eden 4, Hofford 3, Brown 2

	G	IP	GS	CG	W	L	K	BB	SH	SV	ERA
Ed Morris	**63**	**581**	**63**	**63**	39	24	**298**	101	**7**	0	2.35
Pete Meegan	18	146	16	14	7	8	58	38	1	0	3.39
Hank O'Day	12	103	12	10	5	7	36	16	0	0	3.67
Pud Galvin	11	88.1	11	9	3	7	27	7	0	0	3.67
Frank Mountain	5	46	5	5	1	4	7	24	0	0	4.30
John Hofford	3	25	3	3	0	3	21	9	0	0	3.60
Charlie Eden	4	15.2	1	0	1	2	5	3	0	0	5.17
Tom Brown	2	6	0	0	0	0	2	3	0	0	3.00
		1011	111	104	56	55	454	201	8	0	2.92

PHILADELPHIA   Harry Stovey   Jefferson Street Grounds

		G	AB	H	R	2B	3B	HR	RBI	BB	BA	SA
1B	Harry Stovey	112	486	**153**	**130**	27	9	**13**	75	39	.315	.488
CF	Henry Larkin	108	453	149	114	**37**	14	8	88	26	.329	.525
RF	John Coleman	96	398	119	71	15	11	3	70	25	.299	.412
2B	Cub Stricker	106	398	93	71	9	3	1	41	21	.234	.279
SS	Sadie Houck	93	388	99	74	10	9	0	54	10	.255	.327
3B	Fred Corey	94	384	94	61	14	8	1	38	17	.245	.331
LF	Blondie Purcell	66	304	90	71	15	5	0	22	16	.296	.378
C	Jocko Milligan	67	265	71	35	15	4	2	39	7	.268	.377
C	Jack O'Brien	62	225	60	35	9	1	2	30	20	.267	.342
P	Bobby Mathews	48	179	30	22	3	0	0	12	10	.168	.184
Sub	George Strief	44	175	48	19	8	5	0	27	9	.274	.377
Sub	Lon Knight	29	119	25	17	1	1	0	14	9	.210	.235
Sub	Martin Powell	19	75	12	5	0	3	0	5	1	.160	.240
P	Tom Lovett	16	58	13	9	0	1	0	3	3	.224	.259
P	Ed Knouff	14	48	9	5	0	0	0	2	2	.188	.188
P	Ed Cushman	10	37	7	5	1	0	0	2	1	.189	.216
Sub	Marshall Quinton	7	29	6	6	1	0	0	4	1	.207	.241
P	Bill Vinton	7	26	4	5	2	0	0	4	3	.154	.231
P	Billy Taylor	6	21	4	0	0	0	0	2	0	.190	.190
Sub	Ed Fusselbach	5	19	6	2	1	0	0	2	0	.316	.368
P	Bill Hughes	4	16	3	3	1	1	0	1	1	.188	.375
P	Bob Emslie	4	12	1	1	0	0	0	0	0	.083	.083
Sub	Frank Siffel	2	10	1	0	0	0	0	0	0	.100	.100
Sub	Orator Shaffer	2	9	2	1	0	1	0	1	1	.222	.444
P	Jim Conway	2	6	0	2	0	0	0	0	1	.000	.000
P	Phenomenal Smith	1	2	0	0	0	0	0	0	0	.000	.000
		113	4142	**1099**	**764**	**169**	76	**30**	536	223	**.265**	**.365**

1B   Stovey 82, Powell 19, O'Brien 7, Milligan 6
2B   Stricker 106, Strief 7
SS   Houck 93, Strief 10, O'Brien 9, Corey 1
3B   Corey 92, Strief 19, O'Brien 2
OF   Larkin 108, Coleman 93, Purcell 66, Stovey 30, Knight 29, Strief 8, O'Brien 3, Shaffer 2, Milligan 2, Hughes 2, Mathews 1, Lovett 1, Knouff 1, Emslie 1, Vinton 1, Conway 1, Siffel 1
C   Milligan 61, O'Brien 43, Quinton 7, Fusselbach 5, Siffel 2
P   Mathews 48, Lovett 16, Knouff 14, Cushman 10, Coleman 8, Vinton 7, Taylor 6, Emslie 4, Conway 2, Hughes 2, Corey 1, Knight 1, Purcell 1, Smith 1

	G	IP	GS	CG	W	L	K	BB	SH	SV	ERA
Bobby Mathews	48	422.1	48	46	30	17	286	57	2	0	2.43
Tom Lovett	16	138.2	16	15	7	8	56	38	1	0	3.70
Ed Knouff	14	106	13	12	7	6	43	44	0	0	3.65
Ed Cushman	10	87	10	10	3	7	37	17	0	0	3.52
John Coleman	8	60.1	3	3	2	2	12	5	0	0	3.43
Bill Vinton	7	55	7	6	4	3	34	15	2	0	2.45
Billy Taylor	6	52.1	6	6	1	5	11	9	0	0	3.27
Bob Emslie	4	28.2	4	3	0	4	9	6	0	0	6.28
Bill Hughes	2	16.2	2	2	0	2	4	10	0	0	4.86
Jim Conway	2	12.1	2	1	0	1	0	2	0	0	7.30
Fred Corey	1	9	1	1	1	0	3	1	0	0	7.00
Blondie Purcell	1	6	0	0	0	1	3	2	0	0	6.00
Lon Knight	1	5	0	0	0	0	1	2	0	0	1.80
Phenomenal Smith	1	4	1	0	0	1	7	4	0	0	9.00
		1003.1	113	105	55	57	**506**	212	5	0	3.23

BROOKLYN Charlie Hackett (15–22) Charlie Byrne (38–37) **Washington Park (I)**

		G	AB	H	R	2B	3B	HR	RBI	BB	BA	SA
3B	Bill McClellan	112	464	124	85	22	7	0	49	28	.267	.345
2B	George Pinkney	110	447	124	77	16	5	0	42	27	.277	.336
SS	Germany Smith	108	419	108	63	17	11	4	62	10	.258	.379
LF	Ed Swartwood	99	399	106	80	8	9	0	49	36	.266	.331
1B	Bill Phillips	99	391	118	65	16	11	3	63	27	.302	.422
CF	Pete Hotaling	94	370	95	73	9	5	1	34	49	.257	.316
P	Adonis Terry	71	264	45	23	1	3	1	20	10	.170	.208
RF	John Cassidy	54	221	47	36	6	2	1	28	8	.213	.271
P	Henry Porter	54	195	40	28	1	4	0	16	5	.205	.251
P	John Harkins	43	159	42	20	4	2	1	15	9	.264	.333
C	Jimmy Peoples	41	151	30	21	4	1	1	15	5	.199	.258
C	Jackie Hayes	42	137	18	10	3	0	0	10	5	.131	.153
OF	Jim McTamany	35	131	36	21	7	2	1	13	9	.275	.382
Sub	Bill Krieg	17	60	9	7	4	0	1	5	2	.150	.267
Sub	Charlie Robinson	11	40	6	5	2	1	0	4	3	.150	.250
Sub	Frank Bell	10	29	5	5	0	1	0	2	0	.172	.241
Sub	Dave Oldfield	10	25	8	2	1	0	0	2	3	.320	.360
Sub	George McVey	6	21	3	2	0	0	0	1	2	.143	.143
Sub	Mike Hines	3	13	1	1	0	1	0	1	0	.077	.231
Sub	Bill Schenck	1	4	0	0	0	0	0	0	0	.000	.000
P	Phenomenal Smith	1	3	1	0	0	0	0	0	0	.333	.333
		112	3943	966	624	121	65	14	431	238	.245	.319

1B   Phillips 99, Krieg 5, Swartwood 4, McVey 3, Peoples 1
2B   Pinkney 57, McClellan 55
SS   Smith 108, Pinkney 3, Peoples 2, Swartwood 1
3B   McClellan 57, Pinkney 51, Bell 2, Schenck 1, Harkins 1, Terry 1, Peoples 1
OF   Swartwood 95, Hotaling 94, Cassidy 54, Terry 47, McTamany 35, Harkins 9, Bell 4, Oldfield 2, Peoples 1
C   Hayes 42, Peoples 37, Krieg 12, Robinson 11, Oldfield 9, Bell 7, Hines 3, McVey 3, Swartwood 1
P   Porter 54, Harkins 34, Terry 25, Smith 1

	G	IP	GS	CG	W	L	K	BB	SH	SV	ERA
Henry Porter	54	481.2	54	53	33	21	197	107	2	0	2.78
John Harkins	34	293	34	33	14	20	141	56	1	0	3.75
Adonis Terry	25	209	23	23	6	17	96	42	0	1	4.26
Phenomenal Smith	1	8	1	1	0	1	2	6	0	0	12.38
		991.2	112	110	53	59	436	211	3	1	3.46

LOUISVILLE   **Jim Hart**   **Eclipse Park (I)**

		G	AB	H	R	2B	3B	HR	RBI	BB	BA	SA
RF	Chicken Wolf	112	483	141	79	23	17	1	52	11	.292	.416
CF	Pete Browning	112	481	**174**	98	34	10	9	73	25	**.362**	.530
1B	John Kerins	112	456	111	65	9	16	3	51	20	.243	.353
LF	Leech Maskrey	109	423	97	54	8	11	1	46	19	.229	.307
2B	Tom McLaughlin	112	411	87	49	13	9	2	41	15	.212	.302
3B	Phil Reccius	102	402	97	57	8	10	1	38	13	.241	.318
SS	Joe Miller	98	339	62	44	9	5	0	24	28	.183	.239
P	Guy Hecker	72	297	81	48	9	2	2	35	5	.273	.337
C	Amos Cross	35	130	37	11	2	1	0	14	0	.285	.315
C	Joe Crotty	39	129	20	14	2	0	0	7	3	.155	.171
P	Norman Baker	25	87	18	15	2	0	0	5	2	.207	.230
P	Al Mays	17	61	13	8	1	1	0	4	2	.213	.262
Sub	Billy Geer	14	51	6	2	2	0	0	3	2	.118	.157
Sub	Dan Sullivan	13	44	8	3	1	0	0	4	2	.182	.205
Sub	Miah Murray	12	43	8	4	0	0	0	3	2	.186	.186
Sub	Reddy Mack	11	41	10	7	1	0	0	5	2	.244	.268
Sub	Charlie Krehmeyer	7	31	7	4	1	1	0	5	1	.226	.323
P	Toad Ramsey	9	31	4	2	0	0	0	3	0	.129	.129
P	John Connor	4	14	2	0	0	0	0	1	0	.143	.143
Sub	Monk Cline	2	9	2	0	1	0	0	2	0	.222	.333
Sub	Joe Strauss	2	6	1	0	0	0	0	0	0	.167	.167
		112	3969	986	564	126	**83**	19	416	152	.248	.336

1B   Kerins 96, Hecker 17, Murray 2, Krehmeyer 1, Crotty 1
2B   McLaughlin 93, Mack 11, Miller 8
SS   Miller 79, McLaughlin 19, Geer 14
3B   Reccius 97, Miller 11, Maskrey 3, Cline 1, Kerins 1
OF   Browning 112, Wolf 111, Maskrey 108, Kerins 3, Hecker 3, Kremeyer 2, Strauss 1, Cline 1
C   Crotty 38, Cross 35, Kerins 19, Sullivan 13, Murray 12, Krehmeyer 4, Strauss 1
P   Hecker 54, Baker 25, Mays 17, Ramsey 9, Reccius 7, Connor 4, Wolf 1

	G	IP	GS	CG	W	L	K	BB	SH	SV	ERA
Guy Hecker	54	480	53	51	30	23	209	54	2	0	2.18
Norman Baker	25	217	24	24	13	12	79	69	1	0	3.40
Al Mays	17	150	17	17	6	11	61	43	0	0	2.76
Toad Ramsey	9	79	9	9	3	6	83	28	0	0	1.94
Phil Reccius	7	40	5	4	0	4	10	11	0	1	3.83
John Connor	4	35	4	4	1	3	19	12	0	0	4.89
Chicken Wolf	1	1	0	0	0	0	1	0	0	0	9.00
		1002	112	109	53	59	462	217	3	1	2.67

NEW YORK   Jim Gifford   Polo Grounds (I)

		G	AB	H	R	2B	3B	HR	RBI	BB	BA	SA
1B	Dave Orr	107	444	152	76	29	**21**	6	77	8	.342	**.543**
RF	Steve Brady	108	434	128	60	14	5	3	58	25	.295	.371
SS	Candy Nelson	107	420	107	98	12	4	1	30	**61**	.255	.310
CF	Chief Roseman	101	410	114	72	13	14	4	47	25	.278	.407
3B	Frank Hankinson	94	362	81	43	12	2	2	44	12	.224	.285
LF	Eddie Kennedy	96	349	71	35	8	4	2	21	12	.203	.266
C	Charlie Reipschlager	72	268	65	29	11	1	0	21	9	.243	.291
2B	Tom Forster	57	213	47	28	7	2	0	18	17	.221	.272
C	Bill Holbert	56	202	35	13	3	0	0	13	8	.173	.188
2B	Dasher Troy	45	177	39	24	3	3	2	12	5	.220	.305
P	Jack Lynch	44	153	30	16	5	1	0	10	11	.196	.242
P	Ed Cushman	22	69	10	5	1	0	0	3	9	.145	.159
P	Ed Begley	15	52	9	5	1	0	1	3	1	.173	.250
P	Doug Crothers	18	51	8	11	0	0	0	0	8	.157	.157
Sub	Cal Broughton	11	41	6	1	1	0	0	1	1	.146	.171
Sub	Joe Reilly	10	40	7	6	3	0	0	3	2	.175	.250
P	Buck Becannon	10	33	10	3	0	0	0	2	1	.303	.303
Sub	Dick Pierson	3	9	1	1	0	0	0	0	2	.111	.111
Sub	? Jones	1	4	1	0	0	0	0	0	0	.250	.250
		108	3731	921	526	123	57	21	363	217	.247	.327

1B   Orr 107, Brady 4
2B   Forster 52, Troy 42, Reilly 8, Pierson 3, Brady 2, Reipschlager 1
SS   Nelson 107, Troy 1, Reipschlager 1
3B   Hankinson 94, Reipschlager 6, Holbert 5, Reilly 2, Jones 1, Nelson 1, Brady 1
OF   Brady 105, Roseman 101, Kennedy 96, Holbert 13, Reipschlager 6, Forster 5, Begley 4, Troy 2
C   Reipschlager 59, Holbert 39, Broughton 11
P   Lynch 44, Cushman 22, Crothers 18, Begley 15, Becannon 10, Orr 3, Roseman 1, Hankinson 1

	G	IP	GS	CG	W	L	K	BB	SH	SV	ERA
Jack Lynch	44	379	43	43	23	21	177	42	1	0	3.61
Ed Cushman	22	191	22	22	8	14	133	33	0	0	2.78
Doug Crothers	18	154	18	18	7	11	40	49	1	0	5.08
Ed Begley	15	115	14	10	4	9	44	48	0	0	4.93
Buck Becannon	10	85	10	10	2	8	13	24	0	0	6.25
Dave Orr	3	10	0	0	0	0	1	5	0	0	7.20
Frank Hankinson	1	2	0	0	0	0	0	1	0	0	4.50
Chief Roseman	1	1	1	0	0	1	0	2	0	0	27.00
	937	108	103	44	64	408	204	2	0	4.15

BALTIMORE   Billy Barnie   Oriole Park (I)

		G	AB	H	R	2B	3B	HR	RBI	BB	BA	SA
LF	Joe Sommer	110	471	118	84	23	6	1	44	24	.251	.331
3B	Mike Muldoon	102	410	103	47	20	6	2	52	20	.251	.344
UT	Oyster Burns	78	321	74	47	11	6	5	37	16	.231	.349
SS	Jimmy Macullar	100	320	61	52	7	6	3	26	49	.191	.278
CF	Dennis Casey	63	264	76	50	10	5	3	29	21	.288	.398
C	Bill Traffley	69	254	39	27	4	5	1	20	17	.154	.220
1B	Dan Stearns	67	253	47	40	3	8	1	29	38	.186	.273
P	Hardie Henderson	61	229	51	23	5	2	1	21	12	.223	.275
RF	Ed Greer	56	211	42	32	7	0	0	21	8	.199	.232
2B	Gid Gardner	44	170	37	22	5	4	0	17	12	.218	.294
2B	Tim Manning	43	157	32	17	8	1	0	16	10	.204	.268
Sub	Jim Field	38	144	30	16	3	2	0	10	13	.208	.257

		G	AB	H	R	2B	3B	HR	RBI	BB	BA	SA
Sub	Sam Trott	21	88	24	12	2	2	0	12	5	.273	.341
Sub	Tom York	22	87	23	6	4	2	0	12	8	.264	.356
Sub	Jake Evans	20	77	17	18	1	1	0	7	7	.221	.260
P	Bob Emslie	13	51	12	6	1	1	0	4	0	.235	.294
Sub	Harry Jacoby	11	43	6	4	2	0	0	1	2	.140	.186
P	John Henry	10	34	9	4	3	0	0	3	1	.265	.353
Sub	Phil Powers	9	34	4	6	1	0	0	2	1	.118	.147
Sub	Tom O'Brien	8	33	7	4	3	0	0	5	2	.212	.303
Sub	Gene Derby	10	31	4	4	0	0	0	2	1	.129	.129
Sub	Sandy Nava	8	27	5	2	1	0	0	4	1	.185	.222
Sub	George Mappes	6	19	4	2	0	1	0	0	1	.211	.316
P	Joe Brown	5	19	3	2	0	0	0	0	0	.158	.158
P	Billy Mountjoy	7	18	1	5	0	0	0	0	7	.056	.056
P	Frank Foreman	3	14	4	4	0	1	0	2	0	.286	.429
Sub	Joe Visner	4	13	3	2	0	0	0	2	2	.231	.231
Sub	Oscar Walker	4	13	0	1	0	0	0	1	0	.000	.000
P	Shorty Wetzel	2	7	0	0	0	0	0	1	1	.000	.000
Sub	Charlie Levis	1	4	1	2	0	0	0	0	0	.250	.250
Sub	John Tener	1	4	0	0	0	0	0	0	0	.000	.000
Sub	Tom McDermott	1	0	0	0	0	0	0	0	0	—	—
		110	3820	837	541	124	59	17	380	**279**	.219	.296

1B Stearns 63, Field 38, O'Brien 6, Burns 1, Levis 1, Gardner 1, Sommer 1
2B Manning 41, Gardner 39, Jacoby 11, Mappes 6, Burns 6, Traffley 3, Trott 2, O'Brien 2, McDermott 1, Brown 1, Henderson 1, Muldoon 1
SS Macullar 98, Burns 10, Sommer 2, Trott 1
3B Muldoon 101, Burns 6, Manning 3, Sommer 2
OF Sommer 107, Casey 63, Greer 47, Burns 45, York 22, Evans 20, Traffley 10, Gardner 5, Visner 4, Walker 4, Trott 4, Stearns 3, Emslie 2, Macullar 2, Powers 1, Derby 1, Foreman 1, Mountjoy 1, Henderson 1, Tener 1, Henry 1
C   Traffley 61, Trott 17, Greer 12, Derby 9, Nava 8, Powers 8, Stearns 2
P   Henderson 61, Burns 15, Emslie 13, Henry 9, Mountjoy 6, Brown 4, Foreman 3, Wetzel 2, Sommer 2, Gardner 1

	G	IP	GS	CG	W	L	K	BB	SH	SV	ERA
Hardie Henderson	61	539.1	61	59	25	**35**	263	**117**	0	0	3.19
Bob Emslie	13	107	13	11	3	10	27	30	0	0	4.29
Oyster Burns	15	105.2	11	10	7	4	30	21	1	**3**	3.58
John Henry	9	71	9	9	2	7	31	13	0	0	4.31
Billy Mountjoy	6	53	6	6	2	4	15	13	1	0	5.43
Joe Brown	4	38	4	4	0	4	9	4	0	0	5.68
Frank Foreman	3	27	3	2	2	1	11	9	0	0	6.00
Shorty Wetzel	2	17	1	2	0	2	6	9	0	0	8.47
Gid Gardner	1	9	1	1	0	1	3	6	0	0	10.00
Joe Sommer	2	3	0	0	0	0	0	0	0	1	9.00
		971	110	103	41	68	395	222	2	**4**	3.90

1886
THE ASSOCIATION ATTAINS
ITS PINNACLE

In 1886 confusion continued to reign as to how many times a pitcher should be allowed to miss the mark before a batter was granted a walk. The National League again hiked the number of balls to seven while the American Association went in the opposite direction, reducing to six the number of inaccurate tosses needed for a walk. Both loops were in accord, however, that the pitcher's box should be lengthened by a foot and that a rule the League had dispensed with the previous year, requiring a pitcher to have both feet on the ground while delivering the ball, should be permanently abolished.

Lengthening the pitcher's box aided hurlers such as Guy Hecker who liked to crank up by getting a running start, and other tossers were delighted that they would not be restricted from dancing about as they launched the ball. These rule changes, coming on the heels of the legalization of overhand pitching, resulted in a sudden and alarming profusion of strikeouts, but further modifications in the years ahead removed much of the edge that pitchers gained on hitters in the mid-1880s. The new rule in 1886 that would have the most enduring influence had come into existence the previous fall during a joint meeting between the League and the Association to draft a new National Agreement. With the Union Association challenge now dead and virtually every player bound by the Reserve Clause, magnates in both circuits compacted to put a $2,000 ceiling on player salaries.

Even though the salary limit was ignored initially when too many owners lacked the courage to impose it, the threat it embodied drew players to take a fresh look at the notion of unionizing. Early in 1885, Bill Voltz, a Philadelphia sportswriter who'd helped start several minor leagues, proposed creating a professional baseball player's benevolent association or "Brotherhood" to provide health insurance and emergency funds for injured or needy players. Voltz found little interest in his plan until he approached the New York National League club. Giants captain Monte Ward not only liked Voltz's Brotherhood idea but expanded upon it to make it a trade union. On October 2, 1885, just days before the $2,000 salary limit became law, Ward and several other Giants, notably Tim Keefe and

Buck Ewing, formed the first chapter of the Brotherhood of Professional Baseball Players. By the close of the 1886 season the Brotherhood had over 100 members and chapters in every League city.

Included under Ward's aegis were players in Washington and Kansas City, the League's two newest entries. After the Providence and Buffalo franchises fell into bankruptcy and folded following the 1885 season, Nick Young, who had replaced Abraham Mills as National League president, presided over Washington's formal admission on January 16, 1886. A month later Kansas City was accepted as a compromise when a clandestine plot to fill the vacancy with a team from the American Association (Cincinnati was the most coveted candidate) fell through.

Blissfully unaware of the League's behind-the-scenes machinations, the Association for the first time began a new season with the same eight-team crew that had voyaged under its banner the previous year. The junior circuit was not without internal strife, though, as president Denny McKnight was deposed in late March over his inept handling of a contract wrangle involving Sam Barkley that had been preceded by an ill-conceived attempt to oust the New York Mets from the Association. When the Mets refused to cede their spot and Barkley, unable to get along with St. Louis Browns owner Chris Von Der Ahe, ended up with Pittsburgh, overriding Billy Barnie's vehement protest that he belonged to Baltimore, McKnight was ordered to turn over his papers to Wheeler Wyckoff, moving up from Association secretary to the top job.

Barkley's addition solidified Pittsburgh's infield and helped make Horace Phillips's club the top defensive unit in the Association, but the defending-champion Browns were only a

In 1886 the Detroit Wolverines played .707 ball just two years after finishing last with a .250 winning percentage. It may have been the quickest, and most remarkable, rebuilding job ever, but it left the Wolves still in search of their first pennant. In this Lorillard Tobacco Card, right side of horseshoe from top: Jack Rowe, Charlie Bennett, Pete Conway, Dan Brouthers and Deacon White. Left side: Lady Baldwin, George Wood, Sam Thompson, Charlie Ganzel and Hardy Richardson. Center: Ned Hanlon.

SUPER SEASON FOR SOUTHPAWS

Until the late 1870s analysts believed there was only one position on the diamond that a lefthander could not play successfully. It was not shortstop or catcher. There were plenty of southpaws at those positions in the nineteenth century, and there were also lots of lefty third basemen and second basemen. But the game, even as late as the beginning of the 1880 season, had never seen a lefthanded pitcher of much note. The record for the most wins in a season by a southpaw still belonged to John McMullin, who registered 12 victories for Troy in the National Association's first season. In the National League's maiden 1876 season, in contrast, not a single decision was recorded by a lefthanded pitcher.

Exactly ten years later, though, the myth that a southpaw could never be a great pitcher was dispelled once and for all. Actually, the 1886 season was probably the richest ever for lefthanded pitching feats. Rookie Baltimore southpaw Matt Kilroy rang up an all-time record 513 strikeouts and Louisville's lefty ace, Toad Ramsey, was only a hair less awesome with 499 K's in his first full season. The third-best strikeout total in the majors in 1886 belonged to another Association southpaw, Ed Morris of Pittsburgh, and fourth on the majors' K list was Detroit's Lady Baldwin, who also threw from the port side. In addition, Baldwin in 1886 set the National League record for most wins by a lefty with 42, breaking Morris's year-old major league mark of 39. The following season Kilroy would establish the all-time record for a lefthander when he won 46 games for Baltimore, but Morris would turn out to be the most enduring of the four southpaw stars in 1886, winning 171 games, the most of any lefty in the last century.

fraction less stingy at giving up unearned runs. Since St. Louis also owned both the Association's best offensive unit and best pitching staff by far, it meant an easy repeat pennant. Without a single batter among the loop leaders the previous year, in 1886 Comiskey boosted three .300 hitters in Tip O'Neill, Bob Caruthers and Arlie Latham. Along with swatting .334, Caruthers also led the Association in wins, and Latham set a new loop record by tallying 152 runs. Latham and his teammates carved their reputation, though, more on their daring base running, rowdy base-coaching and umpire-baiting than on their statistics.

Chicago, the 1885 League champion, also won its second straight flag but only after another down-to-the-wire battle. The challenge on this occasion came from the Detroit Wolverines, a perennial loser suddenly shot to prominence by the arrival of the four core members of the Buffalo Bisons the Michigan club had attempted to annex the previous fall. So central to Detroit's improvement was the quartet of Dan Brouthers, Deacon White, Jack Rowe and Hardy Richardson that they begged comparison to the four stars Chicago had pilfered from Boston ten years earlier and were christened the second "Big Four." The new foursome, together with emerging star Sam Thompson and Charlie Bennett, the game's

The 1886 St. Louis Maroons were aka the "Black Diamonds" because so many of them were blacklisted for playing in the Union Association. Top: Al Bauers, Charlie Sweeney, Jerry Denny, Emmett Seery, Patsy Cahill and Jack Glasscock. Middle: Henry Boyle, Jack McGeachy, Egyptian Healy, manager Gus Schmelz, Tom Dolan, John Kirby and Alex McKinnon. Bottom: Joe Quinn, Fred Dunlap and George Myers. On a train trip to Detroit in July 1886, Denny undressed after a night of imbibing and crawled into what he thought was his berth in the sleeping car. When he saw a slumbering form already there, he thought it was Kirby pulling a prank, and whacked him hard on the bottom. Only it was a teenage girl and her father nearly throttled the mortified Denny.

finest all-around catcher in the mid-1880s, aided pitchers Lady Baldwin and Charlie Getzein to post a composite 72–23 record after winning just 23 games between them in 1885. Still, the pair was a step behind Chicago, which got 66 wins from John Clarkson and Jim McCormick while rookie flash Jocko Flynn chipped in another 23 victories. After leading the league race all summer, Detroit stumbled in August, winning just 10 of 23 games while Chicago was victorious in 17 of 23. For the rest of the season the Wolverines played catchup but never quite regained the lost ground, finishing two and a half games in arrears.

Before embarking on their second consecutive World's Series confrontation with Chicago, the Browns tuned up by sweeping four straight games from the League Maroons to snare bragging rights to St. Louis. The city series with the Browns was the Maroons's last gasp before dissolving and turning over most of their players to a replacement franchise in Indianapolis, and it was nearly the death knell for the Browns' season too when Caruthers hurt his knee against the Maroons and was unable to pitch the opening game at Chicago. Comiskey turned instead to Dave Foutz, but after the White Stockings tapped Foutz for two runs in the bottom of the first, Clarkson waltzed to a 6–0 win.

Caruthers recovered sufficiently by the following afternoon to douse McCormick, 12–0, but when he tried to hurl two days in a row, Chicago blasted him 11–4. The teams then journeyed to St. Louis with the Browns down 2–1 in the best-of-seven fray. Clarkson and McCormick had been drained by the arduous pennant race, though, as in 1885, and Flynn's

JOCKO

The 1886 Chicago White Stockings.
Top: Billy Sunday, Abner Dalrymple, Ned Williamson, Jimmy Ryan, Flynn and Tom Burns. Middle: King Kelly, George Gore, Prunes Moolic, Fred Pfeffer and Silver Flint. Bottom: John Clarkson, Cap Anson and Jim McCormick.

Cocky, insouciant, Jocko Flynn stands beside fellow rookie Jimmy Ryan in the 1886 Chicago White Stockings' team picture. It is our lone enduring image of perhaps the greatest one-year wonder in major league history. Flynn, a native of Lawrence, Massachusetts, arrived in Chicago in the spring of 1886 as a twenty-two-year-old rookie pitcher-outfielder together with his minor league batterymate Prunes Moolic, who also made his home in Lawrence. Over the next five months Flynn won 23 games so quickly that it was said of him: "On the street he looks like one of your lawn-tennis dudes. On the field he is, to quote everybody, a perfect terror." The words had hardly appeared in print than Flynn blew out his arm. Not a great one for taking care of himself, he never pitched again in the majors, though he did play part of one game as an outfielder early the following season. Flynn holds the all-time record for the most wins in the majors by a one-year pitcher. A list of nineteenth-century players who won 12 or more games in the only seasons they were major league pitchers:

	YEAR	TEAM	W	L	PCT	ERA
Jocko Flynn	1886	Chi-NL	23*	6	.793	2.24
Parke Swartzel	1889	KC-AA	19	27	.413	4.32
Fred Smith	1890	Tol-AA	19	13	.594	3.27
John Keefe	1890	Syr-AA	17	24	.415	4.32
Fleury Sullivan	1884	Pit-AA	16	35	.314	4.20
Perry Werden	1884	StL-UA	12	1	.923	1.97
Bob Hart	1890	StL-AA	12	8	.600	3.67
Doc Landis	1882	Phi/Bal-AA	12	28	.300	3.32

*The 1996 edition of Macmillan still credits Flynn with 24 wins.

The NL's leading hitter in 1886, King Kelly, whose bat was just part of his value. Kelly won a key 1886 game against Boston in the bottom of the ninth when he led off with a walk and stole second after Cap Anson popped out. Fred Pfeffer then tapped a slow roller between Jack Burdock and John Morrill, and as the umpire raced to first to cover what promised to be a close play, Kelly cut across the diamond about halfway to third. Though the crowd yelled, by the time the umpire spun around Kelly had streaked across the plate with the game-winning run.

arm was so sore he was left behind in Chicago. Short of pitching, the White Stockings were forced to use Clarkson for a second day in a row and then had to put shortstop Ned Williamson in the box. After losing both contests by lopsided scores, Cap Anson suddenly found his team down 3–2 and on the verge of elimination. For Game Six, Anson again summoned Clarkson, making his fourth start in six days. Clarkson gave it a valiant effort and took a 3–0 lead into the bottom of the eighth, but a critical misplay by leftfielder Abner Dalrymple on Latham's long fly tied the count. The 3–3 deadlock was broken when Curt Welch led off the tenth with a single, only the Browns' fourth hit off Clarkson. Welch took second on Foutz's infield hit and then was sacrificed to third by Yank Robinson. With third base coach Arlie Latham heckling him and Welch scampering up and down the line, as if threatening to steal home, perhaps Clarkson grew rattled. In any event, he threw a pitch to Doc Bushong that eluded Chicago catcher King Kelly, and Welch raced home. Whether Welch slid or scored standing up will be forever debated as will whether his run came on a wild pitch or a passed ball. Kelly later offered little illumination when he said, "I signaled Clarkson for a low ball on one side and when it came it was high upon the other. It struck my hand as I tried to get it and I would say it was a passed ball. You can give it to me if you want to. Clarkson told me that it slipped from his hands."

The Browns' post-Series victory parade seemed at the time as if it would be only the first of many such celebrations for the American Association, but there was never another moment nearly as good. Even as National League moguls were congratulating their Association brethren on a victory well done, they were gearing up for a new war.

THE WORST HITTING TEAM EVER

Matt Kilroy's single season strikeout record of 513 in 1886 is all the more remarkable in that he achieved it without the benefit of facing his own Baltimore Orioles teammates, who happened to be the worst assemblage of hitters in major league history. The 1886 Orioles not only batted an execrable .204, the poorest average ever by a team playing a full schedule, but managed to collect only 183 extra base hits in 139 games. Consequently, Kilroy's teammates also compiled the second-lowest slugging average ever at .258.* Rightfielder Jack Manning led the Orioles in virtually every offensive department despite hitting a meager .223. His 18 doubles tied for the team lead, his seven triples were only one behind leader Mike Muldoon, and he tied for second in homers with one. Manning's 159 total bases also led Baltimore by a substantial margin. Indeed, only four Orioles—Manning, Joe Sommer, Milt Scott and Muldoon—collected as many as 100 total bases. Scott set an all-time record for the fewest total bases by a first baseman with 400 or more at bats (117) and by the end of the season usually batted behind the pitcher. Actually, manager Bill Barnie so despaired of getting any run production from his regulars that he frequently batted his pitchers in the middle of the order. Here are the Orioles' 1886 team "leaders" in each major batting department:

AT BATS:	Joe Sommer 560
HITS:	Jack Manning 124
RUNS:	Joe Sommer 79
DOUBLES:	Joe Sommer 18, Jack Manning 18
TRIPLES:	Mike Muldoon 8
HOME RUNS:	Milt Scott 2
TOTAL BASES:	Jack Manning 159
WALKS:	Jack Manning 50
BA:	Jack Manning .223
SA:	Jack Manning .286
OBP:	Jack Manning .291
STOLEN BASES:	Joe Sommer 31
RBI:	Milt Scott 52, Joe Sommer 52

*The Orioles' 1882 entry holds the record with a .257 SA.

THE SEASONAL RECORD

NATIONAL LEAGUE

	W	L	PCT	HOME	ROAD	GB
1. Chicago White Stockings	90	34	.726	52–10	38–24	—
2. Detroit Wolverines	87	36	.707	47–12	40–24	2.5
3. New York Giants	75	44	.630	47–12	28–32	12.5
4. Philadelphia Phillies	71	43	.623	45–14	26–29	14
5. Boston Beaneaters	56	61	.479	32–26	24–35	30.5
6. St. Louis Maroons	43	79	.352	27–34	16–45	46
7. Kansas City Cowboys	30	91	.248	18–42	12–49	58.5
8. Washington Nationals	28	92	.233	19–43	9–49	60

	Chi	Det	NY	Phi	Bos	StL	KC	Was	
Chicago	—	11	10	10	12	13	17	17	90
Detroit	7	—	11	10	11	15	16	17	87
New York	8	7	—	8	11	15	15	11	75
Philadelphia	7	7	8	—	10	12	14	13	71
Boston	6	6	6	3	—	11	11	13	56
St. Louis	4	2	3	6	6	—	12	10	43
Kansas City	1	2	3	2	6	5	—	11	30
Washington	1	1	3	4	5	8	6	—	28
	34	36	44	43	61	79	91	92	480

SEASON LEADERS

Batting Average (300 ABs)

1.	Kelly, Chicago	.388
2.	Anson, Chicago	.371
3.	Brouthers, Detroit	.370
4.	Connor, New York	.355
5.	H. Richardson, Detroit	.351

On–Base Percentage

1.	Kelly, Chicago	.483
2.	Brouthers, Detroit	.445
3.	Gore, Chicago	.434
4.	Anson, Chicago	.433
5.	Connor, New York	.405

Home Runs

1.	H. Richardson, Detroit	11
	Brouthers, Detroit	11
3.	Anson, Chicago	10
4.	Hines, Washington	9
	Denny, St. Louis	9

Hits

1.	H. Richardson, Detroit	189
2.	Anson, Chicago	187
3.	Brouthers, Detroit	181
4.	Kelly, Chicago	175
5.	Connor, New York	172

Slugging Average

1.	Brouthers, Detroit	.581
2.	Anson, Chicago	.544
3.	Connor, New York	.540
4.	Kelly, Chicago	.534
5.	H. Richardson, Detroit	.504

Total Bases

1.	Brouthers, Detroit	284
2.	Anson, Chicago	274
3.	H. Richardson, Detroit	271
4.	Connor, New York	262
5.	Kelly, Chicago	241

RBI

1.	Anson, Chicago	147
2.	Pfeffer, Chicago	95
3.	Thompson, Detroit	89
4.	Rowe, Detroit	87
5.	Ward, New York	81

Runs

1.	Kelly, Chicago	155
2.	Gore, Chicago	150
3.	Brouthers, Detroit	139
4.	H. Richardson, Detroit	125
5.	Anson, Chicago	117

Bases on Balls

1.	Gore, Chicago	102
2.	Kelly, Chicago	83
3.	Willamson, Chicago	80
4.	Brouthers, Detroit	66
5.	Radford, Kansas City	58

Stolen Bases

1.	Andrews, Philadelphia	56
2.	Kelly, Chicago	53
3.	Hanlon, Detroit	50
4.	H. Richardson, Detroit	42
5.	Radford, Kansas City	39

Strikeouts

1.	Seery, St. Louis	82
2.	Morrill, Boston	81
3.	Lillie, Kansas City	80
4.	Cahill, St. Louis	79
5.	Wood, Philadelphia	75

PITCHING

Wins

1.	Keefe, New York	42
	Baldwin, Detroit	42
3.	Clarkson, Chicago	36
4.	Welch, New York	33
5.	McCormick, Chicago	31

Innings

1.	Keefe, New York	535
2.	Radbourn, Boston	509.1
3.	Welch, New York	500
4.	Baldwin, Detroit	487
5.	Clarkson, Chicago	466.2

Strikeouts

1.	Baldwin, Detroit	323
2.	Clarkson, Chicago	313
3.	Keefe, New York	297
4.	Welch, New York	272
5.	Stemmeyer, Boston	239

ERA (140 innings)

1.	Boyle, St. Louis	1.76
2.	Ferguson, Philadelphia	1.98
3.	Baldwin, Detroit	2.24
	Flynn, Chicago	2.24
5.	Clarkson, Chicago	2.41
	Casey, Philadelphia	2.41

Losses

1.	Weidman, Kansas City	36
2.	Whitney, Kansas City	32
3.	Radbourn, Boston	31
	Shaw, Washington	31
5.	Kirby, St. Louis	26

Complete Games

1.	Keefe, New York	62
2.	Radbourn, Boston	57
3.	Welch, New York	56
4.	Baldwin, Detroit	55
5.	Clarkson, Chicago	50

Winning Percentage (25 decisions)

1.	Flynn, Chicago	.793
2.	Ferguson, Philadelphia	.769
3.	Baldwin, Detroit	.764
4.	McCormick, Chicago	.738
5.	Getzein, Detroit	.732

Lowest On–Base Percentage

1.	Baldwin, Detroit	.243
2.	Ferguson, Philadelphia	.244
3.	Flynn, Chicago	.257
4.	Boyle, St. Louis	.261
5.	Clarkson, Chicago	.264

FIELDING

Total Chances

1B	McQuery, Kansas City	1388
2B	Dunlap, StL–Detroit	784
3B	Denny, St. Louis	505
SS	Glasscock, St. Louis	605
OF	Johnston, Boston	305
C	Bennett, Detroit	533
P	Radbourn, Boston	158

Fielding Average

Farrar, Philadelphia	.980
Bastian, Philadelphia	.945
Esterbrook, New York	.895
Glasscock, St. Louis	.906
Dalrymple, Chicago	.953
Bennett, Detroit	.955
Baldwin, Detroit	.969

CHICAGO   **Cap Anson**   **West Side Park (I)**

		G	AB	H	R	2B	3B	HR	RBI	BB	SB	BA	SA
1B	Cap Anson	125	504	187	117	35	11	10	**147**	55	29	.371	.544
2B	Fred Pfeffer	118	474	125	88	17	8	7	95	36	30	.264	.378
UT	King Kelly	118	471	175	**155**	32	11	4	79	83	53	**.388**	.534
3B	Tom Burns	112	445	123	64	18	10	3	65	14	15	.276	.382
CF	George Gore	118	444	135	150	20	12	6	63	**102**	23	.304	.444
SS	Ned Williamson	121	430	93	69	17	8	6	58	80	13	.216	.335
LF	Abner Dalrymple	82	331	77	62	7	12	3	26	33	16	.233	.353
RF	Jimmy Ryan	84	327	100	58	17	6	4	53	12	10	.306	.431
P	John Clarkson	55	210	49	21	9	1	3	23	0	2	.233	.329
P	Jocko Flynn	57	205	41	40	6	2	4	19	18	9	.200	.307
P	Jim McCormick	42	174	41	17	9	2	2	21	2	1	.236	.345
C	Silver Flint	54	173	35	30	6	2	1	13	12	1	.202	.277
Sub	Billy Sunday	28	103	25	16	2	2	0	6	7	10	.243	.301
Sub	Prunes Moolic	16	56	8	9	3	0	0	2	2	0	.143	.196
Sub	Lew Hardie	16	51	9	4	0	0	0	3	4	1	.176	.176
		126	4378	1223	**900**	198	87	53	673	460	213	.279	**.401**

1B   Anson 125, Kelly 9, Flint 3, Pfeffer 1
2B   Pfeffer 118, Kelly 6, Ryan 5
SS   Williamson 121, Ryan 6, Kelly 5
3B   Burns 112, Kelly 8, Ryan 6, Hardie 1
OF   Gore 118, Dalrymple 82, Ryan 70, Kelly 56, Sunday 28, Flynn 28, Clarkson 5, McCormick 4, Moolic 2, Hardie 2
C   Flint 54, Kelly 53, Moolic 15, Hardie 13, Anson 12, Williamson 4
P   Clarkson 55, McCormick 42, Flynn 32, Ryan 5, Williamson 2

	G	IP	GS	CG	W	L	K	BB	SH	SV	ERA
John Clarkson	55	466.2	55	50	36	17	313	86	3	0	2.41
Jim McCormick	42	347.2	42	38	31	11	172	100	2	0	2.82
Jocko Flynn	32	257	29	28	23	6	146	63	2	1	2.24
Jimmy Ryan	5	23.1	0	0	0	0	15	13	0	1	4.63
Ned Williamson	2	3	0	0	0	0	1	0	0	1	0.00
*One combined shutout on May 28: McCormick 3 innings, Flynn 6 innings											
	1097.2	126	116	90	34	**647**	262	7	3	2.54	

DETROIT   Bill Watkins   Recreation Park

		G	AB	H	R	2B	3B	HR	RBI	BB	SB	BA	SA
LF	Hardy Richardson	125	**538**	**189**	125	27	11	**11**	61	46	42	.351	.504
RF	Sam Thompson	122	503	156	101	18	13	8	89	35	13	.310	.445
CF	Ned Hanlon	126	494	116	105	6	6	4	60	57	50	.235	.296
3B	Deacon White	124	491	142	65	19	5	1	76	31	9	.289	.354
1B	Dan Brouthers	121	489	181	139	**40**	15	**11**	72	66	21	.370	**.581**
SS	Jack Rowe	111	468	142	97	21	9	6	87	26	12	.303	.425
C	Charlie Bennett	72	235	57	37	13	5	4	34	48	4	.243	.391
C	Charlie Ganzel	57	213	58	28	7	2	1	31	7	5	.272	.338
P	Lady Baldwin	57	204	41	25	6	3	0	25	18	3	.201	.260
2B	Fred Dunlap	51	196	56	32	8	3	4	37	16	13	.286	.418
Sub	Sam Crane	47	185	26	24	2	2	1	12	8	8	.141	.189
P	Charlie Getzein	43	165	29	14	3	3	0	19	6	3	.176	.230
Sub	Jim Manning	26	97	18	14	2	3	0	7	6	7	.186	.268
Sub	Harry Decker	14	54	12	2	1	0	0	5	2	0	.222	.241
P	Pete Conway	12	43	8	10	1	0	2	3	1	0	.186	.349
P	Bill Smith	10	38	7	2	2	0	0	4	1	0	.184	.237
Sub	Jack McGeachy	6	27	9	3	0	1	0	4	0	2	.333	.407
Sub	Billy Shindle	7	26	7	4	0	0	0	4	0	2	.269	.269
Sub	Larry Twitchell	4	16	1	0	0	0	0	0	0	0	.063	.063
Sub	Tom Gillen	2	10	4	2	0	0	0	4	0	0	.400	.400
P	Phenomenal Smith	3	9	1	0	0	0	0	1	0	0	.111	.111
		126	4501	**1260**	829	176	81	**53**	635	374	194	**.280**	.390

1B   Brouthers 121, Ganzel 5
2B   Dunlap 51, Richardson 42, Crane 38, Hanlon 1
SS   Rowe 110, Crane 8, Shindle 7, Richardson 3, Bennett 1, Manning 1
3B   White 124, Richardson 2
OF   Hanlon 126, Thompson 122, Richardson 80, Manning 26, McGeachy 6, Ganzel 7, Crane 4, Bennett 4, Baldwin 2, Twitchell 2, Dunlap 1, Decker 1, B. Smith 1, Conway 1, Getzein 1
C   Bennett 69, Ganzel 45, Decker 14, Rowe 3, Gillen 2
P   Baldwin 56, Getzein 43, Conway 11, B. Smith 9, Richardson 4, Twitchell 4, P. Smith 3

	G	IP	GS	CG	W	L	K	BB	SH	SV	ERA
Lady Baldwin	56	487	56	55	**42**	13	**323**	100	**7**	0	2.24
Charlie Getzein	43	386.2	43	42	30	11	172	85	1	0	3.03
Pete Conway	11	91	11	11	6	5	35	25	0	0	3.36
Bill Smith	9	77	9	9	5	4	36	30	0	0	4.09
Larry Twitchell	4	25	4	2	0	2	6	12	0	0	6.48
Phenomenal Smith	3	25	3	3	1	1	15	8	0	0	2.16
Hardy Richardson	4	12	0	0	3	0	5	10	0	0	4.50
		1103.2	126	**122**	87	36	592	270	8	0	2.85

NEW YORK   Jim Mutrie   Polo Grounds (I)

		G	AB	H	R	2B	3B	HR	RBI	BB	SB	BA	SA
SS	Monte Ward	122	491	134	82	17	5	2	81	19	36	.273	.340
1B	Roger Connor	118	485	172	105	29	**20**	7	71	41	17	.355	.540
3B	Dude Esterbrook	123	473	125	62	20	6	3	43	8	13	.264	.351
RF	Mike Dorgan	118	442	129	61	19	4	2	79	29	9	.292	.367
UT	Jim O'Rourke	105	440	136	106	26	6	1	34	39	14	.309	.402
2B	Joe Gerhardt	123	426	81	44	11	7	0	40	22	8	.190	.249
LF	Pete Gillespie	97	396	108	65	13	8	0	58	16	17	.273	.346
C	Buck Ewing	73	275	85	59	11	7	4	31	16	18	.309	.444
CF	Danny Richardson	68	237	55	43	9	1	1	27	17	12	.232	.291
P	Mickey Welch	59	213	46	17	4	2	0	18	7	3	.216	.254
P	Tim Keefe	64	205	35	26	10	1	1	20	17	3	.171	.244

		G	AB	H	R	2B	3B	HR	RBI	BB	SB	BA	SA
Sub	Pat Deasley	41	143	38	18	6	1	0	17	4	2	.266	.322
Sub	Bill Finley	13	44	8	2	0	0	0	5	1	2	.182	.182
Sub	Gene Begley	5	16	2	1	0	0	0	1	1	1	.125	.125
Sub	Ed Caskin	1	4	2	1	0	0	0	1	0	0	.500	.500
Sub	Larry Corcoran	1	4	0	0	0	0	0	0	0	0	.000	.000
Sub	Jim Devine	1	3	0	0	0	0	0	0	0	0	.000	.000
P	Jim Devlin	1	1	0	0	0	0	0	1	0	0	.000	.000
		124	4298	1156	692	175	67	22	527	237	155	.269	.356

1B Connor 118, Dorgan 3, Ewing 2, O'Rourke 2
2B Gerhardt 123, Richardson 1
SS Ward 122, Richardson 1, Caskin 1
3B Esterbrook 123, Richardson 1
OF Dorgan 116, Gillespie 97, Richardson 64, O'Rourke 63, Ewing 23, Deasley 15, Foster 14, Finley 8, Welch 3, Begley 2, Keefe 1, Corcoran 1, Devine 1
C   Ewing 50, O'Rourke 47, Deasley 30, Finley 8, Begley 3
P   Keefe 64, Welch 59, Richardson 5, Devlin 1

	G	IP	GS	CG	W	L	K	BB	SH	SV	ERA
Tim Keefe	**64**	**535**	**64**	**62**	**42**	20	297	102	2	0	2.53
Mickey Welch	59	500	59	56	33	22	272	**163**	1	0	2.99
Danny Richardson	5	25	1	1	0	2	17	11	0	0	5.76
Jim Devlin	1	2	0	0	0	0	2	4	0	1	18.00
		1062	124	119	75	44	588	280	3	1	2.86

PHILADELPHIA   **Harry Wright**   **Recreation Park**

		G	AB	H	R	2B	3B	HR	RBI	BB	SB	BA	SA
OF	George Wood	106	450	123	81	18	15	4	50	23	9	.273	.407
1B	Sid Farrar	118	439	109	55	19	7	5	50	16	10	.248	.358
CF	Ed Andrews	107	437	109	93	15	4	2	28	31	**56**	.249	.316
3B	Joe Mulvey	107	430	115	71	16	10	2	53	15	27	.267	.365
SS	Arthur Irwin	101	373	87	51	6	6	0	34	35	24	.233	.282
2B	Charlie Bastian	105	373	81	46	9	11	2	38	33	29	.217	.316
UT	Ed Daily	79	309	70	40	17	1	4	50	7	23	.227	.327
RF	Jim Fogarty	77	280	82	54	13	5	3	47	42	30	.293	.407
P	Charlie Ferguson	72	261	66	56	9	1	2	25	37	9	.253	.318
C	Jack Clements	54	185	38	15	5	1	0	11	7	4	.205	.243
C	Deacon McGuire	50	167	33	25	7	1	2	18	19	2	.198	.287
P	Dan Casey	44	151	23	11	4	1	0	9	9	0	.152	.192
Sub	Tony Cusick	29	104	23	10	5	1	0	4	3	1	.221	.288
Sub	Jack Farrell	17	60	11	7	0	1	0	3	3	1	.183	.217
Sub	Tommy McCarthy	8	27	5	6	2	1	0	3	2	1	.185	.333
P	Cannonball Titcomb	5	16	1	0	0	0	0	1	0	0	.063	.063
P	John Strike	3	7	0	0	0	0	0	0	0	0	.000	.000
Sub	Charlie Ganzel	1	3	0	0	0	0	0	0	0	0	.000	.000
		119	4072	976	621	145	66	26	424	282	**226**	.240	.327

1B Farrar 118, Cusick 1
2B Bastian 87, Farrell 17, Fogarty 13, Andrews 3
SS Irwin 100, Bastian 10, Wood 6, Fogarty 3
3B Mulvey 107, Bastian 8, Fogarty 3, Wood 3, Irwin 1
OF Andrews 104, Wood 97, Fogarty 60, Daily 56, Ferguson 27, McCarthy 8, Clements 7, Casey 5, Cusick 3, McGuire 1, Strike 1, Mulvey 1
C   McGuire 49, Clements 47, Cusick 25, Ganzel 1
P   Ferguson 48, Casey 44, Daily 27, Titcomb 5, Strike 2, McCarthy 1, Fogarty 1

	G	IP	GS	CG	W	L	K	BB	SH	SV	ERA
Charlie Ferguson	48	395.2	45	43	30	9	212	69	4	**2**	**1.98**
Dan Casey	44	369	44	39	24	18	193	104	4	0	2.41
Ed Daily	27	218	23	22	16	9	95	59	1	0	3.06
Cannonball Titcomb	5	41	5	5	0	5	24	24	0	0	3.73
John Strike	2	15	2	1	1	1	11	7	0	0	4.80
Jim Fogarty	1	6	0	0	0	1	4	0	0	0	0.00
Tommy McCarthy	1	1	0	0	0	0	1	1	0	0	0.00
	*One combined shutout on Oct. 4: Ferguson 2 innings, Daily 7 innings										
	1045.2	119	110	71	43	540	264	**10**	2	**2.45**	

BOSTON   **John Morrill**   **South End Grounds (I)**

		G	AB	H	R	2B	3B	HR	RBI	BB	SB	BA	SA
UT	Ezra Sutton	116	499	138	83	21	6	3	48	26	18	.277	.361
SS	John Morrill	117	430	106	86	25	6	7	69	56	9	.247	.381
LF	Joe Hornung	94	424	109	67	12	2	2	40	10	16	.257	.309
3B	Billy Nash	109	417	117	61	11	8	1	45	24	16	.281	.353
CF	Dick Johnston	109	413	99	48	18	9	1	57	3	11	.240	.334
1B	Sam Wise	96	387	112	71	19	12	4	72	33	31	.289	.432
RF	Tom Poorman	96	371	97	72	16	6	3	41	19	31	.261	.361
P	Hoss Radbourn	66	253	60	30	5	1	2	22	17	5	.237	.289
2B	Jack Burdock	59	221	48	26	6	1	0	25	11	3	.217	.253
C	Con Daily	50	180	43	25	4	2	0	21	19	2	.239	.283
P	Charlie Buffinton	44	176	51	27	4	1	1	30	6	3	.290	.341
P	Bill Stemmeyer	41	148	41	24	3	2	0	20	12	3	.277	.324
Sub	Pop Tate	31	106	24	13	3	1	0	3	7	0	.226	.274
Sub	Tom Gunning	27	98	22	15	2	1	0	7	3	3	.224	.265
Sub	Pat Dealey	15	46	15	9	1	1	0	3	4	5	.326	.391
P	Charlie Parsons	2	8	3	0	1	0	0	0	0	0	.375	.500
Sub	Myron Allen	1	3	0	0	0	0	0	0	0	0	.000	.000
		118	4180	1085	657	151	59	24	503	250	156	.260	.341

1B	Wise 57, Morrill 42, Buffinton 19
2B	Burdock 59, Morrill 20, Wise 20, Sutton 18, Allen 1
SS	Morrill 55, Sutton 28, Wise 18, Nash 17
3B	Nash 90, Sutton 28
OF	Johnston 109, Poorman 96, Hornung 94, Sutton 43, Buffinton 9, Radbourn 9, Dealey 1
C	Daily 50, Tate 31, Gunning 27, Dealey 14
P	Radbourn 58, Stemmeyer 41, Buffinton 18, Parsons 2, Morrill 1

	G	IP	GS	CG	W	L	K	BB	SH	SV	ERA
Hoss Radbourn	58	509.1	58	57	27	31	218	111	3	0	3.00
Bill Stemmeyer	41	348.2	41	41	22	18	239	144	0	0	3.02
Charlie Buffinton	18	151	17	16	7	10	47	39	0	0	4.59
Charlie Parsons	2	16	2	2	0	2	5	4	0	0	3.94
John Morrill	1	4	0	0	0	0	2	0	0	0	0.00
		1029	118	116	56	61	511	298	3	0	3.24

ST. LOUIS   Gus Schmelz   Union Park

		G	AB	H	R	2B	3B	HR	RBI	BB	SB	BA	SA
1B	Alex McKinnon	122	491	148	75	24	7	8	72	21	10	.301	.428
SS	Jack Glasscock	121	486	158	96	29	7	3	40	38	38	.325	.432
3B	Jerry Denny	119	475	122	58	24	6	9	62	14	16	.257	.389
RF	Patsy Cahill	125	463	92	43	17	6	1	32	9	16	.199	.268
LF	Emmett Seery	126	453	108	73	22	6	2	48	57	24	.238	.327
C	George Myers	79	295	56	26	7	3	0	27	18	6	.190	.234
2B	Fred Dunlap	71	285	76	53	15	2	3	32	28	7	.267	.365
CF	Joe Quinn	75	271	63	33	11	3	1	21	8	12	.232	.306
Sub	Jack McGeachy	59	226	46	31	12	3	2	24	1	8	.204	.310
P	Egyptian Healy	43	145	14	10	5	0	0	5	2	0	.097	.131
C	Frank Graves	43	138	21	7	2	0	0	9	7	11	.152	.167
P	John Kirby	42	136	15	10	4	0	0	5	3	0	.110	.140
Sub	Sam Crane	39	116	20	10	3	1	0	7	13	6	.172	.216
P	Henry Boyle	30	108	27	8	2	2	1	13	5	0	.250	.333
P	Charlie Sweeney	17	64	16	4	2	0	0	7	3	0	.250	.281
Sub	Tom Dolan	15	44	11	8	3	0	0	1	7	2	.250	.318
P	Joe Murphy	4	14	3	0	1	0	0	1	0	0	.214	.286
Sub	George Mappes	6	14	2	1	0	0	0	0	1	0	.143	.143
P	Al Bauers	4	12	2	1	0	0	0	0	0	0	.167	.167
Sub	Red Connally	2	7	0	0	0	0	0	0	0	0	.000	.000
P	Jim Reardon	1	4	1	0	0	0	0	0	0	0	.250	.250
Sub	Lou Pelouze	1	3	0	0	0	0	0	0	0	0	.000	.000
		126	4250	1001	547	183	46	30	406	235	156	.236	.321

1B   McKinnon 119, Quinn 7
2B   Dunlap 71, Crane 39, Quinn 15, McGeachy 2, Mappes 1
SS   Glasscock 120, Denny 3, Quinn 2, Sweeney 2, Cahill 1
3B   Denny 117, Quinn 4, McGeachy 2, Mappes 2, Cahill 1, Myers 1
OF   Seery 126, Cahill 124, McGeachy 55, Quinn 48, Boyle 6, Myers 6, Sweeney 4, Kirby 3, Graves 3, McKinnon 3, Connally 2, Healy 1, Glasscock 1, Murphy 1, Pelouze 1
C   Meyers 72, Graves 41, Dolan 15, Mappes 3
P   Healy 42, Kirby 41, Boyle 25, Sweeney 11, Murphy 4, Bauers 4, Cahill 2, Seery 2, Graves 1, Reardon 1

	G	IP	GS	CG	W	L	K	BB	SH	SV	ERA
Egyptian Healy	42	353.2	41	39	17	23	213	118	3	0	2.88
John Kirby	41	325	41	38	11	26	129	134	1	0	3.30
Henry Boyle	25	210	24	23	9	15	101	46	2	0	**1.76**
Charlie Sweeney	11	93	11	11	5	6	28	39	0	0	4.16
Joe Murphy	4	33	4	3	0	4	11	16	0	0	8.18
Al Bauers	4	28.2	4	3	0	4	13	27	0	0	5.97
Patsy Cahill	2	12	0	0	1	0	2	3	0	0	3.00
Jim Reardon	1	8	1	1	0	1	0	5	0	0	6.75
Emmett Seery	2	7	0	0	0	0	2	3	0	0	7.71
Frank Graves	1	7	0	0	0	0	2	1	0	0	9.00
		1077.1	126	118	43	79	501	392	6	0	3.24

KANSAS CITY Dave Rowe   **Association Park**

		G	AB	H	R	2B	3B	HR	RBI	BB	SB	BA	SA
RF	Paul Radford	122	493	113	78	17	5	0	20	58	39	.229	.284
2B	Al Myers	118	473	131	69	22	9	4	51	22	3	.277	.387
1B	Mox McQuery	122	449	111	62	27	4	4	38	36	4	.247	.352
3B	Jim Donnelly	113	438	88	51	11	3	0	38	36	16	.201	.240
CF	Dave Rowe	105	429	103	53	24	8	3	57	15	2	.240	.354
LF	Jim Lillie	114	416	73	37	9	0	0	22	11	13	.175	.197
SS	Charlie Bassett	90	342	89	41	19	8	2	32	36	6	.260	.380
P	Jim Whitney	67	247	59	25	13	3	2	23	29	5	.239	.340
C	Mert Hackett	62	230	50	18	8	3	3	25	4	1	.217	.317
C	Fatty Briody	56	215	51	14	10	3	0	29	3	0	.237	.312
P	Pete Conway	51	194	47	22	8	2	1	18	5	3	.242	.320
P	Stump Weidman	51	179	30	13	2	0	0	7	5	3	.168	.179
Sub	Frank Ringo	16	56	13	6	7	0	0	7	5	0	.232	.357
Sub	Dan Dugdale	12	40	7	4	0	0	0	2	2	1	.175	.175
P	Silver King	7	22	1	0	0	0	0	1	2	0	.045	.045
P	Larry McKeon	3	9	0	0	0	0	0	0	0	0	.000	.000
Sub	George Baker	1	4	1	1	0	0	0	0	0	0	.250	.250
		126	4236	967	494	177	48	19	370	269	96	.228	.306

1B	McQuery 122, Briody 1
2B	Myers 118, Rowe 4, Radford 1
SS	Bassett 82, Radford 30, Rowe 11
3B	Donnelly 113, Bassett 8, Whitney 1, Ringo 1
OF	Lillie 114, Radford 92, Rowe 90, Conway 31, Whitney 22, Hackett 13, Dugdale 6, Weidman 3, Ringo 2, King 2, Briody 2
C	Briody 54, Hackett 52, Ringo 13, Dugdale 7, Baker 1
P	Weidman 51, Whitney 46, Conway 23, King 5, McKeon 3, Lillie 1

	G	IP	GS	CG	W	L	K	BB	SH	SV	ERA
Stump Weidman	51	427.2	51	48	12	**36**	168	112	1	0	4.52
Jim Whitney	46	393	44	42	12	32	167	55	3	0	4.49
Pete Conway	23	180	20	19	5	15	81	61	0	0	5.75
Silver King	5	39	5	5	1	3	23	9	0	0	4.85
Larry McKeon	3	21	3	3	0	2	3	8	0	0	10.71
Jim Lillie	1	6	0	0	0	0	0	1	0	0	4.50
—3 forfeit Ls vs Washington on October 7, October 8 and October 9—											
	1066.2	123	117	30	88	442	**246**	4	0	4.84	

WASHINGTON Mike Scanlon (13–67)   **John Gaffney (15–25)**   **Swampoodle Grounds**

		G	AB	H	R	2B	3B	HR	RBI	BB	SB	BA	SA
CF	Paul Hines	121	487	152	80	30	8	9	56	35	21	.312	.462
2B	Jim Knowles	115	443	94	43	16	11	3	35	15	20	.212	.318
LF	Cliff Carroll	111	433	99	73	11	6	2	22	44	31	.229	.296
1B	Phil Baker	81	325	72	37	6	5	1	34	20	16	.222	.280
RF	Cannonball Crane	80	292	50	20	11	3	0	20	13	8	.171	.229
C	Barney Gilligan	81	273	52	23	9	2	0	17	39	6	.190	.238
SS	Davy Force	68	242	44	26	5	1	0	16	17	9	.182	.211
SS	Sadie Houck	52	195	42	14	3	0	0	14	2	4	.215	.231
2B	Jack Farrell	47	171	41	24	11	4	2	18	15	12	.240	.386
3B	Buck Gladman	44	152	21	17	5	3	1	15	12	5	.138	.230
P	Dupee Shaw	45	148	13	13	2	0	0	6	14	0	.088	.101
1B	Joe Start	31	122	27	10	4	1	0	17	5	4	.221	.270
Sub	Bill Krieg	27	98	25	11	6	3	1	15	3	2	.255	.408
Sub	George Shoch	26	95	28	11	2	1	1	18	2	2	.295	.368

		G	AB	H	R	2B	3B	HR	RBI	BB	SB	BA	SA
Sub	Jackie Hayes	26	89	17	8	3	0	3	9	4	0	.191	.326
Sub	Larry Corcoran	21	81	15	9	2	1	0	3	7	3	.185	.235
P	Bob Barr	23	79	13	6	2	0	0	2	4	0	.165	.190
Sub	Dave Oldfield	21	71	10	2	2	0	0	2	5	0	.141	.169
P	Tony Madigan	14	48	4	2	1	0	0	2	1	0	.083	.104
Sub	Connie Mack	10	36	13	4	2	1	0	5	0	0	.361	.472
P	Frank Gilmore	9	29	0	2	0	0	0	0	2	0	.000	.000
Sub	Harry Decker	5	23	5	0	1	1	0	2	1	0	.217	.348
Sub	Ed Whiting	6	21	0	0	0	0	0	0	1	0	.000	.000
P	Hank O'Day	6	19	1	0	0	0	0	0	0	0	.053	.053
Sub	Walt Goldsby	6	18	4	0	1	0	0	1	2	0	.222	.278
P	One Arm Daily	6	16	2	2	0	0	0	1	2	0	.125	.125
Sub	John McGlone	4	15	1	2	0	0	0	1	0	0	.067	.067
P	John Henry	4	14	5	3	0	0	0	0	0	0	.357	.357
P	George Keefe	4	14	0	1	0	0	0	0	0	0	.000	.000
Sub	Tom Kinslow	3	8	2	1	0	0	0	1	0	0	.250	.250
P	Ed Fuller	2	7	1	0	0	0	0	0	0	0	.143	.143
Sub	Jim Gallagher	1	5	1	1	0	0	0	0	0	0	.200	.200
P	George Winkelman	1	5	1	0	0	0	0	0	0	0	.200	.200
P	John Fox	1	3	1	0	0	0	0	0	0	0	.333	.333
P	Bill Wise	1	3	0	0	0	0	0	0	0	0	.000	.000
P	Joe Yingling	1	2	0	0	0	0	0	0	0	0	.000	.000
Sub	? Joyce	1	0	0	0	0	0	0	0	0	0	—	—
		125	4082	856	445	135	51	23	332	265	143	.210	.285

1B	Baker 56, Start 31, Krieg 27, Hines 10
2B	Knowles 62, Farrell 47, Force 8, Hines 3, Houck 1, Hayes 1
SS	Force 56, Houck 51, Corcoran 9, Hines 5, Gilligan 1, Shoch 1, Decker 1, Gallagher 1
3B	Knowles 53, Gladman 44, Hines 15, McGlone 4, Force 4, Decker 2, Gilligan 1
OF	Carroll 111, Hines 92, Crane 68, Shoch 25, Baker 21, Gilligan 14, Hayes 12, Corcoran 11, Oldfield 9, Goldsby 6, Shaw 1, Madigan 1, Winkelman 1, Fuller 1, Joyce 1
C	Gilligan 71, Baker 16, Hayes 14, Oldfield 12, Mack 10, Whiting 6, Decker 4, Crane 4, Kinslow 3
P	Shaw 45, Barr 23, Madigan 14, Crane 10, Gilmore 9, O'Day 6, Daily 6, Keefe 4, Henry 4, Fuller 2, Corcoran 2, Wise 1, Winkelman 1, Yingling 1, Fox 1

	G	IP	GS	CG	W	L	K	BB	SH	SV	ERA
Dupee Shaw	45	385.2	44	43	13	31	177	91	1	0	3.34
Bob Barr	23	191.2	23	21	3	18	80	54	1	0	4.41
Tony Madigan	14	114.2	13	13	1	13	29	44	0	0	4.87
Frank Gilmore	9	75	9	9	4	4	75	22	1	0	2.52
Cannonball Crane	10	70	8	7	1	7	39	53	1	0	7.20
One Arm Daily	6	49	6	6	0	6	15	40	0	0	7.35
Hank O'Day	6	49	6	6	2	2	47	17	0	0	1.65
George Keefe	4	31.1	4	4	0	3	5	15	0	0	5.17
John Henry	4	27.2	4	4	1	3	19	15	0	0	4.23
Larry Corcoran	2	14	1	1	0	1	3	4	0	0	5.79
Ed Fuller	2	13	1	1	0	1	3	5	0	0	6.92
John Fox	1	8	1	1	0	1	3	11	0	0	9.00
George Winkelman	1	6	1	0	0	1	4	5	0	0	10.50
Bill Wise	1	3	1	0	0	1	0	2	0	0	9.00
Joe Yingling	1	3	0	0	0	0	1	1	0	0	12.00
	—3 forfeit Ws on: October 7, 8 and 9 vs Kansas City—										
	1041	122	116	25	92	500	379	4	0	4.30

WORLD'S SERIES

St. Louis (AA) defeated Chicago (NL) 4 games to 2

Game 1 at West Side Park (Chi), Oct. 18: Chi (Clarkson) 6, StL (Foutz) 0
Game 2 at West Side Park (Chi), Oct. 19: StL (Caruthers) 12, Chi (McCormick) 0
Game 3 at West Side Park (Chi), Oct. 20: Chi (Clarkson) 11, StL (Caruthers) 4
Game 4 at Sportsman's Park (StL), Oct. 21: StL (Foutz) 8, Chi (Clarkson) 5
Game 5 at Sportsman's Park (StL), Oct. 22: StL (Hudson) 10, Chi (Williamson) 3
Game 6 at Sportsman's Park (StL), Oct. 23: StL (Caruthers) 4, Chi (Clarkson) 3 (10 innings)

ST. LOUIS

		G	AB	H	R	2B	3B	HR	RBI	BB	BA	SA
1B	Charlie Comiskey	6	24	7	2	1	0	0	2	0	.292	.333
P/RF	Bob Caruthers	6	24	6	6	1	2	0	5	1	.250	.458
SS	Bill Gleason	6	24	5	3	0	0	0	5	1	.250	.250
3B/C	Arlie Latham	6	23	4	4	0	1	0	3	3	.174	.261
LF	Tip O'Neill	6	20	8	4	0	2	2	2	4	**.400**	**.900**
CF	Curt Welch	6	20	7	7	2	0	0	1	3	.350	.450
2B	Yank Robinson	6	19	6	5	1	1	0	3	2	.316	.474
C	Doc Bushong	6	16	3	4	1	0	0	2	4	.188	.250
P/RF	Dave Foutz	4	15	3	2	1	1	0	3	0	.200	.400
P/RF	Nat Hudson	2	6	1	1	0	1	0	0	1	.167	.500
		7	191	50	38	7	8	2	29	19	.262	.414

	G	IP	GS	CG	W	L	K	BB	SH	SV	ERA
Bob Caruthers	3	26	3	3	2	1	12	6	1	0	2.42
Dave Foutz	2	15	2	2	1	1	7	6	0	0	3.60
Nat Hudson	1	7	1	1	1	0	3	3	0	0	2.57
		48	6	6	4	2	22	15	1	0	2.81

CHICAGO

		G	AB	H	R	2B	3B	HR	RBI	BB	BA	SA
C/UT	King Kelly	6	24	5	4	0	0	1	1	2	.208	.333
CF	George Gore	6	23	4	4	0	0	1	2	3	.174	.304
2B	Fred Pfeffer	6	21	6	7	0	0	1	4	2	.286	.429
3B/RF	Tom Burns	6	21	6	2	2	1	0	1	0	.286	.476
1B/C	Cap Anson	6	21	5	3	1	0	0	1	4	.238	.286
LF	Abner Dalrymple	6	21	4	2	1	1	0	2	0	.190	.333
RF/UT	Jimmy Ryan	6	20	5	4	1	0	0	2	0	.250	.300
SS/UT	Ned Williamson	6	18	1	2	0	1	0	3	4	.056	.167
P/RF	John Clarkson	4	15	1	0	0	0	0	1	0	.067	.067
C	Silver Flint	1	3	0	0	0	0	0	1	0	.000	.000
P	Jim McCormick	1	3	0	0	0	0	0	0	0	.000	.000
		6	190	37	28	5	3	3	18	15	.195	.257

	G	IP	GS	CG	W	L	K	BB	SH	SV	ERA
John Clarkson	4	31.1	4	3	2	2	28	12	1	0	2.01
Jim McCormick	1	8	1	1	0	1	4	2	0	0	6.75
Jimmy Ryan	1	5	0	0	0	0	4	4	0	0	9.00
Ned Williamson	2	2	1	0	0	1	2	1	0	0	4.50
		46.1	6	4	2	4	38	19	1	0	3.69

AMERICAN ASSOCIATION

	W	L	PCT	HOME	ROAD	GB
1. St. Louis Browns	93	46	.669	52–18	41–28	—
2. Pittsburgh Alleghenys	80	57	.584	45–28	35–29	12
3. Brooklyn Grays	76	61	.555	45–25	31–36	16
4. Louisville Colonels	66	70	.485	37–30	29–40	25.5
5. Cincinnati Reds	65	73	.471	40–31	25–42	27.5
6. Philadelphia Athletics	63	72	.467	37–31	26–41	28
7. New York Metropolitans	53	82	.393	30–33	23–49	38
8. Baltimore Orioles	48	83	.366	30–32	18–51	41

	StL	Pit	Bro	Lou	Cin	Phi	NY	Bal	
St. Louis	—	12	13	9	15	15	16	13	93
Pittsburgh	8	—	12	12	13	11	12	12	80
Brooklyn	7	8	—	13	13	11	10	14	76
Louisville	10	7	7	—	10	9	11	12	66
Cincinnati	5	7	7	10	—	10	13	13	65
Philadelphia	5	8	7	11	10	—	12	10	63
New York	4	8	9	8	7	8		9	53
Baltimore	7	7	6	7	5	8	8	—	48
	46	57	61	70	73	72	82	83	544

SEASON LEADERS

Batting Average (300 ABs)

1.	Hecker, Louisville	.341
2.	Browning, Louisville	.340
3.	Orr, New York	.338
4.	Caruthers, St. Louis	.334
5.	O'Neill, St. Louis	.328

On–Base Percentage

1.	Caruthers, St. Louis	.463
2.	Hecker, Louisville	.402
3.	Larkin, Philadelphia	.390
4.	Browning, Louisville	.389
5.	O'Neill, St. Louis	.385

Home Runs

1.	McPhee, Cincinnati	8
2.	Stovey, Philadelphia	7
	Orr, New York	7
4.	Fennelly, Cincinnati	6
5.	F. Carroll, Pittsburgh	5
	Roseman, New York	5
	C. Jones, Cincinnati	5
	Milligan, Philadelphia	5

Hits

1.	Orr, New York	193
2.	O'Neill, St. Louis	190
3.	Larkin, Philadelphia	180
4.	Latham, St,. Louis	174
5.	Phillips, Brooklyn	160

Slugging Average

1.	Orr, New York	.5271
2.	Caruthers, St. Louis	.5268
3.	Larkin, Philadelphia	.450
4.	Hecker, Louisville	.446
5.	Browning, Louisville	.441

Total Bases

1.	Orr, New York	301
2.	O'Neill, St. Louis	255
3.	Larkin, Philadelphia	254
4.	Welch, St. Louis	221
5.	McPhee, Cincinnati	217

Stolen Bases

1.	Stovey, Philadelphia	68
2.	Latham, St. Louis	60
3.	Welch, St. Louis	59
4.	Robinson, St. Louis	51
5.	McClellan, Brooklyn	43

Runs

1.	Latham St. Louis	152
2.	McPhee, Cincinnati	139
3.	Larkin, Philadelphia	133
4.	McClellan, Brooklyn	131
5.	Pinkney, Brooklyn	119

Bases on Balls

1.	Swartwood, Brooklyn	70
	Pinkney, Brooklyn	70
3.	Mack, Louisville	68
4.	Kerins, Louisville	66
5.	Four with	64

RBI

1.	O'Neill, St. Louis	107
2.	Corkhill, Cincinatti	97
3.	Welch, St. Louis	95
4.	Orr, New York	91
5.	Reilly, Cincinnati	79

PITCHING

Wins

1.	Morris, Pittsburgh	41
	Foutz, St. Louis	41
3.	Ramsey, Louisville	38
4.	Mullane, Cincinnati	33
5.	Caruthers, St. Louis	30

Losses

1.	Kilroy, Baltimore	34
2.	Lynch, New York	30
3.	Mays, New York	27
	Mullane, Cincinnati	27
	Ramsey, Louisville	27

Innings

1.	Ramsey, Louisville	588.2
2.	Kilroy, Baltimore	583
3.	Morris, Pittsburgh	555.1
4.	Mullane, Cincinnati	529.2
5.	Foutz, St. Louis	504

Complete games

1.	Ramsey, Louisville	66
	Kilroy, Baltimore	66
3.	Morris, Pittsburgh	63
4.	Mullane, Cincinnati	55
	Foutz, St. Louis	55

Strikeouts

1.	Kilroy, Baltimore	513
2.	Ramsey, Louisville	499
3.	Morris, Pittsburgh	326
4.	Foutz, St. Louis	283
5.	Mullane, Cincinnati	250

Winning Percentage (25 decisions)

1.	Foutz, St. Louis	.719
2.	Caruthers, St. Louis	.682
3.	Morris, Pittsburgh	.672
4.	Hudson, St. Louis	.615
5.	Atkinson, Philadelphia	.595

ERA (140 Innings)

1.	Foutz, St. Louis	2.11
2.	Caruthers, St. Louis	2.32
3.	Ramsey, Louisville	2.45
	Morris, Pittsburgh	2.45
5.	Galvin, Pittsburgh	2.67

Lowest On–Base Percentage

1.	Morris, Pittsburgh	.258
2.	Caruthers, St. Louis	.263
3.	Ramsey, Louisville	.269
4.	Foutz, St. Louis	.274
	Kilroy, Baltimore	.274

FIELDING

Total Chances

1B	Orr, New York	1507
2B	McPhee, Cincinnati	1058
3B	Hankinson, New York	469
SS	Fennelly, Cincinnati	771
OF	Welch, St. Louis	332
C	Bushong, St. Louis	829
P	Kilroy, Baltimore	176

Fielding Average

	Orr, New York	.981
	McPhee, Cincinnati	.939
	Whitney, Pittsburgh	.906
	P. Smith, Pittsburgh	.895
	Welch, St. Louis	.952
	Bushong, St. Louis	.942
	Foutz, St. Louis	.949

ST. LOUIS   **Charlie Comiskey**   **Sportsman's Park (I)**

		G	AB	H	R	2B	3B	HR	RBI	BB	SB	BA	SA
LF	Tip O'Neill	138	579	190	106	28	14	3	**107**	47	9	.328	.440
3B	Arlie Latham	134	578	174	**152**	23	8	1	47	55	60	.301	.374
1B	Charlie Comiskey	131	578	147	95	15	9	3	76	10	41	.254	.327
CF	Curt Welch	138	563	158	114	31	13	2	95	29	59	.281	.393
SS	Bill Gleason	125	524	141	97	18	5	0	61	43	19	.269	.323
2B	Yank Robinson	133	481	132	89	26	9	3	71	64	51	.274	.385
P	Dave Foutz	102	414	116	66	18	9	3	59	9	17	.280	.389
C	Doc Bushong	107	386	86	56	8	0	1	31	31	12	.223	.251
P	Bob Caruthers	87	317	106	91	21	14	4	61	64	26	.334	.527
RF	Hugh Nicol	67	253	52	44	6	3	0	19	26	38	.206	.253
P	Nate Hudson	43	150	35	16	4	1	0	17	11	2	.233	.273
Sub	Rudy Kemmler	35	123	17	13	2	0	0	6	8	0	.138	.154
P	Jumbo McGinnis	10	37	7	4	2	0	0	4	3	1	.189	.243
Sub	Trick McSorley	5	20	3	1	3	0	0	0	0	0	.150	.300
Sub	Lou Harding	1	3	1	0	1	0	0	1	0	0	.333	.667
P	Joe Murphy	1	3	0	0	0	0	0	0	0	1	.000	.000
		139	5009	**1365**	**944**	**206**	85	20	655	400	**336**	**.273**	**.360**

1B   Comiskey 122, Foutz 11, Kemmler 3, Hudson 3, Bushong 1
2B   Robinson 125, Comiskey 9, Nicol 4, Welch 2, Caruthers 2, Latham 1
SS   Gleason 125, Nicol 8, McSorley 5, Robinson 1
3B   Latham 133, Robinson 6
OF   Welch 138, O'Neill 138, Nicol 57, Caruthers 43, Foutz 34, Hudson 12, Comiskey 2, Robinson 1
C   Bushong 106, Kemmler 32, Harding 1
P   Foutz 59, Caruthers 44, Hudson 29, McGinnis 10, Murphy 1, Robinson 1

	G	IP	GS	CG	W	L	K	BB	SH	SV	ERA
Dave Foutz	59	504	57	55	**41**	16	283	144	11	**1**	**2.11**
Bob Caruthers	44	387.1	43	42	30	14	166	86	2	0	2.32
Nat Hudson	29	234.1	27	25	16	10	100	62	0	1	3.03
Jumbo McGinnis	10	87.2	10	10	5	5	30	27	1	0	3.80
Yank Robinson	1	9	1	1	0	1	1	7	0	0	3.00
Joe Murphy	1	7	1	1	1	0	3	3	0	0	3.86
		1229.1	139	134	93	46	583	329	14	**2**	**2.49**

PITTSBURGH Horace Phillips **Recreation Park**

		G	AB	H	R	2B	3B	HR	RBI	BB	SB	BA	SA
3B	Art Whitney	136	511	122	70	13	4	0	55	51	15	.239	.280
C	Fred Carroll	122	486	140	92	28	11	5	64	52	20	.288	.422
SS	Pop Smith	126	483	105	75	20	9	2	57	42	38	.217	.308
UT	Willie Kuehne	117	481	98	73	16	17	1	49	19	26	.204	.314
2B	Sam Barkley	122	478	127	77	31	8	1	69	58	22	.266	.370
RF	Tom Brown	115	460	131	106	11	11	1	51	56	30	.285	.363
CF	Fred Mann	116	440	110	85	16	14	2	60	45	26	.250	.364
C	Doggie Miller	83	317	80	70	15	1	2	36	43	35	.252	.325
LF	Ed Glenn	71	277	53	32	6	5	0	26	17	19	.191	.249
1B	Otto Schomberg	72	246	67	53	6	6	1	29	57	7	.272	.358
P	Ed Morris	64	227	38	26	8	3	1	24	10	6	.167	.242
P	Pud Galvin	50	194	49	24	7	2	0	21	3	8	.253	.309
Sub	Frank Ringo	15	56	12	3	2	2	0	5	1	0	.214	.321
P	Frank Mountain	18	55	8	6	1	1	0	2	13	3	.145	.200
P	Jim Handiboe	14	44	5	10	1	0	0	2	6	1	.114	.136
Sub	John Coleman	11	43	15	3	2	1	0	9	2	1	.349	.442
P	John Hofford	9	34	10	4	3	1	0	5	3	2	.294	.441
Sub	Tom Quinn	3	11	0	1	0	0	0	0	0	0	.000	.000
P	Bill Bishop	2	7	1	0	0	0	0	0	0	0	.143	.143
Sub	Dan Sullivan	1	4	0	0	0	0	0	0	0	0	.000	.000
		140	4854	1171	810	186	**96**	16	564	**478**	260	.241	.329

1B Schomberg 72, Carroll 25, Kuehne 18, Mountain 16, Ringo 9, Barkley 2
2B Barkley 112, Smith 28, Miller 1
SS Smith 98, Whitney 42, Carroll 1
3B Whitney 95, Kuehne 47
OF Mann 116, Brown 115, Glenn 71, Kuehne 54, Carroll 27, Miller 23, Coleman 11, Barkley 8, Handiboe 2
C Carroll 70, Miller 61, Ringo 6, Quinn 3, Smith 1, Sullivan 1
P Morris 64, Galvin 50, Handiboe 14, Hofford 9, Mountain 2, Bishop 2, Whitney 1, Brown 1

	G	IP	GS	CG	W	L	K	BB	SH	SV	ERA
Ed Morris	64	555.1	63	63	**41**	20	326	118	**12**	1	2.45
Pud Galvin	50	434.2	50	49	29	21	72	75	2	0	2.67
Jim Handiboe	14	114	14	12	7	7	83	33	1	0	3.32
John Hofford	9	81	9	9	3	6	25	40	0	0	4.33
Bill Bishop	2	17	2	2	0	1	4	11	0	0	3.18
Frank Mountain	2	16	2	2	0	2	2	14	0	0	7.88
Art Whitney	1	6	0	0	0	0	2	3	0	0	3.00
Tom Brown	1	2	0	0	0	0	1	5	0	0	9.00
		1226	140	137	80	57	515	**299**	15	1	2.83

BROOKLYN Charlie Byrne **Washington Park (I)**

		G	AB	H	R	2B	3B	HR	RBI	BB	SB	BA	SA
3B	George Pinkney	141	**597**	156	119	22	7	0	37	**70**	32	.261	.322
2B	Bill McClellan	141	595	152	131	33	9	1	71	56	43	.255	.346
1B	Bill Phillips	141	585	160	68	26	15	0	72	33	13	.274	.369
RF	Ed Swartwood	122	471	132	95	13	10	3	58	70	37	.280	.369
LF	Ernie Burch	113	456	119	78	22	6	2	72	39	16	.261	.349
SS	Germany Smith	105	426	105	66	17	6	2	45	19	22	.246	.329
CF	Jim McTamany	111	418	106	86	23	10	2	56	54	18	.254	.371
C	Jimmy Peoples	93	340	74	43	7	3	3	38	20	20	.218	.282
P	Adonis Terry	75	299	71	34	8	9	2	39	10	17	.237	.344
C	Bob Clark	71	269	58	37	8	2	0	26	17	14	.216	.260
P	Henry Porter	48	184	33	20	4	0	0	13	4	3	.179	.201

		G	AB	H	R	2B	3B	HR	RBI	BB	SB	BA	SA
P	John Harkins	41	142	32	18	4	2	1	15	17	2	.225	.303
P	Steve Toole	14	57	20	7	4	0	0	9	1	3	.351	.421
Sub	Dave Oldfield	14	55	13	7	1	0	0	5	2	1	.236	.255
P	Hardie Henderson	14	50	9	9	2	0	0	6	5	0	.180	.220
Sub	Joe Strauss	9	36	9	6	1	1	0	5	1	4	.250	.333
Sub	Jim McCauley	11	30	7	5	1	0	0	3	11	2	.233	.267
Sub	Eddie Kennedy	6	22	4	1	0	0	0	2	2	1	.182	.182
Sub	Pop Schriver	8	21	1	2	0	0	0	0	2	0	.048	.048
		141	5053	1261	832	196	80	16	572	433	248	.250	.330

1B Phillips 141
2B McClellan 141
SS Smith 105, Peoples 14, Terry 13, Clark 12, Oldfield 1
3B Pinkney 141, Peoples 1
OF Swartwood 122, Burch 113, McTamany 111, Terry 32, Clark 17, Peoples 8, Harkins 8, Strauss 7, Kennedy 6, Schriver 5, Toole 3, Oldfield 1, Smith 1
C   Peoples 76, Clark 44, Oldfield 13, McCauley 11, Schriver 3, Strauss 2, Swartwood 1, Smith 1
P   Porter 48, Harkins 34, Terry 34, Henderson 14, Toole 13, Pinkney 1

	G	IP	GS	CG	W	L	K	BB	SH	SV	ERA
Henry Porter	48	424	48	48	27	19	163	120	1	0	3.42
John Harkins	34	292.1	33	33	15	16	118	114	0	0	3.60
Adonis Terry #	34	288.1	34	32	18	16	162	115	5	0	3.09
Hardie Henderson	14	124	14	14	10	4	49	51	0	0	2.90
Steve Toole	13	104	12	11	6	6	48	64	0	0	4.41
George Pinkney	1	2	0	0	0	0	0	0	0	0	4.50
		1234.2	141	138	76	61	540	464	6	0	3.42

No-hit game 1–0 vs St. Louis, July 24

LOUISVILLE   Jim Hart   Eclipse Park (I)

		G	AB	H	R	2B	3B	HR	RBI	BB	SB	BA	SA
3B	Joe Werrick	136	561	140	75	20	14	3	62	33	19	.250	.351
SS	Bill White	135	557	143	96	17	10	1	66	37	14	.257	.329
RF	Chicken Wolf	130	545	148	93	17	12	3	61	27	23	.272	.363
C	John Kerins	120	487	131	113	19	9	4	50	66	26	.269	.370
2B	Reddy Mack	137	483	118	82	23	11	1	56	68	13	.244	.344
CF	Pete Browning	112	467	159	86	29	6	2	68	30	26	.340	.441
P	Guy Hecker	84	343	117	76	14	5	4	48	32	25	**.341**	.446
LF	Joe Strauss	74	297	64	36	5	6	1	31	8	25	.215	.283
C	Amos Cross	74	283	78	51	14	6	1	42	44	13	.276	.378
1B	Paul Cook	66	262	54	28	5	2	0	14	10	6	.206	.240
P	Toad Ramsey	67	241	58	29	8	1	0	28	6	1	.241	.282
Sub	Lou Sylvester	45	154	35	41	5	3	0	17	29	3	.227	.299
Sub	Hub Collins	27	101	29	12	3	2	0	10	5	7	.287	.356
Sub	Bones Ely	10	32	5	5	0	0	0	6	2	1	.156	.156
P	Tom Sullivan	9	27	3	1	0	0	0	0	4	0	.158	.211
Sub	Leech Maskrey	5	19	3	1	1	0	0	2	0	1	.158	.211
P	Icebox Chamberlain	6	19	3	2	0	0	0	1	4	0	.158	.158
Sub	Phil Reccius	5	13	4	4	1	1	0	1	3	0	.308	.538
P	Ted Kennedy	4	13	1	1	1	0	0	0	1	0	.077	.154
Sub	John Heinzman	1	5	0	1	0	0	0	0	0	0	.000	.000
P	Joe Neale	2	5	0	0	0	0	0	0	0	0	.000	.000
Sub	Tom Terrell	1	4	1	0	0	0	0	0	0	0	.250	.250
Sub	Clarence Murphy	1	3	0	0	0	0	0	0	0	0	.000	.000
		138	4921	1294	833	182	88	20	564	410	202	.263	.348

1B   Kerins 47, Cook 43, Hecker 22, Cross 20, Wolf 8, Heinzman 1, Collins 1
2B   Mack 137, Wolf 1, Collins 1
SS   White 135, Kerins 1, Cross 2, Collins 1
3B   Werrick 136, Collins 2
OF   Wolf 122, Browning 112, Strauss 73, Sylvester 45, Collins 24, Hecker 17, Kerins 7, Maskrey 5, Reccius 5, Ely 5, Cook 2, Chamberlain 2, Neale 2, Cross 1, Sullivan 1, Murphy 1, Terrell 1
C   Kerins 65, Cross 51, Cook 21, Wolf 3, Strauss 1, Terrell 1
P   Ramsey 67, Hecker 52, Sullivan 9, Ely 6, Chamberlain 4, Kennedy 4, Strauss 2, Reccius 1, White 1, Wolf 1, Neale 1, Reccius 1

	G	IP	GS	CG	W	L	K	BB	SH	SV	ERA
Toad Ramsey	67	**588.2**	67	**66**	38	27	499	**207**	3	0	2.45
Guy Hecker	52	420.2	48	45	26	23	133	118	2	0	2.87
Tom Sullivan	9	75	9	8	2	7	27	33	0	0	3.96
Bones Ely	6	44	4	4	0	4	28	26	0	1	5.32
Ted Kennedy	4	32	4	4	0	4	14	16	0	0	5.34
Icebox Chamberlain	4	31.1	4	4	0	3	18	17	0	0	6.61
Joe Neale	1	7	1	0	0	1	0	7	0	0	7.71
Joe Strauss	2	4	0	0	0	0	0	3	0	1	4.50
Chicken Wolf	1	3	0	0	0	0	0	0	0	0	15.00
Phil Reccius	1	3	1	0	0	1	0	3	0	0	9.00
Bill White	1	1	0	0	0	0	1	2	0	0	9.00
		1209.2	138	131	66	70	720	432	5	**2**	3.07

CINCINNATI   Opie Caylor   American Park

		G	AB	H	R	2B	3B	HR	RBI	BB	SB	BA	SA
2B	Bid McPhee	140	560	150	139	23	12	**8**	70	59	40	.268	.395
RF	Pop Corkhill	129	540	143	81	9	7	5	97	23	24	.265	.333
LF	Charley Jones	127	500	135	87	22	10	6	68	61	3	.270	.390
SS	Frank Fennelly	132	497	124	113	13	17	6	72	60	32	.249	.380
3B	Hick Carpenter	111	458	101	67	8	5	2	61	18	8	.221	.273
1B	Long John Reilly	115	441	117	92	12	11	4	79	31	19	.265	.370
CF	Fred Lewis	77	324	103	72	14	6	2	32	20	8	.318	.417
P	Tony Mullane	91	324	73	59	12	5	0	39	25	20	.225	.293
C	Kid Baldwin	87	315	72	41	8	7	3	32	8	12	.229	.327
C	Pop Snyder	60	220	41	33	8	3	0	28	13	11	.186	.250
Sub	Jim Keenan	44	148	40	31	4	3	3	24	18	0	.270	.399
P	George Pechiney	41	144	30	14	4	2	1	21	6	1	.208	.285
Sub	Leech Maskrey	27	98	19	7	3	1	0	10	5	4	.194	.245
P	Larry McKeon	19	75	19	9	2	3	0	9	0	0	.253	.360
P	Abner Powell	19	74	17	13	1	1	0	8	4	0	.230	.270
Sub	Lou Sylvester	17	55	10	10	0	0	3	8	7	2	.182	.345
Sub	Lee Richmond	8	29	8	3	0	0	0	3	3	0	.276	.276
Sub	Lefty Marr	8	29	8	2	1	1	0	2	1	1	.276	.379
P	Elmer Smith	9	28	8	6	1	1	0	2	9	0	.286	.393
P	Joe Murphy	5	18	0	0	0	0	0	0	0	0	.000	.000
P	Will White	3	9	1	1	0	0	0	1	1	0	.111	.111
P	Bill Irwin	2	6	0	0	0	0	0	0	1	0	.000	.000
P	Clarence Stephens	1	5	3	0	0	0	0	0	0	0	.600	.600
Sub	Jack Boyle	1	5	1	0	0	0	0	0	0	0	.200	.200
P	? Smith	1	4	1	1	0	0	0	0	0	0	.250	.250
P	Dan Bickham	1	3	1	2	0	0	0	0	1	0	.333	.333
Sub	Farmer Vaughn	1	3	0	0	0	0	0	0	0	0	.000	.000
P	Jim Reardon	1	3	0	0	0	0	0	0	0	0	.000	.000
		141	4915	1225	883	145	95	**45**	666	374	185	.249	.345

1B   Reilly 110, Snyder 19, Corkhill 7, Keenan 4, Mullane 4, McKeon 2
2B   McPhee 140, Mullane 1, McKeon 1
SS   Fennelly 132, Powell 6, Corkhill 3, Mullane 1
3B   Carpenter 111, Baldwin 13, Corkhill 12, Keenan 5, Maskrey 2, Mullane 2, Lewis 1
OF   Jones 127, Corkhill 112, Lewis 76, Mullane 27, Maskrey 26, Sylvester 17, Powell 13, Marr 8, Richmond 7, Keenan 7, Reilly 6, Baldwin 6, Pechiney 4, Snyder 1, Reardon 1, E. Smith 1
C   Baldwin 71, Snyder 41, Keenan 30, Boyle 1, Vaughn 1
P   Mullane 63, Pechiney 40, McKeon 19, E. Smith 9, Murphy 5, Powell 4, Richmond 3, White 3, Keenan 2, Irwin 2, Bickham 1, Reardon 1, Stephens 1, Corkhill 1, ? Smith 1

	G	IP	GS	CG	W	L	K	BB	SH	SV	ERA
Tony Mullane	63	529.2	56	55	33	27	250	166	1	0	3.70
George Pechiney	40	330.1	40	35	15	21	110	133	2	0	4.14
Larry McKeon	19	156	19	16	8	8	46	54	0	0	5.08
Elmer Smith	9	72.2	9	8	4	4	40	44	0	0	3.96
Joe Murphy	5	46	5	5	2	3	11	21	0	0	4.89
Will White	3	26	3	3	1	2	6	10	0	0	4.15
Lee Richmond	3	18	2	1	0	2	6	11	0	0	8.00
Bill Irwin	2	17	2	2	0	2	6	8	0	0	5.82
Abner Powell	4	15.1	1	1	0	1	4	9	0	0	4.70
? Smith	1	9	1	1	0	1	1	10	0	0	2.00
Dan Bickham	1	9	1	1	1	0	6	3	0	0	3.00
Jim Keenan	2	8	0	0	0	1	2	3	0	0	3.38
Clarence Stephens	1	8	1	1	1	0	6	5	0	0	5.63
Jim Reardon	1	2	1	0	0	1	0	4	0	0	18.00
Pop Corkhill	1	0.2	0	0	0	0	1	0	0	0	13.50
	1247.2	141	129	65	73	495	481	3	0	4.18	

PHILADELPHIA   **Lew Simmons (41–55)**   **Bill Sharsig (22–17)**   **Jefferson Street Grounds**

		G	AB	H	R	2B	3B	HR	RBI	BB	SB	BA	SA
LF	Henry Larkin	139	565	180	133	**36**	16	2	74	59	32	.319	.450
2B	Lou Bierbauer	137	522	118	56	17	5	2	47	21	19	.226	.289
RF	John Coleman	121	492	121	67	18	16	0	65	33	28	.246	.348
1B	Harry Stovey	123	489	144	115	28	11	7	59	64	**68**	.294	.440
UT	Jack O'Brien	105	423	107	65	25	7	0	56	38	23	.253	.345
C	Wilbert Robinson	87	342	69	57	11	3	1	30	21	33	.202	.260
C	Jocko Milligan	75	301	76	52	17	3	5	45	21	18	.252	.379
3B	Jack Gleason	77	299	56	39	8	7	1	31	16	8	.187	.271
SS	Chippy McGarr	71	267	71	41	9	3	2	31	9	17	.266	.345
CF	Ed Greer	71	264	51	33	5	3	1	20	8	12	.193	.246
Sub	Joe Quest	42	150	31	14	4	1	0	10	20	5	.207	.247
P	Al Atkinson	45	148	18	27	1	1	0	9	26	4	.122	.142
Sub	Denny Lyons	32	123	26	22	3	1	0	11	8	7	.211	.252
P	Bobby Mathews	24	88	21	16	3	0	0	10	3	1	.239	.273
Sub	Orator Shaffer	21	82	22	15	3	3	0	8	8	3	.268	.378
P	Bill Hart	22	73	10	3	1	1	0	1	3	1	.137	.178
P	Ted Kennedy	20	68	3	3	0	0	0	0	3	0	.044	.044
P	Cyclone Miller	21	66	9	8	2	0	0	1	14	3	.136	.167
Sub	George Bradley	13	48	4	1	0	1	0	1	1	2	.083	.125
Sub	John Irwin	3	13	3	4	1	0	0	1	0	0	.231	.308
P	Sam Weaver	2	7	1	0	0	0	0	0	0	0	.143	.143
P	Jake Aydelott	2	6	0	0	0	0	0	0	1	0	.000	.000
P	Charlie Gessner	1	4	1	1	0	0	0	0	0	0	.250	.250
P	Rex Smith	1	4	0	0	0	0	0	0	0	0	.000	.000
P	Jim Hyndman	1	4	0	0	0	0	0	0	0	0	.000	.000
P	Jim Brown	1	3	0	0	0	0	0	0	0	0	.000	.000

		G	AB	H	R	2B	3B	HR	RBI	BB	SB	BA	SA
Sub	Charlie Kelly	1	3	0	0	0	0	0	0	0	0	.000	.000
P	Ed Clark	1	2	0	0	0	0	0	0	1	0	.000	.000
		139	4856	1142	772	192	82	21	510	378	284	.235	.321

1B   Stovey 62, Milligan 29, O'Brien 24, Robinson 22, Coleman 6, Weaver 1
2B   Bierbauer 133, O'Brien 7, Quest 2, Coleman 1
SS   McGarr 71, Quest 41, Bradley 13, O'Brien 10, Bierbauer 2, Irwin 2, Kelly 1
3B   Gleason 77, Lyons 32, O'Brien 27, Milligan 3, Irwin 1
OF   Larkin 139, Coleman 115, Greer 69, Stovey 63, Shaffer 21, Milligan 5, Robinson 5, O'Brien 3, Hyndman 1, Miller 1, Mathews 1
C   Robinson 61, Milligan 40, O'Brien 36, Bierbauer 4, Greer 2
P   Atkinson 45, Mathews 24, Hart 22, Kennedy 20, Miller 19, Coleman 3, Weaver 2, Aydelott 2, Bierbauer 2, Stovey 1, Gessner 1, Clark 1, Smith 1, Brown 1, Hyndman 1

	G	IP	GS	CG	W	L	K	BB	SH	SV	ERA
Al Atkinson #	45	396.2	45	44	25	17	154	101	1	0	3.95
Bobby Mathews	24	197.2	24	22	13	9	93	53	0	0	3.96
Bill Hart	22	186	22	22	9	13	78	66	2	0	3.19
Ted Kennedy	20	172.2	19	19	5	15	68	65	0	0	4.53
Cyclone Miller	19	169.2	19	19	10	8	99	59	1	0	2.97
John Coleman	3	20.2	1	1	1	1	2	5	0	0	2.61
Jake Aydelott	2	18	2	2	0	2	5	12	0	0	4.00
Sam Weaver	2	11	2	1	0	2	2	2	0	0	14.73
Lou Bierbauer	2	10.2	0	0	0	0	1	5	0	0	4.22
Rex Smith	1	9	1	1	0	1	4	5	0	0	7.00
Jim Brown	1	8	1	1	0	1	4	3	0	0	3.24
Charlie Gessner	1	8	1	1	0	1	0	5	0	0	9.00
Ed Clark	1	8	1	1	0	1	2	2	0	0	6.75
Jim Hyndman	1	2	1	0	0	1	1	5	0	0	27.00
Harry Stovey	1	0.1	0	0	0	0	0	0	0	0	27.00
		1218.2	139	134	63	72	513	388	4	0	3.97

No-hit game 3–2 vs New York, May 1

NEW YORK   **Jim Gifford (5–12)**   **Bob Ferguson (48–70)**   **St. George Grounds**

		G	AB	H	R	2B	3B	HR	RBI	BB	SB	BA	SA
1B	Dave Orr	136	571	**193**	93	25	**31**	7	91	17	16	.338	**.527**
LF	Chief Roseman	134	559	127	90	19	10	5	53	24	6	.227	.324
3B	Frank Hankinson	136	522	126	66	14	5	2	63	49	10	.241	.299
RF	Steve Brady	124	466	112	56	8	5	0	39	35	16	.240	.279
SS	Candy Nelson	109	413	93	89	7	2	0	24	64	14	.225	.252
2B	Tom Forster	67	251	49	33	3	2	1	20	20	9	.195	.235
Sub	Tom McLaughlin	74	250	34	27	3	1	0	16	26	13	.136	.156
C	Charlie Reipschlager	65	232	49	21	8	3	0	25	9	2	.211	.280
CF	Steve Behel	59	224	46	32	5	2	0	17	22	16	.205	.246
Sub	John Meister	45	186	44	35	7	3	2	21	4	1	.237	.339
Sub	Jim Donahue	49	186	37	14	0	0	0	9	10	1	.199	.199
C	Bill Holbert	48	171	35	8	4	2	0	13	6	4	.205	.251
P	Jack Lynch	51	169	27	17	5	0	0	9	15	4	.160	.189
P	Al Mays	41	135	16	11	3	1	1	10	4	2	.119	.178
P	Ed Cushman	38	126	19	10	1	0	0	5	9	0	.151	.159
Sub	Elmer Foster	35	125	23	16	0	1	0	7	7	3	.184	.200
Sub	Joe Crotty	14	47	8	6	0	1	0	2	4	3	.170	.213
P	John Shaffer	8	25	6	3	0	0	0	1	4	0	.240	.240
Sub	Chief Zimmer	6	19	3	1	0	0	0	1	1	0	.158	.158

		G	AB	H	R	2B	3B	HR	RBI	BB	SB	BA	SA
Sub	Pete Connell	1	5	0	0	0	0	0	0	0	0	.000	.000
P	Harry Brooks	1	1	0	0	0	0	0	0	0	0	.000	.000
		137	4683	1047	628	108	72	18	426	330	120	.224	.289

- 1B Orr 136, Brady 1
- 2B Forster 62, Meister 45, Foster 21, McLaughlin 10
- SS Nelson 73, McLaughlin 63, Forster 1, Holbert 1
- 3B Hankinson 136, Connell 1
- OF Roseman 134, Brady 123, Behel 59, Nelson 36, Donahue 32, Foster 14, Reipschlager 9, Forster 4, Holbert 3, Brooks 1, McLaughlin 1
- C Reipschlager 57, Holbert 45, Donahue 19, Crotty 14, Zimmer 6
- P Lynch 51, Mays 41, Cushman 38, Shaffer 8, Brooks 1, Roseman 1

	G	IP	GS	CG	W	L	K	BB	SH	SV	ERA
Jack Lynch	51	432.2	50	50	20	30	193	116	1	0	3.95
Al Mays	41	350	40	39	11	27	163	140	1	0	3.39
Ed Cushman	38	325.2	38	37	17	21	167	99	2	0	3.12
John Shaffer	8	69	8	8	5	3	36	29	1	0	1.96
Chief Roseman	1	7	0	0	0	0	0	0	0	0	5.14
Harry Brooks	1	2	1	0	0	1	0	2	0	0	36.00
		1186.1	137	134	53	82	559	386	5	0	3.50

BALTIMORE   Billy Barnie   Oriole Park (I)

		G	AB	H	R	2B	3B	HR	RBI	BB	SB	BA	SA
LF	Joe Sommer	139	560	117	79	18	4	1	52	24	31	.209	.261
RF	Jack Manning	137	556	124	78	18	7	1	45	50	24	.223	.286
1B	Milt Scott	137	484	92	48	11	4	2	52	22	11	.190	.242
2B	Mike Muldoon	101	381	76	57	13	8	0	23	34	12	.199	.276
UT	Joe Farrell	73	301	63	36	8	3	1	31	12	5	.209	.266
C	Chris Fulmer	80	270	66	54	9	3	1	30	48	29	.244	.311
SS	Jimmy Macullar	85	268	55	49	7	5	1	26	49	23	.205	.239
Sub	Sadie Houck	61	260	50	29	8	1	0	17	4	25	.192	.231
P	Matt Kilroy	68	218	38	33	3	1	0	11	21	20	.174	.197
3B	Jumbo Davis	60	216	42	23	5	2	1	20	11	12	.194	.250
Sub	Pat O'Connell	42	166	30	20	3	2	0	8	11	10	.181	.223
CF	Buster Hoover	40	157	34	25	2	6	0	10	16	15	.217	.306
C	Tom Dolan	38	125	19	13	3	2	0	12	8	8	.152	.208
Sub	Blondie Purcell	26	85	19	17	0	1	0	8	17	13	.224	.247
Sub	Bill Traffley	25	85	18	15	0	1	0	7	10	8	.212	.235
P	Jumbo McGinnis	26	85	16	7	5	0	1	6	4	3	.188	.282
Sub	Jim Clinton	23	83	15	8	1	0	0	6	4	3	.181	.193
Sub	Len Sowders	23	76	20	10	3	1	0	14	12	6	.263	.329
P	Hardie Henderson	19	68	16	5	2	2	0	14	6	0	.235	.324
P	Billy Taylor	10	39	12	4	0	1	0	8	1	1	.308	.359
Sub	Abner Powell	11	39	7	4	2	1	0	7	1	4	.179	.282
Sub	Ed Greer	11	38	5	2	1	0	0	4	2	4	.132	.158
P	Dick Conway	9	34	7	5	2	0	0	3	3	1	.206	.265
Sub	Bill Conway	7	14	2	4	0	0	0	3	7	0	.143	.143
Sub	Ned Bligh	3	9	0	0	0	0	0	0	1	0	.000	.000
Sub	Billy Barnie	1	6	0	0	0	0	0	0	1	0	.000	.000
Sub	Sandy Nava	2	5	1	0	0	0		0	0	1	.200	.200
Sub	Tony Hellman	1	3	0	0	0	0	0	0	0	0	.000	.000
P	Frank Houseman	1	4	1	0	0	0	0	0	0	0	.250	.250
P	Ed Knouff	1	3	0	0	0	0	0	0	0	0	.000	.000
P	? Zay	1	1	0	0	0	0	0	0	0	0	.000	.000
		139	4639	945	625	124	51	8	417	379	269	.204	.258

1B   Scott 137, Taylor 1, O'Connell 1, Sowders 1
2B   Muldoon 57, Farrell 45, Sommer 32, Houck 5, Macullar 1
SS   Macullar 82, Houck 55, Sommer 3, Nava 1, Purcell 1
3B   Davis 60, Muldoon 44, Farrell 27, Sommer 11
OF   Manning 137, Sommer 95, O'Connell 41, Hoover 40, Purcell 26, Clinton 23, Sowders 23, Fulmer 12, Greer
     10, Powell 4, Dolan 3, Macullar 2, Kilroy 2, McGinnis 2, Zay 1, D. Conway 1, Houck 1, Farrell 1, Purcell 1,
     Barnie 1
C   Fulmer 68, Dolan 35, Traffley 25, B. Conway 7, Bligh 3, Barnie 1, Greer 1, Taylor 1, Nava 1, Hellman 1
P   Kilroy 68, McGinnis 26, Henderson 19, D. Conway 9, Taylor 8, Powell 7, Knouff 1, Scott 1, Macullar 1,
     Zay 1, Sommer 1, Fulmer 1, Houseman 1, O'Connell 1, Purcell 1

	G	IP	GS	CG	W	L	K	BB	SH	SV	ERA
Matt Kilroy #	**68**	583	**68**	**66**	29	**34**	**513**	182	5	0	3.37
Jumbo McGinnis	26	209.1	25	24	11	13	70	48	0	0	3.48
Hardie Henderson	19	171.1	19	19	3	15	88	66	0	0	4.62
Dick Conway	9	76.2	9	8	2	7	64	43	0	0	6.81
Billy Taylor	8	72.1	8	8	1	6	37	20	0	0	5.72
Abner Powell	7	60	7	7	2	5	15	26	0	0	5.10
Ed Knouff	1	9	1	1	0	1	8	5	0	0	2.00
Frank Houseman	1	8	1	1	0	1	5	1	0	0	3.38
Joe Sommer	1	4	0	0	0	0	1	3	0	0	18.00
Milt Scott	1	3	0	0	0	0	0	2	0	0	3.00
Pat O'Connell	1	3	0	0	0	0	1	2	0	0	6.00
? Zay	1	2	1	0	0	1	2	4	0	0	9.00
Jimmy Macullar	1	2	0	0	0	0	1	0	0	0	9.00
Chris Fulmer	1	2	0	0	0	0	0	1	0	0	4.50
Blondie Purcell	1	1	0	0	0	0	0	0	0	0	9.00
		1206.2	139	134	48	83	**805**	403	5	0	4.08

No-hit game 6–0 vs Pittsburgh, October 6

1887
THE LONG, LONG SEASON

When the two major leagues met in the fall of 1886 to hammer out wrinkles in the National Agreement and the playing rules, it was as equals. But the American Association failed to grasp that the National League had a hidden agenda. Soon after that seemingly peaceful meeting the senior circuit twisted the spat between Pittsburgh and the Association to its own ends by luring the Allegheny club to bolt to the League in place of the floundering Kansas City franchise.

Notwithstanding this brazen theft of its second strongest team in 1886, the Association continued to act the dove and to honor its commitment to be governed henceforward by the same playing rules as the League. That agreement meant having to draft virtually a whole new rulebook. Never before and never again did the game undergo as many changes as occurred in 1887. Among the myriad of innovations were establishing the stolen base as an official statistic, making the hit-batsman rule a universal part of the game, allowing the home club captain to be the sole judge of the fitness of his field for resuming play after a rain delay (which led to obvious abuses whenever rain came with the home team trailing), mandating that a team could no longer play with fewer than nine men (previously teams had sometimes played with eight, usually after a substitute for an injured player was denied by the opposing captain), and requiring every potential participant in a game to be on the bench in full uniform (previously substitutes were sometimes drafted from the crowd and occasionally even allowed to play in streetclothes). These revisions were slight, though, compared to the new guidelines that pitchers and batters were made to digest. Beginning in 1887, the position a pitcher had to assume when he delivered the ball was depicted laboriously in the rulebook. The intention was twofold. Along with restricting a pitcher to a single step before he released the ball, thereby eliminating the running starts favored by Guy Hecker and other hurlers in the mid-1880s, the game's designers also sought to end the chicanery many pitchers like Dave Foutz and Larry McKeon used to deceive batters and baserunners as to when and where they would throw the ball. The end result was that a pitcher was required to have his rear foot on the back line of the box, thereby establishing

A preseason view of the 1887 Philadelphia Phillies. Cannonball Titcomb was cut before the campaign started and Tony Cusick exited shortly after it was underway. Cusick was behind the bat in Wilmington the day that Union Association umpire Pat Dutton nearly became the first on-field fatality in major league history.

TOP 10 NATIONAL LEAGUE HITTERS IN 1887

SPORTING LIFE'S FINAL AVERAGES			CURRENT FINAL AVERAGES		
Anson	Chicago	.421	Thompson	Detroit	.372
Brouthers	Detroit	.411*	Anson	Chicago	.347
Thompson	Detroit	.406	Brouthers	Detroit	.338
Kelly	Boston	.394	Ward	New York	.338
Schomberg	Indianapolis	.389	Wise	Boston	.334
Connor	New York	.382	Carroll	Pittsburgh	.328
Wise	Boston	.380	Andrews	Philadelphia	.325
Carroll	Pittsburgh	.380	Denny	Indianapolis	.324
Ward	New York	.371	Kelly	Boston	.322
Williamson	Chicago	.371	Rowe	Detroit	.318

Sporting Life credited Brouthers 239 hits in 570 at bats but miscalculated his average; it should have been .419. His current final average, of course, excludes his walks.

The huge disparity seen above made both major leagues wish they had heeded a Brooklyn *Eagle* reporter who wrote on the eve of the 1887 season: "Whatever advantage there was in making this rule as an extra penalty for wild pitching, the advantage is offset by the drawback of its rendering the batting statistics valueless as a criterion of a batsman's skill so far as base hits are concerned . . . I think the League and the American Association will mutually agree to rescind this rule of base hits on called balls before the regular championship season sets in."

The reigning major league champion Detroit Wolverines in 1888. Top: Deacon White, Sy Sutcliffe, Dan Brouthers, Sam Thompson, Charlie Ganzel and Lady Baldwin. Middle: Pete Conway, Jack Rowe, Ned Hanlon, manager Bill Watkins, Charlie Getzein, Larry Twitchell and Charlie Bennett. Bottom: Henry Gruber, Hardy Richardson and Eb Beatin. A veteran team, loaded with many of the top players of the era, the Wolves got an added bonus in 1888 when 21-year-old Conway won 30 games. Yet, rather than successfully defend their title, they finished a distant fifth.

a firm pitching distance (55'6") for the first time. In a further attempt to restore the delicate balance between batter and pitcher, which had continued to tip dangerously toward the latter in 1886, the rules committee granted a batter four strikes in 1887 and agreed to award him his base after only five called balls. Yet more, they decreed that a batter would be credited with both a hit and time at bat every time he coaxed a walk. Finally, as if someone belatedly realized that pitchers deserved at least one break, in 1887 a batter was no longer permitted to call for either a high or a low pitch and the strike zone now encompassed the entire area between his knees and shoulders.

Amid the blizzard of off-season franchise shifts and rule changes, followers of the game were made to absorb still another enormous innovation. Fed up with trying to discipline the incorrigible and high-living King Kelly, Chicago club president Al Spalding peddled the League's 1886 batting titlist to Boston. Kelly's $10,000 sale price shattered records but would soon be equaled when Spalding decided to clean his clubhouse of troublemakers completely and at the close of the 1887 season talked Boston out of another ten grand for the high-strung John Clarkson, whose mammoth ego was rivaled on the club only by manager Cap Anson's. Along with ridding themselves of Kelly, the White Stockings sent center fielder George Gore to the New York Giants. Although a much lesser transaction in terms of money and publicity, Gore's departure cut nearly as deeply. In 1887, while the League batted 18 points higher as a whole, Chicago's team batting average fell eight points below its 1886 mark as Anson's new outfield duo of future evangelist Billy Sunday and rookie Marty Sullivan could not begin to replace Gore and Kelly.

As a result, the White Stockings, traditionally a quick starter, went just 11–15 in the early weeks of the 1887 season and ended May nine games behind Detroit's 21–7 start. Chicago gained six and a half games on the Wolverines in June and July but then fell back again in August. A late surge by the Philadelphia Phillies, which won their last 16 decisions, swept them past Chicago into second place but left them still three and a half lengths behind Detroit at the tape.

FORFEIT I

By 1887 forfeited games, rare in the previous decade, had become commonplace. That season there were four forfeits declared in the American Association alone, two of which involved the Philadelphia Athletics. The first, on July 22 at Philadelphia, coincided with an historic event—the appearance of Fred Chapman, the youngest player ever to participate in a major league game. Chapman, just 14 years old, started in the box against Cleveland's Mike Morrison and trailed 6–2 after five innings. He was spared the loss, though, when Philadelphia scored two runs in the sixth and Cleveland then clashed with umpire Mitchell (first name unknown) over whether Henry Larkin of the A's interfered with Blues catcher Pop Snyder, allowing Harry Stovey to escape a run-down and get safely to third base. According to *Sporting Life,* "while the matter was being discussed, Mr. Mitchell, to the surprise of everyone, gave the Athletics the game (by forfeit)."

Exactly three weeks later, on August 12, the A's were embroiled in the 1887 season's most bizarre forfeit. Finding himself behind 9–7 in a seesaw game with the New York Mets, A's rookie pitching star Gus Weyhing hit a low liner that ricocheted off rightfielder Eddie Hogan's foot. Weyhing made third base on the hit but was ordered back to second by umpire Jerry Sullivan, who said Weyhing was entitled only to a groundruled double as per the Mets' park rule because his hit had rolled into the "Fall of Babylon" scenery in deep right field. A's manager Frank Bancroft argued vigorously that Hogan's intervening foot should make the hit a home run, if anything. Mets manager Opie Caylor meanwhile stood behind the two, gleefully fanning the flames. When Bancroft refused to leave the field after Sullivan pulled out his watch, Caylor's Mets were made the beneficiaries of one of their infrequent wins in 1887, but Weyhing, unlike Chapman, was tagged with a loss since his team trailed when the forfeit occurred. In *The Great Encyclopedia of Nineteenth-Century Major League Baseball* forfeits are only listed in team pitching charts when no pitching wins or losses were assigned.

THE UNKNOWN RBI KING

Sam Thompson uncorks one of the hits that made him the now-recognized 1887 NL batting king. At the time Cap Anson was awarded the crown.

No scorekeepers kept track of RBI in 1887. Runs batted in would not become an official statistic until 1920. Nevertheless some attention was paid in the last century to players who were good at driving home baserunners. We know now that Sam Thompson set the nineteenth-century season RBI record in 1887 when his bat scored 166 teammates, and even though Detroit manager Bill Watkins could not have fully appreciated what a prize he had, certainly he was aware that Thompson was doing something special that year. Anyway, he had Thompson hitting cleanup most of the time.

It is doubtful, though, that Philadelphia Phillies manager Harry Wright had more than an inkling that his roster had someone nearly as efficient as Thompson. In 1887, Charlie Ferguson drove in 85 runs for the Phils in just 264 at bats. Ferguson's ratio of one RBI for every 3.1 at bats would, by projection, have given him 175 RBI had he batted as many times as Thompson did (545). Why didn't Ferguson bat more often? Because he was mainly a pitcher prior to 1887, though Wright also considered him a potentially outstanding outfielder. Toward the end of the 1887 season Wright began to comprehend that Ferguson was too valuable to be sitting on the bench when he wasn't pitching. During the final eight weeks Wright finally gave up on Barney McLaughlin and Charlie Bastian, who hit a combined .214, and began playing Ferguson every day at second base. The move helped the Phillies to squeak past Chicago and grab second place by compiling 16 wins and a tie in their last 17 games. That streak would prove to be Ferguson's last 17 games in the majors. The following spring, a few days after his 25th birthday, he came down with typhoid fever and died on the eve of the 1888 season in his home at 2512 North Broadstreet in Philadelphia with many of his teammates at his bedside.

Charlie Ferguson collected 99 wins in his first four seasons, but it was with his bat that he probably would have left his biggest imprint on the game if he had not died just 12 days after his 25th birthday.

Detroit's first and only major league pennant in the nineteenth century came just three years after the club had been on the brink of disbanding following an abysmal last-place finish. In the interim the Wolverines had so thoroughly re-vamped under new owner Frederick Stearns that only catcher Charlie Bennett, center fielder Ned Hanlon, and two pitch-ers, Charlie Getzein and Stump Weidman, remained from the 1884 cellar-dweller. But though Stearns had rebuilt his team with speed and elan, he was thwarted from reaping the benefits he had anticipated. Since Detroit in the 1880s had a small population by big league standards, Stearns planned to make the Wolverines a great road attraction and earn most of his profits on visits to Chicago, New York, Philadelphia and Boston. But team owners in those cities, led by Spalding and Boston's Arthur Soden, changed the rules governing the di-vision of gate receipts when they fathomed Stearns's strategy.

By the close of the 1887 season Stearns must have wished he had followed the advice of his manager, Bill Watkins. Some months earlier, after Pittsburgh defected to the League, Watkins had attended an emergency American Association meeting to select a replacement team (which turned out to be Cleveland) and volunteered his Detroit club. When Association leaders questioned Watkins's sincerity, he cabled Stearns for permission to make a formal bid for admission to the Association. Stearns refused Watkins, claiming the Wolverines would stay in the National League because it was about to capitulate to all his demands, but less than two years later his fellow League moguls had helped put Stearns in so deep a financial hole that Detroit was forced to give up its franchise and would be with-out major league ball for the rest of the century.

Still thinking he could make money on his slugging Wolverines, Stearns challenged St. Louis Browns owner Chris Von Der Ahe to a 15-game World's Series, with the two teams traveling in a special train of parlor cars and playing not just in Detroit and St. Louis but in all major league cities. Von Der Ahe further agreed to hike the Series admission price to one dollar and to Stearns's novel idea of using two umpires, "Honest John" Kelly and "Honest John" Gaffney, the game's two most prominent arbiters at the time. Von Der Ahe found all of Stearns's lavish suggestions appealing in part because he had a flair for extravagance

A Kalamazoo Bat Card of Tim Keefe, the NL's most difficult pitcher to reach base safely against in 1887. In 1888, Keefe became the first to pitch in a World's Series for both an NL and an AA flag winner. Two years later Keefe jumped to the Players League. Participating in three different major leagues enabled him to hurl winning games in an all-time record 47 different major league parks.

himself but more because his Browns also had suffered a disappointing season at the gate in 1887. Much of the reason was winning a third straight pennant by a huge 14-game margin against the likes of teams like newcomer Cleveland, which could bag only one of 19 contests with Von Der Ahe's club. Owing to the multitude of rule changes and the one-sided pennant race. The Association season had so many contretemps and so little drama that Tip O'Neill's towering offensive performance was nearly obscured. In 1887, O'Neill became the only man ever to lead a major league in batting average, slugging average, hits, runs, total bases, doubles, triples, home runs, RBI and on-base percentage. But for years O'Neill's .490 batting average and indeed his entire 1887 season was looked upon as simply a statistical freak owing to the rule that year that bases on balls counted as hits. Only long after the fact—when O'Neill's walks were deducted from his hit and at bat totals and it was found that he still batted .435—did his extraordinary performance in 1887 begin to receive its due.

In the World's Series, however, O'Neill came a cropper, as did virtually all of the Browns. After achieving a split in the first two games at Sportsman's Park, St. Louis dropped the third contest at Detroit, 2–1 in 13 innings, when the usually sure-handed Charlie Comiskey bobbled a throw to first, allowing Charlie Ganzel to score the winning run. At that point the two teams took to the road for the remainder of their 15-game extravaganza, playing every day in a different big league city, but the Series could effectively have ended when Detroit took Game Four in Pittsburgh, 8–0, and certainly should have ended after the Wolverines bagged all but one of the next five games to lead 7–2 after nine contests were down. But instead the sorry show continued for the full 15 games. The long, long season ended at last in St. Louis in front of only 659 diehards on October 26, the latest closing date in history to that point.

THE SEASONAL RECORD

NATIONAL LEAGUE

	W	L	PCT	HOME	ROAD	GB
1. Detroit Wolverines	79	45	.637	44–17	35–28	—
2. Philadelphia Phillies	75	48	.610	38–23	37–25	3.5
3. Chicago White Stockings	71	50	.587	44–18	27–32	6.5
4. New York Giants	68	55	.553	36–26	32–29	10.5
5. Boston Beaneaters	61	60	.504	39–22	22–38	16.5
6. Pittsburgh Alleghenys	55	69	.444	31–33	24–36	24
7. Washington Nationals	46	76	.377	26–32	20–44	32
8. Indianapolis Hoosiers	37	89	.294	24–39	13–50	43

	Det	Phi	Chi	NY	Bos	Pit	Was	Ind	
Detroit	—	10	8	10	11	13	13	14	79
Philadelphia	8	—	6	10	9	12	13	17	75
Chicago	10	12	—	10	9	5	11	13	71
New York	8	7	6	—	10	12	10	15	68
Boston	7	90	61	7	—	11	10	11	61
Pittsburgh	4	61	12	6	7	—	9	11	54
Washington	4	3	7	8	7	9	0	8	46
Indianapolis	4	1	5	3	7	7	10	—	37
	45	48	50	55	60	69	76	89	492

SEASON LEADERS

Batting Average (300 ABs)

1.	Thompson, Detroit	.372
2.	Anson, Chicago	.347
3.	Brouthers, Detroit	.338
	Ward, New York	.338
5.	Wise, Boston	.334

On–Base Percentage

1.	Brouthers, Detroit	.426
2.	Anson, Chicago	.422
3.	Thompson, Detroit	.416
4.	Schomberg, Indianapolis	.397
5.	Kelly, Boston	.393

Home Runs

1.	O'Brien, Washington	19
2.	Connor, New York	17
3.	Pfeffer, Chicago	16
4.	Wood, Detroit	14
5.	Brouthers, Detroit	12
	Morrill, Boston	12

Slugging Average

1.	Thompson, Detroit	.571
2.	Brouthers, Detroit	.562
3.	Connor, New York	.541
4.	Wise, Boston	.522
5.	Anson, Chicago	.517

Total Bases

1.	Thompson, Detroit	311
2.	Brouthers, Detroit	281
3.	H. Richardson, Detroit	263
4.	Denny, Indianapolis	256
5.	Connor, New York	255

RBI

1.	Thompson, Detroit	166
2.	Connor, New York	104
	Anson, Chicago	102
4.	Brouthers, Detroit	101
5.	Denny, Indianapolis	97

Hits

1.	Thompson, Detroit	203
2.	Ward, New York	184
3.	H. Richardson, Detroit	178
4.	Rowe, Detroit	171
5.	Brouthers, Detroit	169

Stolen Bases

1.	Ward, New York	111
2.	Fogarty, Philadelphia	102
3.	Kelly, Boston	84
4.	Hanlon, Detroit	69
5.	Glasscock, Indianapolis	62

Bases on Balls

1.	Fogarty, Philadelphia	82
2.	Connor, New York	75
3.	Williamson, Chicago	73
4.	Seery, Indianapolis	71
	Brouthers, Detroit	71

Runs

1.	Brouthers, Detroit	153
2.	Rowe, Detroit	135
3.	H. Richardson, Detroit	131
4.	Kelly, Boston	120
5.	Thompson, Detroit	118
	Wood, Philadelphia	118

Strikeouts

1.	Morrill, Boston	86
2.	Seery, Indianapolis	68
3.	Brown, Pitt–Ind	65
4.	Williamson, Chicago	57
5.	Sullivan, Chicago	53

PITCHING

Wins

1.	Clarkson, Chicago	38
2.	Keefe, New York	35
3.	Getzein, Detroit	29
4.	Galvin, Pittsburgh	28
	Casey, Philadelphia	28

Innings

1.	Clarkson, Chicago	523
2.	Keefe, New York	476.2
3.	Galvin, Pittsburgh	440.2
4.	Radbourn, Boston	425
5.	Whitney, Washington	404.2

Strikeouts

1.	Clarkson, Chicago	237
2.	Keefe, New York	189
3.	M. Baldwin, Chicago	164
4.	Buffinton, Philadelphia	160
5.	Whitney, Washington	146

ERA (140 innings)

1.	Casey, Philadelphia	2.86
2.	Conway, Detroit	2.90
3.	Ferguson, Philadelphia	3.00
4.	Clarkson, Chicago	3.08
5.	Keefe, New York	3.12

Losses

1.	Healy, Indianapolis	29
2.	Boyle, Indianapolis	24
3.	Radbourn, Boston	23
	McCormick, Pittsburgh	23
5.	Morris, Pittsburgh	22

Complete Games

1.	Clarkson, Chicago	56
2.	Keefe, New York	54
3.	Radbourn, Boston	48
4.	Galvin, Pittsburgh	47
5.	Whitney, Washington	46

Winning Percentage (25 decisions)

1.	Getzein, Detroit	.690
2.	Ferguson, Philadelphia	.688
3.	Casey, Philadelphia	.683
4.	Keefe, New York	.648
5.	Clarkson, Chicago	.644

Lowest On–Base Percentage

1.	Keefe, New York	.276
2.	Clarkson, Chicago	.281
3.	Whitney, Washington	.284
4.	Ferguson, Philadelphia	.289
5.	Galvin, Pittsburgh	.299

FIELDING

Total Chances		
1B	Connor, New York	1379
2B	Pfeffer, Chicago	867
3B	Nash, Boston	508
SS	Glasscock, Indianapolis	777
OF	Johnston, Boston	400
C	Mack, Washington	563
P	Clarkson, Chicago	166

Fielding Average	
Connor, New York	.993
Bassett, Indianapolis	.931
Whitney, Pittsburgh	.924
Ward, New York	.919
Hornung, Boston	.935*
Daly, Chicago	.935
Getzein, Detroit	.964

*Pete Gillespie of New York had a .946 FA but played only 76 games.

DETROIT   Bill Watkins   Recreation Park

		G	AB	H	R	2B	3B	HR	RBI	BB	SB	BA	SA
RF	Sam Thompson	127	**545**	**203**	118	29	**23**	11	**166**	32	22	**.372**	**.571**
UT	Hardy Richardson	120	543	178	131	25	18	8	94	31	29	.328	.484
SS	Jack Rowe	124	537	171	135	30	10	6	96	39	22	.318	.445
1B	Dan Brouthers	123	500	169	**153**	**36**	20	12	101	71	34	.338	.562
CF	Ned Hanlon	118	471	129	79	13	7	4	69	30	69	.274	.357
3B	Deacon White	111	449	136	71	20	11	3	75	26	20	.303	.416
2B	Fred Dunlap	65	272	72	60	13	10	5	45	25	15	.265	.441
LF	Larry Twitchell	65	264	88	44	14	6	0	51	8	12	.333	.432
C	Charlie Ganzel	57	227	59	40	6	5	0	20	8	3	.260	.330
C	Charlie Bennett	46	160	39	26	6	5	3	20	30	7	.244	.400
P	Charlie Getzein	43	156	29	19	4	5	1	14	10	2	.186	.295
C	Fatty Briody	33	128	29	24	6	1	1	26	9	6	.227	.313
P	Pete Conway	24	95	22	16	5	1	1	7	2	0	.232	.337
P	Lady Baldwin	24	85	23	15	0	1	0	11	10	4	.271	.294
Sub	Billy Shindle	22	84	24	17	3	2	0	12	7	13	.286	.369
P	Stump Weidman	21	82	17	12	2	0	0	7	3	6	.207	.232
Sub	Jim Manning	13	52	10	5	1	0	0	3	5	3	.192	.212
P	Henry Gruber	7	24	4	3	0	1	0	0	6	0	.167	.250
P	Turk Burke	2	8	2	1	0	0	0	1	0	0	.250	.250
P	Eb Beatin	2	7	0	0	0	0	0	0	0	0	.000	.000
		127	4689	**1404**	**969**	**213**	**126**	55	**818**	352	267	**.299**	**.434**

1B   Brouthers 123, White 2, Ganzel 2, Bennett 1
2B   Dunlap 65, Richardson 64
SS   Rowe 124, Manning 3
3B   White 106, Shindle 21, Ganzel 1
OF   Thompson 125, Hanlon 118, Richardson 59, Twitchell 53, Manning 10, Conway 8, Ganzel 4, White 3, Bennett 1, Getzein 1, Weidman 1, Burke 1, Shindle 1
C   Ganzel 51, Bennett 45, Briody 33
P   Getzein 43, Baldwin 24, Weidman 21, Conway 17, Twitchell 15, Gruber 7, Burke 2, Beatin 2, Dunlap 1

	G	IP	GS	CG	W	L	K	BB	SH	SV	ERA
Charlie Getzein	43	366.2	42	41	29	13	135	106	2	0	3.73
Lady Baldwin	24	211	24	24	13	10	60	61	1	0	3.84
Stump Weidman	21	183	21	20	13	7	56	60	0	0	5.36
Pete Conway	17	146	17	16	8	9	40	47	0	0	2.90
Larry Twitchell	15	112.1	12	11	11	1	24	36	0	**1**	4.33
Henry Gruber	7	62.1	7	7	4	3	12	21	0	0	2.74
Eb Beatin	2	18	2	2	1	1	6	8	0	0	4.00
Turk Burke	2	15	2	1	0	1	3	5	0	0	6.00
Fred Dunlap	1	2	0	0	0	0	1	0	0	0	4.50
		1116.1	127	122	79	45	337	344	3	1	3.95

PHILADELPHIA **Harry Wright** **Philadelphia Baseball Grounds**

		G	AB	H	R	2B	3B	HR	RBI	BB	SB	BA	SA
RF	Jim Fogarty	126	495	129	113	26	12	8	50	**82**	102	.261	.410
LF	George Wood	113	491	142	118	22	19	14	66	40	19	.289	.497
3B	Joe Mulvey	111	474	136	93	21	6	2	78	21	43	.287	.369
CF	Ed Andrews	104	464	151	110	19	7	4	67	21	57	.325	.422
1B	Sid Farrar	116	443	125	83	20	9	4	72	42	24	.282	.395
SS	Arthur Irwin	100	374	95	65	14	8	2	56	48	19	.254	.350
P	Charlie Buffinton	66	269	72	34	12	1	1	46	11	8	.268	.331
P	Charlie Ferguson	72	264	89	67	14	6	3	85	34	13	.337	.470
C	Jack Clements	66	246	69	48	13	7	1	47	9	7	.280	.402
Sub	Charlie Bastian	60	221	47	33	11	1	1	21	19	11	.213	.285
2B	Barney McLaughlin	50	205	45	26	8	3	1	26	11	2	.220	.302
P	Dan Casey	45	164	27	22	3	0	1	17	6	1	.165	.201
C	Deacon McGuire	41	150	46	22	6	6	2	23	11	3	.307	.467
Sub	Ed Daily	26	106	30	18	11	1	1	17	3	8	.283	.434
Sub	Tom Gunning	28	104	27	22	6	1	1	16	5	18	.260	.365
Sub	Tommy McCarthy	18	70	13	7	4	0	0	6	2	15	.186	.243
P	Al Maul	16	56	17	15	2	2	1	4	15	5	.304	.464
Sub	Tony Cusick	7	24	7	3	1	0	0	5	3	0	.292	.333
P	Jim Devlin	2	6	2	2	0	0	0	0	1	0	.333	.333
Sub	Harry Lyons	1	4	0	0	0	0	0	0	1	0	.000	.000
		128	4630	1269	901	213	89	47	702	385	355	.274	.389

1B   Farrar 116, Buffinton 10, Cusick 3, Maul 2, Andrews 1
2B   McLaughlin 50, Bastian 39, Ferguson 27, Andrews 7, McCarthy 5, Wood 3, Fogarty 1, Cusick 1
SS   Irwin 100, Bastian 18, Clements 3, Wood 3, McCarthy 3, Fogarty 2
3B   Mulvey 111, Ferguson 5, Bastian 4, Clements 4, Wood 3, Fogarty 2, McCarthy 2
OF   Fogarty 123, Wood 104, Andrews 99, Buffinton 22, Daily 22, Maul 8, McCarthy 8, Ferguson 6, Casey 1, Lyons 1
C   Clements 59, McGuire 41, Gunning 28, Cusick 4
P   Casey 45, Buffinton 40, Ferguson 37, Maul 7, Daily 6, Devlin 2, Fogarty 1

	G	IP	GS	CG	W	L	K	BB	SH	SV	ERA
Dan Casey	45	390.1	45	43	28	13	119	115	**4**	0	**2.86**
Charlie Buffinton	40	332.1	38	35	21	17	160	92	1	0	3.66
Charlie Ferguson	37	297.1	33	31	22	10	125	47	2	**1**	3.00
Al Maul	7	50.1	5	4	4	2	18	15	0	0	5.54
Ed Daily	6	41.1	5	4	0	4	7	25	0	0	7.19
Jim Devlin	2	18	2	2	0	2	6	10	0	0	6.00
Jim Fogarty	1	3	0	0	0	0	0	1	0	0	9.00
		1132.2	128	119	75	48	435	305	**7**	1	3.47

CHICAGO   Cap Anson   West Side Park (I)

		G	AB	H	R	2B	3B	HR	RBI	BB	SB	BA	SA
CF	Jimmy Ryan	126	508	145	117	23	10	11	74	53	50	.285	.435
2B	Fred Pfeffer	123	479	133	95	21	6	16	89	34	57	.278	.447
1B	Cap Anson	122	472	164	107	33	13	7	102	60	27	.347	.517
LF	Marty Sullivan	115	472	134	98	13	16	7	77	36	35	.284	.424
3B	Ned Williamson	127	439	117	77	20	14	9	78	73	45	.267	.437
SS	Tom Burns	115	424	112	57	20	10	3	60	34	32	.264	.380
C	Tom Daly	74	256	53	45	10	4	2	17	22	29	.207	.301
P	John Clarkson	63	215	52	40	5	5	6	25	11	6	.242	.395
RF	Billy Sunday	50	199	58	41	6	6	3	32	21	34	.291	.427
C	Silver Flint	49	187	50	22	8	6	3	21	4	7	.267	.422
P	George Van Haltren	45	172	35	30	4	0	3	17	15	12	.203	.279
Sub	Del Darling	38	141	45	28	7	4	3	20	22	19	.319	.489
P	Mark Baldwin	41	139	26	18	1	1	4	17	10	4	.187	.295
Sub	Bob Pettit	32	138	36	29	3	3	2	12	8	16	.261	.370
Sub	Patsy Tebeau	20	68	11	8	3	0	0	10	4	8	.162	.206
P	Shadow Pyle	4	16	3	1	1	0	1	4	0	1	.188	.438
P	Charlie Sprague	3	13	2	0	0	0	0	0	0	0	.154	.154
P	Emil Geiss	3	12	1	0	0	0	0	0	0	0	.083	.083
Sub	Jocko Flynn	1	0	0	0	0	0	0	0	0	0	—	—
		127	4350	1177	813	178	98	**80**	655	**407**	382	.271	.412

1B   Anson 122, Daly 2, Flint 2, Baldwin 1, Geiss 1, Pettit 1
2B   Pfeffer 123, Ryan 3, Daly 2, Geiss 1
SS   Williamson 127, Daly 2
3B   Burns 107, Tebeau 20
OF   Ryan 122, Sullivan 115, Sunday 50, Pettit 32, Van Haltren 27, Darling 20, Daly 8, Burns 8, Clarkson 5, Baldwin 5, Pfeffer 2, Pyle 1, Sprague 1, Flynn 1
C   Daly 64, Flint 47, Darling 20, Anson 1, Pettit 1
P   Clarkson 60, Baldwin 40, Van Haltren 20, Ryan 8, Pyle 4, Sprague 3, Geiss 1, Pettit 1, Wiliamson 1, Sullivan 1

	G	IP	GS	CG	W	L	K	BB	SH	SV	ERA
John Clarkson	**60**	**523**	**59**	**56**	**38**	21	**237**	92	2	0	3.08
Mark Baldwin	40	334	39	35	18	17	164	122	1	**1**	3.40
George Van Haltren	20	161	18	18	11	7	76	66	1	**1**	3.86
Jimmy Ryan	8	45	3	2	2	1	14	17	0	0	4.20
Shadow Pyle	4	26.2	4	3	1	3	5	21	0	0	4.73
Charlie Sprague	3	22	3	2	1	0	9	13	0	0	4.91
Emil Geiss	1	9	1	1	0	1	4	3	0	0	8.00
Marty Sullivan	1	2.1	0	0	0	0	1	1	0	0	7.71
Ned Williamson	1	2	0	0	0	0	0	1	0	0	9.00
Bob Pettit	1	1	0	0	0	0	0	2	0	**1**	0.00
		1126	127	117	71	50	**510**	338	4	**3**	**3.46**

NEW YORK   Jim Mutrie   Polo Grounds (I)

		G	AB	H	R	2B	3B	HR	RBI	BB	SB	BA	SA
SS	Monte Ward	129	**545**	184	114	16	5	1	53	29	**111**	.338	.391
1B	Roger Connor	127	471	134	113	26	22	17	104	75	43	.285	.541
CF	George Gore	111	459	133	95	16	5	1	49	42	39	.290	.353
2B	Danny Richardson	122	450	125	79	19	10	3	62	36	41	.278	.384
LF	Mike Tiernan	103	407	117	82	13	12	10	62	32	28	.287	.452
UT	Jim O'Rourke	103	397	113	73	15	13	3	88	36	46	.285	.411
3B	Buck Ewing	77	318	97	83	17	13	6	44	30	26	.305	.497
RF	Pete Gillespie	76	295	78	40	9	3	3	37	12	37	.264	.346

		G	AB	H	R	2B	3B	HR	RBI	BB	SB	BA	SA
Sub	Mike Dorgan	71	283	73	41	10	0	0	34	15	22	.258	.293
P	Tim Keefe	56	191	42	27	7	6	2	23	20	2	.220	.351
C	Willard Brown	49	170	37	17	3	2	0	25	10	10	.218	.259
P	Mickey Welch	40	148	36	16	4	2	2	15	6	2	.243	.338
Sub	Pat Deasley	30	118	37	12	5	0	0	23	9	3	.314	.356
Sub	John Rainey	17	58	17	6	3	0	0	12	5	0	.293	.345
Sub	Pat Murphy	17	56	12	4	2	0	0	4	2	1	.214	.250
P	Bill George	13	53	9	6	0	0	0	5	1	2	.170	.170
P	Mike Mattimore	8	32	8	5	1	0	0	4	0	1	.250	.281
P	Cannonball Titcomb	9	29	2	1	0	0	0	1	1	1	.069	.069
Sub	Gil Hatfield	2	7	3	2	1	0	0	3	0	0	.429	.571
P	Bill Swabach	2	7	0	0	0	0	0	0	0	0	.000	.000
Sub	Buck Becannon	1	5	0	0	0	0	0	0	0	0	.000	.000
P	John Roach	1	4	1	0	0	0	0	1	0	0	.250	.250
Sub	Joe Gerhardt	1	4	0	0	0	0	0	0	0	0	.000	.000
Sub	Roger Carey	1	4	0	0	0	0	0	2	0	0	.000	.000
P	Stump Weidman	1	3	1	0	0	0	0	0	0	0	.333	.333
Sub	Candy Nelson	1	2	0	0	0	0	0	0	0	0	.000	.000
		129	4516	1259	816	167	93	48	651	361	**415**	.279	.389

1B Connor 127, Dorgan 2
2B Richardson 108, Ewing 19, O'Rourke 2, Carey 1
SS Ward 129, Deasley 1
3B Ewing 51, O'Rourke 38, Richardson 14, Rainey 17, Deasley 7, Brown 3, Hatfield 2, Gillespie 1, Nelson 1, Becannon 1, Gerhardt 1
OF Gore 111, Tiernan 103, Gillespie 76, Dorgan 69, O'Rourke 28, Mattimore 2, Brown 2, Keefe 2, Welch 1, George 1
C   Brown 46, O'Rourke 40, Deasley 24, Murphy 17, Ewing 8,
P   Keefe 56, Welch 40, George 13, Titcomb 9, Mattimore 7, Tiernan 5, Swabach 2, Roach 1, Weidman 1, Richardson 1

	G	IP	GS	CG	W	L	K	BB	SH	SV	ERA
Tim Keefe	56	476.2	56	54	35	19	189	108	2	0	3.12
Mickey Welch	40	346	40	39	22	15	115	91	2	0	3.36
Bill George	13	108	13	11	3	9	49	89	0	0	5.25
Cannonball Titcomb	9	72	9	9	4	3	34	37	0	0	4.13
Mike Mattimore	7	57.1	7	6	3	3	12	28	1	0	2.35
Mike Tiernan	5	19.2	0	0	1	2	3	7	0	1	8.69
Bill Swabach	2	16	2	2	0	2	6	6	0	0	5.06
John Roach	1	8	1	1	0	1	3	4	0	0	11.25
Stump Weidman	1	8	1	1	0	1	4	2	0	0	1.13
Danny Richardson	1	0	0	0	0	0	0	1	0	0	—
		1113.2	129	123	68	55	415	373	5	1	3.58

BOSTON   King Kelly (49–43)   John Morrill (12–17)   South End Grounds (I)

		G	AB	H	R	2B	3B	HR	RBI	BB	SB	BA	SA
CF	Dick Johnston	127	507	131	87	13	20	5	77	16	52	.258	.393
1B	John Morrill	127	504	141	79	32	6	12	81	37	19	.280	.438
RF	King Kelly	116	484	156	120	34	11	8	63	55	84	.322	.488
3B	Billy Nash	121	475	140	100	24	12	6	94	60	43	.295	.440
SS	Sam Wise	113	467	156	103	27	17	9	92	36	43	.334	.522
LF	Joe Hornung	98	437	118	85	10	6	5	49	17	41	.270	.355
UT	Ezra Sutton	77	326	99	58	14	9	3	46	13	17	.304	.429
2B	Jack Burdock	65	237	61	36	6	0	0	29	18	19	.257	.283
C	Pop Tate	60	231	60	34	5	3	0	27	8	7	.260	.307
P	Hoss Radbourn	51	175	40	25	2	2	1	24	18	6	.229	.280
Sub	Bobby Wheelock	47	166	42	32	4	2	2	15	15	20	.253	.337
P	Dick Conway	42	145	36	20	4	1	0	10	16	5	.248	.290
P	Kid Madden	37	132	32	23	2	3	1	10	12	6	.242	.326
C	Con Daily	36	120	19	12	5	0	0	13	9	7	.158	.200
Sub	Tom O'Rourke	22	78	12	12	3	0	0	10	7	4	.154	.192
P	Bill Stemmeyer	15	47	12	5	0	2	1	9	3	0	.255	.404
		127	4531	1255	831	185	94	53	649	340	373	.277	.394

1B	Morrill 127
2B	Burdock 65, Kelly 30, Wise 16, Sutton 13, Wheelock 4
SS	Wise 72, Sutton 37, Wheelock 20, Kelly 2
3B	Nash 117, Sutton 11, Kelly 2, O'Rourke 1
OF	Johnston 127, Hornung 98, Kelly 61, Wheelock 28, Wise 27, Sutton 18, Conway 16, Tate 8, Nash 5, Radbourn 2, Madden 1, O'Rourke 1
C	Tate 53, Daily 36, Kelly 24, O'Rourke 21
P	Radbourn 50, Madden 37, Conway 26, Stemmeyer 15, Kelly 2

	G	IP	GS	CG	W	L	K	BB	SH	SV	ERA
Hoss Radbourn	50	425	50	48	24	23	87	133	1	0	4.55
Kid Madden	37	321	37	36	21	14	81	122	3	0	3.79
Dick Conway	26	222.1	26	25	9	15	45	86	0	0	4.66
Bill Stemmeyer	15	119.1	14	14	6	8	41	41	0	1	5.20
King Kelly	2	13	0	0	1	0	0	14	0	0	3.46
		1100.2	127	123	61	60	254	396	4	1	4.41

PITTSBURGH   Horace Phillips   Recreation Park

		G	AB	H	R	2B	3B	HR	RBI	BB	SB	BA	SA
RF	John Coleman	115	475	139	75	21	11	2	54	31	25	.293	.396
2B	Pop Smith	122	456	98	69	12	7	2	54	30	30	.215	.285
3B	Art Whitney	119	431	112	57	11	4	0	51	55	10	.260	.304
UT	Fred Carroll	102	421	138	71	24	15	6	54	36	23	.328	.499
SS	Willie Kuehne	102	402	120	68	18	15	1	41	14	17	.299	.425
LF	Abner Dalrymple	92	358	76	45	18	5	2	31	45	29	.212	.307
C	Doggie Miller	88	342	83	58	17	4	1	34	35	33	.243	.325
1B	Sam Barkley	89	340	76	44	10	4	1	35	30	6	.224	.285
1B	Alex McKinnon	48	200	68	26	16	4	1	30	8	6	.340	.475
P	Pud Galvin	49	193	41	10	7	3	2	22	2	5	.212	.311
CF	Tom Brown	47	192	47	30	3	4	0	6	11	12	.245	.302
Sub	Ed Beecher	41	169	41	15	8	0	2	22	7	8	.243	.325
Sub	Jocko Fields	43	164	44	26	9	2	0	17	7	7	.268	.348
P	Jim McCormick	36	136	33	12	7	0	0	18	2	9	.243	.294
P	Ed Morris	38	126	25	15	2	0	0	10	5	1	.198	.214
P	Bill Bishop	3	9	0	0	0	0	0	0	1	0	.000	.000
		125	4414	1141	621	183	78	20	479	319	221	.258	.349

1B   Barkley 53, McKinnon 48, Carroll 17, Kuehne 4, Fields 3, Coleman 2
2B   Smith 89, Barkley 36
SS   Kuehne 91, Smith 33, Carroll 1
3B   Whitney 119, Kuehne 4, Miller 1, Fields 1
OF   Coleman 115, Dalrymple 92, Brown 47, Carroll 46, Beecher 41, Fields 27, Miller 14, Kuehne 3, Galvin 1
C   Miller 73, Carroll 40, Fields 14
P   Galvin 49, Morris 38, McCormick 36, Bishop 3, Fields 1

	G	IP	GS	CG	W	L	K	BB	SH	SV	ERA
Pud Galvin	49	440.2	48	47	28	21	76	67	3	0	3.29
Jim McCormick	36	322.1	36	36	13	23	77	84	0	0	4.30
Ed Morris	38	317.2	38	37	14	22	91	71	1	0	4.31
Bill Bishop	3	27	3	3	0	3	4	22	0	0	13.33
Jocko Fields	1	1	0	0	0	0	0	2	0	0	0.00
		1108.2	125	123	55	69	248	**246**	4	0	4.12

WASHINGTON   John Gaffney   Swampoodle Grounds

		G	AB	H	R	2B	3B	HR	RBI	BB	SB	BA	SA
CF	Paul Hines	123	478	147	83	32	5	10	72	48	46	.308	.458
1B	Billy O'Brien	113	453	126	71	16	12	**19**	73	21	11	.278	.492
3B	Jim Donnelly	117	425	85	51	9	6	1	46	16	42	.200	.256
LF	Cliff Carroll	103	420	104	79	17	4	4	37	17	40	.248	.336
2B	Al Myers	105	362	84	45	9	5	2	36	40	18	.232	.301
SS	Jack Farrell	87	339	75	40	14	9	0	41	20	31	.221	.316
C	Connie Mack	82	314	63	35	6	1	0	20	8	26	.201	.226
RF	Ed Daily	78	311	78	39	6	10	2	36	14	26	.251	.354
Sub	George Shoch	70	264	63	47	9	1	1	18	21	29	.239	.292
Sub	Pat Dealey	58	212	55	33	8	2	1	18	8	36	.259	.330
P	Jim Whitney	54	201	53	29	9	6	2	22	18	10	.264	.398
P	Hank O'Day	36	116	23	10	3	0	0	7	7	1	.198	.224
Sub	Bill Krieg	25	95	24	9	4	1	2	17	7	2	.253	.379
P	Frank Gilmore	28	93	6	4	0	0	0	1	7	2	.065	.065
Sub	Barney Gilligan	28	90	18	7	2	0	1	6	5	2	.200	.256
P	Dupee Shaw	21	70	13	7	2	0	0	3	8	1	.186	.214
Sub	John Irwin	8	31	11	6	2	0	2	3	3	6	.355	.613
Sub	Sam Crane	7	30	9	6	1	1	0	1	1	5	.300	.400
Sub	Jerry O'Brien	1	4	0	0	0	0	0	0	0	0	.000	.000
Sub	Bill Wright	1	3	2	0	0	0	0	0	0	0	.667	.667
P	George Keefe	1	3	0	0	0	0	0	0	0	0	.000	.000
		126	4314	1039	601	149	63	47	457	269	334	.241	.337

1B   B. O'Brien 104, Krieg 16, Hines 7
2B   Myers 78, Farrell 40, Hines 5, B. O'Brien 2, Mack 2, J. O'Brien 1, Shoch 1
SS   Farrell 48, Myers 27, Dealey 23, Crane 7, Shoch 6, O'Day 6, Irwin 5, Hines 4, Gilligan 3, Donnelly 2
3B   Donnelly 115, Dealey 5, B. O'Brien 4, Irwin 4
OF   Hines 109, Carroll 103, Daily 77, Shoch 63, Krieg 9, Whitney 7, Dealey 5, Mack 5, B. O'Brien 4, O'Day 2, Gilligan 1
C   Mack 76, Dealey 28, Gilligan 26, Wright 1
P   Whitney 47, Gilmore 30, O'Day 30, Shaw 21, Daily 1, Keefe 1

	G	IP	GS	CG	W	L	K	BB	SH	SV	ERA
Jim Whitney	47	404.2	47	46	24	21	146	42	2	0	3.22
Hank O'Day	30	254.2	30	29	8	20	86	109	0	0	4.17
Frank Gilmore	30	234.2	27	27	7	20	114	92	1	0	3.87
Dupee Shaw	21	181.1	20	20	7	13	47	46	0	0	6.45
George Keefe	1	8	1	1	0	1	0	4	0	0	9.00
Ed Daily	1	7	1	1	0	1	3	6	0	0	7.71
		1090.1	126	**124**	46	76	396	299	3	0	4.19

INDIANAPOLIS **Watch Burnham (6–22)**   **Fred Thomas (11–18)**   **Horace Fogel (20–49)**
Athletic Park (I)

		G	AB	H	R	2B	3B	HR	RBI	BB	SB	BA	SA
3B	Jerry Denny	122	510	165	86	34	12	11	97	13	29	.324	.502
SS	Jack Glasscock	122	483	142	91	18	7	0	40	41	62	.294	.360
LF	Emmett Seery	122	465	104	104	18	15	4	28	71	48	.224	.353
2B	Charlie Bassett	119	452	104	41	14	6	1	47	25	25	.230	.294
1B	Otto Schomberg	112	419	129	91	18	16	5	83	56	21	.308	.463
CF	Jack McGeachy	99	405	109	49	17	3	1	56	5	27	.269	.333
RF	Patsy Cahill	68	263	54	22	4	3	0	26	9	34	.205	.243
C	George Myers	69	235	51	25	8	1	1	20	22	36	.217	.272
C	Tug Arundel	43	157	31	13	4	0	0	13	8	8	.197	.223
C	Mert Hackett	42	147	35	12	6	3	2	10	7	4	.238	.361
P	Henry Boyle	41	141	27	17	9	1	2	13	9	2	.191	.312
Sub	Tom Brown	36	140	25	20	3	0	0	9	8	13	.179	.243
P	Egyptian Healy	41	138	24	14	4	2	3	14	4	7	.174	.297
Sub	Mark Polhemus	20	75	18	6	1	0	0	8	2	4	.240	.253
Sub	Gid Gardner	18	63	11	8	1	0	1	8	12	7	.175	.238
P	Lev Shreve	14	49	13	6	1	0	0	4	3	2	.265	.286
Sub	Bill Johnson	11	42	8	3	0	0	0	3	0	5	.190	.190
P	Sam Moffett	11	41	5	6	1	0	0	1	1	2	.122	.146
Sub	Henry Jackson	10	38	10	1	1	0	0	3	0	2	.263	.289
P	John Kirby	8	29	4	3	0	1	0	2	0	0	.138	.207
P	Doc Leitner	8	27	4	3	0	0	0	0	0	1	.148	.148
P	Hank Morrison	7	26	3	4	0	0	0	3	2	2	.115	.115
P	? Fast	4	11	2	1	0	0	0	0	0	1	.182	.182
P	Larry Corcoran	3	10	2	2	0	0	0	0	2	2	.200	.200
P	John Sowders	1	2	0	0	0	0	0	0	0	0	.000	.000
		127	4368	1080	628	162	70	33	488	300	334	.247	.339

1B   Schomberg 112, Jackson 10, Myers 6, Hackett 1, Arundel 1
2B   Bassett 119, Gardner 7, Denny 1
SS   Glasscock 122, Denny 4, Cahill 1, Seery 1
3B   Denny 116, Cahill 9, McGeachy 1, Myers 1
OF   Seery 122, McGeachy 98, Cahill 56, Brown 36, Polhemus 20, Myers 15, Gardner 11, Johnson 11, Moffett 5, Boyle 4, Kirby 3, Corcoran 2, Arundel 2, Hackett 2, Schomberg 1, Denny 1, Morrison 1, Sowders 1, Fast 1
C   Myers 50, Arundel 42, Hackett 40
P   Healy 41, Boyle 38, Shreve 14, Leitner 8, Kirby 8, Morrison 7, Moffett 6, Cahill 6, Fast 4, Corcoran 2, Glasscock 1, McGeachy 1, Sowders 1

	G	IP	GS	CG	W	L	K	BB	SH	SV	ERA
Egyptian Healy	41	341	41	40	12	**29**	75	108	3	0	5.17
Henry Boyle	38	328	38	37	13	24	85	69	0	0	3.65
Lev Shreve	14	122	14	14	5	9	22	65	1	0	4.72
Doc Leitner	8	65	8	8	2	6	27	41	0	0	5.68
John Kirby	8	62	8	5	1	6	7	43	0	0	6.10
Hank Morrison	7	57	7	5	3	4	13	27	0	0	7.58
Sam Moffett	6	50	6	6	1	5	3	23	0	0	3.78
Patsy Cahill	6	22	1	1	0	2	5	19	0	0	14.32
? Fast	4	15.2	2	1	0	1	0	8	0	1	10.34
Larry Corcoran	2	15	2	1	0	2	4	19	0	0	12.60
Jack McGeachy	1	6.1	0	0	0	1	3	4	0	0	11.37
John Sowders	1	3	0	0	0	0	0	5	0	0	21.00
Jack Glasscock	1	1	0	0	0	0	1	0	0	0	0.00
		1088	127	118	37	89	245	431	4	1	5.24

WORLD'S SERIES

Detroit (NL) defeated St. Louis (AA) 10 games to 5

Game 1 at Sportsman's Park (StL), Oct. 10: StL (Caruthers) 6, Det (Getzein) 1
Game 2 at Sportsman's Park (StL), Oct. 11: Det (Conway) 5, StL (Foutz) 3
Game 3 at Recreation Park (Det), Oct. 12: Det (Getzein) 2, StL (Caruthers) 1 (13 inn.)
Game 4 at Recreation Park (Pit), Oct. 13: Det (Baldwin) 8, StL (King) 0
Game 5 at Washington Park (Bro), Oct. 14: StL (Caruthers) 5, Det (Conway) 2
Game 6 at Polo Grounds (NY), Oct. 15: Det (Getzein) 9, StL (Foutz) 0
Game 7 at Baseball Grounds (Phi), Oct. 17: Det (Baldwin) 3, StL (Caruthers) 1
Game 8 at South Side Grounds (Bos), Oct.18: Det (Getzein) 9, StL (Caruthers) 2
Game 9 at Baseball Grounds (Phi), Oct. 19: Det (Conway) 4, StL (King) 2
Game 10 at Swampoodle Grounds (Was), Oct. 21 (AM): StL (Caruthers) 11, Det (Getzein) 4
Game 11 at Oriole Park (Bal), Oct. 21 (PM): Det (Baldwin) 13, StL (Foutz) 3
Game 12 at Washington Park (Bro), Oct. 22: StL (King) 5, Det (Conway) 1
Game 13 at Recreation Park (Det), Oct. 24: Det (Baldwin) 6, StL (Caruthers) 3
Game 14 at West Side Park (Chi), Oct. 25: Det (Getzein) 4, StL (King) 3
Game 15 at Sportsman's Park (StL), Oct.26: StL (Caruthers) 9, Det (Getzein) 2

DETROIT

		G	AB	H	R	2B	3B	HR	RBI	BB	BA	SA
UT	Hardy Richardson	15	66	13	12	5	2	1	4	1	.197	.348
SS	Jack Rowe	15	63	21	12	1	1	0	7	2	.333	.397
RF	Sam Thompson	15	58	21	8	2	0	2	7	3	**.362**	**.621**
1B/C	Charlie Ganzel	14	58	13	5	1	0	0	2	1	.224	.241
3B/1B	Deacon White	15	58	12	8	1	1	0	3	2	.207	.259
CF	Ned Hanlon	15	50	11	5	1	1	0	4	5	.220	.280
C/1B	Charlie Bennett	11	42	11	6	2	1	0	9	3	.262	.357
2B	Fred Dunlap	11	40	6	5	0	1	0	1	0	.150	.175
P	Charlie Getzein	6	20	6	5	2	0	0	2	3	.300	.400
LF	Larry Twitchell	6	20	5	5	1	0	1	3	0	.250	.300
P	Lady Baldwin	5	17	4	1	1	0	0	1	2	.235	.294
P	Pete Conway	4	12	0	0	0	0	0	0	0	.000	.000
1B/C	Sy Sutcliffe	4	11	1	1	0	0	0	0	1	.091	.091
1B	Dan Brouthers	1	3	2	0	0	0	0	0	0	.667	.667
		15	518	126	73	17	7	4	43	23	.243	.326

		G	IP	GS	CG	W	L	K	BB	SH	SV	ERA
	Charlie Getzein	6	58	6	6	4	2	17	15	1	0	2.48
	Lady Baldwin	5	42	5	5	4	1	4	10	1	0	1.50
	Pete Conway	4	33	4	4	2	2	10	6	0	0	3.00
			133	15	15	10	5	31	31	2	0	2.30

ST. LOUIS

		G	AB	H	R	2B	3B	HR	RBI	BB	BA	SA
LF	Tip O'Neill	15	65	13	7	2	1	1	5	0	.200	.308
1B/OF	Charlie Comiskey	15	62	19	8	2	0	0	2	1	.306	.339
UT	Dave Foutz	15	59	10	4	2	1	0	1	2	.169	.237
3B	Arlie Latham	15	58	17	12	1	0	0	1	9	.293	.310
CF	Curt Welch	15	58	12	6	3	1	1	6	0	.207	.345
SS	Bill Gleason	13	49	8	3	0	0	0	1	3	.163	.163
2B	Yank Robinson	15	46	15	5	5	1	0	4	10	.326	.478
P/OF	Bob Caruthers	10	46	11	2	0	0	0	3	1	.239	.239
C	Doc Bushong	9	29	7	3	0	0	0	1	4	.241	.241
C	Jack Boyle	6	24	5	1	0	0	0	1	0	.208	.208
P	Silver King	4	14	1	0	0	0	0	0	0	.071	.071
SS	Harry Lyons	2	7	2	3	0	0	0	0	1	.286	.286
		15	517	120	54	15	4	2	25	31	.232	.288

	G	IP	GS	CG	W	L	K	BB	SH	SV	ERA
Bob Caruthers	8	71.2	8	8	4	4	19	12	0	0	2.13
Silver King	4	31	4	4	1	3	21	2	0	0	2.03
Dave Foutz	3	26	3	3	0	6	6	9	0	0	3.46
		128.2	15	15	5	10	46	23	0	0	2.38

AMERICAN ASSOCIATION

	W	L	PCT	HOME	ROAD	GB
1. St. Louis Browns	95	40	.704	58–15	37–25	—
2. Cincinnati Reds	81	54	.600	46–27	35–27	14
3. Baltimore Orioles	77	58	.570	42–21	35–37	18
4. Louisville Colonels	76	60	.559	45–23	31–37	19.5
5. Philadelphia Athletics	64	69	.481	41–27	23–42	30
6. Brooklyn Grays	60	74	.448	37–38	23–36	34.5
7. New York Metropolitans	44	89	.331	25–33	19–56	50
8. Cleveland Blues	39	92	.298	22–36	17–56	54

	StL	Cin	Bal	Lou	Phi	Bro	NY	Cle	
St. Louis	—	6	16	13	12	16	14	18	95
Cincinnati	12	—	9	8	11	13	17	11	81
Baltimore	3	11	—	7	14	10	15	17	77
Louisville	7	12	11	—	11	12	12	11	76
Philadelphia	8	9	6	8	—	8	11	14	64
Brooklyn	4	7	9	8	10	—	9	13	60
New York	5	3	4	8	7	9	—	8	44
Cleveland	1	6	3	8	4	6	11	—	39
	40	54	58	60	69	74	89	92	536

SEASON LEADERS

Batting Average (325 ABs)

1	O'Neill, St. Louis	.435
2.	Browning, Louisville	.402
3.	Orr, New York	.368
4.	Lyons, Philadelphia	.367
5.	Caruthers, St. Louis	.357

On–Base Percentage

1.	O'Neill, St. Louis	.490
2.	Browning, Louisville	.464
3.	Caruthers, St. Louis	.463
4.	Robinson, St. Louis	.445
5.	Lyons, Philadelphia	.421

Home Runs

1.	O'Neill, St. Louis	14
2.	Reilly, Cincinnati	10
3.	Burns, Baltimore	9
4.	Caruthers, St. Louis	8
	Davis, Baltimore	8
	Fennelly, Cincinnati	8

Hits

1.	O'Neill, St. Louis	225
2.	Browning, Louisville	220
3.	Lyons, Philadelphia	209
4.	Latham, St. Louis	198
5.	Burns, Baltimore	188

Bases on Balls

1.	Radford, New York	106
2.	Robinson, St. Louis	92
3.	Nicol, Cincinnati	86
4.	Mack, Louisville	83
5.	Fennelly, Cincinnati	82

Slugging Average

1.	O'Neill, St. Louis	.691
2.	Caruthers, St. Louis	.547
	Browning, Louisville	.547
4.	Lyons, Philadelphia	.523
5.	Burns, Baltimore	.519

Total Bases

1.	O'Neill, St. Louis	357
2.	Browning, Louisville	299
3.	Lyons, Philadelphia	298
4.	Burns, Baltimore	286
5.	Reilly, Cincinnati	263

Stolen Bases

1.	Nicol, Cincinnati	138
2.	Latham, St. Louis	129
3.	Comiskey, St. Louis	117
4.	Browning, Louisville	103
5.	McPhee, Cincinnati	95

Runs

1.	O'Neill, St. Louis	167
2.	Latham, St. Louis	163
3.	Griffin, Baltimore	142
4.	Poorman, Philadelphia	140
5.	Comiskey, St. Louis	139

RBI

1.	O'Neill, St. Louis	123
2.	Browning, Louisville	118
3.	Davis, Baltimore	109
4.	Welch, St. Louis	108
	Foutz, St. Louis	108

PITCHING

Wins

1.	Kilroy, Baltimore	46
2.	Ramsey, Louisville	37
3.	E. Smith, Cincinnati	34
4.	King, St. Louis	32
5.	Mullane, Cincinnati	31

Innings

1.	Kilroy, Baltimore	589.1
2.	Ramsey, Louisville	561
3.	P. Smith, Baltimore	491.1
4.	Seward, Philadelphia	470.2
5.	Weyhing, Philadelphia	466.1

Losses

1.	Mays, New York	34
2.	Crowell, Cleveland	31
3.	P. Smith, Baltimore	30
4.	Weyhing, Philadelphia	28
5.	Ramsey, Louisville	27

Complete Games

1.	Kilroy, Baltimore	66
2.	Ramsey, Louisville	61
3.	P. Smith, Baltimore	54
4.	Weyhing, Philadelphia	53
5.	Seward, Philadelphia	52

Strikeouts

1.	Ramsey, Louisville	355
2.	Kilroy, Baltimore	217
3.	P. Smith, Baltimore	206
4.	Weyhing, Philadelphia	193
5.	E. Smith, Cincinnati	176

ERA (140 Innings)

1.	E. Smith, Cincinnati	2.94
2.	Kilroy, Baltimore	3.07
3.	Mullane, Cincinnati	3.24
4.	Caruthers, St. Louis	3.30
5.	Ramsey, Louisville	3.43

Winning Percentage (24 decisions)

1.	Caruthers, St. Louis	.763
2.	King, St. Louis	.727
3.	Kilroy, Baltimore	.708
4.	Foutz, St. Louis	.676
5.	E. Smith, Cincinnati	.667

Lowest On–Base Percentage

1.	E. Smith, Cincinnati	.286
2.	Caruthers, St. Louis	.287
3.	Ramsey, Louisville	.299
4.	Kilroy, Baltimore	.306
	Foutz, St. Louis	.306

FIELDING

Total Chances

1B	Tucker, Baltimore	1431
2B	McPhee, Cincinnati	948
3B	Pinkney, Brooklyn	546
SS	White, Louisville	731
OF	Welch, St. Louis	388
C	Baldwin, Cincinnati	625
P	Kilroy, Baltimore	224

Fielding Average

Phillips, Brooklyn	.982
Greenwood, Baltimore	.928
Pinkney, Brooklyn	.890
G. Smith, Brooklyn	.886
Corkhill, Cincinnati	.952
Boyle, St. Louis	.890
Caruthers, St. Louis	.971

ST. LOUIS Charlie Comiskey Sportsman's Park (I)

		G	AB	H	R	2B	3B	HR	RBI	BB	SB	BA	SA
3B	Arlie Latham	136	**627**	198	163	35	10	2	86	45	129	.316	.413
SS	Bill Gleason	135	578	172	135	19	1	0	76	41	23	.288	.323
CF	Curt Welch	131	544	151	98	32	7	3	108	25	89	.278	.379
1B	Charlie Comiskey	125	538	180	139	22	5	4	103	27	117	.335	.416
LF	Tip O'Neill	124	517	**225**	**167**	**52**	**19**	**14**	**123**	50	30	**.435**	**.691**
2B	Yank Robinson	125	430	131	102	32	4	1	74	92	75	.305	.405
UT	Dave Foutz	102	423	151	79	26	13	4	108	23	22	.357	.508
RF	Bob Caruthers	98	364	130	102	23	11	8	73	66	49	.357	.547
C	Jack Boyle	88	350	66	48	3	1	2	41	20	7	.189	.220
P	Silver King	62	222	46	28	6	1	0	19	24	10	.207	.243
C	Doc Bushong	53	201	51	35	4	0	0	26	11	14	.254	.274
Sub	Lou Sylvester	29	112	25	20	4	3	1	18	13	13	.223	.339
P	Ed Knouff	15	56	10	4	1	2	0	6	1	1	.179	.268
P	Nat Hudson	13	48	12	7	2	1	0	3	4	0	.250	.333
Sub	Harry Lyons	2	8	1	2	0	0	0	1	0	2	.125	.125
P	Joe Murphy	1	6	1	0	0	0	0	0	0	0	.167	.167
Sub	Mike Goodfellow	1	4	0	0	0	0	0	0	0	0	.000	.000
		138	5048	**1550**	**1131**	**261**	**78**	**39**	**862**	442	**581**	**.307**	**.413**

1B	Comiskey 116, Foutz 15, Caruthers 7, Boyle 2, Welch 1
2B	Robinson 117, Comiskey 9, Welch 8, Latham 5, Sylvester 1, Lyons 1
SS	Gleason 135, Robinson 2
3B	Latham 132, Robinson 6, Bushong 2, Boyle 1
OF	O'Neill 124, Welch 123, Caruthers 54, Foutz 50, Sylvester 29, King 17, Knouff 9, Hudson 6, Comiskey 3, Robinson 2, Boyle 2, Bushong 2, Lyons 1
C	Boyle 86, Bushong 52, Latham 2, Robinson 1, Goodfellow 1
P	King 46, Foutz 40, Caruthers 39, Hudson 9. Knouff 9, Murphy 1, Robinson 1

	G	IP	GS	CG	W	L	K	BB	SH	SV	ERA
Silver King	46	390	44	43	32	12	128	109	2	1	3.78
Bob Caruthers	39	341	39	39	29	9	74	61	2	0	3.30
Dave Foutz	40	339.1	38	36	25	12	94	90	1	0	3.87
Nat Hudson	9	67	9	7	4	4	15	20	0	0	4.97
Ed Knouff	6	50	6	6	4	2	18	36	1	0	4.50
Joe Murphy	1	9	1	1	1	0	5	4	0	0	5.00
Yank Robinson	1	3	0	0	0	0	0	3	0	1	3.00
		—1 forfeit L vs Louisville on July 3—								
		1199.1	137	132	95	39	334	323	6	2	3.77

CINCINNATI   Gus Schmelz   American Park

		G	AB	H	R	2B	3B	HR	RBI	BB	SB	BA	SA
1B	Long John Reilly	134	551	170	106	35	14	10	96	22	50	.309	.477
CF	Pop Corkhill	128	541	168	79	19	11	5	97	14	30	.311	.414
2B	Bid McPhee	129	540	156	137	20	**19**	2	87	55	95	.289	.407
SS	Frank Fennelly	134	526	140	133	15	16	8	97	82	74	.266	.401
3B	Hick Carpenter	127	498	124	70	12	6	1	50	19	44	.249	.303
RF	Hugh Nicol	125	475	102	122	18	2	1	34	86	**138**	.215	.267
C	Kid Baldwin	96	388	98	46	15	10	1	57	6	13	.253	.351
LF	White Wings Tebeau	85	318	94	57	12	5	4	33	31	37	.296	.403
P	Tony Mullane	56	199	44	35	6	3	3	23	16	20	.221	.327
P	Elmer Smith	52	186	47	26	10	6	0	23	11	5	.253	.371
Sub	Jim Keenan	47	174	44	19	4	1	0	17	11	7	.253	.287
Sub	Charley Jones	41	153	48	28	7	4	2	40	19	7	.314	.451
P	Billy Serad	22	79	14	9	1	2	0	5	3	0	.177	.241
Sub	Heinie Kappel	23	78	22	11	3	2	0	15	2	3	.282	.372
Sub	Jack O'Connor	12	40	4	4	0	0	0	1	2	3	.100	.100
P	Jumbo McGinnis	8	31	6	8	2	1	0	2	1	1	.194	.323
P	Mike Shea	2	8	2	1	0	0	0	0	1	0	.250	.250
P	Mother Watson	2	8	1	1	0	0	0	0	1	0	.125	.125
P	Bill Widner	1	4	1	0	0	0	0	1	0	0	.250	.250
		136	4797	1285	892	179	**102**	37	678	382	527	.268	.371

- 1B   Reilly 127, Keenan 11
- 2B   McPhee 129, Kappel 6
- SS   Fennelly 134, Kappel 1
- 3B   Carpenter 127, Kappel 9
- OF   Corkhill 128, Nicol 125, Tebeau 84, Jones 41, Reilly 9, Mullane 9, Kappel 7, O'Connor 7, Baldwin 2, Smith 2, Serad 1, Watson 1
- C   Baldwin 96, Keenan 38, O'Connor 5
- P   Smith 52, Mullane 48, Serad 22, McGinnis 8, Corkhill 5, Shea 2, Watson 2, Widner 1, Tebeau 1

	G	IP	GS	CG	W	L	K	BB	SH	SV	ERA
Elmer Smith	52	447.1	52	49	34	17	176	126	3	0	**2.94**
Tony Mullane	48	416.1	48	47	31	17	97	121	**6**	0	3.24
Billy Serad	22	187.1	21	20	10	11	34	80	2	1	4.08
Jumbo McGinnis	8	69.1	8	8	3	5	18	43	0	0	5.45
Mike Shea	2	16.2	2	2	1	1	0	10	0	0	7.02
Pop Corkhill	5	14.2	0	0	1	0	3	5	0	0	5.52
Mother Watson	2	14	2	1	0	1	1	6	0	0	5.79
Bill Widner	1	9	1	1	1	0	0	2	0	0	5.00
White Wings Tebeau	1	8	1	1	0	1	1	3	0	0	13.50
		—1 forfeit L vs Louisville on April 30—								
		1182.2	135	129	81	53	330	396	**11**	1	**3.58**

BALTIMORE   **Billy Barnie**   **Oriole Park (I)**

		G	AB	H	R	2B	3B	HR	RBI	BB	SB	BA	SA
RF	Blondie Purcell	140	567	142	101	25	8	4	96	48	88	.250	.344
SS	Oyster Burns	140	551	188	122	33	**19**	9	99	63	58	.341	.519
CF	Mike Griffin	136	532	160	142	32	13	3	94	55	94	.301	.427
1B	Tommy Tucker	136	524	144	114	15	9	6	84	29	85	.275	.372
2B	Bill Greenwood	118	495	130	114	16	6	0	65	54	71	.263	.319
3B	Jumbo Davis	130	485	150	81	23	**19**	8	109	28	49	.309	.485
LF	Joe Sommer	131	463	123	88	11	5	0	65	63	29	.266	.311
C	Sam Trott	85	300	77	44	16	3	0	37	27	8	.257	.330
P	Matt Kilroy	72	239	59	46	5	6	0	25	31	12	.247	.318
P	Phenomenal Smith	64	205	48	37	7	6	1	18	26	7	.234	.341
C	Chris Fulmer	56	201	54	52	11	4	0	32	36	35	.269	.363
Sub	Law Daniels	48	165	41	23	5	1	0	32	8	7	.248	.291
P	Ed Knouff	9	31	9	4	0	0	0	3	1	1	.290	.290
Sub	Jackie Hayes	8	28	4	2	3	0	0	3	0	0	.143	.250
P	Lev Shreve	6	24	4	3	0	1	0	2	1	1	.167	.250
P	Bill Gardner	4	11	3	2	0	0	0	1	1	0	.273	.273
P	Ed Keating	1	4	1	0	0	0	0	0	0	0	.250	.250
		141	4825	1337	975	202	100	31	765	**469**	545	.277	.380

1B   Tucker 136, Daniels 4, Trott 2
2B   Greenwood 117, Sommer 13, Trott 11, Daniels 2, Burns 1
SS   Burns 98, Davis 43, Sommer 2, Gardner 1, Daniels 1, Trott 1, Kilroy 1
3B   Davis 87, Burns 42, Sommer 10, Hayes 3, Daniels 1, Gardiner 1
OF   Purcell 140, Griffin 136, Sommer 110, Daniels 15, Fulmer 8, Smith 7, Kilroy 4, Hayes 4, Trott 3, Knouff 3, Shreve 2, Greenwood 1
C   Trott 69, Fulmer 48, Daniels 26, Hayes 1
P   Kilroy 69, Smith 58, Knouff 9, Shreve 5, Gardner 3, Burns 3, Keating 1, Sommer 1, Purcell 1

	G	IP	GS	CG	W	L	K	BB	SH	SV	ERA
Matt Kilroy	**69**	**589.1**	**69**	**66**	**46**	19	217	157	**6**	0	3.07
Phenomenal Smith	58	491.1	55	54	25	30	206	176	1	0	3.79
Ed Knouff	9	63	9	6	2	6	27	41	0	0	7.57
Lev Shreve	5	38	5	4	3	1	13	19	1	0	3.79
Bill Gardner	3	13	2	1	0	1	3	10	0	0	11.08
Oyster Burns	3	11.1	0	0	1	0	2	4	0	0	9.53
Ed Keating	1	9	1	1	0	1	0	6	0	0	11.00
Blondie Purcell	1	4	0	0	0	0	2	4	0	0	15.75
Joe Sommer	1	1	0	0	0	0	0	1	0	0	9.00
		1220	141	132	77	58	470	418	8	0	3.87

LOUISVILLE   **Honest John Kelly**   **Eclipse Park (I)**

		G	AB	H	R	2B	3B	HR	RBI	BB	SB	BA	SA
RF	Chicken Wolf	137	569	160	103	27	13	2	102	34	45	.281	.385
LF	Hub Collins	130	559	162	122	22	8	1	66	39	71	.290	.363
CF	Pete Browning	134	547	220	137	35	16	4	118	55	103	.402	.547
3B	Joe Werrick	136	533	152	90	21	13	7	99	38	49	.285	.413
SS	Bill White	132	512	129	85	7	9	2	79	47	41	.252	.313
2B	Reddy Mack	128	478	147	117	23	8	1	69	83	22	.308	.395
1B	John Kerins	112	476	140	101	18	**19**	5	57	38	49	.294	.443
P	Guy Hecker	91	370	118	89	21	6	4	50	31	48	.319	.441
P	Toad Ramsey	65	225	43	19	4	0	0	24	19	2	.191	.209
C	Paul Cook	61	223	55	34	4	2	0	17	11	15	.247	.283
C	Lave Cross	54	203	54	32	8	3	0	26	15	15	.266	.335
P	Icebox Chamberlain	37	131	26	14	1	1	1	16	12	2	.198	.244

		G	AB	H	R	2B	3B	HR	RBI	BB	SB	BA	SA
Sub	Phil Reccius	11	37	9	9	2	0	0	4	8	3	.243	.297
Sub	Amos Cross	8	28	3	0	0	0	0	0	1	0	.107	.107
P	Joe Neale	5	19	1	3	0	0	0	1	3	1	.053	.053
Sub	Ducky Hemp	1	3	1	1	1	0	0	0	1	0	.333	.667
P	Peekaboo Veach	1	3	0	0	0	0	0	0	1	0	.000	.000
		139	4916	1420	956	194	98	27	728	436	466	.289	.385

1B Kerins 74, Hecker 43, Wolf 11, Collins 8, Cook 6, A. Cross 2
2B Mack 128, Collins 10
SS White 132, Collins 4, Reccius 1
3B Werrick 136, Collins 1
OF Browning 134, Wolf 128, Collins 109, Hecker 16, L. Cross 10, Reccius 10, Kerins 5, Chamberlain 2, A. Cross 1, Hemp 1
C Cook 55, L. Cross 44, Kerins 35, A. Cross 5
P Ramsey 65, Hecker 43, Chamberlain 36, Neale 5, Veach 1

	G	IP	GS	CG	W	L	K	BB	SH	SV	ERA
Toad Ramsey	65	561	64	61	37	27	**355**	167	0	0	3.43
Guy Hecker	34	285.1	32	32	18	12	58	50	2	1	4.16
Icebox Chamberlain	36	309	36	35	18	16	118	117	1	0	3.79
Joe Neale	5	41.1	4	4	1	4	11	15	0	0	6.97
Peekaboo Veach	1	9	1	1	0	1	2	8	0	0	4.00
—2 forfeit Ws: vs Cincinnati on April 30 and vs St. Louis on July 3—
	1205.2	137	**133**	74	60	**544**	357	3	1	3.82

PHILADELPHIA **Charlie Mason (38–40)** **Frank Bancroft (26–29)** **Jefferson Street Grounds**

		G	AB	H	R	2B	3B	HR	RBI	BB	SB	BA	SA
RF	Tom Poorman	135	585	155	140	18	**19**	4	61	35	88	.265	.381
3B	Denny Lyons	137	570	209	128	43	14	6	102	47	73	.367	.523
SS	Chippy McGarr	137	536	158	93	23	6	1	63	23	84	.295	.366
2B	Lou Bierbauer	126	530	144	74	19	7	1	82	13	40	.272	.340
LF	Henry Larkin	126	497	154	105	22	12	3	88	48	37	.310	.421
CF	Harry Stovey	124	497	142	125	31	12	4	77	56	74	.286	.421
1B	Jocko Milligan	95	377	114	54	27	4	2	50	21	8	.302	.411
P	Ed Seward	74	266	50	31	10	0	5	28	16	14	.188	.282
C	Wilbert Robinson	68	264	60	28	6	2	1	24	14	15	.227	.277
OF	Fred Mann	55	229	63	42	14	6	0	32	15	16	.275	.389
P	Gus Weyhing	57	209	42	19	6	1	0	16	6	8	.201	.239
C	George Townsend	31	109	21	12	3	0	0	14	3	8	.193	.220
Sub	Ed Flanagan	19	80	20	12	5	0	1	10	3	3	.250	.350
Sub	Chief Roseman	21	73	16	16	2	1	0	8	10	3	.219	.274
P	Al Atkinson	16	59	12	8	2	0	1	5	5	3	.203	.288
P	Bob Mathews	7	25	5	5	0	0	0	0	4	0	.200	.200
P	Bill Hart	3	13	1	0	0	0	0	0	0	0	.077	.077
Sub	Ed Greer	3	11	2	1	0	0	0	0	0	2	.182	.182
P	Cannonball Titcomb	3	10	0	0	0	0	0	0	2	0	.000	.000
Sub	Jim Roxburgh	3	8	1	0	0	0	0	0	0	0	.125	.125
P	Billy Taylor	1	4	1	0	0	0	0	1	0	0	.250	.250
P	Fred Chapman	1	2	0	0	0	0	0	0	0	0	.000	.000
P	Bill Casey	1	0	0	0	0	0	0	0	0	0	—	—
		137	4954	1370	893	231	84	29	661	321	476	.277	.375

1B   Milligan 50, Stovey 46, Larkin 23, Flanagan 19, Robinson 3
2B   Bierbauer 126, Larkin 10, Poorman 2, Roxburgh 1
SS   McGarr 137
3B   Lyons 137
OF   Poorman 135, Larkin 93, Stovey 80, Mann 55. Seward 21, Roseman 21, Atkinson 4, Weyhing 3, Townsend 3, Greer 3, Milligan 1, Robinson 1
C   Robinson 67, Milligan 47, Townsend 28, Roxburgh 2
P   Seward 55, Weyhing 55, Atkinson 15, Mathews 7, Titcomb 3, Hart 3, Chapman 1, Taylor 1, Casey 1, Bierbauer 1, Poorman 1

	G	IP	GS	CG	W	L	K	BB	SH	SV	ERA
Ed Seward	55	470.2	52	52	25	25	155	140	3	0	4.13
Gus Weyhing	55	466.1	55	53	26	28	193	167	2	0	4.27
Al Atkinson	15	124.2	15	11	6	8	34	54	0	0	5.92
Bobby Mathews	7	58	7	7	3	4	9	25	0	0	6.67
Bill Hart	3	26	3	3	1	2	4	17	0	0	4.50
Cannonball Titcomb	3	24	3	3	1	2	16	19	0	0	6.00
Billy Taylor	1	9	1	1	1	0	0	7	0	0	3.00
Fred Chapman	1	5	1	1	0	0	4	2	0	0	7.20
Bill Casey	1	1	0	0	0	0	0	1	0	0	18.00
Lou Bierbauer	1	1	0	0	0	0	1	0	0	1	0.00
Tom Poorman	1	0.2	0	0	0	0	1	1	0	0	40.50
—1 forfeit W vs Cleveland on July 22—											
		1186.1	137	131	63	69	417	433	5	1	4.59

BROOKLYN   Charlie Byrne   Washington Park (I)

		G	AB	H	R	2B	3B	HR	RBI	BB	SB	BA	SA
3B	George Pinkney	138	580	155	133	26	6	3	69	61	59	.267	.348
2B	Bill McClellan	136	548	144	109	24	6	1	53	80	70	.263	.344
1B	Bill Phillips	132	533	142	82	34	11	2	101	45	16	.266	.383
CF	Jim McTamany	134	520	134	123	22	10	1	68	76	66	.258	.344
SS	Germany Smith	103	435	128	79	19	16	4	72	13	26	.294	.439
RF	Ed Swartwood	91	363	92	72	14	8	1	54	46	29	.253	.344
P	Adonis Terry	86	352	103	56	6	10	3	65	16	27	.293	.392
LF	Ed Greer	91	327	83	49	13	2	2	48	25	33	.254	.324
C	Jimmy Peoples	73	268	68	36	14	2	1	38	16	22	.254	.332
Sub	Ernie Burch	49	188	55	47	4	4	2	26	29	15	.293	.388
C	Bob Clark	48	177	47	24	3	1	0	18	7	15	.266	.294
P	Henry Porter	40	146	29	16	2	4	1	12	10	6	.199	.288
Sub	Jack O'Brien	30	123	28	18	4	1	1	17	6	8	.228	.301
P	Steve Toole	26	103	24	19	6	0	1	13	3	4	.233	.320
Sub	Billy Otterson	30	100	20	16	4	1	2	15	8	8	.200	.320
P	John Harkins	27	98	23	10	5	0	0	16	7	4	.235	.286
P	Hardie Henderson	13	41	5	10	0	0	0	3	6	1	.122	.122
P	Bert Cunningham	3	8	0	3	0	0	0	0	2	0	.000	.000
Sub	Chief Roseman	1	3	1	2	0	0	0	1	0	0	.333	.333
		138	4913	1281	904	200	82	25	689	456	409	.261	.350

1B   Phillips 132, Peoples 4, Toole 3
2B   McClellan 136, O'Brien 1, Peoples 1, Harkins 1
SS   Smith 101, Otterson 30, Peoples 4, Terry 2, Pinkney 2
3B   Pinkney 136, Smith 2
OF   McTamany 134, Swartwood 91, Greer 76, Burch 49, Terry 49, Peoples 8, Harkins 4, O'Brien 4, Clark 3, Porter 1, Roseman 1
C   Peoples 57, Clark 45, O'Brien 25, Greer 16
P   Porter 40, Terry 40, Harkins 24, Toole 24, Henderson 13, Cunningham 3

	G	IP	GS	CG	W	L	K	BB	SH	SV	ERA
Henry Porter	40	339.2	40	38	15	24	74	96	1	0	4.21
Adonis Terry	34	318	35	35	16	16	138	99	1	**3**	4.02
John Harkins	24	199	24	22	10	14	36	77	0	0	6.02
Steve Toole	24	194	24	22	14	10	48	106	1	0	4.31
Hardie Henderson	13	111.2	12	12	5	8	28	63	0	0	3.95
Bert Cunningham	3	23	3	3	0	2	8	13	0	0	5.09
		1185.1	138	132	60	74	332	454	3	3	4.47

NEW YORK   **Bob Ferguson (6–24)**   **Dave Orr (3–5)**   **Opie Caylor (35–60)**
St. George Grounds

		G	AB	H	R	2B	3B	HR	RBI	BB	SB	BA	SA
LF	Darby O'Brien	127	522	157	97	30	15	5	73	40	49	.301	.437
3B	Frank Hankinson	127	512	137	79	29	11	1	71	38	19	.268	.373
SS	Paul Radford	128	486	129	127	15	5	4	45	**106**	73	.265	.342
1B	Dave Orr	84	345	127	63	25	10	2	66	22	17	.368	.516
2B	Joe Gerhardt	85	307	68	40	13	2	0	27	24	15	.221	.277
Sub	Candy Nelson	68	257	63	61	5	1	0	24	48	29	.245	.272
C	Bill Holbert	60	255	58	20	4	3	0	32	7	12	.227	.267
CF	Charley Jones	62	247	63	30	11	3	3	29	12	8	.255	.360
RF	Chief Roseman	60	241	55	30	10	1	1	27	9	3	.228	.290
P	Al Mays	62	221	45	23	15	4	2	23	10	7	.204	.335
C	Jim Donahue	60	220	62	33	4	1	1	29	21	6	.282	.323
Sub	John Meister	39	158	35	24	6	2	1	21	16	9	.222	.304
Sub	Tom O'Brien	31	129	25	13	3	2	0	18	2	10	.194	.248
Sub	Eddie Hogan	32	120	24	22	6	1	0	5	30	12	.200	.267
C	Pete Sommers	33	116	21	9	3	0	1	12	7	6	.181	.233
Sub	Dude Esterbrook	20	101	17	11	1	0	0	7	6	8	.168	.178
P	Ed Cushman	27	93	23	14	4	2	0	9	10	2	.247	.333
P	Jack Lynch	23	83	14	4	1	0	0	6	7	3	.169	.181
Sub	Jimmy Knowles	16	60	15	12	1	1	0	6	1	6	.250	.300
Sub	Clarence Cross	16	55	11	9	2	1	0	5	2	0	.200	.273
P	John Shaffer	13	48	8	4	1	1	0	3	1	1	.167	.229
P	Stump Weidman	14	46	7	5	1	1	0	1	4	2	.152	.217
Sub	Jon Morrison	9	34	4	7	0	0	0	3	6	0	.118	.118
Sub	Sadie Houck	10	33	5	3	1	0	0	0	3	2	.152	.182
Sub	Cyclone Ryan	8	32	7	4	1	0	0	3	3	1	.219	.250
Sub	Fred O'Neill	6	26	8	4	1	1	0	3	1	3	.308	.423
P	Bill Fagan	6	21	3	0	0	0	0	0	0	0	.143	.143
P	Charlie Parsons	4	15	3	3	0	0	0	0	1	1	.200	.200
P	George McMullen	3	12	1	2	0	0	0	0	0	0	.083	.083
Sub	Charlie Hall	3	12	1	1	0	0	0	0	2	1	.083	.083
Sub	Tom Kinslow	2	6	0	0	0	0	0	0	0	0	.000	.000
Sub	Hugh Collins	1	4	1	0	0	0	0	0	0	0	.250	.250
Sub	Lip Pike	1	4	0	0	0	0	0	0	0	0	.000	.000
		138	4820	1197	754	193	66	20	549	439	305	.248	.328

1B   Orr 81, T. O'Brien 20, D. O'Brien 10, Esterbrook 9, Holbert 8, Ryan 8, Donahue 4, Roseman 3, Lynch 2, Sommers 1, Mays 1, Jones 1

2B   Gerhardt 84, Radford 18, Knowles 16, Meister 14, Esterbrook 5, T. O'Brien 2, Holbert 1, Donahue 1, Nelson 1, Houck 1

SS   Radford 76, Nelson 32, Cross 13, Houck 10, Esterbrook 5, Hogan 4, D. O'Brien 2, Holbert 2, Meister 1

3B   Hankinson 127, Cross 4, Meister 3, T. O'Brien 2, Gerhardt 1, D. O'Brien 1, Donahue 1, Hogan 1, Knowles 1

OF   D. O'Brien 121, Jones 62, Roseman 59, Nelson 37, Radford 37, Hogan 29, Meister 22, Mays 11, Morrison 9, T. O'Brien 8, Esterbrook 7, O'Neill 6, Donahue 5, Weidman 3, Hall 3, Orr 3, Sommers 1, Cushman 1, McMullen 1, Pike 1

C   Holbert 60, Donahue 51, Sommers 31, Kinslow 2, Collins 1

P   Mays 52, Cushman 26, Lynch 21, Shaffer 13, Weidman 12, Fagan 6, Parsons 4, McMullen 3, Jones 2, Radford 2, Roseman 2, Ryan 2, D. O'Brien 1, T. O'Brien 1

	G	IP	GS	CG	W	L	K	BB	SH	SV	ERA
Al Mays	52	441.1	52	50	17	34	124	136	0	0	4.73
Ed Cushman	26	220	26	25	10	15	64	83	0	0	5.97
Jack Lynch	21	187	21	21	7	14	45	36	0	0	5.10
John Shaffer	13	112	13	13	2	11	22	53	0	0	6.19
Stump Weidman	12	97	12	11	4	8	37	25	1	0	4.64
Bill Fagan	6	45	6	6	1	4	12	24	0	0	4.00
Charlie Parsons	4	34	4	4	1	1	5	6	0	0	4.50
George McMullen	3	21	3	2	2	1	2	19	0	0	7.71
Chief Roseman	2	8	0	0	0	0	1	5	0	0	7.88
Paul Radford	2	5	0	0	0	0	4	3	0	0	18.00
Darby O'Brien	1	3.2	0	0	0	0	0	5	0	0	7.36
Charley Jones	2	3	0	0	0	0	0	4	0	0	3.00
Cyclone Ryan	2	2.1	1	0	0	1	0	6	0	0	23.14
Tom O'Brien	1	1	0	0	0	0	0	1	0	0	0.00
		1180.1	138	132	44	89	316	406	1	0	5.28

CLEVELAND   **Jimmy Williams**   **Association Park (II)**

		G	AB	H	R	2B	3B	HR	RBI	BB	SB	BA	SA
SS	Ed McKean	132	539	154	97	16	3	2	54	60	76	.286	.375
2B	Cub Stricker	131	534	141	122	9	4	2	53	53	86	.264	.326
CF	Pete Hotaling	126	505	151	108	28	13	3	94	53	43	.299	.424
LF	Myron Allen	117	463	128	66	22	10	4	77	36	26	.276	.393
1B	Jim Toy	109	423	94	56	20	5	1	56	17	8	.222	.300
C	Pop Snyder	74	282	72	33	12	6	0	27	9	5	.255	.340
RF	Fred Mann	64	259	80	45	15	7	2	41	23	25	.309	.444
C	Charlie Reipschlager	63	231	49	20	8	3	0	17	11	7	.212	.273
3B	Phil Reccius	62	229	47	23	6	3	0	29	24	9	.205	.258
Sub	Scrappy Carroll	57	216	43	30	5	1	0	19	15	19	.199	.231
P	Billy Crowell	45	156	22	15	1	0	0	6	10	5	.141	.147
P	Mike Morrison	41	141	27	23	6	8	1	12	11	5	.191	.241
Sub	Charlie Sweeney	36	133	30	22	4	4	0	19	21	11	.226	.316
P	Bob Gilks	22	83	26	12	2	0	0	13	3	5	.313	.337
Sub	John McGlone	21	79	20	14	2	1	0	10	7	15	.253	.304
Sub	Jimmy Say	16	64	24	9	5	3	0	12	1	0	.375	.547
Sub	John Munyan	16	58	14	9	1	1	0	6	3	4	.241	.293
P	One Arm Daily	16	58	4	1	0	0	0	1	3	0	.069	.069
Sub	Chief Zimmer	14	52	12	9	5	0	0	4	4	1	.231	.327
Sub	Ed Herr	11	44	12	6	2	0	0	6	6	2	.273	.318
P	George Pechiney	10	36	9	6	1	0	0	2	2	0	.250	.278
Sub	Ed Flynn	7	27	5	0	1	0	0	4	1	3	.185	.222
P	John Kirby	5	18	3	0	0	1	0	0	0	0	.167	.278
Sub	Hank Simon	3	10	1	1	0	0	0	0	0	0	.100	.100
P	Frank Scheibeck	3	9	2	2	0	0	0	0	2	0	.222	.222
		133	4649	1170	729	178	77	14	562	375	355	.252	.332

1B   Toy 82, Sweeney 20, Reipschlager 16, Snyder 13, Gilks 6, Zimmer 2
2B   Stricker 126, McKean 8, Morrison 1, Gilks 1, Carroll 1
SS   McKean 123, Stricker 6, Toy 3, Allen 2, Sweeney 2, Scheibeck 1
3B   Reccius 62, McGlone 21, Say 16, Herr 11, Toy 8, Flynn 6, Carroll 3, Allen 3, Sweeney 2, Munyan 2, Morrison 1, Scheibeck 1
OF   Hotaling 126, Allen 115, Mann 64, Carroll 54, Munyan 12, Toy 11, Sweeney 10, McKean 4, Morrison 4, Gilks 3, Simon 3, Flynn 1
C   Snyder 63, Reipschlager 48, Zimmer 12, Toy 10, Munyan 3
P   Crowell 45, Morrison 40, Daily 16, Gilks 13, Pechiney 10, Kirby 5, Stricker 3, Sweeney 3, Allen 2, Scheibeck 1, Reccius 1

	G	IP	GS	CG	W	L	K	BB	SH	SV	ERA
Billy Crowell	45	389.1	45	45	14	31	72	138	1	0	4.88
Mike Morrison	40	316.2	40	35	12	25	158	**205**	0	0	4.92
One Arm Daily	16	139.2	16	16	4	12	30	44	0	0	3.67
Bob Gilks	13	108	13	12	7	5	28	42	1	0	3.08
George Pechiney	10	86	10	10	1	9	24	44	0	0	7.12
John Kirby	5	41	5	5	0	5	6	28	0	0	9.00
Charlie Sweeney	3	24	3	3	0	3	8	13	0	0	8.25
Myron Allen	2	9.2	0	0	1	0	1	3	0	0	1.86
Frank Scheibeck	1	9	1	1	0	1	3	4	0	0	12.00
Phil Reccius	1	7	0	0	0	0	0	5	0	0	7.71
Cub Stricker	3	5.2	0	0	0	0	2	7	0	1	3.18
—1 forfeit L vs Philadelphia on July 22—											
	1136	133	127	39	91	332	533	2	1	4.99	

1888
GOTHAM WINS ITS FIRST
WORLD CHAMPIONSHIP

Following the 1887 season, Chicago White Stockings owner and president Al Spalding pushed hard for a new major league alignment. Spalding proposed that the American Association drop its two weakest franchises, Cleveland and the New York Mets, while his colleagues shed the National League's two perennial tailenders, Washington and Indianapolis. The six teams left in each circuit would then merge into a single 12-team federation called the "American League."

The time was not yet ripe for Spalding's plan. Nor would the game's foremost observer, Henry Chadwick, have any better luck with the innovation he posited in *Sporting Life*. In January 1888, Chadwick railed against the increasing numbers of switchhitters such as Tommy Tucker, Cliff Carroll and Charlie Ferguson who jumped from one batter's box to the other while a pitcher was in the midst of his windup. Chadwick advocated a rule against switching sides of the plate once a pitcher went into motion, but it would be another 20 years before his suggestion was heeded.

Actually, 1888 saw the fewest franchise transfers and rule changes of any season during the decade. Only the New York Mets disappeared from the scene, replaced in the Association by a new Kansas City entry, and the lone revisions on the playing field of major import restored the three strikes-and-out rule and dispensed with counting a base on balls as both a time at bat and a hit. Yet never before and never again would such a seemingly small adjustment in the game's rules have so great an impact on the way it was played. Batting averages in the National League tumbled an average of 27 points, the average pitcher's ERA shrank from 4.05 to 2.83 and the loop strikeout total rose from 2,837 to 3,998 while walks dropped from 2,732 to 2,093. In the American Association the effect was even more pronounced. Batters hit an average of 35 points less, pitchers lopped an average of 1.23 runs off their ERAs, walks fell from 3,320 to 2,634 and strikeouts soared 38 percent from 3,075 to 4,234.

Most important of all, by again tipping the scales in the pitchers' favor the rulesmakers

The NL's newcomers in 1889, the Cleveland Blues, weren't nearly as crisp on the playing field as they looked here in arguably the handsomest team photo of the period. Nevertheless, they improved by ten and a half games over their .379 (50-82) sixth-place finish in 1888, their last year in the AA. Standing—Jim McAleer, Patsy Tebeau, Jersey Bakely and Pop Snyder. Seated—Cub Stricker, Darby O'Brien, Jay Faatz, Paul Radford, Larry Twitchell, manager Tom Loftus, Sy Sutcliffe, Eb Beatin and Ed McKean.

triggered an enormous decrease in run production. League teams dipped to 4,937 tallies in 1887 after producing 6,180 the previous year, and the Association went from 7,234 runs to 5,691. The sharp decline in offense changed priorities and resulted in a new champion being crowned in the League. Traditionally strong in the box and on defense, the New York Giants finally emerged in 1888. Though injuries nagged center fielder George Gore most of the season and shortstop Monte Ward lost 87 points off his batting average and led the League in errors, manager Jim Mutrie got ample compensation from his crack battery of Tim Keefe and Buck Ewing. In 1888, for the first time in his career, Ewing was hale enough to play 100 games, and Keefe was unquestionably the League's most dominant hurler as he not only won the pitching Triple Crown by leading in wins, strikeouts and ERA but also topped his cohorts in shutouts and winning percentage.

Second to the Giants were the Chicago White Stockings, spearheaded by southpaw rookie Gus Krock's 25 wins, center fielder Jimmy Ryan's 16 homers—the most in the majors—and first baseman Cap Anson, who won his last batting title. A length back in third were the Philadelphia Phillies, who survived a woeful .225 team batting average. But no team in the majors had less clout in 1888 than Washington. The last-place Nationals hit just

The 1888 world champion Giants. Front: Stump Weidman, Bill George, Cannonball Crane, Cannonball Titcomb, Monte Ward, Elmer Foster, manager Jim Mutrie, Danny Richardson, Jim O'Rourke, Mike Tiernan (behind O'Rourke), Mickey Welch, Elmer Cleveland and Mike Slattery. Rear: Tim Keefe (behind George), Pat Murphy, Roger Connor, unknown, Buck Ewing, Willard Brown, Gil Hatfield and George Gore.

.208, and rookie center fielder Dummy Hoy at .274 was the only regular above .225. Meanwhile, Detroit, the defending champion, tumbled out of the race in August after losing 16 straight games. The Wolverines eventually finished fifth when only Dan Brouthers of their six .300 hitters in 1887 managed to top the mark again.

The St. Louis Browns appeared certain to suffer an even worse decline than Detroit. Over the winter owner Chris Von Der Ahe almost totally dismantled his three-time American Association pennant winner. Bill Gleason, the only shortstop the Browns had known in their six-year history, was dealt to the Philadelphia Athletics, together with Curt Welch, the game's best defensive center fielder. To further ravage his team up the middle, Von Der Ahe sold the Brooklyn Bridegrooms his star pitching tandem of Bob Caruthers and Dave Foutz, plus Doc Bushong, who in 1886 had become the first man ever to catch 100 games in a season. Since Caruthers and Foutz had combined for 198 victories during the Browns' 1885–87 pennant run, and Von Der Ahe planned to use as his catcher Jack Boyle, a .189 hitter in 1887, and would ultimately replace Gleason and Welch with Bill White and Harry Lyons, who hit .175 and .194, respectively, for the Browns in 1888, St. Louis seemingly had no chance to tie the 1872–75 Boston Red Stockings' record of four straight pennants. In his preseason forecast, Opie Caylor gleefully opined, "I will be wonderfully surprised if the new St. Louis team will figure at all among the leaders in the race."

FORFEIT II

In 1888, Philadelphia was third in the NL despite finishing 14th in batting among the 16 ML teams. George Wood was part of the problem, hitting just .229. Wood's RBI totals in the 1880s cast heavy doubt on the reliability of RBI data in that era. In almost every season Wood is credited with suspiciously few RBI given his relatively high number of extra base hits and total bases.

Shortly past noon on October 13, 1888, Cap Anson stared out the window of his hotel room in Philadelphia. It was the closing day of the season, a Saturday, and Anson had no overwhelming desire to change into his uniform and ride out to the Phillies park that gray afternoon. He had the League batting title wrapped up and his White Stockings had clinched second place. So he watched the sky, hoping. Eventually, when the weather still hadn't cooperated, he changed into his uniform.

Finally, around 2:30, it began to rain, lightly at first and then harder and harder. Though he was already dressed to play, Anson remained at his hotel window even after the rain stopped a few minutes short of 3:30. He later said he hadn't bothered to take his team to the park because he'd been certain the game would be called. But the field at the Phillies park, in the opinion of umpire Charlie Daniels, was playable. With his team there in uniform and some 1,500 on hand to watch them warming up, Philadelphia manager Harry Wright pressed Daniels when game-time came and went, but there was still no sign of the White Stockings. Given no other choice, Daniels finally forfeited the game to Philadelphia.

The undeserved win gave the Phillies third place. Had Philadelphia played that day and lost, the Boston Beaneaters would have finished third. Three years later, when the Beaneaters and White Stockings became embroiled in arguably the most controversial pennant race in the nineteenth century, people around the National League would remember the day Anson and his team hadn't even bothered to show up.

SINISTER SECOND BASEMEN AND SHORTSTOPS

One glance at the 1888 season stats and anyone would assume that trouble at second base cost Brooklyn the American Association pennant. When your man there during the entire second half of the season hits only .122 and scores just 15 runs in 70 games, the evidence is overwhelming. The lone enduring mystery is why Brooklyn's rookie manager Bill McGunnigle benched Bill McClellan, the team's incumbent second baseman who'd scored 109 runs in 1887, and gave his job to Jack Burdock. In 1888, Burdock was 36 years old and hadn't played regularly since 1884.

The Brooklyn Bridegrooms would have been the AA's best team in 1888 if baseball were an eight-man game. Unhappily for manager Bill McGunnigle, every other team had a second baseman, so he had to find one too. His choice was Jack Burdock. Top: Bob Clark, Burdock, Doc Bushong, Dave Foutz, Bob Caruthers and Paul Radford. Bottom: George Pinkney, Jimmy Peoples, Germany Smith, Darby O'Brien, Dave Orr, Adonis Terry, Mickey Hughes and Bill McClellan.

When Boston released him early in the season, his career seemed over. Instead he found himself in the middle of the Association's first decent pennant race in four years.

What made Brooklyn quit on McClellan and go with Burdock? McGunnigle died in 1899 without ever having been asked that question, at least not for publication, but we can reasonably surmise that his answer would have made something of the fact that McClellan threw with his left arm. By 1888 lefthanded second basemen, shortstops and third basemen—fairly common earlier in the decade—were on the wane everywhere, not just in the majors. It probably did not escape McGunnigle, either, that the last team to win a pennant with a southpaw at one of those three infield positions was Cincinnati in 1882. In the interim a host of throwers from the sinister side who began their careers as middle infielders had found some other spot on the diamond to play. Roger Connor, for instance. Connor was exclusively a third baseman with Troy in 1879, his rookie year. He later served most of a season at second base. By 1888, though, he was settled for good at first base.

Hick Carpenter was among the very few lefthanded infielders who never made the switch to another location. In 1889, Carpenter became the first southpaw to play

1,000 major league games as an infielder. He also became the first man ever to play as many as 1,000 games in the majors at third base. Although Carpenter was 34 in 1889, it was probably not altogether age that caused that season to be his major league coda. For the 1889 season was not only the last for Carpenter but the next to last for virtually every lefty infielder. Since Bill Greenwood in 1890, no man who threw from the sinister side has ever played 100 or more games in a major league season at second base, shortstop or third base. A list of known lefthanders who served as regulars at one of the three infield positions from 1871 through today:

	YEAR	TEAM	REG. POS.
Ed Pinkham	1871	Chi-NA	3B
Jimmy Hallinan	1876	NY-NL	SS
" "	1877	Cin-NL	2B
Billy Redmond	1878	Mil-NL	SS
Bill McClellan	1878	Chi-NL	2B
" "	1881	Pro-NL	SS
" "	1883	Phi-NL	SS
" "	1884	Phi-NL	SS
" "	1885	Bro-AA	3B
" "	1886	Bro-AA	2B
" "	1887	Bro-AA	2B
Jimmy Macullar	1879	Syr-NL	SS
" "	1884	Bal-AA	SS
" "	1885	Bal-AA	SS
" "	1886	Bal-AA	SS
Roger Connor	1880	Tro-NL	3B
" "	1884	NY-NL	2B
Hick Carpenter	1880	Cin-NL	3B
" "	1882	Cin-AA	3B
" "	1883	Cin-AA	3B
" "	1884	Cin-AA	3B
" "	1885	Cin-AA	3B
" "	1886	Cin-AA	3B
" "	1887	Cin-AA	3B
" "	1888	Cin-AA	3B
" "	1889	Cin-AA	3B
Jack Leary	1883	Lou-AA	SS
Sam Trott	1883	Det-NL	2B*
Tom Evers	1884	Was-UA	2B
Bill Greenwood	1884	Bro-AA	2B
" "	1887	Bal-AA	2B
" "	1888	Bal-AA	2B
" "	1889	Col-AA	2B
" "	1890	Roc-AA	2B
Lefty Marr	1889	Col-AA	3B
" "	1890	Cin-NL	3B
Billy Hulen	1896	Phi-LA	SS**

*Also caught 34 games
**The last lefty to play second, short or third in more than 50 percent of his team's games.

Caylor, who loathed Von Der Ahe, then had to writhe in agony during the closing months of the season when the Browns, though most of them liked Von Der Ahe no better than Caylor, overtook heavily favored Brooklyn and sped home first by six and a half games. St. Louis's main cogs were repeat batting champion Tip O'Neill and Silver King, who was even more spectacular than Keefe in 1888. King's major league leading 45 wins represented nearly half of the Browns' total of 92, and his 1.64 ERA was made all the more impressive than Keefe's 1.74 by the fact that the Association had no other pitchers below 2.00 while the League had three besides Keefe.

Since the season in both circuits ran until mid-October, the World's Series could not begin until October 16. Having learned next to nothing from the previous year's postseason debacle, Von Der Ahe pushed for a 10-game Series to be played in its entirety even if one team had a prohibitive lead. He then agreed to Giants owner John Day's plan to play the first six games in the East and again assented to a double-umpire team of "Honest John" Gaffney and "Honest John" Kelly.

MR. ROBINSON

The 1888 season was the last in which a batter had to look at five bad pitches before he received a walk. Bases on balls, accordingly, were still hard to come by and usually went to sluggers like Roger Connor—the National League leader in 1888—or else tiny leadoff-man types such as Hugh Nicol and Dummy Hoy. The American Association walk leader in 1888 was neither a leadoff type nor a slugger; he hit all of .231 that year and had a .314 slugging average. Nevertheless he collected 116 walks to establish a new major league record. Even more remarkably, he totaled 11 more walks than he did hits. His name was Yank Robinson, and in 1888 he also established another major league record for the lowest batting average by a player who led his league in on-base percentage. Robinson either had the most phenomenal eye or the most phenomenal good luck of anyone in the last century. Three times during his relatively short career he collected 100 or more walks and totaled more walks than he did hits. Only one other nineteenth-century player ever did that even once, a man who in his way was as inimitable as Robinson.

	YEAR	TEAM	AB	H	BB	BA	OBP
Yank Robinson	1889	StL-AA	455	105	116	.231	.400
Yank Robinson	1889	StL-AA	452	94	118	.208	.376
Yank Robinson	1890	Pit-PL	306	70	101	.178	.328
Jack Crooks	1892	StL-LA	445	95	136	.213	.400*
Jack Crooks	1893	StL-LA	448	106	121	.237	.408

*The lowest BA ever by a player with a .400 or better OBP
Note: As a rookie in 1890 with Brooklyn of the Players League, Bill Joyce collected the same number of walks as hits—123.

THE WORST MAJOR LEAGUER IN THE NINETEENTH CENTURY

Deeming a player the best or worst anything always initiates a wild debate, but *The Great Encyclopedia of Nineteenth-Century Major League Baseball* hauls off and steps to the end of the limb. The worst major leaguer in the nineteenth century was Frank Gilmore. He wins by a landslide. In his three seasons with the Washington Nationals (1886–88), Gilmore compiled stats that rank him high among the all-time worst hitters as well as pitchers, and he was no marvel in the field either. Perhaps the best gauge of a pitcher's worth as a fielder is how many chances he handles. In 49 games as a boxman Gilmore had just 63 total chances. To help assess those figures: In 1888 Gilmore's pitching teammate Hank O'Day, considered a good fielder, collected 90 chances in 46 games, and Washington's top pitcher in 1886, Dupee Shaw, picked up 86 chances in 45 outings. The lists below offer ample assessment of Gilmore's pitching and hitting prowess, although certainly the former at least was affected by Washington's general ineptness in those years.

NINETEENTH-CENTURY WORST CAREER WINNING PERCENTAGE
(MINIMUM 45 DECISIONS)

	YEARS	W	L	ERA	PCT
Bill Stearns	1871–75	13	64	4.98	.169
Kirtley Baker	1890/1893–94/1898–99	9	38	6.28	.191
George Cobb	1892	10	37	4.86	.213
John Coleman	1883–90	23	72	4.68	.242
Jack Neagle	1879/1883–84	16	50	4.59	.242
Blondie Purcell	1879–87	15	43	3.73	.259
John Kirby	1884–88	18	50	4.09	.265
Jim Hughey	1891/1893/1896–00	29	80	4.87	.266
Frank Gilmore	1886–88	12	33	4.26	.267

ALL-TIME WORST CAREER BATTING AVERAGE
(MINIMUM 100 AT BATS)

	YEARS	AB	H	BA	SA
Ron Herbel	1963–71	206	6	.026	.039
Frank Gilmore	1886–88	163	7	.043	.043
Andy McGaffigan	1981–91	126	6	.048	.071
Ed Klepfer	1911–19	125	6	.048	.048
Bill Butler	1969–77	117	6	.051	.051
Taylor Phillips	1956–63	113	6	.053	.053
Bill Trotter	1937–44	109	6	.055	.064
Don Carman	1983–92	209	12	.057	.057
Don Johnson	1947–58	155	9	.058	.065
Luke Walker	1965–74	188	11	.059	.059
Buster Narum	1963–67	118	7	.059	.136

NINETEENTH-CENTURY WORST CAREER BATTING AVERAGE
(MINIMUM 100 AT BATS)

	YEARS	AB	H	BA	SA
Frank Gilmore	1886–88	163	7	.043	.043
Ted Kennedy	1885–86	117	7	.060	.068
Gus Shallix	1884–85	128	8	.065	.065
Mike Jordan	1890	125	12	.096	.104
Cannonball Titcomb	1886–90	224	22	.098	.112
John Kirby	1884–88	256	27	.105	.137
John Dolan	1890–95	109	12	.110	.193
Bill Vinton	1884–85	134	15	.112	.134
Ren Deagle	1883–84	128	15	.117	.141
John Hanna	1884	143	18	.126	.154
Frank Cox	1884	102	13	.127	.176

Note: In 1890, his lone big league season, Charlie McCullough gave Gilmore stiff competition, hitting .032 in 95 at bats and posting a .179 winning percentage in 28 decisions.

Some two weeks later, after the Giants won five of the six games in the East to render the four games in St. Louis nearly superfluous, Von Der Ahe openly accused Gaffney and Kelly of crooked work and his own shortstop White of subhuman play. The two umpires and White had little effect, though, on the outcome. The fifth postseason clash between the two leagues belonged almost entirely to Tim Keefe. In 35 innings Keefe allowed just 18 hits and two earned runs. It was only justice that he claimed four wins, including the Series clincher in Game Eight at St. Louis.

THE SEASONAL RECORD

NATIONAL LEAGUE

	W	L	PCT	HOME	ROAD	GB
1. New York Giants	84	47	.641	44–23	40–24	—
2. Chicago White Stockings	77	58	.570	43–27	34–31	9
3. Philadelphia Phillies	69	61	.531	37–29	32–32	14.5
4. Boston Beaneaters	70	64	.522	36–30	34–34	15.5
5. Detroit Wolverines	68	63	.519	40–26	28–37	16
6. Pittsburgh Alleghenys	66	68	.493	37–30	29–38	19.5
7. Indianapolis Hoosiers	50	85	.370	31–35	19–50	36
8. Washington Nationals	48	86	.358	26–38	22–48	37.5

	NY	Chi	Phi	Bos	Det	Pit	Ind	Was	
New York	—	8	14	12	11	10	14	15	84
Chicago	11	—	8	12	10	9	14	13	77
Philadelphia	5	10	—	10	7	14	13	10	69
Boston	8	7	9	—	10	10	11	15	70
Detroit	7	10	11	8	—	10	11	11	68
Pittsburgh	7	11	6	8	10	—	14	10	66
Indianapolis	5	6	4	9	8	6	—	12	50
Washington	4	6	9	5	7	9	8	—	48
	47	58	61	64	63	68	85	86	537

SEASON LEADERS

Batting Average (375 ABs)

1.	Anson, Chicago	.344
2.	Ryan, Chicago	.332
3.	Kelly, Boston	.318
4.	Brouthers, Detroit	.307
5.	Ewing, New York	.306

On–Base Percentage

1.	Anson, Chicago	.400
2.	Brouthers, Detroit	.399
3.	Connor, New York	.389
4.	Ryan, Chicago	.377
5.	Hoy, Washington	.374

Home Runs

1.	Ryan, Chicago	16
2.	Connor, New York	14
3.	Johnston, Boston	12
	Denny, Indianapolis	12
	Anson, Chicago	12

Slugging Average

1.	Ryan, Chicago	.515
2.	Anson, Chicago	.499
3.	Connor, New York	.480
	Kelly, Boston	.480
5.	Johnston, Boston	.472

Total Bases

1.	Ryan, Chicago	283
2.	Johnston, Boston	276
3.	Anson, Chicago	257
4.	Brouthers, Detroit	242
5.	Connor, New York	231

RBI

1.	Anson, Chicago	84
2.	Nash, Boston	75
3.	Rowe, Detroit	74
4.	Williamson, Chicago	73
5.	Connor, New York	71
	White, Detroit	71
	Kelly, Boston	71

Hits

1.	Ryan, Chicago	182
2.	Anson, Chicago	177
3.	Johnston, Boston	173
4.	Brouthers, Detroit	160
5.	White, Detroit	157

Stolen Bases

1.	Hoy, Washington	82
2.	Seery, Indianapolis	80
3.	Sunday, Pittsburgh	71
4.	Pfeffer, Chicago	64
5.	Ryan, Chicago	60

Bases on Balls

1.	Connor, New York	73
2.	Hoy, Washington	69
3.	Brouthers, Detroit	68
4.	Williamson, Chicago	65
5.	Seery, Indianapolis	64

Runs

1.	Brouthers, Detroit	118
2.	Ryan, Chicago	115
3.	Johnston, Boston	102
4.	Anson, Chicago	101
5.	Connor, New York	98

Strikeouts

1.	Denny, Indianapolis	79
2.	P. Smith, Pittsburgh	78
3.	Seery, Indianapolis	73
4.	Williamson, Chicago	71
5.	B. O'Brien, Washington	70

PITCHING

Wins

1.	Keefe, New York	35
2.	Clarkson, Boston	33
3.	Conway, Detroit	30
4.	Morris, Pittsburgh	29
5.	Buffinton, Philadelphia	28

Innings

1.	Clarkson, Boston	483.1
2.	Morris, Pittsburgh	480
3.	Galvin, Pittsburgh	437.1
4.	Keefe, New York	434.1
5.	Welch, New York	425.1

Strikeouts

1.	Keefe, New York	335
2.	Clarkson, Chicago	223
3.	Getzein, Detroit	202
4.	Buffinton, Philadelphia	199
5.	O'Day, Washington	186

ERA (140 innings)

1.	Keefe, New York	1.74
2.	Sanders, Philadelphia	1.90
3.	Buffinton, Philadelphia	1.91
4.	Welch, New York	1.93
5.	Sowders, Boston	2.07

Losses

1.	O'Day, Washington	29
2.	Getzein, Detroit	25
	Galvin Pittsburgh	25
4.	Healy, Indianapolis	24
	Shreve, Indianapolis	24

Complete Games

1.	Morris, Pittsburgh	54
2.	Clarkson, Boston	53
3.	Galvin, Pittsburgh	49
4.	Keefe, New York	48
5.	Welch, New York	47

Winning Percentage (25 decisions)

1.	Keefe, New York	.745
2.	Conway, Detroit	.682
3.	Sanders, Philadelphia	.655
4.	Krock, Chicago	.641
5.	Clarkson, Boston	.623

Lowest On–Base Percentage

1.	Conway, Detroit	.243
	Keefe, New York	.243
3.	Buffinton, Philadelphia	.244
4.	Gruber, Detroit	.249
5.	Titcomb, New York	.253

FIELDING

Total Chances

1B	Morrill, Boston	1501
2B	Pfeffer, Chicago	943
3B	Burns, Chicago	516
SS	Irwin, Philadelphia	642
OF	Sunday, Pittsburgh	345
C	Ewing, New York	645
P	Buffinton, Boston	163

Fielding Average

Anson, Chicago	.986
D. Richardson, New York	.942
Nash, Boston	.913
Glasscock, Indianapolis	.901
O'Rourke, New York	.960
Bennett, Detroit	.966
Morris, Pittsburgh	.940

NEW YORK **Jim Mutrie** **Polo Grounds (I)**

		G	AB	H	R	2B	3B	HR	RBI	BB	SB	BA	SA
2B	Danny Richardson	135	561	127	82	16	7	8	61	15	35	.226	.323
SS	Monte Ward	122	510	128	70	14	5	2	49	9	38	.251	.310
1B	Roger Connor	134	481	140	98	15	17	14	71	**73**	27	.291	.480
RF	Mike Tiernan	113	443	130	75	16	8	9	52	42	52	.293	.427
C	Buck Ewing	103	415	127	83	18	15	6	58	24	53	.306	.465
LF	Jim O'Rourke	107	409	112	50	16	6	4	50	24	25	.274	.372
CF	Mike Slattery	103	391	96	50	12	6	1	35	13	26	.246	.315
3B	Art Whitney	90	328	72	28	1	4	1	28	8	7	.220	.256
Sub	George Gore	64	254	56	37	4	4	2	17	30	11	.220	.291
P	Tim Keefe	51	181	23	10	3	0	2	8	4	3	.127	.177
P	Mickey Welch	47	169	32	16	5	0	2	10	1	4	.189	.254
Sub	Elmer Foster	37	136	20	15	3	2	0	10	9	13	.147	.199
Sub	Pat Murphy	28	106	18	11	1	0	0	4	6	3	.170	.179
Sub	Gil Hatfield	28	105	19	7	1	0	0	9	2	8	.181	.190
P	Cannonball Titcomb	23	82	10	6	1	0	0	5	1	5	.122	.134
Sub	Willard Brown	20	59	16	4	1	0	0	6	1	1	.271	.288
P	Bill George	9	39	9	7	1	0	1	6	0	1	.231	.333
P	Cannonball Crane	12	37	6	3	2	0	1	2	3	1	.162	.297
Sub	Elmer Cleveland	9	34	8	6	0	2	2	5	3	1	.235	.529
P	Stump Weidman	2	7	0	1	0	0	0	1	2	0	.000	.000
		138	4747	1149	659	130	76	55	487	270	314	.242	.336

1B	Connor 133, O'Rourke 4
2B	Richardson 135, Connor 1, Hatfield 1
SS	Ward 122, Hatfield 13, Ewing 4
3B	Whitney 90, Ewing 21, Hatfield 14, Cleveland 9, O'Rourke 2, Titcomb 1, Foster 1
OF	Tiernan 113, Slattery 103, O'Rourke 87, Gore 64, Foster 37, George 6, Hatfield 1, Keefe 1
C	Ewing 78, Murphy 28, Brown 20, O'Rourke 15
P	Keefe 51, Welch 47, Titcomb 23, Crane 12, George 4, Weidman 2, Ewing 2

	Games	IP	GS	CG	W	L	K	BB	SH	SV	ERA
Tim Keefe	51	434.1	51	48	**35**	12	**335**	90	**8**	0	**1.74**
Mickey Welch	47	425.1	47	47	26	19	167	108	5	0	1.93
Cannonball Titcomb	23	197	23	22	14	8	129	46	4	0	2.24
Cannonball Crane	12	92.2	11	11	5	6	58	40	2	1	2.43
Bill George	4	33.2	3	3	2	1	26	11	1	0	1.34
Stump Weidman	2	18	2	2	1	1	5	8	0	0	3.50
Buck Ewing	2	7	0	0	0	0	6	4	0	0	2.57
		—1 forfeit W vs Pittsburgh on May 31—									
	1208	137	133	83	47	**726**	308	**20**	1	**1.96**	

CHICAGO   **Cap Anson**   **West Side Park (1)**

		G	AB	H	R	2B	3B	HR	RBI	BB	SB	BA	SA
CF	Jimmy Ryan	129	549	**182**	115	33	10	**16**	64	35	60	.332	**.515**
2B	Fred Pfeffer	135	517	129	90	22	10	8	57	32	64	.250	.377
1B	Cap Anson	134	515	177	101	20	12	12	**84**	47	28	**.344**	.499
3B	Tom Burns	134	483	115	60	12	6	3	70	26	34	.238	.306
SS	Ned Williamson	132	452	113	75	9	14	8	73	65	25	.250	.385
UT	George Van Haltren	81	318	90	46	9	14	4	34	22	21	.283	.437
LF	Marty Sullivan	75	314	74	40	12	6	7	39	15	9	.236	.379
RF	Hugh Duffy	71	298	84	60	10	4	7	41	9	13	.282	.413
C	Duke Farrell	64	241	56	34	6	3	3	19	4	8	.232	.320
C	Tom Daly	65	219	42	34	2	6	0	29	10	10	.192	.256
Sub	Bob Pettit	43	169	43	23	1	4	4	23	7	7	.254	.379
P	Gus Krock	39	134	22	9	0	0	1	11	5	1	.164	.187
P	Mark Baldwin	30	106	16	11	1	2	1	5	5	4	.151	.226
Sub	Silver Flint	22	77	14	6	3	0	0	3	1	1	.182	.221
Sub	Del Darling	20	75	16	12	3	1	2	7	3	0	.213	.360
P	John Tener	13	46	9	4	1	0	0	1	1	1	.196	.217
P	George Borchers	10	33	2	3	2	0	0	2	1	1	.061	.121
P	Ad Gumbert	7	24	8	3	0	1	0	2	0	0	.333	.417
P	Frank Dwyer	5	21	4	2	1	0	0	2	0	0	.190	.238
P	Charlie Brynan	3	11	2	1	0	1	0	1	0	0	.182	.364
P	Dad Clarke	2	7	2	4	0	1	1	2	1	0	.286	1.000
P	Willard Mains	2	7	1	1	0	0	0	0	1	0	.143	.143
		136	4616	1201	**734**	147	**95**	**77**	569	290	287	.260	**.383**

1B	Anson 134, Farrell 1
2B	Pfeffer 135
SS	Williamson 132, Duffy 3
3B	Burns 134, Duffy 1
OF	Ryan 128, Sullivan 75, Duffy 67, Van Haltren 57, Pettit 43, Farrell 31, Daly 4, Baldwin 3, Borchers 3, Gumbert 2, Tener 1, Mains 1, Clarke 1, Brynan 1
C	Daly 62, Farrell 33, Flint 22, Darling 20
P	Krock 39, Baldwin 30, Van Haltren 30, Tener 12, Borchers 10, Ryan 8, Gumbert 6, Dwyer 5, Brynan 3, Mains 2, Clarke 2

	G	IP	GS	CG	W	L	K	BB	SH	SV	ERA
Gus Krock	39	339.2	39	39	25	14	161	45	4	0	2.44
Mark Baldwin	30	251	30	27	13	15	157	99	2	0	2.76
George Van Haltren	30	245.2	24	24	13	13	139	60	4	1	3.52
John Tener	12	102	12	11	7	5	39	25	1	0	2.74
George Borchers	10	67	10	7	4	4	26	29	1	0	3.49
Ad Gumbert	6	48.2	6	5	3	3	16	10	0	0	3.14
Frank Dwyer	5	42	5	5	4	1	17	9	1	0	1.07
Jimmy Ryan	8	38.1	2	1	4	0	11	12	0	0	3.05
Tod Brynan	3	25	3	2	2	1	11	7	0	0	6.48
Dad Clarke	2	16	2	1	1	0	6	6	0	0	5.06
Willard Mains	2	11	2	1	1	1	5	6	0	0	4.91
		—1 forfeit L vs Philadelphia on October 13—									
		1186.1	135	123	77	57	588	308	13	1	2.96

PHILADELPHIA Harry Wright   **Philadelphia Baseball Grounds**

		G	AB	H	R	2B	3B	HR	RBI	BB	SB	BA	SA
CF	Ed Andrews	124	528	126	75	14	4	3	44	21	35	.239	.297
1B	Sid Farrar	131	508	124	53	24	7	1	53	31	21	.244	.325
RF	Jim Fogarty	121	454	107	72	14	6	1	35	53	58	.236	.300
SS	Arthur Irwin	125	448	98	51	12	4	0	28	33	19	.219	.263
LF	George Wood	106	433	99	67	19	6	6	15	39	20	.229	.342
3B	Joe Mulvey	100	398	86	37	12	3	0	39	9	18	.216	.261
C	Jack Clements	86	326	80	26	8	4	1	32	10	3	.245	.304
Sub	Ed Delahanty	74	290	66	40	12	2	1	31	12	38	.228	.293
2B	Charlie Bastian	80	275	53	30	4	1	1	17	27	12	.193	.225
P	Ben Sanders	57	236	58	26	11	2	1	25	8	13	.246	.322
P	Charlie Buffinton	46	160	29	14	4	1	0	12	7	1	.181	.219
Sub	Pop Schriver	40	134	26	15	5	2	1	23	7	2	.194	.284
P	Dan Casey	33	118	18	11	2	1	0	5	3	2	.153	.186
P	Kid Gleason	24	83	17	4	2	0	0	5	3	3	.205	.229
Sub	Bill Hallman	18	63	13	5	4	1	0	6	1	1	.206	.302
Sub	Deacon McGuire	12	51	17	7	4	2	0	11	4	0	.333	.490
Sub	Woodie Wagenhorst	2	8	1	2	0	0	0	0	0	0	.125	.125
Sub	John Grim	2	7	1	0	0	0	0	0	0	0	.143	.143
Sub	Cupid Childs	2	4	0	0	0	0	0	0	0	0	.000	.000
Sub	Gid Gardner	1	3	2	0	0	0	0	1	0	0	.667	.667
P	Jim Tyng	1	1	0	0	0	0	0	0	0	0	.000	.000
		132	4528	1021	535	151	46	16	418	268	246	.225	.290

1B   Farrar 131
2B   Bastian 65, Delahanty 56, Hallman 4, Irwin 3, Childs 2, Grim 1, Gardner 1
SS   Irwin 122, Schriver 6, Bastian 1, Fogarty 1, Hallman 1
3B   Mulvey 100, Bastian 14, Schriver 6, Fogarty 5, McGuire 2, Wagenhorst 2, Wood 2, Hallman 1, Sanders 1
OF   Andrews 124, Fogarty 117, Wood 104, Sanders 25, Delahanty 17, Hallman 3, Clements 1, Buffinton 1,
     Casey 1, Schriver 1, Gleason 1, Grim 1
C   Clements 85, Schriver 27, McGuire 10, Hallman 10
P   Buffinton 46, Casey 33, Sanders 31, Gleason 24, Wood 2, Tyng 1

	G	IP	GS	CG	W	L	K	BB	SH	SV	ERA
Charlie Buffinton	46	400.1	46	43	28	17	199	59	6	0	1.91
Dan Casey	33	285.2	33	31	14	18	108	48	2	0	3.15
Ben Sanders	31	275.1	29	28	19	10	121	33	8	0	1.90
Kid Gleason	24	199.2	23	23	7	16	89	53	0	0	2.84
Jim Tyng	1	4	0	0	0	0	2	2	0	1	4.50
George Wood	2	2	0	0	0	0	0	1	0	2	4.40
		—1 forfeit W vs Chicago on October 13—									
	1167	131	125	68	61	519	196	16	3	2.38

BOSTON   **John Morrill**   **South End Grounds (1)**

		G	AB	H	R	2B	3B	HR	RBI	BB	SB	BA	SA
CF	Dick Johnston	135	**585**	173	102	31	**18**	12	68	15	35	.296	.472
3B	Billy Nash	135	526	149	71	18	15	4	75	50	20	.283	.397
1B	John Morrill	135	486	96	60	18	7	4	39	55	21	.198	.288
C	King Kelly	107	440	140	85	22	11	9	71	31	56	.318	.480
LF	Joe Hornung	107	431	103	61	11	7	3	53	16	29	.239	.318
RF	Tom Brown	107	420	104	62	10	7	9	49	30	46	.248	.369
SS	Sam Wise	105	417	100	66	19	12	4	40	34	33	.240	.372
Sub	Irv Ray	50	206	51	26	2	3	2	26	6	7	.248	.316
P	John Clarkson	55	205	40	20	9	1	1	17	7	5	.195	.263
2B	Joe Quinn	38	156	47	19	8	3	4	29	2	12	.301	.468
C	Pop Tate	41	148	34	18	7	1	1	6	8	3	.230	.311
P	Bill Sowders	36	122	18	14	2	0	0	6	3	1	.148	.164
Sub	Ezra Sutton	28	110	24	16	3	1	1	16	7	10	.218	.291
Sub	Billy Klusman	28	107	18	9	4	0	2	11	5	3	.168	.262
P	Hoss Radbourn	24	79	17	6	1	0	0	6	3	4	.215	.228
Sub	Jack Burdock	22	79	16	5	0	0	0	4	2	1	.203	.203
Sub	Tom O'Rourke	20	74	13	3	0	0	0	4	1	2	.176	.176
P	Kid Madden	20	67	11	7	0	0	0	5	1	4	.164	.164
Sub	Ed Glenn	20	65	10	8	0	2	0	3	2	0	.154	.215
Sub	Bill Higgins	14	54	10	5	1	0	0	4	1	1	.185	.204
P	Dick Conway	7	25	4	2	0	0	0	1	1	0	.160	.160
Sub	Mike Hines	4	16	2	3	0	1	0	2	2	0	.125	.250
Sub	Pete Sommers	4	13	3	1	1	0	0	0	0	0	.231	.308
Sub	Nick Wise	1	3	0	0	0	0	0	0	0	0	.000	.000
		137	4834	1183	669	167	89	56	535	282	293	.245	.351

1B   Morrill 133, S. Wise 5
2B   Quinn 38, Nash 31, Klusman 28, Burdock 22, Higgins 14, Ray 3, Morrill 2, S. Wise 2
SS   S. Wise 89, Ray 48, Sutton 1
3B   Nash 105, Sutton 27, S. Wise 6, Glenn 1
OF   Johnston 135, Brown 107, Hornung 107, Kelly 34, Glenn 19, S. Wise 4, Hines 3, N. Wise 1, Tate 1, Clarkson 1, Conway 1, O'Rourke 1
C   Kelly 76, Tate 41, O'Rourke 20, Sommers 4, N. Wise 1, Hines 1
P   Clarkson 54, Sowders 36, Radbourn 24, Madden 20, Conway 6

	G	IP	GS	CG	W	L	K	BB	SH	SV	ERA
John Clarkson	54	**483.1**	54	53	33	20	223	**119**	3	0	2.76
Bill Sowders	36	317	35	34	19	15	132	73	2	0	2.07
Hoss Radbourn	24	207	24	24	7	16	64	45	1	0	2.87
Kid Madden	20	165	18	17	7	11	53	24	1	0	2.95
Dick Conway	6	53	6	6	4	2	12	8	0	0	2.38
		1225.1	137	134	70	64	484	269	7	0	2.61

DETROIT **Bill Watkins (49–44)** **Bob Leadley (19–19)** **Recreation Park**

		G	AB	H	R	2B	3B	HR	RBI	BB	SB	BA	SA
3B	Deacon White	125	527	157	75	22	5	4	71	21	12	.298	.381
LF	Larry Twitchell	131	524	128	71	19	4	5	67	28	14	.244	.324
1B	Dan Brouthers	129	522	160	**118**	**33**	11	9	66	68	34	.307	.464
CF	Ned Hanlon	109	459	122	64	6	8	5	39	15	38	.266	.346
SS	Jack Rowe	105	451	125	62	19	8	2	74	19	10	.277	.368
C	Charlie Ganzel	95	386	96	45	13	5	1	46	14	12	.249	.316
2B	Hardy Richardson	58	266	77	60	18	2	6	32	17	13	.289	.440
C	Charlie Bennett	74	258	68	32	12	4	5	29	31	4	.264	.399
RF	Count Campau	70	251	51	28	5	3	1	18	19	27	.203	.259
Sub	Sam Thompson	56	238	67	51	10	8	6	40	23	5	.282	.466
Sub	Sy Sutcliffe	49	191	49	17	5	3	0	23	5	6	.257	.314
P	Pete Conway	46	167	46	28	4	2	3	23	8	1	.275	.377
P	Charlie Getzein	46	167	41	14	2	2	1	10	12	6	.246	.299
Sub	Ted Scheffler	27	94	19	17	3	1	0	4	9	4	.202	.255
P	Henry Gruber	27	92	13	8	2	1	0	4	6	0	.141	.185
Sub	Parson Nicholson	24	85	22	11	2	3	1	9	2	6	.259	.388
Sub	Jake Wells	16	57	9	5	1	0	0	2	0	0	.158	.175
P	Eb Beatin	16	56	14	8	1	2	2	9	6	1	.250	.456
P	Lady Baldwin	6	23	6	5	0	0	0	3	3	0	.261	.261
Sub	Deacon McGuire	3	13	0	0	0	0	0	0	0	0	.000	.000
Sub	Sam LaRoque	2	9	4	1	0	0	0	2	1	0	.444	.444
Sub	Barney Gilligan	1	5	1	1	0	0	0	0	0	0	.200	.200
Sub	Frank Scheibeck	1	4	0	0	0	0	0	0	0	0	.000	.000
Sub	Cal Broughton	1	4	0	0	0	0	0	0	0	0	.000	.000
		134	4849	**1275**	721	177	72	51	571	**307**	193	**.263**	.361

1B	Brouthers 129, Sutcliffe 5, Ganzel 1, Bennett 1
2B	Richardson 58, Ganzel 49, Nicholson 24, LaRoque 2, Sutcliffe 2
SS	Rowe 105, Sutcliffe 24, Ganzel 3, Beatin 2, Scheibeck 1
3B	White 125, Ganzel 9
OF	Twitchell 131, Hanlon 109, Campau 70, Thompson 56, Scheffler 27, Ganzel 5, Sutcliffe 4, Beatin 2, Baldwin 1, Conway 1
C	Bennett 73, Ganzel 28, Wells 16, Sutcliffe 14, McGuire 3, Broughton 1, Gilligan 1
P	Getzein 46, Conway 45, Gruber 27, Beatin 12, Baldwin 6, Twitchell 2

	G	IP	GS	CG	W	L	K	BB	SH	SV	ERA
Charlie Getzein	46	404	46	45	19	25	202	54	2	0	3.05
Pete Conway	45	391	45	43	30	14	176	57	4	0	2.26
Henry Gruber	27	240	25	25	11	14	71	41	3	0	2.29
Eb Beatin	12	107	12	12	5	7	44	16	1	0	2.86
Lady Baldwin	6	53	6	5	3	3	26	15	0	0	5.43
Larry Twitchell	2	4	0	0	0	0	3	0	0	1	6.75
		1199	134	130	68	63	522	**183**	10	1	2.74

PITTSBURGH　　**Horace Phillips**　　**Recreation Park**

		G	AB	H	R	2B	3B	HR	RBI	BB	SB	BA	SA
3B	Willie Kuehne	138	524	123	60	22	11	3	62	9	34	.235	.336
CF	Billy Sunday	120	505	119	69	14	3	0	15	12	71	.236	.275
SS	Pop Smith	131	481	99	61	15	2	4	52	22	37	.206	.270
RF	John Coleman	116	438	101	49	11	4	0	26	29	15	.231	.274
C	Doggie Miller	103	404	112	50	17	5	0	36	18	27	.277	.344
C	Fred Carroll	97	366	91	62	14	5	2	48	32	18	.249	.331
2B	Fred Dunlap	82	321	84	41	12	4	1	36	16	24	.262	.333
1B	Jake Beckley	71	283	97	35	15	3	0	27	7	20	.343	.417
UT	Al Maul	74	259	54	21	9	4	0	31	21	9	.208	.274
LF	Abner Dalrymple	57	227	50	19	9	2	0	14	6	7	.220	.278
P	Ed Morris	55	189	19	12	0	2	0	6	3	2	.101	.122
P	Pud Galvin	50	175	25	6	1	1	1	3	1	4	.143	.177
Sub	Jocko Fields	45	169	33	22	7	2	1	15	8	9	.195	.278
Sub	Elmer Cleveland	30	108	24	10	2	1	2	11	5	3	.222	.315
Sub	Pete McShannic	26	98	19	5	1	0	0	5	1	3	.194	.204
P	Harry Staley	25	85	11	6	1	0	0	1	1	2	.129	.141
Sub	Sam Nichol	8	22	1	3	0	0	0	0	2	0	.045	.045
Sub	Cliff Carroll	5	20	0	1	0	0	0	0	0	2	.000	.000
P	Hardie Henderson	5	18	5	2	0	0	0	3	0	0	.278	.278
P	Phil Knell	3	11	1	0	0	0	0	0	0	0	.091	.091
Sub	Henry Yaik	2	6	2	0	0	0	0	1	1	0	.333	.333
Sub	Bill Farmer	2	4	0	0	0	0	0	0	0	0	.000	.000
		139	4713	1070	534	150	49	14	392	194	287	.227	.289

1B	Beckley 71, Maul 38, Coleman 25, F. Carroll 5
2B	Dunlap 82, Smith 56
SS	Smith 75, Kuehne 63
3B	Kuehne 75, Cleveland 30, McShannic 26, Miller 4, Fields 3, F. Carroll 1
OF	Sunday 120, Coleman 91, Dalrymple 57, F. Carroll 38, Maul 34, Miller 32, Fields 29, Nichol 8, C. Carroll 5, Galvin 1, Henderson 1, Yaik 1, Farmer 1
C	Miller 68, F. Carroll 54, Fields 14, Farmer 1, Yaik 1
P	Morris 55, Galvin 50, Staley 25, Henderson 5, Maul 3, Knell 3

	G	IP	GS	CG	W	L	K	BB	SH	SV	ERA
Ed Morris	**55**	480	**55**	**54**	29	23	135	74	5	0	2.31
Pud Galvin	50	437.1	50	49	23	25	107	53	6	0	2.63
Harry Staley	25	207.1	24	24	12	12	89	53	2	0	2.69
Hardie Henderson	5	35.1	5	4	1	3	9	20	0	0	5.35
Phil Knell	3	26.1	3	3	1	2	15	18	0	0	3.76
Al Maul	3	17	1	1	0	2	12	5	0	0	6.35
		—1 Forfeit L vs New York on May 31—									
		1203.1	138	**135**	66	67	367	223	13	0	2.67

INDIANAPOLIS Harry Spence   **Athletic Park (II)**

		G	AB	H	R	2B	3B	HR	RBI	BB	SB	BA	SA
3B	Jerry Denny	126	524	137	92	27	7	12	63	9	32	.261	.408
CF	Paul Hines	133	513	144	84	26	3	4	58	41	31	.281	.366
LF	Emmett Seery	133	500	110	87	20	10	5	50	64	80	.220	.330
2B	Charlie Bassett	128	481	116	58	20	3	2	60	32	24	.241	.308
RF	Jack McGeachy	118	452	99	45	15	2	0	30	5	49	.219	.261
SS	Jack Glasscock	113	442	119	63	17	3	1	45	14	48	.269	.328
C	Dick Buckley	71	260	71	28	9	3	5	22	6	4	.273	.388
Sub	George Myers	66	248	59	36	9	0	2	16	16	28	.238	.298
1B	Dude Esterbrook	64	246	54	21	8	0	0	17	2	11	.220	.252
C	Con Daily	57	202	44	14	6	1	0	14	10	15	.218	.257
Sub	Jumbo Schoeneck	48	169	40	15	4	0	0	20	9	11	.237	.260
P	Egyptian Healy	37	131	30	14	9	0	1	13	1	5	.229	.321
P	Henry Boyle	37	125	18	13	2	0	1	6	6	1	.144	.184
P	Lev Shreve	36	115	21	10	3	0	0	2	4	5	.183	.209
Sub	Otto Schomberg	30	112	24	11	5	1	1	10	10	6	.214	.304
P	Bill Burdick	21	68	10	6	0	0	0	1	2	0	.147	.147
P	Sam Moffett	10	35	4	6	0	0	0	0	5	0	.114	.114
		136	4623	1100	603	**180**	33	34	427	236	**350**	.238	.313

1B   Esterbrook 61, Schoeneck 48, Schomberg 15, Hines 6, Daily 5, Myers 1, Boyle 1, Buckley 1
2B   Bassett 128, Denny 5, Glasscock 3, Daily 1
SS   Glascock 110, Denny 25, Hines 2, McGeachy 1, Seery 1
3B   Denny 96, Buckley 22, Myers 14, Daily 5, Esterbrook 3, Glasscock 3
OF   Seery 133, Hines 125, McGeachy 117, Schomberg 15, Myers 10, Daily 5, Moffett 3, Shreve 1, Healy 1,
      Burdick 1, Denny 1, Buckley 1
C   Buckley 51, Myers 47, Daily 42
P   Boyle 37, Healy 37, Shreve 35, Burdick 20, Moffett 7, Schoeneck 2, Denny 1, Glasscock 1, McGeachy 1

	G	IP	GS	CG	W	L	K	BB	SH	SV	ERA
Henry Boyle	37	323	37	36	15	22	98	58	3	0	3.26
Egyptian Healy	37	321.1	37	36	12	24	124	87	1	0	3.89
Lev Shreve	35	297.2	35	34	11	24	101	93	1	0	4.63
Bill Burdick	20	176	20	20	10	10	55	43	0	0	2.81
Sam Moffett	7	56	7	6	2	5	7	17	1	0	4.66
Jack McGeachy	1	5	0	0	0	0	0	3	0	0	7.20
Jumbo Schoeneck	2	4.1	0	0	0	0	1	1	0	0	0.00
Jerry Denny	1	4	0	0	0	0	1	4	0	0	9.00
Jack Glasscock	1	0.1	0	0	0	0	1	2	0	0	54.00
		1187.2	136	132	50	85	388	308	6	0	3.81

WASHINGTON   **Walter Hewett (10–29)**   **Ted Sullivan (38–57)**   **Swampoodle Grounds**

		G	AB	H	R	2B	3B	HR	RBI	BB	SB	BA	SA
1B	Billy O'Brien	133	528	119	42	15	2	9	66	9	10	.225	.313
CF	Dummy Hoy	136	503	138	77	10	8	2	29	69	82	.274	.338
2B	Al Myers	132	502	104	46	12	7	2	46	37	20	.207	.271
LF	Walt Wilmot	119	473	106	61	16	9	4	43	23	46	.224	.321
RF	Ed Daily	110	453	102	56	8	4	7	39	7	44	.225	.307
3B	Jim Donnelly	122	428	86	43	9	4	0	23	20	44	.201	.241
SS	George Shoch	90	317	58	46	6	3	2	24	25	23	.183	.240
C	Connie Mack	85	300	56	49	5	6	3	29	17	31	.187	.273
Sub	Shorty Fuller	49	170	31	11	5	2	0	12	10	6	.182	.235
P	Hank O'Day	47	166	23	6	2	0	0	6	4	3	.139	.151
P	Jim Whitney	42	141	24	13	0	0	1	17	7	3	.170	.191
Sub	Pat Deasley	34	127	20	6	1	0	0	4	2	2	.157	.165
Sub	John Irwin	37	126	28	14	5	2	0	8	5	15	.222	.294
P	Bill Widner	15	60	12	4	0	0	0	6	0	1	.200	.200
Sub	Tug Arundel	17	51	10	2	0	1	0	3	5	1	.196	.235
Sub	Pete Sweeney	11	44	8	3	0	1	0	5	0	0	.182	.227
P	George Keefe	13	42	9	2	3	0	0	6	2	0	.214	.286
Sub	Miah Murray	12	42	4	1	1	0	0	3	1	0	.095	.119
P	Frank Gilmore	13	41	1	0	0	0	0	2	0	0	.024	.024
Sub	Perry Werden	3	10	3	0	0	0	0	2	1	0	.300	.300
P	Dupee Shaw	3	10	0	0	0	0	0	0	0	0	.000	.000
P	George Haddock	2	5	1	0	0	0	0	0	1	0	.200	.200
Sub	Gid Gardner	2	4	1	0	0	0	0	0	1	0	.250	.250
P	John Greening	1	3	0	0	0	0	0	0	0	0	.000	.000
Sub	Jim Banning	1	0	0	0	0	0	0	0	0	0	.000	.000
		136	4546	944	482	98	49	30	373	246	331	.208	.271

1B   O'Brien 132, Murray 2, Mack 1, Daily 1, Whitney 1
2B   Myers 132, Fuller 2, Gardner 1, Shoch 1, Deasley 1
SS   Shoch 52, Fuller 47, Irwin 27, Donnelly 5, O'Day 2, Mack 1, Gardner 1, Deasley 1
3B   Donnelly 117, Irwin 10, Sweeney 8, O'Brien 1
OF   Hoy 136, Wilmot 119, Daily 100, Shoch 37, Mack 4, Whitney 3, Werden 3, Sweeney 3, Widner 2, Gilmore 1, Deasley 1
C   Mack 79, Deasley 31, Arundel 17, Murray 10, Gilmore 1, Banning 1
P   O'Day 46, Whitney 39, Widner 13, Keefe 13, Gilmore 12, Daily 9, Shaw 3, Haddock 2, Greening 1, Shoch 1

	G	IP	GS	CG	W	L	K	BB	SH	SV	ERA
Hank O'Day	46	403	46	46	16	**29**	186	117	2	0	3.10
Jim Whitney	39	325	39	37	18	21	79	54	3	0	3.05
Bill Widner	13	115	13	13	5	7	33	22	0	0	2.82
George Keefe	13	114	13	13	6	7	52	43	1	0	2.84
Frank Gilmore	12	95.2	11	10	1	9	23	29	0	0	6.59
Ed Daily	9	73.2	8	8	2	7	20	19	0	0	4.89
Dupee Shaw	3	25	3	3	0	3	8	7	0	0	6.48
George Haddock	2	16	2	2	0	2	3	2	0	0	2.25
John Greening	1	9	1	1	0	1	2	4	0	0	11.00
George Shoch	1	3	0	0	0	0	0	1	0	0	0.00
		1179.1	136	133	48	86	406	298	6	0	3.54

WORLD'S SERIES

New York (NL) defeated St. Louis (AA) 6 games to 4

Game 1 at Polo Grounds (NY), Oct. 16: NY (Keefe) 2, StL (Caruthers) 1
Game 2 at Polo Grounds (NY), Oct. 17: StL (Chamberlain) 3, NY (Welch) 0
Game 3 at Polo Grounds (NY), Oct. 18: NY (Keefe) 4, StL (King) 2
Game 4 at Washington Park (Bro), Oct. 19: NY (Crane) 6, StL (Chamberlain) 3
Game 5 at Polo Grounds (NY), Oct. 20: NY (Keefe) 6, StL (King) 4
Game 6 at Baseball Grounds (Phi), Oct. 22: NY (Welch) 12, StL (Chamberlain) 5
Game 7 at Sportsman's Park (StL), Oct. 24: StL (King) 7, NY (Crane) 5
Game 8 at Sportsman's Park (StL), Oct. 25: NY (Keefe) 11, StL (Chamberlain) 3
Game 9 at Sportsman's Park (StL), Oct. 26: StL (Devlin) 14, NY (George) 11 (10 inn.)
Game 10 at Sportsman's Park (StL), Oct. 27: StL (Chamberlain) 18, NY (Titcomb) 11

NEW YORK

		G	AB	H	R	2B	3B	HR	RBI	BB	BA	SA
CF/2B	Mike Slattery	10	39	8	6	2	0	0	5	0	.205	.256
RF	Mike Tiernan	10	38	13	8	0	0	1	6	8	.342	.421
3B/LF	Art Whitney	10	37	12	7	0	1	0	12	1	.324	.378
UT	Jim O'Rourke	10	36	8	4	0	0	0	1	4	.222	.222
2B	Danny Richardson	9	36	6	6	2	0	0	6	3	.167	.222
SS	Monte Ward	8	29	11	4	1	0	0	6	1	.379	.414
C/1B	Buck Ewing	7	26	9	5	0	2	1	6	1	.346	**.615**
1B	Roger Connor	7	23	7	7	1	2	0	3	4	.333	.522
LF/3B	George Gore	3	11	5	5	1	0	0	0	2	.455	.545
P	Tim Keefe	4	11	1	2	0	0	0	0	2	.091	.091
C	Pat Murphy	3	10	1	1	0	0	0	1	0	.100	.100
P/1B	Bill George	2	9	3	2	1	0	1	4	0	.333	.778
C	Willard Brown	2	8	3	1	1	0	0	0	0	.375	.500
UT	Gil Hatfield	2	8	2	2	0	0	0	1	1	.250	.250
P	Mickey Welch	2	7	2	2	0	0	0	1	0	.286	.286
P	Cannonball Crane	2	7	1	1	0	0	0	2	0	.143	.143
P/OF	Cannonball Titcomb	1	4	2	1	1	0	0	1	0	.500	.750
		10	339	94	64	10	5	3	55	27	.277	.363

	G	IP	GS	CG	W	L	K	BB	SH	SV	ERA
Tim Keefe	4	35	4	4	4	0	30	9	0	0	0.51
Cannonball Crane	2	17	2	2	1	1	12	6	0	0	2.12
Mickey Welch	2	17	2	2	1	1	2	9	0	0	2.65
Bill George	1	10	1	1	0	1	4	3	0	0	7.20
Gil Hatfield	1	5	0	0	0	0	3	2	0	0	12.60
Cannonball Titcomb	1	4	1	0	0	1	2	2	0	0	6.75
		88	10	9	6	4	52	32	0	0	2.97

ST. LOUIS

		G	AB	H	R	2B	3B	HR	RBI	BB	BA	SA
1B/CF	Charlie Comiskey	10	41	11	6	1	1	0	3	1	.268	.341
RF	Tommy McCarthy	10	41	10	10	1	0	1	9	0	.244	,341
3B	Arlie Latham	10	40	10	10	0	0	0	3	5	.250	.250
LF	Tip O'Neill	10	37	9	8	1	0	2	11	6	.243	.432
2B	Yank Robinson	10	36	9	7	2	1	0	7	6	.250	.361
SS	Bill White	10	35	5	4	1	0	0	4	3	.143	.171
C/1B	Jocko Milligan	8	25	10	5	2	1	0	4	3	**.400**	.560
CF	Harry Lyons	5	17	2	0	0	0	0	1	1	.118	.118
C/CF	Jack Boyle	4	16	7	4	0	1	0	4	2	.438	.563
P	Silver King	5	15	1	1	0	0	0	0	1	.067	.067
P	Icebox Chamberlain	5	13	0	3	0	0	0	0	4	.000	.000
CF	Ed Herr	3	11	1	2	0	0	0	0	0	.091	.091
P	Jim Devlin	1	3	0	0	0	0	0	0	0	.000	.000
		10	330	75	60	8	4	3	46	32	.227	.303

	G	IP	GS	CG	W	L	K	BB	SH	SV	ERA
Icebox Chamberlain	5	44	5	5	2	3	13	16	1	0	5.32
Silver King	5	35	5	4	1	3	12	9	0	0	2.31
Jim Devlin	1	7	0	0	1	0	5	2	0	0	2.57
		86	10	9	4	6	30	27	1	0	3.87

AMERICAN ASSOCIATION

	W	L	PCT	HOME	ROAD	GB
1. St. Louis Browns	92	43	.681	60–21	32–22	—
2. Brooklyn Bridegrooms	88	52	.629	53–20	35–32	6.5
3. Philadelphia Athletics	81	52	.609	55–20	26–32	10
4. Cincinnati Reds	80	54	.597	55–24	25–30	11.5
5. Baltimore Orioles	57	80	.416	30–26	27–54	36
6. Cleveland Blues	50	82	.379	34–27	16–55	40.5
7. Louisville Colonels	48	87	.356	27–30	21–57	44
8. Kansas City Cowboys	43	89	.326	23–34	20–55	47.5

	StL	Bro	Phi	Cin	Bal	Cle	Lou	KC	
St. Louis	—	10	10	10	14	16	16	16	92
Brooklyn	10	—	12	14	12	16	13	11	88
Philadelphia	7	8	—	10	14	13	15	14	81
Cincinnati	8	6	10	—	14	10	17	15	80
Baltimore	6	8	5	6	—	10	11	11	57
Cleveland	4	4	7	7	9	—	9	10	50
Louisville	4	7	5	3	9	8	—	12	48
Kansas City	4	9	3	4	8	9	6	—	43
	43	52	52	54	80	82	87	89	539

SEASON LEADERS

Batting Average

1.	O'Neill, St. Louis	.335
2.	Reilly, Cincinnati	.321
3.	Browning, Louisville	.313
4.	Collins, Lou–Brook	.307
5.	Orr, Brooklyn	.305

On–Base Percentage

1.	Robinson, St. Louis	.400
2.	O'Neill, St. Louis	.390
3.	Browning, Louisville	.380
4.	Collins, Lou–Brook	.373
5.	Stovey, Philadelphia	.365

Home Runs

1.	Reilly, Cincinnati	13
2.	Stovey, Philadelphia	9
3.	Larkin, Philadelphia	7
4.	Tucker, Baltimore	6
	Lyons, Philadelphia	6
	Comiskey, St. Louis	6
	McKean, Cleveland	6

Hits

1.	O'Neill, St. Louis	177
2.	Reilly, Cincinnati	169
3.	McKean, Cleveland	164
4.	Collins, Lou–Brook	162
5.	Corkhill, Cin–Brook	160

Stolen Bases

1.	Latham St. Louis	109
2.	Nicol, Cincinnati	103
3.	Welch, Philadelphia	95
4.	McCarthy, St. Louis	93
5.	Stovey, Philadelphia	87

Slugging Average

1.	Reilly, Cincinnati	.501
2.	Stovey, Philadelphia	.460
3.	O'Neill, St. Louis	.446
4.	Browning, Louisville	.436
5.	O. Burns, Balt–Brook	.435

Total Bases

1.	Reilly, Cincinnati	264
2.	Stovey, Philadelphia	244
3.	O'Neill, St. Louis	236
4.	McKean, Cleveland	233
5.	O. Burns, Balt–Brook	230

RBI

1.	Reilly, Cincinnati	103
2.	Larkin, Philadelphia	101
3.	Foutz, Brooklyn	99
4.	O'Neill, St. Louis	98
5.	Corkhill, Cin–Brook	93

Runs

1.	Pinkney, Brooklyn	134
2.	Collins, Lou–Brook	133
3.	Stovey, Philadelphia	127
4.	Welch, Philadelphia	125
5.	Latham, St. Louis	119

Bases on Balls

1.	Robinson, St. Louis	116
2.	Fennelly, Cin–Phil	72
3.	Nicol, Cincinnati	67
	McTamany, Kansas City	67
5.	Pinkney, Brooklyn	66

PITCHING

Wins

1.	King, St. Louis	45
2.	Seward, Philadelphia	35
3.	Caruthers, Brooklyn	29
4.	Weyhing, Philadelphia	28
5.	Viau, Cincinnati	27

Losses

1.	Porter, Kansas City	37
2.	Bakely, Cleveland	33
3.	Ramsey, Louisville	30
4.	Cunningham, Baltimore	29
5.	Kilroy, Baltimore	21
	King, St. Louis	21

Innings

1.	King, St. Louis	585.2
2.	Bakely, Cleveland	532.2
3.	Seward, Philadelphia	518.2
4.	Porter, Kansas City	474
5.	Cunningham, Baltimore	453.1

Complete Games

1.	King, St. Louis	64
2.	Bakely, Cleveland	60
3.	Seward, Philadelphia	57
4.	Porter, Kansas City	53
5.	Cunningham, Baltimore	50

Strikeouts

1.	Seward, Philadelphia	272
2.	King, St. Louis	258
3.	Ramsey, Louisville	228
4.	Bakely, Cleveland	212
5.	Weyhing, Philadelphia	204

Winning Percentage (25 decisions)

1.	Hudson, St. Louis	.714
2.	Chamberlain, Lou–StL	.694
3.	King, St. Louis	.682
4.	Caruthers, Brooklyn	.659
	Viau, Cincinnati	.659

ERA (140 Innings)

1.	King, St. Louis	1.64
2.	Seward, Philadelphia	2.01
3.	Terry, Brooklyn	2.03
4.	Hughes, Brooklyn	2.13
5.	Chamberlain, Lou–StL	2.19

Lowest On–Base Percentage

1.	King, St. Louis	.237
2.	Caruthers, Brooklyn	.255
3.	Seward, Philadelphia	.258
4.	Foutz, Brooklyn	.262
	Hughes, Brooklyn	.262

FIELDING

Total Chances

1B	Phillips, Kansas City	1563
2B	Bierbauer, Philadelphia	809
3B	Shindle, Baltimore	605
SS	White, Louis–StL	601
OF	Corkhill, Cinci–Brook	335
C	Robinson, Philadelphia	609
P	Porter, Kansas City	160

Fielding Average

Faatz, Cleveland	.989
McPhee, Cincinnati	.940
Shindle, Baltimore	.922
Easterday, Kansas City	.888
Corkhill, Cinci–Brook	.961
Boyle, St. Louis	.932
Chamberlain, Louis–StL	.963

ST. LOUIS   Charlie Comiskey   Sportsman's Park (I)

		G	AB	H	R	2B	3B	HR	RBI	BB	SB	BA	SA
1B	Charlie Comiskey	137	**576**	157	102	22	5	6	83	12	72	.273	.359
3B	Arlie Latham	133	570	151	119	19	5	2	31	43	**109**	.265	.326
LF	Tip O'Neill	130	529	**177**	96	24	10	5	98	44	26	**.335**	.446
RF	Tommy McCarthy	131	511	140	107	20	3	1	68	38	93	.274	.331
CF	Harry Lyons	123	499	97	66	10	5	4	63	20	36	.194	.259
2B	Yank Robinson	134	455	105	111	17	6	3	53	**116**	56	.231	.314
SS	Bill White	76	275	48	31	2	3	2	30	21	6	.175	.225
C	Jack Boyle	71	257	62	33	8	1	1	23	13	11	.241	.292
C	Jocko Milligan	63	219	55	19	6	2	5	37	17	3	.251	.365
P	Silver King	66	207	43	25	4	6	1	14	40	6	.208	.300
P	Nate Hudson	56	196	50	27	7	0	2	28	18	9	.255	.321
Sub	Ed Herr	43	172	46	21	7	1	3	43	11	9	.267	.372
Sub	Chippy McGarr	34	132	31	17	1	0	0	13	6	25	.235	.242
P	Icebox Chamberlain	14	50	5	6	0	0	1	2	3	3	.100	.160
P	Jim Devlin	11	37	11	7	1	0	0	3	4	2	.297	.324
Sub	Tom Dolan	11	36	7	1	1	0	0	1	1	1	.194	.222
P	Ed Knouff	9	31	3	1	0	0	0	1	3	1	.097	.097
P	Julie Freeman	1	3	1	0	0	0	0	0	0	0	.333	.333
		137	4755	1189	789	149	47	**36**	591	410	468	**.250**	.324

1B   Comiskey 133, Milligan 5, Hudson 3
2B   Robinson 102, McGarr 33, Comiskey 3, White 2, Lyons 1
SS   White 74, Robinson 34, Herr 28, McGarr 1, Hudson 1, Latham 1, Lyons 1
3B   Latham 133, Herr 4, Lyons 2
OF   McCarthy 131, O'Neill 130, Lyons 122, Hudson 16, Herr 11, Comiskey 5, King 2, Chamberlain 1, Boyle 1
C   Boyle 70, Milligan 58, Dolan 11
P   King 66, Hudson 39, Chamberlain 14, Devlin 11, Knouff 9, McCarthy 2, Freeman 1,

	G	IP	GS	CG	W	L	K	BB	SH	SV	ERA
Silver King	**66**	**585.2**	**65**	**64**	**45**	21	258	76	**6**	0	**1.64**
Nat Hudson	39	333	37	36	25	10	130	59	5	0	2.54
Icebox Chamberlain	14	112	14	13	11	2	57	27	1	0	1.61
Jim Devlin	11	90.1	11	10	6	5	45	20	0	0	3.19
Ed Knouff	9	81	9	9	5	4	25	37	0	0	2.67
Julie Freeman	1	6.1	1	0	0	1	1	4	0	0	4.26
Tommy McCarthy	2	4.1	0	0	0	0	1	2	0	0	4.15
		1212.2	137	132	92	43	517	**225**	12	0	**2.09**

BROOKLYN   Bill McGunnigle   Washington Park (I)

		G	AB	H	R	2B	3B	HR	RBI	BB	SB	BA	SA
3B	George Pinkney	143	575	156	**134**	18	8	4	52	66	51	.271	.351
RF	Dave Foutz	140	563	156	91	20	13	3	99	28	35	.277	.375
LF	Darby O'Brien	136	532	149	105	27	6	2	65	30	55	.280	.365
SS	Germany Smith	103	402	86	47	10	7	3	61	22	27	.214	.296
1B	Dave Orr	99	394	120	57	20	5	1	59	7	11	.305	.388
P	Bob Caruthers	95	335	77	58	10	5	5	53	45	23	.230	.334
CF	Paul Radford	90	308	67	48	9	3	2	29	35	33	.218	.286
Sub	Bill McClellan	74	278	57	33	7	3	0	21	40	13	.205	.252
C	Doc Bushong	69	253	53	23	5	1	0	16	5	9	.209	.237
2B	Jack Burdock	70	246	30	15	1	2	1	8	8	9	.122	.154
Sub	Oyster Burns	52	204	58	40	9	6	2	25	14	21	.284	.417
C	Bob Clark	45	150	36	23	5	3	1	20	9	11	.240	.333
P	Mickey Hughes	40	139	19	10	5	0	0	10	7	1	.137	.173
P	Adonis Terry	30	115	29	13	6	0	0	8	5	7	.252	.304
Sub	Jimmy Peoples	32	103	20	15	5	3	0	17	8	10	.194	.301
Sub	Pop Corkhill	19	71	27	17	4	3	1	19	4	3	.380	.563
P	Al Mays	18	63	5	4	1	1	0	5	5	2	.079	.127
Sub	Bill Holbert	15	50	6	4	1	0	0	1	2	0	.120	.140
Sub	Ed Silch	14	48	13	5	4	0	0	3	4	4	.271	.354
Sub	Hub Collins	12	42	13	16	**5**	1	0	3	9	9	.310	.476
		143	4871	1177	758	172	70	25	574	353	334	.242	.321

1B   Orr 99, Foutz 42, Terry 2, Clark 1
2B   Burdock 70, McClellan 56, Collins 12, Radford 2, Burns 3, Smith 1
SS   Smith 103, Burns 36, Peoples 5
3B   Pinkney 143
OF   O'Brien 136, Radford 88, Foutz 78, Caruthers 51, Corkhill 19, McClellan 18, Burns 14, Silch 14, Clark 8, Terry 7, Peoples 2, Mays 1
C   Bushong 69, Clark 36, Peoples 25, Holbert 15
P   Caruthers 44, Hughes 40, Terry 23, Foutz 23, Mays 18

	G	IP	GS	CG	W	L	K	BB	SH	SV	ERA
Bob Caruthers	44	391.2	43	42	29	15	140	53	4	0	2.39
Mickey Hughes	40	363	40	40	25	13	159	98	2	0	2.13
Adonis Terry #	23	195	23	20	13	8	138	67	2	0	2.03
Dave Foutz	23	176	19	19	12	7	73	35	0	0	2.51
Al Mays	18	160.2	18	17	9	9	67	32	1	0	2.80
		1286.1	143	**138**	88	52	577	285	9	0	2.33

No-hit game 4–0 vs Louisville, May 27

PHILADELPHIA **Bill Sharsig** **Jefferson Street Grounds**

		G	AB	H	R	2B	3B	HR	RBI	BB	SB	BA	SA
CF	Curt Welch	136	549	155	125	22	8	1	61	33	95	.282	.357
1B	Henry Larkin	135	546	147	92	28	12	7	101	33	20	.269	.403
2B	Lou Bierbauer	134	535	143	83	20	9	0	80	25	34	.267	.338
LF	Harry Stovey	130	530	152	127	25	**20**	9	65	65	87	.287	.460
SS	Bill Gleason	123	499	112	55	10	2	0	61	12	27	.224	.253
3B	Denny Lyons	111	456	135	93	22	5	6	83	41	39	.296	.406
RF	Tom Poorman	97	383	87	76	16	6	2	44	31	46	.227	.316
C	Wilbert Robinson	66	254	62	32	7	2	1	31	9	11	.244	.299
P	Ed Seward	64	225	32	27	3	3	2	14	18	12	.142	.209
P	Gus Weyhing	48	184	40	19	6	8	1	14	1	5	.217	.353
C	George Townsend	42	161	25	13	6	0	0	12	4	2	.155	.193
P	Mike Mattimore	41	142	38	22	6	5	0	12	12	16	.268	.380
Sub	Mike Sullivan	28	112	31	20	5	6	1	19	3	10	.277	.455
Sub	Tom Gunning	23	92	18	18	0	0	0	5	2	14	.196	.196
Sub	Blondie Purcell	18	66	11	10	3	1	0	6	5	10	.167	.242
Sub	Frank Fennelly	15	47	11	13	2	2	1	12	9	5	.234	.426
P	Bill Blair	4	13	4	1	1	0	0	1	1	0	.308	.385
Sub	Bill Farmer	3	12	2	0	0	0	0	1	0	0	.167	.167
P	Phenomenal Smith	3	9	3	1	1	0	0	2	1	1	.333	.444
Sub	Frank Zinn	2	7	0	0	0	0	0	0	1	0	.000	.000
P	Bob Gamble	1	3	1	0	0	0	0	0	0	0	.000	.000
Sub	Whitey Gibson	1	3	0	0	0	0	0	0	0	0	.000	.000
		136	4828	**1209**	827	**183**	89	31	**624**	303	434	**.250**	**.344**

1B	Larkin 122, Stovey 13, Robinson 1, Gleason 1
2B	Bierbauer 121, Larkin 14, Welch 3
SS	Gleason 121, Fennelly 15
3B	Lyons 111, Bierbauer 13, Sullivan 10, Gleason 1, Purcell 1
OF	Welch 135, Stovey 118, Poorman 97, Sullivan 18, Purcell 18, Mattimore 16, Seward 7, Weyhing 2, Blair 1
C	Robinson 65, Townsend 42, Gunning 23, Farmer 3, Zinn 2, Gibson 1
P	Seward 57, Weyhing 47, Mattimore 26, Blair 4, Smith 3, Gamble 1, Bierbauer 1

	G	IP	GS	CG	W	L	K	BB	SH	SV	ERA
Ed Seward #	57	518.2	57	57	35	19	**272**	127	**6**	0	2.01
Gus Weyhing ##	47	404	47	45	28	18	204	111	3	0	2.25
Mike Mattimore	26	221	24	24	15	10	80	65	4	0	3.38
Bill Blair	4	31	4	3	1	3	16	8	0	0	2.61
Phenomenal Smith	3	22	3	3	2	1	19	10	0	0	2.86
Bob Gamble	1	9	1	1	0	1	2	3	0	0	8.00
Lou Bierbauer	1	3	0	0	0	0	3	0	0	0	0.00
		1208.2	136	133	81	52	596	324	**13**	0	2.41

No hit game 12–2 vs Cincinnati, July 26
No hit game 4–0 vs Kansas City, July 31

CINCINNATI　　**Gus Schmelz**　　**American Park**

		G	AB	H	R	2B	3B	HR	RBI	BB	SB	BA	SA
3B	Hick Carpenter	136	551	147	68	14	5	3	67	5	59	.267	.327
RF	Hugh Nicol	135	548	131	112	10	2	1	35	67	103	.239	.270
1B	Long John Reilly	127	527	169	112	28	14	**13**	**103**	17	82	.321	**.501**
CF	Pop Corkhill	118	490	133	68	11	9	1	74	15	27	.271	.337
2B	Bid McPhee	111	458	110	88	12	10	4	51	43	54	.240	.336
SS	Frank Fennelly	120	448	88	64	8	7	2	56	63	43	.196	.259
LF	White Wings Tebeau	121	411	94	72	12	12	3	51	61	37	.229	.338
C	Jim Keenan	85	313	73	38	9	8	1	40	22	9	.233	.323
C	Kid Baldwin	67	271	59	27	11	3	1	25	3	4	.218	.292
P	Tony Mullane	51	175	44	27	4	4	1	16	8	12	.251	.337
P	Leon Viau	43	149	13	16	1	2	0	8	11	5	.087	.121
Sub	Heinie Kappel	36	143	37	18	4	4	1	15	2	20	.259	.364
Sub	Jack O'Connor	36	137	28	14	3	1	1	17	6	12	.204	.263
P	Elmer Smith	40	129	29	15	4	1	0	9	20	2	.225	.271
P	John Weyhing	8	23	3	2	0	0	0	0	1	0	.130	.130
P	Billy Serad	6	23	3	4	1	0	0	4	1	0	.130	.174
Sub	Ned Bligh	3	5	0	0	0	0	0	0	0	0	.000	.000
		137	4801	1161	745	132	82	32	571	345	**469**	.242	.323

1B　Reilly 117, Keenan 16, Mullane 4, Baldwin 1, Corkhill 1
2B　McPhee 109, Nicol 12, Kappel 10, Fennelly 4, Mullane 2, Corkhill 1
SS　Fennelly 112, Kappel 25, Nicol 1
3B　Carpenter 136, McPhee 1, Kappel 1
OF　Nicol 125, Tebeau 121, Corkhill 116, O'Connor 34, Reilly 10, Fennelly 4, Mullane 3, Smith 2, Baldwin 2, Bligh 1, Viau 1, McPhee 1,
C　Keenan 69, Baldwin 65, O'Connor 2, Bligh 2
P　Mullane 44, Viau 42, Smith 40, Weyhing 8, Serad 6, Corkhill 2

	G	IP	GS	CG	W	L	K	BB	SH	SV	ERA
Tony Mullane	44	380.1	42	41	26	16	186	75	4	**1**	2.84
Leon Viau	42	387.2	42	42	27	14	164	110	1	0	2.65
Elmer Smith	40	348.1	40	37	22	17	154	89	5	0	2.74
John Weyhing	8	65.2	8	7	3	4	30	17	0	0	1.23
Billy Serad	6	50.2	5	5	2	3	4	19	0	0	3.55
Pop Corkhill	2	5	0	0	0	0	1	0	0	**1**	10.80
		1237.2	137	132	80	54	539	310	10	**2**	2.73

BALTIMORE   **Billy Barnie**   **Oriole Park (I)**

		G	AB	H	R	2B	3B	HR	RBI	BB	SB	BA	SA
CF	Mike Griffin	137	542	139	103	21	11	0	46	55	46	.256	.336
1B	Tommy Tucker	136	520	149	74	17	12	6	61	16	43	.287	.400
3B	Billy Shindle	135	514	107	61	14	8	1	53	20	52	.208	.272
2B	Bill Greenwood	115	409	78	69	13	1	0	29	30	46	.191	.227
RF	Blondie Purcell	101	406	96	53	9	4	2	39	27	16	.236	.293
SS	Jack Farrell	103	398	81	72	19	5	4	36	26	29	.204	.307
LF	Oyster Burns	79	325	97	54	18	9	4	42	24	23	.298	.446
Sub	Joe Sommer	79	297	65	31	10	0	0	35	18	13	.219	.253
Sub	Jack O'Brien	57	196	44	25	11	5	0	18	17	14	.224	.332
P	Bert Cunningham	51	177	33	17	3	2	1	9	5	2	.186	.243
C	Chris Fulmer	52	166	31	20	5	1	0	10	21	10	.187	.229
Sub	Walt Goldsby	45	165	39	13	1	1	0	14	8	17	.236	.255
P	Matt Kilroy	43	145	26	13	5	2	0	19	19	10	.179	.241
Sub	Bart Cantz	37	126	21	7	2	1	0	9	2	0	.167	.198
P	Phenomenal Smith	35	109	27	16	3	4	1	12	11	2	.248	.376
Sub	Sam Trott	31	108	30	19	11	4	0	22	4	1	.278	.454
P	Sam Shaw	6	20	3	3	0	0	0	0	2	1	.150	.150
P	George Walker	4	13	1	1	0	0	0	1	0	0	.077	.077
P	Pat Whitaker	2	6	0	0	0	0	0	0	0	0	.000	.000
Sub	John Peltz	1	4	1	1	0	0	0	0	0	1	.250	.250
P	Mike Kilroy	1	4	0	0	0	0	0	0	0	0	.000	.000
P	John Harkins	1	3	0	1	0	0	0	0	1	0	.000	.000
Sub	George Bradley	1	3	0	0	0	0	0	0	0	0	.000	.000
		137	4656	1068	653	162	70	19	455	298	326	.229	.306

1B   Tucker 129, O'Brien 7, Purcell 1, Trott 1, Sommer 1
2B   Greenwood 86, Farrell 52, Sommer 2, Burns 1, Trott 1
SS   Farrell 54, Sommer 34, Greenwood 28, Burns 23, Purcell 2, Bradley 1
3B   Shindle 135, Burns 2, Trott 1
OF   Griffin 137, Purcell 100, Burns 56, Goldsby 45, Sommer 44, O'Brien 13, Tucker 7, Fulmer 7, Matt Kilroy 7, Cantz 4, Trott 3, Greenwood 1, Cunningham 1, Smith 1, Peltz 1
C   Fulmer 45, O'Brien 37, Cantz 33, Trott 27
P   Cunningham 51, Matt Kilroy 40, Smith 35, Shaw 6, Burns 5, Walker 4, Whitaker 2, Harkins 1, Mike Kilroy 1, Tucker 1

	G	IP	GS	CG	W	L	K	BB	SH	SV	ERA
Bert Cunningham	51	453.1	51	50	22	29	186	157	0	0	3.39
Matt Kilroy	40	321	40	35	17	21	135	79	2	0	4.04
Phenomenal Smith	35	292	32	31	14	19	152	137	0	0	3.61
Sam Shaw	6	53	6	6	2	4	22	15	0	0	3.40
George Walker	4	35	4	4	1	3	18	14	1	0	5.91
Pat Whitaker	2	14	2	2	1	1	5	6	0	0	5.14
Oyster Burns	5	12.2	0	0	0	1	2	3	0	0	4.26
Mike Kilroy	1	9	1	1	0	1	1	5	0	0	8.00
John Harkins	1	8	1	1	0	1	2	3	0	0	6.75
Tommy Tucker	1	2.1	0	0	0	0	2	0	0	0	3.86
		1200.1	137	130	57	80	525	419	3	0	3.78

CLEVELAND Jimmy Williams (20–44)   Tom Loftus (30–38)   Association Park (II)

		G	AB	H	R	2B	3B	HR	RBI	BB	SB	BA	SA
SS	Ed McKean	131	548	164	94	21	15	6	68	28	52	.299	.425
2B	Cub Stricker	127	493	115	80	13	6	1	33	50	60	.233	.290
LF	Bob Gilks	119	484	111	59	14	4	1	63	7	16	.229	.281
1B	Jay Faatz	120	470	124	73	10	2	0	51	12	64	.264	.294
CF	Pete Hotaling	98	403	101	67	7	6	0	55	26	35	.251	.298
3B	Gus Alberts	102	364	75	51	10	6	1	48	41	26	.206	.275
Sub	Mike Goodfellow	68	269	66	24	7	0	0	29	11	7	.245	.271
RF	Ed Hogan	78	269	61	60	16	6	0	24	50	30	.227	.331
C	Pop Snyder	64	237	51	22	7	3	0	14	6	9	.215	.270
C	Chief Zimmer	65	212	51	27	11	4	0	22	18	15	.241	.330
Sub	John McGlone	55	203	37	22	1	3	1	22	16	26	.182	.232
P	Jersey Bakely	61	194	26	19	0	1	1	9	26	1	.134	.160
P	Darby O'Brien	32	109	20	13	1	0	0	9	4	2	.183	.193
Sub	Deacon McGuire	26	94	24	15	1	3	1	13	7	2	.255	.362
Sub	Bill McClellan	22	72	16	6	0	0	0	5	6	6	.222	.222
P	Billy Crowell	18	58	5	5	2	0	0	3	3	1	.086	.121
Sub	Dick Van Zant	10	31	8	1	1	0	0	1	1	1	.258	.290
P	George Proeser	7	23	7	5	2	0	0	1	1	0	.304	.391
P	Ed Keas	6	23	2	1	0	0	0	0	0	0	.087	.087
P	Mike Morrison	4	17	4	2	0	0	0	0	0	0	.235	.235
P	Doc Oberlander	3	14	3	3	2	0	0	4	0	0	.214	.357
P	Bill Stemmeyer	3	10	4	2	1	0	0	1	1	0	.400	.500
P	Ed Knouff	2	6	1	0	1	0	0	0	1	0	.167	.333
		135	4603	1076	651	128	59	12	475	315	353	.234	.295

1B Faatz 120, McGuire 6, Snyder 4, Goodfellow 3, Zimmer 3, Stemmeyer 1
2B Stricker 122, McKean 9, McClellan 5, Knouff 1, Gilks 1
SS McKean 78, Alberts 53, Gilks 4, McClellan 2, Zimmer 1, Bakely 1, Goodfellow 1
3B Alberts 49, McGlone 48, Gilks 28, Van Zant 10, McKean 1
OF Hotaling 98, Gilks 87, Hogan 78, Goodfellow 62, McKean 48, McClellan 15, McGlone 7, Stricker 6, McGuire 3, Zimmer 3, Snyder 3, O'Brien 2, Crowell 1
C Zimmer 59, Snyder 58, McGuire 17, Goodfellow 4
P Bakely 61, O'Brien 30, Crowell 18, Proeser 7, Keas 6, Gilks 4, Morrison 4, Oberlander 3, Knouff 2, Stricker 2. Stemmeyer 2

	G	IP	GS	CG	W	L	K	BB	SH	SV	ERA
Jersey Bakely	61	532.2	61	60	25	33	212	128	4	0	2.97
Darby O'Brien	30	259	30	30	11	19	135	99	1	0	3.30
Billy Crowell	18	150.2	18	16	5	13	61	61	0	0	5.79
George Proeser	7	59	7	7	3	4	20	30	1	0	3.81
Ed Keas	6	51	6	6	3	3	18	12	0	0	2.29
Mike Morrison	4	35	4	4	1	3	14	19	0	0	5.40
Doc Oberlander	3	25.2	3	3	1	2	23	18	0	0	5.26
Bob Gilks	4	21	2	2	0	2	3	8	0	1	8.14
Bill Stemmeyer	2	16	2	2	0	2	7	9	0	0	9.00
Cub Stricker	2	12	0	0	1	0	5	2	0	0	4.50
Ed Knouff	2	9	2	1	0	1	2	3	0	0	1.00
		1171	135	131	50	82	500	389	6	1	3.72

LOUISVILLE Honest John Kelly (10–29)   John Kerins (3–4)   **Mordecai Davidson (35–54)**
Eclipse Park (I)

		G	AB	H	R	2B	3B	HR	RBI	BB	SB	BA	SA
RF	Chicken Wolf	128	538	154	80	28	11	0	67	25	41	.286	.379
LF	Hub Collins	116	485	149	117	**26***	11	2	50	41	62	.307	.419
2B	Reddy Mack	112	446	97	77	13	5	3	34	52	18	.217	.289
3B	Joe Werrick	111	413	89	49	12	7	0	51	30	15	.215	.278
CF	Pete Browning	99	383	120	58	22	8	3	72	37	36	.313	.436
UT	John Kerins	83	319	75	38	11	4	2	41	25	16	.235	.313
P	Scott Stratton	67	249	64	35	8	1	1	29	12	10	.257	.309
P	Guy Hecker	56	211	48	32	9	2	0	29	11	20	.227	.289
1B	Skyrocket Smith	58	206	49	27	9	4	1	31	24	5	.238	.335
SS	Bill White	49	198	55	35	6	5	1	30	7	15	.278	.374
Sub	Farmer Vaughn	51	189	37	15	4	2	1	21	4	4	.196	.254
C	Paul Cook	57	185	34	20	2	0	0	13	5	9	.184	.195
C	Lave Cross	47	181	41	20	3	0	0	15	2	10	.227	.243
P	Toad Ramsey	42	142	17	12	6	0	0	9	9	0	.120	.162
Sub	Harry Raymond	32	123	26	8	2	0	0	13	1	7	.211	.228
Sub	Phil Tomney	34	120	18	15	3	0	0	4	7	11	.150	.175
Sub	Farmer Weaver	26	112	28	12	1	1	0	8	3	12	.250	.277
P	Icebox Chamberlain	26	94	18	11	4	2	0	3	6	8	.191	.277
Sub	Dude Esterbrook	23	93	21	9	6	0	0	7	3	5	.226	.290
Sub	Wally Andrews	26	93	18	12	6	3	0	6	13	5	.194	.323
P	John Ewing	21	79	16	6	1	1	0	5	1	7	.203	.241
Sub	Phil Reccius	2	9	2	0	1	0	0	4	1	0	.222	.333
Sub	Ed Fusselbach	1	4	1	0	0	0	0	1	0	0	.250	.250
Sub	Hercules Burnett	1	4	0	1	0	0	0	0	1	1	.000	.000
P	Billy Crowell	1	3	0	0	0	0	0	0	1	1	.000	.000
Sub	? Long	1	2	0	0	0	0	0	0	1	0	.000	.000
		139	4881	1177	689	**183**	67	14	543	322	318	.241	.315

1B	Smith 58, Hecker 30, Andrews 26, Esterbrook 23, Kerins 4, Wolf 1
2B	Mack 112, Collins 19, Werrick 8, Kerins 1
SS	Wolf 39, White 38, Tomney 34, Collins 15, Werrick 11, Cross 2, Cook 1
3B	Werrick 89, Raymond 31, White 11, Wolf 4, Reccius 2, Kerins 2
OF	Browning 99, Wolf 85, Collins 82, Kerins 47, Stratton 38, Vaughn 28, Weaver 26, Cross 12, Cook 4, Chamberlain 4, Ramsey 4, Werrick 3, Hecker 1, Raymond 1, Fusselbach 1, Burnett 1, Long 1
C	Cook 53, Cross 37, Kerins 33, Vaughn 25, Wolf 3
P	Ramsey 40, Stratton 33, Hecker 28, Chamberlain 24, Ewing 21, Crowell 1

	G	IP	GS	CG	W	L	K	BB	SH	SV	ERA
Toad Ramsey	40	342.1	40	37	8	30	228	86	1	0	3.42
Scott Stratton	33	269.2	28	28	10	17	97	53	2	0	3.64
Guy Hecker	28	223.1	25	25	8	17	63	43	0	0	3.39
Icebox Chamberlain	24	196	24	21	14	9	119	59	1	0	2.53
John Ewing	21	191	21	21	8	13	87	34	2	0	2.83
Billy Crowell	1	9	1	1	0	1	5	6	0	0	6.00
		1231.1	139	133	48	87	**599**	281	6	0	3.25

KANSAS CITY   Dave Rowe (14–36)   Sam Barkley (21–36)   Bill Watkins (8–17)
Association Park (I)

		G	AB	H	R	2B	3B	HR	RBI	BB	SB	BA	SA
CF	Jim McTamany	130	516	127	94	12	10	4	41	67	55	.246	.331
1B	Bill Phillips	129	509	120	57	20	10	1	56	27	10	.236	.320
3B	Jumbo Davis	121	491	131	70	22	8	3	61	20	42	.267	.363
2B	Sam Barkley	116	482	104	67	21	6	4	51	26	15	.216	.309
SS	Henry Easterday	115	401	76	42	7	6	3	37	31	23	.190	.259
C	Jim Donahue	88	337	79	29	11	3	1	28	21	12	.234	.394
RF	Monk Cline	73	293	69	45	13	2	0	19	20	29	.235	.294
Sub	Law Daniels	61	218	45	32	2	0	2	28	14	20	.206	.243
P	Henry Porter	55	195	28	12	3	0	0	10	8	1	.144	.159
Sub	Frank Hankinson	37	155	27	20	4	1	1	20	11	2	.174	.232
LF	Myron Allen	37	136	29	23	6	4	0	10	9	4	.213	.316
Sub	Billy Hamilton	35	129	34	21	4	4	0	11	4	19	.264	.357
Sub	Dave Rowe	32	122	21	14	3	4	0	13	6	2	.172	.262
Sub	Jim Brennan	34	118	20	5	2	0	0	6	3	3	.169	.186
P	Tom Sullivan	28	92	10	10	1	0	0	5	9	7	.109	.120
Sub	Jim Burns	15	66	20	13	0	0	0	4	1	6	.303	.303
P	Bill Fagan	18	65	14	5	3	0	0	4	2	0	.215	.262
P	Red Ehret	17	63	12	4	4	0	0	4	1	1	.190	.254
P	Steve Toole	13	48	10	6	2	2	0	7	1	2	.208	.233
Sub	Fatty Briody	13	48	10	1	1	0	0	8	1	0	.208	.229
P	Frank Hoffman	12	39	6	6	1	0	0	2	4	2	.154	.179
Sub	Charley Jones	6	25	4	2	0	1	0	5	1	1	.160	.240
P	John Kirby	5	16	1	1	0	0	0	0	0	0	.063	.063
Sub	Charlie Hoover	3	10	3	0	0	0	0	1	0	0	.300	.300
Sub	Ed Glenn	3	8	0	0	0	0	0	0	0	1	.000	.000
P	Frank Hafner	2	6	0	0	0	0	0	0	1	0	.000	.000
		132	4588	1000	579	142	61	19	431	288	257	.218	.288

1B   Phillips 129, Hankinson 2, Ehret 1
2B   Barkley 116, Hankinson 13, Cline 3, Donahue 1, Ehret 1
SS   Easterday 115, Hankinson 9, Davis 8, Daniels 1
3B   Davis 113, Hankinson 7, Brennan 5, Donahue 5, Daniels 2, Cline 1
OF   McTamany 130, Cline 70, Allen 35, Hamilton 35, Rowe 32, Daniels 30, Donahue 18, Burns 15, Ehret 10,
       Hankinson 7, Jones 6, Brennan 5, Sullivan 4, Glenn 3, Porter 2, Fagan 2, Toole 2
C   Donahue 67, Daniels 29, Brennan 25, Briody 13, Hoover 3
P   Porter 55, Sullivan 24, Fagan 17, Hoffman 12, Toole 12, Ehret 7, Kirby 5, Hafner 2, Allen 2

	G	IP	GS	CG	W	L	K	BB	SH	SV	ERA
Henry Porter #	55	474	54	53	18	**37**	145	120	4	0	4.16
Tom Sullivan	24	214.2	24	24	8	16	84	68	0	0	3.40
Bill Fagan	17	142.1	17	15	5	11	49	75	0	0	5.69
Frank Hoffman	12	104	12	12	3	9	38	42	0	0	2.77
Steve Toole	12	91.2	10	10	5	6	35	50	0	0	6.68
Red Ehret	7	52	6	5	3	2	12	22	0	0	3.98
John Kirby	5	43	5	5	1	4	11	7	0	0	4.19
Myron Allen	2	18	2	2	0	2	2	1	0	0	2.50
Frank Hafner	2	18	2	2	0	2	5	16	0	0	7.00
		1157.2	132	128	43	89	381	401	4	0	4.29

No-hit game 4–0 vs Baltimore, June 6

1889

CLARKSON WINS EVERYTHING
BUT THE PENNANT

Though no one realized it at the time, 1889 was a landmark season. Frightened by the abrupt offensive deterioration the previous year, the rules committee shaved the number of called balls needed for a walk to four. It was as if a magic formula had been discovered. Years of tinkering with the number of balls and strikes were suddenly ended when the four-ball, three-strike ratio worked so well in 1889 that it has remained constant ever since.

A second rule change in 1889 permitted each team to substitute for one player per game for any reason at the end of a completed inning. Embellishments to this new rule would soon create more jobs on the major league level by opening the way for the use of pinch hitters and pinch runners as well as the more liberal use of relief pitchers, but players were preoccupied at that moment by a much more immediate concern. In 1888 the Reserve Clause had been extended to minor league teams. Given this added hold on players, National League owners revived the salary limitation plan they had enacted three years earlier but then backed off from enforcing. First they waited until Al Spalding took an "all-American" team on a world tour following the 1888 season. Spalding's contingent was comprised of players from his own Chicago club sprinkled with stars from other League teams, including New York Giants shortstop Monte Ward, the president of the players' Brotherhood. With Ward conveniently out of the country, Indianapolis owner John "Tooth" Brush proposed a salary classification plan based on both a player's performance and his much less tangible "personal conduct." Brush's plan ranked players from A to E with a $250 salary differential for each of the five classifications, ranging from a $2,500 peak to a $1,500 low. Former League president Abraham Mills opposed the scheme, claiming that a manager "who can't handle salary with the powerful reserve rule at his command ought to have a wet-nurse," but his was virtually the lone executive voice of dissent.

Ward heard of the plan when the all-American team reached Europe and immediately asked to be released from his tour contract so he could return to the United States and confront the owners. His pleas that Brush's plan robbed players of initiative and paid them less than their worth on an open market were ignored, but earlier on the tour, in Egypt, the

370

notion of a "Players League" had first been hatched. During the 1889 season Ward covertly began putting together his Players League and had most of the pieces in place by fall.

Ward's extensive off-field activities did not impair his play. In 1889 he actually hiked his batting average 48 points and reduced his errors from 86 to 68. When first baseman Roger Connor rebounded from two subpar years to lead the league in RBI and pitcher Tim Keefe and catcher Buck Ewing again had fine years for the Giants, Jim Mutrie's club was in control of its own destiny at Cleveland on October 5, the final day of the season. A win by Keefe against Henry Gruber would clinch the Giants' second straight pennant. The Blues, which had deserted the American Association after the 1888 campaign to take Detroit's spot in the League, stood to gain fifth place by beating the Giants in the finale. Though the motivation was there for Cleveland, Gruber was 7–15 going into the game and Keefe 27–13; it seemed a lock for New York. Meanwhile, if New York stumbled, in Pittsburgh warming up was John Clarkson, set to claim the pennant for Boston by beating Pud Galvin. Pittsburgh also could capture fifth place with a victory coupled with a Cleveland loss, and unlike Gruber, Galvin was formidable. Already he had 22 wins and the previous year had become the first hurler to achieve 300 career victories. Clarkson, though, was unreal in 1889. He had the most dominant season of any pitcher in major league history. With the pitching Triple Crown already firmly in hand, he was shooting to become the only twirler besides Al Spalding to win 50 or more games twice during his career.

Clarkson lost on October 5 to Galvin, 5–1, but it affected only his individual stats. When

Keefe topped Gruber 5–3, it meant that even if Clarkson had achieved his fiftieth win, Boston would have tied New York in won-lost differential (84–44 to 83–43) but would still have finished three percentage points behind at .656 to the Giants' .659. As it was, Clarkson compiled 21 more wins, 22 more complete games and 200 more innings than any other League pitcher. All are major league records for the greatest margin of difference between a leader and a runner-up.

The American Association race, though it ended with Brooklyn two games in front, was even more

John Clarkson nearly carried an unimposing Boston team to the NL pennant in 1889. Not only did he lead the loop in every major pitching department, but he led most by landslide margins. Clarkson's erratic temperament was forgiven by teammates while he was winning big, but many worked to hasten his departure when he began to slip.

tumultuous. Owing to schedule vagaries and a rule then that teams could decide for themselves whether to make up tie games or postponed games, the St. Louis Browns were poised to cop their fifth straight pennant by sweeping a doubleheader from Cincinnati on October 15, the Association's official closing date, and then taking three straight makeup games from the Philadelphia Athletics. A loss in the opener of the twinbill at Cincinnati rendered the nightcap and the makeup games moot and made the events of September 7 to September 10 in Brooklyn loom all the more decisive. Over that four-day stretch the Browns had been slated to play their last three games of the season against Bill McGunnigle's Bridegrooms and needed to win them all to wrest first place from Brooklyn. But of the three games only one was actually played, and even it was never finished.

FAMOUS FIRSTS VI

In 1889, Baltimore Orioles first baseman Tommy Tucker became the first switchhitter to win a major league batting crown. Eleven years later, when the century ended, he was still the only batting titlist who hit from both sides of the plate. That distinction remained Tucker's until 1956. He had another important distinction that will always remain his. Tucker is the only man to play 1,500 or more games at first base in the nineteenth century and not make the Hall of Fame. At the moment he still owns yet a third distinction. No other switchhitter has ever surpassed his .372 batting average in 1889. Given the rest of Tucker's stats that year, one would expect him to have a fourth distinction—the nineteenth-century record for the most hits in a season by switchhitter—but, surprisingly, that is not the case. Here is an evolutionary chart of the nineteenth-century record for the most hits in a season by a switchhitter.

	YEAR	TEAM	HITS
Bob Ferguson	1871	NY-NA	38
Bob Ferguson	1872	Atl-NA	45
Bob Ferguson	1873	Atl-NA	59
Bob Ferguson	1874	Atl-NA	63
Bob Ferguson	1875	Har-NA	88
Bob Ferguson	1878	Chi-NL	91
Bob Ferguson	1881	Tro-NL	96
Cliff Carroll	1884	Pro-NL	118*
Bill Greenwood	1887	Bal-AA	130**
Tommy Tucker	1887	Bal-AA	144
Tommy Tucker	1888	Bal-AA	149
Tommy Tucker	1889	Bal-AA	196
Walt Wilmot	1894	Chi-LA	197

*Fred Lewis, who collected 106 hits in 1884, is listed as a switchhitter by some sources, but the preponderance of evidence is that he batted lefty just a few times as an experiment; Monte Ward did the same thing in 1888 from the right side.
**Greenwood is here because he as well as Tucker broke the former record in 1887.

With his team ahead 4–2 on Saturday, September 7, at Washington Park, Browns manager Charlie Comiskey ordered his troops off the field in the ninth inning when umpire Fred Goldsmith would not agree that it was too dark to continue play. Goldsmith then forfeited the game to Brooklyn. Enraged at Comiskey and owner Chris Von Der Ahe, who had lit candles and arranged them like footlights around the Browns' bench to emphasize how dark it was, the Brooklyn crowd fired beer steins at the Browns as they ran for their buggy outside the park.

Von Der Ahe refused to play the following day even though a huge Sunday crowd of 17,000 was expected unless Goldsmith would rescind the forfeit. Goldsmith demurred and then also forfeited Sunday's game to Brooklyn when the Browns did not show up. Two days later, for the scheduled finale of the Series, the Browns overcame their fear of another crowd assault and journeyed to Washington Park, but a heavy rainstorm washed out the game.

Saturday's forfeit was ultimately overturned and the game was awarded to St. Louis, 4–2, the score at the time it was halted. But Sunday's forfeit was upheld. The inane compromise appeased no one but the Browns and the Columbus Solons, Cleveland's replacement in 1889, which also had suffered a controversial forfeit loss in Brooklyn earlier in the season.

THE LONG-LIVED LYNCH

After umpiring in the National League in 1889, Tom Lynch was selected to officiate the World's Series together with John Gaffney. When Lynch held out at the last minute for an $800 Series appearance fee, he was replaced by Bob Ferguson and became a pariah as far as most league owners were concerned. Lynch, a former outfielder with the Phillies and the 1884 Wilmingtons of the Union Association, decided to make a comeback as a player. He dropped down to the minors in 1890. Returning to his home in Cohoes, New York, after the season, he encountered a jack-spinner in a local mill named Richard Doyle on the morning of October 27. Lynch and Doyle had quarreled three years earlier, and tempers quickly heated again. Doyle pulled out a pistol and shot Lynch in the chest close to his heart. After being carried to his house on Lancaster Street, Lynch was despaired of by everyone including *Sporting Life*, which headlined its report of the incident:

THE BALL PLAYER FATALLY WOUNDED DURING A SALOON ROW IN COHOES.

Lynch managed to hang on a while longer, though. He was the chief spokesman for National League umpires for a time in the early part of the twentieth century. Later he ran a theatrical booking agency in Hartford but was lured back into baseball in 1910 to become National League president after Harry Pulliam committed suicide. Lynch's tour as league president lasted only until 1913, but he still had a ways to go. When he finally died at his Cohoes home in 1955 at age 94, he was the next-to-last surviving participant in the Union Association's lone major league season.

ONE-GAMER IV

When Baltimore manager Billy Barnie made out his lineup on June 17, 1889, he wrote in George Goetz's name. As might be expected, Goetz was never seen again after he fanned in all four of his plate appearances. No one else has ever come up so empty offensively in his only big league game, but Goetz's hitting stats—or lack of them—were only part of what fans saw about him in the box score in their favorite papers the following morning. Goetz also pitched nine innings against Louisville and then was inexplicably removed in the bottom of the tenth after Baltimore tallied four runs in the top of the frame to go ahead, 10–6. Goetz's premature departure deprived him of gaining a complete-game victory in his lone major league outing. A list of men who hurled complete-game wins at the 50-foot distance in their only major league pitching appearances:

	DATE	TEAM	INN	K	BB	ERA
George Snyder	Sept. 30, 1882	Phi-AA	9	0	2	0.00
Fred Andrus	July 4, 1884	Chi-NL	9	2	2	2.00
Dan Bickham	Aug. 13, 1886	Cin-AA	9	6	3	3.00
Harry Raymond	July 27, 1889	Lou-AA	9	1	11	1.00
Bill Price	Apr. 27, 1890	Phi-AA	9	1	7	2.00
Babe Doty	Aug. 18, 1890	Tol-AA	9	4	1	1.00

Meanwhile all of Brooklyn was indignant with the verdict, screaming that it was yet one more proof that Comiskey's team of foul mouths and rule-benders would always get their way, and the mood in which it left the city bore heavily on Bridegrooms owner Charlie Byrne's mind over the winter.

For the moment, though, Byrne cared only that his team had at last broken the Browns' chokehold on the Association pennant. Moreover, his Bridegrooms had set a new nineteenth-century attendance record and were assured a hefty World's Series cut, for their opponents would be none other than the New York Giants, making for the first ever postseason battle between two teams from the same urban sector.

In 1889, Hick Carpenter became the first major leaguer to play 1,000 games at third base as well as the only lefty to play that many games at any infield position other than first base.

MYERS AND MANNING

With batting averages plummeting everywhere in 1888 to new record lows, it went unremarked that Washington second baseman Al Myers set a new negative standard for players with 500 or more at bats when he hit just .207. All such arcane records were almost completely ignored not only in the 1880s but until very recently. Anyway, we now know that the record Myers broke had formerly belonged to Joe Sommer of the 1886 Baltimore Orioles, the worst-hitting team in history. Myers's mark lasted all of one year. In 1889 player-manager Jim Manning of the Kansas City Cowboys hit just .204 in 506 at bats while dividing his duties between second base and the outfield. Manning's record was as short-lived as his Cowboys. It lasted just two years as the Cowboys too survived only two seasons in the Association after replacing the New York Mets. A list of nineteenth-century players who hit below .225 with 500 or more at bats:

	YEAR	POS	TEAM	AB	H	R	BA	OBP	SA
Germany Smith	1891	SS	Cin-NL	512	103	50	.201	.258	.260
Jim Manning	1889	OF/2B	KC-AA	506	103	68	.204	.297	.281
Lou Bierbauer	1891	2B	Pit-NL	500	103	60	.206	.252	.262
Al Myers	1888	2B	Was-NL	502	104	46	.207	.270	.271
Billy Shindle	1888	3B	Bal-AA	514	107	61	.208	.249	.272
Joe Sommer	1886	OF	Bal-AA	560	117	79	.209	.245	.261
Mike Lehane	1890	1B	Col-AA	512	108	54	.211	.276	.268
Shorty Fuller	1891	SS	StL-AA	576	122	105	.212	.296	.271
Bones Ely	1898	SS	Pit-LA	519	110	49	.212	.247	.270
Bob Gilks	1890	OF	Cle-NL	544	116	65	.213	.265	.243
Will Smalley	1890	3B	Cle-NL	502	107	62	.213	.303	.239
Duke Farrell	1892	3B	Pit-LA	605	130	96	.215	.276	.314
Mike Lehane	1891	1B	Col-AA	511	110	59	.215	.268	.272
Cub Stricker	1891	2B	Bos-AA	514	111	96	.216	.309	.261
Joe Quinn	1892	2B	Bos-LA	532	116	63	.218	.275	.254
Emmett Seery	1888	OF	Ind-NL	500	110	87	.220	.316	.330
Kid Gleason	1898	2B	NY-LA	570	126	78	.221	.278	.253
Hughie Jennings	1892	SS	Lou-LA	594	132	65	.222	.270	.273
Jack Manning	1886	OF	Bal-AA	556	124	78	.224	.291	.286

It should have been the greatest interleague clash in the last century, especially when Byrne and Giants owner John Day both learned enough from the 1887 and 1888 Series fiascos to stipulate that their best-of-11 affair would cease as soon as the winner had been decided. And indeed the 1889 Series began as if it would be a classic, drawing swarms of sportswriters and spectators to the first two games. But the audience and the media both soured when the Bridegrooms borrowed a page from the Browns, stalling whenever they got ahead and wheedling the two umpires, Bob Ferguson and John Gaffney, that it was too dark to continue. After Brooklyn won three of the first four games and all of its victories were abbreviated by darkness, Day and Ewing, the Giants' field captain, told Byrne that they didn't "care to run any chance of losing another game on account of darkness or intentional delays" and would compete no more "against a club that insists on playing dirty ball." Alarmed at a possible huge revenue loss, Byrne hastily agreed to move up the starting time for the rest of the Series games so they could be played to completion.

The Giants then won five straight games to go up 6–3 and eliminate the need for a 10th or 11th game. Making their turnabout all the more remarkable was the negligible contribution from their two aces, Keefe and Mickey Welch. After collecting 55 wins between them during the regular season, each was hammered in an early Series loss and never given another start. Convinced the two were exhausted by the pennant drive, Mutrie turned instead

A preseason glimpse of the 1889 Columbus Solons and their tony uniforms. Several of these fresh faces, such as Phil Lawless, never played in the majors, but burly Dave Orr (seated, fourth from left) certainly did. Line shots came off Orr's .342 career bat so wickedly that judicious infielders played him back on the outfield grass. Others are: Lefty Marr, left of Orr; Wild Bill Widner, right of Orr; Jimmy Peoples, right of Widner; Henry Easterday, top far left; and Hank Gasright, front and center, holding the team attack cat under tight restraint.

to Cannonball Crane and Hank O'Day. McGunnigle likewise was forced to call on secondary hurlers when 40-game winner Bob Caruthers was equally as ineffective as Keefe and Welch. The difference was that Crane and O'Day, a combined 25–21 in 1889, won six of seven decisions in the postseason while McGunnigle's stand-ins for Caruthers produced a composite 7.44 ERA. A year after becoming the first man to pilot a World's Series entrant from each major league, Mutrie also found himself the first to win two straight Series championships.

These grand celebrants are the first repeat world champions—the 1889 New York Giants. Top: Art Whitney, Tim Keefe, Mike Tiernan, Mickey Welch, Roger Connor, Willard Brown and Buck Ewing. Bottom: Pat Murphy, Cannonball Crane, Monte Ward, Jim Mutrie, Danny Richardson, Bill George and Jim O'Rourke.

THE SEASONAL RECORD

NATIONAL LEAGUE

	W	L	PCT	HOME	ROAD	GB
1. New York Giants	83	43	.659	47-15	36-28	—
2. Boston Beaneaters	83	45	.648	48-17	35-28	1
3. Chicago White Stockings	67	65	.508	37-30	30-35	19
4. Philadelphia Phillies	63	64	.496	43-24	20-40	20
5. Pittsburgh Alleghenys	61	71	.462	40-28	21-43	20.5
6. Cleveland Spiders	61	72	.459	33-35	28-37	25.5
7. Indianapolis Hoosiers	59	75	.440	32-36	27-39	28
8. Washington Nationals	41	83	.331	24-29	17-54	41

	NY	Bos	Chi	Phil	Pit	Cle	Ind	Was	
New York	—	6	13	12	12	14	13	13	83
Boston	8	—	10	13	16	12	10	14	83
Chicago	5	7	—	9	10	11	13	12	67
Philadelphia	7	6	10	—	9	9	13	9	63
Pittsburgh	7	3	9	9	—	13	10	10	61
Cleveland	4	8	9	10	7	—	9	14	61
Indianapolis	7	10	7	4	10	10	—	11	59
Washington	5	5	7	7	7	3	7	—	41
	43	45	65	64	71	72	75	83	518

SEASON LEADERS

Batting Average

1.	Brouthers, Boston	.373
2.	Glasscock, Indianapolis	.352
3.	Tiernan, New York	.335
4.	F. Carroll, Pittsburgh	.330
5.	Ewing, New York	.327

On-Base Percentage

1.	F. Carroll, Pittsburgh	.486
2.	Brouthers, Boston	.462
3.	Tiernan, New York	.447
4.	Connor, New York	.426
5.	Gore, Chicago	.416

Home Runs

1.	Thompson, Philadelphia	20
2.	Denny, Indianapolis	18
3.	Ryan, Chicago	17
4.	Connor, New York	13
5.	Duffy, Chicago	12

Slugging Average

1.	Connor, New York	.528
2.	Brouthers, Boston	.507
3.	Ryan, Chicago	.498
4.	Tiernan, New York	.497
5.	Thompson, Philadelphia	.492

Total Bases

1.	Ryan, Chicago	287
2.	Glasscock, Indianapolis	272
3.	Thompson, Philadelphia	262
	Connor, New York	262
5.	Tiernan, New York	248

RBI

1.	Connor, New York	130
2.	Brouthers, Boston	118
3.	Anson, Chicago	117
4.	Denny, Indianapolis	112
5.	Thompson, Philadelphia	111

Hits

1.	Glasscock, Indianapolis	205
2.	Brouthers, Boston	181
3.	Ryan, Chicago	177
4.	Duffy, Chicago	172
5.	Van Haltren, Chicago	168

Stolen Bases

1.	Fogarty, Philadelphia	99
2.	Kelly, Boston	68
3.	Brown, Boston	63
4.	Ward, New York	62
5.	Glasscock, Indianapolis	57

Runs

1.	Tiernan, New York	147
2.	Duffy, Chicago	144
3.	Ryan, Chicago	140
4.	Gore, New York	132
5.	Glasscock, Indianapolis	128

Strikeouts

1.	Denny, Indianapolis	63
2.	Wise, Washington	62
	Ryan, Chicago	62
4.	Johnston, Boston	60
	Fogarty, Philadelphia	60

PITCHING

Wins

1.	Clarkson, Boston	49
2.	T. Keefe, New York	28
	Buffinton, Philadelphia	28
4.	Welch, New York	27
5.	Galvin, Pittsburgh	23

Innings

1.	Clarkson, Boston	620
2.	Staley, Pittsburgh	420
3.	Buffinton, Philadelphia	380
4.	Boyle, Indianapolis	378.2
5.	Welch, New York	375

Strikeouts

1.	Clarkson, Boston	284
2.	T. Keefe, New York	225
3.	Staley, Pittsburgh	159
4.	Buffinton, Philadelphia	153
5.	Getzein, Indianapolis	139

ERA (140 innings)

1.	Clarkson, Boston	2.73
2.	Bakely, Cleveland	2.96
3.	Welch, New York	3.02
4.	Buffinton, Philadelphia	3.24
5.	T. Keefe, New York	3.31

Losses

1.	Staley, Pittsburgh	26
2.	Boyle, Indianapolis	23
3.	Getzein, Indianapolis	22
	Bakely, Cleveland	22
5.	Clarkson, Boston	19
	Haddock, Washington	19

Complete Games

1.	Clarkson, Boston	68
2.	Staley, Pittsburgh	46
3.	Welch, New York	39
	O'Brien, Cleveland	39
	T. Keefe, New York	39

Winning Percentage (25 decisions)

1.	Clarkson, Boston	.721
2.	Welch, New York	.692
3.	T. Keefe, New York	.683
4.	Radbourn, Boston	.645
5.	Buffinton, Philadelphia	.636

Lowest On-Base Percentage

1.	Clarkson, Boston	.305
2.	Radbourn, Boston	.306
3.	Staley, Pittsburgh	.309
4.	Welch, New York	.310
5.	T. Keefe, New York	.311

FIELDING

Total Chances		
1B	Anson, Chicago	1515
2B	Pfeffer, Chicago	991
3B	Burns, Chicago	598
SS	Glasscock, Indianapolis	791
OF	Fogarty, Philadelphia	358
C	B. Ewing, New York	718
P	Clarkson, Boston	235

Fielding Average	
Anson, Chicago	.982
Dunlap, Pittsburgh	.950
Denny, Indianapolis	.913
Glasscock, Indianapolis	.915
Fogarty, Philadelphia	.961
Bennett, Boston	.955
Radbourn, Boston	.975

NEW YORK   Jim Mutrie   St. George Grounds (23 games)   Polo Grounds (II)   (38 games)

		G	AB	H	R	2B	3B	HR	RBI	BB	SB	BA	SA
LF	Jim O'Rourke	128	502	161	89	36	7	3	81	40	33	.321	.438
RF	Mike Tiernan	122	499	167	**147**	23	14	10	73	**96**	33	.335	.497
2B	Danny Richardson	125	497	139	88	22	8	7	100	46	32	.280	.398
1B	Roger Connor	131	496	157	117	32	17	13	**130**	93	21	.317	**.528**
CF	George Gore	120	488	149	132	21	7	7	54	84	28	.305	.420
SS	Monte Ward	114	479	143	87	13	4	1	67	27	62	.299	.349
3B	Art Whitney	129	473	103	71	12	2	1	59	56	19	.218	.258
C	Buck Ewing	99	407	133	91	23	13	4	87	37	34	.327	.477
P	Mickey Welch	45	156	30	20	5	1	0	12	5	0	.192	.237
P	Tim Keefe	47	149	23	17	5	2	0	8	8	2	.154	.215
C	Willard Brown	40	139	36	16	10	0	1	29	9	6	.259	.353
Sub	Gil Hatfield	32	125	23	21	2	0	1	12	9	9	.184	.224
P	Cannonball Crane	29	103	21	16	1	0	2	11	13	6	.204	.272
Sub	Mike Slattery	12	48	14	7	2	0	1	12	4	2	.292	.396
P	Hank O'Day	10	31	3	5	0	0	0	2	4	2	.097	.097
Sub	Pat Murphy	9	28	10	5	1	1	1	4	2	0	.357	.571
Sub	Harry Lyons	5	20	2	1	0	1	0	2	2	0	.100	.200
Sub	Bill George	3	15	4	1	0	0	0	0	0	1	.267	.267
P	Cannonball Titcomb	3	12	1	2	0	0	0	0	0	0	.083	.083
Sub	Elmer Foster	2	4	0	2	0	0	0	0	3	2	.000	.000
		131	4671	1319	**935**	208	**77**	52	**743**	538	292	**.282**	**.393**

1B	Connor 131, Crane 1
2B	Richardson 125, Ward 7
SS	Ward 108, Hatfield 24
3B	Whitney 129, Hatfield 2, Connor 1
OF	O'Rourke 128, Tiernan 122, Gore 120, Slattery 12, Lyons 5, George 3, Brown 3, Foster 2, Ewing 1
C	Ewing 97, Brown 37, Murphy 9, O'Rourke 2
P	Keefe 47, Welch 45, Crane 29, O'Day 10, Hatfield 6, Ewing 3, Titcomb 3, Whitney 1

	G	IP	GS	CG	W	L	K	BB	SH	SV	ERA
Mickey Welch	45	375	41	39	27	12	125	149	3	**2**	3.02
Tim Keefe	47	364	45	38	28	13	225	151	3	1	3.31
Cannonball Crane	29	230	25	23	14	10	130	136	0	0	3.68
Hank O'Day	10	78	10	8	9	1	28	35	0	0	4.27
Gil Hatfield	6	52	5	5	2	4	28	25	0	0	3.98
Cannonball Titcomb	3	26	3	3	1	2	7	16	0	0	6.58
Buck Ewing	3	20	2	2	2	0	12	8	0	0	4.05
Art Whitney	1	6	0	0	0	1	3	3	0	0	3.00
		1151	131	118	83	43	**558**	523	6	3	3.47

BOSTON   **Jim Hart**   **South End Grounds (I)**

		G	AB	H	R	2B	3B	HR	RBI	BB	SB	BA	SA
CF	Dick Johnston	132	539	123	80	16	4	5	67	41	34	.228	.301
2B	Hardy Richardson	132	536	163	122	33	10	6	79	48	47	.304	.437
RF	King Kelly	125	507	149	120	**41**	5	9	78	65	68	.294	.448
1B	Dan Brouthers	126	485	181	105	26	9	7	118	66	22	**.373**	.507
3B	Billy Nash	129	481	132	84	20	2	3	76	79	26	.274	.343
SS	Joe Quinn	112	444	116	57	13	5	2	69	25	24	.261	.327
LF	Tom Brown	90	362	84	93	10	5	2	24	59	63	.232	.304
UT	Charlie Ganzel	73	275	73	30	3	5	1	43	15	13	.265	.324
P	John Clarkson	73	262	54	36	9	3	2	23	11	8	.206	.286
C	Charlie Bennett	82	247	57	42	8	2	4	28	21	7	.231	.328
SS	Pop Smith	59	208	54	21	13	4	0	32	23	11	.260	.361
P	Hoss Radbourn	35	122	23	17	1	0	1	13	9	3	.189	.221
P	Kid Madden	24	86	25	7	1	0	0	14	3	4	.291	.302
Sub	Irv Ray	9	33	10	8	1	0	0	2	4	1	.303	.333
P	Bill Daley	9	20	3	2	1	0	0	0	1	0	.150	.200
P	Bill Sowders	7	17	4	2	0	0	0	1	1	0	.235	.235
Sub	Jerry Hurley	1	4	0	0	0	0	0	0	0	0	.000	.000
		133	4628	1251	826	196	54	42	667	471	**331**	.270	.363

1B   Brouthers 126, Ganzel 7
2B   Richardson 86, Quinn 47
SS   Quinn 63, Smith 59, Ganzel 6, Ray 5
3B   Nash 128, Ray 4, Quinn 2, Ganzel 1, Clarkson 1, Radbourn 1
OF   Johnston 132, Kelly 113, Brown 90, Richardson 46, Ganzel 26, Clarkson 2, Radbourn 2, Madden 2, Hurley 1
C   Bennett 82, Ganzel 39, Kelly 23, Hurley 1
P   Clarkson 73, Radbourn 33, Madden 22, Daley 9, Sowders 7, Nash 1

	G	IP	GS	CG	W	L	K	BB	SH	SV	ERA
John Clarkson	**73**	**620**	**72**	**68**	**49**	19	**284**	203	8	1	**2.73**
Hoss Radbourn	33	277	31	28	20	11	99	72	1	0	3.67
Kid Madden	22	178	19	18	10	10	64	71	1	1	4.40
Bill Daley	9	48	7	4	3	3	40	43	0	0	4.31
Bill Sowders	7	42	4	3	1	2	10	23	0	2*	5.14
Billy Nash	1	1	0	0	0	0	0	1	0	0	0.00
		1166	133	121	83	45	497	413	**10**	4	3.36

CHICAGO   Cap Anson   West Side Park (I)

		G	AB	H	R	2B	3B	HR	RBI	BB	SB	BA	SA
RF	Hugh Duffy	136	**584**	172	144	21	7	12	89	46	52	.295	.416
CF	Jimmy Ryan	135	576	177	140	31	14	17	72	70	45	.307	.498
LF	George Van Haltren	134	543	168	126	20	10	9	81	82	28	.309	.433
2B	Fred Pfeffer	134	531	121	85	15	7	7	77	53	45	.228	.322
3B	Tom Burns	136	525	127	64	27	6	4	66	32	18	.242	.339
1B	Cap Anson	134	518	161	100	32	7	7	117	86	27	.311	.440
C	Duke Farrell	101	407	101	66	19	7	11	75	41	13	.248	.410
SS	Ned Williamson	47	173	41	16	3	1	1	30	23	2	.237	.283
SS	Charlie Bastian	46	155	21	19	0	0	0	10	25	1	.135	.135
P	Ad Gumbert	41	153	44	30	3	2	7	29	11	2	.288	.471
P	John Tener	42	150	41	18	4	2	1	19	7	2	.273	.347
P	Frank Dwyer	36	135	27	14	1	1	1	6	4	0	.200	.244
P	Bill Hutchison	37	133	21	14	1	1	1	7	7	2	.158	.203
Sub	Del Darling	36	120	23	14	1	1	0	7	25	5	.192	.217
Sub	Silver Flint	15	56	13	6	1	0	1	9	3	1	.232	.304
Sub	Pete Sommers	12	45	10	5	5	0	0	8	2	0	.222	.333
P	Gus Krock	7	24	4	4	0	0	0	2	0	0	.167	.167
P	Egyptian Healy	5	20	2	2	0	0	0	1	0	0	.100	.100
P	Bill Bishop	2	1	0	0	0	0	0	0	1	0	.000	.000
		136	4849	1274	867	184	66	**79**	705	518	243	.263	.377

1B   Anson 134, Tener 2
2B   Pfeffer 134, Bastian 1, Van Haltren 1
SS   Williamson 47, Bastian 45, Ryan 29, Duffy 10, Van Haltren 3, Dwyer 2
3B   Burns 136
OF   Van Haltren 130, Duffy 126, Ryan 106, Farrell 25, Gumbert 13, Tener 6, Dwyer 3, Sommers 1, Hutchison 1
C   Farrell 76, Darling 36, Flint 15, Sommers 11
P   Hutchison 37, Tener 35, Dwyer 32, Gumbert 31, Krock 7, Healy 5, Bishop 2

	G	IP	GS	CG	W	L	K	BB	SH	SV	ERA
Bill Hutchison	37	318	36	33	16	17	136	117	3	0	3.54
John Tener	35	287	30	28	15	15	105	105	1	0	3.64
Frank Dwyer	32	276	30	27	16	13	63	72	0	0	3.59
Ad Gumbert	31	246.1	28	25	16	13	91	76	2	0	3.62
Gus Krock	7	60.2	7	5	3	3	16	14	0	0	4.90
Egyptian Healy	5	46	5	5	1	4	22	18	0	0	4.50
Bill Bishop	2	3	0	0	0	0	1	6	0	2	18.00
		1237	136	123	67	65	434	408	6	2	3.73

PHILADELPHIA   Harry Wright   Philadelphia Baseball Grounds

		G	AB	H	R	2B	3B	HR	RBI	BB	SB	BA	SA
3B	Joe Mulvey	129	544	157	77	21	9	6	77	23	23	.289	.393
RF	Sam Thompson	128	533	158	103	36	4	**20**	111	36	24	.296	.492
CF	Jim Fogarty	128	499	129	107	15	17	3	54	65	**99**	.259	.375
1B	Sid Farrar	130	477	128	70	22	2	3	58	52	28	.268	.342
SS	Bill Hallman	119	462	117	67	21	8	2	60	36	20	.253	.346
LF	George Wood	97	422	106	77	21	4	5	53	53	17	.251	.355
C	Jack Clements	78	310	88	51	17	1	4	35	29	3	.284	.384
2B	Al Myers	75	305	82	52	14	2	0	28	36	8	.269	.328
Sub	Ed Delahanty	56	246	72	37	13	3	0	27	14	19	.293	.370
C	Pop Schriver	51	211	56	24	10	0	1	19	16	5	.265	.327
P	Ben Sanders	44	169	47	21	8	2	0	21	6	4	.278	.349
P	Charlie Buffinton	47	154	32	16	2	0	0	21	9	0	.208	.221
P	Kid Gleason	30	99	25	11	5	0	0	8	8	4	.253	.303
Sub	Art Irwin	18	73	16	9	5	0	0	10	6	6	.219	.288
P	Dan Casey	20	68	15	5	2	0	0	8	0	0	.221	.250

		G	AB	H	R	2B	3B	HR	RBI	BB	SB	BA	SA
Sub	Ed Andrews	10	39	11	10	1	0	0	7	2	7	.282	.308
Sub	Harry Decker	11	30	3	4	0	0	0	2	2	1	.100	.100
Sub	Piggy Ward	7	25	4	0	1	0	0	4	0	1	.160	.200
P	Dave Anderson	5	11	2	1	1	0	0	0	0	0	.182	.273
P	Bill Day	4	10	0	0	0	0	0	0	0	0	.000	.000
P	Pete Wood	3	8	0	0	0	0	0	2	0	0	.000	.000
		130	4695	1248	742	215	52	44	605	393	269	.266	.362

1B Farrar 130
2B Myers 75, Delahanty 24, Hallman 13, Decker 7, Ward 6, Schriver 6, Gleason 2, Andrews 1
SS Hallman 106, Irwin 18, Delahanty 1, G. Wood 6
3B Mulvey 129, Schriver 1
OF Thompson 128, Fogarty 128, G. Wood 92, Delahanty 31, Andrews 9, Sanders 3, Buffinton 1, Gleason 1, Decker 1, Ward 1
C   Clements 78, Schriver 48, Decker 3, Hallman 1
P   Buffinton 47, Sanders 44, Gleason 29, Casey 20, Anderson 5, Day 4, Fogarty 4, P. Wood 3, G. Wood 1

	G	IP	GS	CG	W	L	K	BB	SH	SV	ERA
Charlie Buffinton	47	380	43	37	28	16	153	121	2	0	3.24
Ben Sanders	44	349.2	39	34	19	18	123	96	1	1	3.55
Kid Gleason	29	205	21	15	9	15	64	97	0	1	5.58
Dan Casey	20	152.2	20	15	6	10	65	72	1	0	3.77
Dave Anderson	5	23	2	1	0	1	8	14	0	0	7.43
Bill Day	4	19	3	2	0	3	20	23	0	0	5.21
Pete Wood	3	19	2	2	1	1	8	3	0	0	5.21
Jim Fogarty	4	4	0	0	0	0	0	2	0	0	9.00
George Wood	1	1	0	0	0	0	2	0	0	0	18.00
		1153.1	130	106	63	64	443	428	4	2	4.00

PITTSBURGH **Horace Phillips (28-43)** **Fred Dunlap (7-10)** **Ned Hanlon (26-18)**
Recreation Park

		G	AB	H	R	2B	3B	HR	RBI	BB	SB	BA	SA
1B	Jake Beckley	123	522	157	91	24	10	9	97	29	11	.301	.437
CF	Ned Hanlon	116	461	110	81	14	10	2	37	58	53	.239	.325
2B	Fred Dunlap	121	451	106	59	19	0	2	65	42	21	.235	.290
C	Doggie Miller	104	422	113	77	25	3	6	56	31	16	.268	.384
3B	Willie Kuehne	97	390	96	43	20	5	5	57	9	15	.246	.362
RF	Billy Sunday	81	321	77	62	10	6	2	25	27	47	.240	.327
UT	Fred Carroll	91	318	105	80	21	11	2	51	85	19	.330	.484
SS	Jack Rowe	75	317	82	57	14	3	2	32	22	5	.259	.341
Sub	Jocko Fields	75	289	90	41	22	5	2	43	29	7	.311	.443
Sub	Pop Smith	72	258	54	26	10	2	5	27	24	12	.209	.322
LF	Al Maul	68	257	71	37	6	6	4	44	29	18	.276	.393
Sub	Deacon White	55	225	57	35	10	1	0	26	16	2	.253	.307
P	Harry Staley	51	186	30	11	3	1	0	8	4	1	.161	.188
P	Pud Galvin	41	150	28	15	7	2	0	16	3	2	.187	.260
P	Ed Morris	21	72	7	2	1	0	0	4	4	1	.097	.111
P	Bill Sowders	15	48	13	4	1	0	0	4	3	0	.271	.292
Sub	Chuck Lauer	4	16	3	2	0	0	0	1	0	0	.188	.188
P	Bill Garfield	4	13	0	0	0	0	0	0	0	0	.000	.000
P	Pete Conway	3	10	1	2	0	0	1	2	1	1	.100	.400
P	Andy Dunning	2	7	0	0	0	0	0	0	0	0	.000	.000
P	Alex Beam	2	6	1	0	1	0	0	0	0	0	.167	.333
P	Alex Jones	1	5	1	1	1	0	0	1	0	0	.200	.400
P	Al Krumm	1	4	0	0	0	0	0	0	0	0	.000	.000
		134	4748	1202	726	209	65	42	596	420	231	.253	.351

1B   Beckley 122, Carroll 7, White 3, Kuehne 2
2B   Dunlap 121, Smith 9, Kuehne 5
SS   Rowe 75, Smith 58, Kuehne 2
3B   Kuehne 75, White 52, Miller 3, Smith 3, Carroll 1
OF   Hanlon 116, Sunday 81, Maul 64, Fields 60, Carroll 41, Miller 27, Kuehne 13, Smith 3, Staley 2, Sowders 2, Conway 1, Beckley 1, Lauer 1
C   Miller 76, Carroll 43, Fields 16, Lauer 3
P   Staley 49, Galvin 41, Morris 21, Sowders 13, Maul 6, Garfield 4, Conway 3, Dunning 2, Beam 2, Jones 1, Krumm 1

	G	IP	GS	CG	W	L	K	BB	SH	SV	ERA
Hank Staley	49	420	47	46	21	**26**	159	116	1	1	3.51
Pud Galvin	41	341	40	38	23	16	77	78	4	0	4.17
Ed Morris	21	170	21	18	6	13	40	48	0	0	4.13
Bill Sowders	13	52.2	11	9	6	5	33	29	0	0	7.35
Al Maul	6	42	4	4	1	4	11	28	0	0	9.86
Bill Garfield	4	29	2	2	0	2	4	17	0	0	7.76
Pete Conway	3	22	3	2	2	1	2	16	0	0	4.91
Andy Dunning	2	18	2	2	0	2	4	16	0	0	7.00
Alex Beam	2	18	2	2	1	1	1	15	0	0	6.50
Alex Jones	1	9	1	1	1	0	10	1	0	0	3.00
Al Krumm	1	9	1	1	0	1	4	10	0	0	10.00
		1130.2	134	125	61	71	345	**374**	5	1	4.51

CLEVELAND   **Tom Loftus**   **National League Park (II)**   **(formerly Association Park)**

		G	AB	H	R	2B	3B	HR	RBI	BB	SB	BA	SA
2B	Cub Stricker	136	566	142	83	10	4	1	47	58	32	.251	.288
LF	Larry Twitchell	134	549	151	73	16	11	4	95	29	17	.275	.366
3B	Patsy Tebeau	136	521	147	72	20	6	8	76	37	26	.282	.390
SS	Ed McKean	123	500	159	88	22	8	4	75	42	35	.318	.418
RF	Paul Radford	136	487	116	94	21	5	1	46	91	30	.238	.308
CF	Jimmy McAleer	110	447	105	66	6	6	1	35	30	37	.235	.282
1B	Jay Faatz	117	442	102	50	12	5	2	38	17	27	.231	.294
C	Chief Zimmer	84	259	67	47	9	9	1	21	44	14	.259	.375
Sub	Bob Gilks	53	210	50	17	5	2	0	18	7	6	.238	.281
C	Sy Sutcliffe	46	161	40	17	3	2	1	21	14	5	.248	.311
P	Darby O'Brien	41	140	35	13	1	0	0	18	12	2	.250	.257
P	Eb Beatin	37	121	14	13	0	0	1	8	14	0	.116	.140
P	Jersey Bakely	36	111	15	9	1	1	1	8	17	1	.135	.189
Sub	Pop Snyder	22	83	16	5	3	0	0	12	2	4	.193	.229
P	Henry Gruber	25	69	7	7	2	0	0	4	14	0	.101	.130
P	Charlie Sprague	2	7	1	2	0	0	0	1	1	1	.143	.143
		136	4673	1167	656	131	59	25	523	429	237	.250	.319

1B   Faatz 117, Gilks 10, Sutcliffe 8, Zimmer 3
2B   Stricker 135, McKean 1, Gilks 1
SS   McKean 122, Gilks 13, Stricker 1
3B   Tebeau 136, Radford 1
OF   Radford 136, Twitchell 134, McAleer 110, Gilks 29, Sutcliffe 1, Beatin 1, Bakely 1
C   Zimmer 81, Sutcliffe 37, Snyder 22
P   O'Brien 41, Bakely 36, Beatin 36, Gruber 25, Sprague 2, Twitchell 1

	G	IP	GS	CG	W	L	K	BB	SH	SV	ERA
Darby O'Brien	41	346.2	41	39	22	17	122	167	1	0	4.15
Eb Beatin	36	317.2	36	35	20	15	126	141	3	0	3.57
Jersey Bakely	36	304.1	34	33	12	22	105	106	2	0	2.96
Henry Gruber	25	205	23	23	7	16	74	94	0	1	3.64
Charlie Sprague	2	17	2	2	0	2	8	10	0	0	8.47
Larry Twitchell	1	1	0	0	0	0	0	1	0	0	0.00
		1191.2	136	**132**	61	72	435	519	6	1	3.66

INDIANAPOLIS Frank Bancroft (25-43) Jack Glasscock (34-32) **Athletic Park (II)**

		G	AB	H	R	2B	3B	HR	RBI	BB	SB	BA	SA
SS	Jack Glasscock	134	582	**205**	128	40	3	7	85	31	57	.352	.467
3B	Jerry Denny	133	578	163	96	24	0	18	112	27	22	.282	.417
RF	Jack McGeachy	131	532	142	83	32	1	2	63	9	37	.267	.342
LF	Emmett Seery	127	526	165	123	26	12	8	59	67	19	.314	.454
1B	Paul Hines	121	486	148	77	27	1	6	72	49	34	.305	.401
2B	Charlie Bassett	127	477	117	64	12	5	4	68	37	15	.245	.317
C	Dick Buckley	68	260	67	35	11	0	8	41	15	5	.258	.392
CF	Marty Sullivan	69	256	73	45	11	3	4	35	50	15	.285	.398
C	Con Daily	62	219	55	35	6	2	0	26	28	14	.251	.297
Sub	Ed Andrews	40	173	53	32	11	0	0	22	5	7	.306	.370
P	Henry Boyle	46	155	38	17	10	0	1	17	9	4	.245	.329
Sub	George Myers	43	149	29	22	3	0	0	12	17	12	.195	.215
P	Charlie Getzein	45	139	25	20	4	2	2	14	15	2	.180	.281
P	Amos Rusie	33	103	18	15	3	1	0	4	2	3	.175	.223
Sub	Pete Sommers	23	84	21	12	2	2	2	14	1	2	.250	.393
Sub	Jumbo Schoeneck	16	62	15	3	2	2	0	8	3	1	.242	.339
P	Jim Whitney	10	32	12	6	4	1	0	4	5	2	.375	.563
P	Jack Fee	7	21	3	2	0	0	0	0	0	0	.143	.143
P	Bill Burdick	10	17	2	1	0	0	0	1	4	0	.118	.118
P	Gus Krock	4	14	5	2	0	0	0	4	2	1	.357	.357
P	Lev Shreve	3	7	0	1	0	0	0	0	1	0	.000	.000
P	Varney Anderson	2	5	0	0	0	0	0	0	0	0	.000	.000
P	Jack Fanning	1	1	0	0	0	0	0	0	0	0	.000	.000
Sub	Pete Weckbecker	1	1	0	0	0	0	0	2	0	0	.000	.000
		135	4879	**1356**	819	**228**	35	62	663	377	252	.278	.377

1B Hines 109, Schoeneck 16, Daily 6, Sullivan 5, Buckley 1, Myers 1
2B Bassett 127, Denny 7, Glasscock 2, Andrews 1
SS Glasscock 132, Denny 5
3B Denny 123, Buckley 12, Daily 1, Boyle 1
OF McGeachy 131, Seery 127, Sullivan 64, Andrews 40, Myers 23, Hines 12, Daily 6, Sommers 2, Buckley 1, Whitney 1
C Buckley 55, Daily 51, Sommers 21, Myers 18, Weckbecker 1
P Boyle 46, Getzein 45, Rusie 33, Burdick 10, Whitney 9, Fee 7, Krock 4, Shreve 3, McGeachy 3, Anderson 2, Glasscock 1, Fanning 1

	G	IP	GS	CG	W	L	K	BB	SH	SV	ERA
Henry Boyle	46	378.2	45	38	21	23	97	95	2	0	3.92
Charlie Getzein	45	349	44	36	18	22	139	100	0	1	4.54
Amos Rusie	33	225	22	19	12	10	109	116	1	0	5.32
Jim Whitney	9	70	8	7	2	7	16	19	0	0	6.81
Bill Burdick	10	45.2	4	2	2	4	16	13	0	1	4.53
Jack Fee	7	40	3	2	2	2	10	31	0	0	4.27
Gus Krock	4	32	4	3	2	2	10	14	0	0	7.31
Lev Shreve	3	15.2	3	1	0	3	5	12	0	0	13.79
Varney Anderson	2	12	1	1	0	1	3	9	0	0	4.50
Jack McGeachy	3	4.2	0	0	0	0	3	6	0	0	11.57
Jack Fanning	1	1	1	0	0	1	0	2	0	0	18.00
Jack Glasscock	1	0.2	0	0	0	0	0	3	0	0	0.00
		1174.1	135	109	59	75	408	420	3	2	4.85

WASHINGTON   **John Morrill (13-38)**   **Arthur Irwin (28-45)**   **Swampoodle Grounds**

		G	AB	H	R	2B	3B	HR	RBI	BB	SB	BA	SA
CF	Dummy Hoy	127	507	139	98	11	6	0	39	75	35	.274	.320
2B	Sam Wise	121	472	118	79	15	8	4	62	61	24	.250	.341
LF	Walt Wilmot	108	432	125	88	19	**19**	9	57	51	40	.289	.484
UT	Connie Mack	98	386	113	51	16	1	0	42	15	26	.293	.339
SS	Arthur Irwin	85	313	73	49	10	5	0	32	42	9	.233	.297
1B	John Carney	69	273	63	25	7	0	1	29	14	12	.231	.267
C	Tom Daly	71	250	75	39	13	5	1	40	38	18	.300	.404
3B	John Irwin	58	228	66	42	11	4	0	25	25	10	.289	.373
Sub	Pete Sweeney	49	193	44	13	7	3	1	23	11	8	.228	.311
RF	Ed Beecher	42	179	53	20	9	0	0	30	5	3	.296	.346
Sub	Al Myers	46	176	46	24	3	0	0	20	22	10	.261	.278
Sub	John Morrill	44	146	27	20	5	0	2	16	30	12	.185	.260
Sub	Spider Clark	38	145	37	19	7	2	3	22	6	8	.255	.393
P	Alex Ferson	35	114	13	6	3	1	0	3	10	1	.114	.158
P	George Haddock	34	112	25	13	3	0	2	14	19	3	.223	.304
Sub	George Shoch	30	109	26	12	2	0	0	11	20	9	.239	.257
P	George Keefe	30	98	16	7	2	1	0	1	8	2	.163	.204
Sub	Hi Ebright	16	59	15	7	2	2	1	6	3	1	.254	.407
P	Egyptian Healy	13	45	10	7	2	0	1	4	0	0	.222	.333
P	Hank O'Day	13	44	8	1	1	0	0	5	3	0	.182	.205
Sub	John Riddle	11	37	8	3	3	0	0	3	2	0	.216	.297
P	Gus Krock	6	23	2	3	0	0	0	3	0	0	.087	.087
P	Mike Sullivan	9	19	1	2	0	0	0	0	1	0	.053	.053
Sub	Jim Donnelly	4	13	2	3	0	0	0	0	2	1	.154	.154
Sub	Billy O'Brien	2	8	0	1	0	0	0	0	1	0	.000	.000
Sub	Art McCoy	2	6	0	0	0	0	0	0	2	0	.000	.000
P	John Thornton	1	4	0	0	0	0	0	1	0	0	.000	.000
Sub	Harry Clarke	1	3	0	0	0	0	0	0	0	0	.000	.000
Sub	Jim Banning	2	1	0	0	0	0	0	0	0	0	.000	.000
		127	4395	1105	632	151	57	25	488	466	232	.251	.329

1B   Carney 53, Morrill 40, Mack 22, Daly 8, Beecher 3, O'Brien 2
2B   Wise 72, Myers 46, Daly 4, Clark 2, McCoy 2, A. Irwin 1, Sweeney 1, Morrill 1
SS   A. Irwin 85, Wise 26, Clark 13, Ebright 3, Shoch 1, Daly 1
3B   J. Irwin 58, Sweeney 47, Wise 13, Donnelly 4, Morrill 3, Clark 2
OF   Hoy 127, Wilmot 108, Beecher 39, Mack 34, Shoch 29, Carney 16, Wise 10, Clark 9, Ebright 4, Daly 3,
     Haddock 3, Riddle 2, Keefe 1, Sweeney 1, Clarke 1
C   Daly 57, Mack 45, Clark 14, Riddle 9, Ebright 9, Banning 2
P   Ferson 36, Haddock 33, Keefe 30, O'Day 13, Healy 13, Sullivan 9, Krock 6, A. Irwin 1, Morrill 1, Thornton 1

	G	IP	GS	CG	W	L	K	BB	SH	SV	ERA
Alex Ferson	36	288.1	34	28	17	17	85	105	1	0	3.90
George Haddock	33	276.1	31	30	11	19	106	123	0	0	4.20
George Keefe	30	230	28	24	8	18	90	143	0	0	5.13
Hank O'Day	13	108	13	11	2	10	23	57	0	0	4.33
Egyptian Healy	13	101	12	10	1	11	49	38	0	0	6.24
Gus Krock	6	48	6	6	2	4	17	22	0	0	5.25
Mike Sullivan	9	41	3	3	0	3	15	32	0	0	7.24
John Thornton	1	9	1	1	0	1	3	7	0	0	5.00
Arthur Irwin	1	1	0	0	0	0	0	0	0	0	0.00
John Morrill	1	0.1	0	0	0	0	0	0	0	0	0.00
		1103	127	113	41	83	388	527	1	0	4.68

WORLD'S SERIES

New York (NL) defeated Brooklyn (AA) 6 games to 3

Game 1 at Polo Grounds (NY), Oct. 18: Bro (Terry) 12, NY (Keefe) 10
Game 2 at Washington Park (Bro), Oct. 19: NY (Crane) 6, Bro (Caruthers) 2
Game 3 at Polo Grounds (NY), Oct. 22: Bro (Hughes) 8, NY (Welch) 7
Game 4 at Washington Park (Bro), Oct. 23: Bro (Terry) 10, NY (Crane) 7
Game 5 at Washington Park (Bro), Oct. 24: NY (Crane) 11, Bro (Caruthers) 3
Game 6 at Polo Grounds (NY), Oct. 25: NY (O'Day) 2, Bro (Terry) 1 (11 inn.)
Game 7 at Polo Grounds (NY), Oct. 26: NY (Crane) 11, Bro (Lovett) 7
Game 8 at Washington Park (Bro), Oct. 28: NY (Crane) 17, Bro (Terry) 7
Game 9 at Polo Grounds (NY), Oct. 29: NY (O'Day) 3, Bro (Terry) 2

NEW YORK

		G	AB	H	R	2B	3B	HR	RBI	BB	BA	SA
RF	Mike Tiernan	9	38	11	12	1	1	1	5	5	.289	.447
SS	Monte Ward	9	36	15	10	0	1	0	7	5	**.417**	.444
LF	Jim O'Rourke	9	36	14	7	2	2	2	7	2	.389	**.722**
C	Buck Ewing	8	36	9	5	4	0	0	7	2	.250	.361
1B	Roger Connor	9	35	12	9	2	2	0	12	3	.343	.514
2B	Danny Richardson	9	35	11	8	1	1	3	8	3	.314	.657
3B	Art Whitney	9	35	8	4	2	1	0	3	1	.229	.343
CF	George Gore	5	21	7	5	1	1	0	1	3	.333	.476
P	Cannonball Crane	5	18	5	3	1	1	1	5	1	.278	.611
CF	Mike Slattery	4	16	3	6	0	0	0	1	3	.188	.188
P	Hank O'Day	3	6	1	0	0	0	0	0	2	.167	.167
C	Willard Brown	1	5	3	3	0	0	1	2	0	.600	1.167
P	Tim Keefe	2	4	2	1	1	0	0	0	1	.500	.750
P	Mickey Welch	1	3	1	0	1	0	0	0	0	.333	.667
			324	102	73	16	10	8	58	31	.315	.500

	G	IP	GS	CG	W	L	K	BB	SH	SV	ERA
Cannonball Crane	5	38.2	5	4	4	1	19	32	0	0	3.72
Hank O'Day	3	23	2	2	2	0	12	14	0	0	1.17
Tim Keefe	2	11	1	1	0	1	4	2	0	1	8.18
Mickey Welch	1	5	1	0	0	1	1	3	0	0	9.00
		77.2	9	7	6	3	36	51	0	1	3.94

BROOKLYN

		G	AB	H	R	2B	3B	HR	RBI	BB	BA	SA
2B	Hub Collins	9	35	13	13	3	0	1	2	7	.371	.543
1B/P	Dave Foutz	9	35	10	7	2	0	1	9	4	.286	.429
RF	Oyster Burns	9	35	8	8	3	0	2	11	5	.229	.486
3B	George Pinkney	9	31	8	2	2	0	0	3	4	.258	.323
LF	Darby O'Brien	9	31	5	8	0	1	0	4	12	.161	.226
SS	Germany Smith	8	29	5	2	2	1	0	2	3	.172	.310
CF	Pop Corkhill	9	24	5	4	1	0	1	5	6	.208	.333
P/1B	Adonis Terry	5	18	3	1	0	0	0	1	1	.167	.167
C/OF	Joe Visner	5	16	2	2	1	0	0	0	2	.125	.188
C	Bob Clark	4	12	5	3	2	0	0	3	2	.417	.583
P	Bob Caruthers	4	8	2	1	0	0	0	1	3	.250	.250
C	Doc Bushong	3	8	0	0	0	0	0	0	1	.000	.000
SS	Jumbo Davis	1	4	0	0	0	0	0	0	0	.000	.000
P	Mickey Hughes	1	3	1	1	1	0	0	0	1	.333	.667
P	Tom Lovett	1	1	0	0	0	0	0	0	0	.000	.000
		9	290	67	52	17	2	5	41	51	.231	.355

	G	IP	GS	CG	W	L	K	BB	SH	SV	ERA
Adonis Terry	5	37.2	5	4	2	3	14	18	0	0	5.97
Bob Caruthers	4	24	2	2	0	2	6	6	0	1	3.75
Mickey Hughes	1	7	1	1	1	0	3	3	0	0	7.71
Dave Foutz	1	5	0	0	0	0	2	2	0	0	7.20
Tom Lovett	1	3	1	0	0	1	1	2	0	0	24.00
		76.2	9	7	3	6	26	31	0	1	6.22

AMERICAN ASSOCIATION

	W	L	PCT	HOME	ROAD	GB
1. Brooklyn Bridegrooms	93	44	.679	50-19	43-25	—
2. St. Louis Browns	90	45	.667	51-18	39-27	2
3. Philadelphia Athletics	75	58	.564	46-22	29-36	16
4. Cincinnati Reds	76	63	.547	47-26	29-37	18
5. Baltimore Orioles	70	65	.519	40-24	30-41	22
6. Columbus Solons	60	78	.435	36-33	24-45	33.5
7. Kansas City Cowboys	55	82	.401	33-35	20-47	38
8. Louisville Colonels	27	111	.196	18-46	9-65	66.5

	Bro	StL	Phi	Cin	Bal	Col	KC	Lou	
Brooklyn	—	8	12	15	12	11	16	19	93
St. Louis	11	—	9	12	12	14	14	18	90
Philadelphia	7	8	—	11	11	12	12	14	75
Cincinnati	5	8	9	—	11	11	14	18	76
Baltimore	8	7	8	8	—	12	11	16	70
Columbus	8	6	7	9	8	—	9	13	60
Kansas City	4	6	8	6	7	11	—	13	55
Louisville	1	2	5	2	4	7	6	—	27
	44	45	58	63	65	78	82	111	546

SEASON LEADERS

Batting Average

1.	Tucker, Baltimore	.372
2.	O'Neill, St. Louis	.335
3.	Lyons, Philadelphia	.329
4.	Orr, Columbus	.327
5.	Holliday, Cincinnati	.321

On-Base Percentage

1.	Tucker, Baltimore	.450
2.	Larkin, Philadelphia	.428
3.	Lyons, Philadelphia	.426
4.	O'Neill, St. Louis	.419
5.	Hamilton, Kansas City	.413

Home Runs

1.	Stovey, Philadelphia	19
	Holliday, Cincinnati	19
3.	Duffee, St. Louis	15
4.	Milligan, St. Louis	12
5.	Lyons, Philadelphia	9
	O'Neill, St. Louis	9

Hits

1.	Tucker, Baltimore	196
2.	Orr, Columbus	183
3.	Holliday, Cincinnati	181
4.	O'Neill, St. Louis	179
5.	Shindle, Baltimore	178

Stolen Bases

1.	Hamilton, Kansas City	111
2.	O'Brien, Brooklyn	91
3.	Long, Kansas City	89
4.	Nicol, Cincinnati	80
5.	Latham, St. Louis	69

Slugging Average

1.	Stovey, Philadelphia	.527
2.	Holliday, Cincinnati	.497
3.	Tucker, Baltimore	.484
4.	O'Neill, St. Louis	.478
5.	Lyons, Philadelphia	.469

Total Bases

1.	Stovey, Philadelphia	293
2.	Holliday, Cincinnati	280
3.	Tucker, Baltimore	255
	O'Neill, St. Louis	255
5.	Orr, Columbus	250

RBI

1.	Stovey, Philadelphia	119
2.	Foutz, Brooklyn	113
3.	O'Neill, St. Louis	110
4.	Bierbauer, Philadelphia	105
5.	Holliday, Cincinnati	104

Runs

1.	Stovey, Philadelphia	152
	Griffin, Baltimore	152
3.	D. O'Brien, Brooklyn	146
4.	Hamilton, Kansas City	144
5.	Collins, Brooklyn	139

Strikeouts

1.	Duffee, St. Louis	81
2.	Fennelly, Philadelphia	78
3.	O'Brien, Brooklyn	76
4.	Hornung, Baltimore	72
5.	Greenwood, Columbus	71

PITCHING

Wins

1.	Caruthers, Brooklyn	40
2.	King, St. Louis	33
3.	Duryea, Cincinnati	32
	Chamberlain, St. Louis	32
5.	Weyhing, Philadelphia	30

Losses

1.	M. Baldwin, Columbus	34
2.	Ewing, Louisville	30
3.	Ehret, Louisville	29
4.	Swartzel, Kansas City	27
5.	Kilroy, Baltimore	25

Innings

1.	Baldwin, Columbus	513.2
2.	Kilroy, Baltimore	480.2
3.	King, St. Louis	458
4.	Weyhing, Philadelphia	449
5.	Caruthers, Brooklyn	445

Strikeouts

1.	Baldwin, Columbus	368
2.	Kilroy, Baltimore	217
3.	Weyhing, Philadelphia	213
4.	Chamberlain, St. Louis	202
5.	King, St. Louis	188

ERA (140 innings)

1.	Stivetts, St. Louis	2.25
2.	Duryea, Cincinnati	2.56
3.	Kilroy, Baltimore	2.85
4.	Weyhing, Philadelphia	2.95
5.	Chamberlain, St. Louis	2.97

Complete Games

1.	Kilroy, Baltimore	55
2.	Baldwin, Columbus	54
3.	Weyhing, Philadelphia	50
4.	King, St. Louis	47
5.	Caruthers, Brooklyn	46

Winning Percentage (25 decisions)

1.	Caruthers, Brooklyn	.784
2.	King, St. Louis	.686
3.	Chamberlain, St. Louis	.681
4.	Lovett, Brooklyn	.630
5.	Duryea, Cincinnati	.627

Lowest On-Base Percentage

1.	Stivetts, St. Louis	.285
2.	Caruthers, Brooklyn	.299
3.	Duryea, Cincinnati	.303
4.	Conway, Kansas City	.306
	Foreman, Baltimore	.306

FIELDING

Total Chances

1B	Stearns, Kansas City	1503
2B	McPhee, Cincinnati	925
3B	Shindle, Baltimore	636
SS	Long, Kansas City	931
OF	J. Burns, Kansas City	366
C	O'Connor, Columbus	577
P	Swartzel, Kansas City	175

Fielding Average

Reilly, Cincinnati	.984
McPhee, Cincinnati	.946
Pinkney, Brooklyn	.897
Fuller, St. Louis	.913
Corkhill, Brooklyn	.949
O'Connor, Columbus	.955
Caruthers, Brooklyn	.969

BROOKLYN   Bill McGunnigle   Washington Park (I)*

		G	AB	H	R	2B	3B	HR	RBI	BB	SB	BA	SA
LF	Darby O'Brien	136	567	170	146	30	11	5	80	61	91	.300	.418
2B	Hub Collins	138	560	149	139	18	3	2	73	80	65	.266	.320
1B	Dave Foutz	138	553	152	118	19	8	6	113	64	43	.275	.371
3B	George Pinkney	138	545	134	103	25	7	4	82	59	47	.246	.339
CF	Pop Corkhill	138	537	134	91	21	9	8	78	42	22	.250	.367
RF	Oyster Burns	131	504	153	105	19	13	5	100	68	32	.304	.423
SS	Germany Smith	121	446	103	89	22	3	3	53	40	35	.231	.314
C	Joe Visner	80	295	76	56	12	10	8	68	36	13	.258	.447
C	Bob Clark	53	182	50	32	5	2	0	22	26	18	.275	.324
P	Bob Caruthers	59	172	43	45	8	3	2	31	44	9	.250	.366
P	Adonis Terry	49	160	48	29	6	6	2	26	14	8	.300	.450
P	Tom Lovett	29	100	19	18	1	3	2	19	2	2	.190	.320
Sub	Doc Bushong	25	84	13	15	1	0	0	8	9	2	.155	.167
P	Mickey Hughes	20	68	12	4	0	0	0	5	4	0	.176	.176
Sub	Charlie Reynolds	12	42	9	5	1	1	0	3	1	2	.214	.286
		140	4815	1265	**995**	188	79	47	**761**	**550**	389	.263	.364

The park grandstand burned down on May 19. A new grandstand was quickly built.

```
1B   Foutz 134, Terry 10, Caruthers 2, Corkhill 1
2B   Collins 138
SS   Smith 120, Burns 19, Corkhill 1
3B   Pinkney 138
OF   Corkhill 138, O'Brien 136, Burns 113, Visner 29, Caruthers 3, Hughes 1, Smith 1
C    Visner 53, Clark 53, Bushong 25, Reynolds 12
P    Caruthers 56, Terry 41, Lovett 29, Hughes 20, Foutz 12
```

	G	IP	GS	CG	W	L	K	BB	SH	SV	ERA
Bob Caruthers	56	445	50	46	**40**	11	118	104	**7**	1	3.13
Adonis Terry	41	326	39	35	22	15	186	126	2	0	3.29
Tom Lovett	29	229	28	23	17	10	92	65	1	0	4.32
Mickey Hughes	20	153	17	13	9	8	54	86	0	0	4.35
Dave Foutz	12	59.2	4	3	3	0	21	19	0	0	4.37
—Two forfeit Ws: vs Columbus on June 24; vs St. Louis on September 8—											
	1212.2	140	120	91	44	471	400	**400**	**10**	1	3.61

ST. LOUIS   Charlie Comiskey   Sportsman's Park (I)

		G	AB	H	R	2B	3B	HR	RBI	BB	SB	BA	SA
RF	Tommy McCarthy	140	**604**	176	136	24	7	2	63	46	57	.291	.364
1B	Charlie Comiskey	137	587	168	105	28	10	3	102	19	65	.286	.383
LF	Tip O'Neill	134	534	179	123	33	8	9	110	72	28	.335	.478
SS	Shorty Fuller	140	517	117	91	18	6	0	51	52	38	.226	.284
3B	Arlie Latham	118	512	126	110	13	3	4	49	42	69	.246	.307
CF	Charlie Duffee	137	509	124	93	15	11	16	86	60	21	.244	.411
2B	Yank Robinson	132	452	94	97	17	3	5	70	118	39	.208	.292
C	Jack Boyle	99	347	85	54	11	5	3	42	21	5	.245	.331
C	Jocko Milligan	72	273	100	53	30	2	12	76	16	2	.366	.623
P	Silver King	56	189	43	37	7	3	0	30	22	3	.228	.296
P	Icebox Chamberlain	53	171	34	18	8	3	2	31	12	3	.199	.316
P	Jack Stivetts	27	79	18	12	2	2	0	7	3	0	.228	.304
P	Nat Hudson	13	52	13	6	1	1	1	10	2	1	.250	.365
Sub	Pete Sweeney	9	38	14	8	2	0	0	8	1	2	.368	.421
P	Jim Devlin	9	26	5	4	0	0	0	0	1	1	.192	.192
P	Toad Ramsey	5	17	5	2	1	0	0	4	1	0	.294	.353
Sub	Tom Gettinger	4	16	7	2	0	0	1	2	2	0	.438	.625
Sub	Jim Gill	2	8	2	2	1	0	0	1	1	0	.250	.375
Sub	Jumbo Davis	2	4	0	1	0	0	0	0	1	0	.000	.000
Sub	Dad Meek	2	2	1	2	0	0	0	1	0	1	.500	.500
Sub	Jack Bellman	1	2	1	1	0	0	0	0	1	0	.500	.500
		141	4939	1312	957	211	64	**58**	743	493	336	.266	.370

```
1B   Comiskey 134, Milligan 9, Boyle 4, Hudson 2, King 2
2B   Robinson 132, Latham 3, Comiskey 3, McCarthy 2, Duffee 2, Boyle 1, Chamberlain 1, Gill 1
SS   Fuller 140, Davis 1
3B   Latham 116, Boyle 12, Sweeney 8, Duffee 5,
OF   McCarthy 140, O'Neill 134, Duffee 132, Hudson 6, Boyle 5, Gettinger 4, Comiskey 3, King 1, Stivetts 1,
     Sweeney 1, Davis 1, Gill 1
C    Boyle 80, Milligan 66, Meek 2, Bellman 1
P    King 56, Chamberlain 53, Stivetts 26, Devlin 9, Hudson 9, Ramsey 5, McCarthy 1, Comiskey 1
```

	G	IP	GS	CG	W	L	K	BB	SH	SV	ERA
Silver King	56	458	53	47	34	16	188	125	2	1	3.14
Icebox Chamberlain	53	421.1	51	44	32	15	202	165	3	1	2.97
Jack Stivetts	26	191.2	20	18	13	7	143	68	2	1	**2.25**
Jim Devlin	9	60	8	5	5	3	37	24	0	0	2.40
Nat Hudson	9	60	5	4	3	2	13	15	0	0	4.20
Toad Ramsey	5	41	3	3	3	1	33	10	0	0	3.95
Tommy McCarthy	1	5	0	0	0	0	1	6	0	0	7.20
Charlie Comiskey	1	0.1	0	0	0	0	0	0	0	0	0.00
		—1 forfeit L vs Brooklyn on September 8—									
	1237.2	140	121	90	44	**617**	413	7	3	**3.00**

PHILADELPHIA   Bill Sharsig   Jefferson Street Grounds

		G	AB	H	R	2B	3B	HR	RBI	BB	SB	BA	SA
LF	Harry Stovey	137	556	171	**152**	38	13	**19**	**119**	77	63	.308	**.527**
2B	Lou Bierbauer	130	549	167	80	27	7	7	105	29	17	.304	.417
1B	Henry Larkin	133	516	164	105	23	12	3	74	83	11	.318	.426
CF	Curt Welch	125	516	140	134	**39**	6	0	39	67	66	.271	.370
SS	Frank Fennelly	138	513	132	70	20	5	1	64	65	15	.257	.322
3B	Denny Lyons	131	510	168	135	36	4	9	82	79	10	.329	.469
RF	Blondie Purcell	129	507	160	72	19	7	0	85	50	22	.316	.381
C	Wilbert Robinson	69	264	61	31	13	2	0	28	6	9	.231	.295
C	Lave Cross	55	199	44	22	8	2	0	23	14	11	.221	.281
P	Gus Weyhing	54	191	25	16	2	0	0	12	9	4	.131	.141
P	Ed Seward	46	143	31	22	5	3	2	17	22	6	.217	.336
Sub	Jim Brennan	31	113	25	12	4	0	0	15	10	1	.221	.257
P	Sadie McMahon	30	104	16	9	2	1	0	4	4	3	.154	.192
Sub	Mike Mattimore	23	73	17	10	1	2	1	8	9	6	.233	.342
Sub	Tom Gunning	8	24	6	3	0	1	1	1	4	3	.250	.458
P	George Bausewine	7	21	1	1	0	0	0	0	4	2	.048	.048
P	John Coleman	6	19	1	1	0	0	0	1	1	1	.053	.053
Sub	Barney Graham	4	18	3	0	0	0	0	0	0	0	.167	.167
P	Phenomenal Smith	5	16	3	3	1	0	0	0	3	0	.188	.250
P	Ed Knouff	3	12	3	2	1	0	0	2	1	1	.250	.333
Sub	Bill Collins	1	4	1	0	0	0	0	1	1	1	.250	.250
		138	4868	**1339**	880	**239**	65	43	680	534	252	**.275**	.377

1B   Larkin 131, Mattimore 7, Lyons 1, Stovey 1
2B   Bierbauer 130, Brennan 7, Larkin 1, Seward 1
SS   Fennelly 138
3B   Lyons 130, Graham 4, Brennan 4, Larkin 1
OF   Stovey 137, Purcell 129, Welch 125, Mattimore 12, Seward 8, Brennan 7, McMahon 2, Coleman 1, Weyhing 1
C   Robinson 69, Cross 55, Brennan 13, Gunning 8, Collins 1, Bierbauer 1
P   Weyhing 54, Seward 39, McMahon 28, Bausewine 7, Mattimore 5, Smith 5, Coleman 5, Knouff 3

	G	IP	GS	CG	W	L	K	BB	SH	SV	ERA
Gus Weyhing	54	449	53	50	30	21	213	212	4	0	2.95
Ed Seward	39	320	38	35	21	15	102	101	3	0	3.97
Sadie McMahon	28	242	27	27	14	12	117	102	2	0	3.53
George Bausewine	7	55.1	6	6	1	4	18	33	0	0	3.90
Phenomenal Smith	5	43	5	5	2	3	12	25	0	0	4.40
John Coleman	5	34	5	4	3	2	6	14	0	0	2.91
Mike Mattimore	5	31	1	1	2	1	6	13	0	1	5.81
Ed Knouff	3	25	3	2	2	0	5	9	0	0	3.96
	1199.1	138	**130**	75	58	479	509	9	1	3.53

CINCINNATI   **Gus Schmelz**   **American Park**

		G	AB	H	R	2B	3B	HR	RBI	BB	SB	BA	SA
CF	Bug Holliday	135	563	181	107	28	7	**19**	104	43	46	.321	.497
SS	Ollie Beard	141	558	159	96	13	14	1	77	35	36	.285	.364
2B	Bid McPhee	135	540	145	109	25	7	5	57	60	63	.269	.368
LF	White Wings Tebeau	135	496	125	110	21	11	7	70	69	61	.252	.381
3B	Hick Carpenter	123	486	127	67	23	6	0	63	18	47	.261	.333
RF	Hugh Nicol	122	474	121	82	7	8	2	58	54	80	.255	.316
1B	Long John Reilly	111	427	111	84	24	13	5	66	34	43	.260	.412
C	Jim Keenan	87	300	86	52	10	11	6	60	48	18	.287	.453
C	Kid Baldwin	60	223	55	34	14	2	1	34	5	7	.247	.341
P	Tony Mullane	63	196	58	53	16	4	0	29	27	24	.296	.418
Sub	Billy Earle	53	169	45	37	4	7	4	31	30	26	.266	.444
P	Jesse Duryea	54	162	44	37	6	3	0	17	11	5	.272	.346
P	Leon Viau	47	147	21	14	2	1	0	9	11	4	.143	.170
P	Elmer Smith	29	83	23	12	3	1	2	17	7	1	.277	.410
P	Charlie Petty	5	20	6	3	1	1	0	4	0	1	.300	.450
P	Ted Conovar	1	0	0	0	0	0	0	0	0	0	—	—
		141	4844	1307	897	197	**96**	52	696	452	462	.270	**.382**

1B Reilly 109, Keenan 21, Earle 5, Mullane 4, Carpenter 2, Tebeau 1, Baldwin 1
2B McPhee 135, Nicol 7
SS Beard 141
3B Carpenter 121, Mullane 18, Nicol 3, McPhee 1, Keenan 1, Baldwin 1
OF Holliday 135, Tebeau 134, Nicol 115, Earle 26, Mullane 12, Baldwin 4, Duryea 3, Reilly 2, Viau 1
C Keenan 66, Baldwin 55, Earle 23
P Duryea 53, Viau 47, Mullane 33, Smith 29, Petty 5, Conovar 1

	G	IP	GS	CG	W	L	K	BB	SH	SV	ERA
Jesse Duryea	53	401	48	38	32	19	183	127	2	1	2.56
Leon Viau	47	373	42	38	22	20	152	136	1	1	3.79
Tony Mullane	33	220	24	17	11	9	112	89	0	**5**	2.99
Elmer Smith	29	203	22	16	9	12	104	101	0	0	4.88
Charlie Petty	5	44	5	5	2	3	10	20	0	0	5.52
Ted Conovar	1	2	0	0	0	0	1	2	0	1	13.50
		1243	141	114	76	63	562	475	3	**8**	3.50

BALTIMORE   **Billy Barnie**   **Oriole Park (1)**

		G	AB	H	R	2B	3B	HR	RBI	BB	SB	BA	SA
3B	Billy Shindle	138	567	178	122	24	7	3	64	42	56	.314	.397
LF	Joe Hornung	135	533	122	73	13	9	1	78	22	34	.229	.293
CF	Mike Griffin	137	531	148	152	21	14	4	48	91	39	.279	.394
1B	Tommy Tucker	134	527	196	103	22	11	5	99	42	63	**.372**	.484
2B	Reddy Mack	136	519	125	84	24	7	1	87	60	23	.241	.320
RF	Joe Sommer	106	386	85	51	13	2	1	36	42	18	.220	.272
C	Pop Tate	72	253	46	28	6	3	1	27	13	4	.182	.241
P	Matt Kilroy	65	208	57	32	3	6	1	26	23	13	.274	.361
C	Tom Quinn	55	194	34	18	2	1	1	15	19	6	.175	.211
P	Frank Foreman	54	181	26	18	2	1	1	11	12	7	.144	.182
SS	Jack Farrell	42	157	33	25	3	0	1	26	15	14	.210	.248
SS	Will Holland	40	143	27	13	1	2	0	16	9	4	.189	.224
P	Bert Cunningham	41	131	27	10	4	2	0	18	4	3	.206	.267
Sub	Irv Ray	26	106	36	20	4	1	0	17	7	12	.340	.396
Sub	Joe Dowie	20	75	17	12	5	0	0	8	2	5	.227	.293
Sub	Bart Cantz	20	69	12	6	2	0	0	8	4	2	.174	.203
Sub	Chris Fulmer	16	58	15	11	3	1	0	13	6	2	.259	.345
Sub	John Kerins	16	53	15	7	2	0	0	12	2	2	.283	.321
Sub	Dusty Miller	11	40	6	4	1	1	0	6	2	3	.150	.225
Sub	George Wood	3	10	2	1	0	0	0	1	0	1	.200	.200
Sub	Chippy McGarr	3	7	1	1	0	0	0	0	1	0	.143	.143
P	Pat Whitaker	1	4	1	0	0	0	0	2	0	0	.250	.250
P	George Goetz	1	4	0	0	0	0	0	0	0	0	.000	.000
		139	4756	1209	791	155	68	20	618	418	311	.254	.328

1B   Tucker 123, Tate 10, Kerins 9
2B   Mack 135, Griffin 5
SS   Farrell 42, Holland 39, Griffin 25, Ray 20, Miller 8, McGarr 3, Kerins 1, Sommer 1, Cunningham 1
3B   Shindle 138, Hornung 1
OF   Hornung 134, Griffin 109, Sommer 105, Dowie 20, Fulmer 14, Tucker 12, Kilroy 8, Ray 6, Foreman 3, Miller 3, Wood 3, Kerins 2, Cantz 2, Cunningham 2, Holland 1, Mack 1
C   Tate 62, Quinn 55, Cantz 18, Kerins 4, Fulmer 2
P   Kilroy 59, Foreman 51, Cunningham 39, Goetz 1, Whitaker 1

	G	IP	GS	CG	W	L	K	BB	SH	SV	ERA
Matt Kilroy	59	480.2	56	**55**	29	25	217	142	5	0	2.85
Frank Foreman	51	414	48	43	23	21	180	137	5	0	3.52
Bert Cunningham	39	279.1	33	29	16	19	140	141	0	1	4.87
George Goetz	1	9	1	0	1	0	2	0	0	0	4.00
Pat Whitaker	1	9	1	1	1	0	1	4	0	0	2.00
		1192	139	128	70	65	540	424	**10**	1	3.56

COLUMBUS   Al Buckenberger   Recreation Park (II)

		G	AB	H	R	2B	3B	HR	RBI	BB	SB	BA	SA
LF	Ed Daily	136	578	148	105	22	8	3	70	38	60	.256	.337
1B	Dave Orr	134	560	183	70	31	12	4	87	9	12	.327	.446
3B	Lefty Marr	139	546	167	110	26	15	1	75	87	29	.306	.414
CF	Jim McTamany	139	529	146	113	21	7	4	52	116	40	.276	.365
RF	Spud Johnson	116	459	130	91	14	10	2	79	39	34	.283	.370
2B	Bill Greenwood	118	414	93	62	7	10	3	49	58	37	.225	.312
C	Jack O'Connor	107	398	107	69	17	7	4	60	33	26	.269	.377
SS	Henry Easterday	95	324	56	43	5	8	4	34	41	10	.173	.275
P	Mark Baldwin	64	208	39	19	6	5	2	25	16	2	.188	.293
Sub	Heinie Kappel	46	173	47	25	7	5	3	21	21	10	.272	.422
P	Bill Widner	41	133	28	16	3	0	2	10	2	5	.211	.278
Sub	Jimmy Peoples	29	100	23	13	6	2	1	16	6	3	.230	.360
P	Hank Gastright	32	94	17	5	0	1	0	11	3	2	.181	.202
Sub	Ned Bligh	28	93	13	6	1	1	0	5	4	2	.140	.172
P	Al Mays	21	54	7	4	1	0	0	4	11	1	.130	.148
Sub	Jack Crooks	12	43	14	13	2	3	0	7	10	10	.326	.512
Sub	Jack Doyle	11	36	10	6	1	1	0	3	6	9	.278	.361
Sub	Rudy Kemmler	8	26	3	2	0	0	0	0	3	0	.115	.115
Sub	Charlie Reilly	6	23	11	5	1	0	3	6	2	9	.478	.913
Sub	Bill George	5	17	4	1	0	0	0	3	1	1	.235	.235
P	John Easton	4	7	0	0	0	0	0	0	0	2	.000	.000
Sub	Sparrow McCaffrey	2	1	1	1	0	0	0	0	1	0	1.000	1.000
P	John Weyhing	1	0	0	0	0	0	0	0	0	0	—	—
		140	4816	1247	779	171	95	36	617	507	304	.259	.356

1B Orr 134, O'Connor 3, Johnson 2, Marr 1, Widner 1
2B Greenwood 118, Crooks 12, Easterday 5, O'Connor 4, Doyle 2, Peoples 2
SS Easterday 89, Marr 26, Kappel 23, Johnson 1, Peoples 1
3B Marr 66, Johnson 44, Kappel 23, Reilly 6, Easterday 1
OF McTamany 139, Daily 136, Johnson 69, Marr 47, O'Connor 19, Peoples 5, George 4, Doyle 3, Mays 2, Baldwin 1, Widner 1,
C O'Connor 84, Bligh 28, Peoples 22, Kemmler 8, Doyle 7, McCaffrey 2, Marr 1
P Baldwin 63, Widner 41, Gastright 32, Mays 21, Easton 4, George 2, Daily 2, Weyhing 1

	G	IP	GS	CG	W	L	K	BB	SH	SV	ERA
Mark Baldwin	63	513.2	59	54	27	34	368	274	6	1	3.61
Bill Widner	41	294	34	25	12	20	63	85	2	1	5.20
Hank Gastright	32	222.2	26	21	10	16	115	104	0	0	4.57
Al Mays	21	140	19	13	10	7	52	56	1	0	4.82
Jack Easton	4	18	1	1	1	0	7	21	0	1	3.50
Bill George	2	8	0	0	0	0	3	3	0	0	7.88
Ed Daily	2	1.2	0	0	0	0	2	4	0	1	21.60
John Weyhing	1	1	0	0	0	0	0	4	0	0	27.00
—1 forfeit L vs Brooklyn on June 24—											
		1199	139	114	60	77	610	551	9	4	4.39

KANSAS CITY   Bill Watkins   Exposition Park

		G	AB	H	R	2B	3B	HR	RBI	BB	SB	BA	SA
CF	Jim Burns	134	579	176	103	23	11	5	97	20	56	.304	.408
SS	Herman Long	136	574	158	137	32	6	3	60	64	89	.275	.368
1B	Dan Stearns	139	560	160	96	24	12	3	87	56	67	.286	.387
RF	Billy Hamilton	137	534	161	144	17	12	3	77	87	**111**	.301	.395
LF	Jim Manning	132	506	103	68	16	7	3	68	54	58	.204	.281
C	Charlie Hoover	71	258	64	44	2	5	1	25	29	9	.248	.306
C	Jim Donahue	67	252	59	30	5	4	0	32	21	12	.234	.286
3B	Jumbo Davis	62	241	64	40	4	3	0	30	17	25	.266	.307
Sub	John Pickett	53	201	45	20	7	0	0	12	11	7	.224	.259
Sub	Bill Alvord	50	186	43	23	8	9	0	18	10	3	.231	.371
2B	Sam Barkley	45	176	50	36	6	2	0	23	15	8	.284	.341
P	Parke Swartzel	51	174	25	19	4	0	0	20	18	7	.144	.167
P	Jim Conway	41	149	31	14	2	2	0	12	2	1	.208	.248
Sub	Joe Gunson	34	122	24	15	3	1	0	12	3	2	.197	.238
Sub	Chippy McGarr	25	108	31	22	3	0	0	16	6	12	.287	.315
P	John Sowders	28	87	19	11	3	0	0	6	4	1	.218	.253
P	John McCarty	20	79	18	12	0	1	0	12	1	3	.228	.253
Sub	Mike Mattimore	19	75	12	6	1	1	0	5	3	0	.160	.200
P	Tom Sullivan	10	33	5	8	1	0	0	1	5	0	.152	.182
Sub	Red Bittman	4	14	4	2	0	0	0	2	1	1	.286	.286
P	Frank Pears	3	11	1	0	0	0	0	1	0	0	.091	.091
P	Henry Porter	4	10	1	0	0	0	0	1	1	0	.100	.100
P	Charlie Bell	2	6	1	1	1	0	0	3	2	0	.167	.333
Sub	Charlie Reynolds	1	4	1	1	0	0	0	1	0	0	.250	.250
P	John Bates	1	4	0	0	0	0	0	0	0	0	.000	.000
Sub	Steve Ladew	2	4	0	0	0	0	0	0	0	0	.000	.000
		139	4947	1256	852	162	76	18	621	430	**472**	.254	.328

1B   Stearns 135, Barkley 4
2B   Manning 63, Barkley 41, Pickett 11, Long 8, Alvord 8, McGarr 5, Bittman 4
SS   Long 128, Alvord 8, McGarr 3, Manning 1
3B   Davis 62, Alvord 34, Pickett 14, McGarr 11, Donahue 10, Stearns 4, Hoover 4, Gunson 1, Manning 1, Burns 1
OF   Hamilton 137, Burns 134, Manning 69, Pickett 28, Mattimore 19, Donahue 14, McGarr 6, McCarty 6, Swartzel 4, Sowders 3, Hoover 3, Long 1, Gunson 1, Pears 1, Bell 1, Ladew 1
C   Hoover 66, Donahue 46, Gunson 32, Reynolds 4
P   Swartzel 48, Conway 41, Sowders 25, McCarty 15, Sullivan 10, Porter 4, Pears 3, Bell 1, Bates 1, Mattimore 1, Ladew 1

	G	IP	GS	CG	W	L	K	BB	SH	SV	ERA
Parke Swartzel	48	410.1	47	45	19	27	147	117	0	1	4.32
Jim Conway	41	335	37	33	19	19	115	90	0	0	3.25
John Sowders	25	185	23	20	6	16	104	105	0	1	4.82
John McCarty	15	119.2	14	13	8	6	36	61	0	0	3.91
Tom Sullivan	10	87.1	10	10	2	8	24	48	0	0	5.67
Henry Porter	4	23	4	3	0	3	9	14	0	0	12.52
Frank Pears	3	22	2	2	0	2	5	9	0	0	4.91
Charlie Bell	1	9	1	1	1	0	3	3	0	0	1.00
John Bates	1	8	1	1	0	1	3	5	0	0	13.50
Mike Mattimore	1	3	0	0	0	0	1	2	0	0	3.00
Steve Ladew	1	2	0	0	0	0	0	3	0	0	4.50
		1204.1	139	128	55	82	447	457	0	2	4.36

LOUISVILLE   Dude Esterbrook (2-8)   Chicken Wolf (14-51)   Dan Shannon (10-46)
Jack Chapman (1-6)   Eclipse Park (I)

		G	AB	H	R	2B	3B	HR	RBI	BB	SB	BA	SA
RF	Chicken Wolf	130	546	159	72	20	9	3	57	29	18	.291	.377
3B	Harry Raymond	130	515	123	58	12	9	0	47	19	19	.239	.297
CF	Farmer Weaver	124	499	145	62	17	6	0	60	40	21	.291	.349
2B	Dan Shannon	121	498	128	90	22	12	4	48	42	26	.257	.373
SS	Phil Tomney	112	376	80	61	8	5	4	38	46	26	.213	.293
UT	Farmer Vaughn	90	360	86	39	11	5	3	45	7	13	.239	.322
1B	Guy Hecker	81	327	93	42	17	5	1	36	18	17	.284	.376
LF	Pete Browning	83	324	83	39	19	5	2	32	34	21	.256	.364
C	Paul Cook	81	286	65	34	10	1	0	15	15	11	.227	.269
P	Red Ehret	67	258	65	27	6	6	1	31	4	4	.252	.333
P	Scott Stratton	62	229	66	30	7	5	4	34	13	10	.288	.415
P	John Ewing	41	134	23	12	2	0	0	6	9	5	.172	.187
Sub	John Galligan	31	120	20	6	0	2	0	7	6	1	.167	.200
Sub	Fred Carl	25	99	20	13	2	2	0	13	16	0	.202	.263
Sub	Ed Flanagan	23	88	22	11	7	3	0	8	7	1	.250	.398
Sub	John Ryan	21	79	14	8	1	0	0	2	3	2	.177	.190
Sub	Bill Gleason	16	58	14	6	2	0	0	5	4	1	.241	.276
P	Toad Ramsey	18	57	15	3	1	0	0	3	1	1	.263	.281
Sub	Dude Esterbrook	11	44	14	8	3	0	0	9	5	6	.318	.386
P	Mike McDermott	9	33	6	7	2	0	0	3	2	0	.182	.242
Sub	John Kerins	2	9	3	2	1	0	0	3	0	0	.333	.444
P	Bill Robinson	1	3	1	2	0	0	0	0	0	0	.333	.333
Sub	Harry Scherer	1	3	1	0	0	0	0	0	0	0	.333	.333
Sub	Harry Smith	1	2	1	0	0	0	0	1	0	0	.500	.500
Sub	? Fisher	1	2	1	0	0	0	0	0	0	0	.500	.500
Sub	John Traffley	1	2	1	0	0	0	0	0	0	0	.500	.500
Sub	Mike Gaule	1	2	0	0	0	0	0	0	0	0	.000	.000
P	Ed Springer	1	2	0	0	0	0	0	0	0	0	.000	.000
		140	4955	1249	632	170	75	22	503	320	203	.252	.330

1B   Hecker 65, Flanagan 23, Vaughn 18, Stratton 17, Wolf 16, Easterbrook 8, Cook 1, Ewing 1
2B   Shannon 121, Wolf 13, Carl 6, Weaver 1, Ehret 1
SS   Tomney 112, Gleason 16, Wolf 10, Cook 1, Ehret 1, Esterbrook 1
3B   Raymond 129, Wolf 7, Vaughn 3, Ryan 2, Weaver 1, Ehret 1, Carl 1
OF   Weaver 128, Wolf 88, Browning 83, Galligan 31, Stratton 29, Ehret 22, Vaughn 20, Carl 18, Cook 7,
      Ryan 4, Esterbrook 2, Kerins 2, Gaule 1, Traffley 1, Scherer 1, Fisher 1, Hecker 1, Raymond 1, Smith 1
C   Cook 74, Vaughn 54, Ryan 15, Weaver 2, Kerins 1, Smith 1
P   Ehret 45, Ewing 40, Hecker 19, Stratton 19, Ramsey 18, McDermott 9, Springer 1,
      Raymond 1, Robinson 1

	G	IP	GS	CG	W	L	K	BB	SH	SV	ERA
Red Ehret	45	364	38	35	10	29	135	115	1	0	4.80
John Ewing	40	331	39	37	6	30	155	147	1	0	4.87
Guy Hecker	19	151.1	16	15	5	13	33	47	0	0	5.59
Scott Stratton	19	133.2	17	13	3	13	42	42	0	1	3.23
Toad Ramsey	18	140	18	15	1	16	60	71	0	0	5.59
Mike McDermott	9	84.1	9	9	1	8	22	34	0	0	4.16
Harry Raymond	1	9	1	1	1	0	1	11	0	0	1.00
Bill Robinson	1	8	1	1	0	1	2	6	0	0	10.23
Ed Springer	1	5	1	1	0	1	1	2	0	0	9.00
		1226.1	140	127	27	111	451	475	2	1	4.81

1890
THE PLAYERS' REBELLION

On November 4, 1889, just six days after he helped the Giants win their second straight World's Series, Brotherhood president Monte Ward and his war committee severed ties with the National League and formed a new federation named the Players League largely because it was owned and operated by National League players. Ward's rebel loop eventually embraced many of the American Association's leading lights also, including St. Louis Browns player-manager Charlie Comiskey, Louisville's mercurial Pete Browning and Harry Stovey, the soul of the Philadelphia Athletics.

Ward's ex-Giants teammate, Tim Keefe, furnished the Brotherhood's official ball, which was made by his Manhattan sporting goods firm and was much livelier than the Spalding (NL) or Reach (AA) balls. Other significant points of departure by the Brotherhood from the two established major leagues were having two umpires work each of its games and lengthening the pitcher's box six inches to increase the pitching distance to 57 feet. Ward's creation also had several major differences in the way it did business. The Players League abolished the Reserve Clause, replacing it with an absolute one-year contract that contained, much like today's player contracts, a two-year option to renew or a three-year bond. In addition, a player could not be traded without his consent, and before a manager could release a player the board of directors on his team had to give its approval.

Yet if Ward was revolutionary in some areas, he was overly conservative in others. The Players League chose to pattern itself after the National League in banning the sale of alcohol in its parks and unofficially prohibiting black players. When it also rejected playing on Sunday and thereby cut itself off from the six-day-week proletariat, the *Sporting Times*, an organ published by former New York Mets owner Erastus Wiman, said "the sentimental Brotherhood Labor-Unionists" were now assured of getting little support from their "falsely founded sympathy for the Brotherhood among factory hands, mill hands and laborers." Still, Ward's product consistently showed itself to be the most popular of the three varieties of major league baseball operating in 1890. On Memorial Day, after four double-

The Chicago Pirates were the preseason pick to win the PL flag largely because they were piloted by first sacker Charlie Comiskey, who had previously led the St. Louis Browns to four consecutive AA pennants and brought several of his Browns teammates with him, including Silver King, Arlie Latham, Jack Boyle and Tip O'Neill. Weak stickwork by its infielders, especially Comiskey, Latham and Ned Williamson, doomed the Chicago entry to 4th place. Clockwise, from the top— Comiskey, Hugh Duffy, Latham, Duke Farrell, Charlie Bastian, King, Williamson, Del Darling, Charlie Bartson, O'Neill, Boyle and Mark Baldwin. Center— Jimmy Ryan, Fred Pfeffer and Frank Dwyer.

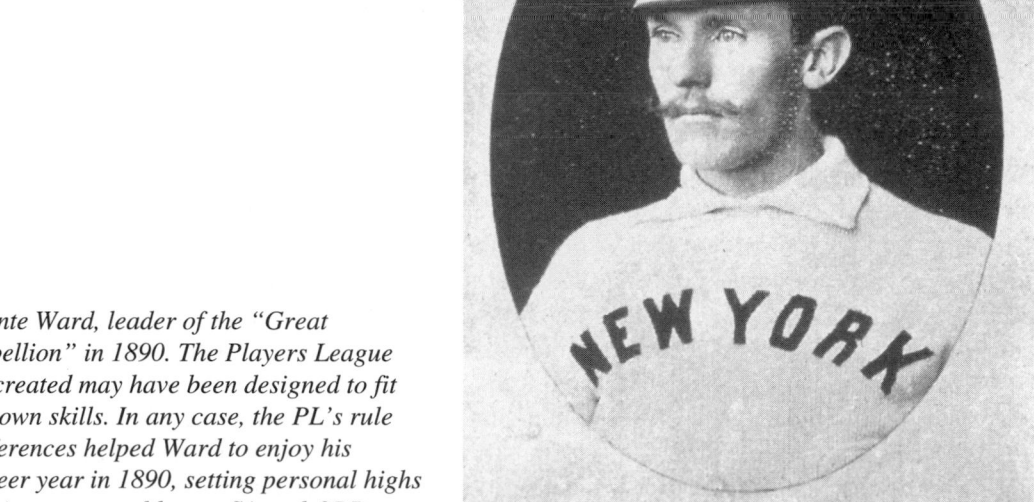

Monte Ward, leader of the "Great Rebellion" in 1890. The Players League he created may have been designed to fit his own skills. In any case, the PL's rule differences helped Ward to enjoy his career year in 1890, setting personal highs in hits, runs, total bases, SA and OBP.

THE APATHETIC ATHLETICS

In September 1890, after most of the Philadelphia Athletics jumped ship when club treasurer William Whittaker claimed there was no money left to pay them, manager Bill Sharsig was sent on the club's last western road trip with $245 in his purse and a patchwork crew that finished the season with 22 straight losses. Among Sharsig's cast of nonentities were both the nineteenth-century record-holder and runner-up for the most career pitching losses without a win. Two other members of the winless list were with Pittsburgh, the 1890 National League basement finisher which lost 113 games to break Louisville's year-old major league record of 111 defeats. A list of winless nineteenth-century pitchers with five or more career losses:

	LOSSES	WORST YEAR
Charlie Stecher	10	1890 Phi-AA (0–10)
Ed O'Neill	8	1890 Tol/Phi-AA (0–8)
Tommy McCarthy	7	1884 Bos-UA (0–7)*
Joe McDermott	7	1872 Eck-NA (0–7)
Charlie Heard	6	1890 Pit-NL (0–6)
Tom Ford	6	1890 Col/Bro-AA (0–6)
Carney Flynn	5	1896 NY/Was-LA (0–3)
Fred Osborne	5	1890 Pit-NL (0–5)
Bones Ely	5	1886 Lou-AA (0–4)*
Henry Oberbeck	5	1884 Bal/KC-UA (0–5)
Frank Beck	5	1884 Pit-AA/Bal-UA (0–5)
Harry Maupin	5	1899 Cle-LA (0–3)

*McCarthy and Ely later enjoyed success in the majors but only after they gave up pitching.

headers were played in each loop, the attendance figures read: PL 39,080; NL 28,166; and AA 20,546.

The Brotherhood continued to outdraw the two entrenched circuits throughout the summer while the Association's attendance problems multiplied. Some of the Association's plight could be traced to redoubled efforts in 1890 by Sabbatarians to cut the lifelines of teams that tried to play on Sunday. The Association season was marred by frequent near-riots when anti-Sunday forces besieged its parks bent on halting games, but Association owners had a much larger hurdle to overcome than Sabbatarians or the Players League. On November 12, 1889, little more than a week after the Players League was officially born, Brooklyn and Cincinnati quit the Association and joined the National League amidst a bitter fight to elect a new Association president to replace Wheeler Wyckoff. When the two clubs exited, with them went Baltimore and Kansas City, trimming the Association to just four teams. Franchises in Syracuse, Rochester and Toledo were hastily annexed, but the eight-team composition was not restored until 22-year-old Jim Kennedy posted the necessary $10,000 bond for a club of his own creation called the Brooklyn Gladiators.

The Gladiators were a dismal mix of has-beens Kennedy coaxed out of retirement and amateurs he siphoned off the Brooklyn sandlots, and the other three newcomers were little

Bill Van Dyke (batting) and Harry Sage with Des Moines in 1889. The two minor leaguers were given an unexpected opportunity by Toledo when there were suddenly three major leagues in 1890. Van Dyke was third in the AA in stolen bases and Sage led all AA catchers in assists. He also hit .149, the third lowest season mark of any 19th-century player who collected 250 or more at bats. Sage trails Will White (.136 in 1879) and Charley Bassett (.144 in 1885).

better. With the Browns riddled by Players League defections, the Philadelphia Athletics and the Columbus Solons appeared to have the inside track on the 1890 American Association flag. But Solons manager Gus Schmelz had too many rookies to blend with the few experienced veterans the Players League raiders spared and the Athletics, after leading the loop on July 4, the traditional date to separate pretenders from genuine contenders, saw the bottom fall out of their season when front office mismanagement left manager Bill Sharsig without any money to pay his players. The Athletics tumbled to seventh place after most of the team quit rather than agree to be paid on a per diem basis when and if funds were available, and the door to the penthouse was opened for Louisville. After finishing last in 1889 and losing a record 26 straight games, the Falls City team triumphed in 1890 almost by default when it lost few key performers to the Players League if only because it had few men Ward's raiders coveted.

The Brooklyn Bridegrooms and Cincinnati Reds, in contrast, took an aggressive tack once the war with the players loomed. Both eliminated the specter by signing most of their regulars for 1890 before Ward formed his rebel circuit. As a result, immediately upon joining the National League, they became its two classiest teams. Cincinnati in particular dominated the early going. Behind rookie pitcher Billy Rhines and Long John Reilly's booming bat, the Reds took a five-game lead over the pack on July 4. But Reilly then went into a protracted slump and though Rhines continued to shine, Tony Mullane, Jesse Duryea and the rest of manager Tom Loftus's veteran hurlers had lackluster seasons, causing Cincinnati to fade badly. Brooklyn also got poor work from several veterans, especially leftfielder Pop Corkhill, but when center fielder Darby O'Brien tore tendons in his hand in early July, ne-

The 1890 Syracuse Stars, an interim AA team in 1890, with Joe Battin, back in the majors after hitting a whopping .169 for Syracuse's minor league entry in 1889. Top: Battin, unknown, Mox McQuery and Bones Ely. Middle: Mike Dorgan, Dan Casey, Rasty Wright, Mike Morrison and Toby Lyons. Bottom: ? Ramsey, Grant Briggs and Barney McLaughlin. Missing is the Stars' "star," Cupid Childs, and also Ramsey's first name. Could Toad have snuck into this scrappy-looking team shot?

cessity made a genius of manager Bill McGunnigle. He began using pitcher Adonis Terry in the outfield, spelled by pitcher Bob Caruthers in the games Terry hurled. Both Terry and Caruthers were capable all-around players, but the time when pitchers were expected to perform elsewhere on their days off was nearing its end. McGunnigle extended it for one more season and in so doing became the only skipper to win pennants in back-to-back seasons in two different major leagues. His Bridegrooms grabbed the National League lead in early August, vaulting past the Philadelphia Phillies, which had taken over first place a few weeks earlier. Philadelphia, the Chicago Colts and the Boston Beaneaters each took a turn on the second rung down the home stretch, but Brooklyn held fast to the top of the ladder. Besides deploying his pitchers judiciously in the outfield, McGunnigle used them well in the box. Other teams in recent years had gone to a three-man pitching rotation, but only the Browns in 1887 had won a pennant by dividing their box work equally among three hurlers. Caruthers, Terry and Tom Lovett made Brooklyn the first National League flag winner with a three-man rotation, as each of the trio won 23 or more games and worked at least 300 innings.

Brooklyn's victory meant the American Association's 1889 champion would face its 1889 basement dweller in the World's Series, not an appetizing prospect. Many observers felt the postseason clash should properly have been a three-team affair, involving the Players League champion Boston Reds. Certainly the Reds with Hoss Radbourn, Dan Brouthers, Hardy Richardson, Harry Stovey, and, most of all, catcher-manager King Kelly, boasted more marquee players than Brooklyn, to say nothing of Louisville. Indeed, not a single member of the Louisville team at World's Series time had ever before played on a pennant winner in the major leagues, and only rookie second baseman Tim Shinnick could

WHY THE AA LOST THE ATTENDANCE WAR IN 1890

Reliable attendance figures for the 1890 season should be available one day. Try Doomsday. Each of the three major leagues that year lied through its teeth, but the Players League probably had the least to lie about thanks mostly to its champion Boston Reds, which drew around 200,000. Pittsburgh, the National League's netherworld tenant, stood at the opposite end of the spectrum, bringing in just 16,064 fans all year, but on the whole, senior loop teams fared nearly as well as Players League entrants, and both circuits so far outstripped the American Association that it put its attendance figures in a time capsule after the season, never to be opened until Pete Browning makes the Hall of Fame. An 1890 population chart of cities with major league teams that year quickly explains why the Association lost the head-count race.

AA		NL		PL	
New York	2,492,591	New York	2,492,591	New York	2,492,591
Phila.	1,046,964	New York	2,492,591	New York	2,492,591
St. Louis	451,770	Chicago	1,099,850	Chicago	1,099,850
Baltimore	434,439	Phila.	1,046,964	Phila.	1,046,964
Louisville	161,129	Boston	448,477	Boston	448,477
Rochester	133,896	Cincinnati	296,908	Cleveland	261,353
Columbus	88,150	Cleveland	261,353	Pittsburgh	238,617
Syracuse	88,143	Pittsburgh	238,617	Buffalo	255,664

New York City's population includes Brooklyn, which was a separate city in 1890, but the two were closely yoked once the Brooklyn Bridge was finished in 1883. Since the National League and the Players League had teams in both New York City and Brooklyn, New York's population figure appears twice in their columns. All three leagues had teams in Brooklyn in 1890, though it may be a stretch to believe that with the brand of ball they played the Association Gladiators ever lured anyone from the Manhattan side of the Brooklyn Bridge.

The one and only Players League titlist—the 1890 Boston Reds. Top: Dick Johnston, Matt Kilroy, Dan Brouthers, Harry Stovey, Tom Brown and Pop Swett. Middle: Billy Nash, Joe Quinn, Arthur Irwin, King Kelly, Hoss Radbourn, Ad Gumbert and Hardy Richardson. Bottom: Bill Daley, Morg Murphy and Kid Madden.

claim success at any level. Shinnick bragged that he had never played on anything but championship teams since his days at Philips Exeter Academy in the mid-1880s, but his streak seemed certain to end when Louisville fell behind 2–0 in the best-of-nine Series by dropping the first two contests at home.

Following a 7–7 tie in Game Three, Red Ehret salvaged the finale in the Falls City for the Louisvilles by nipping Lovett, 5–4. Two days of rain enabled a rested Lovett to win the opener in Brooklyn, but Ehret prevented Brooklyn from applying the clincher by saving Game Six in relief of Scott Stratton. The next afternoon Ehret bested Lovett again, 6–2, to knot matters at three-all. Miraculously, the least promising matchup in the seven-year history of the interleague World's Series had suddenly turned into the most exciting scuffle since 1886. Alas, it was never finished. Increasingly miserable weather and ever dwindling attendance figures persuaded the combatants to call the 1890 World's Series a 3-3 draw. McGunnigle and Louisville manager Jack Chapman talked of finishing it the following spring before the start of the 1891 season, but by then the two circuits were at each other's throats. There would never be another postseason match between the National League and the American Association.

FAMOUS FIRSTS VII

The Cleveland Infants led the Players League in hitting but nevertheless barely dodged the cellar. Pitching was the culprit. Two of the Infants' few bright moments were provided by Charlie Dewald. On September 20 the rookie lefty, just arrived from Jamestown of the New York–Penn League, beat Monte Ward's Brooklyn Players League runner-up, 4–3, in his big-league debut. Five days later Dewald outlasted King Kelly's pennant-bound Boston team, 10–9. Dewald never pitched again in the majors, exiting with the distinction of being the first pitcher ever to knock off his league's two best teams in his only two appearances. In addition, Dewald is one of only four men in the nineteenth century who collected two or more career wins without a loss and the lone member of the select list who was a true pitcher.

	WINS	BEST YEAR
Roger Bresnahan	4	1897 Was-NL (4–0)
Hardy Richardson	3*	1886 Det-NL (3–0)
Charlie Dewald	2	1890 Cle-PL (2–0)
Cub Stricker	2	1882 Phi-AA (1–0)/1888 Cle-AA (1–0)

*Disputed. Some sources credit him with only two wins in 1886.

TEAM NICKNAMES

In March, 1890, a terrible cyclone in the Louisville area did massive property damage and killed over 100. When Louisville manager Jack Chapman arranged a benefit game for the disaster victims, it was snowed out. Since the Colonels were coming off a ghastly last-place finish, the jinx began to seem so pervasive that people began calling the team the Cyclones.

The name hung on for a year or so and then Louisville became the Colonels again. It's uncertain when, just as it's not too certain when they started to be known as the Colonels rather than by their original name—the Eclipse. Probably it happened about the time someone noticed most of the original cast members who'd played with the Eclipse semipro team before it joined the American Association were no longer around. In any case, Louisville's nickname history is typical. It's impossible, for almost every nineteenth-century major league team, to pin down exactly when or why or by whom it first began to be called the Phillies instead of the Quakers or the Reds instead of the Red Stockings or whatever. As a result, throughout *The Great Encyclopedia of Nineteenth-Century Major League Baseball* the team nicknames in the Annual Record are often open to debate. Based on new information, some of them will no doubt be changed by the next edition.

The Pittsburgh Burghers, with Ned Hanlon (#12), then in his first full season as a helmsman. Hanlon skippered the Smoke City PL club to a 6th place finish. Others in numerical order from #1 to #15 are: Harry Staley, Jake Beckley (without his trademark mustache), Jocko Fields, Jerry Hurley, Willie Kuehne, Ed Morris (the only known picture of him with a mustache), Yank Robinson, Al Maul, Joe Visner, Tommy Corcoran, Tom Quinn, Hanlon, John Tener, Fred Carroll and Pud Galvin.

THE SEASONAL RECORD

NATIONAL LEAGUE

	W	L	PCT	HOME	ROAD	GB
1. Brooklyn Bridegrooms	86	43	.667	58–16	28–27	—
2. Chicago Colts	84	53	.613	48–24	36–29	6
3. Philadelphia Phillies	78	54	.591	54–22	24–32	9.5
4. Cincinnati Reds	77	55	.583	50–23	27–32	10.5
5. Boston Beaneaters	76	57	.571	43–23	33–34	12
6. New York Giants	63	68	.481	37–27	26–41	24
7. Cleveland Spiders	44	88	.333	30–37	14–51	43.5
8. Pittsburgh Infants	23	113	.169	14–25	9–88	66.5

	Bro	Chi	Phi	Cin	Bos	NY	Cle	Pit	
Brooklyn	—	11	10	9	11	10	17	18	86
Chicago	9	—	9	12	11	13	13	17	84
Philadelphia	8	10	—	9	9	11	14	17	78
Cincinnati	7	8	11	—	8	14	13	16	77
Boston	6	8	11	11	—	11	13	16	76
New York	8	6	6	6	8	—	12	17	63
Cleveland	3	7	5	4	7	6	—	12	44
Pittsburgh	2	3	2	4	3	3	6	—	23
	43	53	54	55	57	68	88	113	531

SEASON LEADERS

Batting Average (350 ABs)

1.	Glasscock, New York	.336
2.	Hamilton, Philadelphia	.325
3.	Clements, Philadelphia	.315
4.	O'Brien, Brooklyn	.314
5.	Thompson, Philadelphia	.313

On–Base Percentage

1.	Anson, Chicago	.443
2.	Hamilton, Philadelphia	.430
3.	Pinkney, Brooklyn	.411
4.	McKean, Cleveland	.401
5.	Glasscock, New York	.395

Home Runs

1.	Wilmot, Chicago	13
	Tiernan, New York	13
	O. Burns, Brooklyn	13
4.	Long, Boston	8
5.	Six with	7

Slugging Average

1.	Tiernan, New York	.495
2.	Clements, Philadelphia	.472
	Reilly, Cincinnati	.472
4.	O. Burns, Brooklyn	.464
5.	Burkett, New York	.461

Total Bases

1.	Tiernan, New York	274
2.	Reilly, Cincinnati	261
3.	Thompson, Philadelphia	243
4.	Wilmot, Chicago	239
5.	Glasscock, New York	225

RBI

1.	O. Burns, Brooklyn	128
2.	Anson, Chicago	107
3.	Thompson, Philadelphia	102
4.	Wilmot, Chicago	99
5.	Foutz, Brooklyn	98

Hits

1.	Thompson, Philadelphia	172
	Glasscock, New York	172
3.	Tiernan, New York	168
4.	Reilly, Cincinnati	166
	C. Carroll, Chicago	166

Runs

1.	Collins, Brooklyn	148
2.	C. Carroll, Chicago	134
3.	Hamilton, Philadelphia	133
4.	Tiernan, New York	132
5.	McPhee, Cincinnati	125

Stolen Bases

1.	Hamilton, Philadelphia	102
2.	Collins, Brooklyn	85
3.	Sunday, Pit–Phil	84
4.	Wilmot, Chicago	76
5.	Tiernan, New York	56

Strikeouts

1.	P. Smith, Boston	81
2.	Hutchison, Chicago	63
3.	Denny, New York	62
4.	Bennett, Boston	56
5.	Allen, Philadelphia	54
	Zimmer, Cleveland	54

PITCHING

Wins

1.	Hutchison, Chicago	42
2.	Gleason, Philadelphia	38
3.	Lovett, Brooklyn	30
4.	Rusie, New York	29
5.	Rhines, Cincinnati	28

Losses

1.	Rusie, New York	34
2.	Beatin, Cleveland	30
3.	Hutchison, Chicago	25
4.	Vickery, Philadelphia	22
5.	Nichols, Boston	19
	Baker, Pittsburgh	19

Innings

1.	Hutchison, Chicago	603
2.	Rusie, New York	548.2
3.	Gleason, Philadelphia	506
4.	Beatin, Cleveland	474.1
5.	Nichols, Boston	424

Complete Games

1.	Hutchison, Chicago	65
2.	Rusie, New York	56
3.	Gleason, Philadelphia	54
4.	Beatin, Cleveland	53
5.	Nichols, Boston	47

Strikeouts

1.	Rusie, New York	341
2.	Hutchison, Chicago	289
3.	Nichols, Boston	222
	Gleason, Philadelphia	222
5.	Terry, Brooklyn	185

Winning Percentage (25 decisions)

1.	Lovett, Brooklyn	.732
2.	Gleason, Philadelphia	.691
3.	Luby, Chicago	.690
4.	Caruthers, Brooklyn	.676
5.	Hutchison, Chicago	.627

ERA (140 innings)

1.	Rhines, Cincinnati	1.95
2.	Nichols, Boston	2.23
3.	Mullane, Cincinnati	2.24
4.	Rusie, New York	2.56
5.	Gleason, Philadelphia	2.63

Lowest On–Base Percentage

1.	Rhines, Cincinnati	.282
2.	Nichols, Boston	.284
3.	Hutchison, Chicago	.287
4.	Getzein, Boston	.292
5.	Duryea, Cincinnati	.295

FIELDING

Total Chances

1B	Reilly, Cincinnati	1463
2B	McPhee, Cincinnati	886
3B	Smalley, Cleveland	632
SS	Allen, Philadelphia	906
OF	Wilmot, Chicago	369
C	Zimmer, Cleveland	713
P	Hutchison, Chicago	186

Fielding Average

Tucker, Boston	.979
Bassett, New York	.952
McGarr, Boston	.933
Cooney, Chicago	.936
O'Brien, Brooklyn	.960
Bennett, Boston	.959
Luby, Chicago	.964

BROOKLYN   **Bill McGunnigle**   **Washington Park**

		G	AB	H	R	2B	3B	HR	RBI	BB	SB	BA	SA
2B	Hub Collins	129	510	142	**148**	32	7	3	69	85	85	.278	.386
1B	Dave Foutz	129	509	154	106	25	13	5	98	52	42	.303	.432
3B	George Pinkney	126	485	150	115	20	9	7	83	80	47	.309	.431
SS	Germany Smith	129	481	92	76	6	5	1	47	42	24	.191	.231
RF	Oyster Burns	119	472	134	102	22	12	**13**	**128**	51	21	.284	.464
P	Adonis Terry	99	363	101	63	17	9	4	59	40	32	.278	.408
CF	Darby O'Brien	85	350	110	78	28	6	2	63	32	38	.314	.446
C	Tom Daly	82	292	71	55	9	4	5	43	32	20	.243	.353
P	Bob Caruthers	71	238	63	46	7	4	1	29	47	13	.265	.340
LF	Pop Corkhill	51	204	46	23	4	2	1	21	15	6	.225	.279
P	Tom Lovett	44	164	33	22	4	0	1	20	12	6	.201	.244
C	Bob Clark	43	151	33	24	3	3	0	15	15	10	.219	.278
Sub	Patsy Donovan	28	105	23	17	5	1	0	8	5	3	.219	.286
Sub	Doc Bushong	16	55	13	5	2	0	0	7	6	2	.236	.273
P	Mickey Hughes	9	26	1	2	0	0	0	1	1	0	.038	.038
Sub	George Stallings	4	11	0	1	0	0	0	0	1	0	.000	.000
P	Lady Baldwin	2	3	0	1	0	0	0	0	1	0	.000	.000
		129	4419	1166	**884**	184	75	43	**691**	517	**349**	.264	**.369**

1B	Foutz 113, Daly 12, Corkhill 6, Terry 1
2B	Collins 129
SS	Smith 129
3B	Pinkney 126, Burns 3
OF	Burns 116, O'Brien 85, Terry 54, Corkhill 48, Caruthers 39, Donovan 28, Foutz 13, Bushong 1, Lovett 1, Clark 1, Daly 1
C	Daly 69, Clark 42, Bushong 15, Stallings 4
P	Terry 46, Lovett 44, Caruthers 37, Hughes 9, Foutz 5, Baldwin 2

	G	IP	GS	CG	W	L	K	BB	SH	SV	ERA
Tom Lovett	44	372	41	39	30	11	124	141	4	0	2.78
Adonis Terry	46	370	44	38	26	16	185	133	1	0	2.94
Bob Caruthers	37	300	33	30	23	11	64	87	2	0	3.09
Mickey Hughes	9	66.1	8	6	4	4	22	30	0	0	5.16
Dave Foutz	5	29	2	2	2	1	4	6	0	**2**	1.86
Lady Baldwin	2	7.2	1	0	1	0	4	4	0	0	7.04
		1145	129	115	86	43	403	401	7	2	3.05

CHICAGO **Cap Anson** **West Side Park (I)**

		G	AB	H	R	2B	3B	HR	RBI	BB	SB	BA	SA
LF	Cliff Carroll	136	**582**	166	134	16	6	7	65	53	34	.285	.369
SS	Jimmy Cooney	135	574	156	114	19	10	4	52	73	45	.272	.361
CF	Walt Wilmot	139	571	159	114	15	13	**13**	99	64	76	.278	.419
3B	Tom Burns	139	538	149	86	17	6	5	86	57	44	.277	.359
1B	Cap Anson	139	504	157	95	14	5	7	107	**113**	29	.312	.401
UT	Howard Earl	92	384	95	57	10	3	7	51	18	17	.247	.344
C	Mal Kittridge	96	333	67	46	8	3	3	35	39	7	.201	.270
P	Bill Hutchison	71	261	53	28	7	2	2	27	13	6	.203	.268
2B	Bob Glenalvin	66	250	67	43	10	3	4	26	19	30	.268	.380
RF	Jim Andrews	53	202	38	32	4	2	3	17	23	11	.188	.272
Sub	Tom Nagle	38	144	39	21	5	1	1	11	7	4	.271	.340
P	Pat Luby	36	116	31	27	5	3	3	17	9	3	.267	.440
Sub	Pete O'Brien	27	106	30	15	7	0	3	16	5	4	.283	.434
Sub	Elmer Foster	27	105	26	20	4	2	5	23	9	18	.248	.467
P	Ed Stein	20	59	9	4	1	0	0	7	7	1	.153	.169
P	Mike Sullivan	12	40	5	1	1	0	0	7	2	0	.125	.150
Sub	Jake Stenzel	11	41	11	3	1	0	0	3	1	0	.268	.293
P	Roscoe Coughlin	11	39	10	5	1	1	0	1	2	0	.256	.333
Sub	Ed Hutchinson	4	17	1	0	1	0	0	0	0	0	.059	.118
Sub	Chuck Lauer	2	8	2	1	1	0	0	0	2	0	.250	.375
P	Robert Gibson	1	4	0	0	0	0	0	0	1	0	.000	.000
Sub	Pop Lytle	1	4	0	1	0	0	0	0	0	0	.000	.000
Sub	Marty Honan	1	3	0	0	0	0	0	1	0	0	.000	.000
P	Fred Demarais	1	2	0	0	0	0	0	0	0	0	.000	.000
Sub	Pat Wright	1	2	0	0	0	0	0	0	1	0	.000	.000
P	Ed Eiteljorge	1	1	0	0	0	0	0	0	0	0	.000	.000
P	Ossie France	1	1	0	0	0	0	0	0	0	0	.000	.000
		139	4891	**1271**	847	147	60	**67**	653	516	329	.260	.356

1B Anson 135, Earl 3, Luby 2
2B Glenalvin 66, Earl 39, O'Brien 27, Hutchinson 4, Anson 2, Wright 1
SS Cooney 135, Earl 4
3B Burns 139
OF Wilmot 139, Carroll 136, Andrews 53, Earl 49, Foster 27, Nagle 6, Stenzel 6, Lytle 1
C Kittridge 96, Nagle 33, Stenzel 6, Anson 3, Lauer 2, Honan 1, Cooney 1
P Hutchison 71, Luby 34, Stein 20, Sullivan 12, Coughlin 11, France 1, Gibson 1, Eiteljorge 1, Demarais 1

	G	IP	GS	CG	W	L	K	BB	SH	SV	ERA
Bill Hutchison	71	**603**	**66**	**65**	**42**	25	289	199	5	**2**	2.70
Pat Luby	34	267.2	31	26	20	9	85	95	0	1	3.19
Ed Stein	20	160.2	18	14	12	6	65	83	1	0	3.81
Mike Sullivan	12	96	12	10	5	6	33	58	0	0	4.59
Roscoe Coughlin	11	95	10	10	4	6	29	40	0	0	4.26
Robert Gibson	1	9	1	1	1	0	1	2	0	0	0.00
Ed Eiteljorge	1	2	1	0	0	1	1	1	0	0	22.50
Fred Demarais	1	2	0	0	0	0	1	1	0	0	0.00
Ossee France	1	2	0	0	0	0	0	2	0	0	13.50
		1237.1	139	126	84	53	504	481	6	**3**	3.24

PHILADELPHIA   **Harry Wright (36–31)**   **Jack Clements (13–6)**   **Al Reach (4–7)**
Bob Allen (25–10)   **Philadelphia Baseball Grounds**

		G	AB	H	R	2B	3B	HR	RBI	BB	SB	BA	SA
RF	Sam Thompson	132	549	**172**	116	**41**	9	4	102	42	25	.313	.443
LF	Billy Hamilton	123	496	161	133	13	9	2	49	83	**102**	.325	.399
2B	Al Myers	117	487	135	95	29	7	2	81	57	44	.277	.378
3B	Ed Mayer	117	484	117	49	25	5	1	70	22	20	.242	.320
SS	Bob Allen	133	456	103	69	15	11	2	57	87	13	.226	.320
CF	Eddie Burke	100	430	113	85	16	11	4	50	49	38	.263	.379
1B	Al McCauley	116	418	102	63	25	7	1	42	57	8	.244	.344
C	Jack Clements	97	381	120	64	23	8	7	74	45	10	.315	.472
P	Kid Gleason	63	224	47	22	3	0	0	17	12	10	.210	.223
Sub	Pop Schriver	57	223	61	37	9	6	0	35	22	9	.274	.368
P	Tom Vickery	46	159	33	15	4	0	0	11	7	12	.208	.233
Sub	Bill Grey	34	128	31	20	8	4	0	21	6	5	.242	.367
Sub	Billy Sunday	31	119	31	26	3	1	0	6	18	28	.261	.303
P	Phenomenal Smith	26	86	24	19	4	0	0	19	10	6	.279	.326
Sub	Harry Decker	5	19	7	5	1	0	0	2	4	4	.368	.421
P	Duke Esper	5	19	3	2	1	0	0	2	0	0	.158	.211
P	Bill Day	4	10	1	1	0	0	0	1	0	0	.100	.100
P	Dave Anderson	3	9	1	1	0	0	0	0	0	0	.111	.111
P	Jack McFetridge	1	4	3	0	0	0	0	1	0	0	.750	.750
P	Sumner Bowman	1	4	2	0	0	0	0	1	0	0	.500	.500
Sub	Frank Motz	1	2	0	1	0	0	0	0	1	1	.000	.000
P	John Coleman	1	0	0	0	0	0	0	0	0	0	—	—
		133	4707	1267	823	**220**	78	23	631	522	335	**.269**	.364

1B   McCauley 116, Schriver 10, Clements 5, Decker 2, Grey 1, Motz 1
2B   Myers 117, Grey 8, Burke 4, Schriver 3, Gleason 2
SS   Allen 133
3B   Mayer 117, Schriver 8, Grey 8
OF   Thompson 132, Hamilton 123, Burke 96, Sunday 31, Grey 10, Smith 3, Decker 2, Coleman 2, Schriver 2
C   Clements 91, Schriver 34, Grey 7, Decker 1
P   Gleason 60, Vickery 46, Smith 24, Esper 5, Day 4, Anderson 3, Coleman 1, McFetridge 1, Bowman 1

	G	IP	GS	CG	W	L	K	BB	SH	SV	ERA
Kid Gleason	60	506	55	54	38	17	222	167	6	**2**	2.63
Tom Vickery	46	382	46	41	24	22	162	184	2	0	3.44
Phenomenal Smith	24	204	20	19	8	12	81	89	1	0	4.28
Duke Esper	5	41	5	4	5	0	18	16	0	0	3.07
Bill Day	4	23.2	2	2	1	1	9	12	0	0	3.04
Dave Anderson	3	19.1	2	1	1	1	7	11	0	0	7.45
Jack McFetridge	1	9	1	1	1	0	4	2	0	0	1.00
Sumner Bowman	1	8	1	0	0	0	2	2	0	0	7.88
John Coleman	1	1.2	1	0	0	1	2	3	0	0	21.60
		1194.2	133	122	78	54	507	486	9	2	3.32

CINCINNATI   Tom Loftus   League Park (1) (formerly American Park)

		G	AB	H	R	2B	3B	HR	RBI	BB	SB	BA	SA
1B	Long John Reilly	132	553	166	114	25	**26**	6	86	16	29	.300	.472
2B	Bid McPhee	132	528	135	125	16	22	3	39	82	55	.256	.386
3B	Lefty Marr	130	527	157	91	17	12	1	73	46	44	.298	.381
CF	Bug Holliday	131	518	140	93	18	14	4	75	49	50	.270	.382
SS	Ollie Beard	122	492	132	64	17	15	3	72	44	30	.268	.382
LF	Joe Knight	127	481	150	67	26	8	4	67	38	17	.312	.424
P	Tony Mullane	81	286	79	41	9	8	0	34	39	19	.276	.364
C	Jerry Harrington	65	236	58	25	7	1	1	23	15	4	.246	.297
C	Jim Keenan	54	202	28	21	4	2	3	19	19	5	.139	.223
RF	Hugh Nicol	50	186	39	28	1	4	0	19	19	24	.210	.258
Sub	Arlie Latham	41	164	41	35	6	2	0	15	23	20	.250	.311
P	Billy Rhines	46	154	29	14	1	2	0	11	7	2	.188	.221
P	Jesse Duryea	33	99	15	13	1	1	1	6	19	9	.152	.212
P	Frank Foreman	25	75	10	13	1	3	1	7	10	0	.133	.267
Sub	Kid Baldwin	22	72	11	5	0	0	0	10	3	2	.153	.153
P	Leon Viau	13	36	5	2	0	0	0	1	3	2	.139	.139
Sub	Billy Clingman	7	27	7	2	1	0	0	5	1	0	.259	.296
P	John Dolan	2	8	1	0	0	0	0	1	0	0	.125	.125
		134	4644	1203	753	150	**120**	27	563	433	312	.259	.360

1B	Reilly 132, Keenan 2, Mullane 1
2B	McPhee 132, Clingman 1, Nicol 1
SS	Beard 113, Mullane 10, Clingman 6, Nicol 3, Marr 3
3B	Marr 63, Latham 41, Mullane 21, Beard 9, Keenan 1
OF	Holliday 131, Knight 127, Marr 64, Nicol 46, Mullane 28, Baldwin 2, Foreman 1, Keenan 1, Duryea 1, Reilly 1, Latham 1
C	Harrington 65, Keenan 50, Baldwin 20
P	Rhines 46, Duryea 33, Mullane 25, Foreman 25, Viau 13, Dolan 2

	G	IP	GS	CG	W	L	K	BB	SH	SV	ERA
Billy Rhines	46	401.1	45	45	28	17	182	113	6	0	**1.95**
Jesse Duryea	33	274	32	29	16	12	108	60	2	0	2.92
Tony Mullane	25	209	21	21	12	10	91	96	0	1	2.24
Frank Foreman	25	198.1	24	20	13	10	57	89	0	0	3.95
Leon Viau	13	90	10	7	7	5	41	39	1	0	4.50
John Dolan	2	18	2	2	1	1	9	10	0	0	4.50
		1190.2	134	124	77	55	488	407	9	1	**2.79**

BOSTON   Frank Selee   South End Grounds (I)

		G	AB	H	R	2B	3B	HR	RBI	BB	SB	BA	SA
1B	Tommy Tucker	132	539	159	104	17	8	1	62	56	43	.295	.362
RF	Steve Brodie	132	514	152	77	19	9	0	67	66	29	.296	.368
LF	Marty Sullivan	121	505	144	82	19	7	6	61	56	33	.285	.386
3B	Chippy McGarr	121	487	115	68	12	7	1	51	34	39	.236	.296
2B	Pop Smith	134	463	106	82	16	12	1	53	80	39	.229	.322
SS	Herman Long	101	431	108	95	15	3	8	52	40	49	.251	.355
C	Charlie Bennett	85	281	60	59	17	2	3	40	72	6	.214	.320
CF	Paul Hines	69	273	72	41	12	3	2	48	32	9	.264	.352
Sub	Bobby Lowe	52	207	58	35	13	2	2	21	26	15	.280	.391
Sub	Lew Hardie	47	185	42	17	8	0	3	17	18	4	.227	.319
P	Kid Nichols	49	174	43	18	5	1	0	23	11	2	.247	.287
P	John Clarkson	45	173	43	18	6	3	2	26	8	2	.249	.353
Sub	Charlie Ganzel	38	163	44	21	7	3	0	24	5	1	.270	.350
P	Charlie Getzein	41	147	34	27	9	2	2	25	16	4	.231	.361

		G	AB	H	R	2B	3B	HR	RBI	BB	SB	BA	SA
Sub	Patsy Donovan	32	140	36	17	0	0	0	9	8	10	.257	.257
Sub	Art Schellhase	9	29	4	1	0	0	0	1	1	0	.138	.138
P	John Taber	2	6	0	1	0	0	0	0	0	0	.000	.000
P	Tony Von Fricken	1	3	0	0	0	0	0	0	0	0	.000	.000
P	Al Lawson	1	2	0	0	0	0	0	0	1	0	.000	.000
		134	4722	1220	763	175	62	31	580	**530**	285	.258	.341

1B Tucker 132, Hardie 1, Hines 1
2B Smith 134, Ganzel 1
SS Long 101, Lowe 24, McGarr 5, Ganzel 3, Smith 1, Schellhase 1, Hardie 1
3B McGarr 115, Lowe 12, Hardie 7, Schellhase 1, Sullivan 1
OF Brodie 132, Sullivan 120, Hines 69, Donovan 32, Lowe 15, Hardie 15, Ganzel 15, Lowe 15, Schellhase 5, Nichols 2, Clarkson 1, Getzein 1, McGarr 1
C Bennett 85, Hardie 25, Ganzel 22, Schellhase 2
P Nichols 48, Clarkson 44, Getzein 40, Taber 2, Lawson 1, Von Fricken 1

	G	IP	GS	CG	W	L	K	BB	SH	SV	ERA
Kid Nichols	48	424	47	47	27	19	222	112	**7**	0	2.23
John Clarkson	44	383	44	43	26	18	138	140	2	0	3.27
Charlie Getzein	40	350	40	39	23	17	140	82	4	0	3.19
John Taber	2	13	1	1	0	1	3	8	0	1	4.15
Al Lawson	1	9	1	1	0	1	1	4	0	0	4.00
Tony Von Fricken	1	8	1	1	0	1	2	8	0	0	10.13
		1187	134	**132**	76	57	506	**354**	**13**	1	2.93

NEW YORK   **Jim Mutrie**   **Polo Grounds (II)**

		G	AB	H	R	2B	3B	HR	RBI	BB	SB	BA	SA
CF	Mike Tiernan	133	533	168	132	25	21	**13**	59	68	56	.304	**.495**
LF	Joe Hornung	120	513	122	62	18	5	0	65	12	39	.238	.292
SS	Jack Glasscock	124	512	**172**	91	32	9	1	66	41	54	**.336**	.439
3B	Jerry Denny	114	437	93	50	18	7	3	42	28	11	.213	.307
2B	Charlie Bassett	100	410	98	52	13	8	0	54	29	14	.239	.310
RF	Jesse Burkett	111	401	124	67	23	13	4	60	33	14	.309	.461
UT	Archie Clarke	101	395	89	55	12	8	0	49	32	44	.225	.296
P	Amos Rusie	73	284	79	31	13	6	0	28	7	6	.278	.366
C	Dick Buckley	70	266	68	39	11	0	2	26	23	3	.256	.320
1B	Dude Esterbrook	45	197	57	29	14	1	0	29	10	12	.289	.371
1B	Lew Whistler	45	170	49	27	9	7	2	29	20	8	.288	.459
Sub	John Henry	37	144	35	19	6	0	0	16	7	12	.243	.285
P	Mickey Welch	37	123	22	15	4	0	0	10	9	1	.179	.211
Sub	Pat Murphy	32	119	28	14	5	1	0	9	14	3	.235	.294
P	John Sharrott	32	109	22	16	3	2	0	14	0	6	.202	.266
Sub	Shorty Howe	19	64	11	4	0	0	0	4	3	3	.172	.172
Sub	Pete Sommers	17	47	5	4	1	1	0	1	4	0	.106	.170
Sub	George McMillan	10	35	5	4	0	0	0	1	7	1	.143	.143
P	Ed Daily	4	15	2	1	1	0	0	1	0	0	.133	.200
Sub	Sam Crane	4	12	0	0	0	0	0	0	0	1	.000	.000
Sub	Mort Scanlan	3	10	0	0	0	0	0	0	2	1	.000	.000
P	Bob Murphy	3	9	1	0	0	0	0	0	0	0	.111	.111
Sub	Tom O'Rourke	2	7	0	1	0	0	0	0	1	0	.000	.000
		135	4832	1250	713	208	89	25	563	350	289	.259	.354

1B   Whistler 45, Esterbrook 45, Hornung 36, Sommers 5, Scanlon 3, Crane 1
2B   Bassett 100, Howe 18, Clarke 15, Crane 2, Denny 1
SS   Glasscock 124, Denny 7, Hornung 2, Clarke 1, P. Murphy 1
3B   Denny 106, Clarke 16, Buckley 8, Hornung 5, Howe 1
OF   Tiernan 133, Burkett 90, Hornung 77, Henry 37, Clarke 33, Rusie 14, McMillan 10, Sharrott 9, Daily 3, P. Murphy 3, Sommers 2, Crane 1
C   Buckley 62, Clarke 36, P. Murphy 29, Sommers 11, O'Rourke 2
P   Rusie 67, Welch 37, Sharrott 25, Burkett 21, B. Murphy 3, Daily 2

	G	IP	GS	CG	W	L	K	BB	SH	SV	ERA
Amos Rusie	67	548.2	62	56	29	**34**	341	289	4	1	2.56
Mickey Welch	37	292.1	37	33	17	14	97	122	2	0	2.99
Jack Sharrott	25	184	19	18	11	10	84	88	0	0	2.89
Jesse Burkett	21	118	14	6	3	10	82	92	0	0	5.57
Bob Murphy	3	18	2	1	1	0	8	10	0	0	5.50
Ed Daily	2	16	1	1	2	0	0	6	0	0	2.25
		1177	135	115	63	68	**612**	607	6	1	3.06

CLEVELAND   Gus Schmelz (21–55)   Bob Leadley (23–33)   National League Park (I)

		G	AB	H	R	2B	3B	HR	RBI	BB	SB	BA	SA
LF	Bob Gilks	130	544	116	65	10	3	0	41	32	17	.213	.243
SS	Ed McKean	136	530	157	95	15	14	7	61	87	23	.296	.417
CF	George Davis	136	526	139	98	22	9	6	73	53	22	.264	.375
3B	Will Smalley	136	502	107	62	11	1	0	42	60	10	.213	.239
C	Chief Zimmer	125	444	95	54	16	6	2	57	46	15	.214	.291
2B	Joe Ardner	84	323	72	28	13	1	0	35	17	9	.223	.269
RF	Vince Dailey	64	246	71	41	5	7	0	32	33	17	.289	.366
1B	Peekaboo Veach	64	238	56	24	10	5	0	32	33	9	.235	.319
1B	Jake Virtue	62	223	68	39	6	5	2	25	49	9	.305	.404
P	Ed Beatin	54	191	27	25	4	3	1	21	12	2	.141	.209
Sub	Tom Dowse	38	159	33	20	2	1	0	9	12	3	.208	.233
Sub	Buck West	37	151	37	20	6	1	2	29	7	4	.245	.338
Sub	Bill Delaney	36	116	22	16	1	1	1	7	21	5	.190	.241
P	Jack Wadsworth	20	68	12	6	2	0	0	7	2	1	.176	.206
P	Cy Young	17	65	8	6	2	0	0	4	0	1	.123	.154
P	Ezra Lincoln	15	51	8	4	1	0	0	0	2	0	.157	.176
Sub	Ratsy Wright	13	45	5	7	1	0	0	2	12	3	.111	.133
P	Leon Viau	13	43	7	6	1	0	0	2	4	2	.163	.186
Sub	Pat Lyons	11	38	2	2	1	0	0	1	4	0	.053	.079
Sub	Joe Sommer	9	35	8	4	1	0	0	0	2	0	.229	.257
Sub	Pete Sommers	9	34	7	4	1	1	0	1	2	0	.206	.294
P	Bill Garfield	9	26	4	0	0	0	0	2	3	0	.154	.154
P	Edgar Smith	8	24	7	2	0	1	0	4	4	0	.292	.375
Sub	Len Stockwell	2	7	2	2	1	0	0	0	0	0	.286	.429
P	Charlie Parsons	2	4	3	0	0	0	0	2	0	0	.750	.750
		136	4633	1073	630	132	59	21	489	497	152	.232	.299

1B   Veach 64, Virtue 62, Dowse 10, Stockwell 1
2B   Ardner 84, Delaney 36, Lyons 11, McKean 3, Davis 2, Gilks 2
SS   McKean 134, Gilks 3, Davis 1
3B   Smalley 136
OF   Davis 133, Gilks 123, Dailey 64, West 37, Dowse 26, Wright 13, Sommer 9, Smith 2, Sommers 1, Stockwell 1
C   Zimmer 125, Sommers 8, Dowse 3
P   Beatin 54, Wadsworth 20, Young 17, Lincoln 15, Viau 13, Garfield 9, Smith 6, Gilks 4, Parsons 2, Dailey 2, Dowse 1, Sommer 1

	G	IP	GS	CG	W	L	K	BB	SH	SV	ERA
Eb Beatin	54	474.1	54	53	22	30	155	186	1	0	3.83
Jack Wadsworth	20	169.2	19	19	2	16	26	81	0	0	5.20
Cy Young	17	147.2	16	16	9	7	39	30	0	0	3.47
Ezra Lincoln	15	118	15	13	3	11	22	53	0	0	4.42
Leon Viau	13	107	13	13	4	9	30	42	1	0	3.36
Bill Garfield	9	70	8	7	1	7	16	35	0	0	4.89
Edgar Smith	6	44	6	5	1	4	11	10	0	0	4.30
Bob Gilks	4	31.2	3	3	2	2	5	9	0	0	4.26
Charlie Parsons	2	9	1	0	0	1	2	6	0	0	6.00
Vince Dailey	2	7	1	0	0	1	0	7	0	0	7.71
Tom Dowse	1	5	0	0	0	0	0	1	0	0	5.40
Joe Sommer	1	1	0	0	0	0	0	2	0	0	0.00
		1184.1	136	129	44	88	306	462	2	0	4.13

PITTSBURGH   **Guy Hecker**   **Recreation Park**

		G	AB	H	R	2B	3B	HR	RBI	BB	SB	BA	SA
3B	Doggie Miller	138	549	150	85	24	3	4	66	68	32	.273	.350
2B	Sam Laroque	111	434	105	59	20	4	1	40	35	27	.242	.313
CF	Tun Berger	101	391	104	64	18	4	0	40	35	11	.266	.332
RF	Billy Sunday	86	358	92	58	9	2	1	33	32	56	.257	.302
C	Harry Decker	92	354	97	52	14	3	5	38	26	8	.274	.373
1B	Guy Hecker	86	340	77	43	13	9	0	38	19	13	.226	.318
UT	Bill Wilson	83	304	65	30	11	3	0	21	22	5	.214	.270
Sub	Fred Roat	57	215	48	18	2	0	2	17	16	7	.223	.260
LF	John Kelty	59	207	49	24	10	2	1	27	22	10	.237	.319
SS	Ed Sales	51	189	43	19	7	3	1	23	16	3	.228	.312
Sub	Fred Osborne	43	168	40	24	8	3	1	14	6	0	.238	.339
Sub	Mike Jordan	37	125	12	8	1	0	0	6	15	5	.096	.104
Sub	Eddie Burke	31	124	26	17	5	2	1	7	14	6	.210	.306
Sub	Paul Hines	31	121	22	11	1	0	0	9	11	6	.182	.190
Sub	Sam Crane	22	82	16	3	3	0	0	3	0	5	.195	.232
Sub	Ducky Hemp	21	81	19	9	0	2	0	4	8	3	.235	.284
P	Kirtley Baker	25	68	10	6	0	0	0	0	10	1	.147	.147
Sub	Fred Dunlap	17	64	11	9	1	1	0	3	7	2	.172	.219
Sub	Pop Lytle	15	55	8	2	1	0	0	0	8	0	.145	.164
P	Bill Sowders	17	50	9	3	0	0	0	4	2	1	.180	.180
Sub	Henry Youngman	13	47	6	6	1	1	0	4	6	1	.128	.191
P	Bill Phillips	14	46	11	6	2	0	0	2	3	0	.239	.283
P	Charlie Heard	12	43	8	2	2	0	0	0	1	0	.186	.233
P	Dave Anderson	13	42	3	4	0	0	0	0	1	0	.071	.071
P	Billy Gumbert	10	37	9	8	3	0	1	7	2	1	.243	.405
P	Sumner Bowman	11	36	10	7	1	0	0	3	4	0	.278	.306
P	Crazy Schmit	11	33	2	4	0	0	0	0	5	2	.061	.061
Sub	Peekaboo Veach	8	30	9	6	1	1	2	5	8	0	.300	.600
P	Bill Day	6	23	1	1	0	0	0	2	0	0	.043	.043
P	Phenomenal Smith	5	17	7	3	0	0	0	3	1	0	.412	.412
P	Charlie Gray	5	15	3	1	1	0	0	3	0	0	.200	.267
P	Bob Gibson	3	13	3	1	0	0	0	1	0	0	.231	.231
P	Pete Daniels	4	12	4	1	1	0	0	2	0	0	.333	.417
P	John Coleman	3	11	2	1	0	0	0	0	3	1	.182	.182
P	Henry Jones	5	9	2	0	0	0	0	0	0	1	.222	.222
Sub	Harry Gilbert	2	8	2	1	0	0	0	0	0	0	.250	.250
Sub	John Gilbert	2	8	0	0	0	0	0	0	0	0	.000	.000
P	Duke Esper	2	7	1	0	0	0	0	0	0	0	.143	.143
Sub	Phil Routcliffe	1	4	1	1	0	0	0	1	0	1	.250	.250
P	Al Lawson	2	4	0	0	0	0	0	0	0	0	.000	.000

		G	AB	H	R	2B	3B	HR	RBI	BB	SB	BA	SA
Sub	Frank McGinn	1	4	0	0	0	0	0	0	0	0	.000	.000
Sub	Fred Truax	1	3	1	0	0	0	0	1	1	0	.333	.333
Sub	Reddy Gray	1	3	0	0	0	0	0	0	0	0	.000	.000
P	George Ziegler	1	2	0	0	0	0	0	0	0	0	.000	.000
P	John Heyner	1	2	0	0	0	0	0	0	0	0	.000	.000
Sub	Ed Clements	1	1	0	0	0	0	0	0	0	0	.000	.000
		138	4739	1088	597	160	43	20	427	408	208	.230	.294

1B	Hecker 69, Wilson 18, Hines 17, Decker 16, Roat 9, Veach 8, Laroque 2, Gumbert 1
2B	Laroque 78, Dunlap 17, Crane 15, Lytle 8, Miller 6, Youngman 6, Berger 6, H. Gilbert 2, Decker 1
SS	Sales 51, Berger 33, Laroque 31, Miller 13, Crane 7, J. Gilbert 2, Decker 1, Wilson 1, R. Gray 1, Clements 1
3B	Miller 88, Roat 44, Youngman 7, Berger 1
OF	Sunday 86, Kelty 59, Berger 41, Jordan 37, Osborne 35, Burke 31, Miller 25, Wilson 25, Hemp 21, Hines 14, Hecker 7, Lytle 7, Heard 6, Decker 4, Roat 4, Phillips 4, Gibson 2, Sowders 2, Bowman 2, Coleman 2, Laroque 1, Truax 1, McGinn 1, Routcliffe 1
C	Decker 70, Wilson 38, Berger 21, Miller 10
P	Baker 25, Sowders 15, Hecker 14, Anderson 13, Schmit 11, Gumbert 10, Phillips 10, Bowman 9, Osborne 8, Day 6, Heard 6, Smith 5, Jones 5, C. Gray 5, Daniels 4, Gibson 3, Esper 2, Coleman 2, Lawson 2, Heyner 1, Sunday 1, Ziegler 1

	G	IP	GS	CG	W	L	K	BB	SH	SV	ERA
Kirtley Baker	25	178.1	21	19	3	19	76	86	2	0	5.60
Guy Hecker	14	119.2	12	11	2	9	32	44	0	0	5.11
Dave Anderson	13	108	13	13	2	11	41	49	0	0	4.67
Bill Sowders	15	106	11	9	3	8	30	24	0	0	4.42
Crazy Schmit	11	83.1	10	9	1	9	35	42	1	0	5.83
Bill Phillips	10	82	10	9	1	9	25	29	0	0	7.57
Billy Gumbert	10	79.1	10	8	4	6	18	31	0	0	5.22
Sumner Bowman	9	70.2	7	6	2	5	22	50	0	0	6.62
Fred Osborne	8	58	5	5	0	5	14	45	0	0	8.38
Bill Day	6	50	6	6	0	6	10	24	0	0	5.22
Charlie Heard	6	44	6	5	0	6	13	32	0	0	8.39
Phenomenal Smith	5	44	5	5	1	3	15	13	0	0	3.07
Henry Jones	5	31	4	2	2	1	13	14	0	0	3.48
Charlie Gray	5	31	4	3	1	4	10	24	0	0	7.55
Pete Daniels	4	28	4	3	1	2	8	12	0	0	7.07
Duke Esper	2	17	2	2	0	2	9	10	0	0	5.29
John Coleman	2	14	2	1	0	2	3	6	0	0	9.64
Robert Gibson	3	12	3	2	0	3	3	23	0	0	17.25
Al Lawson	2	10	2	1	0	2	2	10	0	0	9.00
George Ziegler	1	6	1	0	0	1	1	0	0	0	10.50
John Heyner	1	4	0	0	0	0	1	5	0	0	13.50
Billy Sunday	1	0	0	0	0	0	0	0	0	0	—
		1176.1	138	119	23	113	381	573	3	0	5.97

WORLD'S SERIES

Brooklyn (NL) tied Louisville (AA) 3 games to 3 with 1 tie game

Game 1 at Eclipse Park (Lou), Oct. 17: Bro (Terry) 9, Lou (Stratton) 0
Game 2 at Eclipse Park (Lou), Oct. 18: Bro (Lovett) 5, Lou (Daily) 3
Game 3 at Eclipse Park (Lou), Oct. 20: Bro (Terry) 7, Lou (Meakim) 7
Game 4 at Eclipse Park (Lou), Oct. 21: Lou (Ehret) 5, Bro (Terry) 4
Game 5 at Washington Park (Bro), Oct. 25: Bro (Lovett) 7, Lou (Daily) 2
Game 6 at Washington Park (Bro), Oct. 27: Lou (Stratton) 9, Bro (Terry) 8
Game 7 at Washington Park (Bro), Oct. 28: Lou (Ehret) 6, Bro (Lovett) 2

LOUISVILLE

		G	AB	H	R	2B	3B	HR	RBI	BB	BA	SA
1B	Harry Taylor	7	30	9	6	1	0	0	2	2	.300	.333
CF	Farmer Weaver	7	27	7	4	1	0	0	4	1	.259	.296
SS/3B	Harry Raymond	7	27	4	5	1	1	0	1	2	.148	.185
LF	Charlie Hamburg	7	26	7	3	1	0	0	2	0	.269	.308
3B/RF	Jimmy Wolf	7	25	9	4	3	1	0	8	3	.360	**.560**
2B	Tim Shinnick	7	24	7	3	1	1	0	3	2	.292	.417
RF/P	Ed Daily	6	22	3	1	1	1	0	3	1	.136	.272
C	John Ryan	6	19	1	0	0	0	0	2	0	.053	.053
P/RF	Scott Stratton	4	9	2	4	1	0	0	0	2	.222	.333
P	Red Ehret	3	7	3	1	0	1	0	0	0	.429	.571
SS	Phil Tomney	2	5	1	1	0	0	0	0	3	.200	.200
C	Pete Weckbecker	1	4	0	0	0	0	0	0	0	.000	.000
C	Ned Bligh	2	3	0	0	0	0	0	0	0	.000	.000
P	George Meakim	1	2	1	0	0	0	0	0	0	.500	.500
			230	54	32	10	5	0	25	16	.235	.322

		G	IP	GS	CG	W	L	K	BB	SH	SV	ERA
Red Ehret		3	20	2	2	2	0	13	6	0	1	1.35
Scott Stratton		3	19	3	1	1	1	8	4	0	0	2.36
Ed Daily		2	17	2	2	0	2	5	8	0	0	2.65
George Meakim		1	4	0	0	0	0	1	1	0	0	0.00
			60	7	5	3	3	27	19	0	1	1.95

BROOKLYN

		G	AB	H	R	2B	3B	HR	RBI	BB	BA	SA
1B/OF	Dave Foutz	7	30	9	6	2	1	0	4	0	.300	.433
2B	Hub Collins	7	29	9	7	0	1	0	1	3	.310	.379
SS	Germany Smith	7	29	8	3	0	2	0	7	0	.276	.414
RF/3B	Oyster Burns	7	27	6	6	2	0	1	5	3	.222	.407
LF	Darby O'Brien	6	24	3	3	0	1	0	3	1	.125	.208
C/1B	Tom Daily	6	22	4	1	2	0	0	3	0	.182	.273
P/OF	Adonis Terry	6	20	5	1	1	0	0	0	6	.250	.300
CF	Patsy Donovan	5	17	8	5	1	0	0	3	2	**.471**	.529
P/OF	Tom Lovett	5	15	1	0	0	0	0	0	0	.067	.067
3B	George Pinkney	4	14	5	4	0	2	0	3	2	.357	.643
RF	Bob Caruthers	2	6	0	0	0	0	0	0	2	.000	.000
C	Doc Bushong	2	6	0	0	0	0	0	0	0	.000	.000
C	Bob Clark	1	3	2	2	0	1	0	1	0	.667	1.333
		7	242	56	42	8	8	1	30	19	.231	.343

	G	IP	GS	CG	W	L	K	BB	SH	SV	ERA
Tom Lovett	4	35	4	4	2	2	14	6	0	0	2.83
Adonis Terry	3	25	3	3	1	1	8	10	1	0	3.60
		60	7	7	3	3	22	16	1	0	3.15

AMERICAN ASSOCIATION

	W	L	PCT	HOME	ROAD	GB
1. Louisville Colonels	88	44	.667	57–13	31–31	—
2. Columbus Solons	79	55	.590	47–22	32–33	10
3. St. Louis Browns	77	58	.570	44–25	33–33	12.5
4. Toledo Maumees	68	64	.515	40–27	28–37	20
5. Rochester Hop Bitters	63	63	.500	40–22	23–41	22
6. Baltimore Orioles	15	19	.441	8–11	7–8	24
7. Syracuse Stars	55	72	.433	30–30	25–42	30.5
8. Philadelphia Athletics	54	78	.409	36–36	18–42	34
9. Brooklyn Gladiators	26	72	.265	15–22	11–50	45

	Lou	Col	StL	Tol	Roc	Bal	Syr	Phi	Bro	
Louisville	—	8	9	14	11	2	14	17	13	88
Columbus	10	—	12	13	10	4	10	11	9	79
St. Louis	11	8	—	9	12	5	10	13	9	77
Toledo	6	7	7	—	11	3	11	14	9	68
Rochester	6	9	8	6	—	1	11	12	10	63
Baltimore	1	2	2	2	5	—	1	2	*	15
Syracuse	5	7	9	9	4	2	—	7	12	55
Philadelphia	3	9	7	6	7	2	10	—	10	54
Brooklyn	2	5	4	5	3	*	5	2	—	26
	44	55	58	64	63	19	72	78	72	525

*Teams did not play one another

SEASON LEADERS

Batting Average (325 ABs)

1.	Wolf, Louisville	.363
2.	Lyons, Philadelphia	.354
3.	McCarthy, St. Louis	.350
4.	S. Johnson, Columbus	.346
5.	Childs, Syracuse	.345

Slugging Average

1.	Lyons, Philadelphia	.531
2.	Childs, Syracuse	.481
3.	Wolf, Louisville	.479
4.	McCarthy, St. Louis	.467
5.	S. Johnson, Columbus	.461

On–Base Percentage

1.	Lyons, Philadelphia	.458
2.	Swartwood, Toledo	.444
3.	Childs, Syracuse	.434
4.	McCarthy, St. Louis	.430
5.	Wright, Syracuse	.428

Total Bases

1.	Wolf, Louisville	260
2.	McCarthy, St. Louis	256
3.	S. Johnson, Columbus	248
4.	Childs, Syracuse	237
5.	Werden, Toledo	227

Home Runs

1.	Campau, St. Louis	9
2.	Cartwright, St. Louis	8
3.	Stivetts, St. Louis	7
	Lyons, Philadelphia	7
5.	Werden, Toledo	6
	McCarthy, St. Louis	6

Stolen Bases

1.	McCarthy, St. Louis	83
2.	Scheffler, Rochester	77
3.	Van Dyke, Toledo	73
4.	Welch, Phila-Balt	72
5.	Daily, Brook–Louis	62
	Shinnick, Louisville	62

Hits

1.	Wolf, Louisville	197
2.	McCarthy, St. Louis	192
3.	S. Johnson, Columbus	186
4.	Childs, Syracuse	170
5.	Taylor, Louisville	169

Runs

1.	McTamany, Columbus	140
2.	McCarthy, St. Louis	137
3.	Fuller, St. Louis	118
4.	Sneed, Tol–Colum	117
5.	Welch, Phila-Balt	116

RBI

1.	Johnson , Columbus	113
2.	Wolf, Louisville	98
3.	Childs, Syracuse	89
4.	Knowles, Rochester	84
5.	Shinnick, Louisville	82

PITCHING

Wins

1.	McMahon, Phila–Balt	36
2.	Stratton, Louisville	34
3.	Gastright, Columbus	30
4.	Barr, Rochester	28
5.	Stivetts, St. Louis	27

Losses

1.	Barr, Rochester	24
	J. Keefe, Syracuse	24
3.	McCullough, Brook-Syr	23
4.	Casey, Syracuse	22
5.	Healy, Toledo	21
	Cushman, Toledo	21
	McMahon, Phila–Balt	21

Innings

1.	McMahon, Phila–Balt	509
2.	Barr, Rochester	493.1
3.	Stratton, Louisville	431
4.	Stivetts, St. Louis	419.1
5.	Gastright, Columbus	401.1

Complete games

1.	McMahon, Phila–Balt	55
2.	Barr, Rochester	52
3.	Stratton, Louisville	44
	Healy, Toledo	44
5.	Gastright, Columbus	41
	Stivetts, St. Louis	41

Strikeouts

1.	McMahon, Phila–Balt	291
2.	Stivetts, St. Louis	289
3.	Ramsey, St. Louis	257
4.	Healy, Toledo	225
5.	Barr, Rochester	209

Winning Percentage (25 decisions)

1.	Stratton, Louisville	.708
2.	Gastright, Columbus	.682
	Chamberlain, StL–Col	.682
4.	Ehret, Louisville	.641
5.	McMahon, Phila–Balt	.632

ERA (140 Innings)

1.	Stratton, Louisville	2.36
2.	Ehret, Louisville	2.53
3.	Knauss, Columbus	2.81
4.	Chamberlain, StL–Col	2.83
5.	Healy, Toledo	2.89

Lowest On–Base Percentage

1.	Stratton, Louisville	.270
2.	Gastright, Columbus	.282
3.	Knauss, Columbus	.290
4.	Healy, Toledo	.293
5.	Ehret, Louisville	.296

FIELDING

Total Chances		
1B	Lehane, Columbus	1530
2B	Gerhardt, Brook–StL	815
3B	Reilly, Columbus	616
SS	Scheibeck, Toledo	786
OF	H. Lyons, Rochester	314
C	O'Connor, Columbus	712
P	McMahon, Phila–Balt	194

Fielding Average	
Lehane, Columbus	.982
Gerhardt, Brook-StL	.940
D. Lyons, Philadelphia	.909
McLaughlin, Syracuse	.902
Shaffer, Philadelphia	.958
O'Connor, Columbus	.962
Stratton, Louisville	.977

LOUISVILLE   Jack Chapman   Eclipse Park (I)

		G	AB	H	R	2B	3B	HR	RBI	BB	SB	BA	SA
CF	Farmer Weaver	130	557	161	101	27	9	3	67	29	45	.289	.386
1B	Harry Taylor	134	553	169	115	7	7	0	53	68	45	.306	.344
RF	Chicken Wolf	134	543	**197**	100	29	11	4	98	43	46	**.363**	.479
3B	Harry Raymond	123	521	135	91	7	4	2	51	22	18	.259	.299
2B	Tim Shinnick	133	493	126	87	16	11	1	82	62	62	.256	.339
LF	Charlie Hamburg	133	485	132	93	22	2	3	77	69	46	.272	.344
SS	Phil Tomney	108	386	107	72	21	7	1	58	43	27	.277	.376
C	John Ryan	93	337	73	43	16	4	0	35	12	6	.217	.288
P	Scott Stratton	55	189	61	29	3	5	0	24	16	8	.323	.392
P	Phil Ehret	43	146	31	11	2	1	0	10	1	1	.212	.240
Sub	Pete Weckbecker	32	101	24	17	1	0	0	11	8	7	.238	.248
P	Ed Daily	23	80	20	24	0	2	0	9	13	13	.250	.300
Sub	Ned Bligh	24	73	15	9	0	0	1	9	9	1	.205	.247
P	George Meakim	29	72	11	6	0	0	0	6	8	8	.153	.153
P	Herb Goodall	19	45	19	10	2	0	0	5	1	0	.422	.467
Sub	Dan Phelan	8	32	8	4	1	1	0	4	0	1	.250	.344
Sub	Dan O'Connor	6	26	12	3	1	1	0	5	1	5	.462	.577
Sub	Henry Easterday	7	24	2	2	0	0	0	1	2	1	.083	.083
P	Mickey Jones	3	9	4	1	0	0	0	2	2	0	.444	.444
Sub	Chief Roseman	2	8	2	0	0	0	0	0	0	0	.250	.250
Sub	Pete Sweeney	2	7	1	1	1	0	0	1	1	1	.143	.286
		136	4687	**1310**	819	156	65	15	608	410	341	**.279**	.350

1B	Taylor 118, Phelan 8, O'Connor 6, Roseman 2, Ryan 1
2B	Shinnick 130, Taylor 4
SS	Tomney 108, Taylor 12, Easterday 6, Raymond 4, Sweeney 2, Weaver 2, Ryan 1
3B	Raymond 119, Wolf 12, Shinnick 3, Weaver 1, Easterday 1
OF	Hamburg 133, Weaver 127, Wolf 123, Daily 11, Stratton 5, Ryan 3, Meakim 1, Goodall 1
C	Ryan 89, Weckbecker 32, Bligh 24, Taylor 1
P	Stratton 50, Ehret 43, Meakim 28, Goodall 18, Daily 12, Jones 3

	G	IP	GS	CG	W	L	K	BB	SH	SV	ERA
Scott Stratton	50	431	49	44	34	14	207	61	4	0	**2.36**
Red Ehret	43	359	38	35	25	14	174	79	4	2	2.53
George Meakim	28	192	21	16	12	7	123	63	3	1	2.91
Herb Goodall	18	109	13	8	8	5	46	51	1	**4**	3.39
Ed Daily	12	93	10	9	6	3	31	30	1	0	1.94
Mickey Jones	3	22	3	2	2	0	6	9	0	0	3.27
—1 forfeit W vs St. Louis on April 20; 1 forfeit L vs Syracuse on August 3—											
	1206	134	114	87	43	587	**293**	13	7	**2.57**	

COLUMBUS   **Al Buckenberger**   **Recreation Park (II)**

		G	AB	H	R	2B	3B	HR	RBI	BB	SB	BA	SA
LF	Spud Johnson	135	538	186	106	23	18	1	**113**	48	43	.346	.461
3B	Charlie Reilly	137	530	141	75	23	3	4	77	35	43	.266	.343
1B	Mickey Lehane	140	512	108	54	19	5	0	56	43	13	.211	.268
2B	Jack Crooks	135	485	107	86	5	4	1	62	96	57	.221	.254
RF	Jack Sneed	128	484	141	114	13	15	2	65	63	39	.291	.393
CF	Jim McTamany	125	466	120	**140**	27	7	1	48	**112**	43	.258	.352
C	Jack O'Connor	121	457	148	89	14	10	2	66	38	29	.324	.411
Sub	Jack Doyle	77	298	80	47	17	7	2	44	13	27	.268	.393
SS	Henry Easterday	58	197	31	25	5	1	1	17	23	5	.157	.208
SS	Bobby Wheelock	52	190	45	24	6	1	1	16	25	34	.237	.295
P	Hank Gastright	48	169	36	18	2	2	0	21	13	1	.213	.249
P	John Easton	41	107	19	14	0	2	0	6	10	6	.178	.215
P	Frank Knauss	37	106	24	18	0	2	1	14	12	6	.226	.292
P	Icebox Chamberlain	25	65	15	8	3	0	0	4	7	2	.231	.277
Sub	Sam Nichol	14	56	9	7	0	0	0	4	2	3	.161	.161
P	Bill Widner	13	41	8	3	0	0	0	2	2	2	.195	.195
Sub	Ned Bligh	8	29	6	2	2	0	0	5	2	0	.207	.276
Sub	John Munyan	2	7	1	1	0	0	0	0	0	0	.143	.143
P	Al Mays	1	3	0	0	0	0	0	0	1	0	.000	.000
P	Tom Ford	1	1	0	0	0	0	0	0	0	0	.000	.000
		140	4741	1225	831	159	77	16	620	**545**	353	.258	.335

1B   Lehane 140
2B   Crooks 133, Doyle 6, O'Connor 2, Reilly 1, Easton 1
SS   Easterday 58, Wheelock 52, Doyle 25, O'Connor 8, Sneed 2, Easton 2
3B   Reilly 130, Doyle 3, Crooks 2, O'Connor 1
OF   Johnson 135, Sneed 126, McTamany 125, Nichol 14, Doyle 9, O'Connor 9, Munyan 2, Easton 2, Crooks 1
C   O'Connor 106, Doyle 38, Bligh 8
P   Gastright 48, Easton 37, Knauss 37, Chamberlain 25, Widner 13, Mays 1, Ford 1

	G	IP	GS	CG	W	L	K	BB	SH	SV	ERA
Hank Gastright	48	401.1	45	41	30	14	199	135	4	0	2.94
Frank Knauss	37	275.2	34	28	17	12	148	106	3	2	2.81
Jack Easton	37	255.2	29	23	15	14	147	125	0	1	3.52
Icebox Chamberlain	25	175	21	19	12	6	114	70	6*	0	2.21
Bill Widner	13	96	10	8	4	8	14	24	1	0	3.28
Al Mays	1	9	1	1	0	1	2	8	0	0	8.00
Tom Ford	1	2	0	0	0	0	0	3	0	0	0.00
		—1 forfeit W vs Brooklyn on July 27—									
		1214.2	140	120	78	55	624	471	**14**	3	2.99

ST. LOUIS   **Tommy McCarthy (14–10)**   **Chief Roseman (17–18)**   **Count Campau (26–14)**
Joe Gerhardt (20–16)   **Sportsman's Park (I)**

		G	AB	H	R	2B	3B	HR	RBI	BB	SB	BA	SA
RF	Tommy McCarthy	133	548	192	137	28	9	6	69	66	83	.350	.467
SS	Shorty Fuller	130	526	146	118	9	9	1	40	73	60	.278	.335
CF	Charlie Duffee	98	378	104	68	11	7	3	54	37	20	.275	.365
C	John Munyan	96	342	91	61	15	7	4	42	32	11	.266	.386
LF	Count Campau	75	314	101	68	9	12	9	75	26	36	.322	.513
Sub	Chief Roseman	80	302	103	47	26	0	2	58	30	7	.341	.447
1B	Ed Cartwright	75	300	90	70	12	4	8	60	29	26	.300	.447
2B	Bill Higgins	67	258	65	39	6	2	0	35	24	7	.252	.291
Sub	Tom Gettinger	58	227	54	31	7	5	3	30	20	8	.238	.352
P	Jack Stivetts	67	226	65	36	15	6	7	43	16	2	.288	.500
3B	Pete Sweeney	49	190	34	23	3	2	0	10	17	8	.179	.216
P	Toad Ramsey	44	145	33	17	6	1	0	11	5	0	.228	.283
Sub	Joe Gerhardt	37	125	32	15	0	0	1	11	9	5	.256	.280
Sub	Jake Wells	30	105	25	17	3	0	0	12	10	1	.238	.267
Sub	Dusty Miller	26	96	21	17	5	3	1	10	8	4	.219	.365
P	Bob Hart	27	78	15	7	1	0	1	8	9	1	.192	.244
Sub	Billy Earle	22	73	17	16	3	1	0	12	7	6	.233	.301
Sub	Jumbo Davis	21	71	18	8	3	1	0	13	9	5	.254	.324
Sub	Billy Klusman	15	65	18	9	4	1	1	11	1	1	.277	.415
Sub	John Kerins	18	63	8	8	2	0	0	3	8	2	.127	.159
Sub	Pat Hartnett	14	53	10	6	2	1	0	4	6	1	.189	.264
Sub	Mike Trost	17	51	13	10	2	0	1	7	6	4	.255	.353
P	Bill Whitrock	16	48	7	7	3	0	0	3	2	0	.146	.208
Sub	Jim Donnelly	11	42	14	11	0	0	0	3	8	5	.333	.333
Sub	Ed Herr	12	41	9	5	2	1	0	1	5	2	.220	.317
P	Joe Neale	11	30	2	4	0	0	0	1	3	0	.067	.067
Sub	Jerry Kane	8	25	5	3	0	0	0	2	2	0	.200	.200
Sub	Dad Meek	4	16	5	3	0	0	0	1	0	1	.313	.313
P	Icebox Chamberlain	5	15	2	1	0	0	0	2	0	0	.133	.133
Sub	Gus Creely	4	15	0	0	0	0	0	0	0	1	.000	.000
Sub	Ed Pabst	4	14	2	1	0	1	0	0	0	0	.143	.286
P	George Nicol	3	7	2	4	1	0	0	1	4	0	.286	.429
Sub	Joe Burke	2	6	4	3	0	0	0	2	1	0	.667	.667
Sub	Jim Adams	1	4	1	0	0	0	0	0	0	0	.250	.250
Sub	Frank Millard	1	1	0	0	0	0	0	0	1	0	.000	.000
		139	4800	1308	870	178	73	48	634	474	307	.273	**.370**

1B Cartwright 75, Roseman 22, Kerins 17, Hartnett 14, Kane 5, Stivetts 3, Sweeney 3, Campau 1
2B Higgins 67, Sweeney 23, Gerhardt 20, Klusman 15, Herr 7, Munyan 5, Earle 1, McCarthy 1, Millard 1
SS Fuller 130, Creely 4, Miller 3, Duffee 1, Munyan 1, Earle 1
3B Duffee 33, McCarthy 32, Sweeney 21, Davis 21, Gerhardt 17, Donnelly 11, Munyan 3, Burke 2, Earle 1, Campau 1, Herr 1
OF McCarthy 102, Campau 74, Duffee 66, Roseman 58, Gettinger 58, Miller 24, Stivetts 10, Munyan 7, Herr 4, Trost 4, Pabst 4, Wells 3, Earle 3, Sweeney 2, Neale 1, Whitrock 1, Hart 1
C   Munyan 83, Wells 28, Earle 18, Trost 13, Meek 4, Kane 4, Kerins 1, Adams 1
P   Stivetts 54, Ramsey 44, Hart 26, Whitrock 16, Neale 10, Chamberlain 5, Nicol 3

	G	IP	GS	CG	W	L	K	BB	SH	SV	ERA
Jack Stivetts	54	419.1	46	41	27	21	289	179	3	0	3.52
Toad Ramsey	44	348.2	40	34	23	17	257	102	1	0	3.69
Bob Hart	26	201.1	24	20	12	8	95	66	0	0	3.67
Bill Whitrock	16	105	11	10	5	6	39	40	0	1	3.51
Joe Neale	10	69	9	8	5	3	23	15	0	0	3.39
Icebox Chamberlain	5	35	5	3	3	1	14	26	0*	0	5.91
George Nicol	3	17	3	2	2	1	16	19	0	0	4.76
—1 forfeit L vs Louisville on April 20—											
	1195.1	138	118	77	57	**733**	447	4	1	3.67	

TOLEDO   Charlie Morton   Speranza Park

		G	AB	H	R	2B	3B	HR	RBI	BB	SB	BA	SA
2B	Parson Nicholson	134	523	140	78	16	11	4	72	42	46	.268	.363
LF	Bill Van Dyke	129	502	129	74	14	11	2	54	25	73	.257	.341
1B	Perry Werden	128	498	147	113	22	**20**	6	72	78	59	.295	.456
3B	Billy Alvord	116	495	135	69	13	16	2	52	22	21	.273	.376
SS	Frank Scheibeck	134	485	117	72	13	5	1	49	76	57	.241	.295
RF	Ed Swartwood	126	462	151	106	23	11	3	64	80	53	.327	.444
CF	White Wings Tebeau	94	381	102	71	16	10	1	36	51	55	.268	.370
C	Harry Sage	81	275	41	40	8	4	2	25	29	10	.149	.229
P	Charlie Sprague	55	199	47	25	5	6	1	19	16	10	.236	.337
P	Egyptian Healy	48	156	34	27	7	4	1	10	15	7	.218	.333
P	Ed Cushman	40	130	13	9	0	2	0	10	10	4	.100	.131
P	Fred Smith	38	126	21	11	7	1	0	10	8	4	.167	.238
C	Emmett Rogers	34	110	19	18	3	3	0	7	14	2	.173	.255
Sub	Tub Welch	35	108	31	15	3	1	1	14	8	7	.287	.361
Sub	John Peltz	20	73	18	8	2	2	0	13	3	7	.247	.329
Sub	Jack Sneed	9	30	6	3	0	0	0	4	8	5	.200	.200
P	Ed O'Neill	2	9	0	0	0	0	0	0	0	0	.000	.000
P	Dan Abbott	3	7	1	0	0	1	0	1	0	1	.143	.429
P	Babe Doty	1	3	0	0	0	0	0	0	1	0	.000	.000
Sub	Floyd Ritter	1	3	0	0	0	0	0	0	0	0	.000	.000
		134	4575	1152	739	152	**108**	24	512	486	**421**	.252	.348

1B   Werden 124, Welsh 10, Healy 2
2B   Nicholson 134, Van Dyke 2
SS   Scheibeck 134
3B   Alvord 116, Van Dyke 18
OF   Swartwood 126, Van Dyke 110, Tebeau 94, Sprague 40, Peltz 20, Sneed 9, Werden 5, Smith 3, Sage 1, Rogers 1
C   Sage 80, Rogers 34, Welsh 25, Ritter 1, Nicholson 1, Van Dyke 1
P   Healy 46, Cushman 40, Smith 35, Sprague 19, Abbott 3, O'Neil 2, Swartwood 1, Doty 1, Tebeau 1

	G	IP	GS	CG	W	L	K	BB	SH	SV	ERA
Egyptian Healy	46	389	46	44	22	21	225	127	2	0	2.89
Ed Cushman	40	315.2	38	34	17	21	125	107	0	1	4.19
Fred Smith	35	286	34	31	19	13	116	90	2	0	3.27
Charlie Sprague	19	122.2	12	9	9	5	59	78	0	0	3.89
Ed O'Neil	2	16	2	2	0	1	2	13	0	0	7.88
Dan Abbott	3	13	1	1	0	2	1	8	0	1	6.23
Babe Doty	1	9	1	1	1	0	4	1	0	0	1.00
White Wings Tebeau	1	5	0	0	0	0	0	5	0	0	9.00
Ed Swartwood	1	3	0	0	0	0	1	0	0	0	3.00
—1 forfeit L vs Philadelphia on July 2—											
	1159.1	134	122	68	63	533	429	4	2	3.56	

ROCHESTER Pat Powers   **Culver Field (I)**

		G	AB	H	R	2B	3B	HR	RBI	BB	SB	BA	SA
LF	Harry Lyons	133	**584**	152	83	11	11	3	58	27	47	.260	.332
3B	Jimmy Knowles	123	491	138	83	12	8	5	84	59	55	.281	.369
RF	Ted Scheffler	119	445	109	111	12	6	3	34	78	77	.245	.319
2B	Bill Greenwood	124	437	97	76	11	6	2	41	48	40	.222	.288
CF	Sandy Griffin	107	407	125	85	28	4	5	53	50	21	.307	.432
C	Deacon McGuire	87	331	99	46	16	4	4	53	21	8	.299	.408
1B	Tom O'Brien	73	273	52	36	6	5	0	31	30	6	.190	.249
SS	Marr Phillips	64	257	53	18	8	0	0	34	16	10	.206	.237
C	Dave McKeough	62	218	49	38	5	0	0	20	29	14	.225	.248
P	Bob Barr	57	201	36	22	2	0	2	15	13	1	.179	.219
Sub	John Grim	50	192	51	30	6	9	2	34	7	14	.266	.422
Sub	Jim Field	52	188	38	30	7	5	4	25	21	8	.202	.356
P	Will Callahan	48	159	23	16	4	2	1	14	8	2	.145	.214
Sub	Leo Smith	35	112	21	11	1	3	0	11	14	1	.188	.250
Sub	Dan Burke	32	102	22	14	1	0	0	9	17	2	.216	.225
P	Cannonball Titcomb	21	75	8	3	0	1	0	6	3	0	.107	.133
P	Bob Miller	15	40	6	3	1	0	0	2	3	0	.150	.175
P	John Fitzgerald	11	31	6	1	0	0	0	2	2	1	.194	.194
P	Henry Blauvelt	2	6	3	3	0	0	0	1	0	3	.500	.500
Sub	Phil Reccius	1	4	0	0	0	0	0	1	0	0	.000	.000
		133	4553	1088	709	131	64	31	528	446	310	.239	.316

1B	O'Brien 68, Field 51, McGuire 15, Grim 2, Burke 2
2B	Greenwood 123, O'Brien 8, Grim 4, McKeough 2, Titcomb 1, Griffin 1
SS	Phillips 64, Smith 35, Grim 21, McKeough 13, Greenwood 1
3B	Knowles 123, Grim 8, Lyons 2, McKeough 1, Titcomb 1
OF	Lyons 132, Scheffler 119, Griffin 107, Burke 29, Callahan 13, McGuire 3, Miller 3, Grim 3, Reccius 1
C	McGuire 71, McKeough 47, Grim 15, Burke 4, Scheffler 1, Lyons 1
P	Barr 57, Callahan 37, Titcomb 20, Miller 13, Fitzgerald 11, Field 2, Blauvelt 2, McGuire 1, Grim 1, Lyons 1

	G	IP	GS	CG	W	L	K	BB	SH	SV	ERA
Bob Barr	57	493.1	54	52	28	**24**	209	**219**	3	0	3.25
Will Callahan	37	296.1	36	31	18	15	127	125	0	0	3.28
Cannonball Titcomb #	20	168.2	19	19	10	9	73	97	1	0	3.74
Bob Miller	13	92.1	12	11	3	7	20	26	0	1	4.29
John Fitzgerald	11	78	11	8	3	8	35	45	1	1	4.04
Henry Blauvelt	2	12.1	0	0	0	0	5	8	0	0	10.22
Jim Field	2	9.2	1	1	1	0	2	4	0	1	2.79
Deacon McGuire	1	4	0	0	0	0	1	1	0	0	6.75
Harry Lyons	1	3.2	0	0	0	0	2	1	0	0	12.27
John Grim	1	3.1	0	0	0	0	3	4	0	0	0.00
		1161.2	133	**122**	63	63	477	530	5	2	3.56

No-hit game 7–0 vs Syracuse, September 15

BALTIMORE   **Billy Barnie**   **Oriole Park (II)**

		G	AB	H	R	2B	3B	HR	RBI	BB	SB	BA	SA
SS	Irv Ray	38	139	50	28	6	2	1	20	15	11	.360	.453
LF	Joe Sommer	38	129	33	13	4	2	0	23	13	10	.256	.318
1B	Tom Power	38	125	26	11	3	1	0	6	13	6	.208	.248
3B	Pete Gilbert	29	100	28	25	2	1	1	18	10	12	.280	.350
RF	Bill Johnson	24	95	28	15	2	3	0	6	7	8	.295	.379
2B	Reddy Mack	26	95	27	14	3	5	0	11	10	7	.284	.421
CF	Dan Long	21	77	12	19	0	0	0	2	14	16	.156	.156
Sub	Pop Tate	19	71	13	7	1	1	0	6	4	3	.183	.225
Sub	Curt Welch	19	68	9	16	4	0	0	5	9	8	.132	.191
C	George Townsend	18	67	16	6	4	1	0	9	4	3	.239	.328
P	Les German	17	51	6	7	1	0	0	3	8	5	.118	.137
Sub	Wilbert Robinson	14	48	13	7	1	0	0	4	3	1	.271	.292
P	Sadie McMahon	12	39	4	4	0	0	0	1	1	2	.103	.103
Sub	Joe McGuckin	11	37	4	2	0	0	0	2	6	3	.108	.108
Sub	Belden Hill	9	30	5	3	2	0	0	2	3	6	.167	.233
P	Mike O'Rourke	8	26	3	5	1	0	0	1	5	0	.115	.154
P	Mike Morrison	4	9	1	0	0	0	0	0	0	0	.111	.111
P	Norm Baker	2	7	0	0	0	0	0	0	0	0	.000	.000
		38	1213	278	182	34	16	2	119	125	101	.229	.289

1B   Power 26, Tate 8, Robinson 3, Welch 2
2B   Mack 26, Power 12
SS   Ray 38
3B   Gilbert 29, Hill 9
OF   Sommer 38, Johnson 24, Long 21, Welch 17, McGuckin 11, O'Rourke 3
C   Townsend 18, Robinson 11, Tate 11
P   German 17, McMahon 12, O'Rourke 5, Morrison 4, Baker 2

	G	IP	GS	CG	W	L	K	BB	SH	SV	ERA
Les German	17	132.1	16	15	5	11	37	54	0	0	4.83
Sadie McMahon	**12***	**99***	**11***	**11***	**7***	3	**66***	33	1	0	3.00
Mike O'Rourke	5	41	5	5	1	2	8	10	0	0	3.95
Mike Morrison	4	26	4	3	1	2	13	20	0	0	3.81
Norm Baker	2	17	2	2	1	1	10	6	0	0	3.71
		315.1	38	36	15	19	134	123	1	0	4.03

SYRACUSE   George Frazier (51–65)   Wally Fessenden (4–7)   Star Park (II)

		G	AB	H	R	2B	3B	HR	RBI	BB	SB	BA	SA
LF	Bones Ely	119	496	130	72	16	6	0	64	31	44	.262	.319
2B	Cupid Childs	126	493	170	109	33	14	2	89	72	56	.345	.481
1B	Mox McQuery	122	461	142	64	17	6	2	55	53	26	.308	.384
CF	Ratsy Wright	88	348	106	82	10	6	0	29	69	30	.305	.368
3B	Tim O'Rourke	87	332	94	48	13	6	1	46	36	22	.283	.367
SS	Barney McLaughlin	86	329	87	43	8	1	2	40	47	13	.264	.313
C	Grant Briggs	86	316	57	44	6	5	0	21	16	7	.180	.231
RF	Pat Friel	62	261	65	51	8	2	3	21	17	34	.249	.330
P	Dan Casey	46	160	26	11	5	2	0	11	6	3	.163	.219
P	John Keefe	43	157	30	10	0	0	0	5	3	0	.191	.191
Sub	Hank Simon	38	156	47	33	5	3	2	23	17	12	.301	.410
C	Tom O'Rourke	41	153	33	16	8	0	0	12	12	2	.216	.268
Sub	Mike Dorgan	33	139	30	19	8	0	0	18	16	8	.216	.273
P	Mike Morrison	34	120	29	17	3	4	1	12	6	3	.242	.358
Sub	Joe Battin	29	119	25	15	2	1	0	13	8	8	.210	.244
Sub	Herman Pitz	29	95	21	17	0	0	0	3	13	14	.221	.221
Sub	Pat Dealey	18	66	12	9	1	0	0	4	5	4	.182	.197
Sub	George Proeser	13	53	13	11	1	1	1	6	10	1	.245	.358
P	Ed Mars	16	51	14	9	1	1	0	9	5	0	.275	.333
Sub	Ducky Hemp	9	33	5	1	1	0	0	1	0	1	.152	.182
Sub	John Leighton	7	27	8	6	2	0	0	0	3	2	.296	.370
P	Bill Sullivan	6	22	2	2	0	0	0	1	1	0	.091	.091
Sub	Dan Burke	9	20	0	1	0	0	0	0	5	0	.000	.000
Sub	John Peltz	5	17	3	2	1	1	0	2	3	0	.176	.353
P	Toby Lyons	3	12	4	3	0	0	0	0	0	0	.333	.333
P	Charlie McCullough	3	9	1	1	0	0	0	0	3	2	.111	.111
P	Ezra Lincoln	3	8	0	0	0	0	0	0	0	0	.000	.000
P	Frank Keffer	2	7	1	1	0	0	0	0	0	0	.143	.143
Sub	Louis Graff	1	5	2	0	1	0	0	3	0	0	.400	.600
Sub	Bill Higgins	1	4	1	1	1	0	0	1	0	0	.250	.500
		128	4469	1158	698	151	59	14	487	457	292	.259	.329

1B   McQuery 122, Ely 4, Tom O'Rourke 1
2B   Childs 125, Ely 2, Higgins 1
SS   McLaughlin 86, Ely 36, Briggs 4, Childs 1, Morrison 1, Pitz 1
3B   Tim O'Rourke 87, Battin 29, Dealey 6, Briggs 5, Ely 1
OF   Wright 88, Ely 78, Friel 62, Simon 38, Dorgan 33, Briggs 33, Morrison 16, Proeser 13, Hemp 9, Leighton 7, Peltz 5, Dealey 2, Casey 1, Pitz 1, Sullivan 1
C   Briggs 46, Tom O'Rourke 40, Pitz 27, Dealey 10, Burke 9, Graff 1
P   Casey 45, Keefe 43, Morrison 17, Mars 16, Sullivan 6, McCullough 3, Lyons 3, Lincoln 3, Keffer 2, Ely 1

	G	IP	GS	CG	W	L	K	BB	SH	SV	ERA
Dan Casey	45	360.2	42	40	19	22	169	165	2	0	4.14
John Keefe	43	352.1	41	36	17	**24**	120	148	2	0	4.32
Mike Morrison	17	127	14	13	6	9	69	81	1	0	5.88
Ed Mars	16	121.1	14	14	9	5	59	49	0	0	4.67
Bill Sullivan	6	42	6	4	1	4	13	27	0	0	7.93
Charlie McCullough	3	26	3	3	1	2	8	14	0	0	7.27
Toby Lyons	3	22.1	3	2	0	2	6	21	0	0	10.48
Ezra Lincoln	3	20	3	2	0	3	6	4	0	0	10.35
Frank Keffer	2	16	1	1	1	1	4	9	0	0	5.63
Bones Ely	1	2	0	0	0	0	0	0	0	0	22.50
	—1 forfeit W vs Louisville on August 3—										
	1089.2	127	115	54	72	454	518	5	0	4.98

PHILADELPHIA Bill Sharsig **Jefferson Street Grounds**

		G	AB	H	R	2B	3B	HR	RBI	BB	SB	BA	SA
LF	Blondie Purcell	110	463	128	110	28	3	2	59	43	48	.276	.363
1B	Jack O'Brien	109	433	113	80	24	14	4	80	52	31	.261	.409
SS	Ben Conroy	117	404	69	45	13	1	0	21	45	17	.171	.208
CF	Curt Welch	103	396	106	100	21	4	2	40	49	64	.268	.356
RF	Orator Shaffer	100	390	110	55	15	5	1	58	47	29	.282	.354
3B	Denny Lyons	88	339	120	79	29	5	7	73	57	21	.354	**.531**
C	Wilbert Robinson	82	329	78	32	13	4	4	42	16	20	.237	.337
2B	Taylor Shaffer	69	261	45	28	3	4	0	21	28	19	.172	.215
Sub	Joe Kappel	56	208	50	29	8	1	1	22	20	12	.240	.303
P	Sadie McMahon	49	175	40	27	5	1	2	19	7	2	.229	.303
P	Ed Green	39	126	15	15	1	1	0	5	13	7	.119	.143
Sub	George Carman	28	97	17	9	2	0	0	7	8	5	.175	.196
Sub	Kid Baldwin	24	90	21	5	1	2	0	12	4	2	.233	.289
Sub	John Riddle	27	85	7	7	0	1	0	2	17	4	.082	.106
Sub	Joe Daly	21	75	21	8	4	1	0	7	3	1	.280	.360
Sub	Andy Knox	21	75	19	6	3	0	0	8	9	5	.253	.293
P	Ed Seward	26	72	10	7	4	0	0	2	8	3	.139	.194
Sub	Henry Easterday	19	68	10	17	1	0	1	3	10	4	.147	.206
P	Duke Esper	18	61	18	11	2	2	0	11	2	1	.295	.393
Sub	Pete Sweeney	14	49	8	5	1	1	0	0	7	0	.163	.224
Sub	Al Sauters	14	41	4	1	0	0	0	0	11	0	.098	.098
Sub	Charlie Snyder	9	33	9	5	1	0	0	4	2	0	.273	.303
P	Ed O'Neil	10	31	5	0	0	0	0	2	3	0	.125	.125
P	Charlie Stecher	10	29	7	3	0	1	0	0	1	0	.241	.310
Sub	Ed Pabst	8	25	10	7	2	0	0	3	5	3	.400	.480
Sub	Bart Cantz	5	22	1	1	0	0	0	1	0	0	.045	.045
P	Jim Whitney	7	21	5	3	0	0	0	1	1	0	.238	.238
Sub	Henry Meyers	5	19	3	2	0	0	0	1	1	2	.158	.158
Sub	George Crawford	5	17	2	1	0	0	0	3	0	1	.118	.118
P	Mickey Hughes	6	16	2	2	0	0	0	1	2	2	.125	.125
Sub	Dennis Fitzgerald	2	8	2	0	0	0	0	0	0	0	.250	.250
Sub	Pete Hasney	2	7	1	1	0	0	0	0	1	0	.143	.143
Sub	Sam Campbell	2	5	0	0	0	0	0	0	1	0	.000	.000
P	Billy Price	1	4	1	0	0	0	0	0	0	0	.250	.250
P	Horace Helmbold	1	3	0	1	0	0	0	0	0	1	.000	.000
P	Harry Stine	1	3	0	0	0	0	0	0	1	0	.000	.000
Sub	Bob Stafford	1	2	0	0	0	0	0	0	0	0	.000	.000
Sub	John McBride	1	2	0	0	0	0	0	0	0	0	.000	.000
P	John Sterling	1	2	0	0	0	0	0	0	0	0	.000	.000
Sub	Ham Sweigert	1	1	0	0	0	0	0	0	1	1	.000	.000
Sub	Bill Collins	1	1	0	0	0	0	0	0	0	0	.000	.000
Sub	? Macey	1	1	0	0	0	0	0	0	0	0	.000	.000
Sub	? Lackey	1	1	0	0	0	0	0	0	0	0	.000	.000
		132	4490	1057	702	**181**	51	24	508	475	305	.235	.314

1B O'Brien 109, Knox 21, O. Shaffer 3, McMahon 1
2B T. Shaffer 69, Conroy 42, Sweeney 9, Green 2, Kappel 2, Carman 2, Campbell 2, Sauters 2, Riddle 2
SS Conroy 74, Easterday 19, Kappel 18, Carman 15, Green 3, Fitzgerald 2, Collins 1, Crawford 1
3B Lyons 88, Sauters 11, Kappel 11, Green 10, Meyers 5, Baldwin 5, Sweeney 2, O'Neil 1, Stecher 1, Carman 1, Riddle 1
OF Purcell 110, Welch 103, O. Shaffer 98, Kappel 23, Daly 14, Riddle 12, Carman 10, Pabst 8, Seward 6, Snyder 5, Crawford 4, Sweeney 4, O'Neil 3, Sauters 2, Hasney 2, Conroy 1, O'Brien 1, Whitney 1, Sweigert 1, Stafford 1, McBride 1, Hughes 1
C Robinson 82, Baldwin 19, Riddle 13, Daly 9, Snyder 5, Cantz 5, Kappel 3, O'Brien 1, Macey 1
P McMahon 48, Green 25, Seward 21, Esper 18, Stecher 10, O'Neil 6, Hughes 6, Whitney 6, Helmbold 1, Stine 1, Price 1, Sterling 1, Welch 1, Lackey 1

	G	IP	GS	CG	W	L	K	BB	SH	SV	ERA
Sadie McMahon	48*	410*	46*	44*	29*	18	225*	133	0	1	3.34
Ed Green	25	191	22	20	7	15	56	94	1	1	5.80
Ed Seward	21	154	19	15	5	12	55	72	1	0	4.73
Duke Esper	18	143.2	16	14	8	9	61	67	1	0	4.89
Charlie Stecher	10	68	10	9	0	10	18	60	0	0	10.32
Ed O'Neil	6	52	6	6	0	6	17	32	0	0	9.69
Mickey Hughes	6	41.1	5	4	1	3	15	21	0	0	5.44
Jim Whitney	6	40	4	3	2	2	6	11	0	0	5.18
Bill Price	1	9	1	1	1	0	1	7	0	0	2.00
Harry Stine	1	8	1	1	0	1	1	4	0	0	9.00
Horace Helmbold	1	7	1	1	0	1	3	6	0	0	14.14
John Sterling	1	5	1	1	0	1	1	4	0	0	21.60
? Lackey	1	2	0	0	0	0	1	3	0	0	9.00
Curt Welch	1	1	0	0	0	0	1	0	0	0	54.00
			—1 forfeit W vs Toledo on July 2—								
	1132	132	119	54	78	461	514	3	2	5.22

BROOKLYN   Jim Kennedy   Ridgewood Park (through June 8)
Polo Grounds (II) (starting June 9)

		G	AB	H	R	2B	3B	HR	RBI	BB	SB	BA	SA
RF	Ed Daily	91	394	94	68	15	7	1	39	24	49	.239	.320
1B	Billy O'Brien	96	388	108	47	25	8	4	67	28	5	.278	.415
CF	John Peltz	98	384	87	55	9	6	1	33	32	10	.227	.289
LF	Hank Simon	89	373	96	66	17	11	0	38	34	23	.257	.362
2B	Joe Gerhardt	99	369	75	34	10	4	2	40	30	9	.203	.268
UT	Frank Bowes	61	232	51	28	5	2	0	24	7	11	.220	.259
SS	Candy Nelson	60	223	56	44	3	2	0	12	35	12	.251	.283
C	Herman Pitz	61	189	26	26	0	0	0	6	45	25	.138	.138
Sub	Frank Fennelly	45	178	44	40	8	3	2	18	30	6	.247	.360
C	Jim Toy	44	160	29	11	3	0	0	7	11	2	.181	.200
3B	Jumbo Davis	38	142	43	33	9	2	2	28	15	10	.303	.437
P	Mike Mattimore	33	129	17	14	1	1	0	7	16	11	.132	.155
P	Charlie McCullough	26	86	2	2	0	0	0	1	3	1	.023	.023
Sub	Fred Siefke	16	58	8	1	2	0	0	3	5	2	.138	.172
P	Bob Murphy	16	50	9	4	2	0	1	0	3	0	.180	.280
Sub	Pat O'Connell	11	40	9	7	2	1	0	3	7	3	.225	.325
P	Tom Ford	10	30	1	1	0	0	0	0	1	1	.033	.033
P	Steve Toole	6	20	6	2	3	0	0	2	0	0	.300	.450
P	Jim Powers	4	13	2	5	0	0	0	0	1	1	.154	.154
Sub	Hi Church	3	9	1	1	0	0	0	0	0	0	.111	.111
P	Jack Lynch	1	4	3	2	2	0	0	0	1	0	.750	1.250
P	Gus Williams	2	4	2	1	0	0	0	0	0	1	.500	.500
		100	3475	769	492	116	47	13	328	328	182	.221	.293

1B   O'Brien 96, Bowes 3, O'Connell 1
2B   Gerhardt 99, Pitz 1
SS   Nelson 57, Fennelly 38, Ford 4, Bowes 2, Pitz 1
3B   Davis 38, Siefke 16, Pitz 16, Bowes 13, O'Connell 10, Fennelly 7
OF   Peltz 98, Simon 89, Daily 64, Bowes 19, Mattimore 14, Pitz 9, Murphy 5, Nelson 4, Church 3
C   Toy 44, Pitz 34, Bowes 25
P   Daily 27, McCullough 26, Mattimore 19, Murphy 12, Ford 7, Toole 6, Powers 4, Williams 2, Lynch 1

	G	IP	GS	CG	W	L	K	BB	SH	SV	ERA
Ed Daily	27	235.2	27	27	10	15	82	93	0	0	4.05
Charlie McCullough	26	215.2	25	24	4	21	61	102	0	0	4.59
Mike Mattimore	19	178.1	19	19	6	13	33	76	0	0	4.54
Bob Murphy	12	96	12	10	3	9	26	46	0	0	5.72
Steve Toole	6	53.1	6	6	2	4	10	39	0	0	4.05
Tom Ford	7	49	6	6	0	6	12	32	0	0	5.14
Jim Powers	4	30	2	2	1	2	3	16	0	0	5.70
Gus Williams	2	12	2	1	0	1	2	12	0	0	7.50
Jack Lynch	1	9	1	1	0	1	1	5	0	0	12.00
—1 forfeit L vs Columbus on July 27—											
		879	100	96	26	72	230	421	0	0	4.71

PLAYERS LEAGUE

	W	L	PCT	HOME	ROAD	GB
1. Boston Reds	81	48	.628	48–21	33–27	—
2. Brooklyn Ward's Wonders	76	56	.576	46–19	30–37	6.5
3. New York Giants	74	57	.565	47–19	27–38	8
4. Chicago Pirates	75	62	.547	46–23	29–39	10
5. Philadelphia Quakers	68	63	.519	35–30	33–33	14
6. Pittsburgh Burghers	60	68	.469	37–28	23–40	20.5
7. Cleveland Infants	55	75	.423	31–30	24–45	26.5
8. Buffalo Bisons	36	96	.273	23–42	13–54	46.5

	Bos	Bro	NY	Chi	Phi	Pit	Cle	Buf	
Boston	—	11	12	12	10	10	12	14	81
Brooklyn	7		7	10	14	14	12	12	76
New York	8	10	—	9	5	14	11	17	74
Chicago	8	9	9	—	10	11	13	15	75
Philadelphia	6	6	12	10	—	7	11	16	68
Pittsburgh	5	6	6	9	12	—	9	13	60
Cleveland	8	8	8	7	8	7	—	9	55
Buffalo	6	6	3	5	4	5	7	—	36
	48	56	57	62	63	68	75	96	525

SEASON LEADERS

Batting Average (330 ABs)

1.	Browning, Cleveland	.3732
2.	Orr, Brooklyn	.3728
3.	O'Rourke, New York	.360
4.	Connor, New York	.349
5.	Ryan, Chicago	.340

Slugging Average

1.	Connor, New York	.548
2.	Ewing, New York	.545
3.	Orr, Brooklyn	.537
4.	Beckley, Pittsburgh	.535
5.	Browning, Cleveland	.517

On–Base Percentage

1.	Brouthers, Boston	.466
2.	Browning, Cleveland	.459
3.	Connor, New York	.450
4.	Y. Robinson, Pittburgh	.434
5.	Gore, New York	.432

Total Bases

1.	Shindle, Philadelphia	281
2.	Duffy, Chicago	280
3.	Beckley, Pittsburgh	276
4.	H. Richardson, Boston	274
5.	Connor, New York	265

Home Runs

1. Connor, New York	14
2. H. Richardson, Boston	13
3. Stovey, Boston	12
4. Shindle, Philadelphia	10
Gore, New York	10

Hits

1. Duffy, Chicago	191
2. Ward, Brooklyn	189
3. Shindle, Philadelphia	188
4. Browning, Cleveland	184
5. H. Richardson, Boston	181

Stolen Bases

1. Stovey, Boston	97
2. T. Brown, Boston	79
3. Duffy, Chicago	78
4. Hanlon, Pittsburgh	65
5. Ward, Brooklyn	63

RBI

1. H. Richardson, Boston	146
2. Orr, Brooklyn	124
3. Beckley, Pittsburgh	120
4. O'Rourke, New York	115
5. Larkin, Cleveland	112

Runs

1. Duffy, Chicago	161
2. T. Brown, Boston	146
3. Stovey, Boston	142
4. Ward, Brooklyn	134
5. Connor, New York	133

Strikeouts

1. Brown, Boston	84
2. Joyce, Brooklyn	77
3. Fields, Pittsburgh	52
4. M. Baldwin, Chicago	51
5. Fogarty, Philadelphia	50

PITCHING

Wins

1. M. Baldwin, Chicago	34
2. King, Chicago	30
Weyhing, Brooklyn	30
4. Radbourn, Boston	27
5. Gumbert, Boston	23

Innings

1. M. Baldwin, Chicago	501
2. King, Chicago	461
3. Weyhing, Brooklyn	390
4. Staley, Pittsburgh	387.2
5. Gruber, Cleveland	383.1

Strikeouts

1. M. Baldwin, Chicago	211
2. King, Chicago	185
3. Weyhing, Brooklyn	177
4. Ewing, New York	145
Staley, Pittsburgh	145

ERA (140 Innings)

1. King, Chicago	2.69
2. Staley, Pittsburgh	3.23
3. M. Baldwin, Chicago	3.31
Radbourn, Boston	3.31
5. T. Keefe, New York	3.38

Losses

1. Haddock, Buffalo	26
2. Staley, Pittsburgh	25
Bakely, Cleveland	25
4. M. Baldwin, Chicago	24
Cunningham, Phila-Buff	24

Complete games

1. M. Baldwin, Chicago	54
2. King, Chicago	48
3. Staley, Pittsburgh	45
4. Gruber, Cleveland	39
5. Weyhing, Brooklyn	38

Winning Percentage (25 decisions)

1. B. Daley, Boston	.720
2. Radbourn, Boston	.692
3. Knell, Philadelphia	.667
4. Gumbert, Boston	.657
5. Weyhing, Brooklyn	.652

Lowest On–Base Percentage

1. Staley, Pittsburgh	.290
2. King, Chicago	.301
3. Radbourn, Boston	.310
4. T. Keefe, New York	.318
5. Sanders, Philadelphia	.320

FIELDING

Total Chances

1B	Connor, New York		1436
2B	Bierbauer, Brooklyn		906
3B	Nash, Boston		583
SS	Ward, Brooklyn		858
OF	Brown, Boston		338
C	Mack, Buffalo		637
P	M. Baldwin, Chicago		187

Fielding Average

Connor, New York	.985
Quinn, Boston	.942
P. Tebeau, Cleveland	.872
Rowe, Buffalo	.901
Fogarty, Philadelphia	.963
B. Ewing, New York	.949
D. O'Brien, Cleveland	.9642
King, Chicago	.9640

BOSTON   King Kelly   Congress Street Grounds

		G	AB	H	R	2B	3B	HR	RBI	BB	SB	BA	SA
LF	Hardy Richardson	130	555	181	126	26	14	13	**146**	52	42	.326	.494
CF	Tom Brown	128	543	150	146	23	14	4	61	86	79	.276	.392
2B	Joe Quinn	130	509	153	87	19	8	7	82	44	29	.301	.411
3B	Billy Nash	129	488	130	103	28	6	5	90	88	26	.266	.379
RF	Harry Stovey	118	481	143	142	25	11	12	83	81	**97**	.297	.470
1B	Dan Brouthers	123	460	152	117	36	9	1	97	99	28	.330	.454
SS	Arthur Irwin	96	354	92	60	17	1	0	45	57	16	.260	.314
C	King Kelly	89	340	111	83	18	6	4	66	52	51	.326	.450
C	Morg Murphy	68	246	56	38	10	2	2	32	24	16	.228	.309
P	Hoss Radbourn	42	154	39	20	6	0	0	16	9	7	.253	.292
P	Ad Gumbert	44	145	35	23	7	1	3	20	18	5	.241	.366
P	Bill Daley	37	110	17	14	1	0	2	7	9	1	.155	.218
Sub	Pop Swett	37	94	18	16	4	3	1	12	16	4	.191	.330
P	Matt Kilroy	31	93	20	11	1	1	0	8	12	11	.215	.247
P	Kid Madden	13	38	7	5	2	0	0	4	3	0	.184	.237
Sub	Dick Johnston	2	9	1	0	0	0	0	0	0	0	.111	.111
Sub	John Morrill	2	7	1	1	0	0	0	2	2	0	.143	.143
		130	4626	1306	992	**223**	76	54	768	**652**	**412**	.282	.398

1B Brouthers 123, Kelly 4, Stovey 1, Richardson 1, Radbourn 1, Morrill 1
2B Quinn 130
SS Irwin 96, Kelly 27, Richardson 6, Murphy 2, Kilroy 1, Madden 1, Morrill 1
3B Nash 129, Kelly 2, Kilroy 1, Murphy 1
OF Brown 128, Richardson 124, Stovey 117, Gumbert 7, Kelly 6, Radbourn 4, Swett 3, Daley 3, Madden 2, Johnston 2, Kilroy 2, Murphy 1
C Murphy 67, Kelly 56, Swett 34
P Radbourn 41, Gumbert 39, Daley 34, Kilroy 30, Madden 10, Nash 1, Kelly 1

	G	IP	GS	CG	W	L	K	BB	SH	SV	ERA
Hoss Radbourn	41	343	38	36	27	12	80	100	1	0	3.31
Ad Gumbert	39	277.1	33	27	23	12	81	86	1	0	3.96
Bill Daley	34	235	25	19	18	7	110	167	2	2	3.60
Matt Kilroy	30	217.2	27	18	9	15	48	87	0	0	4.26
Kid Madden	10	62	7	5	3	2	24	25	1	0	4.79
King Kelly	1	2	0	0	1	0	2	2	0	0	4.50
Billy Nash	1	0.1	0	0	0	0	0	0	0	0	0.00
	—One combined shutout on July 16: Gumbert 2 innings, Kilroy 7 innings—										
	1137.1	130	105	81	48	345	467	6	2	3.79

BROOKLYN   **Monte Ward**   **Eastern Park**

		G	AB	H	R	2B	3B	HR	RBI	BB	SB	BA	SA
2B	Lou Bierbauer	133	589	180	128	31	11	7	99	40	16	.306	.431
SS	Monte Ward	128	561	189	134	15	12	4	60	51	63	.337	.428
3B	Bill Joyce	133	489	123	121	18	18	1	78	**123**	43	.252	.368
1B	Dave Orr	107	464	173	89	32	13	6	124	30	10	.373	.537
RF	Jack McGeachy	104	443	108	84	24	4	1	65	19	21	.244	.323
CF	Ed Andrews	94	395	100	84	14	2	3	38	40	21	.253	.322
LF	Emmett Seery	104	394	88	78	12	7	1	50	70	44	.223	.297
UT	George Van Haltren	92	376	126	84	8	9	5	54	41	35	.335	.444
C	Tom Kinslow	64	242	64	30	11	6	4	46	10	2	.264	.409
C	Paul Cook	58	218	55	32	3	3	0	31	14	7	.252	.294
C	Con Daily	46	168	42	20	6	3	0	35	15	6	.250	.321
P	Gus Weyhing	49	165	27	21	2	3	1	15	16	2	.164	.230
P	John Sowders	40	132	25	14	3	0	1	20	10	0	.189	.235
Sub	Art Sunday	24	83	22	26	5	1	0	13	15	0	.265	.349
P	Con Murphy	23	69	15	11	2	0	0	7	5	1	.217	.246
P	George Hemming	19	57	9	5	0	1	0	8	1	1	.158	.193
Sub	Jackie Hayes	12	42	8	3	0	0	0	5	2	0	.190	.190
		133	4887	1354	964	186	93	34	748	502	272	.277	.374

1B   Orr 107, Cook 21, Daily 6
2B   Bierbauer 133, Hayes 1
SS   Ward 128, Hayes 3, Van Haltren 3
3B   Joyce 133
OF   McGeachy 104, Seery 104, Andrews 94, Van Haltren 67, Sunday 24, Hayes 6, Murphy 3, Sowders 3, Daily 1, Hemming 1, Cook 1
C   Kinslow 64, Daily 40, Cook 36, Hayes 2
P   Weyhing 49, Sowders 39, Van Haltren 28, Murphy 20, Hemming 19

	G	IP	GS	CG	W	L	K	BB	SH	SV	ERA
Gus Weyhing	49	390	46	38	30	16	177	179	3	0	3.60
John Sowders	39	309	37	28	19	16	91	161	1	0	3.82
George Van Haltren	28	223	25	23	15	10	48	89	0	2	4.28
Con Murphy	20	139	14	11	4	10	29	82	0	2	4.79
George Hemming	19	123	11	11	8	4	32	59	0	**3***	3.80
	1184	133	111	76	56	377	570	4	**7**	3.95

NEW YORK   **Buck Ewing**   **Polo Grounds (III)**

		G	AB	H	R	2B	3B	HR	RBI	BB	SB	BA	SA
SS	Danny Richardson	124	528	135	102	12	9	4	80	37	37	.256	.335
1B	Roger Connor	123	484	169	133	24	15	**14**	103	88	22	.349	**.548**
RF	Jim O'Rourke	111	478	172	112	37	5	9	115	33	23	.360	.515
3B	Art Whitney	119	442	97	71	12	3	0	45	64	8	.219	.260
LF	Mike Slattery	97	411	126	80	20	11	5	67	27	18	.307	.445
CF	George Gore	93	399	127	132	26	8	10	55	77	28	.318	.499
C	Buck Ewing	83	352	119	98	19	15	8	72	39	36	.338	.545
2B	Dan Shannon	83	324	70	59	7	8	3	44	25	21	.216	.315
Sub	Dick Johnston	77	306	74	37	9	7	1	43	18	7	.242	.327
Sub	Gil Hatfield	71	287	80	32	13	6	2	37	17	12	.279	.387
Sub	Willard Brown	60	230	64	47	8	4	4	43	13	5	.278	.400
Sub	Farmer Vaughn	44	166	44	27	7	0	1	22	10	6	.265	.325
P	Hank O'Day	43	150	34	24	2	1	1	23	10	1	.227	.273
P	Cannonball Crane	43	146	46	27	5	4	0	16	10	5	.315	.404
P	John Ewing	35	114	24	18	2	1	2	17	5	2	.211	.298
P	Tim Keefe	30	92	10	18	1	0	2	11	13	0	.109	.185
Sub	Fred Dunlap	1	4	2	1	0	0	0	0	0	0	.500	.500
		132	4913	**1393**	**1018**	204	97	**66**	**793**	486	231	.284	**.405**

1B Connor 123, Brown 9
2B Shannon 77, Richardson 56, Brown 2, Vaughn 1, B. Ewing 1, Dunlap 1
SS Richardson 68, Whitney 31, Hatfield 27, Shannon 6, Johnston 2
3B Whitney 88, Hatfield 42, Brown 3, Vaughn 1
OF O'Rourke 111, Slattery 97, Gore 93, Johnston 76, Brown 13, Vaughn 12, Hatfield 1
C   B. Ewing 81, Brown 34, Vaughn 30
P   Crane 43, O'Day 43, J. Ewing 35, Keefe 30, Hatfield 3, B. Ewing 1

	G	IP	GS	CG	W	L	K	BB	SH	SV	ERA
Cannonball Crane	43	330.1	35	28	16	19	117	210	0	0	4.63
Hank O'Day	43	329	35	32	22	13	94	163	1	**3**	4.21
John Ewing	35	267.1	31	27	18	12	145	104	1	2	4.24
Tim Keefe	30	229	30	23	17	11	88	85	1	0	3.38
Buck Ewing	1	9	1	1	0	1	2	3	0	0	4.00
Gil Hatfield	3	7.2	0	0	1	1	3	4	0	1	3.52
	1172.1	132	111	74	57	449	569	3	6	4.17

CHICAGO Charlie Comiskey South Side Park (II)

		G	AB	H	R	2B	3B	HR	RBI	BB	SB	BA	SA
RF	Hugh Duffy	137	**596**	**191**	161	36	16	7	82	59	78	.320	.470
LF	Tip O'Neill	137	577	174	112	20	16	3	75	65	29	.302	.407
2B	Fred Pfeffer	124	499	128	86	21	8	5	80	44	27	.257	.361
CF	Jimmy Ryan	118	486	165	99	32	5	6	89	60	30	.340	.463
C	Duke Farrell	117	451	131	79	21	12	2	84	42	8	.290	.404
1B	Charlie Comiskey	88	377	92	53	11	3	0	59	14	34	.244	.289
UT	Jack Boyle	100	369	96	56	9	5	1	49	44	11	.260	.320
SS	Charlie Bastian	80	283	54	38	10	5	0	29	33	4	.191	.261
3B	Ned Williamson	73	261	51	34	7	3	2	26	36	3	.195	.268
Sub	Del Darling	58	221	57	45	12	4	2	39	29	5	.258	.376
P	Mark Baldwin	59	215	45	27	4	6	1	25	15	4	.209	.298
3B	Arlie Latham	52	214	49	47	7	2	1	20	22	32	.229	.294
P	Silver King	58	185	31	24	2	5	1	16	13	3	.168	.249
Sub	Frank Shugart	29	106	20	8	5	5	0	15	5	5	.189	.330
P	Charlie Bartson	25	75	13	7	1	0	0	6	11	2	.173	.187
P	Frank Dwyer	16	53	14	10	2	0	0	11	0	1	.264	.302
		138	4968	1311	886	200	95	31	705	492	276	.264	.361

1B Comiskey 88, Darling 29, Farrell 22, Boyle 7, King 1
2B Pfeffer 124, Bastian 12, Darling 3
SS Bastian 64, Shugart 25, Williamson 21, Boyle 16, Darling 15
3B Williamson 52, Latham 52, Boyle 30, Bastian 4, Darling 2
OF Duffy 137, O'Neill 137, Ryan 118, Farrell 10, Darling 7, Shugart 5, Dwyer 4, Boyle 2, King 1
C   Farrell 90, Boyle 50, Darling 9
P   Baldwin 59, King 56, Bartson 25, Dwyer 12

	G	IP	GS	CG	W	L	K	BB	SH	SV	ERA
Mark Baldwin	**59**	**501**	**57**	**54**	**34**	24	**211**	249	1	0	3.31
Silver King #	56	461	56	48	30	22	185	163	**4**	0	**2.69**
Charlie Bartson	25	188	19	16	8	10	47	66	0	1	4.26
Frank Dwyer	12	69.1	6	6	3	6	17	25	0	1	6.23
	1219.1	138	124	75	62	**460**	503	5	2	**3.39**

No-hit game 0–1 vs Brooklyn, June 21 (8 innings)

PHILADELPHIA   **Jim Fogarty (7–9)**   **Charlie Buffinton (61–54)**   **Forepaugh Park**

		G	AB	H	R	2B	3B	HR	RBI	BB	SB	BA	SA
SS	Billy Shindle	132	584	188	127	21	21	10	90	40	51	.322	.481
LF	George Wood	132	539	156	115	20	14	9	102	51	20	.289	.429
3B	Joe Mulvey	120	519	149	96	26	15	6	87	27	20	.287	.430
CF	Mike Griffin	115	489	140	127	29	6	6	54	64	30	.286	.407
1B	Sid Farrar	127	481	122	84	17	11	1	69	51	9	.254	.341
2B	John Pickett	100	407	114	82	7	9	4	64	40	12	.280	.371
UT	Bill Hallman	84	356	95	59	16	7	1	37	33	6	.267	.360
RF	Jim Fogarty	91	347	83	71	17	6	4	58	59	36	.239	.357
C	Lave Cross	63	245	73	42	7	8	3	47	12	5	.298	.429
C	Jocko Milligan	62	234	69	38	9	3	3	57	19	2	.295	.397
P	Ben Sanders	52	189	59	31	6	6	0	30	10	2	.312	.407
P	Charlie Buffinton	42	150	41	24	3	2	1	24	9	1	.273	.340
P	Phil Knell	36	132	29	19	3	3	0	18	7	3	.220	.288
Sub	Dan Shannon	19	75	18	15	5	1	1	16	4	4	.240	.373
P	Bill Husted	18	56	6	5	0	0	0	5	3	1	.107	.107
P	Bert Cunningham	15	52	6	6	1	1	0	3	2	1	.115	.173
		132	4855	1348	941	187	**113**	49	761	431	203	.278	.393

1B	Farrar 127, Milligan 3, Buffinton 3
2B	Pickett 100, Shannon 19, Hallman 14
SS	Shindle 130, Hallman 2
3B	Mulvey 120, Hallman 10, Shindle 2, Wood 1, Fogarty 1
OF	Wood 132, Griffin 115, Fogarty 91, Hallman 34, Cross 15, Sanders 10, Buffinton 5, Knell 2, Cunningham 1
C	Milligan 59, Cross 49, Hallman 26
P	Sanders 43, Buffinton 36, Knell 35, Husted 18, Cunningham 14

	G	IP	GS	CG	W	L	K	BB	SH	SV	ERA
Ben Sanders	43	346.2	40	37	19	18	107	69	2	1	3.76
Phil Knell	35	286.2	31	30	22	11	99	166	2	0	3.83
Charlie Buffinton	36	283.1	33	28	19	15	89	126	0	1	3.81
Bill Husted	18	129	17	12	5	10	33	67	0	0	4.88
Bert Cunningham	14	108.2	11	11	3	9	33	67	0	0	5.22
	1154.1	132	118	68	63	361	495	4	2	4.05

PITTSBURGH   **Ned Hanlon**   **Exposition Park (II)**

		G	AB	H	R	2B	3B	HR	RBI	BB	SB	BA	SA
3B	Willie Kuehne	126	528	126	66	21	12	5	73	28	21	.239	.352
LF	Jocko Fields	126	526	149	101	18	20	9	86	57	24	.283	.445
RF	Joe Visner	127	521	138	110	15	**22**	3	71	76	18	.265	.395
1B	Jake Beckley	121	516	167	109	38	**22**	9	120	42	18	.324	.535
SS	Tommy Corcoran	123	503	117	80	14	13	1	61	38	43	.233	.318
CF	Ned Hanlon	118	472	131	106	16	6	1	44	80	65	.278	.343
C	Fred Carroll	111	416	124	95	20	7	2	71	75	35	.298	.394
2B	Yank Robinson	98	306	70	59	10	3	0	38	101	17	.229	.281
C	Tom Quinn	55	207	44	23	4	3	1	15	17	1	.213	.275
P	Harry Staley	47	164	34	25	3	2	1	25	13	0	.207	.268
P	Al Maul	45	162	42	31	6	2	0	21	22	5	.259	.321
P	Pud Galvin	26	97	20	8	2	1	0	12	6	1	.206	.247
P	John Tener	18	63	12	7	0	0	2	5	7	1	.190	.286
P	Ed Morris	18	63	9	7	0	0	0	5	5	0	.143	.143
Sub	Jerry Hurley	8	22	6	5	1	0	0	2	2	0	.273	.318
Sub	Reddy Gray	2	9	2	3	0	0	1	3	0	0	.222	.556
P	Fred Doe	1	2	1	0	0	0	0	0	0	0	.500	.500
		128	4577	1192	835	168	**113**	35	652	569	249	.260	.369

1B   Beckley 121, Carroll 7
2B   Robinson 98, Fields 30, Gray 2
SS   Corcoran 123, Fields 4, Maul 1
3B   Kuehne 126, Tener 2
OF   Visner 127, Hanlon 118, Fields 80, Carroll 49, Maul 15, Tener 2, Staley 1, Hurley 1
C   Carroll 56, Quinn 55, Fields 15, Hurley 7
P   Staley 46, Maul 30, Galvin 26, Morris 18, Tener 14, Doe 1

	G	IP	GS	CG	W	L	K	BB	SH	SV	ERA
Harry Staley	46	387.2	46	44	21	25	145	74	3	0	3.23
Al Maul	30	246.2	28	26	16	12	81	104	2	0	3.79
Pud Galvin	26	217	25	23	12	13	35	49	1	0	4.35
Ed Morris	18	144.1	15	15	8	7	25	35	1	0	4.86
John Tener	14	117	14	13	3	11	30	70	0	0	7.31
Fred Doe	1	4	0	0	0	0	2	2	0	0	4.50
		1116.2	128	121	60	68	318	**334**	7	0	4.22

CLEVELAND   Henry Larkin (34–45)   Patsy Tebeau (21–30)   Brotherhood Park

		G	AB	H	R	2B	3B	HR	RBI	BB	SB	BA	SA
2B	Cub Stricker	127	544	133	93	19	8	2	65	54	24	.244	.320
SS	Ed Delahanty	115	517	154	107	26	13	3	64	24	25	.298	.416
1B	Henry Larkin	125	506	168	93	32	15	5	112	65	5	.332	.484
LF	Pete Browning	118	493	184	112	**40**	8	5	93	75	35	**.373**	.517
RF	Paul Radford	122	466	136	98	24	12	2	62	82	25	.292	.408
3B	Patsy Tebeau	110	450	135	86	26	6	5	74	34	14	.300	.418
C	Sy Sutcliffe	99	386	127	62	14	8	2	60	33	10	.329	.422
CF	Jimmy McAleer	86	341	91	58	8	7	1	42	37	21	.267	.340
C	Jim Brennan	59	233	59	32	3	7	0	26	13	8	.253	.326
Sub	Larry Twitchell	56	233	52	33	6	3	2	36	17	4	.223	.300
P	Henry Gruber	50	163	36	21	3	3	0	9	26	0	.221	.276
P	Jersey Bakely	43	138	28	10	3	0	0	9	11	0	.203	.225
P	Darby O'Brien	26	96	15	12	1	1	0	6	2	0	.156	.188
Sub	Jack Carney	25	89	31	15	5	3	0	21	14	6	.348	.472
P	Willie McGill	24	68	10	10	2	0	0	6	21	0	.147	.176
Sub	Pop Snyder	13	48	9	5	1	0	0	12	1	1	.188	.208
P	George Hemming	3	11	2	1	0	0	0	1	0	2	.182	.182
P	Charlie Dewald	2	8	3	1	0	0	0	3	0	0	.375	.375
Sub	Neil Stynes	2	8	0	0	0	0	0	0	0	0	.000	.000
Sub	? Budd	1	4	0	0	0	0	0	0	0	0	.000	.000
P	Bill Gleason	1	2	0	0	0	0	0	0	0	0	.000	.000
		131	4804	1373	849	213	94	27	701	509	180	**.286**	.386

1B   Larkin 125, Carney 6, Delahanty 1
2B   Stricker 109, Delahanty 20, Radford 4
SS   Delahanty 76, Radford 36, Stricker 20, Sutcliffe 4
3B   Tebeau 110, Brennan 14, Radford 7, Delahanty 3, Sutcliffe 2, Gruber 1
OF   Browning 118, McAleer 86, Radford 80, Twitchell 56, Carney 19, Delahanty 18, Sutcliffe 15, Brennan 6, Gruber 3, Budd 1, McGill 1, Bakely 1, O'Brien 1, Larkin 1
C   Sutcliffe 84, Brennan 42, Snyder 13, Stynes 2
P   Gruber 48, Bakely 43, O'Brien 25, McGill 24, Hemming 3, Dewald 2, Gleason 1, Radford 1

	G	IP	GS	CG	W	L	K	BB	SH	SV	ERA
Henry Gruber	48	383.1	44	39	22	23	110	204	1	0	4.27
Jersey Bakely	43	326.1	38	32	12	25	67	147	0	0	4.47
Darby O'Brien	25	206.1	25	22	8	16	54	93	0	0	3.40
Willie McGill	24	183.2	20	19	11	9	82	96	0	0	4.12
George Hemming	3	21	1	1	0	1	3	19	0	0*	6.86
Charlie Dewald	2	14	2	2	2	0	6	5	0	0	0.64
Paul Radford	1	5	0	0	0	0	3	1	0	0	3.60
Bill Gleason	1	4	1	0	0	1	0	6	0	0	27.00
		1143.2	131	115	55	75	325	571	1	0	4.23

BUFFALO   **Jack Rowe (33–72)**   **Jay Faatz (9–24)**   **Olympic Park (II)**

		G	AB	H	R	2B	3B	HR	RBI	BB	SB	BA	SA
LF	Ed Beecher	126	536	159	69	22	10	3	90	29	14	.297	.392
2B	Sam Wise	119	505	148	95	29	11	6	102	46	19	.293	.430
SS	Jack Rowe	125	504	126	77	22	7	2	76	48	10	.250	.333
C	Connie Mack	123	503	134	95	15	12	0	53	47	16	.266	.344
CF	Dummy Hoy	122	493	147	107	17	8	1	53	94	39	.298	.371
1B	Deacon White	122	439	114	62	13	4	0	47	67	3	.260	.308
3B	John Irwin	77	308	72	62	11	4	0	34	43	18	.234	.295
Sub	Spider Clark	69	260	69	45	11	1	1	25	20	8	.265	.327
RF	Jocko Halligan	57	211	53	28	9	2	3	33	20	7	.251	.355
P	Larry Twitchell	44	172	38	24	3	1	2	17	23	4	.221	.285
Sub	John Rainey	42	166	39	29	5	1	1	20	24	12	.235	.295
P	George Haddock	42	146	36	21	11	0	0	24	24	3	.247	.322
Sub	Jay Faatz	32	111	21	18	0	2	1	16	9	2	.189	.252
Sub	Jack Carney	28	107	29	11	3	0	0	13	7	2	.271	.299
P	Bert Cunningham	28	101	23	11	5	1	0	11	6	0	.228	.297
P	George Keefe	25	79	16	15	1	0	0	7	13	0	.203	.215
P	General Stafford	15	49	7	11	1	0	0	3	7	2	.143	.163
P	Alex Ferson	11	32	7	4	0	0	0	2	6	1	.219	.219
P	Lady Baldwin	7	28	8	4	1	0	0	2	2	0	.286	.321
P	John Buckley	4	15	0	1	0	0	0	0	2	0	.000	.000
P	Gus Krock	4	12	1	1	0	0	0	1	1	0	.083	.083
P	? Lewis	1	5	1	1	0	0	0	0	0	0	.200	.200
P	Bill Duzen	2	4	1	2	0	0	0	1	3	0	.250	.500
P	Dan Cotter	1	4	0	0	0	0	0	0	0	0	.000	.000
Sub	Jim Gillespie	1	3	0	0	0	0	0	0	0	0	.000	.000
P	Fred Doe	1	2	0	0	0	0	0	0	0	0	.000	.000
		134	4795	1249	793	180	64	20	630	541	160	.260	.337

1B   White 57, Faatz 32, Carney 24, Irwin 12, Clark 6, Mack 5, Twitchell 3
2B   Wise 119, Clark 13, Rainey 2, Irwin 1, Hoy 1
SS   Rowe 125, Rainey 7, Clark 1, White 1
3B   J. Irwin 64, White 64, Rainey 6, Clark 3
OF   Beecher 126, Hoy 122, Halligan 43, Clark 34, Twitchell 32, Rainey 28, Mack 9, Haddock 7, Carney 4,
     Stafford 4, Cunningham 3, Ferson 1, Gillespie 1, Lewis 1
C   Mack 112, Halligan 16, Clark 14
P   Haddock 35, Cunningham 25, Keefe 25, Twitchell 12, Stafford 12, Ferson 10, Baldwin 7, Krock 4, Buckley 4,
     Duzen 2, Doe 1, Lewis 1, Cotter 1, Clark 1, White 1, Beecher 1

	G	IP	GS	CG	W	L	K	BB	SH	SV	ERA
George Haddock	35	290.2	34	31	9	**26**	123	149	0	0	5.76
Bert Cunningham	25	211	25	24	9	15	78	134	2	0	5.84
George Keefe	25	196	22	22	6	16	55	138	0	0	6.52
Larry Twitchell	12	104.1	12	12	5	7	29	72	0	0	4.57
General Stafford	12	98	12	11	3	9	21	43	0	0	5.14
Alex Ferson	10	71	10	7	1	7	13	40	0	0	5.45
Lady Baldwin	7	62	7	7	2	5	13	24	0	0	4.50
John Buckley	4	34	4	4	1	3	4	16	0	0	7.68
Gus Krock	4	25	3	3	0	3	5	15	0	0	6.12
Bill Duzen	2	13	2	2	0	2	5	14	0	0	13.85
Dan Cotter	1	9	1	1	0	1	0	7	0	0	14.00
Deacon White	1	8	0	0	0	0	0	2	0	0	9.00
Fred Doe	1	6	1	1	0	1	2	7	0	0	12.00
Ed Beecher	1	6	0	0	0	0	0	3	0	0	12.00
Spider Clark	1	4	0	0	0	0	2	2	0	0	6.75
? Lewis	1	3	1	0	0	1	1	7	0	0	60.00
		1141	134	**125**	36	96	351	673	2	0	6.11

1891

THE AMERICAN ASSOCIATION'S LAST HURRAH

By the close of the 1890 campaign several Players League teams were in such deep financial distress that they could no longer meet their payrolls. Thanks to expert subterfuge by Al Spalding and other National League owners, Monte Ward and his war committee failed to realize that many National League and American Association teams were in even worse shape. After a lot of brave talk that it would continue the battle, Ward's rebel organization finally knuckled under on January 14, 1891.

The National League, as part of its peace settlement with the Brotherhood, agreed to allow new American Association franchises in Boston and Chicago in 1891 provided that all reserved players on defunct Brotherhood teams returned to their former clubs. Instead of following the League's bidding, the Association took on the Players League champion Boston Reds virtually intact, plus the core of the Philadelphia Brotherhood team, and then laid plans to form a new franchise in Chicago the following year. The defiant move meant that although the Players League was officially dead, two remnants of it would survive at least one more year.

The Philadelphia Brotherhood team orchestrated a merger with the disheveled Philadelphia Athletics franchise that kept long-time manager Bill Sharsig at the club's helm—for the moment anyway—while the Boston Reds were among the replacements for Rochester, Syracuse, Toledo and the Brooklyn Gladiators, the Association's four interim clubs in the 1890 war year. Brooklyn had actually departed the previous August, giving way to Baltimore when Orioles manager Billy Barnie and owner Henry Von der Horst, after a short sojourn in the minor league Atlantic Association, patched up their differences with the American Association and returned to the fold. To complete the Association's composition for 1891 a team from Washington was added and King Kelly was coaxed into becoming the front man for a new franchise in Cincinnati that would bear his name: Kelly's Killers.

Cornering Kelly and the ex-League stars on the Boston Reds such as Dan Brouthers, Charlie Buffinton, Hardy Richardson and Hugh Duffy helped the Association make up for

Kid Gleason led the Phils in wins in 1891. He also outhit about half the regulars on the team. When his hillwork deteriorated after the pitching distance was lengthened in 1893, he was converted to a second baseman. Gleason was the last man in major league history to have a season in which he pitched 500 innings and also one in which he collected 500 at bats.

the multitude of players it lost to the League either through defection or the Brotherhood war. Among the missing by 1891 were Pete Browning, Tommy Tucker, Billy Shindle, Silver King, Mark Baldwin, Billy Hamilton and Herman Long as well as four entire teams—Pittsburgh, Cleveland and finally the two casualties of the 1889 battle for the Association presidency, Cincinnati and the Brooklyn Bridegrooms. Owing to a paperwork gaffe by the Philadelphia Athletics, the Association stood to lose two more luminaries when the Boston National League team claimed Harry Stovey and Pittsburgh snatched Lou Bierbauer, arguing that both were free agents because the A's had omitted them from their reserve list. A Board of Control comprised of Philadelphia Phillies owner John I. Rogers, newly elected American Association president Allan W. Thurman and Louis Krauthoff, a former executive of the Kansas City Association team, which was now in the Western Association, convened to settle the dispute. Association monarchs expected Krauthoff and Thurman to tip the scale their way, but Thurman stunned them by voting instead with Rogers and awarding Stovey and Bierbauer to the National League.

Thurman's decision triggered the American Association to impeach him and then to withdraw from the National Agreement, throwing the two major leagues into war again and jeopardizing the possibility of staging an eighth annual World's Series at the end of the season. It was unfortunate for the

Bill Hutchison, the only pitcher not in the Hall of Fame despite leading the majors in wins three years running. Hutchison also won more games after age 30 than any other 19th-century hurler. He denied that the increased pitching distance hurt him, but his post-1892 hill stats argue differently.

Association. The Boston Reds were one of the strongest teams in the last century. Ex-League shortstop Arthur Irwin, who was given the Reds' reins when Kelly left to start the new Cincinnati franchise, got some competition early in the summer from the St. Louis Browns, which had Charlie Comiskey back at their helm, but by July the Reds had full charge of the pennant race and streaked home eight and a half games in front. The Reds

A MANAGER'S TALE

No established manager suffered more during the Players League war than Jim Mutrie. After winning back-to-back championships, Mutrie watched powerlessly while most of his New York Giants stars joined Monte Ward in the Brotherhood revolt, leaving his team a shambles. Even garnering Jack Glasscock, Jerry Denny and rookie fireballer Amos Rusie from the defunct Indianapolis team could not save Mutrie's Giants in 1890. So few fans came to their games that owner John Day needed a quick financial fix. Other National League owners, including Al Spalding and Arthur Soden, rescued Day by buying a piece of the Giants and then eventually squeezed him out of his controlling interest in the club.

Regaining most of the players he'd lost to the Brotherhood helped Mutrie pilot the Giants to the league lead in June of 1891, but his team was "in frightfully crippled condition." Catcher Buck Ewing had hurt his arm making a throw on a damp spring day and it idled him most of the season. Ewing's brother John had a "lump" on his pitching arm, causing him to miss time. Rusie was forced to go home to Indianapolis in June when his father lost a leg in a railway accident. Glasscock had to leave the team when his father died. John Sharrott dislocated his shoulder sliding into a base. Finally, all of Mutrie's lineup juggling left only Dick Buckley to catch despite a sore hand. The Giants soon ceded the League lead to Chicago, but they still had a voice in whether Chicago won the pennant. Five of Boston's 18 straight victories at the end of the 1891 season came at the Giants' expense, while Mutrie kept Buck Ewing on the bench for all five contests, played slugging first baseman Roger Connor in just one of the games, and persisted in pitching Mickey Welch and Mike Sullivan, winners of just seven games between them in 1891, rather than Rusie and John Ewing, who combined for 54 wins. Mutrie contended Buck Ewing's arm was dead and the others just happened to need a rest while Boston was in town, but Cap Anson's veiled accusations that the Giants had deliberately thrown the games to the Beaneaters compelled other League owners to investigate the charge. Anson was a notorious cry baby, though, and what was more, memories of some of his own past actions ran long. To no one's surprise the committee the League appointed whitewashed the Giants of any wrongdoing and officially awarded Boston the pennant in early November. Mutrie nonetheless was relieved of his post at the Giants helm and never managed again in the majors.

The unsung Jack Crooks. His .957 fielding average for Columbus in 1891 set a new standard for second basemen. The following year, despite hitting just .213, Crooks set a major league record for walks that lasted until 1911.

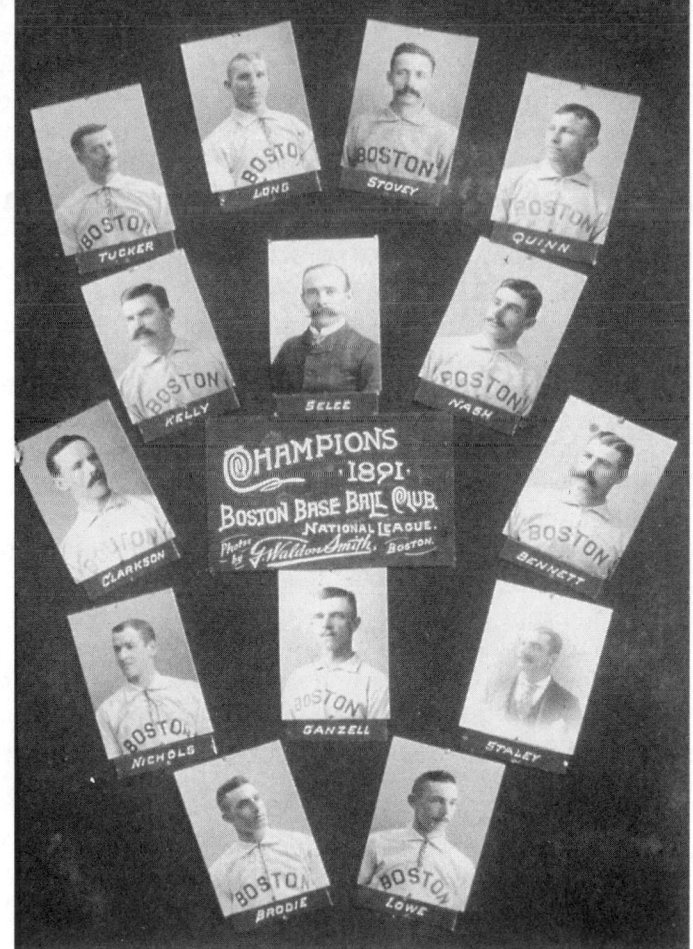

Frank Selee's first pennant winner. Coming in only Selee's second season as Boston's manager, it was built largely through his flair for blending players acquired from here, there and everywhere. Only Brodie, Nichols and Lowe—all of them rookies Selee installed when he took over the club in 1890—cut their major league teeth in a Boston Nationals uniform.

missed the team Triple Crown by only a single percentage point, losing out in fielding average to Columbus .935 to .934. But while Brouthers won the batting title, third baseman Duke Farrell bagged the homer crown and shared the RBI lead with teammate Hugh Duffy, center fielder Tom Brown took honors in hits, runs, total bases and stolen bases, and Irwin's twin aces Buffinton and George Haddock combined for 63 wins, the Association's finest all-around player in 1891 was St. Louis's Jack Stivetts. In only his second full big league season the 23-year-old righthander not only won 33 games but also hit .305 while taking an occasional turn in the outfield.

On the whole, though, the Browns were not in Boston's class. To add insult, the Reds procured King Kelly as their field captain after his Cincinnati franchise was disbanded in mid-August and awarded to Milwaukee of the crumbling Western Association. With Kelly as an

---

ANOTHER MANAGER'S TALE

Bill McGunnigle, the lone manager to win back-to-back pennants in two different major leagues, is also the only manager to lose his job after winning two straight pennants. After piloting the 1890 Players League entry in Brooklyn, Monte Ward liked the taste of command so much that he wanted to do it again. The New York Giants, his old League team, then let him work out a deal to play for and manage the Brooklyn National League team. But what about McGunnigle, the Bridegrooms' extraordinarily successful current manager? Owner Charlie Byrne had the solution—fire him.

Under Ward's command the Bridegrooms behaved like chumps rather than defending champs. Typical was an incident on July 4 at Chicago. While Tom Daly, the Bridegrooms regular catcher in 1890, was dozing on the outfield grass between games of the holiday doubleheader, Oyster Burns stabbed him in the leg with a penknife. Burns swore he'd only meant to prick his sleeping teammate for a laugh, but Daly woke with a jolt and turned into the blade, severing a tendon that put him out of action.

Sixteen days later, in a game against Jim Mutrie's New York Giants at Brooklyn's Eastern Park, Ward saw any lingering hope of resuscitating his comatose team come to an abrupt end when Roger Connor of the Giants hit a short fly ball to right field. A train passing the park at that moment prevented Burns in right field or second baseman Hub Collins from hearing Ward's cry for which of them to take the pop up. Burns hollered for Collins to get it, but unable to hear him, Collins hesitated a step and then continued his pursuit. The two met head-on in a collision that witnesses swore was the worst ever seen on a ball field. Burns went home in a cab, battered but intact, but Collins was unconscious for several hours and never regained any memory of the incident. Ward's immediate choice to replace Collins at second base was Jack Burdock, out of the majors ever since 1888 when he doomed the chances of McGunnigle's first Bridegrooms team for a pennant by hitting .122.

TOM BROWN I

There are about a hundred different lists of unusual nineteenth-century records or record combinations that are headed by Tom Brown. The reason is because Brown's performances fluctuated so wildly from one season to the next that his overall career looks as if it ought to belong to three or four different players. Brown mirrored almost exactly the quality of the team for which he played. Put on a champion, as happened in 1891, he was named the Boston Reds' most valuable player by local writers after he scored a then-record 177 runs; four years earlier, shipped in mid-season to the last-place Indianapolis Hoosiers, he hit .179. Here is one list Brown heads, and it's an important one. No other player in major league history scored more career runs on fewer than 2,000 hits. Significantly, the first seven men on the list and nine of the first dozen were nineteenth-century players.

	RUNS	HITS
Tom Brown	1521	1952
Harry Stovey	1492	1770
Arlie Latham	1478	1833
Mike Griffin	1405	1759
King Kelly	1357	1813
George Gore	1327	1612
Mike Tiernan	1313	1834
Donie Bush	1280	1804
Bobby Bonds	1258	1886
Sam Thompson	1256	1979
Eddie Yost	1215	1863
Cupid Childs	1214	1720

added draw, the Reds began hearing that Cap Anson, whose Chicago Colts seemed nearly as certain to win the National League flag, might be persuaded even in the absence of a National Agreement to meet them in a World's Series. That rumor caused a crisis in the League camp, leading to a secret strategy session. What grew out of it will never be known, but subsequent events tend to support Anson's contention that his club was robbed of the 1891 pennant.

In any case, after only four games with the Reds, Kelly jumped ship and rejoined his old League team, the Boston Beaneaters. The Beaneaters were Chicago's only remaining challenger, but when they suffered a second straight loss to the Colts on September 15, the *Sporting News* proclaimed they "might as well give up all hope of flying the flag." The following day, though, with just 20 games left to go, Kid Nichols beat Chicago for the first time in 1891 to launch an 18-game winning streak that enabled Boston to overtake Chicago at the wire and capture the pennant. Knowing that a postseason clash could only benefit the Association, particularly if the Reds were to win it, the Beaneaters were not about to meet their crosstown rival in a World's Series and instructed League president Nick Young to rebuff Association president Zach Phelps's formal challenge when it was issued on October 9. Instead of what might have been a glorious postseason match, the 1891 season was allowed to dwindle away in a string of late-autumn exhibition games. In December, at the Bates House hotel in Indianapolis, League and Association potentates met for a week in closed session to thrash out their differences. Out of that conference came an end to war, a revived National Agreement and a new major league.

THE SEASONAL RECORD

NATIONAL LEAGUE

	W	L	PCT	HOME	ROAD	GB
1. Boston Beaneaters	87	51	.630	51–20	36–31	—
2. Chicago Colts	82	53	.607	43–22	39–31	3.5
3. New York Giants	71	61	.538	39–28	32–33	13
4. Philadelphia Phillies	68	69	.496	35–34	33–35	18.5
5. Cleveland Spiders	65	74	.468	40–28	25–46	22.5
6. Brooklyn Bridegrooms	61	76	.445	41–31	20–45	25.5
7. Cincinnati Reds	56	81	.409	26–41	30–40	30.5
8. Pittsburgh Pirates	55	80	.407	32–34	23–46	30.5

	Bos	Chi	NY	Phi	Cle	Bro	Cin	Pit	
Boston	—	7	15	12	11	15	11	16	87
Chicago	13	—	5	9	16	13	14	12	82
New York	5	13	—	9	13	11	13	7	71
Philadelphia	7	10	10	—	10	8	11	12	68
Cleveland	9	4	6	10	—	9	13	14	65
Brooklyn	5	7	8	12	11	—	9	9	61
Cincinnati	9	6	5	9	7	10	—	10	56
Pittsburgh	3	6	12	8	6	10	10	—	55
	51	53	61	69	74	76	81	80	545

SEASON LEADERS

Batting Average

1.	Hamilton, Philadelphia	.340
2.	Holliday, Cincinnati	.319
3.	Browning, Pit–Cin	.317
4.	Clements, Philadelphia	.310
5.	Tiernan, New York	.306

On–Base Percentage

1.	Hamilton, Philadelphia	.453
2.	Connor, New York	.399
3.	Childs, Cleveland	.395
	Browning, Pit–Cin	.395
5.	Tiernan, New York	.388

Slugging Average

1.	Stovey, Boston	.498
2.	Tiernan, New York	.494
3.	Holliday, Cincinnati	.473
4.	Connor, New York	.449
5.	Ryan, Chicago	.434

Total Bases

1.	Stovey, Boston	271
2.	Tiernan, New York	268
3.	Long, Boston	235
4.	Davis, Cleveland	233
5.	Beckley, Pittsburgh	232

Home Runs

1.	Tiernan, New York	16
	Stovey, Boston	16
3.	Wilmot, Chicago	11
4.	Holliday, Cincinnati	9
	Dahlen, Chicago	9
	Ryan, Chicago	9
	Long, Boston	9

Hits

1.	Hamilton, Philadelphia	179
2.	McKean, Cleveland	170
3.	Tiernan, New York	166
4.	Davis, Cleveland	165
5.	O'Rourke, New York	164

Stolen Bases

1.	Hamilton, Philadelphia	111
2.	Latham, Cincinnati	87
3.	Griffin, Brooklyn	65
4.	Long, Boston	60
5.	Stovey, Boston	57
	Ward, Brooklyn	57

RBI

1.	Anson, Chicago	120
2.	Stovey, Boston	95
	O'Rourke, New York	95
	Nash, Boston	95
5.	Connor, New York	94

Runs

1.	Hamilton, Philadelphia	141
2.	Long, Boston	129
3.	Childs, Cleveland	120
4.	Latham, Cincinnati	119
5.	Stovey, Boston	118

Strikeouts

1.	Stovey, Boston	69
2.	M. Baldwin, Pittsburgh	67
3.	H. Collins, Brooklyn	63
4.	Hutchison, Chicago	62
5.	Bennett, Boston	61

PITCHING

Wins

1.	Hutchison, Chicago	44
2.	Rusie, New York	33
3.	Clarkson, Boston	33
4.	Nichols, Boston	30
5.	Young, Cleveland	27

Innings

1.	Hutchison, Chicago	561
2.	Rusie, New York	500.1
3.	Clarkson, Chicago	460.2
4.	M. Baldwin, Pittsburgh	437.2
5.	Mullane, Cincinnati	426.1

Strikeouts

1.	Rusie, New York	337
2.	Hutchison, Chicago	261
3.	Nichols, Boston	240
4.	M. Baldwin, Pittsburgh	197
5.	King, Pittsburgh	160

Losses

1.	King, Pittsburgh	29
2.	M. Baldwin, Pittsburgh	28
3.	Mullane, Cincinnati	26
4.	Rhines, Cincinnati	24
5.	Young, Cleveland	22
	Gruber, Cleveland	22
	Gleason, Philadelphia	22

Complete Games

1.	Hutchison, Chicago	56
2.	Rusie, New York	52
3.	M. Baldwin, Pittsburgh	48
4.	Clarkson, Boston	47
5.	Nichols, Boston	45

Winning Percentage (25 dec.)

1.	J. Ewing, New York	.724
2.	Hutchison, Chicago	.698
3.	Staley, Pit–Bos	.649
4.	Nichols, Boston	.638
5.	Clarkson, Boston	.635

ERA (140 innings)

1. J. Ewing, New York		2.27
2. Nichols, Boston		2.39
3. Rusie, New York		2.55
4. Staley, Pit–Bos		2.58
5. M. Baldwin, Pittsburgh		2.76

Lowest On–Base Percentage

1. Staley, Pit–Bos		.292
2. Hutchison, Chicago		.293
3. Nichols, Boston		.296
4. J. Ewing, New York		.305
Clarkson, Boston		.305

FIELDING

Total Chances

1B	Virtue, Cleveland	1553
2B	Pfeffer, Chicago	980
3B	Latham, Cincinnati	622
SS	Long, Boston	871
OF	Griffin, Brooklyn	400
C	Zimmer, Cleveland	702
P	Clarkson, Boston	154

Fielding Average

W. Brown, Philadelphia	.989
McPhee, Cincinnati	.954
Bassett, New York	.908
Cooney, Chicago	.917
Griffin, Brooklyn	.960
Bennett, Boston	.960
Mullane, Cincinnati	.958

BOSTON Frank Selee South End Grounds (I)

		G	AB	H	R	2B	3B	HR	RBI	BB	SB	BA	SA
SS	Herman Long	139	577	163	129	21	12	9	76	80	60	.282	.407
1B	Tommy Tucker	140	548	148	103	16	5	2	69	37	26	.270	.328
RF	Harry Stovey	134	544	152	118	31	**20**	**16**	95	78	57	.279	**.498**
3B	Billy Nash	140	537	148	92	24	9	5	95	74	28	.276	.282
CF	Steve Brodie	133	523	136	84	13	6	2	78	63	25	.260	.319
2B	Joe Quinn	124	508	122	70	8	10	3	63	28	24	.240	.313
LF	Bobby Lowe	125	497	129	92	19	5	6	74	53	43	.260	.354
C	Charlie Ganzel	70	263	68	33	18	5	1	29	12	7	.259	.376
C	Charlie Bennett	75	256	55	35	9	3	5	39	42	3	.215	.332
P	John Clarkson	55	187	42	28	7	4	0	26	18	2	.225	.305
P	Kid Nichols	52	183	36	21	6	0	0	27	12	1	.197	.230
P	Harry Staley	31	102	17	7	4	0	1	16	8	0	.167	.235
Sub	Marty Sullivan	17	67	15	15	1	0	2	7	5	7	.224	.328
Sub	King Kelly	16	52	12	7	1	0	0	5	6	6	.231	.250
Sub	Joe Kelley	12	45	11	7	1	1	0	3	2	0	.244	.311
P	Charlie Getzein	14	41	7	4	2	1	1	6	7	0	.171	.341
Sub	George Rooks	5	16	2	1	0	0	0	0	4	0	.125	.125
Sub	Fred Lake	5	7	1	1	0	0	0	0	2	0	.143	.143
P	John Kiley	1	2	0	0	0	0	0	0	1	0	.000	.000
P	Cyclone Ryan	1	1	0	0	0	0	0	0	0	0	.000	.000
P	Charlie Brynan	1	0	0	0	0	0	0	0	0	0	—	—
P	Jim Sullivan	1	0	0	0	0	0	0	0	0	0	—	—
		140	4956	1264	**847**	181	81	53	**708**	**532**	289	.255	.356

1B Tucker 140, Stovey 1
2B Quinn 124, Lowe 17
SS Long 139, Lowe 2
3B Nash 140. Lowe 1
OF Stovey 134, Brodie 133, Lowe 107, Sullivan 17, Ganzel 13, Kelley 12, Kelly 6, Rooks 5, Getzein 3, Lake 1, Clarkson 1
C Bennett 75, Ganzel 59, Kelly 11, Lake 4
P Clarkson 55, Nichols 52, Staley 31, Getzein 11, Kiley 1, Ryan 1, Sullivan 1, Brynan 1, Lowe 1, Tucker 1

	G	IP	GS	CG	W	L	K	BB	SH	SV	ERA
John Clarkson	55	460.2	51	47	33	19	141	154	3	**3**	2.79
Kid Nichols	52	425.1	48	45	30	17	240	103	5	**3**	2.39
Harry Staley	31	252.1	30	26	20	8	114	69	1	0	2.50
Charlie Getzein	11	89	9	7	4	5	29	23	0	0	3.84
John Kiley	1	8	1	1	0	1	1	5	0	0	6.75
Cyclone Ryan	1	3	0	0	0	0	0	1	0	0	0.00
Charlie Brynan	1	1	1	0	0	1	0	3	0	0	54.00
Bobby Lowe	1	1	0	0	0	0	0	1	0	0	9.00
Tommy Tucker	1	1	0	0	0	0	0	0	0	0	9.00
Jim Sullivan	1	0.1	0	0	0	0	0	5	0	0	81.00
		1241.2	140	**126**	87	51	525	**364**	9	**6**	**2.76**

CHICAGO   **Cap Anson**   **South Side Park (II) 36 games**   **West Side Park (1) 31 games**

		G	AB	H	R	2B	3B	HR	RBI	BB	SB	BA	SA
3B	Bill Dahlen	135	549	143	114	18	13	9	76	67	21	.260	.390
1B	Cap Anson	136	540	157	81	24	8	8	**120**	75	17	.291	.409
RF	Cliff Carroll	130	515	132	87	20	8	7	80	50	31	.256	.367
CF	Jimmy Ryan	118	505	140	110	22	15	9	66	53	27	.277	.434
LF	Walt Wilmot	121	498	139	102	14	10	11	71	55	42	.279	.414
2B	Fred Pfeffer	137	498	123	93	12	9	7	77	79	40	.247	.349
SS	Jimmy Cooney	118	465	114	84	15	3	0	42	48	21	.245	.290
C	Mal Kittridge	79	296	62	26	8	5	2	27	17	4	.209	.291
Sub	Tom Burns	59	243	55	36	8	1	1	17	21	18	.226	.280
P	Bill Hutchison	67	243	45	27	4	2	2	25	17	5	.185	.242
P	Ad Gumbert	34	105	32	18	7	4	0	16	13	4	.305	.448
P	Pat Luby	32	98	24	19	2	4	2	24	8	3	.245	.408
Sub	Pop Schriver	27	90	30	15	1	4	1	21	10	1	.333	.467
Sub	Bill Bowman	15	45	4	2	1	0	0	5	5	0	.089	.111
P	Ed Stein	14	43	7	4	1	0	0	4	3	0	.163	.186
Sub	Bill Merritt	11	42	9	4	1	0	0	4	2	0	.214	.238
P	Tom Vickery	14	39	7	3	1	0	0	1	0	3	.179	.205
Sub	Tom Nagle	8	25	3	3	0	0	0	1	1	0	.120	.120
Sub	Elmer Foster	4	16	3	3	0	0	1	1	1	1	.188	.375
Sub	Marty Honan	5	12	2	1	0	1	0	3	1	0	.167	.333
P	George Nicol	3	6	2	0	0	1	0	3	0	0	.333	.667
		137	4873	1233	832	159	88	**60**	684	526	238	.253	.359

1B   Anson 136, Schriver 2, Merritt 1, Luby 1, Gumbert 1
2B   Pfeffer 137
SS   Cooney 118, Dahlen 15, Burns 4, Ryan 2, Vickery 1
3B   Dahlen 84, Burns 53
OF   Carroll 130, Wilmot 121, Ryan 117, Dahlen 37, Foster 4, Burns 2, Luby 2, Gumbert 1, Nagle 1, Hutchison 1
C   Kittridge 79, Schriver 27, Bowman 15, Merritt 11, Nagle 7, Honan 5, Anson 2
P   Hutchison 66, Gumbert 32, Luby 30, Vickery 14, Stein 14, Nicol 3, Ryan 2

	G	IP	GS	CG	W	L	K	BB	SH	SV	ERA
Bill Hutchison	**66**	**561**	**58**	**56**	**44**	19	261	178	4	1	2.81
Ad Gumbert	32	256.1	31	24	17	11	73	90	1	0	3.58
Pat Luby	30	206	24	18	8	11	52	94	0	1	4.76
Ed Stein	14	101	10	9	7	6	38	57	1	0	3.74
Tom Vickery	14	79.2	12	7	6	5	39	44	0	0	4.07
George Nicol	3	11	2	0	0	1	12	10	0	0	4.91
Jimmy Ryan	2	5.2	0	0	0	0	2	2	0	1	1.59
		1220.2	137	114	82	53	477	475	6	3	3.47

NEW YORK Jim Mutrie **Polo Grounds (III)**

		G	AB	H	R	2B	3B	HR	RBI	BB	SB	BA	SA
LF	Jim O'Rourke	136	555	164	92	28	7	5	95	26	19	.295	.398
RF	Mike Tiernan	134	542	166	111	30	12	**16**	73	69	53	.306	.494
CF	George Gore	130	528	150	103	22	7	2	48	74	19	.284	.364
3B	Charlie Bassett	130	524	136	60	19	8	4	68	36	16	.260	.349
2B	Danny Richardson	114	516	139	85	18	5	4	51	33	28	.269	.347
1B	Roger Connor	129	479	139	112	29	13	7	94	83	27	.290	.449
SS	Jack Glasscock	97	369	89	46	12	6	0	55	36	29	.241	.306
Sub	Lew Whistler	72	265	65	39	8	7	3	38	24	4	.245	.362
C	Dick Buckley	75	253	55	23	9	1	4	31	11	3	.217	.308
P	Amos Rusie	62	220	54	30	5	2	0	15	3	2	.245	.286
C	Archie Clarke	48	174	33	17	2	2	0	21	15	5	.190	.224
P	John Ewing	33	113	23	10	1	0	0	8	3	4	.204	.212
P	Mickey Welch	22	71	10	4	0	0	0	4	3	0	.141	.141
Sub	Buster Burrell	15	53	5	1	0	0	0	1	3	2	.094	.094
Sub	Buck Ewing	14	49	17	8	2	1	0	18	5	5	.347	.429
P	Jack Sharrott	10	30	10	5	2	0	1	7	1	3	.333	.500
P	Roscoe Coughlin	8	23	3	3	1	1	0	1	5	1	.130	.261
P	Tim Keefe	8	21	2	2	0	0	0	1	3	1	.095	.095
Sub	Jerry Denny	4	16	4	0	1	0	0	1	0	2	.250	.313
P	Bob Barr	5	11	1	0	0	0	0	0	2	0	.091	.091
P	Mike Sullivan	3	10	2	3	0	0	0	0	0	1	.200	.200
P	Dad Clarkson	5	9	4	0	0	0	0	0	2	0	.444	.444
P	Jack Taylor	1	2	0	0	0	0	0	0	1	0	.000	.000
P	Andy Dunning	1	0	0	0	0	0	0	0	0	0	—	—
		136	4833	1271	754	189	72	46	630	438	224	**.263**	**.360**

1B	Connor 129, Whistler 7
2B	Richardson 114, Bassett 9, B. Ewing 8, Whistler 6
SS	Glasscock 97, Whistler 33, Richardson 9
3B	Bassett 121, Whistler 5, Clarke 5, Denny 4, Buckley 1
OF	Tiernan 134, Gore 130, O'Rourke 126, Whistler 22, Clarke 2, Rusie 1, Burrell 1
C	Buckley 74, Clarke 42, Burrell 15, O'Rourke 14, B. Ewing 6
P	Rusie 61, J. Ewing 33, Welch 22, Sharrott 10, Keefe 8, Coughlin 8, Clarkson 5, Barr 5, Sullivan 3, Dunning 1, Taylor 1

	G	IP	GS	CG	W	L	K	BB	SH	SV	ERA
Amos Rusie #	61	500.1	57	52	33	20	**337**	262	**6**	1	2.55
John Ewing	33	269.1	30	28	21	8	138	105	5	0	**2.27**
Mickey Welch	22	160	15	14	5	9	46	97	0	1	4.28
Jack Sharrott	10	69.1	9	6	5	5	41	35	0	1	2.60
Roscoe Coughlin	8	61	7	6	3	4	22	23	0	0	3.84
Tim Keefe	8	55	7	4	2	5	29	27	0	0	5.24
Dad Clarkson	5	28	2	1	1	2	11	18	0	0	2.89
Bob Barr	5	27	4	2	0	4	11	12	0	0	5.33
Mike Sullivan	3	24	3	3	1	2	11	8	0	0	3.38
Jack Taylor	1	8	1	1	0	1	3	3	0	0	1.13
Andy Dunning	1	2	1	0	0	1	2	3	0	0	4.50
		1204	136	117	71	61	**651**	593	**11**	3	2.99

No-hit game 6–0 vs Brooklyn, July 31

PHILADELPHIA   **Harry Wright**   **Philadelphia Baseball Grounds**

		G	AB	H	R	2B	3B	HR	RBI	BB	SB	BA	SA
RF	Sam Thompson	133	554	163	108	23	10	8	90	52	29	.294	.415
CF	Ed Delahanty	128	543	132	92	19	9	4	86	33	25	.243	.333
LF	Billy Hamilton	133	527	**179**	**141**	23	7	2	60	**102**	111	**.340**	.421
2B	Al Myers	135	514	118	67	27	2	2	69	69	8	.230	.302
1B	Willard Brown	115	441	107	62	20	4	0	50	34	7	.243	.306
SS	Bob Allen	118	438	97	46	7	4	1	51	43	12	.221	.263
C	Jack Clements	107	423	131	58	29	4	4	75	43	3	.310	.426
3B	Billy Shindle	103	415	87	68	13	1	0	38	33	17	.210	.246
Sub	Ed Mayer	68	268	50	24	2	4	0	31	14	7	.187	.224
P	Kid Gleason	65	214	53	31	5	2	0	17	20	6	.248	.290
P	Duke Esper	39	123	27	18	4	1	0	9	7	1	.220	.268
P	John Thornton	39	123	17	7	3	0	0	6	2	1	.138	.163
Sub	Bill Grey	23	75	18	11	0	0	0	7	3	3	.240	.240
Sub	Jerry Denny	19	73	21	5	1	1	0	11	4	1	.288	.329
P	Bill Kling	13	31	6	3	0	0	0	2	7	0	.194	.194
Sub	Jocko Fields	8	30	7	4	2	1	0	5	4	0	.233	.367
P	Tim Keefe	11	29	5	0	0	1	0	1	4	0	.172	.241
Sub	Lou Graulich	7	26	8	2	0	0	0	3	1	0	.308	.308
Sub	Joe Donohue	6	22	7	2	1	0	0	2	1	0	.318	.364
P	Ed Cassian	6	17	2	0	0	0	0	1	0	0	.118	.118
Sub	Harry Morelock	4	14	1	1	0	0	0	0	3	0	.071	.071
P	Phenomenal Smith	3	8	3	0	0	0	0	2	2	1	.375	.375
P	John Schultze	6	6	1	3	1	0	0	0	0	0	.167	.333
Sub	Walter Plock	2	5	2	2	0	0	0	0	0	0	.400	.400
P	Mike Kilroy	3	5	2	1	0	0	1	1	1	0	.400	.400
P	Joe Gormley	1	4	0	0	0	0	0	0	0	0	.000	.000
P	Phil Saylor	1	1	0	0	0	0	0	0	0	0	.000	.000
Sub	Charlie Bastian	1	0	0	0	0	0	0	0	0	0	—	—
		138	4929	1244	756	180	51	21	617	482	232	.252	.322

1B   Brown 97, Delahanty 27, Denny 12, Graulich 3, Clements 2
2B   Myers 135, Delahanty 3, Mayer 1
SS   Allen 118, Mayer 7, Morelock 4, Gleason 4, Shindle 3, Grey 3, Donohue 2
3B   Shindle 100, Mayer 31, Denny 7, Grey 1
OF   Thompson 133, Hamilton 133, Delahanty 97, Mayer 29, Grey 10, Gleason 9, Donohue 4, Thornton 3, Brown 2, Plock 2, Kling 1
C   Clements 107, Brown 19, Grey 11, Fields 8, Graulich 4
P   Gleason 53, Esper 39, Thornton 37, Kling 12, Keefe 11, Cassian 6, Schultze 6, Smith 3, Kilroy 3, Gormley 1, Saylor 1

	G	IP	GS	CG	W	L	K	BB	SH	SV	ERA
Kid Gleason	53	418	44	40	24	22	100	165	1	1	3.51
Duke Esper	39	296	36	25	20	15	108	121	1	1	3.56
John Thornton	37	269	32	23	15	16	52	115	1	2	3.68
Tim Keefe	11	76.1	10	9	3	6	35	28	0	1	3.91
Bill Kling	12	75	7	4	4	2	26	32	0	0	4.32
Ed Cassian	6	38	4	3	1	3	10	16	0	0	2.84
Phenomenal Smith	3	19	2	0	1	1	3	8	0	0	4.26
John Schultze	6	15	1	0	0	1	4	11	0	0	6.60
Mike Kilroy	3	10	1	0	0	2	3	4	0	0	9.90
Joe Gormley	1	8	1	1	0	1	2	5	0	0	5.63
Phil Saylor	1	3	0	0	0	0	0	0	0	0	6.00
		1229.1	138	105	68	69	343	505	3	5	3.73

CLEVELAND   Bob Leadley (34–34)   Patsy Tebeau (34–40)   **League Park (I)**

		G	AB	H	R	2B	3B	HR	RBI	BB	SB	BA	SA
SS	Ed McKean	141	603	170	115	13	12	6	69	64	14	.282	.373
CF	George Davis	136	570	165	115	35	12	3	89	53	42	.289	.409
LF	Jimmy McAleer	136	565	134	97	16	11	1	61	49	51	.237	.310
2B	Cupid Childs	141	551	155	120	21	12	2	83	97	39	.281	.374
1B	Jake Virtue	139	517	135	82	19	14	2	72	75	15	.261	.364
C	Chief Zimmer	116	440	112	55	21	4	3	69	33	15	.255	.341
RF	Spud Johnson	80	327	84	49	8	3	1	46	22	16	.257	.309
Sub	Jack Doyle	69	250	69	43	14	4	0	43	26	24	.276	.364
3B	Patsy Tebeau	61	249	65	38	8	3	1	41	16	12	.261	.329
P	Cy Young	55	174	29	23	5	2	1	18	11	2	.167	.236
Sub	Jesse Burkett	42	167	45	29	7	4	0	13	23	1	.269	.359
P	Leon Viau	45	144	23	15	3	2	0	6	12	2	.160	.208
P	Henry Gruber	46	141	23	17	3	2	1	20	21	0	.163	.234
Sub	Jerry Denny	36	138	31	17	5	0	0	21	12	3	.225	.261
Sub	John Shearon	30	124	30	10	1	1	0	13	1	6	.242	.266
Sub	Billy Alvord	13	59	17	7	2	2	1	7	0	0	.288	.341
P	Ed Seward	7	19	4	2	2	0	0	1	3	0	.211	.316
P	Ed Beatin	5	13	1	0	0	0	0	0	0	0	.077	.077
P	Frank Knauss	3	6	1	1	0	0	0	0	0	0	.167	.167
Sub	Marty Sullivan	1	4	1	0	0	0	0	1	0	0	.250	.250
P	Charlie Getzein	1	4	0	0	0	0	0	0	0	0	.000	.000
Sub	Bill Collins	2	3	0	0	0	0	0	0	0	0	.000	.000
P	Henry Killeen	1	3	0	0	0	0	0	0	1	0	.000	.000
Sub	Joe Daly	1	3	0	0	0	0	0	0	1	0	.000	.000
		141	5074	**1294**	835	183	88	22	673	519	242	.255	.339

1B   Virtue 139, Seward 1, Johnson 1
2B   Childs 141
SS   McKean 141, Doyle 1
3B   Tebeau 61, Denny 29, Davis 22, Doyle 20, Alvord 13, Zimmer 1
OF   McAleer 136, Davis 116, Johnson 79, Burkett 42, Shearon 28, Doyle 21, Denny 8, Seward 3, Gruber 2, Viau 1, Collins 1, Sullivan 1, Daly 1, Tebeau 1
C   Zimmer 116, Doyle 29, Collins 1
P   Young 55, Viau 45, Gruber 44, Shearon 6, Beatin 5, Knauss 3, Seward 3, Davis 3, Getzein 1, Killeen 1

	G	IP	GS	CG	W	L	K	BB	SH	SV	ERA
Cy Young	55	423.2	46	43	27	22	147	140	0	2	2.85
Henry Gruber	44	348.2	40	35	17	22	79	119	1	0	4.13
Leon Viau	45	343.2	38	31	18	17	130	138	0	0	3.01
John Shearon	6	46	5	4	1	3	19	24	0	0	3.52
Ed Beatin	5	29	4	2	0	3	4	21	0	0	5.28
Ed Seward	3	16.1	3	0	2	1	4	1	0	0	3.86
Frank Knauss	3	15	3	1	0	3	6	8	0	0	7.20
Charlie Getzein	1	9	1	1	0	1	4	4	0	0	8.00
Henry Killeen	1	8.2	1	1	0	1	3	8	0	0	6.23
George Davis	3	4	0	0	0	1	4	3	0	1	15.75
		1244	141	118	65	74	400	476	1	3	3.50

BROOKLYN   **Monte Ward**   **Eastern Park**

		G	AB	H	R	2B	3B	HR	RBI	BB	SB	BA	SA
CF	Mike Griffin	134	521	139	106	**36**	9	3	65	57	65	.271	.392
1B	Dave Foutz	130	521	134	87	26	8	2	73	40	48	.257	.349
3B	George Pinkney	135	501	137	80	19	6	2	71	66	44	.273	.347
RF	Oyster Burns	123	470	134	75	24	13	4	83	53	21	.285	.417
SS	Monte Ward	105	441	122	85	13	5	0	39	36	57	.277	.329
2B	Hub Collins	107	435	120	82	16	5	23	31	59	32	.276	.356
LF	Darby O'Brien	103	395	100	79	18	6	5	57	39	31	.253	.367
C	Tom KInslow	61	228	54	22	6	0	0	33	9	3	.237	.263
C	Con Daily	60	206	66	25	10	1	0	30	15	7	.320	.379
Sub	Tom Daly	58	200	50	29	11	5	2	27	21	7	.250	.385
P	Bob Caruthers	56	171	48	24	5	3	2	23	25	4	.281	.380
Sub	John O'Brien	43	167	41	22	4	2	0	26	12	4	.246	.293
P	Tom Lovett	44	153	25	14	1	2	0	17	7	4	.163	.196
Sub	Bones Ely	31	111	17	9	0	1	0	11	7	4	.153	.171
P	Adonis Terry	30	91	19	10	7	1	0	6	9	4	.209	.308
P	George Hemming	27	82	13	11	3	2	0	10	6	2	.159	.244
P	Bert Inks	13	35	10	3	1	0	0	0	2	0	.286	.314
Sub	Jack Burdock	3	12	1	1	0	0	0	1	1	0	.083	.083
Sub	Dude Esterbrook	3	8	3	1	0	0	0	0	0	0	.375	.375
		137	4748	1233	765	**200**	69	23	603	464	337	.260	.345

1B   Foutz 124, Daly 15, Daily 1
2B   Collins 72, O'Brien 43, Ward 18, Burdock 3, Esterbrook 1, Ely 1, Caruthers 1
SS   Ward 87, Ely 28, Daly 11, Burns 6, Pinkney 5, Daily 2, Foutz 1
3B   Pinkney 130, Burns 5, Ely 2
OF   Griffin 134, Burns 113, O'Brien 103, Collins 35, Caruthers 17, Daly 7, Terry 5, Daily 3, Esterbrook 2
C   Kinslow 61, Daily 55, Daly 26
P   Lovett 44, Caruthers 38, Hemming 27, Terry 25, Inks 13, Foutz 6

	G	IP	GS	CG	W	L	K	BB	SH	SV	ERA
Tom Lovett #	44	365.2	43	39	23	19	129	129	3	0	3.69
Bob Caruthers	38	297	32	29	18	14	69	107	2	1	3.12
George Hemming	27	199.2	22	19	8	15	83	84	1	1	4.96
Adonis Terry	25	194	22	18	6	16	65	80	1	1	4.22
Bert Inks	13	96.1	13	11	3	10	47	43	1	0	4.02
Dave Foutz	6	52	5	5	3	2	14	16	0	0	3.29
		1204.2	137	121	61	76	407	459	8	3	3.86

No-hit game 4–0 vs New York, September 22

CINCINNATI   **Tom Loftus**   **League Park (I)**

		G	AB	H	R	2B	3B	HR	RBI	BB	SB	BA	SA
2B	Bid McPhee	138	562	144	107	14	16	6	38	74	33	.256	.370
1B	Long John Reilly	135	546	132	60	20	13	4	64	9	22	.242	.348
3B	Arlie Latham	135	533	145	119	20	10	7	53	74	87	.272	.386
SS	Germany Smith	138	512	103	50	11	5	3	53	38	16	.201	.260
CF	Bug Holliday	111	442	141	74	21	10	9	84	37	30	.319	.473
C	Jerry Harrington	92	333	76	25	10	5	2	41	19	4	.228	.306
RF	Lefty Marr	72	286	74	32	9	7	0	32	25	16	.259	.339
C	Jim Keenan	75	252	51	30	7	5	4	33	33	2	.202	.317
Sub	Jocko Halligan	61	247	77	43	13	6	3	44	24	5	.312	.449
LF	Pete Browning	55	216	74	29	10	3	0	33	24	12	.343	.417
P	Tony Mullane	64	209	31	16	1	2	0	10	18	4	.148	.172
OF	Mike Slattery	41	158	33	24	3	2	1	16	10	1	.209	.272
P	Billy Rhines	48	148	18	10	3	1	0	5	7	1	.122	.155
Sub	Ervin Curtis	27	108	29	11	3	3	1	13	9	3	.269	.380
P	Hoss Radbourn	29	96	17	11	2	2	0	10	4	1	.177	.240
Sub	Bob Clark	16	54	6	2	0	0	0	3	6	3	.111	.111
P	Cannonball Crane	15	46	5	3	0	0	0	2	3	3	.109	.109
P	Jesse Duryea	10	32	1	0	0	0	0	3	0	1	.031	.031
Sub	Frank Foreman	1	4	1	0	1	0	0	0	0	0	.250	.500
Sub	Pop Corkhill	1	4	0	0	0	0	0	0	0	0	.000	.000
P	Clarence Stephens	1	3	0	0	0	0	0	0	0	0	.000	.000
		138	4791	1158	646	148	**90**	40	537	414	244	.242	.335

1B	Reilly 100, Keenan 41
2B	McPhee 138
SS	Smith 138
3B	Latham 135, Mullane 3, Radbourn 1, Harrington 1, Keenan 1
OF	Holliday 111, Marr 72, Halligan 61, Browning 55, Slattery 41, Reilly 36, Curtis 27, Mullane 12, Radbourn 2, Corkhill 1, Foreman 1
C	Harrington 92, Keenan 34, Clark 16, Latham 1
P	Mullane 51, Rhines 48, Radbourn 26, Crane 15, Duryea 10, Stephens 1

	G	IP	GS	CG	W	L	K	BB	SH	SV	ERA
Tony Mullane	51	426.1	47	42	23	26	124	187	1	0	3.23
Billy Rhines	48	372.2	43	40	17	24	138	124	1	1	2.87
Hoss Radbourn	26	218	24	23	11	13	54	62	2	0	4.25
Cannonball Crane	15	116.2	13	11	4	8	51	64	1	0	4.09
Jesse Duryea	10	77	10	8	1	9	23	25	0	0	5.38
Clarence Stephens	1	8	1	1	0	1	3	3	0	0	7.88
— One combined shutout on April 27; Mullane 3 innings, Rhines 6 innings —											
		1218.2	138	125	56	81	393	465	5	1	3.55

PITTSBURGH	Ned Hanlon (31–47)			Bill McGunnigle (24–33)				Exposition Park				
	G	AB	H	R	2B	3B	HR	RBI	BB	SB	BA	SA
1B Jake Beckley	133	554	162	94	20	19	4	73	44	13	.292	.422
UT Doggie Miller	135	548	156	80	19	6	4	57	59	35	.285	.363
2B Lou Bierbauer	121	500	103	60	13	6	1	47	28	12	.206	.262
CF Ned Hanlon	119	455	121	87	12	8	0	60	48	54	.266	.327
3B Charlie Reilly	114	415	91	43	8	5	3	44	29	20	.219	.284
RF Fred Carroll	91	353	77	55	13	4	4	48	48	22	.218	.312
SS Frank Shugart	75	320	88	57	19	8	3	33	20	21	.275	.412
C Connie Mack	75	280	60	43	10	0	0	29	19	4	.214	.250
LF Pete Browning	50	203	59	35	14	1	4	28	27	4	.291	.429
P Mark Baldwin	53	177	27	11	3	2	1	12	15	1	.153	.209
P Al Maul	47	149	28	15	2	4	0	14	20	4	.188	.255
P Silver King	49	148	25	12	2	3	0	9	14	0	.169	.223
OF Pop Corkhill	41	145	33	16	1	1	3	20	7	7	.228	.310
OF Bud Lally	41	143	32	24	6	2	1	17	16	0	.224	.315
Sub Tun Berger	43	134	32	15	2	2	1	14	12	4	.239	.291
P Pud Galvin	33	109	18	11	0	0	0	7	3	0	.165	.165
Sub Jocko Fields	23	75	18	10	3	0	0	5	10	1	.240	.280
P Harry Staley	9	31	7	4	0	1	0	3	3	0	.226	.290
Sub Piggy Ward	5	18	6	3	0	0	0	2	3	3	.333	.333
Sub John Newell	5	18	2	1	0	0	0	2	0	0	.111	.111
P Scott Stratton	2	8	1	1	0	0	0	0	0	0	.125	.125
Sub Ed Spurney	3	7	2	2	1	0	0	0	2	0	.286	.429
Sub Sam Laroque	1	4	0	0	0	0	0	0	0	0	.000	.000
	137	4794	1148	679	148	71	29	524	427	205	.239	.318

1B   Beckley 133, Mack 3, Miller 1
2B   Bierbauer 121, Berger 17
SS   Shugart 75, Miller 37, Reilly 11, Fields 8, Berger 6, Spurney 3, Hanlon 1
3B   Reilly 99, Miller 34, Newell 5, Laroque 1, King 1
OF   Hanlon 119, Carroll 91, Browning 50, Corkhill 41, Lally 41, Maul 40, Miller 24, Ward 5, Reilly 4, Kelley 2, Berger 2
C   Mack 72, Miller 41, Berger 18, Fields 15
P   Baldwin 53, King 48, Galvin 33, Staley 9, Maul 8, Stratton 2

	G	IP	GS	CG	W	L	K	BB	SH	SV	ERA
Mark Baldwin	53	437.2	50	48	22	28	197	227	2	0	2.76
Silver King	48	384.1	44	40	14	29	160	144	3	1	3.11
Pud Galvin	33	246.2	31	23	14	14	46	62	2	0	2.88
Harry Staley	9	71.2	7	6	4	5	25	11	0	0	2.89
Al Maul	8	39	3	3	1	2	13	16	0	1	2.31
Scott Stratton	2	18.1	2	2	0	2	5	5	0	0	2.45
		1197.2	137	122	55	80	446	465	7	2	2.89

AMERICAN ASSOCIATION

	W	L	PCT	HOME	ROAD	GB
1. Boston Reds	93	42	.689	51–17	42–25	—
2. St. Louis Browns	85	51	.625	52–20	33–31	8.5
3. Milwaukee Brewers	21	15	.583	16–5	5–10	22.5
4. Baltimore Orioles	71	64	.526	44–24	27–40	22
5. Philadelphia Athletics	73	66	.525	43–26	30–40	22
6. Columbus Solons	61	76	.445	34–29	27–47	33
7. Cincinnati Kelly's Killers	43	57	.430	24–20	19–37	32.5
8. Louisville Colonels	54	83	.394	40–32	14–51	40
9. Washington Nationals	44	91	.326	28–40	16–51	49

	Bos	StL	Bal	Phi	Col	Cin/Mil	Lou	Was	
Boston	—	8	12	13	15	8/5	14	18	93
St. Louis	10	—	12	10	11	14/0	11	17	85
Baltimore	8	7	—	9	12	7/3	14	11	71
Philadelphia	7	10	10	—	11	8/5	12	10	73
Columbus	5	9	7	9	—	7/0	12	12	61
Cincinnati	5	5	5	4	8	—	7	9	43
Milwaukee	2	1	3	3	5	—	3	4	21
Louisville	3	9	6	8	8	9/1	—	10	54
Washington	2	2	9	10	6	4/1	10	—	44
	42	52	64	66	76	57/15	84	91	559

SEASON LEADERS

Batting Average (325 ABs)

1. Brouthers, Boston	.350
2. Duffy, Boston	.336
3. O'Neill, St. Louis	.323
4. T. Brown, Boston	.321
5. Van Haltren, Baltimore	.318

On–Base Percentage

1. Brouthers, Boston	.471
2. D. Lyons, St. Louis	.445
3. Hoy, St. Louis	.424
4. Seery, Cincinnati	.423
5. Duffy, Boston	.408

Home Runs

1. Farrell, Boston	12
2. Milligan, Philadelphia	11
D. Lyons, St. Louis	11
4. O'Neill, St. Louis	10
Duffee, Columbus	10
Larkin, Philadelphia	10
Canavan, Cin–Mil	10

Slugging Average

1. Brouthers, Boston	.512
2. Milligan, Philadelphia	.505
3. Farrell, Boston	.474
4. T. Brown, Boston	.469
5. L. Cross, Philadelphia	.458

Total Bases

1. T. Brown, Boston	276
2. Van Haltren, Baltimore	251
3. Brouthers, Boston	249
4. Duffy, Boston	243
5. Werden, Baltimore	234

RBI

1. Farrell, Boston	110
Duffy, Boston	110
3. Brouthers, Boston	109
4. Milligan, Philadelphia	106
5. Werden, Baltimore	104

Hits

1. T. Brown, Boston	189
2. Duffy, Boston	180
Van Haltren, Baltimore	180
4. McCarthy, St. Louis	176
5. Brouthers, Boston	170

Stolen Bases

1. T. Brown, Boston	106
2. Duffy, Boston	85
3. Van Haltren, Baltimore	75
4. Hoy, St Louis	59
5. Radford, Boston	55

Runs

1. T. Brown, Boston	177
2. Van Haltren, Baltimore	136
3. Hoy, St. Louis	134
Duffy, Boston	134
5. McCarthy, St. Louis	124

Strikeouts

1. Brown, Boston	96
2. Gilbert, Baltimore	77
Lehane, Columbus	77
4. Weyhing, Philadelphia	65
5. Werden, Baltimore	59

PITCHING

Wins

1. McMahon, Baltimore	35
2. Haddock, Boston	34
3. Stivetts, St. Louis	33
4. Weyhing, Philadelphia	31
5. Buffinton, Boston	29

Innings

1. McMahon, Baltimore	503
2. Knell, Columbus	462
3. Weyhing, Philadelphia	450
4. Stivetts, St. Louis	440
5. Carsey, Washington	415

Strikeouts

1. Stivetts, St. Louis	259
2. Knell, Columbus	228
3. Weyhing, Philadelphia	219
McMahon, Baltimore	219
5. Chamberlain, Philadelphia	204

ERA (140 Innings)

1. Crane, Cincinnati	2.45
2. Haddock, Boston	2.49
3. Buffinton, Boston	2.55
4. McMahon, Baltimore	2.81
5. Stivetts, St. Louis	2.86

Losses

1. Carsey, Washington	37
2. Knell, Columbus	27
3. McMahon, Baltimore	25
4. Chamberlain, Philadelphia	23
Dwyer, Cin–Mil	23

Complete Games

1. McMahon, Baltimore	53
2. Weyhing, Philadelphia	51
3. Knell, Columbus	47
4. Carsey, Washington	46
5. Chamberlain, Philadelphia	44

Winning Percentage (25 decisions)

1. Buffinton, Boston	.763
2. Haddock, Boston	.756
3. Weyhing, Philadelphia	.608
4. Stivetts, St. Louis	.600
5. McMahon, Baltimore	.593

Lowest On–Base Percentage

1. Buffinton, Boston	.285
2. Haddock, Boston	.299
3. McMahon, Baltimore	.306
4. Weyhing, Philadelphia	.311
Stivetts, St. Louis	.317

FIELDING

Total Chances			Fielding Average	
1B	Comiskey, St. Louis	1511	Lehane, Columbus	.981
2B	Stricker, Boston	874	Crooks, Columbus	.957
3B	Gilbert, Baltimore	609	Whitney, Cin–StL	.902
SS	Corcoran, Philadelphia	806	Corcoran, Philadelphia	.911
OF	Weaver, Louisville	342	Weaver, Louisville	.956
C	Murphy, Boston	681	Murphy, Boston	.954
P	Knell, Columbus	169	Meekin, Louisville	.960

BOSTON   **Arthur Irwin**   **Congress Street Grounds**

		G	AB	H	R	2B	3B	HR	RBI	BB	SB	BA	SA
CF	Tom Brown	137	**589**	**189**	**177**	30	**21**	5	71	70	**106**	.321	.469
RF	Hugh Duffy	127	536	180	134	20	8	9	**110**	61	85	.336	.453
2B	Cub Stricker	139	514	111	96	15	4	0	46	63	54	.216	.261
1B	Dan Brouthers	130	486	170	117	26	19	5	108	87	31	**.350**	**.512**
UT	Duke Farrell	122	473	143	108	19	13	**12**	**110**	59	21	.302	.474
SS	Paul Radford	133	456	118	102	11	5	0	65	96	55	.259	.305
C	Morg Murphy	106	402	87	60	11	4	4	54	36	17	.216	.294
LF	Hardy Richardson	74	278	71	45	9	4	7	51	40	16	.255	.392
3B	Bill Joyce	65	243	75	76	9	15	3	51	63	36	.309	.506
P	George Haddock	58	185	45	30	4	1	3	23	21	3	.243	.324
P	Charlie Buffinton	58	181	34	16	2	1	1	16	19	0	.188	.227
Sub	Jack McGeachy	41	178	45	26	2	1	1	21	12	11	.253	.292
P	Darby O'Brien	41	128	30	19	1	0	0	10	8	3	.234	.242
Sub	John Irwin	19	72	16	6	2	2	0	15	6	6	.222	.306
P	Bill Daley	20	59	10	5	0	1	0	9	1	1	.169	.203
P	Clark Griffith	10	23	4	6	1	1	1	3	6	1	.174	.435
Sub	Arthur Irwin	6	17	2	1	0	0	0	0	2	0	.118	.118
Sub	King Kelly	4	15	4	2	0	0	1	4	0	1	.267	.467
P	John Fitzgerald	6	14	1	0	1	0	0	1	0	0	.071	.143
Sub	Tom Cotter	6	12	3	1	0	0	0	4	1	0	.250	.250
Sub	Tommy Dowd	4	11	1	1	0	0	0	0	0	0	.091	.091
Sub	Tim Donahue	4	7	0	0	0	0	0	0	0	0	.000	.000
Sub	Frank Quinlan	2	5	0	0	0	0	0	0	0	0	.000	.000
P	Kid Madden	1	3	2	0	0	0	0	1	0	0	.667	.667
Sub	Mike Flynn	1	2	0	0	0	0	0	0	0	0	.000	.000
		139	4889	**1341**	**1028**	163	100	52	**773**	651	447	**.274**	**.380**

1B	Brouthers 130, Farrell 4, Buffinton 4, Richardson 3, Joyce 1
2B	Stricker 139
SS	Radford 131, A. Irwin 6, Richardson 4, Duffy 1, J. Irwin 1
3B	Farrell 66, Joyce 64, Richardson 9, Duffy 3, J. Irwin 2
OF	Brown 137, Duffy 124, Richardson 60, McGeachy 41, Farrell 23, J. Irwin 17, Buffinton 10, Haddock 8, Dowd 4, Radford 4, Griffith 3, Murphy 2, Daley 2, Cotter 1, Quinlan 1
C	Murphy 104, Farrell 37, Cotter 5, Kelly 4, Donahue 4, Quinlan 1, Flynn 1
P	Haddock 51, Buffinton 48, O'Brien 40, Daley 19, Griffith 7, Fitzgerald 6, Radford 1, Madden 1

	G	IP	GS	CG	W	L	K	BB	SH	SV	ERA
George Haddock	51	379.2	47	37	**34**	11	169	137	**5**	1	2.49
Charlie Buffinton	48	363.2	43	33	29	9	158	120	4	1	2.55
Darby O'Brien	40	268.2	30	22	18	13	87	127	0	**2**	3.65
Bill Daley	19	126.2	11	10	8	6	68	81	0	**2**	2.98
Clark Griffith	7	40	4	3	3	1	20	15	0	0	5.62
John Fitzgerald	6	32	3	2	1	1	16	11	0	1	5.63
Kid Madden	1	8	1	1	0	1	6	6	0	0	6.75
Paul Radford	1	1	0	0	0	0	0	0	0	0	0.00

— Two combined shutouts: July 18, Buffinton 6 innings, Fitzgerald 3 innings; July 22, Buffinton 7 innings, O'Brien 2 innings —

		1219.2	139	108	93	42	524	497	**9**	7	3.03

ST. LOUIS Charlie Comiskey Sportsman's Park (I)

		G	AB	H	R	2B	3B	HR	RBI	BB	SB	BA	SA
SS	Shorty Fuller	135	576	122	105	14	7	2	61	67	42	.212	.271
1B	Charlie Comiskey	139	572	148	84	16	2	2	88	33	38	.259	.304
RF	Tommy McCarthy	134	570	176	124	21	6	8	92	49	37	.309	.409
CF	Dummy Hoy	139	559	163	134	13	5	5	66	**117**	59	.292	.360
LF	Tip O'Neill	127	514	166	111	28	4	10	95	61	25	.323	.451
3B	Denny Lyons	120	451	142	124	24	3	11	84	88	9	.315	.455
C	Jack Boyle	121	434	122	76	18	8	5	79	44	18	.281	.394
P	Jack Stivetts	85	302	92	45	10	2	7	54	10	4	.305	.421
2B	Bill Eagan	82	297	65	49	11	4	4	43	44	21	.219	.323
Sub	John Munyan	60	176	41	41	4	3	0	19	41	13	.233	.290
P	Willie McGill	35	83	13	12	1	1	0	4	25	2	.157	.193
P	Clark Griffith	27	77	12	11	1	0	1	8	8	2	.156	.208
Sub	Del Darling	17	53	7	9	1	3	0	9	10	0	.132	.264
P	Joe Neale	15	51	6	6	0	1	1	8	3	1	.118	.216
P	George Rettger	15	42	3	5	0	0	1	2	5	1	.071	.143
P	Jack Easton	9	28	5	5	0	0	0	2	3	2	.179	.179
Sub	Joe Visner	6	27	4	2	0	1	0	1	0	0	.148	.222
Sub	Paul Cook	7	25	5	3	0	0	0	1	1	0	.200	.200
P	Harry Burrell	8	20	4	2	1	0	0	3	0	0	.200	.250
Sub	John Ricks	5	18	3	3	0	0	0	0	0	0	.167	.167
Sub	Paul McSweeney	3	12	3	2	1	0	0	2	0	1	.250	.333
P	Ted Breitenstein	6	12	0	0	0	0	0	0	2	1	.000	.000
Sub	Marty McQuaid	4	11	4	1	2	0	0	1	0	1	.364	.545
P	Jesse Duryea	3	11	4	3	0	1	0	2	0	2	.364	.545
Sub	Art Whitney	3	11	0	0	0	0	0	0	1	0	.000	.000
Sub	Bill Zies	2	3	1	0	0	0	0	0	0	0	.333	.333
Sub	Yank Robinson	1	3	0	0	0	0	0	0	0	0	.000	.000
Sub	John Schultz	1	2	0	0	0	0	0	0	0	0	.000	.000
Sub	Harry Fuller	1	2	0	0	0	0	0	0	0	0	.000	.000
		139	4942	1310	959	166	51	**57**	722	612	279	.265	.354

1B Comiskey 139, Boyle 3
2B Eagan 82, S. Fuller 38, McCarthy 14, McQuaid 3, Boyle 3, McSweeney 3, Darling 2, Robinson 1
SS S. Fuller 102, Boyle 25, McCarthy 12, Munyan 5, Darling 1
3B Lyons 120, Boyle 7, Ricks 5, Whitney 3, Munyan 3, McCarthy 2, H. Fuller 1, McSweeney 1
OF Hoy 139, O'Neill 127, McCarthy 112, Stivetts 24, Munyan 12, Visner 6, Boyle 3, Easton 2, Comiskey 2, Burrell 1, Rettger 1, McQuaid 1
C Boyle 91, Munyan 43, Darling 17, Cook 7, Zies 2, Schultz 1
P Stivetts 64, McGill 33, Griffith 27, Neale 15, Rettger 14, Burrell 7, Easton 7, Breitenstein 6, Duryea 3, McCarthy 1

	G	IP	GS	CG	W	L	K	BB	SH	SV	ERA
Jack Stivetts	**64**	440	56	40	33	22	**259**	232	3	1	2.86
Willie McGill	33	232.2	31	22	18	9	144	126	1	1	2.97
Clark Griffith	27	186.1	17	12	11	8	68	58	0	0	3.33
Jack Easton	7	47.2	6	4	3	2	22	23	0	0	5.10
Joe Neale	15	110.1	11	9	6	4	24	36	1	1	4.24
George Rettger	14	92.2	12	10	7	3	49	51	1	1	3.40
Harry Burrell	7	43	4	3	4	2	19	21	0	0	4.81
Ted Breitenstein	6	28.2	1	1	2	0	13	14	1	1	2.20
Jesse Duryea	3	24	3	2	1	1	13	10	0	0	3.38
Tommy McCarthy	1	1	0	0	0	0	0	0	0	0	9.00
	— One combined shutout on April 28: Stivetts 7 innings, Breitenstein 2 innings —										
		1206.1	139	101	85	51	**614**	576	7	5	3.27

No-hit game 8–0 vs Louisville, October 4

MILWAUKEE   Charlie Cushman   Athletic Field

		G	AB	H	R	2B	3B	HR	RBI	BB	SB	BA	SA
CF	Eddie Burke	35	144	34	31	9	0	2	21	12	7	.236	.340
2B	Jimmy Canavan	35	142	38	33	2	4	3	21	16	7	.268	.401
LF	Abner Dalrymple	32	135	42	31	7	5	1	22	7	6	.311	.459
RF	Howard Earl	31	129	32	21	5	2	1	17	5	3	.248	.341
SS	George Shoch	34	127	40	29	7	1	1	16	18	12	.315	.409
UT	John Grim	29	119	28	14	5	1	1	14	2	1	.235	.319
1B	Jack Carney	31	110	33	22	5	2	3	23	13	5	.300	.464
C	Farmer Vaughn	25	99	33	13	7	0	0	9	4	1	.333	.404
Sub	Bob Pettit	22	80	14	10	4	0	1	5	7	2	.175	.263
3B	Gus Alberts	12	41	4	6	0	0	0	2	7	1	.098	.098
P	Frank Dwyer	10	40	9	1	1	0	0	2	1	1	.225	.250
P	George Davies	12	37	9	4	2	0	0	4	6	0	.243	.297
P	Frank Killen	11	35	8	8	3	0	0	5	8	0	.229	.314
Sub	Tom Letcher	6	21	4	3	1	0	0	2	0	1	.190	.238
P	Jim Hughey	2	7	1	0	0	0	0	1	0	0	.143	.143
P	Willard Mains	2	5	3	1	0	0	0	0	1	0	.600	.600
		36	1271	332	227	58	15	13	164	107	47	.261	.361

1B	Carney 31, Vaughn 4, Earl 2
2B	Canavan 24, Pettit 9, Grim 3
SS	Shoch 25, Canavan 11
3B	Alberts 12, Grim 10, Shoch 9, Pettit 6
OF	Burke 35, Dalrymple 32, Earl 30, Pettit 7, Letcher 6, Vaughn 1
C	Vaughn 20, Grim 16
P	Davies 12, Killen 11, Dwyer 10, Mains 2, Hughey 2

	G	IP	GS	CG	W	L	K	BB	SH	SV	ERA
George Davies	12	102	12	12	7	5	61	35	1	0	2.65
Frank Killen	11	96.2	11	11	7	4	38	51	2	0	1.68
Frank Dwyer	10	86	10	10	6	4	27	21	0	0	2.20
Jim Hughey	2	15	1	1	1	0	9	3	0	0	3.00
Willard Mains	2	10	2	1	0	2	2	10	0	0	10.80
		309.2	36	35	21	15	137	120	3	0	2.50

BALTIMORE **Billy Barnie** **Oriole Park (II) 14 games** **Union Park 56 games**

		G	AB	H	R	2B	3B	HR	RBI	BB	SB	BA	SA
LF	George Van Haltren	139	566	180	136	14	15	9	83	71	75	.318	.443
1B	Perry Werden	139	552	160	102	20	18	6	104	52	46	.290	.424
CF	Curt Welch	132	514	138	122	22	10	3	55	77	50	.268	.368
3B	Pete Gilbert	139	513	118	81	15	7	3	72	37	31	.230	.304
RF	Bill Johnson	129	480	130	101	13	14	2	79	89	32	.271	.369
SS	Irv Ray	103	418	116	72	17	5	0	58	54	28	.278	.342
2B	Sam Wise	103	388	96	70	14	5	1	48	62	33	.247	.317
C	Wilbert Robinson	93	334	72	25	8	5	2	46	16	18	.216	.287
P	Sadie McMahon	61	210	43	31	2	4	1	15	7	6	.205	.267
Sub	George Townsend	61	204	39	29	5	4	0	18	20	3	.191	.255
Sub	John McGraw	41	115	31	17	3	5	0	14	12	4	.270	.383
P	Kid Madden	38	107	29	18	2	2	1	15	9	2	.271	.355
Sub	Joe Walsh	26	100	21	14	0	1	1	10	6	4	.210	.260
P	Bert Cunningham	31	100	15	17	3	1	1	11	13	4	.150	.230
P	Egyptian Healy	23	64	9	4	2	0	0	6	8	1	.141	.172
Sub	Lew Hardie	15	56	13	7	0	3	0	1	8	3	.232	.339
Sub	John O'Connell	8	29	5	2	1	0	0	7	3	2	.172	.207
P	Jersey Bakely	8	21	2	2	1	0	0	1	7	0	.095	.143
		139	4771	1217	850	142	99	30	643	551	342	.255	.345

1B   Werden 139
2B   Wise 99, Welch 21, Walsh 13, O'Connell 3, Van Haltren 2
SS   Van Haltren 59, Ray 40, McGraw 29, Walsh 13, O'Connell 3, Wise 3, Welch 2, Cunningham 1
3B   Gilbert 139, McGraw 3
OF   Johnson 129, Welch 113, Van Haltren 81, Ray 64, Hardie 15, McGraw 9, Madden 7, Townsend 3, McMahon 2, Cunningham 2, O'Connell 2, Robinson 1
C   Robinson 92, Townsend 58
P   McMahon 61, Madden 32, Cunningham 30, Healy 23, Bakely 8, Van Haltren 6

	G	IP	GS	CG	W	L	K	BB	SH	SV	ERA
Sadie McMahon	61	503	58	53	35	24	219	149	5	1	2.81
Bert Cunningham	30	237.2	25	21	11	14	59	138	0	0	4.01
Kid Madden	32	224	27	20	13	12	56	88	1	1	4.10
Egyptian Healy	23	170.1	22	19	8	10	54	57	0	0	3.75
Jersey Bakely	8	59	6	5	4	2	13	30	0	0	2.29
George Van Haltren	6	23	1	0	0	1	7	10	0	0	5.09
		—1 forfeit L vs Washington on October 5—									
		1217	139	118	71	63	408	472	6	2	3.43

PHILADELPHIA   Bill Sharsig (6–11)   George Wood (67–55)   **Forepaugh Park**

		G	AB	H	R	2B	3B	HR	RBI	BB	SB	BA	SA
2B	Bill Hallman	141	587	166	112	21	13	6	69	38	18	.283	.394
LF	George Wood	132	528	163	105	18	14	3	61	72	22	.309	.413
1B	Henry Larkin	133	526	147	94	27	14	10	93	66	2	.279	.441
SS	Tommy Corcoran	133	511	130	84	11	15	7	71	29	30	.254	.376
C	Jocko Milligan	118	455	138	75	35	12	11	106	56	2	.303	.505
3B	Joe Mulvey	113	453	115	62	9	13	5	66	17	11	.254	.364
Sub	Lave Cross	110	402	121	66	20	14	5	52	38	14	.301	.458
CF	Pop Corkhill	83	349	73	50	7	7	0	31	26	12	.209	.269
Sub	Jim McTamany	58	218	49	57	6	3	3	21	43	13	.225	.321
RF	Jack McGeachy	50	201	46	24	4	3	2	13	6	9	.229	.308
P	Gus Weyhing	54	198	22	11	5	1	0	11	7	2	.111	.146
P	Icebox Chamberlain	54	176	33	21	3	5	2	19	21	3	.188	.295
P	Ben Sanders	40	156	39	24	6	4	1	19	7	2	.250	.359
Sub	Ed Beecher	16	71	15	9	2	4	0	7	3	7	.211	.352
P	Will Callahan	15	56	11	6	1	0	0	4	5	0	.196	.214
Sub	Dave McKeough	15	54	14	4	1	1	0	3	8	0	.259	.315
P	Sumner Bowman	14	54	13	8	4	0	0	2	2	1	.241	.315
P	George Meakim	6	15	3	2	1	0	0	1	2	0	.200	.267
Sub	Bill Clymer	3	11	0	0	0	0	0	0	1	1	.000	.000
Sub	Pat Friel	2	8	2	2	1	0	0	0	0	0	.250	.375
P	Mike Sullivan	2	7	0	0	0	0	0	0	0	0	.000	.000
Sub	Bob Matthews	1	3	1	1	0	0	0	0	0	0	.333	.333
		143	5039	1301	817	**182**	**123**	55	649	447	149	.258	.376

1B   Larkin 111, Milligan 32
2B   Hallman 141, Cross 1
SS   Corcoran 133, Wood 5, Clymer 3, Callahan 1, Cross 1, McKeough 1
3B   Mulvey 113, Cross 24, Wood 6, Callahan 1
OF   Wood 122, Corkhill 83, McTamany 58, McGeachy 50, Cross 43, Larkin 23, Sanders 22, Beecher 16, Chamberlain 6, Bowman 6, Friel 2, Weyhing 2, Matthews 1
C   Milligan 87, Cross 43, McKeough 14
P   Weyhing 52, Chamberlain 49, Sanders 19, Callahan 13, Bowman 8, Meakim 5, Sullivan 2

	G	IP	GS	CG	W	L	K	BB	SH	SV	ERA
Gus Weyhing	52	450	51	51	31	20	219	161	3	0	3.18
Icebox Chamberlain	49	405.2	46	44	22	23	204	206	0	0	4.22
Ben Sanders	19	145	18	15	11	5	40	37	0	0	3.79
Will Callahan	13	112	11	11	6	6	28	47	0	0	6.43
Sumner Bowman	8	68	8	8	2	5	22	37	0	0	3.44
George Meakim	5	35	6	4	1	4	13	22	0	0	6.94
Mike Sullivan	2	18	2	2	0	2	7	10	0	0	3.50
		—1 forfeit L vs Louisville on September 20—									
		1233.2	142	**135**	73	65	533	520	3	0	4.01

COLUMBUS   Gus Schmelz   **Recreation Park (II)**

		G	AB	H	R	2B	3B	HR	RBI	BB	SB	BA	SA
LF	Charlie Duffee	137	552	166	86	28	4	10	90	42	41	.301	.420
2B	Jack Crooks	138	519	127	110	19	13	0	46	103	50	.245	.331
1B	Mike Lehane	137	511	110	59	12	7	1	52	34	16	.215	.272
SS	Bobby Wheelock	136	498	114	82	15	1	0	39	78	52	.229	.263
RF	Jon Sneed	99	366	94	66	9	6	1	61	55	24	.257	.322
CF	Jim McTamany	81	304	76	59	17	9	3	35	58	20	.250	.395

		G	AB	H	R	2B	3B	HR	RBI	BB	SB	BA	SA
C	Jim Donahue	77	280	61	27	4	3	0	35	31	2	.218	.254
3B	Willie Kuehne	68	261	56	32	9	0	2	22	10	21	.215	.272
C	Jack O'Connor	56	229	61	28	12	3	0	37	11	10	.266	.345
Sub	Larry Twitchell	57	224	62	32	9	4	2	35	20	10	.277	.379
P	Phil Knell	66	215	34	25	2	3	0	19	8	4	.158	.195
Sub	Tom Dowse	55	201	45	24	7	0	0	22	13	2	.224	.259
Sub	Tim O'Rourke	34	136	38	22	1	3	0	12	15	9	.279	.331
P	Hank Gastright	35	117	23	11	2	4	0	10	12	2	.197	.282
P	John Dolan	28	78	7	6	3	0	1	8	8	1	.090	.167
P	Jack Easton	25	74	15	11	4	1	0	8	3	4	.203	.284
Sub	Jim Donnelly	17	54	13	6	0	0	0	9	13	7	.241	.241
Sub	Elmer Cleveland	12	41	7	12	0	0	0	4	12	4	.171	.171
P	Jack Leiper	6	21	3	2	0	0	0	3	0	0	.143	.143
P	Dad Clarke	4	9	1	2	1	0	0	0	2	0	.111	.222
P	Jim Sullivan	1	4	0	0	0	0	0	0	0	0	.000	.000
P	Bill Lyston	1	2	0	0	0	0	0	0	1	1	.000	.000
P	Ed Clark	1	1	0	0	0	0	0	0	0	0	.000	.000
		138	4697	1113	702	154	61	20	547	529	280	.237	.308

1B   Lehane 137, Donahue 1
2B   Crooks 138, Knell 1
SS   Wheelock 136, Duffee 2
3B   Kuehne 68, O'Rourke 34, Donnelly 17, Cleveland 12, Duffee 7
OF   Duffee 128, Sneed 99, McTamany 81, Twitchell 56, O'Connor 40, Knell 9, Dowse 5, Easton 5, Donahue 1, Dolan 1
C   Donahue 75, Dowse 51, O'Connor 21
P   Knell 58, Gastright 35, Dolan 27, Easton 20, Leiper 6, Twitchell 6, Clarke 4, Sullivan 1, Lyston 1, Clark 1

	G	IP	GS	CG	W	L	K	BB	SH	SV	ERA
Phil Knell	58	462	52	47	28	27	228	226	5	0	2.92
Hank Gastright	35	283.2	33	28	12	19	109	136	1	0	3.78
John Dolan	27	203.1	24	19	12	11	68	84	0	0	4.16
Jack Easton	20	150.1	18	15	5	12	65	63	0	0	4.43
Jack Leiper	6	45	5	4	2	2	19	39	0	0	5.40
Larry Twitchell	6	31	1	1	1	1	8	13	0	0	4.06
Dad Clarke	4	21	3	2	1	2	2	16	0	0	6.86
Jim Sullivan	1	9	1	1	0	1	1	5	0	0	4.00
Bill Lyston	1	6	1	1	0	1	1	6	0	0	10.50
Ed Clark	1	2	0	0	0	0	1	0	0	0	0.00
		1213.1	138	118	61	76	502	588	6	0	3.75

CINCINNATI King Kelly   **Pendleton Park**

		G	AB	H	R	2B	3B	HR	RBI	BB	SB	BA	SA
SS	Jimmy Canavan	101	426	97	74	13	14	7	66	27	21	.228	.373
CF	Dick Johnston	99	376	83	59	11	2	6	51	38	12	.221	.309
RF	Emmett Seery	97	372	106	77	15	10	4	36	81	19	.285	.411
1B	Jack Carney	99	367	102	47	10	8	3	43	35	15	.278	.373
LF	Ed Andrews	83	356	75	47	7	4	0	26	33	22	.211	.253
3B	Art Whitney	93	347	69	42	6	1	3	33	31	8	.199	.248
2B	Yank Robinson	97	342	61	48	9	4	1	37	68	23	.178	.237
C	King Kelly	82	283	84	56	15	7	1	53	51	22	.297	.410
Sub	Farmer Vaughn	51	175	45	21	7	1	1	14	14	7	.257	.326
P	Frank Dwyer	40	141	40	24	4	3	0	18	5	4	.284	.355P
	Cannonball Crane	34	110	17	13	0	0	1	7	8	4	.155	.182
P	Willard Mains	31	90	22	14	3	2	1	10	5	2	.244	.356
Sub	Lefty Marr	14	57	11	9	1	0	0	4	7	2	.193	.211
Sub	Jerry Hurley	24	66	14	10	3	2	0	6	12	2	.212	.318
P	Matt Kilroy	8	20	3	2	0	0	0	0	4	0	.150	.150
P	Willie McGill	8	20	2	4	0	0	0	0	9	0	.100	.100
Sub	Billy Clingman	1	5	1	0	1	0	0	0	0	0	.200	.400
P	Charlie Bell	1	4	2	1	0	0	0	1	0	0	.500	.500
P	Kid Keenan	1	4	2	1	0	0	0	1	0	1	.500	.500
Sub	Joe Burke	1	4	1	0	0	0	0	1	0	0	.250	.250
P	Bill Widner	1	4	1	0	0	0	0	0	0	0	.250	.250
Sub	Charlie Bastian	1	4	0	0	0	0	0	0	0	0	.000	.000
P	John Slagle	1	1	0	0	0	0	0	0	0	0	.000	.000
		102	3574	838	549	105	58	28	407	428	164	.234	.320

1B	Carney 99, Kelly 5, Vaughn 2, Hurley 1
2B	Robinson 97, Kelly 6, Dwyer 2, Burke 1, Clingman 1, Bastian 1
SS	Canavan 101, Kelly 1
3B	Whitney 93, Kelly 8, Vaughn 2
OF	Johnston 99, Seery 97, Andrews 83, Marr 14, Kelly 7, Vaughn 6, Dwyer 4, Crane 3, Mains 1, Kilroy 1, Hurley 1
C	Kelly 66, Hurley 24, Vaughn 44
P	Dwyer 35, Crane 32, Mains 30, McGill 8, Kilroy 7, Kelly 3, Bell 1, Widner 1, Keenan 1, Vaughn 1, Slagle 1

	G	IP	GS	CG	W	L	K	BB	SH	SV	ERA
Frank Dwyer	35	289	31	29	13	19	101	124	1	0	4.52
Cannonball Crane	32	250	31	25	14	14	122	139	1	0	2.45
Willard Mains	30	204	23	19	12	12	76	107	0	0	2.69
Willie McGill	8	65	8	6	2	5	19	37	0	0	4.98
Matt Kilroy	7	45.1	6	4	1	4	6	19	0	0	2.98
King Kelly	3	15.1	0	0	0	1	0	7	0	0	5.28
Charlie Bell	1	9	1	1	1	0	1	3	0	0	0.00
Kid Keenan	1	8	1	1	0	1	5	4	0	0	0.00
Bill Widner	1	8	1	1	0	1	0	4	0	0	7.88
Farmer Vaughn	1	7	0	0	0	0	0	1	0	0	3.86
John Slagle	1	1.1	0	0	0	0	1	1	0	1	0.00
		901	102	86	43	57	331	446	2	1	3.43

LOUISVILLE   Jack Chapman   Eclipse Park (I)

		G	AB	H	R	2B	3B	HR	RBI	BB	SB	BA	SA
CF	Farmer Weaver	133	556	157	74	24	7	1	53	33	30	.282	.356
RF	Chicken Wolf	136	528	135	67	17	8	1	81	42	13	.256	.324
2B	Tim Shinnick	126	436	96	77	9	11	1	52	54	36	.220	.298
LF	Patsy Donovan	105	439	141	73	10	3	2	53	30	27	.321	.371
C	Tom Cahill	119	430	109	68	17	7	3	44	41	39	.253	.347
SS	Hughie Jennings	88	351	103	53	10	8	1	58	17	12	.293	.376
1B	Harry Taylor	91	348	103	80	7	3	2	35	55	15	.296	.351
3B	Ollie Beard	68	257	62	35	4	5	0	24	33	7	.241	.296
C	John Ryan	75	253	57	24	5	4	2	25	15	3	.225	.300
Sub	Willie Kuehne	39	152	41	25	3	1	1	17	7	9	.277	.327
C	Paul Cook	45	153	35	21	3	1	0	23	11	4	.229	.261
P	Scott Stratton	34	115	27	9	2	0	0	8	11	8	.235	.252
P	John Fitzgerald	33	108	19	15	2	2	1	10	13	3	.176	.250
P	Jouett Meekin	32	94	21	14	0	3	1	10	15	4	.216	.309
P	Red Ehret	26	91	22	9	2	1	0	9	5	3	.242	.286
Sub	Monk Cline	19	70	21	11	3	1	0	11	16	2	.300	.371
P	Ed Daily	22	64	16	10	2	0	0	8	8	4	.250	.281
Sub	Harry Raymond	14	59	12	4	2	0	0	2	5	3	.203	.237
Sub	John Irwin	14	55	15	7	1	1	0	7	5	1	.273	.327
P	John Doran	15	53	10	5	2	0	0	0	1	0	.189	.226
Sub	Sam Laroque	10	35	11	6	2	1	1	8	5	1	.314	.514
P	Charlie Bell	10	28	1	3	0	0	0	0	6	0	.036	.036
Sub	Jim Long	6	25	6	5	0	0	0	4	3	1	.240	.240
Sub	Art Schellhase	6	16	2	3	0	0	0	0	1	2	.125	.125
Sub	Paddy Fox	6	19	2	1	0	1	0	2	2	0	.105	.211
P	George Boone	4	6	2	0	0	0	0	0	0	0	.333	.333
Sub	Joe Gerhardt	2	6	0	0	0	0	0	0	1	0	.000	.000
Sub	Pat Pettee	2	5	0	1	0	0	0	0	3	1	.000	.000
Sub	Jack Wentz	1	4	1	0	0	0	0	0	0	0	.250	.250
Sub	Grant Briggs	1	4	1	0	0	0	0	0	0	0	.250	.250
Sub	Jack Darragh	1	2	1	0	0	0	0	0	0	0	.500	.500
Sub	Nick Reeder	1	2	0	0	0	0	0	0	0	0	.000	.000
		139	4764	1229	698	130	69	17	544	438	226	.258	.324

1B Taylor 90, Jennings 17, Ryan 11, Cook 10, Stratton 8, Wolf 5, Meekin 1, Darragh 1, Laroque 1
2B Shinnick 118, Laroque 10, Cahill 6, Ryan 3, Pettee 2, Gerhardt 2, Taylor 1, Wentz 1
SS Jennings 70, Cahill 49, Raymond 14, Beard 7, Shinick 1
3B Beard 61, Kuehne 39, Irwin 14, Shinnick 7, Fox 6, Ryan 6, Cahill 3, Jennings 3, Taylor 1, Wolf 1, Reeder 1
OF Wolf 131, Weaver 130, Donovan 105, Cline 19, Cahill 12, Daily 7, Stratton 6, Long 6, Ryan 4, Meekin 3, Fitzgerald 1
C Cahill 55, Ryan 56, Cook 35, Schellhase 6, Weaver 4, Briggs 1, Taylor 1
P Fitzgerald 32, Meekin 28, Ehret 26, Stratton 20, Doran 15, Daily 15, Bell 10, Boone 4

	G	IP	GS	CG	W	L	K	BB	SH	SV	ERA
John Fitzgerald	32	267	31	28	14	17	110	89	3	0	3.44
Jouett Meekin	28	221	25	24	9	16	141	106	2	0	4.44
Red Ehret	26	220.2	24	23	13	13	76	70	2	0	3.47
Scott Stratton	20	172	20	20	6	13	52	34	1	0	4.08
John Doran	15	126	14	12	5	10	55	75	1	0	5.43
Ed Daily	15	111.1	14	11	4	8	27	48	0	0	5.74
Charlie Bell	10	77	9	8	2	6	16	20	0	0	4.68
George Boone	4	15	1	0	0	0	4	9	0	1	7.80
		—1 forfeit W vs Philadelphia on September 20—									
	1210	138	126	53	83	481	451	9	1	4.27

WASHINGTON   Sam Trott (4–7)   Pop Snyder (23–46)   Dan Shannon (15–34)
Sandy Griffin (2–4)   **Boundary Field**

		G	AB	H	R	2B	3B	HR	RBI	BB	SB	BA	SA
SS	Gil Hatfield	134	500	128	83	11	8	1	48	50	43	.256	.316
2B	Tommy Dowd	112	464	120	66	9	10	1	44	19	39	.259	.328
C	Deacon McGuire	114	413	125	55	22	10	3	66	43	10	.303	.426
RF	Larry Murphy	101	400	106	73	15	3	1	35	63	29	.265	.325
3B	Billy Alvord	81	312	73	28	8	3	0	30	11	3	.234	.279
1B	Mox McQuery	68	261	63	40	9	4	2	37	18	3	.241	.330
LF	Ed Beecher	58	235	57	35	11	3	2	28	27	17	.243	.340
1B	Al McCauley	59	206	58	36	5	8	1	31	30	9	.282	.398
CF	Paul Hines	54	206	58	25	7	5	0	31	21	6	.282	.364
Sub	Sy Sutcliffe	53	201	71	29	8	3	2	33	17	8	.353	.453
P	Kid Carsey	61	187	28	25	5	2	0	15	19	2	.150	.198
P	Frank Foreman	50	153	34	26	4	5	4	19	23	6	.222	.392
Sub	Pete Lohman	32	109	21	18	1	4	1	11	16	1	.193	.303
Sub	Ervin Curtis	29	103	26	17	3	2	0	12	13	2	.252	.320
Sub	Pop Smith	27	90	16	13	2	2	0	13	13	2	.178	.244
Sub	Jim Burns	20	82	26	15	6	0	0	10	6	2	.317	.390
Sub	Ed Daily	21	79	18	13	2	0	0	6	11	8	.228	.253
Sub	Patsy Donovan	17	70	14	9	1	0	0	3	4	1	.200	.214
Sub	Sandy Griffin	20	69	19	15	4	2	0	10	10	2	.275	.391
Sub	Joe Visner	18	68	19	13	2	3	1	7	8	2	.279	.441
Sub	Dan Shannon	19	67	9	7	2	0	0	3	6	3	.134	.164
Sub	Mike Slattery	15	60	17	8	1	0	0	5	4	6	.283	.300
P	Jersey Bakely	13	45	10	2	1	0	0	4	3	0	.222	.244
Sub	Jumbo Davis	12	44	14	7	3	2	0	9	7	8	.318	.477
Sub	Tom McLaughlin	14	41	11	9	0	1	0	3	7	3	.268	.317
Sub	Will Smalley	11	38	6	5	0	1	0	3	5	0	.158	.211
Sub	Pop Snyder	8	27	5	4	0	1	0	2	0	0	.185	.259
P	Ed Cassian	7	26	9	4	1	1	0	4	0	0	.346	.462
P	Ed Eiteljorg	8	26	5	3	1	0	0	4	1	0	.192	.231
Sub	Fred Dunlap	8	25	5	4	1	1	0	4	5	3	.200	.320
Sub	Tom Hart	8	24	3	1	0	0	0	2	2	1	.125	.125
P	Buck Freeman	5	18	4	1	1	0	0	1	2	0	.222	.278
P	Bob Miller	7	18	2	1	0	0	0	2	0	0	.111	.111
P	George Keefe	5	14	2	1	0	0	0	1	3	0	.143	.143
P	Bill Quarles	3	11	0	0	0	0	0	0	0	0	.000	.000
P	Martin Duke	4	9	1	0	1	0	0	0	0	0	.111	.222
Sub	Miah Murray	2	8	0	0	0	0	0	0	0	0	.000	.000
P	Harry Mace	3	6	0	0	0	0	0	0	1	0	.000	.000
		139	4715	1183	691	147	84	19	536	468	219	.251	.330

1B   McQuery 68, McCauley 59, Hines 10, Snyder 4, McGuire 1
2B   Dowd 107, Smith 19, Dunlap 8, Shannon 5, Smalley 2, Lohman 1
SS   Hatfield 105, McLaughlin 14, Shannon 14, Smith 5, Sutcliffe 3, Carsey 2, Burns 1, Lohman 1
3B   Alvord 81, Hatfield 27, Davis 12, Smalley 9, Lohman 4, Smith 4, McGuire 3, Sutcliffe 3, Visner 1
OF   Murphy 101, Beecher 58, Hines 47, Sutcliffe 35, Curtis 29, Daily 21, Griffin 20, Burns 20, McGuire 18, Donovan 17, Visner 17, Slattery 15, Lohman 8, Foreman 8, Carsey 7, Dowd 5, Hatfield 3, Hart 3, Snyder 1
C   McGuire 98, Sutcliffe 22, Lohman 21, Hart 5, Snyder 3, Murray 2, Visner 1
P   Carsey 54, Foreman 43, Bakely 13, Eiteljorg 8, Cassian 7, Miller 7, Keefe 5, Freeman 5, Duke 4, Hatfield 4, Mace 3, Quarles 3,

	G	IP	GS	CG	W	L	K	BB	SH	SV	ERA
Kid Carsey	54	415	53	46	14	**37**	174	161	1	0	4.99
Frank Foreman	43	345.1	41	39	18	20	170	142	1	1	3.73
Jersey Bakely	13	104.1	12	11	2	10	32	60	0	0	5.35
Ed Eiteljorge	8	67.1	7	6	1	5	23	41	0	0	6.16
Ed Cassian	7	53	5	5	2	4	14	35	0	0	5.60
Buck Freeman	5	44	4	4	3	2	28	33	0	0	3.89
Bob Miller	7	42	7	3	2	5	13	24	0	0	4.29
George Keefe	5	37	4	4	0	3	11	17	0	1	2.68
Martin Duke	4	23	3	2	0	3	5	19	0	0	7.43
Bill Quarles	3	22	2	2	1	1	10	12	0	0	8.18
Gil Hatfield	4	18	0	0	0	0	3	14	0	0	11.00
Jimmy Mace	3	16	1	1	0	1	3	8	0	0	7.31
		—1 forfeit W vs Baltimore on Oct. 5—									
		1181	139	123	43	**91**	486	566	2	2	4.83

THE LEAGUE-ASSOCIATION ERA
(1892-1900)

After ten year of intermittent war, the National League and the American Association threw down their arms once and for all on December 18, 1891, and consolidated into a single 12-team league. St. Louis, Baltimore, Washington and Louisville bonded with the eight existing National League franchises to form the new circuit and then representatives of the Association clubs left homeless were asked to submit their buyout prices. Ultimately the undomiciled franchises were awarded around $135,000, with each of the 12 surviving major league clubs committed to contribute 10 percent of its gate receipts to a general fund until the debt was paid off.

Though the Association ceased to function as an independent entity, its influence on the game remained strong. Not only were eight of the 12 surviving major league teams direct descendants of American Association franchises, but the new League drafted a constitution remarkably similar to the controversial one the Association sired ten years earlier. Paramount among its amendments were a 25-cent minimum admission price in any cities that wished it, Sunday ball in all locales where the law allowed it (although no club would be compelled to play on Sunday), and each club to have the right to decide for itself whether to sell alcoholic beverages in its home park. Many National League teams that heretofore had loyally adhered to the party line that the Sabbath should be properly observed instantly embraced Sunday ball, especially Chicago, whose magnates had waited impatiently ever since 1888 when a minor league team in the windy City, playing on Sunday, had piled up several new local attendance records. By 1899, although many Eastern clubs still preserved vestiges of the Victorian era, if only because local laws forbade baseball on the Sabbath in most Eastern cities, the Boston Beaneaters were alone in refusing to play Sunday games even on the road.

So it came to pass that three of the Association's founding principles were made part and parcel of the fabric of our national pastime in 1892. When peace became certain, the National League was willing to incorporate almost all of the Association's legacy, even its name. The consolidation committee originally recommended the new 12-team confedera-

These New York Giants look capable enough, but they brought up the rear among the eight veteran NL teams in 1892. However, the Giants beat out all four AA newcomers to finish eighth overall in the 12-team LA's first season. Top: Eddie Burke, Jack Boyle, Charlie Bassett, Amos Rusie, manager Pat Powers, Buck Ewing, Cannonball Crane, Mike Tiernan, George Gore and Jim O'Rourke. Bottom: Danny Murphy, Jocko Fields, Harry Lyons, team mascot Shorty Fuller, Mickey Welch and Jack Sharrott.

tion be called "The American League," but old guard owners found this name combination abhorrent because it meant putting the Association's contribution first. A second logical name combination—"The National Association"—was nearly as unpalatable because it would have revived the name of a major league that had already failed.

After long debate, the new alliance was christened the "National League and American Association of Base Ball Clubs." The ponderous title was used only on official documents. Most newspapers obediently carried the loop's standings for several years under the heading "League-Association," but by the late 1890s they began referring to it again as simply "the League." Long before then the disappearance of the Association had signaled a change in the type of men who owned major league clubs. Gone were the "sporting men" like Charlie Mason who operated pool halls and breweries and rubbed elbows with fans of their teams at their taverns and bookie joints. In their stead were industrialists, bankers and streetcar-company owners such as John Brush, the Robison brothers and Andrew Freedman. Politicos and early-day owners like Boss Tweed had got into the game to win votes, brewers like Chris Von Der Ahe and Henry Von der Horst got into it to sell beer, but capitalists like Brush and the Robisons used their teams to sell their program that they were on a common ground with their employees. Brush, the Robisons and the impossibly repressive Freedman would carry the game into the new century and "The Deadball Era." Von Der Ahe, the prototype of the freewheelers who had flourished in baseball's "Golden Age," would be out of the game by 1898, his like not to be seen again for nearly half a century.

1892

THE SPLIT SEASON

The National League and American Association of Base Ball Clubs officially commenced business on April 12, 1892. Of the four surviving Association teams, only Louisville won its inaugural game in the new league. When Louisville raced to a 7–2 start, only a game off the pace set by early leader Boston, the *Sporting News* thought that Louisville's pennant chances "ar now very gilt-edged."

But the Colonels soon faded, though they continued to be the best of the new loop's four Association addenda. Unhappily in 1892 that meant finishing with the fourth-worst record in a 12-team league. For the Colonels came home eleventh in the first half of the season and ninth in the second leg but finished ninth overall when Washington, nearly a first-division team in the first half, tumbled to the cellar the second time around the course. Much of the reason the American Association alums made such a poor showing in 1892 owed to their having been outfoxed by many of the National League clubs before the peace treaty was written. Almost as soon as the 1891 season ended, teams like Boston, Brooklyn and Philadelphia anticipated the merger and began looting players from the Association. Chris Von Der Ahe's St. Louis Browns were the hardest hit. By the time the debris was cleared, Von Der Ahe had been pillaged of every member of his starting nine in 1891. Boston was the chief beneficiary, garnering 33-game winner Jack Stivetts. Meanwhile the Philadelphia Phillies made off with three core members of the Philadelphia Association team—Gus Weyhing, Lave Cross and Bill Hallman—and Brooklyn emerged with another Philadelphia Association stalwart, shortstop Tommy Corcoran, as well as Dan Brouthers, Bill Joyce and George Haddock from the Association's final champion, the Boston Reds.

These three teams headed the pack in the first half-season, helped in no small part by their Association acquisitions. Stivetts won 35 games in 1892, Brouthers collected his fifth batting title, and Weyhing became the only pitcher ever to post three consecutive 30-win seasons in three different major leagues. Defending champion Boston needed little more assistance than Stivetts provided to retain its supremacy, but Brooklyn and Philadelphia had both been sub-.500 teams in 1891. So surprising were the Bridegrooms in their second

Action pictures from the 19th century are about as commonly seen as perfect games. Here appears to be a rundown play at the plate. The setting supposedly is Louisville's Eclipse Park sometime in the 1890s, but the year is unknown. If we were able to see beyond the pitcher more clearly, we could at least judge whether it was post-1892, the last season the pitching area was flat and box-shaped.

season under Monte Ward that they pursued Boston down to the finish line in the first-half race before finally succumbing by two and a half games.

When both Brooklyn and Philadelphia slumped in the second half, the fear was that Boston would win again, killing interest in a postseason "Pennant Series." Few paid any attention to the Cleveland Spiders, the early second-half leader, because the Spiders visibly were the same team that had finished a poor fifth the year before. But the Spiders had something less visible going for them—youth. In 1892 second baseman Cupid Childs, leftfielder Jesse Burkett, shortstop Ed McKean, third baseman-manager Patsy Tebeau and the all-purpose George Davis still had most of their careers ahead of them, and the Spiders' most valuable asset of all, Cy Young, was only in the third season of what would be a 22-year career. Young's third season was arguably his best. In 1892 he won 36 games, just one less than leader Bill Hutchison of Chicago, and topped the League-Association in both ERA and winning percentage. For support, rookie Nig Cuppy supplied 28 wins and John Clarkson was good for 17 after being shipped Cleveland's way when he grieved at a pay cut on top of being no better than third fiddle in Boston behind Stivetts and Kid Nichols.

Though there were rumblings that Boston slacked off in the second half so Cleveland could win and create a true Pennant Series between two co-champions, the likelihood is that Cleveland simply matured into a solid team as the season progressed. Young, Clarkson and Cuppy ranked first, third and fourth in ERA, and the Spiders fourth starter, George Davies, ranked sixth. Yet it was not as if no one else had pitching in 1892. Actually, every team except St. Louis had at least one 20-game winner, and even the Browns staff consisted of seven hurlers who won a combined 1,361 games in the majors or an average of nearly 200 apiece. The pitching depth that virtually every team enjoyed stemmed from the disappearance of roughly a quarter of the pitchers employed in the majors in 1891. With the shrinkage from 16 to 12 teams, managers could afford to be very selective about which players they kept. Though the weaker hitters were discarded as well, it was the pitching side of the scale that again became disturbingly heavier.

Jim Canavan (seen here with the 1894 Cincinnati Reds) hit .166 for Chicago in 1892, the lowest average ever by a big leaguer with 400 or more at bats. Top: Jack McCarthy, Farmer Vaughn, Bug Holliday, Morg Murphy and Dummy Hoy. Middle: Frank Motz, Frank Dwyer, Charlie Comiskey, Icebox Chamberlain and Arlie Latham. Bottom: Lem Cross, Tom Parrott, Canavan, Bid McPhee and Germany Smith.

Another corollary of the reduction in jobs now that the American Association was dead was a reduction in pay, since players no longer had any option but to take what they were given. When attendance figures began dropping among teams that were certain to bring up the rear in 1892, several clubs trimmed salaries a few months into the season so that the war debt owed to the Association clubs the peace settlement orphaned could be more quickly paid off. Charlie Buffinton, already disgusted at being stuck on the last-place Baltimore Orioles in the consolidation process, quit the game rather than accept a midyear pay cut. Buffinton's departure was but one of many unpleasantries Henry Von der Horst's team endured. Jocko Halligan, expected to put some sorely needed punch into the Orioles' attack when he was picked up from Cincinnati, instead put his punch into teammate Cub Stricker. When Stricker's jaw was fractured, sending him to the hospital, Ned Hanlon, the club's third different manager in 1892, kicked Halligan off the team. St. Louis meanwhile went through five managers, Washington and Pittsburgh employed three each, and even Jack Chapman lost his job less than two years after steering Louisville to its only major league pennant. Chapman's replacement was second baseman Fred Pfeffer, whom Cap Anson had

THE SWITCHHITTING BOOM

In 1882 there were only three switchhitters playing regularly in the major leagues and two of them, Tony Mullane and Will White, were pitchers. Just ten years later nearly every team had at least one switchhitting regular. The reason for the explosion no doubt was the proliferation in the mid-1880s of lefthanded pitchers. Here are the leading switchhitters and their teams in 1892.

Boston—Tommy Tucker, 1B; Kid Nichols, P
Cleveland—George Davis, Utilityman; Jake Virtue, 1B
Brooklyn—Tom Daly, Utilityman
Philadelphia—Charlie Reilly, 3B
Cincinnati—Tony Mullane, P
Pittsburgh—Duke Farrell, 3B
Chicago—Walt Wilmot, LF; Jimmy Cooney, 2B
New York—none
Louisville—none
Washington—none
St. Louis—Cliff Carroll, LF; Kid Gleason, P
Baltimore—none

Later in the decade these dozen switchhitters were joined by Jake Gettman, Doc Casey, Claude Ritchey, Billy Clingman, Candy LaChance, Dan McGann, John Anderson, Tom McCreery and Tuck Turner, among others.

Jake Virtue, one of the flood of switchhitters to debut in the early 1890s and just about the only batsman who declined when the pitching distance was lengthened. The Cleveland first sacker hit a very respectable .282 in 1892 but dropped to .265 the following year when averages everywhere else soared.

allowed to leave Chicago in 1892 so he could finish his career in his home town. Anson had expected Jimmy Canavan would replace Pfeffer, but he was proven wrong when Canavan hit just .166, the worst job ever by a major leaguer in 400 or more at bats. Anson's own bat was also culpable in Chicago's tumble into the second division after nearly winning the pennant the previous year. But his .272 batting average was still 36 points better than that of Jake Beckley, another future Hall of Fame first baseman, and Beckley's .236, in turn, was 47 points above King Kelly's .189.

Concern over the offensive decay, rampant by the time the season ended, was temporarily allayed by the forthcoming best-of-nine postseason clash for the League-Association pennant. There had been talk of staging the affair in San Francisco where the weather was certain to be better than what late October usually delivered to Cleveland and Boston, but the plan fell flat when several players balked at the notion of traveling so far. So it was Cleveland's League Park that hosted the opening game of the first series in history for a major league title. That game produced the most memorable postseason pitchers' duel in the nineteenth century. Young and Stivetts battled to a 0-0 stalemate, halted by darkness after 11 innings. Cleveland's failure to come up with key hits continued in the next two games, resulting in a pair of one-run losses. Hugh Duffy meanwhile furnished practically all of the offense and defense for both sides. In Game Three, Duffy drove in three of Boston's four tallies and speared a ninth-inning liner to help a Cleveland rally fall a run short. Moving to Boston, Duffy's two-run homer was all Nichols needed in Game Four as he posted a 4-0 shutout. Down 3-0 in games, Cleveland tried Clarkson in the box the following day and scored six runs in the third frame, but the Beaneaters then riddled their former ace for 12

1892 ATTENDANCE LEADER

Of the 12 teams in the League-Association's first season of 1892, Cincinnati had the highest percentage of ex-American Association players. With the exception of pitchers Mike Sullivan and Billy Rhines, every one of the Reds regular position players and pitchers in 1892 played at least one full season in the Association, and many were among the Association's greatest stars. If an all-time American Association all-star team were named, certainly Tony Mullane, Tip O'Neill, Bid McPhee and Pete Browning, Curt Welch, Germany Smith and Arlie Latham would be on it somewhere, and Charlie Comiskey would be the manager. All were with the Reds in 1892, along with Bug Holliday, the Association record holder for the most home runs in a season. Actually, Holliday, O'Neill and Browning were the Reds regular outfield for most of the year until Browning got hurt and was replaced by Curt Welch. That's three of the Association's greatest hitters and its greatest flychaser in the same outfield. It may be only a fluke that Cincinnati, just a fifth-place team in 1892, nevertheless led the new combined League-Association in attendance. We will never know.

runs over the next five innings and won 12-7. On the verge of elimination, Cleveland again took an early lead in Game Six, scoring three off Nichols in the top of the third, and the Beaneaters again came back quickly against Young. Nichols aided his own cause by driving home the tying and go-ahead runs in the fourth inning and then blanking the Spiders the rest of the way. Boston's 5-0 sweep erased all dispute over who the true champion was in 1892, for there could always have been the argument that the Beaneaters had the best overall record during the regular season if Cleveland had won.

ONE-MAN SHOWS

Bill Hutchison dominated major league pitching departments for three straight seasons (1890–92) as no other pitcher has before or since for a period of comparable length. In 1892, Hutchison accomplished something that was done for the last time when he won 37 of Chicago's 70 victories. No pitcher since 1892 has collected half or more of his team's wins—not even Steve Carlton when he won 27 games in 1972 for the last-place Phillies. However, Hutchison was not alone in his achievement.

Frank Killen, toiling for tenth-place Washington in 1892, rang up exactly half of the Nationals' 58 victories. Killen's 29 wins remained the most by a pitcher for a Washington major league entry until 1912 when someone named Johnson collected 33. The following is a list of pitchers who won half or more of their team's victories since 1886 when major league teams first began playing schedules of more than 120 games, making it virtually impossible for one pitcher to do most of the work:

Frank Killen won 65 games in his first two full major league seasons and later became the National League's last southpaw 30-game winner to date; yet he collected only 164 wins in a spectacularly uneven career.

	YEAR	TEAM	WINS	PCT. TEAM WINS
Tim Keefe	1886	NY-NL	42	45
Ed Morris	1886	Pit-AA	41	51
Tony Mullane	1886	Cin-AA	33	51
Toad Ramsey	1886	Lou-AA	38	58
Matt Kilroy	1886	Bal-AA	29	60*
John Clarkson	1887	Chi-NL	38	54
Tim Keefe	1887	NY-NL	35	51
Pud Galvin	1887	Pit-NL	28	51
Jim Whitney	1887	Was-NL	24	52
Matt Kilroy	1887	Bal-AA	46	60*
Jersey Bakely	1888	Cle-AA	25	50
John Clarkson	1889	Bos-NL	49	59
Bill Hutchison	1890	Chi-NL	42	50
Eb Beatin	1890	Cle-NL	22	50
Sadie McMahon	1890	Phi-AA	29	54
Bill Hutchison	1891	Chi-NL	44	54
Bill Hutchison	1892	Chi-LA	37	52
Frank Killen	1892	Was-LA	29	58

* In the early years several pitchers collected all of their team's victories in a season, and as late as 1884 some still earned well over three-quarters. Kilroy is the only pitcher since 1886 to be credited with as many as 60 percent of his team's wins. Astonishingly, he did it in back-to-back seasons.

THE SEASONAL RECORD

	W	L	PCT	HOME	ROAD	GB
1. Boston Beaneaters	102	48	.680	54–21	48–27	—
2. Cleveland Spiders	93	56	.624	54–24	39–32	8.5
3. Brooklyn Bridegrooms	95	59	.615	51–24	44–35	9
4. Philadelphia Phillies	87	66	.569	55–26	32–40	16.5
5. Cincinnati Reds	82	68	.547	45–32	37–36	20
6. Pittsburgh Pirates	80	73	.523	52–34	28–39	23.5
7. Chicago Colts	70	76	.479	36–31	34–45	30
8. New York Giants	71	80	.470	42–36	29–44	31.5
9. Louisville Colonels	63	89	.414	37–31	26–58	40
10. Washington Nationals	58	93	.384	34–36	24–57	44.5
11. St. Louis Browns	56	94	.373	37–36	19–58	46
12. Baltimore Orioles	46	101	.313	29–46	17–55	54.5

FIRST HALF		W	L	PCT	GB
1.	Bos	52	22	.703	—
2.	Bro	51	26	.662	2.5
3.	Phi	46	30	.605	7
4.	Cin	44	31	.587	8.5
5.	Cle	40	33	.548	11.5
6.	Pit	37	39	.487	16
7.	Was	35	41	.460	18
8.	Chi	31	39	.443	19
9.	StL	31	42	.425	20.5
10.	NY	31	43	.419	21
11.	Lou	30	47	.390	23.5
12.	Bal	20	55	.267	32.5

SECOND HALF		W	L	PCT	GB
1.	Cle	53	23	.697	—
2.	Bos	50	26	.658	3
3.	Bro	44	33	.571	9.5
4.	Pit	43	34	.558	10.5
5.	Phi	41	36	.532	12.5
6.	NY	40	37	.519	13.5
7.	Chi	39	37	.513	14
8.	Cin	38	37	.507	14.5
9.	Lou	33	42	.440	19.5
10.	Bal	26	46	.361	25
11.	StL	25	52	.325	28.5
12.	Was	23	52	.307	29.5

	Bos	Cle	Bro	Phi	Cin	Pit	Chi	NY	Lou	Was	StL	Bal	
Boston	—	8	9	6	8	7	10	11	12	11	7	13	102
Cleveland	6	—	6	10	9	7	9	8	13	6	8	11	93
Brooklyn	5	8	—	9	6	10	10	7	9	10	9	12	95
Philadelphia	7	4	5	—	9	8	9	9	10	9	7	10	87
Cincinnati	5	5	8	5	—	5	7	8	7	10	10	10	82
Pittsburgh	6	7	4	6	9	—	7	10	6	6	10	9	80
Chicago	4	3	4	5	6	7	—	10	5	12	7	7	70
New York	3	5	7	5	6	4	4	—	10	9	9	9	71
Louisville	2	1	5	4	6	8	9	4	—	8	9	7	63
Washington	3	8	4	5	3	8	2	4	6	—	8	7	58
St. Louis	7	5	5	7	2	4	5	4	5	6	—	6	56
Baltimore	0	2	2	4	4	5	4	5	6	6	8	—	46
	48	56	59	66	68	73	76	80	89	93	94	101	802

SEASON LEADERS

Batting Average (400 ABs)

1.	Brouthers, Brooklyn	.335
2.	Hamilton, Philadelphia	.330
3.	Childs, Cleveland	.317
4.	O. Burns, Brooklyn	.315
5.	Delahanty, Philadelphia	.306

On–Base Percentage

1.	Childs, Cleveland	.443
2.	Brouthers, Brooklyn	.432
3.	Hamilton, Philadelphia	.423
4.	Connor, Philadelphia	.420
5.	Crooks, St. Louis	.400

Home Runs

1.	Holliday, Cincinnati	13
2.	Connor, Philadelphia	12
3.	Ryan, Chicago	10
	Beckley, Pittsburgh	10
5.	Thompson, Philadelphia	9

Slugging Average

1.	Delahanty, Philadelphia	.495
2.	Brouthers, Brooklyn	.480
3.	Connor, Philadelphia	.463
4.	O. Burns, Brooklyn	.454
5.	Holliday, Cincinnati	.449

Total Bases

1.	Brouthers, Brooklyn	282
2.	Holliday, Cincinnati	270
3.	Thompson, Philadelphia	263
4.	Connor, Philadelphia	261
5.	Duffy, Boston	251

RBI

1.	Brouthers, Brooklyn	124
2.	Thompson, Philadelphia	104
3.	Larkin, Washington	96
	O. Burns, Brooklyn	96
	Beckley, Pittsburgh	96

Hits

1.	Brouthers, Brooklyn	197
2.	Thompson, Philadelphia	186
3.	Duffy, Boston	184
4.	Hamilton, Philadelphia	183
5.	Long, Boston	181

Stolen Bases

1.	Ward, Brooklyn	88
2.	Brown, Louisville	78
3.	Latham, Cincinnati	66
4.	Hoy, Washington	60
	Dahlen, Chicago	60

Runs

1.	Childs, Cleveland	136
2.	Hamilton, Philadelphia	132
3.	Duffy, Boston	125
4.	Connor, Philadelphia	123
5.	Brouthers, Brooklyn	121

Strikeouts

1.	Brown, Louisville	94
2.	Virtue, Cleveland	68
3.	Weyhing, Philadelphia	67
4.	T. Daly, Brooklyn	61
	Killen, Washington	61

PITCHING

Wins

1.	Hutchison, Chicago	37
2.	Young, Cleveland	36
3.	Stivetts, Boston	35
	Nichols, Boston	35
5.	Weyhing, Philadelphia	32

Innings

1.	Hutchison, Chicago	627
2.	Rusie, New York	532
3.	Weyhing, Philadelphia	469.2
4.	Killen, Washington	459.2
5.	Nichols, Boston	453
	Young, Cleveland	453

Strikeouts

1.	Hutchison, Chicago	316
2.	Rusie, New York	288
3.	Weyhing, Philadelphia	202
4.	Stein, Brooklyn	190
5.	Nichols, Boston	187

ERA (154 innings)

1.	Young, Cleveland	1.93
2.	Keefe, Philadelphia	2.36
3.	J. Clarkson, Bos–Cle	2.48
4.	Cuppy, Cleveland	2.51
5.	Terry, Bal–Pit	2.57

Losses

1.	Cobb, Baltimore	37
2.	Hutchison, Chicago	36
3.	Rusie, New York	31
4.	Baldwin, Pittsburgh	27
5.	Killen, Washington	26

Complete Games

1.	Hutchison, Chicago	67
2.	Rusie, New York	58
3.	Nichols, Boston	49
4.	Young, Cleveland	48
5.	Killen, Washington	46
	Weyhing, Philadelphia	46

Winning Percentage (25 decisions)

1.	Young, Cleveland	.750
2.	Terry, Bal-Pit	.692
3.	Haddock, Brooklyn	.690
4.	Staley, Boston	.688
5.	Nichols, Boston	.686
	Stivetts, Boston	.686

Lowest On–Base Percentage

1.	Young, Cleveland	.266
2.	Nichols, Boston	.283
3.	Stratton, Louisville	.286
4.	Keefe, Philadelphia	.287
5.	Mullane, Cincinnati	.290

FIELDING

Total Chances

1B	Beckley, Pittsburgh	1693
2B	Bierbauer, Pittsburgh	989
3B	Shindle, Baltimore	660
SS	Jennings, Louisville	970
OF	Brown, Louisville	422
C	Clements, Philadelphia	599
P	Hutchison, Chicago	190

Fielding Average

Connor, Philadelphia	.985
Quinn, Boston	.951
Nash, Boston	.898
D. Richardson, Washington	.931
Griffin, Brooklyn	.986
Mack, Pittsburgh	.951
Nichols, Boston	.966

BOSTON   **Frank Selee**   **South End Grounds (I)**

		G	AB	H	R	2B	3B	HR	RBI	BB	SB	BA	SA
SS	Herman Long	151	646	181	115	33	6	6	77	44	57	.280	.378
CF	Hugh Duffy	147	612	184	125	28	12	5	81	60	51	.301	.410
RF	Tommy McCarthy	152	603	146	119	19	5	4	63	93	53	.242	.310
1B	Tommy Tucker	149	542	153	85	15	7	1	62	45	22	.282	.341
2B	Joe Quinn	143	532	116	63	14	1	1	59	35	17	.218	.254
3B	Billy Nash	135	526	137	94	25	5	4	95	59	31	.260	.350
LF	Bobby Lowe	124	475	115	79	16	7	3	57	37	36	.242	.324
C	King Kelly	78	281	53	40	7	0	2	41	39	24	.189	.235
P	Jack Stivetts	70	240	71	40	14	2	3	36	27	8	.296	.408
C	Charlie Ganzel	54	198	53	25	9	3	0	25	18	7	.268	.343
P	Kid Nichols	58	197	39	21	6	2	2	21	16	3	.198	.279
Sub	Harry Stovey	38	146	24	21	8	1	0	12	14	20	.164	.233
P	Harry Staley	38	122	16	9	2	0	1	9	9	2	.131	.172
C	Charlie Bennett	35	114	23	19	4	0	1	16	27	6	.202	.263
P	John Clarkson	16	57	13	7	3	0	1	13	3	1	.228	.333
Sub	Dan Burke	1	4	0	0	0	0	0	0	0	0	.000	.000
P	Dad Clarkson	1	3	0	0	0	0	0	0	0	0	.000	.000
P	Leon Viau	1	3	0	0	0	0	0	0	0	0	.000	.000
Sub	Joe Daly	1	0	0	0	0	0	0	0	0	0	—	—
		152	5301	1324	862	203	51	34	668	526	338	.250	.327

1B	Tucker 149, Kelly, 2, Ganzel 1, Stivetts 1
2B	Quinn 143, Lowe 10
SS	Long 141, Lowe 13
3B	Nash 135, Lowe 14, Kelly 2, Duffy 2, Long 1
OF	McCarthy 152, Duffy 146, Lowe 90, Stovey 38, Stivetts 18, Long 12, Nichols 5, Ganzel 2, Kelly 2, Staley 1, Nash 1
C	Kelly 72, Ganzel 51, Bennett 35, Daly 1, Burke 1
P	Stivetts 58, Nichols 53, Staley 37, J. Clarkson 16, Viau 1, D. Clarkson 1, Kelly 1

	G	IP	GS	CG	W	L	K	BB	SH	SV	ERA
Kid Nichols	53	453	51	49	35	16	187	121	5	0	2.84
Jack Stivetts #	54	415.2	48	45	35	16	180	171	3	1	3.03
Harry Staley	37	299.2	35	31	22	10	93	97	3	0	3.03
John Clarkson	16	145.2	16	15	8	6	48	60	4	0	2.35
Leon Viau	1	9	1	1	1	0	1	4	0	0	0.00
Dad Clarkson	1	7	1	1	1	0	0	3	0	0	1.29
King Kelly	1	6	0	0	0	0	0	4	0	0	1.50
		1336	152	142	102	48	509	460	**15**	1	2.86

No–hit game 11–0 vs Brooklyn, August 6

CLEVELAND   **Patsy Tebeau**   **League Park (I)**

		G	AB	H	R	2B	3B	HR	RBI	BB	SB	BA	SA
LF	Jesse Burkett	145	608	167	119	15	14	6	66	67	36	.275	.375
3B	George Davis	144	597	144	95	27	12	5	82	58	36	.241	.352
RF	Jack O'Connor	140	572	142	71	22	5	1	58	25	17	.248	.309
CF	Jimmy McAleer	149	571	136	92	26	7	4	70	63	40	.238	.329
2B	Cupid Childs	145	558	177	**136**	14	11	3	53	117	26	.317	.398
1B	Jake Virtue	147	557	157	98	15	20	2	89	84	14	.282	.391
SS	Ed McKean	129	531	139	76	14	10	0	93	49	19	.262	.326
C	Chief Zimmer	111	413	108	63	29	13	1	64	32	18	.262	.402
UT	Patsy Tebeau	86	340	83	47	13	3	2	49	23	6	.244	.318
P	Cy Young	53	196	31	14	5	0	1	15	7	3	.158	.199
P	Nig Cuppy	50	168	36	15	11	0	0	24	7	2	.214	.280
P	John Clarkson	29	101	14	8	0	0	0	4	8	2	.139	.139
Sub	Jack Doyle	24	88	26	17	4	1	1	14	6	5	.295	.398
P	George Davies	26	87	12	3	1	0	0	6	3	1	.138	.149
P	George Rettger	6	15	2	0	0	0	0	0	3	0	.133	.133
P	Tom Williams	3	10	1	1	0	0	0	0	0	0	.100	.100
P	Leon Viau	1	0	0	0	0	0	0	0	0	0	—	—
		153	5412	1375	855	196	96	26	687	552	225	.254	.340

1B	Virtue 147, Tebeau 4, Doyle 1
2B	Childs 145, Tebeau 5, Davis 3
SS	McKean 129, Davis 20, Tebeau 3, Doyle 1
3B	Davis 79, Tebeau 74
OF	McAleer 149, Burkett 145, O'Connor 106, Davis 44, Doyle 12, Cuppy 3, Williams 1
C	Zimmer 111, O'Connor 34, Doyle 9
P	Young 53, Cuppy 47, Clarkson 29, Davies 26, Rettger 6, Williams 2, Viau 1

	G	IP	GS	CG	W	L	K	BB	SH	SV	ERA
Cy Young	53	453	49	48	36	12	168	118	**9**	0	**1.93**
Nig Cuppy	47	376	42	38	28	13	103	121	1	1	2.51
John Clarkson	29	243.1	28	27	17	10	91	72	1	1	2.55
George Davies	26	215.2	26	23	10	16	95	69	0	0	2.59
George Rettger	6	38	5	3	1	3	12	31	0	0	4.26
Tom Williams	2	9	1	1	1	0	3	1	0	0	3.00
Leon Viau	1	1	1	0	0	1	0	1	0	0	36.00
	—1 forfeit L vs Pittsburgh on October 12—										
	1336	152	140	93	55	472	**413**	11	2	**2.41**

BROOKLYN   Monte Ward   Eastern Park

		G	AB	H	R	2B	3B	HR	RBI	BB	SB	BA	SA
2B	Monte Ward	148	614	163	109	13	3	1	47	82	**88**	.265	.306
SS	Tommy Corcoran	151	613	145	77	11	6	1	74	34	39	.237	.279
1B	Dan Brouthers	152	588	**197**	121	30	20	5	**124**	84	31	**.335**	.480
RF	Oyster Burns	141	542	171	88	27	18	4	96	65	33	.315	.454
LF	Darby O'Brien	122	490	119	72	14	5	1	56	29	57	.243	.298
CF	Mike Griffin	129	452	125	103	17	11	3	66	68	49	.277	.383
UT	Tom Daly	124	446	114	76	15	6	4	51	64	34	.256	.343
3B	Bill Joyce	97	372	91	89	15	12	6	45	82	23	.245	.398
C	Con Daily	80	278	65	38	10	1	0	28	38	18	.234	.277
C	Tom Kinslow	66	246	75	37	6	11	2	40	13	4	.305	.443
Sub	Dave Foutz	61	220	41	33	5	3	1	26	14	19	.186	.250
P	George Haddock	47	158	28	23	6	1	0	11	12	2	.177	.228
P	Ed Stein	48	144	31	18	2	1	0	8	17	0	.215	.243
P	Bill Hart	37	125	24	14	3	4	2	17	7	4	.192	.328
Sub	Hub Collins	21	87	26	17	5	1	0	17	14	4	.299	.379
P	Brickyard Kennedy	26	85	14	12	3	2	0	11	4	3	.165	.247
P	Bert Inks	9	25	10	8	1	0	0	2	2	1	.400	.440
		158	5485	**1439**	**935**	183	105	30	**719**	629	409	**.262**	.350

1B   Brouthers 152, Foutz 6
2B   Ward 148, Daly 10
SS   Corcoran 151, Burns 5, Griffin 2
3B   Joyce 94, Daly 57, Burns 7
OF   Burns 129, Griffin 127, O'Brien 122, Daly 30, Foutz 29, Collins 21, Daily 13, Hart 12, Joyce 3, Kennedy 1, Haddock 1
C   Daily 68, Kinslow 66, Daly 27
P   Stein 48, Haddock 46, Foutz 29, Hart 28, Kennedy 26, Inks 9

	G	IP	GS	CG	W	L	K	BB	SH	SV	ERA
George Haddock	46	381.1	44	39	29	13	153	163	3	1	3.14
Ed Stein	48	377.1	42	38	27	16	190	150	6	1	2.84
Dave Foutz	29	203	20	17	13	8	56	63	0	1	3.41
Bill Hart	28	195	23	16	9	12	65	96	2	1	3.28
Brickyard Kennedy	26	191	21	18	13	8	108	95	0	1	3.86
Bert Inks	9	58	8	4	4	2	25	33	1	0	3.88
		1405.2	158	132	95	59	597	600	12	**5**	3.25

PHILADELPHIA   Harry Wright   Philadelphia Baseball Grounds

		G	AB	H	R	2B	3B	HR	RBI	BB	SB	BA	SA
RF	Sam Thompson	153	609	186	109	28	11	9	104	59	28	.305	.432
2B	Bill Hallman	138	586	171	106	27	10	2	84	32	19	.292	.382
1B	Roger Connor	155	564	166	123	**37**	11	12	73	116	22	.294	.463
SS	Bob Allen	152	563	128	77	20	14	2	64	61	15	.227	.323
LF	Billy Hamilton	139	554	183	132	21	7	3	53	81	57	.330	.410
UT	Lave Cross	140	541	149	84	15	10	4	69	39	18	.275	.362
CF	Ed Delahanty	123	477	146	79	30	**21**	6	91	31	29	.306	**.495**
C	Jack Clements	109	402	106	50	25	6	8	76	43	7	.264	.415
3B	Charlie Reilly	91	331	65	42	7	3	1	24	18	13	.196	.245
P	Gus Weyhing	66	214	29	14	5	0	0	13	11	2	.136	.159
P	Kid Carsey	44	131	20	8	2	1	1	10	9	1	.153	.206
P	Tim Keefe	39	117	10	6	2	0	1	3	13	1	.085	.128
Sub	Joe Mulvey	25	98	14	9	1	1	0	4	6	2	.143	.173
P	Duke Esper	23	70	17	8	2	0	1	11	2	1	.243	.314
Sub	Tom Dowse	16	54	10	3	0	0	0	6	2	1	.185	.185

		G	AB	H	R	2B	3B	HR	RBI	BB	SB	BA	SA
Sub	Dummy Stephenson	8	37	10	4	3	0	0	5	0	0	.270	.351
P	Phil Knell	11	34	3	4	0	0	0	1	3	0	.088	.088
P	John Thornton	5	13	5	1	0	0	0	2	0	0	.385	.385
P	Jack Taylor	3	12	2	1	0	0	0	0	1	0	.167	.167
Sub	Jerry Connors	1	3	0	0	0	0	0	0	0	0	.000	.000
Sub	Harry Morelock	1	3	0	0	0	0	0	0	0	0	.000	.000
		155	5413	1420	860	**225**	95	**50**	693	528	216	**.262**	.367

1B Connor 155
2B Hallman 138, Cross 14, Reilly 4
SS Allen 152, Cross 5
3B Reilly 70, Cross 65, Mulvey 25, Delahanty 4, Morelock 1
OF Thompson 153, Hamilton 139, Delahanty 121, Cross 25, Reilly 15, Stephenson 8, Weyhing 7, Carsey 2, Thornton 2, Connors 1, Esper 1
C   Clements 109, Cross 39, Dowse 15
P   Weyhing 59, Carsey 43, Keefe 39, Esper 21, Knell 11, Thornton 3, Taylor 3

	G	IP	GS	CG	W	L	K	BB	SH	SV	ERA
Gus Weyhing	59	469.2	49	46	32	21	202	168	6	**3**	2.66
Kid Carsey	43	317.2	36	30	19	16	76	104	1	1	3.12
Tim Keefe	39	313.1	38	31	19	16	127	100	3	0	2.36
Duke Esper	21	160.1	18	14	11	6	45	58	0	1	3.42
Phil Knell	11	80	9	7	5	5	43	35	0	0	4.05
Jack Taylor	3	26	3	2	1	0	7	10	0	0	1.38
John Thornton	3	12	2	1	0	2	2	17	0	0	12.75
	* One combined shutout on July 21: Keefe 7 innings, Weyhing 2 innings										
	1379	155	131	87	66	502	492	10	**5**	2.93

CINCINNATI   **Charlie Comiskey**   **League Park (I)**

		G	AB	H	R	2B	3B	HR	RBI	BB	SB	BA	SA
3B	Arlie Latham	152	622	148	111	20	4	0	44	60	66	.238	.283
RF	Bug Holliday	152	602	176	114	23	16	**13**	91	57	43	.292	.449
2B	Bid McPhee	144	573	157	111	19	12	4	60	84	44	.274	.370
1B	Charlie Comiskey	141	551	125	61	14	6	3	71	32	30	.227	.290
SS	Germany Smith	139	506	121	58	13	6	8	63	42	19	.239	.336
LF	Tip O'Neill	109	419	105	63	14	6	2	52	53	11	.251	.327
C	Farmer Vaughn	91	346	88	45	10	5	2	50	16	10	.254	.329
CF	Pete Browning	83	307	93	47	12	5	3	52	40	8	.303	.404
C	Morg Murphy	74	234	46	29	8	2	2	24	25	4	.197	.274
P	Icebox Chamberlain	53	160	36	13	3	1	2	15	7	1	.225	.294
P	Frank Dwyer	40	129	21	15	0	2	0	6	4	2	.163	.194
P	Tony Mullane	39	118	20	14	3	1	0	9	9	4	.169	.212
Sub	Frank Genins	35	110	20	12	4	0	0	7	12	7	.182	.218
Sub	George Wood	30	107	21	10	2	4	0	14	10	4	.196	.290
Sub	Jocko Halligan	26	101	29	14	4	0	2	12	12	3	.287	.386
Sub	Curt Welch	25	94	19	14	0	2	1	7	7	7	.202	.277
P	Mike Sullivan	21	74	13	5	1	1	0	5	0	0	.176	.216
Sub	Jerry Harrington	22	61	13	6	1	0	0	3	6	0	.213	.230
Sub	Buster Hoover	14	51	9	7	0	0	0	2	5	1	.176	.176
Sub	Eddie Burke	15	41	6	6	1	0	0	4	9	2	.146	.171
P	Billy Rhines	13	30	5	2	0	1	1	4	3	0	.167	.333
P	Jesse Duryea	9	27	3	3	1	0	0	0	5	0	.111	.148
Sub	Willie Kuehne	6	24	5	3	1	0	1	4	1	0	.208	.375
Sub	Dan Mahoney	5	21	4	1	0	1	0	1	1	0	.190	.286
P	George Rettger	2	8	1	1	1	0	0	3	1	0	.125	.250

		G	AB	H	R	2B	3B	HR	RBI	BB	SB	BA	SA
P	Willie McGill	3	7	2	1	0	0	0	1	0	1	.286	.286
P	Dan Daub	4	7	0	0	0	0	0	0	0	0	.000	.000
P	George Meakim	3	5	0	0	0	0	0	0	0	0	.000	.000
Sub	Tom Dowse	1	4	0	0	0	0	0	0	0	0	.000	.000
P	George Hemming	1	3	1	0	0	0	0	0	0	0	.333	.333
P	Frank Knauss	1	3	1	0	0	0	0	0	1	0	.333	.333
P	Bumpus Jones	1	2	0	0	0	0	0	0	1	0	.000	.000
P	Clarence Stephens	1	2	0	0	0	0	0	0	0	0	.000	.000
		155	5349	1288	766	155	75	44	604	503	270	.241	.322

1B Comiskey 141, Vaughn 14, Mullane 2, Browning 2, Harrington 1
2B McPhee 144, Latham 9, Kuehne 2
SS Smith 139, Genins 17
3B Latham 142, Vaughn 6, Kuehne 4, Genins 4, Burke 1
OF Holliday 152, O'Neill 109, Browning 82, Wood 30, Halligan 26, Welch 25, Hoover 14, Burke 14, Genins 14, Vaughn 11, Dwyer 6, Chamberlain 1, Rhines 1, Rettger 1, Latham 1
C Murphy 74, Vaughn 67, Harrington 22, Mahoney 5, Dowse 1
P Chamberlain 52, Mullane 37, Dwyer 33, Sullivan 21, Rhines 12, Duryea 9, Daub 4, Meakim 3, McGill 3, Stephens 1, Rettger 1, Hemming 1, Jones 1, Knauss 1, Holliday 1

	G	IP	GS	CG	W	L	K	BB	SH	SV	ERA
Icebox Chamberlain	52	406.1	49	43	19	23	169	170	2	0	3.39
Tony Mullane	37	295	34	30	21	13	109	127	3	1	2.59
Frank Dwyer	33	259.1	27	24	19	10	45	49	3	1	2.33
Mike Sullivan	21	166.1	16	15	12	4	56	74	0	0	3.08
Billy Rhines	12	83.2	10	7	4	7	12	36	0	0	5.06
Jesse Duryea	9	68	7	5	2	5	21	26	0	0	3.57
Dan Daub	4	25	3	2	1	2	7	13	0	0	2.88
Willie McGill	3	17	3	1	1	1	7	5	0	0	5.29
George Meakim	3	13.2	3	1	1	1	4	9	0	0	8.56
George Rettger	1	9	1	1	1	0	1	10	0	0	4.00
Bumpus Jones #	1	9	1	1	1	0	3	4	0	0	0.00
Frank Knauss	1	8	0	0	0	0	2	5	0	0	3.38
Clarence Stephens	1	7	1	0	0	1	1	4	0	0	1.29
George Hemming	1	6	0	0	0	1	0	2	0	0	7.50
Bug Holliday	1	4	0	0	0	0	0	1	0	0	11.25
		1377.1	155	130	82	68	437	535	8	2	3.17

No hit game 7–1 vs Pittsburgh, October 15

PITTSBURGH **Al Buckenberger (53–41)** **Tom Burns (27–32)** **Exposition Park**

		G	AB	H	R	2B	3B	HR	RBI	BB	SB	BA	SA
2B	Lou Bierbauer	152	649	153	81	20	9	8	65	25	11	.236	.331
UT	Doggie Miller	149	623	158	103	15	12	2	59	69	28	.254	.326
1B	Jake Beckley	151	614	145	102	21	19	10	96	31	30	.236	.381
3B	Duke Farrell	152	605	130	96	10	13	8	77	46	20	.215	.314
SS	Frank Shugart	137	554	148	94	19	4	0	62	47	28	.267	.352
LF	Elmer Smith	138	511	140	86	16	14	4	63	82	22	.274	.384
RF	Patsy Donovan	90	388	114	77	15	3	2	26	20	40	.294	.363
C	Connie Mack	97	346	84	39	9	4	1	31	21	11	.243	.301
Sub	Pop Corkhill	68	256	47	23	1	4	0	25	12	6	.184	.219
CF	Joe Kelley	56	205	49	26	7	7	0	28	17	8	.239	.341
P	Mark Baldwin	56	178	18	11	2	0	1	13	13	1	.101	.129
P	Red Ehret	40	132	34	12	2	0	0	19	7	1	.258	.273
P	Adonis Terry	31	100	16	10	0	4	2	11	10	2	.160	.300
Sub	George Van Haltren	13	55	11	10	2	2	0	5	6	6	.200	.309

		G	AB	H	R	2B	3B	HR	RBI	BB	SB	BA	SA
Sub	Harry Raymond	12	49	4	4	0	1	0	2	4	1	.082	.122
Sub	Ed Swartwood	13	42	10	8	1	0	0	4	13	1	.238	.262
P	Pud Galvin	12	41	5	4	1	0	0	4	2	0	.122	.146
Sub	Tom Burns	12	39	8	7	0	0	0	4	3	1	.205	.205
P	Billy Gumbert	7	18	2	2	0	1	0	1	0	2	.111	.222
P	Fred Woodcock	5	15	3	2	0	1	0	1	1	0	.200	.333
Sub	Billy Earle	5	13	7	5	2	0	0	3	4	2	.538	.692
P	Kid Camp	4	11	1	0	0	0	0	0	0	0	.091	.091
Sub	Jake Stenzel	3	9	0	0	0	0	0	0	1	1	.000	.000
P	Duke Esper	3	9	0	0	0	0	0	1	0	0	.000	.000
Sub	Bobby Cargo	2	4	1	0	0	0	0	0	0	0	.250	.250
P	Jock Menefee	1	3	0	0	0	0	0	0	0	0	.000	.000
P	Will Thompson	1	0	0	0	0	0	0	0	1	0	—	—
		155	5469	1288	802	143	108	38	600	435	222	.236	.322

1B Beckley 151, Mack 1
2B Bierbauer 152
SS Shugart 134, Miller 19, Cargo 2
3B Farrell 133, Raymond 12, Burns 8, Miller 2,
OF Smith 124, Donovan 90, Miller 76, Corkhill 68, Kelley 56, Farrell 20, Van Haltren 13, Swartwood 13, Mack 3, Burns 3, Stenzel 2, Shugart 1, Terry 1, Gumbert 1, Menefee 1
C Mack 92, Miller 63, Earle 5, Shugart 2, Stenzel 1
P Baldwin 56, Ehret 39, Terry 30, Smith 17, Galvin 12, Gumbert 6, Woodcock 5, Camp 4, Esper 3, Thompson 1, Menefee 1

	G	IP	GS	CG	W	L	K	BB	SH	SV	ERA
Mark Baldwin	56	440.1	53	45	26	27	157	194	0	0	3.47
Red Ehret	39	316	36	32	16	20	101	83	0	0	2.65
Adonis Terry	30	240	26	24	18	7	95	106	2	1	2.51
Elmer Smith	17	134	13	12	6	7	51	58	1	0	3.63
Pud Galvin	12	96	12	10	5	6	29	28	0	0	2.63
Billy Gumbert	6	39.2	3	2	3	2	3	23	0	0	1.36
Fred Woodcock	5	33	4	3	1	2	8	17	0	0	3.55
Kid Camp	4	23	1	1	0	1	6	9	0	0	6.26
Duke Esper	3	18.1	3	1	2	0	5	12	0	0	5.40
Jock Menefee	1	4	0	0	0	0	0	2	0	0	11.25
Will Thompson	1	3	1	0	0	1	0	5	0	0	3.00
—3 forfeit Ws: vs New York on May 10; vs Chicago on September 22 and vs Cleveland on October 12—											
	1347.1	152	130	77	73	455	537	3	1	3.10

CHICAGO   Cap Anson   South Side Park (I)

		G	AB	H	R	2B	3B	HR	RBI	BB	SB	BA	SA
SS	Bill Dahlen	143	581	169	114	23	19	5	58	45	60	.291	.422
1B	Cap Anson	146	559	152	62	25	9	1	74	67	13	.272	.354
CF	Jimmy Ryan	128	505	148	105	21	11	10	65	61	27	.293	.438
2B	Jimmy Canavan	118	439	73	48	10	11	0	32	48	33	.166	.239
RF	Sam Dungan	113	433	123	46	19	7	0	53	35	15	.284	.360
LF	Walt Wilmot	92	380	82	47	7	7	2	35	40	31	.216	.287
3B	Jiggs Parrott	78	333	67	38	8	5	2	22	8	7	.201	.273
C	Pop Schriver	92	326	73	40	10	6	1	34	27	4	.224	.301
Sub	George Decker	78	291	66	32	6	7	1	28	20	9	.227	.306
P	Bill Hutchison	77	263	57	23	10	5	1	22	10	8	.217	.304
SS	Jimmy Cooney	65	238	41	18	1	0	0	20	23	10	.172	.176
C	Mal Kittridge	69	229	41	19	5	0	0	10	11	2	.179	.201
P	Ad Gumbert	52	178	42	18	1	2	1	8	14	5	.236	.281
P	Pat Luby	45	163	31	14	3	2	2	20	12	3	.190	.270
Sub	Charlie Newman	16	61	10	4	0	0	0	2	1	2	.164	.164
Sub	Jim Connor	9	34	2	0	0	0	0	0	1	0	.059	.059
Sub	Fred Roat	8	31	6	4	0	1	0	2	2	2	.194	.258
P	Harry DeMiller	4	10	3	2	0	0	0	5	2	2	.300	.300
P	George Meakim	1	5	2	1	0	0	0	2	0	0	.400	.400
P	John Hollison	1	3	0	0	0	0	0	0	0	0	.000	.000
P	Frank Griffith	1	1	0	0	0	0	0	0	0	0	.000	.000
		147	5063	1188	635	149	92	26	492	427	233	.235	.316

1B   Anson 146
2B   Canavan 112, Decker 16, Connor 9, Roat 8, Dahlen 1
SS   Dahlen 72, Cooney 65, Ryan 9, Canavan 2
3B   Parrott 78, Dahlen 68
OF   Ryan 120, Dungan 113, Wilmot 92. Decker 62, Newman 16, Luby 16, Schriver 10, Gumbert 7, Canavan 4, Hutchison 2, Dahlen 2
C   Schriver 82, Kittridge 69
P   Hutchison 75, Gumbert 46, Luby 31, DeMiller 4, Griffith 1, Hollison 1, Meakim 1

	G	IP	GS	CG	W	L	K	BB	SH	SV	ERA
Bill Hutchison	**75**	**627**	**71**	**67**	**37**	36	**316**	187	5	0	2.74
Ad Gumbert	46	382.2	45	39	22	19	118	107	0	0	3.41
Pat Luby	31	247.1	26	24	10	16	64	106	1	1	3.13
Harry DeMiller	4	24	2	2	1	1	15	16	0	0	6.38
George Meakim	1	9	1	1	0	1	0	2	0	0	11.00
Frank Griffith	1	4	1	0	0	1	3	6	0	0	11.25
John Hollison	1	4	0	0	0	0	2	0	0	0	2.25
	—2 forfeit Ls: vs Louisville on April 23; vs Pittsburgh on September 22—										
	1298	146	133	70	74	518	424	6	1		3.16

NEW YORK   **Pat Powers**   **Polo Grounds (III)**

		G	AB	H	R	2B	3B	HR	RBI	BB	SB	BA	SA
SS	Shorty Fuller	141	508	115	74	11	4	1	48	52	37	.226	.270
RF	Mike Tiernan	116	450	129	79	16	10	5	66	57	20	.287	.400
LF	Jim O'Rourke	115	448	136	62	28	5	0	56	30	16	.304	.388
C	Jack Boyle	120	436	80	52	8	8	0	32	36	10	.183	.239
CF	Harry Lyons	96	411	98	67	5	2	0	53	33	25	.238	.260
1B	Buck Ewing	105	393	122	58	10	15	8	76	38	42	.310	.473
3B	Denny Lyons	108	389	100	71	16	7	8	51	59	11	.257	.396
UT	Jack Doyle	90	366	109	61	22	1	5	55	18	42	.298	.404
2B	Eddie Burke	89	363	94	81	10	5	6	41	46	42	.259	.364
P	Amos Rusie	69	252	53	18	6	4	1	26	3	4	.210	.278
Sub	Hardy Richardson	64	248	53	36	11	5	2	34	21	14	.214	.323
OF	George Gore	53	193	49	47	11	2	0	11	49	20	.254	.332
P	Silver King	52	167	35	27	3	4	2	23	16	1	.210	.311
P	Cannonball Crane	48	163	40	20	1	0	0	14	11	2	.245	.264
Sub	Jack McMahon	40	147	33	21	5	7	1	24	10	3	.224	.374
Sub	Charlie Bassett	35	130	27	9	2	3	0	16	6	0	.208	.269
Sub	Jocko Fields	21	66	18	8	4	2	0	5	9	2	.273	.394
Sub	Jimmy Knowles	16	59	9	9	1	0	0	7	6	2	.153	.169
Sub	Willie Keeler	14	53	17	7	3	0	0	6	3	5	.321	.377
Sub	Danny Murphy	8	26	3	2	0	0	0	0	5	0	.115	.115
Sub	Charlie Newman	3	12	4	1	0	0	0	1	2	3	.333	.333
Sub	John Sharrott	4	8	1	1	0	0	0	0	0	0	.125	.125
P	Mickey Welch	1	3	1	0	0	0	0	0	0	0	.333	.333
		153	5291	1326	811	173	85	39	645	510	301	.251	.338

1B   Ewing 73, Boyle 40, McMahon 36, Richardson 9, O'Rourke 1
2B   Burke 59, Richardson 33, Doyle 31, Bassett 30, Ewing 2
SS   Fuller 141, Doyle 7, Richardson 6, Boyle 2, Knowles 1
3B   D. Lyons 108, Knowles 15, Keeler 14, Doyle 13, Bassett 5
OF   Tiernan 116, O'Rourke 111, H. Lyons 96, Gore 53, Burke 30, Richardson 17, Doyle 17, Fields 11, Rusie 4, Sharrott 3, Newman 3, Boyle 2, Crane 1
C   Boyle 79, Ewing 30, Doyle 26, Fields 10, Murphy 8, McMahon 5, O'Rourke 4,
P   Rusie 64, King 52, Crane 47, Sharrott 1, Welch 1

	G	IP	GS	CG	W	L	K	BB	SH	SV	ERA
Amos Rusie	64	532	62	58	31	31	288	**267**	2	0	2.88
Silver King	52	419.1	47	46	23	24	177	174	1	0	3.24
Cannonball Crane	47	364.1	43	35	16	24	174	189	2	1	3.80
Mickey Welch	1	5	1	0	0	0	1	4	0	0	14.40
John Sharrott	1	2	0	0	0	0	1	1	0	0	4.50
—1 forfeit W vs Baltimore on April 20; 1 forfeit L vs Pittsburgh on May 10—											
	1322.2	153	139	70	79	**641**	635	5	1	3.29	

LOUISVILLE   **Jack Chapman (21–33)**   **Fred Pfeffer (42–56)**   **Eclipse Park (I)**

		G	AB	H	R	2B	3B	HR	RBI	BB	SB	BA	SA
CF	Tom Brown	153	**660**	150	105	16	8	2	45	47	78	.227	.285
SS	Hughie Jennings	152	594	132	65	16	4	2	61	30	28	.222	.273
LF	Farmer Weaver	138	551	140	58	15	4	0	57	40	30	.254	.296
RF	Harry Taylor	125	493	128	66	7	1	0	34	58	24	.260	.278
2B	Fred Pfeffer	124	470	121	78	14	9	2	76	67	27	.257	.338
C	John Grim	97	370	90	40	16	4	1	36	13	18	.243	.316
Sub	Charlie Bassett	79	313	67	36	5	5	2	35	15	16	.214	.281
3B	Willie Kuehne	76	287	48	22	4	5	0	36	13	6	.167	.216
1B	Lew Whistler	80	285	67	42	4	7	5	34	30	14	.235	.351
P	Scott Stratton	63	219	56	22	2	9	0	23	17	9	.256	.347
P	Ben Sanders	54	198	54	30	12	2	3	18	16	6	.273	.399
Sub	Bill Merritt	46	168	33	22	4	2	1	13	11	3	.196	.262
Sub	Emmett Seery	42	154	31	18	6	1	0	15	24	6	.201	.253
Sub	Tom Dowse	41	145	21	10	2	0	0	7	2	1	.145	.159
P	Fritz Clausen	24	84	13	4	1	0	0	3	5	0	.155	.167
Sub	Pete Browning	21	77	19	10	4	0	0	4	12	5	.247	.299
P	Leon Viau	21	66	13	5	2	0	0	5	7	2	.197	.227
P	Jouett Meekin	20	64	5	7	1	0	0	3	6	1	.078	.094
P	Alex Jones	18	55	8	6	0	0	0	2	7	0	.145	.145
Sub	Alex McFarlan	14	42	7	2	0	0	0	1	8	1	.167	.167
P	John Fitzgerald	4	15	2	1	1	0	0	1	1	0	.133	.200
P	George Hemming	4	13	1	0	0	0	0	0	2	0	.077	.077
P	Egyptian Healy	2	7	2	0	1	0	0	0	1	0	.286	.429
Sub	Jack Dooms	1	4	0	0	0	0	0	0	1	0	.000	.000
		154	5334	1208	649	133	61	18	509	433	275	.226	.284

1B	Whistler 72, Taylor 34, Sanders 15, Dowse 11, Grim 11, Weaver 10, Pfeffer 10, Stratton 6
2B	Pfeffer 116, Taylor 14, Whistler 10, Grim 10, Bassett 6, McFarlan 2, Dowse 1
SS	Jennings 152, Taylor 2, Grim 1
3B	Kuehne 76, Bassett 73, Taylor 5, Grim 1
OF	Brown 153, Weaver 122, Taylor 73, Seery 42, Browning 21, Stratton 17, McFarlan 12, Sanders 9, Grim 8, Viau 5, Dowse 3, Dooms 1, Pfeffer 1, Meekin 1
C	Grim 69, Merritt 46, Dowse 29, Weaver 15
P	Stratton 42, Sanders 31, Clausen 24, Meekin 19, Jones 18, Viau 16, Fitzgerald 4, Hemming 4, Healy 2, Pfeffer 1

	G	IP	GS	CG	W	L	K	BB	SH	SV	ERA
Scott Stratton	42	351.2	40	39	21	19	93	70	2	0	2.92
Ben Sanders #	31	268.1	31	30	12	19	77	62	3	0	3.22
Fritz Clausen	24	200	24	24	9	13	94	87	2	0	3.06
Jouett Meekin	19	156.1	18	17	7	10	67	78	0	0	4.03
Alex Jones	18	146.2	16	13	5	11	44	56	1	0	3.31
Leon Viau	16	130.2	15	14	4	11	36	56	1	0	3.99
George Hemming	4	35	4	4	2	2	12	17	0	0	4.63
John Fitzgerald	4	34	4	4	1	3	3	11	0	0	4.24
Egyptian Healy	2	18.1	2	2	1	1	4	5	0	0	1.96
Fred Pfeffer	1	5	0	0	0	0	0	5	0	0	1.80
—1 forfeit W vs Chicago on April 23—											
	1346	154	**147**	62	89	430	447	9	0	3.34

\# No-hit game 6–2 vs Baltimore, August 22

WASHINGTON Billy Barnie (0–2) Arthur Irwin (46–60) Danny Richardson (12–31)
Boundary Field

		G	AB	H	R	2B	3B	HR	RBI	BB	SB	BA	SA
CF	Dummy Hoy	152	593	166	108	19	8	3	75	86	60	.280	.354
2B	Tommy Dowd	144	584	142	94	9	10	1	50	34	49	.243	.298
SS	Danny Richardson	142	551	132	48	13	4	3	58	25	25	.240	.294
RF	Paul Radford	137	510	130	93	19	4	1	37	86	35	.255	.314
LF	Charlie Duffee	132	492	122	64	12	11	6	51	36	28	.248	.354
1B	Henry Larkin	119	464	130	76	13	7	8	96	39	21	.280	.390
C	Jocko Milligan	88	323	89	40	20	9	4	43	26	2	.276	.430
C	Deacon McGuire	97	315	73	46	14	4	4	43	61	7	.232	.340
3B	Yank Robinson	67	218	39	26	4	3	0	19	38	11	.179	.225
Sub	Larry Twitchell	51	192	42	20	9	5	0	20	11	8	.219	.318
P	Frank Killen	65	186	37	27	4	4	4	23	26	2	.199	.328
Sub	Patsy Donovan	40	163	39	29	3	3	0	12	11	16	.239	.294
Sub	Tun Berger	26	97	14	9	2	1	0	3	7	3	.144	.186
P	Bert Abbey	27	75	9	5	1	0	0	3	9	2	.120	.133
P	Phil Knell	22	68	8	8	0	0	0	1	3	0	.118	.118
P	Jesse Duryea	18	50	6	4	1	0	0	3	2	0	.120	.140
P	Jouett Meekin	14	45	6	7	0	0	2	7	3	0	.133	.267
Sub	Hardy Richardson	10	37	4	2	0	0	0	0	5	2	.108	.108
Sub	Jake Drauby	10	34	7	3	0	1	0	3	2	0	.206	.265
P	Hank Gastright	12	29	4	1	1	1	0	2	5	0	.138	.241
P	Frank Foreman	11	28	13	5	2	2	1	3	3	0	.464	.786
Sub	Tom Dowse	7	27	7	5	1	0	0	2	0	0	.259	.296
Sub	Jimmy Cooney	6	25	4	5	0	1	0	4	4	1	.160	.240
Sub	George Ulrich	6	24	7	1	1	0	0	0	0	2	.292	.333
Sub	Harry Raymond	4	15	1	2	0	0	0	0	3	1	.067	.067
P	John Dolan	5	13	3	1	0	0	0	1	2	0	.231	.231
P	Alex Jones	4	11	3	0	0	0	0	1	1	1	.273	.273
P	Bert Inks	3	10	3	1	1	0	0	0	0	0	.300	.400
P	Matt Kilroy	4	10	2	0	0	0	0	0	1	0	.200	.200
Sub	Dan Potts	1	4	1	0	0	0	0	0	0	0	.250	.250
Sub	Hal O'Hagan	1	4	1	1	0	0	0	0	0	0	.250	.250
Sub	Frank Shannon	1	4	1	0	0	0	0	2	0	0	.250	.250
Sub	Kohly Miller	1	3	0	0	0	0	0	0	0	0	.000	.000
		153	5204	1245	731	149	78	37	562	529	276	.239	.319

1B Larkin 117, Milligan 28, McGuire 8, Duffee 4

2B Dowd 98, D. Richardson 49, Robinson 4, Radford 2, H. Richardson 1

SS D. Richardson 93, Radford 20, Berger 18, Dowd 6, Cooney 6, Robinson 5, Twitchell 3, Ulrich 2, Miller 1, Shannon 1

3B Robinson 58, Radford 54, Dowd 18, Drauby 10, Duffee 6, Raymond 4, Ulrich 3, Twitchell 1, H. Richardson 2, D. Richardson 1

OF Hoy 152, Duffee 125, Radford 62, Twitchell 48, Donovan 40, Dowd 23, H. Richardson 7, Dowse 4, Larkin 2, Killen 2, McGuire 1

C McGuire 89, Milligan 59, Berger 9, Dowse 3, Ulrich 2, O'Hagan 1, Potts 1

P Killen 60, Abbey 27, Knell 22, Duryea 18, Meekin 14, Gastright 11, Foreman 11, Dolan 5, Kilroy 4, Jones 4, Inks 3

	G	IP	GS	CG	W	L	K	BB	SH	SV	ERA
Frank Killen	60	459.2	52	46	29	26	147	182	2	0	3.31
Bert Abbey	27	195.2	23	19	5	18	77	76	0	1	3.45
Phil Knell	22	170	21	17	9	13	74	76	1	0	3.65
Jesse Duryea	18	127	15	13	3	11	48	45	1	2	2.41
Jouett Meekin	14	112	14	13	3	10	58	48	1	0	3.46
Hank Gastright	11	79.2	7	6	3	3	32	38	0	0	5.08
Frank Foreman	11	60	7	4	2	4	16	37	0	0	3.30
John Dolan	5	37	4	3	2	2	8	15	0	0	4.38
Alex Jones	4	27	4	3	0	3	7	14	0	0	4.00
Matt Kilroy	4	26.1	3	2	1	1	1	15	0	0	2.39
Bert Inks	3	21	3	3	1	2	11	10	0	0	5.14
		1315.1	153	129	58	93	479	556	5	3	3.46

ST. LOUIS   Jack Glasscock (1–3)   Cub Stricker (6–17)   Jack Crooks (27–33)
George Gore (6–9)   Bob Caruthers (16–32)   Sportsman's Park (I)

		G	AB	H	R	2B	3B	HR	RBI	BB	SB	BA	SA
CF	Steve Brodie	154	602	152	85	10	9	4	60	52	28	.252	.319
1B	Perry Werden	149	598	154	73	22	6	8	84	59	20	.258	.355
SS	Jack Glasscock	139	566	151	83	27	5	3	72	44	26	.267	.348
RF	Bob Caruthers	143	513	142	76	16	8	3	69	86	24	.277	.357
2B	Jack Crooks	128	445	95	82	7	4	7	38	**126**	23	.213	.294
C	Dick Buckley	121	410	93	43	17	4	5	52	22	7	.227	.324
LF	Cliff Carroll	101	407	111	82	14	8	4	49	47	30	.273	.376
3B	George Pinkney	78	290	50	31	3	2	0	25	36	4	.172	.197
P	Kid Gleason	66	233	50	35	4	2	3	25	34	7	.215	.288
Sub	Gene Moriarty	47	177	31	20	4	1	3	19	4	7	.175	.260
Sub	Llewellyn Camp	42	145	30	19	3	1	2	13	17	12	.207	.283
P	Ted Breitenstein	47	131	16	16	1	1	0	6	16	4	.122	.145
Sub	Cub Stricker	28	98	20	12	1	0	0	11	10	5	.204	.214
Sub	Bill Moran	24	81	11	2	1	0	0	5	2	0	.136	.148
Sub	George Gore	20	73	15	9	0	1	0	4	18	2	.205	.233
P	Pink Hawley	20	71	12	3	1	0	1	5	1	0	.169	.225
Sub	Grant Briggs	22	55	4	2	1	0	0	1	5	2	.073	.091
Sub	Frank Genins	15	51	10	5	1	0	0	4	1	3	.196	.216
Sub	Frank Bird	17	50	10	9	3	1	1	1	6	2	.200	.360
P	Charlie Getzein	13	45	9	3	0	0	1	4	3	0	.200	.267
P	Bill Hawke	15	45	4	2	0	0	0	1	0	0	.089	.089
P	Pud Galvin	12	39	2	2	0	0	0	1	1	0	.051	.051
P	Frank Dwyer	10	25	2	4	0	0	0	0	4	0	.080	.080
Sub	Willie Kuehne	6	24	4	1	1	0	0	0	0	1	.167	.208
P	Jack Easton	5	17	3	1	1	0	0	2	0	1	.176	.235
Sub	Bill Van Dyke	4	16	2	2	0	0	0	1	0	0	.125	.125
Sub	Chicken Wolf	3	14	2	1	0	0	0	1	0	0	.143	.143
Sub	Jim McCormick	3	11	0	0	0	0	0	0	1	0	.000	.000
Sub	Ed Haigh	1	4	1	0	0	0	0	0	0	0	.250	.250
Sub	Kohly Miller	1	4	0	0	0	0	0	0	0	0	.000	.000
Sub	Hick Carpenter	1	3	1	0	0	0	0	0	1	0	.333	.333
Sub	Heinie Peitz	1	3	0	0	0	0	0	0	0	0	.000	.000
Sub	John Thornton	1	3	0	0	0	0	0	0	0	0	.000	.000
Sub	Mark McGrillis	1	3	0	0	0	0	0	0	0	0	.000	.000
Sub	? Collins	1	2	0	0	0	0	0	0	0	0	.000	.000
P	Joe Young	1	1	0	0	0	0	0	0	0	0	.000	.000
Sub	? Leonard	1	0	0	0	0	0	0	0	0	1	—	—
		155	5259	1187	703	138	53	45	553	607	209	.226	.298

1B   Werden 149, Caruthers 4, Buckley 2, Gleason 1
2B   Crooks 101, Stricker 27, Brodie 16, Gleason 10, Caruthers 6, McCormick 2
SS   Glasscock 139, Genins 14, Kuehne 1, Stricker 1
3B   Pinkney 78, Camp 39, Crooks 25, Kuehne 6, Brodie 2, McCormick 1, McGrillis 1, Miller 1, Carpenter 1
OF   Brodie 137, Caruthers 122, Carroll 101, Moriarty 47, Gore 20, Gleason 11, Breitenstein 10, Briggs 8, Van Dyke 4, Camp 3, Wolf 3, Crooks 2, Hawke 1, Easton 1, Haigh 1, Collins 1, Genins 1, Thornton 1, Leonard 1
C   Buckley 119, Moran 24, Bird 17, Briggs 15, Peitz 1, Gleason 1
P   Gleason 47, Breitenstein 39, Hawley 20, Caruthers 16, Hawke 14, Getzein 13, Galvin 12, Dwyer 10, Easton 5, Young 1

	G	IP	GS	CG	W	L	K	BB	SH	SV	ERA
Kid Gleason	47	400	45	43	20	24	133	151	2	0	3.33
Ted Breitenstein	39	282.1	32	28	9	19	126	148	1	0	4.69
Pink Hawley	20	166.1	20	18	6	14	63	63	0	0	3.19
Charlie Getzein	13	108	13	12	5	8	32	31	0	0	5.67
Bob Caruthers	16	101.2	10	10	2	10	21	27	0	1	5.84
Bill Hawke	14	97.1	11	10	5	5	55	45	1	0	3.70
Pud Galvin	12	92	12	10	5	6	27	26	0	0	3.23
Frank Dwyer	10	64	10	6	2	8	16	24	0	0	5.63
Jack Easton	5	31	2	2	2	0	4	26	0	0	6.39
Joe Young	1	2	0	0	0	0	1	2	0	0	22.50
		1344.2	155	139	56	94	478	543	4	1	4.20

BALTIMORE   George Van Haltren (1–10)   John Waltz (2–6)   Ned Hanlon (43–85)   Union Park

		G	AB	H	R	2B	3B	HR	RBI	BB	SB	BA	SA
3B	Billy Shindle	143	619	156	100	20	18	3	50	35	24	.252	.357
RF	George Van Haltren	135	556	168	105	20	12	7	57	70	49	.302	.419
C	Wilbert Robinson	90	330	88	36	14	4	2	57	15	5	.267	.352
C	Joe Gunson	89	314	67	35	10	5	0	32	16	2	.213	.277
UT	George Shoch	76	308	85	42	15	3	1	50	24	14	.276	.354
UT	John McGraw	79	286	77	41	13	2	1	26	32	15	.269	.339
LF	Harry Stovey	74	283	77	58	14	11	4	55	40	20	.272	.442
1B	Sy Sutcliffe	66	276	77	41	10	7	1	27	14	12	.279	.377
2B	Cub Stricker	75	269	71	45	5	5	3	37	32	13	.264	.353
SS	Tim O'Rourke	63	239	74	40	8	4	0	35	24	12	.310	.377
CF	Curt Welch	63	237	56	42	1	3	1	22	36	14	.236	.278
Sub	Lew Whistler	52	209	47	32	6	6	2	21	18	12	.225	.340
Sub	Piggy Ward	56	186	54	28	6	5	1	33	31	10	.290	.392
Sub	Jocko Halligan	46	178	47	38	4	7	2	43	30	8	.264	.399
P	Sadie McMahon	49	177	25	12	1	2	0	18	7	0	.141	.169
P	George Cobb	57	172	36	20	4	5	1	13	22	2	.209	.308
Sub	John Pickett	36	141	30	13	2	3	1	12	7	2	.213	.291
Sub	George Wood	21	76	17	9	1	1	0	10	10	1	.224	.263
P	Tom Vickery	24	74	18	6	2	1	0	4	5	3	.243	.297
Sub	Monte Cross	15	50	8	5	0	0	0	2	4	2	.160	.160
Sub	Sun Daly	13	48	12	5	0	2	0	7	1	0	.250	.333
P	Charlie Buffinton	13	43	15	7	1	1	0	4	3	1	.349	.419
Sub	Ned Hanlon	11	43	7	3	1	1	0	2	3	0	.163	.233
Sub	Joe Kelley	10	33	7	3	0	0	0	4	4	2	.212	.212
P	Egyptian Healy	9	27	6	3	0	1	0	1	2	0	.222	.296
P	Frank Foreman	7	23	4	2	1	1	0	1	3	1	.174	.304
P	Crazy Schmit	7	19	2	1	0	0	0	0	3	1	.105	.105
Sub	Pete Gilbert	4	15	3	0	0	0	0	0	1	1	.200	.200
Sub	Bill Johnson	4	15	2	2	0	0	0	2	2	0	.133	.133
Sub	John Godar	5	14	3	2	0	0	0	1	2	1	.214	.214
P	Ben Stephens	5	13	0	2	0	0	0	0	2	0	.000	.000

		G	AB	H	R	2B	3B	HR	RBI	BB	SB	BA	SA
P	Bill Gilbert	2	6	2	0	1	0	0	1	0	0	.333	.500
P	Adonis Terry	1	4	0	0	0	0	0	0	0	0	.000	.000
P	Bill Kling	2	4	1	1	0	1	0	1	1	0	.250	.750
P	Alex Ferson	2	4	0	0	0	0	0	0	0	0	.000	.000
P	Harry Ely	1	3	0	0	0	0	0	0	0	0	.000	.000
Sub	Tom Hess	1	2	0	0	0	0	0	0	0	0	.000	.000
		152	5296	1342	779	160	111	30	628	499	227	.253	.343

1B Sutcliffe 66, Whistler 51, Halligan 19, Stovey 10, Van Haltren 2, Robinson 2, Gunson 2, McMahon 1

2B Stricker 75, Pickett 36, McGraw 34, Ward 7, Gunson 1

SS O'Rourke 58, Shoch 57, Cross 15, Shindle 9, McGraw 8, Ward 5, Van Haltren 2

3B Shindle 134, Shoch 7, P. Gilbert 4, Van Haltren 3, McGraw 3, O'Rourke 1

OF Van Haltren 129, Stovey 64, Welch 63, Ward 43, McGraw 34, Halligan 22, Wood 21, Gunson 20, Daly 13, Shoch 12, Hanlon 11, Kelley 10, Cobb 6, Foreman 5, Godar 5, Johnson 4, O'Rourke 4, Robinson 1, Schmit 1, Whistler 1

C   Robinson 87, Gunson 67, Halligan 5, Ward 1, Hess 1

P   Cobb 53, McMahon 48, Vickery 24, Buffinton 13, Healy 9, Schmit 6, Stephens 5, Van Haltren 4, Foreman 4, Kling 2, Ferson 2, B. Gilbert 2, Terry 1, Ely 1

	G	IP	GS	CG	W	L	K	BB	SH	SV	ERA
Sadie McMahon	48	397	46	44	20	25	118	145	2	1	3.24
George Cobb	53	394.1	47	42	10	**37**	159	140	0	0	4.86
Tom Vickery	24	176	21	17	8	10	49	87	0	0	3.53
Charlie Buffinton	13	97	13	9	3	8	30	46	0	0	4.92
Egyptian Healy	9	68.1	8	5	3	6	24	21	0	0	4.74
Crazy Schmit	6	47.1	6	6	1	4	17	26	0	0	3.23
Ben Stephens	5	29	2	2	1	1	7	9	0	1	2.79
Frank Foreman	4	25	3	2	0	3	5	11	0	0	6.84
George Van Haltren	4	14.2	0	0	0	0	5	7	0	0	9.20
Bill Gilbert	2	14	1	1	0	1	5	17	0	0	5.79
Bill Kling	3	11	2	0	0	2	7	7	0	0	11.45
Alex Ferson	2	9	1	1	0	1	8	6	0	0	11.00
Adonis Terry	1	9	1	1	0	1	3	7	0	0	4.00
Harry Ely	1	7	1	1	0	1	0	7	0	0	7.71
		—1 forfeit L vs New York on April 20—									
		1298.2	152	131	46	100	437	536	2	1	4.28

PENNANT SERIES

Boston (NL) beat Cleveland (NL) 5 games to 0 with 1 tie game

Game 1 at League Park (Cle), Oct. 17: Cle (Young) 0, Bos (Stivetts) 0 11 innings
Game 2 at League Park (Cle), Oct. 18: Bos (Staley) 4, Cle (Clarkson) 3
Game 3 at League Park (Cle), Oct. 19: Bos (Stivetts) 3, Cle (Young) 2
Game 4 at South End Grounds (Bos), Oct. 21: Bos (Nichols) 4, Cle (Cuppy) 0
Game 5 at South End Grounds (Bos), Oct. 22: Bos (Stivetts) 12, Cle (Clarkson) 7
Game 6 at South End Grounds (Bos), Oct. 24: Bos (Nichols) 8, Cle (Young) 3

BOSTON

		G	AB	H	R	2B	3B	HR	RBI	BB	BA	SA
SS	Herman Long	6	27	6	4	0	0	0	1	0	.222	.222
CF	Hugh Duffy	6	26	12	3	3	2	1	9	1	**.462**	**.769**
3B	Billy Nash	6	24	4	3	0	0	0	4	2	.167	.167
1B	Tommy Tucker	6	23	6	2	0	0	1	2	0	.261	.391
LF	Bobby Lowe	6	23	3	8	0	0	0	0	1	.130	.130
RF	Tommy McCarthy	6	21	8	2	2	0	0	2	6	.381	.476
2B	Joe Quinn	6	21	6	2	1	1	0	4	1	.286	.429
p	Jack Stivetts	3	12	3	3	1	1	0	1	0	.250	.500
C	Charlie Ganzel	2	8	4	1	0	0	0	2	1	.500	.500
C	King Kelly	2	8	0	0	0	0	0	0	0	.000	.000
C	Charlie Bennett	2	7	2	2	0	0	1	1	0	.286	.714
P	Kid Nichols	2	7	2	0	0	0	0	2	0	.286	.286
P	Harry Staley	1	4	0	0	0	0	0	0	0	.000	.000
			211	56	31	7	4	3	28	12	.265	.379

	G	IP	GS	CG	W	L	K	BB	SH	SV	ERA
Jack Stivetts	3	29	3	3	2	0	17	7	1	0	0.93
Kid Nichols	2	18	2	2	2	0	13	4	1	0	1.00
Harry Staley	1	9	1	1	1	0	0	1	0	0	3.00
		56	6	6	5	0	30	12	2	0	1.29

CLEVELAND

		G	AB	H	R	2B	3B	HR	RBI	BB	BA	SA
SS	Ed McKean	6	25	11	2	0	0	0	6	1	.440	.440
LF	Jesse Burkett	6	25	8	3	1	0	0	1	0	.320	.360
1B	Jake Virtue	6	24	3	1	0	0	0	0	2	.125	.125
C	Chief Zimmer	6	23	6	2	1	1	0	2	0	.261	.391
2B	Cupid Childs	6	22	9	3	0	2	0	0	5	.409	.591
CF	Jimmy McAleer	6	22	4	0	0	0	0	1	2	.182	.182
RF	Jack O'Connor	6	22	3	1	0	0	0	0	2	.136	.136
3B	Patsy Tebeau	5	18	0	1	0	0	0	0	0	.000	.000
P	Cy Young	3	11	1	1	0	0	0	0	0	.091	.091
P	John Clarkson	2	8	2	1	0	0	1	3	0	.250	.625
3B/2B	George Davis	2	6	1	0	0	0	0	0	0	.167	.167
P	Nig Cuppy	1	3	0	0	0	0	0	0	0	.000	.000
		6	209	48	15	2	3	1	13	12	.230	.282

	G	IP	GS	CG	W	L	K	BB	SH	SV	ERA
Cy Young	3	27	3	3	0	2	9	3	1	0	3.00
John Clarkson	2	17	2	2	0	2	9	5	0	0	5.29
Nig Cuppy	1	8	1	1	0	1	1	4	0	0	1.13
		52	6	6	0	5	19	12	1	0	3.46

1893
60'6"

Tracing poor attendance in 1892 to too many low-scoring games, the League-Association rules committee enacted the greatest change in the geometry of the playing field since 1881 when the pitching distance had been lengthened by five feet. For the 1893 season the pitching distance was again lengthened, this time from 50 feet to 60 feet 6 inches. There are various stories to account for the odd six inches, even one attributing them to a surveyor's error, but in any case only another five feet were actually added to the distance between the batter and the point where a pitcher would now release the ball. Since 1887 a pitcher had been required to start with his rear or pitching foot on a back line 55' 6" from the plate. Beginning in 1893 a hurler had to plant his pitching foot five feet farther from his target. Allowed one stride before delivery, the average pitcher would now be approximately 55 feet from the plate at his release point.

Yet the increased distance was only part of the new rule. Commencing also in 1893, the pitcher's boundary, rather than being a rectangular box, was a white rubber plate 12 inches long and 4 inches wide. The rubber plate was as much an added impediment as the extra distance, for a pitcher was required to take his position facing the batter with both feet on the ground and keep one foot in contact with the plate at all times in the act of delivering the ball. In an effort to lighten the pitcher's new burden rulesmakers allowed the pitcher's plate to be implanted in an elevated area (or mound) if teams so chose and also abolished bats with one flat side that some players had found useful for bunting or tapping balls foul without penalty until they got a pitch to their liking. But these concessions to pitchers were small compensation for the sudden and enormous revisions they were forced to make to the style in which they performed their craft.

It was the rubber plate far more than the extra five feet or so that spelled the ruin of many of the game's most lustrous pitchers prior to 1893. Some men actually seemed to improve at the added distance. Amos Rusie, the League-Association's walk king, decreased his walks from 267 to 212, and Frank Killen, who had the fifth-highest walk total in 1892, dropped from 182 to 140. Rusie and Killen, with their intimidating fastballs at a 50-foot distance, were two of the

FAMOUS FIRSTS VI

Ted Breitenstein, the LA's surprise ERA leader in the landmark 1893 season, in a preseason collage of the 1894 St. Louis Browns. Top: Duff Cooley, Tom Hannigan (who's he?), Dewey McDougal, Tommy Dowd and Roger Connor. Middle: Heinie Peitz, Marty Hogan, Harry Staley, Art Twineham and Breitenstein. Bottom: Bones Ely and Tom Brown.

On the final day of the 1892 season Bumpus Jones, making his first major league appearance for Cincinnati, tossed a no-hitter against Pittsburgh's Mark Baldwin. It was the last no-hit game in the majors from a rectangular pitcher's box set at a 50-foot distance from home plate, but Jones was not the first pitcher to throw a no-hitter in his first start. The previous year, on the St. Louis Browns' final day of play in the American Association, Ted Breitenstein had turned in the Association's last no-hit game in his first starting assignment for the Browns.

Though they launched their careers in an almost identical fashion, Breitenstein and Jones went very different directions in 1893 when the pitching rules changed dramatically. Jones began the year in Cincinnati but was cut when he was bombed in five starts and a relief appearance. The New York Giants gave him one starting chance to display his pre-1893 form and then cut him too when he lasted just four innings. Jones departed with a 10.19 ERA for 1893 and never pitched again in the majors. As for the direction Breitenstein went, see the chart below comparing major league pitchers in 1892 and 1893.

1893 ERA QUALIFIERS/1892 COMPARISON (126 Innings Minimum)

		G	IP	ERA
1.	Ted Breitenstein	48	382.2	**3.18**
	1892	39	282.1	4.69
2.	Amos Rusie	**56**	**482**	3.23
	1892	64	532	2.88
3.	Cy Young	53	422.2	3.36
	1892	53	453	**1.93**
4.	Red Ehret	39	314.1	3.44
	1892	39	316	2.65
5.	Dad Clarkson (R)	24	186.1	3.48
6.	Kid Nichols	52	425	3.52
	1892	53	453	2.84
7.	Frank Killen	55	415	3.64
	1892	60	459.2	3.31

		G	IP	ERA
8.	Brickyard Kennedy	46	382.2	3.72*
	1892	26	191	3.86
9.	Icebox Chamberlain	34	241	3.73
	1892	52	406.1	3.39
10.	Ed Stein	37	298.1	3.77
	1892	48	377.1	2.84
11.	Edgar McNabb (R)	21	142	4.12
12.	Mark Baldwin	46	333.2	4.15
	1892	56	440.1	3.47
13.	Frank Dwyer	37	287.1	4.13
	1892	33	259.1	2.33
14.	Les German(**)	20	152	4.14
15.	Jack Taylor (R)	25	170	4.24
16.	Jock Menefee (R)	15	129.1	4.24
17.	Sadie McMahon	43	346.1	4.37
	1892	48	397	3.24
18.	Tim Keefe	22	178	4.40
	1892	39	313.1	2.36
19.	Jack Stivetts	38	283.2	4.41
	1892	58	415.2	3.03
20.	Hal Mauck (R)	23	143	4.41
21.	Tony Mullane	49	367	4.44
	1892	37	295	2.59
22.	Adonis Terry	26	170	4.45
	1892	31	249	2.51
23.	John Clarkson	36	295	4.45
	1892	45	389	2.48
24.	Nig Cuppy	31	243.2	4.47
	1892	47	376	2.51
25.	Tom Parrott (R)	26	181	4.48
26.	Pink Hawley	31	227	4.60
	1892	20	166.1	3.19
27.	Willie McGill(**)	39	302.2	4.61
28.	Kid Gleason	48	380.1	4.61
	1892	47	400	3.33
29.	Duke Esper	42	334.1	4.71
	1892	24	178.2	3.63
30.	Gus Weyhing	42	345.1	4.74
	1892	59	469.2	2.66
31.	Bill Hutchison	44	348.1	4.75
	1892	**75**	**627**	2.74
32.	Bill Hawke	30	230.1	4.77
	1892	14	97.1	3.70
33.	Kid Carsey	39	318.1	4.81
	1892	43	317.2	3.12
35.	Jouett Meekin	31	245	4.96
	1892	33	268.1	3.79
36.	Mike Sullivan	27	183.2	5.05
	1892	21	166.1	3.08
37.	George Hemming	41	332	5.10
	1892	5	41	5.05
38.	Harry Staley	36	263	5.13
	1892	37	299.2	3.03
39.	Ad Gumbert	22	162.2	5.15
	1892	46	382.2	3.41
40.	Al Maul (**)	37	297	5.30
41.	Scott Stratton	37	314.2	5.43
	1892	42	351.2	2.92

		G	IP	ERA
42.	Hank Gastright	28	215	5.44
	1892	11	79.2	5.08
43.	George Haddock	23	151	5.60
	1892	46	381.1	3.14
44.	Silver King	24	154	6.08
	1892	52	419.1	3.24
45.	Bill Rhodes (R)	20	151.2	7.60

Notes: Numbers in bold led the league. An (R) in parenthesis designates a rookie, and
(**) designates a pitcher active in the majors prior to 1893 but out of the majors in 1892.

* Kennedy was the only pitcher besides Breitenstein to improve his ERA in 1893. The
likely reason for their improvement is that both were rookies in 1892, but that doesn't
even begin to explain how Breitenstein could have improved so much.

hurlers most responsible for the new pitching rules. Yet another was Bill Hutchison, the
League-Association strikeout leader in 1892 and its top winner for the past three years running,
but unlike Rusie and Killen, who continued to thrive under the new restrictions, Hutchison was
severely hampered. Other big winners whose totals plummeted when they were made to an-
chor one foot to a rubber plate were Gus Weyhing, Scott Stratton, Silver King and George
Haddock. King's pet pitch, a sidearm crossfire that he started in the back left corner of the

pitcher's box and finished by stepping to his
right and firing the ball over his left shoulder,
was eradicated by the new pitching rubber,
and his career was effectively ended.

Obviously, for every King or Hutchison
who suffered from the new rule there was a
hitter who benefitted. In 1893 the League-
Association batting average jumped 35 points
and teams scored an average of 1.47 more
runs per game. The increase in scoring had the
desired effect. Attendance rose markedly in
almost every city, and especially in the two
most crucial ones, Chicago and New York.
Though the schedule was reduced from 154 to
132 games, giving each team 11 fewer home
dates, Chicago drew 223,500, up from
109,067, and New York's figures soared from
130,566 to 290,000.

*Gus Weyhing had 177 wins in his first six
major league seasons and was just 26 years
old. His seventh year came in 1893 when the
pitching rules were drastically altered. Unable
to adapt, Weyhing won only 87 more games.*

League-Association moguls, along with shaving 22 games off the schedule in response to complaints that the 1892 season had been too long, also scrapped the split-season experiment for fear that fans would continue to suspect the first-half winner of laying down on the back leg to make extra money by forcing a postseason playoff. It meant that all the pennant winner had to show at the end of the season was temporary possession of the Dauvray Cup, first donated to the World's Series winner in 1887 by actress Helen Dauvray, then Monte Ward's wife. Harry Wright, who had yet to win the Dauvray Cup or anything else since 1878, craved one last pennant before his health made him step down from the Philadelphia Phillies managership, and he looked to have every chance. By 1893 the Phillies had assembled the best everyday lineup in the game, headed by outfielders Billy Hamilton, Sam Thompson and Ed Delahanty, catcher Jack Clements and shortstop Bob Allen. Wright's team, as a result, topped the League-Association in batting, slugging and scoring and set a new fielding average standard of .944. The Phillies came across as a group of underachievers, though, when they finished fourth. Some of the problem was that under the new pitching restrictions Weyhing, their former ace, did not adapt as well as other front-line hurlers, but the Phils' real downfall was an inability to beat Boston and St. Louis. Losing the season series to Boston, winner of the last two pennants, was understandable, but the Phils self-destructed by losing eight of their 12 contests with the tenth-place Browns. Cleveland, a notch above the Phils in the standings, nevertheless lost nine of 12 to Philadelphia, but hammered the team right above it, Pittsburgh, nine of 12. Pittsburgh in turn took six of ten from Boston, the team right above it in the standings.

The strange proclivity to do well against the team above it but flounder against the team right beneath it in the standings ended with Boston, which had no one above it on closing day. Frank Selee's third successive pennant at the Beaneaters helm came rather routinely,

EARLY BURNOUTS

At the close of the 1892 season Silver King had 180 career wins. He was just 24 years old and his arm seemed sound. But after the new pitching restrictions were imposed on him, King won just 24 more games for a total of 204, all of them before he turned 30. Four other pitchers besides King have won 200 career games before their thirtieth birthdays and none thereafter. Each of the five collected all of his wins in the nineteenth century, and four of the five were active in 1893, though one, Bob Caruthers, was no longer a pitcher by then.

	WINS	LAST WIN	AGE AT LAST WIN
Amos Rusie	245	1893	27
Bob Caruthers	218	1892	28
Al Spalding	205	1897	26
Silver King	204	1897	29
Jack Stivetts	203	1897	29

Kid Nichols had only one pitch—a fastball. It was enough to make him the biggest winner in the majors during the decade of the 1890s. Nichols collected 310 victories between his inaugural season in 1890 and the turn of the century.

Pittsburgh provoked the ill-advised Temple Cup experiment by finishing a close second in 1893. William Temple, the cup's sire, was married to the daughter of Jimmy Wood, the NA star who lost his leg in 1874. Temple's daughter in turn married major leaguer Del Mason, a pitcher with Cincinnati. Top: Denny Lyons, Elmer Smith and Doggie Miller. Middle: Red Ehret, Joe Sugden, Jake Beckley, George Van Haltren, Frank Killen, Connie Mack and Jack Glasscock. Bottom: Lou Bierbauer, Patsy Donovan, Adonis Terry, Manager Al Buckenberger, Tom Colcolough, Billy Earle and Jake Stenzel.

SULLIVAN THE SIEVE

In 1893 two shortstops, Joe Sullivan of the Washington Nationals and Herman Long of the Boston Beaneaters, became the last major leaguers to make 100 errors in a season. Moreover, Sullivan's .860 fielding average reached a nadir for shortstops that has not been surpassed since. it was not fielders but their gloves that suddenly got better after 1893. Although two players of note, Bid McPhee and Jerry Denny, continued to balk at the notion of using a glove, others had long since surrendered to the advantages a glove could give them. When some began designing contraptions resembling butterfly nets, in 1895 a rule was inserted limiting fielders to gloves not over ten ounces in weight and more than 14 inches in circumference around the palm of the hand. Catchers and first basemen were exempted from any restrictions on the size or weight of their gloves but were made to switch to a fielder's glove if they played another position. In the early 1890s it was not unusual to see Lave Cross, for one, playing third base with a catcher's glove. Joe Sullivan's glove of choice in 1893 ought to have been a bushel basket. A list of major leaguers who made 100 or more errors in a season:

	YEAR	PO	TEAM	ERRORS	FA
Lew Say	1884	SS	Bal/KC-UA	102	.808*
Frank Fennelly	1886	SS	Cin-AA	117	.848
Yank Robinson	1886	2B	StL-AA	103	.883
Bill McClellan	1887	2B	Bro-AA	105	.879
Ed McKean	1887	SS	Cle-AA	105	.849
Frank Fennelly	1888	SS	Cin/Phi-AA	106	.862
Jumbo Davis	1888	3B	KC-AA	100	.841
Herman Long	1889	SS	KC-AA	122	.876
Phil Tomney	1889	SS	Lou-AA	114	.857
Billy Shindle	1890	SS	Phi-PL	122	.854
Bill Joyce	1890	3B	Bro-PL	107	.811
Monte Ward	1890	SS	Bro-PL	105	.878
Jimmy Canavan	1891	SS	Cin/Mil-AA	113	.860
Herman Long	1892	SS	Bos-LA	102	.889
Frank Shugart	1892	SS	Pit-LA	100	.887
Joe Sullivan	1893	SS	Was-LA	102	.860
Herman Long	1893	SS	Bos-LA	100	.885

* Along with being the first major leaguer to make 100 errors in a season, Say may also have been the first infielder to pull the hidden-ball trick while playing for Albany in an International Association game against Worcester on September 26, 1879. Say's "first" was denied him, however, to Henry Chadwick's indignation when the umpire refused to allow the out, claiming there was nothing in the rules that made the ploy permissible.

though it is hard to see why. In 1893, Selee's only two significant roster changes were to get rid of King Kelly and Joe Quinn. Kelly's going meant more work for Boston's other two backstoppers, Charlie Bennett and Charlie Ganzel, while Bobby Lowe was brought in from the outfield to replace Quinn at second base. But Bennett, who caught the most games, hit just .191 and Cliff Carroll, acquired from St. Louis to fill Lowe's outfield slot, had the worst year of any League-Association regular with 400 or more at bats, hitting .224. Though Kid Nichols adapted so well to the new pitching dimensions that he finished at 34-14, Jack Stivetts, Harry Staley and Hank Gastright, Boston's other three regular starters, never regained their pre-1893 form.

Killen won a loop-high 36 games for Pittsburgh after coming to the Pirates from Washington when he and Duke Farrell swapped uniforms. Another deal, with St. Louis in midsummer, brought manager Al Buckenberger the only nineteenth-century shortstop to win a batting title in Jack Glasscock. When Glasscock hit .341 in his half-season for Pittsburgh, Elmer Smith completed his conversion from a sore-armed former 30-game winner to a hard-hitting outfielder by leading all full-season Pirates with a .343 mark, and part-timer Jake Stenzel smoked the ball at a .362 pace. Buckenberger suddenly had the League-Association's strongest all-around team. Statistically anyway, In 1893 the Pirates outstripped Boston in every department—hitting, pitching and fielding—and though they scored fewer runs than the Beaneaters, they also gave up fewer.

The difference was Selee, a master at putting together a team better than the sum of its parts. Still, the Pirates—and the Beaneaters too, for that matter—were left with a hollow feeling at the close of the season. Winning the pennant somehow did not seem like enough. There ought to be something more to achieve. William Temple, Pittsburgh's president, proposed a plan whereby the second-place team at the end of each future season would challenge the first-place team to a best-of-seven series. He then ordered a cup in his name for $800 from New York jeweler A. E. Thrall and stipulated that permanent possession of the "Temple Cup" would go to the first team to win it three times. Unfortunately for Pittsburgh, Temple's plan was not implemented until the following season. Many wished it had never been implemented at all.

THE SEASONAL RECORD

	W	L	PCT	HOME	ROAD	GB
1. Boston Beaneaters	86	43	.667	49–15	37–28	—
2. Pittsburgh Pirates	81	48	.628	54–19	27–29	5
3. Cleveland Spiders	73	55	.570	47–22	26–33	12.5
4. Philadelphia Phillies	72	57	.558	43–22	29–35	14
5. New York Giants	68	64	.515	49–20	19–44	19.5
6. Brooklyn Bridegrooms	65	63	.508	43–24	22–39	20.5
7. Cincinnati Reds	65	63	.508	37–27	28–36	20.5
8. Baltimore Orioles	60	70	.462	36–24	24–46	26.5
9. Chicago Colts	56	71	.441	38–34	18–37	29
10. St. Louis Browns	57	75	.432	40–30	17–45	30.5
11. Louisville Colonels	50	75	.400	24–28	26–47	34
12. Washington Nationals	40	89	.310	21–27	19–62	46

	Bos	Pit	Cle	Phi	NY	Bro	Cin	Bal	Chi	StL	Lou	Was	
Boston	—	4	7	8	8	8	6	10	8	10	10	7	86
Pittsburgh	6	—	3	5	8	4	9	11	9	9	8	9	81
Cleveland	5	9	—	3	6	7	5	4	8	9	6	11	73
Philadelphia	4	7	9	—	5	5	9	7	6	4	8	8	72
New York	4	4	6	7	—	6	6	8	5	8	7	7	68
Brooklyn	4	8	5	6	6	—	4	2	7	8	7	8	65
Cincinnati	6	3	6	1	6	8	—	8	7	7	6	7	65
Baltimore	2	1	8	5	4	10	4	—	5	9	5	7	60
Chicago	3	3	4	6	7	3	5	7	—	3	6	9	56
St. Louis	2	3	3	8	4	4	5	3	9	—	8	8	57
Louisville	2	4	3	4	5	5	6	5	4	4	—	8	50
Washington	5	2	1	4	5	3	4	5	3	4	4	—	40
	43	48	55	57	64	63	63	70	71	75	75	89	773

SEASON LEADERS

Batting Average (350 ABs)

1.	Hamilton, Philadelphia	.380
2.	Thompson, Philadelphia	.370
3.	Delahanty, Philadelphia	.368
4.	Duffy, Boston	.363
5.	Davis, New York	.355

On–Base Percentage

1.	Hamilton, Philadelphia	.490
2.	Childs, Cleveland	.463
3.	Burkett, Cleveland	.459
4.	McGraw, Baltimore	.454
5.	E. Smith, Pittsburgh	.435

Slugging Average

1.	Delahanty, Philadelphia	.583
2.	Davis, New York	.554
3.	Thompson, Philadelphia	.530
4.	E. Smith, Pittsburgh	.525
5.	Hamilton, Philadelphia	.524

Total Bases

1.	Delahanty, Philadelphia	347
2.	Thompson, Philadelphia	318
3.	Davis, New York	304
4.	E. Smith, Pittsburgh	272
5.	McKean, Cleveland	258
	Duffy, Boston	258

Home Runs

1.	Delahanty, Philadelphia	19
2.	Clements, Philadelphia	17
3.	Tiernan, New York	14
	Lowe, Boston	14
5.	Davis, New York	11
	Connor, New York	11
	Thompson, Philadelphia	11

Hits

1.	Thompson, Philadelphia	222
2.	Delahanty, Philadelphia	219
3.	Duffy, Boston	203
4.	Davis, New York	195
5.	Ward, New York	193

Stolen Bases

1.	T. Brown, Louisville	66
2.	Dowd, St. Louis	59
3.	Latham, Cincinnati	57
4.	Burke, New York	54
5.	Brodie, StL–Bal	49

RBI

1.	Delahanty, Philadelphia	146
2.	McKean, Cleveland	133
3.	Thompson, Philadelphia	126
4.	Nash, Boston	123
5.	Ewing, Cleveland	122

Runs

1.	Long, Boston	149
2.	Duffy, Boston	147
3.	Delahanty, Philadelphia	145
	Childs, Cleveland	145
	Burkett, Cleveland	145

Strikeouts

1.	Daly, Brooklyn	65
2.	T. Brown, Louisville	63
3.	Treadway, Baltimore	50
4.	Kelley, Baltimore	44
5.	Radford, Washington	42

PITCHING

Wins

1.	Killen, Pittsburgh	36
2.	Young, Cleveland	34
	Nichols, Boston	34
4.	Rusie, New York	33
5.	Kennedy, Brooklyn	25

Innings

1.	Rusie, New York	482
2.	Nichols, Boston	425
3.	Young, Cleveland	422.2
4.	Killen, Washington	415
5.	Breitenstein, St. Louis	382.2
	Kennedy, Brooklyn	382.2

Strikeouts

1.	Rusie, New York	208
2.	Kennedy, Brooklyn	107
3.	Young, Cleveland	102
	Breitenstein, St. Louis	102
5.	Weyhing, Philadelphia	101

Losses

1.	Esper, Washington	28
2.	Breitenstein, St. Louis	24
	Hutchison, Chicago	24
4.	Stratton, Louisville	23
5.	Gleason, St. Louis	22
	Mullane, Cin–Bal	22

Complete Games

1.	Rusie, New York	50
2.	Nichols, Boston	43
3.	Young, Cleveland	42
4.	Kennedy, Brooklyn	40
5.	Killen, Pittsburgh	38
	Hutchison, Chicago	38
	Breitenstein, St. Louis	38

Winning Percentage (25 decisions)

1.	Gastright, Bos–Pit	.750
2.	Killen, Pittsburgh	.720
3.	Nichols, Boston	.708
4.	Young, Cleveland	.680
5.	Staley, Boston	.643

ERA (140 innings)

1. Breitenstein, St. Louis   3.18
2. Rusie, New York   3.23
3. Young, Cleveland   3.36
4. Ehret, Pittsburgh   3.44
5. D. Clarkson, St. Louis   3.48

Lowest On–Base Percentage

1. Young, Cleveland   .308
   Nichols, Boston   .308
3. Killen, Pittsburgh   .312
4. Breitenstein, St. Louis   .316
5. Stein, Brooklyn   .323

FIELDING

Total Chances

1B	Connor, New York	1546
2B	McPhee, Cincinnati	892
3B	Lyons, Pittsburgh	563
SS	Allen, Philadelphia	815
OF	T. Brown, Louisville	407
C	Farrell, Washington	481
P	Rusie, New York	152

Fielding Average

W. Brown, Bal–Lou	.988
Bierbauer, Pittsburgh	.959
Nash, Boston	.923
G. Smith, Cincinnati	.934
Griffin, Brooklyn	.965
Vaughn, Cincinnati	.969
Gumbert, Pittsburgh	1.000

BOSTON   Frank Selee   South End Grounds (I)

		G	AB	H	R	2B	3B	HR	RBI	BB	SB	BA	SA
CF	Hugh Duffy	131	560	203	147	23	7	6	118	50	44	.363	.461
SS	Herman Long	128	552	159	**149**	22	6	6	58	73	38	.288	.382
2B	Bobby Lowe	126	526	157	130	19	5	14	89	55	22	.298	.433
1B	Tommy Tucker	121	486	138	83	13	2	7	91	27	8	.284	.362
3B	Billy Nash	128	485	141	115	27	6	10	123	85	30	.291	.433
LF	Tommy McCarthy	116	462	160	107	28	6	5	111	64	46	.346	.465
RF	Cliff Carroll	120	438	98	80	7	5	2	54	88	29	.224	.276
C	Charlie Ganzel	73	281	75	50	10	2	1	48	22	6	.267	.327
C	Charlie Bennett	60	191	40	34	6	0	4	27	40	5	.209	.304
P	Kid Nichols	53	177	39	25	3	2	2	26	15	4	.220	.294
P	Jack Stivetts	50	172	51	32	5	6	3	25	12	6	.297	.448
Sub	Bill Merritt	39	141	49	30	6	3	3	26	13	3	.348	.496
P	Harry Staley	36	113	30	13	5	0	2	21	10	1	.265	.363
P	Hank Gastright	20	68	13	11	3	0	0	10	6	0	.191	.235
Sub	Bill Van Dyke	3	12	3	2	1	0	0	1	0	1	.250	.333
P	Bill Quarles	3	9	2	0	0	0	0	0	1	0	.222	.222
P	Bill Coyle	2	4	0	0	0	0	0	0	0	0	.000	.000
P	Jim Garry	1	1	0	0	0	0	0	0	0	0	.000	.000
		131	4678	1358	1008	178	50	65	828	**561**	243	.290	.391

1B   Tucker 121, Ganzel 10
2B   Lowe 121, McCarthy 7, Long 5
SS   Long 123, Lowe 5, McCarthy 3
3B   Nash 128, Stivetts 3
OF   Duffy 131, Carroll 120, McCarthy 108, Ganzel 23, Stivetts 8, Van Dyke 3, Merritt 2, Nichols 1, Gastright 1
C   Bennett 60, Ganzel 40, Merritt 37
P   Nichols 52, Stivetts 38, Staley 36, Gastright 19, Quarles 3, Coyle 2, Garry 1

	G	IP	GS	CG	W	L	K	BB	SH	SV	ERA
Kid Nichols	52	425	44	43	34	14	94	118	1	1	3.52
Jack Stivetts	38	283.2	34	29	20	12	61	115	1	1	4.41
Harry Staley	36	263	31	23	18	10	61	81	0	0	5.13
Hank Gastright	19	156	18	16	12	4	27	76	0	0	5.13
Bill Quarles	3	27	3	3	2	1	6	5	0	0	4.67
Bill Coyle	2	8	1	0	0	1	2	3	0	0	9.00
Jim Garry	1	1	0	0	0	1	2	4	0	0	63.00
		1163.2	131	**114**	86	43	253	402	2	2	4.43

PITTSBURGH   Al Buckenberger   Exposition Park

		G	AB	H	R	2B	3B	HR	RBI	BB	SB	BA	SA
1B	Jake Beckley	131	542	164	108	32	19	5	106	54	15	.303	.459
CF	George Van Haltren	124	529	179	129	14	11	3	79	75	37	.338	.423
2B	Lou Bierbauer	128	528	150	84	19	11	4	94	36	11	.284	.384
LF	Elmer Smith	128	518	179	121	26	23	7	103	77	26	.346	.525
RF	Patsy Donovan	113	499	158	114	5	8	2	56	42	46	.317	.371
3B	Denny Lyons	131	490	150	103	19	16	3	105	97	19	.306	.429
SS	Jack Glasscock	66	293	100	49	7	11	1	74	17	16	.341	.451
Sub	Jake Stenzel	60	224	81	57	13	4	4	37	24	16	.362	.509
SS	Frank Shugart	52	210	55	37	7	3	1	32	19	12	.262	.338
P	Frank Killen	55	171	47	35	6	6	4	30	22	1	.275	.450
C	Doggie Miller	41	154	28	23	6	1	0	17	17	3	.182	.234
P	Red Ehret	40	136	24	16	3	0	1	17	10	1	.176	.221
C	Connie Mack	37	133	38	22	3	1	0	15	10	4	.286	.323
C	Billy Earle	27	95	24	21	4	4	2	15	7	1	.253	.442
P	Ad Gumbert	29	95	21	17	3	3	0	10	10	0	.221	.316
C	Joe Sugden	27	92	24	20	4	3	0	12	10	1	.261	.370
P	Adonis Terry	26	71	18	9	4	3	0	11	3	1	.254	.394
P	Hank Gastright	9	24	1	2	0	0	0	0	2	0	.042	.042
P	Tom Colcolough	8	14	2	3	0	0	0	1	5	0	.143	.143
Sub	Reddy Gray	2	9	4	0	1	0	0	2	0	0	.444	.556
Sub	Sam Gillen	3	6	0	0	0	0	0	0	0	0	.000	.000
P	Mark Baldwin	1	1	0	0	0	0	0	0	0	0	.000	.000
		131	4834	1447	970	176	**127**	37	816	537	210	.299	.411

1B Beckley 131
2B Bierbauer 128, Van Haltren 2, Stenzel 1
SS Glasscock 66, Shugart 51, Van Haltren 12, Gillen 3, Gray 2, Stenzel 1
3B Lyons 131
OF Smith 128, Donovan 112, Van Haltren 111, Stenzel 45, Gumbert 7, Shugart 1
C   Miller 40, Mack 37, Sugden 27, Earle 27, Stenzel 12
P   Killen 55, Ehret 39, Terry 26, Gumbert 22, Gastright 9, Colcolough 8, Baldwin 1

	G	IP	GS	CG	W	L	K	BB	SH	SV	ERA
Frank Killen	55	415	48	38	**36**	14	99	140	2	0	3.64
Red Ehret	39	314.1	35	32	18	18	70	115	**4**	0	3.44
Adonis Terry	26	170	19	14	12	8	52	99	0	0	4.45
Ad Gumbert	22	162.2	20	16	11	7	40	78	2	0	5.15
Hank Gastright	9	59	5	3	3	1	12	39	0	0	6.25
Tom Colcolough	8	43.2	3	1	1	0	7	32	0	2	4.12
Mark Baldwin	1	2.1	1	0	0	0	0	1	0	0*	11.57
		1167	131	104	81	48	280	504	**8**	2	4.08

CLEVELAND Patsy Tebeau   League Park (I)

		G	AB	H	R	2B	3B	HR	RBI	BB	SB	BA	SA
SS	Ed McKean	125	545	169	103	29	24	4	133	50	16	.310	.473
LF	Jesse Burkett	125	511	178	145	25	15	6	82	98	39	.348	.491
RF	Buck Ewing	116	500	172	117	28	15	6	122	41	47	.344	.496
UT	Patsy Tebeau	116	486	160	90	32	8	2	102	32	19	.329	.440
2B	Cupid Childs	124	485	158	145	19	10	3	65	120	23	.326	.425
C	Jack O'Connor	96	384	110	72	23	1	4	75	29	29	.286	.383
1B	Jake Virtue	97	378	100	87	16	10	1	60	54	11	.265	.368
CF	Jimmy McAleer	91	350	83	63	5	1	2	41	35	32	.237	.274
3B	Chippy McGarr	63	249	77	38	12	0	0	28	20	24	.309	.357
C	Chief Zimmer	57	227	70	27	13	7	2	41	16	4	.308	.454
P	Cy Young	53	187	44	23	4	0	1	27	4	2	.235	.273
P	John Clarkson	37	131	27	18	6	2	1	17	4	2	.206	.305
P	Nig Cuppy	32	109	27	14	6	2	0	14	8	1	.248	.339
Sub	Joe Gunson	21	73	19	11	1	0	0	9	6	0	.260	.274
P	Charlie Hastings	16	39	7	6	0	2	0	1	8	1	.179	.282
Sub	Ed McFarland	8	22	9	5	2	1	0	6	1	0	.409	.551
P	Tom Williams	8	18	5	5	0	0	0	2	4	2	.278	.278
Sub	Billy Alvord	3	12	2	2	0	0	0	2	0	0	.167	.167
P	Chauncey Fisher	2	8	2	0	0	0	0	0	0	0	.250	.250
Sub	Jim Gilman	2	7	2	1	0	0	0	1	0	0	.286	.286
P	Jack Scheible	2	7	1	0	0	0	0	1	1	0	.143	.143
P	George Davies	3	6	2	1	0	0	0	1	0	0	.333	.333
Sub	Frank Boyd	2	5	1	3	1	0	0	3	1	0	.200	.400
P	John Stafford	2	4	0	0	0	0	0	0	0	0	.000	.000
Sub	Pete Allen	1	4	0	0	0	0	0	0	0	0	.000	.000
		129	4747	1425	976	222	98	32	833	532	252	.300	.408

1B Virtue 73, Tebeau 57, Ewing 1
2B Childs 123, Ewing 5, Tebeau 3, Gilman 2
SS McKean 125, Virtue 5
3B McGarr 63, Tebeau 56, Virtue 5, Alvord 3, McFarland 2, Zimmer 1
OF Burkett 125, Ewing 112, McAleer 91, O'Connor 44, Virtue 13, McFarland 5, Williams 3, Cuppy 2, Clarkson 1, Hastings 1, Stafford 1
C Zimmer 56, O'Connor 56, Gunson 21, Boyd 2, McFarland 1, Ewing 1, Allen 1
P Young 53, Clarkson 36, Cuppy 31, Hastings 15, Williams 5, Davies 3, Stafford 2, Scheible 2, Fisher 2, Virtue 1

	G	IP	GS	CG	W	L	K	BB	SH	SV	ERA
Cy Young	53	422.2	46	42	34	16	102	103	1	1	3.36
John Clarkson	36	295	35	31	16	17	62	95	0	0	4.45
Nig Cuppy	31	243.2	30	24	17	10	39	75	0	0	4.47
Charlie Hastings	15	92	9	6	4	5	14	33	0	1	4.70
Tom Williams	5	24	2	2	1	1	6	10	0	0	4.88
Jack Scheible	2	18	2	2	1	1	1	11	1	0	2.00
Chauncey Fisher	2	18	2	2	0	2	9	9	0	0	5.50
George Davies	3	15	3	1	0	2	3	10	0	0	11.40
John Stafford	2	7	0	0	0	1	4	7	0	0	14.14
Jake Virtue	1	5	0	0	0	0	2	3	0	0	1.80
		1140.1	129	110	73	55	242	**356**	2	2	4.20

PHILADELPHIA   Harry Wright   Philadelphia Baseball Grounds

		G	AB	H	R	2B	3B	HR	RBI	BB	SB	BA	SA
RF	Sam Thompson	131	**600**	222	130	**37**	13	11	126	50	18	.370	.530
2B	Bill Hallman	132	596	183	119	28	7	5	76	51	22	.307	.403
LF	Ed Delahanty	132	595	219	145	35	18	**19**	**146**	47	37	.368	**.583**
1B	Jack Boyle	124	504	144	105	29	9	4	81	41	22	.286	.403
SS	Bob Allen	124	471	126	86	19	12	8	90	71	8	.268	.410
3B	Charlie Reilly	104	416	102	64	16	7	4	56	33	13	.245	.346
UT	Lave Cross	96	415	124	81	17	6	4	78	26	18	.299	.398
C	Jack Clements	94	376	107	64	20	3	17	80	39	3	.285	.489
CF	Billy Hamilton	82	355	135	110	22	7	5	44	63	43	**.380**	.524
Sub	Tuck Turner	36	155	50	32	4	3	1	13	9	7	.323	.406
P	John Sharrott	50	152	38	25	4	3	1	22	8	6	.250	.336
P	Gus Weyhing	43	147	22	14	3	0	0	11	14	1	.150	.170
P	Kid Carsey	39	145	27	12	1	1	0	10	5	2	.186	.207
P	Jack Taylor	31	93	20	11	5	1	0	18	1	1	.215	.290
P	Tim Keefe	22	79	18	10	4	0	0	6	9	1	.228	.278
P	Tom Vickery	15	35	11	1	1	0	0	4	1	0	.314	.343
P	Gus McGinnis	5	15	3	1	1	0	0	1	0	0	.200	.267
P	Frank O'Connor	3	2	2	1	0	0	1	3	0	0	1.000	2.500
		133	5151	**1553**	**1011**	**246**	90	80	865	468	202	**.301**	**.431**

1B   Boyle 112, Hallman 12, Delahanty 6, Cross 6, Clements 1, Thompson 1
2B   Hallman 120, Delahanty 15, Boyle 2, Vickery 1
SS   Allen 124, Cross 10,
3B   Reilly 104, Cross 30
OF   Thompson 131, Delahanty 117, Hamilton 82, Turner 36, Sharrott 33, Cross 10, Taylor 3, Weyhing 1
C   Clements 92, Cross 40, Boyle 6
P   Weyhing 42, Carsey 39, Taylor 25, Keefe 22, Vickery 13, Sharrott 12, McGinnis 5, O'Connor 3

	G	IP	GS	CG	W	L	K	BB	SH	SV	ERA
Gus Weyhing	42	345.1	40	33	23	16	101	145	2	0	4.74
Kid Carsey	39	318.1	35	30	20	15	50	124	1	0	4.81
Tim Keefe	22	178	22	17	10	7	53	79	0	0	4.40
Jack Taylor	25	170	16	14	10	9	41	77	0	1	4.24
Tom Vickery	13	80	11	7	4	5	15	37	0	0	5.40
John Sharrott	12	56	4	2	4	2	11	33	0	0	4.50
Gus McGinnis	5	37.1	4	4	1	3	12	17	1	0	4.34
Frank O'Connor	3	4	1	0	0	0	0	9	0	1	11.25
		1189	133	107	72	57	283	521	4	2	4.68

NEW YORK   Monte Ward   Polo Grounds (III)

		G	AB	H	R	2B	3B	HR	RBI	BB	SB	BA	SA
2B	Monte Ward	135	588	193	129	27	9	2	77	47	46	.328	.415
3B	George Davis	133	549	195	112	22	27	11	119	42	37	.355	.554
LF	Eddie Burke	135	537	150	122	23	10	9	80	51	54	.279	.410
RF	Mike Tiernan	125	511	158	114	19	12	14	102	72	26	.309	.476
1B	Roger Connor	135	511	156	111	25	8	11	105	91	24	.305	.450
SS	Shorty Fuller	130	474	112	78	14	8	0	51	60	26	.236	.300
C	Jack Doyle	82	318	102	56	17	5	1	51	27	40	.321	.415
CF	General Stafford	67	281	79	58	7	4	5	27	25	19	.281	.388
P	Amos Rusie	56	212	57	32	3	4	3	27	3	0	.269	.363
Sub	Harry Lyons	47	187	51	27	5	2	0	21	14	10	.273	.321
C	Jocko Milligan	42	147	34	16	5	6	1	25	14	2	.231	.367
P	Mark Baldwin	45	134	17	12	4	2	0	9	8	2	.127	.187
C	Parke Wilson	31	114	28	16	4	1	2	21	7	5	.246	.351
P	Les German	22	74	23	10	0	1	0	15	5	1	.311	.338
Sub	King Kelly	20	67	18	9	1	0	0	15	6	3	.269	.284
Sub	Jack McMahon	11	30	10	5	2	1	0	4	2	0	.333	.467
P	Cannonball Crane	12	26	12	8	1	0	0	3	7	0	.462	.500
Sub	Willie Keeler	7	24	8	5	2	1	1	7	5	3	.333	.625
P	Charlie Petty	9	22	7	5	0	0	1	4	4	0	.318	.455
P	Silver King	7	17	3	8	0	0	0	3	7	0	.176	.176
P	George Davies	5	12	4	4	1	0	0	0	5	0	.333	.417
P	Crazy Schmit	4	9	4	2	0	0	0	0	0	0	.444	.444
Sub	Shorty Howe	1	5	3	1	0	0	0	2	0	1	.600	.600
Sub	? Kinsler	1	3	0	1	0	0	0	0	1	0	.000	.000
P	Frank Foreman	2	3	0	0	0	0	0	0	0	0	.000	.000
P	Red Donahue	2	2	0	0	0	0	0	0	0	0	.000	.000
P	Seth Sigsby	1	1	0	0	0	0	0	0	0	0	.000	.000
P	Bumpus Jones	1	0	0	0	0	0	0	0	1	0	—	—
		136	4858	1424	941	182	101	61	768	504	**299**	.293	.410

1B	Connor 135, Crane 1, Doyle 1
2B	Ward 134, Keeler 2
SS	Fuller 130, Doyle 4, Keeler 2, Davis 1
3B	Davis 133, Doyle 3, Howe 1, Connor 1, German 1
OF	Burke 135, Tiernan 125, Stafford 67, Lyons 47, Doyle 29, Keeler 3, Kelly 1, German 1, Crane 1, Kinsler 1
C	Doyle 48, Milligan 42, Wilson 31, Kelly 17, McMahon 11
P	Rusie 56, Baldwin 45, German 20, Crane 10, Petty 9, King 7, Davies 5, Schmit 4, Foreman 2, Donahue 2, Jones 1, Sigsby 1

	G	IP	GS	CG	W	L	K	BB	SH	SV	ERA
Amos Rusie	**56**	**482**	52	**50**	33	21	**208**	218	**4**	1	3.23
Mark Baldwin	45	331.1	39	33	16	20	100	141	2	**2***	4.10
Les German	20	152	18	14	8	8	35	70	0	0	4.14
Cannonball Crane	10	68.1	7	4	2	4	11	41	0	0	5.93
Charlie Petty	9	54	6	4	5	2	12	28	0	0	3.33
Silver King	7	49	7	4	3	4	13	26	0	0	8.63
George Davies	5	36.1	1	1	1	1	7	13	0	0	6.19
Crazy Schmit	4	20.2	4	1	0	2	5	17	0	0	7.40
Frank Foreman	2	5.2	1	0	0	1	0	10	0	0	27.00
Red Donahue	2	5	0	0	0	0	1	3	0	1	9.00
Bumpus Jones	1	4	1	0	0	1	1	10	0	0	11.25
Seth Sigsby	1	3	0	0	0	0	2	4	0	0	9.00
		1209.7	136	111	68	64	**395**	581	6	4	4.29

BROOKLYN   Dave Foutz   **Eastern Park**

		G	AB	H	R	2B	3B	HR	RBI	BB	SB	BA	SA
LF	Dave Foutz	130	557	137	91	20	10	7	67	32	39	.246	.355
2B	Tom Daly	126	470	136	94	21	14	8	70	76	32	.289	.445
SS	Tommy Corcoran	115	459	126	61	11	10	2	58	27	14	.275	.355
RF	Oyster Burns	109	415	112	68	22	8	7	60	36	14	.270	.412
CF	Mike Griffin	95	362	103	85	21	7	6	59	59	30	.285	.431
3B	George Shoch	94	327	86	53	17	1	2	54	48	9	.263	.339
C	Tom Kinslow	78	312	76	38	8	4	4	45	11	4	.244	.333
1B	Dan Brouthers	77	282	95	57	21	11	2	59	52	9	.337	.511
C	Con Daily	61	215	57	33	4	2	1	32	20	13	.265	.316
Sub	Danny Richardson	54	206	46	36	6	2	0	27	13	7	.223	.272
Sub	Harry Stovey	48	175	44	43	6	6	1	29	44	22	.251	.371
P	Brickyard Kennedy	46	157	39	25	6	2	0	16	8	4	.248	.312
Sub	Gil Hatfield	34	120	35	24	3	3	2	19	17	9	.292	.417
P	Ed Stein	37	118	25	12	1	0	0	14	8	1	.212	.220
P	George Haddock	29	85	24	21	1	2	1	7	8	2	.282	.376
Sub	Willie Keeler	20	80	25	14	1	1	1	9	4	2	.313	.387
P	Tom Lovett	18	50	9	8	1	0	0	5	3	0	.180	.200
P	Dan Daub	12	42	8	6	0	0	0	4	4	2	.190	.190
P	George Sharrott	13	39	9	4	1	0	1	4	1	0	.231	.333
Sub	Candy LaChance	11	35	6	1	1	0	0	6	2	0	.171	.200
P	Cannonball Crane	3	5	2	1	1	0	0	0	0	0	.400	.600
		130	4511	1200	775	173	83	45	644	473	213	.266	.371

1B   Brouthers 77, Foutz 54, Lovett 1
2B   Daly 82, Richardson 46, Shoch 3, Griffin 2
SS   Corcoran 115, Shoch 11, Richardson 3, Burns 1
3B   Daly 45, Shoch 37, Hatfield 34, Keeler 12, Richardson 5
OF   Burns 108, Griffin 93, Foutz 77, Stovey 48, Shoch 46, Daily 9, Keeler 8, Haddock 7, LaChance 5, Lovett 4, Kinslow 2, Crane 1
C   Kinslow 76, Daily 51, LaChance 6
P   Kennedy 46, Stein 37, Haddock 23, Lovett 14, Sharrott 13, Daub 12, Foutz 6, Crane 2

	G	IP	GS	CG	W	L	K	BB	SH	SV	ERA
Brickyard Kennedy	46	382.2	44	40	25	20	107	168	2	1	3.72
Ed Stein	37	298.1	34	28	19	15	81	119	1	0	3.77
George Haddock	23	151	20	12	8	9	37	89	0	0	5.60
Dan Daub	12	103	12	12	6	6	25	61	0	0	3.84
Tom Lovett	14	96	8	6	3	5	15	35	0	1	6.56
George Sharrott	13	95	10	10	4	6	24	58	0	1	5.87
Dave Foutz	6	18	0	0	0	0	3	8	0	0	7.50
Cannonball Crane	2	10	2	1	0	2	5	9	0	0	13.50
		1154	130	109	65	63	297	547	3	3	4.55

CINCINNATI Charlie Comiskey League Park (I)

		G	AB	H	R	2B	3B	HR	RBI	BB	SB	BA	SA
3B	Arlie Latham	127	531	150	101	18	6	2	49	62	57	.282	.350
CF	Bug Holliday	126	500	155	108	24	10	5	89	73	32	.310	.428
SS	Germany Smith	130	500	118	63	18	6	4	56	38	14	.236	.320
2B	Bid McPhee	127	491	138	101	17	11	3	68	94	25	.281	.379
C	Farmer Vaughn	121	483	135	68	17	12	1	108	35	16	.280	.371
LF	Jimmy Canavan	121	461	104	65	13	7	5	64	51	31	.226	.317
1B	Charlie Comiskey	64	259	57	38	12	1	0	26	11	9	.220	.274
C	Morg Murphy	57	200	47	25	5	1	1	19	14	1	.235	.285
RF	Jack McCarthy	49	195	55	28	8	3	0	22	22	6	.282	.354
Sub	Frank Motz	43	156	40	16	7	1	2	25	19	3	.256	.353
Sub	Piggy Ward	41	150	42	44	4	1	0	10	37	27	.280	.320
P	Frank Dwyer	38	120	24	22	1	2	1	17	9	2	.200	.267
P	Icebox Chamberlain	34	97	19	9	4	1	0	10	5	3	.196	.258
Sub	George Henry	21	83	23	11	3	0	0	13	11	2	.277	.313
P	Mike Sullivan	27	79	16	7	2	0	1	7	2	2	.203	.266
P	Tom Parrott	24	68	13	5	1	1	1	9	1	0	.191	.279
P	Tony Mullane	16	52	15	11	0	0	1	6	5	1	.288	.346
Sub	Bob Caruthers	13	48	14	14	2	0	1	8	15	4	.292	.396
Sub	Jud Smith	17	43	10	7	1	0	1	5	9	1	.233	.326
P	Silver King	17	37	6	5	1	1	0	1	8	0	.162	.243
Sub	Connie Murphy	6	17	3	3	1	0	0	2	1	0	.176	.235
P	Bumpus Jones	6	16	4	3	1	1	0	0	1	1	.250	.438
Sub	Charlie Duffee	4	12	2	3	1	0	0	0	5	0	.167	.250
P	George Darby	4	10	3	1	0	0	0	1	1	0	.300	.300
P	Lem Cross	3	6	2	1	0	0	0	0	2	0	.333	.333
Sub	George Ulrich	1	3	0	0	0	0	0	0	0	1	.000	.000
		131	4617	1195	759	161	65	29	615	532	238	.259	.341

1B Comiskey 64, Motz 43, Vaughn 21, McCarthy 2, Ward 1, M. Murphy 1, Holliday 1, Dwyer 1
2B McPhee 127, Canavan 5
SS G. Smith 130, J. Smith 1
3B Latham 127, J. Smith 6, Mullane 1, Canavan 1
OF Holiday 125, Canavan 116, McCarthy 47, Ward 40, Vaughn 23, Henry 21, Caruthers 13, J. Smith 9, Duffee 4, Ulrich 1, Dwyer 1, Parrott 1
C Vaughn 80, M. Murphy 56, C. Murphy 4
P Dwyer 37, Chamberlain 34, Sullivan 27, Parrott 22, King 17, Mullane 15, Jones 6, Darby 4, Cross 3

	G	IP	GS	CG	W	L	K	BB	SH	SV	ERA
Frank Dwyer	37	287.1	30	28	18	15	53	93	1	2	4.13
Icebox Chamberlain	34	241	27	19	16	12	59	112	1	0	3.73
Mike Sullivan	27	183.2	18	14	8	11	40	103	0	1	5.05
Tom Parrott	22	154	17	11	10	7	33	70	1	0	4.09
Tony Mullane	15	122.1	13	11	6	6	24	65	0	1*	4.41
Silver King	17	105	15	8	5	6	30	56	1	1	4.89
George Darby	4	29	3	2	1	1	6	18	0	0	7.76
Bumpus Jones	6	28.2	5	2	1	3	6	23	0	0	10.05
Lem Cross	3	21	3	2	0	2	7	9	0	0	5.57
		1172	131	97	65	63	258	549	4	5	4.55

BALTIMORE   Ned Hanlon   Union Park

		G	AB	H	R	2B	3B	HR	RBI	BB	SB	BA	SA
3B	Billy Shindle	125	521	136	100	22	11	1	75	66	17	.261	.351
CF	Joe Kelley	125	502	153	120	27	16	9	76	77	33	.305	.476
2B	Heinie Reitz	130	490	140	90	17	13	1	76	65	24	.286	.380
SS	John McGraw	127	480	154	123	9	10	5	64	101	38	.321	.413
RF	George Treadway	115	458	119	78	16	17	1	67	57	24	.260	.376
1B	Harry Taylor	88	360	102	50	9	1	1	54	32	24	.283	.322
C	Wilbert Robinson	95	359	120	49	21	3	3	57	26	17	.334	.435
LF	Jim Long	55	226	48	31	8	1	2	25	16	23	.212	.283
Sub	Boileryard Clarke	49	183	32	23	1	3	1	24	19	2	.175	.230
P	Sadie McMahon	43	148	36	13	3	0	0	22	4	1	.243	.264
Sub	Tim O'Rourke	31	135	49	22	4	1	0	19	12	5	.363	.407
P	Tony Mullane	38	114	26	15	2	1	0	14	5	5	.228	.263
Sub	Jocko Milligan	24	102	25	19	5	2	1	19	5	2	.245	.363
Sub	Steve Brodie	25	97	35	18	7	2	0	19	12	8	.361	.474
P	Bill Hawke	29	93	16	8	2	0	1	9	7	0	.172	.226
P	Edgar McNabb	21	67	13	11	1	1	0	8	4	1	.194	.239
Sub	Bob Gilks	15	64	17	10	2	0	0	7	0	3	.266	.297
P	Kirtley Baker	19	57	17	9	1	1	0	6	8	1	.298	.351
Sub	Hughie Jennings	16	55	14	6	0	0	1	6	4	0	.255	.309
Sub	Piggy Ward	11	49	12	11	1	3	0	5	5	4	.245	.388
Sub	Willard Brown	7	32	4	5	3	0	0	5	1	0	.125	.219
Sub	Harry Stovey	8	26	4	4	2	0	0	5	8	1	.154	.231
P	Crazy Schmit	9	21	5	4	1	0	0	2	2	0	.238	.286
P	Jack Wadsworth	3	7	3	0	0	0	0	0	1	0	.429	.429
P	Stub Brown	2	5	1	1	0	0	0	1	0	0	.200	.200
		130	4651	1281	820	164	86	27	665	537	233	.275	.365

1B Taylor 88, Milligan 22, Clarke 11, Brown 7, Ward 2, Robinson 1, Mullane 1
2B Reitz 130
SS McGraw 117, Jennings 15, O'Rourke 1
3B Shindle 125, O'Rourke 5
OF Kelley 125, Treadway 115, Long 55, Brodie 25, O'Rourke 25, Gilks 15, McGraw 11, Ward 9, Stovey 7, Baker 3, Mullane 2, Jennings 1
C   Robinson 93, Clarke 38, Milligan 1
P   McMahon 43, Mullane 34, Hawke 29, McNabb 21, Baker 15, Schmit 9, Wadsworth 3, Brown 2

	G	IP	GS	CG	W	L	K	BB	SH	SV	ERA
Sadie McMahon	43	346.1	40	35	23	18	79	156	0	1	4.37
Tony Mullane	34	244.2	26	23	12	16	71	124	0	1*	4.45
Bill Hawke #	29	225	29	22	11	16	69	108	1	0	4.76
Edgar McNabb	21	142	14	12	8	7	18	53	0	0	4.12
Kirtley Baker	15	91.2	12	8	3	8	26	58	0	0	8.44
Crazy Schmit	9	49	6	4	3	2	10	22	0	0	6.61
Jack Wadsworth	3	16	3	0	0	3	2	8	0	0	11.25
Stub Brown	2	9	0	0	0	0	0	5	0	0	6.00
		1123.2	130	104	60	70	275	534	1	2	4.97

No-hit game 5–0 vs Washington, August 16

CHICAGO **Cap Anson** **South Side Park (II) (8 games)** **West Side Park (II) (after May 23)**

		G	AB	H	R	2B	3B	HR	RBI	BB	SB	BA	SA
SS	Bill Dahlen	116	485	146	113	28	15	5	64	58	31	.301	.452
2B	Bill Lange	117	469	132	92	8	7	8	88	52	47	.281	.380
RF	Sam Dungan	107	465	138	86	23	7	2	64	29	11	.297	.389
3B	Jiggs Parrott	110	455	111	54	10	9	1	65	13	25	.244	.312
1B	Cap Anson	103	398	125	70	24	2	0	91	68	13	.314	.384
LF	Walt Wilmot	94	392	118	69	14	14	3	61	40	39	.301	.431
CF	Jimmy Ryan	83	341	102	82	21	7	3	30	59	8	.299	.428
Sub	George Decker	81	328	89	57	9	8	2	48	24	22	.271	.366
C	Mal Kittridge	70	255	59	32	9	5	2	30	17	3	.231	.329
C	Pop Schriver	64	229	65	49	8	3	4	34	14	4	.284	.397
P	Bill Hutchison	46	162	41	14	7	3	0	25	7	2	.253	.333
Sub	Llewellyn Camp	38	156	41	37	7	7	2	17	19	30	.263	.436
P	Willie McGill	40	124	29	18	4	0	0	13	20	5	.234	.266
Sub	Charlie Irwin	21	82	25	14	6	2	0	13	10	4	.305	.427
Sub	Bob Glenalvin	16	61	21	11	3	1	0	12	7	7	.344	.426
P	Hal Mauck	23	61	9	2	0	0	0	4	3	0	.148	.148
P	Fritz Clausen	10	33	4	2	0	0	0	0	2	0	.121	.121
P	Tom Parrott	7	27	7	4	1	0	0	3	1	0	.259	.296
P	Bert Abbey	7	26	6	2	1	0	0	2	2	0	.231	.269
P	Gus McGinnis	13	25	6	8	0	0	0	7	9	0	.240	.240
Sub	Bill Eagan	6	19	5	3	0	0	0	2	5	4	.263	.263
P	Frank Donnelly	8	18	8	4	1	2	0	3	2	0	.444	.722
Sub	John O'Brien	4	14	5	3	0	1	0	1	2	0	.357	.500
Sub	Henry Lynch	4	14	3	0	2	0	0	2	1	0	.214	.357
P	Clark Griffith	4	11	2	1	0	0	0	2	0	0	.182	.182
P	Sam Shaw	2	7	2	1	0	0	0	1	0	0	.286	.286
Sub	Bob Caruthers	1	3	0	0	0	0	0	0	1	0	.000	.000
P	Jim Hughey	2	2	0	1	0	0	0	0	1	0	.000	.000
P	Gus Yost	1	1	0	0	0	0	0	0	0	0	.000	.000
P	Doc Parker	1	1	0	0	0	0	0	0	0	0	.000	.000
P	Abe Johnson	1	0	0	0	0	0	0	0	0	0	—	—
		128	4664	1299	829	186	93	32	682	465	255	.279	.379

1B   Anson 101, Decker 27, T. Parrott 1
2B   Lange 57, Decker 20, Glenalvin 16, Dahlen 10, Camp 9, J. Parrott 7, Eagan 6, O'Brien 4, T. Parrott 1
SS   Dahlen 88, Irwin 21, Ryan 10, Lange 7, Camp 3, Decker 2
3B   J. Parrott 99, Camp 16, Lange 8, Dahlen 3, T. Parrott 2
OF   Dungan 107, Wilmot 93, Ryan 73, Lange 40, Decker 33, Dahlen 17, Camp 11, Schriver 5, J. Parrott 4, Lynch 4, Hutchison 2, Caruthers 1, McGinnis 1
C   Kittridge 70, Schriver 56, Lange 7
P   Hutchison 44, McGill 39, Mauck 23, McGinnis 13, Clausen 10, Donnelly 8, Abbey 7, T. Parrott 4, Griffith 4, Hughey 2, Shaw 2, Parker 1, Ryan 1, Johnson 1, Yost 1

	G	IP	GS	CG	W	L	K	BB	SH	SV	ERA
Bill Hutchison	44	348.1	40	38	16	24	80	156	2	0	4.75
Willie McGill	39	302.2	34	26	17	18	91	181	1	0	4.61
Hal Mauck	23	143	18	12	8	10	23	60	1	0	4.41
Fritz Clausen	10	76	9	8	6	2	31	39	0	1	3.08
Gus McGinnis	13	67.1	5	3	2	5	13	31	0	0	5.35
Bert Abbey	7	56	7	5	2	4	6	20	0	0	5.46
Frank Donnelly	7	42	5	3	3	1	6	17	0	2	5.36
Tom Parrott	4	27	3	2	0	3	7	17	0	0	6.67
Clark Griffith	4	19.2	2	2	1	1	9	5	0	0	5.03
Sam Shaw	2	16	2	1	1	0	1	13	0	0	5.63
Jim Hughey	2	9	2	1	0	1	4	3	0	0	11.00
Jimmy Ryan	1	4.2	0	0	0	0	1	0	0	0	0.00

	G	IP	GS	CG	W	L	K	BB	SH	SV	ERA
Gus Yost	1	2.2	1	0	0	1	1	8	0	0	13.50
Doc Parker	1	2	0	0	0	0	0	1	0	1	13.50
Abe Johnson	1	1	0	0	0	0	0	2	0	1	36.00
	1117.1	128	101	56	71	273	553	4	5	4.81

ST. LOUIS   Bill Watkins   Sportsman's Park (II)

		G	AB	H	R	2B	3B	HR	RBI	BB	SB	BA	SA
RF	Tom Dowd	132	581	164	114	18	7	1	54	49	59	.282	.343
2B	Joe Quinn	135	547	126	68	18	6	0	71	33	24	.230	.285
1B	Perry Werden	125	500	138	73	22	**29**	1	94	49	11	.276	.442
CF	Steve Brodie	107	469	149	71	16	8	2	79	33	41	.318	.399
3B	Jack Crooks	128	448	106	93	10	9	1	48	121	31	.237	.306
C	Heinie Peitz	96	362	92	53	12	9	1	45	54	12	.254	.345
UT	Frank Shugart	59	246	69	41	10	4	0	28	22	13	.280	.354
P	Kid Gleason	59	199	51	25	6	4	0	20	19	2	.256	.327
SS	Jack Glasscock	48	195	56	32	8	1	1	26	25	20	.287	.354
SS	Bones Ely	44	178	45	25	1	6	0	16	17	2	.253	.326
LF	Charlie Frank	40	164	55	29	6	3	1	17	18	8	.335	.427
P	Ted Breitenstein	49	160	29	20	1	1	1	14	18	3	.181	.219
Sub	Joe Gunson	40	151	41	20	5	0	0	15	6	0	.272	.305
Sub	Duff Cooley	29	107	37	20	2	3	0	21	8	8	.346	.421
Sub	Jimmy Bannon	26	107	36	9	3	4	0	15	4	8	.336	.439
Sub	Sandy Griffin	23	92	18	9	1	1	0	9	16	2	.196	.228
P	Pink Hawley	31	91	26	10	7	3	0	17	11	1	.286	.429
P	Dad Clarkson	25	75	10	8	1	0	0	5	9	0	.133	.147
Sub	Art Twineham	14	48	15	8	2	0	0	11	1	0	.313	.354
Sub	Lew Whistler	10	38	9	5	1	0	0	2	3	0	.237	.263
Sub	Bill Goodenough	10	31	5	4	1	0	0	2	3	2	.161	.194
Sub	Dennie O'Neill	7	25	3	3	0	0	0	2	4	3	.120	.120
Sub	Dick Buckley	9	23	4	2	1	0	0	1	0	0	.174	.217
Sub	Pat McCauley	5	16	1	0	0	0	0	0	0	0	.063	.063
Sub	Jud Smith	4	13	1	1	0	0	0	0	1	0	.077	.077
P	John Dolan	3	7	1	1	0	0	1	3	0	0	.143	.571
P	Bill Hawke	1	3	1	0	0	0	0	1	0	0	.333	.333
P	Frank Pears	1	2	0	0	0	0	0	0	0	0	.000	.000
Sub	Kid Summers	2	1	0	1	0	0	0	0	0	0	.000	.000
		135	4879	1288	745	152	98	10	616	524	250	.264	.341

1B   Werden 124, O'Neill 7, Peitz 5, Whistler 1
2B   Quinn 135, Dowd 1
SS   Glasscock 48, Ely 44, Shugart 23, Peitz 11, Cooley 5, Crooks 4, Bannon 2, Gleason 1
3B   Crooks 123, Shugart 9, Smith 4
OF   Dowd 132, Brodie 107, Frank 40, Shugart 28, Bannon 24, Griffin 23, Cooley 15, Gleason 11, Peitz 10, Goodenough 10, Whistler 9, Gunson 5, Breitenstein 2, Summers 1, Werden 1, Clarkson 1
C   Peitz 74, Gunson 35, Twineham 14, Cooley 10, Buckley 9, McCauley 5, Summers 1, Crooks 1
P   Breitenstein 48, Gleason 48, Hawley 31, Clarkson 24, Dolan 3, Hawke 1, Pears 1, Bannon 1

	G	IP	GS	CG	W	L	K	BB	SH	SV	ERA
Ted Breitenstein	48	382.2	42	38	19	24	102	156	1	1	**3.18**
Kid Gleason	48	380.1	45	37	21	22	86	187	1	1	4.61
Pink Hawley	31	227	24	21	5	17	73	103	0	1	4.60
Dad Clarkson	24	186.1	21	17	12	9	37	79	1	0	3.48
John Dolan	3	17.1	1	1	0	1	1	7	0	1	4.15
Bill Hawke	1	5.1	1	0	0	1	1	3	0	0	5.06
Jimmy Bannon	1	4	1	0	0	1	1	5	0	0	22.50
Frank Pears	1	3.1	0	0	0	0	0	2	0	0	13.50
		1207	135	**114**	57	75	301	542	3	4	**4.06**

LOUISVILLE   Billy Barnie   Eclipse Park (II)

		G	AB	H	R	2B	3B	HR	RBI	BB	SB	BA	SA
CF	Tom Brown	122	529	127	104	15	7	5	54	56	**66**	.240	.323
2B	Fred Pfeffer	125	508	129	85	29	12	3	75	51	32	.254	.376
1B	Willard Brown	111	461	140	80	23	7	1	85	50	9	.304	.390
3B	George Pinkney	118	446	105	64	12	6	1	62	50	12	.235	.296
RF	Farmer Weaver	106	439	128	79	17	7	2	49	27	17	.292	.376
C	John Grim	99	415	111	68	19	8	3	54	12	15	.267	.373
SS	Tim O'Rourke	92	352	99	80	8	4	0	53	77	22	.281	.327
LF	Pete Browning	57	220	78	38	11	3	1	37	44	8	.355	.445
P	Scott Stratton	60	277	49	34	8	5	0	16	25	6	.226	.309
Sub	Larry Twitchell	45	187	58	37	11	3	2	31	17	7	.310	.433
Sub	Jerry Denny	44	175	43	22	5	4	1	22	9	4	.246	.337
P	George Hemming	45	158	32	17	5	2	0	19	12	0	.203	.259
Sub	Hughie Jennings	23	88	12	6	3	0	0	9	3	0	.136	.170
P	Jock Menefee	22	73	20	10	2	1	0	12	13	2	.274	.329
P	Bill Rhodes	20	70	9	6	1	2	0	7	8	0	.129	.200
Sub	Lew Whistler	13	47	10	5	1	1	0	9	5	1	.213	.277
Sub	Curt Welch	14	47	8	5	1	0	0	2	16	1	.170	.191
Sub	Jerry Harrington	10	36	4	4	1	0	0	6	3	0	.111	.139
Sub	Bob Clark	12	28	3	3	1	0	0	3	5	0	.107	.143
P	Bill Whitrock	8	25	7	5	0	1	0	4	1	1	.280	.360
P	Matt Kilroy	5	16	7	4	3	0	0	3	1	0	.438	.625
P	Fritz Clausen	5	14	3	2	0	0	0	2	0	0	.214	.214
P	Billy Rhines	5	11	1	0	0	0	0	0	0	0	.091	.091
P	Con Lucid	2	3	1	1	0	0	0	0	0	0	.333	.333
P	Billy Gumbert	1	1	1	0	1	0	0	2	0	0	1.000	2.000
		126	4566	1185	759	177	73	19	616	485	203	.260	.343

1B Brown 111, Whistler 13, Grim 3, Stratton 1
2B Pfeffer 125, Grim 2
SS O'Rourke 60, Denny 42, Jennings 23, Clark 1, Grim 1
3B Pinkney 118, O'Rourke 6, Denny 2
OF Brown 122, Weaver 85, Browning 57, Twtichell 45, O'Rourke 26, Stratton 23, Welch 14, Menefee 7, Hemming 4, Clark 1, Whitrock 1, Grim 1
C Grim 92, Weaver 21, Clark 10, Harrington 10, Brown 1
P Hemming 41, Stratton 37, Rhodes 20, Menefee 15, Whitrock 8, Clausen 5, Rhines 5, Kilroy 5, Lucid 2, Gumbert 1

	G	IP	GS	CG	W	L	K	BB	SH	SV	ERA
George Hemming	41	332	32	32	18	17	79	176	1	1	5.10
Scott Stratton	37	314.2	35	34	12	23	43	100	1	0	5.43
Bill Rhodes	20	151.2	19	17	5	12	22	66	0	0	7.60
Jock Menefee	15	129.1	15	14	8	7	30	40	1	0	4.24
Bill Whitrock	8	46.2	8	5	2	5	8	18	0	0	8.10
Matt Kilroy	5	35	5	5	3	2	4	23	1	0	9.00
Fritz Clausen	5	33	5	3	1	4	4	22	0	0	6.00
Billy Rhines	5	31	5	3	1	4	0	19	0	0	8.71
Con Lucid	3	6	1	0	0	1	0	10	0	0	15.00
Billy Gumbert	1	0.2	1	0	0	0	0	5	0	0	27.00
		1080	126	113	50	75	190	479	4	1	5.90

WASHINGTON   **Jim O'Rourke**   **Boundary Field**

		G	AB	H	R	2B	3B	HR	RBI	BB	SB	BA	SA
CF	Dummy Hoy	130	564	138	106	12	6	0	45	66	48	.245	.287
LF	Jim O'Rourke	129	547	157	75	22	5	2	95	49	15	.287	.356
2B	Sam Wise	122	521	162	102	27	17	5	77	49	20	.311	.457
C	Duke Farrell	124	511	143	84	13	13	4	75	47	11	.280	.380
SS	Joe Sullivan	128	508	135	72	16	13	2	64	36	7	.266	.360
RF	Paul Radford	124	464	106	87	18	3	2	34	105	32	.228	.293
1B	Henry Larkin	81	319	101	54	20	3	4	73	50	1	.317	.436
C	Deacon McGuire	63	237	62	29	14	3	1	26	26	3	.262	.359
3B	Joe Mulvey	55	226	53	21	9	4	0	19	7	2	.235	.310
Sub	Cub Stricker	59	218	40	28	7	1	0	20	20	4	.183	.225
P	Duke Esper	42	143	41	15	6	3	0	24	14	0	.287	.371
P	Al Maul	44	134	34	10	8	4	0	12	33	1	.254	.373
Sub	Charlie Abbey	31	116	30	11	1	4	0	12	12	9	.259	.336
P	Jouett Meekin	33	113	29	15	3	2	3	20	4	0	.257	.398
P	Jesse Duryea	17	47	13	6	4	0	0	6	3	0	.277	.362
P	Otis Stocksdale	12	40	12	7	0	2	0	6	2	1	.300	.400
P	Ben Stephens	9	29	3	0	0	0	0	0	1	0	.103	.103
P	John Graff	2	5	1	0	0	0	0	0	0	0	.200	.200
		130	4742	1260	722	180	83	23	608	524	154	.266	.354

1B	Larkin 81, O'Rourke 33, McGuire 12, Farrell 3, Radford 1, Stocksdale 1
2B	Wise 91, Stricker 39, Radford 1
SS	Sullivan 128, Stricker 4
3B	Mulvey 55, Farrell 41, Wise 31, Stricker 4
OF	Hoy 130, Radford 123, O'Rourke 87, Abbey 31, Stricker 12, Maul 7, Meekin 3, Stocksdale 1
C	Farrell 81, McGuire 50, O'Rourke 9
P	Esper 42, Maul 37, Meekin 31, Duryea 17, Stocksdale 11, Stephens 9, Graff 2, Radford 1

	G	IP	GS	CG	W	L	K	BB	SH	SV	ERA
Duke Esper	42	334.1	36	34	12	**28**	78	156	0	0	4.71
Al Maul	37	297	33	29	12	21	72	144	1	0	5.30
Jouett Meekin	31	245	28	24	10	15	91	140	1	0	4.96
Jesse Duryea	17	117	15	9	4	10	20	56	0	0	7.54
Otis Stocksdale	11	69	11	7	2	8	12	32	0	0	8.22
Ben Stephens	9	63.2	6	6	0	6	14	31	0	0	5.80
John Graff	2	12	1	1	0	1	4	13	0	0	11.25
Paul Radford	1	1	0	0	0	0	1	2	0	0	18.00
		1139	130	110	40	89	292	574	2	0	5.56

1894
THE BIRDS SOAR

Rulesmakers, weary of watching batters bunt pitches foul without penalty until they got one they liked, in 1894 declared that a foul hit, other than a foul tip, resulting from a bunt attempt was now a strike. In a similar vein, the sacrifice rule was refined to award a batter a sacrifice hit if he bunted to advance a runner with none out as well as with one out. There were no other significant rule changes in 1894. Yet that season unleashed the greatest offensive deluge in history. The League-Association batted .309 as a whole, and each game featured an average of 15 runs and over 22 hits.

Why it was that hitters really feasted the second year—rather than the first year—that the pitching distance was lengthened will probably never be fully explicable, but the fans definitely seemed to respond to the accent on offense. Attendance figures rose again in 1894 and would continue to climb until 1896. Yet while many team owners were turning a handsome profit, they were not about to share it. The 1890 Players League war had helped hike major league salaries to a $2,000 minimum, but by 1894 the Philadelphia Phillies had a salary max of $1,800 and rookies with every major league club got between $600 and $700. What was more, some owners revived the old penny-pinching tactic of forcing substitutes to double as ticket takers and groundskeepers. Unable to take out their frustration anywhere else, players vented it on the field. By 1893 only 54 of the 128 players active in the Players League were still in the majors, many having quit because they found the changes in the game too disheartening. In their stead came a new breed of player who thrived on rowdyism and intimidation. The 1894 season was the first to demonstrate that the roughhouse style could pay dividends in the standings if not necessarily at the box office. The Baltimore Orioles, expert at spiking, tripping and grabbing the belts of enemy base runners when an umpire was not looking, were the surprise pennant winner. Meanwhile, the Cleveland Spiders, equally adept at taunting opponents and terrorizing umpires, drew the second fewest home fans in the majors despite finishing in the first division.

By the spring of 1894 the Orioles had just three regulars who were with them two years

Somehow the ephemeral Charlie Dewald got into this collage of the 1894 Cleveland Spiders. Top: Dewald, Cy Young, Nig Cuppy, Jack O'Connor and Jimmy McAleer. Middle: Cupid Childs, Chippy McGarr, Patsy Tebeau, Ed McKean and Chauncey Fisher. Bottom: Jake Virtue, John Clarkson, Buck Ewing, Chief Zimmer and Jesse Burkett. Dewald didn't throw a single pitch for Cleveland in 1894, but one not here who did was Frank Griffith, a southpaw quarterback at Northwestern before he joined the Spiders.

earlier when the two major leagues merged. Most of the other starters had been acquired by manager Ned Hanlon via a string of deft trades, but since Baltimore had finished last in 1892 and just eighth the following year, little was anticipated in 1894. Hence the Orioles caught the rest of the League-Association napping when the campaign opened and held a four-game lead on June 25 after winning 24 of their first 34 games. A collective hitting slump sent the Orioles into a tailspin that left them five games behind Boston by the end of July. Hanlon then attempted to stop Boston's three-year championship reign by appointing third baseman John McGraw his cleanup hitter and hard-hitting Joe Kelley his leadoff man. Even though McGraw had little power and compiled the fewest RBI of any Baltimore regular, it got the desired result. With Kelley (who scored 74 runs in the last 47 games of the season) at the top of the order and McGraw at the heart of it, the Orioles regained first place on August 30 and held it the rest of the way by reeling off 18 straight wins and taking 28 of their last 31 games.

Though the Orioles collectively batted .343 and scored 1,171 runs, they won not on their hitting but on their exceptional defense and good health. The former was a particularly im-

Baltimore's first big league pennant winner—the 1894 Orioles. Top: Ned Hanlon, Henry Von der Horst and Herman Von der Horst. Middle: Steve Brodie, George Hemming, Wilbert Robinson, Dan Brouthers, Sadie McMahon, Boileryard Clarke, Stub Brown, Duke Esper and Joe Kelley. Bottom: Heinie Reitz, Kid Gleason, Frank Bonner, John McGraw, Hughie Jennings, Willie Keeler and Bill Hawke. These O's pounded a 19th-century-record 150 triples and had five 100-RBI men, but students of the mid-1890s game find it even more telling that after finishing last in 1892 with a league-worst 4.28 ERA, Baltimore came home first in 1894 despite posting a 5.00 ERA, still the highest ever by a pennant winner.

GOOD HIT, NO PITCH

The Chicago Colts finished in the second division for the third year in a row in 1894. Offense was not their trouble. Cap Anson, at age 42, hit .388 and fell just one RBI short of being the only player ever to drive in 100 runs in under 350 at bats. A trio of Colts—Bill Hutchison, Adonis Terry and Scott Stratton—produced this composite line of batting stats:

AB	H	2B	3B	HR	RBI	BA	SA
327	111	14	6	9	56	.339	.502

The three were pitchers, however, and when they worked at their primary trade, their composite line showed just 24 wins and 32 losses with 303 walks, 121 strikeouts and an ERA around 6.00. Hutchison and Stratton never got it back together after the pitching distance was lengthened, but the following year Terry became the only pitcher ever to win 20 games in a major league that still forbade overhand pitching—the American Association in 1884—and one that espoused the sixty foot six inch pitching distance.

Hugh Duffy, the only man to forge .300 seasons in four different major leagues. His record-setting .440 BA in 1894 is still disputed by some authorities. Many more authorities are unhappy that major league baseball still credits him with the 1893 batting title even though Billy Hamilton outhit him by 17 points (.380 to .363).

portant asset in 1894 since games saw an average of only four strikeouts and around seven walks, meaning the ball was almost constantly in play. Baltimore's .944 fielding average topped the loop by nine points, and Hanlon could rejoice too that his team alone among the contenders was spared any serious injuries. with all eight regulars available almost every day, Hanlon needed to use only two substitutions all season, Boileryard Clarke and Frank Bonner. Clarke served as the Orioles backup catcher and first baseman, and Bonner filled in everywhere else. Baltimore's pitching was another story. The Orioles were last in the League in complete games and lacked a real staff ace as no fewer than six of Hanlon's hurlers worked 100 or more innings and ten all told collected at least one decision.

The second-place New York Giants, in contrast, used just five pitchers all year and posted a staff ERA of 3.83 that was 1.14 runs per game lower than any other team's. But player-manager Monte Ward, in his last season, hit just .265, and Ward's keystone partner, Shorty Fuller, batted .283. Both their marks were well below the League-Association average, as was Mike Tiernan's .276. Tiernan, normally the Giants' most reliable run producer, shouldered most of the blame for New York's failure to catch Baltimore, but the fault really lay with the front office. While Hanlon, realizing he needed pitching help, was busy in the second half of the season plugging holes in his thin hill staff by trading for such as Duke Esper, who went 10-2 for the Orioles down the stretch, the Giants continued to rely almost exclusively on their Big Two of Amos Rusie and Jouett Meekin. The pair were awesome in 1894, posting 69 victories and a combined .758 winning percentage, but New York's other three hurlers won 50 fewer games than Rusie and Meekin while losing the same amount (22).

Boston, eight games back in third place, had a similar deficiency. Kid Nichols and Jack Stivetts were a combined 58-27 for the Beaneaters, but Frank Selee got just an aggregate

25-22 performance from the rest of his staff. Pitching shorts, plus the loss of catcher Charlie Bennett who lost both legs in an offseason accident, stymied the highest scoring team in major league history. Thanks in large measure to Hugh Duffy's matchless season and a nineteenth-century team-record .484 slugging average, Boston tallied a record 1,220 runs. The Beaneaters were also the only club to win a season series from Baltimore, taking eight of the 12 games the pair played, but a 40-20 mark against the bottom five teams was a full ten games poorer than Baltimore's 50-10 against the same crew of tailenders and accounted as much as anything else for the difference between the two in the standings.

The League-Association's underachievers once again were the Philadelphia Phillies, 18 games off the pace even though they batted an all-time record .349. The Phils had an injury excuse, though, losing shortstop Bob Allen, the key to the League-Association's stingiest defense in 1893, to a beaning. Allen's replacement was Joe Sullivan, coming off a year in which he made 102 errors. Sullivan hit .352 for the Phils, but more offense was the last thing manager Arthur Irwin needed. In early August, Baltimore came to Philadelphia for a

---

ON THE ROAD AGAIN WITH DUKE

In 1894 Giants catcher Duke Farrell became the only major leaguer ever to compile 100 or more hits six years in a row for six different teams. Though his whirlwind odyssey was about to slow down, his career would become no less strange. Farrell played 11 more years in the majors during which he only changed teams three more times, but just once again was he able to achieve as many as 100 hits in a season. Meanwhile he developed into the game's first great pinch hitter. At the close of his career in 1905, Farrell held the major league career records for both the most pinch hits (23) and the highest batting average in pinch roles (.389). Nothing he did in 1894 offered any hint of what was ahead. Farrell ended that season hitless in his only career pinch-hit at bat to that point. An evolutionary chart of the record for the most pinch hits in a season at the time Farrell retired:

	TEAM	LEAGUE	YEAR	PH's
Jack Doyle	Cleveland	LA	1892	1
Connie Mack	Pittsburgh	LA	1892	1
Charlie Reilly	Philadelphia	LA	1892	1
John Sharrott	Philadelphia	LA	1893	2
Kid Gleason	Baltimore	LA	1894	2
Frank Connaughton	Boston	LA	1894	2
Jack Stivetts	Boston	LA	1894	2
Mike Grady	Philadelphia	LA	1894	2
Tom Parrott	Cincinnati	LA	1894	2
Tuck Turner	Philadelphia	LA	1895	2
Win Mercer	Washington	LA	1895	2
Doggie Miller	Louisville	LA	1896	6
Duke Farrell	Washington	LA	1897	8
Sammy Strang	New York	NL	1905	8

The average man here, pitchers included, hit .349. Yes, it's the greatest hitting machine of all time—the 1894 Philadelphia Phillies. Top: Nixey Callahan, Bob Allen, Ed Delahanty, Jack Boyle, Sam Thompson, Jack Taylor and Charlie Reilly. Middle: Jack Clements, Gus Weyhing, Bill Hallman, manager Arthur Irwin, Kid Carsey, Billy Hamilton and George Haddock. Bottom: Fred Hartman, John Sharrott, Tuck Turner and Mike Grady.

LUCKY TUCK

Tuck Turner was doubly blessed. As a rookie in 1893, he debuted in the season the pitching distance was increased to sixty feet six inches and he also happened to wear the uniform of the Phillies, the most potent offensive force in the majors. Turner joined the parade, hitting .323. In 1894, when the Phillies' team batting average went through the stratosphere, Turner jumped to the head of the parade, leading the club at .416. Since the Phils' other three outfielders—Sam Thompson, Ed Delahanty and Billy Hamilton—also hit around .400 and were better fielders and base runners than Turner, he saw only spot duty. The same thing happened in 1895 when he hit .386 but got just 210 at bats.

Still, Turner finished the 1895 season as the first player in history to compile a .380-plus career batting average in his first 800 at bats in the majors. Only one other player in the years since—Joe Jackson—has ever matched Turner's meteoric start.

three-game series that represented the Phils' last realistic chance to climb back into the race. Jack Taylor won the opener of a twin bill for Philadelphia on August 3, beating Esper 14-4, but George Harper and Gus Weyhing were drubbed in the nightcap, 16-3. The following day, after blasting Kid Carsey to win a 19-12 donnybrook, the Orioles left town having gained a notch on the Phils despite surrendering 29 runs in the three games because the Phils had surrendered 39. It was a typical series for Irwin when he matched forces with Selee, Ward and Hanlon, the managers of the three teams that finished ahead of his Phils.

In the first Temple Cup series the proposed division of the players' share from the gate receipts was 65 percent to the winning team and 35 percent to the losers, but the Orioles vetoed that arrangement. Feeling that the pennant was Baltimore's regardless and the match

THE FIRST GREAT FIREMAN

Even after the pitching distance was lengthened in 1893, starting pitchers were still expected to finish what they began. many teams, regardless of the score, stubbornly refused to lift a starter, and in consequence relief pitching was still an undiscovered art. The Cleveland Spiders were one of the first clubs to break with tradition after manager Patsy Tebeau realized he had something of a find in Nig Cuppy. In 1894, Cuppy won 24 games total but only 16 as a starter. His other eight relief victories came in relief stints. Those eight bonus wins set a post-1893 record for relief victories that lasted until 1915. What made Cuppy's feat even more spectacular is that he was unbeaten as a fireman in 1894 and at one point in his career was a perfect 14-0 in relief roles.

Unlike almost every other player in the 1890s, Nig Cuppy didn't mind playing in Baltimore, where fans were notoriously vicious toward visitors. Cuppy reveled in being hissed and would deliberately stall on the mound to invite spectators to boo and "count time" on him between pitches.

was little more than a series of exhibition games, each Orioles starter made a secret fifty/fifty deal with his counterpart on the Giants. The best-of-seven series then became a travesty as the Giants won four straight one-sided games with Rusie and Meekin bagging two victories each. Though the Giants were now officially the League-Association champions, no one outside of New York bought the fact that their victory meant anything, a problem that would haunt promoters of the Temple Cup series in each year of its short existence.

TRADER NED

No provision was made for player trades between teams in the original National Agreement. Accordingly, there were few deals as such until after the National League and the American Association merged, and prior to then players customarily changed teams during periods of interleague war—as in 1884–85, 1889–90 and 1891–92—or when they were released, sold or otherwise wore out their welcome.

By 1893 the climate and the rules had changed, and Baltimore's Ned Hanlon was quick to take advantage. His 1894–97 Orioles were the first dynasty to be assembled to a large extent via the trade route. Here's how Hanlon gathered the key members of his 1894 flock.

Holdovers from the 1891 AA Orioles: 3B, John McGraw; C, Wilbert Robinson; P, Sadie McMahon

From Pittsburgh: LF, Joe Kelley and $2,000 cash in a September, 1892, trade for George Van Haltren (the only deal where Hanlon gave up a player of equal value)

From Louisville: (1) SS, Hughie Jennings (along with Harry Taylor) in a June 1893 trade for Tim O'Rourke and cash. (2) P, George Hemming (a 20-game winner in 1895) in a late 1894 trade for Bert Inks and cash

From Brooklyn: LF, Willie Keeler and 1B, Dan Brouthers in a January 1894 trade for George Treadway and Billy Shindle

From St. Louis: (1) P, Bill Hawke, an early-season gift in 1893 (2) CF, Steve Brodie, a late-season gift in 1893 (3) P, Kid Gleason for a song early in 1894

From Washington: P, Duke Esper for two notes of a song in mid-1894

From the minors: 2B, Heinie Reitz in 1894

THE SEASONAL RECORD

	W	L	PCT	HOME	ROAD	GB
1. Baltimore Orioles	89	39	.695	52–15	37–24	—
2. New York Giants	88	44	.667	49–17	39–27	3
3. Boston Beaneaters	83	49	.629	44–19	39–30	8
4. Philadelphia Phillies	71	57	.555	48–20	23–37	18
5. Brooklyn Bridegrooms	70	61	.534	42–24	28–37	20.5
6. Cleveland Spiders	68	61	.527	35–24	33–37	21.5
7. Pittsburgh Pirates	65	65	.500	46–28	19–37	25
8. Chicago Colts	57	75	.432	35–30	22–45	34
9. St. Louis Browns	56	76	.424	34–32	22–44	35
10. Cincinnati Reds	55	75	.423	38–28	17–47	35
11. Washington Nationals	45	87	.341	32–30	13–57	46
12. Louisville Colonels	36	94	.277	24–37	12–57	54

	Bal	NY	Bos	Phi	Bro	Cle	Pit	Chi	StL	Cin	Was	Lou	
Baltimore	—	6	4	6	8	9	6	9	10	10	11	10	89
New York	6	—	6	5	7	9	8	11	7	7	10	12	88
Boston	8	6	—	6	6	9	8	7	6	8	9	10	83
Philadelphia	4	7	6	—	7	5	8	5	5	8	8	8	71
Brooklyn	4	5	6	5	—	6	7	6	8	6	9	8	70
Cleveland	3	3	3	7	5	—	4	10	9	8	8	8	68
Pittsburgh	4	4	4	4	5	8	—	6	6	7	8	9	65
Chicago	3	1	5	7	6	2	6	—	6	6	7	8	57
St. Louis	2	5	6	7	4	3	6	6	—	5	6	6	56
Cincinnati	2	5	4	3	6	3	5	6	7	—	7	7	55
Washington	1	2	3	4	3	4	4	5	6	5	—	8	45
Louisville	2	0	2	3	4	3	3	4	6	5	4	—	36
	39	44	49	57	61	61	65	75	76	75	87	94	781

SEASON LEADERS

Batting Average (350 ABs)

1.	Duffy, Boston	.440
2.	Delahanty, Philadelphia	.407
	Thompson, Philadelphia	.407
4.	Hamilton, Philadelphia	.404
5.	Kelley, Baltimore	.393

On–Base Percentage

1.	Hamilton, Philadelphia	.523
2.	Kelley, Baltimore	.502
	Duffy, Boston	.502
4.	Joyce, Washington	.496
5.	Delahanty, Philadelphia	.478

Home Runs

1.	Duffy, Boston	18
2.	Lowe, Boston	17
	Joyce, Washington	17
4.	Dahlen, Chicago	15
5.	Six with	13

Slugging Average

1.	Duffy, Boston	.694
2.	Thompson, Philadelphia	.686
3.	Joyce, Washington	.648
4.	Kelley, Baltimore	.602
5.	Delahanty, Philadelphia	.585

Total Bases

1.	Duffy, Boston	372
2.	Lowe, Boston	319
3.	Kelley, Baltimore	305
	Keeler, Baltimore	305
5.	Stenzel, Pittsburgh	303

RBI

1.	Duffy, Boston	145
2.	Thompson, Philadelphia	141
3.	Delahanty, Philadelphia	131
4.	Wilmot, Chicago	130
5.	McKean, Cleveland	128
	Brouthers, Baltimore	128

Hits

1.	Duffy, Boston	237
2.	Hamilton, Philadelphia	220
3.	Keeler, Baltimore	219
4.	Lowe, Boston	212
5.	Brodie, Baltimore	210

Stolen Bases

1.	Hamilton, Philadelphia	98
2.	McGraw, Baltimore	78
3.	Wilmot, Chicago	74
4.	T. Brown, Louisville	66
5.	Lange, Chicago	65

Runs

1.	Hamilton, Philadelphia	192
2.	Kelley, Baltimore	165
	Keeler, Baltimore	165
4.	Duffy, Boston	160
5.	Lowe, Boston	158

Strikeouts

1.	T. Brown, Louisville	73
2.	Treadway, Brooklyn	43
	Cartwright, Washington	43
4.	Daly, Brooklyn	42
	Bannon, Boston	42

PITCHING

Wins

1.	Rusie, New York	36
2.	Meekin, New York	33
3.	Nichols, Boston	32
4.	Breitenstein, St. Louis	27
5.	Stein, Brooklyn	26
	Stivetts, Boston	26
	Young, Cleveland	26

Innings

1.	Breitenstein, St. Louis	447.1
2.	Rusie, New York	444
3.	Meekin, New York	409
4.	Young, Cleveland	408.2
5.	Nichols, Boston	407

Strikeouts

1.	Rusie, New York	195
2.	Breitenstein, St. Louis	140
3.	Meekin, New York	133
4.	Hawley, St. Louis	120
5.	Nichols, Boston	113

ERA (140 innings)

1.	Rusie, New York	2.78
2.	Meekin, New York	3.70
3.	Mercer, Washington	3.85
4.	Young, Cleveland	3.94
5.	Taylor, Philadelphia	4.08

Losses

1.	Hawley, St. Louis	26
2.	Menefee, Lou-Pitt	25
3.	Breitenstein, St. Louis	23
	Mercer, Washington	23
5.	Dwyer, Cincinnati	22

Complete Games

1.	Breitenstein, St. Louis	46
2.	Rusie, New York	45
3.	Young, Cleveland	44
4.	Nichols, Boston	40
	Meekin, New York	40

Winning Percentage (25 decisions)

1.	Meekin, New York	.786
2.	McMahon, Baltimore	.758
3.	Rusie, New York	.735
4.	Nichols, Boston	.711
5.	Stein, Brooklyn	.659
	Stivetts, Boston	.659

Lowest On–Base Percentage

1.	Rusie, New York	.331
2.	Meekin, New York	.333
3.	J. Clarkson, Cleveland	.336
4.	Young, Cleveland	.338
5.	Nichols, Boston	.346

FIELDING

Total Chances

1B	Beckley, Pittsburgh	1341
2B	McPhee, Cincinnati	884
3B	Nash, Boston	505
SS	Jennings, Baltimore	869
OF	Abbey, Washington	407
C	Farrell, New York	648
P	Rusie, New York	155

Fielding Average

Anson, Chicago	.990
Reitz, Baltimore	.968
Nash, Boston	.933
Glasscock, Pittsburgh	.933
Thompson, Philadelphia	.977
Zimmer, Cleveland	.963
Cuppy, Cleveland	.975

BALTIMORE   **Ned Hanlon**   **Union Park**

		G	AB	H	R	2B	3B	HR	RBI	BB	SB	BA	SA
RF	Willie Keeler	129	590	219	165	27	22	5	94	40	32	.371	.517
CF	Steve Brodie	129	573	210	134	25	11	3	113	18	42	.366	.464
1B	Dan Brouthers	123	525	182	137	39	23	9	128	67	38	.347	.560
3B	John McGraw	120	512	174	156	18	14	1	92	91	78	.340	.436
LF	Joe Kelley	129	507	199	165	48	20	6	111	107	46	.393	.602
SS	Hughie Jennings	128	501	168	134	28	16	4	109	37	37	.335	.479
2B	Heinie Reitz	108	446	135	86	22	**31**	2	105	42	18	.303	.504
C	Wilbert Robinson	109	414	146	69	21	4	1	98	46	12	.353	.430
P	Sadie McMahon	35	126	36	17	5	1	0	25	9	1	.286	.341
Sub	Frank Bonner	33	118	38	27	10	2	0	24	17	12	.322	.441
Sub	Boileryard Clarke	28	100	24	18	8	0	1	19	16	2	.240	.350
P	Bill Hawke	32	92	28	12	5	1	1	16	3	1	.304	.413
P	Kid Gleason	29	86	30	22	5	1	0	17	7	1	.349	.430
P	Bert Inks	22	57	18	9	3	0	0	6	5	1	.316	.368
P	Tony Mullane	21	53	21	3	3	0	0	9	6	2	.396	.453
P	Duke Esper	16	45	10	9	3	1	0	6	4	0	.222	.333
P	Stub Brown	9	23	2	3	0	0	0	1	0	1	.087	.087
P	George Hemming	6	21	6	4	1	2	0	3	1	0	.286	.524
P	Jack Horner	2	6	1	1	0	1	0	0	0	0	.167	.500
P	Kirtly Baker	2	4	0	0	0	0	0	0	0	0	.000	.000
		129	4799	1647	1171	271	**150**	33	976	516	324	.343	.483

1B	Brouthers 123, Clarke 5, Gleason 1
2B	Reitz 97, Bonner 27, McGraw 6, Keeler 1
SS	Jennings 128, Bonner 1
3B	McGraw 118, Reitz 12, Bonner 2
OF	Kelley 129, Brodie 129, Keeler 128, Bonner 4, Baker 1
C	Robinson 109, Clarke 23
P	McMahon 35, Hawke 32, Inks 22, Gleason 21, Mullane 21, Esper 16, Brown 9, Hemming 6, Horner 2, Baker 1

	G	IP	GS	CG	W	L	K	BB	SH	SV	ERA
Sadie McMahon	35	275.2	33	26	25	8	60	111	0	0	4.21
Bill Hawke	32	206	25	17	16	9	68	78	0	3	5.81
Kid Gleason	21	172	20	19	15	5	35	44	0	0	4.45
Bert Inks	22	133	14	10	9	4	30	54	0	1	5.55
Tony Mullane	21	122.2	15	9	6	9	43	90	0	4	6.31
Duke Esper	16	101	9	8	10	2	25	36	0	2	3.92
Stub Brown	9	49.2	6	3	4	0	8	24	0	0	4.89
George Hemming	6	45.1	6	4	4	0	4	26	0	0	3.57
Jack Horner	2	11	1	1	0	1	2	7	0	1	9.00
Kirtley Baker	1	0	0	0	0	0	1	2	0	0	—
	*One combined shutout on May 7: Mullane 6 innings, Horner 3 innings										
	1116.1	129	97	89	39	275	472	1	**11**	5.00

NEW YORK   **Monte Ward**   **Polo Grounds (III)**

		G	AB	H	R	2B	3B	HR	RBI	BB	SB	BA	SA
LF	Eddie Burke	136	566	172	121	23	11	4	77	37	34	.304	.405
2B	Monte Ward	136	540	143	100	12	5	0	77	34	39	.265	.306
CF	George Van Haltren	137	519	172	109	22	4	7	104	55	43	.331	.430
3B	George Davis	124	477	168	120	26	19	8	91	66	40	.352	.537
RF	Mike Tiernan	112	424	117	84	19	13	5	77	54	28	.276	.417
1B	Jack Doyle	105	422	155	90	30	8	3	100	35	42	.367	.498
C	Duke Farrell	114	401	114	47	20	12	4	66	35	9	.284	.424
SS	Shorty Fuller	93	368	104	81	14	4	2	46	52	32	.283	.359
Sub	Yale Murphy	74	280	76	64	6	2	0	28	51	28	.271	.307
P	Amos Rusie	56	186	52	20	5	4	3	26	5	5	.280	.398
Sub	Parke Wilson	49	175	58	35	5	5	1	32	14	8	.331	.434
P	Jouett Meekin	52	170	48	28	2	7	5	29	7	3	.282	.465
Sub	Roger Connor	22	82	24	10	7	0	1	14	8	2	.293	.415
P	Les German	23	57	17	8	2	0	0	8	3	1	.298	.333
P	Huyler Westervelt	23	56	8	9	1	0	0	7	6	2	.143	.161
Sub	General Stafford	14	46	10	10	1	1	0	4	10	2	.217	.283
P	Dad Clarke	16	37	8	4	2	1	0	3	4	1	.216	.324
		137	4806	1446	940	197	96	43	789	476	319	.301	.409

1B   Doyle 99, Connor 21, Wilson 15, Farrell 4, Stafford 1, Murphy 1
2B   Ward 136, Stafford 1, Murphy 1, Fuller 1
SS   Fuller 89, Murphy 49
3B   Davis 124, Stafford 6, Farrell 5, Murphy 3, Fuller 2
OF   Van Haltren 137, Burke 136, Tiernan 111, Murphy 20, Stafford 5, Fuller 2, Connor 1
C   Farrell 104, Wilson 34, Doyle 6
P   Rusie 54, Meekin 52, Westervelt 23, German 23, Clarke 15

	G	IP	GS	CG	W	L	K	BB	SH	SV	ERA
Amos Rusie	54	444	50	45	36	13	**195**	**200**	**3**	1	**2.78**
Jouett Meekin	52	409	48	40	33	9	133	171	1	2	3.70
Huyler Westervelt	23	141	18	11	7	10	35	76	1	0	5.04
Les German	23	134	15	10	9	8	17	66	0	1	5.78
Dad Clarke	15	84	6	5	3	4	15	26	0	1	4.93
		1212	137	111	88	44	**395**	539	5	5	**3.83**

BOSTON   **Frank Selee**   **South End Grounds (II)***

		G	AB	H	R	2B	3B	HR	RBI	BB	SB	BA	SA
2B	Bobby Lowe	133	**613**	212	158	34	11	17	115	50	23	.346	.520
CF	Hugh Duffy	124	539	**237**	160	**51**	16	**18**	145	66	48	**.440**	**.694**
LF	Tommy McCarthy	127	539	188	118	21	8	13	126	59	43	.349	.490
3B	Billy Nash	132	512	148	132	23	6	8	87	91	20	.289	.404
1B	Tommy Tucker	123	500	165	112	24	6	3	100	53	18	.330	.420
RF	Jimmy Bannon	128	494	166	130	29	10	13	114	62	47	.336	.514
SS	Herman Long	104	475	154	136	28	11	12	79	35	24	.324	.505
C	Charlie Ganzel	70	266	74	51	7	6	3	56	19	1	.278	.383
P	Jack Stivetts	68	244	80	55	12	7	8	64	16	3	.328	.533
C	John Ryan	53	201	54	39	12	7	1	29	13	3	.269	.413
Sub	Frank Connaughton	46	171	59	42	9	2	2	33	16	3	.345	.456
P	Kid Nichols	51	170	50	39	11	2	0	34	16	1	.294	.382
Sub	Fred Tenney	27	86	34	23	7	1	2	21	12	6	.395	.570
P	Harry Staley	28	85	20	12	2	1	2	25	13	0	.235	.353
P	Tom Lovett	15	49	7	4	1	0	1	5	2	0	.143	.224
P	George Hodson	12	30	3	4	0	0	0	4	3	1	.100	.100
Sub	Bill Merritt	10	26	6	3	1	0	0	6	8	0	.231	.269
P	George Stultz	1	3	1	0	0	0	0	0	0	0	.333	.333
P	Scott Hawley	1	3	0	0	0	0	0	0	0	0	.000	.000
P	Henry Lampe	2	2	0	0	0	0	0	0	0	0	.000	.000
P	Tom Smith	2	2	0	1	0	0	0	0	1	0	.000	.000
P	Frank West	1	1	0	1	0	0	0	0	0	0	.000	.000
		133	5011	1658	**1220**	**272**	94	**103**	1043	535	242	.331	**.484**

1B   Tucker 123, Ganzel 7, Stivetts 4, Ryan 2, Tenney 1
2B   Lowe 130, Long 3, McCarthy 1, Ganzel 1
SS   Long 98, Connaughton 33, Duffy 2, Lowe 2, McCarthy 2, Ganzel 2
3B   Nash 132, Lowe 1
OF   Bannon 128, McCarthy 127, Duffy 124, Stivetts 16, Tenney 6, Long 5, Connaughton 4, Ganzel 3, Merritt 1, Nichols 1, Staley 1, Tucker 1
C   Ganzel 59, Ryan 51, Tenney 20, Merritt 8, Connaughton 7
P   Nichols 50, Stivetts 45, Staley 27, Lovett 15, Hodson 12, Smith 2, Lampe 2, Stultz 1, Hawley 1, West 1, Bannon 1, McCarthy 1

	G	IP	GS	CG	W	L	K	BB	SH	SV	ERA
Kid Nichols	50	407	46	40	32	13	113	121	**3**	0	4.75
Jack Stivetts	45	338	39	30	26	14	76	127	0	0	4.90
Harry Staley	27	208.2	21	18	12	10	32	61	0	0	6.81
Tom Lovett	15	104	13	10	8	6	23	36	0	0	5.97
George Hodson	12	74	11	8	4	4	12	35	0	0	5.84
George Stultz	1	9	1	1	1	0	1	5	0	0	0.00
Scott Hawley	1	7	1	1	0	1	1	7	0	0	7.71
Tom Smith	2	6	0	0	0	0	2	6	0	1	15.00
Henry Lampe	2	5.1	1	0	0	1	1	7	0	0	11.81
Frank West	1	3	0	0	0	0	1	2	0	0	9.00
Jimmy Bannon	1	2	0	0	0	0	0	1	0	0	0.00
Tommy McCarthy	1	2	0	0	0	0	0	3	0	0	4.50
		1166	133	108	83	49	262	**411**	3	1	5.41

* Boston's park was completely rebuilt after a fire destroyed the double–decked structure on May 15, 1894; the reconstructed park, known as South End Grounds (II), opened on July 20, 1894, and had only one deck so that it could be insured more cheaply. During the reconstruction Boston played its home games at Congress Street Park.

PHILADELPHIA	Arthur Irwin		Philadelphia Baseball Grounds*									
		G	AB	H	R	2B	3B	HR	RBI	BB	SB	BA	SA
CF	Billy Hamilton	131	544	220	**192**	25	15	4	87	126	**98**	.404	.528
3B	Lave Cross	119	529	204	123	34	9	7	125	29	21	.386	.524
2B	Bill Hallman	119	505	156	107	19	7	0	66	36	36	.309	.374
1B	Jack Boyle	114	495	149	98	21	10	4	88	45	21	.301	.408
LF	Ed Delahanty	114	489	199	147	39	18	4	131	60	21	.407	.585
RF	Sam Thompson	99	437	178	108	29	27	13	141	40	24	.407	.686
OF	Tuck Turner	80	339	141	91	21	9	1	82	23	11	.416	.540
SS	Joe Sullivan	75	304	107	63	10	8	3	63	23	10	.352	.467
C	Mike Grady	60	190	69	45	13	8	0	40	14	3	.363	.516
C	Dick Buckley	43	160	47	18	7	3	1	26	6	0	.294	.394
C	Jack Clements	45	159	55	26	6	5	3	36	24	6	.346	.503
Sub	Bob Allen	40	149	38	26	10	3	0	19	17	4	.255	.362
P	Jack Taylor	41	144	48	20	11	2	0	22	6	4	.333	.438
Sub	Charlie Reilly	39	135	40	21	1	2	0	19	16	9	.296	.333
P	Kid Carsey	35	125	34	30	2	2	0	18	16	3	.272	.320
P	Gus Weyhing	38	115	20	8	2	1	0	10	7	2	.174	.209
P	George Harper	12	40	6	7	2	0	0	3	2	0	.150	.200
P	George Haddock	10	29	5	2	0	2	0	1	3	0	.172	.310
P	Nixey Callahan	9	21	5	4	0	0	0	0	0	0	.238	.238
P	John Johnson	4	16	3	4	0	0	0	3	1	0	.188	.188
P	Jack Fanning	5	13	2	2	0	0	0	0	2	0	.154	.154
P	Al Lukens	3	8	0	0	0	0	0	0	0	0	.000	.000
P	Al Burris	1	4	2	0	0	0	0	0	0	0	.500	.500
P	Alex Jones	1	4	1	1	0	0	0	1	0	0	.250	.250
Sub	Tom Delahanty	1	4	1	0	0	0	0	0	0	0	.250	.250
Sub	Joe Yingling	1	4	1	0	0	0	0	0	0	0	.250	.250
P	Frank Figgemeier	1	3	1	0	0	0	0	0	0	0	.333	.333
Sub	Tom Murray	1	2	0	0	0	0	0	0	0	0	.000	.000
Sub	Arthur Irwin	1	0	0	0	0	0	0	0	0	0	—	—
P	Jack Scheible	1	0	0	0	0	0	0	0	0	0	—	—
		129	4967	**1732**	1143	252	131	40	981	496	273	**.349**	.476

1B   Boyle 114, E. Delahanty 12, Grady 11, Buckley 1, Reilly 1
2B   Hallman 119, E. Delahanty 6, Reilly 4, T. Delahanty 1, Boyle 1, Cross 1
SS   Sullivan 75, Allen 40, E. Delahanty 8, Murray 1, Irwin 1, Yingling 1, Reilly 1, Cross 1
3B   Cross 100, Reilly 28, E. Delahanty 9, Boyle 1
OF   Hamilton 129, Thompson 99, E. Delahanty 88, Turner 78, Reilly 5, Grady 2
C   Clements 45, Grady 44, Buckley 42, Cross 16
P   Taylor 41, Weyhing 38, Carsey 35, Harper 12, Haddock 10, Callahan 9, Fanning 5, Johnson 4, Lukens 3,
     Jones 1, Burris 1, Scheible 1, Turner 1, Figgemeier 1

* The Phillies' park was destroyed by fire on August 6, 1894. Temporary stands reopened on August 18.

	G	IP	GS	CG	W	L	K	BB	SH	SV	ERA
Jack Taylor	41	298	34	31	23	13	76	96	1	1	4.08
Kid Carsey	35	277	31	26	18	12	41	102	0	0	5.56
Gus Weyhing	38	266.1	34	25	16	14	81	116	2	1	5.81
George Harper	12	86.1	9	7	6	6	24	49	0	0	5.32
George Haddock	10	56	7	5	4	3	7	34	0	0	5.79
Nixey Callahan	9	33.2	2	1	1	2	9	17	0	2	9.89
John Johnson	4	32.2	3	2	1	1	10	15	0	0	6.06
Jack Fanning	5	32.1	4	2	1	3	7	20	0	0	8.07
Al Lukens	3	15	2	1	0	1	0	10	0	0	10.20
Alex Jones	1	9	1	1	1	0	2	0	0	0	2.00
Frank Figgemeier	1	8	1	1	0	1	2	4	0	0	11.25
Tuck Turner	1	6	0	0	0	0	3	2	0	0	7.50
Al Burris	1	5	0	0	0	0	0	2	0	0	18.00
Jack Scheible	1	0.1	1	0	0	1	0	2	0	0	189.00
	1125.2	129	102	71	57	262	469	3	4	5.63

BROOKLYN **Dave Foutz** **Eastern Park**

		G	AB	H	R	2B	3B	HR	RBI	BB	SB	BA	SA
SS	Tommy Corcoran	129	576	173	123	21	20	5	92	25	33	.300	.432
RF	Oyster Burns	125	505	179	106	32	14	5	107	44	30	.354	.503
2B	Tom Daly	123	492	168	135	22	10	8	82	77	51	.341	.476
LF	George Treadway	123	479	157	124	27	26	4	102	72	27	.328	.518
3B	Billy Shindle	116	476	141	94	22	9	4	96	29	19	.296	.405
CF	Mike Griffin	107	402	144	122	28	4	5	75	78	39	.358	.485
1B	Dave Foutz	72	293	90	40	12	9	0	51	14	14	.307	.410
1B	Candy LaChance	68	257	83	48	13	8	5	52	16	20	.323	.494
Sub	George Shoch	64	239	77	47	6	5	1	37	26	16	.322	.402C
C	Con Daily	67	234	60	40	14	7	0	32	31	8	.256	.376
C	Tom Kinslow	62	223	68	39	5	6	2	41	20	4	.305	.408
P	Brickyard Kennedy	48	161	49	22	7	3	0	23	3	2	.304	.385
P	Ed Stein	46	147	38	29	8	4	2	30	9	4	.259	.408
P	Dan Daub	34	95	18	12	0	1	0	15	7	1	.189	.211
Sub	John Anderson	17	63	19	14	1	3	1	19	3	7	.302	.460
Sub	Billy Earle	14	50	17	13	6	0	0	6	6	4	.340	.460
P	Hank Gastright	16	41	7	4	3	0	0	2	2	1	.171	.244
P	Con Lucid	10	33	7	4	1	0	0	1	0	0	.212	.242
Sub	Pete Gilbert	6	25	2	1	0	0	0	1	1	2	.080	.080
P	Fred Underwood	7	18	7	3	0	1	0	0	2	0	.389	.500
P	George Sharrott	2	3	1	0	0	0	0	0	0	0	.333	.333
Sub	Pete Browning	1	2	2	1	0	0	0	2	1	0	1.000	1.000
P	Jim Korwan	1	2	0	0	0	0	0	0	0	0	.000	.000
P	Andy Somerville	1	0	0	0	0	0	0	0	0	0	—	—
		134	4816	1507	1021	228	130	42	162	466	282	.313	.440

1B	Foutz 72, LaChance 56, Daily 7, Treadway 1, Kinslow 1
2B	Daly 123, Shoch 9, Gilbert 3, Earle 1
SS	Corcoran 129, Shoch 6
3B	Shindle 116, Shoch 14, Gilbert 3, Anderson 1
OF	Burns 125, Treadway 122, Griffin 106, Shoch 35, Anderson 16, LaChance 3, Browning 1, Stein 1, Daub 1
C	Kinslow 61, Daily 60, Earle 12, LaChance 10
P	Kennedy 48, Stein 44, Daub 34, Gastright 16, Lucid 10, Underwood 7, Sharrott 2, Somerville 1, Korwan 1, Foutz 1

	G	IP	GS	CG	W	L	K	BB	SH	SV	ERA
Brickyard Kennedy	48	360.2	41	34	24	20	107	149	0	2	4.92
Ed Stein	44	350	40	37	26	14	84	170	2	1	4.63
Dan Daub	34	224	27	15	10	12	45	91	0	0	6.11
Hank Gastright	16	93	8	6	2	6	20	55	1	2	6.39
Con Lucid	10	71.1	9	7	5	3	15	44	0	0	6.56
Fred Underwood	7	47	6	5	2	4	10	30	0	0	7.85
George Sharrott	2	9	2	1	0	1	2	5	0	0	7.00
Jim Korwan	1	5	0	0	0	0	2	5	0	0	14.40
Dave Foutz	1	2	0	0	0	0	0	1	0	0	13.50
Andy Sommerville	1	0.1	1	0	0	1	0	5	0	0	162.00
—1 forfeit W vs Washington on May 1—											
	1162.1	134	105	69	61	285	555	3	5	5.51

CLEVELAND   Patsy Tebeau   League Park (I)

		G	AB	H	R	2B	3B	HR	RBI	BB	SB	BA	SA
SS	Ed McKean	130	554	198	116	30	15	8	128	49	33	.357	.509
LF	Jesse Burkett	125	523	187	138	27	14	8	94	84	28	.358	.509
1B	Patsy Tebeau	125	523	158	82	23	7	3	89	35	30	.302	.390
3B	Chippy McGarr	128	523	144	94	24	6	2	74	28	31	.275	.356
2B	Cupid Childs	118	479	169	143	21	12	2	52	107	17	.353	.459
C	Chief Zimmer	90	341	97	55	20	5	4	65	17	14	.284	.408
C	Jack O'Connor	86	330	104	67	23	7	2	51	15	15	.315	.445
RF	Harry Blake	73	296	78	51	15	4	1	51	30	1	.264	.351
CF	Jimmy McAleer	64	253	73	36	15	1	2	40	13	14	.289	.379
OF	Buck Ewing	53	211	53	32	12	4	2	39	24	18	.251	.374
P	Cy Young	52	186	40	24	8	4	2	26	2	4	.215	.333
Sub	White Wings Tebeau	40	150	47	32	9	4	0	25	25	9	.313	.427
P	Nig Cuppy	44	135	35	28	6	3	0	19	15	3	.259	.348
Sub	Jake Virtue	29	89	23	15	4	1	0	10	13	1	.258	.326
P	John Clarkson	22	55	11	8	0	0	1	7	6	1	.200	.255
P	Mike Sullivan	13	44	13	6	1	1	0	8	2	0	.295	.364
P	Frank Griffith	7	24	8	4	2	2	0	9	1	0	.333	.583
P	Bobby Wallace	4	13	2	0	1	0	0	1	0	0	.154	.231
P	Tony Mullane	4	13	1	0	0	0	0	0	4	1	.077	.077
P	Charlie Petty	4	12	1	0	0	0	0	0	0	0	.083	.083
P	Frank Knauss	2	4	0	1	0	0	0	1	1	0	.000	.000
P	Chauncey Fisher	3	4	0	0	0	0	0	1	0	0	.000	.000
P	Bill Lyston	1	2	0	0	0	0	0	0	0	0	.000	.000
P	Tom Thomas	1	0	0	0	0	0	0	0	0	0	—	—
		130	4764	1442	932	241	90	37	790	471	220	.303	.414

1B P. Tebeau 115, W. Tebeau 12, O'Connor 7, Virtue 2
2B Childs 118, P. Tebeau 10, Virtue 3, Ewing 1
SS McKean 130, P. Tebeau 1
3B McGarr 128, P. Tebeau 2, W. Tebeau 1
OF Burkett 125, Blake 73, McAleer 64, Ewing 52, O'Connor 33, W. Tebeau 27, Virtue 21, Clarkson 1, Cuppy 1, Griffith 1
C Zimmer 89, O'Connor 45
P Young 52, Cuppy 43, Clarkson 22, Sullivan 13, Griffith 7, Mullane 4, Wallace 4, Petty 4, Fisher 3, Knauss 2, Lyston 1, Virtue 1, Thomas 1, Burkett 1

	G	IP	GS	CG	W	L	K	BB	SH	SV	ERA
Cy Young	52	408.2	47	44	26	21	108	106	2	1	3.94
Nig Cuppy	43	316	33	29	24	15	65	128	3	0	4.56
John Clarkson	22	150.2	18	13	8	10	28	46	1	0	4.42
Mike Sullivan	13	90.2	11	9	6	5	19	47	0	0	6.35
Frank Griffith	7	42.1	6	3	1	2	15	37	0	0	9.99
Tony Mullane	4	33	4	3	1	2	3	10	0	0	7.64
Charlie Petty	4	27	3	2	0	2	4	14	0	0	8.67
Bobby Wallace	4	26	3	2	2	1	10	20	0	0	5.19
Chauncey Fisher	3	11	2	0	0	2	0	5	0	0	11.45
Frank Knauss	2	11	2	1	0	1	2	14	0	0	5.73
Jesse Burkett	1	4	0	0	0	0	0	1	0	0	4.50
Bill Lyston	1	3.2	1	0	0	0	0	4	0	0	9.82
Tom Thomas	1	0.1	0	0	0	0	0	2	0	0	27.00
Jake Virtue	1	0	0	0	0	0	0	1	0	0	—
		1124.1	130	106	68	61	254	435	6	1	4.97

PITTSBURGH **Al Buckenberger (53–55)** **Connie Mack (12–10)** **Exposition Park**

		G	AB	H	R	2B	3B	HR	RBI	BB	SB	BA	SA
RF	Patsy Donovan	132	576	174	145	21	10	4	76	33	41	.302	.394
1B	Jake Beckley	131	533	183	121	36	18	7	120	43	21	.343	.518
2B	Lou Bierbauer	130	525	159	86	19	13	3	107	26	19	.303	.406
CF	Jake Stenzel	131	522	185	148	39	20	13	121	75	61	.354	.580
LF	Elmer Smith	125	489	174	128	33	19	6	72	65	33	.356	.538
SS	Jack Glasscock	86	332	93	46	10	7	1	63	31	18	.280	.361
3B	Denny Lyons	71	254	82	51	14	4	4	50	42	14	.323	.457
C	Connie Mack	69	228	57	32	7	1	1	21	20	8	.250	.303
3B	Fred Hartman	49	182	58	41	4	7	2	20	16	12	.319	.451
C	Joe Sugden	39	139	.46	23	13	2	2	23	14	3	.331	.496
P	Red Ehret	46	135	23	6	4	1	0	11	8	0	.170	.215
Sub	Farmer Weaver	30	115	40	16	7	2	0	24	6	4	.348	.443
P	Ad Gumbert	38	113	33	18	4	5	1	19	6	1	.292	.442
Sub	Bill Merritt	34	109	30	18	1	2	1	18	15	2	.275	.349
Sub	Frank Scheibeck	28	102	36	20	2	3	1	10	11	7	.353	.461
P	Frank Killen	28	80	21	13	3	1	0	13	6	0	.263	.325
P	Tom Colcolough	22	70	14	10	2	2	0	6	5	1	.200	.286
P	Jock Menefee	13	47	12	6	1	2	0	7	3	2	.255	.362
Sub	Monte Cross	13	43	19	14	1	5	2	13	5	6	.442	.837
Sub	Gene Steere	10	39	8	3	0	0	0	4	2	2	.205	.205
P	George Nicol	8	20	9	8	1	0	0	3	0	0	.450	.500
Sub	Gene Demontreville	2	8	2	0	0	0	0	0	1	0	.250	.250
P	Jack Easton	3	5	0	0	0	0	0	2	0	0	.000	.000
Sub	Jim Ritz	1	4	0	1	0	0	0	0	0	1	.000	.000
P	Harry Jordan	1	3	0	0	0	0	0	0	1	0	.000	.000
P	Phil Knell	1	3	0	1	0	0	0	0	0	0	.000	.000
P	Adonis Terry	1	0	0	0	0	0	0	0	0	0	—	—
		132	4676	1458	955	222	124	48	803	434	256	.312	.443

1B Beckley 131, Merritt 4
2B Bierbauer 130, Scheibeck 2
SS Glasscock 85, Cross 13, Weaver 12, Scheibeck 11, Steere 10, Sugden 3, Demontreville 2
3B Lyons 71, Hartman 49, Weaver 5, Sugden 4, Scheibeck 3, Ritz 1
OF Donovan 132, Stenzel 131, Smith 125, Scheibeck 9, Merritt 2, Sugden 1, Weaver 1
C Mack 69, Sugden 31, Merritt 28, Weaver 14
P Ehret 46, Gumbert 37, Killen 28, Colcolough 22, Menefee 13, Nicol 8, Easton 3, Terry 1, Jordan 1, Knell 1, Smith 1

	G	IP	GS	CG	W	L	K	BB	SH	SV	ERA
Red Ehret	46	346.2	38	31	19	21	102	128	1	0	5.14
Ad Gumbert	37	269	31	26	15	14	65	84	0	0	6.02
Frank Killen	28	204	28	20	14	11	62	86	1	0	4.50
Tom Colcolough	22	146.2	14	11	8	5	29	70	0	0	7.08
Jock Menefee	13	111.2	13	13	5	8	33	39	0	0	5.40
George Nicol	8	44.1	5	3	3	4	11	33	0	0	6.50
Jack Easton	3	19.2	1	1	0	1	1	4	0	0	4.12
Harry Jordan	1	9	1	1	1	0	1	2	0	0	4.00
Phil Knell	1	7	0	0	0	0	0	6	0	0	11.57
Elmer Smith	1	4	0	0	0	0	0	1	0	0	4.50
Adonis Terry	1	0.2	1	0	0	1	0	4	0	0	67.50
		1164.2	132	106	65	65	304	457	2	0	5.60

CHICAGO   Cap Anson   West Side Park (II)

		G	AB	H	R	2B	3B	HR	RBI	BB	SB	BA	SA
LF	Walt Wilmot	133	597	197	134	45	12	5	130	35	74	.330	.471
2B	Jiggs Parrott	124	517	128	82	17	9	3	64	16	30	.248	.333
SS	Bill Dahlen	121	502	179	149	32	14	15	107	76	42	.357	.566
3B	Charlie Irwin	128	498	144	84	24	9	8	95	63	35	.289	.422
RF	Jimmy Ryan	108	474	171	132	37	7	3	62	50	11	.361	.487
CF	Bill Lange	111	442	145	84	16	9	6	90	56	65	.328	.446
UT	George Decker	91	384	120	74	17	6	8	92	24	23	.313	.451
C	Pop Schriver	96	349	96	55	12	3	3	47	29	9	.275	.352
1B	Cap Anson	83	340	132	82	28	4	5	99	40	17	.388	.538
C	Mal Kittridge	51	168	53	36	8	2	0	23	26	2	.315	.387
P	Clark Griffith	46	142	33	27	5	4	0	15	23	6	.232	.324
P	Bill Hutchison	39	136	42	30	3	0	6	16	11	2	.309	.463
P	Scott Stratton	23	96	36	29	5	4	3	23	6	3	.375	.604
P	Adonis Terry	30	95	33	19	4	2	0	17	11	3	.347	.432
P	Willie McGill	27	82	20	10	5	0	0	3	15	1	.244	.305
Sub	Sam Dungan	10	39	9	5	2	0	0	3	7	1	.231	.282
P	Bert Abbey	11	39	5	3	0	0	0	4	2	1	.128	.128
Sub	Llewellyn Camp	8	33	6	1	2	0	0	1	1	0	.182	.242
Sub	John Houseman	4	15	6	5	3	1	0	4	5	2	.400	.733
P	Kid Camp	3	11	0	0	0	0	0	0	0	0	.000	.000
P	Fritz Clausen	1	1	0	0	0	0	0	0	0	0	.000	.000
		135	4960	1555	1041	265	86	65	895	496	**327**	.314	.441

1B   Anson 82, Decker 48, Schriver 2, Stratton 2, Terry 2
2B   Parrott 123, L. Camp 8, Decker 2, Houseman 1, Anson 1
SS   Dahlen 66, Irwin 61, Houseman 3, Schriver 3, Lange 2, Decker 1, Griffith 1
3B   Irwin 67, Dahlen 55, Decker 7, Schriver 3, Parrott 1, Lange 1
OF   Wilmot 133, Lange 109, Ryan 108, Decker 29, Dungan 10, Terry 7, Griffith 7, Stratton 5, Hutchison 4
C   Schriver 88, Kittridge 51
P   Hutchison 36, Griffith 36, McGill 27, Terry 23, Stratton 15, Abbey 11, K. Camp 3, Clausen 1

	G	IP	GS	CG	W	L	K	BB	SH	SV	ERA
Bill Hutchison	36	277.2	34	28	14	16	59	140	0	0	6.06
Clark Griffith	36	261.1	30	28	21	14	71	85	0	0	4.92
Willie McGill	27	208	23	22	7	19	58	117	0	0	5.84
Adonis Terry	23	163.1	21	16	5	11	39	123	0	0	5.84
Scott Stratton	15	119.2	12	11	8	5	23	40	0	0	6.03
Bert Abbey	11	92	11	10	2	7	24	37	0	0	5.18
Kid Camp	3	22	2	2	0	1	6	12	0	0	6.55
Fritz Clausen	1	4.1	1	0	0	1	1	3	0	0	10.38
—1 forfeit L vs Louisville on August 3—											
		1148	134	**117**	57	74	281	557	0	0	5.68

ST. LOUIS Doggie Miller Sportsman's Park (II)

		G	AB	H	R	2B	3B	HR	RBI	BB	SB	BA	SA
CF	Frank Shugart	133	527	154	103	19	18	7	72	38	21	.292	.436
RF	Tom Dowd	123	524	142	92	16	8	4	62	54	31	.271	.355
SS	Bones Ely	127	510	156	85	20	12	12	89	30	23	.306	.463
3B	Doggie Miller	127	481	163	93	9	11	8	86	58	17	.339	.453
2B	Joe Quinn	106	405	116	59	18	1	4	61	24	25	.286	.365
1B	Roger Connor	99	380	122	83	28	25	7	79	51	17	.321	.582
C	Heinie Peitz	99	338	89	52	19	9	3	49	43	14	.263	.399
LF	Charlie Frank	80	319	89	52	12	7	4	42	44	14	.279	.398
Sub	Duff Cooley	54	206	61	35	3	1	1	21	12	7	.296	.335
P	Ted Breitenstein	63	182	40	27	7	2	0	13	31	3	.220	.280
P	Pink Hawley	53	163	43	16	6	6	2	23	5	2	.264	.411
Sub	Art Twineham	38	127	40	22	4	1	1	16	9	2	.315	.386
Sub	Marty Hogan	29	100	28	11	3	4	0	13	3	7	.280	.390
Sub	Dick Buckley	29	89	16	5	1	2	1	3	6	1	.180	.270
P	Dad Clarkson	33	88	16	11	0	1	0	7	16	1	.182	.205
Sub	Tim O'Rourke	18	71	20	10	4	1	0	10	8	2	.282	.366
P	Kid Gleason	9	28	7	3	0	1	0	1	2	0	.250	.321
Sub	Joe Peitz	7	26	11	10	2	3	0	3	6	2	.423	.731
P	Ernie Mason	4	12	3	0	0	0	0	0	1	0	.250	.250
Sub	Paul Russell	3	10	1	1	0	0	0	0	0	0	.100	.100
Sub	Willard Brown	3	9	1	0	0	0	0	0	0	0	.111	.111
Sub	Pete Browning	2	7	1	1	0	0	0	0	0	0	.143	.143
Sub	George Paynter	1	4	0	0	0	0	0	0	1	1	.000	.000
Sub	Art Ball	1	3	1	0	0	0	0	0	0	0	.333	.333
Sub	John Ricks	1	1	0	0	0	0	0	0	0	0	.000	.000
		133	4610	1320	771	171	113	54	650	442	190	.286	.408

1B   Connor 99, H. Peitz 14, Miller 12, Frank 3, Brown 3, Buckley 1, Gleason 1, Cooley 1
2B   Quinn 106, Miller 18, Dowd 7, Ely 1, Russell 1, Ball 1
SS   Ely 126, Shugart 7, Cooley 1, Miller 1
3B   Miller 52, H. Peitz 47, O'Rourke 18, Cooley 13, Shugart 7, Russell 1, Ricks 1, Dowd 1
OF   Shugart 122, Dowd 117, Frank 77, Cooley 39, Hogan 29, J. Peitz 7, Breitenstein 7, Miller 4, Browning 2, Hawley 1, Paynter 1, Russell 1, Mason 1
C   Miller 41, H. Peitz 39, Twineham 38, Buckley 27
P   Breitenstein 56, Hawley 53, Clarkson 32, Gleason 8, Mason 4, Frank 2, Ely 1, H. Peitz 1

	G	IP	GS	CG	W	L	K	BB	SH	SV	ERA
Ted Breitenstein	**56**	**447.1**	50	**46**	27	23	140	191	1	0	4.79
Pink Hawley	53	392.2	41	36	19	27	120	140	0	0	4.90
Dad Clarkson	32	233.1	32	24	8	17	46	117	1	0	6.36
Kid Gleason	8	58	8	6	2	6	9	21	0	0	6.05
Ernie Mason	4	22.2	2	2	0	3	3	10	0	0	7.15
Charlie Frank	2	3	0	0	0	0	1	7	0	0	15.00
Heinie Peitz	1	3	0	0	0	0	0	2	0	0	9.00
Bones Ely	1	1	0	0	0	0	0	3	0	0	0.00
		1161	133	114	56	76	319	500	2	0	5.29

CINCINNATI **Charlie Comiskey** **League Park (II)**

		G	AB	H	R	2B	3B	HR	RBI	BB	SB	BA	SA
3B	Arlie Latham	129	524	164	129	23	6	4	60	60	59	.313	.403
LF	Bug Holliday	122	511	190	119	24	7	13	119	40	29	.372	.523
CF	Dummy Hoy	128	495	148	114	22	13	5	70	87	27	.299	.426
SS	Germany Smith	127	482	127	73	33	5	3	76	41	15	.263	.371
2B	Bid McPhee	126	474	144	107	21	9	5	88	90	33	.304	.418
RF	Jimmy Canavan	101	356	97	77	16	9	13	70	62	13	.272	.478
Sub	Farmer Vaughn	72	284	88	50	15	5	8	64	12	5	.310	.482
C	Morg Murphy	75	255	70	42	9	0	1	37	26	6	.275	.322
P	Tom Parrott	68	229	74	51	12	6	4	40	17	4	.323	.480
1B	Charlie Comiskey	61	220	58	26	8	0	0	33	5	10	.264	.300
P	Frank Dwyer	54	172	46	31	9	2	2	28	15	0	.267	.378
Sub	Jack McCarthy	40	167	45	29	9	1	0	21	17	3	.269	.335
Sub	Bill Merritt	29	113	37	17	6	1	1	21	9	4	.327	.425
P	Icebox Chamberlain	23	70	22	10	7	1	1	7	7	2	.314	.486
Sub	Frank Motz	18	69	14	8	4	0	0	12	9	2	.203	.261
P	Bill Whitrock	18	60	13	8	1	0	0	8	2	1	.217	.233
Sub	Bill Massey	13	53	15	7	3	0	0	5	3	0	.283	.340
P	Chauncey Fisher	11	43	10	5	1	1	1	4	1	0	.233	.372
P	Lem Cross	8	26	6	3	1	1	0	4	1	0	.231	.346
Sub	Marty Hogan	6	23	3	4	0	0	0	3	1	2	.130	.130
P	Henry Fournier	6	19	2	0	0	0	0	1	1	0	.105	.105
P	Jesse Tannehill	5	11	0	0	0	0	0	1	1	0	.000	.000
Sub	Connie Murphy	1	4	0	0	0	0	0	0	1	0	.000	.000
P	? McGuire	1	4	1	0	0	0	0	0	0	0	.250	.250
P	Carney Flynn	2	3	0	0	0	0	0	0	0	0	.000	.000
P	Fred Blank	1	3	0	0	0	0	0	0	0	0	.000	.000
P	Bill Pfann	1	1	0	0	0	0	0	0	0	0	.000	.000
		132	4671	1374	910	224	67	61	772	508	215	.294	.410

1B Comiskey 60, Vaughn 27, Motz 18, McCarthy 15, Parrott 12, Massey 10, Merritt 1, Canavan 1, Holliday 1
2B McPhee 126, Massey 2, Latham 2, Canavan 1, Parrott 1
SS Smith 127, Vaughn 3, Canavan 3, Dwyer 2, M. Murphy 1, Parrott 1
3B Latham 127, Merritt 3, Canavan 2, M Murphy 1, Massey 1, Parrott 1, Whitrock 1
OF Hoy 128, Holliday 119, Canavan 95, McCarthy 25, Parrott 13, Dwyer 10, Vaughn 8, Whitrock 7, Hogan 6, Merritt 1, Comiskey 1,
C M. Murphy 74, Vaughn 43, Merritt 24, C. Murphy 1
P Dwyer 45, Parrott 41, Chamberlain 23, Fisher 11, Whitrock 10, Cross 8, Fournier 6, Tannehill 5, Flynn 2, Pfann 1, Blank 1, McGuire 1

	G	IP	GS	CG	W	L	K	BB	SH	SV	ERA
Frank Dwyer	45	348	40	34	19	22	49	106	1	1	5.07
Tom Parrott	41	308.2	36	31	17	19	61	126	1	1	5.60
Icebox Chamberlain	23	177.2	22	18	10	9	57	91	1	0	5.77
Chauncey Fisher	11	91	11	10	2	8	14	44	0	0	7.32
Bill Whitrock	10	70.1	8	8	2	6	9	39	0	0	6.65
Lem Cross	8	53	7	3	3	4	11	21	0	0	8.49
Henry Fournier	6	45	4	4	1	3	5	20	0	0	5.40
Jesse Tannehill	5	29	1	1	1	0	7	16	0	1	7.14
Fred Blank	1	8	1	1	0	1	1	9	0	0	4.50
Carney Flynn	2	7.2	1	0	0	2	4	10	0	0	17.61
? McGuire	1	6	0	0	0	0	1	5	0	0	10.50
Bill Pfann	1	3	1	0	0	1	0	4	0	0	27.00
*One combined shutout on June 30: Tannehill 3 innings, Parrott 6 innings											
	1147.1	132	110	55	75	219	491	4	3	5.99	

WASHINGTON Gus Schmelz   Boundary Field

		G	AB	H	R	2B	3B	HR	RBI	BB	SB	BA	SA
CF	Charlie Abbey	129	523	164	95	26	18	7	101	58	31	.314	.472
1B	Ed Cartwright	132	507	149	88	35	13	12	106	57	31	.294	.485
RF	Bill Hassamaer	118	494	159	106	33	17	4	90	41	16	.322	.482
C	Deacon McGuire	104	425	130	67	18	6	6	78	33	11	.306	.419
LF	Kip Selbach	97	372	114	69	21	17	7	71	51	21	.306	.511
3B	Bill Joyce	99	355	126	103	25	14	17	89	87	21	.355	.648
2B	Piggy Ward	98	347	105	86	11	7	0	36	80	41	.303	.375
UT	Paul Radford	95	325	78	61	13	5	0	49	65	24	.240	.311
Sub	White Wings Tebeau	61	222	50	41	10	6	0	28	37	17	.225	.324
SS	Frank Scheibeck	52	196	45	49	2	4	0	17	45	11	.230	.281
P	Win Mercer	53	164	48	29	5	2	2	29	9	9	.293	.384
Sub	Dan Dugdale	38	134	32	19	4	2	0	16	13	7	.239	.299
P	Al Maul	41	125	30	23	3	3	2	20	14	1	.240	.360
P	Otis Stocksdale	24	71	23	10	1	0	0	6	2	2	.324	.338
Sub	Joe Sullivan	17	60	15	7	3	0	0	5	6	3	.250	.300
P	Mike Sullivan	20	57	9	4	1	1	1	7	2	0	.158	.263
P	Duke Esper	19	54	14	7	3	1	1	4	4	0	.259	.407
P	Charlie Petty	16	41	8	5	0	1	0	3	4	0	.195	.244
Sub	Tim O'Rourke	7	25	5	4	2	1	0	2	2	0	.200	.360
P	Jake Boyd	6	21	3	1	0	0	0	1	1	2	.143	.143
P	George Haddock	5	16	3	4	2	0	0	3	1	1	.188	.313
P	John Malarkey	4	14	1	1	0	0	0	0	0	0	.071	.071
Sub	Kid Mohler	3	9	1	0	0	0	0	0	2	0	.111	.111
P	Varney Anderson	2	7	3	2	0	0	0	0	0	0	.429	.429
Sub	Count Campau	2	7	1	1	0	0	0	0	1	0	.143	.143
P	Ben Stephens	3	4	1	0	0	0	0	0	0	0	.250	.250
P	Rip Egan	1	3	0	0	0	0	0	1	1	0	.000	.000
P	Bill Wynne	1	3	0	0	0	0	0	0	1	0	.000	.000
		132	4581	1317	882	218	118	59	762	**617**	249	.287	.425

1B   Cartwright 132
2B   Ward 79, Radford 25, Hassamaer 14, J. Sullivan 8, O'Rourke 4, Mohler 3, Stocksdale 2
SS   Scheibeck 52, Radford 47, Selbach 19, J. Sullivan 6, Hassamaer 4, Ward 3, O'Rourke 3, Stocksdale 1
3B   Joyce 99, Hassamaer 31, Dugdale 3, Ward 1, Stocksdale 1, J. Sullivan 1
OF   Abbey 129, Selbach 80, Hassamaer 68, Tebeau 61, Radford 24, Ward 12, Maul 14, Stocksdale 4, Mercer 4, Boyd 3, Campau 2, Dugdale 2, Haddock 1, J. Sullivan 1, Malarkey 1, Esper 1, M. Sullivan 1
C   McGuire 104, Dugdale 33
P   Mercer 50, Maul 29, M. Sullivan 20, Esper 18, Stocksdale 18, Petty 16, Haddock 4, Stephens 3, Boyd 3, Malarkey 3, Anderson 2, Wynne 1, Egan 1

	G	IP	GS	CG	W	L	K	BB	SH	SV	ERA
Win Mercer	50	336.1	38	29	17	23	72	126	0	3	3.85
Al Maul	29	204.2	27	21	11	15	34	73	0	0	5.94
Mike Sullivan	20	117.2	12	11	2	10	21	74	0	1	6.58
Otis Stocksdale	18	117.1	14	11	5	9	10	42	0	0	5.06
Charlie Petty	16	103	12	8	3	8	14	32	0	0	5.59
Duke Esper	18	116	14	7	5	10	24	39	0	0	7.45
George Haddock	4	29	4	4	0	4	1	17	0	0	8.69
John Malarkey	3	26	3	3	2	1	3	5	0	0	4.15
Jake Boyd	3	19	3	3	0	3	3	14	0	0	8.53
Varney Anderson	2	14	2	2	0	2	3	6	0	0	7.07
Ben Stephens	3	11	2	1	0	0	1	8	0	0	4.91
Bill Wynne	1	8	1	1	0	1	2	8	0	0	6.75
Rip Egan	1	5	0	0	0	0	2	2	0	0	10.80
—1 forfeit L vs Brooklyn on May 1—											
		1107	132	101	45	86	190	446	0	4	5.51

LOUISVILLE   Billy Barnie   Eclipse Park (II)

		G	AB	H	R	2B	3B	HR	RBI	BB	SB	BA	SA
CF	Tom Brown	129	536	136	122	22	14	9	57	60	66	.254	.397
SS	Danny Richardson	116	430	109	51	17	2	1	40	35	8	.253	.309
C	John Grim	108	410	122	66	27	7	7	70	16	14	.298	.449
2B	Fred Pfeffer	104	409	126	68	12	14	5	59	30	31	.308	.443
LF	Fred Clarke	76	310	83	54	11	7	7	48	25	25	.268	.416
1B	Luke Lutenberg	69	250	48	42	10	4	0	23	23	4	.192	.264
Sub	Farmer Weaver	64	244	54	19	5	2	3	24	7	3	.221	.295
3B	Jerry Denny	60	221	61	26	11	7	0	32	13	10	.276	.389
Sub	Tim O'Rourke	55	220	61	46	3	3	0	27	23	9	.277	.318
Sub	Larry Twitchell	52	210	56	28	16	3	2	32	15	8	.267	.400
Sub	Pat Flaherty	38	145	43	15	5	3	0	15	9	2	.297	.372
RF	Ollie Smith	38	134	40	26	6	1	3	20	27	13	.299	.425
P	George Hemming	36	131	33	20	2	6	2	10	5	2	.252	.405
P	Phil Knell	32	113	31	10	2	4	1	13	0	1	.274	.389
Sub	George Nicol	27	108	38	12	6	4	0	19	2	4	.352	.481
Sub	Pete Gilbert	28	108	33	13	3	1	1	14	5	2	.306	.380
P	Jock Menefee	29	79	13	7	1	0	0	4	8	2	.165	.177
P	Jack Wadsworth	22	74	19	9	5	1	0	10	4	0	.257	.351
Sub	Billy Earle	22	65	23	10	1	0	0	7	9	2	.354	.369
Sub	Willard Brown	13	48	10	5	2	0	0	9	5	1	.208	.250
Sub	Fred Zahner	13	45	9	7	0	1	0	3	3	2	.200	.244
Sub	Fred Lake	16	42	12	8	2	0	1	10	11	2	.286	.405
P	Scott Stratton	13	37	12	9	1	2	0	4	4	1	.324	.459
Sub	Sam Dungan	8	32	11	6	1	0	0	3	4	2	.344	.375
Sub	Henry Cote	10	31	9	7	2	2	0	3	5	2	.290	.484
P	Bert Inks	8	27	12	4	0	0	0	3	1	0	.444	.444
P	Matt Kilroy	8	17	2	2	0	0	0	1	1	1	.118	.118
P	Bill Peppers	2	4	0	0	0	0	0	0	0	0	.000	.000
P	Bill Whitrock	1	2	0	0	0	0	0	0	0	0	.000	.000
		130	4482	1206	692	173	88	42	560	350	217	.269	.375

1B Lutenberg 67, O'Rourke 30, Brown 13, Weaver 10, Grim 7, Zahner 1, Earle 1, Hemming 1
2B Pfeffer 90, Grim 24, Richardson 10, Lake 6, Lutenberg 2, O'Rourke 2, Earle 1, Weaver 1
SS Richardson 107, Pfeffer 15, Weaver 12, Lake 5, O'Rourke 3, Menefee 1
3B Denny 60, Flaherty 38, Gilbert 28, O'Rourke 3, Grim 1, Earle 1
OF Brown 129, Clarke 76, Twitchell 51, O. Smith 38, Weaver 35, Nicol 26, O'Rourke 18, Dungan 8, Stratton 5, Zahner 2, Earle 1
C   Grim 77, Earle 18, Weaver 17, Cote 10, Zahner 10, Lake 5
P   Hemming 35, Knell 32, Menefee 28, Wadsworth 22, Inks 8, Kilroy 8, Stratton 7, Peppers 2, Whitrock 1, Twitchell 1, Nicol 1, Pfeffer 1

	G	IP	GS	CG	W	L	K	BB	SH	SV	ERA
George Hemming	35	294.1	32	32	13	19	66	133	1	1	4.37
Phil Knell	32	247	28	25	7	21	67	104	0	0	5.32
Jock Menefee	28	211.2	24	20	8	17	43	50	1	0	4.29
Jack Wadsworth	22	173	22	20	4	18	57	103	0	0	7.60
Bert Inks	8	59.2	8	8	2	6	8	34	0	0	6.49
Scott Stratton	7	43	5	4	1	5	3	13	0	0	8.37
Matt Kilroy	8	37	7	3	0	5	11	20	0	0	3.89
George Nicol	1	9	1	1	0	1	3	5	0	0	15.00
Bill Peppers	2	8	1	0	0	1	0	4	0	0	6.75
Fred Pfeffer	1	7	0	0	0	0	0	6	0	0	2.57
Bill Whitrock	1	4	1	0	0	1	0	2	0	0	9.00
Larry Twitchell	1	3	0	0	0	0	0	1	0	0	6.00
		—1 forfeit W vs Chicago on August 3—									
		1096.2	129	113	35	94	258	475	2	1	5.45

1895

THE WINNER AGAIN BUT STILL
NOT THE CHAMPION

In 1895 the 12 teams in the League-Association hit a composite .296, down 13 points from the previous year. The reason for the marked decrease is as difficult to fathom as the unprecedented hitting barrage in 1894. The few significant rule changes in 1895 if anything should have further aided the offense. For the first time gloves were specifically addressed by rulesmakers with limitations imposed on their size and design. Another newcomer to the umpire's manual was the first infield fly rule. After years of having to watch infielders engineer double plays and sometimes even triple plays by deliberately dropping routine pop flies to trap helpless baserunners into darting to the next base where they were easy force-out victims, umpires in 1895 were mandated to declare a batter automatically out if he hit a fair pop fly that could be caught by an infielder while first and second bases were occupied or first, second and third bases, with less than two out. These additional advantages to the team on offense were countered to some extent by a rule enlarging the pitcher's plate or "rubber" to 24 by 6 inches, but there was still little reason to expect the scale to begin to tilt the pitchers' way again in 1895.

What was expected was that rules authorizing umpires to impose heavy fines on players who "kicked" unduly at their decisions would curb rowdyism. Knowing, though, that inflicting a stiff penalty would only heighten a poorly paid player's animosity, most umpires backed off from levying fines. The game, as a result, grew all the more raucous in 1895, forcing rulesmakers to give umpires a freer rein the following year in ejecting offending players. But for the moment the chief promulgators of rowdy-ball, the Baltimore Orioles and Cleveland Spiders, continued to flourish, although there were other reason too for their success. In recapping the 1895 season, the Spalding Guide ventured: "The New York club had able pitchers, the Philadelphia club had 'heavy hitters'; but these counted for little against the superiority in team-work strength of the teams of the Baltimore and Cleveland clubs."

Baltimore's successful bid for a second consecutive pennant was definitely a team effort. Lucky with injuries the previous year, Orioles manager Ned Hanlon had to go to his bench

536

Cap Anson's 1895 Chicago Colts with the vaunted Bill Lange and two of that year's top rookies—
Bill Everett and Ace Stewart. Everett's name, spelled correctly here, so seldom was that eventually
he gave up fighting it and played as Everett. Stewart's name was mud after he clashed too often
with Anson. He was banished to the minors in the closing weeks of the season and never played up
top again. Top: Bill Moran, Adonis Terry, Bert Abbey, Lange, Everitt and Stewart. Seated: Bill
Dahlen, George Decker, Cap Anson, Bill Hutchison and Walt Wilmot. Front: Jimmy Ryan, Mal
Kittridge, Charlie Irwin, Clark Griffith and Tim Donahue.

constantly in 1895. Hanlon's first problem was to find a new hill leader when Sadie
McMahon, his 1894 ace, continued to be plagued by a lame arm. Hanlon chose Bill Hoffer,
up from the Eastern League, and was rewarded with the only 30-win season by a rookie
since the sixty-foot six-inch distance was adopted. Aging first sacker Dan Brouthers, verg-
ing on 37, was Hanlon's next chore. Brouthers's job went to good-field, no-hit rookie
Scoops Carey. No sooner had Hanlon patched up that hole than second baseman Heinie
Reitz broke his collarbone, opening a spot for converted pitcher Kid Gleason. Later catcher
Wilbert Robinson was idled for a long stretch when he had to have part of finger amputated
and third sacker John McGraw fell prey to malaria. On each occasion Hanlon had a solution.

   After a rocky start, Baltimore occupied first place on July 4, percentage points ahead of
Pittsburgh, the early leader. The race was so close, though, that Philadelphia, in eighth
place, was just three and a half games from first. Cleveland, at home most of July, won 17
of its next 23 to wrest the lead from the Orioles, but Hanlon spurred his men to a 23-4 mark
in August and regained the top perch. Further help for Baltimore arrived when McMahon's
arm mended in time to win ten late-season games and John Clarkson's younger brother Dad,
a bust with St. Louis, scrambled to 12 wins in 15 decisions after Hanlon rescued him from
the hapless Browns in a June trade.

By Labor Day, although nine of the 12 teams were still playing better than .500 ball, the race had narrowed to Cleveland and Baltimore. The Orioles put some daylight behind them by taking two of three at home from the Spiders in the second week of September, but the race was not officially decided until Baltimore's last series of the season against New York. Demoralized by having slipped to ninth after finishing second in 1894, the Giants mounted

THE 1895 BATTING RACE

Record-keeping was still rudimentary in 1895. Compounding the problem for official statisticians was lax and in some cities willfully wrong scorekeeping. Here is commentary on Willie Keeler's march to the batting crown in 1897:

"John Heydler, who is one of the best known baseball scribes in the business, says exception should be taken to this overgenerous scoring and that Keeler's figures of .432 will not agree with any private accounts. Frank Houseman of St. Louis also has objections to Baltimore scoring methods. He says: 'Down in Baltimore, one day, Keeler sent two flies to Lally (left fielder Dan Lally of the St. Louis Browns), who muffed both of them. Then he hit to Hartman (Browns third baseman Fred Hartman) and the latter fumbled and then threw wild. Then Keeler made a good single. The next morning four hits appeared to Keeler's credit in the Baltimore papers. Talk about Cleveland stuffing Burkett's average, why, they are not in it with the oyster scribes of Baltimore.'"

Keeler's batting average was reduced to .424 when differences were later discovered in his hit and at bat totals. Jesse Burkett suffered a similar reduction in 1895, albeit posthumously. Nevertheless some historians believe that National League president Nick Young's stats—bad math and all—are more reliable than those of modern researchers.

Top 10 Hitters in 1894

	As of 1997				As Issued on October 12, 1895, by Young		
		H/AB	BA			H/AB	BA
1.	Burkett, Cleve	225/550	.409	1.	Burkett, Cleve	235/555	.423
2.	Delahanty, Phi	194/480	.404	2.	Delahanty, Phi	192/481	.399
3.	Clements, Phi	127/322	.394	3.	Keeler, Balt	221/560	.394
4.	Thompson, Phi	211/538	.392	4.	Thompson, Phi	210/533	.394
5.	Lange, Chicago	186/478	.389	5.	Hamilton, Phi	203/517	.393
6.	Jennings, Balt	204/529	.386	6.	Clements, Phi	126/324	.389
7.	Keeler, Balt	221/565	.377	7.	Lange, Chicago	186/479	.388
8.	Stenzel, Pitt	192/514	.374	8.	Jennings, Balt	204/528	.386
9.	Everett, Chicago	197/550	.358	9.	Stenzel, Pitt	200/520	.384
10.	Duffy, Boston	187/531	.352	10.	McGraw, Balt	144/385	.374

The 1895 Cincinnati Reds: Top: Phillips, Grey, Vaughn, Parrott, Rhines, Spies. Middle: Holliday, McPhee, Merritt, Murphy, Ewing, Hoy, Miller, Smith, Dwyer. Bottom: Foreman, Latham (with team mascot Trilby), Hogriever. In 1895 the Reds got this production from one spot in their batting order.

AB	H	R	2B	3B	HR	RBI	BB	SB	BA	SA
573	170	94	29	15	6	98	30	15	.297	.426

Those totals, had they been achieved by just one man, would have ranked second on the team in almost every department. They were jointly accomplished by the six Reds pitchers in 1895 who most of the time batted last. This sort of production ought to have been noticed by manager Buck Ewing, and evidently it was. Ewing used Tom Parrott, his best-hitting pitcher, at first base and in the outfield on occasion. However, he never called on Parrott to pinch hit. Ewing appeared not to believe in pinch hitters. He used only one in 1895. Pennant-winning Baltimore, in contrast, had eleven pinch hit at bats in 1895 but logged only one successful pinch hit. Perhaps that was what influenced Ewing. In 1895 the license to use a pinch hitter still seemed more a frill than a way to help win ball games.

TOM BROWN AGAIN

After setting the nineteenth-century major league record the previous year for the lowest batting average by an outfielder in 600 or more at bats (.227), in 1893 Tom Brown hit .240 to head the list for the lowest batting average of any regular that season with 500 or more at bats. Brown lost his chance to repeat his 1893 dubious achievement when he batted .2537 in 1894, .0002 points better than Danny Richardson's .2535. However, Brown got back in the groove in 1895 by hitting .223 to beat out Shorty Fuller by two points for the honor of having the lowest BA of any major league regular. It was Brown's last noteworthy dubious achievement. His team suddenly improved and, predictably, so did he. Playing for Washington's two best major league clubs in the last century, Brown closed out his career as a regular with two straight .290-plus seasons in 1896–97.

A Gotham sheet-music company's rendering of the 1895 New York Giants. The Big Apple entry slipped all the way from second to ninth in 1895 but still finished above .500 thanks to have-nots Washington, St. Louis and Louisville, which compiled an aggregate .295 winning percentage.

little resistance. Hoffer won the pennant-clinching game on September 28, and in the season finale McGraw homered to beat Amos Rusie, enabling the Orioles to finish three games ahead of Cleveland.

Two afternoons later Baltimore appeared at Cleveland's League Park for the opening game of the second Temple Cup series. Having little appetite for the affair anyway, the Orioles lost all stomach for it when they found themselves facing a hostile crowd that pelted them with fruit and vegetables. McMahon put up a good battle before losing the first game 5-4 to Cy Young, but the Spiders then had "it all their own way in Cleveland." By the time the series moved to Baltimore on October 7, the Orioles were down 3-0. Buoyed by a home crowd just as obstreperous as Cleveland's, Duke Esper staved off elimination and gave Baltimore its first Temple Cup victory in eight tries by blanking Nig Cuppy, 5-0. The next day, though, Young beat Hoffer 5-2 to hand Cleveland possession of the cup for the next year.

After their final-game victory, the Spiders fled Baltimore's Union Park behind a police wall, $580 richer per man, though again there were rumors of a prearranged fifty/fifty split. Upon returning from Baltimore, the victors were given a banquet by the Cleveland Elks

THE MANAGER VANISHES

Arthur Irwin.

In 1895 the Philadelphia Phillies set the nineteenth-century attendance record by attracting 474,971 fans. Much of the Phils' appeal was their heavy artillery, but when they again failed to win a pennant despite leading the majors in batting for the third year in a row, manager Arthur Irwin was bounced. Unfazed, he moved on to piloting the New York Giants for a while and then to promoting boxing matches, roller hockey games and marathon bike races. He also bought and sold several minor league teams and served as the New York Yankees head scout.

Irwin liked to think of himself as an original. He claimed he invented the first fielders mitt, took part in the first squeeze play, was the first full-time college baseball coach and organized the first pro football team. There is some evidence to support each of these claims. In any case, Irwin was a wealthy man by 1921. Then 63, he began telling people he was dying of stomach cancer (although the doctor who gave him this dire news was never found) and booked passage on the steamer *Calvin Austin*, bound for his Boston home from New York on the night of July 13.

When the ship docked in Boston the next morning, Irwin was no longer aboard. The presumption was that he had committed suicide by jumping into the Atlantic, but two questions haunted his wife and son Arthur Herbert. What became of the $5,000 Irwin had withdrawn from a bank before leaving New York and why did he, an impeccable dresser, wear a baggy, ill-fitting suit on his last night that was the only thing he left behind in his stateroom on the *Calvin Austin*?

After going to Hartford to settle his father's estate, Arthur Herbert made an unpleasant discovery. His father had another wife and son in New York. Further investigation unearthed that Irwin had taken both women on road trips at different times while managing in the minor leagues. Even in the face of this clear evidence that Irwin was leading a double life, his Boston family continued to believe his death was suicide, but many other people believed he was murdered for the $5,000 and his body thrown overboard.

There of course is another possible explanation for Irwin's abrupt disappearance. The Baseball Hall of Fame in Cooperstown has a letter written in 1922 by a pitcher who knew Irwin. His letter queried: "How can Arthur Irwin be dead? I just saw him in Oklahoma."

THE ALL-TIME WORST PITCHERS

Here are four top-ten lists of pitchers with the all-time worst career ERAs for a specified minimum number of innings. In every instance except one the leader is a pitcher who was active in the mid-1890s. The 1895 season is particularly well represented. The worst pitching staff that year probably belonged either to last-place Louisville or eleventh-place St. Louis, but third-place Philadelphia certainly had the most wretched pitching staff of any contender in history. Of the ten pitchers the Phils employed in 1895, the four who were most often used were merely bad, but the other six had a composite ERA of around 8.00. Several of them appear on one or more of the four lists.

WORST CAREER ERA, MINIMUM 100 INNINGS

	YEARS	W/L	INNINGS	ERA
Dewey McDougal	1895–96	4–11	124.2	8.30
Bill Rhodes	1893	5–12	151.2	7.60
Jake Boyd	1894–96	3–16	136.1	7.20
Chet Nichols	1926–32	1–8	122.2	7.19
Luther Roy	1924–29	6–12	170.2	7.17
Lauren Pepper	1954–57	2–8	109.2	7.06
Bill Kissinger	1895–97	7–25	319.1	6.99
Hal Elliott	1929–32	11–24	322.1	6.95
Carl Doyle	1935–40	6–15	222.2	6.95
Hector Fajardo	1991–95	5–9	124.1	6.95

WORST CAREER ERA, MINIMUM 250 INNINGS

	YEARS	W/L	INNINGS	ERA
Bill Kissinger	1895–97	7–25	319.1	6.99
Hal Elliott	1929–32	11–24	322.1	6.95
Jack Wadsworth	1890–95	6–38	367.2	6.85
Jack Knight	1922–27	10–18	255	6.85
Jim Walkup	1934–39	16–38	462.1	6.74
Kirtley Baker	1890–99	9–38	371	6.28
Otis Stocksdale	1893–96	15–31	347	6.20
Mike McDermott	1895–97	11–33	355.2	6.17
Les Sweetland	1927–31	33–58	740.2	6.10
Lefty Mills	1934–40	15–30	435	6.06

WORST CAREER ERA, MINIMUM 600 INNINGS

	YEARS	W/L	INNINGS	ERA
Les Sweetland	1927–31	33–58	740.2	6.10
Claude Willoughby	1925–31	38–58	841.1	5.84
Russ Van Atta	1933–39	33–41	712.1	5.60
Bert Inks	1891–96	27–46	603.2	5.52
Les German	1890–97	34–63	849.1	5.49
Roxie Lawson	1930–40	47–39	851.2	5.37
Tom Parrott	1893–96	39–48	795	5.33
Lynn Nelson	1930–40	33–42	676.2	5.25
Jay Hook	1957–64	29–62	752.2	5.23
Mike Sullivan	1889–99	54–66	1105.1	5.14

WORST CAREER ERA, MINIMUM 1000 INNINGS				
	YEARS	W/L	INNINGS	ERA
Mike Sullivan	1889–99	54–66	1105.1	5.14
Chief Hogsett	1929–38/44	63–87	1222	5.02
Roy Mahaffey	1926–36	67–49	1056	5.01
Jack Knott	1933–46	82–103	1557	4.97
Kid Carsey	1891–1901	116–138	2222	4.95
Buck Ross	1936–45	56–95	1365.1	4.94
Alex Ferguson	1918–29	61–85	1238.2	4.90
Carl Scheib	1943–54	45–65	1070.2	4.88
Gordon Rhodes	1929–36	43–74	1070.2	4.85
Jesse Jefferson	1973–81	39–81	1085.2	4.81

Club. Set at each table was a four-foot-square design of a baseball diamond with a spider on each base, a spider at the pitcher's mound and an open oyster midway between home and first, representing the city of Baltimore, with four spiders warming over it and gobbling it up.

Once again, though, only in the victorious city was possession of the Temple Cup taken seriously. Everywhere else the postseason series had begun to be viewed as an artificial effort to kindle fan interest in a 12-team battle that usually winnowed down to two or three teams by August. Another problem with the Temple Cup was that it was anticlimactic after a close pennant race, as in 1895, and the pennant winner entered the series with nothing to gain and everything to lose. Alternatives to the Temple Cup were proposed, but no one seemed to want to look at the most logical solution. The 12 teams could have been split into two divisions, East and West, which would have saved travel costs, heightened geographic rivalries and created two bonafide qualifiers for the postseason series.

THE SEASONAL RECORD

		W	L	PCT	HOME	ROAD	GB
1.	Baltimore Orioles	87	43	.669	54–12	33–31	—
2.	Cleveland Spiders	84	46	.646	47–13	37–33	3
3.	Philadelphia Phillies	78	53	.595	51–21	27–32	9.5
4.	Chicago Colts	72	58	.554	43–26	29–32	15
5.	Boston Beaneaters	71	60	.542	48–19	23–41	16.5
6.	Brooklyn Bridegrooms	71	60	.542	43–22	28–38	16.5
7.	Pittsburgh Pirates	71	61	.538	44–21	27–40	17
8.	Cincinnati Reds	66	64	.508	42–22	24–42	21
9.	New York Giants	66	65	.504	40–27	26–38	21.5
10.	Washington Nationals	43	85	.336	31–34	12–51	43
11.	St. Louis Browns	39	92	.298	25–41	14–51	48.5
12.	Louisville Colonels	35	96	.267	19–38	16–58	52.5

	Ba	Cl	Phi	Ch	Bos	Br	Pt	Ci	NY	Wa	StL	Lo	
Baltimore	—	5	8	8	10	7	7	8	9	9	6	10	87
Cleveland	6	—	7	5	6	10	7	6	7	9	11	10	84
Philadelphia	4	5	—	6	7	7	8	8	8	8	7	10	78
Chicago	4	6	6	—	5	6	8	5	4	9	10	9	72
Boston	2	6	5	7	4	—	7	5	8	9	9	9	71
Brooklyn	5	2	5	6	—	7	7	5	9	5	9	11	71
Pittsburgh	5	5	4	4	5	5	—	8	8	8	9	10	71
Cincinnati	4	6	4	7	7	7	4	—	4	8	9	6	66
New York	3	5	3	8	4	3	4	8	—	8	11	9	66
Washington	3	3	4	2	3	7	4	2	4	—	5	6	43
St. Louis	6	1	5	2	3	3	3	3	1	6	—	6	39
Louisville	1	2	2	3	3	1	2	6	3	6	6	—	35
	43	46	53	58	60	60	61	64	65	85	92	96	783

SEASON LEADERS

Batting Average (350 ABs)

1.	Burkett, Cleveland	.409
2.	Delahanty, Philadelphia	.404
3.	Thompson, Philadelphia	.392
4.	Lange, Chicago	.389
5.	Jennings, Baltimore	.386

On–Base Percentage

1.	Delahanty, Philadelphia	.500
2.	Hamilton, Philadelphia	.490
3.	Burkett, Cleveland	.486
4.	McGraw, Baltimore	.459
5.	Lange, Chicago	.456
	Kelley, Baltimore	.456

Slugging Average

1.	Thompson, Philadelphia	.654
2.	Delahanty, Philadelphia	.617
3.	Lange, Chicago	.575
4.	Kelley, Baltimore	.546
5.	Stenzel, Pittsburgh	.539

Total Bases

1.	Thompson, Philadelphia	352
2.	Delahanty, Philadelphia	296
3.	Burkett, Cleveland	288
4.	McKean, Cleveland	283
	Kelley, Baltimore	283

Home Runs

1.	Thompson, Philadelphia	18
2.	Joyce, Washington	17
3.	Clements, Philadelphia	13
4.	Delahanty, Philadelphia	11
5.	McGuire, Washington	10
	Lange, Chicago	10
	Nash, Boston	10
	Kelley, Baltimore	10
	Miller, Cincinnati	10

Hits

1.	Burkett, Cleveland	225
2.	Keeler, Baltimore	213
3.	Thompson, Philadelphia	211
4.	Jennings, Baltimore	204
5.	Hamilton, Philadelphia	201

Stolen Bases

1.	Hamilton, Philadelphia	97
2.	Lange, Chicago	67
3.	McGraw, Baltimore	61
4.	Kelley, Baltimore	54
5.	Jennings, Baltimore	53
	Stenzel, Pittsburgh	53

RBI

1.	Thompson, Philadelphia	165
2.	Kelley, Baltimore	134
	Brodie, Baltimore	134
4.	Jennings, Baltimore	125
5.	McKean, Cleveland	119

Runs

1.	Hamilton, Philadelphia	166
2.	Keeler, Baltimore	162
3.	Jennings, Baltimore	159
4.	Burkett, Cleveland	153
5.	Delahanty, Philadelphia	149

Strikeouts

1.	T. Brown, StL–Wash	60
2.	Joyce, Washington	54
3.	Daly, Brooklyn	52
4.	Dahlen, Chicago	51
5.	LaChance, Brooklyn	48

PITCHING

Wins

1.	Young, Cleveland	39
2.	Hoffer, Baltimore	31
	Hawley, Pittsburgh	31
4.	Griffith, Chicago	26
	Nichols, Boston	26
	Cuppy, Cleveland	26
	Taylor, Philadelphia	26

Innings

1.	Hawley, Pittsburgh	441.1
2.	Breitenstein, St. Louis	429.2
3.	Rusie, New York	393.1
4.	Nichols, Boston	379.2
5.	Young, Cleveland	369.2

Strikeouts

1.	Rusie, New York	201
2.	Hawley, Pittsburgh	142
3.	Nichols, Boston	140
4.	Breitenstein, St. Louis	127
5.	Young, Cleveland	121

Losses

1.	Breitenstein, St. Louis	30
2.	Rusie, New York	23
	Mercer, Washington	23
4.	Hawley, Pittsburgh	22
5.	Hutchison, Chicago	21
	Weyhing, Phi-Pit-Lou	21

Complete Games

1.	Breitenstein, St. Louis	46
2.	Hawley, Pittsburgh	44
3.	Rusie, New York	42
	Nichols, Boston	42
5.	Griffith, Chicago	39

Winning Percentage (25 decisions)

1.	Hoffer, Baltimore	.838
2.	Young, Cleveland	.778
3.	Rhines, Cincinnati	.655
4.	Cuppy, Cleveland	.650
	Griffith, Chicago	.650
	Taylor, Philadelphia	650

ERA (140 innings)

1.	Maul, Washington	2.45
2.	Hawley, Pittsburgh	3.18
3.	Hoffer, Baltimore	3.21
4.	B. Foreman, Pittsburgh	3.22
5.	Young, Cleveland	3.26

Lowest On–Base Percentage

1.	Young, Cleveland	.294
2.	Maul, Washington	.309
3.	Nichols, Boston	.316
4.	Hawley, Pittsburgh	.320
5.	Cuppy, Cleveland	.323

FIELDING

Total Chances

1B	Beckley, Pittsburgh	1425
2B	Quinn, St. Louis	792
3B	L. Cross, Philadelphia	531
SS	Jennings, Baltimore	938
OF	F. Clarke, Louisville	413
C	McGuire, Washington	627
P	Breitenstein, St. Louis	157

Fielding Average

Carey, Baltimore	.987
Crooks, Washington	.956
L. Cross, Philadelphia	.940
Jennings, Baltimore	.940
Griffin, Brooklyn	.969
Robinson, Baltimore	.979
Stein, Brooklyn	.974

BALTIMORE Ned Hanlon Union Park

		G	AB	H	R	2B	3B	HR	RBI	BB	SB	BA	SA
RF	Willie Keeler	131	**565**	213	162	24	15	4	78	37	47	.377	.494
SS	Hughie Jennings	131	529	204	159	41	7	4	125	24	53	.386	.512
CF	Steve Brodie	131	528	184	85	27	10	2	134	26	35	.348	.449
LF	Joe Kelley	131	518	189	148	26	19	10	134	77	54	.365	.546
1B	Scoops Carey	123	490	128	59	21	6	1	75	27	2	.261	.335
2B	Kid Gleason	112	421	130	90	14	12	0	74	33	19	.309	.399
3B	John McGraw	96	388	143	110	13	6	2	48	60	61	.369	.448
C	Wilbert Robinson	77	282	74	38	19	1	0	48	12	11	.262	.337
Sub	Heinie Reitz	70	245	72	45	15	5	0	29	18	15	.294	.396
C	Boileryard Clarke	67	241	70	38	15	3	0	35	13	8	.290	.378
P	Bill Hoffer	41	126	27	22	3	1	0	9	8	0	.214	.254
P	George Hemming	35	117	33	19	10	2	1	16	2	0	.282	.427
P	Duke Esper	34	90	16	7	2	0	0	2	4	0	.178	.200
P	Dad Clarkson	20	57	8	10	1	0	1	4	5	0	.140	.211
P	Sadie McMahon	15	51	16	5	1	0	0	5	3	1	.314	.333
Sub	Frank Bonner	11	42	14	9	1	1	0	7	5	4	.333	.405
Sub	Dan Brouthers	5	23	6	2	2	0	0	5	1	0	.261	.348
P	Arlie Pond	7	6	2	0	0	1	0	0	0	0	.333	.667
P	Bill Kissinger	2	5	1	1	0	0	0	0	0	0	.200	.200
Sub	Frank Bowerman	1	1	0	0	0	0	0	0	0	0	.000	.000
		132	4725	1530	1009	235	89	25	828	355	310	.324	.427

1B	Carey 123, Clarke 6, Brouthers 5
2B	Gleason 85, Reitz 48, McGraw 1
SS	Jennings 131, Reitz 1, Carey 1
3B	McGraw 95, Reitz 18, Gleason 12, Bonner 11, Carey 1
OF	Keeler 131, Kelley 131, Brodie 131, Gleason 4, Pond 1, Carey 1
C	Robinson 75, Clarke 60, Bowerman 1
P	Hoffer 41, Esper 34, Hemming 34, Clarkson 20, McMahon 15, Gleason 9, Pond 6, Kissinger 2

	G	IP	GS	CG	W	L	K	BB	SH	SV	ERA
Bill Hoffer	41	314	38	32	31	6	80	124	**4**	0	3.21
George Hemming	34	262.1	31	26	20	13	43	96	1	0	4.05
Duke Esper	34	218.1	25	16	10	12	39	79	1	1	3.92
Dad Clarkson	20	142	14	10	12	3	23	64	0	0	3.87
Sadie McMahon	15	122.1	15	15	10	4	37	32	**4**	0	2.94
Kid Gleason	9	50.1	5	3	2	4	6	21	0	1	6.97
Arlie Pond	6	13.2	1	1	0	1	13	12	0	2	5.93
Bill Kissinger	2	11.1	2	1	1	0	3	2	0	0	3.97
	—1 forfeit W vs Pittsburgh on August 28—										
	1134.1	131	104	86	43	244	430	**10**	4	**3.80**

CLEVELAND   **Patsy Tebeau**   **League Park (I)**

		G	AB	H	R	2B	3B	HR	RBI	BB	SB	BA	SA
SS	Ed McKean	131	**565**	193	131	32	17	8	119	45	12	.342	.501
LF	Jesse Burkett	131	550	**225**	153	22	13	5	83	74	41	**.409**	.524
CF	Jimmy McAleer	131	528	143	84	17	2	0	68	38	32	.271	.311
2B	Cupid Childs	119	462	133	96	15	3	4	90	74	20	.288	.359
3B	Chippy McGarr	112	419	111	85	14	2	2	59	34	19	.265	.322
C	Jack O'Connor	89	340	99	51	14	10	0	58	30	11	.291	.391
Sub	White Wings Tebeau	91	337	110	57	16	6	0	68	50	12	.326	.409
C	Chief Zimmer	88	315	107	60	21	2	5	56	33	14	.340	.467
RF	Harry Blake	84	315	87	50	10	1	3	45	30	11	.276	.343
1B	Patsy Tebeau	63	264	84	50	13	2	2	52	16	8	.318	.405
P	Nig Cuppy	47	140	40	36	9	3	0	25	20	2	.286	.393
P	Cy Young	47	140	30	20	5	2	0	13	11	0	.214	.279
P	Bobby Wallace	30	98	21	16	2	3	0	10	6	0	.214	.296
Sub	Ed Gremminger	20	78	21	10	1	0	0	15	5	0	.269	.282
P	Phil Knell	20	55	11	9	2	1	0	5	1	1	.200	.273
P	Zeke Wilson	8	18	2	2	0	0	0	3	1	3	.111	.111
P	Mike Sullivan	4	15	2	2	1	0	0	1	0	0	.133	.200
Sub	Fred Donovan	3	12	1	1	0	0	0	1	1	0	.083	.083
Sub	Pussy Tebeau	2	6	3	3	0	0	0	1	2	1	.500	.500
Sub	Tom O'Meara	1	1	0	1	0	0	0	0	1	0	.000	.000
		131	4658	1423	917	194	67	29	772	472	187	.305	.395

1B P. Tebeau 49, W. Tebeau 42, O'Connor 41, Zimmer 3
2B Childs 119, P. Tebeau 9, McGarr 4
SS McKean 131
3B McGarr 108, Gremminger 20, P. Tebeau 6, O'Connor 1
OF Burkett 131, McAleer 131, Blake 83, W. Tebeau 49, P. Tabeau 2
C   Zimmer 84, O'Connor 47, Donovan 3, O'Meara 1
P   Young 47, Cuppy 47, Wallace 30, Knell 20, Wilson 8, Sullivan 4

	G	IP	GS	CG	W	L	K	BB	SH	SV	ERA
Cy Young	47	369.2	40	36	**35**	10	121	75	**4**	0	3.26
Nig Cuppy	47	353	40	36	26	14	91	95	1	2	3.54
Bobby Wallace	30	228.2	28	22	12	14	63	87	1	1	4.09
Phil Knell	20	116.2	13	9	7	5	30	53	0	0	5.40
Zeke Wilson	8	44.2	7	3	3	1	16	20	0	0	4.23
Mike Sullivan	4	31	3	2	1	2	5	16	0	0	8.42
	1143.2	131	108	84	46	326	346	**346**	6	3	3.91

PHILADELPHIA   **Arthur Irwin**   **Philadelphia Baseball Grounds (II)**

		G	AB	H	R	2B	3B	HR	RBI	BB	SB	BA	SA
1B	Jack Boyle	133	**565**	143	90	17	4	0	67	35	13	.253	.297
2B	Bill Hallman	124	539	169	94	26	5	1	91	34	16	.314	.386
RF	Sam Thompson	119	538	211	131	45	21	18	**165**	31	27	.392	**.654**
3B	Lave Cross	125	535	145	95	26	9	2	101	35	21	.271	.364
CF	Billy Hamilton	123	517	201	**166**	22	6	7	74	96	97	.389	.495
LF	Ed Delahanty	116	480	194	149	**49**	10	11	106	86	46	.404	.617
SS	Joe Sullivan	94	373	126	75	7	3	2	50	24	15	.338	.389
C	Jack Clements	88	322	127	64	27	2	13	75	22	3	.394	.612
OF	Tuck Turner	59	210	81	51	8	6	2	43	25	14	.386	.510
Sub	Charlie Reilly	49	179	48	28	6	1	0	25	13	7	.268	.313
P	Jack Taylor	42	155	45	26	11	2	3	35	7	3	.290	.445
P	Kid Carsey	44	141	41	24	2	0	0	20	15	2	.291	.305
Sub	Mike Grady	46	123	40	21	3	1	1	23	14	5	.325	.390
Sub	Dick Buckley	38	112	28	20	6	1	0	14	9	2	.250	.321
P	Willie McGill	20	63	14	7	6	0	0	11	6	0	.222	.317
P	Al Orth	11	45	16	8	4	0	1	13	1	0	.356	.511
Sub	Art Madison	10	34	12	6	3	0	0	8	1	4	.353	.441
P	Tom Smith	11	33	8	1	1	0	0	3	3	0	.242	.273
P	Con Lucid	10	29	10	8	3	1	0	5	3	0	.345	.517
P	Henry Lampe	7	16	2	1	0	1	0	0	2	0	.125	.250
P	Ernie Beam	10	11	2	2	0	0	0	0	0	1	.182	.182
P	Deke White	3	8	1	0	0	0	0	1	0	0	.125	.125
P	George Hodson	4	5	0	1	0	0	0	0	1	0	.000	.000
P	Gus Weyhing	2	4	0	0	0	0	0	0	0	0	.000	.000
		133	5037	**1664**	**1068**	**272**	73	61	**930**	463	276	**.330**	**.450**

1B Boyle 133, Grady 1
2B Hallman 122, Delahanty 6, Reilly 3, Madison 3
SS Sullivan 89, Reilly 34, Delahanty 9, Madison 6, Hallman 3
3B Cross 125, Reilly 11, Madison 2, Grady 1, Delahanty 1
OF Hamilton 123, Thompson 118, Delahanty 103, Turner 55, Sullivan 6, Grady 5, Reilly 1, Taylor 1, Beam 1
C Clements 88, Grady 38, Buckley 38
P Carsey 44, Taylor 41, McGill 20, Orth 11, Smith 11, Lucid 10, Beam 9, Lampe 7, Hodson 4, White 3, Weyhing 2

	G	IP	GS	CG	W	L	K	BB	SH	SV	ERA
Kid Carsey	44	342.1	40	35	24	16	64	118	0	1	4.92
Jack Taylor	41	335	37	33	26	14	93	83	1	1	4.49
Willie McGill	20	146	20	13	10	8	70	81	0	0	5.55
Al Orth	11	88	10	9	8	1	25	22	0	1	3.89
Con Lucid	10	69.2	10	7	6	3	19	35	1	0	5.94
Tom Smith	11	68	7	4	2	3	21	53	0	0	6.88
Henry Lampe	7	44	3	2	0	2	18	33	0	0	7.57
Ernie Beam	9	24.2	1	1	0	2	3	25	0	**3**	11.31
Deke White	3	17.1	1	1	1	0	6	13	0	1	9.87
George Hodson	4	17	2	1	1	2	6	9	0	0	9.53
Gus Weyhing	2	9	2	0	0	2	5	13	0	0	20.00
		1161	133	106	78	53	330	485	2	**7**	5.47

CHICAGO   Cap Anson   West Side Park (II)

		G	AB	H	R	2B	3B	HR	RBI	BB	SB	BA	SA
3B	Bill Everett	133	550	197	129	16	10	3	88	33	47	.358	.440
SS	Bill Dahlen	129	516	131	106	19	10	7	62	61	38	.254	.370
CF	Bill Lange	123	478	186	120	27	16	10	98	55	67	.389	.575
1B	Cap Anson	122	474	159	87	23	6	2	91	55	12	.335	.422
LF	Walt Wilmot	108	466	132	86	16	6	8	72	30	28	.283	.395
RF	Jimmy Ryan	108	438	139	83	22	8	6	49	48	18	.317	.445
2B	Ace Stewart	97	365	88	52	8	10	8	76	39	14	.241	.384
Sub	George Decker	73	297	82	51	9	7	2	41	17	11	.276	.374
C	Tim Donahue	63	219	59	29	9	1	2	36	20	5	.269	.347
C	Mal Kittridge	60	212	48	30	6	3	3	29	16	6	.226	.325
P	Clark Griffith	43	144	46	20	3	0	1	27	16	2	.319	.361
P	Adonis Terry	40	137	30	18	3	2	1	10	2	1	.219	.292
P	Bill Hutchison	38	126	25	12	3	3	0	11	5	1	.198	.270
Sub	Harry Truby	33	119	40	17	3	0	0	16	10	7	.336	.361
Sub	Bill Moran	15	55	9	8	2	1	1	9	3	2	.164	.291
P	Scott Stratton	10	24	7	3	1	1	0	2	4	1	.292	.417
P	Walter Thornton	8	22	7	4	1	0	1	7	3	0	.318	.500
P	Doc Parker	7	22	7	3	0	1	0	2	1	0	.318	.409
P	Danny Friend	5	17	4	4	0	0	0	1	1	0	.235	.235
Sub	Charlie Irwin	3	10	2	4	0	0	0	0	2	0	.200	.200
P	Monte McFarland	2	7	1	0	0	0	0	0	0	0	.143	.143
Sub	Jiggs Parrott	3	4	1	0	0	0	0	0	0	0	.250	.250
P	Bert Abbey	1	3	1	0	0	0	0	0	0	0	.333	.333
P	John Dolan	2	3	0	0	0	0	0	0	1	0	.000	.000
		133	4708	1401	866	171	85	55	727	422	260	.298	.405

1B   Anson 122, Decker 11, Thornton 1, Parrott 1
2B   Stewart 97, Truby 33, Everett 3, Decker 1
SS   Dahlen 129, Irwin 3, Terry 1, Decker 1, Parrott 1
3B   Everett 130, Decker 3
OF   Lange 123, Ryan 108, Wilmot 108, Decker 57, Stratton 4, Dahlen 1, Griffith 1, Parrott 1, Terry 1
C   Donahue 63, Kittridge 59, Moran 15
P   Griffith 42, Hutchison 38, Terry 38, Thornton 7, Parker 7, Stratton 5, Friend 5, McFarland 2, Dolan 2, Abbey 1

	G	IP	GS	CG	W	L	K	BB	SH	SV	ERA
Clark Griffith	42	353	41	39	26	14	79	91	0	0	3.93
Adonis Terry	38	311.1	34	31	21	14	88	131	0	0	4.80
Bill Hutchison	38	291	35	30	13	21	85	129	2	0	4.73
Doc Parker	7	51.1	6	5	4	2	9	9	1	0	3.68
Danny Friend	5	41	5	5	2	2	10	14	0	0	5.27
Walter Thornton	7	40	2	2	2	0	13	31	0	1	6.07
Scott Stratton	5	30	5	3	2	3	4	14	0	0	9.60
Monte McFarland	2	14	2	2	2	0	5	5	0	0	5.14
John Dolan	2	11	2	1	0	1	1	6	0	0	6.55
Bert Abbey	1	8	1	1	0	1	3	2	0	0	4.50
		1150.2	133	**119**	72	58	297	432	3	1	4.67

BOSTON   **Frank Selee**   **South End Grounds (II)**

		G	AB	H	R	2B	3B	HR	RBI	BB	SB	BA	SA
SS	Herman Long	124	535	169	109	23	10	9	75	31	35	.316	.447
CF	Hugh Duffy	130	531	187	110	30	6	9	100	63	42	.352	.482
3B	Billy Nash	132	508	147	97	23	6	10	108	74	18	.289	.417
RF	Jimmy Bannon	124	489	171	101	35	5	6	74	54	28	.350	.479
1B	Tommy Tucker	125	462	115	87	19	6	3	73	61	15	.249	.335
LF	Tommy McCarthy	117	452	131	90	13	2	2	73	72	18	.290	.341
2B	Bobby Lowe	99	412	122	101	12	7	7	62	40	24	.296	.410
C	Charlie Ganzel	80	277	73	38	2	5	1	52	24	1	.264	.318
C	John Ryan	49	189	55	22	7	0	0	18	6	3	.291	.328
Sub	Fred Tenney	49	173	47	35	9	1	1	21	24	6	.272	.353
P	Jack Stivetts	46	158	30	20	6	4	0	24	6	1	.190	.278
P	Kid Nichols	49	157	37	23	3	2	0	18	14	0	.236	.280
P	Jim Sullivan	22	85	15	14	3	0	0	8	7	2	.176	.212
P	Cozy Dolan	26	83	20	12	4	1	0	7	6	3	.241	.313
Sub	Joe Harrington	18	65	18	21	0	2	2	13	7	3	.277	.431
Sub	Jimmy Collins	11	38	8	10	3	0	1	8	4	0	.211	.368
Sub	Charlie Nyce	9	35	8	7	5	0	2	9	4	0	.229	.543
P	Frank Sexton	9	22	5	2	0	0	0	2	1	0	.227	.227
P	Zeke Wilson	6	19	6	3	0	0	1	6	0	0	.316	.474
P	Otis Stocksdale	5	15	4	3	0	0	0	1	1	0	.267	.267
Sub	Jack Warner	3	7	1	2	0	0	0	1	1	0	.143	.143
P	Bill Banks	1	3	0	0	0	0	0	0	0	0	.000	.000
		132	4715	1369	907	197	57	54	753	500	199	.290	.391

1B   Tucker 125, Stivetts 5, Ganzel 2, Stocksdale 2
2B   Lowe 99, Harrington 18, McCarthy 9, Ryan 5, Long 2, Sexton 1
SS   Long 122, Nyce 9, Ganzel 2
3B   Nash 132
OF   Duffy 130, Bannon 122, McCarthy 109, Tenney 28, Collins 10, Stivetts 2, Ryan 1, Sexton 1, Nichols 1, Dolan 1, Sullivan 1
C   Ganzel 76, Ryan 43, Tenney 21, Warner 3
P   Nichols 48, Stivetts 38, Dolan 25, Sullivan 21, Sexton 7, Wilson 6, Stocksdale 4, Banks 1, Bannon 1

	G	IP	GS	CG	W	L	K	BB	SH	SV	ERA
Kid Nichols	47	379.2	42	42	26	16	140	86	1	3	3.41
Jack Stivetts	38	291	34	30	17	17	111	89	0	0	4.64
Cozy Dolan	25	198.1	21	18	11	7	47	67	3	1	4.27
Jim Sullivan	21	179.1	19	16	11	9	46	58	0	0	4.82
Frank Sexton	7	49	5	4	1	5	14	22	0	0	5.69
Zeke Wilson	6	45	6	4	2	4	5	27	0	0	5.20
Otis Stocksdale	4	23	4	1	2	2	2	8	0	0	5.87
Bill Banks	1	7	1	1	1	0	4	4	0	0	0.00
Jimmy Bannon	1	3	0	0	0	0	1	2	0	0	6.00
		1175.1	132	116	71	60	370	363	4	4	4.27

BROOKLYN   **Dave Foutz**   **Eastern Park**

		G	AB	H	R	2B	3B	HR	RBI	BB	SB	BA	SA
1B	Candy LaChance	127	536	167	99	22	8	8	108	29	37	.312	.427
SS	Tommy Corcoran	127	535	142	81	17	10	2	69	23	17	.265	.346
CF	Mike Griffin	131	519	173	140	38	7	4	65	93	27	.333	.457
3B	Billy Shindle	118	477	133	91	21	2	3	69	47	17	.279	.350
2B	Tom Daly	120	455	128	89	17	8	2	68	52	28	.281	.367
LF	John Anderson	102	419	120	76	11	14	9	87	12	24	.286	.444
RF	George Treadway	86	339	87	54	14	3	7	54	33	9	.257	.378
C	John Grim	93	329	92	54	17	5	0	44	13	9	.280	.362
Sub	George Shoch	61	216	56	49	9	7	0	29	32	7	.259	.366
Sub	Con Daily	40	142	30	17	3	2	1	11	10	3	.211	.282
P	Brickyard Kennedy	40	127	39	18	3	1	0	21	4	0	.307	.346
Sub	Dave Foutz	31	115	34	14	4	1	0	21	4	1	.296	.348
P	Ed Stein	32	104	26	12	3	2	0	14	5	0	.250	.317
P	Ad Gumbert	34	97	35	21	6	0	2	13	7	0	.361	.485
Sub	Oyster Burns	20	76	14	7	0	1	0	7	8	0	.184	.211
P	Dan Daub	25	71	14	8	0	0	0	8	8	3	.197	.197
P	Con Lucid	21	53	13	14	0	3	0	10	7	0	.245	.358
Sub	Joe Mulvey	13	49	15	8	4	1	0	8	2	1	.306	.429
Sub	Buster Burrell	12	28	4	7	0	0	1	5	4	0	.143	.250
P	Bert Abbey	8	19	5	4	0	1	0	1	2	0	.263	.368
Sub	Hunkey Hines	2	8	2	3	0	0	0	1	2	0	.250	.250
P	John Cronin	2	2	1	1	0	1	0	2	0	0	.500	1.500
P	Sandy McDougal	1	1	0	0	0	0	0	0	0	0	.000	.000
		133	4717	1330	867	189	77	39	715	397	183	.282	.379

1B LaChance 125, Foutz 8, Grim 1
2B Daly 120, Shoch 13
SS Corcoran 127, Shoch 6, Griffin 1
3B Shindle 116, Mulvey 13, Shoch 3
OF Griffin 131, Anderson 101, Treadway 86, Shoch 39, Foutz 20, Burns 19, LaChance 3, Hines 2, Grim 1,
     Daily 1, Gumbert 1
C   Grim 91, Daily 39, Burrell 12
P   Kennedy 39, Gumbert 33, Stein 32, Daub 25, Lucid 21, Abbey 8, Cronin 2, McDougal 1

	G	IP	GS	CG	W	L	K	BB	SH	SV	ERA
Brickyard Kennedy	39	279.2	33	26	19	12	39	93	2	2	5.12
Ed Stein	32	255.1	27	24	15	13	55	93	1	1	4.72
Ad Gumbert	33	234	26	20	11	16	45	69	0	1	5.08
Dan Daub	25	184.2	21	16	10	10	36	51	0	0	4.29
Con Lucid	21	137	19	12	10	7	24	72	2	0	5.52
Bert Abbey	8	52	6	5	5	2	14	9	0	0	4.33
Jack Cronin	2	5	0	0	0	0	1	3	0	2	10.80
Sandy McDougal	1	3	0	0	0	0	2	5	0	1	12.00
		—1 forfeit W vs Louisville on May 23—									
		1150.2	132	103	70	60	216	395	5	6	4.94

PITTSBURGH   **Connie Mack**   **Exposition Park**

		G	AB	H	R	2B	3B	HR	RBI	BB	SB	BA	SA
1B	Jake Beckley	129	530	174	104	31	19	5	110	24	20	.328	.487
RF	Patsy Donovan	125	519	160	114	17	6	1	58	47	36	.308	.370
CF	Jake Stenzel	129	514	192	114	38	13	7	97	57	53	.374	.539
LF	Elmer Smith	124	480	145	88	14	12	1	81	55	34	.302	.388
2B	Lou Bierbauer	117	466	120	53	13	11	0	69	19	18	.258	.333
SS	Monte Cross	108	393	101	67	14	13	3	54	38	39	.257	.382
3B	Billy Clingman	106	382	99	69	16	4	0	45	41	19	.259	.322
Sub	Frank Genins	73	252	63	43	8	0	2	24	22	19	.250	.306
C	Bill Merritt	67	239	68	32	5	1	0	27	18	2	.285	.314
P	Pink Hawley	57	185	57	33	14	3	5	42	3	1	.308	.497
C	Joe Sugden	49	155	48	28	4	1	1	17	16	4	.310	.368
P	Bill Hart	36	106	25	8	5	2	0	11	1	1	.236	.321
Sub	Bill Stuart	19	77	19	5	3	0	0	10	2	2	.247	.286
Sub	Tom Kinslow	19	62	14	10	2	0	0	5	2	1	.226	.258
Sub	Connie Mack	14	49	15	12	2	0	0	4	7	1	.306	.347
P	Brownie Foreman	19	46	3	6	0	0	0	4	7	2	.065	.065
P	Frank Killen	14	38	13	7	0	1	0	5	6	2	.342	.395
Sub	Billy Niles	11	37	8	2	0	0	0	0	5	2	.216	.216
P	Jim Gardner	11	34	9	5	2	0	0	3	3	1	.265	.324
P	Sam Moran	11	26	4	5	0	1	1	1	1	0	.154	.346
Sub	John Corcoran	6	20	3	0	0	0	0	1	0	0	.150	.150
P	Tom Colcolough	7	15	5	4	1	2	0	3	2	0	.333	.667
P	Harry Jordan	2	7	2	0	0	0	0	1	0	0	.286	.286
P	Jake Hewitt	4	6	1	0	0	0	0	0	0	0	.167	.167
P	Gus Weyhing	1	4	1	2	1	0	0	1	0	0	.250	.500
P	Gussie Gannon	1	2	0	0	0	0	0	0	0	0	.000	.000
P	Dave Wright	1	1	0	0	0	0	0	0	0	0	.000	.000
P	Jock Menefee	2	0	0	0	0	0	0	0	0	0	—	—
		134	4645	1349	811	190	89	26	673	376	257	.290	.386

1B   Beckley 129, Genins 2, Merritt 2, Mack 1
2B   Bierbauer 117, Genins 16, Stuart 2, Cross 1, Niles 1
SS   Cross 107, Stuart 17, Genins 8, Corcoran 4
3B   Clingman 106, Genins 16, Niles 10, Corcoran 2
OF   Stenzel 129, Donovan 125, Smith 123, Genins 29
C   Merritt 63, Sugden 49, Kinslow 18, Mack 12
P   Hawley 56, Hart 36, Foreman 19, Killen 13, Gardner 11, Moran 10, Colcolough 6, Hewitt 4, Menefee 2, Jordan 2, Wright 1, Weyhing 1, Gannon 1

	G	IP	GS	CG	W	L	K	BB	SH	SV	ERA
Pink Hawley	**56**	**444.1**	**50**	44	31	22	142	122	**4**	1	3.18
Bill Hart	36	261.2	29	24	14	17	85	135	0	1	4.75
Brownie Foreman	19	139.2	16	12	8	6	54	64	0	2	3.22
Frank Killen	13	95	11	6	5	5	25	57	0	0	5.49
Jim Gardner	11	85.1	10	8	8	2	31	27	0	0	2.64
Sam Moran	10	62.2	6	6	2	4	19	51	0	0	7.47
Tom Colcolough	6	35.1	5	2	1	1	15	21	0	0	5.60
Harry Jordan	2	17	2	2	0	2	4	6	0	0	4.24
Jake Hewitt	4	13	2	1	1	0	4	2	0	2	4.15
Gus Weyhing	1	9	1	1	1	0	3	5	0	0	1.00
Gussie Gannon	1	5	0	0	0	0	0	2	0	0	1.80
Dave Wright	1	2	0	0	0	0	0	1	0	0	27.00
Jock Menefee	2	1.2	1	0	0	1	0	7	0	0	16.20
—1 forfeit L vs Baltimore on August 28—											
	1171.2	133	106	71	60	382	500	4	6	4.05	

CINCINNATI   **Buck Ewing**   **League Park (II)**

		G	AB	H	R	2B	3B	HR	RBI	BB	SB	BA	SA
RF	Dusty Miller	132	529	177	103	31	16	10	112	33	43	.335	.510
SS	Germany Smith	127	503	151	75	23	6	4	74	34	13	.300	.394
3B	Arlie Latham	112	460	143	93	14	6	2	69	42	48	.311	.380
1B	Buck Ewing	105	434	138	90	24	13	5	94	30	34	.318	.468
2B	Bid McPhee	115	432	129	107	24	12	1	75	73	30	.299	.417
LF	Dummy Hoy	107	429	119	93	21	12	3	55	52	50	.277	.403
C	Farmer Vaughn	92	334	102	60	23	5	1	48	17	15	.305	.413
CF	George Hogriever	69	239	65	61	8	7	2	34	36	41	.272	.389
Sub	Eddie Burke	56	228	61	52	8	6	1	25	22	19	.268	.368
P	Tom Parrott	64	201	69	35	13	7	3	41	11	10	.343	.522
Sub	Bill Grey	52	181	55	24	17	4	1	29	15	4	.304	.459
Sub	Bug Holliday	32	127	38	25	9	2	0	20	10	6	.299	.402
P	Frank Dwyer	37	113	30	14	3	5	1	16	5	2	.265	.407
P	Billy Rhines	38	113	25	20	2	2	0	23	8	0	.221	.274
P	Frank Foreman	32	94	29	14	7	0	2	11	4	1	.309	.447
Sub	Morg Murphy	25	82	22	15	2	0	0	16	11	6	.268	.293
Sub	Bill Merritt	22	79	14	9	2	0	0	12	6	2	.177	.203
Sub	Harry Spies	14	50	11	2	0	1	0	5	3	0	.220	.260
P	Bill Phillips	19	48	15	9	3	1	0	6	2	1	.313	.417
P	King Bailey	1	4	2	2	1	0	0	1	0	1	.500	.750
Sub	Mike Kahoe	3	4	0	0	0	0	0	0	0	0	.000	.000
		132	4684	1395	903	235	**105**	36	766	414	**326**	.298	.416

1B   Ewing 105, Vaughn 15, Parrott 14, Latham 3, Spies 2
2B   McPhee 115, Grey 16, Hogriever 3, Vaughn 1, Latham 1, Merritt 1
SS   Smith 127, Grey 5
3B   Latham 108, Grey 27, Vaughn 1
OF   Miller 132, Hoy 107, Hogriever 66, Burke 56, Holliday 32, Parrott 9, Grey 1
C   Vaughn 77, Murphy 25, Merritt 20, Spies 12, Grey 5, Kahoe 3
P   Parrott 41, Rhines 38, Dwyer 37, Foreman 32, Phillips 18, Bailey 1

	G	IP	GS	CG	W	L	K	BB	SH	SV	ERA
Frank Dwyer	37	280.1	31	23	18	15	46	74	2	0	4.24
Billy Rhines	38	267.2	33	25	19	10	72	76	0	0	4.81
Tom Parrott	41	263.1	31	23	11	18	57	76	0	**3**	5.47
Frank Foreman	32	219	27	19	11	14	55	92	0	1	4.11
Bill Phillips	18	109	9	6	6	7	15	44	0	2	6.03
King Bailey	1	8	1	1	1	0	0	0	0	0	5.63
		1147.1	132	97	66	64	245	362	2	6	4.81

NEW YORK George Davis (16–17) Jack Doyle (32–31) Harvey Watkins (18–17)
Polo Grounds (III)

		G	AB	H	R	2B	3B	HR	RBI	BB	SB	BA	SA
CF	George Van Haltren	131	521	177	113	23	19	8	103	57	32	.340	.503
RF	Mike Tiernan	120	476	165	127	23	21	7	70	66	36	.347	.527
2B	General Stafford	124	463	129	79	12	5	3	73	40	42	.279	.346
SS	Shorty Fuller	126	458	103	82	11	3	0	32	64	15	.225	.262
3B	George Davis	110	430	146	108	36	9	5	101	55	48	.340	.500
1B	Jack Doyle	82	319	100	52	21	3	1	66	24	35	.313	.408
C	Duke Farrell	90	312	90	38	16	9	1	58	38	11	.288	.407
Sub	Parke Wilson	67	238	56	32	9	0	0	30	14	11	.235	.273
Sub	Yale Murphy	51	184	37	35	6	2	0	16	27	7	.201	.255
P	Amos Rusie	53	179	44	14	3	1	1	19	0	2	.246	.291
LF	Eddie Burke	39	167	43	38	6	2	1	12	7	14	.257	.335
Sub	Tom Bannon	37	159	43	33	6	2	0	8	7	20	.270	.333
P	Dad Clarke	37	121	29	16	2	1	0	10	8	0	.240	.273
LF	Oyster Burns	33	114	35	21	5	3	1	25	14	10	.307	.430
P	Les German	35	111	29	16	2	2	2	16	9	1	.261	.369
P	Jouett Meekin	31	96	28	16	4	3	1	16	3	2	.292	.427
Sub	Pop Schriver	24	92	29	16	2	1	1	16	9	3	.315	.391
Sub	Willie Clark	23	88	23	9	3	2	0	16	5	1	.261	.341
Sub	Harry Davis	7	24	7	1	0	1	0	6	2	1	.292	.375
Sub	Frank Butler	5	22	6	5	1	0	0	2	1	0	.273	.318
P	Andy Boswell	5	16	3	1	0	0	0	1	1	1	.188	.188
P	Ed Doheny	3	10	1	0	0	1	0	3	1	0	.100	.300
Sub	Larry Battam	2	4	1	0	0	0	0	0	2	0	.250	.250
P	Frank Knauss	1	1	0	0	0	0	0	0	0	0	.000	.000
		132	4605	1324	852	191	90	32	699	454	292	.288	.389

1B Doyle 58, Clark 23, Bannon 16, G. Davis 14, Wilson 11, H. Davis 7, Schriver 6, Farrell 2, Burns 1
2B Stafford 110, Doyle 13, G. Davis 10, Murphy 1
SS Fuller 126, Murphy 8
3B G. Davis 81, Farrell 24, German 11, Murphy 8, Doyle 6, Wilson 3, Battam 2, Stafford 2
OF Van Haltren 131, Tiernan 119, Burke 39, Murphy 33, Burns 32, Bannon 21, Stafford 12, G. Davis 7, Butler 5, Rusie 1
C Farrell 62, Wilson 53, Schriver 18, Doyle 4
P Rusie 49, Clarke 37, Meekin 29, German 25, Boswell 5, Doheny 3, Van Haltren 1, Knauss 1

	G	IP	GS	CG	W	L	K	BB	SH	SV	ERA
Amos Rusie	49	393.1	47	42	23	23	**201**	159	**4**	0	3.73
Dad Clarke	37	281.2	30	27	18	15	67	60	1	1	3.39
Jouett Meekin	29	225.2	29	24	16	11	76	73	1	0	5.30
Les German	25	178.1	18	16	7	11	36	78	0	0	5.96
Andy Boswell	5	34	4	3	2	2	18	22	0	0	5.82
Ed Doheny	3	25.2	3	3	0	3	9	19	0	0	6.66
George Van Haltren	1	5	0	0	0	0	1	2	0	0	12.60
Frank Knauss	1	3.2	1	0	0	0	1	2	0	0	17.18
		1147.1	132	115	66	65	**409**	415	6	1	4.51

WASHINGTON Gus Schmelz **Boundary Field**

		G	AB	H	R	2B	3B	HR	RBI	BB	SB	BA	SA
C	Deacon McGuire	132	533	179	89	30	8	10	97	40	16	.336	.478
LF	Kip Selbach	129	516	166	115	21	**22**	6	55	69	31	.322	.483
CF	Charlie Abbey	132	511	141	102	14	10	8	84	43	28	.276	.389
3B	Bill Joyce	126	474	148	110	25	13	17	95	96	29	.312	.527
1B	Ed Cartwright	122	472	156	95	34	17	3	90	54	50	.331	.494

		G	AB	H	R	2B	3B	HR	RBI	BB	SB	BA	SA
2B	Jack Crooks	117	409	114	80	19	8	6	57	68	36	.279	.408
RF	Bill Hassamaer	85	358	100	42	18	4	1	60	26	8	.279	.360
P	Win Mercer	63	196	50	26	9	1	1	26	12	7	.255	.327
SS	Frank Scheibeck	48	167	31	17	5	2	0	25	17	5	.186	.240
P	Jake Boyd	51	157	42	29	5	1	1	16	20	2	.268	.331
OF	Tom Brown	34	134	32	25	8	3	2	16	18	8	.239	.388
SS	Jack Glasscock	25	100	23	20	2	0	0	10	7	3	.230	.250
P	Varney Anderson	35	97	28	22	2	3	0	16	10	0	.289	.371
Sub	Dan Coogan	26	77	17	9	2	1	0	7	13	1	.221	.273
P	Otis Stocksdale	25	74	23	12	4	2	0	15	3	1	.311	.419
P	Al Maul	22	72	18	9	5	2	0	16	6	0	.250	.375
Sub	Gene Demontreville	12	46	10	7	1	3	0	9	3	5	.217	.370
Sub	Parson Nicholson	10	38	7	7	2	1	0	5	7	6	.184	.289
P	John Malarkey	22	37	5	2	0	0	0	4	2	0	.135	.135
P	John Gilroy	12	29	7	8	1	0	0	4	1	0	.241	.276
Sub	Billy Lush	5	18	6	2	0	0	0	2	2	0	.333	.333
P	Joe Corbett	7	15	2	1	0	0	0	1	0	0	.133	.133
P	Andy Boswell	7	14	4	4	0	0	0	1	1	1	.286	.286
Sub	Dan Mahoney	6	12	2	2	0	0	0	1	0	0	.167	.167
P	Doc McJames	2	7	1	1	0	0	0	1	0	0	.143	.143
P	Carlton Molesworth	4	7	1	0	0	0	0	0	0	0	.143	.143
Sub	Joe Woerlin	1	3	1	1	0	0	0	0	0	0	.333	.333
Sub	Bill McCauley	1	2	0	0	0	0	0	0	0	0	.000	.000
P	Ed Buckingham	1	1	0	0	0	0	0	0	0	0	.000	.000
P	Oscar Purner	1	1	0	0	0	0	0	0	0	0	.000	.000
Sub	Phil Wisner	1	0	0	0	0	0	0	0	0	0	—	—
		132	4577	1314	837	207	101	55	713	**518**	237	.287	.412

1B Cartwright 122, Hassamaer 9, Boswell 1, Mahoney 1
2B Crooks 117, Boyd 10, Selbach 5, Scheibeck 2, Mercer 1
SS Scheibeck 44, Glasscock 25, Coogan 18, Demontreville 12, Nicholson 10, Boyd 8, Mercer 7, Selbach 6, Corbett 2, Woerlin 1, Wisner 1, McGuire 1, Hassamaer 1, McCauley 1
3B Joyce 126, Mercer 3, Scheibeck 2, Hassamaer 1, Boyd 1, Coogan 1, Gilroy 1
OF Abbey 132, Selbach 118, Hassamaer 75, Brown 34, Boyd 21, Mercer 5, Lush 5, Maul 4, Gilroy 3, Coogan 2, Corbett 2, Stocksdale 2, Anderson 1
C McGuire 132, Coogan 5, Mahoney 2
P Mercer 43, Anderson 29, Malarkey 22, Stocksdale 20, Maul 16, Boyd 14, Gilroy 8, Boswell 6, Molesworth 4, Corbett 3, McJames 2, Buckingham 1, Purner 1

	G	IP	GS	CG	W	L	K	BB	SH	SV	ERA
Win Mercer	43	311	38	32	13	23	84	96	0	2	4.46
Varney Anderson	29	204.2	25	18	9	16	35	97	0	0	5.89
Otis Stocksdale	20	136	17	11	6	11	23	52	0	1	6.09
Al Maul	16	135.2	16	14	10	5	34	37	0	0	**2.45**
John Malarkey	22	100.2	8	5	0	8	32	60	0	2	5.99
Jake Boyd	14	85.1	12	8	2	11	16	35	0	0	7.07
John Gilroy	8	41.1	4	2	1	4	2	24	0	0	6.53
Andy Boswell	6	30	3	3	1	2	12	19	0	0	6.00
Joe Corbett	3	19	3	3	0	2	3	9	0	0	5.68
Doc McJames	2	17	2	2	1	1	9	16	0	0	1.59
Carlton Molesworth	4	16	3	1	0	2	7	15	0	0	14.63
Ed Buckingham	1	3	1	0	0	0	1	2	0	0	6.00
Oscar Purner	1	2	0	0	0	0	0	3	0	0	9.00
		1101.2	132	99	43	85	258	465	0	5	5.28

ST. LOUIS   **Al Buckenberger (16–34)**   **Chris Von Der Ahe (1–0)**   **Joe Quinn (11–28)**
Lew Phelan (11–30)   **Sportsman's Park (II)**

	G	AB	H	R	2B	3B	HR	RBI	BB	SB	BA	SA
LF	Duff Cooley	132	563	191	106	9	20	7	75	36	27	.339	.464
2B	Joe Quinn	134	543	169	84	19	9	2	74	36	22	.311	.390
RF	Tommy Dowd	129	505	163	95	19	17	7	74	30	30	.323	.469
3B	Doggie Miller	121	490	143	81	15	4	5	74	25	18	.292	.369
SS	Bones Ely	117	467	121	68	16	2	1	46	19	28	.259	.308
1B	Roger Connor	104	398	131	78	29	9	8	77	63	9	.329	.508
CF	Tom Brown	83	350	76	72	11	4	1	31	48	34	.217	.280
C	Heinie Peitz	90	334	95	44	14	12	2	65	29	9	.284	.416
P	Ted Breitenstein	72	218	42	25	2	0	0	18	29	5	.193	.202
Sub	Biff Sheehan	52	180	57	24	3	6	1	18	20	7	.317	.417
3B	Denny Lyons	33	129	38	24	6	0	2	25	14	3	.295	.388
P	Bill Kissinger	33	97	24	8	6	1	0	8	0	1	.247	.330
P	Red Ehret	37	96	21	13	2	1	1	9	6	0	.219	.292
Sub	Joe Otten	26	87	21	8	0	0	0	8	5	2	.241	.241
Sub	Ike Samuls	34	74	17	5	2	0	0	5	5	5	.230	.257
P	Harry Staley	23	67	9	4	0	2	0	1	4	1	.134	.194
Sub	Frank Bonner	15	59	8	3	0	1	1	8	1	2	.136	.220
P	Dewey McDougal	18	41	6	1	1	0	0	6	8	0	.146	.171
P	Dad Clarkson	7	23	1	0	0	0	0	0	3	0	.043	.043
Sub	Marty Hogan	5	18	3	2	1	0	0	2	3	2	.167	.222
Sub	Guy McFadden	4	14	3	1	0	0	0	2	0	0	.214	.214
Sub	Joe Connor	2	7	0	0	0	0	0	1	0	0	.000	.000
Sub	Henry Adkinson	1	5	2	1	0	0	0	0	0	0	.400	.400
P	John Coleman	1	5	1	0	0	0	0	0	0	0	.200	.200
Sub	Walt Kinlock	1	3	1	0	0	0	0	0	0	0	.333	.333
Sub	Fred Fagin	1	3	1	0	0	0	0	2	0	0	.333	.333
P	Red Donahue	1	3	0	0	0	0	0	0	0	0	.000	.000
Sub	John Ryan	2	2	0	0	0	0	0	0	0	0	.000	.000
		135	4781	1344	747	155	88	38	629	384	205	.281	.374

1B   Connor 103, Sheehan 11, Peitz 11, Miller 6, McFadden 4
2B   Quinn 134, Dowd 2
SS   Ely 117, Miller 9, Kissinger 4, Samuls 3, Cooley 3
3B   Miller 46, Lyons 33, Samuls 31, Dowd 17, Peitz 10, Bonner 10, Cooley 5, Ryan 2, Connor 2, Kinlock 1, Kissinger 1
OF   Cooley 124, Dowd 115, Brown 83, Sheehan 41, Miller 21, Breitenstein 16, Bonner 5, Hogan 5, Kissinger 4, Otten 2, Adkinson 1
C   Peitz 71, Miller 46, Otten 24, Bonner 1, Fagin 1, Cooley 1
P   Breitenstein 54, Ehret 37, Kissinger 24, Staley 23, McDougal 18, Clarkson 7, Donahue 1, Coleman 1

	G	IP	GS	CG	W	L	K	BB	SH	SV	ERA
Ted Breitenstein	54	429.2	50	46	19	30	127	178	1	1	4.44
Red Ehret	37	231.2	32	18	6	19	55	88	0	0	6.02
Harry Staley	23	158.2	16	13	6	13	28	39	0	0	5.22
Bill Kissinger	24	140.2	14	9	4	12	31	51	0	0	6.72
Dewey McDougal	18	114.2	14	10	3	10	23	46	0	0	8.32
Dad Clarkson	7	61	7	7	1	6	9	26	0	0	7.38
Red Donahue	1	8	1	1	0	1	2	3	0	0	6.75
John Coleman	1	8	1	1	0	1	5	8	0	0	13.50
		1152.1	135	105	39	92	280	439	1	1	5.76

LOUISVILLE   John McCloskey   Eclipse Park (II)

		G	AB	H	R	2B	3B	HR	RBI	BB	SB	BA	SA
LF	Fred Clarke	132	550	191	96	21	5	4	82	34	40	.347	.425
2B	John O'Brien	128	539	138	82	10	4	1	50	45	15	.256	.295
SS	Frank Shugart	113	473	125	61	14	13	4	70	31	14	.264	.374
3B	Jimmy Collins	96	373	104	65	17	5	6	49	33	12	.279	.399
1B	Harry Spies	74	276	74	42	14	7	2	35	11	4	.268	.391
RF	Tom Gettinger	63	260	70	28	11	5	2	32	8	6	.269	.373
C	Jack Warner	67	232	62	20	4	2	1	20	11	10	.267	.315
CF	Joe Wright	60	228	63	30	10	4	1	30	12	7	.276	.368
Sub	Walter Preston	50	197	55	42	6	4	1	24	17	11	.279	.365
Sub	Ducky Holmes	40	161	60	33	10	2	3	20	12	9	.373	.516
C	Tub Welch	47	153	37	18	4	1	1	8	13	2	.242	.301
P	Tom McCreery	31	108	35	18	3	1	0	10	8	3	.324	.370
P	Bert Cunningham	32	100	30	14	7	3	0	13	9	0	.300	.430
1B	Dan Brouthers	24	97	30	13	10	1	2	15	11	1	.309	.495
Sub	Bill Hassamaer	23	96	20	7	2	2	0	14	3	0	.208	.271
OF	Dan Sweeney	22	90	24	18	5	0	1	16	17	2	.267	.356
P	Gus Weyhing	28	89	20	9	2	0	1	10	11	1	.225	.281
P	Bert Inks	28	84	21	9	4	0	0	7	6	0	.250	.298
P	Mike McDermott	33	82	13	12	2	3	0	4	13	1	.159	.256
Sub	Jack Glasscock	18	74	25	9	3	1	1	6	3	1	.338	.446
Sub	Ambrose McGann	20	73	21	9	5	2	0	9	8	6	.288	.411
P	Pat Luby	19	53	15	6	2	2	0	9	8	2	.283	.396
Sub	Fred Zahner	21	49	11	7	1	1	0	6	6	0	.224	.286
Sub	Fred Pfeffer	11	45	13	8	1	0	0	5	5	2	.289	.311
Sub	Billie Kemmer	11	38	7	5	0	0	1	3	2	0	.184	.263
Sub	Dan Minnehan	8	34	13	6	0	0	0	6	1	0	.382	.382
Sub	Henry Cote	10	33	10	10	0	0	0	5	3	2	.303	.303
P	Phil Knell	10	26	6	3	2	1	0	6	1	1	.231	.385
Sub	Tom Morrison	6	22	6	3	0	2	0	4	1	0	.273	.455
P	Dan McFarlan	7	21	5	2	1	0	0	1	0	0	.238	.286
Sub	Hercules Burnett	5	17	7	6	0	1	2	3	2	2	.412	.882
Sub	Gil Hatfield	5	16	3	3	0	0	0	1	1	0	.188	.188
Sub	Barry McCormick	3	12	3	2	0	1	0	0	0	1	.250	.417
Sub	Mike Trost	3	12	1	1	0	0	0	1	0	1	.083	.083
P	Jack Wadsworth	2	4	1	0	0	0	0	0	0	0	.250	.250
P	George Meakim	1	3	1	1	0	0	0	0	0	0	.333	.333
Sub	Grant Briggs	1	3	0	0	0	0	0	0	0	0	.000	.000
P	Bill Kling	1	1	0	0	0	0	0	0	0	0	.000	.000
P	George Borchers	1	0	0	0	0	0	0	0	0	0	—	—
P	Bill Childers	1	0	0	0	0	0	0	0	0	0	—	—
		133	4724	1320	698	171	73	34	574	346	156	.279	.368

1B   Spies 47, Brouthers 24, Hassamaer 21, Welch 20, Glasscock 5, Luby 5, Warner 3, O'Brien 3, Trost 3, Pfeffer 3, Kemmer 2, McCreery 1, Burnett 1

2B   O'Brien 125, Pfeffer 3, Collins 2, Warner 1, McCormick 1, Hassamaer 1

SS   Shugart 88, Glasscock 13, McGann 8, Holmes 8, Pfeffer 5, McCreery 4, Morrison 3, McCormick 2, Hatfield 2, Collins 1, Hassamaer 1, Spies 1

3B   Collins 77, Preston 25, Kemmer 9, Minnehan 7, McGann 6, Holmes 4, Hatfield 3, Morrison 3, McCreery 1

OF   Clarke 132, Gettinger 63, Wright 59, Holmes 29, Shugart 27, Preston 26, Sweeney 22, McCreery 18, Collins 18, McGann 5, Burnett 4, Minnehan 2, Luby 2, Cunningham 1

C   Warner 64, Welch 28, Spies 26, Zahner 21, Cote 10, Briggs 1, Wright 1

P   McDermott 33, Cunningham 31, Weyhing 28, Inks 28, Luby 11, Knell 10, McCreery 8, McFarlan 7, Wadsworth 2, Holmes 2, Gettinger 2, Meakim 1, Borchers 1, Kling 1, Childers 1

	G	IP	GS	CG	W	L	K	BB	SH	SV	ERA
Bert Cunningham	31	231	28	24	11	16	49	104	1	0	4.75
Gus Weyhing	28	213	25	22	7	19	53	66	1	0	5.41
Mike McDermott	33	207.1	26	18	4	19	42	103	0	0	5.99
Bert Inks	28	205.1	27	21	7	20	42	78	0	0	6.40
Pat Luby	11	71.1	6	5	1	5	12	19	0	0	6.81
Phil Knell	10	56.2	6	3	0	6	19	21	0	0	6.51
Tom McCreery	8	48.2	4	3	3	1	14	38	1	1	5.36
Dan McFarlan	7	46	7	6	0	7	10	15	0	0	6.65
Ducky Holmes	2	14	1	1	1	0	0	4	0	0	5.79
Jack Wadsworth	2	9	0	0	0	1	2	7	0	0	16.00
George Meakim	1	7	1	1	1	0	2	4	0	0	2.57
Tom Gettinger	2	6.1	0	0	0	0	0	1	0	0	7.11
Bill Kling	1	1	0	0	0	0	0	1	0	0	0.00
George Borchers	1	0.2	1	0	0	1	0	3	0	0	27.00
Bill Childers	1	0	0	0	0	0	0	6	0	0	—
		—1 forfeit L vs Brooklyn on May 23—									
		1117.1	132	104	35	95	245	470	3	1	5.90

1896

BREAK UP THE BIRDS

Commencing in 1896, the decision rested with the head umpire, rather than the home team captain, when and if to resume play following a rain delay. That same year rules originated that the home team had to have at least a dozen balls on hand for each scheduled contest and that only players in uniform, the manager and the club president were allowed to occupy their team's bench during the course of a game. Otherwise the 1896 season brought remarkably few changes. Yet batting marks continued to plummet, dropping another six points per player, and the average pitcher's ERA fell from 4.76 to 4.38. So acutely had the scale again begun to tip toward the defensive side that the St. Louis Browns' loop worst ERA in 1896 of 5.33 was just .01 runs above the League-Association average two years earlier.

The pitching resurgence initially seemed as if it might halt the Baltimore Orioles' pennant skein. At the end of the first month of the 1896 season, the standings looked as if they had been printed upside down. Kingpin Baltimore sat in ninth place and Cleveland, the 1895 runner-up, was anchored in the tenth berth while the Pittsburgh Pirates in their second full season with catcher-manager Connie Mack at their helm, ruled the harbor after an 8-2 April.

But apart from Pink Hawley and Frank Killen, who in 1896 became the last National League southpaw to win 30 games, Pittsburgh had no pitchers of consequence. Cleveland, after acquiring Zeke Wilson from Boston, had a third solid starter behind Cy Young and Nig Cuppy and began to come on strong in May. Baltimore likewise reverted to form when rookie righthander Arlie Pond showed evidence of compensating for Sadie McMahon's chronic sore arm and erratic work from George Hemming and Duke Esper. Following on the heels of Bill Hoffer, Pond gave Orioles pilot Ned Hanlon his second outstanding yearling hurler in two seasons, but Hanlon was still not out of the woods. Although Heinie Reitz mended from his fractured collarbone, freeing the Orioles to swap interim second baseman Kid Gleason to New York for first sacker Jack Doyle, a hole suddenly opened at third base

SAD SPIDERS

Cleveland's keystone partners, Cupid Childs (left) and Ed McKean. Ironically, the only other two middle infielders who had .300 career BAs with at least 1,500 hits but failed to make the Hall of Fame were Cecil Travis and Buddy Myer, who also were keystone partners with Washington in the 1930s.

There are only four middle infielders in all of major league history who are not in the Hall of Fame despite compiling .300 career batting averages while achieving over 1,500 hits, and two of them played side by side for the Cleveland Spiders in the 1890s. Even allowing for the fact that batting marks in the mid-1890s are somewhat suspect, Cupid Childs and Ed McKean are still worthy candidates. They are not in the Hall of Fame for one reason. Cleveland never won a pennant with them and everyone discounts the Spiders' Temple Cup triumph in 1895. There are a number of explanations for Cleveland's failure to beat out Boston or Baltimore at least once in the 1890s, but one stands out above all others. Jesse Burkett was among the best outfielders of his day; the other two men Cleveland had out there with him most of the time were stiffs. The evidence of that is overpowering. Between 1893, the year the pitching distance was increased, and the end of the century, the three men who saw the most outfield duty in Cleveland livery were Burkett, Harry Blake and Jimmy McAleer. Burkett had the third highest BA of any player during that period who collected at least 1,000 at bats. His .376 mark for the eight seasons between 1893 and 1900 trails only Willie Keeler's .382 and Ed Delahanty's .377. Blake and McAleer are leading members of the exact opposite list.

THE WORST-HITTING OUTFIELDERS (1893–1900), MINIMUM 1000 AT BATS

	AB	H	BA
Harry Blake	1877	473	.252
Tom Brown	2508	645	.257
Dick Harley	1467	362	.260
Jimmy McAleer	2043	537	.263

Brown and Harley had some excuse. They played most of the time with rotten teams. Blake and McAleer had no excuse. They were poor hitters who would have posted some of the lowest outfield batting averages in history if they had played ten years earlier or ten years later. Cleveland had no excuse either. McAleer arguably could have been carried for his glove, but not to find someone better than Blake cost the Spiders a pennant or two and cost either Childs or McKean—or possibly both—a spot in Cooperstown.

after John McGraw was downed by typhoid fever during spring training. As a stopgap, Hanlon turned to Jim Donnelly, a perennial minor leaguer following three straight seasons in the mid-1880s when he hit .201 or less. Given unexpected life, Donnelly blossomed, batting .328 to exactly match the Orioles' loop-leading team average.

Still, Baltimore could not shed Cleveland. Moreover, the two preseason favorites were receiving a surprisingly stiff challenge from the Cincinnati Reds. Barely a .500 team in 1895, the Reds were steered by local favorite Buck Ewing, now nearly through as a player but still strong on the fundamentals of the game and good at teaching them. With Bid McPhee at second base, wide-ranging Germany Smith at short and Dummy Hoy in center field, Ewing's team was particularly strong up the middle, and it was reflected in the 1896 fielding stats. McPhee, in the first full season he wore a glove, set a new fielding-average record for second basemen and the Reds became the first team in major league history to average fewer than two errors a game. At the end of July, Cincinnati sat atop the League-Association throne at 61-29, two games up on Baltimore and three and a half ahead of Cleveland. Two Achilles' heels then overturned the Reds. Bug Holliday, after undergoing a near fatal appendectomy the previous year, could play only 29 games in 1896, and Ewing was never able to replace his run production. Cincinnati's second hindrance was encroaching age. The oldest of the three contending teams, the Reds tired and won just 16 of 37 games in the last two months of the season.

A 19-7 run in August enabled Baltimore to open up a five-and-a-half-game bulge on Cincinnati. The Orioles moved out of reach by sweeping a Labor Day tripleheader from last-place Louisville and then taking a twin bill from the Colonels the following day. On September 10, the Spiders, after nipping at Cincinnati's heels for most of the month, finally passed their interstate rivals and gained the right to oppose Baltimore in the Temple Cup series.

For the second year in a row Cleveland's Jesse Burkett paced the League-Association in batting and hits. Burkett also led in total bases, but most of the other offensive honors went to Ed Delahanty of

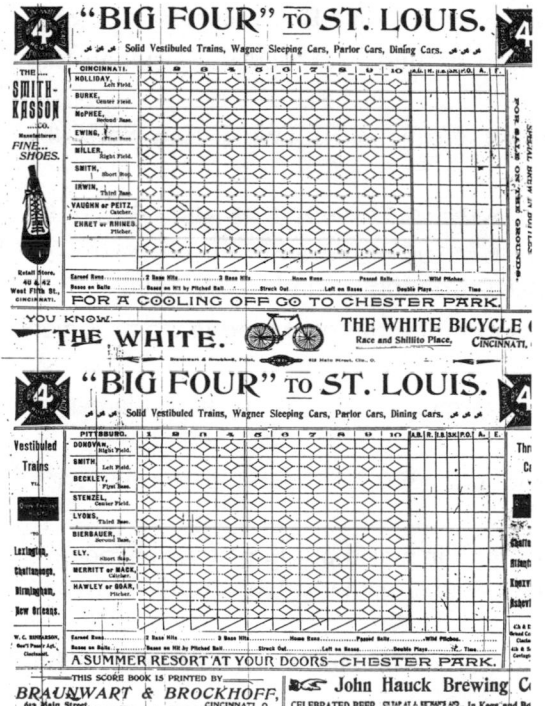

A page from an 1896 Cincinnati scorecard. Jot Goar must have been thrilled when he came to the park that day and saw himself listed as a likely starting pitcher since he never got to start a single game in the majors.

Philadelphia. Delahanty's day against Adonis Terry of Chicago on July 13 typified the Phillies' disappointing year when he became the only slugger prior to 1986 to hit four home runs in a losing cause. A preseason trade that brought Billy Nash from Boston for Billy Hamilton proved particularly costly for the Phils when Nash, plagued by injuries and dual responsibilities as the club's manager and third baseman, hit just .247 while Hamilton was hitting 118 points higher, topping the League-Association in walks and scoring 152 runs. Nor did it help the Phils soothe their fans when they went 0-12 for the season against the Orioles and finished eighth. Philadelphia's slide resulted in a drop of over 100,000 in atten-

FAMOUS FIRST VIII

In 1895, Deacon McGuire of Washington became the first catcher in the post-1893 era to lead his team in hitting as well as the last catcher until 1944 to lead his team in at bats. Another remarkably underpublicized catching first occurred in 1896. That year, for the first time ever, a 45-year-old man caught as many as ten games in a major league season. It was not done by McGuire, though he would later become the first to catch as many as 100 games after age 40. It was done by none other than the player-manager of the Chicago Colts, one Cap Anson. A list of some other significant catching firsts in the last century:

first rookie regular catcher on a pennant winner—Mike Hines, Boston NL, 1883

First post-1876 catcher to lead his team in batting—Cal McVey, Cincinnati NL, 1877; John Clapp, St. Louis NL, 1877

First catcher to lead a major league in home runs—Buck Ewing, New York NL, 1883

First to catch 100 or more games in a season—Doc Bushong, St. Louis AA, 1886

First to catch 100 or more games and collect 100 or more hits in the same season—Connie Mack, Buffalo PL, and Jack O'Connor, Columbus AA, 1890

First to catch 100 or more games in a season for a National League team—Chief Zimmer, Cleveland, 1890

First lefthander to catch 100 or more games in a season—Jack Clements, Philadelphia NL, 1891

First to catch 100 or more games and bat .300 in the same season—Jack O'Connor, Columbus AA, 1890 (.324)

First post–1876 player to be a regular at a middle infield position after serving one or more years as a regular catcher—Jack Rowe, regular catcher 1880–84, regular shortstop 1885–90

First regular catcher to lead his team in stolen bases—King Kelly, Boston NL, 1888

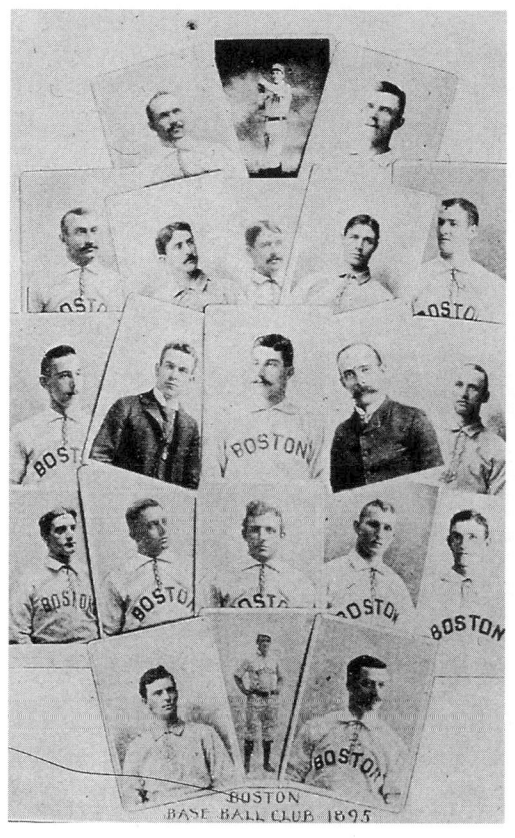

Billy Nash, seen here in 1895, his last season with Boston, flopped as Philadelphia's player-manager in 1896. Though he was one of the top third basemen in the last century, more is known about most one-gamers than is known about him. Nash died of a heart attack in 1929 while visiting the Board of Health building in East Orange, New Jersey. All we know about his life at the time is that he was working as a hospital orderly in Wrentham, Massachusetts. Top: John Ryan, Frank Sexton, Charlie Ganzel. Row four: Jack Stivetts, Zeke Wilson, George Hodson, Jimmy Collins, Kid Nichols. Middle row: Bobby Lowe, Hugh Duffy, Nash, Frank Selee, Jack Warner. Row two: Cozy Dolan, Tommy McCarthy, Jimmy Bannon, Herman Long, Jim Sullivan. Bottom: Charlie Nyce, Fred Tenney, Tommy Tucker.

Four of the six Hall of Famers who were the heart of the 1894–96 Baltimore dynasty. Back: Willie Keeler and John McGraw. Front: Joe Kelley and Hughie Jennings. Missing from this elegant study are Wilbert Robinson and the moving force behind the dynasty, manager Ned Hanlon, who was not selected to the Hall of Fame until 1996.

Though the 1896 Brooklyn Bridegrooms dressed to kill for their team pic, they played far beneath their potential and finished deep in the second division. By the end of the 1896 season only player-manager Dave Foutz and Tom Daly remained to remind Brooklyn fans of the team's 1889–90 mini-dynasty. Foutz died before the 1897 campaign began and Daly was released. Daly later returned, however, and became the lone man to play for both Brooklyn's 1889–90 and 1899–1900 mini-dynasties. Top: Burrell, Yeager, Bonner, Griffin, Harper, McCarthy, Payne, Gumbert and Shoch. Middle: Daly, Smith, Corcoran, Jones, Kennedy, Abbey and Daub. Seated: Daily, Anderson, Foutz, Grim, LaChance, Stein.

dance, but the Phils drew almost treble the number of customers last-place Louisville did. Bad as the Colonels were, though, they produced three of the year's most exciting new-comers as freshman fireballers Chick Fraser and Still Bill Hill finished one-two in the League-Association in walks and Tom McCreery, in his first full season, topped all League-Association batters in strikeouts but nonetheless fell just four points short of the nineteenth-century National League record for the highest batting average by a switchhitter in 400 or more at bats when he rapped .351.

Brooklyn also produced a fine rookie in right fielder Fielder Jones, whose .354 mark fell only four points short of the record established the previous year by Chicago's Bill Everett for the highest batting average ever by a rookie in 400 or more at bats. Notwithstanding Jones's debut, the Bridegrooms plummeted to tie with Washington for ninth place and posted their lowest winning percentage (.443) since 1884, their inaugural major league season. Brooklyn's co-tenant in the nation's largest metropolitan area, the New York Giants, also dropped below .500 when Amos Rusie sat out the entire season after team owner Andrew Freedman fined him $200 for "indifference" and tried to slash his salary.

Freedman claimed the climate of the times justified his closefisted tactics with Rusie and other Giants stars and could point to the 1896 Temple Cup series as an example. For the second year in a row poor crowds turned out in both Cleveland and Baltimore. Severely lashed after their previous two embarrassing Temple Cup losses, the Orioles decided to take the postseason proceeding a little more seriously this time. Hoffer cruised to a 7-1 win over Young in the opener. When Spiders manager Patsy Tebeau turned to Bobby Wallace, his fourth-strong pitcher, in Game Two, Hanlon countered with Joe Corbett. The younger brother of heavyweight champ Jim Corbett, the 20-year-old righthander had been used sparingly during the regular season. Corbett won Game Two, 7-2, and Hanlon, hoping to spark fan interest, called on him again in Game Four after Hoffer breezed to another win in the third contest to give the Orioles a commanding 3-0 lead. But only around 1,500 shuffled through the League Park turnstiles on October 8 to watch Corbett and Nig Cuppy duel through six scoreless innings. Baltimore then tallied two runs in the seventh and three more in the eighth to give Corbett a 5-0 verdict and seal the second dull 4-0 sweep in the Temple Cup's brief three-year history. Each winning Oriole got around $200 while the Spiders took home only $117 per man. Even in a time of miserably small salaries and low player morale, the meager payoff for playing in raw weather to determine a winner few took seriously seemed hardly worth the effort.

THE SEASONAL RECORD

	W	L	PCT	HOME	ROAD	GB
1. Baltimore Orioles	90	39	.698	49–16	41–23	—
2. Cleveland Spiders	80	48	.625	43–19	37–29	9.5
3. Cincinnati Reds	77	50	.606	51–15	26–35	12
4. Boston Beaneaters	74	57	.565	42–24	32–33	17
5. Chicago Colts	71	57	.555	42–24	29–33	18.5
6. Pittsburgh Pirates	66	63	.512	35–31	31–32	24
7. New York Giants	64	67	.489	39–26	25–41	27
8. Philadelphia Phillies	62	68	.477	42–27	20–41	28.5
9. Brooklyn Bridegrooms	58	73	.443	35–28	23–45	33
Washington Nationals	58	73	.443	38–29	20–44	33
11. St. Louis Browns	40	90	.308	27–34	13–56	50.5
12. Louisville Colonels	38	93	.290	25–37	13–56	53

	Ba	Cl	Cin	Bo	Ch	Pi	NY	Ph	Was	Br	StL	Lo	
Baltimore	—	3	10	5	7	9	9	12	10	60	91	10	90
Cleveland	8	—	5	7	9	4	7	6	9	7	10	8	80
Cincinnati	2	6	—	6	6	5	6	8	7	10	12	9	77
Boston	7	5	5	—	3	7	7	7	7	10	8	8	74
Chicago	4	2	4	9	—	11	5	4	8	6	9	9	71
Pittsburgh	2	8	7	5	1	—	8	6	6	5	8	10	66
New York	3	5	6	5	7	4	—	3	6	8	9	8	64
Philadelphia	0	6	4	5	8	6	8	—	8	4	8	5	62
Washington	2	3	4	5	4	6	6	4	—	8	7	9	58
Brooklyn	6	5	2	2	6	6	4	8	4	—	7	8	58
St. Louis	3	2	0	4	3	3	3	3	5	5	—	9	40
Louisville	2	3	3	4	3	2	4	7	3	4	3	—	38
	39	48	50	57	57	63	67	68	73	73	90	93	778

SEASON LEADERS

Batting Average (350 ABs)

1.	Burkett, Cleveland	.410
2.	Jennings, Baltimore	.401
3.	Delahanty, Philadelphia	.397
4.	Keeler, Baltimore	.386
5.	Tiernan, New York	.369

On–Base Percentage

1.	Hamilton, Philadelphia	.477
2.	Delahanty, Philadelphia	.472
	Jennings, Baltimore	.472
4.	Joyce, Wash–NY	.470
5.	Kelley, Baltimore	.469

Home Runs

1.	Delahanty, Philadelphia	13
	Joyce, Wash–NY	13
3.	Thompson, Philadelphia	12
4.	Connor, St. Louis	11
5.	Dahlen, Chicago	9
	Clarke, Louisville	9

Hits

1.	Burkett, Cleveland	240
2.	Keeler, Baltimore	210
3.	Jennings, Baltimore	209
4.	Delahanty, Philadelphia	198
5.	Van Haltren, New York	197

Stolen Bases

1.	Kelley, Baltimore	87
2.	Lange, Chicago	84
3.	Hamilton, Boston	83
4.	Miller, Cincinnati	76
5.	Doyle, Baltimore	73

Slugging Average

1.	Delahanty, Philadelphia	.631
2.	Dahlen, Chicago	.553
3.	McCreery, Louisville	.546
4.	Kelley, Baltimore	.543
5.	Burkett, Cleveland	.541

Total Bases

1.	Burkett, Cleveland	317
2.	Delahanty, Philadelphia	315
3.	Kelley, Baltimore	282
4.	Van Haltren, New York	272
5.	Keeler, Baltimore	270

RBI

1.	Delahanty, Philadelphia	126
2.	Jennings, Baltimore	121
3.	Duffy, Boston	113
4.	McKean, Cleveland	112
5.	Childs, Cleveland	106
	Reitz, Baltimore	106

Runs

1.	Burkett, Cleveland	160
2.	Keeler, Baltimore	153
3.	Hamilton, Philadelphia	152
4.	Kelley, Baltimore	148
5.	Dahlen, Chicago	137

Strikeouts

1.	McCreery, Louisville	58
2.	Clingman, Louisville	51
3.	Lush, Washington	49
	T. Brown, Washington	49
5.	M. Cross, St. Louis	48

PITCHING

Wins

1.	Nichols, Boston	30
	Killen, Pittsburgh	30
3.	Young, Cleveland	28
4.	Meekin, New York	26
5.	Mercer, Washington	25
	Cuppy, Cleveland	25
	Hoffer, Baltimore	25

Losses

1.	Hart, St. Louis	29
2.	Hill, Louisville	28
3.	Fraser, Louisville	27
4.	Breitenstein, St. Louis	26
5.	D. Clarke, New York	24
	Donahue, St. Louis	24

Innings

1.	Killen, Pittsburgh	432.1
2.	Young, Cleveland	414.1
3.	Hawley, Pittsburgh	378
4.	Nichols, Boston	372.1
5.	Mercer, Washington	366.1

Strikeouts

1.	Young, Cleveland	140
2.	Hawley, Pittsburgh	137
3.	Killen, Pittsburgh	134
4.	Breitenstein, StL	114
5.	Meekin, New York	110

ERA (140 innings)

1.	Rhines, Cincinnati	2.45
2.	Nichols, Boston	2.83
3.	Cuppy, Cleveland	3.12
4.	Dwyer, Cincinnati	3.15
5.	Young, Cleveland	3.24

Complete Games

1.	Killen, Pittsburgh	44
2.	Young, Cleveland	42
3.	Mercer, Washington	38
4.	Nichols, Boston	37
	Hawley, Pittsburgh	37
	Hart, St. Louis	37
	Breitenstein, St. Louis	37

Winning Percentage (25 decisions)

1.	Hoffer, Baltimore	.781
2.	Dwyer, Cincinnati	.686
3.	Nichols, Boston	.682
4.	Griffith, Chicago	.676
5.	Wilson, Cleveland	.653

Lowest On–Base Percentage

1.	Rhines, Cincinnati	.311
2.	Cuppy, Cleveland	.314
3.	Young, Cleveland	.317
	Nichols, Boston	.317
5.	Esper, Baltimore	.319

FIELDING

Total Chances

1B	P. Tebeau, Cleveland	1436
2B	Childs, Cleveland	915
3B	Clingman, Louisville	507
SS	Jennings, Baltimore	919
OF	Lange, Chicago	355
C	McGuire, Washington	466
P	Young, Cleveland	165

Fielding Average

Connor, St. Louis	.988
McPhee, Cincinnati	.978
C. Irwin, Cincinnati	.931
Jennings, Baltimore	.928
Thompson, Philadelphia	.974
Zimmer, Cleveland	.972
Nichols, Boston	1.000

BALTIMORE   **Ned Hanlon**   **Union Park**

		G	AB	H	R	2B	3B	HR	RBI	BB	SB	BA	SA
RF	Willie Keeler	127	544	210	153	22	13	4	82	37	67	.386	.496
SS	Hughie Jennings	130	521	209	125	27	9	0	121	19	70	.401	.488
LF	Joe Kelley	131	519	189	148	31	19	8	100	91	87	.364	.543
CF	Steve Brodie	132	516	153	98	19	11	2	87	36	25	.297	.388
1B	Jack Doyle	118	487	165	116	29	4	1	101	42	73	.339	.421
2B	Heinie Reitz	120	464	133	76	15	6	4	106	49	28	.287	.371
3B	Jim Donnelly	106	396	130	70	14	10	0	71	34	38	.328	.414
C	Boileryard Clarke	80	300	89	48	14	7	2	71	14	7	.297	.410
C	Wilbert Robinson	67	245	85	43	9	6	2	38	14	9	.347	.457
P	Bill Hoffer	35	125	38	23	7	4	0	15	12	8	.304	.424
P	George Hemming	30	97	25	16	6	5	0	11	4	4	.258	.423
Sub	Joe Quinn	24	82	27	22	1	1	0	5	6	6	.329	.366
P	Arlie Pond	28	81	19	10	2	0	0	8	8	1	.235	.259
Sub	John McGraw	23	77	25	20	2	2	0	14	11	13	.325	.403
P	Sadie McMahon	22	73	9	6	2	0	0	4	1	1	.123	.151
P	Duke Esper	20	66	13	7	3	1	0	5	1	0	.197	.273
Sub	Bill Keister	15	58	14	8	3	0	0	5	3	4	.241	.293
P	Joe Corbett	9	22	6	0	1	1	0	3	0	0	.273	.409
P	Dad Clarkson	7	18	5	4	0	0	0	2	2	0	.278	.278
Sub	Frank Bowerman	4	16	2	0	0	0	0	4	1	0	.125	.125
P	Jerry Nops	3	9	1	1	0	0	0	1	1	0	.111	.111
P	Otis Stocksdale	2	3	1	1	0	1	0	0	0	0	.333	1.000
		132	4719	**1548**	**995**	207	**100**	23	**854**	386	**441**	**.328**	**.429**

1B	Doyle 118, Clarke 14, Hemming 1, Bowerman 1, McGraw 1
2B	Reitz 118, Quinn 8, Keister 8, Doyle 1
SS	Jennings 130, Reitz 3, Quinn 1
3B	Donnelly 106, McGraw 18, Keister 6, Quinn 5, Corbett 1
OF	Brodie 132, Kelley 130, Keeler 127, Quinn 8, Hemming 2
C	Robinson 67, Clarke 67, Bowerman 3
P	Hoffer 35, Pond 28, Hemming 25, McMahon 22, Esper 20, Corbett 8, Clarkson 7, Nops 3, Stocksdale 1

	G	IP	GS	CG	W	L	K	BB	SH	SV	ERA
Bill Hoffer	35	309	35	32	25	7	93	95	3	0	3.38
Arlie Pond	28	214.1	26	21	16	8	80	57	2	0	3.49
George Hemming	25	202	21	20	15	6	33	54	3	0	4.19
Sadie McMahon	22	175.2	22	19	11	9	33	55	0	0	3.48
Duke Esper	20	155.2	18	14	14	5	19	39	1	0	3.58
Dad Clarkson	7	47	4	3	4	2	7	18	0	0	4.98
Joe Corbett	8	41	3	3	3	0	28	17	0	1	2.20
Jerry Nops	3	22	3	3	2	1	8	2	0	0	6.14
Otis Stocksdale	1	1.2	0	0	0	1	1	2	0	0	16.20
		1168.1	132	115	90	39	302	339	9	1	3.67

CLEVELAND **Patsy Tebeau** **League Park (I)**

		G	AB	H	R	2B	3B	HR	RBI	BB	SB	BA	SA
LF	Jesse Burkett	133	**586**	**240**	**160**	27	16	6	72	49	34	.410	.541
SS	Ed McKean	133	571	193	100	29	12	7	112	45	13	.338	.468
1B	Patsy Tebeau	132	543	146	56	22	6	2	94	21	20	.269	.343
2B	Cupid Childs	132	498	177	106	24	9	1	106	100	25	.355	.446
CF	Jimmy McAleer	116	455	131	70	16	4	1	54	47	24	.288	.347
3B	Chippy McGarr	113	455	122	68	16	4	1	53	22	16	.268	.327
RF	Harry Blake	104	383	92	66	12	5	1	43	46	10	.240	.305
C	Chief Zimmer	91	336	93	46	18	3	3	46	31	4	.277	.375
Sub	Jack O'Connor	68	256	76	41	11	1	1	43	15	15	.297	.359
P	Cy Young	53	180	52	31	11	3	3	28	4	1	.289	.433
P	Bobby Wallace	45	149	35	19	6	3	1	17	11	2	.235	.336
P	Nig Cuppy	47	141	38	29	5	2	1	20	20	1	.270	.355
P	Zeke Wilson	33	100	27	18	3	2	0	13	5	1	.270	.340
Sub	John Shearon	16	64	11	6	0	1	0	3	4	3	.172	.203
Sub	Tom Delahanty	16	56	13	11	4	0	0	4	8	4	.232	.304
Sub	Tom O'Meara	12	33	5	5	0	0	0	0	5	0	.152	.152
Sub	Sport McAllister	8	27	6	2	2	0	0	1	0	1	.222	.296
P	Dale Gear	4	15	6	5	1	1	0	3	1	0	.400	.600
Sub	Lou Criger	2	5	0	0	0	0	0	0	1	1	.000	.000
P	Icebox Chamberlain	2	3	0	1	0	0	0	0	1	0	.000	.000
		135	4856	1463	840	207	72	28	712	436	175	.301	.391

1B Tebeau 122, O'Connor 17, Young 3, Wallace 1, Gear 1, O'Meara 1
2B Childs 132, Tebeau 5
SS McKean 133, Tebeau 1, Blake 1
3B McGarr 113, Delahanty 10, Tebeau 7, Zimmer 1
OF Burkett 133, McAleer 116, Blake 103, Wallace 23, Shearon 16, O'Connor 12, McAllister 4, Cuppy 1
C Zimmer 91, O'Connor 37, O'Meara 9, McAllister 2, Criger 1, McGarr 1
P Young 51, Cuppy 46, Wilson 33, Wallace 22, Gear 3, Chamberlain 2, McAllister 1, Tebeau 1

	G	IP	GS	CG	W	L	K	BB	SH	SV	ERA
Cy Young	51	414.1	46	42	28	15	**140**	62	**5**	3	3.24
Nig Cuppy	46	358	40	35	25	14	86	75	1	1	3.12
Zeke Wilson	33	240	29	20	17	9	56	81	1	1	4.01
Bobby Wallace	22	145.1	16	13	10	7	46	49	2	0	3.34
Dale Gear	3	23	2	2	0	2	6	6	0	0	5.48
Icebox Chamberlain	2	11	2	1	0	1	2	5	0	0	7.36
Sport McAllister	1	4	0	0	0	0	0	2	0	0	6.75
Patsy Tebeau	1	0	0	0	0	0	0	0	0	0	—
		1195.2	135	113	80	48	336	**280**	9	**5**	**3.46**

CINCINNATI   Buck Ewing   League Park (II)

		G	AB	H	R	2B	3B	HR	RBI	BB	SB	BA	SA
LF	Eddie Burke	122	521	177	120	24	9	1	52	41	53	.340	.426
RF	Dusty Miller	125	504	162	91	38	12	4	93	33	76	.321	.468
3B	Charlie Irwin	127	476	141	77	16	6	1	67	26	31	.296	.361
SS	Germany Smith	120	456	131	65	21	9	3	71	28	22	.287	.393
CF	Dummy Hoy	121	443	132	120	23	7	4	57	65	50	.298	.409
2B	Bid McPhee	117	433	132	81	18	7	1	87	51	48	.305	.386
UT	Farmer Vaughn	114	433	127	71	20	9	2	66	16	7	.293	.395
1B	Buck Ewing	69	263	73	41	14	4	1	38	29	41	.278	.373
C	Heinie Peitz	68	211	63	33	12	5	2	34	30	7	.299	.431
Sub	Bill Grey	46	121	25	15	2	1	0	17	19	6	.207	.240
P	Frank Dwyer	36	110	29	17	4	4	0	15	11	3	.264	.373
P	Red Ehret	34	102	20	10	2	0	1	20	10	2	.196	.245
Sub	Bug Holliday	29	84	27	17	4	0	0	8	9	1	.321	.369
P	Frank Foreman	27	74	18	9	2	0	0	8	4	2	.243	.270
P	Chauncey Fisher	27	57	14	10	3	0	0	9	6	1	.246	.298
P	Billy Rhines	19	52	10	4	1	0	0	6	2	0	.192	.212
P	Brownie Foreman	4	10	2	0	0	0	0	0	1	0	.200	.200
P	Bert Inks	3	7	0	1	0	0	0	0	1	0	.000	.000
P	Hank Gastright	1	2	0	0	0	0	0	0	0	0	.000	.000
P	Wiley Davis	2	1	0	1	0	0	0	0	0	0	.000	.000
		128	4360	1283	783	204	73	20	648	382	350	.294	.388

1B   Ewing 69, Vaughn 57, Holliday 5, Grey 2, Ehret 1
2B   McPhee 117, Grey 12
SS   Smith 120, Grey 8, Holliday 1
3B   Irwin 127, Grey 1
OF   Miller 125, Burke 122, Hoy 120, Holliday 16, Grey 3
C   Peitz 67, Vaughn 57, Grey 11
P   Dwyer 36, Ehret 34, F. Foreman 27, Fisher 27, Rhines 19, B. Foreman 4, Inks 3, Davis 2, Gastright 1, Holliday 1

	G	IP	GS	CG	W	L	K	BB	SH	SV	ERA
Frank Dwyer	36	288.2	34	30	24	11	57	60	3	1	3.15
Red Ehret	34	276.2	33	29	18	14	60	74	2	0	3.42
Frank Foreman	27	185.2	22	17	14	7	33	62	0	1	3.97
Chauncey Fisher	27	159.2	15	13	10	7	25	36	2	2	4.45
Billy Rhines	19	143	17	11	8	6	32	48	3	0	**2.45**
Brownie Foreman	4	23	4	3	1	3	9	16	1	0	11.35
Bert Inks	3	20	3	2	1	1	2	9	0	0	4.50
Hank Gastright	1	6	0	0	0	0	0	1	0	0	4.50
Wiley Davis	2	4.1	0	0	1	1	1	2	0	0	8.31
Bug Holliday	1	1	0	0	0	0	0	2	0	0	0.00
*One combined shutout on May 24: Rhines 3 innings, F. Foreman 6 innings											
	1108	128	105	77	50	219	310	**12**	4	3.67	

BOSTON   **Frank Selee**   **South End Grounds (II)**

		G	AB	H	R	2B	3B	HR	RBI	BB	SB	BA	SA
LF	Hugh Duffy	131	527	158	97	16	8	5	112	52	39	.300	.389
CF	Billy Hamilton	131	523	191	152	24	9	3	52	110	83	.365	.463
SS	Herman Long	120	501	172	105	26	8	6	100	26	36	.343	.463
1B	Tommy Tucker	122	474	144	74	27	5	2	72	30	6	.304	.395
UT	Fred Tenney	88	348	117	64	14	3	2	49	36	18	.336	.411
RF	Jimmy Bannon	89	343	86	52	9	5	0	50	32	16	.251	.306
2B	Bobby Lowe	73	305	98	59	11	4	2	48	20	15	.321	.403
3B	Jimmy Collins	84	304	90	48	10	9	1	46	30	10	.296	.398
C	Marty Bergen	65	245	66	39	6	4	4	37	11	6	.269	.376
P	Jack Stivetts	67	221	76	42	9	6	3	49	12	4	.344	.480
Sub	Joe Harrington	53	198	39	25	5	3	1	25	19	2	.197	.268
C	Charlie Ganzel	75	179	47	28	2	0	1	18	9	2	.263	.291
Sub	Dan McGann	43	171	55	25	6	7	2	30	12	2	.322	.474
P	Kid Nichols	51	147	28	27	3	3	1	24	12	2	.190	.272
P	Jim Sullivan	31	88	19	9	3	0	1	9	2	0	.216	.284
P	Fred Klobedanz	11	41	13	4	1	0	2	8	0	0	.317	.488
Sub	John Ryan	8	32	3	2	1	0	0	0	0	0	.094	.125
P	Willard Mains	10	22	6	2	1	0	0	4	0	0	.273	.318
P	Ted Lewis	6	18	2	1	1	0	0	2	0	0	.111	.167
P	Cozy Dolan	6	14	2	4	0	0	0	0	0	0	.143	.143
P	Bill Banks	4	11	3	0	0	0	0	0	1	0	.273	.273
Sub	George Yeager	2	5	1	1	0	0	0	0	0	0	.200	.200
		132	4717	1416	860	175	74	36	735	414	241	.300	.392

1B Tucker 122, Stivetts 5, Ganzel 3, Yeager 2, Bergen 1
2B Lowe 73, McGann 43, Duffy 9, Bannon 6, Harrington 1
SS Long 120, Bannon 5, Collins 4, Harrington 4, Duffy 2, Ganzel 2
3B Collins 80, Harrington 49, Bannon 3, Stivetts 1
OF Hamilton 131, Duffy 126, Bannon 76, Tenney 60, Stivetts 12, Nichols 2
C   Bergen 63, Ganzel 41, Tenney 27, Ryan 8
P   Nichols 49, Stivetts 42, Sullivan 31, Klobedanz 10, Mains 8, Lewis 6, Dolan 6, Banks 4

	G	IP	GS	CG	W	L	K	BB	SH	SV	ERA
Kid Nichols	49	372.1	43	37	**30**	14	102	101	3	1	2.83
Jack Stivetts	42	329	36	31	22	14	71	99	2	0	4.10
Jim Sullivan	31	225.1	26	21	11	12	33	68	1	1	4.03
Fred Klobedanz	10	80.2	9	9	6	4	26	31	0	0	3.01
Willard Mains	8	42.2	5	3	3	2	13	31	0	1	5.48
Ted Lewis	6	41.2	5	4	1	4	12	27	0	0	3.24
Cozy Dolan	6	41	5	3	1	4	14	27	0	0	4.83
Bill Banks	4	23	3	2	0	3	6	13	0	0	10.57
		1155.2	132	110	74	57	277	397	6	3	3.78

CHICAGO **Cap Anson** **West Side Park (II)**

		G	AB	H	R	2B	3B	HR	RBI	BB	SB	BA	SA
3B	Bill Everett	132	575	184	130	16	13	2	46	41	46	.320	.403
RF	Jimmy Ryan	128	489	149	83	24	10	3	86	46	29	.305	.413
SS	Bill Dahlen	125	474	167	137	30	19	9	74	64	51	.352	.553
CF	Bill Lange	122	469	153	114	21	16	4	92	65	84	.326	.465
LF	George Decker	107	421	118	68	23	11	5	61	23	20	.280	.423
1B	Cap Anson	108	402	133	72	18	2	2	90	49	24	.331	.400
2B	Fred Pfeffer	94	360	88	45	16	7	2	52	23	22	.244	.344
C	Mal Kittridge	65	215	48	17	4	1	1	19	14	6	.223	.265
C	Tim Donahue	57	188	41	27	10	1	0	20	11	11	.218	.282
Sub	Barry McCormick	45	168	37	22	3	1	1	23	14	9	.220	.268
P	Clark Griffith	38	135	36	22	5	2	1	16	9	3	.267	.356
P	Danny Friend	37	126	30	12	3	3	1	10	3	2	.238	.333
Sub	Harry Truby	29	109	28	13	2	2	2	31	6	4	.257	.367
Sub	George Flynn	29	106	27	15	1	2	0	4	11	12	.255	.302
P	Adonis Terry	30	99	26	14	4	2	0	15	8	4	.263	.343
P	Buttons Briggs	26	78	10	5	0	2	0	6	7	0	.128	.179
Sub	Josh Reilly	9	42	9	6	1	0	0	2	1	2	.214	.238
P	Doc Parker	10	36	10	4	0	1	0	4	1	0	.278	.333
Sub	Algie McBride	9	29	7	2	1	1	1	7	7	0	.241	.448
Sub	Con Daily	9	27	2	1	0	0	0	1	1	1	.074	.074
P	Walter Thornton	9	22	8	6	0	1	0	1	5	2	.364	.455
P	Monte McFarland	4	12	0	0	0	0	0	0	0	0	.000	.000
		132	4582	1311	815	182	97	34	660	409	332	.286	.390

1B Anson 98, Decker 36
2B Pfeffer 94, Truby 28, Reilly 8, McCormick 3
SS Dahlen 125, McCormick 6, Reilly 1
3B Everett 97, McCormick 35
OF Ryan 128, Lange 121, Decker 71, Everett 35, Flynn 29, McBride 9, Thornton 3, McCormick 1, Parker 1, Briggs 1, Friend 1
C Kittridge 64, Donahue 57, Anson 10, Daily 9, Decker 1, Lange 1
P Griffith 36, Friend 36, Terry 30, Briggs 26, Parker 9, Thornton 5, McFarland 4, Kittridge 1

	G	IP	GS	CG	W	L	K	BB	SH	SV	ERA
Clark Griffith	36	317.2	35	35	23	11	81	70	0	0	3.54
Danny Friend	36	290.2	33	28	18	14	86	139	1	0	4.74
Adonis Terry	30	235.1	28	25	15	14	74	88	1	0	4.28
Buttons Briggs	26	194	21	19	12	8	84	108	0	1	4.31
Doc Parker	9	73	7	7	1	5	15	27	0	0	6.16
Monte McFarland	4	25	3	2	0	4	3	21	0	0	7.20
Walter Thornton	5	23.2	5	2	2	1	10	13	0	0	5.70
Mal Kittridge	1	1.2	0	0	0	0	0	1	0	0	5.40
		1161	132	**118**	71	57	353	467	2	1	4.41

PITTSBURGH   Connie Mack   **Exposition Park**

		G	AB	H	R	2B	3B	HR	RBI	BB	SB	BA	SA
RF	Patsy Donovan	131	573	183	113	20	5	3	59	35	48	.319	.387
SS	Bones Ely	128	537	153	85	15	9	3	77	33	18	.285	.363
LF	Elmer Smith	122	484	175	121	21	14	6	94	74	33	.362	.500
CF	Jake Stenzel	114	479	173	104	26	14	2	82	32	57	.361	.486
3B	Denny Lyons	118	436	134	77	25	6	4	71	67	13	.307	.420
C	Joe Sugden	80	301	89	42	5	7	0	36	19	5	.296	.359
C	Bill Merritt	77	282	82	26	8	2	1	42	18	3	.291	.344
2B	Lou Bierbauer	59	258	74	33	10	6	0	39	5	7	.287	.372
2B	Dick Padden	61	219	53	33	4	8	2	24	14	8	.242	.361
1B	Jake Beckley	59	217	55	44	7	5	3	32	22	8	.253	.373
P	Frank Killen	55	173	40	29	4	5	2	25	26	1	.231	.347
Sub	Harry Davis	44	168	32	24	5	6	0	23	13	9	.190	.292
P	Pink Hawley	50	163	39	19	9	4	1	21	1	1	.239	.362
Sub	Connie Mack	33	120	26	9	4	1	0	16	5	0	.217	.267
P	Jim Hughey	25	65	14	4	1	0	0	5	5	0	.215	.231
Sub	Joe Wright	15	52	16	5	2	1	0	6	1	1	.308	.385
P	Charlie Hastings	17	37	8	5	1	0	0	3	4	0	.216	.243
Sub	Jud Smith	10	35	12	6	2	1	0	4	2	3	.343	.457
Sub	Harry Truby	8	32	5	1	0	0	0	3	2	1	.156	.156
Sub	Abel Lizotte	7	29	3	3	0	0	0	3	2	1	.103	.103
P	Brownie Foreman	9	20	3	2	0	0	0	2	7	0	.150	.150
P	Elmer Horton	2	7	0	1	0	0	0	0	0	0	.000	.000
P	Jot Goar	3	6	1	0	0	0	0	0	0	0	.167	.167
Sub	Eddie Boyle	2	5	0	0	0	0	0	0	0	0	.000	.000
Sub	Tom Delahanty	1	3	1	1	0	0	0	0	0	0	.333	.333
		131	4701	1371	787	169	94	27	667	387	217	.292	.385

1B   Beckley 56, Davis 35, Mack 28, Sugden 7, Lizotte 7, Merritt 3, Stenzel 1
2B   Padden 61, Bierbauer 59, Truby 8, Merritt 3, Beckley 1
SS   Ely 128, Merritt 2, Delahanty 1, Davis 1
3B   Lyons 116, Smith 10, Merritt 5, Wright 1
OF   Donovan 131, Smith 122, Stenzel 114, Wright 12, Davis 10, Sugden 4, Beckley 3
C   Sugden 70, Merritt 62, Mack 5, Boyle 2
P   Killen 52, Hawley 49, Hughey 25, Hastings 17, Foreman 9, Goar 3, Horton 2

	G	IP	GS	CG	W	L	K	BB	SH	SV	FRA
Frank Killen	52	432.1	50	44	30	18	134	119	5	0	3.41
Pink Hawley	49	378	43	37	22	21	137	157	2	0	3.57
Jim Hughey	25	155	14	11	6	8	48	67	0	0	4.99
Charlie Hastings	17	104	13	9	5	10	19	44	0	1	5.88
Brownie Foreman	9	61.2	9	5	3	3	18	35	0	0	6.57
Elmer Horton	2	15	2	2	0	2	3	9	0	0	9.60
Jot Goar	3	13.1	0	0	0	1	3	8	0	0	16.88
*One combined shutout on August 8: Hughey 3 innings, Hawley 6 innings											
		1159.1	131	108	66	63	362	439	8	1	4.30

NEW YORK   **Arthur Irwin (36–53)**   **Bill Joyce (28–14)**   **Polo Grounds (III)**

		G	AB	H	R	2B	3B	HR	RBI	BB	SB	BA	SA
CF	George Van Haltren	133	562	197	136	18	21	5	74	55	39	.351	.484
2B	Kid Gleason	133	541	162	79	17	5	4	89	42	46	.299	.372
RF	Mike Tiernan	133	521	192	132	24	16	7	89	77	35	.369	.516
3B	George Davis	124	494	158	98	25	12	6	99	50	48	.320	.455
SS	Frank Connaughton	88	315	82	53	3	2	2	43	25	22	.260	.302
C	Parke Wilson	75	253	60	33	2	0	0	23	13	9	.237	.245
1B	Willie Clark	72	247	72	38	12	4	0	33	15	8	.291	.372
Sub	Harry Davis	64	233	64	43	11	10	2	50	31	16	.275	.433
LF	General Stafford	59	230	66	28	9	1	0	40	13	15	.287	.335
Sub	Duke Farrell	58	191	54	23	7	3	1	37	19	2	.283	.366
Sub	Jake Beckley	46	182	55	37	8	4	5	38	9	11	.302	.473
Sub	Bill Joyce	49	165	61	36	9	2	5*	43	34	13	.370	.539
P	Dad Clarke	49	147	30	11	0	1	0	10	12	0	.204	.218
P	Jouett Meekin	43	144	43	27	6	5	2	16	12	2	.299	.451
P	Mike Sullivan	25	77	16	10	1	0	0	5	1	0	.208	.221
Sub	Shorty Fuller	18	72	12	10	0	0	0	7	14	4	.167	.167
Sub	Dave Zearfoss	19	60	13	5	1	1	0	6	5	2	.217	.267
Sub	Jack Warner	19	54	14	9	1	0	0	3	3	1	.259	.278
Sub	George Ulrich	14	45	8	4	1	0	0	1	1	0	.178	.200
P	Ed Doheny	17	40	6	5	1	0	0	3	4	1	.150	.175
P	Cy Seymour	12	32	7	2	0	0	0	0	0	0	.219	.219
Sub	Fred Pfeffer	4	14	2	1	0	0	0	4	1	0	.143	.143
P	Sal Campfield	6	12	2	2	1	0	0	3	1	0	.167	.250
P	Charlie Gettig	6	9	3	3	1	0	0	0	0	0	.333	.444
Sub	Tom Bannon	2	7	1	1	1	0	0	0	1	0	.143	.286
P	Bill Reidy	2	5	0	1	0	0	0	0	0	0	.000	.000
P	Carney Flynn	3	4	2	1	0	0	1	3	0	0	.500	1.250
P	Cy Bowen	2	3	1	1	0	0	0	1	1	0	.333	.333
PH	Reddy Foster	1	1	0	0	0	0	0	0	0	0	.000	.000
P	Les German	1	1	0	0	0	0	0	0	0	0	.000	.000
		133	4661	1383	829	159	87	40	720	439	274	.297	.394

1B	Clark 65, Beckley 45, H. Davis 23, G. Davis 3, Wilson 2
2B	Gleason 130, Pfeffer 4
SS	Connaughton 54, G. Davis 45, Fuller 18, Farrell 13, Stafford 6
3B	G. Davis 74, Joyce 49, Farrell 7, Gleason 3, Ulrich 3
OF	Tiernan 133, Stafford 53, H. Davis 40, Connaughton 30, Ulrich 11, G. Davis 3, Bannon 2, Beckley 2, Gleason 1, Seymour 1
C	Wilson 71, Farrell 34, Warner 19, Zearfoss 19
P	Clarke 48, Meekin 42, Sullivan 25, Doheny 17, Seymour 11, Campfield 6, Gettig 4, Flynn 3, Reidy 2, Bowen 2, Van Haltren 2, German 1

	G	IP	GS	CG	W	L	K	BB	SH	SV	ERA
Dad Clarke	48	351	40	33	17	24	66	60	1	1	4.26
Jouett Meekin	42	334.1	41	34	26	14	110	127	0	0	3.82
Mike Sullivan	25	185.1	22	18	10	13	42	71	0	0	4.66
Ed Doheny	17	108.1	15	9	6	7	39	59	0	0	4.49
Cy Seymour	11	70.1	8	4	2	4	33	51	0	0	6.40
Sal Campfield	6	27	2	2	1	1	6	6	0	0	4.00
Charlie Gettig	4	14	1	1	1	0	5	8	0	1	9.64
Bill Reidy	2	13	1	1	0	1	1	2	0	0	7.62
Cy Bowen	2	12	1	1	0	1	3	9	0	0	6.00
Carney Flynn	3	10.2	2	1	0	2	4	8	0	0	11.81
George Van Haltren	2	8	0	0	1	0	3	1	0	0	2.25
Les German	1	2.2	0	0	0	0	0	1	0	0	13.50
		1136.2	133	104	64	67	312	403	1	2	4.54

PHILADELPHIA   **Billy Nash**   **Philadelphia Baseball Grounds (II)**

		G	AB	H	R	2B	3B	HR	RBI	BB	SB	BA	SA
RF	Sam Thompson	119	517	154	103	28	7	12	100	28	12	.298	.449
LF	Ed Delahanty	123	499	198	131	**44**	17	**13**	**126**	62	37	.397	**.631**
2B	Bill Hallman	120	469	150	82	21	3	2	83	45	16	.320	.390
UT	Lave Cross	106	406	104	63	23	5	1	73	32	8	.256	.345
SS	Billy Hulen	88	339	90	87	18	7	0	38	55	23	.265	.360
CF	Duff Cooley	64	287	88	63	6	4	2	22	18	18	.307	.376
C	Mike Grady	72	242	77	49	20	7	1	44	16	10	.318	.471
3B	Billy Nash	65	227	56	29	9	1	3	30	34	3	.247	.335
1B	Dan Brouthers	57	218	75	42	13	3	1	41	44	7	.344	.445
Sub	Joe Sullivan	48	191	48	45	5	3	2	24	18	9	.251	.340
C	Jack Clements	57	184	66	35	5	7	5	45	17	2	.359	.543
Sub	Nap Lajoie	39	175	57	36	12	7	4	42	1	7	.326	.543
P	Jack Taylor	47	157	29	10	6	0	0	18	9	0	.185	.223
Sub	Jack Boyle	40	145	43	17	4	1	1	28	6	3	.297	.359
Sub	Sam Mertes	37	143	34	20	4	4	0	14	8	19	.238	.322
P	Al Orth	25	82	21	12	3	3	1	13	3	2	.256	.402
P	Kid Carsey	27	81	18	13	2	2	0	7	11	1	.222	.296
Sub	Phil Geier	17	56	13	12	0	1	0	6	6	3	.232	.268
P	Harry Keener	16	51	16	6	4	0	0	7	1	3	.314	.392
Sub	Bill Gallagher	14	49	15	9	2	0	0	6	10	0	.306	.347
P	Ad Gumbert	11	34	9	7	1	1	1	7	0	1	.265	.441
Sub	Tuck Turner	13	32	7	12	2	0	0	0	8	6	.219	.281
P	Willie McGill	12	29	6	4	1	1	0	2	2	0	.207	.310
P	Con Lucid	5	16	2	0	0	0	0	0	0	1	.125	.125
Sub	Ben Ellis	4	16	1	0	0	0	0	0	3	0	.063	.063
P	George Wheeler	3	9	1	1	0	0	0	0	0	0	.111	.111
Sub	Dan Leahy	2	6	2	0	1	0	0	1	1	0	.333	.500
P	Ned Garvin	2	6	0	0	0	0	0	1	0	0	.000	.000
P	Bert Inks	3	5	1	1	0	0	0	0	0	0	.200	.200
P	Jerry Nops	1	4	0	0	0	0	0	0	0	0	.000	.000
P	Bill Whitrock	2	3	0	0	0	0	0	0	0	0	.000	.000
P	Charlie Jordan	2	2	1	1	0	0	0	0	0	0	.500	.500
		130	4680	1382	890	**234**	84	**49**	778	438	191	.295	.413

1B   Brouthers 57, Lajoie 39, Delahanty 22, Boyle 12
2B   Hallman 120, Cross 6, Geier 3, Hulen 2, Delahanty 1, Mertes 1
SS   Hulen 73, Cross 37, Gallagher 14, Sullivan 2, Ellis 2, Leahy 2, Mertes 1
3B   Nash 65, Cross 61, Grady 7, Ellis 2, Sullivan 1
OF   Thompson 119, Delahanty 99, Cooley 64, Sullivan 45, Mertes 35, Hulen 12, Geier 12, Turner 8, Cross 2, Taylor 2
C   Grady 61, Clements 53, Boyle 28, Geier 2, Cross 1
P   Taylor 45, Carsey 27, Orth 25, Keener 16, McGill 12, Gumbert 11, Lucid 5, Inks 3, Wheeler 3, Jordan 2, Garvin 2, Whitrock 2, Nops 1, Hallman 1

	G	IP	GS	CG	W	L	K	BB	SH	SV	ERA
Jack Taylor	45	359	41	35	20	21	97	112	1	1	4.79
Al Orth	25	196	23	19	15	10	23	46	0	0	4.41
Kid Carsey	27	187.1	21	18	11	11	36	72	1	1	5.62
Harry Keener	16	113.1	13	11	3	11	28	39	0	0	5.88
Willie McGill	12	79.2	11	7	5	4	29	53	0	0	5.31
Ad Gumbert	11	77.1	10	7	5	3	14	23	1	0	4.54
Con Lucid	5	42	5	5	1	4	3	17	0	0	8.36
George Wheeler	3	16.1	2	2	1	1	2	5	0	0	3.86
Ned Garvin	2	13	1	1	0	1	4	7	0	0	7.62
Bert Inks	3	10.1	1	0	0	1	2	5	0	0	7.84
Bill Whitrock	2	9	1	1	0	1	1	3	0	0	3.00
Jerry Nops	1	7	1	1	1	0	1	1	0	0	5.14
Charlie Jordan	2	4.2	0	0	0	0	3	2	0	0	7.71
Bill Hallman	1	2	0	0	0	0	0	2	0	0	18.00
		1117	130	107	62	68	243	387	3	2	5.20

BROOKLYN   **Dave Foutz**   **Eastern Park**

		G	AB	H	R	2B	3B	HR	RBI	BB	SB	BA	SA
SS	Tommy Corcoran	132	532	154	63	15	7	3	73	15	16	.289	.361
3B	Billy Shindle	131	516	144	75	24	9	1	61	24	24	.279	.366
CF	Mike Griffin	122	493	152	101	27	9	4	51	48	23	.308	.424
UT	John Anderson	108	430	135	70	23	17	1	55	18	37	.314	.453
RF	Fielder Jones	104	395	140	82	10	8	3	46	48	18	.354	.443
LF	Tommy McCarthy	103	377	94	62	8	4	3	47	34	22	.249	.316
1B	Candy LaChance	89	348	99	60	10	13	7	58	23	17	.284	.448
C	John Grim	81	281	75	32	13	1	2	35	12	7	.267	.342
Sub	George Shoch	76	250	73	36	7	4	1	28	33	11	.292	.364
2B	Tom Daly	67	224	63	43	13	6	3	29	33	19	.281	.433
C	Buster Burrell	62	206	62	19	11	3	0	23	15	1	.301	.383
P	Brickyard Kennedy	42	122	23	12	2	0	0	10	2	1	.189	.205
P	Harley Payne	38	98	21	5	4	1	0	10	9	0	.214	.276
P	Dan Daub	32	84	19	9	1	2	0	14	10	1	.226	.286
P	Bert Abbey	25	63	12	7	1	2	0	7	6	0	.190	.270
P	Ed Stein	17	39	10	3	1	0	0	2	2	0	.256	.282
P	George Harper	16	37	6	5	0	1	0	3	8	0	.162	.216
Sub	Frank Bonner	9	34	6	8	2	0	0	5	2	1	.176	.235
P	Ad Gumbert	5	11	2	0	1	0	0	0	1	0	.182	.273
Sub	Dave Foutz	2	8	2	0	1	0	0	0	1	0	.250	.375
		133	4548	1292	692	174	87	28	557	344	198	.284	.379

1B   LaChance 89, Anderson 42, Grim 5, Foutz 1
2B   Daly 66, Shoch 62, Bonner 9
SS   Corcoran 132, Shoch 1
3B   Shindle 131, Shoch 3
OF   Griffin 122, Jones 103, McCarthy 103, Anderson 68, Shoch 10, Payne 1, Foutz 1
C   Grim 77, Burrell 60, Daly 1
P   Kennedy 42, Payne 34, Daub 32, Abbey 25, Stein 17, Harper 16, Gumbert 5

	G	IP	GS	CG	W	L	K	BB	SH	SV	ERA
Brickyard Kennedy	42	305.2	38	28	17	20	76	130	1	1	4.42
Harley Payne	34	241.2	28	24	14	16	52	58	2	0	3.39
Dan Daub	32	225	24	18	12	11	53	63	0	0	3.60
Bert Abbey	25	164.1	18	12	8	8	37	48	0	0	5.15
Ed Stein	17	90.1	10	6	3	6	16	51	0	0	4.88
George Harper	16	86	11	7	4	8	22	39	0	0	5.55
Ad Gumbert	5	31	4	2	0	4	3	11	0	0	3.77
		1144	133	97	58	73	259	400	3	1	4.25

WASHINGTON   **Gus Schmelz**   **Boundary Field**

		G	AB	H	R	2B	3B	HR	RBI	BB	SB	BA	SA
SS	Gene Demontreville	133	533	183	94	24	5	8	77	29	28	.343	.452
1B	Ed Cartwright	133	499	138	76	15	10	1	62	54	28	.277	.353
LF	Kip Selbach	127	487	148	100	17	13	5	100	76	49	.304	.423
CF	Tom Brown	116	435	128	87	17	6	2	59	58	28	.294	.375
C	Deacon McGuire	108	389	125	60	25	3	2	70	30	12	.321	.416
RF	Billy Lush	97	352	87	74	9	11	4	45	66	28	.247	.369
3B	Bill Joyce	81	310	97	85	16	10	8*	51	67	32	.313	.506
Sub	Charlie Abbey	79	301	79	47	12	6	1	49	27	16	.262	.352
2B	John O'Brien	73	270	72	38	6	3	4	33	27	4	.267	.356
P	Win Mercer	49	156	38	23	1	1	1	14	9	9	.244	.282
Sub	Jim Rogers	38	154	43	21	6	4	1	30	10	3	.279	.390
Sub	Harvey Smith	36	131	36	21	7	2	0	17	12	9	.275	.359
Sub	Duke Farrell	37	130	39	18	7	3	1	30	7	2	.300	.423
P	Doc McJames	37	111	18	8	1	0	0	5	3	1	.162	.171
Sub	Jack Crooks	25	84	24	20	3	0	3	20	16	2	.286	.429
Sub	Pat McCauley	26	84	21	14	3	0	3	11	7	3	.250	.393
P	Les German	30	70	16	11	1	0	1	6	5	3	.229	.286
P	Silver King	22	58	16	9	6	0	0	12	8	1	.276	.379
P	Al Maul	8	28	8	6	1	1	0	5	3	0	.286	.393
P	Elisha Norton	8	19	4	2	0	1	0	0	0	0	.211	.316
P	Jake Boyd	4	13	1	1	0	0	0	1	1	0	.077	.077
Sub	Zeke Wrigley	5	9	1	1	0	0	0	2	1	0	.111	.111
P	Carney Flynn	4	8	2	0	0	0	0	0	0	0	.250	.250
P	Varney Anderson	2	5	3	1	1	0	0	2	0	0	.600	.800
P	John Malarkey	1	2	1	1	1	0	0	1	0	0	.500	1.000
P	John Gilroy	1	1	0	0	0	0	0	0	0	0	.000	.000
		133	4639	1328	818	179	79	45	702	**516**	258	.286	.388

1B   Cartwright 133, McGuire 1
2B   O'Brien 73, Joyce 33, Crooks 20, Rogers 6, Lush 3, Wrigley 3
SS   Demontreville 133, Wrigley 1
3B   Joyce 48, Smith 36, Rogers 32, Farrell 14, Crooks 4, German 1
OF   Selbach 126, Brown 116, Lush 91, Abbey 78, Rogers 1, McCauley 1, German 1, Mercer 1
C   McGuire 98, McCauley 24, Farrell 18
P   Mercer 46, McJames 37, German 28, King 22, Maul 8, Norton 8, Boyd 4, Flynn 4, Anderson 2, Abbey 1, Malarkey 1, Gilroy 1

	G	IP	GS	CG	W	L	K	BB	SH	SV	ERA
Win Mercer	46	366.1	45	38	25	18	94	117	2	0	4.13
Doc McJames	37	280.1	33	29	12	20	103	135	0	1	4.27
Les German	28	166.2	20	14	2	20	20	74	0	1	6.32
Silver King	22	145.1	16	12	10	7	35	43	0	1	4.09
Al Maul	8	62	8	7	5	2	18	20	0	0	3.63
Effie Norton	8	44	5	2	3	1	13	14	0	0	3.07
Jake Boyd	4	32	2	2	1	2	6	15	0	0	6.75
Carney Flynn	4	20	1	1	0	1	3	10	0	0	8.55
Varney Anderson	2	9	2	1	0	1	0	3	0	0	13.00
John Malarkey	1	7	1	0	0	1	0	3	0	0	1.29
John Gilroy	1	2	0	0	0	0	0	1	0	0	0.00
Charlie Abbey	1	2	0	0	0	0	0	0	0	0	4.50
		1136.2	133	106	58	73	292	435	2	3	4.61

ST. LOUIS   **Harry Diddlebock (7–10)**   **Arlie Latham (0–3)**   **Chris Von Der Ahe (0–2)**
Roger Connor (8–37)   **Tommy Dowd (25–38)**   **Sportsman's Park (II)**

		G	AB	H	R	2B	3B	HR	RBI	BB	SB	BA	SA
2B	Tommy Dowd	126	521	138	93	17	11	5	46	42	40	.265	.369
1B	Roger Connor	126	483	137	71	21	9	11	72	52	10	.284	.433
CF	Tom Parrott	118	474	138	62	13	12	7	70	11	12	.291	.414
3B	Bert Myers	122	454	116	47	12	8	0	37	40	8	.256	.317
SS	Monte Cross	125	427	104	66	10	6	6	52	58	40	.244	.337
LF	Klondike Douglass	81	296	78	42	6	4	1	28	35	18	.264	.321
C	Ed McFarland	83	290	70	48	13	4	3	36	15	7	.241	.345
Sub	Joe Sullivan	51	212	62	25	4	2	2	21	9	5	.292	.358
RF	Tuck Turner	51	203	50	30	7	8	1	27	14	6	.246	.374
Sub	Joe Quinn	48	191	40	19	6	1	1	17	9	8	.209	.267
C	Morg Murphy	49	175	45	12	5	2	0	11	8	1	.257	.309
Sub	Duff Cooley	40	166	51	29	5	3	0	13	7	12	.307	.373
P	Ted Breitenstein	51	162	42	21	5	2	0	12	13	8	.259	.315
P	Bill Hart	49	161	30	9	4	5	0	15	3	7	.186	.273
P	Red Donahue	33	107	17	5	2	0	0	9	3	1	.159	.178
P	Bill Kissinger	23	73	22	8	4	0	0	12	0	0	.301	.356
Sub	Tom Niland	18	68	12	3	0	1	0	3	5	0	.176	.206
Sub	Arlie Latham	8	35	7	3	0	0	0	5	4	2	.200	.200
Sub	Biff Sheehan	6	19	3	0	0	0	0	1	4	0	.158	.158
P	Dewey McDougal	3	3	0	0	0	0	0	0	0	0	.000	.000
P	John Wood	1	0	0	0	0	0	0	0	0	0	—	—
		131	4520	1162	593	134	78	37	487	332	185	.257	.346

1B   Connor 126, Parrott 6
2B   Dowd 78, Quinn 48, Sullivan 7
SS   Cross 125, Niland 5, Douglass 2, Myers 1
3B   Myers 121, Latham 8, Kissinger 1, Sullivan 1
OF   Parrott 108, Douglass 74, Turner 51, Dowd 48, Sullivan 45, Cooley 40, Niland 13, Breitenstein 8, Hart 8, Sheehan 6, Kissinger 3, McFarland 2, Donahue 1
C   McFarland 80, Murphy 48, Douglass 6
P   Breitenstein 44, Hart 42, Donahue 32, Kissinger 20, Parrott 7, McDougal 3, Wood 1

	G	IP	GS	CG	W	L	K	BB	SH	SV	ERA
Ted Breitenstein	44	339.2	43	37	18	26	114	138	1	0	4.48
Bill Hart	42	336	41	37	12	**29**	65	141	0	0	5.12
Red Donahue	32	267	32	28	7	24	70	98	0	0	5.80
Bill Kissinger	20	136	12	11	2	9	22	55	0	1	6.49
Tom Parrott	7	42	2	2	1	1	8	18	0	0	6.21
Dewey McDougal	3	10	1	0	0	1	0	4	0	0	8.10
John Wood	1	0	0	0	0	0	0	2	0	0	—
		1130.2	131	115	40	90	279	456	1	1	5.33

LOUISVILLE   **John McCloskey (2–17)**   **Bill McGunnigle (36–76)**   **Eclipse Park (II)**

		G	AB	H	R	2B	3B	HR	RBI	BB	SB	BA	SA
LF	Fred Clarke	131	517	168	96	15	18	9	79	43	34	.325	.476
RF	Tom McCreery	115	441	155	87	23	**21**	7	65	42	26	.351	.546
3B	Billy Clingman	121	423	99	57	10	2	2	37	57	19	.234	.281
C	Charlie Dexter	107	402	112	65	18	7	3	37	17	21	.279	.381
UT	Doggie Miller	98	324	89	54	17	4	1	33	27	16	.275	.361
1B	Jim Rogers	72	290	75	39	8	6	0	38	15	13	.259	.328
2B	John O'Brien	49	186	63	24	9	1	2	24	13	4	.339	.430

		G	AB	H	R	2B	3B	HR	RBI	BB	SB	BA	SA
Sub	Pete Cassidy	50	184	39	16	1	1	0	12	7	5	.212	.228
CF	Ollie Pickering	45	165	50	28	6	4	1	22	12	13	.303	.406
SS	Joe Dolan	44	165	35	14	2	1	3	18	9	6	.212	.291
P	Chick Fraser	45	146	22	12	3	2	0	6	7	1	.151	.199
Sub	Ducky Holmes	47	141	38	22	3	2	0	18	13	8	.270	.319
2B	Jack Crooks	39	122	29	19	5	1	2	15	20	8	.238	.344
P	Bill Hill	34	116	24	11	0	0	0	5	5	1	.207	.207
Sub	Frank Shannon	41	115	18	14	1	1	1	15	13	3	.157	.209
Sub	Jack Warner	33	110	25	9	1	1	0	10	10	3	.227	.255
Sub	Herm McFarland	30	110	21	11	4	1	1	12	9	4	.191	.273
Sub	Bill Hassamaer	30	106	26	8	5	0	2	14	14	1	.245	.349
Sub	Frank Eustace	25	100	17	18	2	2	1	11	6	0	.170	.260
P	Bert Cunningham	29	88	22	11	3	2	2	15	5	4	.250	.398
Sub	Abbie Johnson	25	87	20	10	2	1	0	14	4	0	.230	.276
Sub	Sammy Strang	14	46	12	6	0	0	0	7	6	4	.261	.261
P	Tom Smith	15	39	8	3	1	1	0	1	4	0	.205	.282
P	Art Herman	14	36	5	3	0	0	0	2	0	0	.139	.139
P	Mike McDermott	12	27	8	6	2	0	0	1	2	0	.296	.370
Sub	Tom Morrison	8	27	4	3	1	0	0	0	4	0	.148	.185
Sub	Tom Kinslow	8	25	7	4	0	1	0	7	1	0	.280	.360
P	Gus Weyhing	5	15	2	2	0	0	0	1	2	1	.133	.133
Sub	Eddie Boyle	3	9	0	0	0	0	0	0	2	0	.000	.000
Sub	Joe Wright	2	7	2	0	0	0	0	0	0	0	.286	.286
Sub	George Treadway	2	7	1	0	0	0	0	1	1	0	.143	.143
Sub	Larry Freund	2	5	1	1	0	0	0	0	1	0	.200	.200
P	Fritz Clausen	2	4	0	0	0	0	0	0	0	0	.000	.000
P	Charlie Emig	1	3	0	0	0	0	0	0	0	0	.000	.000
P	Joe Kostal	2	0	0	0	0	0	0	0	0	0		
		134	4588	1197	653	142	80	37	520	371	195	.261	.351

1B Rogers 60, Cassidy 38, Hassamaer 29, Smith 4, Miller 3, Treadway 1, Kinslow 1, Warner 1
2B O'Brien 49, Crooks 39, Miller 25, Johnson 25, Eustace 3, McCreery 1, Holmes 1
SS Dolan 44, Shannon 28, Eustace 22, Strang 14, Rogers 12, Cassidy 11, Miller 2, Cunningham 1, Morrison 1, Holmes 1
3B Clingman 121, Miller 8, Morrison 5, Shannon 3, German 1
OF Clarke 131, McCreery 111, Dexter 47, Pickering 45, Holmes 33, McFarland 28, Miller 8, Fraser 2, Wright 2, Morrison 2, Treadway 1, German 1
C Dexter 55, Miller 48, Warner 32, Kinslow 5, Boyle 3, Freund 2, McFarland 1
P Fraser 43, Hill 34, German 28, Cunningham 27, Herman 14, McDermott 12, Smith 11, Weyhing 5, Clausen 2, Holmes 2, Kostal 2, Emig 1, McCreery 1

	G	IP	GS	CG	W	L	K	BB	SH	SV	ERA
Chick Fraser	43	349.1	38	36	12	27	91	**166**	0	1	4.87
Bill Hill	34	319.2	39	32	9	28	104	155	0	2	4.31
Bert Cunningham	27	189.1	20	17	7	14	37	74	0	1	5.09
Art Herman	14	94.1	12	9	4	6	13	36	0	0	5.63
Mike McDermott	12	65	10	4	2	7	12	44	1	0	7.34
Tom Smith	11	55	5	4	2	3	14	25	0	0	5.40
Gus Weyhing	5	42	5	4	2	3	9	15	0	0	6.64
Ducky Holmes	2	12	1	0	0	1	3	8	0	0	7.50
Fritz Clausen	2	11	2	1	0	2	4	6	0	0	6.55
Charlie Emig	1	8	1	1	0	1	1	7	0	0	7.88
Joe Kostal	2	2	0	0	0	0	0	0	0	0	0.00
Tom McCreery	1	1	1	0	0	1	0	5	0	0	36.00
		1148.2	134	108	38	93	288	541	1	4	5.12

1897
THE GOOD GUYS WIN

By 1897, League-Association monarchs were at their wit's end. Led by the Baltimore Orioles and the Cleveland Spiders, the roughhouse style of play had grown so pervasive that Boston sportswriter Tim Murnane, himself an early-day player, observed, "The time will soon come when no person above the rank of garrotter can be secured to umpire a game." In the 1895 season alone 59 different men served as umpires in championship games, causing League-Association president Nick Young to grow so frantic to fill the constant vacancies that he hired most of his arbiters sight unseen or else took on ex-players with no officiating experience who were down on their luck. Young's only new weapon of consequence in 1897 in the war against rowdyism was a rule authorizing an umpire to fine any player who deliberately defaced or discolored a ball in play five dollars.

But even though the roughhouse element was little perturbed by such rules, the game underwent a number of changes in 1897. Some were seemingly paradoxical. The League-Association batting average, which had been shrinking every year since 1894, went up two points to .292, yet pitchers achieved 54 more complete games and strikeout totals likewise swelled while walks dipped. Since scoring also dropped despite more base hits being produced, it suggested that the quality of pitching had improved overall. The improvement was reflected most in the mound depth that all of the better teams now enjoyed. Although several managers in recent years had experimented with a four-man pitching rotation, most of them, like John McCloskey with last-place Louisville in 1895, had employed four pitchers for the lack of one or two outstanding ones. Baltimore's Ned Hanlon in 1897 was the first winning manager to spread his mound duties evenly among four men. The four Orioles—Joe Corbett, Bill Hoffer, Arlie Pond and Jerry Nops, Hanlon's third rookie hill find in three years—all won between 18 and 24 games while working between 221 and 313 innings.

For a time Hanlon's latest stratagem seemed destined to bring Baltimore a fourth straight pennant. After the first two weeks of the season, the Orioles were 7-1 and tied for first place with the Philadelphia Phillies, which could be guaranteed to fold soon because, while they

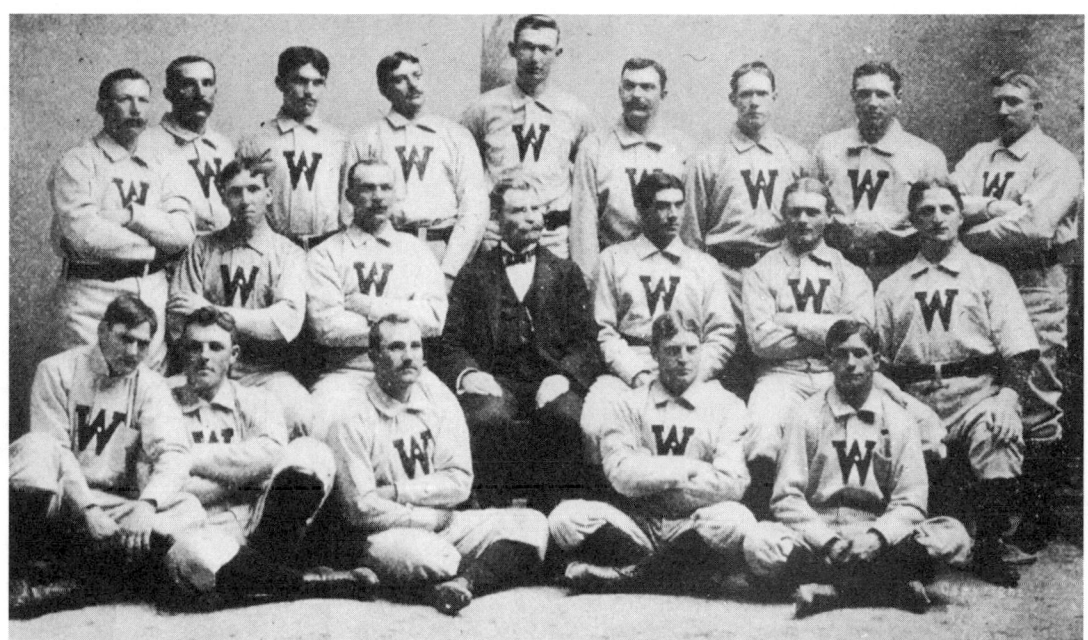

The 1897 Washingtons. Tom Brown replaced Gus Schmelz as manager when the club got off to a woeful 9-25 start. Somehow Brown prodded his charges to win 52 of their last 98 games, making for the longest stretch in the last century that a Washington major league team played better than .500 ball. Standing: Charlie Reilly, Ed Cartwright, Doc McJames, Al Maul, Cy Swaim, Duke Farrell, ? Ashe, Brown and Les German. Seated: ? Kimble, Deacon McGuire, Schmelz, Win Mercer, Billy Lush and Elisha Norton. Front: Gene Demontreville, John O'Brien, Kip Selbach, Charlie Abbey and Zeke Wrigley.

had a new firebrand manager in George Stallings, they still lacked pitching strength. Occupying last place on May 1 at 1-6 were the Boston Beaneaters, another team that looked to have pitching woes when Jack Stivetts and Jim Sullivan, two of manager Frank Selee's top three pitchers in 1896, developed ailing arms. But Boston owner Arthur Soden thought the trouble lay elsewhere. Deploring the "kicking" many of his players had been doing and claiming it had a deleterious effect on the team, he swore that from now on offenders fined for browbeating umpires would pay out of their own pockets rather than having their fines clandestinely paid by the team. As if to prove Soden right, Boston went on a 22-2 tear in June and surged into the lead after taking two games out of three from Baltimore at home late in the month. Hanlon contended that the key to the turnabout was injuries, forcing each of his four regular infielders, plus catcher Wilbert Robinson, to miss part of the season, but some close to the Orioles cited dissension, especially between first baseman Jack Doyle and third baseman John McGraw. The pair loathed each other and fought in the clubhouse on several occasions, and McGraw also tangled in July with the not notably fractious Willie Keeler after accusing the little right fielder of costing the team the game when he let his mind wander on the field. Still other observers blamed the Orioles' midseason sag on cen-

Frank Selee's 1897 Boston Beaneaters. Top: Jim Sullivan, Jack Stivetts, Bob Allen, Charlie Ganzel, Fred Klobedanz, Ted Lewis and Fred Lake. Middle: Herman Long, Kid Nichols, George Yeager, Selee, Hugh Duffy, Fred Tenney and Billy Hamilton. Bottom: Jimmy Collins, Chick Stahl and Bobby Lowe.

ter field, now occupied by Jake Stenzel whose acquisition from Pittsburgh in a trade for Steve Brodie and Jim Donnelly had broken up what many believed was the best outfield corps yet seen in Keeler, Brodie and Joe Kelley.

But the good-guy Beaneaters had their share of disruptions, too, as Selee replaced popular long-time first baseman Tommy Tucker with Fred Tenney, gave Jimmy Bannon's right-field post to rookie Chick Stahl, made Jimmy Collins, who had split hot-corner duty in 1896 with Joe Harrington, his full-time third baseman and turned over Stivetts's and Sullivan's spots in the pitching rotation to two recruits who had joined Boston late the previous season, Ted Lewis and Fred Klobedanz.

Lewis, Klobedanz and veteran ace Kid Nichols won 78 games among them in 1897 against just 30 losses. With every regular except catcher Marty Bergen hitting at least .309 and Stivetts slamming .367 as a combination pitcher-outfielder, the Beaneaters batted .319 and became the last team until 1930 to score in quadruple digits. When Boston also allowed the fewest runs in the majors and posted the best fielding average, the pennant seemed assured. But the dissension-ridden and injury-plagued Orioles refused to submit. When Boston came to Baltimore's Union Park on September 24 for the final three games of the season between the two combatants, the Beaneaters trailed by a single percentage point. Nichols won the series opener on Friday, 6-4, but Hoffer beat Klobedanz the following afternoon to put the Orioles back into first place. Sunday was an off day since local blue laws still forbade baseball on the Sabbath in Baltimore, but on Monday an overflow throng of nearly 25,000 came out to watch Corbett, the Orioles leading winner, duel Nichols, with both pitching on just two days' rest. The capacity crowd sat stunned as Boston bats pummeled Corbett and three other Orioles—indeed every pitcher Hanlon had in uniform that day except Pond—and won 19-10 to leave town with a game and a half lead.

The season was over for all intents and purposes. When it officially ended a week later

Billy Barnie with the last major league team that he piloted for a full season—the 1897 Brooklyn Bridegrooms. One of the keenest baseball minds of his day, Barnie finished above .500 just four times in the 14-odd seasons he managed in the bigs. He simply never had the horses, and 1897 was no exception. Brooklyn nevertheless snuck into the first division despite ending up 10 games below .500. Top row: Jack Dunn, Aleck Smith, Fielder Jones, Ed Stein and George Shoch. Third row: Harley Payne, Candy LaChance, Chauncey Fisher, Brickyard Kennedy, John Anderson and Pat Hannifan. Second row: Danny Daub, John Grim, Mike Griffin, Barnie, Buster Burrell, Sadie McMahon and Billy Shindle. Front: Jimmy Canavan and Germany Smith.

A SECOND REASON CLEVELAND NEVER WON A PENNANT IN THE 1890S

After playing for the Temple Cup two years in a row, Cleveland finished just a few games over .500 in 1897 and was clearly a team on the decline. The Spiders outfield actually improved when regulars Jimmy McAleer and Harry Blake lost time to injuries, forcing manager Patsy Tebeau to substitute Ollie Pickering and Lou Sockalexis, the first outstanding Native-American player, but Cy Young was barely a .500 pitcher and Nig Cuppy tumbled from 25 wins to just 11. The real weak spot, though, was shortstop, where Ed McKean aged quickly. Meanwhile the League-Association's best shortstop was hitting .353 in 1897 and setting an RBI mark for the position that would stand until 1948. His name was George Davis and he played in New York. Cleveland could sure have used Davis in 1897. The thing is, Cleveland had him for the first three years of his career. Unable to figure out whether his proper position was center field, third base or shortstop, the Spiders traded Davis to New York after the 1892 season for ancient Buck Ewing. They traded a man who had about 2,200 hits ahead of him and several fielding records for a man who would turn 35 before his first year in Cleveland was out. It was the worst trade in the 1890s. All during the decade Cleveland was weak at third base and center field, and by 1897 the Spiders also had troubles at shortstop. Had they kept Davis they would have had one less weakness and probably two or three pennants.

on October 3, the Beaneaters had extended their lead over Baltimore by another half-length to two games. The New York Giants, surviving even more internal squabbles than Baltimore, finished third, and Cincinnati, Cleveland, Brooklyn and Washington completed the first division, with the latter two teams tying for the sixth and final rung in the League-Association's upper echelon. In the basement, for the first time in their 16-year history, were the St. Louis Browns with a dismal .221 winning percentage. While the other 11 teams were striving to develop a four-man rotation, the Browns struggled to find even one quality pitcher. St. Louis's team ERA of 6.21 was the worst in the League-Association by 1.54 runs and Red Donahue, the staff "ace," was beaten 35 times to set a mark for the most losses at the sixty-foot six-inch distance.

The Temple Cup series was once again a sloppy, careless, one-sided affair, and for the third time in its four-year history, it was won by the challenging or second-place team. After dropping the opener 13-12, Baltimore swept the next four games. If the pitching truly had improved in 1897, it was never manifested in the postseason. The Orioles batted .382, and even in losing Boston hit .362 and tallied 41 runs in the five contests. As proof of how little the prospect of losing the Temple Cup concerned him, in the final game Selee called on Piano Legs Hickman, who had never before started a game in the majors.

Ugly play, minuscule crowds and the usual rumors that both teams had conspired before the series to split the take fifty/fifty finally induced moguls to call a merciful halt to the Temple Cup experiment when they met in Philadelphia in November. The only dissenting vote came from Hanlon, whose team needed only one more postseason win to take permanent possession of William Temple's cup. Instead it resides today in the Hall of Fame at Cooperstown.

ANOTHER DAVIS

While George Davis was setting an RBI record for shortstops in 1897 that would last for over 50 years, another Davis was setting a mark that will almost certainly never be broken. The other Davis—Harry—played for Pittsburgh and led the League-Association in triples with 28, a remarkably high total even for the 1890s when triples were fairly plentiful. But what was really remarkable was that he had just 10 doubles. No one else—before or since—has ever compiled 18 more triples than doubles in a season. Later in his career Harry Davis led the American League in home runs four years running. No one else—before or since—has ever done that either without making the Hall of Fame. A list of major leaguers who collected 20 or more triples in a season and had at least five more triples than doubles:

	YEAR	TEAM	3B	2B	DIFF
Harry Davis	1897	Pit-LA	28	10	18
Chief Wilson	1912	Pit-NL	36	19	17
Duff Cooley	1895	StL-LA	20	9	11
Heinie Reitz	1894	Bal-LA	31	22	9
Tommy Leach	1902	Pit-NL	22	14	8
Dale Mitchell	1949	Cle-AL	23	16	7
Dick Johnston	1887	Bos-NL	20	13	7
Joe Visner	1890	Pit-PL	22	15	7
Perry Werden	1893	StL-LA	29	22	7
Jake Daubert	1922	Cin-NL	22	15	7
Dave Orr	1886	NY-AA	31	25	6
Bid McPhee	1890	Cin-NL	22	16	6
Buck Freeman	1899	Was-LA	25	19	6
Vic Saier	1913	Chi-NL	21	15	6
Buck Ewing	1884	NY-NL	20	15	5
Jake Virtue	1892	Cle-LA	20	15	5
George Davis	1893	NY-LA	27	22	5

THE WEAKEST POSITION IN THE 1890S

Nap Lajoie taking a practice cut in 1901, the year he hit a twentieth-century record .426. In 1897, Lajoie shattered several 1893–1900 batting records for first basemen. The following year, moved to the position where he would achieve immortality, Lajoie set a period RBI record for second basemen.

Playing his first full season in the majors in 1897, Nap Lajoie set 1893–1900 era records for the most total bases and the highest slugging average of any player at his position. Lajoie also fell just a few points short of the era mark for the highest batting average. Since Lajoie was an extraordinary hitter, it should be no surprise to learn that he set all those marks even so early in his career. The surprise may be to learn that in 1897 Lajoie—arguably the greatest second baseman in history—played first base. Another surprise may be to learn that even though nineteenth-century first baseman are overrepresented in the Hall of Fame, in the 1893–1900 era more teams were weak at first base than at any other position. Here are lists, by position, of both the best and the worst hitting performances of the 1893–1900 era with 400 and 500 at-bat minimums.

	BEST	
	RBI	TOTAL BASES
	1B	
400	101, Jack Doyle, Baltimore, 1896	255, Roger Connor, NY-StL, 1894
500	128, Dan Brouthers, Baltimore, 1894	310, Nap Lajoie, Philadelphia, 1897
	2B	
400	106, done by three different players	230, Nap Lajoie, Philadelphia, 1900
500	127, Nap Lajoie, Philadelphia, 1898	319, Bobby Lowe, Boston, 1894

RBI

			TOTAL BASES

3B

RBI

| 400 | 123, Billy Nash, Boston, 1893 |
| 500 | 132, Jimmy Collins, Boston, 1897 |

SS

| 400 | 100, Jack Glasscock, StL-Pitt, 1894 |
| 500 | 136, George Davis, New York, 1897 |

OF

| 400 | 141, Sam Thompson, Philadelphia, 1894 |
| 500 | 165, Sam Thompson, Philadelphia, 1895 |

C

| 400 | 108, Farmer Vaughn Cincinnati, 1893 |
| 500 | 97, Deacon McGuire, Washington, 1895 |

TOTAL BASES

256, George Davis, New York, 1894
328, Jimmy Williams, Pittsburgh, 1899

240, Herman Long, Boston, 1894
283, Ed McKean, Cleveland, 1895

300, Sam Thompson, Philadelphia, 1894
374, Hugh Duffy, Boston, 1894

184, John Grim, Louisville, 1894
255, Deacon McGuire, Washington, 1895

RUNS

1B

| 400 | 116, Jack Doyle, New York, 1896 |
| 500 | 137, Dan Brouthers, Baltimore, 1894 |

2B

| 400 | 145, Cupid Childs, Cleveland, 1893 |
| 500 | 158, Bobby Lowe, Boston, 1894 |

3B

| 400 | 123, John McGraw, Baltimore, 1894 |
| 500 | 156, John McGraw Baltimore, 1894 |

SS

| 400 | 137, Bill Dahlen, Chicago, 1896 |
| 500 | 159, Hughie Jennings, Baltimore, 1895 |

OF

| 400 | 149, Ed Delahanty, Philadelphia, 1894 |
| 500 | 192, Billy Hamilton, Philadelphia, 1894 |

C

| 400 | 69, Wilbert Robinson, Baltimore, 1894 |
| 500 | 89, Deacon McGuire, Washington, 1895 |

HOME RUNS

11, Roger Connor, St. Louis, 1896
12, Ed Cartwright, Washington, 1894

8, done by three different players
17, Bobby Lowe, Boston, 1894

17, Bill Joyce, Washington, 1895
15, Jimmy Collins, Boston, 1898

12, Herman Long, Boston, 1894, 1900
15, Bill Dahlen, Chicago, 1894

13, done by three different players
25, Buck Freeman, Washington, 1899

7, John Grim, Louisville, 1894
10, Deacon McGuire, Washington, 1895

	HITS		ON-BASE PERCENTAGE
		1B	
400	165, Jack Doyle, New York, 1896		.420, Jack Doyle, New York, 1894
500	209, Fred Tenney Boston, 1899		.425, Dan Brouthers, Baltimore, 1894
		2B	
400	177, Cupid Childs, Cleveland, 1896		.475, Cupid Childs, Cleveland, 1894
500	212, Bobby Lowe Boston, 1894		.401, Bobby Lowe, Boston, 1894
		3B	
400	168, George Davis, New York, 1894		.470, Bill Joyce, Wash-NY, 1896
500	219, Jimmy Williams, Pittsburgh, 1899		.475, John McGraw, Baltimore, 1898
		SS	
400	167, Bill Dahlen, Chicago, 1896		.463, Hughie Jennings, Baltimore, 1897
500	209, Hughie Jennings, Baltimore, 1896		.472, Hughie Jennings, Baltimore, 1896
		OF	
400	199, Ed Delahanty, Philadelphia, 1894		.500, Ed Delahanty, Philadelphia, 1895
500	240, Jesse Burkett, Cleveland, 1896		.523, Billy Hamilton, Philadelphia, 1894
		C	
400	146, Wilbert Robinson, Baltimore, 1894		.421, Wilbert Robinson, Baltimore, 1894
500	179, Deacon McGuire, Washington, 1895		.388, Deacon McGuire, Washington, 1895

	BATTING AVERAGE		SLUGGING AVERAGE
		1B	
400	.366, Jack Doyle, New York, 1894		.552, Roger Connor, NY-StL, 1894
500	.361, Nap Lajoie, Philadelphia, 1897		.569, Nap Lajoie, Philadelphia, 1897
		2B	
400	.355, Cupid Childs, Cleveland, 1896		.510, Nap Lajoie, Philadelphia, 1900
500	.346, Bobby Lowe, Boston, 1894		.520 Bobby Lowe, Boston, 1894
		3B	
400	.352, George Davis, New York, 1984		.537, George Davis, New York, 1894
500	.386, Lave Cross, Philadelphia, 1894		.554, George Davis, New York, 1893
		SS	
400	.355, Hughie Jennings, Baltimore, 1897		.533, Bill Dahlen, Chicago, 1896
500	.401, Hughie Jennings, Baltimore, 1896		.566, Bill Dahlen, Chicago, 1894
		OF	
400	.407, done by two different players in 1894		.631, Ed Delahanty, Philadelphia, 1896
500	.440 Hugh Duffy, Boston, NL, 1894		.694, Hugh Duffy, Boston, NL, 1894

C

400	.353, Wilbert Robinson, Baltimore, 1894		.449, John Grim, Louisville, 1894
500	.336, Deacon McGuire, Washington, 1895		.478, Deacon McGuire, Washington, 1895

WORST

	RBI		TOTAL BASES
		1B	
400	31, Duff Cooley, Philadelphia, 1899		135, Tommy Tucker, Cleveland, 1899
500	48, Klondike Douglass, Philadelphia, 1898		164, Jack Doyle, New York, 1900
		2B	
400	29, Kid Gleason, New York, 1900		109, John O'Brien, Balt-Pitt, 1899
500	44, Cupid Childs, Chicago, 1900		144, Kid Gleason, New York, 1898
		3B	
400	37, Bert Myers, St. Louis, 1896		124, Billy Shindle, Brooklyn, 1898
500	45, Doc Casey, Wash-Brook, 1899		148, Bill Grey, Pittsburgh, 1898
		SS	
400	29, Germany Smith, Brooklyn, 1897		109, Germany Smith, Brooklyn, 1897
500	43, Harry Lochhead, Cleveland, 1899		140, Bones Ely, Pittsburgh, 1898
		OF	
400	31, Sport McAllister, Cleveland, 1899		121, Cliff Carroll, Boston, 1893
500	32, Tommy Dowd, St. Louis, 1898		162, Dummy Hoy, Washington, 1893
		C	
400	37, Charlie Dexter, Louisville, 1896		155, Frank Bowerman, Pittsburgh, 1899
500	75, Duke Farrell, Washington, 1893		194, Duke Farrell, Washington, 1893

	RUNS		ON-BASE PERCENTAGE
		1B	
400	40, Tommy Tucker, Cleveland, 1899		.292, Jack O'Connor, Cleveland, 1898
500	53, Tommy Tucker, Brook-StL, 1898		.299, Candy LaChance, Brooklyn, 1898
		2B	
400	40, done by two different players		.284, John O'Brien, Balt-Pitt, 1899
500	51, Jim Connor, Chicago, 1898		.274, Jiggs Parrott, Chicago, 1894
		3B	
400	37, Suter Sullivan, Cleveland, 1899		.249, Billy Shindle, Brooklyn, 1898
500	56, Bill Grey, Pittsburgh, 1898		.282, Bill Grey, Pittsburgh, 1898

SS

400	47, Germany Smith, Brooklyn, 1897	.233, Germany Smith, Brooklyn, 1897
500	49, Bones Ely, Pittsburgh, 1898	.247, Bones Ely, Pittsburgh, 1898

OF

400	29, Sport McAllister, Cleveland, 1899	.273, Sport McAllister, Cleveland, 1899
500	70, Tommy Dowd, St. Louis, 1898	.287, Tommy Dowd, St. Louis, 1898

C

400	49, Frank Bowerman, Pittsburgh, 1899	.286, Frank Bowerman, Pittsburgh, 1899
500	84, Duke Farrell, Washington, 1893	.346, Duke Farrell, Washington, 1893

BATTING AVERAGE   SLUGGING AVERAGE

1B

400	.241, Tommy Tucker, Cleveland, 1899	.296, Tommy Tucker, Cleveland, 1899
500	.247, Candy LaChance, Brooklyn, 1898	.297, Jack Boyle, Philadelphia, 1895

2B

400	.215, John O'Brien, Balt-Pitt, 1899	.263, John O'Brien, Balt-Pitt, 1899
500	.221, Kid Gleason, New York, 1898	.253, Kid Gleason, New York, 1898

3B

400	.225, Billy Shindle, Brooklyn, 1898	.266, Billy Shindle, Brooklyn, 1898
500	.229, Bill Grey, Pittsburgh, 1898	.280, Bill Grey, Pittsburgh, 1898

SS

400	.201, Germany Smith, Brooklyn, 1897	.255, Germany Smith, Brooklyn, 1897
500	.212, Bones Ely, Pittsburgh, 1898	.261, Harry Lochhead, Cleveland, 1899

OF

400	.223, Tom Brown, StL-Wash, 1895	.276, Cliff Carroll, Boston, 1893
500	.240, Tom Brown, Louisville, 1893	.287, Dummy Hoy, Washington, 1893

C

400	.259, Frank Bowerman, Pittsburgh, 1899	.323, Deacon McGuire, Washington, 1898
500	.280, Duke Farrell, Washington, 1893	.380, Duke Farrell, Washington, 1893

THE SEASONAL RECORD

	W	L	PCT	HOME	ROAD	GB
1. Boston Beaneaters	93	39	.705	54–12	39–27	—
2. Baltimore Orioles	90	40	.692	51–15	39–25	2
3. New York Giants	83	48	.634	51–19	32–29	9.5
4. Cincinnati Reds	76	56	.576	49–18	27–38	17
5. Cleveland Spiders	69	62	.527	49–16	20–46	23.5
6. Brooklyn Bridegrooms	61	71	.462	38–29	23–42	32
7. Washington Nationals	61	71	.462	40–26	21–45	32
8. Pittsburgh Pirates	60	71	.458	38–27	22–44	32.5
9. Chicago Colts	59	73	.447	36–30	23–43	34
10. Philadelphia Phillies	55	77	.417	32–34	23–43	38
11. Louisville Colonels	52	78	.400	34–31	18–47	40
12. St. Louis Browns	29	102	.221	18–41	11–61	63.5

	Bos	Ba	NY	Ci	Cl	Br	Wa	Pi	Ch	Ph	Lo	StL	
Boston	—	6	8	9	7	9	7	10	8	10	9	10	93
Baltimore	6	—	5	6	7	9	9	9	9	10	10	10	90
New York	4	7	—	5	9	9	9	8	7	7	6	12	83
Cincinnati	3	6	7	—	7	5	8	5	7	8	9	11	76
Cleveland	5	4	3	5	—	5	8	6	8	9	5	11	69
Brooklyn	3	3	3	7	7	—	7	7	6	6	5	7	61
Washington	5	3	3	4	4	5	—	7	5	8	8	9	61
Pittsburgh	2	3	3	7	6	5	5	—	6	7	8	8	60
Chicago	4	3	5	5	4	6	7	6	—	5	6	8	59
Philadelphia	2	2	5	4	3	6	4	5	7	—	9	8	55
Louisville	3	1	6	3	7	7	4	4	6	3	—	8	52
St. Louis	2	2	0	1	1	5	3	4	4	4	3	—	29
	39	40	48	56	62	71	71	71	73	77	78	102	788

SEASON LEADERS

Batting Average (350 ABs)

1. Keeler, Baltimore	.424
2. F. Clarke, Louisville	.390
3. Burkett, Cleveland	.383
4. Delahanty, Philadelphia	.377
5. Kelley, Baltimore	.362

On–Base Percentage

1. McGraw, Baltimore	.471
2. Burkett, Cleveland	.468
3. Keeler, Baltimore	.464
4. Jennings, Baltimore	.463
5. F. Clarke, Louisville	.462

Home Runs

1. Duffy, Boston	11
2. Davis, New York	10
3. Lajoie, Philadelphia	9
4. Beckley, NY–Cin	8
5. Grady, Phil–StL	7
Stafford, NY–StL	7

Slugging Average

1. Lajoie, Philadelphia	.569
2. Keeler, Baltimore	.539
3. Delahanty, Philadelphia	.538
4. F. Clarke, Louisville	.533
5. Davis, New York	.509

Total Bases

1. Lajoie, Philadelphia	310
2. Keeler, Baltimore	304
3. Delahanty, Philadelphia	285
4. F. Clarke, Louisville	276
5. Duffy, Boston	265

RBI

1. Davis, New York	136
2. Collins, Boston	132
3. Duffy, Boston	129
4. Lajoie, Philadelphia	127
5. Kelley, Baltimore	118

Hits

1.	Keeler, Baltimore	239
2.	F. Clarke, Louisville	202
3.	Delahanty, Philadelphia	200
4.	Burkett, Cleveland	198
5.	Lajoie, Philadelphia	197

Runs

1.	Hamilton, Boston	152
2.	Keeler, Baltimore	145
3.	Griffin, Brooklyn	136
4.	Jones, Brooklyn	134
5.	Jennings, Baltimore	133

Stolen Bases

1.	Lange, Chicago	73
2.	Stenzel, Baltimore	69
3.	Hamilton, Boston	66
4.	Davis, New York	65
5.	Keeler, Baltimore	64

PITCHING

Wins

1.	Nichols, Boston	31
2.	Rusie, New York	28
3.	Klobedanz, Boston	26
4.	Corbett, Baltimore	24
5.	Breitenstein, Cincinnati	23

Losses

1.	Donahue, St. Louis	35
2.	Hart, St. Louis	27
3.	McJames, Washington	23
	Killen, Pittsburgh	23
5.	Kennedy, Brooklyn	20
	Mercer, Washington	20
	Taylor, Philadelphia	20

Innings

1.	Nichols, Boston	368
2.	Donahue, St. Louis	348
3.	Griffith, Chicago	343.2
4.	Kennedy, Brooklyn	343.1
5.	Mercer, Washington	342

Complete Games

1.	Killen, Pittsburgh	38
	Donahue, St. Louis	38
	Griffith, Chicago	38
4.	Nichols, Boston	37
5.	Kennedy, Brooklyn	36

Strikeouts

1.	McJames, Washington	156
2.	Seymour, New York	149
	Corbett, Baltimore	149
4.	Rusie, New York	135
5.	Nichols, Boston	127

Winning Percentage (25 decisions)

1.	Klobedanz, Boston	.788
2.	Nops, Baltimore	.769
3.	Corbett, Baltimore	.750
4.	Nichols, Boston	.738
5.	Rusie, New York	.737

ERA (140 innings)

1.	Rusie, New York	2.54
2.	Nichols, Boston	2.64
3.	Nops, Baltimore	2.81
4.	Corbett, Baltimore	3.11
5.	Powell, Cleveland	3.16

Lowest On-Base Percentage

1.	Nichols, Boston	.291
2.	Rusie, New York	.308
3.	Cuppy, Cleveland	.314
4.	Young, Cleveland	.318
5.	Nops, Baltimore	.319

FIELDING

Total Chances

1B	Werden, Louisville	1457
2B	Padden, Pittsburgh	819
3B	Collins, Boston	564
SS	M. Cross, St. Louis	913
OF	Hoy, Cincinnati	395
C	Warner, New York	672
P	Seymour, New York	133

Fielding Average

Tebeau, Cleveland	.994
McPhee, Cincinnati	.966
Clingman, Louisville	.947
Jennings, Baltimore	.933
Brodie, Pittsburgh	.983
Peitz, Cincinnati	.979
Donahue, St. Louis	.976

BOSTON   **Frank Selee**   **South End Grounds (II)**

		G	AB	H	R	2B	3B	HR	RBI	BB	SB	BA	SA
1B	Fred Tenney	132	**566**	180	125	24	3	1	85	49	34	.318	.376
LF	Hugh Duffy	134	550	187	130	25	10	**11**	129	52	41	.340	.482
3B	Jimmy Collins	134	529	183	103	28	13	6	132	41	14	.346	.482
CF	Billy Hamilton	127	507	174	**152**	17	5	3	61	105	66	.343	.414
2B	Bobby Lowe	123	499	154	87	24	8	5	106	32	16	.309	.419
RF	Chick Stahl	114	469	166	112	30	13	4	97	38	18	.354	.499
SS	Herman Long	107	450	145	89	32	7	3	69	23	22	.322	.444
C	Marty Bergen	87	327	81	47	11	3	2	45	18	5	.248	.318
P	Jack Stivetts	61	199	73	41	9	9	2	37	15	2	.367	.533
P	Fred Klobedanz	48	148	48	29	8	5	1	20	5	1	.324	.466
P	Kid Nichols	46	147	39	20	5	0	3	28	7	4	.265	.361
Sub	Bob Allen	34	119	38	33	5	0	1	24	18	1	.319	.387
P	Ted Lewis	38	113	28	15	0	1	0	8	6	3	.248	.265
Sub	Charlie Ganzel	30	105	28	15	4	3	0	14	4	2	.267	.362
Sub	George Yeager	30	95	23	20	2	3	2	15	7	2	.242	.389
Sub	Fred Lake	19	62	15	2	4	0	0	5	1	2	.242	.306
P	Jim Sullivan	13	33	6	3	0	0	0	3	0	0	.182	.182
Sub	Tommy Tucker	4	14	3	0	2	0	0	4	2	0	.214	.357
P	Piano Legs Hickman	2	3	2	1	0	0	1	2	0	0	.667	1.667
Sub	Mike Mahoney	2	2	1	1	0	0	0	1	0	0	.500	.500
		135	4937	1574	**1025**	230	83	**45**	885	423	233	.319	**.426**

1B   Tenney 128, Tucker 4, Ganzel 2, Stivetts 2
2B   Lowe 123, Duffy 6, Yeager 4, Stivetts 2, Allen 1
SS   Long 107, Allen 32, Duffy 2
3B   Collins 134, Yeager 1
OF   Duffy 129, Hamilton 126, Stahl 111, Stivetts 29, Yeager 10, Tenney 4, Klobedanz 2, Long 1, Bergen 1, Allen 1
C   Bergen 85, Ganzel 27, Lake 18, Yeager 13, Mahoney 1, Allen 1
P   Nichols 46, Klobedanz 38, Lewis 38, Stivetts 18, Sullivan 13, Hickman 2, Mahoney 1

	G	IP	GS	CG	W	L	K	BB	SH	SV	ERA
Kid Nichols	46	**368**	40	37	**31**	11	127	68	2	**3**	2.64
Fred Klobedanz	38	309.1	37	30	26	7	92	125	2	0	4.60
Ted Lewis	38	290	34	30	21	12	65	125	2	1	3.85
Jack Stivetts	18	129.1	15	10	11	4	27	43	0	0	3.41
Jim Sullivan	13	89	9	8	4	5	17	26	1	2	3.94
Piano Legs Hickman	2	7.2	0	0	0	0	0	5	0	1	5.87
Mike Mahoney	1	1	0	0	0	0	1	1	0	0	18.00
* One combined shutout on Sept. 22: Stivetts 5 innings, Sullivan 2 innings											
	1194.1	135	115	93	39	329	393	**8**	**7**	3.65	

BALTIMORE   **Ned Hanlon**   **Union Park**

		G	AB	H	R	2B	3B	HR	RBI	BB	SB	BA	SA
RF	Willie Keeler	129	564	**239**	**145**	27	19	0	74	35	64	**.424**	.539
CF	Jake Stenzel	131	536	189	113	**43**	7	4	116	36	69	.353	.481
LF	Joe Kelley	131	505	183	113	31	9	5	118	70	44	.362	.489
2B	Heinie Reitz	128	477	138	76	15	6	2	84	50	23	.289	.358
1B	Jack Doyle	114	460	163	91	29	4	2	87	29	62	.354	.448
SS	Hughie Jennings	117	439	156	133	26	9	2	79	42	60	.355	.469
3B	John McGraw	106	391	127	90	15	3	0	48	99	44	.325	.379
Sub	Joe Quinn	75	285	74	33	11	4	1	45	13	12	.260	.337
C	Boileryard Clarke	64	241	65	32	7	1	1	38	9	5	.270	.320
C	Wilbert Robinson	48	181	57	25	9	0	0	23	8	0	.315	.365
P	Joe Corbett	42	150	37	27	6	1	0	22	4	4	.247	.300
Sub	Tom O'Brien	50	147	37	25	6	0	0	32	20	7	.252	.293
P	Bill Hoffer	42	139	33	20	8	1	1	16	6	2	.237	.331
Sub	Frank Bowerman	38	130	41	16	5	0	1	21	1	3	.315	.377
P	Jerry Nops	30	92	18	7	2	2	0	7	3	0	.196	.261
P	Arlie Pond	33	90	22	16	3	0	0	6	11	2	.244	.278
P	Doc Amole	11	28	3	1	0	0	0	5	1	0	.107	.107
P	George Blackburn	5	13	1	1	0	0	0	0	0	0	.077	.077
P	Al Maul	2	3	1	0	0	0	0	0	0	0	.333	.333
P	Dick Cogan	1	1	0	0	0	0	0	0	0	0	.000	.000
		136	4872	**1584**	964	**243**	66	19	821	**437**	**401**	**.325**	.414

1B   Doyle 114, O'Brien 25, Clarke 4, Quinn 2
2B   Reitz 128, Quinn 11
S   Jennings 116, Quinn 21. Kelley 3, Corbett 1
3B   McGraw 105, Quinn 37, Kelley 2
OF   Stenzel 131, Kelley 130, Keeler 129, O'Brien 24, Quinn 6, Hoffer 4, Pond 1, Corbett 1
C   Clarke 59, Robinson 48, Bowerman 36
P   Hoffer 38, Corbett 37, Pond 32, Nops 30, Amole 11, Blackburn 5, Maul 2, Cogan 1

	G	IP	GS	CG	W	L	K	BB	SH	SV	ERA
Joe Corbett	37	313	37	34	24	8	149	115	1	0	3.11
Bill Hoffer	38	303.1	33	29	22	11	62	104	1	0	4.30
Arlie Pond	32	248	28	23	18	9	59	72	0	0	3.52
Jerry Nops	30	220.2	25	23	20	6	69	52	1	0	2.81
Doc Amole	11	70	7	6	4	4	19	17	0	0	2.57
George Blackburn	5	33	4	3	2	2	1	12	0	0	6.82
Al Maul	2	7.2	2	0	0	0	2	8	0	0	7.04
Dick Cogan	1	2	0	0	0	0	0	2	0	0	13.50
		1197.2	136	118	90	40	361	382	3	0	3.55

NEW YORK   **Bill Joyce**   **Polo Grounds (III)**

		G	AB	H	R	2B	3B	HR	RBI	BB	SB	BA	SA
CF	George Van Haltren	129	564	186	117	22	9	3	64	40	50	.330	.417
2B	Kid Gleason	131	540	172	85	16	4	1	106	26	43	.319	.369
RF	Mike Tiernan	127	528	174	123	29	10	5	72	61	40	.330	.451
SS	George Davis	130	519	183	112	31	10	10	**136**	41	65	.353	.509
1B	Willie Clark	116	431	122	63	17	12	1	75	37	18	.283	.385
C	Jack Warner	110	397	109	50	6	3	2	51	26	8	.275	.320
3B	Bill Joyce	109	388	118	109	15	13	3	64	78	33	.304	.433
LF	Ducky Holmes	79	306	82	51	8	6	1	44	18	30	.268	.343
Sub	Tom McCreery	49	177	53	36	8	5	1	27	22	15	.299	.418
Sub	Parke Wilson	46	154	46	29	9	3	0	22	15	5	.299	.396
P	Amos Rusie	40	144	40	25	1	3	0	22	3	1	.278	.326
P	Jouett Meekin	42	137	41	22	6	1	0	10	5	3	.299	.358
P	Cy Seymour	44	137	33	13	5	1	2	14	4	3	.241	.336
Sub	Jim Donnelly	23	85	16	19	3	0	0	11	9	6	.188	.224
P	Charlie Gettig	22	75	15	8	6	0	0	12	6	3	.200	.280
Sub	Jake Beckley	17	68	17	8	2	3	1	11	2	2	.250	.412
P	Mike Sullivan	23	66	18	6	1	0	0	8	2	0	.273	.288
P	Ed Doheny	10	35	7	5	1	0	0	0	1	2	.200	.229
Sub	Walt Wilmot	11	34	9	8	2	0	1	4	2	1	.265	.412
Sub	General Stafford	7	23	2	0	0	0	0	3	3	0	.087	.087
P	Dad Clarke	7	18	3	4	0	0	0	1	1	0	.167	.167
Sub	Dave Zearfoss	5	10	3	1	0	1	0	0	0	0	.300	.500
Sub	Yale Murphy	5	8	0	1	0	0	0	1	2	0	.000	.000
		137	4844	1449	895	188	84	31	758	404	328	.299	.392

1B   Clark 107, Beckley 17, Wilson 10, Joyce 2, Clarke 1
2B   Gleason 129, Gettig 6, McCreery 3, Murphy 2, Wilson 1
SS   Davis 130, Gleason 3, Gettig 3, Murphy 3, Stafford 2, Holmes 1
3B   Joyce 106, Donnelly 23, Gettig 7, Clark 1
OF   Van Haltren 129, Tiernan 127, Holmes 77, McCreery 45, Wilmot 9, Clark 7, Seymour 6, Stafford 5, Wilson 4, Gettig 3
C   Warner 110, Wilson 30, Zearfoss 5
P   Rusie 38, Seymour 38, Meekin 37, Sullivan 23, Doheny 10, Clarke 6, Gettig 3

	G	IP	GS	CG	W	L	K	BB	SH	SV	ERA
Amos Rusie	38	322.1	37	35	28	10	135	87	2	0	**2.54**
Jouett Meekin	37	303.2	34	30	20	11	83	99	2	0	3.76
Cy Seymour	38	277.2	33	28	18	14	149	**164**	2	1	3.37
Mike Sullivan	23	148.2	16	11	8	7	35	71	1	2	5.09
Ed Doheny	10	85	10	10	4	4	37	45	0	0	2.12
Dad Clarke	6	31	4	2	2	1	10	11	0	0	6.10
Charlie Gettig	3	19	2	2	1	1	7	9	0	0	5.21
	*One combined shutout on July 5: Rusie 7 innings, Sullivan 2 innings										
	—2 forfeit Ws: vs Washington on May 3; vs Pittsburgh on June 1—										
	1187.1	136	118	83	48	**456**	486	8	3	**3.47**

CINCINNATI   **Buck Ewing**   **League Park (II)**

		G	AB	H	R	2B	3B	HR	RBI	BB	SB	BA	SA
3B	Charlie Irwin	134	505	146	89	26	6	0	74	47	27	.289	.364
CF	Dummy Hoy	128	497	145	87	24	6	2	42	54	37	.292	.376
UT	Tommy Corcoran	109	445	128	76	30	5	3	57	13	15	.288	.398
RF	Dusty Miller	119	440	139	83	27	1	4	70	48	29	.316	.409
LF	Eddie Burke	95	387	103	71	17	1	1	41	29	22	.266	.323
1B	Jake Beckley	97	365	126	76	17	9	7	76	18	23	.345	.499
SS	Claude Ritchey	101	337	95	58	12	4	0	41	42	11	.282	.341
2B	Bid McPhee	81	282	85	45	13	7	1	39	35	9	.301	.408
C	Heinie Peitz	78	266	78	35	11	7	1	44	18	3	.293	.398
Sub	Farmer Vaughn	54	199	58	21	13	5	0	30	2	2	.291	.407
Sub	Bug Holliday	61	195	61	50	9	4	2	20	27	6	.313	.431
C	Pop Schriver	61	178	54	29	12	4	1	30	19	3	.303	.433
P	Ted Breitenstein	41	124	33	16	4	6	0	23	6	5	.266	.395
P	Billy Rhines	41	107	17	4	1	1	0	8	9	0	.159	.187
P	Frank Dwyer	37	94	25	13	1	1	0	10	5	0	.266	.298
P	Red Ehret	34	66	13	6	2	0	0	6	4	2	.197	.227
P	Bill Damman	16	31	5	4	0	2	0	6	4	0	.161	.290
P	Stub Brown	2	5	0	0	0	0	0	0	0	0	.000	.000
Sub	Buck Ewing	1	1	0	0	0	0	0	0	0	0	.000	.000
		134	4524	1311	763	219	69	22	617	380	194	.290	.383

1B	Beckley 97, Vaughn 35, Holliday 3, Ewing 1
2B	McPhee 81, Corcoran 47, Ritchey 8, Holliday 3
SS	Ritchey 70, Corcoran 63, Holliday 4
3B	Irwin 134
OF	Hoy 128, Miller 119, Burke 95, Holliday 42, Ritchey 22
C	Peitz 71, Schriver 53, Vaughn 15,
P	Rhines 41, Breitenstein 40, Dwyer 37, Ehret 34, Damman 16, Brown 2, Peitz 2

	G	IP	GS	CG	W	L	K	BB	SH	SV	ERA
Ted Breitenstein	40	320.1	39	32	23	12	98	91	2	0	3.62
Billy Rhines	41	288.2	32	26	21	15	65	86	1	0	4.08
Frank Dwyer	37	247.1	31	22	18	13	41	56	0	0	3.78
Red Ehret	34	184.1	19	11	8	10	43	47	0	2	4.78
Bill Damman	16	95	11	7	6	4	21	37	1	0	4.74
Stub Brown	2	13	1	1	0	1	2	8	0	0	4.15
Heinie Peitz	2	8	1	1	0	1	0	4	0	0	7.88
		1156.2	134	100	76	56	270	329	4	2	4.09

CLEVELAND **Patsy Tebeau** **League Park (I)**

		G	AB	H	R	2B	3B	HR	RBI	BB	SB	BA	SA
SS	Ed McKean	125	523	143	83	21	14	2	78	40	15	.273	.379
LF	Jesse Burkett	128	517	198	129	28	7	2	60	76	28	.383	.476
3B	Bobby Wallace	131	516	173	99	33	21	4	112	48	14	.335	.504
2B	Cupid Childs	114	444	150	105	15	9	1	61	74	25	.338	.419
1B	Patsy Tebeau	109	412	110	62	15	9	0	59	30	11	.267	.347
UT	Jack O'Connor	103	397	115	49	21	4	2	69	26	20	.290	.378
C	Chief Zimmer	80	294	93	50	22	3	0	40	25	8	.316	.412
RF	Louis Sockalexis	66	278	94	43	9	8	3	42	18	16	.338	.460
CF	Ollie Pickering	46	182	64	33	5	2	1	22	11	18	.352	.418
P	Cy Young	48	153	34	14	4	3	0	19	2	4	.222	.288
Sub	Lou Criger	39	138	31	15	4	1	0	22	23	5	.225	.268
Sub	Sport McAllister	43	137	30	23	5	1	0	11	12	3	.219	.270
Sub	Harry Blake	32	117	30	17	3	1	1	15	12	5	.256	.325
P	Zeke Wilson	37	116	26	16	0	1	0	9	8	3	.224	.241
P	Jack Powell	28	97	20	10	1	0	0	12	6	0	.206	.216
Sub	Jim McAleer	24	91	20	6	2	0	0	10	7	4	.220	.242
P	Nig Cuppy	21	55	8	5	0	1	0	3	5	0	.145	.182
Sub	Ira Belden	8	30	8	5	0	2	0	4	2	0	.267	.400
P	Mike McDermott	9	25	8	0	1	0	0	5	0	0	.320	.400
P	Henry Clarke	7	25	7	3	0	0	0	3	2	0	.280	.280
Sub	Dale Gear	7	24	4	3	1	0	0	2	3	2	.167	.208
Sub	Fred Cooke	5	17	5	2	2	0	0	3	3	0	.294	.412
P	Charlie Brown	4	11	3	1	1	0	0	1	0	0	.273	.364
P	John Pappalau	2	5	0	0	0	0	0	1	2	0	.000	.000
		132	4604	1374	773	192	88	16	663	435	181	.298	.389

1B Tebeau 92, O'Connor 36, McAllister 3, Criger 2, Young 2, Wilson 1
2B Childs 114, Tebeau 18, McAllister 1, Pickering 1
SS McKean 125, McAllister 4, Tebeau 1
3B Wallace 130, Tebeau 2
OF Burkett 127, Sockalexis 66, O'Connor 52, Pickering 46, Blake 32, McAllister 28, McAleer 24, Belden 8, Gear 6, Cooke 5, Clarke 2, Wilson 2, Powell 1, Wallace 1
C   Zimmer 80, Criger 37, O'Connor 13, McAllister 2
P   Young 46, Wilson 34, Powell 27, Cuppy 19, McDermott 9, Clarke 5, McAllister 4, Brown 4, Pappalau 2

	G	IP	GS	CG	W	L	K	BB	SH	SV	ERA
Cy Young #	46	335.2	38	35	21	19	88	49	2	0	3.78
Zeke Wilson	34	263.2	30	26	16	11	69	83	1	0	4.16
Jack Powell	27	225	26	24	15	10	61	62	2	0	3.16
Nig Cuppy	19	138	17	13	10	6	23	26	1	0	3.20
Mike McDermott	9	62	7	4	4	5	12	25	0	0	4.50
Henry Clarke	5	30.2	4	3	0	4	3	12	0	0	6.16
Sport McAllister	4	28	3	3	1	2	10	9	0	0	4.50
Charlie Brown	4	24.1	4	2	1	2	8	17	0	0	7.77
John Pappalau	2	12	1	1	0	1	3	6	0	0	10.50
—1 forfeit W vs Philadelphia on July 24; 2 forfeit Ls: vs Louisville on August 4; vs Washington on September 8—											
		1119.1	130	111	68	60	277	**289**	6	0	3.96

No-hit game 6–0 vs Cincinnati, September 18

BROOKLYN   **Billy Barnie**   **Eastern Park**

		G	AB	H	R	2B	3B	HR	RBI	BB	SB	BA	SA
RF	Fielder Jones	135	548	172	134	15	10	1	49	61	48	.314	.383
3B	Billy Shindle	134	542	154	83	32	6	4	105	35	23	.284	.387
CF	Mike Griffin	134	534	169	136	25	11	2	56	81	16	.316	.416
1B	Candy LaChance	126	520	160	86	28	16	4	90	15	26	.308	.446
LF	John Anderson	117	492	160	93	28	12	4	85	17	29	.325	.455
SS	Germany Smith	112	428	86	47	17	3	0	29	14	1	.201	.255
C	John Grim	80	290	72	26	10	1	0	25	1	3	.248	.290
2B	George Shoch	85	284	79	42	9	2	0	38	49	6	.278	.324
2B	Jimmy Canavan	63	240	52	25	9	3	2	34	26	9	.217	.304
Sub	Aleck Smith	66	237	71	36	13	1	1	39	4	12	.300	.376
P	Brickyard Kennedy	45	147	40	10	4	3	1	18	3	0	.272	.361
P	Jack Dunn	36	131	29	20	4	0	0	17	4	2	.221	.252
P	Harley Payne	41	110	26	13	0	1	0	11	8	0	.236	.255
Sub	Buster Burrell	33	103	25	15	2	0	2	18	10	1	.243	.320
P	Chauncey Fisher	20	59	12	7	0	1	0	8	6	0	.203	.237
Sub	Jimmy Sheckard	13	49	14	12	3	2	3	14	6	5	.286	.612
P	Dan Daub	19	49	11	11	3	0	0	4	9	2	.224	.286
P	Sadie McMahon	9	25	5	2	0	0	0	2	1	0	.200	.200
Sub	Pat Hannifan	10	20	5	4	0	0	0	2	1	4	.250	.250
P	John Brown	1	2	1	0	0	0	0	0	0	0	.500	.500
		136	4810	1343	802	202	72	24	644	351	187	.279	.366

1B   LaChance 126, A. Smith 6, Burrell 4, Anderson 3
2B   Shoch 68, Canavan 63, Dunn 4, Hannifan 2
SS   G. Smith 112, Shoch 13, Sheckard 11, Dunn 1
3B   Shindle 134, Dunn 3
OF   Jones 135, Griffin 134, Anderson 115, A. Smith 18, Shoch 4, Hannifan 3, Dunn 3, Sheckard 2, Payne 1
C   Grim 77, A. Smith 43, Burrell 27
P   Kennedy 44, Payne 40, Dunn 25, Fisher 20, Daub 19, McMahon 9, Brown 1

	G	IP	GS	CG	W	L	K	BB	SH	SV	ERA
Brickyard Kennedy	44	343.1	40	36	18	20	81	149	2	1	3.91
Harley Payne	40	280	38	30	14	17	86	71	1	0	4.63
Jack Dunn	25	216.2	21	21	14	9	26	66	0	0	4.57
Chauncey Fisher	20	149	13	11	9	7	31	43	1	1	4.23
Dan Daub	19	137.2	16	11	6	11	19	48	0	0	6.08
Sadie McMahon	9	63	7	5	0	6	13	29	0	0	5.86
John Brown	1	5	1	0	0	1	0	4	0	0	7.20
		1194.2	136	114	61	71	256	410	4	2	4.60

WASHINGTON   **Gus Schmelz (9–25)**   **Tom Brown (52–46)**   **Boundary Field**

		G	AB	H	R	2B	3B	HR	RBI	BB	SB	BA	SA
SS	Gene Demontreville	133	**566**	193	92	27	8	3	93	21	30	.341	.433
LF	Kip Selbach	124	486	152	113	25	16	5	59	80	46	.313	.461
CF	Tom Brown	116	469	137	91	17	2	5	45	52	25	.292	.369
Sub	Zeke Wrigley	104	388	110	65	14	8	3	64	21	5	.284	.384
1B	Tommy Tucker	93	352	119	52	18	5	5	61	27	18	.338	.460
3B	Charlie Reilly	101	351	97	64	18	3	2	60	34	18	.276	.362
C	Deacon McGuire	93	327	112	51	17	7	4	53	21	9	.343	.474
2B	John O'Brien	86	320	78	37	12	2	3	45	19	6	.244	.322
RF	Charlie Abbey	80	300	78	52	14	8	3	34	27	9	.260	.390
C	Duke Farrell	78	261	84	41	9	6	0	53	17	8	.322	.402
Sub	Jake Gettman	36	143	45	28	7	3	3	29	7	8	.315	.469
P	Win Mercer	50	139	44	23	2	5	0	19	6	7	.317	.403
Sub	Ed Cartwright	33	124	29	19	4	0	0	15	8	9	.234	.266
P	Doc McJames	44	124	21	12	1	2	0	13	5	1	.169	.210
P	Cy Swaim	26	71	16	7	1	0	0	9	1	3	.225	.239
P	Silver King	24	57	11	8	2	0	0	7	12	0	.193	.228
Sub	Tom Leahy	19	52	20	12	2	1	0	7	9	6	.385	.462
P	Les German	19	44	15	8	2	0	0	3	3	0	.341	.386
P	Elisha Norton	7	18	5	0	2	1	0	2	0	0	.278	.500
P	Roger Bresnahan	6	16	6	1	0	0	0	3	1	0	.375	.375
Sub	Bill Fox	4	14	4	4	0	0	0	0	1	0	.286	.286
Sub	Billy Lush	3	12	0	1	0	0	0	0	2	0	.000	.000
P	Al Maul	1	1	0	0	0	0	0	0	0	0	.000	.000
P	Joe Stanley	1	1	0	0	0	0	0	0	0	0	.000	.000
		135	4636	1376	781	194	77	36	674	374	208	.297	.395

1B	Tucker 93, Cartwright 33, McGuire 6, Farrell 1
2B	O'Brien 86, Demontreville 33, Wrigley 9, Leahy 3, Fox 2, German 2
SS	Demontreville 99, Wrigley 33, Fox 2
3B	Reilly 101, Wrigley 30, Leahy 5, German 1
OF	Selbach 124, Brown 115, Abbey 80, Wrigley 36, Gettman 36, Leahy 10, Lush 3, Norton 3, Bresnahan 1
C	McGuire 73, Farrell 63, Leahy 1, Mercer 1
P	Mercer 47, McJames 44, Swaim 27, King 23, German 15, Bresnahan 6, Norton 4, Maul 1, Stanley 1

	G	IP	GS	CG	W	L	K	BB	SH	SV	ERA
Win Mercer	**47**	342	**43**	35	21	20	91	104	**3**	**3**	3.18
Doc McJames	44	323.2	39	33	15	23	**156**	137	**3**	2	3.61
Cy Swaim	26	184	19	14	9	11	52	59	0	0	4.60
Silver King	23	154	19	12	6	9	32	45	0	1	4.79
Les German	15	83.2	5	4	3	5	2	33	0	0	5.59
Roger Bresnahan	6	41	3	3	4	0	12	10	1	0	3.95
Effie Norton	4	17	2	1	2	1	3	11	0	0	6.88
Al Maul	1	2	1	0	0	1	0	1	0	0	9.00
Joe Stanley	1	0.2	0	0	0	0	0	0	0	0	0.00
—1 forfeit W vs Cleveland on September 8; 1 forfeit L vs New York on May 3—
		1148	135	102	60	70	348	400	7	6	4.01

PITTSBURGH   **Patsy Donovan**   **Exposition Park**

		G	AB	H	R	2B	3B	HR	RBI	BB	SB	BA	SA
2B	Dick Padden	134	517	146	84	16	10	2	58	38	18	.282	.364
SS	Bones Ely	133	516	146	63	20	8	2	74	25	10	.283	.364
RF	Patsy Donovan	120	479	154	82	16	7	0	57	25	34	.322	.384
LF	Elmer Smith	123	467	145	99	19	17	6	54	70	25	.310	.463
1B	Harry Davis	111	429	131	70	10	**28**	2	63	26	21	.305	.473
CF	Steve Brodie	100	370	108	47	7	12	2	53	25	11	.292	.392
C	Joe Sugden	84	288	64	31	6	4	0	38	18	9	.222	.271
C	Bill Merritt	62	209	55	21	6	1	1	26	9	2	.263	.316
3B	Jesse Hoffmeister	48	188	58	33	6	9	3	36	8	6	.309	.484
P	Jesse Tannehill	56	184	49	22	8	2	0	22	18	4	.266	.332
3B	Jim Donnelly	44	161	31	22	4	0	0	14	16	14	.193	.217
Sub	Denny Lyons	39	131	27	22	6	4	2	17	22	5	.206	.359
P	Pink Hawley	40	130	30	10	3	1	0	9	4	0	.231	.269
P	Frank Killen	42	129	32	16	4	0	1	7	17	2	.248	.302
Sub	Jack Rothfuss	32	115	36	20	3	1	2	18	5	3	.313	.409
Sub	Tom Leahy	24	92	24	10	3	3	0	12	7	3	.261	.359
P	Jim Gardner	27	76	12	13	2	1	1	8	9	3	.158	.250
P	Jim Hughey	25	63	8	4	1	0	0	3	5	0	.127	.143
P	Charlie Hastings	16	43	10	7	0	0	1	6	11	0	.233	.302
Sub	Charlie Kuhns	1	3	0	0	0	0	0	0	1	0	.000	.000
		135	4590	1266	676	140	**108**	25	575	379	170	.276	.370

1B   Davis 64, Rothfuss 32, Lyons 32, Merritt 7, Sugden 3
2B   Padden 134, Gardner 1
3B   Hoffmeister 48, Donnelly 44, Davis 32, Gardner 6, Leahy 6, Lyons 2, Kuhns 1
SS   Ely 133, Davis 1
OF   Smith 123, Donovan 120, Brodie 100, Tannehill 33, Davis 14, Leahy 13, Gardner 6
C   Sugden 81, Merritt 53, Leahy 6
P   Killen 42, Hawley 40, Hughey 25, Tannehill 21, Hastings 16, Gardner 14

	G	IP	GS	CG	W	L	K	BB	SH	SV	ERA
Frank Killen	42	337.1	41	**38**	17	23	99	76	1	0	4.46
Pink Hawley	40	311.1	39	33	18	18	88	94	0	0	4.80
Jim Hughey	25	149.1	17	13	6	10	38	45	0	1	5.06
Jesse Tannehill	21	142	16	11	9	9	40	24	1	1	4.25
Charlie Hastings	16	118	10	9	5	4	42	47	0	0	4.58
Jim Gardner	14	95.1	11	8	5	5	35	32	0	0	5.19
—2 forfeit Ls: vs New York on June 1; vs Philadelphia on June 4—											
		1153.1	134	112	60	71	342	318	2	2	4.67

CHICAGO   Cap Anson   West Side Park (II)

		G	AB	H	R	2B	3B	HR	RBI	BB	SB	BA	SA
RF	Jimmy Ryan	136	520	156	103	33	17	5	85	50	27	.300	.458
CF	Bill Lange	118	479	163	119	24	14	5	83	48	73	.340	.480
LF	George Decker	111	428	124	72	12	7	5	63	24	11	.290	.386
1B	Cap Anson	114	424	121	67	17	3	3	75	60	11	.285	.361
Sub	Barry McCormick	101	419	112	87	8	10	2	55	33	44	.267	.348
3B	Bill Everett	92	379	119	63	14	7	5	39	36	26	.314	.427
UT	Nixey Callahan	96	360	105	60	18	6	3	47	10	12	.292	.400
2B	Jim Connor	77	285	83	40	10	5	3	38	24	10	.291	.393
SS	Bill Dahlen	75	276	80	67	18	8	6	40	43	15	.290	.478
UT	Walter Thornton	75	265	85	39	9	6	0	55	30	13	.321	.400
C	Mal Kittridge	79	262	53	25	5	5	1	30	22	9	.202	.271
C	Tim Donahue	58	188	45	28	7	3	0	21	9	3	.239	.309
P	Clark Griffith	46	162	38	27	8	4	0	21	18	2	.235	.333
Sub	Fred Pfeffer	32	114	26	10	0	1	0	11	12	5	.228	.246
P	Danny Friend	25	88	25	12	5	0	0	9	5	1	.284	.341
P	Buttons Briggs	22	81	13	5	0	1	0	5	3	1	.160	.185
P	Roger Denzer	12	39	6	4	1	0	0	1	1	0	.154	.179
Sub	Tom Hernon	4	16	1	2	0	0	0	2	0	1	.063	.063
P	Jim Korwan	5	12	0	0	0	0	0	0	1	0	.000	.000
P	Dave Wright	1	3	1	1	0	0	0	1	1	0	.333	.333
P	Adonis Terry	1	3	0	1	0	0	0	0	0	0	.000	.000
		138	4803	1356	832	189	97	38	681	430	264	.282	.386

1B   Anson 103, Decker 38, Donahue 1, Griffith 1
2B   Connor 76, Pfeffer 32, Callahan 30, McCormick 1, Decker 1
SS   Dahlen 75, McCormick 46, Callahan 18, Griffith 2, Donahue 2
3B   Everett 83, McCormick 56, Callahan 2, Griffith 1
OF   Ryan 136, Lange 118, Decker 75, Thornton 59, Callahan 21, Everett 8, Hernon 4, Griffith 2, Friend 1
C   Kittridge 79, Donahue 55, Anson 11
P   Griffith 41, Friend 24, Callahan 23, Briggs 22, Thornton 16, Denzer 12, Korwan 5, Terry 1, Wright 1

	G	IP	GS	CG	W	L	K	BB	SH	SV	ERA
Clark Griffith	41	343.2	38	**38**	21	18	102	86	1	1	3.72
Danny Friend	24	203	24	23	12	11	58	86	0	0	4.52
Nixey Callahan	23	189.2	22	21	12	9	52	55	1	0	4.03
Buttons Briggs	22	186.2	22	21	4	17	60	85	0	0	5.26
Walter Thornton	16	130.1	16	15	6	7	55	51	0	0	4.70
Roger Denzer	12	94.2	10	8	2	8	17	34	0	0	5.13
Jim Korwan	5	34	4	3	1	2	12	28	0	0	5.82
Adonis Terry	1	8	1	1	0	1	1	6	0	0	10.13
Dave Wright	1	7	1	1	1	0	4	2	0	0	15.43
		1197	138	**131**	59	73	361	433	2	1	4.53

PHILADELPHIA		George Stallings		Philadelphia Baseball Grounds (II)								
		G	AB	H	R	2B	3B	HR	RBI	BB	SB	BA	SA
CF	Duff Cooley	133	**566**	186	124	14	13	4	40	51	31	.329	.420
1B	Nap Lajoie	126	545	197	107	40	23	9	127	15	20	.361	**.569**
LF	Ed Delahanty	129	530	200	109	40	15	5	96	60	26	.377	.538
RF	Tommy Dowd	91	391	114	68	14	4	0	43	19	30	.292	.348
2B	Lave Cross	88	344	89	37	17	5	3	51	10	10	.259	.363
3B	Billy Nash	104	337	87	45	20	2	0	39	60	4	.258	.329
UT	Phil Geier	92	316	88	51	6	2	1	35	56	19	.278	.320
C	Jack Boyle	75	288	73	37	9	1	2	36	19	3	.253	.313
SS	Sam Gillen	75	270	70	32	10	3	0	27	35	2	.259	.319
C	Jack Clements	55	185	44	18	4	2	6	36	12	3	.238	.378
Sub	Frank Shugart	40	163	41	20	8	2	5	25	8	5	.252	.417
P	Al Orth	53	152	50	26	7	4	1	17	3	5	.329	.447
P	Jack Taylor	43	139	35	12	6	1	1	17	7	0	.252	.331
Sub	Ed McFarland	38	130	29	18	3	5	1	16	14	2	.223	.346
Sub	Bill Hallman	31	126	33	16	3	0	0	15	8	1	.262	.286
P	George Wheeler	26	79	16	11	7	0	0	0	4	2	.203	.291
P	Jack Fifield	27	77	18	11	3	0	2	6	9	0	.234	.351
P	Davey Dunkle	7	23	4	2	1	0	0	1	2	0	.174	.217
Sub	Sam Thompson	3	13	3	2	0	1	0	3	1	0	.231	.385
P	Kid Carsey	4	13	3	1	0	0	0	1	0	0	.231	.231
Sub	Mike Grady	4	13	2	1	0	0	0	0	1	0	.154	.154
P	Youngy Johnson	5	13	1	0	0	0	0	0	0	0	.077	.077
Sub	Kohly Miller	3	11	2	2	0	0	0	1	2	0	.182	.182
Sub	Ed Abbaticchio	3	10	3	0	0	0	0	0	1	0	.300	.300
Sub	George Stallings	2	9	2	1	1	0	0	0	0	0	.222	.333
P	Bob Becker	5	9	1	1	0	0	0	1	2	0	.111	.111
P	Tully Sparks	1	3	0	0	0	0	0	0	0	0	.000	.000
P	Tom Lipp	1	1	1	0	0	0	0	0	0	0	1.000	1.000
		134	4756	1392	752	213	83	40	633	399	163	.293	.398

1B   Lajoie 108, Boyle 24, Cooley 2, Delahanty 1, Stallings 1
2B   Cross 38, Geier 37, Hallman 31, Dowd 19, Nash 4, Abbaticchio 3, Miller 3
SS   Gillen 69, Shugart 40, Nash 19, Geier 6, Cross 1
3B   Nash 79, Cross 47, Gillen 6, Lajoie 2, Geier 2
OF   Cooley 131, Delahanty 129, Dowd 73, Geier 45, Lajoie 19, Orth 6, Thompson 3, Cross 2, Stallings 1, Taylor 1
C   Boyle 50, Clements 49, McFarland 37, Grady 3
P   Taylor 40, Orth 36, Fifield 27, Wheeler 26, Dunkle 7, Becker 5, Johnson 5, Carsey 4, Sparks 1, Lipp 1

	G	IP	GS	CG	W	L	K	BB	SH	SV	ERA
Jack Taylor	40	317.1	37	35	16	20	88	76	2	2	4.23
Al Orth	36	282.1	34	29	14	19	64	82	2	0	4.62
Jack Fifield	27	210.2	26	21	5	18	38	80	0	0	5.51
George Wheeler	26	191	19	17	11	10	35	62	0	0	3.96
Davey Dunkle	7	62	7	7	5	2	9	23	0	0	3.48
Youngy Johnson	5	29	2	1	1	2	7	12	0	0	4.66
Kid Carsey	4	28	4	2	2	1	1	16	0	0	5.14
Bob Becker	5	24	2	2	0	2	10	7	0	0	5.63
Tully Sparks	1	8	1	1	0	1	0	4	0	0	10.13
Tom Lipp	1	3	1	0	0	1	1	2	0	0	15.00
—1 forfeit W vs Pittsburgh on June 4; 1 forfeit L vs Cleveland on July 24—											
		1155.1	133	115	54	76	253	364	4	2	4.60

LOUISVILLE   Jim Rogers (17–24)   Fred Clarke (35–54)   Eclipse Park (II)

		G	AB	H	R	2B	3B	HR	RBI	BB	SB	BA	SA
LF	Fred Clarke	128	518	202	120	30	13	6	67	45	57	.390	.533
1B	Perry Werden	131	506	153	76	21	14	5	83	40	14	.302	.429
SS	General Stafford	111	432	120	68	16	5	7	53	31	14	.278	.387
3B	Billy Clingman	113	395	90	59	14	7	2	47	37	14	.228	.314
C	Bill Wilson	105	381	81	43	12	4	1	41	18	9	.213	.273
RF	Tom McCreery	89	338	96	55	5	6	4	40	38	13	.284	.370
Sub	Charlie Dexter	76	257	72	43	12	5	2	46	21	12	.280	.389
CF	Ollie Pickering	63	246	62	34	5	2	1	20	25	20	.252	.301
Sub	Honus Wagner	61	237	80	37	17	4	2	39	15	19	.338	.468
Sub	Abbie Johnson	48	161	39	16	6	1	0	23	13	2	.242	.292
2B	Jim Rogers	41	150	22	22	3	2	2	22	22	4	.147	.233
Sub	Joe Dolan	36	133	28	10	2	2	0	7	8	6	.211	.256
Sub	Doc Nance	35	120	29	25	5	3	3	17	20	3	.242	.408
P	Chick Fraser	36	112	18	10	1	0	2	11	10	2	.161	.223
P	Bert Cunningham	31	93	22	13	0	1	2	10	1	1	.237	.323
Sub	Heinie Smith	21	76	20	7	3	0	1	7	3	1	.263	.342
P	Bill Hill	27	74	7	5	0	1	0	4	4	1	.095	.122
P	Bill Magee	22	62	13	4	1	0	0	9	4	0	.210	.226
Sub	Irv Hach	16	51	11	5	2	0	0	3	5	1	.216	.255
Sub	Dick Butler	10	38	7	3	0	0	0	2	0	1	.184	.184
P	George Hemming	10	28	5	5	1	0	0	2	2	0	.179	.214
P	Roy Evans	9	23	3	1	0	0	0	3	2	0	.130	.130
P	Dad Clarke	7	22	5	0	0	0	0	2	0	0	.227	.227
Sub	Bill Clark	4	16	3	2	0	0	0	2	1	1	.188	.188
P	Pete Dowling	4	10	2	1	1	0	0	0	0	0	.200	.300
Sub	Frank Martin	2	8	2	1	0	0	0	0	0	0	.250	.250
P	Art Herman	3	6	2	1	1	0	0	1	3	0	.333	.500
P	Burt Miller	4	6	1	0	0	0	0	0	0	0	.167	.167
P	Rube Waddell	2	6	0	0	0	0	0	0	0	0	.000	.000
P	Jim Jones	2	4	1	2	1	0	0	0	1	0	.250	.500
Sub	Tom Delahanty	1	4	1	1	1	0	0	2	0	0	.250	.500
Sub	Ducky Holmes	2	4	0	0	0	0	0	0	1	0	.000	.000
Sub	Ossee Schreckengost	1	3	0	0	0	0	0	0	0	0	.000	.000
		134	4520	1197	669	160	70	40	563	370	195	.265	.358

1B Werden 131, Rogers 3, Hemming 1
2B Rogers 39, Johnson 33, Smith 21, Dolan 18, Hach 9, Wagner 9, Clark 3, Martin 2, Delahanty 1
SS Stafford 103, Dolan 18, Johnson 12, Dexter 2, Holmes 1
3B Clingman 113, Dexter 14, Hach 7, Clark 1, Wilson 1, Stafford 1
OF F. Clarke 127, McCreery 89, Pickering 62, Wagner 52, Nance 35, Dexter 32, Stafford 7, Cunningham 2, Fraser 1
C   Wilson 103, Dexter 23, Butler 10, Schreckengost 1
P   Fraser 35, Cunningham 29, Hill 27, Magee 22, Hemming 9, Evans 9, D. Clarke 7, Dowling 4, Miller 4, Herman 3, Waddell 2, Jones 1

	G	IP	GS	CG	W	L	K	BB	SH	SV	ERA
Chick Fraser	35	286.1	34	32	15	19	70	133	0	0	4.09
Bert Cunningham	29	234.2	27	25	14	13	49	72	0	0	4.14
Bill Hill	27	199	26	20	7	17	55	69	1	0	3.62
Bill Magee	22	155.1	16	13	4	12	44	99	1	0	5.39
George Hemming	9	67	8	7	3	4	7	25	0	0	5.10
Roy Evans	9	59.1	8	6	5	4	20	24	0	0	4.10
Dad Clarke	7	54.2	6	6	2	4	7	10	0	0	3.95
Pete Dowling	4	26	4	2	1	2	3	8	0	0	5.88

	G	IP	GS	CG	W	L	K	BB	SH	SV	ERA
Art Herman	3	18	2	1	0	1	4	5	0	0	4.00
Burt Miller	4	17	1	1	0	1	3	3	0	0	7.94
Rube Waddell	2	14	1	1	0	1	5	6	0	0	3.21
Jim Jones	1	6.2	0	0	0	0	0	5	0	0	18.90
		—1 forfeit W vs Cleveland on August 4—									
		1138	133	114	51	78	267	459	2	0	4.42

ST. LOUIS   Tommy Dowd (6–22)   Hugh Nicol (8–32)   Bill Hallman (13–36)
Chris Von Der Ahe (2–12)   Sportsman's Park (II)

	G	AB	H	R	2B	3B	HR	RBI	BB	SB	BA	SA
C	Klondike Douglass	125	516	170	77	15	3	6	50	52	12	.329	.405
3B	Fred Hartman	124	516	158	67	21	8	2	67	26	18	.306	.390
SS	Monte Cross	131	462	132	59	17	11	4	55	62	38	.286	.396
RF	Tuck Turner	103	416	121	58	17	12	2	41	35	8	.291	.404
LF	Bud Lally	87	355	99	56	15	5	2	42	9	12	.279	.366
CF	Dick Harley	89	330	96	43	6	4	3	35	36	23	.291	.361
1B	Mike Grady	83	322	90	48	11	3	7	45	26	7	.280	.398
2B	Bill Hallman	79	298	66	31	6	2	0	26	24	12	.221	.255
Sub	John Houseman	80	278	68	34	6	6	0	21	28	16	.245	.309
C	Morg Murphy	62	207	35	13	2	0	0	12	6	1	.169	.179
P	Bill Hart	46	156	39	14	1	2	2	14	1	4	.250	.321
P	Red Donahue	51	155	33	11	7	2	1	14	4	1	.213	.303
Sub	Tommy Dowd	35	145	38	25	9	1	0	9	6	11	.262	.338
Sub	Ed McFarland	31	107	35	14	5	2	1	17	8	2	.327	.439
Sub	Roger Connor	22	83	19	13	3	1	1	12	13	3	.229	.325
Sub	Lou Bierbauer	12	46	10	1	0	0	0	1	0	2	.217	.217
P	Kid Carsey	13	43	13	2	2	2	0	5	1	1	.302	.442
P	Willie Sudhoff	11	42	10	7	1	0	0	3	1	0	.238	.262
P	Bill Kissinger	14	39	13	7	3	2	0	6	3	0	.333	.513
P	Percy Coleman	12	28	6	2	0	0	0	3	1	0	.214	.214
P	Duke Esper	8	25	8	2	0	0	0	3	1	0	.320	.320
P	Bill Hutchison	6	18	5	1	0	1	0	0	1	0	.278	.389
P	Con Lucid	6	17	3	2	0	0	0	1	4	0	.176	.176
Sub	Ed Beecher	3	12	4	1	0	0	0	1	0	1	.333	.333
P	Mike McDermott	4	9	2	0	1	0	0	0	0	0	.222	.333
Sub	Frank Huelsman	2	7	2	0	1	0	0	0	0	0	.286	.429
P	John Grimes	3	7	2	0	0	0	0	1	3	0	.286	.286
P	Roy Evans	3	3	0	0	0	0	0	0	3	0	.000	.000
		132	4642	1277	588	149	67	31	484	354	172	.275	.356

1B Grady 83, Connor 22, Douglass 17, Murphy 8, McFarland 3, Lally 3, Hallman 3, Donahue 1, Hart 1
2B Hallman 77, Houseman 41, Bierbauer 12, Dowd 5, McFarland 1
SS Cross 131, Houseman 5, Douglass 1
3B Hartman 124, Douglass 7, Houseman 3
OF Turner 102, Harley 89, Lally 84, Douglass 43, Houseman 33, Dowd 30, Kissinger 7, Hart 6, Beecher 3, McFarland 3, Huelsman 2, Donahue 2, Grady 1
C Douglass 61, Murphy 53, McFarland 23
P Donahue 46, Hart 39, Coleman 12, Carsey 12, Sudhoff 11, Esper 8, Kissinger 7, Hutchison 6, Lucid 6, McDermott 4, Grimes 3, Evans 3

	G	IP	GS	CG	W	L	K	BB	SH	SV	ERA
Red Donahue	**46**	348	42	**38**	10	**35**	64	106	1	1	6.13
Bill Hart	39	294.2	38	31	9	27	67	148	0	0	6.26
Kid Carsey	12	99	11	11	3	8	14	31	0	0	6.00
Willie Sudhoff	11	92.2	9	9	2	7	19	21	0	0	4.47
Duke Esper	8	61.1	8	7	1	6	8	12	0	0	5.28
Percy Coleman	12	57.1	4	2	1	2	10	32	0	0	8.16
Con Lucid	6	49	6	5	1	5	4	26	0	0	3.67
Bill Hutchison	6	40	5	2	1	4	5	22	0	0	6.08
Bill Kissinger	7	31.1	4	2	0	4	5	15	0	0	11.49
Mike McDermott	4	21.1	4	1	1	2	3	19	0	0	9.28
John Grimes	3	19.2	1	1	0	2	4	8	0	0	5.95
Roy Evans	3	13	0	0	0	0	4	13	0	0	9.69
		1127.1	132	109	29	102	207	453	1	1	6.21

1898
THE GREATEST TEAM
OF THE 1890S

The sinking of the USS *Maine* on February 15, 1898, plunged the nation into war with Spain. It was the first war to impact on a major league season, and though it was over by midsummer, its effect was blamed for falling attendance in virtually every League-Association city. After the hordes that witnessed the crucial three-game series in Baltimore between the Orioles and the Boston Beaneaters near the close of the 1897 season, only 6,500 showed up for the Orioles' home opener in 1898 and it proved to be their biggest crowd all year. Though the schedule was increased in 1898 to 154 games, giving each team 11 more home dates, Baltimore drew just 123,416.

Attendance problems were even more acute in Cleveland, owing to bitter strife between the local populace and the Robison brothers, who owned both the Spiders and a Forest City streetcar company. When the Robisons hired non-union strikebreakers to operate their car lines, virtually every Cleveland labor group protested the use of scabs by boycotting the Spiders and forcing the Robisons to put their team on the road most of the last half of the season. Cleveland, as a result, played 114 of its 156 games outside of northern Ohio after transferring many of its home dates to rival cities. Among the beneficiaries was Chicago, which got to be the host team 89 times in its 152 outings. The extra home dates enabled the Colts to shatter all Windy City records and lead the majors in attendance with 424,352, a figure made all the more phenomenal in that for the first season in the team's 23-year history it took the field without Cap Anson. Betrayed by Al Spalding, who had promised him a controlling interest in the Colts and then reneged, Anson "orphaned" Chicago and abandoned his first-base spot at West Side Park for a nonplaying managerial post in New York, where he also quickly grew disenchanted after a few weeks of dealing with Giants owner Andrew Freedman.

On Opening Day in 1898 the game was not only missing Anson but several other legacies from its infancy. Gone was a rule giving an official scorer the option to credit a player with a stolen base if he went from first to third on a single or otherwise took an extra base. The new, stricter rule for what constituted a steal, combined with a more liberal balk rule,

The cleaner lost Zeke Wilson's uniform the day the 1898 Cleveland Spiders had their picture snapped. Shortly thereafter Cleveland lost most of the men here. This pic was shot late in the season, just days before Young, Burkett and all of the team's other stars played their last games in a Spiders uniform. Standing: Frank, Heidrick, Young, Wilson and McKean. Seated: Cuppy, Blake, Tebeau, Burkett, Wallace and Criger. Front: Powell, O'Connor and Fraser.

to sharply reduce the number of thefts—in 1898, Ed Delahanty topped the League-Association with just 58 steals, the fewest since 1886 by a leader—and is the ancestor of the current definition of a stolen base. Another rule revision terminated the ancient custom of players mingling with the crowd by forbidding any player not in the game from sitting or standing anywhere in the park but his team's bench. But perhaps the most telling change in 1898 was a new rule which imposed further restrictions on a pitcher's pickoff move and barred him from standing on the rubber with a base or bases occupied and the ball not in his possession in an effort to beguile a runner into falling for the hidden-ball trick.

But if the rulesmakers sensed that pitchers were about to regain the upper hand, their attempt to tip the scale back the other way came too late. In 1898 the League-Association batting average dwindled 21 points to .271, and for the first time in major league history the slugging average leader had a sub–.300 batting average. One reason for the drastic offen-

WHO ARE THEY?

There are two Hall of Fame pitchers who were both born in 1871. Both won over 240 games in the majors. Both began their careers in the nineteenth century and finished in the twentieth century. Both spent most of their careers in the same major league, yet they never pitched against each other in a championship game. Both spent most of their careers with the same major league team, yet they were never teammates. The younger of the two achieved his last major league victory in 1898 before the older of the two achieved his first major league victory. Who are they? See the photo caption on page 808 for the answer.

FORFEIT III

Though just 27, Amos Rusie won his last major league game around the time this picture of the 1898 New York Giants was taken. Clarence Foster had just played his first major league game shortly before and was still too green to know you don't wear your glove to the team pic. Though just 20, he was called Pop. The 1898 Giants were called Freedman's Folly by Cap Anson, who walked out on the club after just three weeks at its helm. Standing: Gleason, Van Haltren, Rusie, Carrick, Foster, Seymour, Grady. Seated: Davis, Meekin, Doyle, Doheny, Warner, Gettig

Prior to the 1898 season John Brush, now the owner of the Cincinnati Reds, decided enough time had passed that he could float another "Brush Rule" past his confreres. This one was no better received by the players than his 1889 edict limiting their salaries. Brush's 1898 rule proclaimed that any player who addressed an umpire or a fellow player in a "villainously filthy" manner would be brought before a three-man disciplinary board and banished for life if deemed guilty.

No one ever had his career terminated for violating Brush's latest creation. Few players were even fined. There were some famous incidents, though. Only July 25, 1898, in the fourth inning of a 1-1 game between Baltimore and New York at the Polo Grounds, Orioles outfielder Ducky Holmes was jeered by local fans after he fanned and heard himself told that the Giants—for whom he'd played the previous year—were well rid of him. According to one report, Holmes hollered he was glad at least that he wasn't working "for a Sheeny" anymore. The reference was to the ethnicity of Giants owner Andrew Freedman. It was unclear whether Freedman actually heard the remark himself or imagined its nature from the crowd's reaction. In any case, Freedman demanded that umpire Tom Lynch eject Holmes from the game. When Lynch claimed not to have heard Holmes say anything "villainous," Freedman had Giants manager Bill Joyce pull his team off the field, impelling Lynch to forfeit the game to Baltimore.

Whereupon the angry New York crowd surrounded Freedman and cowed him into refunding their money. Orioles manager Ned Hanlon later declined Freedman's demand to give back Baltimore's share of the gate receipts for the truncated game and urged the League-Association's four-man board of control to fine the Giants $1,000 for deliberately forfeiting the contest. Freedman, hot to get redress somewhere, next demanded that Holmes be suspended for the rest of the season. Loop president Nick Young, never renown for brave stances, initially did both, fining Freedman and suspending Holmes. Beginning to fear that he was holding a losing hand, Freedman allowed himself to be persuaded to take a long vacation in Europe. While he was out of the country, a grateful Young rescinded his fine and reinstated Holmes.

When the Orioles next visited the Polo Grounds in September, Holmes was back in the Birds lineup. Meanwhile, Freedman formally protested to no avail every game for the rest of the year in which his maligner appeared.

---

sive decline was that most standout pitchers like Cy Young and Kid Nichols had long since adapted to the new pitching distance and the requirement to stand in a fixed spot as they began their delivery. A second, even more primary reason low-scoring games were about to become the norm again was that a whole new crop of pitchers who had trained on a pitching rubber sixty feet six inches from the plate were beginning to arrive in the majors.

Foremost among the newcomers in 1898 was Vic Willis, whose appearance meant 25 wins and the last piece Boston manager Frank Selee needed to fashion the most powerful team in the 1890s. Selee's 1898 Beaneaters tied his 1892 team's nineteenth-century record for wins with 102, but it was not their sheer number of victories so much as their triumph only after a hard battle against a team nearly their equal that signaled their greatness. In 1898, Baltimore skipper Ned Hanlon had his best-balanced team yet as his hitters paced the loop in batting, scoring and stolen bases and his pitchers were second only to Chicago in ERA despite the loss of three of his key 1897 staff members. The war with Spain took Arlie Pond to the Medical Corps in the Philippines when he got his medical degree, a holdout battle took Joe Corbett back to the West Coast, and a poor start in 1898 took Bill Hoffer to Pittsburgh. To replace the trio's 64 wins in 1897, Hanlon for the fourth year in a row found an exceptional rookie pitcher and for perhaps the dozenth time during the decade made a bold trade. Jim Hughes, the rookie hurler, debuted by tossing a shutout in his first start and a no-hitter in his second, and the trade, with Washington, brought Doc McJames, the 1897 strikeout king, along with second baseman Gene DeMontreville for a slipping Heinie Reitz and a petulant Jack Doyle. Hanlon's third mound discovery in 1898 was a tale from the Twilight Zone. Desperate for a fourth starter, he resurrected Al Maul, who was approaching 33 and had never before been a big winner or overly durable in an astoundingly uneven career that stretched back to the Union Association. In 1898, Maul finished 26 of his 28 starts and won 20 of them with a 2.10 ERA. With the most improbable 20-game winner of the decade and 50 victories from McJames and Hughes, plus 24 wins from Jerry Nops and Frank Kitson, another rookie find, Hanlon had 94 games in the bank and got one more from Pond before he left for a military medical career and another in July via a forfeit, courtesy of Giants owner Andrew Freedman.

In a normal year 96 wins would have restored the Orioles to the top rung and given Hanlon his fourth pennant in five seasons. But 1898 was an extraordinary year. Boston, by

THE BAD, BAD BROWNS

The St. Louis Browns finished in the League-Association cellar for the second year in a row in 1898. Chris Von Der Ahe disintegrated personally and financially and virtually gave away the club—not that there was much left of it by then. About the only area in which the Browns improved in 1898 was that they stuck to the same manager all season. Tim Hurst took a year away from the most harrowing profession there was in the 1890s—major league umpire—and then decided he'd stepped into something even more hazardous to his health. In 1899, Hurst went back to umpiring and the Browns went off in another direction too, but that's a story for another day. The story here is that the 1897–98 Browns set a record for the worst two-year run of any team in major league history that played a season schedule of at least 80 games. And guess what? Their 1896–98 performance was also the worst three-year run. The Browns had some competition, though, in the 1890s and actually had to work fairly hard to break both the two-year- and three-year-worst marks. Here is a list of their competitors for the title of the baddest team of all time.

Guess why Jack Clements looks ready to slug the cameraman. He's just been photographed with one of the worst teams ever—the 1898 St. Louis Browns. Team pilot Tim Hurst, ever ready to slug someone, preferably a player who questioned one of his calls when he umpired, elected to skip the event instead. Standing: Tucker, Hughey, Smith, Stenzel, Quinn, Carsey. Seated: Harley, Sugden, Cross, Dowd, Clements

WORST TEAMS OVER A TWO-YEAR PERIOD

	LEAGUE	YEARS	W	L	PCT
St. Louis Browns	LA	1897–98	68	213	.242
Philadelphia Athletics	AL	1915–16	79	305	.259
Philadelphia Quakers	NL	1883–84	56	154	.267
Louisville Colonels	LA	1894–95	71	190	.272
Louisville Colonels	AA	1888–89	75	198	.275
Baltimore Orioles	AA	1882–83	47	122	.278
Philadelphia Phillies	NL	1941–42	85	220	.279
Washington Senators	AL	1903–04	81	207	.281
New York Mets	NL	1962–63	91	231	.283
Philadelphia Athletics	AL	1919–20	84	210	.286

Note: Several National Association teams had worse records over two-year or three-year periods, as did the 1876–77 Cincinnati Red Stockings (24-98 .197), when the schedule still called for fewer than 80 games.

WORST TEAMS OVER A THREE-YEAR PERIOD

	LEAGUE	YEARS	W	L	PCT
St. Louis Browns	LA	1896–98	108	303	.263
Louisville Colonels	LA	1894–96	109	283	.278
Philadelphia Athletics	AL	1915–17	134	324	.293
Philadelphia Phillies	NL	1940–42	135	323	.295
New York Mets	NL	1962–64	144	340	.298
Philadelphia Athletics	AL	1919–21	137	310	.306
Boston Doves	NL	1909–11	142	315	.311
St. Louis Browns	AL	1937–39	144	316	.313
Boston Red Sox	AL	1925–27	144	315	.314
Pittsburgh Pirates	NL	1952–54	145	317	.314

a margin of only one victory, missed becoming the first team ever to have four 20-game winners. As it was, Selee's four-man rotation accounted for all but one of the Beaneaters' 102 wins and for 144 of the team's 149 decisions. Yet Boston did not by any means have the race to itself. Cincinnati, with the first successful five-man pitching rotation yet seen and still the best keystone pairing in Bid McPhee and Tommy Corcoran, occupied first place from May 11 to the afternoon of August 16 when the Beaneaters finally crept ahead.

The Reds recovered the lead near the end of the month but for a few days, and after that Boston took charge. Still, Hanlon's Orioles hung right on Selee's tail until the first week in October when the two titans met in a three-game series at Boston. After the Beaneaters won the first two rounds, the third was rained out, killing Baltimore's last hope of catching up. When the season ended on October 15, the Orioles had slipped to six games off the pace. Nevertheless, Hanlon could look back upon the past five years at a team that had played .679 ball, the highest winning percentage by any major league club ever over a comparable span. He might also have liked to look ahead to a forthcoming Temple Cup battle with Boston, but in that wish he would have been alone. After the previous year's postseason debacle, the Beaneaters were well satisfied just to take their hard-won pennant home for the winter.

SOUTHPAW CATCHERS

Jack Clements was approaching his fifteenth season in the majors in the spring of 1898 and was nearly 34 years old, ancient in that era for a catcher. He was coming off a season in which he'd hit .238, but the St. Louis Browns were hungry for name players in 1898. So they made Clements their regular backstopper and got 86 games behind the plate out of him. He thereupon became the last lefty in major league history to serve as a regular catcher. Here is the list of lefties who caught at least 25 games in the majors in the nineteenth century:

	GAMES	YEARS ACTIVE
Jack Clements	1073	1884–1900
Sam Trott	272	1880–85/1887–88
Pop Tate	202	1885–90
Sy Sutcliffe	186	1884–92
Fergy Malone	173	1871–76/1884
Bill Harbidge	128	1875–80/1882–84
Mike Hines	99	1883–85/1888
John Humphries	75	1883–84
Fred Tenney	69	1894–1900*
Art Twineham	52	1893–94
Dave Oldfield	35	1883/1885–86

*Though he broke in as a catcher, Tenney played most of his career at first base; however, he caught two additional games in the 20th century, giving him 71 games behind the bat altogether. The 20th-century record for most games caught by a southpaw is held by Jiggs Donahue with 43; Donahue also caught two games prior to 1901.

Note: For many catchers in the nineteenth century, it is unknown as yet with which arm they threw. The same is true for many players at other positions and even for some pitchers like Tom Lovett who were major figures. Among the unknown catchers, the leading candidate for being a lefty thrower is Con Daily.

SLOW BALL TO STARDOM

After winning 22 games as a rookie with Baltimore of the American Association in 1888, Bert Cunningham pitched without distinction for the next ten years. He even spent three seasons in the minors after the Association and the National League merged in 1892, reducing jobs. Then in 1898, out of nowhere, the junk-balling Cunningham catapulted Louisville to sudden respectability when he won 28 games. In the process he set the record for the most wins in a season at the 60'6" distance without throwing a shutout and the post–1876 record for the fewest strikeouts by a pitcher with 25 or more wins. The list of post–1876 leaders in fewest strikeouts by a 25-game winner:

	YEAR	TEAM	WINS	K
Bert Cunningham	1898	Lou-LA	28	34
Al Spalding	1876	Chi-NL	47	39
Eddie Rommel	1922	Phi-AL	27	54
Sadie McMahon	1894	Bal-LA	25	60
Pink Hawley	1898	Cin-LA	27	69
Carl Mays	1921	NY-AL	27	70
Ted Lewis	1898	Bos-LA	26	72
Jim Bagby	1920	Cle-AL	31	73
Joe McGinnity	1899	Bal-LA	28	74
Joe McGinnity	1901	Bal-AL	26	75

The list of all-time leaders in most wins without throwing a shutout:

	YEAR	TEAM	WINS
Toad Ramsey	1887	Lou-AA	37
George Zettlein	1873	Phi-NA	36
Dick McBride	1874	Ath-NA	33
Bert Cunningham	1898	Lou-LA	28
Cy Young	1891	Cle-NL	27
Mark Baldwin	1892	Pit-LA	26
Clark Griffith	1895	Chi-LA	26*
Jouett Meekin	1896	NY-LA	26
Jack Stivetts	1894	Bos-LA	26
Hardie Henderson	1885	Bal-AA	25
Bobby Mathews	1872	NY-NA	25
Sadie McMahon	1894	Bal-LA	25

*Record-holder for the most consecutive 20-win seasons—three (1894–96)—without throwing a shutout, reputedly in part because he believed that shutouts brought bad luck.

The 1898 Louisville Colonels, missing 28-game winner Bert Cunningham, the man who at long last made them respectable. Here, however, is Bill Magee, the shadowy Canadian hurler who contrived to lose three games to the impossibly awful 1899 Cleveland Spiders, each while pitching with a different team. Standing: Mal Kittridge, Charlie Dexter, Dummy Hoy, Fred Clarke, Nick Altrock, Heinie Smith, Claude Ritchey and Topsy Hartsel. Seated: Bill Magee, Pete Dowling, Honus Wagner, George Decker, Billy Clingman and Mike Powers.

THE SEASONAL RECORD

		W	L	PCT	HOME	ROAD	GB
1.	Boston Beaneaters	102	47	.685	62–15	40–32	—
2.	Baltimore Orioles	96	53	.644	58–15	38–38	6
3.	Cincinnati Reds	92	60	.605	58–28	34–32	11.5
4.	Chicago Orphans	85	65	.567	58–31	27–34	17.5
5.	Cleveland Spiders	81	68	.544	36–18	45–50	21
6.	Philadelphia Phillies	78	71	.523	49–31	29–40	24
7.	New York Giants	77	73	.513	45–28	32–45	25.5
8.	Pittsburgh Pirates	72	76	.486	39–35	33–41	29.5
9.	Louisville Colonels	70	81	.464	43–34	27–47	33
10.	Brooklyn Bridegrooms	54	91	.372	30–41	24–50	46
11.	Washington Nationals	51	101	.336	34–44	17–57	52.5
12.	St. Louis Browns	39	111	.260	21–44	18–67	63.5

	Bos	Ba	Ci	Ch	Cl	Ph	NY	Pi	Lo	Br	Wa	StL	
Boston	—	7	9	9	6	10	10	9	8	11	11	12	102
Baltimore	5	—	8	9	8	10	10	10	9	8	7	12	96
Cincinnati	4	6	—	8	8	7	6	12	9	11	9	12	92
Chicago	5	5	6	—	7	6	9	7	9	10	11	10	85
Cleveland	7	6	5	7	—	7	6	5	9	7	12	10	81
Philadelphia	4	3	7	7	7	—	7	6	10	6	12	9	78
New York	4	3	8	5	8	6	—	5	8	11	9	10	77
Pittsburgh	5	4	2	4	8	8	9	—	9	5	9	9	72
Louisville	6	5	5	5	5	4	6	4	—	10	10	10	70
Brooklyn	2	5	3	4	6	6	3	9	2	—	7	7	54
Washington	3	7	5	3	2	2	4	5	4	6	—	10	51
St. Louis	2	2	2	4	3	5	3	4	4	6	4	—	39
	47	53	60	65	68	71	73	76	81	91	101	111	897

SEASON LEADERS

Batting Average (400 ABs)

1.	Keeler, Baltimore	.385
2.	Hamilton, Boston	.369
3.	McGraw, Baltimore	.342
	E. Smith, Cincinnati	.342
5.	Burkett, Cleveland	.341

On–Base Percentage

1.	Hamilton, Boston	.480
2.	McGraw, Baltimore	.475
3.	Jennings, Baltimore	.454
4.	Flick, Philadelphia	.430
5.	Delahanty, Philadelphia	.426

Home Runs

1.	Collins, Boston	15
2.	Joyce, New York	10
	Wagner, Louisville	10
4.	Anderson, Brk-Wash-Brk	9
	McKean, Cleveland	9

Slugging Average

1.	Anderson, Brk-Wash-Brk	.494
2.	Collins, Boston	.479
3.	Lajoie, Philadelphia	.461
4.	Delahanty, Philadelphia	.454
5.	Hamilton, Boston	.453

Total Bases

1.	Collins, Boston	286
2.	Lajoie, Philadelphia	280
3.	Van Haltren, New York	270
4.	Anderson, Brk-Wash-Brk	257
5.	Cooley, Philadelphia	256

RBI

1.	Lajoie, Philadelphia	127
2.	Collins, Boston	111
3.	Kelley, Baltimore	110
4.	Duffy, Boston	108
5.	McGann, Baltimore	106

Hits

1.	Keeler, Baltimore	216
2.	Burkett, Cleveland	213
3.	Van Haltren, New York	204
4.	Lajoie, Philadelphia	197
5.	Collins, Boston	196
	Cooley, Philadelphia	196

Runs

1.	McGraw, Baltimore	143
2.	Jennings, Baltimore	135
3.	Van Haltren, New York	129
4.	Keeler, Baltimore	126
5.	Cooley, Philadelphia	123

Stolen Bases

1.	Delahanty, Philadelphia	58
2.	Hamilton, Boston	54
3.	Demontreville, Baltimore	49
4.	Dexter, Louisville	44
5.	McGraw, Baltimore	43

PITCHING

Wins

1.	Nichols, Boston	31
2.	Cunningham, Louisville	28
3.	McJames, Baltimore	27
	Hawley, Cincinnati	27
5.	Lewis, Boston	26

Losses

1.	Taylor, St. Louis	29
2.	Sudhoff, St. Louis	27
3.	Weyhing, Washington	26
4.	Hughey, St. Louis	24
5.	Kennedy, Brooklyn	22
	Yeager, Brooklyn	22

Innings

1.	Taylor, St. Louis	397.1
2.	Nichols, Boston	388
3.	Young, Cleveland	377.2
4.	McJames, Baltimore	374
5.	Cunningham, Louisville	362

Complete Games

1.	Taylor, St. Louis	42
2.	Cunningham, Louisville	41
3.	Young, Cleveland	40
	Nichols, Boston	40
	McJames, Baltimore	40

Strikeouts

1.	Seymour, New York	239
2.	McJames, Baltimore	178
3.	Willis, Boston	160
4.	Nichols, Boston	138
5.	Piatt, Philadelphia	121

Winning Percentage (25 decisions)

1.	Lewis, Boston	.765
2.	Maul, Baltimore	.741
3.	Nichols, Boston	.721
4.	Hawley, Cincinnati	.711
5.	Griffith, Chicago	.706

ERA (154 innings)

1.	Griffith, Chicago	1.88
2.	Maul, Baltimore	2.10
3.	Nichols, Boston	2.13
4.	McJames, Baltimore	2.36
5.	Callahan, Chicago	2.46

Lowest On-Base Percentage

1.	Nichols, Boston	.272
2.	Maul, Baltimore	.275
3.	Young, Cleveland	.288
4.	Griffith, Chicago	.294
5.	McJames, Baltimore	.297

FIELDING

Total Chances		
1B	Everett, Chicago	1631
2B	Lajoie, Philadelphia	894
3B	Collins, Boston	617
SS	M. Cross, Philadelphia	1003
OF	Cooley, Philadelphia	389
C	Warner, New York	697
P	Taylor, St. Louis	184

Fielding Average		
Decker, St. L-Louis		.985
Reitz, Washington		.959
L. Cross, St. Louis		.945
Ely, Pittsburgh		.943
Griffin, Brooklyn		.974
Clements, St. Louis		.971
Hill, Cincinnati		.986

BOSTON   Frank Selee   South End Grounds (II)

		G	AB	H	R	2B	3B	HR	RBI	BB	SB	BA	SA
3B	Jimmy Collins	152	597	196	107	35	5	**15**	111	40	12	.328	.479
SS	Herman Long	144	589	156	99	21	10	6	99	39	20	.265	.365
LF	Hugh Duffy	152	568	169	97	13	3	8	108	59	29	.298	.373
2B	Bobby Lowe	147	559	152	65	11	7	4	94	29	12	.272	.338
1B	Fred Tenney	117	488	160	106	25	5	0	62	33	23	.328	.400
RF	Chick Stahl	125	467	144	72	21	8	3	52	46	6	.308	.407
C	Marty Bergen	120	446	125	62	16	5	3	60	13	9	.280	.359
CF	Billy Hamilton	110	417	154	110	16	5	3	50	87	54	.369	.453
Sub	George Yeager	68	221	59	37	13	1	3	24	16	1	.267	.376
P	Kid Nichols	51	158	38	26	3	3	2	23	4	0	.241	.335
P	Ted Lewis	42	131	37	17	6	0	0	18	6	0	.282	.328
P	Fred Klobedanz	43	127	27	12	2	1	3	15	1	0	.213	.315
Sub	General Stafford	37	123	32	21	2	0	1	8	4	3	.260	.301
P	Vic Willis	41	117	17	9	0	0	0	6	11	0	.145	.145
Sub	Jack Stivetts	41	111	28	16	1	1	2	16	10	1	.252	.333
P	Piano Legs Hickman	29	58	15	4	2	0	0	7	1	0	.259	.293
Sub	Dave Pickett	14	43	12	3	1	0	0	3	6	2	.279	.302
Sub	Bill Keister	10	30	5	5	2	0	0	4	0	0	.167	.233
Sub	Stub Smith	3	10	1	1	0	0	0	0	0	0	.100	.100
Sub	Kitty Bransfield	5	9	2	2	0	1	0	1	0	0	.222	.444
Sub	Hi Ladd	1	4	1	1	0	0	0	0	0	0	.250	.250
P	Mike Sullivan	3	3	1	0	0	0	0	0	0	0	.333	.333
		152	5276	1531	872	190	55	**53**	761	405	172	.290	**.377**

1B	Tenney 117, Yeager 17, Stivetts 10, Hickman 6, Klobedanz 6, Bergen 2, Duffy 1, Nichols 1, Stafford 1, Bransfield 1
2B	Lowe 145, Keister 4, Stivetts 2, Long 2, Lewis 1
SS	Long 142, Stivetts 4, Keister 4, Smith 3, Lowe 2, Yeager 2
3B	Collins 152, Duffy 1
OF	Duffy 152, Stahl 125, Hamilton 110, Stafford 35, Pickett 14, Stivetts 14, Yeager 9, Hickman 7, Klobedanz 2, Keister 1, Ladd 1
C	Bergen 117, Yeager 37, Bransfield 4, Tenney 1, Duffy 1
P	Nichols 50, Lewis 41, Willis 41, Klobedanz 35, Hickman 6, Sullivan 3, Stivetts 2

	G	IP	GS	CG	W	L	K	BB	SH	SV	ERA
Kid Nichols	**50**	388	42	40	**31**	12	138	85	5	**4**	2.13
Ted Lewis	41	313.1	33	29	26	8	72	109	1	2	2.90
Vic Willis	41	311	38	29	25	13	160	148	1	0	2.84
Fred Klobedanz	35	270.2	33	25	19	10	51	99	0	0	3.89
Piano Legs Hickman	6	33	3	3	1	2	9	13	1	2	2.18
Mike Sullivan	3	12	2	0	0	1	1	9	0	0	12.00
Jack Stivetts	2	12	1	1	0	1	1	7	0	0	8.25
* One combined shutout on Aug. 18: Lewis 5 innings, Hickman 4 innings											
	1340	152	127	102	47	432	470	8		**8**	2.98

BALTIMORE **Ned Hanlon** **Union Park**

		G	AB	H	R	2B	3B	HR	RBI	BB	SB	BA	SA
2B	Gene Demontreville	151	567	186	93	19	2	0	86	52	49	.328	.369
RF	Willie Keeler	128	561	**216**	126	7	2	1	44	31	28	.385	.410
1B	Dan McGann	145	535	161	99	18	8	5	106	53	33	.301	.393
SS	Hughie Jennings	143	534	175	135	25	11	1	87	78	28	.328	.421
3B	John McGraw	143	515	176	**143**	8	10	0	53	112	43	.342	.396
CF	Joe Kelley	124	464	149	71	18	15	2	110	56	24	.321	.438
LF	Ducky Holmes	113	442	126	54	10	9	1	64	23	25	.285	.355
C	Wilbert Robinson	79	289	80	29	12	2	0	38	16	3	.277	.332
C	Boileryard Clarke	82	285	69	26	5	2	0	27	4	2	.242	.274
P	Jim Hughes	52	164	37	23	7	4	2	20	12	0	.226	.354
P	Doc McJames	45	149	27	12	7	1	0	14	5	2	.181	.242
Sub	Jake Stenzel	35	138	35	33	5	2	0	22	12	4	.254	.319
Sub	Steve Brodie	23	98	30	12	3	2	0	19	5	3	.306	.378
P	Al Maul	29	93	19	21	3	2	0	10	16	1	.204	.280
P	Jerry Nops	33	91	20	11	1	2	0	8	10	0	.220	.275
P	Frank Kitson	31	86	27	13	1	3	0	16	5	2	.314	.395
Sub	Art Ball	32	81	15	7	2	0	0	8	7	2	.185	.210
Sub	Tom O'Brien	18	60	13	9	0	0	0	14	10	0	.217	.217
Sub	Joe Quinn	12	32	8	5	1	0	0	5	1	0	.250	.281
P	Bill Hoffer	8	24	5	2	1	0	0	4	4	0	.208	.250
Sub	Frank Bowerman	5	16	7	5	1	0	0	1	2	1	.438	.500
Sub	Mike Heydon	3	9	1	2	0	0	0	1	2	0	.111	.111
P	Arlie Pond	3	7	2	2	0	0	0	0	2	0	.286	.286
Sub	Henry Wilson	1	2	0	0	0	0	0	0	1	0	.000	.000
		154	5242	**1584**	**933**	154	77	12	**757**	519	**250**	**.302**	.368

1B	McGann 145, Clarke 10
2B	Demontreville 123, Jennings 27, Ball 2, Quinn 1
SS	Jennings 115, Demontreville 28, Ball 14
3B	McGraw 137, Ball 15, Quinn 8, Kelley 2, Keeler 1
OF	Keeler 128, Kelley 122, Holmes 113, Stenzel 35, Brodie 23, O'Brien 16, Hughes 15, Kitson 11, Hoffer 4, McGraw 3, Jennings 1, Ball 1, Quinn 1, Maul 1
C	Robinson 77, Clarke 70, Bowerman 4, Heydon 3, Wilson 1
P	McJames 45, Hughes 38, Nops 33, Maul 28, Kitson 17, Hoffer 4, Pond 3

	G	IP	GS	CG	W	L	K	BB	SH	SV	ERA
Doc McJames	45	374	42	40	27	15	178	113	2	0	2.36
Jim Hughes #	38	300.2	35	31	23	12	81	100	5	0	3.20
Al Maul	28	239.2	28	26	20	7	31	49	1	0	2.10
Jerry Nops	33	235	29	23	16	9	91	78	2	0	3.56
Frank Kitson	17	119.1	13	13	8	5	32	35	1	0	3.24
Bill Hoffer	4	34.1	4	4	0	4	5	16	0	0	7.34
Arlie Pond	3	20	2	1	1	1	4	9	1	0	0.45
—1 forfeit W vs New York on July 25—											
		1323	153	138	95	54	422	400	12	0	2.90

No-hit game 8-0 vs Boston, April 22

CINCINNATI Buck Ewing League Park (II)

		G	AB	H	R	2B	3B	HR	RBI	BB	SB	BA	SA
SS	Tommy Corcoran	153	619	155	80	28	15	2	87	26	19	.250	.354
RF	Dusty Miller	152	586	175	99	24	12	3	90	38	32	.299	.396
3B	Charlie Irwin	136	501	120	77	14	5	3	55	31	18	.240	.305
LF	Elmer Smith	123	486	166	79	21	10	1	66	69	20	.342	.432
CF	Algie McBride	120	486	147	94	14	12	2	43	51	16	.302	.393
2B	Bid McPhee	133	486	121	72	26	9	1	60	66	21	.249	.346
1B	Jake Beckley	118	459	135	86	20	12	4	72	28	6	.294	.416
C	Heinie Peitz	105	330	90	49	15	5	1	43	35	9	.273	.358
Sub	Harry Steinfeldt	88	308	91	47	18	6	0	43	27	9	.295	.393
Sub	Farmer Vaughn	78	275	84	35	12	4	1	46	11	4	.305	.389
P	Pink Hawley	43	130	24	17	2	1	1	16	5	1	.185	.238
P	Ted Breitenstein	41	121	26	16	2	1	0	17	16	0	.215	.248
Sub	Bob Wood	39	109	30	14	6	0	0	16	9	1	.275	.330
Sub	Bug Holliday	30	106	25	21	2	1	0	7	14	5	.236	.274
P	Bill Hill	33	98	13	10	1	0	0	3	5	0	.133	.143
P	Frank Dwyer	31	85	12	11	1	1	0	5	7	1	.141	.176
P	Bill Damman	35	82	16	14	0	4	0	7	10	0	.195	.293
Sub	Herm McFarland	19	64	18	10	1	3	0	11	7	3	.281	.391
P	Percy Coleman	1	3	0	0	0	0	0	1	0	0	.000	.000
P	Jot Goar	1	0	0	0	0	0	0	0	0	0	—	—
		157	5334	1448	831	207	**101**	19	688	455	165	.271	.359

1B John Beckley 118, Vaughn 39, Steinfeldt 4, Wood 1
2B McPhee 130, Steinfeldt 31
SS Corcoran 153, Steinfeldt 5
3B Irwin 136, Steinfeldt 22
OF Miller 152, Smith 123, McBride 120, Steinfeldt 29, Holliday 28, McFarland 17, McPhee 3, Breitenstein 2, Wood 1
C Peitz 101, Vaughn 33, Wood 29
P Hawley 43, Breitenstein 39, Damman 35, Hill 33, Dwyer 31, Coleman 1, Goar 1, Smith 1

	G	IP	GS	CG	W	L	K	BB	SH	SV	ERA
Pink Hawley	43	331	37	32	27	11	69	91	3	0	3.37
Ted Breitenstein #	39	315.2	37	32	20	14	68	123	3	0	3.42
Bill Hill	33	262	32	26	13	14	75	119	2	0	3.98
Frank Dwyer	31	240	28	24	16	10	29	42	0	0	3.04
Bill Damman	35	224.2	22	16	16	10	51	67	2	2	3.61
Percy Coleman	1	9	1	1	0	1	2	3	0	0	3.00
Jot Goar	1	2	0	0	0	0	0	1	0	0	9.00
Elmer Smith	1	1	0	0	0	0	0	3	0	0	18.00
		1385.1	157	131	92	60	294	449	10	2	3.50

No-hit game 11-0 vs Pittsburgh, April 22

CHICAGO   Tom Burns   **West Side Park (II)**

		G	AB	H	R	2B	3B	HR	RBI	BB	SB	BA	SA
1B	Bill Everett	149	596	190	102	15	6	0	69	53	28	.319	.364
LF	Jimmy Ryan	144	572	185	122	32	13	4	79	73	29	.323	.446
3B	Barry McCormick	137	530	131	76	15	9	2	78	47	15	.247	.321
SS	Bill Dahlen	142	521	151	96	35	8	1	79	58	27	.290	.393
2B	Jim Connor	138	505	114	51	9	9	0	67	42	11	.226	.279
CF	Bill Lange	113	442	141	79	16	11	5	69	36	22	.319	.439
C	Tim Donahue	122	396	87	52	12	3	0	39	49	17	.220	.265
RF	Sam Mertes	83	269	80	45	4	8	1	47	34	27	.297	.383
P	Walter Thornton	62	210	62	34	5	2	0	14	22	8	.295	.338
Sub	Danny Green	47	188	59	26	4	3	4	27	7	12	.314	.431
P	Nixey Callahan	43	164	43	27	7	5	0	22	4	3	.262	.366
UT	Frank Isbell	45	159	37	17	4	0	0	8	3	3	.233	.258
P	Walt Woods	48	154	27	16	1	0	0	8	4	3	.175	.182
Sub	Frank Chance	53	147	41	32	4	3	1	14	7	7	.279	.367
P	Clark Griffith	38	122	20	15	2	3	0	15	13	1	.164	.230
P	Matt Kilroy	26	96	22	20	4	1	0	10	13	0	.229	.292
Sub	Harry Wolverton	13	49	16	4	1	0	0	2	1	1	.327	.347
Sub	Art Nichols	14	42	12	7	1	0	0	6	4	6	.286	.310
P	Jack Taylor	5	15	3	4	2	0	0	2	3	0	.200	.333
P	Buttons Briggs	4	14	6	2	1	0	0	1	0	0	.429	.500
P	Bill Phyle	3	9	1	1	0	0	0	0	2	0	.111	.111
P	Danny Friend	2	7	2	0	1	0	0	0	0	0	.286	.429
P	Henry Clarke	2	4	1	0	0	0	0	0	1	0	.250	.250
P	John Katoll	2	4	0	0	0	0	0	0	0	0	.000	.000
Sub	Frank Martin	1	4	0	0	0	0	0	0	0	0	.000	.000
		152	5219	1431	828	175	84	18	656	476	220	.274	.350

1B   Everett 149, Chance 3, Mertes 2, Lange 2, Callahan 1
2B   Connor 138, Woods 6, Mertes 4, Isbell 3, Martin 1, McCormick 1, Callahan 1
SS   Dahlen 142, Mertes 14, Woods 3, Isbell 2, McCormick 1, Callahan 1
3B   McCormick 136, Wolverton 13, Isbell 3, Woods 3
OF   Ryan 144, Lange 111, Mertes 60, Green 47, Thornton 34, Isbell 28, Chance 17, Kilroy 12, Woods 11, Callahan 9, Clarke 1
C   Donahue 122, Chance 33, Nichols 14
P   Griffith 38, Callahan 31, Thornton 28, Woods 27, Isbell 13, Kilroy 13, Taylor 5, Briggs 4, Phyle 3, Katoll 2, Friend 2, Clarke 1

	G	IP	GS	CG	W	L	K	BB	SH	SV	ERA
Clark Griffith	38	325.2	38	36	24	10	97	64	4	0	**1.88**
Nixey Callahan	31	274.1	31	30	20	10	73	71	2	0	2.46
Walter Thornton #	28	215.1	25	21	13	10	56	56	2	0	3.34
Walt Woods	27	215	22	18	9	13	26	59	3	0	3.14
Matt Kilroy	13	100.1	11	10	6	7	18	30	0	0	4.31
Frank Isbell	13	81	9	7	4	7	16	42	0	0	3.56
Jack Taylor	5	41	5	5	5	0	11	10	0	0	2.20
Buttons Briggs	4	30	4	3	1	3	14	10	0	0	5.70
Bill Phyle	3	23	3	3	2	1	4	6	2	0	0.78
Danny Friend	2	17	2	2	0	2	4	10	0	0	5.29
Jack Katoll	2	11	1	1	0	1	3	1	0	0	0.82
Henry Clarke	1	9	1	1	1	0	1	5	0	0	2.00
	—1 forfeit L vs Philadelphia on September 16—										
	1342.2	152	137	85	64	323	364	**13**	0	**2.83**

No-hit game 2-0 vs Brooklyn, August 22

CLEVELAND   Patsy Tebeau   League Park (I)

		G	AB	H	R	2B	3B	HR	RBI	BB	SB	BA	SA
LF	Jesse Burkett	150	624	213	114	18	9	0	42	69	19	.341	.399
SS	Ed McKean	151	604	172	89	23	1	9	94	56	11	.285	.371
3B	Bobby Wallace	154	593	160	81	25	13	3	99	63	7	.270	.371
UT	Jack O'Connor	131	478	119	50	17	4	1	56	26	8	.249	.308
1B	Patsy Tebeau	125	477	123	53	11	4	1	63	53	5	.258	.304
RF	Harry Blake	136	474	116	65	18	7	0	58	69	12	.245	.312
2B	Cupid Childs	110	413	119	90	9	4	1	31	69	9	.288	.337
CF	Jim McAleer	106	366	87	47	3	0	0	48	46	7	.238	.246
C	Lou Criger	84	287	80	43	13	4	1	32	40	2	.279	.362
P	Cy Young	47	154	39	20	4	1	2	13	8	2	.253	.331
P	Jack Powell	42	136	18	15	3	1	0	9	11	0	.132	.169
P	Zeke Wilson	37	118	21	11	2	1	0	9	5	0	.178	.212
Sub	Emmett Heidrick	19	76	23	10	2	2	0	8	3	3	.303	.382
Sub	Louis Sockalexis	21	67	15	11	2	0	0	10	1	0	.224	.254
C	Chief Zimmer	20	63	15	5	2	0	0	4	5	2	.238	.270
P	Sport McAllister	17	57	13	8	3	1	0	9	5	0	.228	.316
Sub	Fred Frank	17	53	11	3	1	1	0	3	4	1	.208	.264
P	Nig Cuppy	18	48	5	2	0	0	0	0	3	1	.104	.104
Sub	Jimmy Burke	13	38	4	1	1	0	0	1	2	1	.105	.132
Sub	Ossee Schreckengost	10	35	11	5	2	3	0	10	0	1	.314	.543
P	Cowboy Jones	9	28	2	1	0	0	0	1	3	1	.071	.071
Sub	Ed Beecher	8	25	5	1	2	0	0	0	0	0	.200	.280
P	Chick Fraser	6	16	4	2	1	0	0	2	0	1	.250	.313
P	Frank Bates	4	9	1	2	0	0	0	1	3	0	.111	.111
P	George Kelb	3	5	1	1	0	0	0	0	0	0	.200	.200
P	Pete McBride	1	2	2	0	0	0	0	2	1	0	1.000	1.000
		156	5246	1379	730	162	56	18	605	545	93	.263	.325

1B Tebeau 91, O'Connor 69, Blake 2
2B Childs 110, Tebeau 34, Wallace 13, McAleer 2
2B McKean 151, Tebeau 7
3B Wallace 141, Burke 13, Tebeau 3
OF Burkett 150, Blake 136, McAleer 104, Heidrick 19, Frank 17, Sockalexis 16, O'Connor 15, McAllister 8, Beecher 8, Wilson 3
C   Criger 82, O'Connor 48, Zimmer 19, Schreckengost 9
P   Young 46, Powell 42, Wilson 33, Cuppy 18, McAllister 9, Jones 9, Fraser 6, Bates 4, Kelb 3, McBride 1

	G	IP	GS	CG	W	L	K	BB	SH	SV	ERA
Cy Young	46	377.2	41	40	25	13	101	41	1	0	2.53
Jack Powell	42	342	41	36	23	15	93	112	6	0	3.00
Zeke Wilson	33	254.2	31	28	13	18	45	51	1	0	3.60
Nig Cuppy	18	128	15	13	9	8	27	25	1	0	3.30
Cowboy Jones	9	72	9	7	4	4	26	29	0	0	3.00
Sport McAllister	9	65.1	7	6	3	4	9	23	0	0	4.55
Chick Fraser	6	42	6	6	2	3	19	12	0	0	5.57
Frank Bates	4	29	4	4	2	1	5	11	0	0	3.10
George Kelb	3	16.1	1	1	0	1	8	1	0	0	4.41
Pete McBride	1	7	1	1	0	1	6	4	0	0	6.43
		1334	156	142	81	68	339	309	9	0	3.20

PHILADELPHIA   George Stallings (19–27)   Bill Shettsline (59–44)
Philadelphia Baseball Grounds (II)

		G	AB	H	R	2B	3B	HR	RBI	BB	SB	BA	SA
CF	Duff Cooley	149	629	196	123	24	12	4	55	48	17	.312	.407
2B	Nap Lajoie	147	608	197	113	**43**	11	6	**127**	21	25	.324	.461
1B	Klondike Douglass	146	582	150	105	26	4	2	48	55	18	.258	.326
LF	Ed Delahanty	144	548	183	115	36	9	4	92	77	**58**	.334	.454
SS	Monte Cross	149	525	135	68	25	5	1	50	55	20	.257	.330
RF	Elmer Flick	134	453	137	84	16	13	8	81	86	23	.302	.448
C	Ed McFarland	121	429	121	65	21	5	3	71	44	4	.282	.375
3B	Billy Lauder	97	361	95	42	14	7	2	67	19	6	.263	.357
P	Al Orth	38	123	36	17	6	4	1	14	3	1	.293	.431
P	Wiley Piatt	41	122	32	19	2	1	0	9	6	0	.262	.295
P	Red Donahue	35	112	16	8	0	1	0	10	4	1	.143	.161
Sub	Ed Abbaticchio	25	92	21	9	4	0	0	14	7	4	.228	.272
Sub	Morg Murphy	25	86	17	6	3	0	0	11	6	0	.198	.233
Sub	Billy Nash	20	70	17	9	2	1	0	9	11	0	.243	.300
P	Jack Fifield	21	64	7	5	1	1	0	4	5	1	.109	.156
Sub	Sam Thompson	14	63	22	14	5	3	1	15	4	2	.349	.571
Sub	Dave Fultz	19	55	10	7	2	2	0	5	6	1	.182	.291
P	George Wheeler	15	43	8	5	1	0	0	3	3	0	.186	.209
Sub	Kid Elberfeld	14	38	9	1	4	0	0	7	5	0	.237	.342
P	Davey Dunkle	12	28	6	2	1	0	0	1	1	0	.214	.250
Sub	Ike Fisher	9	26	3	0	1	0	0	0	0	1	.115	.154
Sub	Jack Boyle	6	22	2	0	0	1	0	3	1	0	.091	.182
P	Bill Duggleby	9	21	5	4	1	0	1	6	4	0	.238	.429
P	Ed Murphy	7	14	5	0	0	0	0	3	0	0	.357	.357
P	Bert Conn	1	3	1	1	0	1	0	1	0	0	.333	1.000
P	Bob Becker	1	1	0	0	0	0	0	0	0	1	0	.000	.000
Sub	George Stallings	1	0	0	1	0	0	0	0	0	0	—	—
		150	5118	1431	823	**238**	81	33	706	472	182	.280	**.377**

1B   Douglass 146, Boyle 4, Lajoie 1
2B   Lajoie 146, Abbaticchio 4, Fultz 3
SS   Cross 149, Fultz 1
3B   Lauder 97, Abbaticchio 20, Nash 20, Elberfeld 14, Fisher 1
OF   Cooley 149, Delahanty 144, Flick 133, Fultz 14, Thompson 14, Abbaticchio 1, Orth 1
C   McFarland 121, M. Murphy 25, Fisher 8, Boyle 3
P   Piatt 39, Donahue 35, Orth 32, Fifield 21, Wheeler 15, Dunkle 12, Duggleby 9, E. Murphy 7, Conn 1, Becker 1

	G	IP	GS	CG	W	L	K	BB	SH	SV	ERA
Wiley Piatt	39	306	37	33	24	14	121	97	**6**	0	3.18
Red Donahue #	35	284.1	35	33	16	17	57	80	1	0	3.55
Al Orth	32	250	28	25	15	13	52	53	1	0	3.02
Jack Fifield	21	171.1	21	18	11	9	31	60	2	0	3.31
George Wheeler	15	112.1	13	10	6	8	20	36	0	0	4.17
Davey Dunkle	12	68.1	7	4	1	4	21	38	0	0	6.98
Bill Duggleby	9	54	5	4	3	3	12	18	0	0	5.50
Ed Murphy	7	30	3	2	1	2	8	10	0	0	5.10
Bert Conn	1	7	1	0	0	1	3	2	0	0	6.43
Bob Becker	1	5	0	0	0	0	0	5	0	0	10.80
		—1 forfeit W vs Chicago on September 16—									
	1288.1	150	129	78	71	325	399	10	0	3.72

No-hit game 5-0 vs Boston, July 8

NEW YORK   Bill Joyce (68–50)   Cap Anson (9–13)   Polo Grounds (III)

		G	AB	H	R	2B	3B	HR	RBI	BB	SB	BA	SA
CF	George Van Haltren	156	**654**	204	129	28	16	2	68	59	36	.312	.413
2B	Kid Gleason	150	570	126	78	8	5	0	62	39	21	.221	.253
1B	Bill Joyce	145	508	131	91	20	9	10	91	88	34	.258	.392
SS	George Davis	121	486	149	80	20	5	2	86	32	26	.307	.381
3B	Fred Hartman	123	475	129	57	16	11	2	88	25	11	.272	.364
LF	Mike Tiernan	103	415	116	90	15	11	5	49	43	19	.280	.405
C	Jack Warner	110	373	96	40	14	5	0	42	22	9	.257	.322
RF	Jack Doyle	82	297	84	42	15	3	1	43	12	14	.283	.364
P	Cy Seymour	80	297	82	41	5	2	4	23	9	8	.276	.347
Sub	Mike Grady	93	287	85	64	19	5	3	49	38	20	.296	.429
P	Charlie Gettig	64	196	49	30	6	2	0	26	15	5	.250	.301
Sub	Walt Wilmot	35	138	33	16	4	2	2	22	9	4	.239	.341
P	Amos Rusie	41	138	29	23	2	4	0	8	1	2	.210	.283
P	Jouett Meekin	38	129	27	16	5	1	0	12	9	0	.209	.264
Sub	Tom McCreery	35	121	24	15	4	3	1	17	19	3	.198	.306
Sub	Pop Foster	32	112	30	10	6	1	0	9	0	0	.268	.329
P	Ed Doheny	28	86	14	11	1	1	2	11	4	0	.163	.267
P	Bill Carrick	5	18	3	0	1	0	0	2	1	0	.167	.222
Sub	Tacks Latimer	5	17	5	1	1	0	0	1	0	0	.294	.353
Sub	John Puhl	2	9	2	1	0	0	0	1	0	0	.222	.222
Sub	Joe Regan	2	5	1	1	0	0	0	2	0	0	.200	.200
P	Jock Menefee	1	5	0	0	0	0	0	0	0	0	.000	.000
Sub	Ed Glenn	2	4	1	1	0	0	0	0	3	1	.250	.250
Sub	Jack Gilbert	1	4	1	0	0	0	0	0	0	1	.250	.250
Sub	Parke Wilson	1	4	0	0	0	0	0	0	0	0	.000	.000
Sub	Dave Zearfoss	1	1	1	0	0	0	0	0	0	0	1.000	1.000
		157	5349	1422	837	190	86	34	712	428	214	.266	.353

1B	Joyce 130, Doyle 24, Grady 7, Gettig 2, Rusie 1
2B	Gleason 144, Gettig 12, Joyce 2, Seymour 1
SS	Davis 121, Doyle 15, Gettig 9, Gleason 6, Grady 3, Glenn 2, Foster 2
3B	Hartman 123, Joyce 14, Foster 10, Doyle 5, Gettig 4, Puhl 2
OF	Van Haltren 156, Tiernan 103, Doyle 38, Seymour 35, McCreery 35, Wilmot 34, Grady 30, Gettig 21, Foster 21, Latimer 2, Regan 2, Gilbert 1, Warner 1, Wilson 1, Rusie 1
C	Warner 109, Grady 57, Latimer 4, Doyle 2, Zearfoss 1, Gettig 1
P	Seymour 45, Meekin 38, Rusie 37, Doheny 28, Gettig 17, Carrick 5, Menefee 1

	G	IP	GS	CG	W	L	K	BB	SH	SV	ERA
Cy Seymour	45	356.2	43	39	25	19	**239**	213	4	0	3.18
Jouett Meekin	38	320	37	34	16	18	82	108	1	0	3.77
Amos Rusie	37	300	36	33	20	11	114	103	4	1	3.03
Ed Doheny	28	213	27	23	7	19	96	101	0	0	3.68
Charlie Gettig	17	115	8	7	6	3	14	39	0	0	3.83
Bill Carrick	5	39.2	4	4	3	1	10	21	0	0	3.40
Jock Menefee	1	9.1	1	1	0	1	3	2	0	0	4.82
—1 forfeit L vs Baltimore on July 25—											
		1353.2	156	141	77	72	**558**	587	9	1	3.44

PITTSBURGH   **Bill Watkins**   **Exposition Park**

		G	AB	H	R	2B	3B	HR	RBI	BB	SB	BA	SA
RF	Patsy Donovan	147	610	184	112	16	9	0	37	34	41	.302	.357
LF	Jack McCarthy	137	537	155	75	13	12	4	78	34	7	.289	.380
3B	Bill Grey	137	528	121	56	17	5	0	67	28	5	.229	.280
SS	Bones Ely	148	519	110	49	14	5	2	44	24	6	.212	.270
2B	Dick Padden	128	463	119	61	7	6	2	43	35	11	.257	.311
CF	Tom O'Brien	107	413	107	53	10	8	1	45	25	13	.259	.329
C	Pop Schriver	95	315	72	25	15	3	0	32	23	0	.229	.295
C	Frank Bowerman	69	241	66	17	6	3	0	29	7	4	.274	.324
1B	Harry Davis	58	222	65	31	9	13	1	24	12	7	.293	.464
1B	Willie Clark	57	209	64	29	9	7	1	31	22	0	.306	.431
Sub	Tom McCreery	53	190	59	33	5	7	2	20	26	3	.311	.442
Sub	Steve Brodie	42	156	41	15	5	0	0	21	6	3	.263	.295
P	Jesse Tannehill	60	152	44	25	9	3	1	17	7	4	.289	.408
P	Billy Rhines	31	100	15	7	1	1	0	5	6	0	.150	.180
P	Jim Gardner	35	91	14	8	0	0	0	3	14	1	.154	.154
P	Frank Killen	24	65	17	6	1	0	0	4	6	0	.262	.277
Sub	Bill Eagan	19	61	20	14	2	3	0	5	8	1	.328	.459
P	Bill Hart	16	50	12	4	0	1	0	3	1	1	.240	.280
Sub	John Ganzel	15	45	6	5	0	0	0	2	4	0	.133	.133
P	Charlie Hastings	19	43	10	5	0	1	0	4	7	0	.233	.279
Sub	Morg Murphy	5	16	2	0	0	0	0	2	1	0	.125	.125
Sub	Fred Lake	3	13	1	1	0	0	0	1	2	0	.077	.077
P	Sam Leever	5	12	3	2	0	0	0	1	1	0	.250	.250
P	Bill Hoffer	4	11	1	0	0	1	0	0	0	0	.091	.273
P	John Cronin	4	10	1	1	1	0	0	1	2	0	.100	.200
P	Zeke Rosebraugh	4	8	3	0	0	0	0	1	1	0	.375	.375
Sub	Joe Rickert	2	6	1	0	0	0	0	0	0	0	.167	.167
Sub	Hi Ladd	1	1	0	0	0	0	0	0	0	0	.000	.000
		152	5087	1313	634	140	88	14	520	336	107	.258	.328

1B   Clark 57, Davis 53, O'Brien 21, Ganzel 12, Bowerman 9, Lake 3, Schriver 1
2B   Padden 128, Eagan 17, O'Brien 7, Gardner 1
SS   Ely 148, O'Brien 4
3B   Grey 137, O'Brien 8, Gardner 8
OF   Donovan 147, McCarthy 137, O'Brien 69, McCreery 51, Brodie 42, Tannehill 7, Davis 6, Rickert 2
C   Schriver 92, Bowerman 59, Murphy 5
P   Tannehill 43, Rhines 31, Gardner 25, Killen 23, Hastings 19, Hart 16, Leever 5, Rosebraugh 4, Hoffer 4, Cronin 4, Ganzel 1

	G	IP	GS	CG	W	L	K	BB	SH	SV	ERA
Jesse Tannehill	43	326.2	38	34	25	13	93	63	5	2	2.95
Billy Rhines	31	258	29	27	12	16	48	61	2	0	3.52
Jim Gardner	25	185.1	22	19	10	13	41	48	1	0	3.21
Frank Killen	23	177.2	23	17	10	11	48	41	0	0	3.75
Charlie Hastings	19	137.1	13	12	4	10	40	52	0	0	3.41
Bill Hart	16	125	15	13	5	9	19	44	1	1	4.82
Sam Leever	5	33	3	2	1	0	15	5	0	0	2.45
Bill Hoffer	4	31	3	3	3	0	11	15	0	0	1.74
Jack Cronin	4	28	4	2	2	2	9	8	1	0	3.54
Zeke Rosebraugh	4	21.2	2	2	0	2	6	9	0	0	3.32
		1323.2	152	131	72	76	330	346	10	3	3.41

LOUISVILLE   **Fred Clarke**   **Eclipse Park (II)**

		G	AB	H	R	2B	3B	HR	RBI	BB	SB	BA	SA
LF	Fred Clarke	149	599	184	116	23	12	3	47	48	40	.307	.401
1B	Honus Wagner	151	588	176	80	29	3	10	105	31	27	.299	.410
CF	Dummy Hoy	148	582	177	104	15	16	6	66	49	37	.304	.416
SS	Claude Ritchey	151	551	140	65	10	4	5	51	46	19	.254	.314
3B	Billy Clingman	154	538	138	65	12	6	0	50	51	15	.257	.301
RF	Charlie Dexter	112	421	132	76	13	5	1	66	26	44	.314	.375
C	Mal Kittridge	86	287	70	27	8	5	1	31	15	9	.244	.317
Sub	General Stafford	49	181	54	26	3	0	1	25	19	7	.298	.331
Sub	George Decker	42	148	44	27	4	3	0	19	9	9	.297	.365
P	Bert Cunningham	44	140	32	21	3	1	1	16	10	1	.229	.286
Sub	Harry Davis	37	138	30	18	5	2	1	16	7	6	.217	.304
2B	Heinie Smith	35	121	23	14	4	0	0	13	6	6	.190	.223
P	Bill Magee	38	111	14	10	1	0	0	5	2	2	.126	.135
P	Pete Dowling	36	107	21	9	4	4	0	9	6	1	.196	.308
Sub	Bill Wilson	29	102	17	5	1	2	1	13	5	3	.167	.245
Sub	Mike Powers	34	99	27	13	4	3	1	19	5	1	.273	.404
P	Chick Fraser	26	78	13	8	0	2	0	3	6	2	.167	.218
Sub	Doc Nance	22	76	24	13	5	0	1	16	12	2	.316	.421
Sub	Topsy Hartsel	22	71	23	11	0	0	0	9	11	2	.324	.324
Sub	Cooney Snyder	17	61	10	4	0	0	0	6	3	0	.164	.164
P	Red Ehret	13	40	9	3	3	1	0	4	1	0	.225	.350
Sub	Scoops Carey	8	32	6	1	1	1	0	1	1	0	.188	.281
P	Nick Altrock	11	29	7	4	0	0	0	2	2	1	.241	.241
Sub	Billy Taylor	9	24	6	2	1	0	0	2	1	1	.250	.292
Sub	Josh Clarke	6	18	3	0	0	0	0	0	1	0	.167	.167
Sub	Tom Stouch	4	16	5	4	1	0	0	6	1	0	.313	.375
Sub	John Richter	3	13	2	1	0	0	0	0	0	0	.154	.154
Sub	Tommy Leach	3	10	3	0	0	0	0	0	0	0	.100	.100
P	Frank Todd	4	5	1	1	0	1	0	1	0	0	.200	.600
P	Lou Mahaffey	1	4	0	0	0	0	0	0	1	0	.000	.000
P	Dad Clarke	1	3	0	0	0	0	0	0	0	0	.000	.000
		154	5193	1389	728	150	71	32	601	375	235	.267	.342

1B   Wagner 75, Davis 34, Decker 32, Carey 8, Powers 6, Wilson 1
2B   Ritchey 71, Smith 33, Stafford 28, Wagner 10, Dexter 8, Stouch 4, Davis 2, Clingman 1, Taylor 1, Leach 1
SS   Ritchey 80, Clingman 74
3B   Clingman 79, Wagner 65, Taylor 7, Leach 3, Richter 3, Stafford 1
OF   F. Clarke 149, Hoy 148, Dexter 95, Stafford 22, Nance 22, Hartsel 21, Decker 6, J. Clarke 5, Clingman 1, Davis 1, Powers 1
C   Kittridge 86, Wilson 28, Powers 22, Snyder 17, Dexter 7
P   Cunningham 44, Magee 38, Dowling 36, Fraser 26, Ehret 12, Altrock 11, Todd 4, D. Clarke 1, Mahaffey 1

	G	IP	GS	CG	W	L	K	BB	SH	SV	ERA
Bert Cunningham	44	362	42	41	28	15	34	65	0	0	3.16
Bill Magee	38	295.1	33	29	16	15	55	129	3	0	4.05
Pete Dowling	36	285.2	32	30	13	20	84	120	0	0	4.16
Chick Fraser	26	203	26	20	7	17	58	100	1	0	5.32
Red Ehret	12	89	10	9	3	7	20	20	0	0	5.76
Nick Altrock	11	70	7	6	3	3	13	21	0	0	4.50
Frank Todd	4	11	2	0	0	2	5	8	0	0	13.91
Dad Clarke	1	9	1	1	0	1	1	2	0	0	5.00
Lou Mahaffey	1	9	1	1	0	1	1	5	0	0	3.00
		1334	154	137	70	81	271	470	4	0	4.24

BROOKLYN   **Billy Barnie (15–20)**   **Mike Griffin (1–3)**   **Charlie Ebbets (38–68)**
Washington Park (II)

		G	AB	H	R	2B	3B	HR	RBI	BB	SB	BA	SA
RF	Fielder Jones	146	596	181	89	15	9	1	69	46	36	.304	.364
CF	Mike Griffin	134	537	161	88	18	6	2	40	60	15	.300	.367
1B	Candy LaChance	136	526	130	62	23	7	5	65	31	23	.247	.346
2B	Bill Hallman	134	509	124	57	10	7	2	63	29	9	.244	.303
3B	Billy Shindle	120	466	105	50	10	3	1	41	10	3	.225	.266
LF	Jimmy Sheckard	105	408	113	51	17	9	4	64	37	8	.277	.392
SS	George Magoon	93	343	77	35	7	0	1	39	30	7	.224	.254
C	John Ryan	87	301	57	39	11	4	0	24	15	5	.189	.252
1B	Tommy Tucker	73	283	79	35	9	4	1	34	12	1	.279	.350
Sub	Aleck Smith	52	199	52	25	6	5	0	23	3	7	.261	.342
C	John Grim	52	178	50	17	5	1	0	11	8	1	.281	.320
P	Jack Dunn	51	167	41	21	0	1	0	19	7	3	.246	.357
P	Brickyard Kennedy	40	135	34	15	7	2	0	13	3	2	.252	.333
P	Joe Yeager	43	134	23	12	5	1	0	15	7	1	.172	.224
Sub	John Anderson	25	90	22	12	5	4*	0	10	6	2	.244	**.389***
Sub	Tom Daly	23	73	24	11	3	1	0	11	14	6	.329	.397
P	Ralph Miller	24	62	12	6	1	0	0	6	4	1	.194	.210
P	Kit McKenna	14	40	9	5	3	0	0	7	2	0	.225	.300
Sub	Butts Wagner	11	38	9	2	1	1	0	3	2	0	.237	.316
P	Ed Stein	3	10	4	1	0	0	0	1	1	0	.400	.400
P	Harry Howell	2	8	2	1	0	0	0	1	1	0	.250	.250
P	Welcome Gaston	2	8	1	2	0	1	0	1	0	0	.125	.375
P	Harley Payne	1	4	3	1	0	0	0	3	0	0	.750	.750
P	Elmer Horton	1	4	1	0	0	0	0	0	0	0	.250	.250
P	Lefty Hopper	2	4	0	1	0	0	0	0	0	0	.000	.000
P	F.C. Hansford	1	3	0	0	0	0	0	0	0	0	.000	.000
		149	5126	1314	638	156	66	17	563	328	130	.256	.322

1B   LaChance 74, Tucker 73, Anderson 2, Ryan 1, Smith 1
2B   Hallman 124, Daly 23, Smith 2, Yeager 1
SS   Magoon 93, LaChance 48, Dunn 4, Jones 2, Yeager 2
3B   Shindle 120, Wagner 11, Hallman 10, Ryan 4, Dunn 2, Smith 2, Sheckard 1
OF   Jones 144, Griffin 134, Sheckard 105, Smith 26, Anderson 22, LaChance 13, Yeager 4, Dunn 4, Miller 1
C   Ryan 84, Grim 52, Smith 20
P   Dunn 41, Kennedy 40, Yeager 36, Miller 23, McKenna 14, Stein 3, Howell 2, Gaston 2, Hopper 2, Horton 1, Hansford 1, Payne 1

	G	IP	GS	CG	W	L	K	BB	SH	SV	ERA
Brickyard Kennedy	40	339.1	39	38	16	22	73	123	0	0	3.37
Jack Dunn	41	322.2	37	31	16	21	66	82	0	0	3.60
Joe Yeager	36	291.1	33	32	12	22	70	80	0	0	3.65
Ralph Miller	23	151.2	21	16	4	14	43	86	0	0	5.34
Kit McKenna	14	100.2	9	7	2	6	27	57	0	0	5.63
Ed Stein	3	23	2	2	0	2	6	9	0	0	5.48
Harry Howell	2	18	2	2	2	0	2	11	0	0	5.00
Welcome Gaston	2	16	2	2	1	1	0	9	0	0	2.81
Lefty Hopper	2	11	2	2	0	2	5	5	0	0	4.91
Harley Payne	1	9	1	1	1	0	2	3	0	0	4.00
Elmer Horton	1	9	1	1	0	1	0	6	0	0	10.00
F.C. Hansford	1	7	0	0	0	0	0	5	0	0	3.86
		*One combined shutout on Sept. 30: Kennedy 3 innings, Dunn 5 innings									
		1298.2	149	134	54	91	294	476	1	0	4.01

WASHINGTON   Tom Brown (12–26)   Jack Doyle (8–9)   Deacon McGuire (21–47)
Arthur Irwin (10–19)   Boundary Field

		G	AB	H	R	2B	3B	HR	RBI	BB	SB	BA	SA
RF	Jake Gettman	142	567	157	75	16	5	5	47	29	32	.277	.349
LF	Kip Selbach	132	515	156	88	28	11	3	60	64	25	.303	.417
2B	Heinie Reitz	132	489	148	62	20	2	2	47	32	11	.303	.364
C	Deacon McGuire	131	489	131	59	18	3	1	57	24	10	.268	.323
CF	John Anderson	110	430	131	70	28	18*	9	71	23	18	.305	.516*
SS	Zeke Wrigley	111	400	98	50	9	10	2	39	20	10	.245	.333
C	Duke Farrell	99	338	106	47	12	6	1	53	34	12	.314	.393
P	Win Mercer	80	249	80	38	3	5	2	25	18	14	.321	.398
3B	Jud Smith	66	234	71	33	7	5	3	28	22	11	.303	.415
Sub	Butts Wagner	63	223	50	20	11	2	1	31	14	4	.224	.305
1B	Jack Doyle	43	177	54	26	2	2	2	26	7	9	.305	.373
P	Gus Weyhing	46	141	25	12	3	0	0	5	8	2	.177	.199
Sub	Doc Casey	28	112	31	13	2	0	0	15	3	15	.277	.295
Sub	Bert Myers	31	110	29	14	1	4	0	13	13	2	.264	.345
Sub	Buck Freeman	29	107	39	19	2	3	3	21	7	2	.364	.523
P	Bill Donovan	39	103	17	11	2	2	2	8	4	2	.165	.282
P	Bill Dinneen	32	80	8	10	0	1	0	3	9	1	.100	.125
Sub	Charlie Carr	20	73	14	6	2	0	0	4	2	2	.192	.219
Sub	Frank Gatins	17	58	13	6	2	0	0	5	3	2	.224	.259
P	Frank Killen	21	55	15	7	2	0	0	7	12	1	.273	.309
Sub	Tom Leahy	15	55	10	10	2	0	0	5	8	6	.182	.218
Sub	Tom Brown	16	55	9	8	1	0	0	2	5	3	.164	.182
P	Cy Swaim	16	35	5	2	0	0	0	4	0	0	.143	.143
Sub	Bob McHale	11	33	6	5	2	0	0	7	1	1	.182	.242
Sub	Jim Field	5	21	2	1	0	0	0	0	0	1	.095	.095
P	Doc Amole	7	20	2	4	0	0	0	0	1	0	.100	.100
P	Roy Evans	7	19	1	2	0	0	0	2	2	0	.053	.053
P	Kirtly Baker	6	18	5	3	0	1	0	3	3	0	.278	.389
Sub	Bill Eagle	4	13	4	0	1	0	0	2	0	0	.308	.385
Sub	Tom Kinslow	3	9	1	0	0	0	0	0	0	0	.111	.111
P	Pop Williams	2	8	3	3	1	0	0	0	0	0	.375	.500
Sub	Jack Gilbert	2	5	1	0	0	0	0	1	1	1	.200	.200
Sub	Marty McQuaid	1	4	0	0	0	0	0	0	0	0	.000	.000
Sub	Ed Glenn	1	4	0	0	0	0	0	0	0	0	.000	.000
P	Jack Sutthoff	2	3	1	0	0	0	0	0	1	0	.333	.333
Sub	Harry Davis	1	3	0	0	0	0	0	0	0	0	.000	.000
P	Charlie Weber	1	2	0	0	0	0	0	0	0	0	.000	.000
		155	5257	1423	704	177	80	36	591	370	197	.271	.355

1B   Doyle 38, McGuire 37, Farrell 28, Carr 20, Anderson 17, Smith 7, Field 5, Gettman 3, Davis 1, McHale 1, Kinslow 1
2B   Reitz 132, Wrigley 11, Doyle 5, Wagner 5, Leahy 3, Smith 1, Mercer 1, Donovan 1
SS   Wrigley 97, Mercer 23, Gatins 17, Smith 10, Wagner 8, Casey 4, Selbach 1, Donovan 1, Glenn 1, McHale 1
3B   Smith 47, Wagner 39, Myers 31, Casey 22, Leahy 12, Mercer 5, Wrigley 1
OF   Gettman 139, Selbach 131, Anderson 93, Freeman 29, Donovan 20, Mercer 19, Brown 15, Wagner 10, McHale 9, Eagle 4, Killen 4, Wrigley 3, Dinneen 2, Gilbert 2, Weyhing 1, McQuaid 1
C   McGuire 93, Farrell 61, Kinslow 3, Casey 3
P   Weyhing 45, Mercer 33, Dinneen 29, Killen 17, Donovan 17, Swaim 16, Evans 7, Amole 7, Baker 6, Sutthoff 2, Williams 2, Weber 1

	G	IP	GS	CG	W	L	K	BB	SH	SV	ERA
Gus Weyhing	45	361	42	39	15	26	92	84	2	0	4.54
Win Mercer	33	233.2	30	24	12	18	52	71	0	0	4.81
Bill Dinneen	29	218.1	27	22	9	16	83	88	0	0	4.00
Frank Killen	17	128.1	16	15	6	9	43	29	0	0	3.58
Cy Swaim	16	101.1	13	9	3	11	30	28	0	1	4.26
Bill Donovan	17	88	7	6	1	6	36	69	0	0	4.30
Roy Evans	7	50.2	6	4	3	3	11	25	0	0	3.38
Doc Amole	7	49.1	5	4	0	6	11	22	0	0	7.84
Kirtley Baker	6	47	5	4	2	3	7	18	0	0	3.06
Pop Williams	2	17	2	2	0	2	3	7	0	0	8.47
Jack Sutthoff	2	8.1	1	0	0	0	3	8	0	0	12.96
Charlie Weber	1	4	1	0	0	1	0	1	0	0	15.75
		1307	155	129	51	101	371	450	0	1	4.52

ST. LOUIS **Tim Hurst** **Sportsman's Park (II)**

		G	AB	H	R	2B	3B	HR	RBI	BB	SB	BA	SA
3B	Lave Cross	151	602	191	71	28	8	3	79	28	14	.317	.405
RF	Tommy Dowd	139	586	143	70	17	7	0	32	30	16	.244	.297
LF	Dick Harley	142	549	135	74	6	5	0	42	34	13	.246	.275
CF	Jake Stenzel	108	404	114	64	15	11	1	33	41	21	.282	.381
UT	Joe Quinn	103	375	94	35	10	5	0	36	24	13	.251	.304
C	Jack Clements	99	335	86	39	19	5	3	41	21	1	.257	.370
C	Joe Sugden	89	289	73	29	7	1	0	34	23	5	.253	.284
1B	George Decker	76	286	74	26	10	0	1	45	20	4	.259	.304
1B	Tommy Tucker	72	252	60	18	7	2	0	20	18	1	.238	.282
2B	Jack Crooks	72	225	52	33	4	2	1	20	40	3	.231	.280
P	Jack Taylor	54	157	38	17	5	2	1	18	12	1	.242	.318
SS	Germany Smith	51	157	25	16	2	1	1	9	24	1	.159	.204
Sub	Suter Sullivan	42	144	32	10	3	0	0	12	13	1	.222	.243
Sub	Russ Hall	39	143	35	13	2	1	0	10	7	1	.245	.273
Sub	Tuck Turner	35	141	28	20	8	0	0	7	14	1	.199	.255
P	Willie Sudhoff	41	120	19	5	2	1	0	4	5	0	.158	.192
P	Kid Carsey	38	105	21	8	0	1	1	10	10	3	.200	.248
Sub	Ducky Holmes	23	101	24	9	1	1	0	0	2	4	.238	.267
P	Jim Hughey	35	97	11	6	0	1	1	6	10	1	.113	.165
Sub	Tom Kinslow	14	53	15	5	2	1	0	4	1	0	.283	.358
P	Duke Esper	11	27	10	1	0	0	0	5	1	0	.370	.370
P	Pete Daniels	10	17	3	1	1	0	0	1	3	0	.176	.235
P	George Gillpatrick	7	16	2	1	0	0	0	1	0	0	.125	.125
Sub	Lou Bierbauer	4	9	0	0	0	0	0	0	1	0	.000	.000
P	Harry Maupin	2	7	3	0	0	0	0	1	0	0	.429	.429
Sub	Mike Mahoney	2	7	0	0	0	0	0	0	0	0	.000	.000
P	Jim Callahan	2	4	0	0	0	0	0	0	0	0	.000	.000
P	Joe Gannon	1	3	0	0	0	0	0	0	0	0	.000	.000
P	Tom Smith	1	2	1	0	0	0	0	0	1	0	.500	.500
Sub	Jim Donnelly	1	1	1	0	0	0	0	0	0	0	1.000	1.000
		154	5214	1290	571	149	55	13	470	383	104	.247	.305

1B	Decker 75, Tucker 72, Sugden 8, Mahoney 2, Kinslow 1, Sullivan 1
2B	Crooks 66, Quinn 62, Carsey 11, Dowd 10, Sullivan 6, Bierbauer 2
SS	G. Smith 51, Quinn 41, Hall 35, Sullivan 23, Cross 2, Crooks 2, Bierbauer 1
3B	Cross 149, Crooks 3, Hall 3, Bierbauer 1, Donnelly 1
OF	Harley 141, Dowd 129, Stenzel 108, Turner 34, Holmes 22, Sugden 15, Sullivan 10, Carsey 8, Taylor 2, Crooks 1, Hall 1, Quinn 1
C	Clements 86, Sugden 60, Kinslow 14
P	Taylor 50, Sudhoff 41, Hughey 35, Carsey 20, Daniels 10, Esper 10, Gillpatrick 7, Maupin 2, Callahan 2, T. Smith 1, Gannon 1, Sullivan 1

	G	IP	GS	CG	W	L	K	BB	SH	SV	ERA
Jack Taylor	**50**	**397.1**	47	**42**	15	**29**	89	83	0	1	3.90
Willie Sudhoff	41	315	38	35	11	27	65	102	0	1	4.34
Jim Hughey	35	283.2	33	31	7	24	74	71	0	0	3.93
Kid Carsey	20	123.2	13	10	2	12	10	37	0	0	6.33
Duke Esper	10	64.2	8	6	3	5	14	22	0	0	5.98
Pete Daniels	10	54.2	6	3	1	6	13	14	0	0	3.62
George Gillpatrick	7	35	3	1	0	2	12	19	0	0	6.94
Harry Maupin	2	18	2	2	0	2	3	3	0	0	5.50
Tom Smith	1	9	1	1	0	1	1	5	0	0	2.00
Joe Gannon	1	9	1	1	0	1	2	5	0	0	11.00
Jim Callahan	2	8.1	2	1	0	2	2	7	0	0	16.20
Suter Sullivan	1	6	0	0	0	0	3	4	0	0	1.50
		1324.1	154	133	39	111	288	372	0	2	4.53

1899

SYNDICATE BALL
SINKS THE SPIDERS

To halt the offensive decline, rulesmakers imposed a new restriction on pitchers prior to the 1899 season, mandating umpires to charge them with a balk any time they threw to a base in a pick-off attempt without first stepping toward that base. Between this restraint and the amendments to the balk rule that had been introduced the previous year League-Association players stole nearly 600 more bases in 1899 than in 1898. More help came the offense's way from other new rules requiring a catcher to stand within the marked lines of his position whenever the pitcher delivered the ball to the batter and awarding a batter his base if a catcher interfered with his attempt to swing at a pitch by "tipping" his bat.

Seemingly the rulesmakers achieved their goal. In 1899 the League-Association batting average jumped eleven points and scoring increased some six percent. These figures are misleading, however, for much of the offensive hike stemmed from the ineptness of one team—namely Cleveland, which surrendered 1,252 runs to shatter all existing records. In truth, it was not any change in baseball's rules but a change in its corporate structure that promoted the temporary offensive revival. The 1899 season will always be underscored by the influence of "syndicate baseball"—two or more clubs with common ownership. Syndicate baseball was not really new in 1899; ever since 1890 several club owners, including John Brush, Al Spalding and Arthur Soden, had owned stock in the New York Giants as well as in their own teams, and St. Louis Browns owner Chris Von Der Ahe had previously owned a piece of several other American Association teams if only to help keep them afloat. But yoking two different clubs under the same management was a new concept, and it was first proposed by Ferd Abell, one of the two gambling casino partners who had owned the Brooklyn franchise ever since its inception in 1884. Needing financial help when his associate, Charlie Byrne, died in 1898, Abell initially explored the possibility of combining his Bridegrooms with Baltimore owner Henry Von der Horst's Orioles. After Von der Horst rebuffed him, Abell next approached Frederick Robison, who owned the Cleveland Spiders together with his brother Stanley. When it appeared that Robison might

Roy Thomas, one of the many rookie prizes who arrived in 1899. He set an all-time frosh record when he tallied 137 runs. Pittsburgh yearling Jimmy Williams collected a rookie-record 27 triples in 1899 and notched 219 hits, a mark that has been surpassed just once by a freshman in all the years since.

welcome the idea, Von der Horst told *Sporting Life* editor Francis Richter, "Robison has a great team and a worthless franchise. Abell has a valuable plant and no team. These elements combined would develop a winner that would be of immense financial profit, as Brooklyn patrons are hungry for good base ball."

Von der Horst suddenly realized that if what he said was true, he was a fool for passing up the opportunity. Sensing that Robison was about to leap at Abell's offer, he grabbed it himself. Robison and his brother then cast longing eyes on the St. Louis Browns, the League-Association's most moribund team despite being based in the nation's fourth largest city at the time. Soon the Robisons gained controlling interest in the Browns and began dressing all of Cleveland's best players in St. Louis livery. The rape stripped the Spiders to a handful of their 1898 benchwarmers, which the Robisons supplemented with undistinguished minor leaguers, rejects from other League-Association teams and fast-fading veterans hoping to hang on for one last season. But the Robisons never imagined their 1899 Cleveland entry would be so wretched. The Spiders lost 134 games, had no pitchers who logged more than four victories and finished 84 games out of first place. All are major league records for futility as is the Spiders' distinction of having to play the vast majority of their games on the road to avoid the wrath of Cleveland's few remaining fans.

Piqued by slumping attendance figures in Baltimore, Von der Horst had a similar plan for his Orioles. Had matters gone as Von der Horst planned, the likelihood is that in 1899 Baltimore would have been nearly as dismal a team as Cleveland. But Von der Horst was thwarted when third baseman John McGraw and catcher Wilbert Robinson refused to accompany manager Ned Hanlon, Willie Keeler, Joe Kelley, Hughie Jennings, Doc McJames and several other Orioles stars to Brooklyn because they had developed business interests in Baltimore. McGraw, who had also recently married a Baltimore woman, won Von der Horst's grudging permission to stay behind and manage the Orioles. Given this reprieve, McGraw then set about rebuilding Baltimore. Shrewd trades, the emergence of Joe McGinnity as Baltimore's fifth rookie pitching sensation in five years, and McGraw's own play kept

Seen for the eighteenth straight year in a Cincinnati team mug shot is the finest second baseman in the last century, Bid McPhee, looking scarcely a day older than he did as a rookie in 1882. Here too is Harry Steinfeldt, perhaps the first big leaguer to wear shinguards. Only Steinfeldt didn't wear them to catch but to play third base. He was snubbed in 1897 by Pittsburgh, which considered him too unmanly ever to make the grade, but Buck Ewing thought his innovation was enterprising. Ewing's good judgment gave the Reds the last of their many infield gems in the nineteenth century. Top: Dwyer, Damman, Miller, Ewing, McPhee, Beckley and Steinfeldt. Center: Corcoran, Peitz, Breitenstein, Vaughn (below Ewing), Hahn, McBride and Smith. Bottom: Hawley, Taylor, Wood, Phillips, Selbach and Irwin.

the Orioles in the first division all season. But not even McGraw's inspiration could match the team Hanlon fielded by combining his ex-Orioles with such Brooklyn stalwarts as Fielder Jones, Brickyard Kennedy and Tom Daly. Jennings's arm injury left Hanlon momentarily without a shortstop, but he sidestepped that obstacle by swapping two players to Chicago for Bill Dahlen, and when McGraw's wife died in late August of a ruptured appendix, removing Baltimore's sparkplug from the lineup for three weeks, Brooklyn ended the month with a nine and a half game bulge on the Orioles and a six-game cushion over the second-place Boston Beaneaters.

Brooklyn's lead was so prohibitive that the closing weeks of the season were just a formality in every city but Louisville. Building on their best League-Association finish to date the previous year, the Colonels played .690 ball in September and ended the campaign only two games below .500. But even with Honus Wagner, Fred Clarke and Dummy Hoy spurring a best-ever .280 team batting average and rookie Deacon Phillippe bagging 21

Baltimore's last NL entry. Wilbert Robinson was ten years older in 1899 than John McGraw and looked it. Ten years later McGraw, who aged swiftly and harshly, would look older than Robinson. The team dispersed to all points on the big league map when the Orioles were dumped after the 1899 season, but many of them reunited with McGraw in Baltimore for the AL's first major league season in 1901.

FORFEIT IV

The last forfeit game in the 12-team League-Association coincided with the last day Baltimore was affiliated with the National League and John McGraw's first of many forfeit losses as a manager. Baltimore was at Brooklyn on October 14, the 1899 season's closing day, with McGraw pitted against his old Orioles boss, Ned Hanlon. In the second inning umpire George Hunt tossed Orioles outfielder Jimmy Sheckard for arguing an out call on a steal attempt too vehemently. When Sheckard ignored the ejection and tried to take his place in the field after the Orioles were retired, Hunt ordered McGraw to remove his outfielder from the game. McGraw refused, compelling Hunt to forfeit the game to Brooklyn. To placate the angry crowd, McGraw and Hanlon then agreed to play a makeup game for an early-season postponement that was called because of darkness after five innings with Brooklyn comfortably ahead. The gift "doubleheader" victory gave Brooklyn a .68243 winning percentage, which is still the franchise record.

FOR WANT OF A SHORTSTOP

Louisville was on the rise in 1899. Only Bert Cunningham's sag to 17 wins after registering 28 the previous year and a mid-June beaning that sidelined shortstop Billy Clingman for a long spell kept the Colonels below .500. Following Clingman's injury, manager Fred Clarke brought Charlie Dexter in from the outfield for two days to man short while awaiting the arrival of rookie Rudy Hulswitt from Syracuse of the Eastern League. But after Hulswitt made four quick errors in his big-league debut on June 16, Clarke threw pitcher Walt Woods into the breach. The following day Christopher Bayer, a Louisvillian who played as Burley Byers, got the assignment but only long enough to make two errors and go hitless in three at bats.

Clarke's next shortstop-for-a-day was Bob Langsford, a career minor leaguer who had been "thrown out of work by the disbanding of the Southern League." Although Langsford handled five chances flawlessly, he was so badly overmatched at the plate that Clarke in disgust played short himself on June 19. Before Clingman was able to return to action, second baseman Claude Ritchey and third baseman Tommy Leach also tried their hands at his job. In all, the Colonels used ten different shortstops in 1899, including two pitchers, Woods and Cunningham. By the end of the season every team member who got into at least half of the Colonels games had taken his shot at the position except centerfielder Dummy Hoy, who never played a single day at short in his 14 year major league career, and a man who would "only" play 1,888 games at short in his 21-year career. His name was Honus Wagner, and in 1899 Clarke had him play everywhere else in the outfield and the infield but shortstop.

wins, Louisville could not surmount the same hurdle that tripped every other also-ran in 1899. Of its 11 season series with rival clubs, Brooklyn won all 11. Defending champion Boston gave Brooklyn a crisp battle for a while but eventually lost eight times in 14 outings, although the Beaneaters ace, Vic Willis, won four of five attempts against Hanlon's crew. Indeed, Willis and Chicago's Nixey Callahan, with three wins, were the only twirlers to take Brooklyn's measure more than twice in 1899.

Von der Horst's and Abell's scheme was a success both artistically and financially. Brooklyn drew just under 270,000, more than doubling its 1898 attendance. The Robison brothers, even with a disappointing fifth-place team, experienced a similar boom in St. Louis as the transferred talent from Cleveland brought a gate increase of more than 220,000. Baltimore and Cleveland had to stomach attendance drops, however, as did Washington with a calamitous team that in any ordinary year would have finished last, and not even the Colonels' late surge could prevent a marked dip of around 30,000 in Louisville, too. With New York Giants owner Andrew Freedman leading the charge, there was a movement in March, 1900, to reduce the League-Association to eight teams. Three of the four legacies from the American Association—Baltimore, Louisville and Washington—were targeted for elimination, along with Cleveland which had in effect given its "National League" blood to St. Louis, the fourth Association legacy. So it happened that the unwieldy 12-team loop was finally judged a failure and could return to calling itself simply the National League. A number of players from the four folding franchises were absorbed by the remaining teams, but many veterans were forced to seek berths in the minor leagues when there was no longer enough room to accommodate them. Waiting eagerly to scoop them up was Ban Johnson, president of the Western League. Now that the National League had severed the last link with the American Association by dropping its name along with its teams, Johnson was also eager to change the title of his circuit to the American League and begin claiming major league status for it. His appetite extended finally to the four cities the National League had abandoned. Johnson satisfied himself, for the moment, with snatching Cleveland—the one the National League was least likely to contest—for his new loop.

THE 1890s ATTENDANCE LEADER

Here we find Bill Duggleby, the only man to hit a grandslam homer in his first major league at bat, and one of the last of the countless dogs that flavored nineteenth-century team pictures. Missing is Billy Goeckel, who may have been no more than a backup first baseman but really knew how to take a picture. He can be found in another 1899 Phils team shot that appeared in the 1900 Spalding Guide. Top: McFarland, Abbatichio, Lojoie, Orth, Donahue, Cooley, Lauder. Middle: Cross, Tifield, Delahanty, Manager Bill Shettsline, Pratt, Douglass. Bottom: Douggleby, Flick, Murphy, Conn.

In the 11-year period between 1890 and 1900 the Cincinnati Reds led the National League in attendance twice (1892 and 1896), the New York Giants also won the attendance battle twice (1894 and 1897), and Chicago drew the top number once, in 1898. The pacesetters in each of the other six seasons were the Philadelphia Phillies, which entered the new century still in search of their first pennant. The Phillies were perennial contenders all during the 1890s, though, so maybe there was a lesson here of some sort. Was it the Phillies in those years that taught a certain man, then in Pittsburgh, who later managed for half a century in Philadelphia, that the ideal team from a box-office standpoint—or so he said—was one that was a perennial contender but never quite won?

HIGH-SCORING SEASONS

John McGraw topped the League-Association with 140 runs in 1899 despite collecting fewer than 400 at bats. Owing to the large number of walks he amassed and his wife's death, which caused him to miss several weeks, McGraw officially came to bat only 399 times. McGraw's average of .351 runs per 1,000 at bats was bettered on three occasions prior to 1899 but never since. In fact, apart from Babe Ruth who did it several times, only one other twentieth-century player—Ted Williams in 1941—compiled an RBA of .290 or better. McGraw, on the other hand, is only one of many men who had .300-plus RBAs during the 1890s. A list of players who scored 100 or more runs and "hit" .300 in runs scored per 1,000 at bats:

	YEAR	TEAM	AB	R	RBA
Ross Barnes	1876	Chi-NL	322	126	.391
Ross Barnes	1873	Bos-NA	322	125	.388
Fred Dunlap	1884	StL-UA	449	160	.356
Billy Hamilton	1894	Phi-LA	544	192	.353
John McGraw	1899	Bal-LA	399	140	.351
Babe Ruth	1920	NY-AL	458	158	.345
King Kelly	1886	Chi-NL	451	155	.344
George Gore	1886	Chi-NL	444	150	.339
George Gore	1890	NY-PL	399	132	.331
Babe Ruth	1921	NY-AL	540	177	.328
Joe Kelley	1894	Bal-LA	507	165	.326
Tip O'Neill	1887	StL-AA	517	167	.323
Billy Hamilton	1895	Phi-LA	517	166	.321
Ed Delahanty	1895	Phi-LA	480	149	.310
Billy Hamilton	1893	Phi-LA	355	110	.310
Dan Brouthers	1887	Det-NL	500	153	.306
John McGraw	1894	Bal-LA	512	156	.305
Babe Ruth	1928	NY-AL	536	163	.304
Mike Griffin	1894	Bro-LA	402	122	.304
Hughie Jennings	1897	Bal-LA	439	133	.303
Ed Delahanty	1894	Phi-LA	489	147	.301
Tom Brown	1891	Bos-AA	589	177	.301
Hughie Jennings	1895	Bal-LA	529	159	.301
Jim McTamany	1890	Col-AA	466	140	.300
Billy Hamilton	1897	Phi-LA	507	152	.300

ONE-GAMER IV

The 1899 season saw a rash of pitchers who disappeared after winning their first and only major league starts, but none was more mysterious—or more effective—than Billy Ging. Chosen by manager Frank Selee to hurl Boston's final game of the season at New York, Ging won a 2-1 nailbiter called by darkness after eight innings. *Sporting Life*'s correspondent reported, "The Giants could do nothing with Ging of New London, and barely averted a shut-out." Ging was the last man in the nineteenth century to hurl a complete-game win in his only major league appearance. A list of nineteenth-century pitchers who matched Ging's feat at the sixty-foot six-inch distance:

	DATE	TEAM	INN	K	BB	ERA
George Stultz	Sept. 22, 1894	Bos-LA	9	1	5	0.00*
King Bailey	Sept. 21, 1895	Cin-LA	8	0	0	5.63
Skel Roach	Aug. 9, 1899	Chi-LA	9	0	1	3.00
Clay Fauver	Sept. 7, 1899	Lou-LA	9	1	2	0.00*
Billy Ging	Sept. 25, 1899	Bos-LA	8	2	5	1.13

*The ERAs are misleading. Neither Stultz nor Fauver pitched a shutout. Fauver actually gave up four runs, and Stultz two, albeit all were unearned.

THE SEASONAL RECORD

	W	L	PCT	HOME	ROAD	GB
1. Brooklyn Bridegrooms	101	47	.682	61–16	40–31	—
2. Boston Beaneaters	95	57	.625	53–26	42–31	8
3. Philadelphia Phillies	94	58	.618	58–25	36–33	9
4. Baltimore Orioles	86	62	.581	51–24	35–38	15
5. St. Louis Perfectos	84	67	.556	50–33	34–34	18.5
6. Cincinnati Reds	83	67	.553	57–29	26–38	19
7. Pittsburgh Pirates	76	73	.510	49–34	27–39	25.5
8. Chicago Orphans	75	73	.507	44–39	31–34	26
9. Louisville Colonels	75	77	.493	33–28	42–49	28
10. New York Giants	60	90	.400	35–38	25–52	42
11. Washington Nationals	54	98	.355	35–43	19–55	49
12. Cleveland Spiders	20	134	.130	9–33	11–101	84

	Br	Bos	Ph	Ba	StL	Ci	Pt	Ch	Lo	NY	Wa	Cl	
Brooklyn	—	8	8	8	8	7	8	8	11	10	11	14	101
Boston	6	—	5	7	8	10	10	5	9	12	12	11	95
Philadelphia	6	9	—	7	7	10	6	9	6	10	12	12	94
Baltimore	6	7	6	—	8	4	9	9	6	10	9	12	86
St. Louis	4	6	7	6	—	8	7	6	9	10	8	13	84
Cincinnati	6	4	4	9	5	—	10	6	8	9	8	14	83
Pittsburgh	6	4	8	3	7	3	—	7	8	7	11	12	76
Chicago	5	7	5	5	8	8	6	—	7	7	4	13	75
Louisville	3	5	7	7	5	6	6	7	—	7	12	10	75
New York	2	2	4	4	4	5	6	6	7	—	7	13	60
Washington	3	2	2	4	6	6	3	9	2	7	—	10	54
Cleveland	0	3	2	2	1	0	2	1	4	1	4	—	20
	47	57	58	62	67	67	73	73	77	90	98	134	903

SEASON LEADERS

Batting Average (400 ABs)

1. Delahanty, Philadelphia .410
2. Burkett, St. Louis .396
3. McGraw, Baltimore .391*
4. Keeler, Baltimore .379
5. Williams, Pittsburgh .355

* 399 ABS but well over 500 plate appearances

On–Base Percentage

1. McGraw, Baltimore .547
2. Delahanty, Philadelphia .464
3. Burkett, St. Louis .463
4. Thomas, Philadelphia .457
5. Stahl, Boston .426

Home Runs

1. Freeman, Washington 25
2. Wallace, St. Louis 12
3. Williams, Pittsburgh 9
   Delahanty, Philadelphia 9
   Mertes, Chicago 9

Hits

1. Delahanty, Philadelphia 238
2. Burkett, St. Louis 221
3. Williams, Pittsburgh 219
4. Keeler, Brooklyn 216
5. Tenney, Boston 209

Stolen Bases

1. Sheckard, Baltimore 77
2. McGraw, Baltimore 73
3. Heidrick, St. Louis 55
4. Holmes, Baltimore 50
5. F. Clarke, Louisville 49

Slugging Average

1. Delahanty, Philadelphia .582
2. Freeman, Washington .563
3. Williams, Pittsburgh .532
4. Burkett, St. Louis .500
5. Wagner, Louisville .494

Total Bases

1. Delahanty, Philadelphia 338
2. Freeman, Washington 331
3. Williams, Pittsburgh 328
4. Stahl, Boston 284
5. Wagner, Louisville 282

RBI

1. Delahanty, Philadelphia 137
2. Freeman, Washington 122
3. Williams, Pittsburgh 116
4. Wagner, Louisville 113
5. Wallace, St. Louis 108

Runs

1. McGraw, Baltimore 140
   Keeler, Brooklyn 140
3. Thomas, Philadelphia 137
4. Delahanty, Philadelphia 135
5. Williams, Pittsburgh 126

PITCHING

Wins

1.	McGinnity, Baltimore	28
	Hughes, Brooklyn	28
3.	Willis, Boston	27
4.	Young, St. Louis	26
5.	Tannehill, Pittsburgh	24

Losses

1.	Hughey, Cleveland	30
2.	Carrick, New York	27
3.	Leever, Pittsburgh	23
4.	Knepper, Cleveland	22
5.	Weyhing, Washington	21
	Taylor, Chicago	21

Innings

1.	Leever, Pittsburgh	379
2.	Powell, St. Louis	373
3.	Young, St. Louis	369.1
4.	McGinnity, Baltimore	366.1
5.	Carrick, New York	361.2

Complete Games

1.	Young, St. Louis	40
	Powell, St. Louis	40
	Carrick, New York	40
4.	Taylor, Chicago	39
5.	McGinnity, Baltimore	38

Strikeouts

1.	Hahn, Cincinnati	145
2.	Seymour, New York	142
3.	Leever, Pittsburgh	121
4.	Willis, Boston	120
5.	Doheny, New York	115

Winning Percentage (25 decisions)

1.	Hughes, Brooklyn	.824
2.	Willis, Boston	.771
3.	Hahn, Cincinnati	.742
4.	Donahue, Philadelphia	.724
5.	Kennedy, Brooklyn	.710

ERA (154 innings)

1.	Willis, Boston	2.50
2.	Young, St. Louis	2.58
3.	McGinnity, Baltimore	2.68
	Hahn, Cincinnati	2.68
	Hughes, Brooklyn	2.68

Lowest On–Base Percentage

1.	Young, St. Louis	.285
2.	Hahn, Cincinnati	.290
3.	Nichols, Boston	.298
4.	Willis, Boston	.303
5.	Kitson, Baltimore	.304

FIELDING

Total Chances

1B	Everett, Chicago	1633
2B	Gleason, New York	918
3B	Williams, Pittsburgh	671
SS	M. Cross, Philadelphia	989
OF	Slagle, Washington	448
C	McGuire, Wash–Brook	564
P	Cunningham, Louisville	143

Fielding Average

McGann, Brook–Wash	.988
Quinn, Cleveland	.962
L. Cross, Cleve–StL	.959
Davis, New York	.945
Brodie, Baltimore	.979
Zimmer, Cleve–Louis	.978
Kitson, Baltimore	.976

BROOKLYN   **Ned Hanlon**   **Washington Park (II)**

		G	AB	H	R	2B	3B	HR	RBI	BB	SB	BA	SA
RF	Willie Keeler	141	570	216	**140**	12	13	1	61	37	45	.379	.451
LF	Joe Kelley	143	538	175	108	21	14	6	93	70	31	.325	.450
3B	Doc Casey	134	525	141	75	14	8	1	43	25	27	.269	.331
2B	Tom Daly	141	498	156	95	24	9	5	88	69	43	.313	.428
UT	John Anderson	117	439	118	65	18	7	4	92	27	25	.269	.369
SS	Bill Dahlen	121	428	121	87	22	7	4	76	67	29	.283	.395
CF	Fielder Jones	102	365	104	75	8	2	2	38	54	18	.285	.334
C	Duke Farrell	80	254	76	40	10	7	2	55	35	6	.299	.417
Sub	Hughie Jennings	67	216	64	42	3	10	0	40	22	18	.296	.403
1B	Dan McGann	63	214	52	49	11	4	2	32	21	16	.243	.360
C	Deacon McGuire	46	157	50	22	12	4	0	23	12	4	.318	.446
P	Jack Dunn	43	122	30	21	2	1	0	16	3	3	.246	.279
P	Doc McJames	37	112	19	8	4	1	0	6	2	1	.170	.223
P	Brickyard Kennedy	40	109	27	14	5	3	0	8	7	1	.248	.349
P	Jim Hughes	35	107	27	17	4	2	0	14	12	1	.252	.327
Sub	Aleck Smith	17	61	11	6	0	1	0	6	2	0	.180	.213
Sub	Zeke Wrigley	15	49	10	4	2	2	0	11	3	2	.204	.327
Sub	John Grim	15	47	13	3	1	0	0	7	1	0	.277	.298
P	Joe Yeager	23	47	9	12	0	1	0	4	6	0	.191	.234
Sub	Erve Beck	8	24	4	2	2	0	0	2	0	0	.167	.250
Sub	Pete Cassidy	6	20	3	2	1	0	0	4	1	1	.150	.200
P	Bill Donovan	5	13	3	2	1	0	0	0	0	0	.231	.308
P	Al Maul	4	11	3	2	0	0	0	0	1	0	.273	.273
P	Bill Hill	2	5	3	1	0	1	0	2	0	0	.600	1.000
P	Bill Reidy	2	3	0	0	0	0	0	0	0	0	.000	.000
P	Dan McFarlan	1	2	0	0	0	0	0	0	0	0	.000	.000
P	Welcome Gaston	1	1	1	0	1	0	0	2	0	0	1.000	2.000
		150	4937	1436	892	178	97	27	723	477	271	.291	.383

1B   McGann 61, Jennings 50, Anderson 41
2B   Daly 141, Beck 6, Jennings 1
SS   Dahlen 110, Wrigley 14, Jennings 12, Yeager 11, Cassidy 2, Beck 2, Dunn 1
3B   Casey 134, Dahlen 11, Cassidy 3, Wrigley 1, Yeager 1
OF   Kelley 143, Keeler 141, Jones 96, Anderson 76, Yeager 1
C   Farrell 78, McGuire 46, Smith 17, Grim 12
P   Dunn 41, Kennedy 40, McJames 37, Hughes 35, Yeager 10, Donovan 5, Maul 4, Reidy 2, Hill 2, Gaston 1, McFarlan 1

	G	IP	GS	CG	W	L	K	BB	SH	SV	ERA
Jack Dunn	41	299.1	34	29	23	13	48	86	2	2	3.70
Jim Hughes	35	291.2	35	30	**28**	6	99	119	3	0	2.68
Brickyard Kennedy	40	277.1	33	27	22	9	55	86	2	2	2.79
Doc McJames	37	275.1	34	27	19	15	105	122	1	1	3.50
Joe Yeager	10	47.2	4	2	2	2	6	16	1	1	4.72
Al Maul	4	26	4	2	2	0	2	6	0	0	4.50
Bill Donovan	5	25	2	2	1	2	11	13	0	1	4.32
Bill Hill	2	11	1	1	1	0	3	6	0	1	0.82
Bill Reidy	2	7	1	1	1	0	2	2	0	1	2.57
Dan McFarlan	1	6	0	0	0	0	0	3	0	0	1.50
Welcome Gaston	1	3	0	0	0	0	0	4	0	0	3.00
—2 forfeit Ws: vs New York on June 16; vs Baltimore on October 14—											
	1269.1	148	121	99	47	331	463	9	**9**	**3.25**

BOSTON   **Frank Selee**   **South End Grounds (II)**

		G	AB	H	R	2B	3B	HR	RBI	BB	SB	BA	SA
1B	Fred Tenney	150	603	209	115	19	17	1	67	63	28	.347	.439
3B	Jimmy Collins	151	599	166	98	28	11	5	92	40	12	.277	.386
LF	Hugh Duffy	147	588	164	103	29	7	5	102	39	26	.279	.378
SS	Herman Long	145	578	153	91	30	8	6	100	45	20	.265	.375
RF	Chick Stahl	148	576	202	122	23	19	7	52	72	33	.351	.493
2B	Bobby Lowe	152	559	152	81	5	9	4	88	35	17	.272	.335
CF	Billy Hamilton	84	297	92	63	7	1	1	33	72	19	.310	.350
C	Marty Bergen	72	260	67	32	11	3	1	34	10	4	.258	.335
C	Boileryard Clarke	60	223	50	25	3	2	2	32	10	2	.224	.283
Sub	General Stafford	55	182	55	29	4	2	3	40	7	9	.302	.396
Sub	Charlie Frisbee	42	152	50	22	4	2	0	20	9	10	.329	.382
P	Kid Nichols	42	136	26	13	3	0	1	12	6	1	.191	.235
P	Vic Willis	41	134	29	14	3	0	0	16	4	0	.216	.239
P	Ted Lewis	29	96	25	9	1	1	0	9	4	1	.260	.292
Sub	Billy Sullivan	22	74	20	10	2	0	2	12	1	2	.270	.378
P	Piano Legs Hickman	19	63	25	15	2	7	0	15	2	1	.397	.651
P	Jouett Meekin	13	41	7	4	1	1	0	4	2	0	.171	.244
P	Frank Killen	12	41	7	3	1	0	0	5	1	0	.171	.195
P	Harvey Bailey	12	34	8	3	2	0	0	2	2	0	.235	.294
Sub	Charlie Kuhns	7	18	5	2	0	0	0	3	2	0	.278	.278
P	Fred Klobedanz	5	11	2	3	0	0	1	3	3	0	.182	.455
Sub	George Yeager	3	8	1	1	0	0	0	0	1	0	.125	.125
P	Oscar Streit	2	7	0	0	0	0	0	0	0	0	.000	.000
Sub	Mike Hickey	1	3	1	0	0	0	0	0	0	0	.333	.333
P	Mike Sullivan	1	3	1	0	0	0	0	0	1	0	.333	.333
Sub	Bill Merritt	1	2	0	0	0	0	0	0	0	0	.000	.000
P	Billy Ging	1	2	0	0	0	0	0	0	0	0	.000	.000
		153	5290	1517	858	178	90	39	741	431	185	.287	.377

1B   Tenney 150, Long 2, Hickman 1
2B   Lowe 148, Stafford 5, Hickey 1
SS   Long 143, Stafford 5, Lowe 4, Kuhns 3
3B   Collins 151, Kuhns 3
OF   Stahl 148, Duffy 147, Hamilton 81, Stafford 41, Frisbee 40, Hickman 7, Yeager 2
C   Bergen 72, Clarke 60, B. Sullivan 22, Yeager 1, Merritt 1
P   Nichols 42, Willis 41, Lewis 29, Meekin 13, Killen 12, Bailey 12, Hickman 11, Klobedanz 5, Streit 2, M. Sullivan 1, Ging 1, Stahl 1

	G	IP	GS	CG	W	L	K	BB	SH	SV	ERA
Kid Nichols	42	343.1	37	37	21	19	108	82	4	1	2.99
Vic Willis #	41	342.2	38	35	27	8	120	117	**5**	2	**2.50**
Ted Lewis	29	234.2	25	23	17	11	60	73	2	0	3.49
Jouett Meekin	13	108	13	12	7	6	23	23	0	0	2.83
Frank Killen	12	99.1	12	11	7	5	23	26	0	0	4.26
Harvey Bailey	12	86.2	11	8	6	4	26	35	0	0	3.95
Piano Legs Hickman	11	66.1	9	5	6	0	14	40	2	1	4.48
Fred Klobedanz	5	33.1	5	4	1	4	8	9	0	0	4.86
Oscar Streit	2	14.2	1	1	1	0	0	15	0	0	6.75
Mike Sullivan	1	9	1	1	1	0	1	4	0	0	5.00
Billy Ging	1	8	1	1	1	0	2	5	0	0	1.13
Chick Stahl	1	2	0	0	0	0	0	3	0	0	9.00
		1348	153	138	95	57	385	432	13	4	3.26

No-hit game 7-1 vs Washington, August 7

PHILADELPHIA	Bill Shettsline				**Philadelphia Baseball Grounds (II)**							
		G	AB	H	R	2B	3B	HR	RBI	BB	SB	BA	SA
3B	Billy Lauder	151	583	156	74	17	6	3	90	34	15	.268	.333
LF	Ed Delahanty	146	581	**238**	135	**55**	9	9	**137**	55	30	**.410**	**.582**
SS	Monte Cross	154	557	143	85	25	6	3	65	56	26	.257	.339
CF	Roy Thomas	150	547	178	137	12	4	0	47	115	42	.325	.362
RF	Elmer Flick	127	485	166	98	22	11	2	98	42	31	.342	.445
1B	Duff Cooley	94	406	112	75	15	8	1	31	29	15	.276	.360
UT	Pearce Chiles	97	338	108	57	28	7	2	76	16	6	.320	.462
C	Ed McFarland	96	324	108	59	22	9	2	57	36	9	.333	.475
2B	Nap Lajoie	76	312	118	70	19	9	6	70	12	13	.378	.554
C	Klondike Douglass	75	275	70	26	6	6	0	27	10	7	.255	.320
Sub	Joe Dolan	61	222	57	27	6	3	1	30	11	3	.257	.324
Sub	Bill Goeckel	37	141	37	17	3	1	0	16	1	6	.262	.298
P	Wiley Piatt	40	122	33	11	2	2	0	10	5	0	.270	.320
P	Chick Fraser	40	117	21	19	4	1	0	11	6	2	.179	.231
P	Red Donahue	35	111	20	12	0	0	0	7	2	2	.180	.180
P	Al Orth	22	62	13	5	3	1	1	5	1	2	.210	.339
P	Bill Bernard	21	54	13	5	1	0	0	2	2	1	.241	.259
P	Jack Fifield	14	35	9	2	0	0	0	2	3	0	.257	.257
P	Bill Magee	9	31	5	0	0	0	0	2	1	0	.161	.161
Sub	Red Owens	8	21	1	0	0	0	0	1	2	0	.048	.048
P	George Wheeler	6	17	4	2	1	0	1	3	1	1	.235	.471
Sub	Harry Croft	2	7	1	0	0	0	0	0	1	0	.143	.143
Sub	Dave Fultz	2	5	2	0	0	0	0	0	0	1	.400	.400
		154	5353	**1613**	**916**	**241**	83	31	**787**	441	212	**.301**	**.395**

1B Cooley 79, Goeckel 36, Chiles 25, Thomas 14, Douglass 4, Fultz 1
2B Lajoie 67, Dolan 61, Chiles 16, Owens 8, Croft 2, Cooley 1, Fultz 1
SS Cross 154, Fultz 1
3B Lauder 151, Douglass 4, Fraser 3
OF Delahanty 143, Thomas 135, Flick 125, Chiles 46, Cooley 14, Lajoie 5, Fraser 2, Orth 1, Douglass 1
C   McFarland 94, Douglass 66
P   Piatt 39, Donahue 35, Fraser 35, Orth 21, Bernard 21, Fifield 14, Magee 9, Wheeler 6

	G	IP	GS	CG	W	L	K	BB	SH	SV	ERA
Wiley Piatt	39	305	38	31	23	15	89	86	2	0	3.45
Red Donahue	35	279	31	27	21	8	51	63	4	0	3.39
Chick Fraser	35	270.2	33	29	21	12	68	85	4	0	3.36
Al Orth	21	144.2	15	13	14	3	35	19	3	1	2.49
Bill Bernard	21	132.1	12	10	6	6	23	36	1	0	2.65
John Fifield	14	92.2	11	9	3	8	8	36	1	1	4.08
Bill Magee	9	70	9	7	3	5	4	32	0	0	5.66
George Wheeler	6	39	5	3	3	1	3	13	0	0	6.00
		1333.1	154	129	94	58	281	370	**15**	2	3.47

BALTIMORE   **John McGraw**   **Union Park**

		G	AB	H	R	2B	3B	HR	RBI	BB	SB	BA	SA
LF	Ducky Holmes	138	553	177	80	31	7	4	66	39	50	.320	.423
RF	Jimmy Sheckard	147	536	158	104	18	10	3	75	56	**77**	.295	.382
CF	Steve Brodie	137	531	164	82	26	1	3	87	31	19	.309	.379
SS	Bill Keister	136	523	172	96	22	16	3	73	16	33	.329	.449
1B	Candy LaChance	125	472	145	65	23	10	1	75	21	31	.307	.405
3B	John McGraw	117	399	156	**140**	13	3	1	33	**124**	73	.391	.446
C	Wilbert Robinson	108	356	101	40	15	2	0	47	31	5	.284	.337
2B	Gene Demontreville	60	240	67	40	13	4	1	36	10	21	.279	.379
Sub	Dave Fultz	57	210	62	31	3	2	0	18	13	17	.295	.329
Sub	George Magoon	62	207	53	26	8	3	0	31	26	7	.256	.324
Sub	Pat Crisham	53	172	50	23	5	3	0	20	4	4	.291	.355
P	Joe McGinnity	50	145	28	21	0	0	0	10	5	4	.193	.193
Sub	John O'Brien	39	135	26	14	4	0	1	17	15	4	.193	.244
P	Frank Kitson	45	134	27	12	7	1	0	8	6	7	.201	.269
Sub	Aleck Smith	41	120	46	17	6	4	0	25	4	7	.383	.500
P	Jerry Nops	34	105	29	6	2	0	0	12	2	0	.276	.295
P	Harry Howell	28	82	12	4	2	2	0	3	3	0	.146	.220
Sub	Charlie Harris	30	68	19	16	3	0	0	1	3	4	.279	.324
P	Bill Hill	8	24	7	2	0	0	0	4	2	0	.292	.292
Sub	Bobby Rothermel	10	21	2	1	0	0	0	3	1	0	.095	.095
P	Kit McKenna	9	17	1	1	1	0	0	0	3	0	.059	.118
P	Ralph Miller	5	11	2	4	1	1	0	2	3	0	.182	.455
Sub	Hughie Jennings	2	8	3	2	0	2	0	2	0	0	.375	.875
Sub	John Ryan	2	4	2	0	1	0	0	1	0	1	.500	.750
		152	5073	1509	827	204	71	17	649	418	**364**	.297	.376

1B	LaChance 125, Crisham 26, Smith 1, Fultz 1, Sheckard 1
2B	Demontreville 60, Keister 46, O'Brien 39, Rothermel 5, Fultz 2, Harris 2, Jennings 2
SS	Keister 90, Magoon 62, Harris 1, Rothermel 1
3B	McGraw 117, Harris 21, Fultz 20, Rothermel 3
OF	Sheckard 146, Holmes 138, Brodie 137, Fultz 31, Harris 3, Smith 2, McGinnity 2, Keister 1, McKenna 1
C	Robinson 105, Smith 36, Crisham 22, Ryan 2
P	McGinnity 48, Kitson 40, Nops 33, Howell 28, McKenna 8, Hill 8, Miller 5

	G	IP	GS	CG	W	L	K	BB	SH	SV	ERA
Joe McGinnity	48	366.1	41	38	**28**	16	74	93	4	2	2.68
Frank Kitson	40	327.2	37	34	22	16	75	65	2	0	2.77
Jerry Nops	33	259	33	26	17	11	60	71	2	0	4.03
Harry Howell	28	209.1	25	21	13	8	58	69	0	1	3.91
Bill Hill	8	61	7	6	3	4	17	18	0	0	3.25
Kit McKenna	8	45	4	4	2	3	7	19	0	1	4.60
Ralph Miller	6	36	4	3	1	3	3	14	0	0	4.50

* One combined shutout on May 26: Kitson 4 innings, Miller 5 innings
—One forfeit L vs Brooklyn on October 14—

	IP	GS	CG	W	L	K	BB	SH	SV	ERA
	1304.1	151	132	86	61	294	349	9	4	3.31

ST. LOUIS   **Patsy Tebeau**   **League Park (formerly Sportsman's Park)**

		G	AB	H	R	2B	3B	HR	RBI	BB	SB	BA	SA
RF	Emmett Heidrick	146	591	194	109	21	14	2	82	34	55	.328	.421
SS	Bobby Wallace	151	577	170	91	28	14	12	108	54	17	.295	.454
LF	Jesse Burkett	141	558	221	116	21	8	7	71	67	25	.396	.500
2B	Cupid Childs	125	464	123	73	11	11	1	48	74	11	.265	.343
3B	Lave Cross	103	403	122	61	14	5	4	64	17	11	.303	.392
CF	Harry Blake	97	292	70	50	9	4	2	41	43	16	.240	.318
C	Jack O'Connor	84	289	73	33	5	6	0	43	15	7	.253	.311
1B	Patsy Tebeau	77	281	69	27	10	3	1	26	18	5	.246	.313
Sub	Ossee Schreckengost	72	277	77	42	12	2	2	37	15	14	.278	.365
Sub	Ed McKean	67	277	72	40	7	3	3	40	20	4	.260	.339
OF	Mike Donlin	66	266	86	49	9	6	6	27	17	20	.323	.470
C	Lou Criger	77	258	66	39	4	5	2	44	28	14	.256	.333
P	Cy Young	44	148	32	22	5	3	1	18	2	1	.216	.311
P	Jack Powell	49	134	27	13	0	1	1	6	12	0	.201	.239
Sub	Jake Stenzel	35	128	35	21	9	0	1	19	16	8	.273	.367
P	Nig Cuppy	21	70	13	6	0	0	0	3	3	0	.186	.186
P	Willie Sudhoff	25	64	14	10	1	1	0	2	8	0	.219	.266
Sub	Dusty Miller	10	39	8	3	1	0	0	3	3	1	.205	.231
Sub	Charlie Hemphill	11	37	9	4	0	0	1	3	6	0	.243	.324
Sub	Tim Flood	10	31	9	0	0	0	0	3	4	1	.290	.290
P	Cowboy Jones	12	29	5	1	3	0	0	0	4	0	.172	.276
P	Pete McBride	12	27	5	2	1	0	1	5	2	0	.185	.333
Sub	Fritz Buelow	7	15	7	4	0	2	0	2	2	0	.467	.733
P	Tom Thomas	4	12	3	0	1	0	0	2	0	0	.250	.333
P	Zeke Wilson	5	10	0	0	0	0	0	0	1	0	.000	.000
P	Jack Sutthoff	3	10	0	0	0	0	0	0	0	0	.000	.000
Sub	Fred Parent	2	8	1	0	0	0	0	1	0	0	.125	.125
Sub	Jimmy Burke	2	6	2	1	0	0	0	0	1	0	.333	.333
P	Frank Bates	2	3	1	2	0	0	0	1	2	0	.333	.333
		155	5304	1514	819	172	88	47	699	468	210	.285	.378

1B   Tebeau 65, Schreckengost 42, O'Connor 26, McKean 15, Donlin 13, Blake 1
2B   Childs 125, McKean 10, Flood 10, Blake 4, Parent 2, Burke 2, Schreckengost 1, Tebeau 1, McBride 1, Burkett 1
SS   Wallace 100, McKean 42, Tebeau 11, Donlin 3, Blake 1
3B   Cross 103, Wallace 52, Tebeau 1
OF   Heidrick 145, Burkett 140, Blake 87, Donlin 51, Stenzel 33, Hemphill 10, Miller 10, Buelow 2, Schreckengost 1, Powell 1
C   Criger 75, O'Connor 57, Schreckengost 25, Buelow 4, Blake 1
P   Powell 48, Young 44, Sudhoff 25, Cuppy 21, Jones 12, McBride 11, Wilson 5, Thomas 4, Donlin 3, Sutthoff 3, Bates 2

	G	IP	GS	CG	W	L	K	BB	SH	SV	ERA
Jack Powell	48	373	**43**	**40**	23	19	87	85	2	0	3.52
Cy Young	44	369.1	42	**40**	26	16	111	44	4	1	2.58
Willie Sudhoff	25	178.1	23	16	12	10	29	62	0	0	4.04
Nig Cuppy	21	171.2	21	18	11	8	25	26	1	0	3.15
Cowboy Jones	12	85.1	12	9	6	5	28	22	0	0	3.59
Pete McBride	11	64	6	4	2	4	26	40	0	0	4.08
Zeke Wilson	5	26	2	2	1	1	3	4	0	0	4.50
Tom Thomas	4	25	2	2	1	1	8	4	0	0	2.52
Jack Sutthoff	3	24	3	3	1	2	8	15	0	0	4.13
Mike Donlin	3	15.1	1	0	0	1	6	14	0	0	7.63
Frank Bates	2	8.2	0	0	0	0	0	5	0	0	1.04
		—1 forfeit W vs New York on May 19—									
	1340.2	155	134	83	67	331	**321**	7	1	3.36	

CINCINNATI   **Buck Ewing**   **League Park (II)**

		G	AB	H	R	2B	3B	HR	RBI	BB	SB	BA	SA
SS	Tommy Corcoran	137	537	149	91	11	8	0	81	28	32	.277	.318
LF	Kip Selbach	140	521	154	104	27	11	3	87	70	38	.296	.407
1B	Jake Beckley	134	513	171	87	27	16	3	99	40	20	.333	.466
UT	Harry Steinfeldt	107	386	94	62	16	8	0	43	40	19	.244	.326
2B	Bid McPhee	111	373	104	60	17	7	1	65	40	18	.279	.370
CF	Elmer Smith	87	339	101	65	13	6	1	24	47	10	.298	.381
RF	Dusty Miller	80	323	81	44	12	5	0	37	9	18	.251	.319
3B	Charlie Irwin	90	314	73	42	4	8	1	52	26	26	.232	.306
C	Heinie Peitz	93	290	79	45	13	2	1	43	45	11	.272	.341
Sub	Algie McBride	64	251	87	57	12	5	1	23	30	5	.347	.446
C	Bob Wood	62	194	61	34	11	7	0	24	25	3	.314	.443
Sub	Kid Elberfeld	41	138	36	23	4	2	0	22	15	5	.261	.319
Sub	Sam Crawford	31	127	39	25	3	7	1	20	2	6	.307	.465
P	Noodles Hahn	38	109	16	12	3	2	0	11	8	3	.147	.211
Sub	Farmer Vaughn	31	108	19	9	1	0	0	2	3	2	.176	.185
P	Ted Breitenstein	33	105	37	18	4	1	1	11	10	1	.352	.438
P	Pink Hawley	34	101	22	11	4	1	0	10	2	1	.218	.277
Sub	Jimmy Barrett	26	92	34	30	2	4	0	10	18	4	.370	.478
P	Bill Phillips	34	92	12	6	0	2	0	7	7	0	.130	.174
Sub	Socks Seybold	22	85	19	13	5	1	0	8	6	2	.224	.306
P	Jack Taylor	24	68	17	3	2	0	0	7	0	0	.250	.279
Sub	Mike Kahoe	14	42	7	2	1	1	0	4	0	1	.167	.238
Sub	Jake Stenzel	9	29	9	5	1	0	0	3	4	2	.310	.345
P	Emil Frisk	9	25	7	5	1	0	0	2	2	0	.280	.320
P	Bill Damman	9	18	1	0	0	0	0	2	2	0	.056	.056
Sub	Fred Houtz	5	17	4	1	0	1	0	0	4	1	.235	.353
P	John Cronin	5	17	2	2	0	0	0	2	2	0	.118	.118
P	Frank Dwyer	5	11	4	0	0	0	0	0	0	0	.364	.364
		156	5225	1439	856	194	105	13	699	**485**	228	.275	.360

1B	Beckley 134, Vaughn 21, Irwin 1, Wood 1
2B	McPhee 106, Steinfeldt 40, Corcoran 14, Irwin 3
SS	Corcoran 123, Elberfeld 24, Steinfeldt 8, Irwin 6
3B	Irwin 78, Steinfeldt 59, Elberfeld 18, Wood 2
OF	Selbach 140, Smith 87, Miller 80, McBride 64, Crawford 31, Barrett 26, Seybold 22, Stenzel 7, Breitenstein 7, Houtz 5, Wood 2, Steinfeldt 2, Phillips 1, Vaughn 1
C	Peitz 91, Wood 53, Kahoe 13, Vaughn 7
P	Hahn 38, Hawley 34, Phillips 33, Breitenstein 26, Taylor 24, Frisk 9, Damman 9, Dwyer 5, Cronin 5, Peitz 1

	G	IP	GS	CG	W	L	K	BB	SH	SV	ERA
Noodles Hahn	38	309	34	32	23	8	**145**	68	4	0	2.68
Pink Hawley	34	250.1	29	25	14	17	46	65	0	1	4.24
Bill Phillips	33	227.2	27	18	17	9	43	71	1	1	3.32
Ted Breitenstein	26	210.2	24	21	13	9	59	71	0	0	3.59
Jack Taylor	24	168.1	18	15	9	10	34	41	2	2	4.12
Emil Frisk	9	68.1	9	9	3	6	17	17	0	0	3.95
Bill Damman	9	48	5	3	2	1	2	11	1	1	4.88
Jack Cronin	5	41	5	5	2	2	9	16	0	0	5.49
Frank Dwyer	5	32.2	5	2	0	5	2	9	0	0	5.51
Heinie Peitz	1	5	0	0	0	0	3	1	0	0	5.40
		1361	156	130	83	67	360	370	8	5	3.70

PITTSBURGH	Bill Watkins (7–15)		Patsy Donovan (69–58)			Exposition Park						
	G	AB	H	R	2B	3B	HR	RBI	BB	SB	BA	SA
3B Jimmy Williams	152	617	219	126	28	**27**	9	116	60	26	.355	.532
LF Jack McCarthy	138	560	171	108	22	17	3	67	39	28	.305	.421
RF Patsy Donovan	121	531	156	82	11	7	1	55	17	26	.294	.347
SS Bones Ely	138	522	145	66	18	6	3	72	22	8	.278	.352
UT Tom McCreery	118	455	147	76	21	9	2	64	47	11	.323	.422
CF Ginger Beaumont	111	437	154	90	15	8	3	38	41	31	.352	.444
C Frank Bowerman	109	424	110	49	16	10	3	53	11	10	.259	.366
C Pop Schriver	91	301	85	31	19	5	1	49	23	4	.282	.389
1B Willie Clark	80	298	85	49	13	10	0	44	35	11	.285	.396
2B John O'Brien	79	279	63	26	2	4	1	33	21	8	.226	.272
P Sam Leever	51	146	33	15	6	4	0	18	8	0	.226	.322
P Jesse Tannehill	47	132	34	17	5	3	0	10	8	2	.258	.341
Sub Heinie Peitz	34	130	34	11	4	2	0	15	10	3	.262	.323
Sub Pop Dillon	30	121	31	21	5	0	0	20	5	5	.256	.298
Sub Art Madison	42	118	32	20	2	4	0	19	11	1	.271	.376
P Bill Hoffer	31	91	18	12	2	0	0	2	1	1	.198	.220
P Tully Sparks	28	62	8	8	2	1	0	5	9	0	.129	.194
P Jack Chesbro	19	58	9	3	0	0	0	3	3	0	.155	.155
Sub Heinie Smith	16	53	15	9	3	1	0	12	5	2	.283	.377
Sub Paddy Fox	13	41	10	4	0	1	1	3	3	2	.244	.366
P Chummy Gray	9	26	1	2	0	0	0	0	3	0	.038	.038
P Billy Rhines	10	23	10	4	1	2	0	2	0	0	.435	.652
P Jim Gardner	6	13	3	3	1	0	0	0	1	0	.231	.308
P Harley Payne	5	10	1	1	0	0	0	0	1	0	.100	.100
P Zeke Rosebraugh	2	2	0	1	0	0	0	0	0	0	.000	.000
P Jay Parker	1	0	0	0	0	0	0	0	0	0	—	—
	154	5450	1574	834	196	**121**	27	700	384	179	.289	.384

1B Clark 78, Dillon 30, Bowerman 28, Fox 9, Schriver 8, Beaumont 2
2B O'Brien 79, Reitz 34, Madison 19, Smith 15, McCreery 7, Ely 6, Madison 2, Hoffer 1
SS Ely 132, Madison 15, McCreery 9, Smith 1
3B Williams 152, Madison 2
OF McCarthy 138, Donovan 121, Beaumont 102, McCreery 97, Hoffer 6, Tannehill 1
C   Bowerman 79, Schriver 78, Fox 3
P   Leever 51, Tannehill 40, Sparks 28, Hoffer 23, Chesbro 19, Rhines 9, Gray 9, Gardner 6, Payne 5, Rosebraugh 2, Parker 1

	G	IP	GS	CG	W	L	K	BB	SH	SV	ERA
Sam Leever	**51**	**379**	39	35	21	23	121	122	4	**3**	3.18
Jesse Tannehill	40	313	35	32	24	14	61	51	3	1	2.73
Tully Sparks	28	170	17	8	8	6	53	82	0	0	3.86
Bill Hoffer	23	163.2	19	15	8	10	44	64	2	0	3.63
Jack Chesbro	19	149	17	15	6	9	28	59	0	0	4.11
Chummy Gray	9	70.2	7	6	3	3	9	24	0	0	3.44
Billy Rhines	9	54	9	4	4	4	6	13	0	0	6.00
Jim Gardner	6	32.1	3	0	1	0	2	13	0	0	7.52
Harley Payne	5	26.1	5	2	1	3	8	4	0	0	3.76
Zeke Rosebraugh	2	6	2	0	0	1	2	3	0	0	9.00
Jay Parker	1	0	1	0	0	0	0	2	0	0	—
		1364	154	117	76	73	334	437	9	4	3.60

CHICAGO   **Tom Burns**   **West Side Park (II)**

		G	AB	H	R	2B	3B	HR	RBI	BB	SB	BA	SA
1B	Bill Everett	136	536	166	87	17	5	1	74	31	30	.310	.366
LF	Jimmy Ryan	125	525	158	91	20	10	3	68	43	9	.301	.394
RF	Danny Green	117	475	140	90	12	11	6	56	35	18	.295	.404
OF	Sam Mertes	117	426	127	83	13	16	9	81	33	45	.298	.467
CF	Bill Lange	107	416	135	81	21	7	1	58	38	41	.325	.416
3B	Harry Wolverton	99	389	111	50	14	11	1	49	30	14	.285	.386
2B	Barry McCormick	102	376	97	48	15	2	2	52	25	14	.258	.324
SS	Gene Demontreville	82	310	87	43	6	3	0	40	17	26	.281	.319
C	Tim Donahue	92	278	69	39	9	3	0	29	34	10	.248	.302
Sub	Jim Connor	69	234	48	26	7	1	0	24	18	6	.205	.244
C	Frank Chance	64	192	55	37	6	2	1	22	15	10	.286	.354
Sub	George Magoon	59	189	43	24	5	1	0	21	24	5	.228	.265
P	Nixey Callahan	47	150	39	21	4	3	0	18	8	9	.260	.327
P	Jack Taylor	42	139	37	25	9	2	0	17	16	0	.266	.360
Sub	Bill Bradley	35	129	40	26	6	1	2	18	12	4	.310	.419
P	Clark Griffith	39	120	31	15	5	0	0	14	14	2	.258	.300
P	Ned Garvin	24	71	11	1	0	0	0	1	1	0	.155	.155
Sub	Art Nichols	17	47	12	5	2	0	1	11	0	3	.255	.362
Sub	Doc Curley	10	37	4	7	0	1	0	2	3	0	.108	.162
Sub	Frank Quinn	12	34	6	6	0	1	0	1	6	1	.176	.235
P	Bill Phyle	10	34	6	2	0	0	0	1	0	0	.176	.176
P	Dick Cogan	8	25	5	4	1	2	0	4	2	0	.200	.400
P	John Katoll	2	7	0	1	0	0	0	0	1	0	.000	.000
P	John Malarkey	1	5	1	0	1	0	0	0	0	0	.200	.400
P	Skel Roach	1	4	0	0	0	0	0	0	0	0	.000	.000
		152	5148	1428	812	173	82	27	661	406	247	.277	.359

1B   Everett 136, Lange 14, Mertes 3, Donahue 1, Chance 1
2B   McCormick 99, Connor 44, Curley 10, Quinn 1, Callahan 1
SS   Demontreville 82, Magoon 59, Bradley 5, McCormick 3, Callahan 2, Griffith 1, Wolverton 1, Mertes 1
3B   Wolverton 98, Bradley 30, Connor 25
OF   Ryan 125, Green 115, Mertes 108, Lange 94, Quinn 10, Callahan 9, Cogan 3, Chance 1
C   Donahue 91, Chance 57, Nichols 15
P   Taylor 41, Griffith 38, Callahan 35, Garvin 34, Phyle 10, Cogan 5, Katoll 2, Roach 1, Malarkey 1

	G	IP	GS	CG	W	L	K	BB	SH	SV	ERA
Jack Taylor	41	354.2	39	39	18	21	67	84	1	0	3.76
Clark Griffith	38	319.2	38	35	22	14	73	65	0	0	2.79
Nixey Callahan	35	294.1	34	33	21	12	77	76	3	0	3.06
Ned Garvin	24	199	23	22	9	13	69	42	4	0	2.85
Bill Phyle	10	83.2	9	9	1	8	10	29	0	1	4.20
Dick Cogan	5	44	5	5	2	3	9	24	0	0	4.30
Jack Katoll	2	18	2	2	1	1	1	4	0	0	6.00
Skel Roach	1	9	1	1	1	0	0	1	0	0	3.00
John Malarkey	1	9	1	1	0	1	7	5	0	0	13.00
		1331.1	152	**147**	75	73	313	330	8	1	3.37

LOUISVILLE   **Fred Clarke**   **Eclipse Park (II)**

		G	AB	H	R	2B	3B	HR	RBI	BB	SB	BA	SA
CF	Dummy Hoy	154	**633**	194	116	17	13	5	49	61	32	.306	.398
LF	Fred Clarke	148	602	206	122	23	9	5	70	49	49	.342	.435
UT	Honus Wagner	148	571	192	98	43	13	7	113	40	37	.336	.494
2B	Claude Ritchey	147	536	161	65	15	7	4	71	49	21	.300	.377
3B	Tommy Leach	106	406	117	75	10	6	5	57	37	19	.288	.379
SS	Billy Clingman	109	366	96	67	15	4	2	44	46	13	.262	.342
RF	Charlie Dexter	80	295	76	47	7	1	1	33	21	21	.258	.298
1B	Mike Kelley	76	282	68	48	11	2	3	33	21	10	.241	.326
C	Chief Zimmer	75	262	78	43	11	3	2	29	22	9	.298	.385
C	Mike Powers	49	169	35	15	8	2	0	22	6	1	.207	.278
P	Bert Cunningham	44	154	40	17	2	0	2	17	5	1	.260	.312
Sub	George Decker	38	135	36	13	8	0	1	18	12	3	.267	.348
C	Mal Kittridge	45	129	26	11	2	1	0	12	26	3	.202	.233
P	Deacon Phillippe	44	128	26	17	5	0	0	10	8	3	.203	.242
P	Walt Woods	42	126	19	15	1	1	1	14	10	5	.151	.198
P	Pete Dowling	34	116	27	10	4	0	0	9	2	1	.233	.267
Sub	Dave Wills	24	94	21	15	3	1	0	12	2	1	.223	.277
Sub	Topsy Hartsel	30	75	18	8	1	1	1	7	11	1	.240	.320
Sub	Fred Ketchum	15	61	18	13	1	0	0	5	0	2	.295	.311
P	Rube Waddell	10	34	8	2	2	0	0	3	0	0	.235	.294
Sub	Tacks Latimer	9	29	8	3	1	0	0	4	2	1	.276	.310
P	Bill Magee	12	27	3	1	1	1	0	5	0	0	.111	.222
P	Patsy Flaherty	7	24	5	3	1	1	0	6	3	0	.208	.333
Sub	Farmer Steelman	4	15	1	2	0	1	0	2	2	0	.067	.200
P	Harry Wilhelm	5	12	3	1	0	1	1	2	1	0	.250	.667
Sub	Tom Messitt	3	11	1	0	0	0	0	0	0	0	.091	.091
Sub	Bob Langsford	1	4	0	0	0	0	0	0	0	0	.000	.000
P	Clay Fauver	1	4	0	0	0	0	0	0	0	0	.000	.000
Sub	Burley Byers	1	3	0	0	0	0	0	0	0	0	.000	.000
P	Roy Brashear	3	2	1	0	0	0	0	0	0	0	.500	.500
PH	Harry Croft	2	2	0	0	0	0	0	0	0	0	.000	.000
Sub	Rudy Hulswitt	1	0	0	0	0	0	0	0	0	0	—	—
		155	5307	1484	827	192	68	40	647	436	233	.280	.364

1B   Kelley 76, Decker 38, Wills 24, Zimmer 11, Powers 7, Wagner 4, Latimer 1
2B   Ritchey 137, Woods 11, Wagner 7, Leach 2
SS   Clingman 109, Leach 25, Ritchey 11, Dexter 6, Clarke 3, Woods 3, Langsford 1, Hulswitt 1, Byers 1, Cunningham 1
3B   Leach 80, Wagner 75
OF   Hoy 154, Clarke 144, Dexter 71, Wagner 61, Hartsel 22, Ketchum 15, Cunningham 3, Phillippe 2, Woods 2, Flaherty 2
C   Zimmer 62, Kittridge 43, Powers 38, Latimer 8, Steelman 4, Messitt 3
P   Phillippe 42, Cunningham 39, Dowling 34, Woods 26, Magee 12, Waddell 10, Flaherty 5, Wilhelm 5, Brashear 3, Fauver 1

	G	IP	GS	CG	W	L	K	BB	SH	SV	ERA
Bert Cunningham	39	323.2	37	33	17	17	36	75	1	0	3.84
Deacon Phillippe #	42	321	38	33	21	17	68	64	2	1	3.17
Pete Dowling	34	289.2	32	29	13	17	88	93	0	0	3.11
Walt Woods	26	186.1	21	17	9	13	21	37	0	0	3.28
Rube Waddell	10	79	9	9	7	2	44	14	1	1	3.08
Bill Magee	12	71	10	6	3	7	13	28	1	0	5.20
Patsy Flaherty	5	39	4	4	2	3	5	5	0	0	2.31
Harry Wilhelm	5	25	3	2	1	1	6	3	0	0	6.12
Clay Fauver	1	9	1	1	1	0	1	2	0	0	0.00
Kitty Brashear	3	8	0	0	1	0	5	2	0	0	4.50
		1351.2	155	134	75	77	287	323	5	2	3.45

No-hit game 7-0 vs New York, May 25

NEW YORK   **John Day (29-35)**   **Fred Hoey (31-55)**   **Polo Grounds (III)**

		G	AB	H	R	2B	3B	HR	RBI	BB	SB	BA	SA
CF	George Van Haltren	151	604	182	117	21	3	2	58	74	31	.301	.356
2B	Kid Gleason	146	576	152	72	14	4	0	59	24	29	.264	.302
LF	Tom O'Brien	150	573	170	100	21	10	6	77	44	23	.297	.400
1B	Jack Doyle	118	448	134	55	15	7	3	76	33	35	.299	.384
SS	George Davis	108	416	140	68	21	5	1	57	37	34	.337	.418
UT	Parke Wilson	97	328	88	49	8	6	0	42	43	16	.268	.329
UT	Mike Grady	86	311	104	47	18	8	2	54	29	20	.334	.463
RF	Pop Foster	84	301	89	48	9	7	3	57	20	7	.296	.402
C	Jack Warner	88	293	78	38	8	1	0	19	15	15	.266	.300
3B	Fred Hartman	50	174	41	25	3	5	1	16	12	2	.236	.328
P	Cy Seymour	50	159	52	25	3	2	2	27	4	2	.327	.409
Sub	Mike Tiernan	35	137	35	17	4	2	0	7	10	2	.255	.314
P	Bill Carrick	44	130	18	7	2	1	0	10	11	1	.138	.169
P	Ed Doheny	35	112	27	13	2	0	0	9	4	2	.241	.259
P	Charlie Gettig	34	97	24	7	3	0	0	9	7	4	.247	.278
Sub	Tom Fleming	22	77	16	9	1	1	0	4	1	1	.208	.247
Sub	Scott Hardesty	22	72	16	4	0	0	0	4	1	2	.222	.222
Sub	Pete Woodruff	20	61	15	11	1	1	2	7	9	3	.246	.393
P	Jouett Meekin	18	58	12	7	2	1	1	4	3	1	.207	.328
Sub	Frank Martin	17	54	14	5	2	0	0	1	2	0	.259	.296
P	Tom Colcolough	14	37	10	3	1	0	0	6	1	0	.270	.297
Sub	Kid Carsey	5	18	6	2	1	0	0	1	2	2	.333	.389
Sub	Ira Davis	6	17	4	3	1	1	0	2	0	1	.235	.412
Sub	Zeke Wrigley	4	15	3	1	0	0	0	1	1	1	.200	.200
Sub	John O'Neill	2	7	0	0	0	0	0	0	0	0	.000	.000
P	Leo Fishel	1	4	1	0	0	0	0	0	0	0	.250	.250
P	Willie Garoni	3	4	0	0	0	0	0	0	0	0	.000	.000
Sub	Bill Stuart	1	3	0	0	0	0	0	0	0	0	.000	.000
Sub	Pete Cregan	1	2	0	0	0	0	0	0	0	0	.000	.000
Sub	John Puhl	1	2	0	0	0	0	0	0	0	0	.000	.000
P	Frank McPartlin	1	1	0	0	0	0	0	0	0	0	.000	.000
P	Youngy Johnson	1	1	0	0	0	0	0	0	0	0	.000	.000
P	Doc Sechrist	1	0	0	0	0	0	0	0	0	0	—	—
		152	5092	1431	734	161	65	23	607	387	234	.281	.352

1B   Doyle 113, Wilson 29, Grady 4, Seymour 3, Warner 3, Gettig 3, I. Davis 2, Hardesty 2, O'Brien 1, Woodruff 1

2B   Gleason 146, Gettig 3, O'Brien 1, Stuart 1

SS   C. Davis 108, Hardesty 20, Wilson 19, I. Davis 3, Carsey 2, O'Brien 2, Foster 1

3B   Hartman 50, Grady 35, O'Brien 21, Martin 17, Wilson 15, Gettig 8, Wrigley 4, Carsey 3, Foster 1, Seymour 1, Puhl 1

OF   Van Haltren 151, O'Brien 127, Foster 84, Tiernan 35, Fleming 22, Woodruff 19, Seymour 8, Wilson 6, Grady 4, Gettig 1, Cregan 1, Colcolough 1

C   Warner 82, Grady 43, Wilson 31, Doyle 5, O'Neill 2

P   Carrick 44, Doheny 35, Seymour 32, Gettig 18, Meekin 18, Colcolough 11, Garoni 3, Fishel 1, Johnson 1, McPartlin 1, Sechrist 1

	G	IP	GS	CG	W	L	K	BB	SH	SV	ERA
Bill Carrick	44	361.2	**43**	**40**	16	27	60	122	3	0	4.65
Cy Seymour	32	268.1	32	31	14	18	142	**170**	0	0	3.56
Ed Doheny	35	265.1	33	30	14	17	115	156	1	0	4.51
Jouett Meekin	18	148.1	18	16	5	11	30	70	0	0	4.37
Charlie Gettig	18	128	15	12	7	8	25	54	0	0	4.43
Tom Colcolough	11	81.2	8	7	4	5	14	41	0	0	3.97
Willie Garoni	3	10	1	1	0	1	2	2	0	0	4.50
Leo Fishel	1	9	1	1	0	1	6	6	0	0	6.00
Frank McPartlin	1	4	0	0	0	0	2	3	0	0	4.50
Youngy Johnson	1	2	0	0	0	0	1	2	0	0	0.00
Doc Sechrist	1	0	0	0	0	0	0	2	0	0	—
		1278.1	151	138	60	88	**397**	628	4	0	4.29

—2 forfeit Ls: vs St. Louis on May 19; vs Brooklyn on June 16—

WASHINGTON	Arthur Irwin		Boundary Field										
		G	AB	H	R	2B	3B	HR	RBI	BB	SB	BA	SA
CF	Jimmy Slagle	147	599	163	92	15	8	0	41	55	22	.272	.324
RF	Buck Freeman	155	588	187	107	19	25	**25**	122	23	21	.318	.563
LF	Jack O'Brien	127	468	132	68	11	5	6	51	31	17	.282	.365
SS	Dick Padden	134	451	125	66	20	7	2	61	24	27	.277	.366
UT	Win Mercer	108	375	112	73	6	7	1	35	32	16	.299	.360
2B	Frank Bonner	85	347	95	41	20	4	2	44	18	6	.274	.372
1B	Dan McGann	76	280	96	65	9	8	5	58	14	11	.343	.486
Sub	Shad Barry	73	247	71	31	7	5	1	33	12	11	.287	.368
3B	Charlie Atherton	65	242	60	28	5	6	0	23	21	2	.248	.318
C	Deacon McGuire	59	199	54	25	3	1	1	12	16	3	.271	.312
Sub	Pete Cassidy	46	178	56	21	13	0	3	32	9	5	.315	.438
C	Mal Kittridge	44	133	20	14	3	0	0	11	10	2	.150	.173
P	Gus Weyhing	43	126	26	13	3	1	0	12	8	2	.206	.246
P	Bill Dinneen	37	119	36	9	2	0	0	4	8	0	.303	.319
Sub	General Stafford	31	118	29	11	5	1	1	14	5	4	.246	.331
Sub	Frank Scheibeck	27	94	27	19	4	1	0	9	11	5	.287	.351
P	Dan McFarlan	32	86	16	6	2	3	0	4	5	0	.186	.279
Sub	Mike Roach	24	78	17	7	1	0	0	7	3	3	.218	.231
Sub	Billy Hulen	19	68	10	10	1	0	0	3	10	5	.147	.162
Sub	Harry Davis	18	64	12	3	2	3	0	8	8	2	.188	.313
Sub	Jake Gettman	19	62	13	5	1	0	0	2	4	4	.210	.226
Sub	Jim Duncan	15	47	11	5	2	0	0	5	4	1	.234	.277
Sub	Mike Powers	14	38	10	3	2	0	0	3	1	0	.263	.316
Sub	Dick Butler	12	36	10	4	0	1	0	1	2	1	.278	.333
Sub	Doc Casey	9	34	4	3	2	0	0	2	2	1	.118	.176
Sub	Bill Coughlin	6	24	3	2	0	1	0	3	1	1	.125	.208
Sub	Frank McManus	7	21	8	3	1	0	0	2	2	3	.381	.429
P	Jack Fifield	7	20	4	0	1	0	0	2	2	0	.200	.250
P	Roy Evans	7	20	4	2	0	0	0	2	1	0	.200	.200
P	Kirtly Baker	12	19	3	1	0	0	0	1	1	0	.158	.158
P	Bill Magee	8	15	5	1	1	0	0	2	1	0	.333	.400
Sub	Duke Farrell	5	12	4	2	1	0	0	1	2	1	.333	.417
P	Davey Dunkle	4	11	3	0	0	0	0	2	0	0	.273	.273
P	Kid Carsey	4	11	0	1	0	0	0	0	0	0	.000	.000
Sub	George Decker	4	9	0	0	0	0	0	0	0	0	.000	.000
Sub	Arlie Latham	6	6	1	1	0	0	0	0	1	0	.167	.167
P	Frank Killen	2	5	1	0	0	0	0	1	0	0	.200	.200
Sub	Mike Heydon	2	3	0	0	0	0	0	0	2	0	.000	.000
P	Lefty Herring	2	1	1	1	0	0	0	0	0	0	1.000	1.000
P	Dorsey Riddlemoser	1	1	0	0	0	0	0	0	0	0	.000	.000
P	Bill Leith	1	1	0	0	0	0	0	0	0	0	.000	.000
		155	5256	1429	743	162	87	**47**	613	350	176	.272	.363

1B McGann 76, Cassidy 37, Barry 22, Davis 18, Roach 3, Decker 2, Gettman 2, Powers 1, McGuire 1, Mercer 1

2B Bonner 85, Padden 48, Stafford 17, Barry 7, Latham 1

SS Padden 85, Scheibeck 27, Hulen 19, Barry 13, Stafford 13, Cassidy 3, Mercer 1

3B Atherton 63, Mercer 62, Barry 13, Casey 9, Coughlin 6, Cassidy 6, O'Brien 4, Stafford 2, Fifield 1

OF Freeman 155, Slagle 146, O'Brien 121, Barry 23, Mercer 16, Gettman 16, Atherton 1, Latham 1, Dinneen 1, Decker 1

C McGuire 56, Kittridge 43, Roach 20, Duncan 14, Powers 12, Butler 11, McManus 7, Farrell 4, Heydon 2

P Weyhing 43, Dinneen 37, McFarlan 32, Mercer 23, Baker 11, Magee 8, Evans 7, Fifield 6, Dunkle 4, Carsey 4, Killen 2, Freeman 2, Herring 2, Leith 1, Riddlemoser 1

	G	IP	GS	CG	W	L	K	BB	SH	SV	ERA
Gus Weyhing	43	334.2	38	34	17	21	96	76	2	0	4.54
Bill Dinneen	37	291	35	30	14	20	91	106	0	0	3.93
Dan McFarlan	32	211.2	28	22	8	18	41	64	1	0	4.67
Win Mercer	23	186	21	21	7	14	28	53	0	0	4.60
Kirtley Baker	11	54	6	3	1	7	6	22	0	0	6.83
Roy Evans	7	54	7	6	3	4	27	25	0	0	5.67
Jack Fifield	6	47	6	6	2	4	12	17	0	0	6.13
Bill Magee	8	42	7	4	1	4	11	28	0	0	8.57
Kid Carsey	4	29	3	2	1	2	3	4	0	0	3.72
Davey Dunkle	4	26	2	2	0	2	9	14	0	0	10.04
Frank Killen	2	12	2	1	0	2	3	4	0	0	6.00
Buck Freeman	2	7	0	0	0	0	0	3	0	0	7.71
Lefty Herring	2	2	0	0	0	0	0	2	0	0	0.00
Dorsey Riddlemoser	1	2	0	0	0	0	0	2	0	0	18.00
Bill Leith	1	2	0	0	0	0	1	2	0	0	18.00
		1300.1	155	131	54	98	328	422	3	0	4.93

CLEVELAND   **Lave Cross (8–30)**   **Joe Quinn (12–104)**   **League Park (I)**

		G	AB	H	R	2B	3B	HR	RBI	BB	SB	BA	SA
2B	Joe Quinn	147	615	176	73	24	6	0	72	21	22	.286	.345
CF	Tommy Dowd	147	605	168	81	17	6	2	35	48	28	.278	.336
LF	Dick Harley	142	567	142	70	15	7	1	50	40	15	.250	.307
SS	Harry Lochhead	148	541	129	52	7	1	1	43	21	23	.238	.261
3B	Suter Sullivan	127	473	116	37	16	3	0	55	25	16	.245	.292
1B	Tommy Tucker	127	456	110	40	19	3	0	40	24	3	.241	.296
RF	Sport McAllister	113	418	99	29	6	8	1	31	19	5	.237	.297
C	Joe Sugden	76	250	69	19	5	1	0	14	11	2	.276	.304
Sub	Charlie Hemphill	55	202	56	23	3	5	2	23	6	3	.277	.371
3B	Lave Cross	38	154	44	15	5	0	1	20	8	2	.286	.338
Sub	Ossee Schreckengost	43	150	47	15	8	3	0	10	6	4	.313	.407
P	Jim Hughey	36	111	18	9	1	0	0	5	5	0	.162	.171
Sub	Jim Duncan	31	105	24	9	2	3	2	9	4	0	.229	.362
P	Charlie Knepper	27	89	12	6	2	1	0	2	4	0	.135	.180
P	Harry Colliflower	23	76	23	5	4	0	0	9	2	0	.303	.355
Sub	Chief Zimmer	20	73	25	9	2	1	2	14	5	1	.342	.479
P	Crazy Schmit	25	70	11	6	0	0	0	1	6	2	.157	.157
P	Frank Bates	21	65	14	5	1	0	0	3	7	0	.215	.231
Sub	Otto Krueger	13	44	10	4	1	0	0	2	8	1	.227	.250
P	Jack Stivetts	18	39	8	8	1	1	0	2	6	0	.205	.282
P	Kid Carsey	12	36	10	5	0	0	0	4	3	0	.278	.278
P	Bill Hill	11	31	4	2	0	0	0	0	1	0	.129	.129
P	Willie Sudhoff	11	31	2	1	0	1	0	6	4	0	.065	.129
Sub	Louis Sockalexis	7	22	6	0	1	0	0	3	1	0	.273	.318
Sub	Jack Clements	4	12	3	1	0	0	0	0	0	0	.250	.250
P	Jack Harper	5	11	2	2	0	0	0	1	4	0	.182	.182
P	Harry Maupin	5	10	0	0	0	0	0	0	0	0	.000	.000
Sub	Charlie Ziegler	2	8	2	2	0	0	0	0	0	0	.250	.250
Sub	George Bristow	3	8	1	0	1	0	0	0	0	0	.125	.250
P	Eddie Kolb	1	4	1	1	0	0	0	0	0	0	.250	.250
P	Highball Wilson	1	3	1	0	1	0	0	0	0	0	.333	.667
		154	5279	1333	529	142	50	12	454	289	127	.253	.305

1B   Tucker 127, Duncan 17, McAllister 6, Colliflower 4, Sullivan 3, Sugden 3, Schreckengost 1
2B   Quinn 147, Sullivan 2, Krueger 2, McAllister 1, Ziegler 1, Lochhead 1
SS   Lochhead 146, Sullivan 3, McAllister 3, Krueger 2, Stivetts 1, Carsey 1, Schreckengost 1, Ziegler 1
3B   Sullivan 101, Cross 38, Krueger 9, McAllister 7, Sugden 1, Stivetts 1

OF Dowd 147, Harley 142, McAllister 79, Hemphill 54, Sullivan 20, Stivetts 7, Schmit 6, Colliflower 6, Sockalexis 5, Sugden 4, Bristow 3, Bates 2, Schreckengost 1
C   Sugden 66, Schreckengost 39, Zimmer 20, McAllister 17, Duncan 14, Sugden 4, Clements 4
P   Hughey 36, Knepper 27, Schmit 20, Bates 20, Colliflower 14, Sudhoff 11, Hill 11, Carsey 10, Stivetts 7, Harper 5, Maupin 5, McAllister 3, Wilson 1, Kolb 1, Lochhead 1

	G	IP	GS	CG	W	L	K	BB	SH	SV	ERA
Jim Hughey	36	283	34	32	4	**30**	54	88	0	0	5.41
Charlie Knepper	27	219.2	26	26	4	22	43	77	0	0	5.78
Frank Bates	20	153	19	17	1	18	13	105	0	0	7.24
Crazy Schmit	20	138.1	19	16	2	17	24	62	0	0	5.86
Harry Colliflower	14	98	12	11	1	11	8	41	0	0	8.17
Willie Sudhoff	11	86.1	10	8	3	8	10	25	0	0	6.98
Kid Carsey	10	77.2	9	8	1	8	11	24	0	0	5.68
Bill Hill	11	72.1	10	7	3	6	26	39	0	0	6.97
Jack Stivetts	7	38	4	3	0	4	5	25	0	0	5.68
Jack Harper	5	37	5	5	1	4	14	12	0	0	3.89
Harry Maupin	5	25	3	2	0	3	3	7	0	0	12.60
Sport McAllister	3	16	1	1	0	1	2	10	0	0	9.56
Highball Wilson	1	8	1	1	0	1	1	5	0	0	9.00
Eddie Kolb	1	8	1	1	0	1	1	5	0	0	10.13
Harry Lochhead	1	3.2	0	0	0	0	0	2	0	0	0.00
		1264	154	138	20	134	215	527	0	0	6.37

1900

MCGINNITY WINS THE
CHRONICLE-TELEGRAPH CUP

After absorbing the American Association in December, 1891, the National League tottered along for eight years with 12 teams. The elimination of Cleveland, Baltimore, Washington and Louisville in March, 1900, streamlined the League to eight entries and created a stable composition that would endure until 1953. One of the very few rule changes legislated in 1900 streamlined the game itself. Home plate was altered from a 12-inch square to a 17-inch-wide five-sided shape. Although the new design did not actually widen home plate, it made an umpire's task in judging whether a pitch was a ball or a strike appreciably easier.

On the surface, redesigning home plate had little immediate impact on the game. The league batting average decreased only three points, and most pitchers actually recorded fewer strikeouts in 1900 than in 1899. But much of the reason that strikeout totals were lower was that the 140-game schedule was restored, and the reduction from 12 major league teams to eight produced a different result than the 1892 diminution that shrank the number of teams from 16 to 12. In 1900, with jobs scarce, weak-hitting catchers and middle infielders were the first to go. One such was 10-year veteran Mal Kittridge, a .176 hitter in 1899 who later returned to the majors for six more seasons but only after bolstering his résumé by catching 127 games and hitting .300 in 1900 for Worcester of the Eastern League.

The chief beneficiaries of the League's decision to trim its size were Brooklyn and Pittsburgh. Since both had been under "syndicate" ownership in 1899, Brooklyn fell heir to most of the remaining cast from the Baltimore Orioles' dynasty, and Barney Dreyfuss, who owned the controlling stock in both the Pittsburgh and Louisville franchises, simply transferred all of the defunct Kentucky club's top players to the Steel City. Among them were pitchers Deacon Phillippe, Jack Chesbro and Rube Waddell, manager-left fielder Fred Clarke, second baseman Claude Ritchey, utilityman Tommy Leach, catcher Chief Zimmer and the enormously talented Honus Wagner.

The 1900 Chicago Orphans. Still around from the salad days when the Chicagos were called the White Stockings and won pennants was Jimmy Ryan, but the team was otherwise in transition. The only faces here who would still be on the club three years later when it emerged from the doldrums to finish in the first division were Jack Taylor and, of course, Frank Chance. In numerical order: Cupid Childs, Charlie Dexter, Bert Cunningham, Taylor, Clark Griffith, Nixey Callahan, Jimmy Ryan, Danny Green, Jack McCarthy, Tim Donahue, Chance, Sam Mertes, Barry McCormick and Jack Doyle.

But Brooklyn's annexation of three Baltimore pitchers—Frank Kitson, Harry Howell and Joe McGinnity, the majors' top winner in 1899—spelled the difference in 1900. The trio joined with holdover Brickyard Kennedy to account for 70 of Brooklyn's 82 wins and lift manager Ned Hanlon's club to its second straight league pennant by a comfortable four and a half games over Pittsburgh. Philadelphia finished eight lengths back in third place, and Boston rounded out the first division despite slipping below .500 for the first time since 1886.

Even more disappointing than Frank Selee's Beaneaters were the St. Louis Cardinals, which had adopted a new nickname along with most of the Cleveland franchise's talent. Prior to the 1900 season the Cardinals also adopted three ex-Baltimore stars—John McGraw, Wilbert Robinson and Bill Keister—by shelling out $15,000 for their contracts when they refused to accompany the rest of the disbanding Orioles to Brooklyn. The trio, particularly McGraw, made for a natural rivalry with the ex-Orioles in Brooklyn, which was heightened by the fact that Brooklyn was the defending League champion. May 12, the date of Brooklyn's first appearance of the season in St. Louis, was marred by a transit-workers' strike that shut down the streetcar system in the Mound City, but some 7,500 nevertheless managed to reach the ballpark. Brooklyn won the opening game of the series behind McGinnity on a ninth-inning throwing error by McGraw and went on to take three out of four in St. Louis. The Cardinals retaliated by sweeping a Decoration Day doubleheader at Brooklyn but then began a slow downward spiral toward the second division. Meanwhile, once Hanlon's Superbas grabbed first place from Philadelphia by going 17-5 in June, they never relinquished it.

At the opposite end of the standings for most of the season was the other Gotham entry, the New York Giants. A miserable start under Buck Ewing's tutelage landed the Giants in

Ned Hanlon's fifth—and last—pennant winner, the 1900 Brooklyn Superbas. The team was re-nicknamed after a vaudeville act called Hanlon's Superbas. Hanlon's own act was soon to crash. American League raiders decimated Brooklyn so thoroughly that by 1905 Hanlon's team was the worst in the majors. In numerical order: Ebbetts, Hanlon, Dahlen, Kelley, Jennings, Yeager, Howell, Demontreville, Jones, McGuire, Kennedy, McGinnity, Farrell, Daly, Kitson, Keeler

Evidently the Robison brothers didn't believe the 1899 Cleveland Spiders pitching staff was as bad as the team's 20-134 record hinted. Three of the hurlers here, with the 1900 St. Louis Cardinals—Jack Harper, Charlie Knepper and Jim Hughey—came courtesy of the Spiders. Harper never won a game for St. Louis in 1900 and Knepper never even pitched in one, but Hughey bagged five wins and tossed eleven complete games to extend his career record for the most complete games without registering a shutout to 100. Top: Schrecken-gost, Jones, Young, Donovan, Knepper and Harper. Middle: Powell, Wallace, Heidrick, Burkett, Donlin, Tebeau, Buelow, Criger, McGann and Dillard. Front: O'Connor, Keister, Cuppy, Cross and Hughey.

WHERE DID THEY GO?

Here, by team, is a list of significant position players or pitchers in 100 or more innings who were active in the League-Association in 1899 and later returned to the majors after either being frozen out or choosing to play elsewhere when the lone major league reduced from twelve to eight teams in 1900.

	1899 TEAM	1900 LOCATION
John Anderson	Brooklyn	American League
Jim Hughes	Brooklyn	California League
Billy Lauder	Philadelphia	Out of baseball
Ducky Holmes	Baltimore	American League
Candy LaChance	Baltimore	American League
Dave Fultz	Baltimore	American League
Steve Brodie	Baltimore	American League
Kid Elberfeld	Cincinnati	American League
Tully Sparks	Pittsburgh	American League
Bill Hoffer	Pittsburgh	American League
George Magoon*	Chicago	American League
Dummy Hoy	Louisville	American League
Pete Dowling	Louisville	American League
Mike Powers	Louisville	American League
Fred Hartman	New York	American League
Dick Padden	Washington	American League
Frank Bonner	Washington	American League
Jack O'Brien	Washington	American League
Mal Kittridge**	Washington	Eastern League
Tommy Dowd	Cleveland	American League
Dick Harley	Cleveland	American League
Sport McAllister	Cleveland	American League
Joe Sugden	Cleveland	American League
Charlie Hemphill	Cleveland	American League
Ossee Schreckengost	Cleveland	American League

*Also with Baltimore in 1899
**Also with Louisville in 1899

the cellar by the end of May. After shortstop George Davis replaced Ewing, New York staged a furious late surge, but closing day found the Giants still a game and a half behind seventh-place Cincinnati. Despite the basement finish, the first in franchise history, New York's attendance increased by some 70,000, but the Cincinnati franchise, which suffered its poorest finish since 1891, dropped to last in the League in attendance.

Because the Louisville contingent needed time to blend with his Pittsburgh holdovers, Dreyfuss's club did not fully begin to gel until the season was nearly over. When the Pirates went 18-9 in September and finished second, it revived unhappy memories of the Temple Cup matches, in which Pittsburgh had never been a participant even though the Cup's founder had been a Pirates club official. Prodded that he ought to do the honorable thing and

WHO WAS THE 1900 STRIKEOUT KING?

TODAY			DECEMBER 31, 1900		
1.	Hahn, Cincinnati	132	1.	Hahn, Cincinnati	134
2.	Waddell, Pittsburgh	130		Waddell, Pittsburgh	134
3.	Young, St. Louis	115	3.	Young, St. Louis	119
4.	Garvin, Chicago	107	4.	Garvin, Chicago	108
	Dinneen, Boston	107	5.	Dinneen, Boston	106
6.	McGinnity, Brooklyn	93	6.	McGinnity, Brooklyn	90
7.	Newton, Cincinnati	88	7.	Newton, Cincinnati	87
8.	Scott, Cincinnati	87	8.	Leever, Pittsburgh	85
9.	Leever, Pittsburgh	84	9.	Scott, Cincinnati	83
10.	Hawley, New York	80	10.	Callahan, Chicago	77

Pitching strikeout totals were no less subject to error or misinformation than batting averages in the last century. Here are both today's 1900 National League strikeout leaders and the "official" leaders as of the final day of the nineteenth century.

Why this picture of the 1899 Indianapolis Hoosiers? Because the Western League club highlighted the only two noteworthy NL rookies in 1900 who were teammates. The cutback to eight major league teams made jobs for newcomers nonexistent—except in Cincinnati, where incoming pilot Bob Allen brought his twin pitching aces, Doc Newton and Ed Scott, with him from Indy. Top: Herm McFarland, Ace Stewart, George Flynn and George Hogriever. Middle: Newton, Frank Motz, Allen, Frank Foreman and Scott. Bottom: Eddie Hickey, Mike Heydon, Win Kellum and Topsy Hartsel, who also joined Allen on the Reds at the end of the 1900 season.

settle all lingering doubts that his team was really superior to Pittsburgh's, Hanlon accepted Dreyfuss's challenge to a best-of-five postseason match, with all the games to be played in Pittsburgh for a silver cup donated by the Pittsburgh *Chronicle-Telegraph*. The Temple Cup imitation opened on October 15 at the Pirates' Exposition Park. Behind McGinnity and Kitson, Hanlon's Superbas took the first two games but then were blanked 10-0 by Phillippe in the third contest.

The following day the Pirates drew McGinnity again, a disaster for them. While the rest of Hanlon's staff won just two of 12 decisions against the Pirates during the regular season, McGinnity beat Pittsburgh six times in seven tries, plus his opening game win in the Chronicle-Telegraph Cup series. On October 18, McGinnity made it eight of nine against the Pirates in 1900 when he breezed to a 6-1 triumph over Sam Leever. Yet McGinnity did not convince every skeptic that the best team had won in the regular League season, for there was a corps of baseball enthusiasts in Chicago who thought that Brooklyn should really have played their American League champion White Stockings in order to determine the nation's best team in 1900. The century would end, though, with those folks still in a very small minority.

"BERGEN'S CRIME"

After serving as Boston's regular catcher for nearly four years, Marty Bergen broke his hip during the 1899 season in a collision at home plate. It was doubtful that he would ever be able to play again. Accordingly, Beaneaters manager Frank Selee hurriedly began grooming rookie receiver Billy Sullivan and in the interim turned to Boileryard Clarke, who had been picked up from Baltimore for insurance.

Bergen's father came to visit his farm near North Brookfield, Massachusetts, one morning in January, 1900, and found that his son had murdered his wife and two young sons with an ax and then taken a razor to himself, slitting his throat. *Sporting Life* sought to run to earth "the underlying motive for the horrid deed," as did all the local Boston papers. One Hub journal was unkind enough to imply that Bergen's crime was due to his shabby treatment by the Beaneaters and assailed the club's statement that Bergen earned $2,400 in 1899 by writing:

> ". . . the proof that when the bodies of himself and wife and little children were found their cupboard was bare, and that all things pointed to the fact that just before the tragedy they were lacking the actual necessities of life. So while Bergen was . . . paid $2,400 . . . three fines of $500 each and those other little fines imposed on him . . . may have . . . placed himself and his family in the winter time on the verge of starvation. That they were found in the latter condition was proved at the Coroner's inquest, and that the player . . . was allowed to get in this condition by the men he had helped to make rich, is now a matter of history."

Ex-Boston player Tim Murnane, writing for a rival paper, took the Beaneaters' side. Murnane argued that Bergen had signed for $2,100 in 1899, plus a $300 bonus if he fulfilled his contract. Since his injury kept him from finishing the season he forfeited the bonus. In addition, Murnane acknowledged, Bergen was fined $50 by Selee in 1899, giving him a total of $2,050 for the season. Then Murnane contended:

> "Three years ago Bergen bought a small farm for something like $2,000, and lived there in the simplest kind of way, raising nearly

everything he used on his own table. There was no reason to believe that he was not leading a pleasant life. In fact, he had decided to give up base ball and take things easy on the farm. The Boston magnates did everything for him that they did for the other men, and, in fact, a great deal more, and are in no way to blame for any misfortune that overtook the player."

Murnane's argument was accepted in most circles and Bergen's crime, though never forgotten, was eventually judged to have been an aberrant act by a deeply disturbed man. Lots of players in the nineteenth century killed themselves because of unhappy love affairs, marital problems, despair, the death of a loved one, drinking too much—all the usual reasons. Apart from its more grisly and obviously more tragic elements, Bergen's decision to end it all seemed to fit the classic pattern. Yet there are several problems with Murnane's view.

Why were there no officials from the Boston club at Bergen's funeral? Had Bergen, only 28, really decided voluntarily to quit the game and what did he intend to do for the rest of his life if he had? And what of Boileryard Clarke's testimony about what it was like to play for Boston in those years? Upon coming to Boston from Baltimore in 1899, Clarke immediately noticed that along with being notoriously stingy, Beaneaters owner Arthur Soden was a remarkably cold fish. Clarke swore that even though he played with Boston for two full seasons Soden never knew he was on the team, let alone his name.

During the 1890s, when there was only one major league and his players were bound to him like chattels, Soden's cheerless mode of operation was masked by Frank Selee's genius as a manager. But after the American League formed as a rival major league, Soden swiftly began to lose most of his star players to aggressive owners from the other loop who were ready to pay them their worth. One of the first to jump to the upstart American League was Clarke. Soon he had been joined by virtually the whole Boston team. By the time the American League and the National League made their peace in 1903, every National League team had suf-

Arthur Soden (left) and Marty Bergen. Was Soden aware how deeply disturbed his star catcher was? Did Soden even know that Bergen was on the team?

fered heavy losses to the American League, but Boston suffered far and away the most. From the majors' best team in the 1890s, the Beaneaters descended so cataclysmically that they finished in the second division in 12 of the first 13 seasons in the twentieth century. Here is a list of where the 1900 Beaneaters regulars and key subs were by 1903:

	1900 POS	1903 LOCATION
Jimmy Collins	3B	Boston AL
Chick Stahl	LF	Boston AL
Buck Freeman	RF	Boston AL
Bill Dinneen	P	Boston AL
Boileryard Clarke	C	Washington AL
Billy Sullivan	C	Chicago AL
Herman Long	SS	New York/Detroit AL
Hugh Duffy	OF	Out of majors (last with Milwaukee AL, 1901)
Ted Lewis	P	Out of majors (last with Boston AL, 1901)
Shad Barry	Sub	Philadelphia NL
Bobby Lowe	2B	Chicago NL
Billy Hamilton	CF	Out of majors (last with Boston NL, 1901)
Kid Nichols	P	Out of majors (last with Boston NL, 1901)
Fred Tenney	1B	Boston NL
Vic Willis	P	Boston NL
Togie Pittenger	P	Boston NL
Frank Selee	Mgr	Chicago, NL

THE SEASONAL RECORD

	W	L	PCT	HOME	ROAD	GB
1. Brooklyn Superbas	82	54	.603	43–26	39–28	—
2. Pittsburgh Pirates	79	60	.568	42–28	37–32	4.5
3. Philadelphia Phillies	75	63	.543	45–23	30–40	8
4. Boston Beaneaters	66	72	.478	42–29	24–43	17
5. Chicago Orphans	65	75	.464	45–30	20–45	19
St. Louis Cardinals	65	75	.464	40–31	25–44	19
7. Cincinnati Reds	62	77	.446	27–34	35–43	21.5
8. New York Giants	60	78	.435	38–31	22–47	23

	Bro	Pit	Phi	Bos	Chi	StL	Cin	NY	
Brooklyn	—	8	10	16	10	13	15	10	82
Pittsburgh	11	—	11	15	12	11	8	11	79
Philadelphia	8	9	—	11	11	12	11	13	75
Boston	4	5	9	—	12	12	13	11	66
Chicago	10	8	9	8	—	9	9	12	65
St. Louis	7	9	8	8	11	—	8	14	65
Cincinnati	4	12	9	7	11	12	—	7	62
New York	10	9	7	7	8	6	13	—	60
	54	60	63	72	75	75	77	78	564

SEASON LEADERS

Batting Average (350 ABs)

1.	Wagner, Pittsburgh	.381
2.	Flick, Philadelphia	.367
3.	Burkett, St. Louis	.363
4.	Keeler, Brooklyn	.362
5.	Beckley, Cincinnati	.341

On–Base Percentage

1.	McGraw, St. Louis	.505*
2.	Thomas, Philadelphia	.451
3.	Hamilton, Boston	.449
4.	Flick, Philadelphia	.441
5.	Wagner, Pittsburgh	.434

* 334 ABs but nearly 450 plate appearances

Home Runs

1.	Long, Boston	12
2.	Flick, Philadelphia	11
3.	Donlin, St. Louis	10
4.	Hickman, New York	9
5.	Sullivan, Boston	8

Hits

1.	Keeler, Brooklyn	204
2.	Burkett, St. Louis	203
3.	Wagner, Pittsburgh	201
4.	Flick, Philadelphia	200
5.	Beckley, Cincinnati	190

Stolen Bases

1.	Van Haltren, New York	45
	Donovan, St. Louis	45
3.	Barrett, Cincinnati	44
4.	Keeler, Brooklyn	41
5.	Wagner, Pittsburgh	38
	Mertes, Chicago	38

Slugging Average

1.	Wagner, Pittsburgh	.573
2.	Flick, Philadelphia	.545
3.	Lajoie, Philadelphia	.510
4.	Kelley, Brooklyn	.485
5.	Hickman, New York	.482

Total Bases

1.	Wagner, Pittsburgh	302
2.	Flick, Philadelphia	297
3.	Burkett, St. Louis	265
4.	Keeler, Brooklyn	253
5.	Beckley, Cincinnati	242

RBI

1.	Flick, Philadelphia	110
2.	Delahanty, Philadelphia	109
3.	Wagner, Pittsburgh	100
4.	Collins, Boston	95
5.	Beckley, Cincinnati	94

Runs

1.	Thomas, Philadelphia	132
2.	Slagle, Philadelphia	115
3.	Van Haltren, New York	114
	Barrett, Cincinnati	114
5.	Wagner, Pittsburgh	107

PITCHING

Wins

1.	McGinnity, Brooklyn	28
2.	Tannehill, Pittsburgh	20
	Dinneen, Boston	20
	Phillippe, Pittsburgh	20
	Kennedy, Brooklyn	20

Innings

1.	McGinnity, Brooklyn	343
2.	Carrick, New York	341.2
3.	Hawley, New York	329.1
4.	Young, St. Louis	321.1
5.	Dinneen, Boston	320.2

Strikeouts

1.	Hahn, Cincinnati	132
2.	Waddell, Pittsburgh	130
3.	Young, St. Louis	115
4.	Garvin, Chicago	107
	Dinneen, Boston	107

ERA (140 innings)

1.	Waddell, Pittsburgh	2.37
2.	Garvin, Chicago	2.41
3.	Taylor, Chicago	2.55
4.	Leever, Pittsburgh	2.71
5.	Phillippe, Pittsburgh	2.84

Losses

1.	Carrick, New York	22
2.	Scott, Cincinnati	20
	Hahn, Cincinnati	20
4.	Young, St. Louis	19
	C. Jones, St. Louis	19

Complete Games

1.	Hawley, New York	34
2.	Dinneen, Boston	33
3.	McGinnity, Brooklyn	32
	Callahan, Chicago	32
	Young, St. Louis	32
	Carrick, New York	32

Winning Percentage (25 decisions)

1.	McGinnity, Brooklyn	.778
2.	Tannehill, Pittsburgh	.769
3.	Fraser, Philadelphia	.625
4.	Phillippe, Pittsburgh	.606
	Kennedy, Brooklyn	.606

Lowest On-Base Percentage

1.	Phillippe, Pittsburgh	.289
2.	Waddell, Pittsburgh	.291
	Young, St. Louis	.291
4.	Garvin, Chicago	.304
5.	Leever, Pittsburgh	.306
	Griffith, Chicago	.306

FIELDING

Total Chances

1B	Beckley, Cincinnati	1512
2B	Childs, Chicago	806
3B	Collins, Boston	620
SS	Dahlen, Brooklyn	893
OF	Burkett, St. Louis	379
C	Zimmer, Pittsburgh	435
P	Scott, Cincinnati	155

Fielding Average

McGann, St. Louis	.990
Lajoie, Philadelphia	.954
L. Cross, StL–Brook	.945
Davis, New York	.944
Stahl, Boston	.968
McFarland, Philadelphia	.963
Nichols, Boston	.985

BROOKLYN   Ned Hanlon   **Washington Park (II)**

		G	AB	H	R	2B	3B	HR	RBI	BB	SB	BA	SA
RF	Willie Keeler	136	563	**204**	106	13	12	4	68	30	41	.362	.449
CF	Fielder Jones	136	552	171	106	26	4	4	54	57	33	.310	.393
SS	Bill Dahlen	133	483	125	87	16	11	1	69	73	31	.259	.344
3B	Lave Cross	117	461	135	73	14	6	4	67	25	20	.293	.375
LF	Joe Kelley	121	454	145	90	23	17	6	91	53	26	.319	.485
1B	Hughie Jennings	112	441	120	61	18	6	1	69	31	31	.272	.347
2B	Tom Daly	97	343	107	72	17	3	4	55	46	27	.312	.414
Sub	Jimmy Sheckard	85	273	82	74	19	10	1	39	42	30	.300	.454
C	Duke Farrell	74	273	75	33	11	5	0	39	11	3	.275	.352
C	Deacon McGuire	69	241	69	20	15	2	0	34	19	2	.286	.365
Sub	Gene Demontreville	69	234	57	34	8	1	0	28	10	21	.244	.286
P	Joe McGinnity	46	145	28	18	4	1	0	16	1	4	.193	.234
P	Brickyard Kennedy	42	123	37	10	8	2	0	15	5	0	.301	.398
P	Frank Kitson	40	109	32	20	5	1	0	16	6	2	.294	.358
P	Harry Howell	22	42	12	6	2	0	1	6	6	1	.286	.405
P	Jack Dunn	10	26	6	2	0	0	0	1	1	0	.231	.231
Sub	Aleck Smith	6	25	6	2	0	0	0	3	1	2	.240	.240
P	Jerry Nops	9	25	4	0	0	0	0	1	3	0	.160	.160
P	Gus Weyhing	8	18	4	2	0	0	0	2	1	0	.222	.222
P	Bill Donovan	5	13	0	0	0	0	0	2	0	0	.000	.000
P	Joe Yeager	3	9	3	0	0	0	0	0	0	0	.333	.333
Sub	Farmer Steelman	1	4	0	0	0	0	0	0	0	0	.000	.000
Sub	Doc Casey	1	3	1	0	0	0	0	1	0	0	.333	.333
		142	4860	1423	**816**	199	81	26	676	421	**274**	**.293**	**.383**

1B   Jennings 112, Kelley 32, Daly 3, Demontreville 1
2B   Daly 93, Demontreville 48, Jennings 2, Keeler 1
SS   Dahlen 133, Demontreville 12
3B   Cross 117, Kelley 13, Demontreville 7, Smith 6, Casey 1, Yeager 1
OF   Keeler 136, Jones 136, Sheckard 78, Kelley 77, Daly 2, McGinnity 1, Kitson 1, Demontreville 1
C   Farrell 74, McGuire 69, Steelman 1, Smith 1
P   McGinnity 44, Kennedy 42, Kitson 40, Howell 21, Dunn 10, Nops 9, Weyhing 8, Donovan 5, Yeager 2

	G	IP	GS	CG	W	L	K	BB	SH	SV	ERA
Joe McGinnity	44	**343**	37	32	**28**	8	93	**113**	1	0	2.94
Brickyard Kennedy	42	292	35	26	20	13	75	111	2	0	3.91
Frank Kitson	40	253.1	30	31	15	13	55	56	2	**4**	4.19
Harry Howell	21	110.1	10	7	6	5	26	36	2	0	3.75
Jerry Nops	9	68	8	6	4	4	22	18	1	0	3.84
Jack Dunn	10	63	7	5	3	4	6	28	0	0	5.57
Gus Weyhing	8	48	8	3	3	4	8	20	0	0	4.31
Bill Donovan	5	31	4	2	1	2	13	18	0	0	6.68
Joe Yeager	2	17	2	2	1	1	2	5	0	0	6.88
—1 forfeit W vs St. Louis on September 19—											
		1225.2	141	104	81	54	300	405	8	**4**	3.89

PITTSBURGH   Fred Clarke   Exposition Park

		G	AB	H	R	2B	3B	HR	RBI	BB	SB	BA	SA
CF	Ginger Beaumont	138	567	158	105	14	9	5	50	40	27	.279	.362
RF	Honus Wagner	135	527	201	107	**45**	**22**	4	100	41	38	**.381**	**.573**
2B	Claude Ritchey	123	476	139	62	17	8	1	67	29	18	.292	.368
SS	Bones Ely	130	475	116	60	6	6	0	51	17	6	.244	.282
3B	Jimmy Williams	106	416	110	73	15	11	5	68	32	18	.264	.389
LF	Fred Clarke	104	399	110	84	15	12	3	32	51	21	.276	.396
UT	Tom O'Brien	102	376	109	61	22	6	3	61	21	12	.290	.404
C	Chief Zimmer	78	271	80	27	7	10	0	35	17	4	.295	.395
1B	Duff Cooley	66	249	50	30	8	1	0	22	14	9	.201	.241
Sub	Tommy Leach	51	160	34	20	1	2	1	16	21	8	.213	.263
C	Jack O'Connor	40	147	35	15	4	1	0	19	3	5	.238	.279
Sub	Tom McCreery	43	132	29	20	4	3	1	13	16	2	.220	.318
P	Jesse Tannehill	29	110	37	19	7	0	0	17	5	2	.336	.400
P	Deacon Phillippe	38	105	19	7	3	1	0	7	1	0	.181	.229
Sub	Pop Schriver	37	92	27	12	7	0	1	12	10	0	.293	.402
P	Sam Leever	30	88	18	9	2	2	1	5	2	1	.205	.307
P	Jack Chesbro	32	85	15	10	4	1	0	9	6	1	.176	.247
P	Rube Waddell	30	81	14	6	2	3	0	9	0	1	.173	.272
Sub	Pop Dillon	5	18	2	3	1	0	0	1	0	0	.111	.167
Sub	Tacks Latimer	4	12	4	1	1	0	0	2	0	0	.333	.417
Sub	Jiggs Donahue	2	10	2	1	0	1	0	3	0	1	.200	.400
P	Patsy Flaherty	4	9	1	0	0	0	0	0	1	0	.111	.111
P	Ed Poole	2	4	2	1	0	1	1	3	0	0	.500	1.750
P	Jouett Meekin	2	4	0	0	0	0	0	0	0	0	.000	.000
P	Bert Husting	2	3	0	0	0	0	0	0	0	0	.000	.000
P	Walt Woods	1	1	0	0	0	0	0	0	0	0	.000	.000
		140	4817	1312	733	185	**100**	26	602	327	174	.272	.368

1B   Cooley 66, O'Brien 65, Dillon 5, Wagner 3, Zimmer 2, O'Connor 2, Schriver 1
2B   Ritchey 123, Leach 7, Wagner 7, O'Brien 4
SS   Ely 130, Leach 8, Williams 4, O'Brien 2
3B   Williams 103, Leach 31, Wagner 9
OF   Beaumont 138, Wagner 118, Clarke 104, McCreery 35, O'Brien 25, Leach 4, Tannehill 4, Chesbro 1, Donahue 1, Poole 1
C   Zimmer 78, O'Connor 40, Schriver 24, Latimer 4, Donahue 2
P   Phillippe 38, Chesbro 32, Leever 30, Waddell 29, Tannehill 29, Flaherty 4, Husting 2, Meekin 2, Woods 1, Poole 1, Wagner 1, McCreery 1

	G	IP	GS	CG	W	L	K	BB	SH	SV	ERA
Deacon Phillippe	38	279	33	29	20	13	75	42	1	0	2.84
Jesse Tannehill	29	234	27	23	20	6	50	43	2	0	2.88
Sam Leever	30	232.2	29	25	15	13	84	48	3	0	2.71
Jack Chesbro	32	215.2	26	20	15	13	56	79	3	1	3.67
Rube Waddell	29	208.2	22	16	8	13	130	55	2	0	**2.37**
Patsy Flaherty	4	22	1	0	0	0	5	9	0	0	6.14
Jouett Meekin	2	13	2	1	0	2	3	8	0	0	6.92
Bert Husting	2	8	0	0	0	0	7	5	0	0	5.63
Ed Poole	1	7	0	0	1	0	3	0	0	0	1.29
Honus Wagner	1	3	0	0	0	0	1	4	0	0	0.00
Tom McCreery	1	3	0	0	0	0	0	1	0	0	12.00
Walt Woods	1	3	0	0	0	0	1	1	0	0	21.00
		1229	140	114	79	60	**415**	295	11	1	**3.06**

PHILADELPHIA   **Bill Shettsline**   **Philadelphia Baseball Grounds (II)**

		G	AB	H	R	2B	3B	HR	RBI	BB	SB	BA	SA
LF	Jimmy Slagle	141	574	165	115	16	9	0	45	60	34	.287	.347
RF	Elmer Flick	138	545	200	106	32	16	11	**110**	56	35	.367	.545
1B	Ed Delahanty	130	539	174	82	32	10	2	109	41	16	.323	.430
CF	Roy Thomas	140	531	168	**132**	4	3	0	33	115	37	.316	.335
SS	Monte Cross	131	466	94	59	11	3	3	62	51	19	.202	.258
2B	Nap Lajoie	102	451	152	95	33	12	7	92	10	22	.337	.510
3B	Harry Wolverton	101	383	108	42	10	8	3	58	20	4	.282	.373
C	Ed McFarland	94	344	105	50	14	8	0	38	29	9	.305	.392
Sub	Joe Dolan	74	257	51	39	7	3	1	27	16	10	.198	.261
Sub	Klondike Douglass	50	160	48	23	9	4	0	25	13	7	.300	.406
P	Al Orth	33	129	40	6	4	1	1	21	2	2	.310	.380
Sub	Pearce Chiles	33	111	24	13	6	2	1	23	6	4	.216	.333
P	Bill Bernhard	32	91	14	7	1	0	0	6	3	0	.154	.165
P	Red Donahue	32	90	20	9	0	0	0	12	3	1	.222	.222
P	Chick Fraser	29	85	22	8	4	1	0	10	5	2	.259	.329
P	Wiley Piatt	22	68	17	8	0	1	0	7	4	1	.250	.279
Sub	Morg Murphy	11	36	10	2	0	1	0	3	0	0	.278	.333
P	Jack Dunn	10	33	10	3	1	0	0	5	0	1	.303	.333
Sub	Bert Myers	7	28	5	5	1	0	0	2	3	1	.179	.214
P	Al Maul	5	15	3	2	0	0	0	1	2	0	.200	.200
Sub	Charlie Ziegler	3	11	3	0	0	0	0	1	0	0	.273	.273
Sub	Fred Jacklitsch	5	11	2	0	1	0	0	3	0	0	.182	.273
P	Bert Conn	6	9	3	4	1	0	0	1	0	0	.333	.444
P	Warren McLaughlin	1	2	1	0	0	0	0	0	1	0	.500	.500
		141	4969	**1439**	810	187	82	29	**694**	**440**	205	.290	.378

1B   Delahanty 130, Chiles 16
2B   Lajoie 102, Dolan 29, Chiles 12
SS   Cross 131, Dolan 12
3B   Wolverton 101, Dolan 31, Myers 7, Ziegler 3, Douglass 2, Lajoie 1, McFarland 1
OF   Slagle 141, Thomas 139, Flick 138, Chiles 3, Orth 3
C   McFarland 93, Douglass 47, Murphy 11, Jacklitsch 3
P   Orth 33, Bernhard 32, Donahue 32, Fraser 29, Piatt 22, Dunn 10, Maul 5, Conn 4, McLaughlin 1, Thomas 1

	G	IP	GS	CG	W	L	K	BB	SH	SV	ERA
Al Orth	33	262	30	24	14	14	68	60	2	1	3.78
Red Donahue	32	240	24	21	15	10	41	50	2	0	3.60
Chick Fraser	29	223.1	33	29	15	9	58	93	1	0	3.14
Bill Bernhard	32	218.2	27	20	15	10	49	74	0	2	4.77
Wiley Piatt	22	160.2	20	16	9	10	47	71	1	0	4.71
Jack Dunn	10	80	9	9	5	5	12	29	1	0	4.84
Al Maul	5	38	4	3	2	3	6	3	0	0	6.16
Bert Conn	4	17.1	1	1	0	2	2	16	0	0	8.31
Warren McLaughlin	1	6	0	0	0	0	1	6	0	0	4.50
Roy Thomas	1	2.2	0	0	0	0	0	0	0	0	3.38
		1248.2	140	116	75	63	284	402	7	3	4.13

BOSTON   **Frank Selee**   **South End Grounds (II)**

		G	AB	H	R	2B	3B	HR	RBI	BB	SB	BA	SA
3B	Jimmy Collins	141	**586**	178	104	25	5	6	95	34	23	.304	.394
LF	Chick Stahl	135	553	163	88	23	16	5	82	34	27	.295	.421
CF	Billy Hamilton	136	520	173	102	20	5	1	47	107	32	.333	.396
SS	Herman Long	125	486	127	80	19	4	**12**	66	44	26	.261	.391
2B	Bobby Lowe	127	474	132	65	11	5	3	71	26	15	.278	.342
1B	Fred Tenney	111	437	122	77	13	5	1	56	39	17	.279	.339
RF	Buck Freeman	117	418	126	58	19	13	6	65	25	10	.301	.452
C	Boileryard Clarke	81	270	85	35	5	2	1	30	9	0	.315	.359
Sub	Shad Barry	81	254	66	40	10	7	1	37	13	9	.260	.366
C	Billy Sullivan	72	238	65	36	6	0	8	41	9	4	.273	.399
Sub	Hugh Duffy	55	181	55	28	5	4	2	31	16	11	.304	.409
P	Bill Dinneen	44	125	35	14	1	0	0	9	9	6	.280	.288
P	Kid Nichols	29	90	18	14	0	0	1	7	7	1	.200	.233
P	Vic Willis	32	88	12	8	2	1	0	11	3	0	.136	.182
P	Ted Lewis	30	73	10	10	0	0	0	5	11	0	.137	.137
P	Togie Pittinger	18	46	6	2	0	0	0	2	0	0	.130	.130
Sub	Jack Clements	16	42	13	6	1	0	1	10	3	0	.310	.405
P	Nig Cuppy	17	42	11	7	3	0	0	6	4	0	.262	.333
Sub	Joe Connor	7	19	4	2	0	0	0	4	2	1	.211	.211
P	Harvey Bailey	4	9	2	2	0	1	0	1	0	0	.222	.444
P	Rome Chambers	1	1	0	0	0	0	0	0	0	0	.000	.000
		142	4952	1403	778	163	68	**48**	676	395	182	.283	.373

1B	Tenney 111, Freeman 19, Barry 10, Clarke 8
2B	Lowe 127, Barry 16, Sullivan 1, Duffy 1
SS	Long 125, Barry 18, Sullivan 1, Collins 1
3B	Collins 141, Barry 1
OF	Hamilton 136, Stahl 135, Freeman 91, Duffy 49, Barry 24
C	Clarke 67, Sullivan 66, Clements 10, Connor 7
P	Dinneen 40, Willis 32, Lewis 30, Nichols 29, Pittinger 18, Cuppy 17, Bailey 4, Chambers 1

	G	IP	GS	CG	W	L	K	BB	SH	SV	ERA
Bill Dinneen	40	320.2	37	33	20	14	107	105	1	0	3.12
Vic Willis	32	236	29	22	10	17	53	106	2	0	4.19
Kid Nichols	29	231.1	27	25	13	16	53	72	**4**	0	3.07
Ted Lewis	30	209	22	19	13	12	66	86	1	0	4.13
Togie Pittinger	18	114	13	8	2	9	27	54	0	0	5.13
Nig Cuppy	17	105.1	13	9	8	4	23	24	0	1	3.08
Harvey Bailey	4	20	1	0	0	0	9	11	0	0	4.95
Rome Chambers	1	4	0	0	0	0	2	5	0	1	11.25
		1240.1	142	116	66	72	340	463	8	2	3.72

CHICAGO Tom Loftus West Side Park (II)

		G	AB	H	R	2B	3B	HR	RBI	BB	SB	BA	SA
2B	Cupid Childs	137	531	128	67	14	5	0	44	57	15	.241	.286
LF	Jack McCarthy	123	503	148	68	16	7	0	48	24	22	.294	.354
UT	Sam Mertes	127	481	142	72	25	4	7	60	42	38	.295	.407
3B	Bill Bradley	122	444	125	63	21	8	5	49	27	14	.282	.399
RF	Jimmy Ryan	105	415	115	66	25	4	5	59	29	19	.277	.393
CF	Danny Green	103	389	116	63	21	5	5	49	17	28	.298	.416
SS	Barry McCormick	109	379	83	35	13	5	3	48	38	8	.219	.303
1B	John Ganzel	78	284	78	29	14	4	4	32	10	5	.275	.394
C	Tim Donahue	67	216	51	21	10	1	0	17	19	8	.236	.292
SS	Billy Clingman	47	159	33	15	6	0	0	11	17	6	.208	.245
C	Frank Chance	56	149	44	26	9	3	0	13	15	8	.295	.396
Sub	Charlie Dexter	40	125	25	7	5	0	2	20	1	2	.200	.288
P	Nixey Callahan	32	115	27	16	3	2	0	9	6	5	.235	.296
Sub	Sammy Strang	27	102	29	15	3	0	0	9	8	1	.284	.314
P	Clark Griffith	30	95	24	16	4	1	1	7	8	2	.253	.347
Sub	Bill Everett	23	91	24	10	4	0	0	17	3	2	.264	.308
P	Ned Garvin	30	91	14	12	1	0	0	4	3	0	.154	.165
P	Jack Taylor	28	81	19	7	3	1	1	6	3	1	.235	.333
Sub	Johnny Kling	15	51	15	8	3	1	0	7	2	0	.294	.392
Sub	Cozy Dolan	13	48	13	5	1	0	0	2	2	2	.271	.292
P	Jock Menefee	17	46	5	5	0	0	0	4	2	0	.109	.109
P	Bert Cunningham	8	27	4	5	1	0	0	1	1	1	.148	.185
Sub	Art Nichols	8	25	5	1	0	0	0	0	3	1	.200	.200
P	Frank Killen	6	20	3	0	0	0	0	2	1	0	.150	.150
Sub	Sam Dungan	6	15	4	1	0	0	0	1	1	0	.267	.267
Sub	Harry Wolverton	3	11	2	2	0	0	0	0	2	1	.182	.182
P	Tom Hughes	3	6	0	0	0	0	0	0	2	0	.000	.000
P	Mal Eason	1	3	0	0	0	0	0	0	0	0	.000	.000
P	Erwin Harvey	2	3	0	0	0	0	0	0	0	0	.000	.000
Sub	Roger Bresnahan	2	2	0	0	0	0	0	0	0	0	.000	.000
		146	4907	1276	635	**202**	51	33	519	343	189	.260	.342

1B	Ganzel 78, Mertes 33, Everett 23, Bradley 15, Chance 1
2B	Childs 137, McCormick 5, Strang 2, Dexter 1, Donahue 1
SS	McCormick 84, Clingman 47, Strang 9, Mertes 7
3B	Bradley 106, McCormick 21, Strang 16, Wolverton 3
OF	McCarthy 123, Ryan 105, Green 101, Mertes 88, Dexter 13, Dolan 13, Dungan 3
C	Donahue 66, Chance 51, Dexter 22, Kling 15, Nichols 7, Bresnahan 1
P	Callahan 32, Griffith 30, Garvin 30, Taylor 28, Menefee 16, Cunningham 8, Killen 6, Hughes 3, Eason 1, Harvey 1

	G	IP	GS	CG	W	L	K	BB	SH	SV	ERA
Nixey Callahan	32	285.1	32	32	13	16	77	74	2	0	3.82
Clark Griffith	30	248	30	27	14	13	61	51	**4**	0	3.05
Ned Garvin	30	246.1	28	25	10	18	107	63	1	0	2.41
Jack Taylor	28	222.1	26	25	10	17	57	58	2	1	2.55
Jock Menefee	16	117	13	11	9	4	30	35	0	0	3.85
Bert Cunningham	8	64	7	7	4	3	7	21	0	0	4.36
Frank Killen	6	54	6	6	3	3	4	11	0	0	4.67
Tom Hughes	3	21	3	3	1	1	12	7	0	0	5.14
Mal Eason	1	9	1	1	1	0	2	3	0	0	1.00
Erwin Harvey	1	4	0	0	0	0	0	1	0	0	0.00
		1271	146	**137**	65	75	357	324	9	1	3.23

ST. LOUIS   Patsy Tebeau (42–50)   Louie Heilbroner (23–25)   League Park

		G	AB	H	R	2B	3B	HR	RBI	BB	SB	BA	SA
LF	Jesse Burkett	141	559	203	88	11	15	7	68	62	32	.363	.474
RF	Patsy Donovan	124	503	159	78	11	1	0	61	38	**45**	.316	.342
2B	Bill Keister	126	497	149	78	26	10	1	72	25	32	.300	.398
SS	Bobby Wallace	126	485	130	70	25	9	4	70	40	7	.268	.381
1B	Dan McGann	121	444	132	79	10	9	4	58	32	26	.297	.387
CF	Emmett Heidrick	85	339	102	51	6	8	2	45	18	22	.301	.383
3B	John McGraw	99	334	115	84	10	4	2	33	85	29	.344	.416
C	Lou Criger	80	288	78	31	8	6	2	38	4	5	.271	.361
Sub	Mike Donlin	78	276	90	40	8	6	10	48	14	14	.326	.507
C	Wilbert Robinson	60	210	52	26	5	1	0	28	11	7	.248	.281
Sub	Pat Dillard	57	183	42	24	5	2	0	12	13	7	.230	.279
P	Cy Young	41	124	22	13	5	1	1	13	3	1	.177	.258
P	Cowboy Jones	39	117	21	12	0	2	0	7	7	0	.179	.214
P	Jack Powell	38	109	31	15	4	4	1	12	10	3	.284	.422
P	Willie Sudhoff	35	106	20	15	1	1	0	6	11	8	.189	.217
Sub	Joe Quinn	22	80	21	12	2	0	1	11	10	4	.263	.325
Sub	Lave Cross	16	61	18	6	1	0	0	6	1	1	.295	.311
P	Jim Hughey	20	41	7	6	0	0	0	2	8	0	.171	.171
Sub	Otto Krueger	12	35	14	8	3	2	1	3	10	0	.400	.686
Sub	Jack O'Connor	10	32	7	4	0	0	0	6	2	0	.219	.219
P	Gus Weyhing	7	21	2	1	0	0	0	0	0	0	.095	.095
Sub	Fritz Buelow	6	17	4	2	0	0	0	3	0	0	.235	.235
P	Tom Thomas	5	11	1	1	0	0	0	0	2	0	.091	.091
Sub	Patsy Tebeau	1	4	0	0	0	0	0	0	0	0	.000	.000
P	Jack Harper	1	1	0	0	0	0	0	0	0	0	.000	.000
Sub	Harry Stanton	1	0	0	0	0	0	0	0	0	0	—	—
		142	4877	1420	744	141	81	36	602	406	243	.291	.375

1B	McGann 121, Donlin 21
2B	Keister 116, Quinn 14, Krueger 12, McGann 1
SS	Wallace 126, Keister 7, Quinn 6, Dillard 3, Tebeau 1
3B	McGraw 99, Dillard 21, Cross 16, Sudhoff 7, Keister 3, Quinn 1, Wallace 1, Criger 1
OF	Burkett 141, Donovan 124, Heidrick 83, Donlin 47, Dillard 26, Sudhoff 12, Buelow 1
C	Criger 75, Robinson 54, O'Connor 10, Buelow 4, Stanton 1
P	Young 41, Jones 39, Powell 38, Hughey 20, Sudhoff 16, Weyhing 7, Thomas 5, Harper 1

	G	IP	GS	CG	W	L	K	BB	SH	SV	ERA
Cy Young	41	321.1	35	32	19	19	115	36	**4**	0	3.00
Cowboy Jones	39	292.2	36	29	13	19	68	82	3	0	3.57
Jack Powell	38	287.2	37	28	17	16	77	77	3	0	4.44
Willie Sudhoff	16	127	14	13	6	8	29	37	2	0	2.76
Jim Hughey	20	112.2	12	11	5	7	23	40	0	0	5.19
Gus Weyhing	7	46.2	5	3	3	2	6	21	0	0	4.63
Tom Thomas	5	26.1	1	1	2	2	7	4	0	0	3.76
Jack Harper	1	3	1	0	0	1	0	2	0	0	12.00
		—1 forfeit L vs Brooklyn on September 19—									
		1217.1	141	117	65	74	325	299	**12**	0	3.76

CINCINNATI **Bob Allen** **League Park (II)***

		G	AB	H	R	2B	3B	HR	RBI	BB	SB	BA	SA
1B	Jake Beckley	141	558	190	98	26	10	2	94	40	23	.341	.434
CF	Jimmy Barrett	137	545	172	114	11	7	5	42	72	44	.316	.389
SS	Tommy Corcoran	127	523	128	64	21	9	1	54	22	27	.245	.325
3B	Harry Steinfeldt	136	510	125	57	29	7	2	66	27	14	.245	.341
RF	Algie McBride	112	436	120	59	15	8	4	59	25	12	.275	.374
LF	Sam Crawford	101	389	101	68	15	15	7	59	28	14	.260	.429
Sub	Charlie Irwin	87	333	91	59	15	6	1	44	14	9	.273	.363
C	Heinie Peitz	93	294	75	34	14	1	2	34	20	5	.255	.330
2B	Joe Quinn	74	266	73	18	5	2	0	25	16	7	.274	.308
C	Mike Kahoe	52	175	33	18	3	3	1	9	4	3	.189	.257
Sub	Bob Wood	45	139	37	17	8	1	0	22	10	3	.266	.338
P	Ted Breitenstein	41	126	24	12	1	1	2	12	9	0	.190	.262
P	Ed Scott	43	123	19	9	3	2	1	11	1	0	.154	.236
P	Noodles Hahn	38	115	24	12	3	1	2	9	2	0	.209	.304
Sub	Phil Geier	30	113	29	18	1	4	0	10	7	3	.257	.336
Sub	Elmer Smith	29	111	31	14	4	4	1	18	18	5	.279	.414
P	Doc Newton	35	86	17	11	0	1	0	7	6	2	.198	.221
P	Bill Phillips	29	79	13	8	0	0	0	3	3	1	.165	.165
Sub	Topsy Hartsel	18	64	21	10	2	1	2	5	8	7	.328	.484
Sub	Dick Harley	5	21	9	2	1	0	0	5	1	4	.429	.476
Sub	Bob Allen	5	15	2	0	1	0	0	1	0	0	.133	.200
P	Archie Stimmel	2	5	1	1	0	0	0	2	0	0	.200	.200
		144	5026	1335	703	178	83	33	591	333	183	.266	.354

1B Beckley 140, Peitz 8
2B Quinn 74, Steinfeldt 64, Corcoran 5, Irwin 3
SS Corcoran 124, Irwin 16, Allen 5, Steinfeldt 2, Kahoe 1
3B Steinfeldt 67, Irwin 61, Wood 15, Geier 2
OF Barrett 137, McBride 109, Crawford 94, Smith 27, Geier 27, Hartsel 18, Breitenstein 12, Irwin 6, Harley 5, Steinfeldt 2, Wood 1
C Peitz 80, Kahoe 51, Wood 18
P Scott 43, Hahn 38, Newton 35, Phillips 29, Breitenstein 24, Stimmel 2

	G	IP	GS	CG	W	L	K	BB	SH	SV	ERA
Ed Scott	43	315	35	31	17	20	87	65	0	1	3.86
Noodles Hahn #	38	311.1	37	29	16	20	**132**	89	**4**	0	3.27
Doc Newton	35	234.2	27	22	9	15	88	100	1	0	4.14
Bill Phillips	29	208.1	24	17	9	11	51	67	3	0	4.28
Ted Breitenstein	24	192.1	20	18	10	10	39	79	1	0	3.65
Archie Stimmel	2	13	1	1	1	1	2	4	0	0	6.92
		1274.2	144	118	62	77	399	404	9	1	3.83

No-hit game 4-0 vs Philadelphia, July 12

*The grandstand burned down on May 28. A month later the park reopened with the infield in what formerly had been the right field corner.

NEW YORK Buck Ewing (21–41) George Davis (39–37) Polo Grounds (III)

		G	AB	H	R	2B	3B	HR	RBI	BB	SB	BA	SA
CF	George Van Haltren	141	571	180	114	30	7	1	51	50	45	.315	.398
LF	Kip Selbach	141	523	176	98	29	12	4	68	72	36	.337	.461
1B	Jack Doyle	133	505	135	69	24	1	1	66	34	34	.267	.325
3B	Piano Legs Hickman	127	473	148	65	19	17	9	91	17	10	.313	.482
SS	George Davis	114	426	136	69	20	4	3	61	35	29	.319	.406
2B	Kid Gleason	111	420	104	60	11	3	1	29	17	23	.248	.295
RF	Elmer Smith	87	312	81	47	9	7	2	34	24	14	.260	.353
C	Frank Bowerman	80	270	65	25	5	3	1	42	6	10	.241	.293
UT	Mike Grady	83	251	55	36	8	4	0	27	34	9	.219	.283
P	Win Mercer	75	248	73	32	4	0	0	27	26	15	.294	.310
P	Pink Hawley	41	123	25	9	1	1	1	11	3	0	.203	.252
P	Bill Carrick	45	115	20	14	1	1	0	5	9	1	.174	.200
Sub	Jack Warner	34	108	27	15	4	0	0	13	8	1	.250	.287
Sub	Pop Foster	31	84	22	19	3	1	0	11	11	0	.262	.321
Sub	Danny Murphy	22	74	20	11	1	0	0	6	8	4	.270	.284
Sub	Curt Bernard	20	71	18	9	2	0	0	8	6	1	.254	.282
P	Ed Doheny	20	54	12	7	3	0	0	7	1	4	.222	.278
P	Cy Seymour	23	40	12	9	0	0	0	2	3	0	.300	.300
P	Dummy Taylor	11	22	3	2	0	0	0	1	1	0	.136	.136
Sub	Charlie Frisbee	4	13	2	2	1	0	0	3	2	0	.154	.231
P	Christy Mathewson	5	11	2	1	2	0	0	1	1	0	.182	.364
P	Dick Cogan	3	8	1	0	0	0	0	0	1	0	.125	.125
Sub	Tommy Sheehan	1	2	0	0	0	0	0	0	0	0	.000	.000
		141	4724	1317	713	177	61	23	564	369	236	.279	.357

1B Doyle 133, Grady 12, Seymour 1
2B Gleason 111, Murphy 22, Foster 5, Mercer 3, Grady 2
SS Davis 114, Grady 11, Foster 7, Mercer 7, Bowerman 2, Sheehan 1, Bernard 1, Cogan 1, Gleason 1
3B Hickman 120, Mercer 19, Grady 7
OF Van Haltren 141, Selbach 141, Smith 83, Bernard 19, Mercer 14, Foster 12, Hickman 7, Seymour 7, Grady 5, Frisbee 4
C Bowerman 75, Grady 41, Warner 31
P Carrick 45, Hawley 41, Mercer 32, Doheny 20, Seymour 13, Taylor 11, Mathewson 5, Cogan 2, Van Haltren 1

	G	IP	GS	CG	W	L	K	BB	SH	SV	ERA
Bill Carrick	45	341.2	41	32	19	22	63	92	1	0	3.53
Pink Hawley	41	329.1	38	34	18	18	80	89	2	0	3.53
Win Mercer	32	242.2	29	26	13	17	39	58	1	0	3.86
Ed Doheny	20	133.2	18	12	4	14	44	96	0	0	5.45
Dummy Taylor	11	62.1	7	6	4	3	16	24	0	0	2.45
Cy Seymour	13	53	7	2	2	1	19	54	0	0	6.96
Christy Mathewson	5	33.2	1	1	0	3	15	20	0	0	5.08
Dick Cogan	2	8	0	0	0	0	1	6	0	0	6.75
George Van Haltren	1	3	0	0	0	0	0	3	0	0	0.00
		1207.1	141	113	60	78	277	442	4	0	3.96

1900 AMERICAN LEAGUE*

	G	W	L	PCT	Home	Road	GB
1. Chicago White Sox	137	82	53	.607	46–24	36–19	—
2. Milwaukee Brewers	139	79	58	.577	44–28	35–30	4
3. Indianapolis Hoosiers	139	71	64	.526	40–25	31–39	11
4. Detroit Wolverines	140	71	68	.511	47–26	24–42	13
5. Kansas City Blues	141	69	70	.496	39–32	30–38	15
6. Cleveland Broncos	141	64	73	.467	34–32	30–41	19
7. Buffalo Bisons	140	61	78	.439	36–32	25–46	23
8. Minneapolis Millers	142	53	86	.381	31–34	22–52	31

	Chi	Mil	Ind	Det	KC	Cle	Buf	Min	
Chicago	—	12	12	10	7	13	11	17	82
Milwaukee	6	—	13	11	15	11	9	14	79
Indianapolis	5	7	—	12	16	5	14	12	71
Detroit	10	9	7	—	11	12	11	11	71
Kansas City	13	5	4	9	—	10	15	13	69
Cleveland	7	8	14	8	9	—	9	9	64
Buffalo	9	11	6	9	5	11	—	10	61
Minneapolis	3	6	8	9	7	11	9	—	53
	53	58	64	68	70	73	78	86	549

* Most of the team vs. team and batting and pitching statistics were furnished by Bob Tiemann, Ray Nemec, and Bob Hoie, who have all done extensive research on the 1900 American League season.

SEASON LEADERS

Batting Average (350 ABs)

1.	Dungan, Kansas City	.337
2.	Harley, Detroit	.325
3.	Pickering, Cleveland	.324
4.	Hemphill, Kansas City	.319
5.	Werden, Minneapolis	.315

Home Runs

1.	Seybold, Indianapolis	9
	Werden, Minneapolis	9
3.	Atherton, Buffalo	6
4.	Hartsel, Indianapolis	5
	Shugart, Chicago	5

Hits

1.	Pickering, Cleveland	194
2.	O'Brien, Kansas City	171
3.	Waldron, Milwaukee	170
4.	Anderson, Milwaukee	168
5.	Genins, Cleveland	166

Slugging Average

1.	Werden, Minneapolis	.468
2.	Seybold, Indianapolis	.453
3.	Dungan, Kansas City	.433
4.	Hartsel, Indianapolis	.429
5.	Fultz, Milwaukee	.423

Total Bases

1.	Werden, Minneapolis	238
2.	Pickering, Cleveland	231
3.	O'Brien, Kansas City	228
4.	Anderson, Milwaukee	224
5.	Waldron, Milwaukee	218

Runs

1.	Pickering, Cleveland	117
2.	Hogriever, Indianapolis	116
3.	Hoy, Chicago	115
4.	Hemphill, Kansas City	113
5.	Anderson, Milwaukee	94

Stolen Bases

1.	Anderson, Milwaukee	63
2.	Pickering, Cleveland	49
3.	Harley, Detroit	47
4.	Hogriever, Indianapolis	46
5.	Wilmot, Minneapolis	42
	Conroy, Milwaukee	42

PITCHING

Wins

1.	Lee, Kansas City	23
2.	Amole, Buffalo	22
3.	Kellum, Indianapolis	20
	Denzer, Chicago	20
5.	Six with	19

Losses

1.	Ehret, Minneapolis	23
2.	Amole, Buffalo	22
	Lee, Kansas City	22
	Cronin, Detroit	22
5.	Patten, Kansas City	20

Innings

1.	Lee, Kansas City	377
2.	Cronin, Detroit	372
3.	Amole, Buffalo	342
4.	Patten, Kansas City	334
5.	Ehret, Minneapolis	315

Complete Games

1.	Cronin, Detroit	36
	Lee, Kansas City	36
3.	Amole, Buffalo	35
4.	Kellum, Indianapolis	34
5.	Ehret, Minneapolis	33

Strikeouts

1.	Cronin, Detroit	121
2.	Dowling, Milwaukee	107
3.	Patten, Kansas City	104
4.	Amole, Buffalo	100
5.	Sparks, Milwaukee	91

Winning Percentage (25 decisions)

1.	Patterson, Chicago	.680
2.	Miller, Detroit	.679
	Reidy, Milwaukee	.679
	Fisher, Chicago	.679
5.	Denzer, Chicago	.667

FIELDING**

Total Chances

1B	Unavailable
2B	Unavailable
3B	Unavailable
SS	Unavailable
OF	Unavailable
C	Unavailable
P	Unavailable

Fielding Average

Carey, Buffalo	.989
Bierbauer, Mil-Cleve-Buff	.954
Coughlin, Kansas City	.920
Smith, Minneapolis	.918
Hoy, Chicago	.976
Spies, Cleve-Mil	.969
Gardner, Indianapolis	1.000

** As yet, complete fielding statistics are unavailable as are accurate team batting and pitching statistics and accurate total games played at each position. Players listed at a fielding position who are followed by a question mark played an unknown number of games at that position. In several instances, owing to fielding data not as yet available, the sum of the individual total number of games played at a position falls short of the actual number of games the team played.

CHICAGO   **Charlie Comiskey**   **South Side Park (III)**

		G	AB	H	R	2B	3B	HR	SB	BA	SA
CF	Dummy Hoy	137	547	139	115	16	6	1	32	.254	.311
2B	Dick Padden	130	482	137	84	24	5	1	36	.284	.361
LF	Herm McFarland	121	460	111	81	23	7	3	31	.241	.341
C	Joe Sugden	121	459	133	47	23	4	0	15	.290	.357
3B	Fred Hartman	116	450	124	71	21	6	1	15	.276	.356
1B	Frank Isbell	109	399	99	49	14	7	1	22	.248	.326
SS	Frank Shugart	98	377	107	54	21	1	5	15	.284	.385
RF	Steve Brodie	64	229	60	41	6	3	0	8	.262	.314
Sub	Dick Buckley	40	139	28	10	6	0	0	0	.201	245
Sub	Bob Wood	36	127	39	15	11	0	1	3	.307	.417
P	Chauncey Fisher	40	120	27	10	5	1	0	0	.225	.283
P	Jack Katoll	38	109	17	6	4	0	0	0	.156	.193
P	Roger Denzer	36	108	23	8	4	0	0	0	.213	.250
Sub	Pat Dillard	28	98	19	13	1	2	0	5	.194	.245
P	Roy Patterson	33	96	19	12	0	1	0	0	.198	.219
Sub	Charlie O'Leary	27	92	15	4	3	0	0	0	.163	.196
Sub	David Brain	8	25	6	3	1	1	0	0	.240	.360
P	Willie McGill	6	15	3	1	0	0	0	0	.200	.200
P	Ed Doheny	6	14	3	3	1	0	0	0	.214	.286
P	Tom Thomas	3 (#KC)	12	2	4	0	0	0	0	.167	.167
Sub	G.E. Clayton	2	9	3	1	0	0	0	0	.333	.333
P	Frank Killen	1	3	0	1	0	0	0	0	.000	.000
P	Cy Seymour	2	3	0	0	0	0	0	0	.000	.000
PH	Eddie Burke	1(#BU/MN)	1	0	0	0	0	0	0	.000	.000
Sub	Tommy Dowd	36	(See MILWAUKEE)							.235	
Sub	John Shearon	34	(See BUFFALO)							.285	
Sub	Dan Lally	10	(See MINNEAPOLIS)							.238	
Sub	Frank McManus	7	(See KANSAS CITY)							.143	
		137								.257	

1B   Isbell 54, Sugden 43, Dowd 26, Lally 7, Buckley 6, Clayton 2
2B   Padden 130, Brain 1, O'Leary 1
SS   Shugart 98, O'Leary 26, Wood 8, Brain 1
3B   Hartman 116, Isbell 15, Brain 7
OF   Hoy 137, McFarland 120, Brodie 64, Shearon 34, Isbell 18, Dillard 16, Dowd 10, Lally 4, McManus 4, Fisher 4, Patterson 3, Katoll 1
C   Sugden 74, Buckley 34, Wood 28
P   Katoll 36, Denzer 36, Fisher 36, Patterson 30, Isbell 10, McGill 6, Doheny 5, Thomas 3, Seymour 2, Killen 1

	G	IP	GS	CG	W	L	K	BB	SH
Chauncy Fisher	36	285	30	27	19	9	63	51	**6**
Jack Katoll	36	282	29	25	16	14	81	60	**6**
Roger Denzer	36	272	29	24	20	10	76	55	3
Roy Patterson	30	232	27	22	17	8	87	53	4
Frank Isbell	10	53	7	4	5	2	5	23	0
Tom Thomas	3 (#KC)	38	5	2	1	2	12	8	0
Willie McGill	6	33	5	3	3	2	6	14	0
Ed Doheny	5	33	4	3	0	4	14	20	0
Cy Seymour	2	10	2	1	1	1	5	9	0
Frank Killen	1	8	1	1	0	1	1	3	0
					82	53			

NOTE: Men who never played in the major leagues are listed by their full names; those who appear elsewhere either in this or other major league encyclopedias are listed by their playing names. For players with two or more teams: Individual statistical breakdowns with each team are not yet available with a few exceptions. Players affected are shown as follows: (See TEAM) means the player's or pitcher's complete statistical achievements will be found under that team because he played the bulk of his games with it.

(#TEAM ABBREVIATION) means the player or pitcher also played with the abbreviated team and part of his statistical achievements were made with it. Innings pitched, games started, complete games, strikeouts, walks and shutouts for pitchers with more than one team unless known for each team appear under the team with which they played the most games, but won-lost totals are presented for each team. Likewise, total games played, at bats, hits, runs, doubles, triples, home runs, stolen bases and slugging averages for players with more than one team unless known for each team appear under the team with which they played the bulk of their games, but batting averages are presented for each team.

MILWAUKEE   Connie Mack   Lloyd Street Ball Park

		G	AB	H	R	2B	3B	HR	SB	BA	SA
CF	Irv Waldron	139	579	170	92	29	8	1	34	.294	.377
1B	John Anderson	134	542	168	94	32	9	2	**63**	.310	.413
2B	Lou Bierbauer	45 (#CL/BU)	481	110	41	21	1	0	6	.229	.277
3B	Jimmy Burke	127	456	112	47	14	4	1	23	.246	.300
SS	Wid Conroy	116	431	101	58	17	5	1	42	.234	.304
UT	Dave Fultz	114	430	128	85	16	13	4	36	.298	.423
Sub	Tommy Dowd	62 (#CHI)	381	100	47	20	3	0	17	.262	.331
OF	James T. Garry	60 (#BUF)	325	82	44	9	2	0	6	.252	.292
OF	Fred Ketchum	73	316	83	42	7	2	0	12	.263	.297
UT	William L. Diggins	63 (#CLE)	285	74	24	13	4	0	4	.260	.333
C	Harry Smith	80	273	71	25	6	7	2	10	.260	.355
P	Pete Dowling	38	105	28	9	5	1	0	1	.267	.333
Sub	Bill Hallman	29	105	23	13	4	0	0	2	.219	.257
P	Tully Sparks	34	104	24	9	6	0	0	1	.231	.288
P	Bill Reidy	32	104	22	7	2	0	0	2	.212	.231
P	George Rettger	29	82	17	11	4	0	1	0	.207	.293
Sub	George Yeager	25	80	31	16	7	1	0	2	.387	.500
Sub	Willie Clark	19	76	20	10	7	1	0	3	.263	.382
P	Rube Waddell	15	49	12	6	1	1	1	0	.245	.367
P	George Wheeler	16	46	8	4	1	0	0	0	.174	.196
Sub	Heinie Peitz	8	27	10	3	2	0	0	0	.370	.444
P	Bert Husting	5	17	2	1	0	0	0	0	.118	.118
Sub	Fred Raymer	1	4	0	0	0	0	0	0	.000	.000
Sub	?, O'Rourke	1	3	0	0	0	0	0	0	.000	.000
Sub	Harry Spies	17		(See CLEVELAND)						.317	
Sub	Ed Abbaticchio	16		(See MINNEAPOLIS)						.180	
		139								.265	

1B   Anderson 90, Clark 19, Dowd 14, Diggins 13, Yeager 9, Abbaticchio 1
2B   Fultz 57, Bierbauer 45, Conroy 27, Abbaticchio 13, Peitz 8, Raymer 1
SS   Conroy 89, Fultz 49, O'Rourke 1
3B   Burke 127, Rettger ?
OF   Waldron 139, Ketcham 73, Garry 60, Dowd 48, Anderson 44, Hallman 29, Wheeler 4?, Dowling 1, Rettger ?
C   Smith 79, Diggins 50, Spies 17, Yeager 16
P   Dowling 37, Sparks 34, Reidy 32, Rettger 22, Waddell 15, Wheeler 12, Husting 5

	G	IP	GS	CG	W	L	K	BB	SH
Pete Dowling	37	293	36	29	16	19	107	95	3
Bill Reidy	32	286	27	27	19	9	41	32	2
Tully Sparks	34	261	30	25	16	12	91	88	1
George Rettger	22	176	17	16	7	11	31	43	1
Rube Waddell	15	129	14	13	10	3	75	20	2
George Wheeler	12	79	10	6	7	3	18	19	0
Bert Husting	5	45	5	5	4	1	32	25	0
					79	58			

INDIANAPOLIS   Bill Watkins   East Washington Street Park

		G	AB	H	R	2B	3B	HR	SB	BA	SA
CF	George Hogriever	138	524	132	116	25	6	2	46	.252	.334
3B	Eddie Hickey	126	454	111	62	16	4	0	30	.244	.297
2B	George Magoon	120	449	139	81	17	8	1	36	.310	.390
RF	Socks Seybold	115	444	135	72	27	6	9	7	.304	.453
1B	Mike Kelley	108	418	86	52	11	7	1	11	.206	.273
C	Mike Powers	110	416	124	42	17	5	1	0	.298	.370
LF	Topsy Hartsel	104	406	122	86	11	13	5	31	.300	.429
SS	Art Madison	98	378	100	51	11	6	1	8	.265	.333
UT	Phil Geier	80	326	105	39	12	6	1	14	.322	.405
C	Mike Heydon	61	208	52	32	4	5	3	1	.250	.361
Sub	George Flynn	53	175	38	29	9	1	0	13	.217	.280
P	Win Kellum	44	127	26	17	5	2	0	0	.205	.276
P	Frederick E. Barnes	32	94	20	10	2	1	0	1	.213	.255
P	Jim Gardner	23	76	20	5	1	0	0	0	.263	.276
P	Bill Damman	27	67	10	6	0	1	0	0	.149	.179
Sub	Bill Grey	18	66	16	10	3	0	0	2	.242	.288
P	Billy Milligan	13	40	9	2	2	0	0	0	.222	.275
P	Jot Goar	10	38	8	7	2	1	1	0	.211	.395
P	Archie Stimmel	11	34	4	2	0	0	0	0	.118	.118
P	Theodore Guese	10	32	8	0	0	1	0	1	.250	.313
P	Warren Sanders	2	3	2	1	0	0	0	0	.667	.667
Sub	Ace Stewart	1	3	1	1	0	0	0	0	.333	.333
P	Norwood Gibson	1	1	0	0	0	0	0	0	.000	.000
P	Jack Doscher	1	0	0	0	0	0	0	0	—	—
		139								.263	

1B Kelley 108, Powers 11, Seybold 8
2B Magoon 120, Flynn ?, Geier ?, Madison 1, Barnes ?, Gardner ?
SS Madison 98, Geier 32, Grey 18, Magoon 1, Flynn ?
3B Hickey 126, Geier ?, Stewart 1
OF Hogriever 138, Hartsel 101, Seybold 107, Flynn 29, Geier 27, Heydon 16, Richter 3, Barnes ?, Gardner ?, Damman 1
C   Powers 99, Heydon 45
P   Kellum 44, Damman 26, Barnes 25, Gardner 20, Milligan 13, Stimmel 11, Goar 10, Guese 10, Sanders 2, Doscher 1

	G	IP	GS	CG	W	L	K	BB	SH
Win Kellum	44	313	38	34	20	18	87	66	5
Frederick E. Barnes	25	208	22	18	13	10	28	37	0
Bill Damman	26	171	19	16	10	12	46	47	0
Jim Gardner	20	157	17	14	8	8	47	47	1
Billy Milligan	13	104	12	11	6	6	38	40	0
Archie Stimmel	11	87	10	9	5	4	21	19	2
Jot Goar	10	83	10	9	7	2	33	29	0
Theodore Guese	10	68	8	5	2	3	16	22	0
Warren Sanders	2	6	1	0	0	0	1	1	0
Norwood Gibson	1	3	1	0	0	0	1	0	0
Jack Doscher	1	1	1	0	0	1	0	2	0
					71	64			

DETROIT **George Stallings** **Bennett Park**

		G	AB	H	R	2B	3B	HR	SB	BA	SA
LF	Dick Harley	123	486	158	77	15	5	0	47	.325	.377
1B	Pop Dillon	123	470	137	57	21	7	2	25	.291	.379
3B	Doc Casey	115	469	122	75	6	8	0	37	.260	.307
2B	John B. Ryan	126	462	119	71	20	6	1	15	.258	.333
RF	Ducky Holmes	113	433	126	64	11	5	2	29	.291	.353
SS	Kid Elberfeld	109	396	104	61	11	5	0	28	.262	.316
UT	Lou McAllister	111	392	120	65	10	7	2	40	.306	.383
C	Al Shaw	88	294	76	60	10	3	1	4	.269	.323
CF	George Nicol	73	283	73	31	8	5	3	10	.258	.353
OF	George Stallings	42	147	37	17	5	3	1	7	.252	.347
P	Joe Yeager	45	141	30	16	0	4	1	5	.213	.291
P	Jack Cronin	46	141	28	21	6	4	3	2	.199	.362
OF	Charlie Jones	32	121	28	14	5	1	1	6	.231	.314
P	Roscoe Miller	30	98	17	7	1	3	0	0	.163	.235
Sub	Bill Grey	21	78	22	8	1	0	0	2	.282	.295
P	Emil Frisk	31	75	21	12	5	1	0	2	.280	.373
Sub	Daniel Sheehan	??	75	17	7	0	1	0	2	.226	.247
Sub	Harry Bay	12	50	10	8	0	0	0	4	.200	.200
P	Ed Siever	4	38	10	4	0	2	0	0	.258	.368
P	Welcome Gaston	8 (#CLE)	21	5	2	0	0	0	0	.167	
P	Bill Hill	5	8	3	0	0	0	0	0	.375	.375
P	John Fifield	5	6	1	0	0	0	0	0	.167	.167
Sub	Ed Wheeler	2	6	0	0	0	0	0	0	.000	.000
P	Frank Owen	4	5	3	2	1	0	0	0	.600	.800
Sub	Suter Sullivan	22	(See CLEVELAND)							.226	
		141								.267	

1B   Dillon 123, Ryan 15, Owen 1, McAllister ?
2B   Ryan 91, McAllister 32, Grey 3, Holmes 2, Yeager ?
SS   Elberfeld 109, Sheehan 19, Grey 4, McAllister ?, Yeager ?
3B   Casey 115, Sullivan 12, Grey 7, Wheeler 2, Dillon 1, McAllister ?
OF   Harley 123, Holmes 111, Nicol 73, Stallings 42, Jones 32, Bay 12, Frisk 11, Grey 9, Cronin 1, McAllister ?, Yeager ?
C   Shaw 87, McAllister 48, Ryan 20
P   Cronin 45, Yeager 32, Miller 30, Frisk 20, Siever 14, Gaston 8, Fifield 5, Hill 5, Owen 3, McAllister 1

	G	IP	GS	CG	W	L	K	BB	SH
Jack Cronin	45	372	40	**36**	19	22	**121**	83	3
Joe Yeager	32	270	31	31	19	12	49	63	**7**
Roscoe Miller	30	241	27	23	19	9	54	56	4
Emil Frisk	20	150	17	14	6	9	46	42	1
Ed Siever	14	111	12	11	6	5	26	20	1
Welcome Gaston	8 (#CLE)	55	5	3	1	4	9	31	0
Bill Hill	5	22	5	2	1	3	7	15	1
Jack Fifield	5	20	3	0	0	2	2	11	0
Frank Owen	3	12	1	1	0	1	6	2	0
Lou McAllister	1	1	0	0	0	0	0	0	0
		—1 forfeit L vs Cleveland on July 15—							
					71	67			

KANSAS CITY **Jim Manning** **Exposition Park**

		G	AB	H	R	2B	3B	HR	SB	BA	SA
CF	Jack O'Brien	140	573	171	81	35	11	0	26	.298	.398
RF	Charlie Hemphill	131	517	165	113	15	**15**	1	26	.319	.412
3B	Bill Coughlin	130	510	134	60	20	7	1	20	.263	.335
LF	John Farrell	125	478	129	88	21	7	1	28	.270	.349
1B	Sam Dungan	117	469	158	63	28	7	1	6	**.337**	.433
2B	Germany Schaefer	110	398	102	62	15	8	1	30	.256	.342
SS	Butts Wagner	76	312	86	58	17	7	0	14	.276	.375
P	Dale Gear	79	252	70	47	11	3	2	5	.278	.369
C	John Gonding	73	246	46	18	4	1	0	4	.187	.211
2B	Ace Stewart	54	190	34	20	5	1	0	13	.179	.216
SS	Billy Clingman	41	155	48	18	4	1	0	5	.310	.348
C	Parke Wilson	42	154	45	17	5	1	0	7	.292	.338
P	Watty Lee	50	150	34	15	7	0	0	0	.227	.273
P	Case Patten	45	136	28	16	4	0	0	0	.206	.235
C	Frank McManus	33 (#CHI)	128	30	21	3	1	0	7	.234	.273
Sub	John Ganzel	22	92	36	15	7	3	1	4	.391	.565
Sub	Otto Thiel	12	45	5	3	1	0	0	0	.111	.133
P	Eli Cates	11	29	5	3	1	0	0	0	.172	.207
Sub	P.G. Nagle	7	25	7	3	2	0	0	0	.280	.360
C	John Sullivan	7	22	5	2	2	0	0	0	.227	.318
P	Danny Daub	8	18	5	0	1	0	0	0	.278	.333
P	Norwood Gibson	8	18	2	4	0	0	0	0	.125	.125
P	Chummy Gray	13 (#BUF)	14	27	5	2	0	0	0	.185	.185
OF	?, Carroll	1	4	0	0	0	0	0	0	.000	.000
P	Kid Carsey	3	(See BUFFALO)							.286	
P	Tom Thomas	2	(See CHICAGO)							?	
		141								.274	

1B Dungan 115, Ganzel 22
2B Schaefer 88, Stewart 54
SS Wagner 76, Clingman 41, Schaefer 25
3B Coughlin 130, Thiel 12
OF O'Brien 140, Hemphill 131, Farrell 124, Gear 34, Nagle 7, Lee 2, Carroll 1, Daub 1, Coughlin 1
C   Gondling 73, Wilson 39, McManus 33, Sullivan 7
P   Lee 48, Patten 45, Gear 37, Gray 13, Cates 11, Gibson 8, Daub 7, Carsey 3, Thomas 2

	G	IP	GS	CG	W	L	K	BB	SH
Watty Lee	48	**377**	**41**	**36**	**23**	22	82	71	1
Case Patten	45	334	40	31	17	20	104	**123**	3
Dale Gear	37	272	27	25	19	11	63	60	2
Chummy Gray	13 (#BUF)	74	12	3	3	3	10	46	0
Eli Cates	11	66	8	5	2	5	18	32	0
Norwood Gibson	8	62	7	5	2	4	17	21	0
Danny Daub	7	36	3	1	2	3	6	16	0
Kid Carsey	3	(See BUFFALO)			1	0			
Tom Thomas	2	(See CHICAGO)			0	2			
					69	70			

CLEVELAND   **Jimmy McAleer**   **League Park**

		G	AB	H	R	2B	3B	HR	SB	BA	SA
CF	Ollie Pickering	140	**599**	**194**	**117**	29	4	0	49	.324	.386
RF	Frank Genins	140	566	166	84	28	4	0	21	.293	.357
1B	Candy LaChance	116	457	138	60	22	10	1	39	.302	.400
2B	Tim Flood	91 (#BUF)	392	98	66	10	7	1	22	.250	.319
UT	Pat Crisham	95	354	90	31	12	2	2	8	.254	.316
3B	Suter Sullivan	66 (#DET)	336	96	49	17	5	1	10	.286	.375
C	Henry Spies	74 (#MIL)	331	78	39	9	7	1	6	.236	.314
LF	Charlie Frisbee	60	233	54	33	3	5	1	12	.232	.300
SS	Danny Shay	61	219	49	29	12	5	0	7	.224	.324
SS	Rodney Viox	49	168	37	20	5	2	0	2	.220	.274
P	Bill Hart	37	135	34	17	8	0	0	3	.252	.326
Sub	Charlie Buelow	31	130	46	24	11	6	0	2	.354	.531
P	Bill Hoffer	43	126	24	19	6	0	0	1	.190	.238
Sub	Jim Jones	27	113	27	12	6	2	0	1	.239	.327
P	Charles Baker	17 (#BUF)	92	25	12	4	0	0	0	.272	.315
Sub	James E. Tamsett	24	85	12	6	5	0	0	3	.141	.200
Sub	Jimmy McAleer	20	77	18	8	0	1	0	0	.233	.260
Sub	John F. White	19	72	20	11	2	0	0	4	.278	.306
Sub	Frank Cross	22	68	17	10	4	0	0	1	.250	.309
P	Kit McKenna	22	66	9	2	1	0	0	1	.136	.152
Sub	Farmer Weaver	11	41	11	13	2	1	0	3	.268	.366
P	Dick Braggins	12	40	8	3	0	0	0	0	.200	.200
P	Clay Fauver	10	34	7	2	1	1	0	0	.206	.294
Sub	John A. "Roxy" Walters	10	32	5	2	0	0	0	0	.156	.156
P	Sam A. Reust	6	21	4	1	0	0	0	0	.190	.190
P	Charlie Chech	7	20	4	0	1	0	0	0	.200	.250
P	Zeke Wilson	6	17	6	2	2	0	0	0	.353	.471
Sub	Frank Martin	3 (#BUF)	17	0	1	0	0	0	0	.000	.000
P	Alfred B. Smythe	6	12	3	1	1	0	0	0	.250	.333
Sub	Tom Delahanty	3	10	2	0	0	0	0	0	.200	.200
P	Bumpus Jones	3	9	2	2	1	0	0	0	.222	.333
Sub	Ed Hilley	2	6	0	0	0	0	0	0	.000	.000
P	Rip Egan	2	4	1	1	1	0	0	0	.250	.250
Sub	Lou Bierbauer	43	(See MILWAUKEE)							.217	
Sub	William L. Diggins	13	(See MILWAUKEE)							.170	
P	Archibald Kern	2	(See BUFFALO)							.143	.143
P	Welcome Gaston	1	(See DETROIT)							.667	.667
		141								.259	

1B   LaChance 116, Crisham 24

2B   Flood 91, Bierbauer 35, Genins ?, Delahanty 3, Viox 1, Hart ?, Hoffer ?

SS   Shay 61, Viox 48, Genins ?, Buelow 9, Bierbauer ?, White 4

3B   Sullivan 66, Tamsett 24, Buelow 22, Genins ?, Walters 10, Bierbauer ?, Martin 3

OF   Pickering 140, Genins 110, Frisbee 60, Crisham 28, Jones 27, McAleer 20, White 15, Hoffer ?, Weaver 8, Braggins 2, Chech 2, Hart ?, McKenna 1

C   Spies 74, Crisham 39, Cross 16, Diggins 13

P   Hart 34, Hoffer 30, McKenna 21, Baker 17, Braggins 10, Fauver 10, Smythe 6, Reust 6, Wilson 6, Chech 5, Jones 3, Egan 2, Kern 2, Gaston 1

	G	IP	GS	CG	W	L	K	BB	SH
Bill Hart	34	294	33	32	18	15	86	101	2
Bill Hoffer	30	252	29	27	16	12	72	50	3
Charles Baker	17 (#BUF)	221	22	16	6	7	66	69	1
Kit McKenna	21	172	20	18	8	10	37	83	1
Dick Braggins	10	94	9	8	5	5	17	41	0
Clay Fauver	10	85	10	9	4	6	9	14	1
Sam A. Reust	6	52	6	6	2	4	14	15	0
Zeke Wilson	6	44	5	4	1	4	8	12	0
Alfred B. Smythe	6	35	4	2	0	3	3	10	0
Charlie Chech	5	35	3	3	0	2	3	10	0
Bumpus Jones	3	22	3	2	2	1	6	8	0
Rip Egan	2	11	2	1	1	1	1	5	0
Archibald Kern	2	(See BUFFALO)			0	2			
Welcome Gaston	1	(See DETROIT)			0	1			
		—1 forfeit W vs Detroit on July 15—							
					63	73			

BUFFALO   Dan Shannon   Olympic Park II

		G	AB	H	R	2B	3B	HR	SB	BA	SA
1B	Scoops Carey	135	543	147	66	31	9	3	13	.271	.378
LF	Jocko Halligan	129	534	147	82	28	14	1	13	.275	.386
CF	John Shearon	80 (#CHI)	529	140	67	26	11	1	10	.265	.361
RF	Jake Gettman	121	516	154	82	26	12	2	35	.298	.407
C	Ossee Schreckengost	125	503	142	71	23	9	1	14	.282	.370
2B	Jay A. Andrews	122	456	114	51	21	9	1	15	.250	.342
SS	Bill Hallman	100	397	111	53	23	5	0	11	.280	.363
Sub	Charlie Atherton	49	193	65	38	12	4	6	7	.337	.534
C	George Speer	57	192	45	21	6	0	0	3	.234	.266
Sub	Matt Broderick	45	146	34	12	5	0	0	2	.233	.267
Sub	Warren Hart	34	146	32	17	1	3	0	9	.219	.267
P	Doc Amole	47	134	24	13	3	1	0	0	.179	.216
P	John Kerwin	36	122	33	15	6	2	0	0	.270	.352
P	Charlie Hastings	15 (#MI)	71	14	8	1	1	1	0	.197	.282
P	Buck Hooker	25	61	9	6	3	1	0	0	.145	.230
Sub	Jud Smith	14	57	10	6	2	0	1	2	.175	.263
Sub	Julius "Hub" Knoll	14	56	18	12	3	2	0	2	.321	.446
Sub	Eddie Burke	7 (#CH/MN)	53	11	8	2	0	0	4	.208	.245
P	Frank Foreman	18	50	17	9	2	2	0	1	.340	.460
P	Kid Carsey	11 (#KC)	39	8	7	5	0	0	1	.205	.333
Sub	Jack Crooks	8	30	3	5	2	0	0	0	.100	.167
P	Archibald Kern	8 (#CLE)	20	3	2	0	0	0	0	.150	.150
P	Billy Milligan	7	19	8	1	3	1	0	0	.421	.684
P	Edward P. Fertsch	4	10	1	0	0	0	0	0	.100	.100
P	Dad Clarke	3	7	1	0	0	0	0	0	.143	.143
P	Jacob J. Jimeson	1	4	1	0	0	0	0	0	.250	.250
PH	J. Nelson	1	1	0	0	0	0	0	0	.000	.000
Sub	Lou Bierbauer	40	(See MILWAUKEE)							.295	
Sub	James T. Garry	19	(See MILWAUKEE)							.182	
P	Charles Baker	13	(See CLEVELAND)							.375	
Sub	Tim Flood	12	(See CLEVELAND)							.283	
Sub	Frank Martin	2	(See CLEVELAND)							.000	.000
P	Chummy Gray	1	(See KANSAS CITY)							.000	.000
		140								.265	

1B   Carey 135, Schreckengost 24
2B   Atherton 46, Bierbauer 33, Hallman 20, Flood 12, Crooks 8, Andrews 5, Hart 3, Martin 2
SS   Hallman 80, Broderick 45, Carsey 5, Bierbauer 1
3B   Andrews 117, Smith 14, Bierbauer 6, Atherton 3
OF   Halligan 126, Gettman 121, Shearon 80, Hart 31, Knoll 14, Garry 19, Kerwin 8, Burke 7
C   Schreckengost 95, Speer 57
P   Amole 47, Kerwin 28, Hooker 24, Foreman 15, Hastings 15, Baker 13, Kern 8, Milligan 7, Carsey 4,
      Fertsch 4, Clarke 3, Gray 1, Jimeson 1

	G	IP	GS	CG	W	L	K	BB	SH
Doc Amole#	47	342	**41**	35	22	22	100	115	2
John Kerwin	28	233	26	26	12	14	40	53	2
Charlie Hastings	15 (#MIN)	195	23	17	8	5	47	51	0
Buck Hooker	24	161	19	15	4	13	42	29	1
Frank Foreman	15	118	12	10	7	6	27	35	1
Archibald Kern	8 (#CLE)	55	6	4	3	1	17	15	0
Kid Carsey	11 (#KC)	42	5	3	2	1	7	12	0
Billy Milligan	7	35	5	2	1	4	18	9	0
Edward Fertsch	4	24	3	2	0	3	6	9	0
Dad Clarke	3	23	2	1	0	2	3	3	0
Jacob J. Jimeson	1	9	1	1	0	1	3	5	0
Charles Baker	13	(See CLEVELAND)			2	5			
Chummy Gray	1	(See KANSAS CITY)			0	1			
					61	78			

#No-hit game 8-0 vs Detroit, April 19 (Opening Day)

MINNEAPOLIS   Walt Wilmot   Nicollet Park

		G	AB	H	R	2B	3B	HR	SB	BA	SA
CF	Dan Lally	128 (#CHI)	576	151	71	24	6	1	21	.262	.330
1B	Perry Werden	127	511	161	64	**39**	6	**9**	13	.315	**.468**
LF	Walt Wilmot	129	511	136	76	21	6	2	13	.266	.342
SS	Germany Smith	129	492	127	65	15	5	2	13	.258	.321
3B	Billy Nance	129	483	131	69	25	7	2	14	.268	.364
RF	Lefty Davis	101	418	118	82	14	10	1	22	.282	.371
2B	Ed Abbaticchio	101 (#MIL)	415	96	52	13	9	0	24	.231	.306
C	Newt Fisher	118	401	106	57	17	1	1	15	.264	.319
UT	Erwin Harvey	51	193	58	33	10	4	0	5	.301	.394
Sub	Art Nichols	44	165	42	15	8	0	0	14	.255	.303
P	Red Ehret	44	139	35	14	8	0	0	1	.252	.309
P	Doc Parker	32	93	22	7	0	0	1	0	.237	.269
P	Harvey Bailey	28	91	23	6	3	2	0	0	.253	.330
C	Fred Jacklitsch	32	87	16	21	6	1	2	2	.184	.345
Sub	J. Oscar Bandeline	22	66	17	8	3	0	0	4	.258	.303
P	Gene McCann	24	61	12	4	2	0	0	0	.197	.230
C	Edward J. Dixon	16	48	12	9	1	0	1	1	.250	.333
Sub	John Grim	15	45	14	7	4	0	1	2	.311	.467
Sub	Daniel Higgins	12	44	7	1	0	0	0	0	.159	.159
Sub	David C. McAndrews	8	32	3	2	1	0	0	0	.094	.125
Sub	Joseph E. Schrall	8	30	5	5	0	0	0	0	.167	.167
Sub	William Krouse	9	29	5	2	0	0	0	0	.172	.172
Sub	John T. Burns	5	22	5	1	0	0	0	0	.237	.237
Sub	? Campbell	2	8	3	1	0	0	0	0	.375	.375
PH	J. Nelson	1	1	0	0	0	0	0	0	.000	.000
P	Ted Corbett	1	0	0	0	0	0	0	0	—	—
P	Charlie Hastings	12	(See BUFFALO)							.219	
Sub	Eddie Burke	6	(See BUFFALO)							.348	
		142								.265	

1B   Werden 127, Grim 14, Fisher 4, Lally 1
2B   Abbaticchio 101, Nichols 23, Higgins 11, Krouse 9
SS   Smith 129
3B   Nance 129, McAndrews 8, Campbell 2
OF   Wilmot 129, Lally 127, Davis 101, Harvey 26, Bandeline 16, Schrall 8, Burke 6, Burns 5, Ehret 5, Werden 1
C   Fisher 114, Jacklitsch 25, Nichols 21, Dixon 16
P   Ehret 39, Parker 30, Bailey 27, Harvey 23, McCann 22, Hastings 12, Bandeline 5, Corbett 1

	G	IP	GS	CG	W	L	K	BB	SH
Red Ehret	39	315	36	33	12	**23**	76	80	1
Doc Parker	30	242	27	25	12	15	63	57	0
Harvey Bailey	27	221	25	22	14	11	71	59	1
Erwin Harvey	23	170	22	16	7	14	73	82	1
Gene McCann	22	161	18	16	4	13	29	68	1
J. Oscar Bandeline	5	44	5	5	1	4	12	16	0
Ted Corbett	1	2	0	0	0	0	1	0	0
Charlie Hastings	12	(See BUFFALO)			3	6			
					53	86			

EXPLANATION OF THE PLAYER REGISTER

The player register contains the vital statistics and the six central batting statistics of every man who played in a major league game between 1871 and 1900, excepting some men who were either exclusively or else almost exclusively pitchers. Pitchers found in the player register are there either because they played a significant number of games at other positions or else because their batting statistics merit inclusion.

Within the player register players are organized into subregisters by position. Players who performed at more than one position are found at the position where they played the most games. Players who played an equal number of games at two or more positions are found under the most demanding position they played. In the nineteenth century the positions, in order of difficulty, were: catcher, shortstop, third base, second base, outfield, first base.

The players in each subregister are listed alphabetically by surname and, if two or more players bear the same surname, by given name—i.e., in the Outfielders subregister **Smith, Elmer Ellsworth** is found ahead of **Smith, William E.**, and **Smith, William E.** is found ahead of **Smith, William J.** In quotation marks following a player's given name is the name or names he was known by in the nineteenth century. John McGraw, for instance, was called "Mugsy" in the 1890s but was not dubbed "The Little Napolcan" until the twentieth century. Hence there is no mention in the player register of his most famous nickname. When a man played under a name other than his name at birth, his playing name is followed by the part of his birth name that differed from it—in most cases his surname only.

Following the name of each player is a chronological list of the teams for which he played. See the sample player, **Thomas John Carey**, below, for an explanation of the year abbreviations.

Vital statistics—birth date and birthplace, death date, height, weight, batted, threw—are furnished when known. Gaps in information are indicated either by question marks or by the word "Unknown." Since our knowledge of nineteenth-century baseball is still growing, we expect to eliminate some—if not all—of the gaps in future editions.

BIRTH DATE	BIRTHPLACE	DEATH DATE	B	T	HGT	WGT	G	AB	H	R	BA	SA
Carey, Thomas John "Tom"	b. J.J. Norton	71KekNA	72–73BalNA	74MutNA	75HarNA		76–77HarN	78ProN	79CleN			
?/?/49	Brooklyn, N.Y.	2/13/99	R	R	5'8	145	536	2394	645	404	.269	.320

In the above sample from the subregister of Shortstops, we see first the player's surname of Carey, then his given first and middle names followed in quotation marks by the name he was most commonly called and lastly the name under which he was born. In this case, we know only the initials of Carey's first and middle names at birth. Following Carey's birth name is a chronological list of his major league seasons and teams beginning in 71 (1871) and ending in 79 (1879). See below for a list of the team and league abbreviations that follow the year numerals.

Carey's playing career is followed by his birth date or what part of it we know—here only the year. Next is his place of birth, followed by his death date. We then find that Carey batted right, threw right, stood 5'8" and weighed 145 pounds. In his nine-year career Carey played 536 games, compiled 2394 at bats and 645 hits, scored 404 runs and batted .269 with a .320 slugging average. The reader will note that, as is true for every man who played in both the National Association and another major league, Carey's National Association statistics are integrated into his total major league statistics. Unlike other encyclopedias, *The Great Encyclopedia of Nineteenth-Century Major League Baseball* recognizes the National Association as a major league and is not bound by major league baseball's decision to treat its statistics separately. As but one argument against any such separation, the National Association contained most of the best professional players of its time whereas the men who played in the Union Association in 1884 have their statistics integrated into their career totals by major league baseball even though the Union Association was comprised largely of minor leaguers.

Carey played continuously in the major leagues from 1871 through 1879. Here, from the Second Basemen's subregister, is a sample player who had career gaps and an explanation of how they are shown.

BIRTH DATE	BIRTHPLACE	DEATH DATE	B	T	HGT	WGT	G	AB	H	R	BA	SA
Crooks, John Charles "Jack"	89–91ColA	92–93StLN	95–96 WasN	96LouN	98StLN							
11/19/65	St. Paul, Minn.	2/2/18	R	R	5'10	170	794	2780	668	536	.240	.321

Beginning in 1889, Crooks played in the major leagues continuously through 1893. After spending the 1894 season out of the major leagues, he returned in 1895 and stayed with Washington until partway through the 1896 season when he went to Louisville. Crooks was again out of the major leagues in 1897 before returning in 1898 with St. Louis for his final season.

Following the last two numerals of the year in which a man played is an abbreviation of the city where his team resided. The abbreviations follow:

Alt	Altoona	**Mut**	New York Mutuals (NA)
Ath	Philadelphia Athletics (NA)	**Nat**	Washington Nationals (NA)
Atl	Brooklyn Atlantics (NA)	**NH**	New Haven (NA)
Bal	Baltimore	**NY**	New York
Bos	Boston	**Oly**	Washington Olympics (NA)
Bro	Brooklyn	**Phi**	Philadelphia
Buf	Buffalo	**Pit**	Pittsburgh
Cen	Philadelphia Centennials (NA)	**Pro**	Providence
Chi	Chicago	**Reds**	St. Louis Reds (NA)
Cin	Cincinnati	**Res**	Elizabeth Resolutes (NA)
Cle	Cleveland	**Roc**	Rochester
Col	Columbus	**Rok**	Rockford (NA)
Det	Detroit	**StL**	St. Louis
Eck	Brooklyn Eckfords (NA)	**StP**	St. Paul
Har	Hartford	**Syr**	Syracuse
Ind	Indianapolis	**Tol**	Toledo
KC	Kansas City	**Tro**	Troy
Kek	Fort Wayne Kekiongas (NA)	**Vir**	Virginia
Lou	Louisville	**Was**	Washington
Man	Middletown Mansfields (NA)	**Wes**	Keokuk Westerns (NA)
Mar	Maryland (NA)	**Wil**	Wilmington
Mil	Milwaukee	**Wor**	Worchester

Following the year and team information is the abbreviation for the league in which a man played. The abbreviations follow:

NA National Association (1871–75)
N National League (1876–1900)
A American Association (1882–91)
U Union Association (1884)
P Players League (1890)

Note: To simplify the reader's task in following a career line, teams in the player, pitcher and manager registers are designated N during the 1892–99 period when the National League was officially known as the National League and American Association, although elsewhere in the book, when a specific season or achievement is cited, these teams are designated LA.

Other symbols:
* prior to a player's name indicates that he had a brother or brothers who also played in the major leagues, although not always in the nineteenth century.
# prior to a player's name indicates that he had a son or sons who also played in the major leagues, in every case in the twentieth century.

First Basemen

BIRTH DATE	BIRTHPLACE	DEATH DATE	B	T	HGT	WGT	G	AB	H	R	BA	SA
Allison, Andrew K. "Andy"		72EckNA										
?/?/48	New York, N.Y.	Unknown	?	?	5'8	150	22	93	15	11	.161	.194
Andrews, William Walter "Wally"		84LouA	88LouA									
9/18/59	Philadelphia, Pa.	1/20/40	R	R	6'3	170	40	142	28	22	.197	.331
Anson, Adrian Constantine "Cap" "Pop" 71RokNA		72–75AthNA	76–97ChiN									
4/11/52	Marshalltown, Iowa	4/14/22	R	R	6'	227	2523	10277	3416	1996	.332	.445
Baker, Philip "Phil" 83BalA		84WasU	86WasU									
9/19/56	Philadelphia, Pa.	6/4/40	L	L	5'8	152	195	817	212	134	.259	.322
Beckley, Jacob Peter "Jake" "Eagle Eye" 88–89PitN		90PitP	91–96PitN	96–97NYN	97–00CinN							
8/4/67	Hannibal, Mo.	6/25/18	L	L	5'10	200	1602	6456	1998	1200	.309	.452
Bierman, Charles S. "Charlie" 71KekNA												
?/?/45	Hoboken, N.J.	8/4/79	?	?	6'	180	1	2	0	0	.000	.000
Brouthers, Dennis Joseph "Dan" 79–80TroN 81–85BufN 86–88DetN 89BosN 90BosP 91BosA 92–93BroN 94–95BalN 95LouN 96PhiN												
5/8/58	Sylvan Lake, N.Y.	8/2/32	L	L	6'2	207	1671	6706	2296	1523	.342	.519
Brown, Willard "Willard" "California" 87–89NYN 90NYP 91PhiN 93BalN 93–94LouN 94StLN												
?/?/66	San Francisco, Cal.	12/20/97	R	R	6'2	190	418	1589	415	236	.261	.338
Burns, Patrick "Pat" 84BalA		84BalU										
Unknown	Unknown	Unknown	?	?	?	?	7	29	7	3	.241	.379
***Campbell, Michael "Mike"** 73ResNA												
?/?/50	?, Ireland	Unknown	?	?	?	?	21	83	12	9	.145	.145
Carbine, John C. "John" 75WesNA		76LouN										
10/12/55	Syracuse, N.Y.	9/11/15	?	?	6'	187	17	61	7	3	.115	.115
Carey, George C. "Scoops" 95BalN		98LouN										
12/4/70	Pittsburgh, Pa.	12/17/16	R	R	?	175	131	522	134	60	.257	.331
Carleton, James "Jim" 71–72CleNA												
?/?/49	?, N.Y.	Unknown	?	?	5'8	155	36	165	44	39	.267	.345
Carney, John Joseph "Jack" 89WasN		90BufP	90CleP	91CinA	91MilA							
11/10/66	Salem, Mass.	10/19/25	R	R	5'10½	175	252	946	258	120	.273	.354
Carr, Charles Carbitt "Charlie" 98WasN												
12/27/76	Coatsville, Pa.	11/25/32	R	R	6'2	195	20	73	14	6	.192	.219
Cartwright, Edward Charles "Ed" "Jumbo"		90StLA	94–97WasN									
10/6/59	Johnstown, Pa.	9/3/33	R	R	5'10	220	495	1902	562	348	.295	.432
Cassidy, Peter Francis "Pete" 96LouN		99BroN	99WasN									
4/8/73	Wilmington, Del.	7/9/29	R	R	5'10	165	101	382	98	39	.257	.325
***Clapp, Aaron Bronson "Aaron"** 79TroN												
7/?/56	Ithaca, N.Y.	1/13/14	?	R	5'8	175	36	146	39	24	.267	.370
Clark, William Otis "Willie" "Wee Willie" 95–97NYN		98–99PitN										
8/16/72	Pittsburgh, Pa.	11/13/32	L	?	?	?	348	1273	366	188	.288	.390
Cogswell, Edward "Ed" 79BosN		80TroN	82WorN									
2/25/54	?, England	7/27/88	R	R	5'8	150	109	496	146	102	.294	.349
Comiskey, Charles Albert "Charlie" "Commie" 82–89StLA		90ChiP	91StLA	92–94CinN								
8/15/59	Chicago, Ill.	10/26/31	R	R	6'	180	1388	5788	1527	992	.264	.337
Connor, Edward "Ned" 71TroNA												
?/?/50	?, N.Y.	Unknown	?	?	5'9	156	7	33	7	6	.212	.212

First Basemen

BIRTH DATE	BIRTHPLACE	DEATH DATE	B	T	HGT	WGT	G	AB	H	R	BA	SA
*Connor, Roger "Roger" 80–82TroN 83–89NYN 90NYP 91NYN 92PhiN 93–94NYN 94–97StLN												
7/1/57	Waterbury, Conn.	1/4/31	L	L	6'3	220	1997	7794	2467	1620	.317	.486
Crisham, Patrick J. "Pat" 99BalN												
6/4/77	Amesbury, Mass.	6/12/15	?	?	6'	168	53	172	50	23	.291	.355
Croft, Arthur F. "Art" 75RedsNA 77StLN 78IndN												
1/23/55	St. Louis, Mo.	3/16/84	?	?	?	?	133	517	101	50	.195	.230
Cudworth, James Alaric "Jim" "Cuddy" 84KCU												
8/22/58	Fairhaven, Mass.	12/21/43	R	R	6'	165	32	116	17	7	.147	.190
Darragh, James S. "Jack" 91LouA												
7/17/66	Ebensburg, Pa.	8/12/39	?	?	?	?	1	2	1	0	.500	.500
Davis, Harry H. "Harry" "Jasper" 95–96NYN 96–98PitN 98LouN 98–99WasN												
7/19/73	Philadelphia, Pa.	8/11/47	R	R	5'10	180	340	1281	341	190	.266	.411
Dehlman, Herman J. "Herman" "Dutch" 72–74AtlNA 75StLNA 76–77StLN												
?/?/50	Catasauqua, Pa.	3/13/85	?	?	?	?	307	1222	261	226	.214	.248
Devlin, James Alexander "Jim" 73PhiNA 74–75ChiNA 76–77LouN												
?/?/49	Philadelphia, Pa.	10/10/83	R	R	5'11	175	266	1186	340	180	.287	.352
Dillon, Frank Edward "Pop" 99–00PitN												
10/17/73	Normal, Ill.	9/12/31	L	R	6'1	185	35	139	33	24	.237	.281
Doyle, John Joseph "Jack" "Dirty Jack" 89–90Col A 91–92CleN 92–95NYN 96–97BaltN 98WasN 98–00NYN												
10/25/69	Killorglin, Ireland	12/31/58	R	R	5'9	155	1148	4471	1386	771	.310	.402
Dunn, Stephen B. "Steve" 84StPU												
12/21/58	London, Ont., Canada	5/5/33	?	?	5'9½	173	9	32	8	2	.250	.313
Everett, William Lee "Bill" "Wild Bill" b. Everitt 95–00ChiN												
12/13/68	Fort Wayne, Ind.	1/19/38	L	R	6'1½	185	665	2727	880	521	.323	.395
Faatz, Jayson S. "Jay" 84PitA 88CleA 89CleN 90BufP												
10/24/60	Weedsport, N.Y.	4/10/23	R	R	6'4	?	298	1135	274	159	.241	.292
Farrar, Sydney Douglas "Sid" 83–89PhiN 90PhiP												
8/10/59	Paris Hill, Me.	5/7/35	?	R	5'10	185	943	3573	904	497	.253	.342
Field, James C. "Jim" 83–84ColA 85PitA 85BalA 90RocA 98WasN												
4/24/63	Philadelphia, Pa.	5/13/53	?	?	6'1	170	332	1274	292	180	.229	.316
Fisler, Weston Dickson "Wes" "Icicle" 71–75AthNA 76PhiN												
7/5/41	Camden, N.J.	12/25/22	R	?	5'6	137	273	1334	414	258	.310	.390
Flanagan, Edward J. "Ed" "Sleepy" 87PhiA 89LouA												
9/15/61	Lowell, Mass.	11/10/26	?	R	6'1	190	42	168	42	23	.250	.375
Flynn, William "Clipper" 71TroNA 72OlyNA												
4/29/49	Lansingburgh, N.Y.	11/11/81	?	R	5'7	140	38	182	57	47	.313	.363
Foran, James H. "Jim" 71KekNA												
?/?/48	New York, N.Y.	Unknown	?	?	5'6½	159	19	89	31	21	.348	.461
*Foutz, David Luther "Dave" "Scissors" 84–87StLA 88–89BroA 90–96BroN												
9/7/56	Carroll Co., Md.	3/5/97	R	R	6'2	161	1135	4533	1253	784	.276	.378
Fox, George B. "Paddy" 91LouA 99PitN												
12/1/68	Pottstown, Pa.	5/18/14	?	?	?	?	19	60	12	5	.200	.317
*Ganzel, John Henry "John" 98PitN 00ChiN												
4/7/74	Kalamazoo, Mich.	1/14/59	R	R	6'1½	190	93	329	84	34	.255	.359
Goeckel, William John "Billy" 99PhiN												
9/3/71	Wilkes–Barre, Pa.	11/1/22	R	L	?	?	37	141	37	17	.262	.298

First Basemen

BIRTH DATE	BIRTHPLACE	DEATH DATE	B	T	HGT	WGT	G	AB	H	R	BA	SA
Goodman, Jacob "Jake" 78MilN 82PitA												
9/4/53	Lancaster, Pa.	3/9/90	?	?	6'1¹/₂	?	70	293	75	33	.256	.321
Gorman, John F. "Jack" "Stooping Jack" 83StLA 84KCU 84PitA												
?/?/59	St. Louis, Mo.	9/9/89	?	?	?	?	42	168	42	28	.250	.315
Gould, Charles Harvey "Charlie" 71–72BosNA 74BalNA 75NHNA 76–77CinN												
8/21/47	Cincinnati, Ohio	4/10/17	R	R	6'	172	221	963	248	139	.258	.330
Griffin, Thomas William "Tom" 84MilU												
1/?/57	Titusville, Pa.	4/17/33	?	?	?	?	11	41	9	5	.220	.268
Harris, Frank W. "Frank" 84AltU												
11/2/58	Pittsburgh, Pa.	11/26/39	R	R	?	?	24	95	25	10	.263	.305
Hartnett, Patrick J. "Pat" "Happy" 90StLA												
10/20/63	Boston, Mass.	4/10/35	?	?	6'1	175	14	53	10	6	.189	.264
Hautz, Charles A. "Charlie" 75RedsNA 84PitA												
2/5/52	St. Louis, Mo.	1/24/29	R	R	5'7	150	26	107	30	5	.280	.308
Hecker, Guy Jackson "Guy" 82–89LouA 90PitN												
4/3/56	Youngsville, Pa.	12/3/38	R	R	6'	190	703	2866	810	501	.283	.376
Heifer, Franklin "Frank" "Heck" 75BosNA												
1/18/54	Reading, Pa.	8/29/93	?	?	5'10¹/₂	175	11	50	14	11	.280	.400
Heinzman, John Peter "Jack" 86LouA												
9/27/63	New Albany, Ind.	11/10/14	R	R	?	?	1	5	0	1	.000	.000
Householder, Charles W. "Charlie" 82BalA 84BroA												
?/?/56	Harrisburg, Pa.	12/26/08	L	L	5'11	158	150	580	144	70	.248	.347
Hughes, William R. "Bill" 84WasU 85PhiA												
11/25/66	Bladinsville, Ill.	8/25/43	L	L	?	?	18	65	9	8	.138	.185
Jackson, Henry Everett "Henry" 87IndN												
6/23/61	Union City, Ind.	9/14/32	R	R	6'2	185	10	38	10	1	.263	.289
Joy, Aloysius C. "Pop" 84WasU												
6/11/60	Washington D.C.	6/28/37	?	?	?	?	36	130	28	12	.215	.215
Kane, William Jeremiah "Jerry" 90StLA												
4/?/69	Baltimore, Md.	6/16/49	R	R	6'	175	8	25	5	3	.200	.200
Kavanaugh, ? 72EckNA												
Unknown	Unknown	Unknown	?	?	?	?	5	23	6	3	.261	.304
Kelley, Michael Joseph "Mike" 99LouN												
12/2/75	Templeton, Mass.	6/6/55	R	R	6'	210	76	282	68	48	.241	.326
Kerins, John Nelson "John" 84IndA 85–89LouA 89BalA 90StLA												
7/15/58	Indianapolis, Ind.	9/8/19	R	R	5'10	177	557	2227	561	392	.252	.357
King, Samuel Warren "Sam" 84WasA												
5/17/52	Peabody, Mass.	8/11/22	?	L	6'	?	12	45	8	3	.178	.222
Knox, Andrew Jackson "Andy" "Dasher" 90PhiA												
1/6/64	Philadelphia, Pa.	9/14/40	R	R	?	?	21	75	19	6	.253	.293
LaChance, George Joseph "Candy" 93–98BroN 99BalN												
2/15/70	Putnam, Conn.	8/18/32	B	R	6'1	183	682	2694	790	421	.293	.417
Lane, George M. "Chappy" 82PitA 84TolA												
Unknown	Pittsburgh, Pa.	Unknown	R	?	?	165	114	429	87	52	.203	.303
Larkin, Henry E. "Henry" "Ted" 84–89PhiA 90CleP 91PhiA 92–93WasN												
1/12/60	Reading, Pa.	1/31/42	R	R	5'10	175	1184	4718	1430	925	.303	.440

First Basemen

BIRTH DATE	BIRTHPLACE	DEATH DATE	B	T	HGT	WGT	G	AB	H	R	BA	SA
Latham, George Warren "Juice" "Jumbo" 75BosNA 75NHNA 77LouN 82PhiA 83–84LouA												
9/6/52	Utica, N.Y.	5/26/14	R	R	5'8	210	334	1431	353	209	.247	.295
Lehane, Michael Patrick "Mike" "Mickey" 84WasU 90–91ColA												
4/15/65	New York, N.Y.	Unknown	R	?	6'1½	180	280	1035	222	114	.214	.272
Levis, Charles H. "Charlie" 84BalU 84WasU 84IndA 85BalA												
6/21/60	St. Louis, Mo.	10/16/26	R	?	?	?	92	390	88	61	.226	.321
Libby, Stephen Augustus "Steve" 79BufN												
12/8/53	Scarborough, Me.	3/31/35	?	?	6'1½	168	1	2	0	0	.000	.000
Lizotte, Abel "Abel" 96PitN												
4/13/70	Lewiston, Me.	12/4/26	?	?	5'8	174	7	29	3	3	.103	.103
Luff, Henry T. "Henry" 75NHN 82DetN 82CinA 83LouA 84PhiU 84KCU												
9/14/56	Philadelphia, Pa.	10/11/16	?	?	5'11	175	106	450	111	42	.247	.331
Lutenberg, Charles William "Luke" 94LouN												
10/4/64	Quincy, Ill.	12/24/38	R	R	6'2	225	69	250	48	42	.192	.264
Mahoney, George W. "Mike" "Big Mike" 97BosN 98StLN												
12/5/73	Boston, Mass.	1/3/40	R	?	6'4	220	4	9	1	1	.111	.111
Massey, William Harry "Bill" "Big Bill" 94CinN												
1/?/71	Philadelphia, Pa.	10/9/40	R	R	5'11	168	13	53	15	7	.283	.340
McAtee, Michael James "Bub" 71ChiNA 72TroNA												
3/?/45	Troy, N.Y.	10/18/76	?	R	6'1	160	51	264	65	64	.246	.311
McCauley, Allen A. "Al" 84IndA 90PhiN 91WasA												
3/4/63	Indianapolis, Ind.	8/24/17	L	L	6'	180	188	677	170	106	.251	.352
McFadden, Guy G. "Guy" 95StLN												
9/3/72	Topeka, Kan.	3/10/11	?	?	?	?	4	14	3	1	.214	.214
McGann, Dennis Lawrence "Dan" 96BosN 98BalN 99BroN 99WasN 00StLN												
7/15/71	Shelbyville, Ky.	12/13/10	B	R	6'	190	448	1644	496	317	.302	.411
McGuinness, John James "John" 76NYN 79SyrN 84PhiU												
?/?/57	?, Ireland	12/19/16	?	?	5'10½	150	66	275	67	32	.244	.291
McKinnon, Alexander J. "Alex" 84NYN 85–86StLN 87PitN												
8/14/56	Boston, Mass.	7/24/87	R	?	5'11½	170	386	1572	465	209	.296	.412
McMahon, John Henry "Jack" 92–93NYN												
10/15/69	Waterbury, Conn.	12/30/94	R	L	5'10	185	51	177	43	26	.243	.390
McQuery, William Thomas "Mox" 84CinU 85DetN 86KCN 90SyrA 91WasA												
6/28/61	Garrard Co., Ky.	6/12/00	?	?	6'4	?	417	1581	429	231	.271	.365
McSorley, John Bernard "Trick" 75RedsNA 84TolA 85StLN 86StLA												
12/16/52	St. Louis, Mo.	2/9/36	R	R	5'4	142	28	94	23	15	.245	.298
McVey, Calvin Alexander "Cal" 71–72BosNA 73BalNA 74–75BosNA 76–77ChiN 78–79CinN												
8/30/50	Montrose, Iowa	8/20/26	R	R	5'9	170	530	2513	869	565	.346	.450
Mills, Everett "Everett" "Ev" 71OlyNA 72–73BalNA 74–75HarNA 76HarN												
1/20/45	Newark, N.J.	6/22/08	?	?	6'1	174	337	1525	433	283	.284	.358
*Moffett, Joseph W. "Joe" 84TolA												
6/?/59	Wheeling, W.Va.	Unknown	?	?	6'	179	56	204	41	17	201	.255
Morrill, John Francis "John" "Honest John" 76–88BosN 89WasN 90BosP												
2/19/55	Boston, Mass.	4/2/32	R	R	5'10½	155	1265	4912	1275	821	.260	.367
Motz, Frank H. "Frank" 90PhiN 93–94CinN												
10/1/68	Freeburg, Pa.	3/18/44	?	?	6'	160	62	227	54	25	.238	.322

First Basemen

BIRTH DATE	BIRTHPLACE	DEATH DATE	B	T	HGT	WGT	G	AB	H	R	BA	SA
Murnane, Timothy Hayes "Tim"	72ManNA	73–74AthNA	75PhiNA	76–77BosN	78ProN	84BosU						
6/4/52	Naugatuck, Conn.	2/7/17	L	R	5'9½	172	384	1635	427	338	.261	.300
O'Brien, William Smith "Billy"	84StPU	84KCU	87–89WasN	90BroA								
3/14/60	Albany, N.Y.	5/26/11	R	?	6'	185	356	1424	364	164	.256	.395
O'Connor, Daniel Cornelius "Dan"	90LouA											
8/?/68	Guelph, Ont. Can.	3/3/42	L	R	6'2	185	6	26	12	3	.462	.577
O'Neill, Dennis "Dennie"	93StLN											
11/22/66	Holyoke, Mass.	11/15/12	L	L	6'2½	200	7	25	3	3	.120	.120
Orr, David L. "Dave"	83NYA	83NYN	83–87NYA	88BroA	89ColA	90BroP						
9/29/59	New York, N.Y.	6/3/15	R	R	5'11	250	791	3289	1126	536	.342	.502
Phelan, Daniel T. "Dan"	90LouA											
7/23/64	Thomaston, Conn.	12/7/45	?	?	?	?	8	32	8	4	.250	.344
Phillips, William B. "Bill"	79–84CleN	85–87BroA	88KCA									
?/?/57	St. John, N.B., Can.	10/7/00	R	R	?	202	1038	4255	1130	562	.266	.374
Powell, James Edwin "Jim"	84VirA											
8/30/59	Richmond, Va.	11/20/29	?	?	5'10	170	41	151	37	23	.245	.351
Powell, Martin J. "Martin" "Mart"	81–83DetN	84CinU	85PhiA									
3/25/56	Fitchburg, Mass.	2/5/88	L	L	6'	170	298	1238	341	218	.275	.340
Power, Thomas E. "Tom"	90BalA											
Unknown	San Francisco, Ca.	2/25/98	?	?	5'11	164	38	125	26	11	.208	.248
Pratt, Thomas J. "Tom"	71AthNA											
1/24/44	Chelsea, Mass.	9/28/08	?	L	5'7½	150	1	6	2	2	.333	.333
Prince, Walter Farr "Walter"	83LouA	84DetN	84WasA	84WasU								
5/9/61	Amherst, N.H.	3/2/38	L	R	5'9	150	55	202	42	23	.208	.257
Reilly, John Good "John" "Long John"	80CinN	83–89CinA	90–91CinN									
10/5/58	Cincinnati, Ohio	5/31/37	R	R	6'3	178	1142	4684	1352	898	.289	.438
Rogers, James F. "Jim"	96WasN	96–97LouN										
4/9/72	Hartford, Conn.	1/21/00	?	?	5'7½	180	151	594	140	82	.236	.320
Rothfuss, John Albert "Jack"	97PitN											
4/18/72	Newark, N.J.	4/20/47	R	R	5'11½	195	35	115	36	20	.313	.409
Ryan, Daniel R. "Cyclone"	87NYA	91BosN										
?/?/66	Cappagh White, Ireland	1/30/17	?	R	6'	200	9	33	7	4	.212	.242
Scanlan, Mortimer J. "Mort"	90NYN											
3/18/61	Chicago, Ill.	12/29/28	?	?	6'1	186	3	10	0	0	.000	.000
Schoeneck, Louis N. "Jumbo"	84Chi–PitU	84BalU	88–89IndA									
3/3/62	Chicago, Ill.	1/20/30	R	R	6'3	223	170	657	186	79	.283	.350
Schomberg, Otto H. "Otto" b. Shambrick	86PitA	87–88IndN										
11/14/64	Milwaukee, Wis.	5/3/27	L	L	?	?	214	777	220	155	.283	.407
Scott, Milton Parker "Milt" "Mikado Milt"	82ChiN	84–85DetN	85PitA	86BalA								
1/17/66	Chicago, Ill.	11/3/38	?	R	5'9	160	341	1285	293	107	.228	.288
Smith, John J. "Jack"	82TroN	82WorN										
?/?/58	San Francisco, Cal.	Unknown	?	?	5'11	210	54	219	53	37	.242	.320
Smith, Samuel J. "Skyrocket"	88LouA											
3/19/68	Baltimore, Md.	4/26/16	R	?	6'2	170	58	206	49	27	.238	.335
Spies, Henry "Harry"	95CinN	95LouN										
6/12/66	New Orleans, La.	7/8/42	R	R	5'11½	170	86	326	85	44	.261	.371

First Basemen

BIRTH DATE	BIRTHPLACE	DEATH DATE	B	T	HGT	WGT	G	AB	H	R	BA	SA
Start, Joseph "Joe" "Old Reliable" "Rocks" 71–75MutNA 76NYN 77HarN 78ChiN 79–85ProN 86WasN												
10/14/42	New York, N.Y.	3/27/27	L	L	5'9	165	1071	4747	1418	853	.299	.367
Stearns, Daniel Eckford "Dan" "Ecky" 80BufN 81DetN 82CinA 83–85BalA 85BufN 89KCA												
10/17/61	Buffalo, N.Y.	6/28/44	L	R	6'1	185	509	2025	491	295	.242	.325
Sullivan, John Frank "Chub" 77–78CinN 80WorN												
1/12/56	Boston, Mass.	9/12/81	R	R	6'	164	112	442	114	55	.258	.303
Swan, Andrew J. "Andy" 84WasA 84VirA												
5/11/45	Tewksbury, Mass.	8/27/85	?	?	?	?	8	31	8	5	.258	.290
Sweeney, Jeremiah H. "Jerry" 84KCU												
?/?/60	Boston, Mass.	8/25/91	?	?	5'9½	157	31	129	34	16	.264	.287
Taylor, Harry Leonard "Harry" 90–91LouA 92LouN 93BalN												
4/4/66	Halsey Valley, N.Y.	7/12/55	L	?	6'2	160	438	1754	502	311	.286	.322
Taylor, Zachary H. "Zach" 74BalNA												
Unknown	Unknown	Unknown	?	?	?	?	13	48	12	3	.250	.250
***Tebeau, Oliver Wendell** "Patsy" 87ChiN 89CleN 90CleP 91–98CleN 99–00StLN												
12/5/64	St. Louis, Mo.	5/15/18	R	R	5'8	163	1167	4618	1291	671	.280	.364
Tenney, Frederick "Fred" 94–00BosN												
11/26/71	Georgetown, Mass.	7/3/52	L	L	5'9	155	673	2701	869	545	.322	.398
Tobin, William F. "Bill" 80WorN 80TroN												
10/10/54	Hartford, Conn.	10/10/12	L	?	?	?	38	152	24	15	.158	.178
Toy, James Madison "Jim" 87CleA 90BroA												
2/20/58	Beaver Falls, Pa.	3/13/19	?	?	5'6	160	153	583	123	67	.211	.273
Tucker, Thomas Joseph "Tommy" "Foghorn" 87–89BalA 90–97BosN 97WasN 98BroN 98StLN 99CleN												
10/28/63	Holyoke, Mass.	10/22/35	B	R	5'11	165	1687	6479	1882	1084	.290	.373
Veach, William Walter "Peekaboo" 84KCU 87LouN 90CleN 90PitN												
6/15/62	Indianapolis, Ind.	11/12/37	?	?	?	?	100	353	76	39	.215	.309
Virtue, Jacob Kitchline "Jake" "Guesses" 90–94CleN												
3/2/65	Philadelphia, Pa.	2/3/43	B	L	5'9½	165	474	1764	483	321	.274	.376
Werden, Percival Wheritt "Perry" 84StLU 88WasN 90TolA 91BalA 92–93StLN 97LouN												
7/21/65	St. Louis, Mo.	1/9/34	R	R	6'2	220	693	2740	773	444	.282	.414
Whistler, Lewis W. "Lew" b. Wissler 90–91NYN 92BalN 92–93LouN 93StLN												
3/10/68	St. Louis, Mo.	12/30/59	?	R	5'10½	178	272	1014	247	150	.244	.363
White, William Edward "Bill" 79ProN												
Unknown	Milner, Ga.	Unknown	?	?	?	?	1	4	1	1	.250	.250
Wills, Davis Bowles "Dave" 99LouN												
1/26/77	Charlottesville, Va.	10/12/59	L	L	?	?	24	94	21	15	.223	.277

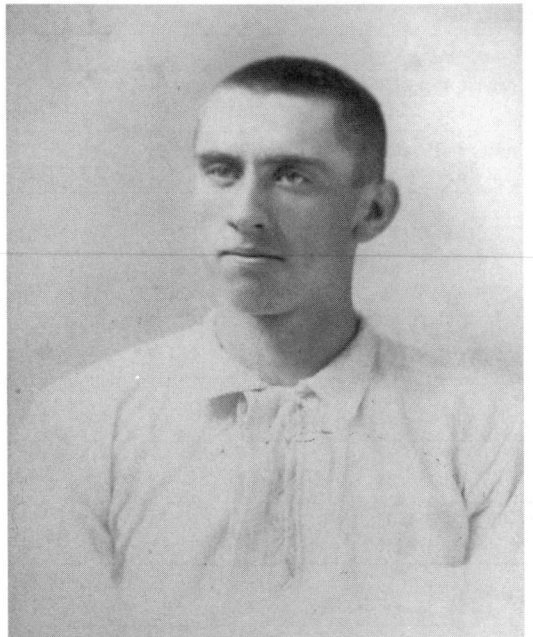

Jack Darragh, a one-gamer whose career line looks intriguing—he hit .500 when he collected a single in his only two major league at bats on May 13, 1891. Darragh was among the many players frozen out when the two major leagues consolidated in 1892, cutting jobs by a quarter.

The 1898 Baltimore Orioles with switchhitting Dan McGann who seemingly solved Ned Hanlon's chronic first-base problem when he joined the O's in 1898 and hit .301 with 106 RBI. The following year, however, he was part of the mass exodus of Baltimore's stars to Brooklyn. McGann developed into possibly the best all-around first sacker in the first decade of the twentieth century before being found dead in 1910 under circumstances that were officially deemed suicide but may have been murder. Top: John McGraw, Willie Keeler, Jerry Nops, Gene Demontreville and Jim Hughes (another mysterious suicide victim). Bottom: Wilbert Robinson, Joe Kelley, Frank Kitson, McGann, Hughie Jennings and Boileryard Clarke.

Second Basemen

BIRTH DATE	BIRTHPLACE	DEATH DATE	B	T	HGT	WGT	G	AB	H	R	BA	SA
Ardner, Joseph A. "Joe" 84CleN 90CleN												
2/27/58	Mt. Vernon, Ohio	9/15/35	R	R	?	160	110	415	88	34	.212	.255
Barkley, Samuel E. "Sam" 84TolA 85StLA 86PitA 87PitN 88–89KCA												
5/24/58	Wheeling, W.Va.	4/20/12	R	R	5'11½	180	582	2329	602	362	.258	.359
Barnes, Roscoe Charles "Ross" 71–75BosNA 76–77ChiN 79CinN 81BosN												
5/8/50	Mt. Morris, Ill.	2/5/15	R	R	5'8½	145	499	2392	858	699	.359	.464
Bassett, Charles Edwin "Charlie" 84–85ProN 86KCN 87–89IndN 90–92NYN 92LouN												
2/9/63	Central Falls, R.I.	5/28/42	R	R	5'10	150	917	3493	806	392	.231	.304
Beavens, E. P. "E.P." (aka Bevens) 71TroNA 72AtlNA												
?/?/48	Troy, N.Y.	Unknown	?	R	5'8	138	13	58	15	13	.257	.293
Beck, Ervin Thomas "Erve" "Dutch" 99BroN												
7/19/78	Toledo, Ohio	12/23/16	R	R	5'10	168	8	24	4	2	.167	.250
Benedict, Arthur Melville "Art" 83PhiN												
3/31/62	Cornwall, Ill.	1/20/48	R	R	?	?	3	15	4	3	.267	.333
Bierbauer, Louis W. "Lou" 86–89PhiA 90BroP 91–96PitN 97–98StLN												
9/28/65	Erie, Pa.	1/31/26	L	R	5'8	140	1383	5706	1521	819	.267	.354
Bittman, Henry Peter "Red" 89KCA												
7/22/62	Cincinnati, Ohio	11/8/29	?	?	?	?	4	14	4	2	.286	.286
Bonner, Frank J. "Frank" 94–95BalN 95StLN 96BroN 99WasN												
8/20/69	Lowell, Mass.	12/31/05	R	R	5'7½	169	153	600	161	88	.268	.370
Bryant, George F. "George" 85DetN												
2/10/57	Bridgeport, Conn.	6/12/07	?	?	?	?	1	4	0	0	.000	.000
Burdock, John Joseph "Jack" 72–73AtlNA 74MutNA 75HarNA 76–77HarN 78–88BosN 88BroA 91BroN												
4/?/52	Brooklyn, N.Y.	11/27/31	R	R	5'9½	158	1187	4916	1230	777	.250	.315
Campbell, Samuel "Sam" 90PhiA												
Unknown	Philadelphia, Pa.	Unknown	?	?	?	?	2	5	0	0	.000	.000
Carey, Roger J. "Roger" 87NYN												
Unknown	Unknown	Unknown	?	?	?	?	1	4	0	0	.000	.000
Childs, Clarence Algernon "Cupid" 88PhiN 90SyrA 91–98CleN 99StLN 00ChiN												
8/14/67	Calvert Co., Md.	11/18/12	L	R	5'8	185	1393	5382	1659	1190	.308	.393
Clark, William Winfield "Bill" 97LouN												
4/11/75	Circleville, Ohio	4/15/59	R	R	5'10	175	4	16	3	2	.188	.188
Collins, Charles Augustine "Chub" 84BufN 84IndA 85DetN												
10/12/57	Dundee, Ont. Can.	5/20/14	B	?	5'11½	165	97	362	71	50	.196	.238
Collins, Hubert B. "Hub" 86–88LouA 88–89BroA 90–92BroN												
4/15/64	Louisville, Ky.	5/21/92	R	R	5'8	160	680	2779	790	653	.284	.369
Connor, James Matthew "Jim" b. O'Connor 92ChiN 97–99ChiN												
5/11/63	Port Jervis, N.Y.	9/3/50	R	R	?	?	293	1058	247	117	.233	.295
Corridan, Philip "Phil" 84Chi–PitU												
Unknown	Fort Wayne, Ind.	Unknown	?	?	?	?	2	7	1	1	.143	.143
Crane, Frederick William Hotchkiss "Fred" 73ResNA 75AtlNA												
11/4/40	Old Saybrook, Conn.	4/27/25	?	?	?	?	22	85	18	7	.212	.224
Crane, Samuel Newhall "Sam" 80BufN 83NYA 84CinU 85–86DetN 86StLN 87WasN 90NYN 90PitN												
1/2/54	Springfield, Mass.	6/26/25	R	R	?	?	373	1359	276	183	.203	.258
Craver, William H. "Bill" 71TroNA 72–73BalNA 74PhiNA 75CenNA 75AthNA 76NYN 77LouN												
6/?/44	Troy, N.Y.	6/17/01	R	R	5'9	160	339	1563	455	320	.290	.375

Second Basemen

BIRTH DATE	BIRTHPLACE	DEATH DATE	B	T	HGT	WGT	G	AB	H	R	BA	SA
Creamer, George W. "George" b. Triebel 78MilN 79SyrN 80–82WorN 83–84PitN												
?/?/55	Philadelphia, Pa.	6/27/86	R	R	6'2	?	500	1862	400	234	.215	.276
Croft, Henry T. "Harry" 99LouN 99PhiN												
8/1/75	Chicago, Ill.	12/11/33	?	?	?	?	4	9	1	0	.111	.111
Cronin, Daniel T. "Dan" 84Chi–PitU 84StLU												
4/1/57	S. Boston, Mass.	11/30/85	?	?	5'8	170	2	9	1	1	.111	.111
Crooks, John Charles "Jack" 89–91ColA 92–93StLN 95–96WasN 96LouN 98StLN												
11/19/65	St. Paul, Minn.	2/2/18	R	R	5'10	170	794	2780	668	536	.240	.321
Curley, Walter James "Doc" 99ChiN												
3/12/74	Upton, Mass.	9/23/20	R	R	?	?	10	37	4	7	.108	.162
*Daly, Thomas Peter "Tom" "Tido" 87–88ChiN 89WasN 90–96BroN 98–00BroN												
2/7/66	Philadelphia, Pa.	10/29/38	B	R	5'7	170	1171	4218	1187	817	.281	.393
Delaney, William L. "Bill" 90CleN												
3/4/63	Cincinnati, Ohio	3/1/42	R	R	?	?	36	116	22	16	.190	.241
*Demontreville, Eugene Napoleon "Gene" (aka Demont) 94PitN 95–97WasN 98BalN 99ChiN 99BalN 00BroN												
3/26/74	St. Paul, Minn.	2/18/35	R	R	5'8	165	642	2504	785	403	.313	.388
Dougherty, Charles William "Charlie" 84AltU												
2/7/62	Darlington, Wis.	2/18/25	?	?	?	?	23	85	22	6	259	.318
Dunlap, Frederick C. "Fred" "Sure Shot" 80–83CleN 84StLU 85–86StLN 86–87DetN 88–90PitN 90NYP 91WasA												
5/21/59	Philadelphia, Pa.	12/1/02	R	R	5'8	165	965	3974	1159	759	.292	.406
Eagan, William "Bill" "Bad Bill" 91StLA 93ChiN 98PitN												
6/1/69	Camden, N.J.	2/13/05	?	?	?	?	107	377	90	66	.239	.342
Evers, Thomas Francis "Tom" 82BalA 84WasU												
3/31/52	Troy, N.Y.	3/23/25	?	L	?	?	110	431	99	54	.230	.248
Fair, George T. "George" 76NYN												
1/14/56	Boston, Mass.	2/12/39	?	?	5'7½	140	1	4	0	0	.000	.000
Farrell, John A. "Jack" 79SyrN 79–85ProN 86PhiN 86–87WasN 88–89BalA												
7/5/57	Newark, N.J.	2/10/14	R	R	5'9	165	884	3613	877	584	.243	.333
Fisher, George C. "George" 84CleN 84WilU												
Unknown	Wilmington, Del.	Unknown	L	?	?	?	14	53	5	2	.094	.094
Fleet, Frank H. "Frank" 71MutNA 72EckNA 73ResNA 74AtlNA 75StLNA 75AtlNA												
?/?/48	New York, N.Y.	6/13/00	?	?	?	?	88	373	85	54	.228	.241
Flood, Timothy A. "Tim" 99StLN												
3/13/77	Montgomery City, Mo.	6/15/29	R	R	5'9	160	10	31	9	0	.290	.290
Forster, Thomas W. "Tom" 82DetN 84PitA 85–86NYA												
5/1/59	New York, N.Y.	7/17/46	R	?	5'9	153	180	666	131	76	.197	.236
Fouser, William C. "Bill" 76PhiN												
10/?/55	Philadelphia, Pa.	3/1/19	?	?	?	?	21	89	12	11	.135	.157
Galvin, John S. "John" 72AtlNA												
?/?/51	Brooklyn, N.Y.	4/20/04	?	?	?	?	1	4	0	0	.000	.000
Gavern, ? 74AtlNA												
Unknown	Unknown	Unknown	?	?	?	?	1	4	0	1	.000	.000

Second Basemen

BIRTH DATE	BIRTHPLACE	DEATH DATE	B	T	HGT	WGT	G	AB	H	R	BA	SA
*Geis, William J. "Bill" b. Geiss 84DetN												
7/15/58	Chicago, Ill.	9/18/24	?	?	5'10	164	75	283	50	22	.177	.265
*Geiss, Emil August "Emil" 87ChiN												
3/20/67	Chicago, Ill.	10/4/11	R	R	5'11	170	3	12	1	0	.083	.083
Gerhardt, John Joseph "Joe" "Move Up Joe" 73WasNA 74BalNA 75MutNA 76–77LouN 78–79CinN 81DetN												
83–84LouA 85–87NYN 87NYA 90BroA 90StLA 91LouA												
2/14/55	Washington, D.C.	3/11/22	R	R	6'	160	1071	4139	939	493	.227	.288
*Gilbert, Harry H. "Harry" 90PitN												
7/7/68	Pottstown, Pa.	12/23/09	?	?	?	?	2	8	2	1	.250	.250
Gill, James C. "Jim" 89StLA												
Unknown	St. Louis, Mo.	Unknown	?	?	?	?	2	8	2	2	.250	.375
*Gleason, William J. "Kid" 88–91PhiA 92–94StLN 94–95BalN 96–00NYN												
10/26/66	Camden, N.J.	1/2/33	B	R	5'7	158	1125	4234	1126	655	.266	.319
Glenalvin, Robert J. "Bob" b. Dowling 90ChiN 93ChiN												
1/17/67	Indianapolis, Ind.	3/24/44	?	R	5'9	160	82	311	88	54	.283	.389
Greenwood, William F. "Bill" 82PhiA 84BroA 87–88BalA 89ColA 90RocA												
?/?/57	Philadelphia, Pa.	5/2/02	B	L	5'7½	180	574	2170	490	381	.226	.287
Hach, Irvin William "Irv" "Major" 97LouN												
6/6/73	Louisville, Ky.	8/13/36	R	R	?	?	16	51	11	5	.216	.255
Haldeman, John Avery "John" 77LouN												
12/2/55	PeeWee Valley, Ky.	9/17/99	L	R	5'10	175	1	4	0	0	.000	.000
Hall, James "Jim" 72AtlNA 74AtlNA 75WesNA												
Unknown	Unknown	1/30/86	?	?	?	?	16	69	20	9	.290	.348
Hallman, William Wilson "Bill" 88–89PhiN 90PhiP 91PhiA 92–97PhiN 97StLN 98BroN												
3/31/67	Pittsburgh, Pa.	9/11/20	R	R	5'8	160	1239	5096	1443	855	.283	.363
Hawkes, Thorndike Proctor "Thorny" 79TroN 84WasA												
10/15/52	Danvers, Mass.	2/3/29	R	R	5'8	135	102	401	94	40	.234	.274
Hellings, ? 75AtlNA												
Unknown	Philadelphia, Pa.	Unknown	?	?	?	?	1	4	1	0	.250	.250
Hengle, Emery J. "Moxie" 84Chi–PitU 84StPU 85BufN												
10/7/57	Chicago, Ill.	12/11/24	R	?	?	?	35	133	24	13	.180	.233
Higgins, William Edward "Bill" 88BosN 90StLA 90SyrA												
9/8/61	Wilmington, Del.	4/25/19	?	R	5'9	155	82	316	76	45	.241	.278
Hiland, John William "John" 85PhiN												
9/?/60	Baltic, R.I.	4/10/01	L	L	5'8½	165	3	9	0	0	.000	.000
Houseman, John Franklin "John" 94ChiN 97StLN												
1/10/70	?, Holland	11/4/22	?	?	?	160	84	293	74	39	.253	.331
Howe, John "Shorty" 90NYN 93NYN												
Unknown	New York, N.Y.	Unknown	?	?	?	?	20	69	14	5	.203	.203
Hutchinson, Edwin Forrest "Ed" 90ChiN												
5/19/67	Pittsburgh, Pa.	7/19/34	L	R	5'11	175	4	17	1	0	.059	.118
Jackson, Samuel "Sam" 71BosNA 72AtlNA												
3/24/49	Ripon, England	8/4/93	R	R	5'5½	160	19	88	19	17	.216	.341
Johnson, Albert L. "Abbie" 96–97LouN												
7/26/72	London, Ont., Can.	Unknown	?	?	5'9½	165	73	248	59	26	.238	.286

Second Basemen

BIRTH DATE	BIRTHPLACE	DEATH DATE	B	T	HGT	WGT	G	AB	H	R	BA	SA
Johnson, Caleb Clark "Caleb" 71CleNA												
5/23/44	Fulton, Ill.	3/7/25	?	?	?	?	16	67	15	10	.224	.239
Jones, Charles F. "Charlie" 84BroA												
Unknown	New York, N.Y.	Unknown	?	?	?	?	25	90	16	10	.178	.189
Jones, Henry Monroe "Henry" "Baldy" 84DetN												
5/10/57	New York, N.Y.	5/31/55	R	?	5'6	149	34	127	28	24	.220	.260
Kearns, Thomas J. "Tom" "Dasher" 80BufN 82DetN 84DetN												
11/9/59	Rochester, N.Y.	12/7/38	R	R	5'7	160	27	99	20	11	.202	.242
Keerl, George Henry "George" 75ChiNA												
4/10/47	Baltimore, Md.	9/13/23	R	R	5'7	145	6	23	3	2	.130	.130
Keister, William Hoffman "Bill" "Wagon Tongue" 96BalN 98BosN 99BalN 00StLN												
8/17/74	Baltimore, Md.	8/19/24	L	R	5'5½	168	287	1108	340	187	.307	.412
Kenney, John "John" 72AtlNA												
Unknown	Unknown	Unknown	?	?	?	?	5	19	0	0	.000	.000
Kernan, Joseph "Joe" 73MarNA												
Unknown	Baltimore, Md.	Unknown	?	?	?	?	2	8	3	1	.375	.375
Kimball, Eugene Boynton "Gene" 71CleN												
8/31/50	Rochester, N.Y.	8/2/82	?	?	5'10	160	29	131	25	18	.191	.198
Klusman, William F. "Billy" 88BosN 90StLA												
3/24/65	Cincinnati, Ohio	6/24/07	R	R	5'10½	185	43	172	36	18	.209	.320
Krueger, Arthur William "Otto" "Oom Paul" 99CleN 00StLN												
9/17/76	Chicago, Ill.	2/20/61	R	R	5'7	165	25	79	24	12	.303	.443
Lajoie, Napoleon "Nap" "Larry" 96–00PhiN												
9/5/74	Woonsocket, R.I.	2/7/59	R	R	6'1	195	492	2091	721	421	.345	.520
LaRoque, Samuel H.J. "Sam" 88DetN 90–91PitN 91LouA												
2/26/63	St. Mathias, Que., Can.	Unknown	?	R	5'11	190	124	482	120	66	.249	.328
Laughlin, Benjamin "Ben" 73ResNA												
Unknown	Unknown	Unknown	?	?	?	?	12	50	12	3	.240	.260
Lowe, Charles "Charlie" 72AtlNA												
Unknown	Baltimore, Md.	Unknown	?	?	?	?	7	31	5	1	.161	.161
Lowe, Robert Lincoln "Bobby" 90–00BosN												
7/10/68	Pittsburgh, Pa.	12/8/51	R	R	5'10	150	1281	5126	1481	952	.289	.390
Lyons, Patrick Jerry "Pat" 90CleN												
3/?/60	?, Canada	1/20/14	?	R	?	?	11	38	2	2	.053	.079
Mack, Joseph "Reddy" b. McNamara 85–88LouA 89–90BalA												
5/2/66	?, Ireland	12/30/16	?	?	?	?	550	2062	524	381	.254	.340
Madison, Arthur "Art" 95PhiN 99PitN												
1/14/71	Clarksburg, Mass.	1/27/33	R	R	5'9	165	53	152	44	26	.289	.375
Manning, Timothy Edward "Tim" 82ProN 83–85BalA 85ProN												
12/3/53	Henley-on-the-Thames, Eng.	6/11/34	R	R	5'10	170	200	730	138	99	.189	.252
Mappes, George Richard "George" "Dick" 85BalA 86StLN												
12/25/65	St. Louis, Mo.	2/20/34	?	?	?	?	12	33	6	3	.182	.242
Martin, Albert "Al" (aka Albert May) 72EckNA 74–75AtlNA												
Unknown	Unknown	Unknown	?	?	?	?	17	73	12	4	.164	.164
Martin, Alphonse Case "Phoney" 72TroNA 72EckNA 73MutNA												
8/4/45	New York, N.Y.	5/24/33	?	?	5'7	148	74	335	79	42	.236	.251

Second Basemen

BIRTH DATE	BIRTHPLACE	DEATH DATE	B	T	HGT	WGT	G	AB	H	R	BA	SA
McClellan, William Henry "Bill" 78ChiN 81ProN 83–84PhiN 85–88BroA 88CleA												
3/22/56	Chicago, Ill.	7/3/29	L	L	5'5½	156	792	3197	773	533	.242	.308
McCormick, James Ambrose "Jim" 92StLN												
11/2/68	Spencer, Mass.	2/1/48	R	R	6'1	160	3	11	0	0	.000	.000
McCoy, Arthur Gray "Art" 89WasN												
7/?/64	Danville, Pa.	3/22/04	?	?	?	168	2	6	0	0	.000	.000
McDermott, Thomas Nathaniel "Sandy" 85BalA												
3/15/56	Zanesville, Ohio	11/23/22	?	?	?	?	1	0	0	0	.000	.000
McGeary, Michael Henry "Mike" 71TroNA 72–74AthNA 75PhiNA 76–77StLN 79–80ProN 80–81CleN 82DetN												
?/?/51	Philadelphia, Pa.	Unknown	R	R	5'7	138	547	2481	684	484	.276	.309
McPhee, John Alexander "Bid" 82–89CinA 90–99CinN												
11/1/59	Massena, N.Y.	1/3/43	R	R	5'8	152	2135	8291	2250	1678	.271	.372
McQuaid, Mortimer Martin "Marty" 91StLA 98WasN												
6/28/61	Chicago, Ill.	3/5/28	?	?	?	?	5	15	4	1	.267	.400
McSweeney, Paul A. "Paul" 91StLA												
4/3/67	St. Louis, Mo.	8/12/51	?	?	?	?	3	12	3	2	.250	.333
Meister, John F. "John" 86–87NYA												
5/10/63	Allentown, Pa.	1/28/23	?	?	5'8	175	84	343	79	59	.230	.324
Merrill, Edward Mason "Ed" 82LouA 82WorN 84IndA												
5/?/60	Maysville, Ky.	8/18/24	?	?	5'11	176	58	204	36	14	.176	.201
Millard, Frank E. "Frank" 90StLA												
7/4/65	E. St. Louis, Ill.	7/4/92	?	?	?	?	1	1	0	0	.000	.000
Miller, Frank A. "Kohly" 92WasN 92StLN 97PhiN												
1/?/74	Cumru Township, Pa.	3/29/51	?	?	?	?	5	18	2	2	.111	.111
Miller, Joseph Wick "Joe" 72NatNA 75WesNA 75ChiNA												
7/24/50	?, Germany	8/30/91	?	?	5'10½	169	29	108	15	5	.139	.148
Mohler, Ernest Follette "Kid" 94WasN												
12/13/74	Oneida, Ill.	11/4/61	R	L	5'4½	145	3	9	1	0	.111	.111
Munn, Horatio B. "Horatio" 75AtlNA												
Unknown	Unknown	Unknown	?	?	?	?	1	4	0	0	.000	.000
Murphy, Daniel Francis "Danny" 00NYN												
8/11/76	Philadelphia, Pa.	11/22/55	R	R	5'9	175	22	74	20	11	.270	.284
Myers, James Albert "Al" "Cod" 84MilU 85PhiN 86KCN 87–89WasN 89–91PhiN												
10/22/63	Danville, Ill.	12/24/27	R	R	5'8½	165	833	3222	788	429	.245	.320
Nicholson, Thomas C. "Parson" 88DetN 90TolA 95WasN												
4/14/63	Blaine, Ohio	2/28/17	?	?	6'6	190	168	646	169	96	.262	.362
O'Brien, Jeremiah "Jerry" 87WasN												
2/2/64	New York, N.Y.	7/4/11	?	?	?	?	1	4	0	0	.000	.000
O'Brien, John J. "John" "Chewing Gum" 91BroN 93ChiN 95–96LouN 96–97WasN 99BalN 99PitN												
7/14/70	St. John, N.B., Can.	5/13/13	L	R	?	175	501	1910	486	246	.254	.316
O'Brien, Peter James "Pete" 90ChiN												
6/16/67	Chicago, Ill.	6/30/37	R	R	5'9½	165	27	106	30	15	.283	.434
O'Brien, Thomas H. "Tom" 82WorN 83BalA 84BosU 85BalA 87NYA 90RocA												
6/22/60	Salem, Mass.	4/21/21	R	R	6'1	185	270	1111	257	158	.231	.323
Owens, Thomas Llewellyn "Red" 99PhiN												
11/1/74	Pottsville, Pa.	8/20/52	R	R	?	?	8	21	1	0	.048	.048
Padden, Richard Joseph "Dick" "Brains" 96–98PitN 99WasN												
9/17/70	Martins Ferry, Ohio	10/31/22	R	R	5'10	165	457	1650	443	244	.268	.349

Second Basemen

BIRTH DATE	BIRTHPLACE	DEATH DATE	B	T	HGT	WGT	G	AB	H	R	BA	SA
Parent, Frederick Alfred "Freddy" 99StLN												
11/25/75	Biddeford, Me.	11/2/72	R	R	5'7	154	2	8	1	0	.125	.125
Peak, Elias "Elias" 84BosU 84PhiU												
5/23/59	Philadelphia, Pa.	12/17/16	?	?	?	?	55	218	44	37	.202	.266
Pettee, Patrick E. "Pat" 91LouA												
1/10/63	Natick, Mass.	10/9/34	R	R	5'10	170	2	5	0	1	.000	.000
Pfeffer, Nathaniel Frederick "Fred" "Fritz" "Dandelion" 82TroN 83–89ChiN 90ChiP 91ChiN 92–95LouN 96NYN 96–97ChiN												
3/17/60	Louisville, Ky.	4/10/32	R	R	5'10½	184	1670	6555	1671	1094	.255	.369
Phelan, James Dickson "Dick" 84BalU 85BufN 85StLN												
12/10/54	Towanda, Pa.	2/13/31	R	?	?	?	107	422	102	66	.242	.318
Pickett, John Thomas "John" 89KCA 90PhiP 92BalN												
2/20/66	Chicago, Ill.	7/4/22	R	R	?	?	189	749	189	115	.252	.326
Pierce, Grayson S. "Gracie" 82LouA 82BalA 83ColA 83NYN 84NYA												
Unknown	New York, N.Y.	8/28/94	R	R	?	?	84	307	57	21	.186	.212
***Pierson, Edmund Dana "Dick" 85NYA**												
10/24/57	Wilkes-Barre, Pa.	7/20/22	?	R	?	?	3	9	1	1	.111	.111
Quest, Joseph L. "Joe" 71CleNA 78IndN 79–82ChiN 83DetN 83–84StLA 84PitA 85DetN 86PhiA												
11/16/52	New Castle, Pa.	11/14/24	R	R	5'6	150	596	2295	499	300	.217	.267
Quinn, Joseph J. "Joe" 84StLU 85–86StLN 88–89BosN 90BosP 91–92BosN 93–96StLN 96–98BalN 98StLN 99CleN 00StLN 00CinN												
12/25/64	Sydney, Australia	11/12/40	R	R	5'7	158	1702	6613	1730	858	.262	.327
Reid, William Alexander "Billy" 83BalA 84PitA												
5/17/57	London, Ont., Can.	6/26/40	L	R	6'	170	43	167	44	25	.263	.293
Reilly, Charles "Josh" 96ChiN												
?/?/68	San Francisco, Ca.	6/13/38	?	?	?	?	9	42	9	6	.214	.238
Reilly, Joseph J. "Joe" 85NYA												
?/?/61	New York, N.Y.	Unknown	?	?	5'10	140	10	40	7	6	.175	.250
Reitz, Henry P. "Heinie" 93–97BalN 98WasN 99PitN												
6/29/67	Chicago, Ill.	11/10/14	L	R	5'7	158	723	2741	800	446	.292	.391
Richardson, ? 84Chi–PitU												
Unknown	Boston, Mass.	Unknown	?	?	5'4	136	1	4	0	0	.000	.000
Richardson, Abram Harding "Hardy" "Old True Blue" 79–85BufN 86–88DetN 89BosN 90BosP 91BosA 92WasN 92NYN												
4/21/55	Clarksboro, N.J.	1/14/31	R	R	5'9½	170	1331	5642	1688	1120	.299	.435
Richardson, Daniel "Danny" 84–89NYN 90NYP 91NYN 92WasN 93BroN 94LouN												
1/25/63	Elmira, N.Y.	9/12/26	R	R	5'8	165	1131	4451	1129	676	.254	.332
Ritchey, Claude Cassius "Claude" "Little All Right" 97CinN 98–99LouN 00PitN												
10/5/73	Emlenton, Pa.	11/8/51	B	R	5'6½	167	522	1900	535	250	.282	.350
Ritter, Charles J. "Charlie" 85BufN												
Unknown	Unknown	Unknown	?	?	?	?	2	6	1	0	.000	.000
***Robinson, Frederic Henry "Fred" 84CinU**												
7/6/56	South Acton, Mass.	12/18/33	R	R	?	?	3	13	3	1	.231	.231
Robinson, William H. "Yank" 82DetN 84BalU 85–89StLA 90PitP 91CinA 91StLA 92WasN												
9/19/59	Philadelphia, Pa.	8/25/94	R	R	5'6½	170	978	3428	825	697	.241	.323
Rothermel, Edward Hill "Bobby" 99BalN												
12/18/70	Fleetwood, Pa.	2/11/27	?	?	?	?	10	21	2	1	.095	.095

Second Basemen

BIRTH DATE	BIRTHPLACE	DEATH DATE	B	T	HGT	WGT	G	AB	H	R	BA	SA
*Shaffer, Taylor "Taylor" 90PhiA												
7/?/70	Philadelphia, Pa.	Unknown	?	?	?	?	69	261	45	28	.172	.215
Shannon, Daniel Webster "Dan" 89LouA 90PhiP 90NYP 91WasA												
3/23/65	Bridgeport, Conn.	10/25/13	?	?	5'9	175	242	964	225	171	.233	.339
Shinnick, Timothy James "Tim" "Dandy" "Good Eye" 90–91LouA												
11/6/67	Exeter, N.H.	5/18/44	B	R	5'9	150	259	929	222	164	.239	.320
Simpson, Martin "Marty" 73MarNA												
Unknown	Baltimore, Md.	Unknown	?	?	?	?	4	15	2	4	.133	.133
Smiley, William B. "Bill" 74BalNA 82StLA 82BalA												
?/?/56	Baltimore, Md.	7/11/84	?	?	?	?	77	308	60	33	.195	.221
Smith, Charles Marvin "Pop" 80CinN 81CleN 81BufN 81WorN 82PhiA 82LouA 83–84ColA 85–86PitA 87–89PitN 89–90BosN 91WasA												
10/12/56	Digby, N.S., Can.	4/18/27	R	R	5'11	170	1112	4238	941	643	.222	.313
Smith, George Henry "Heinie" 97–98LouN 99PitN												
10/24/71	Pittsburgh, Pa.	6/25/39	R	R	5'9½	160	71	250	58	30	.232	.292
Smith, Harry W. "Harry" 77ChiN 77CinN 89LouA												
2/5/56	North Vernon, Ind.	6/4/98	R	R	6'	175	35	132	29	11	.220	.258
Smith, Thomas N. "Tom" 75AtlNA												
?/?/51	Guelph, Ont., Can.	3/28/89	?	?	?	?	3	13	1	0	.077	.077
Somerville, Edward G. "Ed" 75CenNA 75NHNA 76LouN												
3/1/53	Philadelphia, Pa.	10/1/77	R	R	?	?	111	449	90	49	.200	.234
Stewart, Asa "Ace" 95ChiN												
2/14/69	Terre Haute, Ind.	4/17/12	R	R	5'10	176	97	365	88	52	.241	.384
Stouch, Thomas Carl "Tom" 98LouN												
12/2/70	Perrysville, Ohio	10/7/56	R	R	6'2	165	4	16	5	4	.313	.375
Stricker, John A. "Cub" b. Streaker 82–85PhiA 87–88CleA 89CleN 90CleP 91BosA 92StLN 92BalN 93WasN												
6/8/59	Philadelphia, Pa.	11/19/37	R	R	5'3	138	1196	4635	1107	790	.239	.294
Strief, George Andrew "George" 79CleN 82PitA 83–84StLA 84KCU 84Chi–PitU 84CleN 85PhiA												
10/16/56	Cincinnati, Ohio	4/1/46	R	R	5'7	172	362	1360	281	145	.207	.275
Swandell, John Martin "Marty" b. Martin Schwendel 72EckNA 73ResNA												
?/?/45	Brooklyn, N.Y.	10/25/06	?	L	5'10	146	16	64	12	8	.188	.188
Sweasy, Charles Hames "Charlie" b. Swasey 71OlyNA 72CleNA 73BosNA 74BalNA 74AtlNA 75ResNA 76CinN 78ProN												
11/2/47	Newark, N.J.	3/30/08	R	R	5'9	172	166	670	130	67	.194	.219
Troy, John Joseph "Dasher" 81–82DetN 82ProN 83NYN 84–85NYA												
5/8/56	New York, N.Y.	3/30/38	R	R	5'5	154	292	1127	274	166	.243	.327
Truby, Harry Garvin "Harry" "Bird Eye" 95–96ChiN 96PitN												
5/12/70	Ironton, Ohio	3/21/53	?	R	5'11	185	70	260	73	31	.281	.338
Wentz, John George "Jack" b. Wernz 91LouA												
3/4/63	Louisville, Ky.	9/14/07	R	R	5'10½	175	1	4	1	0	.250	.250
West, William Nelson "Billy" 74AtlNA 76NYN												
8/21/40	Philadelphia, Pa.	8/18/91	?	?	?	?	10	39	8	4	.205	.231
Wood, ? 74BalNA												
Unknown	Unknown	Unknown	?	?	?	?	1	5	0	0	.000	.000
Wood, James Leon "Jimmy" 71ChiNA 72TroNA 72EckNA 73PhiNA												
12/1/44	Brooklyn, N.Y.	11/30/86	?	?	5'8½	150	102	487	162	162	.333	.468

Second Basemen

BIRTH DATE	BIRTHPLACE	DEATH DATE	B	T	HGT	WGT	G	AB	H	R	BA	SA
Wright, Patrick Francis "Pat" 90ChiN												
7/5/65	Potsville, Pa.	5/29/43	B	R	6'2	190	1	2	0	0	.000	.000
Yewell, Edwin Leonard "Ed" 84WasA 84WasU												
8/22/62	Washington, D.C.	9/15/40	?	?	?	?	28	97	23	14	.237	.289

Fred Dunlap (left) was paid $6,000 in 1884, an unheard salary for a ballplayer then. John T. Brush devised a plan in 1889 that would have limited the pay for even the game's best second baseman in the 1880s to a max of $2,500.

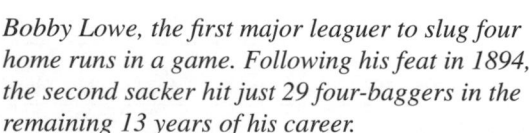

Bobby Lowe, the first major leaguer to slug four home runs in a game. Following his feat in 1894, the second sacker hit just 29 four-baggers in the remaining 13 years of his career.

Third Basemen

BIRTH DATE	BIRTHPLACE	DEATH DATE	B	T	HGT	WGT	G	AB	H	R	BA	SA
Abbaticchio, Edward James "Batty" 97–98PhiN												
4/15/77	Latrobe, Pa.	1/6/57	R	R	5'11	170	28	102	24	9	.235	.275
Ake, John Leckie "John" 84BalA												
8/29/61	Altoona, Pa.	5/11/87	R	R	6'1	180	13	52	10	1	.192	.231
Alberts, Augustus Peter "Gus" 84PitA 84WasU 88CleA 91MilA												
?/?/61	Reading, Pa.	5/7/12	R	R	5'6	180	120	426	84	62	.197	.256
Allen, Cyrus Alban "Jack" 79SyrN 79CleN												
10/2/55	Woodstock, Ill.	4/21/15	R	R	?	160	27	108	16	14	.148	.213
Alvord, William Charles "Billy" "Uncle Bill" 85StLN 89KCA 90TolA 91CleN 91WasA 93CleN												
8/?/63	St. Louis, Mo.	Unknown	?	?	5'10	187	265	1069	270	129	.253	.346
Andrus, William Wiman "Wiman" 85ProN												
10/14/58	Orono, Ontario, Can.	6/17/35	?	?	5'6½	155	1	4	0	0	.000	.000
Atherton, Charles Morgan Herbert "Charlie" "Prexy" 99WasN												
10/19/73	New Brunswick, N.J.	12/19/34	R	R	5'10	160	65	242	60	28	.248	.318
Ball, Arthur Clark "Art" 94StLN 98BalN												
4/?/76	?, Kentucky	12/26/15	?	R	?	168	33	84	16	7	.190	.214
Barber, Charles D. "Charlie" 84CinU												
?/?/54	Philadelphia, Pa.	11/23/10	R	R	?	?	55	204	41	38	.201	.245
Battam, Lawrence J. "Larry" 95NYN												
5/1/78	Brooklyn, N.Y.	1/27/38	?	?	5'11	?	2	4	1	0	.250	.250
Battin, Joseph V. "Joe" 71CleNA 73–74AthNA 75StLNA 76–77StLN 82–84PitA 84Chi–PitU 84BalU 90SyrA												
11/11/51	Philadelphia, Pa.	12/10/37	R	R	?	?	480	1953	439	228	.224	.281
Bellan, Estaban Enrique "Steve" 71–72TroNA 73MutNA												
?/?/50	?, Cuba	8/8/32	?	?	5'6	154	60	274	69	52	.252	.307
Bishop, Frank H. "Frank" 84Chi–PitU												
9/21/60	Belvidere, Ill.	6/18/29	?	?	?	?	4	16	3	1	.188	.250
Bliss, Frank Eugene "Frank" 78MilN												
12/10/52	Chicago, Ill.	1/8/29	?	?	?	?	2	8	1	1	.125	.125
Boland, ? 75AtlNA												
Unknown	Unknown	Unknown	?	?	?	?	1	4	0	0	.000	.000
Bradley, William Joseph "Bill" 99–00ChiN												
2/13/78	Cleveland, Ohio	3/11/54	R	R	6'	185	157	573	165	89	.288	.403
Brannock, Michael J. "Mike" 71ChiNA 75ChiNA												
?/?/53	Guelph, Ont., Canada	Unknown	?	?	5'8	162	5	23	2	4	.087	.087
Brown, Edward P. "Ed" 82StLA 84TolA												
Unknown	Chicago, Ill.	Unknown	?	R	?	178	59	213	38	17	.178	.192
Burke, James Timothy "Jimmy" "Sunset Jimmy" 98CleN 99StLN												
10/12/74	St. Louis, Mo.	3/26/42	R	R	5'7	160	15	44	6	2	.136	.159
Burke, Joseph A. "Joe" 90StLA 91CinA												
Unknown	Cincinnati, Ohio	Unknown	?	?	5'7	160	3	10	5	3	.500	.500
Burns, Thomas Everett "Tom" 80–91ChiN 92PitN												
3/30/57	Honesdale, Pa.	3/19/02	R	R	5'7	152	1251	4920	1299	722	.264	.364
Buttery, Frank "Frank" 72ManNA												
5/13/51	Silvermine, Conn.	12/16/02	?	?	?	?	18	93	24	19	.258	.258
Callahan, Patrick Henry "Pat" 84IndA												
10/15/66	Cleveland, Ohio	2/4/40	?	?	?	?	61	258	67	38	.260	.353

Third Basemen

BIRTH DATE	BIRTHPLACE	DEATH DATE	B	T	HGT	WGT	G	AB	H	R	BA	SA
*Camp, Llewellyn Robert "Lew" 92StLN 93–94ChiN							88	334	77	57	.231	.350
2/22/68	Columbus, Ohio	10/1/48	L	R	6'	175						
Carpenter, Warren William "Hick" 79SyrN 80CinN 81WorN 82–89CinA 92StLN							1118	4637	1202	720	.259	.322
8/16/55	Grafton, Mass.	4/18/37	R	L	5'11	186						
Casey, James Patrick "Doc" 98–99WasN 99–00BroN							172	674	177	91	.263	.318
3/15/70	Lawrence, Mass.	12/31/36	B	R	5'6	157						
Casey, Orrin Robinson "Bob" 82DetN							9	39	9	5	.231	.410
1/26/59	Adolphustown, Ont., Can.	11/28/36	?	?	5'11	190						
Cleveland, Elmer Ellsworth "Elmer" 84CinU 88NYN 88PitN 91ColA							80	298	76	52	.255	.366
9/15/62	Washington, D.C.	10/8/13	R	R	?	?						
Clingman, William Frederick "Billy" 90CinN 91CinA 95PitN 96–99LouN 00ChiN							678	2295	563	334	.245	.306
11/21/69	Cincinnati, Ohio	5/14/58	B	R	5'11	150						
Collins, James Joseph "Jimmy" 95BosN 95LouN 96–00BosN							770	3026	925	535	.306	.425
1/16/70	Buffalo, N.Y.	3/6/43	R	R	5'9	178						
Connell, Peter J. "Pete" 86NYA							1	5	0	0	.000	.000
Unknown	Brooklyn, N.Y.	Unknown	?	?	?	?						
Corey, Frederick Harrison "Fred" 78ProN 80–82WorN 83–85PhiA							432	1738	427	239	.246	.348
?/?/57	S. Kingston, R.I.	11/27/12	R	R	?	?						
Coughlin, William Paul "Bill" "Scranton Bill" 99WasN							6	24	3	2	.125	.208
7/12/78	Scranton, Pa.	5/7/43	R	R	5'9	140						
*Cross, Lafayette Napoleon "Lave" 87–88LouA 89PhiA 90PhiP 91–97PhiN 98StLN 99CleN 99–00StLN 00BroN							1428	5681	1658	891	.292	.372
5/12/66	Milwaukee, Wis.	9/6/27	R	R	5'8½	155						
Davis, James J. "Jumbo" 84KCU 86–87BalA 88–89KCA 89–90StLA 90BroA 91WasA							453	1723	468	266	.272	.379
9/5/61	New York, N.Y.	2/14/21	L	R	5'11	195						
Delahanty, Thomas James "Tom" 94PhiN 96CleN 96PitN 97LouN							19	67	16	13	.239	.313
3/9/72	Cleveland, Ohio	1/10/51	L	R	5'8	175						
Denny, Jeremiah Dennis "Jerry" b. Eldridge 81–85ProN 86StLN 87–89IndN 90–91NYN 91CleN 91PhiN 93–94LouN							1237	4946	1282	714	.260	.384
3/16/59	New York, N.Y.	8/16/27	R	R	5'11½	180						
Donnelly, James B. "Jim" 84KCU 84IndA 85DetN 86KCN 87–89WasN 90StLA 91ColA 96BalN 97PitN 97NYN 98StLN							660	2411	552	324	.229	.278
7/19/65	New Haven, Conn.	3/5/15	R	R	5'10½	155						
#Doscher, John Henry Sr. "Herm" 72–73AtlNA 75WasNA 79TroN 79ChiN 81–82CleN							109	437	98	36	.224	.259
12/20/52	New York, N.Y.	3/20/34	R	R	5'10	182						
Drauby, Jacob C. "Jake" 92WasN							10	34	7	3	.206	.265
?/?/65	Harrisburg, Pa.	Unknown	?	?	5'10	163						
East, Henry H. "Harry" 82BalA							1	4	0	0	.000	.000
4/?/63	St. Louis, Mo.	Unknown	?	?	?	?						
Esterbrook, Thomas Jefferson "Dude" 80BufN 82CleN 83–84NYA 85–86NYN 87NYA 88IndN 88–89LouA 90NYN 91BroN							701	2837	741	387	.261	.334
6/20/57	Staten Isl., N.Y.	4/30/01	R	R	5'11	167						
Farrell, Joseph F. "Joe" 82–84DetN 86BalA							353	1489	345	187	.232	.291
?/?/57	Brooklyn, N.Y.	4/18/93	R	?	5'6	160						
Ferguson, Robert Vavasour "Bob" 71MutNA 72–74AtlNA 75HarNA 76–77HarN 78ChiN 79–82TroN 83PhiN 84PitA							823	3468	918	544	.265	.313
1/31/45	Brooklyn, N.Y.	5/3/94	B	R	5'9½	149						
Fields, George W. "George" 72ManNA							18	87	21	16	.241	.299
7/?/53	Waterbury, Conn.	9/22/33	?	?	?	?						

Third Basemen

BIRTH DATE	BIRTHPLACE	DEATH DATE	B	T	HGT	WGT	G	AB	H	R	BA	SA
Fisher, Charles J. "Charles" b. Fish 84KCU 84Chi–PitU												
3/10/52	Roxford, Mass.	2/18/17	?	?	?	?	11	43	10	4	.233	.279
Flaherty, Patrick Henry "Pat" 94LouN												
1/31/66	St. Louis, Mo.	1/28/46	?	?	5'9	166	38	145	43	15	.297	.372
Flynn, Edward J. "Ed" 87CleA												
6/25/64	Chicago, Ill.	Unknown	L	?	5'9	165	7	27	5	0	.185	.222
Foley, William Brown "Will" 75ChiNA 76–77CinN 78MilN 79CinN 81DetN 84Chi–PitU												
11/15/55	Chicago, Ill.	11/12/16	R	R	5'9½	150	253	982	224	112	.228	.271
***Fuller, Henry W. "Harry" 91StLA**												
12/5/62	Cincinnati, Ohio	12/12/95	?	?	?	?	1	2	0	0	.000	.000
Gilbert, Peter "Pete" 90–91BalA 92BalN 94BroN 94LouN												
9/6/67	Baltic, Conn.	1/1/12	?	R	5'8	180	206	761	184	120	.242	.311
Gilman, James "Jim" 93CleN												
Unknown	Unknown	Unknown	?	?	?	?	2	7	2	1	.286	.286
Gladman, John H. "Buck" 83PhiN 84WasA 86WasN												
?/?/64	Washington, D.C.	Unknown	?	?	?	?	101	380	56	35	.147	.221
***Gleason, John Day "Jack" 77StLN 82–83StLA 83LouA 84StLU 85StLN 86PhiA**												
7/14/54	St. Louis, Mo.	9/4/44	R	R	?	170	343	1425	384	253	.269	.349
Goldsmith, Wallace "Wally" 71KekNA 72OlyNA 73MarNA 75WesNA												
?/?/49	?, Maryland	Unknown	?	?	5'7	146	42	184	34	15	.184	.201
Graham, Barney "Barney" 89PhiA												
Unknown	Philadelphia, Pa.	12/31/96	?	?	?	?	4	18	3	0	.167	.167
Gray, James W. "Jim" 84PitA												
8/7/62	Pittsburgh, Pa.	1/31/38	?	R	?	?	1	2	1	0	.500	.500
Green, James R. "Jim" 84WasU												
Unknown	Cleveland, Ohio	Unknown	?	?	?	?	10	36	5	4	.139	.167
Gremminger, Lorenzo Edward "Ed" "Battleship" 95CleN												
3/30/74	Canton, Ohio	5/26/42	R	R	6'1	200	20	78	21	10	.269	.282
Grey, William Tobin "Bill" 90–91PhiN 95–96CinN 98PitN												
4/15/71	Philadelphia, Pa.	12/8/32	?	?	5'11	175	292	1033	250	126	.242	.315
Hague, William L. "Bill" b. Haug 75StLNA 76–77LouN 78–79ProN												
?/?/52	Philadelphia, Pa.	Unknown	R	R	5'9	164	301	1276	303	134	.237	.264
Hankinson, Frank Edward "Frank" 78–79ChiN 80CleN 81TroN 83–84NYN 85–87NYA 88KCA												
4/29/56	New York, N.Y.	4/5/11	R	R	5'11	168	849	3272	747	410	.228	.301
Harrington, Joseph C. "Joe" 95–96BosN												
12/21/69	Fall River, Mass.	9/13/33	R	R	5'8½	162	72	263	57	46	.217	.308
Harris, Charles Jenkins "Charlie" 99BalN												
10/21/77	Macon, Ga.	3/14/63	R	R	5'8	200	30	68	19	16	.279	.324
Hartman, Frederick Orrin "Fred" "Dutch" 94PitN 97StLN 98–99NYN												
4/25/68	Allegheny, Pa.	11/11/38	R	R	5'8	170	346	1347	386	190	.287	.381
Hickman, Charles Taylor "Charlie" "Piano Legs" 97–99BosN 00NYN												
3/4/76	Taylortown, Pa.	4/19/34	R	R	5'11½	215	167	597	190	85	.318	.528
Hill, Belden L. "Belden" 90BalA												
8/24/64	Kewanee, Ill.	10/22/34	R	R	6'	?	9	30	5	3	.167	.233
Hoffmeister, Jesse H. "Jesse" 97PitN												
Unknown	Toledo, Ohio	Unknown	?	R	?	?	48	188	58	33	.309	.484

Third Basemen

BIRTH DATE	BIRTHPLACE	DEATH DATE	B	T	HGT	WGT	G	AB	H	R	BA	SA
Householder, Charles F. "Charlie" 84Chi–PitU												
?/?/56	Harrisburg, Pa.	Unknown	R	R	5'7	150	83	310	74	32	.239	.319
Irwin, Charles Edwin "Charlie" 93–95ChiN 96–00CinN												
2/15/69	Clinton, Ill.	9/21/25	L	R	5'10	160	726	2719	742	446	.273	.358
*Irwin, John "John" 82WorN 84BosU 86PhiA 87–89WasN 90BufP 91BosA 91LouA												
7/21/61	Toronto, Ont., Can.	2/28/34	L	R	5'10	168	32	1269	312	222	.246	.326
Jacoby, Harry "Harry" 82BalA 85BalA												
Unknown	Philadelphia, Pa.	Unknown	?	?	?	?	42	164	27	21	.165	.213
Jones, ? 85NYA												
Unknown	Unknown	Unknown	?	?	?	?	1	4	1	0	.250	.250
Joyce, William Michael "Bill" "Scrappy" 90BroP 91BosA 92BroN 94–96WasN 96–98NYN												
9/21/65	St. Louis, Mo.	5/8/41	L	R	5'11	185	904	3304	970	820	.294	.467
Kelly, Charles H. "Charlie" 83PhiN 86PhiA												
Unknown	Unknown	Unknown	?	?	?	?	3	10	1	1	.100	.300
Kemmer, William Edward "Bill" b. Kemmerer 95LouN												
11/15/73	?, Pennsylvania	6/8/45	R	R	6'2	?	11	38	7	5	.184	.263
Kennedy, William Edward "Ed" 84CinU												
4/5/61	Bellevue, Ky.	12/22/12	R	R	5'7	160	13	48	10	6	.208	.271
Kinlock, Walter "Walt" 95StLN												
?/?/78	St. Joseph, Mo.	Unknown	?	?	?	?	1	3	1	0	.333	.333
Knowles, James "Jimmy" "Darby" 84PitA 84BroA 86WasN 87NYA 90RocA 92NYN												
9/?/56	Toronto, Ont., Can.	2/11/12	?	?	5'9	160	357	1388	334	185	.241	.329
Kohler, Henry C. "Henry" 71KekNA 73MarNA 74BalNA												
5/5/52	Baltimore, Md.	8/27/34	?	?	?	?	11	41	5	2	.122	.220
Koons, Henry M. "Harry" 84AltU 84Chi–PitU												
?/?/63	Philadelphia, Pa.	Unknown	R	R	5'8	174	22	81	18	8	.222	.272
Kuehne, William J. "Willie" "Bill" b.Knelme 83–84ColA 85–86PitA 87–89PitN 90PitP 91ColA 91–92LouN 92StLN 92CinN												
10/24/58	Leipzig, Germany	10/27/21	R	R	?	185	1085	4277	993	533	.232	.337
Kuhns, Charles B. "Charlie" 97PitN 99BosN												
10/27/77	Freeport, Pa.	7/15/22	?	?	5'9	160	8	21	5	2	.238	.238
Latham, Walter Arlington "Arlie" "Jimmy Fresh" "The Freshest Man on Earth" 80BufN 83–89StLA 90ChiP 90–95CinN 96StLN 99WasN												
3/15/60	W. Lebanon, N.H.	11/29/52	R	R	5'8	150	1623	6820	1833	1477	.269	.341
Lauder, William "Billy" 98–99PhiN												
2/23/74	New York, N.Y.	5/20/33	R	R	5'10	160	248	944	251	116	.266	.342
Leach, Thomas William "Tommy" 98–99LouN 00PitN												
11/4/77	French Creek, N.Y.	9/29/69	R	R	5'6½	150	160	576	152	95	.264	.342
Lyons, Dennis Patrick Aloysius "Denny" 85ProN 86–90PhiA 91StLA 92NYN 93–94PitN 95StLN 96–97PitN												
3/12/66	Cincinnati, Ohio	1/2/29	R	R	5'10	185	1121	4294	1333	932	.310	.443
Martin, Frank "Frank" 97LouN 98ChiN 99NYN												
2/28/79	Chicago, Ill.	9/30/24	?	?	?	?	20	66	16	6	.242	.273
Mayer, Edward H. "Ed" 90–91PhiN												
8/16/66	Marshallville, Ill.	5/18/13	?	?	5'8½	155	185	752	167	73	.222	.286
McCormick, John "Jerry" 83BalA 84PhiU 84WasU												
Unknown	Philadelphia, Pa.	9/19/05	?	?	?	?	202	841	220	104	.262	.328
McCormick, William J. "Barry" 95LouN 96–00ChiN												
12/25/74	Maysville, Ky.	1/28/56	?	R	5'9	?	498	1884	463	270	.246	.320

Third Basemen

BIRTH DATE	BIRTHPLACE	DEATH DATE	B	T	HGT	WGT	G	AB	H	R	BA	SA
McDonald, James "Jim" 84WasU 84PitA 85BufN												
8/6/60	San Francisco, Ca.	9/14/14	?	?	?	?	45	165	24	11	.145	.164
McGarr, James B. "Chippy" 84Chi–PitU 86–87PhiA 88StLA 89KCA 89BalA 90BosN 93–96CleN												
5/10/63	Worcester, Mass.	6/6/04	R	R	5'7	168	826	3253	872	537	.268	.329
McGlone, John T. "John" 86WasN 87–88CleA												
?/?/64	Brooklyn, N.Y.	11/24/27	?	?	5'10	165	80	297	58	38	.195	.242
McGraw, John Joseph "John" "Mugsy" 91BalA 92–99BalN 00StLN												
4/7/73	Truxton, N.Y.	2/25/34	L	R	5'7	155	969	3497	1178	924	.337	.411
McGrillis, Mark A. "Mark" 92StLN												
10/22/72	Philadelphia, Pa.	5/16/35	?	?	?	?	1	3	0	0	.000	.000
McShannic, Peter Robert "Pete" 88PitN												
3/20/64	Pittsburgh, Pa.	11/30/46	B	R	5'7	190	26	98	19	5	.194	.204
Meister, George B. "George" 84TolA												
6/5/64	Dorzbach, Germany	8/24/08	?	?	?	?	34	119	23	9	.193	.244
Metcalf, Al "Al" 75MutNA												
Unknown	Brooklyn, N.Y.	Unknown	?	?	?	?	8	32	7	2	.219	.219
Meyerle, Levi Samuel "Levi" "Long Levi" 71–72AthNA 73PhiNA 74ChiNA 75PhiNA 76PhiN 77CinN 84PhiU												
7/?/45	Philadelphia, Pa.	11/4/21	R	R	6'1	177	307	1443	513	306	.356	.480
Meyers, Henry L. "Henry" 90PhiA												
?/?/60	Philadelphia, Pa.	6/28/98	?	?	?	?	5	19	3	2	.158	.158
Minnehan, Daniel Joseph "Dan" 95LouN												
11/28/65	Troy, N.Y.	8/8/29	R	R	5'10	145	8	34	13	8	.382	.382
Morrison, Thomas J. "Tom" 95–96LouN												
?/?/75	St. Louis, Mo.	Unknown	?	?	5'3	145	14	49	10	6	.204	.306
*Morrissey, John J. "John" 81BufN 82DetN												
12/30/56	Janesville, Wis.	4/29/84	?	?	?	?	14	54	12	4	.222	.259
*Morrissey, Thomas J. "Tom" 84MilU												
?/?/61	Janesville, Wis.	9/23/41	?	?	5'11	180	12	47	8	3	.170	.213
Muldoon, Michael D. "Mike" 82–84CleN 85–86BalA												
?/?/58	?, Ireland	Unknown	?	?	5'8	165	495	1932	450	254	.233	.323
Mulligan, John "John" 84WasU												
Unknown	Philadelphia, Pa.	Unknown	?	?	?	?	1	4	1	2	.250	.250
Mulvey, Joseph H. "Joe" 83ProN 83–89PhiN 90PhiP 91PhiA 92PhiN 93WasN 95BroN												
10/27/58	Providence, R.I.	8/21/28	R	R	5'11½	178	987	4063	1059	598	.261	.355
Myers, James Albert "Bert" 96StLN 98WasN 00PhiN												
4/8/74	Frederick, Md.	10/12/15	R	R	5'10	?	160	592	150	66	.253	.318
Nash, William Mitchell "Billy" 84VirA 85–95BosN 96–98PhiN												
6/24/65	Richmond, Va.	11/15/29	R	R	5'8½	167	1549	5849	1606	1072	.275	.381
Nevin, Alexander Brown "Alexander" 73ResNA												
10/3/50	Allegheny City, Pa.	10/10/21	?	?	?	?	13	53	11	7	.208	.302
Newell, John A. "John" 91PitN												
1/14/68	Wilmington, Del.	1/28/19	R	L	?	?	5	18	2	1	.111	.111
Nichols, Albert H. "Al" 75AtlNA 76NYN 77LouN												
Unknown	Brooklyn, N.Y.	Unknown	?	?	5'11	180	95	361	62	25	.172	.194
Niles, William E. "Bill" 95PitN												
1/11/67	Covington, Ky.	7/3/36	?	?	?	160	11	37	8	2	.216	.216

Third Basemen

BIRTH DATE	BIRTHPLACE	DEATH DATE	B	T	HGT	WGT	G	AB	H	R	BA	SA
O'Rourke, Timothy Patrick "Tim"		"Voiceless Tim"	90SyrA	91ColA	92–93BalN	93–94LouN	94StLN	94WasN				
5/18/64	Chicago, Ill.	4/20/38	L	R	5'10	170	387	1510	440	272	.291	.352
*Parrott, Walter Edward "Jiggs"		92–95ChiN										
7/14/71	Portland, Ore.	4/16/98	?	?	5'11	160	315	1309	307	174	.235	.310
Pierce, Maurice "Maury"	84WasU											
Unknown	Baltimore, Md.	Unknown	?	?	?	?	2	7	1	0	.143	.143
Piercy, Andrew J. "Andy"	81ChiN											
8/?/56	San Jose, Ca.	12/27/32	?	R	?	?	2	8	2	1	.250	.250
Pinkham, Edward "Ed"	71ChiNA											
?/?/49	Brooklyn, N.Y.	Unknown	?	L	5'7	142	24	95	25	27	.263	.453
Pinkney, George Burton "George" (aka Pinckney)		84CleN	85–89BroA	90–91BroN	92StLN	93LouN						
1/11/62	Orange Prairie, Ill.	11/10/26	R	R	5'7	160	1162	4610	1212	874	.263	.338
Popplein, George "George"	73MarNA											
8/?/40	Baltimore, Md.	3/31/01	?	?	?	?	1	4	0	0	.000	.000
Puhl, John G. "John"	98–99NYN											
1/10/76	Brooklyn, N.Y.	8/24/00	?	?	?	?	3	11	2	1	.182	.182
Raymond, Harry H. "Harry" "Jack"		88–91LouN	92PitN	92WasN								
2/20/62	Utica, N.Y.	3/21/25	?	?	5'9	179	315	1282	301	167	.235	.279
*Reccius, Phillip "Phil"	82–87LouA	87CleA	88LouA	90RocA								
6/7/62	Louisville, Ky.	2/15/03	?	?	5'9	163	261	975	225	117	.231	.305
Reeder, Nicholas "Nick" b. Herchenroeder		91LouA										
3/22/67	Louisville, Ky.	9/26/94	R	R	5'9	189	1	2	0	0	.000	.000
Reilly, Charles Thomas "Charlie" "Princeton Charlie" b. O'Reilly			89–90ColA	91PitN	92–95PhiN	97WasN						
2/15/67	Princeton, N.J.	12/16/37	B	R	5'11	190	641	2380	595	342	.250	.325
Richter, John M. "John"	98LouN											
2/8/73	Louisville, Ky.	10/4/27	?	?	6'	178	3	13	2	1	.154	.154
Ricks, John "John"	91StLA	94StLN										
Unknown	Unknown	Unknown	?	?	?	?	6	19	3	3	.158	.158
Ritz, James L. "Jim"	94PitN											
?/?/74	Pittsburgh, Pa.	11/10/96	?	?	?	?	1	4	1	0	.000	.000
Roat, Frederick R. "Fred"	90PitN	92ChiN										
11/10/67	Oregon, Ill.	9/24/13	?	R	?	?	65	246	54	22	.220	.260
Russell, Paul A. "Paul"	94StLN											
?/?/70	Reading, Pa.	Unknown	?	?	?	?	3	10	1	1	.100	.100
Ryan, John J. "John"	95StLN											
Unknown	St. Louis, Mo.	Unknown	?	?	?	?	2	2	0	0	.000	.000
Samuls, Samuel Earl "Ike"	95StLN											
2/20/76	Austria-Hungary	1/1/42	R	R	?	?	24	74	17	5	.230	.257
Sauters, Al "Al"	90PhiA											
Unknown	Philadelphia, Pa.	Unknown	?	?	?	?	14	41	4	1	.098	.098
*Say, James I. "Jimmy"	82LouA	82PhiA	84WilU	84KCU	87CleA							
?/?/62	Baltimore, Md.	6/23/94	?	?	?	?	57	217	57	25	.263	.359
Schafer, Harry C. "Harry" "Silk Stocking"		71–75BosNA	76–78BosN									
8/14/46	Philadelphia, Pa.	2/28/35	R	R	5'9½	143	367	1653	451	338	.273	.332
Schenck, William G. "Bill"	82LouA	84VirA	85BroA									
Unknown	Brooklyn, N.Y.	Unknown	?	?	5'7	171	103	386	91	51	.236	.313

Third Basemen

BIRTH DATE	BIRTHPLACE	DEATH DATE	B	T	HGT	WGT	G	AB	H	R	BA	SA
Selman, Frank C. "Frank" (aka Frank Williams) 71KekNA 72OlyNA 73MarNA 74BalNA 75WasNA												
Unknown	Baltimore, Md.	Unknown	?	?	?	?	37	167	43	27	.259	.347
Shetzline, John Henry "John" 82BalA												
?/?/50	Philadelphia, Pa.	12/15/92	?	?	5'11½	190	73	282	62	23	.220	.270
Shindle, William "Billy" 86–87DetN 88–89BalA 90PhiP 91PhiN 92–93BalN 94–98BroN												
12/5/60	Gloucester, N.J.	6/3/36	R	R	5'8½	155	1422	5807	1560	992	.269	.357
Siefke, Frederick Edwin "Fred" 90BroA												
3/27/70	New York, N.Y.	4/18/93	?	?	5'11	168	16	58	8	1	.138	.172
Siegel, John "John" 84PhiU												
Unknown	York, Pa.	Unknown	?	?	?	?	8	31	7	4	.226	.290
Smalley, William Darwin "Will" "Deacon" 90CleN 91WasA												
6/27/71	Oakland, Ca.	10/11/91	R	R	?	?	147	540	113	67	.209	.237
Smith, Charles J. "Charlie" 71MutNA												
12/11/40	Brooklyn, N.Y.	11/15/97	?	?	5'10½	150	14	72	19	15	.264	.319
Smith, Harvey Fetterhoff "Harvey" 96WasN												
7/14/71	Union Deposit, Pa.	11/12/62	L	R	5'8	160	36	131	36	21	.275	.359
Smith, Judson Grant "Jud" 93CinN 93StLN 96PitN 98WasN												
1/13/69	Green Oak, Mich.	12/7/47	R	R	?	?	97	325	94	47	.289	.394
Stedronsky, John "John" 79ChiN												
Unknown	Cleveland, Ohio	Unknown	?	?	?	?	4	12	1	0	.083	.083
Steinfeldt, Harry M. "Harry" 98–00CinN												
9/29/77	St. Louis, Mo.	8/17/14	R	R	5'9½	180	329	1204	310	166	.257	.350
Sullivan, Patrick J. "Pat" 84KCU												
12/22/62	Milwaukee, Wis.	Unknown	?	R	5'11	165	31	114	22	15	.193	.237
Sullivan, Suter G. "Suter" 98StLN 99CleN												
10/14/72	Baltimore, Md.	4/19/25	?	?	6'	170	169	617	148	47	.240	.280
Sutton, Ezra Ballou "Ezra" 71–72CleNA 73–75AthNA 76PhiN 77–88BosN												
9/17/50	Palmyra, N.Y.	6/20/07	R	R	5'8½	153	1263	5358	1574	992	.294	.386
Sweeney, Peter Jay "Pete" 88–89WasN 89–90StLA 90LouA 90PhiA												
12/31/63	?, California	8/22/01	R	R	?	?	134	521	109	53	.209	.269
Taylor, William H. "Billy" 98LouN												
12/?/70	Butler, Ky.	9/12/05	?	?	5'10	160	9	24	6	2	.250	.292
Trenwith, George "George" 75CenNA												
Unknown	?, Ireland	2/1/90	?	?	?	?	16	70	14	6	.200	.257
Van Zant, Richard "Dick" "Foghorn Dick" 88CleA												
11/?/64	Richmond, Indiana	8/6/12	?	?	?	?	10	31	8	1	.258	.290
Wagenhorst, Ellwood Otto "Woody" 88PhiN												
6/3/63	Kutztown, Pa.	2/12/46	?	?	5'11	165	2	8	1	2	.125	.125
***Wagner, Albert "Butts"** 98WasN 98BroN												
9/17/71	Chartiers, Pa.	11/26/28	R	R	5'10	170	74	261	59	22	.226	.307
Wallace, Rhoderick John "Bobby" 94–98CleN 99–00StLN												
11/4/73	Pittsburgh, Pa.	11/3/60	R	R	5'8	170	640	2431	691	376	.284	.415
Warner, Frederick John Rodney "Fred" 75CenNA 76PhiN 78IndN 79CleN 83PhiN 84BroA												
?/?/55	Philadelphia, Pa.	2/13/86	?	?	5'7	155	257	1034	242	115	.234	.272

Lave Cross (center row, center) broke in as a catcher, but at the close of the nineteenth century he owned the top career fielding average by a third sacker. Here too, with the 1896 Phillies, is Willie McGill, who in 1891 became the youngest 20-game winner ever when he reached the magic circle at the tender age of 17. Top: Boyle, Sullivan, Brouthers, Thompson, Ellis and Orth. Middle: Hallman, Turner, Grady, Clements, Cross, Nash, Lucid, Carsey and McGill. Front: Hulen, Delahanty and Taylor.

Tip O'Neill was only one of several players whose great hitting exploits in 1887 were obscured by the bizarre rules in effect that season. Another was Denny Lyons (left) who was recently discovered to have forged a 52-game hitting streak in 1887, including two games in which he only drew a walk. Since a walk was a hit that year, it should properly have been Lyons's streak that acted as the carrot for Joe DiMaggio in 1941. In 1887, Lyons also set an all-time record for the most putouts by a third baseman (255) as well the nineteenth-century record for the most hits by a hot cornerman (209). Yet more, Lyons's .310 career BA leads all men who played as many as 1,000 games at third base prior to the onset of the "Lively Ball Era" in 1920.

Third Basemen

BIRTH DATE	BIRTHPLACE	DEATH DATE	B	T	HGT	WGT	G	AB	H	R	BA	SA
Waterman, Frederick A. "Fred"	71–72OlyNA	73WasNA	75ChiNA									
12/?/45	New York, N.Y.	12/16/99	?	?	5'7½	148	61	303	101	81	.333	.413
Watkins, William Henry "Bill"	84IndA											
5/5/58	Brantford, Ont., Can.	6/9/37	?	?	5'10	156	34	127	26	16	.205	.236
Werrick, Joseph Abraham "Joe"	84StPU	86–88LouA										
10/25/61	St. Paul, Minn.	5/10/43	R	R	5'9	161	392	1534	383	217	.250	.348
***White, James Laurie "Deacon"**	71–72CleNA	73–75BosNA	76ChiN	77BosN	78–80CinN	81–85BufN	86–88DetN					
89PitN 90BufP												
12/7/47	Caton, N.Y.	7/7/39	L	R	5'11	175	1560	6624	2066	1140	.312	.387
White, William Warren "Warren" (aka William Warren)	71OlyNA	72NatNA	73WasNA	74BalNA	75ChiNA	84WasU						
Unknown	Unknown	Unknown	?	?	5'10½	170	168	727	186	96	.256	.285
***Whitney, Arthur Wilson "Art"**	80WorN	80–81DetN	82ProN	84–86PitA	87PitN	88–89NYN	90NYP	91CinN	91StLA			
1/16/58	Brockton, Mass.	8/15/43	R	R	5'8	155	978	3681	820	475	.223	.269
**Wiley, ? ** 84WasU												
Unknown	Unknown	Unknown	?	?	?	?	1	4	0	0	.000	.000
Williams, James Thomas "Jimmy"	99–00PitN											
12/20/76	St. Louis, Mo.	1/16/65	R	R	5'9	175	258	1033	329	199	.318	.474
Williamson, Edward Nagle "Ned"	78IndN	79–89ChiN	90ChiP									
10/24/57	Philadelphia, Pa.	3/3/94	R	R	5'11	210	1201	4553	1159	809	.255	.384
Wolverton, Harry Sterling "Harry" "Fighting Harry"	98–00ChiN	00PhiN										
12/6/73	Mt. Vernon, Ohio	2/4/37	L	R	5'11	205	216	832	237	90	.285	.375
Woodhead, James "Red"	73MarNA	79SyrN										
7/9/51	Chelsea, Mass.	9/7/81	?	?	5'6	160	35	136	21	5	.154	.162
Youngman, Henry "Henry"	90PitN											
?/?/65	Indiana, Pa.	1/24/36	?	R	?	?	13	47	6	6	.128	.191
Ziegler, Charles W. "Charlie"	99CleN	00PhiN										
1/13/75	Canton, Ohio	4/18/04	?	?	?	?	5	19	5	2	.263	.263

Shortstops

BIRTH DATE	BIRTHPLACE	DEATH DATE	B	T	HGT	WGT	G	AB	H	R	BA	SA
Allen, Robert Gilman "Bob" 90–94PhiN 97BosN 00Cinn												
7/10/67	Marion, Ohio	5/14/43	R	R	5'11	175	606	2211	532	337	.241	.334
Bastian, Charles J. "Charlie" 84WilU 84KCU 85–88PhiN 89ChiN 90ChiP 91CinA 91PhiN												
7/4/60	Philadelphia, Pa.	1/18/32	R	R	5'6½	145	504	1806	342	241	.189	.264
Beard, Oliver Perry "Ollie" 89CinA 90CinN 91LouA												
5/2/62	Lexington, Ky.	5/28/29	R	R	5'11	180	331	1307	353	195	.270	.357
Berger, John Henry "Tun" 90–91PitN 92WasN												
12/6/67	Pittsburgh, Pa.	6/10/07	?	R	?	204	173	622	150	88	.241	.301
Booth, ? 75NHNA												
Unknown	Unknown	Unknown	?	?	?	?	1	2	0	0	.000	.000
Brown, ? 74BalNA												
Unknown	Unknown	Unknown	?	?	?	?	2	9	0	0	.000	.000
Buker, Henry L. "Harry" "Happy" 84DetN												
?/?/59	Chicago, Ill.	8/10/99	?	?	?	?	30	111	15	5	.134	.144
Burke, Michael E. "Mike" 79CinN												
?/?/55	Cincinnati, Ohio	6/9/89	R	R	6'	190	28	117	26	13	.222	.248
Byers, Burley "Burley" b. Christopher A. Bayer 99LouN												
12/19/75	Louisville, Ky.	5/30/33	?	?	?	175	1	3	0	0	.000	.000
Carey, Thomas John "Tom" b. J.J. Norton 71KekNA 72–73BalNA 74MutNA 75HarNA 76–77HarN 78ProN 79CleN												
?/?/49	Brooklyn, N.Y.	2/13/99	R	R	5'8	145	536	2394	645	406	.269	.320
Cargo, Robert J. "Bobby" 92PitN												
10/?/68	Pittsburgh, Pa.	4/27/04	R	R	?	?	2	4	1	0	.250	.250
Carman, George Wartman "George" 90PhiA												
3/29/66	Philadelphia, Pa.	6/16/29	?	?	?	?	28	97	17	9	.175	.196
Caskin, Edward James "Ed" 79–81TroN 83–84NYN 85StLN 86NYN												
12/30/51	Danvers, Mass.	10/9/24	R	R	5'9½	165	482	1871	427	229	.228	.269
Clements, Edward "Ed" 90PitN												
Unknown	Philadelphia, Pa.	Unknown	?	?	?	?	1	1	0	0	.000	.000
Clymer, William Johnston "Bill" "Derby Day Bill" 91PhiA												
12/18/73	Philadelphia, Pa.	12/26/36	?	?	?	?	3	11	0	0	.000	.000
Connaughton, Frank Henry "Frank" 94BosN 96NYN												
1/1/69	Clinton, Mass.	12/1/42	R	R	5'9	165	134	486	141	95	.290	.356
Conroy, Bernard Patrick "Ben" 90PhiA												
3/14/71	Philadelphia, Pa.	11/25/37	?	?	?	160	117	404	69	45	.171	.208
Coogan, Daniel George "Dan" 95WasN												
2/16/75	Philadelphia, Pa.	10/28/42	?	?	?	128	26	77	17	9	.221	.273
#Cooney, James Joseph "Jimmy" 90–92ChiN 92WasN												
7/9/65	Cranston, R.I.	7/1/03	B	R	5'9	155	324	1302	315	221	.242	.300
Corcoran, John A. "John" 95PitN												
?/?/73	Cincinnati, Ohio	11/2/01	?	L	?	?	6	20	3	0	.150	.150
Corcoran, Thomas William "Tommy" "Corky" 90PitP 91PhiA 92–96BroN 97–00CinN												
1/4/69	New Haven, Conn.	6/25/60	R	R	5'9	164	1436	5853	1547	880	.264	.351
Cox, Francis Bernard "Frank" "Runt" 84DetN												
8/29/57	Waltham, Mass.	6/24/28	?	?	5'6	?	27	102	13	6	.127	.176

Shortstops

BIRTH DATE	BIRTHPLACE	DEATH DATE	B	T	HGT	WGT	G	AB	H	R	BA	SA
Creely, August L. "Gus" 90StLA												
6/6/70	Florissant, Mo.	4/22/34	?	?	5'6	150	4	15	0	0	.000	.000
Cross, Montford Montgomery "Monte" 92BalN 94–95PitN 96–97StLN 98–00PhiN												
8/31/69	Philadelphia, Pa.	6/21/34	R	R	5'8½	148	826	2923	736	423	.252	.343
Dahlen, William Frederick "Bill" "Bad Bill" 91–98ChiN 99–00BroN												
1/5/70	Nelliston, N.Y.	12/5/50	R	R	5'9	180	1240	4815	1412	1070	.293	.408
Dailey, John G. "John" 75WasNA 75AtlNA												
Unknown	Brooklyn, N.Y.	1/8/98	?	?	?	?	29	118	21	19	.178	.288
Davis, George Stacey "George" 90–92CleN 93–00NYN												
8/23/70	Cohoes, N.Y.	10/17/40	B	R	5'9	180	1378	5490	1723	1075	.314	.444
Davis, J. Ira "Ira" "Slats" 99NYN												
7/8/70	Philadelphia, Pa.	12/21/42	?	?	?	162	6	17	4	3	.235	.412
*Deasley, John "John" 84WasU 84KCU												
1/?/61	Philadelphia, Pa.	12/25/10	?	?	?	?	44	174	36	23	.207	.236
Dee, James D. "Jim" 84PitA												
Unknown	Buffalo, N.Y.	Unknown	?	?	?	?	12	40	5	0	.125	.125
*Dillon, John "John" 75RedsNA												
Unknown	Unknown	Unknown	?	?	?	?	1	1	0	0	.000	.000
Dolan, Joseph "Joe" 96–97LouN 99–00PhiN												
2/24/73	Baltimore, Md.	3/24/38	?	R	5'10	155	215	777	171	90	.220	.284
*Donnelly, John "John" 73WasNA 74PhiNA												
Unknown	Elizabeth, N.J.	Unknown	?	?	?	?	36	159	40	17	.252	.258
Doyle, Joseph K. "Joe" 72NatNA												
Unknown	Cincinnati, Ohio	Unknown	?	?	?	?	9	41	12	6	.293	.293
Drew, David "Dave" 84PhiU 84WasU												
Unknown	Unknown	Unknown	?	?	?	?	15	62	20	9	.323	.403
Duffy, Edward Charles "Ed" 71ChiN												
?/?/44	?, Ireland	6/21/89	?	R	5'7½	152	26	121	28	30	.231	.273
Easterday, Henry P. "Henry" 84PhiU 88KCA 89–90ColA 90PhiA 90LouA												
9/16/64	Philadelphia, Pa.	3/30/95	R	R	5'6	145	322	1129	203	141	.180	.251
Elberfeld, Norman Arthur "Kid" "The Tabasco Kid" 98PhiN 99CinN												
4/13/75	Pomeroy, Ohio	1/13/44	R	R	5'7	158	55	176	45	24	.256	.330
Ellis, Benjamin Franklin "Ben" 96PhiN												
7/?/70	New York, N.Y.	Unknown	?	?	5'10	165	4	16	1	0	.063	.063
Ely, William Frederick "Bones" 84BufN 86LouA 90SyrA 91BroN 93–95StLN 96–00PitN												
6/7/63	N.Girard, Pa.	1/10/52	R	R	6'1	155	1126	4367	1144	587	.262	.335
Eustace, Frank John "Frank" 96LouN												
11/7/73	New York, N.Y.	10/20/32	?	?	5'9	160	25	100	17	18	.170	.260
Farrell, William "Bill" 82PhiA 83BalA												
Unknown	Bridgeport, Conn.	Unknown	?	?	?	?	4	14	2	2	.143	.214
Fennelly, Francis John "Frank" 84WasA 84–88CinA 88–89PhiA 90BroA												
2/18/60	Fall River, Mass.	8/4/20	R	R	5'8	168	786	3042	781	609	.257	.378
Fitzgerald, Dennis S. "Dennis" 90PhiA												
3/?/65	?, England	10/16/36	?	?	5'10	160	2	8	2	0	.250	.250

Shortstops

BIRTH DATE	BIRTHPLACE	DEATH DATE	B	T	HGT	WGT	G	AB	H	R	BA	SA
Flowers, Charles Richard "Dickie" 71TroNA 72AthNA												
?/?/50	Philadelphia, Pa.	10/5/92	?	?	?	?	24	120	37	40	.308	.417
Force, David W. "Davy" "Wee Davy" 71OlyNA 72TroNA 72–73BalNA 74ChiNA 75AtlNA 76PhiN 76NYN 77StLN 79–85BufN 86WasN												
7/27/49	New York, N.Y.	6/21/18	R	R	5'4	130	1029	4251	1060	653	.249	.296
Ford, Edward L. "Ed" 84VirA												
?/?/62	Richmond, Va.	Unknown	?	?	5'9½	160	2	5	0	0	.000	.000
Fox, William Henry "Bill" 97WasN												
1/15/72	Sturbridge, Mass.	5/7/46	B	R	5'10	180	4	14	4	4	.286	.286
Fuller, William Benjamin "Shorty" 88WasN 89–91StLA 92–96NYN												
10/10/67	Cincinnati, Ohio	4/11/04	R	R	5'6	157	962	3669	862	650	.235	.289
***Fulmer, Charles John "Chick" 71RokNA 72MutNA 73–75PhiNA 76LouN 79–80BufN 82–84CinA 84StLA**												
2/12/51	Philadelphia, Pa.	2/15/40	R	R	6'	158	583	2439	636	360	.261	.324
Gallagher, James E. "Jim" 86WasN												
Unknown	Findlay, Ohio	3/29/94	?	?	?	?	1	5	1	1	.200	.200
Gallagher, William Howard "William" 96PhiN												
2/4/74	Boston, Mass.	3/11/50	?	?	?	?	14	49	15	9	.306	.347
Gatins, Frank Anthony "Frank" 98WasN												
3/6/71	Johnstown, Pa.	11/8/11	?	?	?	?	17	58	13	6	.224	.259
Geer, William Henry Harrison "Billy" b. George Harrison Geer 74MutNA 75NHNA 78CinN 80WorN 84PhiU 84BroA 85LouA												
8/13/49	Syracuse, N.Y.	1/5/22	?	R	5'8	160	232	893	191	128	.214	.279
***Gilbert, John G. "John" 90PitN**												
1/8/64	Pottstown, Pa.	11/12/03	?	?	?	?	2	8	0	0	.000	.000
Gillen, Samuel "Sam" b. Gilleland 93PitN 97PhiN												
1/?/71	Pittsburgh, Pa.	5/13/05	?	?	5'8	?	78	276	70	32	.254	.312
Glasscock, John Wesley "Jack" "Pebbly Jack" 79–84CleN 84CinU 85–86StLN 87–89IndN 90–91NYN 92–93StLN 93–94PitN 95LouN 95WasN												
7/22/59	Wheeling, W.Va.	2/24/47	R	R	5'8	160	1736	7030	2040	1163	.290	.374
***Gleason, William G. "Bill" 82–87StLA 88PhiA 89LouA**												
11/12/58	St. Louis, Mo.	7/21/32	R	R	5'8	170	798	3395	907	613	.267	.327
Glenn, Edward D. "Ed" 98WasN 98NYN												
10/?/75	?, Ohio	12/6/11	R	R	?	?	3	8	1	1	.125	.125
Gray, James D. "Reddy" 90PitP 90PitN 93PitN												
Unknown	Unknown	Unknown	?	R	?	?	5	21	6	3	.286	.476
***Hackett, Walter Henry "Walter" 84BosU 85BosN**												
8/15/57	Cambridge, Mass.	10/2/20	?	?	?	?	138	540	124	79	.230	.376
Hall, Robert Russell "Russ" 98StLN												
9/29/71	Shelbyville, Ky.	7/1/37	?	L	5'10	170	39	143	35	13	.245	.273
Hallinan, James H. "Jimmy" 71KekNA 75WesNA 75MutNA 76NYN 77CinN 77–78ChiN 78IndN												
5/27/49	?, Ireland	10/28/79	L	L	5'9	172	170	760	218	142	.287	.371
Halpin, James Nathaniel "Jim" 82WorN 84WasU 85DetN												
10/4/63	?, England	1/4/93	?	?	?	?	63	230	38	27	.165	.187
Hardesty, Scott Durbin "Scott" 99NYN												
1/26/70	Bellville, Ohio	10/29/44	?	?	?	?	22	72	16	4	.222	.222
***Hatfield, Gilbert "Gil" "Colonel" 85BufN 87–89NYN 90NYP 91WasA 93BroN 95LouN**												
1/27/55	Hoboken, N.J.	5/27/21	?	R	5'9½	168	317	1190	295	173	.248	.319

Shortstops

BIRTH DATE	BIRTHPLACE	DEATH DATE	B	T	HGT	WGT	G	AB	H	R	BA	SA
Herr, Edward Joseph "Ed" 87CleA 88StLA 90StLA												
5/18/62	St. Louis, Mo.	7/18/43	R	R	5'9½	179	66	257	67	32	.261	.354
Holland, Willard A. "Will" 89BalA												
Unknown	Georgetown, Del.	7/19/30	?	?	5'10	180	40	143	27	13	.189	.224
Houck, Sargent Perry "Sadie" 79–80BosN 80ProN 81DetN 83DetN 84–85PhiA 86BalA 86WasN 87NYA												
3/?/56	Washington, D.C.	5/26/19	R	R	5'7	151	641	2659	666	406	.250	.338
Hubbard, Allen "Al" (aka Al West) 83PhiA												
12/9/60	Westfield, Mass.	12/14/30	?	?	?	?	2	6	2	2	.333	.333
Hulen, William Franklin "Billy" 96PhiN 99WasN												
3/12/70	Dixon, Cal.	10/2/47	L	L	5'8	148	107	407	100	97	.246	.327
Hulswitt, Rudolph Edward "Rudy" 99LouN												
2/23/77	Newport, Ky.	1/16/50	R	R	5'8½	165	1	0	0	0	—	—
*Irwin, Arthur Albert "Arthur" 80–82WorN 83–85ProN 86–89PhiN 89WasN 90BosP 91BosA 94PhiN												
2/14/58	Toronto, Ont. Can.	7/16/21	L	R	5'8½	158	1010	3871	934	552	.241	.305
Jennings, Hugh Ambrose "Hughie" 91LouA 92–93LouN 93–98BalN 99BroN 99BalN 99–00BroN												
4/2/69	Pittston, Pa.	2/1/28	R	R	5'8½	165	1112	4279	1360	923	.318	.413
Jones, Frank M. "Frank" 84DetN												
8/25/58	Princeton, Ill.	2/4/36	L	?	?	?	2	8	1	0	.125	.125
Jones, Ryerson L. "Jack" "Ri" "Angel Sleeves" 83LouA 84CinU												
Unknown	Cincinnati, Ohio	Unknown	?	R	?	?	71	279	71	37	.254	.301
^Kappel, Henry "Heinie" 87–88CinA 89ColA												
9/?/63	Philadelphia, Pa.	8/27/05	R	R	5'8	160	105	394	106	54	.269	.391
Kellogg, Nathaniel Monroe "Nate" 85DetN												
9/2/58	Rochester, Iowa	Unknown	?	?	5'9	175	5	17	2	4	.118	.176
Kessler, Henry "Henry" "Lucky" 73–75AtlNA 76–77CinN												
?/?/47	Brooklyn, N.Y.	1/9/00	R	R	5'10	144	105	434	110	51	.253	.272
Kinzie, Walter Harris "Walt" 82DetN 84ChiN 84StLA												
3/16/57	Chicago, Ill.	11/5/09	R	?	5'10	161	34	144	19	9	.132	.208
Langsford, Robert William "Bob" b. Robert Hugo Lankswert 99LouN												
8/5/65	Louisville, Ky.	1/10/07	R	R	?	?	1	4	0	0	.000	.000
Leahy, Daniel C. "Dan" 96PhiN												
8/8/70	Knoxville, Tenn.	12/30/03	?	?	5'9	155	2	6	2	0	.333	.500
Leary, John J. "Jack" 80BosN 81DetN 82PitA 82BalA 83LouA 83BalA 84AltU 84Chi–PitU												
?/?/58	New Haven, Conn.	Unknown	?	L	5'11	186	129	538	125	56	.232	.309
Lochhead, Robert Henry "Harry" 99CleN												
3/29/76	Stockton, Ca.	8/22/09	R	R	5'11	172	148	541	129	52	.238	.261
Long, Herman C. "Herman" "Germany" 89KCA 90–00BosN												
4/13/66	Chicago, Ill.	9/7/09	L	R	5'8½	160	1524	6394	1845	1334	.289	.406
Mack, Dennis Joseph "Denny" b. McGee 71RokNA 72AthNA 73–74PhiNA 76StLN 80BufN 82LouA 83PitA												
?/?/51	Easton, Pa.	4/10/88	R	R	5'7	164	373	1505	343	309	.228	.271
Macullar, James F. "Jimmy" "Little Mac" 79SyrN 82–83CinA 84–86BalA												
1/16/55	Boston, Mass	4/8/24	R	L	5'6	155	449	1541	319	246	.207	.276
Magoon, George Henry "George" "Maggie" 98BroN 99BalN 99ChiN												
3/27/75	St. Albans, Me.	12/6/43	R	R	5'10	160	213	739	173	85	.234	.276
Matthias, Stephen J. "Steve" 84Chi–PitU												
?/?/60	Mitchellville, Md.	Unknown	R	R	5'8	160	37	142	39	24	.275	.338

Shortstops

BIRTH DATE	BIRTHPLACE	DEATH DATE	B	T	HGT	WGT	G	AB	H	R	BA	SA
McCauley, William H. "Bill" 95WasN												
12/20/69	Washington, D.C.	1/27/26	?	?	?	?	1	2	0	0	.000	.000
McDonald, ? 72EckNA												
Unknown	Unknown	Unknown	?	?	?	?	1	4	0	0	.000	.000
McGann, Ambrose "Ambrose" 95LouN												
?/?/75	Baltimore, Md.	Unknown	?	?	?	170	20	73	21	9	.288	.411
McKean, Edwin John "Ed" "Mack" 87–88CleA 89–98CleN 99StLN												
6/6/64	Grafton, Ohio	8/16/19	R	R	5'9	160	1654	6890	2083	1227	.302	.416
***McLaughlin, Bernard "Barney" 84KCU 87PhiN 90SyrA**												
?/?/57	?, Ireland	2/13/21	R	R	?	?	178	696	169	84	.243	.309
***McLaughlin, Francis Edward "Frank" 82WorN 83PitA 84CinU 84Chi–PitU 84KCU**												
6/19/56	Lowell, Mass.	4/5/17	R	R	5'9	160	107	426	97	60	.228	.331
McLaughlin, James "Jim" 84WasU												
Unknown	San Francisco, Ca.	Unknown	?	?	?	?	10	37	7	3	.189	.270
McLaughlin, Thomas "Tom" 83–85LouA 86NYA 91WasA												
3/28/60	Louisville, Ky.	7/21/21	?	R	?	?	340	1183	227	142	.192	.253
#Meinke, Frank Louis "Frank" 84–85DetN												
10/18/63	Chicago, Ill.	11/8/31	R	?	5'10½	172	93	344	56	28	.163	.270
Miller, Joseph A. "Joe" 84TolA 85LouA												
2/17/61	Baltimore, Md.	4/23/28	R	?	5'9½	165	203	762	163	90	.214	.280
Moore, Maurice "Molly" 75AtlNA												
Unknown	Unknown	2/24/81	?	?	?	?	21	86	19	5	.221	.267
Morelock, A. Harry "Harry" 91–92PhiN												
11/?/69	Philadelphia, Pa.	Unknown	?	?	?	?	5	17	1	1	.059	.059
Morris, P. 84WasU												
Unknown	Rockford, Ill.	Unknown	?	?	?	?	1	3	0	0	.000	.000
Moynahan, Michael "Mike" 80BufN 81CleN 81DetN 83–84PhiA 84CleN												
?/?/56	Chicago, Ill.	4/9/99	L	R	?	?	169	688	202	104	.294	.379
Murphy, William Henry "Yale" "Midget" 94–95NYN 97NYN												
11/11/69	Southville, Mass.	2/4/06	L	R	5'3	125	130	472	113	100	.239	.282
Murray, Thomas W. "Tom" 94PhiN												
?/?/66	Savannah, Ga.	Unknown	?	?	?	?	1	2	0	0	.000	.000
Myers, Henry C. "Henry" 81ProN 82BalA 84WilU												
5/?/58	Philadelphia, Pa.	4/18/95	R	R	5'9	159	76	322	56	46	.174	.183
Nelson, John W. "Candy" 72TroNA 72EckNA 73–75MutNA 78IndN 79TroN 81WorN 83–87NYA 87NYN 90BroA												
3/12/54	Portland, Me.	9/4/10	L	R	5'6	145	717	3294	833	648	.253	.298
Newell, T.E. "T.E." 77StLN												
Unknown	St. Louis, Mo.	Unknown	?	?	?	?	1	3	0	0	.000	.000
Nyce, Charles Reiff "Charlie" b. Nice 95BosN												
7/1/70	Philadelphia, Pa.	5/9/08	?	?	5'8	160	9	35	8	7	.229	.543
O'Connell, John Joseph "John" 91BalA												
Unknown	Unknown	5/14/08	?	?	?	?	8	29	5	2	.172	.207
Otterson, William John "Billy" 87BroA												
5/4/62	Pittsburgh, Pa.	9/21/40	R	R	5'7	124	30	100	20	16	.200	.320
Pearce, Richard J. "Dickey" 71–72MutNA 73–74AtlNA 75StLNA 76–77StLN												
2/29/36	Brooklyn, N.Y.	10/12/08	R	R	5'3½	161	291	1326	335	217	.253	.275

Shortstops

BIRTH DATE	BIRTHPLACE	DEATH DATE	B	T	HGT	WGT	G	AB	H	R	BA	SA
Peters, John Paul "John" 74–75ChiNA 76–77ChiN 78MilN 79ChiN 80ProN 81BufN 82–84PitA												
4/8/50	Louisiana, Mo.	1/4/24	R	R	5'7	180	615	2697	748	372	.277	.323
Phillips, Marr B. "Marr" 84IndA 85DetN 85PitA 90RocA												
6/16/57	Pittsburgh, Pa.	4/1/28	R	?	5'6½	164	198	824	197	73	.239	.296
Pirie, James Moir "Jim" 83PhiN												
3/31/53	Ontario, Canada	6/2/34	?	?	5'8	169	5	19	3	1	.158	.158
Quinlan, ? 74PhiNA												
Unknown	Unknown	Unknown	?	?	?	?	1	4	1	0	.000	.000
Radcliff, John Y. "John" 71AthNA 72–73BalNA 74PhiNA 75CenNA												
6/29/48	Philadelphia, Pa.	7/26/11	?	?	5'6	140	157	815	231	198	.283	.353
Ray, Irving Burton "Irv" "Stubby" 88–89BosN 89–91BalA												
1/22/64	Harrington, Me.	2/21/48	L	R	5'6	165	226	902	263	154	.292	.359
***Reach, Robert "Bob"** 72OlyNA 73WasNA												
8/28/43	Williamsburg, N.Y.	5/19/22	?	?	5'5	155	3	13	3	2	.231	.231
Redmond, William T. "Billy" 75RedsNA 77CinN 78MilN												
Unknown	Brooklyn, N.Y.	Unknown	L	L	?	?	70	281	62	29	.221	.260
Richmond, John H. "John" 75AthNA 79SyrN 80–81BosN 82CleN 82PhiA 83–84ColA 85PitA												
?/?/53	?, Pennsylvania	Unknown	?	R	5'9	170	440	1725	410	239	.238	.304
Rickley, Christian "Chris" 84PhiU												
10/7/59	Philadelphia, Pa.	10/25/11	?	?	5'8	160	6	25	5	5	.200	.280
***Rowe, John Charles "Jack"** 79–85BufN 86–88DetN 89PitN 90BufP												
12/8/56	Harrisburg, Pa.	4/25/11	L	R	5'8	170	1044	4386	1256	764	.286	.392
Sager, Samuel B. "Pony" 71RokN												
?/?/47	Marshalltown, Iowa	Unknown	?	?	?	140	8	39	11	9	.282	.282
Sales, Edward A. "Ed" 90PitN												
?/?/61	Harrisburg, Pa.	8/10/12	L	R	?	?	51	189	43	19	.228	.312
Santry, Edward "Ed" 84DetN												
?/?/61	Chicago, Ill.	3/6/99	?	?	?	?	6	22	4	1	.182	.182
***Say, Louis I. "Lou"** 73MarNA 74BalNA 75WasNA 80CinN 82PhiA 83BalA 84BalU 84KCU												
2/4/54	Baltimore, Md.	6/5/30	R	R	5'7	145	298	1239	287	181	.232	.292
Scheibeck, Frank S. "Frank" 87CleA 88DetN 90TolA 94PitN 94–95WasN 99WasN												
6/28/65	Detroit, Mich.	10/22/56	R	R	5'7	145	293	1057	258	180	.244	.303
Sexton, Thomas William "Tom" 84MilU												
3/14/65	Rock Island, Ill.	2/8/34	?	?	?	?	12	47	11	9	.234	.277
Shannon, John Francis "Frank" 92WasN 96LouN												
12/3/73	San Francisco, Ca.	2/37/34	?	?	5'3	155	32	119	19	14	.160	.210
Sheehan, Thomas H. "Tommy" 00NYN												
11/6/77	Sacramento, Ca.	5/22/59	R	R	5'8	160	1	2	0	0	.000	.000
Shoupe, John F. "John" 79TroN 82StLA 84WasU												
9/30/51	Cincinnati, Ohio	2/13/20	L	L	5'7	140	14	55	7	7	.127	.127
Shugart, Frank Harry "Frank" b. Shugarts 90ChiP 91–93Pit 93–94StLN 95LouN 97PhiN												
12/10/66	Luthersburg, Pa.	9/9/44	L	R	5'8	170	638	2599	700	421	.269	.383
Smith, George J. "Germany" 84AltU 84CleN 85–89BroA 90BroN 91–96CinN 97BroN 98StLN												
4/21/63	Pittsburgh, Pa.	12/1/27	R	R	6'	175	1710	6552	1592	907	.243	.332
Smith, James A. "Stub" 98BosN												
11/26/76	Elmwood, Ill.	Unknown	L	R	5'6	145	3	10	1	1	.100	.100

Shortstops

BIRTH DATE	BIRTHPLACE	DEATH DATE	B	T	HGT	WGT	G	AB	H	R	BA	SA
Smith, John "John" 73MarNA 74BalNA 75NHNA												
Unknown	Baltimore, Md.	Unknown	?	?	?	?	12	43	6	3	.140	.163
Smith, Lionel H. "Leo" 90RocA												
5/13/59	Brooklyn, N.Y.	8/30/35	?	?	5'6	142	35	112	21	11	.188	.250
Snyder, James C.A. "Jim" 72EckNA												
9/15/47	Brooklyn, N.Y.	12/1/22	?	?	5'7	130	26	107	28	16	.262	.318
Spencer, ? 72NatNA												
Unknown	Unknown	Unknown	?	?	?	?	1	4	0	1	.000	.000
Spurney, Edward Frederick "Ed" 91PitN												
1/19/72	Cleveland, Ohio	10/12/32	?	?	?	?	3	7	2	2	.286	.429
Steere, Frederick Eugene "Gene" 94PitN												
8/16/72	South Scituate. R.I.	3/13/42	?	?	?	?	10	39	8	3	.205	.205
Strang, Samuel Nicklin "Sammy" "The Dixie Thrush" b. Samuel Strang Nicklin 96LouN 00ChiN												
12/16/76	Chattanooga, Tenn.	3/13/32	B	R	5'8	160	41	148	41	16	.277	.297
Stratton, Asa Evans "Asa" 81WorN												
2/10/53	Grafton, Mass.	8/14/25	?	?	?	?	1	4	1	0	.250	.250
Stuart, William Alexander "Bill" "Chauncey" 95PitN 99NYN												
8/28/73	Boalsburg, Pa.	10/14/28	?	?	5'11	170	20	80	19	5	.237	.275
Sullivan, Joseph Daniel "Joe" 93–94WasN 94–96PhiN 96StLN												
1/6/70	Charlestown, Mass.	11/2/97	?	?	5'10	178	413	1648	493	287	.299	.382
Tomney, Philip Howard "Phil" "Buster" 88–90LouA												
7/7/63	Reading, Pa.	3/18/92	R	R	5'7	155	254	882	205	148	.232	.313
***Treacey, Peter "Pete" 76NYN**												
?/?/52	Brooklyn, N.Y.	Unknown	?	?	?	?	2	5	0	1	.000	.000
Turbidy, Jeremiah "Jerry" 84KCU												
7/4/52	Dudley, Mass.	9/5/20	?	?	5'8	165	13	49	11	5	.224	.306
Wall, Howard "Howard" 73WasNA												
Unknown	Unknown	Unknown	?	?	?	?	1	4	1	1	.250	.250
Walsh, Joseph R. "Joe" "Reddy" 91BalA												
11/5/64	Chicago, Ill.	8/8/11	L	R	?	?	26	100	21	14	.210	.260
Ward, John Montgomery "Monte" "John" 78–82ProN 83–89NYN 90BroP 91–92BroN 93–94NYN												
3/3/60	Bellafonte, Pa.	3/4/25	L	R	5'9	165	1825	7647	2105	1408	.275	.341
Wheelock, Warren H. "Bobby" 87BosN 90–91ColA												
8/6/64	Charlestown, Mass.	3/13/28	R	R	5'8	160	236	854	201	138	.235	.285
White, C.B. "C.B." 83PhiN												
Unknown	Wakeman, Ohio	Unknown	?	?	?	?	1	1	0	0	.000	.000
White, William Dighton "Bill" 84PitA 86–88LouA 88StLA												
5/1/60	Bridgeport, Ohio	12/29/24	?	R	?	?	466	1833	441	272	.241	.312
Whitehead, Milton P. "Milt" 84StLU 84KCU												
?/?/62	?, Canada	8/15/01	B	?	?	?	104	415	86	63	.207	.255
Wise, Samuel Washington "Sam" "Modoc" 81DetN 82–88BosN 89WasN 90BufP 91BalA 93WasN												
8/18/57	Akron, Ohio	1/22/10	L	R	5'10½	170	1175	4715	1281	834	.272	.397
Wisner, Philip N. "Phil" 95WasN												
7/?/69	Washington, D.C.	7/5/36	?	R	?	?	1	0	0	0	.000	.000
Woerlin, Joseph "Joe" 95WasN												
10/9/64	?, France	6/22/19	?	?	?	?	1	3	1	1	.333	.333

Shortstops

BIRTH DATE	BIRTHPLACE	DEATH DATE	B	T	HGT	WGT	G	AB	H	R	BA	SA
Wordsworth, Favel Perry "Favel"		**73ResNA**										
12/22/50	New York, N.Y.	8/12/88	?	?	?	?	12	42	10	5	.238	.262
*Wright, George "George"	**71–75BosN**	**76–78BosN**	**79ProN**	**80–81BosN**	**82ProN**							
1/28/47	Yonkers, N.Y.	8/21/37	R	R	5'9½	150	591	2875	867	665	.302	.395
*Wright, Samuel "Sam"	**75NHNA**	**76BosNA**	**80CinN**	**81BosN**								
11/25/48	New York, N.Y.	5/6/28	R	R	5'7½	146	45	173	29	10	.168	.191
Wrigley, George Watson "Zeke"	**96–98WasN**	**99NYN**	**99BroN**									
1/18/74	Philadelphia, Pa.	9/28/52	?	?	5'8½	150	239	861	222	121	.258	.351
Yingling, Joseph Granville "Joe"	**86WasN**	**94PhiN**										
7/23/66	Westminster, Md.	10/24/46	R	L	5'7½	145	2	6	1	0	.167	.167

Bones Ely, one of several men who played under Connie Mack on two different major league teams—Pittsburgh and the Philadelphia A's. Many other distinctions Ely holds, though, are his alone. For one, he is the only nineteenth-century performer to play over 1,000 games in the majors despite not winning a regular job in top company until he was past 30. Ely, who bowed out in 1902, was also the last member of the Buffalo NL franchise to be active in the majors.

Frank Fennelly looks more like a politician than the game's most underrated shortstop during the 1880s. Later Fennelly did indeed become a politician, in the Massachusetts state legislature, but for some seven season he hit with power, stole loads of bases and scored plenty of runs. Fennelly, Bid McPhee, Hick Carpenter and Long John Reilly were the first infield unit to play together at the same positions for four straight years.

Herman Long (second row, far right) sits with the majors' second-best team in 1899. Boston was aced out of a possible third straight pennant by the Brooklyn-Baltimore combine, but Long had his usual quiet, steady good year. He compiled the most career home runs and RBI of any shortstop active primarily in the nineteenth century. Standing: Clark, Bergen, Nichols, Killen, Willis, Lewis, Hickman. Seated: Tenney, Collins, Stafford, Selee (Mgr.), Duffy (Capt.), Hamilton, Long. Front: Lowe, Stahl

Outfielders

BIRTH DATE	BIRTHPLACE	DEATH DATE	B	T	HGT	WGT	G	AB	H	R	BA	SA
Abbey, Charles S. "Charlie" 93–97WasN												
10/14/66	Falls City, Neb.	4/27/26	L	?	5'8	169	451	1751	492	307	.281	.404
Adams, George "George" 79SyrN												
Unknown	Grafton, Mass.	Unknown	R	R	5'6	175	4	13	3	0	.231	.231
Addy, Robert Edward "Bob" "Magnet" 71RokNA 73PhiNA 73BosNA 74HarNA 75PhiNA 76–77ChiN												
2/?/45	Rochester, N.Y.	4/9/10	L	L	5'8	160	274	1231	342	227	.278	.327
Adkinson, Henry Magee "Henry" 95StLN												
9/1/74	Chicago, Ill.	5/1/23	?	?	?	?	1	5	2	1	.400	.400
Allen, Homer S. "Ham" 72ManNA												
8/?/54	Hamden, Conn.	1/7/92	?	?	?	?	16	66	18	8	.273	.288
Allen, Myron Smith "Myron" "Zeke" 83NYN 86BosN 87CleA 88KCA												
3/22/54	Kingston, N.Y.	3/8/24	R	R	5'8	150	156	606	157	89	.259	.371
***Allison, Arthur Algernon "Art"** 71–72CleNA 73ResNA 75WasNA 75HarNA 76LouN												
1/29/49	Philadelphia, Pa.	2/25/16	?	?	5'8	150	168	736	187	106	.254	.306
Allison, William "Bill" 72EckNA												
9/18/48	Philadelphia, Pa.	6/12/23	?	?	?	?	5	19	3	5	.158	.158
Anderson, John Joseph "John" 94–98BroN 98WasN 98–99BroN												
12/14/73	Sarpsborg, Norway	7/23/49	B	R	6'2	180	596	2363	705	400	.298	.444
Andrews, George Edward "Ed" 84–89PhiN 89IndN 90BroP 91CinA												
4/5/59	Painesville, Ohio	8/12/34	R	R	5'8	160	774	3233	830	602	.257	.320
Andrews, James Pratt "Jim" 90ChiN												
6/5/65	Shelburne Falls, Mass.	12/27/07	?	?	?	?	53	202	38	32	.188	.272
Andrus, Frederick Hotham "Fred" 76ChiN 84ChiN												
8/23/50	Washington, Mich	11/10/37	R	R	6'2	185	9	41	12	9	.293	.366
Annis, William Perley "Bill" 84BosN												
5/24/57	Stoneham, Mass.	6/10/23	R	?	5'7	150	26	96	17	17	.177	.198
Armstrong, Samuel "Sam" 71KekNA												
?/?/50	Baltimore, Md.	Unknown	?	?	6'2	160	12	49	11	9	.224	.306
Arnold, Willis S. "Billy" 72ManNA												
3/2/51	Middletown, Conn.	1/17/99	?	?	?	?	2	7	1	2	.143	.143
Atkinson, Edward "Ed" 73WasNA												
?/?/51	Baltimore, Md.	Unknown	?	?	?	?	8	0	2	0	.000	.000
Austin, Henry C. "Henry" 73ResNA												
?/?/44	Brooklyn, N.Y.	9/3/95	?	?	?	?	23	101	25	10	.248	.337
Bahret, Frank J. "Frank" 84BalU												
Unknown	Poughkeepsie, N.Y.	Unknown	?	?	6'1	184	2	8	0	0	.000	.000
Baker, Charles A. "Charlie" 84 Chi–PitU												
1/15/56	Sterling, Mass.	1/15/37	?	?	?	?	15	57	8	5	.140	.228
***Bannon, James Henry "Jimmy"** "Foxy Grandpa" 93StLN 94–96BosN												
5/5/71	Amesbury, Mass.	3/24/48	R	R	5'5	160	366	1433	459	292	.320	.447
***Bannon, Thomas Edward "Tom"** "Ward Six" 95–96NYN												
5/8/69	Amesbury, Mass.	1/26/50	R	R	5'8	175	39	166	44	34	.265	.331
Barker, Alfred L. "Al" 71RokNA												
1/18/39	Rockford, Ill.	9/15/12	?	?	?	?	1	4	1	0	.250	.250

Outfielders

BIRTH DATE	BIRTHPLACE	DEATH DATE	B	T	HGT	WGT	G	AB	H	R	BA	SA
Barnes, William H. "Bill" 84StPU												
Unknown	Indianapolis, Ind.	Unknown	?	?	?	?	8	30	6	2	.200	.233
Barrett, ? 72AtlNA												
Unknown	Unknown	Unknown	?	?	?	?	8	34	7	7	.206	.235
Barrett, James Erigena "Jimmy" 99–00CinN												
3/28/75	Athol, Mass.	10/24/21	L	R	5'9	170	163	637	206	144	.323	.402
Barrows, Franklin L. "Frank" 71BosNA												
10/22/46	Hudson, Ohio	2/6/22	?	?	?	?	18	86	13	13	.151	.198
Barry, John C. "Shad" 99WasN 00BosN												
10/27/78	Newburgh, N.Y.	11/27/36	R	R	?	?	159	501	137	71	.273	.367
Bass, John E. "John" 71CleNA 72AtlNA 77HarN												
?/?/50	Baltimore, Md.	Unknown	?	?	5'6	150	25	100	29	19	.290	.600
Beach, Stonewall Jackson "Jack" 84WasA												
?/?/62	Alexandria, Va.	7/23/96	?	?	?	?	8	31	3	3	.097	.161
Beals, Thomas L. "Tommy" (aka W. Thomas 1871–73) 71–72OlyNA 73WasNA 74–75BosNA 80ChiN												
8/?/50	New York, N.Y.	10/2/15	R	?	5'5	144	123	539	132	110	.245	.334
Beaumont, Clarence Howeth "Ginger" 99–00PitN												
7/23/76	Rochester, Wis.	4/10/56	L	R	5'8	190	249	1004	312	195	.311	.397
Bechtel, George A. "George" 71AthNA 72MutNA 73–74PhiNA 75CenNA 75AthNA 76LouN 76NYN												
9/2/48	Philadelphia, Pa.	Unknown	?	?	5'11½	165	221	1041	288	215	.277	.354
Beck, Frank J. "Frank" b. Hengstebeck 84PitA 84BalU												
4/29/60	Poughkeepsie, N.Y.	2/8/41	?	R	5'9	141	8	32	6	2	.188	.250
Beecher, Edward "Ed" "Scrap Iron" 97StLN 98CleN												
5/?/76	?, Indiana	?	?	?	?	?	11	37	9	2	.243	.297
Beecher, Edward Harry "Ed" "Harry" 87PitN 89WasN 90BufP 91WasA 91PhiA												
7/2/60	Guilford, Conn.	9/12/35	L	L	5'10	185	283	1190	325	148	.273	.363
Behel, Stephen Arnold Douglas "Steve" 84MilU 86NYA												
11/6/60	Earlville, Ill.	2/15/45	?	?	?	?	68	257	54	37	.210	.249
Belden, Ira Allison "Ira" 97CleN												
4/16/74	Cleveland, Ohio	7/15/16	L	R	5'11	175	8	30	8	5	.267	.400
Benners, Isaac B. "Ike" 84BroA 84WilU												
6/7/56	Philadelphia, Pa.	4/18/32	L	?	?	175	55	211	39	25	.185	.299
Berkelbach, Francis P. "Frank" 84CinA												
Unknown	Philadelphia, Pa.	Unknown	?	?	6'	182	6	25	6	3	.240	.320
Berkenstock, Nathan "Nate" 71AthNA												
?/?/31	?, Pa.	2/23/00	?	?	?	?	1	4	0	0	.000	.000
Bernard, Curtis Henry "Curt" 00NYN												
2/18/78	Parkersburg, W.VA.	4/10/55	L	R	5'10	150	20	71	18	9	.254	.282
Berry, Thomas Haney "Tom" 71AthNA												
12/31/42	Chester, Pa.	6/6/15	?	?	5'6	140	1	4	1	0	.250	.250
Berthrong, Henry W. "Harry" 71OlyNA												
1/1/44	Mumford, N.Y.	4/28/28	?	R	5'6½	140	17	73	17	17	.233	.274
Bielaski, Oscar "Oscar" 72NatNA 73WasNA 74BalNA 75ChiNA 76ChiN												
3/21/47	Washington, D.C.	11/8/11	R	R	5'10½	170	174	746	180	117	.241	.256
Birchall, Adoniram Judson "Jud" 82–84PhiA												
?/?/58	Germantown, Pa.	12/22/87	?	?	?	?	225	1007	254	196	.252	.287

Outfielders

BIRTH DATE	BIRTHPLACE	DEATH DATE	B	T	HGT	WGT	G	AB	H	R	BA	SA
Bird, George Raymond "George" 71RokNA												
6/23/50	Stillman Valley, Ill.	11/9/40	R	R	5'9	160	25	106	28	19	.264	.377
Birdsall, David Solomon "Dave" 71–73BosNA												
7/16/38	New York, N.Y.	12/30/96	R	R	5'9	126	48	240	63	66	.263	.313
Black, Robert Benjamin "Bob" 84KCU												
12/10/62	Cincinnati, Ohio	3/21/33	?	?	5'5	155	38	146	36	25	.247	.390
Blake, Harry Cooper "Harry" 94–98CleN 99StLN												
6/16/74	Portsmouth, Ohio	10/14/19	R	R	5'7	165	526	1877	473	299	.252	.324
Blakiston, Robert J. "Bob" b. Blackstone 82–84PhiA 84IndA												
10/2/55	San Francisco, Cal.	12/25/18	?	?	5'8½	180	154	594	142	87	.239	.276
Blong, Joseph Myles "Joe" 75RedsNA 76–77StLN												
9/17/53	St. Louis, Mo.	9/16/92	R	R	?	?	136	540	119	50	.220	.278
Boardman, Frederick "Frederick" 74BalNA												
Unknown	Chicago, Ill.	Unknown	?	?	?	?	1	4	1	0	.250	.250
Bohn, Charles "Charlie" 82LouA												
?/?/57	Cleveland, Ohio	8/1/03	R	R	5'9	165	4	13	2	0	.154	.154
Booth, Edward H. "Eddie" 72ManNA 72AtlNA 73ResNA 73–74AtlNA 75MutNA 76NYN												
Unknown	Brooklyn, N.Y.	Unknown	?	?	?	?	242	1015	245	128	.241	.292
Boyd, William J. "Bill" 72MutNA 73AtlNA 74HarNA 75AtlNA												
12/22/52	New York, N.Y.	9/30/12	?	?	?	?	147	660	192	93	.291	.388
Bradley, Al "Al" 84WasU												
Unknown	Unknown	Unknown	?	?	5'10	185	1	3	0	0	.000	.000
Brady, ? 75ChiNA												
Unknown	Unknown	Unknown	?	?	?	?	1	4	1	1	.250	.750
Brady, Stephen A. "Steve" 74–75HarNA 75WasNA 83–86NYA												
7/14/51	Worcester, Mass.	11/1/17	?	?	5'9½	165	489	2029	528	311	.260	.305
Briggs, Charles R. "Charlie" 84Chi–PitU												
?/?/61	Batavia, Ill.	Unknown	?	?	5'7	170	49	182	31	29	.170	.253
Bristow, George "George" 99CleN												
5/?/70	Paw Paw, Ill.	Unknown	?	R	?	?	3	8	1	0	.125	.250
Brodie, Walter Scott "Steve" 90–91BosN 92–93StLN 93–96BalN 97–98PitN 98–99BalN												
9/11/68	Warrenton, Va.	10/30/35	L	R	5'11	180	1245	4977	1514	808	.304	.384
Brown, Oliver S. "Oliver" 72AtlNA 75AtlNA												
5/3/49	Brooklyn, N.Y.	9/23/32	?	?	?	?	7	26	1	0	.038	.038
Brown, Thomas Tarlton "Tom" 82BalA 83–84ColA 85–86PitA 87PitN 87IndN 88–89BosN 90BosP 91BosA 92–94LouN 95StLN 95–98WasN												
9/21/60	Liverpool, England	10/25/27	L	R	5'10	168	1786	7363	1952	1521	.265	.361
Browning, Louis Rogers "Pete" "The Gladiator" 82–89LouA 90CleP 91PitN 91CinN 92LouN 92CinN 93LouN 94StLN 94BroN												
6/17/61	Louisville, Ky.	9/10/05	R	R	6'	180	1183	4820	1646	954	.341	.467
Budd, ? 90CleP												
Unknown	Cleveland, Ohio	Unknown	?	?	?	?	1	4	0	0	.000	.000
Bunce, Joshua "Josh" 77HarN												
5/10/47	Brooklyn, N.Y.	4/28/12	?	?	?	?	1	4	0	0	.000	.000
Burch, Earnest W. "Ernie" 84CleN 86–87BroA												
?/?/56	DeKalb Co., Ill.	Unknown	L	?	?	?	194	768	200	134	.260	.341

Outfielders

BIRTH DATE	BIRTHPLACE	DEATH DATE	B	T	HGT	WGT	G	AB	H	R	BA	SA
Burke, Daniel L. "Dan" 90RocA 90SyrA 92BosN												
10/25/68	Abington, Mass.	3/20/33	R	R	5'10	190	42	126	22	15	.175	.183
Burke, Edward D. "Eddie" 90PhiN 90PitN 91MilA 92CinN 92–95NYN 95–97CinN												
10/6/66	Northumberland, Pa.	11/26/07	L	R	5'6	161	853	3508	979	744	.279	.378
Burkett, Jesse Cail "Jesse" "Crab" 90NYN 91–98CleN 99–00StLN												
12/4/68	Wheeling, W.Va	5/27/53	L	L	5'8	155	1359	5604	2001	1258	.357	.470
Burnett, Hercules H. "Hercules" 88LouA 95LouN												
8/13/65	Louisville, Ky.	10/4/36	R	?	?	177	6	21	7	7	.333	.714
Burns, James M. "Jim" 88–89KCA 91WasA												
Unknown	Quincy, Ill.	Unknown	?	?	5'7	168	169	727	222	131	.305	.396
Burns, Richard Simon "Dick" 83DetN 84CinU 85StLN												
12/26/63	Holyoke, Mass.	11/16/37	L	L	5'7	140	130	544	145	97	.267	.388
Burns, Thomas P. "Oyster" 84WilU 84–85BalA 87–88BalA 88–89BroA 90–95BroN 95NYN												
9/6/64	Philadelphia, Pa.	11/11/28	R	R	5'8	183	1187	4637	1389	869	.300	.446
Burroughs, Henry F. "Henry" 71–72OlyNA												
?/?/45	Detroit, Mich.	Unknown	?	?	5'8	147	14	70	16	12	.229	.386
Burt, Frank J. "Frank" 82BalA												
Unknown	Camden, N.J.	Unknown	?	?	?	?	10	36	4	2	.111	.222
Butler, Frank Dean "Frank" "Goldbrick" 95NYN												
7/18/60	Savannah, Ga.	7/10/45	L	L	?	?	5	22	6	5	.273	.318
Butler, Frank Edward "Kid" 84BosU												
5/?/61	Boston, Mass.	4/9/21	?	?	5'6	140	71	255	43	36	.169	.227
Butler, William J. "Bill" 84IndA												
?/?/61	New Orleans, La.	Unknown	?	?	?	?	9	31	7	7	.226	.452
Cahill, John Patrick Parnell "Patsy" 84ColA 86StLN 87IndN												
4/30/65	San Francisco, Ca.	10/31/01	R	R	5'7½	168	252	936	192	93	.205	.260
Callahan, Edward Joseph "Ed" 84StLU 84KCU 84BosU												
12/11/57	Boston, Mass.	2/5/47	?	?	?	?	8	27	9	2	.333	.333
Campau, Charles Columbus "Count" 88DetN 90StLA 94WasN												
10/17/63	Detroit, Mich.	4/3/38	L	R	5'11	160	147	572	153	97	.267	.397
Canavan, James Edward "Jim" 91CinA 91MilA 92ChiN 93–94CinN 97BroN												
11/26/66	New Bedford, Mass.	5/27/49	R	R	5'8	160	539	2064	461	322	.223	.344
Carl, Frederick E. "Fred" 89LouA												
9/8/58	Baltimore, Md.	5/4/19	?	L	5'6	158	25	99	20	13	.202	.263
Carroll, Edward "Chick" 84WasU												
?/?/68	?, Ark.	7/13/08	?	?	?	?	4	16	4	1	.250	.250
Carroll, John E. "Scrappy" 84StPU 85BufN 87CleA												
8/27/60	Buffalo, N.Y.	11/14/42	?	?	5'7½	?	79	287	49	34	.171	.199
Carroll, Samuel Clifford "Cliff" 82–85ProN 86–87WasN 88PitN 90–91ChiN 92StLN 93BosN												
10/18/59	Clay's Grove, Iowa	6/12/23	B	R	5'8½	163	991	3972	995	729	.251	.329
Caruthers, Robert "Bob" "Parisian Bob" 84–87StLA 88–89BroA 90–91BroN 92StLN 93ChiN 93CinN												
1/5/64	Memphis, Tenn.	8/5/11	L	R	5'7	138	705	2465	694	508	.282	.400
*Casey, Dennis Patrick "Dennis" 84WilU 84–85BalA												
3/30/58	Binghampton, N.Y.	1/19/09	L	R	5'9	164	102	421	115	71	.273	.401
Cassidy, John P. "John" 75AtLNA 75NHNA 76–77HarN 78ChiN 79–82TroN 83ProN 84–85BroA												
?/?/57	Brooklyn, N.Y.	7/2/91	R	L	5'8	168	634	2642	650	353	.246	.298

Outfielders

BIRTH DATE	BIRTHPLACE	DEATH DATE	B	T	HGT	WGT	G	AB	H	R	BA	SA
Chapman, John Curtis "Jack"	"Death to Flying Things"	74AtlNA		75StLNA	76LouN							
5/8/43	Brooklyn, N.Y.	6/10/16	?	R	5'11	170	113	504	124	64	.246	.298
Chiles, Pearce Nuget "Pearce"	"What's The Use"	99–00PhiN										
5/28/67	Deepwater, Mo.	Unknown	R	R	5'11	185	130	449	132	70	.294	.430
Church, Hiram Lincoln "Hi"	90BroA											
11/23/63	Central Square, N.Y.	2/23/26	?	?	?	?	3	9	1	1	.111	.111
Clack, Robert S. "Bobby"	b. Clark	74–75AtlNA		76CinN								
6/?/50	?, England	10/22/33	R	R	5'9	153	82	312	48	33	.154	.163
Clark, Owen F. "Spider"	89WasN	90BufP										
9/16/67	Brooklyn, N.Y.	2/8/92	?	R	5'10	150	107	405	106	64	.262	.351
*Clarke, Fred Clifford "Fred"	94–99LouN	00PitN										
10/3/72	Winterset, Iowa	8/14/60	L	R	5'10½	165	869	3495	1144	688	.327	.442
Clarke, Harry Corson "Harry"	89WasN											
?/?/61	Unknown	3/3/23	?	?	?	?	1	3	0	0	.000	.000
*Clarke, Joshua Baldwin "Josh"	98LouN											
3/8/79	Winfield, Kan.	7/2/62	L	R	5'10	180	6	18	3	0	.167	.167
Cline, John P. "Monk"	82BalA	84–85LouA		88KCA	91LouA							
3/3/58	Louisville, Ky.	9/23/16	L	L	5'4	150	232	940	245	165	.261	.334
Clinton, James Lawrence "Jim"	"Big Jim"	72EckNA	73ResNA	74–75AtlNA	76LouN	82WorN	83–83BalA	85CinA				
86BalA												
8/10/50	New York, N.Y.	9/3/21	R	R	5'8½	154	426	1717	439	247	.257	.313
Coleman, John Francis "John"	83–84PhiN	84–86PhiA	86PitA	87–88PitN	89PhiA	90PitN						
3/6/63	Saratoga Springs, N.Y.	5/31/22	L	R	5'9½	170	629	2508	645	332	.257	.345
Collins, ?	92StLN											
Unknown	Unknown	Unknown	?	?	?	?	1	2	0	0	.000	.000
Collins, Daniel Thomas "Dan"	74ChiNA	76LouN										
7/12/54	St. Louis, Mo.	9/21/83	?	?	?	?	10	40	5	4	.125	.150
Collver, William J. "Bill"	85BosN											
3/21/67	Clyde, Ohio	3/24/88	?	?	?	?	1	4	0	0	.000	.000
Cone, Joseph Frederick "Fred"	71BosNA											
5/?/48	Rockford, Ill.	4/13/09	?	?	5'9½	171	19	77	20	17	.260	.325
Connolly, John M. "Red"	86StLN											
?/?/63	New York, N.Y.	3/2/96	?	?	?	?	2	7	0	0	.000	.000
Connors, Jeremiah "Jerry"	92PhiN											
Unknown	Cleveland, Ohio	Unknown	?	?	?	?	1	3	0	0	.000	.000
Cooke, Frederick B. "Fred"	97CleN											
10/?/73	Paulding, Ohio	Unknown	?	?	?	?	5	17	5	2	.294	.512
Cooley, Duff Gordon "Duff"	93–96StLN	96–99PhiN	00PitN									
3/29/73	Leavenworth, Kan.	8/9/37	L	R	5'11	158	695	3179	972	605	.306	.392
Coon, William K. "William"	75AthNA	76PhiN										
3/21/55	?, Pa.	8/30/15	?	?	?	?	57	233	52	31	.223	.253
Corkhill, John Stewart "Pop"	83–88CinA	88–89BroA	90BroN	91PhiA	91CinN	91–92PitN						
4/11/58	Parkesburg, Pa.	4/4/21	L	R	5'10	180	1086	4404	1120	650	.254	.337
Coughlin, Dennis F. "Dennis"	72NatNA											
Unknown	Unknown	Unknown	?	?	?	?	8	37	13	7	.351	.378

Outfielders

BIRTH DATE	BIRTHPLACE	DEATH DATE	B	T	HGT	WGT	G	AB	H	R	BA	SA
Cramer, William B. "Dick" 83NYN												
Unknown	Brooklyn, N.Y.	8/12/85	?	?	?	?	2	6	0	0	.000	.000
Crane, Edward Nicholas "Cannonball" "Ed" 84BosU 85ProN 85BufN 86WasN 88–89NYN 90NYP 91CinA 91CinN												
92–93NYN 93BroN												
5/27/62	Boston, Mass.	9/19/96	R	R	5'10½	204	391	1409	335	199	.238	.329
Crawford, George "George" 90PhiA												
Unknown	Unknown	Unknown	?	?	?	?	5	17	2	1	.118	.118
Crawford, Samuel Earl "Sam" "Wahoo Sam" 99–00CinN												
4/18/80	Wahoo, Neb.	6/15/68	L	L	6'	190	132	516	140	93	.271	.438
Creegan, Martin "Marty" 84WasU												
Unknown	San Francisco, Ca.	Unknown	?	?	?	161	9	33	5	4	.152	.152
Cregan, Peter James "Pete" "Peekskill Pete" 99NYN												
4/13/75	Kingston, N.Y.	5/18/45	R	R	5'7½	150	1	2	0	0	.000	.000
Crowley, William Michael "Bill" 75PhiNA 77LouN 79–80BufN 81BosN 83PhiA 83CleN 84BosN 85BufN												
4/8/57	Philadelphia, Pa.	7/14/91	R	R	5'7½	159	521	2057	540	263	.263	.336
Cullen, John J. "John" 84WilU												
Unknown	Marysville, Ca.	Unknown	?	?	?	?	9	31	6	2	.194	.194
Curtis, Ervin Duane "Ervin" 91CinN 91WasA												
12/27/61	Coldwater, Mich.	2/14/45	L	L	5'8½	157	56	211	55	28	.261	.351
Cuthbert, Edgar Edward "Ned" 71–72AthNA 73PhiNA 74ChiNA 75StLNA 76StLN 77CinN 82–83StLA 84BalU												
6/20/45	Philadelphia, Pa.	2/6/05	R	R	5'6	140	452	2113	537	452	.254	.317
Dailey, Vincent Perry "Vince" 90CleN												
12/25/64	Osceola, Pa.	11/14/19	?	?	6'	200	64	246	71	41	.289	.366
***Daily, Edward M. "Ed"** 85–87PhiN 87–88WasN 89ColA 90BroA 90NYN 90–91LouA 91WasA												
9/7/62	Providence, R.I.	10/21/91	R	R	5'10½	174	640	2573	616	396	.239	.325
Daisey, George K. "George" 84AltU												
Unknown	Altoona, Pa.	Unknown	?	?	5'11	190	1	4	0	0	.000	.000
Dalrymple, Abner Frank "Abner" 78MilN 79–86ChiN 87–88PitN 91MilA												
9/9/57	Warren, Ill.	1/25/39	L	R	5'10½	175	951	4172	1202	813	.288	.410
Daly, James J. "Sun" 92BalN												
1/6/65	Rutland, Vt.	4/30/38	?	?	?	?	13	48	12	5	.250	.333
***Daly, Joseph John "Joe"** 90PhiA 91CleN 92BosN												
9/21/68	Conshohocken, Pa.	3/21/43	?	R	5'8	157	23	78	21	8	.269	.346
Deane, John Henry "Harry" 71KekNA 74BalNA												
5/6/46	Trenton, N.J.	5/31/25	?	?	5'7	150	53	225	54	32	.240	.293
Decker, George A. "George" 92–97ChiN 98StLN 98–99LouN 99WasN												
6/1/69	York, Pa.	6/7/09	L	L	6'1	180	701	2727	753	420	.276	.376
Delahanty, Edward James "Ed" "Big Ed" 88–89PhiN 90CleP 91–00PhiN												
10/30/67	Cleveland, Ohio	7/2/03	R	R	6'1	170	1531	6334	2175	1368	.343	.483
Dexter, Charles Dana "Charlie" 96–99LouN 00ChiN												
6/15/76	Evansville, Ind.	6/9/34	R	R	5'7	155	415	1500	417	238	.278	.357
Dickerson, Lewis Pessano "Buttercup" 78–79CinN 80TroN 80–81WorN 83PitA 84StLU 84BalA 84LouA 85BufN												
10/11/58	Tyaskin, Md.	7/23/20	L	R	5'6	140	408	1762	500	302	.284	.377
Dignan, Stephen E. "Steve" 80BosN 80WorN												
5/16/59	Boston, Mass.	7/11/81	?	?	?	?	11	44	14	5	.318	.386

Outfielders

BIRTH DATE	BIRTHPLACE	DEATH DATE	B	T	HGT	WGT	G	AB	H	R	BA	SA
Dillard, Robert Lee "Pat" 00StLN												
6/12/73	Chattanooga, Tenn.	7/22/07	L	R	6′	180	57	183	42	24	.230	.279
Dolan, Patrick Henry "Cozy" 95–96BosN 00ChiN												
12/3/72	Cambridge, Mass.	3/29/07	L	L	5′10	160	45	145	35	21	.241	.290
Dole, Lester Carrington "Lester" 75NHNA												
7/8/55	Meriden, Conn.	12/10/18	?	?	5′11	?	1	4	2	1	.500	.500
Donlin, Michael Joseph "Mike" "Turkey Mike" 99–00StLN												
5/30/78	Peoria, Ill.	9/24/33	L	L	5′9	170	144	542	176	89	.325	.489
***Donnelly, Peter J. "Pete" 71KekNA**												
10/8/49	Philadelphia, Pa.	10/1/90	?	?	?	?	9	34	7	7	.206	.294
Donohue, Joseph F. "Joe" 91PhiN												
?/?/69	Syracuse, N.Y.	Unknown	?	?	?	?	6	22	7	2	.318	.364
Donovan, Patrick Joseph "Patsy" 90BosN 90BroN 91LouN 91WasN 92WasN 92–99PitN 00StLN												
3/16/65	Queenstown, Ireland	12/25/53	L	L	5′11½	175	1327	5595	1695	1062	.303	.361
Dooms, Henry E. "Jack" "Harry" 92LouN												
1/30/67	St. Louis, Mo.	12/14/99	?	?	?	?	1	4	0	0	.000	.000
***Dorgan, Jeremiah F. "Jerry" 80WorN 82PhiA 84IndA 84BroA 85DetN**												
?/?/56	Meriden, Conn.	6/10/91	L	R	?	165	131	531	150	74	.282	.339
***Dorgan, Michael Cornelius "Mike" 77StLN 79SyrN 80ProN 81WorN 81DetN 83–87NYN 90SyrA**												
10/2/53	Middletown, Conn.	4/26/09	R	R	5′9	180	715	2924	802	443	.274	.340
Dow, Clarence G. "Clarence" 84BosU												
10/11/54	Charlestown, Mass.	3/11/93	?	?	?	?	1	6	2	1	.333	.333
Dowd, Thomas Jefferson "Tommy" "Buttermilk Tommy" 91BosA 91WasA 92WasN 93–97StLN 97PhiN 98StLN 99CleN												
4/20/69	Holyoke, Mass.	7/2/33	R	R	5′8	173	1182	4917	1333	799	.271	.346
Dowie, Joseph E. "Joe" 89BalA												
7/15/65	New Orleans, La.	3/4/17	?	?	5′8	150	20	75	17	12	.227	.293
Doyle, Cornelius J. "Conny" 83PhiN 84PitA												
?/?/62	?, Ireland	7/29/31	?	?	5′10	185	31	126	32	11	.254	.365
Drake, Lyman Daniel "Lyman" 84WasA												
2/9/52	Berea, Ohio	2/6/32	?	?	?	?	2	7	2	0	.286	.429
Duffee, Charles Edward "Charlie" "Home Run" 89–90StLA 91ColA 92WasN 93CinN												
1/27/66	Mobile, Ala.	12/24/94	R	R	?	?	508	1943	518	314	.267	.389
Duffy, Hugh "Hugh" 88–89ChiN 90ChiP 91BosA 92–00BosN												
11/26/66	Cranston, R.I.	10/19/54	R	R	5′7	168	1624	6670	2171	1505	.325	.451
Dungan, Samuel Morrison "Sam" 92–94ChiN 94LouN 00ChiN												
7/29/66	Ferndale, Ca.	3/16/39	R	?	5′11	180	244	984	285	144	.290	.370
Dyler, John F. "John" 82LouA												
6/?/52	Louisville, Ky.	Unknown	?	?	?	?	1	4	0	0	.000	.000
Eagle, William Lycurgus "Bill" 98WasN												
7/25/77	Rockville, Md.	4/27/51	?	?	?	?	4	13	4	0	.308	.385
Earl, Howard J. "Howard" "Slim Jim" 90ChiN 91MilA												
2/25/69	Palmyra, NY	12/23/16	?	?	6′2	180	123	513	127	78	.248	.343
Eden, Charles M. "Charlie" 77ChiN 79CleN 84–85PitA												
1/18/55	Lexington, Ky.	9/17/20	L	L	?	168	226	935	244	118	.261	.372

Outfielders

BIRTH DATE	BIRTHPLACE	DEATH DATE	B	T	HGT	WGT	G	AB	H	R	BA	SA
Egan, James K. "Jim" "The Toy Terrier" 82TroN												
?/?/58	Derby, Conn.	9/26/84	?	L	?	?	30	115	23	15	.200	.261
Eggler, David Daniel "Dave" 71–73MutNA 74PhiNA 75AthNA 76PhiN 77ChiN 79BufN 83BalA 83–85BufN												
4/30/51	Brooklyn, N.Y.	4/5/02	R	R	5'9	165	576	2546	698	492	.274	.331
Eland, ? 73MarNA												
Unknown	Unknown	Unknown	?	?	?	?	1	3	0	0	.000	.000
Ellick, Joseph J. "Joe" 75RedsNA 78MilN 80WorN 84Chi–PitU 84KCU 84BalU												
4/3/54	Cincinnati, Ohio	4/21/23	?	?	5'10	162	116	487	106	77	.218	.242
Evans, ? 75NHNA												
Unknown	Unknown	Unknown	?	?	?	?	1	4	2	1	.500	.500
Evans, Uriah L.P. "Jake" "Bloody Jake" 79–81TroN 82WorN 83–84CleN 85BalA												
9/?/56	Baltimore, Md.	1/16/07	?	R	5'8	154	472	1831	435	215	.238	.300
Ewell, George "George" 71CleNA												
Unknown	Philadelphia. Pa.	Unknown	?	?	?	?	1	3	0	0	.000	.000
Falch, Anton C. "Anton" 84MilU												
12/4/60	Milwaukee, Wis.	3/31/36	?	?	6'6	220	5	18	2	0	.111	.111
Farley, Thomas T. "Tom" 84WasA												
Unknown	Chicago, Ill.	2/26/03	?	?	?	?	14	52	11	5	.212	.288
Farrell, John "Jack" 74HarNA												
1/2/56	Hartford, Conn.	11/15/16	?	?	?	?	3	13	5	3	.385	.385
Fields, John Joseph "Jocko" 87–89PitN 90PitP 91PitN 91PhiN 92NYN												
10/20/64	Cork, Ireland	10/14/50	R	R	5'10	160	341	1319	359	212	.272	.397
Fisher, Charles "Charles" 89LouA												
Unknown	Baltimore, Md.	Unknown	?	?	?	?	1	2	1	0	.500	.500
Flaherty, Martin J. "Martin" 81WorN												
9/24/53	Worcester, Mass.	6/10/20	L	L	?	?	1	2	0	0	.000	.000
Fleming, Thomas Vincent "Tom" "Sleuth" 99NYN												
11/20/73	Philadelphia, Pa.	12/26/57	L	L	5'11	155	22	77	16	9	.208	.247
Fletcher, George Horace Elliot "George" 72EckNA												
4/21/45	Brooklyn, N.Y.	Unknown	?	?	?	?	2	8	3	1	.375	.375
Flick, Elmer Harrison "Elmer" 98–00PhiN												
1/11/76	Bedford, Ohio	1/9/71	L	R	5'9	168	399	1483	503	288	.339	.483
Flynn, George A. "George" "Dibby" 96ChiN												
5/24/71	Chicago, Ill.	12/28/01	?	?	?	?	29	106	27	15	.255	.302
Flynn, Joseph "Joe" 84PhiU 84BosU												
Unknown	Philadelphia, Pa.	Unknown	?	?	?	?	61	240	59	42	.246	.375
*Fogarty, James G. "Jim" 84–89PhiN 90PhiP												
2/12/64	San Francisco, Cal.	5/20/91	R	R	5'10½	180	751	2880	709	508	.246	.343
*Fogarty, Joseph J. "Joe" 85StLN												
11/8/68	San Francisco, Cal.	3/28/18	?	?	?	?	2	8	1	1	.125	.125
Foley, Charles Joseph "Curry" 79–80BosN 81–83BufN												
1/14/56	Milltown, Ireland	10/20/98	?	L	5'10	160	305	1305	373	192	.286	.362
Foley, Thomas J. "Tom" 71ChiNA												
8/16/47	Chicago, Ill.	1/4/96	?	?	5'9½	157	18	84	22	18	.262	.321
Foster, Clarence Francis "Pop" 98–00NYN												
4/8/78	New Haven, Conn.	4/16/44	R	R	5'8½	?	147	497	141	77	.284	.374

Outfielders

BIRTH DATE	BIRTHPLACE	DEATH DATE	B	T	HGT	WGT	G	AB	H	R	BA	SA
Foster, Elmer Ellsworth "Elmer" 84PhiA 84PhiU 86NYA 88–89NYN 90–91ChiN												
8/15/61	Minneapolis, Minn.	7/22/46	R	L	5'10	178	110	400	75	60	.188	.280
Frank, Charles "Charlie" 93–94StLN												
5/30/70	Mobile, Ala.	5/24/22	?	?	5'10	170	120	483	144	81	.298	.408
Frank, Frederick "Fred" 98CleN												
3/11/74	Louisa, Ky.	3/27/50	?	?	?	?	17	53	11	3	.208	.264
Franklin, ? 84WasU												
Unknown	Unknown	Unknown	?	?	?	?	1	3	0	0	.000	.000
Freeman, John Frank "Buck" 91WasA 98–99WasN 00BosN												
10/30/71	Catasauqua, Pa.	6/25/49	L	L	5'9	169	306	1131	356	185	.315	.514
French, William "Bill" 73MarNA												
Unknown	Baltimore, Md.	Unknown	?	?	?	?	6	18	4	3	.222	.222
***Friel, Patrick Henry "Pat"** 90SyrA 91PhiA												
6/11/60	Lewisburg, W.Va.	1/15/24	B	?	5'11	170	64	269	67	53	.249	.331
Frisbee, Charles Augustus "Charlie" "Bunt" 99BosN 00NYN												
2/2/74	Dows, Iowa	11/7/54	B	R	5'9	175	46	165	52	24	.315	.370
***Fulmer, Washington Fayette "Washington"** 75AtlNA												
6/15/40	Philadelphia, Pa.	12/8/07	?	?	?	?	1	4	2	1	.500	.500
Fultz, David Lewis "Dave" 98–99PhiN 99BalN												
5/29/75	Staunton, Va.	10/29/59	R	R	5'11	170	78	270	74	38	.274	.322
Galligan, John T. "John" 89LouA												
?/?/68	Easton, Pa.	7/17/06	?	?	5'10	160	31	120	20	6	.167	.200
Gardner, Frank Washington "Gid" 79TroN 80CleN 83–84BalA 84Chi–PitU 84BalU 85BalA 87IndN 88WasN 88PhiN 88WasN												
6/9/59	Attleboro, Mass.	8/1/14	?	?	?	165	199	765	178	113	.233	.339
Gaule, Michael John "Mike" 89LouA												
8/4/69	Baltimore, Md.	1/24/18	L	L	6'2	?	1	2	0	0	.000	.000
Gear, Dale Dudley "Dale" 96–97CleN												
2/2/72	Lone Elm, Kan.	9/23/51	R	R	5'11	165	11	39	10	8	.256	.359
Gedney, Alfred W. "Al" "Count" 72TroNA 72EckNA 73MutNA 74AthNA 75MutNA												
5/10/49	Brooklyn, N.Y.	3/26/22	?	?	5'9	140	202	836	208	139	.249	.317
Geier, Philip Louis "Phil" 96–97PhiN 00CinN												
11/3/75	Washington, D.C.	9/25/67	L	R	5'7	145	139	485	130	81	.268	.318
Genins, C. Frank "Frank" "Frenchy" 92CinN 92StLN 95PitN												
11/2/66	St. Louis, Mo.	9/30/22	?	R	?	?	123	413	93	60	.225	.266
George, William M. "Bill" 87–89NYN 89ColA												
1/27/65	Bellaire, Ohio	8/23/16	R	L	5'8	165	30	124	26	15	.210	.242
Gettig, Charles Henry "Charlie" 96–99NYN												
12/?/70	Baltimore, Md.	4/11/35	R	?	5'10	172	126	377	91	48	.241	.294
Gettinger, Lewis Thomas Leyton "Tom" b.Gittinger 89–90StLA 95LouN												
12/11/68	Frederick, Md.	7/26/43	L	L	5'10	180	125	503	131	61	.260	.372
Gettman, Jacob John "Jake" 97–99WasN												
10/25/76	Frank, Russia	10/4/56	B	L	5'11	185	197	772	215	108	.278	.361
Gilbert, John Robert "Jack" "Jackrabbit" 98WasN 98NYN												
9/4/75	Rhinecliff, N.Y.	7/7/41	?	?	?	?	3	9	2	0	.222	.222

Outfielders

BIRTH DATE	BIRTHPLACE	DEATH DATE	B	T	HGT	WGT	G	AB	H	R	BA	SA
Gilks, Robert James "Bob" 87–88CleA 89–90CleN 93BalN												
7/2/64	Cincinnati, Ohio	8/21/44	R	R	5'8	178	339	1385	320	163	.231	.270
Gillespie, James Wheatfield "Jim" 90BufP												
9/?/58	?, Canada	9/5/21	L	R	?	?	1	3	0	0	.000	.000
Gillespie, Peter Patrick "Pete" 80–82TroN 83–87NYN												
11/30/51	Carbondale, Pa.	5/5/10	L	R	6'1½	178	714	2927	809	450	.276	.354
Gilman, Pitkin Clark "Pit" 84CleN												
3/14/64	Laporte, Ohio	8/17/50	L	L	?	170	2	10	1	0	.100	.100
Glenn, Edward C. "Ed" "Mouse" 84VirA 86PitA 88KCA 88BosN												
9/19/60	Richmond, Va.	2/10/92	R	R	5'10	160	137	525	106	66	.202	.265
Glenn, John W. "John" 71–72OlyNA 72NatNA 73WasNA 74–75ChiNA 76–77ChiN												
?/?/49	Rochester, N.Y.	11/10/88	R	R	5'8	169	315	1371	366	235	.267	.311
Godar, John Michael "John" 92BalN												
10/25/64	Cincinnati, Ohio	6/23/49	R	R	5'9	160	5	14	3	2	.214	.214
Golden, Michael Henry "Mike" 75WesNA 75ChiNA 78MilN												
9/11/51	Shirley, Mass.	1/11/29	R	R	5'8	168	107	415	90	38	.217	.253
Goldsby, Walton Hugh "Walt" 84StLA 84WasA 84VirA 86WasN 88BalA												
12/31/61	?, Louisiana	1/11/14	L	?	?	?	73	267	65	23	.243	.262
Goodenough, William B. "Bill" 93StLN												
?/?/63	St. Louis, Mo.	5/24/05	?	?	6'1	170	10	31	5	4	.161	.194
Goodfellow, Michael J. "Mike" 87StLA 88CleA												
10/3/66	Port Jervis, N.Y.	2/12/20	R	R	6'	180	69	273	66	24	.242	.267
Gore, George F. "George" "Piano Legs" 79–86ChiN 87–89NYN 90NYP 91–92NYN 92StLN												
5/3/57	Saccarappa, Me.	9/16/33	L	R	5'11	195	1310	5357	1612	1327	.301	.411
Graham, Bernard W. "Bernie" 84Chi–PitU 84BalU												
?/?/60	Beloit, Wis.	10/30/86	L	?	?	?	42	172	46	23	.267	.331
Green, Edward "Danny" 98–00ChiN												
11/6/76	Burlington, N.J.	11/9/14	L	R	?	?	267	1052	315	179	.299	.413
Greer, Edward C. "Ed" 85–86BalA 86–87PhiA 87BroA												
?/?/65	Philadelphia, Pa.	2/4/90	?	R	?	?	232	851	183	117	.215	.268
Griffin, Michael Joseph "Mike" 87–89BalA 90PhiP 91–98BroN												
3/20/65	Utica, N.Y.	4/10/08	L	R	5'7	160	1511	5914	1753	1405	.296	.407
Griffin, Tobias Charles "Sandy" 84NYN 90RocA 91WasA 93StLN												
7/19/58	Fayetteville, N.Y.	6/5/26	R	R	5'10	160	166	630	173	116	.275	.376
Haigh, Edward E. "Ed" 92StLN												
2/7/67	Philadelphia, Pa.	2/13/53	?	?	?	?	1	4	1	0	.250	.250
Hall, Archilbald W. "Al" 79TroN 80CleN												
Unknown	Worcester, Mass.	2/10/85	?	?	?	?	70	314	80	31	.255	.296
Hall, Charles Walter "Charlie" "Doc" 87NYA												
8/24/63	Toulon, Ill.	6/24/21	?	?	?	?	3	12	1	1	.083	.083
Hall, George William "George" 71OlyNA 72–73BalNA 74BosNA 75AthNA 76PhiN 77LouN												
3/29/49	Stepney, England	6/11/23	L	?	5'7	142	363	1691	538	377	.318	.444
Halligan, William E. "Jocko" 90BufP 91–92CinN 92BalN												
12/8/68	Avon, N.Y.	2/13/45	L	?	5'9	166	190	737	206	123	.280	.402
Ham, Ralph A. "Ralph" 71RokNA												
3/?/49	Troy, N.Y.	2/13/05	?	?	5'8	158	25	113	28	25	.248	.283

Outfielders

BIRTH DATE	BIRTHPLACE	DEATH DATE	B	T	HGT	WGT	G	AB	H	R	BA	SA
Hamburg, Charles M. "Charlie" b. Hambrick 90LouA												
11/22/63	Louisville, Ky.	5/18/31	?	?	6'	175	133	485	132	93	.272	.344
Hamilton, William Robert "Billy" "Sliding Billy" 88–89KCA 90–95PhiN 96–00BosN												
2/16/66	Newark, N.J.	12/16/40	L	R	5'6	165	1489	5920	2058	1619	.348	.436
Hanlon, Edward Hugh "Ned" 80CleN 81–88DetN 89PitN 90PitP 91PitN 92BalN												
8/22/57	Montville, Conn.	4/14/37	L	R	5'9½	170	1267	5074	1317	930	.260	.340
Hannifan, Patrick James "Pat" 97BroN												
4/20/66	Nova Scotia, Canada	11/5/08	?	L	?	?	10	20	5	4	.250	.250
Harbidge, William Arthur "Bill" "Yaller Bill" 75HarNA 76–77HarN 78–79ChiN 80TroN 82TroN 83PhiN 84CinU												
3/29/55	Philadelphia, Pa.	3/17/24	L	L	?	162	378	1510	373	200	.247	.303
Harley, Richard Joseph "Dick" 97–98StLN 99CleN 00CinN												
9/25/72	Philadelphia, Pa.	4/3/52	L	R	5'10½	165	378	1467	382	189	.260	.309
Hartsel, Tully Frederick "Topsy" 98–99LouN 00ChiN												
6/26/74	Polk, Ohio	10/14/44	L	L	5'5	155	70	210	62	29	.295	.371
Hasney, Peter James "Pete" 90PhiA												
5/26/65	?, England	5/24/08	?	?	?	?	2	7	1	1	.143	.143
Hassamaer, William Louis "Bill" "Roaring Bill" 94–95WasN 95–96LouN												
7/26/64	St. Louis, Mo.	5/29/10	?	?	6'	180	256	1054	305	163	.289	.408
*Hatfield, John Van Buskirk "John" 71–75MutNA 76NYN												
7/20/47	?, New Jersey	2/20/09	?	?	5'10	165	206	1011	282	218	.279	.343
Hawes, William Hildreth "Bill" 79BosN 84CinU												
11/17/53	Nashua, N.H.	6/16/40	R	R	5'10	155	117	504	128	99	.254	.325
Hayes, Michael "Mike" 76NYN												
?/?/53	Cleveland, Ohio	Unknown	?	?	5'7½	170	5	21	3	1	.143	.333
Heard, Charles "Charlie" 90PitN												
1/30/72	Philadelphia, Pa.	2/20/45	R	R	6'2	190	12	43	8	2	.186	.233
Heidrick, R. Emmet "Emmet" "Snags" 98CleN 99–00StLN												
7/9/76	Queenstown, Pa.	1/20/16	L	R	6'	185	250	1006	170	319	.317	.406
Hemp, William H. "Ducky" 87LouA 90PitN 90SyrA												
12/27/67	St. Louis, Mo.	3/6/23	?	?	?	?	31	117	25	11	.214	.265
Hemphill, Charles Judson "Charlie" "Eagle Eye" 99StLN 99CleN												
4/20/76	Greenville, Mich.	6/22/53	L	L	5'9	160	66	239	65	27	.272	.364
Henry, George Washington "George" 93CinN												
8/10/63	Philadelphia, Pa.	12/30/34	R	R	5'9	180	21	83	23	11	.277	.313
Henry, John Michael "John" 84CleN 85BalA 86WasN 90NYN												
9/2/63	Springfield, Mass.	6/11/39	?	L	?	?	60	218	53	28	.243	.284
Hernon, Thomas H. "Tom" 97ChiN												
11/4/66	E. Bridgewater, Mass.	2/4/02	R	R	?	?	4	16	1	2	.063	.063
Heubel, George A. "George" 71AthNA 72OlyNA 76NYN												
?/?/49	Paterson, N.J.	1/22/96	?	?	5'11½	178	23	102	26	20	.255	.333
Higby, ? 72AtlNA												
Unknown	Unknown	Unknown	?	?	?	?	1	4	0	0	.000	.000
Higham, Richard "Dick" 71MutNA 72BalNA 73–74MutNA 75ChiNA 75MutNA 76HarN 78ProN 80TroN												
7/?/51	?, England	3/18/05	L	R	5'8½	171	372	1787	549	384	.307	.378
Hines, Henry Fred "Hunkey" 95BroN												
9/29/67	Elgin, Ill.	1/2/28	R	R	5'7	165	2	8	2	3	.250	.250

Outfielders

BIRTH DATE	BIRTHPLACE	DEATH DATE	B	T	HGT	WGT	G	AB	H	R	BA	SA
Hines, Paul A. "Paul" 72NatNA 73WasNA 74–75ChiNA 76–77ChiN 78–85ProN 86–87WasN 88–89IndN 90PitN 90BosN 91WasA												
3/1/52	Washington, D.C.	7/10/35	R	R	5'9½	173	1659	7063	2135	1218	.302	.408
Hodes, Charles "Charlie" 71ChiNA 72TroNA 74AtlNA												
?/?/48	New York, N.Y.	2/14/75	?	R	5'11½	175	62	272	63	57	.232	.298
Hogan, Martin F. "Marty" 94CinN 94–95StLN												
10/15/69	Wensbury, England	8/15/23	R	?	5'8	145	40	141	34	17	.241	.326
Hogan, Robert Edward "Eddie" 82StLA 84MilU 87NYA 88CleA												
4/?/60	St. Louis, Mo.	Unknown	R	?	5'7	153	122	429	89	89	.207	.294
Hogriever, George C. "George" 95CinN												
3/17/69	Cincinnati, Ohio	1/26/61	R	R	5'8	160	69	239	65	61	.272	.389
Holdsworth, James "Jim" 72CleNA 72EckNA 73MutNA 74PhiNA 75MutNA 76NYN 77HarN 82TroN 84IndN												
7/14/50	New York, N.Y.	3/22/18	R	R	?	?	318	1481	431	221	.291	.345
Holliday, James Wear "Bug" 89CinA 90–98CinN												
2/8/67	St. Louis, Mo.	2/15/10	R	R	5'11	151	928	3648	1134	728	.311	.448
Hollingshead, John Samuel "Holly" (aka Samuel John Holly) 72NatNA 73WasNA 75WasNA												
1/17/53	Washington, D.C.	10/6/26	?	?	?	?	58	263	70	45	.266	.312
Holmes, James William "Ducky" 95–97LouN 97NYN 98StLN 98–99BalN												
1/28/69	Des Moines, Iowa	8/6/32	L	R	5'6	170	442	1708	507	240	.297	.381
Hooper, Michael H. "Mike" 73MarNA												
2/7/50	Baltimore, Md.	12/1/17	?	?	5'6	165	3	14	3	3	.214	.286
Hoover, William J. "Buster" 84PhiU 84PhiN 86BalA 92CinN												
?/?/63	Philadelphia, Pa.	Unknown	R	R	6'1	178	127	525	151	114	.288	.390
Hornung, Michael Joseph "Joe" "Ubbo Ubbo" 79–80BufN 81–88BosN 89BalA 90NYN												
6/12/57	Carthage, N.Y.	10/30/31	R	R	5'8½	164	1123	4784	1230	788	.257	.350
Hotaling, Peter James "Pete" "Monkey" 79CinN 80CleN 81WorN 82BosN 83–84CleN 85BroA 87–88CleA												
12/16/56	Mohawk, N.Y.	7/3/28	L	R	5'8	166	840	3492	931	590	.267	.353
Houtz, Fred Fritz "Lefty" 99CinN												
9/4/75	Connersville, Ind.	2/15/59	L	L	5'10	170	5	17	4	1	.235	.353
Hoy, William Ellsworth "Dummy" 88–89WasN 90BufP 91StLA 92–93WasN 94–97CinN 98–99LouN												
5/23/62	Houcktown, Ohio	12/15/61	L	R	5'6	160	1590	6298	1806	1264	.287	.371
Huelsman, Frank Elmer "Frank" 97StLN												
6/5/74	St. Louis, Mo.	6/9/59	R	R	6'2	210	2	7	2	0	.286	.429
Hunt, Richard M. "Dick" 72EckNA												
?/?/47	New York, N.Y.	11/20/95	?	?	5'9	145	11	48	15	11	.313	.396
Hurley, William H. "Dick" "Will" 72OlyNA												
?/?/47	Honesdale, Pa.	Unknown	?	?	5'7	160	2	7	0	0	.000	.000
Isbell, William Frank "Frank" "Bald Eagle" 98ChiN												
8/21/75	Delevan, N.Y.	7/15/41	L	R	5'11	190	45	159	37	17	.233	.258
Johns, Thomas Pearce "Tommy" 73MarNA												
9/7/51	Baltimore, Md.	4/13/27	?	?	?	?	1	4	0	0	.000	.000
Johnson, John Ralph "Spud" "Ralph" 89–90ColA 91CleN												
?/?/60	?, Canada	Unknown	L	L	5'9	175	331	1324	400	246	.302	.392
Johnson, William F. "Bill" "Sleepy Bill" 84PhiU 87IndN 90–91BalA 92BalN												
9/?/62	?, New Jersey	7/17/42	L	L	?	140	169	636	168	121	.264	.351
Johnston, Richard Frederick "Dick" 84VirA 85–89BosN 90BosP 90NYP 91CinA												
4/6/63	Kingston, N.Y.	4/4/34	R	R	5'8	155	746	2992	751	453	.251	.366

Outfielders

BIRTH DATE	BIRTHPLACE	DEATH DATE	B	T	HGT	WGT	G	AB	H	R	BA	SA
Jones, L. 73MarNA 74BalNA												
Unknown	Unknown	Unknown	?	?	?	?	3	11	4	0	.364	.364
Jones, ? 84WasA												
Unknown	Johnstown, Pa.	Unknown	?	?	?	?	17	5	2	0	.294	.294
Jones, Charles Wesley "Charley" b. Benjamin Wesley Rippay 75WesNA 75HarNA 76–77CinN 77ChiN 77–78CinN												
79–80BosN 83–87CinA 87NYA 88KCA												
4/30/50	Alamance Co., N.C.	Unknown	R	R	5'11½	202	894	3738	1114	733	.298	.444
Jones, Fielder Allison "Fielder" 96–00BroN												
8/13/71	Shinglehouse, Pa.	3/13/34	L	R	5'11	180	623	2456	768	486	.313	.383
Jordan, Michael Henry "Mike" "Mitty" 90PitN												
2/7/63	Lawrence, Mass.	9/25/40	?	?	5'7½	155	37	125	12	8	.096	.104
Joyce, ? 86WasN												
Unknown	Unknown	Unknown	?	?	?	?	1	0	0	0	—	—
Kalbfus, Charles Henry "Charlie" "Skinny" 84WasU												
12/28/64	Washington, D.C.	11/18/41	R	R	5'11	145	1	5	1	1	.200	.200
*Kappel, Joseph "Joe" 84PhiN 90PhiA												
4/27/57	Philadelphia, Pa.	7/8/29	R	?	5'11	175	60	223	51	30	.229	.287
Keeler, William Henry "Willie" "Wee Willie" b. O'Kelleher 92–93NYN 93BroN 94–98BalN 99–00BroN												
3/3/72	Brooklyn, N.Y.	1/1/23	L	L	5'4½	145	962	4114	1567	1023	.381	.477
Kelley, Joseph James "Joe" 91BosN 92PitN 92–98BalN 99–00BroN												
12/9/71	Cambridge, Mass.	8/14/43	R	R	5'11	190	1113	4290	1449	999	.338	.492
Kelly, Michael Joseph "King" 78–79CinN 80–86ChiN 87–89BosN 90BosP 91CinA 91BosA 91–92BosN 93NYN												
12/31/57	Troy, N.Y.	11/8/94	R	R	5'10	170	1455	5894	1813	1357	.308	.438
Kelly, William J. "Bill" 71KekNA												
Unknown	New York, N.Y.	Unknown	?	?	?	?	18	67	15	16	.224	.269
Kelty, John James "John" "Chief" 90PitN												
6/?/66	Jersey City, N.J.	Unknown	?	?	5'10	175	59	207	49	24	.237	.319
Kennedy, Edward "Ed" 83–85NYA 86BroA												
4/1/56	Carbondale, Pa.	5/20/05	?	?	5'6	150	299	1105	225	142	.204	.259
Ketchum, Frederick L. "Fred" 99LouN												
7/27/75	Elmira, N.Y.	3/12/08	L	R	5'8	157	15	61	18	13	.295	.311
Kienzle, William H. "Bill" 82PhiA 84PhiU												
Unknown	Philadelphia, Pa.	Unknown	L	L	?	?	76	332	87	84	.262	.370
Kiley, John Frederick "John" 84WasA 91BosN												
7/1/59	Dedham, Mass.	12/18/40	L	L	5'7	147	15	58	12	9	.207	.310
King, Marshal Ney "Mart" 71ChiNA 72TroNA												
12/?/49	Troy, N.Y.	10/9/11	?	R	5'9½	176	23	112	21	23	.188	.250
King, Stephen F. "Steve" 71–72TroNA												
?/?/42	Troy, N.Y.	7/8/95	?	?	5'9	175	54	272	96	78	.353	.463
Kinsler, ? 93NYN												
Unknown	Staten Island, N.Y.	Unknown	?	?	?	?	1	3	0	1	.000	.000
Knight, Alonzo P. "Lon" 75AthNA 76PhiN 80WorN 81–82DetN 83–85PhiA 85ProN												
6/16/53	Philadelphia, Pa.	4/23/32	R	R	5'11½	165	545	2288	555	391	.243	.319
Knight, Joseph William "Joe" "Quiet Joe" 84PhiN 90CinN												
9/28/59	Port Stanley, Ont., Can.	10/16/38	L	L	5'11	185	133	505	156	69	.309	.422
Krehmeyer, Charles L. "Charlie" 84StLA 85LouA 85StLN												
7/5/63	St. Louis, Mo.	2/10/26	L	L	5'11	179	29	104	23	7	.221	.269

Outfielders

BIRTH DATE	BIRTHPLACE	DEATH DATE	B	T	HGT	WGT	G	AB	H	R	BA	SA
Ladd, Arthur Clifford "Hi" 98PitN 98BosN												
2/9/70	Willimantic, Conn.	5/7/48	L	R	6'4	180	2	5	1	1	.200	.200
Lafferty, Frank Bernard "Flip" 76PhiN 77LouN												
5/4/54	Scranton, Pa.	2/8/10	?	R	?	?	5	20	1	2	.050	.100
Lally, Daniel J. "Dan" "Bud" 91PitN 97StLN												
8/12/67	Jersey City, N.J.	4/14/36	R	R	5'11½	210	128	498	131	80	.263	.351
Lange, William Alexander "Bill" "Little Eva" 93–99ChiN												
6/6/71	San Francisco, Cal.	7/23/50	R	R	6'1½	190	811	3195	1055	689	.330	.459
Lauer, John Charles "Chuck" 84PitA 89PitN 90ChiN												
?/?/65	Pittsburgh, Pa.	Unknown	?	R	?	?	19	68	10	8	.147	.162
Lavin, John "Johnny" 84StLA												
Unknown	Troy, N.Y.	Unknown	?	?	5'11	175	16	52	11	9	.212	.250
Leahy, Thomas Joseph "Tom" 97PitN 97–98WasN												
6/2/69	New Haven, Conn.	6/11/51	?	R	?	168	58	199	54	32	.271	.347
Lee, Leonidas Pyrrhus "Leonidas" b.Funkhouser 77StLN												
12/13/60	St. Louis, Mo.	6/11/12	?	?	?	?	4	18	5	0	.278	.333
Leighton, John Atkinson "John" 90SyrA												
10/4/61	Peabody, Mass.	10/31/56	?	?	5'11	170	7	27	8	6	.296	.370
Leonard, ? 92StLN												
Unknown	Unknown	Unknown	?	?	?	?	1	0	0	0	—	—
Leonard, Andrew Jackson "Andy" 71OlyNA 72–75BosNA 76–78BosN 80CinN												
6/1/46	County Cavan, Ireland	8/21/03	R	R	5'7	168	501	2391	716	481	.299	.363
Letcher, Frederick Thomas "Tom" "Uncle Tom" 91MilA												
1/?/68	Bryan, Ohio	Unknown	L	?	?	?	6	21	4	3	.190	.238
Lewis, Frederick Miller "Fred" 81BosN 83PhiA 83–84StLA 84StLU 85StLN 86CinA												
10/13/58	Buffalo, N.Y.	6/5/45	R	R	5'10½	194	317	1318	390	224	.296	.378
Lillie, James J. "Jim" "Grasshopper" b. Lilly 83–85BufN 86KCN												
7/27/61	New Haven, Conn.	11/9/90	?	?	?	?	390	1518	332	179	.219	.272
Little, Harry A. "Harry" 77StLN 77LouN												
Unknown	St. Louis, Mo.	Unknown	?	R	?	?	4	15	2	2	.133	.133
Locke, Marshall Pinkney Wilder "Marshall" 84IndA												
3/12/57	Ashland, Ohio	3/6/40	?	?	?	?	7	29	7	5	.241	.310
Lockwood, Milo Hathaway "Milo" 84WasU												
4/7/58	Solon, Ohio	10/9/97	?	?	5'10	180	20	67	14	9	.209	.224
Loftus, Thomas Joseph "Tom" 77StLN 83StLA												
11/15/56	St. Louis, Mo.	4/16/10	R	?	?	168	9	33	6	3	.182	.182
Long, ? 88LouA												
Unknown	Unknown	Unknown	?	?	?	?	1	2	0	0	.000	.000
Long, Daniel W. "Dan" 90BalA												
8/27/67	Boston, Mass.	4/30/29	?	?	?	?	21	77	12	19	.156	.156
Long, James M. "Jim" 91LouA 93BalN												
11/15/62	Louisville, Ky.	12/12/32	?	?	?	?	61	251	54	36	.215	.279
Loughlin, William H. "Bill" 83BalA												
Unknown	Baltimore, Md.	Unknown	?	?	?	?	1	5	2	0	.400	.400
Lovett, Leonard Walker "Len" 73ResNA 75CenNA												
7/17/52	Lancaster Co., Pa.	11/18/22	R	R	?	?	7	26	7	3	.269	.308

Outfielders

BIRTH DATE	BIRTHPLACE	DEATH DATE	B	T	HGT	WGT	G	AB	H	R	BA	SA
Lowry, John D. "John" 75WasNA												
Unknown	Baltimore, Md.	Unknown	?	?	?	?	6	21	3	2	.136	.136
Lush, William Lucas "Billy" 95–97WasN												
11/10/73	Bridgeport, Conn.	8/28/51	B	R	5'8	165	105	382	93	77	.243	.356
Lynch, Henry W. "Henry" 93ChiN												
4/8/66	Worcester, Mass.	11/23/25	?	?	5'7	143	4	14	3	0	.214	.357
Lynch, Thomas James "Tom" 84WilU 84–85PhiN												
4/3/60	Bennington, Vt.	3/28/56	L	R	5'10½	170	42	159	41	20	.258	.358
Lyons, Harry P. "Harry" 87PhiN 87–88StLA 89NYN 90RocA 92–93NYN												
3/25/66	Chester, Pa.	6/30/12	R	R	5'10½	157	407	1713	401	236	.234	.289
Lytle, Edward Benson "Dad" "Pop" 90ChiN 90PitN												
3/10/62	Racine, Wis.	12/21/50	R	R	5'11	160	16	59	8	3	.136	.153
Magner, John T. "John" 79CinN												
?/?/55	St. Louis, Mo.	Unknown	?	?	?	?	1	4	0	0	.000	.000
Maloney, John "John" 76NYN 77HarN												
Unknown	Unknown	Unknown	?	?	?	?	3	11	3	1	.273	.455
Mann, Fred J. "Fred" 82WorN 82PhiA 83–84ColA 85–86PitA 87CleA 87PhiA												
4/1/58	Sutton, Vt.	4/6/16	L	?	5'10½	178	577	2277	597	388	.262	.383
Manning, James H. "Jim" 84–85BosN 85–87DetN 89KCA												
1/31/62	Fall River, Mass.	10/22/29	B	R	5'7	157	364	1384	298	188	.215	.297
Manning, John E. "Jack" 73BosN 74BalNA 74HarNA 75BosNA 76BosN 77CinN 78BosN 80CinN 81BufN 83–85PhiN 86BalA												
12/20/53	Braintree, Mass.	8/15/29	R	R	5'8½	158	834	3510	924	563	.263	.346
***Mansell, John** "John" 82PhiA												
?/?/61	Auburn, N.Y.	2/20/25	L	?	5'10	168	31	126	30	17	.238	.278
***Mansell, Michael R.** "Mike" 79SyrN 80CinN 82–84PitA 84PhiA 84VirA												
1/15/58	Auburn, N.Y.	12/4/02	L	?	5'11	175	371	1471	352	237	.239	.344
***Mansell, Thomas E.** "Tom" "Brick" 79TroN 79SyrN 83DetN 83StLA 84CinA 84ColA												
1/1/55	Auburn, N.Y.	10/6/34	L	R	5'8	160	191	767	199	132	.259	.318
Marr, Charles W. "Lefty" 86CinA 89ColA 90–91CinN 91CinA												
9/19/62	Cincinnati, Ohio	1/11/12	L	L	?	?	363	1445	417	244	.289	.379
***Maskrey, Harry H.** "Harry" 82LouA												
12/21/61	Mercer, Pa.	8/17/30	?	?	?	?	1	4	0	0	.000	.000
***Maskrey, Samuel Leech** "Leech" 82–86LouA 86CinA												
2/11/54	Mercer, Pa.	4/1/22	R	R	5'8	150	418	1601	360	190	.225	.294
Mason, Charles E. "Charlie" 75CenNA 75WasNA 83PhiA												
6/25/53	New Orleans, La.	10/21/36	R	R	?	175	21	82	15	7	.183	.183
Matthews, Robert "Bob" 91PhiA												
Unknown	Camden, N.J.	Unknown	?	?	?	?	1	3	1	1	.333	.333
Mattimore, Michael Joseph "Mike" 87NYN 88–89PhiA 89KCA 90BroA												
?/?/59	Renovo, Pa.	4/28/31	L	L	5'8½	160	124	451	92	57	.204	.273
McAleer, James Robert "Jimmy" "Loafer" 89CleN 90CleP 91–98CleN												
7/10/64	Youngstown, Ohio	4/29/31	R	R	6'	175	1013	3967	1003	619	.253	.310
McAllister, Lewis William "Sport" 96–99CleN												
7/23/74	Austin, Miss.	7/17/62	B	R	5'11	180	181	639	148	62	.232	.293
McBride, Algernon Griggs "Algie" 96ChiN 98–00CinN												
5/23/69	Washington, D.C.	1/10/56	L	L	5'9	162	305	1202	361	212	.300	.399

Outfielders

BIRTH DATE	BIRTHPLACE	DEATH DATE	B	T	HGT	WGT	G	AB	H	R	BA	SA
McBride, John F. "John" 90PhiA												
Unknown	Unknown	Unknown	?	?	?	?	1	2	0	0	.000	.000
McCaffrey, Harry Charles "Harry" 82LouA 82–83StLA 85CinA												
11/25/58	St. Louis, Mo.	4/19/28	R	R	5'10½	185	45	180	44	24	.244	.356
McCarthy, John Arthur "Jack" 93–94CinN 98–99PitN 00ChiN												
3/26/69	Gilbertville, Mass.	9/11/31	L	L	5'9	155	488	1962	574	308	.293	.379
McCarthy, Thomas Francis Michael "Tommy" 84PhiU 85BosN 86–87PhiN 88–91StLA 92–95BosN 96BroN												
7/24/63	Boston, Mass.	8/5/22	R	R	5'7	170	1273	5120	1493	1066	.292	.376
McCarton, Francis "Frank" 72ManNA												
10/6/54	Middletown, Conn.	6/17/07	?	?	?	?	19	85	28	17	.329	.400
McClure, Harold Murray "Hal" "Mac" 82BosN												
8/8/59	Lewisburg, Pa.	3/1/19	R	R	6'	165	2	6	2	1	.333	.333
McCreery, Thomas Livingston "Tom" 95–97LouN 97–98NYN 98–00PitN												
10/19/74	Beaver, Pa.	7/3/41	B	R	5'11	180	533	1962	598	380	.305	.426
McDonald, Daniel "Jack" 72AtlNA												
?/?/47	Brooklyn, N.Y.	11/23/80	?	?	5'11	154	15	62	16	9	.258	.339
*McFarlan, Alexander Shepherd "Alex" 92LouN												
11/11/69	St. Louis, Mo.	3/2/39	?	?	?	?	14	42	7	2	.167	.167
McFarland, Christopher "Chris" 84BaLU												
8/17/61	Fall River, Mass.	5/24/18	?	?	5'9	170	3	14	3	2	.214	.286
McFarland, Hermas Walter "Herm" 96LouN 98CinN												
3/11/70	Des Moines, Iowa	9/21/35	L	R	5'6	150	49	174	39	21	.224	.316
McGeachy, John Charles "Jack" 86DetN 86StLN 87–89IndN 90BroP 91PhiA 91BosA												
5/23/64	Clinton, Mass.	4/5/30	R	R	5'8	165	608	2464	604	345	.245	.314
McGee, Patrick "Pat" 74AtlNA 75MutNA 75AtlNA												
Unknown	Philadelphia, Pa.	6/21/89	?	?	?	?	59	225	38	11	.169	.209
McGinn, Frank J. "Frank" 90PitN												
?/?/69	Cincinnati, Ohio	11/19/97	?	?	?	?	1	4	0	0	.000	.000
McGuckin, Joseph W. "Joe" 90BalA												
3/13/62	Paterson, N.J.	12/31/03	?	?	5'8½	160	11	37	4	2	.108	.108
McGunnigle, William Henry "Bill" "Gunner" 79–80BufN 80WorN 82CleN												
1/1/55	Boston, Mass.	3/9/99	R	R	5'9	155	56	202	35	24	.173	.183
McHale, Robert Emmet "Bob" "Rabbit" 98WasN												
2/7/70	Sacramento, Ca.	6/9/52	?	?	?	?	11	33	6	5	.182	.242
McKee, Frank "Frank" 84WasU												
Unknown	Philadelphia, Pa.	Unknown	?	?	?	?	4	17	3	2	.176	.176
McKelvey, John Wellington "John" 75NHNA												
8/27/47	Rochester, N.Y.	5/31/44	R	R	5'7½	175	43	188	43	26	.230	.255
McKelvy, Russell Errett "Russ" 78IndN 82PitA												
9/8/54	Swissvale, Pa.	10/19/15	R	R	?	?	64	257	57	3	.222	.284
McMillan, George A. "Reddy" 90NYN												
Unknown	Evansville, Ind.	Unknown	?	?	5'8	175	10	35	5	4	.143	.143
McMullin, John F. "John" "Lefty" 71TroNA 72MutNA 73–74AthNA 75PhiNA												
?/?/48	Philadelphia, Pa.	4/11/81	R	L	5'9	160	244	1082	308	234	.285	.348
McRemer, ? 84WasU												
Unknown	Unknown	Unknown	?	?	?	?	1	3	0	0	.000	.000

Outfielders

BIRTH DATE	BIRTHPLACE	DEATH DATE	B	T	HGT	WGT	G	AB	H	R	BA	SA
McTamany, James Edward "Jim" 85–87BroA 88KCA 89–91ColA 91PhiA												
7/1/63	Philadelphia, Pa.	4/6/16	R	R	5'8	190	813	3102	794	693	.256	.355
Mertes, Samuel Blair "Sam" "Sandow" 96PhiN 98–00ChiN												
8/6/72	San Francisco, Ca.	3/11/45	R	R	5'10	185	364	1319	383	220	.290	.412
Miller, Charles Bradley "Dusty" 89BalA 90StLA 95–99CinN 99StLN												
9/10/68	Oil City, Pa.	9/3/45	L	R	5'11½	170	655	2557	769	444	.301	.420
Miller, L. Edward "Ed" 84TolA												
Unknown	Tecumseh, Mich.	Unknown	?	?	?	?	8	24	6	2	.250	.250
Mincher, Edward John "Ed" 71KekNA												
Unknown	Baltimore, Md.	Unknown	?	?	?	?	9	36	8	4	.222	.222
***Moffett, Samuel R. "Sam"** 84CleN 87–88IndN												
3/14/57	Wheeling, W.Va.	5/5/07	R	R	6'	175	88	332	56	38	.169	.220
Moore, Henry S. "Harry" "Henry" 84WasU												
Unknown	Unknown	Unknown	?	?	?	?	111	461	155	77	.336	.414
Morgan, Henry William "Bill" 75RedsNA 78MilN 82PitA 84VirA 84BalU												
10/?/57	Washington, D.C.	Unknown	?	?	?	?	39	151	32	13	.212	.238
Morgan, William "Bill" 83PitA 84WasA												
Unknown	Unknown	Unknown	?	?	?	?	77	276	46	20	.167	.192
Moriarty, Eugene John "Gene" 84BosN 84IndA 85DetN 92StLN												
1/5/65	Holyoke, Mass.	Unknown	L	L	5'8	130	72	269	41	30	.152	.227
Morrison, Jonathan W. "Jon" 84IndA 87NYA												
?/?/59	London, Ont., Canada	Unknown	?	?	5'9½	167	53	216	52	33	.241	.356
Morton, Charles Hazen "Charlie" 82PitA 82StLA 84TolA 85DetN												
10/12/54	Kingsville, Ohio	12/9/21	R	R	?	150	88	325	63	34	.194	.265
Mullen, ? 72CleNA												
Unknown	Unknown	Unknown	?	?	?	?	1	4	0	1	.000	.000
Mullin, Henry J. "Henry" 84WasA 84BosU												
4/?/62	St. John, N.B., Can.	11/8/27	R	?	5'9	160	36	128	17	14	.133	.172
Munce, John Lewis "John" "Big John" 84WilU												
11/18/57	Philadelphia, Pa.	3/15/17	?	?	5'8½	160	7	21	4	1	.190	.190
Murphy, Clarence "Clarence" 86LouA												
Unknown	Unknown	Unknown	?	?	?	?	1	3	0	0	.000	.000
Murphy, Lawrence Patrick "Larry" 91WasA												
Unknown	Unknown	Unknown	L	?	?	?	101	400	106	73	.265	.325
Murphy, William H. "Willie" "Gentle Willie" 84CleN 84WasA												
3/23/64	Springfield, Mass.	Unknown	L	?	5'11	198	47	189	48	21	.254	.317
Nance, William G. "Doc" "Kid" b. Willie G. Cooper 97–98LouN												
8/2/76	Fort Worth, Tex.	5/28/58	R	R	5'7	165	57	196	53	38	.270	.413
Newman, Charles "Charlie" "Decker" 92NYN 92ChiN												
11/5/68	Juda, Wis.	11/23/47	R	R	?	?	19	73	14	5	.192	.192
Nichol, Samuel Anderson "Sam" 88PitN 90ColA												
4/20/69	County Antrim, Ireland	4/19/37	R	R	5'10	178	22	78	10	10	.128	.128
Nicol, George Edward "George" 90StLA 91ChiN 94PitN 94LouN												
10/17/70	Barry, Ill.	8/10/24	?	L	5'7	155	41	141	51	24	.362	.489

Outfielders

BIRTH DATE	BIRTHPLACE	DEATH DATE	B	T	HGT	WGT	G	AB	H	R	BA	SA
Nicol, Hugh "Hugh" "Wee Hugh" 81–82ChiN 83–86StLA 87–89CinA 90CinN												
1/1/58	Campsie, Scotland	6/27/21	R	R	5'4	145	888	3465	812	631	.234	.282
Niland, Thomas James "Tom" "Honest Tom" 96StLN												
4/14/70	Brookfield, Mass.	4/30/50	R	R	5'11	160	18	68	12	3	.176	.206
Noftsker, George Washington "George" 84AltU												
8/24/59	Shippensburg, Pa.	5/8/31	R	R	5'8	135	7	25	1	0	.040	.040
Norton, Frank Prescott "Frank" 71OlyNA												
Unknown	Unknown	Unknown	?	?	?	?	1	1	0	0	.000	.000
Nusz, Emory Moberly "Emory" 84WasU												
4/2/66	Frederick, Md.	8/3/93	?	?	?	?	1	4	0	1	.000	.000
Oberbeck, Henry A. "Henry" 83PitA 83StLA 84BalU 84KCU												
5/17/58	St. Louis, Mo.	8/26/21	?	?	?	?	66	238	42	27	.176	.210
O'Brien, John E. "John" 84BalU												
10/22/51	Columbus, Ohio	12/31/14	?	R	5'11 1/2	187	18	77	19	7	.247	.286
O'Brien, John Joseph "Jack" 99WasN												
2/5/73	Watervliet, N.Y.	6/10/33	L	R	6'1	165	127	468	132	68	.282	.365
O'Brien, Thomas J. "Tom" 97–98BalN 98PitN 99NYN 00PitN												
2/20/73	Verona, Pa.	2/4/01	?	?	?	?	427	1569	436	248	.278	.365
O'Brien, William D. "Darby" 87NYA 88–89BroA 90–92BroN												
9/1/63	Peoria, Ill.	6/15/93	R	R	6'1	186	709	2856	805	577	.282	.387
O'Connell, Patrick H. "Pat" 86BalA 90BroA												
6/10/61	Bangor, Me.	1/24/43	R	R	5'10	175	53	206	39	27	.189	.243
O'Leary, Daniel "Dan" "Hustling Dan" 79ProN 80BosN 81DetN 82WorN 84CinU												
10/22/56	Detroit, Mich.	6/24/22	L	?	5'10	165	45	181	44	18	.243	.298
Olin, Franklin Walter "Frank" 84WasA 84WasU 85DetN												
1/9/60	Woodford, Vt.	5/21/51	L	?	?	?	49	177	56	29	.316	.379
O'Neal, ? "Fancy" 74HarNA												
Unknown	Unknown	Unknown	?	?	?	?	1	3	0	0	.000	.000
O'Neill, Frederick James "Fred" "Tip" 07NYA												
?/?/65	London, Ont., Can.	3/7/92	?	?	5'7	142	6	26	8	4	.308	.423
O'Neill, James Edward "Tip" 83NYN 84–89StLA 90ChiP 91StLA 92CinP												
5/25/58	Woodstock, Ont., Can.	12/31/15	R	R	6'1 1/2	167	1052	4248	1385	879	.326	.458
Oran, Thomas "Tom" 75RedsNA												
?/?/45	Unknown	9/22/86	?	?	?	?	19	81	15	7	.185	.247
*#O'Rourke, James Henry "Jim" "Orator Jim" 72ManNA 73–75BosNA 76–78BosN 79ProN 80BosN 81–84BufN 85–89NYN 90NYP 91–92NYN 93WasN												
9/1/50	Bridgeport, Conn.	1/8/19	R	R	5'8	185	1998	8499	2643	1729	.311	.424
*O'Rourke, John "John" 79–80BosN 83NYA												
8/23/49	Bridgeport, Conn.	6/23/11	L	L	6'	190	230	945	279	148	.295	.442
Osborne, Frederick W. "Fred" 90PitN												
5/?/65	Hampton, Iowa	Unknown	?	L	?	?	41	168	40	24	.238	.339
Pabor, Charles Henry "Charlie" 71–72CleNA 73AtlNA 74PhiNA 75AtlNA 75NHNA												
9/24/46	New York, N.Y.	4/22/13	L	L	5'8	155	170	715	204	101	.285	.340
Pabst, Edward D.A. "Ed" 90PhiA 90StLA												
?/?/68	St. Louis, Mo.	6/19/40	?	R	5'11	170	12	39	12	8	.308	.410
Parks, William Robert "Bill" 75WasNA 75PhiNA 76BosN												
6/4/49	Easton, Pa.	10/10/11	R	R	5'8	150	29	121	21	13	.174	.174

Outfielders

BIRTH DATE	BIRTHPLACE	DEATH DATE	B	T	HGT	WGT	G	AB	H	R	BA	SA
*Parrott, Thomas William "Tom" "Tacky Tom" 93ChiN 93–95CinN 96StLN												
4/10/68	Portland, Ore.	1/1/32	R	R	5'10½	170	281	999	301	157	.301	.438
Parsons, John S. "John" 84CinA												
Unknown	Napoleon, Ohio	Unknown	?	?	5'6	138	1	3	0	0	.000	.000
Patterson, Daniel Thomas "Dan" 71MutNA 72EckNA 74MutNA 75AtlNA												
?/?/46	New York, N.Y.	Unknown	?	L	5'9	143	57	248	50	41	.202	.214
Pattison, George "George" 84PhiU												
Unknown	Unknown	Unknown	?	?	?	?	2	7	1	0	.143	.143
Paynter, George Washington "George" b.Paner 94StLN												
7/6/71	Cincinnati, Ohio	10/1/50	R	R	5'9	125	1	4	0	0	.000	.000
*Peitz, Joseph "Joe" 94StLN												
11/8/69	St. Louis, Mo.	12/4/19	?	?	?	?	7	26	11	10	.423	.731
Pelouze, Louis H. "Louis" 86StLN												
Unknown	Unknown	Unknown	R	R	5'8	170	1	3	0	0	.000	.000
Peltz, John "John" 84IndA 88BalA 90BroA 90SyrA 90TolA												
4/23/61	New Orleans, La.	2/27/06	R	R	?	?	230	871	195	106	.224	.326
Pettit, Robert Henry "Bob" 87–88ChiN 91MilA												
7/19/61	Williamstown, Mass.	11/1/10	L	R	5'9	160	96	387	93	62	.240	.351
Phelps, Cornelius Carmen "Nealy" 71KekNA 73–75MutNA 76NYN 76PhiN												
11/19/40	New York, N.Y.	2/12/85	?	?	?	?	12	46	5	6	.109	.130
Pickering, Oliver Daniel "Ollie" 96–97LouN 97CleN												
4/9/70	Olney, Ill.	1/20/52	L	R	5'11	170	154	593	176	95	.297	.366
Pickett, David T. "Dave" 98BosN												
5/26/74	Brookline, Mass.	4/22/50	?	?	5'7½	170	14	43	12	3	.279	.302
*Pike, Jacob Emanuel "Jay" 77HarN												
Unknown	Brooklyn, N.Y.	Unknown	L	L	?	?	1	4	1	0	.250	.250
*Pike Lipman Emanuel "Lip" 71TroNA 72–73BalNA 74HarNA 75StLNA 76StLN 77–78CinN 78ProN 81WorN 87NYA												
5/25/45	New York, N.Y.	10/10/93	L	L	5'8	158	425	1983	637	433	.321	.463
Plock, Walter S. "Walter" 91PhiN												
7/2/69	Philadelphia, Pa.	4/28/00	?	?	6'3	180	2	5	2	2	.400	.400
Polhemus, Mark "Mark" "Humpty Dumpty" 87IndN												
10/4/62	Brooklyn, N.Y.	11/12/23	?	?	5'6½	185	20	75	18	6	.240	.253
Poorman, Thomas Iverson "Tom" 80BufN 80ChiN 84TolA 85–86BosN 87–88PhiA												
10/14/57	Lock Haven, Pa.	2/18/05	L	R	5'7	135	496	2043	498	396	.244	.335
Porter, Matthew Sheldon "Matt" "Matthew" 84KCU												
Unknown	Kansas City, Mo.	Unknown	?	?	?	?	3	12	1	1	.083	.167
Powell, Charles Abner "Abner" 84WasU 86BalA 86CinA												
12/15/60	Shenandoah, Pa.	8/7/53	L	R	5'7	160	78	304	78	53	.257	.345
Preston, Walter B. "Walt" 95LouN												
?/?/70	Richmond, Va.	Unknown	R	R	6'	175	50	197	55	42	.279	.365
Proeser, George "George" "Yatz" 88CleA 90SyrA												
5/30/64	Cincinnati, Ohio	10/13/41	L	L	5'10	190	20	76	20	16	.263	.368
Purcell, William Aloysius "Blondie" 79SyrN 79–80CinN 81CleN 81–82BufN 83–84PhiN 85PhiA 85BosN 86–88BalA 88–90PhiA												
3/16/54	Paterson, N.J.	2/20/12	R	R	5'9½	159	1097	4563	1217	767	.267	.340

Outfielders

BIRTH DATE	BIRTHPLACE	DEATH DATE	B	T	HGT	WGT	G	AB	H	R	BA	SA
Quinn, Joe "Joe" 77ChiN												
?/?/49	Chicago, Ill.	1/2/09	?	?	5'8½	148	4	14	1	1	.071	.071
Quinn, Frank J. "Frank" 99ChiN												
?/?/76	Grand Rapids, Mich.	2/17/20	?	?	5'8	?	12	34	6	6	.176	.235
Quinn, Patrick "Paddy" 75AtlNA												
Unknown	Unknown	Unknown	?	?	5'8	162	2	8	1	2	.125	.125
*Radbourn, Charles Gardner "Hoss" "Old Hoss" "Charley" 80BufN 81–85ProN 86–89BosN 90BosP 91CinN												
12/11/54	Rochester, N.Y.	2/5/97	R	R	5'9	168	653	2487	585	308	.235	.281
Radford, Paul Revere "Paul" 83BosN 84–85ProN 86KCN 87NYA 88BroA 89CleN 90CleP 91BosA 92–94WasN												
10/14/61	Roxbury, Mass.	2/21/45	R	R	5'6	148	1361	4979	1206	945	.242	.308
Rainey, John Paul "John" 87NYN 90BufP												
7/26/64	Birmingham, Mich.	11/11/12	L	R	5'10	164	59	224	56	35	.250	.308
*Reach, Alfred James "Al" 71–75AthNA												
5/25/40	London, England	1/14/28	L	L	5'6	155	80	393	97	89	.247	.321
*Reccius, John "John" 82–83LouA												
10/29/59	Louisville, Ky.	9/1/30	?	?	5'6½	?	92	329	72	56	.219	.289
Reed, Hugh "Hugh" 74BalNA												
?/?/37	Chicago, Ill.	11/3/83	?	?	?	?	1	4	0	0	.000	.000
Reeder, James Edward "Icicle" 84CinA 84WasU												
5/?/59	Cincinnati, Ohio	Unknown	R	?	6'	?	6	26	4	0	.154	.154
Regan, Joseph Charles "Joe" 98NYN												
7/12/72	Seymour, Conn.	11/18/48	R	R	6'1	?	2	5	1	1	.200	.200
Reising, Charles "Charlie" "Pop" 84IndA												
8/28/61	Lanesville, Ind.	7/26/15	?	?	?	?	2	8	0	0	.000	.000
Remsen, John Jay "Jack" 72–73AtlNA 74MutNA 75HarNA 76HarN 77StLN 78–79ChiN 81CleN 84PhiN 84BroA												
4/?/50	Brooklyn, N.Y.	Unknown	R	R	5'11	189	578	2352	574	366	.244	.317
Ressler, Lawrence P. "Larry" 75WasNA												
8/10/48	?, France	6/12/18	?	?	?	?	27	108	21	17	.194	.204
Reville, Henry "Henry" 74BalNA												
Unknown	Baltimore, Md.	Unknown	?	?	?	?	1	4	0	0	.000	.000
Rexter, William H. "William" 75AtlNA												
Unknown	Brooklyn, N.Y.	Unknown	?	?	?	?	1	4	0	0	.000	.000
Rickert, Joseph Francis "Joe" "Diamond Joe" 98PitN												
12/12/76	London, Ohio	10/15/43	R	R	5'10½	165	2	6	1	0	.167	.167
Riley, William James "Billy" "Pigtail Billy" 75WesNA 79CleN												
?/?/55	Cincinnati, Ohio	11/9/87	R	R	5'10	160	52	198	29	18	.146	.162
Robinson, Alfred Valentine "Val" 72OlyNA												
Unknown	Unknown	Unknown	?	?	?	?	7	30	6	6	.200	.200
Rocap, Adam "Adam" 75AthNA												
?/?/54	Philadelphia, Pa.	3/29/92	?	?	5'9	170	16	69	12	13	.174	.188
Rogers, Fraley W. "Fraley" 72–73 BosNA												
?/?/50	Brooklyn, N.Y.	5/10/81	?	?	5'8	184	46	210	58	40	.276	.338
Rooks, George Brinton McLellan "George" b. Ruckser 91BosN												
10/21/63	Chicago, Ill.	3/11/35	R	R	5'11	170	5	16	2	1	.125	.125
Roseman, James John "Chief" 82TroN 83–86NYA 87PhiA 87NYA 87BroA 90StLA 90LouA												
7/4/56	New York, N.Y.	7/4/38	R	R	5'7	167	681	2761	726	443	.263	.360

Outfielders

BIRTH DATE	BIRTHPLACE	DEATH DATE	B	T	HGT	WGT	G	AB	H	R	BA	SA
Routcliffe, Philip John "Phil" "Chicken" 90PitN												
10/24/70	Oswego, N.Y.	10/4/18	R	R	6'	175	1	4	1	1	.250	.250
*Rowe, David Elwood "Dave" 77ChiN 82CleN 83BalA 84StLU 85StLN 86KCN 88KCA												
10/9/54	Harrisburg, Pa.	12/9/30	R	R	5'9	180	347	1458	383	223	.263	.376
Rudderham, John Edmund "John" 84BosU												
8/30/63	Quincy, Mass.	4/3/42	R	R	5'8	170	1	4	1	0	.250	.250
Ryan, James Edward "Jimmy" "Pony" 85–89ChiN 90ChiP 91–00ChiN												
2/11/63	Clinton, Mass.	10/26/23	R	L	5'9	162	1678	7243	2238	1508	.309	.447
Ryan, John Joseph "Johnny" 73PhiNA 74BalNA 75NHNA 76LouN 77CinN												
10/?/53	Philadelphia, Pa.	3/22/02	?	?	5'7½	175	156	603	125	81	.207	.252
Ryan, John M. "John" 84WasU 84WilU												
Unknown	Washington, D.C.	Unknown	?	?	?	?	9	34	5	2	.147	.206
Ryder, Thomas "Tom" 84StLU												
Unknown	Unknown	Unknown	L	?	?	?	8	28	7	4	.250	.286
Scanlan, Patrick J. "Patrick" 84BosU												
3/25/61	Nova Scotia, Canada	7/17/13	?	?	?	?	6	24	7	2	.292	.333
Scharf, Edward T. "Nick" 82–83BalA												
7/?/58	Baltimore, Md.	5/12/37	?	R	?	?	13	52	10	5	.192	.327
Scheffler, Theodore J. "Ted" 88DetN 90RocA												
4/5/64	New York, N.Y.	2/24/49	R	R	5'10	160	146	539	128	128	.237	.308
Scherer, Harry "Harry" 89LouA												
Unknown	Baltimore, Md.	Unknown	?	?	?	?	1	3	1	0	.333	.333
Scott, ? 84BalU												
Unknown	Unknown	Unknown	?	?	?	?	13	53	12	10	.226	.340
Seery, John Emmett "Emmett" 84BalU 84KCU 85–86StLN 87–89IndN 90BroP 91CinA 92LouN												
2/13/61	Princeville, Ill.	8/7/30	L	R	?	?	916	3547	893	695	.252	.356
Selbach, Albert Karl "Kip" 94–98WasN 99CinN 00NYN												
3/24/72	Columbus, Ohio	2/17/56	R	R	5'7	190	890	3420	1066	687	.312	.450
Sensenderfer, John Phillips Jenkins "Count" 71–74AthNA												
12/28/47	Philadelphia, Pa.	5/3/03	?	?	5'9	170	51	234	70	55	.299	.342
Seward, George E. "George" 75StLNA 76NYN 82StLA												
Unknown	St. Louis, Mo.	Unknown	?	?	5'7	145	64	243	55	35	.226	.247
Seybold, Ralph Orlando "Socks" 99CinN												
11/23/70	Washingtonville, Ohio	12/22/21	R	R	5'11	175	22	85	19	13	.224	.306
Shaffer, ? 75AtlNA												
Unknown	Unknown	Unknown	?	?	?	?	1	4	0	0	.000	.000
Shaffer, Frank "Frank" 84AltU 84KCU 84BalU												
Unknown	Unknown	Unknown	?	?	?	?	66	251	50	30	.199	.235
*Shaffer, George "Orator" 74HarNA 74MutNA 75PhiNA 77LouN 78IndN 79ChiN 80–82CleN 83BufN 84StLU 85StLN 85–86PhiA 90PhiA												
?/?/52	Philadelphia, Pa.	Unknown	L	R	5'9	165	871	3552	1000	601	.282	.367
Shandley, James H. "Jim" 76NYN												
Unknown	New York, N.Y.	11/4/04	?	?	?	?	2	8	1	0	.125	.125
Shearon, John M. "John" 91CleN 96CleN												
?/?/70	Pittsburgh, Pa.	2/1/23	?	?	?	?	46	188	41	16	.218	.245
Sheckard, Samuel James Tilden "Jimmy" 97–98BroN 99BalN 00BroN												
11/23/78	Upper Chanceford, Pa.	1/15/47	L	R	5'9	175	260	1266	367	241	.290	.381

Outfielders

BIRTH DATE	BIRTHPLACE	DEATH DATE	B	T	HGT	WGT	G	AB	H	R	BA	SA
Sheehan, Timothy James "Biff" 95–96StLN												
2/13/69	Hartford, Conn.	10/21/23	?	R	5'9	165	58	199	60	24	.302	.392
Sheppard, John "John" 73MarNA												
Unknown	Baltimore, Md.	Unknown	?	?	?	?	3	11	0	1	.000	.000
Sheridan, ? 75AtlNA												
Unknown	Unknown	Unknown	?	?	?	?	1	4	0	0	.000	.000
Shoch, George Quintus "George" 86–89WasN 91MilA 92BalN 93–97BroN												
1/6/59	Philadelphia, Pa.	9/30/37	R	R	5'6	158	706	2536	671	414	.265	.334
Silch, Edward "Ed" "Baldy" 88BroA												
2/22/65	St. Louis, Mo.	1/15/95	?	R	6'2	180	14	48	13	5	.271	.354
Simmons, Joseph S. "Joe" 71ChiNA 72CleNA 75WasNA												
6/13/45	New York, N.Y.	Unknown	?	?	5'9	166	58	272	60	45	.221	.289
Simon, Henry Joseph "Hank" 87CleA 90BroA 90SyrA												
8/25/62	Hawkinsville, N.Y.	1/1/25	R	R	?	?	130	539	144	100	.267	.371
Skinner, Alexander "Alexander" 84BalU 84Chi–PitU												
8/14/56	Chicago, Ill.	3/5/01	?	?	?	?	2	6	2	1	.333	.333
Sladen, Arthur "Art" 84BosU												
10/28/60	Lowell, Mass.	2/28/14	?	?	?	?	2	7	0	0	.000	.000
Slagle, James Franklin "Jimmy" "Rabbit" 99WasN 00PhiN												
7/11/73	Worthville, Pa.	5/10/56	L	R	5'7	144	288	1173	328	207	.280	.335
Slattery, Michael J. "Mike" 84BosU 88–89NYN 90NYP 91CinN 91WasA												
11/26/66	Boston, Mass.	10/16/04	L	L	6'2	210	374	1481	372	229	.251	.325
Smith, Albert Edgar "Edgar" 83BosN												
10/15/60	North Haven, Conn.	Unknown	?	R	6'	200	30	115	25	10	.213	.313
Smith, Edgar Eugene "Edgar" 83ProN 83PhiN 84WasA 85ProN 90CleN												
6/12/62	Providence, R.I.	11/3/92	R	R	5'10	160	26	98	18	10	.184	.235
Smith, Elmer Ellsworth "Elmer" 86–89CinA 92–97PitN 98–00CinN 00NYN												
3/23/68	Pittsburgh, Pa.	11/3/45	L	L	5'11	178	1214	4623	1444	907	.312	.437
Smith, L. 82BalA												
Unknown	Unknown	Unknown	?	?	?	?	1	3	0	0	.000	.000
Smith, Oliver H. "Ollie" 94LouN												
?/?/68	Mount Vernon, Ohio	Unknown	L	L	?	?	38	134	40	26	.299	.425
Smith, William E. "Bill" 84CleN												
Unknown	Toronto, Canada	8/9/86?	?	?	5'11	178	1	3	0	0	.000	.000
Smith, William J. "Bill" 73MarNA												
Unknown	Baltimore, Md.	Unknown	?	?	?	?	6	23	42	2	.174	.174
Sneed, Jonathan "John" 84IndA 90TolA 90–91ColA												
Unknown	Columbus, Ohio	1/4/99	?	?	5'8	160	263	982	253	197	.268	.347
Snow, Charles M. "Charlie" 74AtlNA												
8/3/49	Lowell, Mass.	Unknown	?	?	?	?	1	1	1	0	1.000	1.000
Snyder, Charles "Charles" 90PhiA												
Unknown	Camden, N.J.	3/10/01	R	R	?	?	9	33	9	5	.273	.303
Snyder, Emanuel Sebastian "Redleg" b. Schneider 76CinN 84WilU												
12/12/54	Camden, N.J.	11/11/33	R	R	5'10	175	72	257	41	14	.160	.179
Snyder, Joshua M. "Josh" 72EckNA												
3/?/44	Brooklyn, N.Y.	4/21/81	?	?	?	?	9	37	6	2	.162	.216

Outfielders

BIRTH DATE	BIRTHPLACE	DEATH DATE	B	T	HGT	WGT	G	AB	H	R	BA	SA
Sockalexis, Louis M. "Chief" 97–99CleN												
10/24/71	Old Town, Me.	12/24/13	L	R	5'11	185	94	367	115	54	.313	.414
Sommer, Joseph John "Joe" 80CinN 82–83CinA 84–89BalA 90CleN 90BalA												
11/20/58	Covington, Ky.	1/16/38	R	R	?	?	920	3675	911	617	.248	.309
*Sowders, Leonard "Len" 86BalA												
6/29/61	Louisville, Ky.	11/19/88	?	?	5'11½	172	23	76	20	10	.263	.329
Sprague, Charles Wellington "Charlie" 87ChiN 89CleN 90TolA												
10/10/64	Cleveland, Ohio	12/31/12	L	L	5'11	150	60	219	50	27	.228	.320
*Stafford, James Joseph "General" "Jamsey" 90BufP 93–97NYN 97–98LouN 98–99BosN 99WasN												
7/9/68	Webster, Mass.	9/18/23	R	R	5'8	165	568	2128	583	341	.274	.350
Stafford, Robert M. "Bob" 90PhiA												
6/26/72	Oak Ridge, N.C.	8/20/16	?	?	?	?	1	2	0	0	.000	.000
Stahl, Charles Sylvester "Chick" 97–00BosN												
1/10/73	Avilla, Ind.	3/28/07	L	L	5'10	160	523	2065	675	394	.327	.503
Stanley, Joseph "Joe" 84BalU												
Unknown	?, New Jersey	Unknown	?	?	?	?	6	21	5	3	.238	.286
Staples, Joseph F. "Joe" 85BufN												
Unknown	Buffalo, N.Y.	Unknown	?	?	?	?	7	22	1	0	.045	.045
Stenzel, Jacob Charles "Jake" b. Stelzle 90ChiN 92–96PitN 97–98BalN 98–99StLN 99CinN												
6/24/67	Cincinnati, Ohio	1/6/19	R	R	5'10	168	766	3024	1042	662	.339	.480
Stephenson, Reuben Crandol "Dummy" 92PhiN												
9/22/69	Petersburg, N.J.	12/1/24	R	R	5'11½	180	8	37	10	4	.270	.351
Stevens, Robert "Bob" 75WasNA												
Unknown	Unknown	Unknown	?	?	?	?	1	4	1	0	.250	.250
Stires, Garrett "Gat" 71RokNA												
10/13/49	Hunterdon Co., N.J.	6/13/33	L	R	5'8	180	25	110	30	23	.273	.473
Stockwell, Leonard Clark "Len" 79CleN 84LouA 90CleN												
8/25/59	Cordova, Ill.	1/28/05	R	R	5'11	165	6	22	3	2	.136	.182
Stoddard, ? 75AtlNA												
Unknown	Unknown	Unknown	?	?	?	?	2	9	1	1	.111	.222
Stovey, Harry Duffield "Harry" b. Stowe 80–82WorN 83–89PhiA 90BosP 91–92BosN 92–93BalN 93BroN												
12/20/56	Philadelphia, Pa.	9/20/37	R	R	5'11½	175	1486	6138	1770	1492	.288	.461
Strauss, Joseph "Joe" "Dutch" "The Socker" b. Strasser 84KCU 85–86LouA 86BroA												
11/16/58	Cincinnati, Ohio	6/24/06	R	R	?	?	101	399	86	46	.216	.281
Studley, Seymour L. "Seem" "Warhorse" 72NatNA												
Unknown	Washington, D.C.	?/?/74	?	?	?	?	5	21	2	3	.095	.095
Sullivan, ? 75NHNA												
Unknown	Bristol, R.I.	Unknown	?	?	?	?	2	8	3	3	.375	.375
Sullivan, Dennis J. "Denny" 79ProN 80BosN												
6/26/58	Boston, Mass.	12/31/25	?	R	5'9	170	6	23	6	6	.261	.348
Sullivan, Martin C. "Marty" 87–88ChiN 89IndN 90–91BosN 91CleN												
10/20/62	Lowell, Mass.	1/6/94	R	R	?	?	398	1618	441	280	.273	.395
Sullivan, Michael Joseph "Mike" 88PhiA												
6/10/60	Webster, Mass.	6/16/29	R	R	5'8½	165	28	112	31	30	.277	.455
Sullivan, Timothy Paul "Ted" 84KCU												
?/?/51	County Clare, Ireland	7/5/29	?	?	?	?	3	9	3	0	.333	.333

Outfielders

BIRTH DATE	BIRTHPLACE	DEATH DATE	B	T	HGT	WGT	G	AB	H	R	BA	SA
Sullivan, William "Bill" 78ChiN												
7/4/53	Holyoke, Mass.	11/13/84	?	?	?	?	2	6	1	1	.167	.167
Sunday, Arthur "Art" b. Wacher 90BroP												
1/21/62	Springfield, Ohio	Unknown	L	L	5'9	193	24	83	22	26	.265	.349
Sunday, William Ashley "Billy" "Parson" 83–87ChiN 88–90PitN 90PhiN												
11/19/62	Ames, Iowa	11/6/35	L	R	5'10	160	499	2007	498	339	.248	.317
Swartwood, Cyrus Edward "Ed" 81BufN 82–84PitA 85–87BroA 90TolA 91PitN												
1/12/59	Rockford, Ill.	5/15/24	L	R	?	198	724	2876	861	607	.299	.400
Sweeney, Daniel J. "Dan" 95LouN												
1/28/68	Philadelphia, Pa.	7/13/13	?	?	5'5	160	22	90	24	18	.267	.356
Sweigert, Hampton "Ham" 90PhiA												
Unknown	Unknown	Unknown	?	?	?	?	1	1	0	0	.000	.000
Sylvester, Louis J. "Lou" 84CinU 86LouA 86CinA 87StLA												
2/14/55	Springfield, Ill.	Unknown	R	R	5'3	165	173	654	159	138	.243	.347
Taylor, Edward S. "Live Oak" 77HarN 84PitA												
Unknown	Unknown	Unknown	?	?	?	?	43	160	35	22	.219	.256
Taylor, James B. "Sandy" 79TroN												
Unknown	Unknown	Unknown	?	?	5'10½	175	24	97	21	10	.216	.258
Tebeau, Charles Alston "Pussy" 95CleN												
2/22/70	Worcester, Mass.	3/25/50	R	R	5'10	175	2	6	3	3	.500	.500
*Tebeau, George E. "George" "White Wings" 87–89CinA 90TolA 94WasN 94–95CleN												
12/26/61	St. Louis, Mo.	2/4/23	R	R	5'9	175	627	2315	622	440	.269	.376
Tenney, Fred Clay "Fred" 84WasU 84BosU 84WilU												
7/9/59	Marlborough, N.H.	6/15/19	?	?	?	?	37	139	30	18	.216	.252
Terry, ? 75WasNA												
Unknown	Attleboro, Pa.	Unknown	?	?	?	?	6	22	4	0	.182	.273
Thake, Albert "Al" 72AtlNA												
9/21/49	Wymondham, England	9/1/72	?	?	6'	?	18	78	23	14	.295	.372
*Thomas, Roy Allen "Roy" 99–00PhiN												
3/24/74	Norristown, Pa.	11/20/59	L	L	5'11	150	290	1078	346	269	.321	.349
Thompson, Frank "Frank" 75AtlNA												
Unknown	Unknown	Unknown	?	?	?	?	1	5	2	1	.400	.400
Thompson, John P. "Tug" 82CinA 84IndA												
Unknown	London, Ont., Can.	Unknown	L	R	5'8	160	25	102	21	10	.206	.235
Thompson, Samuel Luther "Sam" "Big Sam" 85–88DetN 89–98PhiN												
3/5/60	Danville, Ind.	11/7/22	L	L	6'2	207	1399	5953	1972	1252	.331	.506
Thornton, Walter Miller "Walter" 95–98ChiN												
2/18/75	Lewiston, Me.	7/14/60	L	L	6'1	180	154	519	162	83	.312	.382
Tiernan, Michael Joseph "Mike" "Silent Mike" 87–99NYN												
1/21/67	Trenton, N.J.	11/9/18	L	L	5'11	165	1476	5906	1834	1313	.311	.463
Tierney, William J. "Bill" 82CinA 84BalU												
5/14/58	Boston, Mass.	9/21/98	?	?	?	?	2	8	1	1	.125	.125
Tilley, John C. "John" 82CleN 84TolA 84StPU												
Unknown	New York, N.Y.	Unknown	R	?	5'7	154	41	138	19	9	.138	.161
Tipper, James "Jim" 72ManNA 74HarNA 75NHNA												
6/18/49	Middletown, Conn.	4/21/95	?	?	5'5½	148	110	468	116	69	.248	.286

Outfielders

BIRTH DATE	BIRTHPLACE	DEATH DATE	B	T	HGT	WGT	G	AB	H	R	BA	SA
*Traffley, John M. "John" 89LouA												
?/?/62	Chicago, Ill.	5/15/00	?	?	5'9	180	1	2	1	0	.500	.500
*Treacey, Frederick S. "Fred" 71ChiNA 72AthNA 73PhiNA 74ChiNA 75CenNA 75PhiNA 76NYN												
?/?/47	Brooklyn, N.Y.	Unknown	?	?	5'9½	145	269	1232	299	239	.243	.303
Treadway, George T. "George" 93BalN 94–95BroN 96LouN												
11/11/66	Greenup County, Ky.	Unknown	L	?	6'	185	326	1283	364	256	.284	.428
Truax, Frederick W. "Fred" 90PitN												
?/?/68	Unknown	12/18/99	?	?	?	?	1	3	1	0	.333	.333
Trumbull, Edward J. "Ed" b. Trembly 84WasA												
11/3/60	Chicopee, Mass.	1/14/37	?	?	?	?	25	86	10	5	.116	.140
Turner, George A. "Tuck" 93–96PhiN 96–98StLN												
2/13/73	W.New Brighton, N.Y.	7/16/45	B	L	5'6½	165	377	1496	478	294	.320	.429
Twitchell, Lawrence Grant "Larry" 86–88DetN 89CleN 90CleP 90BufP 91ColA 92WasN 93–94LouN												
2/18/64	Cleveland, Ohio	8/23/30	R	R	6'	185	639	2571	676	362	.263	.356
Ulrich, George T. "George" 92WasN 93CinN 96NYN												
6/5/69	Philadelphia, Pa.	Unknown	?	?	?	?	21	72	15	5	.208	.236
Van Dyke, William Jennings "Bill" 90TolA 92StLN 93BosN												
12/15/63	Paris, Ill.	5/5/33	R	R	5'8	170	136	530	134	78	.253	.334
Van Haltren, George Edward Martin "George" "Rip" 87–89ChiN 90BroP 91BalA 92BalN 92–93PitN 93–00NYN												
3/30/66	St. Louis, Mo.	9/29/45	L	L	5'11	170	1741	7110	2255	1501	.317	.425
Visner, Joseph Paul "Joe" b. Vezina 85BalA 89BroA 90PitP 91WasA 91StLA												
9/27/59	Minneapolis, Minn.	6/17/45	L	R	5'11	180	235	924	240	183	.260	.408
*Wagner, John Peter "Honus" "The Flying Dutchman" 97–99LouN 00PitN												
2/24/74	Chartiers, Pa.	12/6/55	R	R	5'11	200	494	1923	649	322	.337	.487
Waitt, Charles C. "Charlie" 75StLNA 77ChiN 82BalA 83PhiN												
10/14/53	Hallowell, Me.	10/21/12	?	?	5'11	165	113	407	67	35	.165	.199
Walker, Oscar "Oscar" 75AtlNA 79–80BufN 82StLA 84BroA 85BalA												
3/18/54	Brooklyn, N.Y.	5/20/89	L	L	5'10	166	282	1128	287	155	.254	.365
*Walker, Welday Wilberforce "Welday" 84TolA												
7/27/60	Steubenville, Ohio	11/23/37	?	?	?	?	5	18	4	1	.222	.278
Ward, Frank Gray "Piggy" 83PhiN 89PhiN 91PitN 92–93BalN 93CinN 94WasN												
4/16/67	Chambersburg, Pa.	10/24/12	B	R	5'9½	196	221	780	223	172	.286	.360
Ward, John E. "John" 84WasU												
Unknown	Washington, D.C.	Unknown	?	?	?	?	1	4	1	0	.250	.250
Weaver, William B. "Farmer" 88–91LouA 92–94LouN 94PitN												
3/23/65	Parkersburg, W.Va.	1/23/43	L	?	?	?	751	3073	853	421	.278	.348
Weber, Joseph Edward "Joe" 84DetN												
2/15/62	Hamilton, Ont., Can.	12/15/21	?	?	?	?	2	8	0	0	.000	.000
Weihe, John Garibaldi "Podgie" 83CinA 84IndA												
11/13/62	Cincinnati, Ohio	4/15/14	R	R	5'11	175	64	260	66	30	.254	.365
Welch, Curtis Benton "Curt" 84TolA 85–87StLA 88–90PhiA 90–91BalA 92BalN 92CinN 93LouN												
2/11/62	E. Liverpool, Ohio	8/29/96	R	R	5'10	175	1107	4385	1152	915	.263	.353
West, Milton Douglas "Buck" 84CinA 90CleN												
8/29/60	Spring Mill, Ohio	1/13/29	L	R	5'10	200	70	282	69	40	.245	.369
Wheeler, Harry Eugene "Harry" 78ProN 79–80CinN 80CleN 82CinA 83ColA 84StLA 84KCU 84Chi–PitU 84BalU												
3/3/58	Versailles, Ind.	10/9/00	R	R	5'11	165	257	1122	256	152	.228	.297

Between 1892 and 1899, Ed Delahanty led the majors in every offensive department except walks at least once. Delahanty and Harry Stovey are the only two nineteenth-century stars to win both a home run and a stolen base crown.

John Ryan, an outfielder with two Union Association teams in 1884. Ryan is often confused with a UA pitcher with the same name, and both have taken turns being wrongly believed to have really been named Daniel Sheehan.

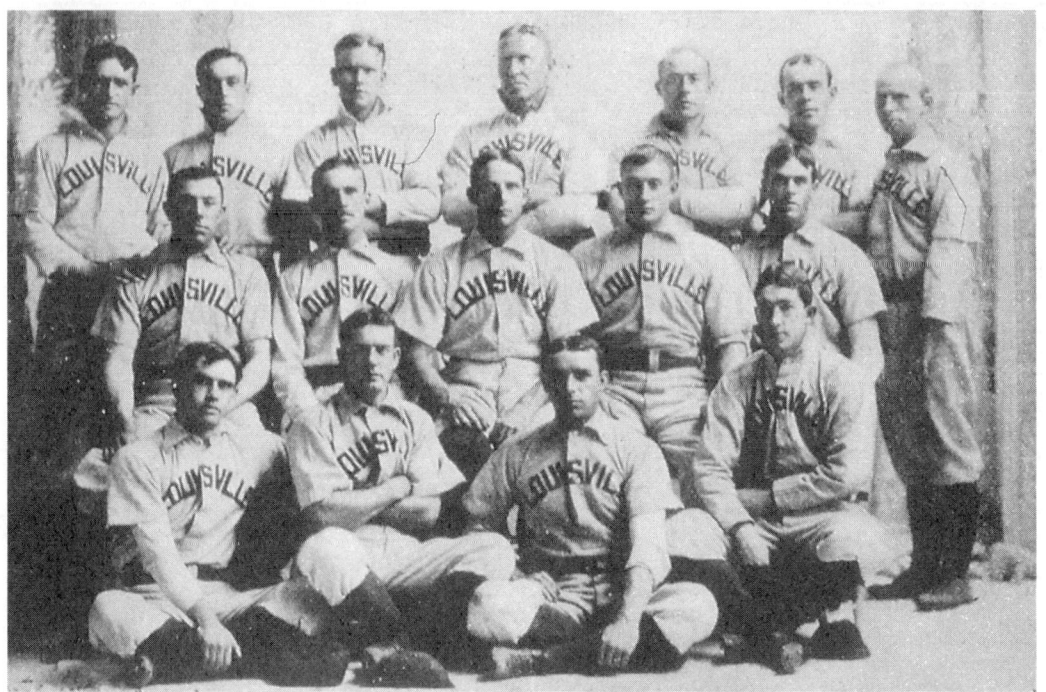

A "rookie card" of Honus Wagner. Why is he in the Outfielders subregister? Because in the last century the game's most renowned shortstop played more games in the outfield than anywhere else. Not until 1901, his fifth season, did Wagner make his first appearance at shortstop. (Wagner shown in the middle row, second from the right.)

Outfielders

BIRTH DATE	BIRTHPLACE	DEATH DATE	B	T	HGT	WGT	G	AB	H	R	BA	SA
White, Elmer "Elmer" 71CleNA												
5/23/50	Caton, N.Y.	3/17/72	?	?	?	?	15	70	18	13	.257	.386
Whitely, Gurdon W. "Gurdon" 84CleN 85BosN												
10/5/59	Ashaway, R.I.	11/24/24	?	?	5'11	190	41	169	30	18	.178	.231
*Whitney, Frank Thomas "Frank" "Jumbo" 76BosN												
2/18/56	Brockton, Mass.	10/30/43	R	R	5'7½	152	34	139	33	27	.237	.302
Williams, Washington J. "Wash" 84VirA 85ChiN												
Unknown	Philadelphia, Pa.	8/9/92	?	?	5'11	180	3	12	3	0	.250	.250
Willigrod, Julius "Julius" 82DetN 82CleN												
Unknown	?, California	11/27/06	L	?	?	?	10	39	6	5	.154	.231
Wills, ? 84WasA 84KCU												
Unknown	Unknown	Unknown	?	?	?	?	9	36	5	3	.139	.222
Wilmot, Walter Robert "Walt" 88–89WasN 90–95ChiN 97–98NYN												
10/18/63	Plover, Wis.	2/1/29	B	R	?	?	960	3981	1100	725	.276	.404
Wilson, George Archer "Tug" "Hickie" 84BroA												
?/?/60	Brooklyn, N.Y.	11/28/14	?	?	5'8	175	24	82	19	13	.232	.280
Winkelman, George Edward "George" 83LouA 86WasN												
6/14/61	Philadelphia, Pa.	5/19/60	L	L	?	?	5	18	1	2	.056	.056
Wolf, William Van Winkle "Jimmy" "Chicken" 82–91LouA 92StLN												
5/12/62	Louisville, Ky.	5/16/03	R	R	5'9	190	1196	4959	1439	779	.290	.388
Wood, George A. "George" "Dandy" 80WorN 81–85DetN 86–89PhiN 89BalA 90PhiP 91PhiA 92BalN 92CinN												
11/9/58	Boston, Mass.	4/4/24	L	R	5'10½	175	1280	5371	1467	965	.273	.403
Woodruff, Peter Frank "Pete" 99NYN												
6/?/73	New York, N.Y.	Unknown	R	R	?	?	20	61	15	11	.246	.393
Worth, Herbert "Herb" 72AtlNA												
5/2/47	Brooklyn, N.Y.	4/27/14	?	?	?	?	1	6	1	1	.200	.400
Woulfe, James Joseph "Jimmy" 84CinA 84PitA												
11/25/59	New Orleans, La.	12/20/24	?	R	5'11	?	23	87	11	10	.126	.161
Wright, Joseph S. "Joe" 95–96LouN 96PitN												
?/?/73	Pittsburgh, Pa.	Unknown	L	L	5'8	175	77	287	81	35	.282	.369
*Wright, William Henry "Harry" 71–75BosNA 76–77BosN												
1/10/35	Sheffield, England	10/3/95	R	R	5'9½	157	180	816	222	183	.272	.338
Wright, William Smith "Rasty" 90SyrA 90CleN												
1/31/63	Birmingham, Mich.	10/14/22	L	?	6'1	185	101	393	111	89	.282	.341
Wylie, James Renwick "Ren" 82PitA												
12/14/61	Elizabeth, Pa.	8/17/51	R	R	5'11	155	1	3	0	0	.000	.000
Wyman, Frank H. "Frank" 84KCU 84Chi–PitU												
5/10/62	Haverhill, Mass.	2/4/16	?	?	?	?	32	132	30	17	.227	.252
Yeatman, William Suter "Bill" 72NatNA												
3/?/39	Alexandria, Va.	4/20/01	?	?	?	?	1	4	0	0	.000	.000
York, Thomas Jefferson "Tom" 71TroNA 72–73BalNA 74PhiNA 75HarNA 76–77HarN 78–82ProN 83CleN 84–85BalN												
7/13/51	Brooklyn, N.Y.	2/17/36	L	?	5'9	165	963	4002	1095	742	.274	.383

Catchers

BIRTH DATE	BIRTHPLACE	DEATH DATE	B	T	HGT	WGT	G	AB	H	R	BA	SA
Adams, James J. "Jim" 90StLA												
?/?/68	E. St. Louis, Ill.	Unknown	?	R	?	?	1	4	1	0	.250	.250
Ahearn, Charles "Charlie" 80TroN												
Unknown	Troy, N.Y.	Unknown	?	?	?	?	1	4	1	1	.250	.250
Alexander, William Henry "Nin" 84KanU 84StLA												
11/24/58	Pana, Ill.	12/22/33	R	R	5'4½	163	20	69	9	2	.130	.130
Allen, Hezekiah "Ki" 84PhiN												
2/25/63	Westport, Conn.	9/21/16	?	?	5'11	160	1	3	2	0	.667	.667
Allen, Jesse Hall "Pete" 93CleN												
5/1/68	Columbiana, Ohio	4/16/46	R	R	5'8½	185	1	4	0	0	.000	.000
***Allison, Douglas L. "Doug" 71OlyNA 72TroNA 72EckNA 73ResNA 73–74MutNA 75HarNA 76–77HarN 78–79ProN 83BalA**												
7/?/45	Philadelphia, Pa.	12/19/16	R	R	5'10½	160	318	1407	381	236	.271	.321
Arundel, John Thomas "Tug" 82PhiA 84TolA 87IndN 88WasN												
6/30/62	Romulus, N.Y.	9/5/12	?	?	?	?	76	260	45	21	.173	.196
Baker, George F. "George" 83BalA 84StLU 85StLN 86KCN												
?/?/59	St. Louis, Mo.	Unknown	?	?	?	?	126	474	74	45	.156	.169
Baldwin, Clarence Geoghan "Kid" 84KCU 84Chi–PitU 85–89CinA 90CinN 90PhiA												
11/1/64	Newport, Ky.	7/10/97	R	R	5'6	147	441	1677	371	186	.221	.299
Bancker, John "Stud" 75NHNA												
Unknown	Philadelphia, Pa	Unknown	?	?	?	?	19	72	11	3	.153	.153
Banning, James M. "Jim" 88WasN												
?/?/66	New York, N.Y.	Unknown	L	R	5'6	150	1	0	0	0	—	—
Barlow, Thomas H. "Tom" 72–73AtlNA 74HarNA 75NHNA 75AtlNA												
Unknown	Unknown	Unknown	?	?	?	?	126	607	174	120	.287	.310
Barnie, William Harrison "Billy" "Bald Billy" 74HarNA 75WesNA 75MutNA 83BalA 86BalA												
1/26/53	New York, N.Y.	7/15/00	?	?	5'7	157	83	321	55	32	.171	.199
Barrett, Martin F. "Marty" 84BosN 84IndA												
11/?/60	Port Henry, N.Y.	1/29/10	R	R	5'9	170	8	19	1	1	.053	.105
Barrett, William "Bill" 71KekNA 72OlyNA 73BalNA												
Unknown	Baltimore, Md.	Unknown	?	?	?	?	3	13	2	1	.154	.231
Beatle, David "Dave" 84DetN												
?/?/61	New York, N.Y.	Unknown	?	?	6'2	180	1	3	0	0	.000	.000
Begley, Eugene T. "Gene" 86NYN												
6/7/61	Brooklyn, N.Y.	Unknown	?	?	?	?	5	16	1	2	.125	.125
Bell, Frank Gustav "Frank" 85BroA												
?/?/63	Cincinnati, Ohio	4/14/91	?	?	6'	?	10	29	5	5	.172	.241
Bellman, John Hutchins "Jack" "Happy Jack" 89StLA												
3/4/64	Taylorsville, Ky.	12/8/31	?	?	?	?	1	2	1	1	.500	.500
Bennett, Charles Wesley "Charlie" 78MilN 80WorN 81–88DetN 89–93BosN												
11/21/54	New Castle, Pa.	2/24/27	R	R	5'11	180	1062	3821	978	549	.256	.387
***Bergen, Martin "Marty" 96–99BosN**												
10/25/71	N. Brookfield, Mass	1/19/00	?	R	5'10	170	344	1278	339	180	.265	.347
Bergh, John Baptist "John" 76PhiN 80BosN												
10/8/57	Boston, Mass.	4/16/83	?	?	?	?	12	44	8	2	.182	.250

Catchers

BIRTH DATE	BIRTHPLACE	DEATH DATE	B	T	HGT	WGT	G	AB	H	R	BA	SA
#Berry, Charles Joseph "Charlie" 84AltU 84KCU 84Chi–PitU												
9/6/60	Elizabeth, N.J.	1/22/40	R	R	5'11	175	43	170	38	21	.224	.300
Bestick, ? 72EckNA												
Unknown	New York, N.Y.	Unknown	?	?	?	?	4	14	4	1	.286	.286
Bignell, George "George" 84MilU												
7/18/58	Taunton, Mass.	1/16/25	?	?	5'9	160	4	9	2	4	.222	.222
Bird, Frank Zepherin "Frank" "Dodo" 92StLN												
3/10/69	Spencer, Mass.	5/20/58	R	R	5'10	195	17	50	10	9	.200	.360
Bligh, Edwin Forrest "Ned" 86BalA 88CinA 89–90ColA 90LouA												
6/30/64	Brooklyn, N.Y.	4/18/92	R	R	5'11	172	66	209	34	17	.163	.201
Blogg, Wesley Collins "Wes" 83PitA												
?/?/55	Norfolk, Va.	3/10/97	?	?	?	?	9	34	5	0	.147	.147
Booth, Amos Smith "Amos" "The Little Darling" 76–77CinN 80CinN 82BalA 82LouA												
9/4/52	Cincinnati, Ohio	7/1/21	R	R	5'9	159	110	438	98	47	.224	.240
Bowerman, Frank Eugene "Frank" 95–98BalN 98–99PitN 00NYN												
12/5/68	Romeo, Mich.	11/30/48	R	R	6'2	190	306	1098	291	112	.265	.338
Bowes, Frank M. "Frank" 90BroA												
?/?/65	Bath, N.Y.	1/21/95	?	R	5'9	160	61	232	51	28	.220	.259
Bowman, William G. "Bill" 91ChiN												
?/?/69	Chicago, Ill.	4/6/18	?	?	5'11	180	15	45	4	2	.089	.111
Boyd, Frank Jay "Frank" 93CleN												
4/2/68	W. Middletown, Pa.	12/16/37	R	R	?	?	2	5	1	3	.200	.400
*Boyle, Edward J. "Eddie" 96LouN 96PitN												
5/8/74	Cincinnati, Ohio	2/9/41	R	R	6'3	200	5	14	0	0	.000	.000
*Boyle, John Anthony "Jack" 86CinA 87–89StLA 90ChiP 91StLA 92NYN 93–98PhiN												
3/22/66	Cincinnati, Ohio	1/7/13	R	R	6'4	190	1084	4217	1066	666	.253	.327
Bransfield, William Edward "Kitty" 98BosN												
1/7/75	Worcester, Mass.	5/1/47	R	R	5'11	207	5	9	2	2	.222	.444
Brennan, James Augustus "Jim" b. John Gottlieb Dorn 84StLU 85StLN 88KCA 89PhiA 90CleP												
?/?/62	St. Louis, Mo.	10/18/04	?	?	?	?	183	705	155	87	.220	.264
Briggs, Grant "Grant" 90SyrA 91LouA 92StLN 95LouN												
3/16/65	Pittsburgh, Pa.	5/31/28	?	?	5'11	170	110	378	62	46	.164	.209
Briody, Charles F. "Fatty" "Alderman" 80TroN 82–84CleN 84CinU 85StLN 86KCN 87DetN 88KCA												
8/13/58	Lansingburgh, N.Y.	6/22/03	?	R	5'8¹/₂	190	323	1186	271	134	.228	.292
Broughton, Cecil Calvert "Cal" 83CleN 83BalA 84MilU 85StLA 85NYA 88DetN												
12/28/60	Magnolia, Wis.	3/15/39	R	R	?	?	40	143	27	10	.189	.231
Brown, Lewis J. "Lew" "Blower" 76–77BosN 78–79ProN 79ChiN 81DetN 81ProN 83BosN 83LouA 84BosU												
2/1/58	Leominster, Mass.	1/16/89	R	R	5'10¹/₂	185	378	1531	379	205	.248	.362
Buckley, Richard D. "Dick" 88–89IndN 90–91NYN 92–94StLN 94–95PhiN												
9/21/58	Troy, N.Y.	12/12/29	?	R	5'10	195	524	1833	449	213	.245	.342
Buelow, Frederick William Alexander "Fritz" 99–00StLN												
2/13/76	Berlin, Germany	12/27/33	R	R	5'10¹/₂	170	13	32	11	6	.344	.469
Bullas, Simeon Edward "Sim" 84TolA												
4/10/61	Cleveland, Ohio	1/14/08	?	?	5'7¹/₂	150	13	45	4	4	.089	.133
Burrell, Frank Andrew "Buster" 91NYN 95–97BroN												
12/22/66	Weymouth, Mass.	5/8/62	R	R	5'10	165	122	390	96	42	.246	.318

Catchers

BIRTH DATE	BIRTHPLACE	DEATH DATE	B	T	HGT	WGT	G	AB	H	R	BA	SA
Bushong, Albert John "Doc" 75AtlNA 76PhiN 80–82WorN 83–84CleN 85–87StLA 88– 90BroN												
9/15/56	Philadelphia, Pa.	8/19/08	R	R	5'11	165	672	2397	514	287	.214	.251
Butler, Richard H. "Dick" 97LouN 99WasN												
Unknown	Brooklyn, N.Y.	Unknown	?	?	?	?	22	74	17	7	.230	.257
Cahill, Thomas H. "Tom" 91LouA												
10/?/68	Fall River, Mass.	12/25/94	?	?	?	?	119	430	109	68	.253	.347
Cantz, Bartholomew L. "Bart" 88–89BalA 90PhiA												
1/29/60	Philadelphia, Pa.	2/12/43	?	?	?	?	62	217	34	14	.157	.184
Carl, Lewis "Lew" 74BalNA												
Unknown	Baltimore, Md.	Unknown	?	?	?	?	1	3	0	0	.000	.000
Carroll, Frederick Herbert "Fred" 84ColA 85–86PitA 87–89PitN 90PitP 91PitN												
7/2/64	Sacramento, Cal.	11/7/04	R	R	5'11	185	754	2892	820	546	.284	.408
Carroll, Patrick "Pat" 84AltU 84PhiU												
3/?/53	Philadelphia, Pa.	2/14/16	?	?	?	?	16	68	16	5	.235	.265
Chance, Frank Leroy "Frank" "Husk" 98–00ChiN												
9/9/77	Fresno, Cal.	9/15/24	R	R	6'	190	173	488	140	95	.287	.371
***Clapp, John Edgar "John"** 72ManNA 73–75AthNA 76–77StLN 78IndN 79BufN 80CinN 81CleN 83NYN												
7/17/51	Ithaca, N.Y.	12/18/04	R	R	5'7	194	588	2523	718	554	.285	.357
Clark, Robert H. "Bob" 86–89BroA 90BroN 91CinN 93LouN												
3/18/63	Covington, Ky.	8/21/19	R	R	5'10	175	288	1011	233	145	.230	.280
Clarke, Arthur Franklin "Artie" 90–91NYN												
5/6/65	Providence, R.I.	11/14/49	R	R	5'8	155	149	569	122	72	.214	.274
Clarke, William Jones "Boileryard" 93–98BalN 99–00BosN												
10/18/68	New York, N.Y.	7/29/59	R	R	5'11½	170	511	1843	484	245	.263	.331
Clements, John J. "Jack" 84PhiU 84–97PhiN 98StLN 99CleN 00BosN												
7/24/64	Philadelphia, Pa.	5/23/41	L	L	5'8½	204	1157	4283	1226	619	.286	.421
Colgan, William H. "Ed" 84PitA												
Unknown	E. St. Louis, Ill.	8/8/95	?	?	?	180	48	161	25	10	.155	.193
Collins, Hugh "Hugh" 87NYA												
Unknown	Unknown	Unknown	?	?	?	150	1	4	1	0	.250	.250
Collins, William J. "Bill" 89–90PhiA 91CleN												
?/?/63	Dublin, Ireland	6/8/93	R	?	?	?	4	8	1	0	.125	.125
Connell, Terence G. "Terry" 74ChiNA												
6/17/55	Philadelphia, Pa.	3/25/24	?	?	?	?	1	4	0	0	.000	.000
***Connor, Joseph Francis "Joe"** 95StLN 00BosN												
12/8/74	Waterbury, Conn.	11/8/57	R	R	6'2	185	9	26	4	2	.154	.154
***Conway, William F. "Bill"** 84PhiN 86BalA												
11/28/61	Lowell, Mass.	12/28/43	R	R	5'8	170	8	18	2	4	.111	.111
Cook, Paul "Paul" 84PhiN 86–89LouA 90BroN 91LouA 91StLA												
5/5/63	Caledonia, N.Y.	5/25/05	R	R	?	?	378	1364	304	172	.223	.256
Corcoran, John H. "Jack" 84BroA												
?/?/60	Lowell, Mass.	Unknown	?	?	?	?	52	185	39	17	.211	.265
Cote, Henry Joseph "Henry" 94–95LouN												
2/19/64	Troy, N.Y.	4/28/40	?	?	5'9½	165	20	64	19	17	.297	.391
Cotter, Thomas B. "Tom" 91BosA												
9/30/66	Waltham, Mass.	11/22/06	R	R	5'10½	149	6	12	3	1	.250	.250

Catchers

BIRTH DATE	BIRTHPLACE	DEATH DATE	B	T	HGT	WGT	G	AB	H	R	BA	SA
Criger, Louis "Lou" 96–98CleN 99–00StLN												
2/3/72	Elkhart, Ind.	5/14/34	R	R	5'10	165	282	976	255	118	.261	.339
***Cross, Amos C. "Amos" 85–87LouA**												
?/?/61	?, Czechoslovakia	7/16/88	?	?	?	?	117	441	118	62	.268	.342
Crotty, Joseph P. "Joe" 82LouA 82StLA 84CinU 85LouA 86NYA												
12/24/60	Cincinnati, Ohio	6/22/26	R	R	?	?	87	308	56	34	.182	.234
Crowley, John A. "John" 84PhiN												
1/12/62	Lawrence, Mass.	9/23/96	?	?	5'10	164	48	168	41	26	.244	.321
Cuff, John J. "John" 84BalU												
6/?/64	Jersey City, N.J.	Unknown	?	?	?	?	3	11	1	1	.091	.182
Curren, Peter "Pete" 76PhiN												
Unknown	Baltimore, Md.	Unknown	?	?	?	175	3	12	4	5	.333	.417
Cusick, Andrew Daniel "Tony" 84WilU 84–87PhiA												
12/?/57	Fall River, Mass.	8/6/29	R	R	5'9 1/2	190	95	332	64	27	.193	.220
***Daily, Cornelius F. "Con" 84PhiU 85ProN 86–87BosN 88–89IndN 90BroP 91–95BroN 96ChiN**												
9/11/64	Blackstone, Mass.	6/14/28	L	?	6'	192	630	2222	541	280	.243	.299
Daniels, Lawrence Long "Law" 87BalA 88KCA												
7/14/62	Newton, Mass.	1/7/29	R	R	5'10	170	109	383	86	55	.225	.264
Darling, Conrad "Dell" 83BufN 87–89ChiN 90ChiP 91StLA												
12/21/61	Erie, Pa.	11/20/04	R	R	5'8	170	175	628	151	109	.240	.354
Dealey, Patrick E. "Pat" 84StPU 85–86BosN 87WasN 90SyrA												
Unknown	Burlington, Vt.	12/16/24	R	R	5'8	145	131	469	113	71	.241	.301
***Deasley, Thomas H. "Pat" 81–82BosN 83–84StLA 85–87NYN 88WasN**												
11/17/57	Philadelphia, Pa.	4/1/43	R	R	5'8 1/2	154	402	1466	358	161	.244	.282
Decker, Earle Henry "Harry" 84IndA 84KCU 86DetN 86WasN 89–90PhiN 90PitN												
9/3/54	Lockport, Ill.	Unknown	R	R	5'11	180	156	570	138	72	.242	.318
Decker, Frank "Frank" 79SyrN 82StLA												
2/26/56	St. Louis, Mo.	2/5/40	R	R	?	?	5	18	3	0	.167	.167
DePangher, Michael Anthony "Mike" 84PhiN												
9/11/58	Marysville, Ca.	7/7/15	L	?	5'8	190	4	10	2	0	.200	.200
Derby, Eugene A. "Gene" 85BalA												
2/3/60	Fitchburg, Mass.	?	?	?	5'7	160	10	31	4	4	.129	.129
***Dillon, Packard Andrew "Packy" 75RedsNA**												
Unknown	St. Louis, Mo.	1/8/90	?	?	?	?	3	13	3	1	.231	.308
Dolan, Thomas J. "Tom" 79ChiN 82BufN 83–84StLA 84StLU 85–86StLN 86BalA 88StLA												
1/10/59	New York, N.Y.	1/16/13	R	R	?	?	225	808	165	95	.204	.256
Donahue, James Augustus "Jim" 86–87NYA 88–89KCA 91ColA												
1/8/62	Lockport, Ill.	4/19/35	R	R	6'	175	341	1275	298	133	.234	.275
***Donahue, John Augustus "Jiggs" 00PitN**												
7/13/79	Springfield, Ohio	7/19/13	L	L	6'1	178	3	10	2	1	.200	.400
Donahue, Timothy Cornelius "Tim" "Bridget" 91BosA 95–00ChiN												
6/8/70	Raynham, Mass.	6/12/02	L	R	5'11	180	463	1492	352	196	.236	.294
Donovan, Frederick Maurice "Fred" 95CleN												
7/4/64	?, New Hampshire	3/7/16	R	R	?	?	3	12	1	1	.083	.083
Douglass, William Bingham "Klondike" 96–97StLN 98–00PhiN												
5/10/72	Boston, Pa.	12/13/53	L	R	6'	200	479	1829	516	273	.282	.354

Catchers

BIRTH DATE	BIRTHPLACE	DEATH DATE	B	T	HGT	WGT	G	AB	H	R	BA	SA
Dowse, Thomas Joseph "Tom" 90CleN 91ColA 92LouN 92CinN 92PhiN 92WasN												
8/12/66	?, Ireland	12/14/46	R	R	5'11	175	160	590	116	62	.197	.220
Drissel, Michael F. "Mike" 85StLA												
12/19/64	St. Louis, Mo.	2/26/13	R	R	5'11	?	6	20	1	0	.050	.050
***Dugan, William H. "Bill"** 84VirA 84KCU												
?/?/64	New York, N.Y.	7/24/21	?	?	?	?	12	34	2	4	.059	.088
Dugdale, Daniel Edward "Dan" 86KCN 94WasN												
10/28/64	Peoria, Ill.	3/9/34	?	?	5'8	180	50	174	39	23	.224	.270
Duncan, James William "Jim" 99WasN 99CleN												
7/1/71	Saltsburg, Pa.	10/16/01	R	R	5'8	140	46	152	35	14	.230	.336
Dwight, Albert Ward "Al" 84KCU												
1/4/56	New York, N.Y.	2/20/03	?	?	?	?	12	43	10	8	.233	.279
Dwyer, John E. "John" 82CleN												
Unknown	Lisbon, Ill.	Unknown	?	?	?	?	1	3	0	0	.000	.000
Earle, William Moffat "Billy" "The Little Globetrotter" 89CinA 90StLA 92–93PitN 94LouN 94BroN												
11/10/67	Philadelphia, Pa.	5/30/46	R	R	5'10½	170	142	465	133	102	.286	.419
Ebright, Hiram C. "Hi" "Buck" 89WasN												
6/12/59	Lancaster Co., Pa.	10/24/16	R	R	?	?	16	59	15	7	.254	.407
Ewing, William "Buck" 80–82TroN 83–89NYN 90NYP 91–92NYN 93–94CleN 95–97CinN												
10/17/59	Hoagland, Ohio	10/20/06	R	R	5'10	188	1315	5363	1625	1129	.303	.456
Fagin, Frederick H. "Fred" 95StLN												
Unknown	Cincinnati, Ohio	Unknown	?	?	?	?	1	3	1	0	.333	.333
Farmer, William "Bill" 88PitN 88PhiA												
12/27/70	Philadelphia, Pa.	Unknown	R	R	5'11½	187	5	16	2	0	.125	.125
Farrell, Charles Andrew "Duke" 88–89ChiN 90ChiP 91BosA 92PitN 93WasN 94–96NYN 96–99WasN 99–00BroN												
8/31/66	Oakdale, Mass.	2/15/25	B	R	6'1	208	1317	4860	1346	756	.277	.389
Farrow, John Jacob "John" 73ResNA 74AtlNA 84BroA												
11/8/53	Verplanck, N.Y.	12/31/14	L	R	?	?	55	228	45	25	.197	.224
Field, Samuel Jay "Sam" 75CenNA 75WasNA 76CinN												
10/12/48	Philadelphia, Pa.	10/28/04	R	R	5'9½	182	12	41	6	2	.146	.146
Finley, William James "Bill" 86NYN												
10/4/63	New York, N.Y.	10/6/12	?	?	5'3	170	13	44	8	2	.182	.182
Fisher, Newton "Newt" "Ike" 98PhiN												
6/28/71	Nashville, Tenn.	2/28/47	R	R	5'9½	171	9	26	3	0	.115	.154
Flint, Frank Sylvester "Silver" 75RedsNA 78IndN 79–89ChiN												
8/3/55	Philadelphia, Pa.	1/14/92	R	R	6'	180	760	2913	687	380	.236	.325
Flynn, Michael J. "Mike" 91BosA												
3/15/72	Co. Kildare, Ireland	6/16/41	?	?	?	?	1	2	0	0	.000	.000
Friend, Frank B. "Frank" b. Frederick Freund 96LouN												
7/5/75	Jeffersonville, Ind.	11/5/33	?	R	5'10	180	2	5	1	1	.200	.200
Fulmer, Christopher "Chris" 84WasU 86–89BalA												
7/4/58	Tamaqua, Pa.	11/9/31	R	R	5'8	165	252	876	216	176	.247	.313
Fusselbach, Edward L. "Eddie" 82StLA 84BalU 85PhiA 88LouA												
7/17/56	Philadelphia, Pa.	4/14/26	R	?	5'6	156	109	462	124	75	.268	.329
***#Ganzel, Charles William "Charlie"** 84StPU 85–86PhiN 86–88DetN 89–97BosN												
6/18/62	Waterford, Wis.	4/7/14	R	R	6'	161	786	2984	774	421	.259	.330

Catchers

BIRTH DATE	BIRTHPLACE	DEATH DATE	B	T	HGT	WGT	G	AB	H	R	BA	SA
Gardner, Alexander "Alex"		**84WasA**										
4/28/61	Toronto, Ont., Can.	6/18/26	?	?	?	?	1	3	0	0	.000	.000
Gastfield, Edward "Ed"	**84–85DetN**	**85ChiN**										
8/1/65	Chicago, Ill.	12/1/99	R	?	5'9½	155	25	88	6	6	.068	.080
Gibson, Leighton P. "Whitey"	**88PhiA**											
10/6/68	Lancaster, Pa.	10/11/07	?	R	5'9	178	1	3	0	0	.000	.000
Gillen, Thomas J. "Tom"	**84PhiU**	**86DetN**										
5/18/62	Philadelphia, Pa.	1/26/89	?	?	5'8	160	31	126	22	7	.175	.190
Gilligan, Andrew Bernard "Barney"	**75AtlNA**	**79–80CleN**	**81–85ProN**	**86–87WasN**	**88DetN**							
1/3/56	Cambridge, Mass.	4/1/34	R	R	5'6½	130	523	1873	388	217	.207	.273
Gilmore, James "Jim"	**75WasNA**											
5/?/53	Baltimore, Md.	11/18/28	?	?	?	?	3	12	3	2	.250	.250
Gilroy, ?	**74ChiNA**	**75AthNA**										
Unknown	Unknown		?	?	?	?	10	44	9	4	.205	.227
Grady, Michael William "Mike"	**94–97PhiN**	**97StLN**	**98–00NYN**									
12/23/69	Kennett Square, Pa.	12/3/43	R	R	5'11	190	526	1739	522	311	.300	.412
Graff, Louis George "Louis" "Chappie"	**90SyrA**											
7/25/66	Philadelphia, Pa.	4/16/55	?	R	?	?	1	5	2	0	.400	.600
Graulich, Lewis "Lew"	**91PhiN**											
Unknown	Camden, N.J.	Unknown	?	?	?	?	7	26	8	2	.308	.308
Graves, Frank M. "Frank"	**86StLN**											
11/2/60	Cincinnati, Ohio	Unknown	?	?	6'	163	43	138	21	7	.152	.167
Grim, John Helm "John"	**88PhiN**	**90RocA**	**91MilA**	**92–94LouN**	**95–99BroN**							
8/9/67	Lebanon, Ky.	7/28/61	R	R	6'2	175	706	2638	705	350	.267	.359
Gross, Emil Michael "Emil" "Em"	**79–81ProN**	**83PhiN**	**84Chi–PitU**									
3/3/58	Chicago, Ill.	8/24/21	R	R	6'	190	248	987	291	141	.295	.427
Guiney, Benjamin Franklin "Ben"	**83–84DetN**											
11/16/58	Detroit, Mich.	12/5/30	B	R	6'	170	3	12	1	1	.083	.083
Gunkle, Frederick W. "Fred"	**79CleN**											
Unknown	Reading, Pa.	Unknown	?	?	?	?	1	3	0	1	.000	.000
Gunning, Thomas Francis "Tom"	**84–86BosN**	**87PhiN**	**88–89PhiA**									
3/4/62	Newmarket, N.H.	3/17/31	R	R	5'10	160	146	537	110	79	.205	.253
Gunson, Joseph Brook "Joe"	**84WasU**	**89KCA**	**92BalN**	**93StLN**	**93CleN**							
3/23/63	Philadelphia, Pa.	11/15/42	R	R	5'6	160	229	826	174	96	.211	.251
*Hackett, Mortimer Martin "Mert"	**83–85BosN**	**86KCN**	**87IndN**									
11/11/59	Cambridge, Mass.	2/22/38	R	R	5'10½	175	256	939	203	87	.216	.318
Haley, Frederick "Fred"	**80TroN**											
6/18/53	Wheeling, W.Va	Unknown	?	R	?	?	2	7	0	0	.000	.000
Hanna, John "John"	**84WasA**	**84VirA**										
11/3/63	Philadelphia, Pa.	11/7/30	?	?	?	?	45	143	18	14	.126	.154
Hardie, Louis W. "Lou"	**84PhiN**	**86ChiN**	**90BosN**	**91BalA**								
8/24/64	New York, N.Y.	3/5/29	?	?	5'11	180	81	300	67	28	.223	.307
Harding, Louis Edward "Lou" "Jumbo"	**86StLA**											
?/?/65	San Francisco, Cal.	Unknown	?	?	5'9½	213	1	3	1	0	.333	.667
Harrington, Jeremiah Peter "Jerry"	**90–92CinN**	**93LouN**										
8/12/69	Keokuk, Iowa	4/16/13	R	R	5'11	220	189	666	151	60	.227	.287

Catchers

BIRTH DATE	BIRTHPLACE	DEATH DATE	B	T	HGT	WGT	G	AB	H	R	BA	SA
Harrison, Washington Ritter "Rit" 75NHNA												
9/16/49	Waterbury, Conn.	11/7/88	?	?	?	?	1	4	2	0	.500	.750
Hart, Thomas Henry "Tom" "Bushy" 91WasA												
6/15/69	Canaan, N.Y.	9/17/39	?	?	5'7	160	8	24	3	1	.125	.125
Hastings, Winfield Scott "Scott" 71RokNA 72CleNA 72–73BalNA 74HarNA 75ChiNA 76LouN 77CinN												
8/10/47	Hillsboro, Ohio	8/14/07	R	R	5'8	161	294	1328	371	264	.279	.325
Hayes, John J. "Jackie" 82WorN 83–84PitA 84–85BroA 86WasN 87BalA 90BroP												
6/27/61	Brooklyn, N.Y.	Unknown	?	R	?	?	300	1148	267	106	.233	.331
Hellman, Anthony J. "Tony" 86BalA												
5/29/61	Cincinnati, Ohio	3/29/98	?	?	?	?	1	3	0	0	.000	.000
Hess, Thomas "Tom" b. Heslin 92BalN												
8/15/75	Brooklyn, N.Y.	12/15/45	?	?	?	?	1	2	0	0	.000	.000
Heydon, Michael Edward "Mike" "Ed" 98BalN 99WasN												
7/15/74	?, Missouri	10/13/13	L	R	6'	?	6	12	1	2	.083	.083
Hicks, Nathaniel Woodhull "Nat" 72–73NYN 74PhiNA 75MutNA 76NYN 77CinN												
4/19/45	Hempstead, N.Y.	4/21/07	R	R	6'1	186	257	1144	301	171	.263	.307
Hines, Michael P. "Mike" 83–85BosN 85BroA 85ProN 88BosN												
9/?/62	?, Ireland	3/14/10	R	L	5'10	176	120	451	91	69	.202	.259
Hoffman, Otto Charles "Hickey" 79CleN												
10/27/56	Cleveland, Ohio	10/27/15	?	?	?	?	2	6	0	0	.000	.000
Holbert, William Henry "Bill" 76LouN 78MilN 79SyrN 79–82TroN 83–87NYA 88BroA												
3/14/55	Baltimore, Md.	3/20/35	R	R	?	197	623	2335	486	182	.208	.232
Honan, Martin Weldon "Marty" 90–91ChiN												
4/?/71	Chicago, Ill.	8/20/08	?	?	?	?	6	15	2	1	.133	.267
Hoover, Charles E. "Charlie" 88–89KCA												
9/21/65	Mound City, Ill.	Unknown	L	R	5'8	?	74	268	67	44	.250	.306
Humphries, John Henry "John" 83NYN 84WasA 84NYN												
11/12/61	N. Gower, Ont., Can.	11/29/33	L	L	6'	185	98	364	52	34	.143	.151
Hunter, William Robert "Bill" 84LouA												
?/?/55	St. Thomas, Ont., Can.	Unknown	?	?	5'7½	160	2	7	1	1	.143	.143
Hurley, Jeremiah Joseph "Jerry" 89BosN 90PitP 91CinA												
6/15/63	Boston, Mass.	9/17/50	R	R	6'	190	33	92	20	15	.217	.304
Ingraham, Charles W. "Charlie" 83BalA												
4/8/60	Chicago, Ill.	2/18/06	?	?	5'11	170	1	4	1	0	.250	.250
Jacklitsch, Frederick Lawrence "Fred" 00PhiN												
5/24/76	Brooklyn, N.Y.	7/18/37	R	R	5'9	180	5	11	2	0	.182	.273
Jennings, Alfred Gorden "Alamazoo" 78MilN												
11/30/50	Newport, Ky.	11/2/94	?	?	?	?	1	2	0	0	.000	.000
Jewett, Nathan W. "Nat" 72EckNA												
12/25/42	New York, N.Y.	2/23/14	?	?	5'6	137	2	8	1	1	.125	.125
Jones, William "Bill" 82BalA 84PhiU												
Unknown	Syracuse, N.Y.	Unknown	?	?	?	?	8	29	3	3	.103	.103
Kahoe, Michael Joseph "Mike" 95CinN 99–00CinN												
9/3/73	Yellow Springs, Ohio	5/14/49	R	R	6'	185	69	221	40	20	.181	.249
Keenan, James William "Jim" 75NHNA 80BufN 82PitA 84IndA 85–89CinA 90–91CinN												
2/10/58	New Haven, Conn.	9/21/26	R	R	5'10	186	527	1886	453	255	.240	.346

Catchers

BIRTH DATE	BIRTHPLACE	DEATH DATE	B	T	HGT	WGT	G	AB	H	R	BA	SA
Kelly, John Francis "Kick" "Father" 82CleN 83BalA 83PhiN 84CinU 84WasU												
3/3/59	Paterson, N.J.	4/13/08	R	R	6'	185	121	465	105	48	.226	.282
Kelly, John O. "Honest John" 79SyrN 79TroN												
10/31/56	New York, N.Y.	3/27/26	?	?	6'1½	185	16	58	9	5	.155	.172
Kemmler, Rudolph "Rudy" b. Kemler 79ProN 81CleN 82CinA 82PitA 83–84ColA 85PitA 86StLA 89ColA												
?/?/60	Chicago, Ill.	6/20/09	R	R	?	?	236	862	168	79	.195	.230
Kennedy, Michael Joseph "Doc" 79–82CleN 83BufN												
8/11/53	Brooklyn, N.Y.	5/23/20	R	R	5'9½	185	160	615	160	67	.260	.319
Kinslow, Thomas F. "Tom" 86WasN 87NYA 90BroP 91–94BroN 95PitN 96LouN 98WasN 98StLN												
1/12/66	Washington, D.C.	2/22/01	R	R	5'10	160	380	1414	376	186	.266	.361
Kittridge, Malachi Jeddidiah "Mal" "Jeddidah" 90–97ChiN 98–99LouN 99WasN												
10/12/69	Clinton, Mass.	6/23/28	R	R	5'7	170	744	2519	547	283	.217	.283
***Kling, John "Johnny" "Noisy"** 00ChiN												
2/25/75	Kansas City, Mo.	1/31/47	R	R	5'9½	160	15	51	15	8	.294	.392
Knowdell, Jacob Augustus "Jake" 74–75AtlNA 78MilN												
7/27/40	Brooklyn, N.Y.	Unknown	?	?	5'7½	148	71	263	47	27	.179	.202
Krieg, William Frederick "Bill" 84Chi–PitU 85ChiN 85BroA 86–87WasN												
1/29/59	Petersburg, Ill.	3/25/30	R	R	5'8	180	141	535	127	62	.237	.344
Lake, Frederick Lovett "Fred" 91BosN 94LouN 97BosN 98PitN												
10/16/66	Nova Scotia, Canada	11/24/31	R	R	5'10	170	45	124	29	12	.234	.306
Latimer, Clifford Wesley "Tacks" 98NYN 99LouN 00PitN												
11/30/77	Loveland, Ohio	4/24/36	R	R	6'	160	18	58	17	5	.293	.345
Lawlor, Michael H. "Mike" 80TroN 84WasU												
3/11/54	Troy, N.Y.	8/3/16	?	R	6'	180	6	16	1	1	.063	.063
Ledwith, Michael "Mike" 74AtlNA												
Unknown	Brooklyn, N.Y.	1/2/29	?	?	?	?	1	4	1	1	.250	.250
Lennon, William F. "Bill" 71KekNA 72NatNA 73MarNA												
?/?/48	Brooklyn, N.Y.	Unknown	?	?	5'7	145	28	121	27	18	.223	.256
Leutz, ? 72EckNA												
Unknown	Unknown	Unknown	?	?	?	?	4	12	1	2	.083	.083
Lohman, George F. "Pete" 91WasA												
10/21/64	Lake Elmo, Minn.	11/21/28	?	?	?	?	32	109	21	18	.193	.303
Loughran, ? 84NYN												
Unknown	New York, N.Y.	Unknown	?	?	?	?	9	29	3	4	.103	.207
Lowe, Richard Alvern "Dick" 84DetN												
1/28/54	Evansville, Wis.	6/28/22	?	?	?	?	1	3	1	0	.333	.333
Macey, ? 90PhiA												
Unknown	Columbus, Ohio	Unknown	?	?	?	?	1	1	0	0	.000	.000
#Mack, Cornelius Alexander "Connie" b. McGillicuddy 86–89WasN 90BufP 91–96PitN												
12/22/62	E. Brookfield, Mass.	2/8/56	R	R	6'1	150	723	2695	659	391	.245	.300
Mahoney, Daniel J. "Dan" 92CinN 95WasN												
3/20/64	Springfield, Mass.	2/1/04	R	R	5'9½	165	11	33	6	3	.182	.242
Malone, Ferguson G. "Fergie" 71–72AthNA 73PhiNA 74ChiNA 75PhiNA 76PhiN 84PhiU												
?/?/42	?, Ireland	1/1/05	R	L	5'8	156	220	1052	288	200	.274	.320
Manlove, Charles Henry Weeks "Charlie" "Chick" 84AltU 84NYN												
10/8/62	Philadelphia, Pa.	2/12/52	R	R	5'9	165	5	17	3	1	.176	.176

Catchers

BIRTH DATE	BIRTHPLACE	DEATH DATE	B	T	HGT	WGT	G	AB	H	R	BA	SA
McCaffrey, Charles P. "Sparrow" 89ColA												
?/?/68	Philadelphia,Pa.	4/29/94	?	?	?	120	2	1	1	1	1.000	1.000
McCauley, James Adelbert "Jim" 84StLA 85BufN 85ChiN 86BroA												
3/24/63	Stanley, N.Y.	9/14/30	L	R	6'	180	39	122	23	10	.189	.230
McCauley, Patrick M. "Pat" 93StLN 96WasN												
6/10/70	Ware, Mass.	1/23/17	?	R	5'10½	156	31	100	22	14	.220	.340
McCloskey, ? 75WasNA												
Unknown	Brooklyn, N.Y.	Unknown	?	?	?	?	11	40	7	1	.175	.175
McCloskey, William George "Bill" 84WilU												
5/?/54	Philadelphia, Pa.	Unknown	?	?	5'8	155	9	30	3	0	.100	.100
McFarland, Edward William "Ed" 93CleN 96–97StLN 97–00PhiN												
8/3/74	Cleveland, Ohio	11/28/59	R	R	5'10	180	471	1646	477	259	.290	.398
McGinley, Timothy S. "Tim" 75CenNA 75NHNA 76BosN												
Unknown	Philadelphia, Pa.	11/2/99	?	?	5'9½	155	54	223	54	23	.242	.274
McGuire, James Thomas "Deacon" 84TolA 85DetN 86–88PhiN 88DetN 88CleA 90RocA 91WasA 92–99WasN 99–00BroN												
11/18/63	Youngstown, Ohio	10/31/36	R	R	6'1	185	1316	4803	1380	661	.287	.391
McKeever, James "Jim" 84BosU												
4/19/61	St. John, N.B., Can.	8/19/97	?	?	5'10	170	16	66	9	13	.136	.136
McKenna, Edward J. "Ed" 74PhiNA 77StLN 84WasU												
Unknown	St. Louis, Mo.	Unknown	?	?	?	?	33	122	23	19	.189	.197
McKeough, David J. "Dave" 90RocA 91PhiA												
12/1/63	Utica, N.Y.	7/11/01	?	?	5'7	158	77	272	63	42	.232	.261
McManus, Francis E. "Frank" 99WasN												
9/21/75	Lawrence, Mass.	9/1/23	?	R	5'10	?	7	21	8	3	.381	.429
McVey, George W. "George" 85BroA												
9/16/65	Port Jervis, N.Y.	5/3/96	R	R	6'1	185	6	21	3	2	.143	.143
Meek, Frank J. "Dad" 89–90StLA												
3/14/67	St. Louis, Mo.	12/22/22	?	?	?	?	6	18	6	5	.333	.333
Merritt, William Henry "Bill" 91ChiN 92LouN 93–94BosN 94PitN 94–95CinN 95–97PitN 99BosN												
7/30/70	Lowell, Mass.	11/17/37	R	R	5'7	160	400	1410	383	182	.272	.334
Messitt, Thomas John "Tom" 99LouN												
7/27/74	Frankfort, Pa.	9/22/34	?	?	5'9	177	3	11	1	0	.091	.091
Meyers, Lewis Henry "Lew" "Crazy Horse" 84CinU												
12/9/59	Cincinnati, Ohio	11/30/20	R	R	5'11	165	2	3	0	1	.000	.000
Miller, George C. "George" 77CinN 84CinA												
2/19/53	Newport, Ky.	7/24/29	R	R	5'5	160	17	57	11	10	.193	.263
Miller, George Frederick "Doggie" "Foghorn" "Calliope" 84–86PitA 87–93PitN 94–95StLN 96LouN												
8/15/64	Brooklyn, N.Y.	4/6/09	R	R	5'6	145	1317	5167	1380	839	.267	.345
Miller, Thomas P. "Tom" "Reddy" 74AthNA 75StLNA												
Unknown	Philadelphia, Pa.	5/29/76	?	?	?	?	59	230	43	19	.187	.196
Milligan, John "Jocko" 84–87PhiA 88–89StLA 90PhiP 91PhiA 92WasN 93BalN 93NYN												
8/8/61	Philadelphia, Pa.	8/29/23	R	R	6'	192	772	2964	848	440	.286	.433
Mills, Charles "Charlie" 71–72MutNA												
Unknown	Brooklyn, N.Y.	4/10/74	?	?	6'	?	38	177	40	33	.226	.282
Monroe, Frank W. "Frank" 84IndA												
Unknown	Hamilton, Ohio	Unknown	?	?	?	?	2	8	0	1	.000	.000

Catchers

BIRTH DATE	BIRTHPLACE	DEATH DATE	B	T	HGT	WGT	G	AB	H	R	BA	SA
Moolic, George Henry "Prunes" 86ChiN												
3/12/65	Lawrence, Mass.	2/19/15	R	R	5'7	145	16	56	8	9	.143	.196
Moore, Jeremiah S. "Jerrie" 84AltU 84CleN 85DetN												
Unknown	Detroit, Mich.	9/26/90	L	?	5'11	170	35	133	35	13	.263	.331
Moran, William L. "Bill" 92StLN 95ChiN												
10/10/69	Joliet, Ill.	4/8/16	?	?	?	175	39	136	20	10	.147	.206
Mullen, John "John" 76PhiN												
Unknown	Philadelphia, Pa.	Unknown	L	L	?	?	1	3	0	0	.000	.000
Mundinger, George "George" 84IndA												
11/20/54	New Orleans, La.	10/12/10	R	R	6'2	200	3	8	2	1	.250	.250
Munyan, John B. "John" 87CleA 90ColA 90–91StLA												
11/14/60	Chester, Pa.	2/18/45	?	?	?	?	174	583	147	112	.252	.345
Murphy, ? 84BosU												
Unknown	Unknown	Unknown	?	?	?	?	1	3	0	0	.000	.000
Murphy, Cornelius David "Connie" "Stone Face" 93–94CinN												
11/1/70	Northfield, Mass.	12/14/45	L	R	5'8	155	7	21	3	3	.143	.190
Murphy, Daniel Joseph "Danny" "Handsome Dan" 92NYN												
9/10/64	Brooklyn, N.Y.	12/14/15	?	?	?	156	8	26	3	2	.115	.115
Murphy, Frank J. "Tony" 84NYA												
?/?/63	Brooklyn, N.Y.	Unknown	?	?	5'6	145	1	3	1	1	.333	.333
Murphy, Morgan Edward "Morg" "Morgan" 90BosP 91BosA 92–95CinN 96–97StLN 98PitN 98PhiN 00PhiN												
2/14/67	E. Providence, R.I.	10/3/38	R	R	5'8	160	557	1939	437	242	.225	.282
Murphy, Patrick J. "Pat" 87–90NYN												
1/2/57	Auburn, Mass.	5/16/27	?	R	5'10	160	86	309	68	34	.220	.272
Murray, Jeremiah J. "Miah" 84ProN 85LouA 88WasN 91WasA												
1/1/65	Boston, Mass.	1/11/22	R	R	5'11½	170	34	120	17	6	.142	.150
Myers, George D. "George" 84–85BufN 86StLN 87–89IndN												
11/13/60	Buffalo, N.Y.	12/14/26	R	R	5'8	170	424	1578	321	183	.203	.250
Nagle, Thomas Edward "Tom" 90–91ChiN												
10/30/65	Milwaukee, Wis.	3/9/46	R	R	5'10	150	46	169	42	24	.249	.308
Nava, Vincent P. "Sandy" b. Irwin Sandy 82–84ProN 85–86BalA												
4/12/50	San Francisco, Cal.	6/15/06	?	?	5'6	155	101	345	61	45	.177	.209
Nichols, Arthur Francis "Art" b. Meikle 98–00ChiN												
7/14/71	Manchester, N.H.	8/9/45	R	R	5'10	175	39	114	29	13	.254	.307
O'Brien, John K. "Jack" "Philadelphia Jack" b. Byrne 82–86PhiA 87BroA 88BalA 90PhiA												
6/12/60	Philadelphia, Pa.	11/20/10	R	R	5'10	184	555	2169	577	366	.266	.369
O'Connor, John Joseph "Jack" "Peach Pie" 87–88CinA 89–91ColA 92–98CleN 99–00StLN 00PitN												
6/2/69	St. Louis, Mo.	11/14/37	R	R	5'10	170	1182	4486	1228	657	.274	.354
O'Donnell, John "John" 84PhiU												
Unknown	Littletown, Pa.	Unknown	?	?	?	?	1	4	1	0	.250	.250
O'Hagen, Harry P. "Hal" 92WasN												
9/30/73	Washington, D.C.	1/14/13	?	?	6'	173	1	4	1	1	.250	.250
Oldfield, David "Dave" 83BalA 85–86BroA 86WasN												
12/18/64	Philadelphia, Pa.	8/28/39	B	L	5'7	175	46	155	31	11	.200	.226
O'Meara, Thomas Edward "Tom" 95–96CleN												
12/12/72	Chicago, Ill.	2/16/02	?	?	?	?	13	34	5	6	.147	.147

Catchers

BIRTH DATE	BIRTHPLACE	DEATH DATE	B	T	HGT	WGT	G	AB	H	R	BA	SA
O'Neill, John J. "John" 99NYN												
Unknown	New York, N.Y.	Unknown	?	R	?	?	2	7	0	0	.000	.000
O'Rourke, Thomas Joseph "Tom" 87–88BosN 90NYN 90SyrA												
10/?/65	New York, NY.	7/19/29	?	R	5'9	158	85	312	58	32	.186	.221
Osterhout, Charles W. "Charlie" 79SyrN												
?/?/56	Syracuse, N.Y.	5/21/33	?	R	?	?	2	8	0	0	.000	.000
Otten, Joseph G. "Joe" 95StLN												
Unknown	Murphysburo, Ill.	Unknown	?	R	?	?	26	87	21	8	.241	.241
Oxley, Henry Havelock "Henry" 84NYN 84NYA												
1/4/58	Covehead, P.E.Isl., Can.	10/12/45	?	?	5'11	163	4	7	0	0	.000	.000
Paul, Louis "Lou" 76PhiN												
Unknown	Unknown	Unknown	R	R	?	?	3	12	2	2	.167	.250
***Peitz, Henry Clement "Heinie" 92–95StLN 96–00CinN**												
11/28/70	St. Louis, Mo.	10/23/43	R	R	5'11	165	720	2428	661	345	.272	.375
Peoples, James Elsworth "Jimmy" 84–85CinA 85–88BroA 89ColA												
10/8/63	Big Beaver, Mich.	8/29/20	?	R	5'8	200	344	1251	264	157	.211	.279
***Pierson, David P. "Dave" 76CinN**												
8/20/55	Wilkes-Barre, Pa.	11/11/22	R	R	5'7	142	57	233	55	33	.236	.262
Pitz, Herman "Herman" 90BroA 90SyrA												
7/18/65	Brooklyn, N.Y.	9/3/24	?	?	5'6	140	90	284	47	43	.165	.165
Potts, Vivian "Dan" 92WasN												
1/?/69	Bristol, Pa.	Unknown	?	?	?	?	1	4	1	0	.250	.250
Powers, Michael Riley "Doc" 98–99LouN 99WasN												
9/22/70	Pittsfield, Mass.	4/26/09	R	R	?	?	97	306	72	31	.235	.291
Powers, Philip B. "Phil" "Grandma" 78ChiN 80BosN 81CleN 82–85CinA 85BalA												
7/26/54	New York, N.Y.	12/22/14	R	R	5'7	166	154	570	103	56	.181	.223
Quinlan, Francis Patrick "Frank" 91BosA												
3/9/69	Marlborough, Mass.	5/4/04	?	?	?	?	2	5	0	0	.000	.000
Quinn, Patrick "Paddy" 81BosN 81WorN												
Unknown	Boston, Mass.	3/?/93	?	?	?	?	3	11	1	0	.091	.091
Quinn, Joseph C. "Joe" 71KekNA												
8/?/49	Chicago, Ill.	1/2/09	?	?	5'8½	148	5	17	4	8	.235	.235
Quinn, Paddy "Paddy" 75WesNA 75HarNA 75ChiNA												
Unknown	Boston, Mass.	3/?/93	?	?	?	?	33	117	31	17	.265	.274
Quinn, Thomas Oscar "Tom" 86PitA 89BalA 90PitP												
4/25/64	Annapolis, Md.	7/24/32	R	R	5'8	180	113	412	78	42	.189	.238
Quinton, Marshall J. "Marshall" 84VirA 85PhiA												
Unknown	Philadelphia, Pa.	Unknown	?	?	5'11	190	33	123	28	18	.228	.276
Reilley, Charles E. "Charlie" 79TroN 80CinBN 81DetN 81WorN 82ProN 84BosU												
?/?/56	Hartford, Conn.	Unknown	R	R	5'10	165	119	439	92	36	.210	.232
Reipschlager, Charles W. "Charlie" 83–86NYA 87CleA												
Unknown	Unknown	Unknown	R	R	5'6½	160	296	1109	246	99	.222	.283
Reynolds, Charles Lawrence "Charlie" 89KCA 89BroA												
5/1/65	Williamsburg, Ind.	7/3/44	?	?	5'9	175	13	46	10	6	.217	.283
Riddle, John H. "John" 89WasN 90PhiA												
2/?/64	?, Pennsylvania	Unknown	R	R	?	?	38	122	15	10	.123	.164

Catchers

BIRTH DATE	BIRTHPLACE	DEATH DATE	B	T	HGT	WGT	G	AB	H	R	BA	SA
Ringo, Frank C. "Frank" 83–84PhiN 84PhiA 85DetN 85–86PitA 86KCN												
10/12/60	Parkville, Mo.	4/12/89	R	?	5'11	175	139	506	97	49	.192	.251
Ritter, Floyd Alexander "Floyd" 90TolA												
6/1/70	Dorset, Ohio	2/7/43	R	R	5'8	155	1	3	0	0	.000	.000
Ritterson, Edward West "Whitey" 76PhiN												
4/26/55	Philadelphia, Pa.	7/28/17	R	R	5'8	?	16	52	13	8	.250	.308
Roach, Michael Stephen "Mike" 99WasN												
12/23/73	New York, N.Y.	11/12/16	?	?	?	?	24	78	17	7	.218	.231
Robinson, Charles Henry "Charlie" 84IndA 85BroA												
7/27/56	Westerly, R.I.	5/18/13	L	R	?	?	31	120	29	16	.242	.292
Robinson, Wilbert "Wilbert" 86–90PhiA 90–91BalA 92–99BalN 00StLN												
6/29/63	Bolton, Mass.	8/8/34	R	R	5'8½	215	1212	4501	1218	567	.271	.341
Rogers, Emmett "Emmett" 90TolA												
?/?/65	Rome, N.Y.	Unknown	B	?	5'10	165	35	110	19	18	.173	.255
Rollinson, William Henry "William" b. Winslow 84WasU												
6/10/56	Fairfield, Me.	9/28/38	?	?	?	?	1	3	0	0	.000	.000
Rowen, W. Edward "Ed" 82BosN 83–84PhiA												
10/22/57	Bridgeport, Conn.	2/22/92	?	?	5'6	195	136	538	130	68	.242	.299
Roxburgh, James A. "Jim" 84BalA 87PhiA												
1/17/58	San Francisco, Ca.	2/21/34	R	R	5'10	170	4	12	3	1	.250	.250
Ryan, John Bernard "Jack" 89–91LouA 94–96BosN 98BroN 99BalN												
11/12/68	Haverhill, Mass.	8/21/52	R	R	5'10½	165	388	1396	315	177	.226	.298
Sage, Harry "Harry" "Doc" 90TolA												
3/16/64	Rock Island, Ill.	5/27/47	R	R	5'10	185	81	275	41	40	.149	.229
Schellhase, Albert Herman "Al" "Schelley" 90BosN 91LouA												
9/13/64	Evansville, Ind.	1/3/19	R	R	5'8	148	15	45	6	4	.133	.133
Schreckengost, Ossee Freeman "Ossee" (aka Ossee Schreck) 97LouN 98–99CleN 99StLN												
4/11/75	New Bethlehem, Pa.	7/9/14	R	R	5'10	180	126	465	135	62	.290	.385
Schriver, William Frederick "Pop" 86BroA 88–90PhiN 91–94ChiN 95NYN 97CinN 98–00PitN												
7/11/65	Brooklyn, N.Y.	12/27/32	R	R	5'9½	172	747	2561	675	350	.264	.353
Schultz, John "John" 91StLA												
Unknown	St. Louis, Mo.	Unknown	L	R	5'11	184	1	2	0	0	.000	.000
Schwartz, William August "Bill" "Pop" "Scooper Bill" 83ColA 84CinU												
4/3/64	Jamestown, Ky.	12/22/40	R	R	6'1	195	31	110	26	14	.236	.300
Siffel, Frank "Frank" 84–85PhiA												
?/?/60	?, Germany	10/26/09	?	?	?	?	10	27	3	4	.148	.185
Sixsmith, Edward "Ed" 84PhiN												
2/26/63	Philadelphia, Pa.	12/12/26	R	R	?	?	1	2	0	0	.000	.000
Smith, Alexander Benjamin "Aleck" "Broadway Aleck" 97–99BroN 99BalN 00BroN												
?/?/71	New York, N.Y.	7/9/19	?	R	?	?	183	642	186	86	.290	.368
Smith, Frank L. "Frank" 84PitA												
11/24/57	?, Canada	10/11/28	?	?	?	?	10	36	9	3	.250	.306
Snyder, Charles N. "Pop" 73WasNA 74BalNA 75PhiNA 76–77LouN 78–79BosN 81BosN 82–86CinA 87–88CleA 89CleN 90CleP 91WasA												
10/6/54	Washington, D.C.	10/29/24	R	R	5'11½	184	930	3644	855	433	.235	.298
Snyder, Frank C. "Cooney" 98LouA												
Unknown	Toronto, Ont., Can.	3/9/17	?	?	6'3	180	17	61	10	4	.164	.164

Catchers

BIRTH DATE	BIRTHPLACE	DEATH DATE	B	T	HGT	WGT	G	AB	H	R	BA	SA
Sommers, Joseph Andrews "Pete" 87NYA 88BosN 89ChiN 89IndN 90NYN 90CleN												
10/26/66	Cleveland, Ohio	7/22/08	R	R	5'11½	181	98	339	67	35	.198	.286
Stallings, George Tweedy "George" 90BroN 97–98PhiN												
11/17/67	Augusta, Ga.	5/13/29	R	R	6'1	187	7	20	2	3	.100	.150
Stanton, Harry Andrew "Harry" 00StLN												
Unknown	St. Louis, Mo.	Unknown	?	R	?	?	1	0	0	0	—	—
Straub, Joseph "Joe" 80TroN 82PhiA 83ColA												
1/19/58	Milwaukee, Wis.	2/13/29	R	R	5'10	160	38	144	22	7	.153	.167
Strick, John Quincy Adams "John" 82LouA												
Unknown	Louisville, Ky.	Unknown	?	?	?	?	32	110	18	17	.164	.236
Struve, Albert "Al" 84StLA												
Unknown	St. Louis, Mo.	Unknown	?	?	?	?	2	7	2	2	.286	.286
Stynes, Cornelius William "Neil" 90CleP												
12/10/68	Arlington, Mass.	3/26/44	R	R	6'	165	2	8	0	0	.000	.000
Suck, Anthony "Tony" b. Charles Anthony Zuck 83BufN 84Chi–PitU 84BalU												
6/11/58	Chicago, Ill.	1/29/95	?	?	5'9	164	58	205	31	21	.151	.161
Sugden, Joseph "Joe" 93–97PitN 98StLN 99CleN												
7/31/70	Philadelphia, Pa.	6/28/59	B	R	5'10	180	444	1514	413	213	.273	.333
Sullivan, Daniel C. "Dan" "Link" 82–85LouA 85StLA 86PitA												
5/9/57	Providence, R.I.	10/26/93	?	R	5'11	194	198	788	183	86	.232	.288
Sullivan, Thomas Jefferson "Sleeper" "Iron Hands" 81BufN 82 83StLA 84StLU												
Unknown	St. Louis, Mo.	9/25/99	R	R	?	175	96	345	64	39	.186	.229
#Sullivan, William Joseph Sr. "Billy" 99–00BosN												
2/1/75	Oakland, Wis.	1/28/65	R	R	5'9	155	94	312	85	46	.272	.394
Summers, William "Kid" 93StLN												
Unknown Toronto, Ont., Can.		10/16/95	?	R	?	?	2	1	0	1	.000	.000
Sutcliffe, Elmer Ellsworth "Sy" 84–85ChiN 85StLN 88DetN 89CleN 90CleP 91WasA 92BalN												
4/15/62	Wheaton, Ill.	2/13/93	L	L	6'2	170	344	1322	381	177	.288	.371
Sweeney, John J. "Rooney" 83BalA 84BalU 85StLN												
?/?/60	New York, N.Y.	Unknown	?	?	5'8	155	76	298	64	51	.215	.275
Swett, William E. "Pop" 90BosP												
4/16/70	San Francisco, Cal.	11/22/34	?	?	6'	175	37	94	18	16	191	.330
Tate, Edward Christopher "Pop" "Dimples" 85–88BosN 89–90BalA												
12/22/60	Richmond, Va.	6/25/32	R	L	5'10	178	227	822	179	101	.218	.274
Terrell, John Thomas "Tom" 86LouA												
6/19/67	Louisville, Ky.	7/9/93	?	?	?	?	1	4	1	0	.250	.250
Thompson, Andrew M. "Andrew" "A.M." 75WasNA												
?/?/45	?, Illinois	Unknown	?	?	?	?	11	41	4	3	.098	.146
Townsend, George Hodson "George" "Sleepy" 87–88PhiA 90–91BalA												
6/4/67	Hartsdale, N.Y.	3/15/30	R	R	5'7½	180	152	541	101	60	.187	.238
***Traffley, William Franklin "Bill"** 78ChiN 83CinA 84–86BalA												
12/21/59	Staten Is., N.Y.	6/23/08	R	R	5'11½	185	179	663	116	85	.175	.235
Tray, James "Jim" 84IndA												
2/14/60	Jackson, Mich.	7/28/05	?	?	5'11	180	6	21	6	2	.286	.286
Trost, Michael J. "Mike" 90StLA 95LouN												
?/?/66	Philadelphia, Pa.	3/24/01	?	R	6'1½	180	20	63	14	11	.222	.302

Catchers

BIRTH DATE	BIRTHPLACE	DEATH DATE	B	T	HGT	WGT	G	AB	H	R	BA	SA
Trott, Samuel W. "Sam" 80BosN 81–83DetN 84–85BalA 87–88BalA												
3/?/59	Washington, D.C.	6/5/25	L	L	5'9	190	360	1354	338	166	.250	.343
Twineham, Arthur W. "Art" "Old Hoss" 93–94StLN												
11/26/66	Galesburg, Ill.	Unknown	L	L	6'1½	190	52	175	55	30	.314	.377
Vadeboncouer, Eugene Onesime "Gene" 84PhiN												
7/5/58	Louiseville, Que., Can.	10/6/35	R	R	5'6	150	4	14	3	1	.214	.214
Valentine, Robert "Bob" 76NYN												
Unknown	Unknown	Unknown	?	?	?	?	1	3	0	0	.000	.000
Vaughn, Harry Francis "Farmer" 86CinA 88–89LouA 90NYP 91CinA 91MilA 92–99CinN												
3/1/64	Ruraldale, Ohio	2/21/14	R	R	6'3	177	915	3454	946	474	.274	.365
Walker, Moses Fleetwood "Moses" "Fleet" 84TolA												
10/7/56	Mt. Pleasant, Ohio	5/11/24	R	R	?	159	42	152	40	23	.263	.316
Walker, Walter S. "Walt" 84DetN												
3/12/60	Berlin, Mich.	2/28/22	?	R	5'10½	162	1	4	1	1	.250	.250
Ward, James H.H. "Jim" 76PhiN												
3/2/55	Boston, Mass.	6/4/86	?	?	?	?	1	4	2	1	.500	.500
Warner, John Joseph "John" 95BosN 95–96LouN 96–00NYN												
8/15/72	New York, N.Y.	12/21/43	L	R	5'11	165	444	1574	412	183	.262	.307
Weber, Harry "Harry" 84IndN												
Unknown	Indianapolis, Ind.	Unknown	?	?	?	?	3	8	0	0	.000	.000
Weckbecker, Peter "Pete" 89IndA 90LouN												
8/30/64	Butler, Pa.	5/16/35	?	?	5'7	150	33	102	24	17	.235	.245
Welch, James T. "Tub" 90TolA 95LouN												
7/3/66	St. Louis, Mo.	Unknown	?	R	5'11	230	82	261	68	33	.261	.326
Wells, Jacob "Jake" 88DetN 90StLA												
8/9/63	Memphis, Tenn.	3/16/27	R	R	5'11	167	46	162	34	22	.210	.235
Whiting, Edward C. "Ed" (aka Harry Zieber) 82BalA 83–84LouA 86WasN												
?/?/60	Philadelphia, Pa.	Unknown	L	R	?	188	180	726	185	94	.255	.347
Wilson, Henry C. "Henry" 98BalN												
4/8/77	Baltimore, Md.	Unknown	?	?	?	?	1	2	0	0	.000	.000
Wilson, Parke Asel "Parke" 93–99NYN												
10/26/67	Keithsburg, Ill.	12/20/34	R	R	5'11	166	366	1266	336	194	.265	.325
Wilson, William G. "Bill" 90PitN 97–98LouN												
11/28/67	Hannibal, Mo.	5/9/24	?	R	?	?	217	787	163	78	.207	.268
Wise, Nicholas Joseph "Nick" 88BosN												
6/15/66	Boston, Mass.	1/15/23	R	R	5'11	194	1	3	0	0	.000	.000
Wolstenholme, Abraham William "Abe" 83PhiN												
3/4/61	Philadelphia, Pa.	3/4/16	?	?	?	?	3	11	1	0	.091	.182
***Wood, Fred S. "Fred" 84DetN 85BufN**												
?/?/63	Hamilton, Ont., Can.	8/23/33	?	?	5'5	150	13	46	3	4	.065	.065
Wood, Robert Lynn "Bob" 98–00CinN												
7/28/65	Thorn Hill, Ohio	5/22/43	R	R	5'8½	153	146	442	128	65	.290	.382
Wright, William Hiram "Bill" 87WasN												
Unknown	Unknown	Unknown	?	?	?	?	1	3	2	0	.667	.667
Yaik, Henry "Henry" 88PitN												
3/1/64	Detroit, Mich.	9/21/35	?	?	5'11	185	2	6	2	0	.333	.333

Catchers

BIRTH DATE	BIRTHPLACE	DEATH DATE	B	T	HGT	WGT	G	AB	H	R	BA	SA
Yeager, George J. "George" "Doc" 96–99BosN												
6/5/74	Cincinnati, Ohio	7/5/40	R	R	5'10	190	103	329	84	59	.255	.371
Zahner, Frederick Joseph "Fred" 94–95LouN												
6/5/70	Louisville, Ky.	7/24/00	?	?	?	?	34	94	20	14	.213	.266
Zearfoss, David William Tilden "Dave" 96–98NYN												
1/1/68	Schenectady, N.Y.	9/12/45	?	R	5'9	?	25	71	17	6	.239	.310
Zies, William "Bill" 91StLA												
Unknown	Unknown	Unknown	L	?	?	?	2	3	1	0	.333	.333
Zimmer, Charles Louis "Chief" 84DetN 86NYA 87–88CleA 89–99CleN 99LouN 00PitN												
11/23/60	Marietta, Ohio	8/22/49	R	R	6'	190	1132	4050	1108	578	.274	.378
Zinn, Frank "Frank" 88PhiA												
12/21/65	Phoenixville, Pa.	5/12/36	?	?	5'8	150	2	7	0	0	.000	.000

Jack Clements, the first man to catch 1,000 major league games. No lefthander since his departure has caught as many as 100 games in the majors. Clements also holds the all-time record for the highest BA in a season by a catcher.

In 1886, Doc Bushong became the first major leaguer to catch 100 games in a season. He was also the first to catch in five World's Series. Bushong's .251 career SA is the lowest of any nineteenth-century player with 2,000 or more at bats.

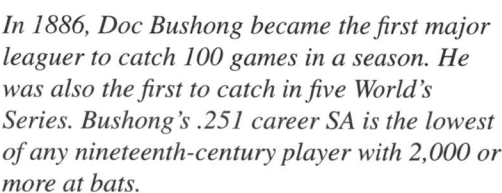

Pitchers As Hitters

Note: The pitchers in this section for the most part either were outstanding hitters or played extensively at other positions but not enough at any one position to be included in the Player Register. Some, like Tim Keefe and John Clarkson, are here to encourage the reader to examine their yearly batting performances in the Annual Record. Keefe collected an astonishing number of walks and Clarkson hit with exceptional power.

BIRTH DATE	BIRTHPLACE	DEATH DATE	B	T	HGT	WGT	G	AB	H	R	BA	SA
Baldwin, Charles Busted "Lady" 84MilU 85–88DetN 90BroN 90BufP												
4/8/59	Oramel, N.Y.	3/7/37	L	L	5'11	160	134	494	114	68	.231	.291
Barr, Robert McClelland "Bob" 83PitA 84WasA 84IndA 88WasN 90RocA 91NYN												
12/?/56	Washington, D.C.	3/11/30	R	R	6'1	192	179	633	117	61	.185	.245
Bond, Thomas Henry "Tommy" 74AtlNA 75HarNA 76HarN 77–81BosN 82WorN 84BosU 84IndA												
4/2/56	Granard, Ireland	1/24/41	R	R	5'7½	160	488	1975	471	213	.238	.277
Boyd, Jacob Henry "Jake" 94–96WasN												
1/19/74	Martinsburg, W.Va	8/12/32	?	L	?	160	61	191	46	31	.241	.293
Bradley, George Washington "George" "Grin" 75StLNA 76StLN 77ChiN 79TroN 80ProN 81DetN 81–83CleN 83PhiA 84CinU 86PhiA 88BalA												
7/13/52	Reading, Pa.	10/2/31	R	R	5'10½	175	567	2258	518	272	.229	.296
Brainard, Asa "Asa" "Count" 71–72OlyNA 72ManNA 73–74BalNA												
?/?/41	Albany, N.Y.	12/29/88	?	R	5'8½	150	108	467	116	71	.248	.272
Breitenstein, Theodore P. "Ted" "Theo" 91StLA 92–96StLN 97–00CinN												
6/1/69	St. Louis, Mo.	5/3/35	L	L	5'9	167	444	1341	289	173	.216	.267
Bresnahan, Roger Philip "Roger" 97WasN 00ChiN												
6/11/79	Toledo, Ohio	12/4/44	R	R	5'9	200	8	18	6	1	.333	.333
Buffinton, Charles G. "Charlie" 82–86BosN 87–89PhiN 90PhiP 91BosA 92BalN												
6/14/61	Fall River, Mass.	9/23/07	R	R	6'1	180	586	2214	543	245	.245	.299
Callahan, James Joseph "Nixey" 94PhiN 97–00ChiN												
3/18/74	Fitchburg, Mass.	10/4/34	R	R	5'10½	180	225	810	219	128	.270	.365
Clarkson, John Gibson "John" 82WorN 84–87ChiN 88–92BosN 92–94CleN												
7/1/61	Cambridge, Mass.	2/4/09	R	R	5'10	155	546	1974	432	254	.219	.319
Dunn, John Joseph "Jack" 97–00BroN 00PhiN												
10/6/72	Meadsville, Pa.	10/22/28	R	R	5'9	?	150	479	116	66	.242	.265
Dwyer, John Francis "Frank" 88–89ChiN 90ChiP 91CinA 91MilA 92StLN 92–99CinN												
3/25/68	Lee, Mass.	2/4/43	R	R	5'8	145	393	1249	287	178	.230	.298
Ferguson, Charles J. "Charlie" 84–87PhiN												
4/17/63	Charlottesville, Va.	4/29/88	B	R	6'	165	257	963	277	191	.288	.372
Fisher, William Charles "Cherokee" 71RokNA 72BalNA 73AthNA 74HarNA 75PhiNA 76CinN 77ChiN 78ProN												
12/?/45	Philadelphia, Pa.	9/26/12	R	R	5'9	164	252	1155	273	179	.236	.285
Flynn, John A. "Jocko" "Jackie" 86–87ChiN												
6/30/64	Lawrence, Mass.	12/30/07	?	R	5'6½	143	58	205	41	40	.200	.307
Foreman, Francis Isiah "Frank" "Monkey" 84Chi–PitU 84KCU 85BalA 89BalA 90–91CinN 91WasA 92WasN 92BalN 93NYN 95–96CinN												
5/1/63	Baltimore, Md.	11/19/57	L	L	6'	160	216	645	140	91	.217	.330
Friend, Daniel Sebastian "Danny" 95–98ChiN												
4/18/73	Cincinnati, Ohio	6/1/42	?	L	5'9	175	69	238	61	28	.256	.332

Pitchers As Hitters

BIRTH DATE	BIRTHPLACE	DEATH DATE	B	T	HGT	WGT	G	AB	H	R	BA	SA
Griffith, Clark Calvin "Clark" 91StLA 91BosA 93–00ChiN												
11/20/69	Clear Creek, Mo.	10/27/55	R	R	5'6½	156	321	1031	246	160	.239	.313
*Gumbert, Addison Courtney "Ad" 88–89ChiN 90BosP 91–92ChiN 93–94PitN 95–96BroN 96PhiN												
10/10/68	Pittsburgh, Pa.	4/23/25	R	R	5'10	200	295	955	261	155	.273	.395
Hawley, Emerson P. "Pink" 92–94StLN 95–97PitN 98–99CinN 00NYN												
12/5/72	Beaver Dam, Wis.	9/19/38	L	R	5'10	185	369	1157	278	128	.240	.344
Hudson, Nathaniel P. "Nat" 86–89StLA												
1/12/59	Chicago, Ill.	3/14/28	R	R	?	?	125	446	110	56	.247	.312
*Hughes, James Jay "Jim" "Jay" 98BalN 99BroN												
1/22/74	Sacramento, Cal.	6/2/24	R	R	?	?	87	271	64	40	.236	.343
Inks, Albert John "Bert" 91–92BroN 92WasN 94BalN 94–95LouN 96CinN 96PhiN												
1/27/71	Ligonier, Ind.	10/3/41	L	L	6'3	175	90	250	75	36	.300	.340
Keefe, Timothy John "Tim" "Sir Timothy" 80–82TroN 83–84NYA 85–89NYN 90NYP 91NYN 91–93PhiN												
1/1/57	Cambridge, Mass.	4/23/33	R	R	5'10½	185	619	2086	390	248	.187	.269
Kennedy, William P. "Brickyard" 92–00BroN												
10/7/67	Bellaire, Ohio	9/23/15	R	R	5'11	160	360	1166	302	139	.259	.331
Kissinger, William Francis "Bill" "Shang" 95BalN 95–97StLN												
8/15/71	Dayton, Ky.	4/20/29	R	R	?	185	72	214	60	24	.280	.369
Kitson, Frank L. "Frank" "Kitty" 98–99BalN 00BroN												
4/11/72	Hopkins, Mich.	4/14/30	L	R	5'11	165	119	329	86	46	.261	.331
Klobedanz, Frederick Augustus "Fred" 96–99BosN												
6/13/71	Waterbury, Conn.	4/12/40	L	L	5'11	190	107	327	90	48	.275	.413
Larkin, Frank S. "Terry" 76NYN 77HarN 78–79ChiN 80TroN 84WasU 84VirA												
Unknown	Unknown	9/16/94	R	R	?	?	240	915	215	116	.235	.303
Luby, John Perkins "Pat" 90–92ChiN 95LouN												
6/?/69	Charleston, S.C.	4/24/99	?	R	6'	185	132	430	101	66	.235	.363
Madden, Michael Joseph "Kid" 87–89BosN 90BosP 91BosA 91BalA												
10/22/66	Portland, Me.	3/16/96	?	L	5'7½	130	133	433	106	60	.243	.298
Mathews, Robert T. "Bobby" 71KekNA 72BalNA 73–75MutNA 76NYN 77CinN 79ProN 81ProN 81–82BosN 83–87PhiA												
11/21/51	Baltimore, Md.	4/17/98	R	R	5'5	140	623	2487	504	318	.203	.230
Maul, Albert Joseph "Al" "Smiling Al" 84PhiU 87PhiN 88–89PitN 90PitP 91PitN 93–97WasN 97–98BalN 99BroN 00PhiN												
10/9/65	Philadelphia, Pa.	5/3/58	R	R	6'	175	408	1369	328	192	.240	.332
Meekin, Jouett "Jouett" 91LouA 92LouN 92–93WasN 94–98NYN 99BosN 99NYN 00PitN												
2/21/67	New Albany, Ind.	12/14/44	R	R	6'1	180	338	1095	267	163	.244	.356
Menefee, John "Jock" 92PitN 93–94LouN 94–95PitN 98NYN 00ChiN												
1/15/68	Rowlesburg, W.Va.	3/11/53	R	R	6'	165	106	253	50	28	.198	.237
Mercer, George Barclay "Win" 94–99WasN 00NYN												
6/20/74	Chester, W.Va.	1/12/03	R	R	5'7	140	480	1527	445	244	.291	.353
Mountain, Frank Henry "Frank" 80TroN 81DetN 82WorN 82PhiA 82WorN 83–84ColA 85–86PitA												
5/17/60	Ft. Edward, N.Y.	11/19/39	R	R	5'11	185	194	717	158	84	.220	.333
Mullane, Anthony John "Tony" "Count" "The Apollo Of The Box" 81DetN 82LouA 83StLA 84TolA 86–89CinA 90–93CinN 93–94BalN 94CleN												
1/20/59	Cork, Ireland	4/25/44	B	B	5'10½	165	784	2720	661	407	.243	.316
Orth, Albert Lewis "Al" "The Curveless Wonder" 95–00PhiN												
9/5/72	Tipton, Ind.	10/8/48	L	R	6'	200	199	593	176	74	.297	.417

Win Mercer was just 19 years old when he posed for his first major league team picture prior to the 1894 season. Mercer was such a fine hitter and excellent all-around player that in between pitching assignments he saw frequent duty at third base and shortstop as well as in the outfield. Top: Charlie Petty, Sam Wise, Joe Mulvey, Bill Hassamaer, Bill Black, Duke Esper, Ed Cartwright and Bill Joyce. Middle: White Wings Tebeau, Ben Stephens, Deacon McGuire, manager Gus Schmelz, Otis Stocksdale, Joe Sullivan and Piggy Ward. Bottom: Kip Selbach, Rip Egan, Jack McMahon, Paul Radford, Dan Dugdale and Mercer.

Pitchers As Hitters

BIRTH DATE	BIRTHPLACE	DEATH DATE	B	T	HGT	WGT	G	AB	H	R	BA	SA
Porter, Henry "Henry" 84KCU 84MilU 85–87BroA 88–89KCA												
6/?/58	Vergennes, Vt.	12/30/06	R	R	?	?	215	782	143	80	.183	.225
Richmond, J. Lee "Lee" 79BosN 80–82WorN 83ProN 86CinA												
5/5/57	Sheffield, Ohio	10/1/29	?	L	5'10	155	251	1018	262	169	.257	.334
Rusie, Amos Wilson "Amos" "The Hoosier Thunderbolt" 89IndN 90–95NYN 97–98NYN												
5/30/71	Mooresville, Ind.	12/6/42	R	R	6'1	200	482	1718	426	208	.248	.320
Sanders, Alexander Bennett "Ben" 88–89PhiN 90PhiP 91PhiA 92LouN												
2/26/65	Catharpin, Va.	8/29/30	R	R	6'	210	247	948	257	132	.271	.366
Seymour, James Bentley "Cy" 96–00NYN												
12/9/72	Albany, N.Y.	9/20/19	L	L	6'	200	209	665	186	95	.280	.350
Sharrott, John Henry "Jack" 90–92NYN 93PhiN												
8/13/69	Bangor, Me.	12/31/27	R	R	5'9	165	96	299	71	47	.237	.321
Spalding, Albert Goodwill "Al" 71–75BosNA 76–78ChiN												
9/2/50	Byron, Ill.	9/9/15	R	R	6'1	170	401	1958	613	417	.313	.382
Stivetts, John Elmer "Jack" "Happy Jack" 89–91StLA 92–98BosN 99CleN												
3/31/68	Ashland, Pa.	4/18/30	R	R	6'2	185	601	1991	592	347	.297	.438

Pitchers As Hitters

BIRTH DATE	BIRTHPLACE	DEATH DATE	B	T	HGT	WGT	G	AB	H	R	BA	SA
Stocksdale, Otis Hinkley "Otis" "Old Gray Fox" 93–95WasN 95BosN 96BalN												
8/7/71	Arcadia, Md.	3/15/33	L	R	5'10½	180	68	203	63	33	.310	.384
Stratton, C. Scott "Scott" 88–90LouA 91PitN 91LouA 92–94LouN 94ChiN 95ChiN												
10/2/69	Campbellsburg, Ky.	3/8/39	L	R	6'	180	389	1383	379	201	.274	.364
Sweeney, Charles J. "Charlie" 82–84ProN 84StLU 85–86StLN 87CleA												
4/13/63	San Francisco, Cal.	4/4/02	R	R	5'10½	181	233	894	224	117	.251	.317
*Tannehill, Jesse Niles "Jesse" "Powder" 94CinN 97–00PitN												
7/14/74	Dayton, Ky.	9/22/56	B	L	5'8	150	202	589	164	83	.278	.360
Taylor, John Budd "Jack" "Brewery Jack" 91NYN 92–97PhiN 98StLN 99CinN												
5/23/73	W. New Brighton, N.Y.	2/7/00	R	R	6'1	190	286	927	234	100	.252	.335
Taylor, William Henry "Billy" "Bollicky Billy" 81WorN 81DetN 81CleN 82–83PitA 84StLU 84–85PhiA 86BalA 87PhiA												
?/?/55	Washington, D.C.	5/14/00	R	R	5'11½	204	274	1164	323	148	.277	.393
Terry, William H. "Adonis" 84–89BroA 90–91BroN 92BalN 92–94PitN 94–97ChiN												
8/7/64	Westfield, Mass.	2/24/15	R	R	5'11½	168	667	2389	594	314	.249	.344
Toole, Stephen John "Steve" 86–87BroA 88KCA 90BroA												
4/9/59	New Orleans, La.	3/28/19	R	L	6'	170	59	228	60	34	.263	.360
Weidman, George E. "Stump" b. Wiedman 80BufN 81–85DetN 86KCN 87DetN 87NYA 87–88NYN												
2/17/61	Rochester, N.Y.	3/2/05	R	R	5'7½	165	379	1401	248	132	.177	.207
Whitney, James Evans "Jim" "Grasshopper" 81–85BosN 86KCN 87–88WasN 89IndN 90PhiA												
11/10/57	Conklin, N.Y.	5/21/91	L	R	6'2	172	550	2144	559	316	.261	.375
Yeager, Joseph F. "Joe" "Little Joe" 98–00BroN												
8/28/75	Philadelphia, Pa.	7/2/37	R	R	5'10	160	69	190	35	24	.184	.232

In 1894, Jack Stivetts compiled 26 wins, 80 hits and a .533 slugging average. No other performer since 1893—not even Babe Ruth—has been both a 20-game winner and so potent a hitter in the same season.

EXPLANATION OF THE PITCHER REGISTER

The pitcher register contains the vital statistics and the six central pitching statistics of every man who pitched in a major league game between 1871 and 1900. Men who played more than half their games at another position besides pitcher or who compiled significant career batting statistics can also be found in one of the player subregisters. However, a man in the pitcher register who also played other positions but spent only one season in the major leagues as a rule does not appear in a player subregister since all of his central career batting statistics are available in the Annual Record section under the team or teams for which he played.

The men in the pitcher register are listed alphabetically by surname and, if two or more players bear the same surname, by given name—i.e., **Sullivan, Michael Joseph** is found ahead of **Sullivan, Thomas**, and **Sullivan, Thomas** is, in turn, ahead of **Sullivan, Thomas Jefferson**. In quotation marks following a pitcher's given name is the name or names he was known by in the nineteenth century. Christy Mathewson, for instance, was called "Matty" as a rookie in 1900 but was not dubbed "The Big Six" until several years later. Hence there is no mention in the pitcher register of his most famous nickname. When a man played under a name other than his name at birth, his playing name is followed by the part of his birth name that differed from it—in most cases his surname only.

Following the name of each pitcher is a chronological list of the teams for which he played. See the sample player, **James J. Lillie**, for an explanation of the year abbreviations.

Vital Statistics—birth date and birthplace, death date, height, weight, batted, threw—are furnished when known. Gaps in information are indicated either by question marks or by the word "Unknown." Since our knowledge of nineteenth-century baseball is still growing, we expect to eliminate some—if not all—of the gaps in future editions.

BIRTH DATE	BIRTHPLACE	DEATH DATE	B	T	HGT	WGT	G	INN	K	W	L	PCT
Lillie, James J. "Jim" "Grasshopper" b. Lilly			83–84BufN		86KCN	(See OF)						
7/27/61	New Haven, Conn.	11/9/90	?	?	?	?	6	31	8	0	2	.000

In the above sample from the pitcher register, we see first the player's surname of Lillie, then his given first and middle names (only Lillie's middle initial is known) followed in quotation marks by the two names he was usually called in order of dominance and last the name under which he was born. Since only Lillie's birth surname differed from the name under which he played, his first name and middle initial are not repeated. Following Lillie's birth name is a chronological list of his major league seasons as a pitcher and the teams for which he pitched. Although Lillie pitched in only six games, there is more to his major league career. The parenthetical note in bold (**See OF**) indicates that Lillie also was an outfielder and his batting record and a complete chronological list of his major league seasons is found in the Outfielders subregister. Other parenthetical position abbreviations that appear in bold in the pitcher register are: 1B=first basemen; 2B=second basemen; SS=shortstops; 3B=third basemen; C=catchers; and P=pitchers as hitters. See below for a list of the team and league abbreviations that follow the year numerals.

Lillie's playing career is followed by his birth date. Next is his place of birth followed by his death date. We then find that the way Lillie batted and threw as well as his height and weight are still unknown. His major league service as a pitcher consisted of six games in which he pitched 31 innings, struck out eight and lost his only two decisions. *The Great Encyclopedia of Nineteenth-Century Major League Baseball* selects strikeouts rather than ERA as a central career pitching statistic in part because strikeout data from the nineteenth century is much less speculative than ERA data but more because we believe strikeout totals in the nineteenth century were less influenced by the quality of the teams for which a pitcher played and thus are more reflective of his performance.

Lillie was primarily an outfielder. Here is an example from the pitcher register of a man who was primarily a pitcher but played one season exclusively at another position, followed by an explanation of how this is shown.

BIRTH DATE	BIRTHPLACE	DEATH DATE	B	T	HGT	WGT	G	INN	K	W	L	PCT
Becannon, James Melvin "Buck" 84–85NYA (87NYN)												
8/22/59	New York, N.Y.	11/5/23	?	?	5'10	165	11	91	15	3	8	.273

In 1884 and 1885 Becannon was exclusively a pitcher. After a career gap in 1886, Becannon returned to the majors in 1887. The (87NYN) in parentheses indicates that he did not pitch in 1887 but played another position. Since his playing time was minimal—in this case only one game at third base—his record for 1887 does not appear in the Third Basemen's subregister since it is available in its entirety in the Annual Record.

Following the last two numerals of the year in which a man played is an abbreviation of the city where his team resided. The abbreviations follow:

Alt	Altoona		**Mut**	New York Mutuals (NA)
Ath	Philadelphia Athletics (NA)		**Nat**	Washington Nationals (NA)
Atl	Brooklyn Atlantics (NA)		**NH**	New Haven (NA)
Bal	Baltimore		**NY**	New York
Bos	Boston		**Oly**	Washington Olympics (NA)
Bro	Brooklyn		**Phi**	Philadelphia
Buf	Buffalo		**Pit**	Pittsburgh
Cen	Philadelphia Centennials (NA)		**Pro**	Providence
Chi	Chicago		**Reds**	St. Louis Reds (NA)
Cin	Cincinnati		**Res**	Elizabeth Resolutes (NA)
Cle	Cleveland		**Roc**	Rochester
Col	Columbus		**Rok**	Rockford (NA)
Det	Detroit		**StL**	St. Louis
Eck	Brooklyn Eckfords (NA)		**StP**	St. Paul
Har	Hartford		**Syr**	Syracuse
Ind	Indianapolis		**Tol**	Toledo
KC	Kansas City		**Tro**	Troy
Kek	Fort Wayne Kekiongas (NA)		**Vir**	Virginia
Lou	Louisville		**Was**	Washington
Man	Middletown Mansfields (NA)		**Wes**	Keokuk Westerns (NA)
Mar	Maryland (NA)		**Wil**	Wilmington
Mil	Milwaukee		**Wor**	Worchester

Following the year and team information is the symbol for the league:

NA	National Association (1871–75)
N	National League (1876–1900)
A	American Association (1882–91)
U	Union Association (1884)
P	Players League (1890)

Note: To simplify the reader's task in following a career line, teams in the player, pitcher and manager registers are designated N during the 1892–99 period when the National League was officially known as the National League and American Association, although elsewhere in the book, when a specific season or achievement is cited, these teams are designated LA.

Other symbols:
*   prior to a pitcher's name indicates that he had a brother or brothers who also played in the major leagues, although not always in the nineteenth century.
\#   prior to a pitcher's name indicates that he had a son or sons who also played in the major leagues, in every case in the twentieth century.

BIRTH DATE	BIRTHPLACE	DEATH DATE	B	T	HGT	WGT	G	INN	K	W	L	PCT
Abbey, Bert Wood "Bert" 92Was 93–95ChiN 95–96BroN												
11/29/69	Essex, Vt.	6/11/62	R	R	5'11	175	79	568	161	22	40	.355
Abbey, Charles S. "Charlie" 96WasN (See OF)												
10/14/66	Falls City, Neb.	4/27/26	L	?	5'8	169	1	2	0	0	0	—
Abbott, Leander Franklin "Dan" 90TolA												
3/16/62	Portage, Ohio	2/13/30	R	R	5'11	190	3	13	1	0	2	.000
Allen, Myron Smith "Myron" "Zeke" 83NYN 87CleA 88KCA (See OF)												
3/22/54	Kingston, N.Y.	3/8/24	R	R	5'8	150	5	35.2	3	1	3	.250
*Allison, Douglas L. "Doug" 78ProN (See C)												
7/?/45	Philadelphia, Pa.	12/19/16	R	R	5'11	160	1	5	0	0	0	—
Altrock, Nicholas "Nick" 98LouN												
9/15/76	Cincinnati, Ohio	1/20/65	B	L	5'10	197	11	70	13	3	3	.500
Amole, Morris George "Doc" 97BalN 98WasN												
7/5/78	Coatesville, Pa.	3/7/12	R	L	5'9	165	18	119.1	30	4	10	.286
Anderson, David S. "Dave" 89–90PhiN 90PitN												
10/10/68	Chester, Pa.	3/22/97	?	L	?	?	21	150.1	56	3	13	.188
Anderson, Varney Small "Varney" "Varn" 89IndN 94–96WasN (See P)												
6/18/66	Geneva, Ill.	11/5/41	R	R	5'10	165	35	239.2	41	9	20	.310
Andrus, Frederick Hotham "Fred" 84ChiN (See OF)												
8/23/50	Washington, Mich	11/10/37	R	R	6'2	185	1	9	2	1	0	1.000
Anson, Adrian Constantine "Cap" "Pop" 83–84ChiN (See 1B)												
4/11/52	Marshalltown, Iowa	4/14/22	R	R	6'	227	3	4	1	0	1	.000
Arundel, Harry "Harry" 75AtlNA 82PitA 84ProN												
2/?/55	Philadelphia, Pa.	3/25/04	R	R	5'6	145	16	130.1	51	5	11	.313
Atkinson, Albert Wright "Al" 84PhiA 84Chi–PitU 84BalU 86–87PhiA												
3/9/61	Clinton, Ill.	6/17/52	R	R	5'11½	165	106	915	435	51	51	.500
Aydelott, Jacob Stuart "Jake" 84IndA 86PhiA												
7/6/61	N. Manchester, Ind.	10/22/26	?	?	6'	180	14	124	35	5	9	.357
Bailey, Harvey Francis "Harvey" 99–00BosN												
11/24/76	Adrian, Mich.	7/10/22	?	L	6'	160	16	106.2	35	6	4	.600
Bailey, Linwood C. "King" 95CinN												
11/?/70	?, Virginia	11/19/17	L	L	6'	185	1	9	0	1	0	1.000
Bakely, Edward Enoch "Jersey" b. Bakeley 83PhiA 84PhiU 84WilU 84KCU 88CleA 89CleN 90CleP 91WasA 91BalA												
4/17/64	Blackwood, N.J.	2/17/15	R	R	?	?	215	1782.2	669	76	125	.378
Baker, Kirtley "Kirtley" "Whitey" 90PitN 93–94BalN 98–99WasN												
6/24/69	Aurora, Ind.	4/15/27	R	R	5'9	160	58	371	115	9	38	.191
Baker, Norman Leslie "Norm" 83PitA 85LouA 90BalA												
10/14/62	Philadelphia, Pa.	2/20/49	?	?	?	?	30	253	94	14	15	.483
Baldwin, Charles Busted "Lady" 84MilU 85–88DetN 90BroN 90BufP (See P)												
4/8/59	Oramel, N.Y.	3/7/37	L	L	5'11	160	118	1017	582	73	41	.640
Baldwin, Clarence Geoghan "Kid" 85CinA (See C)												
11/1/64	Newport, Ky.	7/10/97	R	R	5'6	147	2	4	1	0	0	—
Baldwin, Marcus Elmore "Mark" "Fido" 87–88ChiN 89ColA 90ChiP 91–93PitN 93NYN												
10/29/63	Pittsburgh, Pa.	11/10/29	R	R	6'	190	347	2811.1	1354	156	165	.486

BIRTH DATE	BIRTHPLACE	DEATH DATE	B	T	HGT	WGT	G	INN	K	W	L	PCT
Banks, William John "Bill" b. Yerrick 95–96BosN												
2/26/74	Danville, Pa.	9/8/36	R	R	5'11	150	5	30	10	1	3	.750
*Bannon, James Henry "Jimmy" "Foxy Grandpa" 93StLN 94–95BosN (See OF)												
5/5/71	Amesbury, Mass.	3/24/48	R	R	5'5	160	3	9	2	0	1	.000
Barnes, Roscoe Charles "Ross" 76ChiN (See 2B)												
5/8/50	Mt. Morris, Ill.	2/5/15	R	R	5'8½	145	1	1.1	0	0	0	—
Barr, Robert McClelland "Bob" 83PitA 84WasA 84IndA 86WasN 90RocA 91NYN (See P)												
12/?/56	Washington, D.C.	3/11/30	R	R	6'1	192	159	1328.1	588	49	98	.333
Bartson, Charles Franklin "Charlie" 90ChiP												
3/13/65	Peoria, Ill.	6/9/36	?	?	6'	170	25	188	47	8	10	.444
Bastian, Charles J. "Charlie" 84WilU (See SS)												
7/4/60	Philadelphia, Pa.	1/18/32	R	R	5'6½	145	1	6	2	0	0	—
Bates, Creed Frank "Frank" 98CleN 99StLN 99CleN												
Unknown	Chattanooga, Tenn.	Unknown	?	?	?	?	26	190.2	18	3	19	.136
Bates, John William "John" 89KCA												
5/28/68	?, Ohio	3/24/19	?	?	?	?	1	8	3	0	1	.000
Battin, Joseph V. "Joe" 77StLN 83PitA (See 3B)												
11/11/51	Philadelphia, Pa.	12/10/37	R	R	?	?	3	7.2	1	0	0	—
Bauers, Albert J. "Al" 84ColA 86StLN												
?/?/50	Columbus, Ohio	9/6/13	?	L	?	?	7	53.2	26	1	6	.143
Bausewine, George W. "George" 89PhiA												
3/22/69	Philadelphia, Pa.	7/29/47	?	?	6'2	207	7	55.1	18	1	4	.200
Beam, Alexander Rogers "Alex" 89PitN												
11/21/70	Johnstown, Pa.	4/17/38	?	?	?	?	2	18	1	1	1	.500
Beam, Ernest Joseph "Ernie" 95PhiN												
3/17/67	Mansfield, Ohio	9/12/18	?	R	6'1½	185	9	24.2	3	0	2	.000
Beatin, Ebenezer Ambrose "Eb" 87–88DetN 89–91CleN												
8/10/66	Baltimore, Md.	5/9/25	R	L	5'9	162	109	946	335	48	56	.462
Becannon, James Melvin "Buck" 84–85NYA (87NYN)												
8/22/59	New York, N.Y.	11/5/23	?	?	5'10	165	11	91	15	3	8	.273
Bechtel, George A. "George" 71AthNA 73–74PhiNA 75CenNA 75AthNA (See OF)												
?/?/48	Philadelphia, Pa.	Unknown	?	?	5'11	165	30	243	10	7	20	.259
Beck, Frank J. "Frank" b. Hengstebeck 84PitA 84BalU												
4/29/60	Poughkeepsie, N.Y.	2/8/41	?	R	5'9	141	5	34	18	0	5	.000
Becker, Robert Charles "Bob" 97–98PhiN												
8/15/75	Syracuse, N.Y.	10/11/51	?	L	?	?	6	29	10	0	2	.000
Beecher, Edward H. "Ed" "Harry" 90BufP (See OF)												
7/2/60	Guilford, Conn.	9/12/35	L	L	5'10	185	1	6	0	0	0	—
Begley, Edward N. "Ed" b. Bagley 84NYN 85NYA												
?/?/63	New York, N.Y.	7/24/19	?	?	?	?	46	381	148	16	27	.372
Bell, Charles C. "Charlie" 89KCA 91LouA 91CinA												
8/12/68	Cincinnati, Ohio	2/7/37	?	R	?	?	12	95	20	4	6	.400
Bentley, Clytus G. "Cy" 72ManNA												
11/23/50	East Haven, Conn.	2/26/73	?	?	?	?	18	149	5	2	15	.118
Bernhard, William Henry "Bill" "Strawberry Bill" 99–00PhiN												
3/16/71	Clarence, N.Y.	3/30/49	B	R	6'1	205	53	341	72	21	16	.568

BIRTH DATE	BIRTHPLACE	DEATH DATE	B	T	HGT	WGT	G	INN	K	W	L	PCT
Bickham, Daniel Denison "Dan" 86CinA												
10/31/64	Dayton, Ohio	3/3/51	R	R	5'10	160	1	9	6	1	0	1.000
Bierbauer, Louis W. "Lou" 86–88PhiA (See 2B)												
9/28/65	Erie, Pa.	1/31/26	L	R	5'8	140	4	14.2	5	0	0	—
Bishop, William Robinson "Bill" 86PitA 87PitN 89ChiN												
12/27/69	Adamsburg, Pa.	12/15/32	?	?	?	?	7	47	9	0	4	.000
Black, Robert Benjamin "Bob" 84KCU												
12/10/62	Cincinnati, Ohio	3/21/33	?	?	5'5	155	16	123	93	4	9	.308
Blackburn, George W. "George" "Smiling George" 97BalN												
9/21/71	Ozark, Mo.	Unknown	?	R	5'11	184	5	33	1	2	2	.500
Blair, William Ellsworth "Bill" 88PhiA												
9/17/63	Pittsburgh, Pa.	2/22/90	L	L	5'8½	172	4	31	16	1	3	.250
Blaisdell, Howard Carleton "Dick" 84KCU												
6/18/62	Bradford, Mass.	8/20/86	?	?	?	?	3	26	8	0	3	.000
Blank, Frederick August "Fred" 94CinN												
6/18/74	DeSoto, Mo.	2/5/36	L	L	6'1½	175	1	8	1	0	1	.000
Blauvelt, Henry Russell "Henry" 90RocA												
4/8/73	Nyack, N.Y.	12/28/26	?	?	?	?	2	12.1	5	0	0	—
Blong, Joseph Myles "Joe" 75RedsNA 76–77StL (See OF)												
9/17/53	St. Louis, Mo.	9/16/92	R	R	?	?	41	320.1	65	13	21	.382
Bohn, Charles "Charlie" 82LouA												
?/?/51	Cleveland, Ohio	8/1/03	R	R	5'9	165	2	18	1	1	1	.500
Bond, Thomas Henry "Tommy" 74AtlNA 75HarNA 76HarN 77–81BosN 82WorN 84BosU 84IndA (See P)												
4/2/56	Granard, Ireland	1/24/41	R	R	5'7½	160	417	3628.2	969	234	163	.589
Boone, George Morris "George" 91LouA												
3/1/71	Louisville, Ky.	9/24/10	?	?	?	?	4	15	4	0	0	—
Booth, Amos Smith "Amos" "Darling" 76–77CinN (See C)												
9/14/53	Cincinnati, Ohio	7/1/21	R	R	5'9	159	15	95.2	18	1	8	.111
Booth, Edward H. "Eddie" 76NYN (See OF)												
Unknown	Brooklyn, N.Y.	Unknown	?	?	?	?	1	5	0	0	0	—
Borchers, George Benard "George" "Chief" 88ChiN 95LouN												
4/18/69	Sacramento, Cal.	10/24/38	B	R	5'10	180	11	67.2	26	4	5	.444
Borden, Joseph Emley "Joe" (aka Joseph Emley Josephs) 75PhiNA 76BosN												
5/9/54	Jacobstown, N.J.	10/14/29	R	R	5'9	140	36	284.1	43	13	16	.448
Boswell, Andrew Cottrell "Andy" 95NYN 95WasN												
9/5/74	New Gretna, N.J.	2/3/36	?	R	6'1	165	11	64	30	3	4	.429
Bowen, Sutherland McCoy "Cy" 96NYN												
2/17/71	Kingston, Ind.	1/25/25	R	R	6'	175	2	12	3	0	1	.000
Bowman, Sumner Sallade "Sumner" 90PhiN 90PitN 91PhiA												
2/9/67	Millersburg, Pa.	1/11/54	L	L	6'	160	18	146.2	46	4	10	.286
Boyd, Jacob Henry "Jake" 94–96WasN (See P)												
1/19/74	Martinsburg, W.Va.	8/12/32	?	L	?	160	21	136.1	25	3	16	.158
Boyd, William J. "Bill" 75AtlNA (See OF)												
12/22/52	New York, N.Y.	9/30/12	?	?	?	?	1	1.2	0	0	0	—
Boyle, Henry J. "Henry" "Handsome Henry" 84StLU 85–86StLN 87–89IndN												
9/20/60	Philadelphia, Pa.	5/25/32	?	R	?	?	207	1756.1	602	89	111	.445

BIRTH DATE	BIRTHPLACE	DEATH DATE	B	T	HGT	WGT	G	INN	K	W	L	PCT
Bradley, George H. **"Foghorn"** 76BosN												
7/1/55	Milford, Mass.	4/3/00	R	R	?	?	22	173.1	16	9	10	.474
Bradley, George Washington **"George"** **"Grin"** 75StLNA 76StLN 77ChiN 79TroN 80ProN (81DetN) 81–82CleN												
(83CleN) 83PhiA 84CinU (86PhiA) (88BalA) (See P)												
7/13/52	Reading, Pa.	10/2/31	R	R	5'10½	175	347	2940	671	171	151	.531
Brainard, Asa **"Asa"** **"Count"** 71–72OlyNA 72ManNA 73–74BalNA (See P)												
?/?/41	Albany, N.Y.	12/29/88	?	R	5'8½	150	85	699.2	44	24	53	.312
*Brashear, Norman C. **"Kitty"** 99LouN												
8/27/77	Mansfield, Ohio	12/22/34	R	R	?	?	3	8	5	1	0	1.000
Breitenstein, Alonzo **"Alonzo"** 83PhiN												
11/9/57	Utica, N.Y.	6/19/32	?	?	?	?	1	5	0	0	1	.000
Breitenstein, Theodore P. **"Ted"** **"Theo"** 91StLA 92–96StLN 97–00CinN (See P)												
6/1/69	St. Louis, Mo.	5/3/35	L	L	5'9	167	376	2949.1	886	160	167	.489
Bresnahan, Roger Philip **"Roger"** 97WasN (See P)												
6/11/79	Toledo, Ohio	12/4/44	R	R	5'9	200	6	41	12	4	0	1.000
Briggs, Herbert Theodore **"Buttons"** 96–98ChiN												
7/8/75	Poughkeepsie, N.Y.	2/18/11	R	R	6'1	180	52	410.2	158	17	28	.378
Brill, Francis Hasbrouck **"Frank"** b. Briell 84DetN												
3/30/64	Astoria, N.Y.	11/19/44	R	R	5'8	155	12	103	18	2	10	.167
Britt, James Edward **"Jim"** 72–73AtlNA												
2/25/56	Brooklyn, N.Y.	2/28/23	?	?	?	?	91	816.2	28	26	64	.289
Brooks, Harry Frank **"Harry"** 86NYA												
11/30/65	Philadelphia, Pa.	12/5/45	?	?	?	?	1	2	0	0	1	.000
Brouthers, Dennis Joseph **"Dan"** **"Big Dan"** 79TroN 83BufN (See 1B)												
5/8/58	Sylvan Lake, N.Y.	8/2/32	L	L	6'2	207	4	23	8	0	2	.000
Brown, Charles E. **"Charlie"** 97CleN												
?/?/78	Baltimore, Md.	Unknown	?	L	?	?	4	24.1	8	1	2	.333
Brown, Edward P. **"Ed"** 82StLA 84TolA (See 3B)												
Unknown	Chicago, Ill.	Unknown	?	R	?	180	2	11	2	0	1	.000
Brown, James W.H. **"Jim"** 84AltU 84NYN 84StPU 86PhiA												
12/12/60	Clinton Co., Pa.	4/6/08	?	?	?	?	19	127.1	65	2	15	.118
Brown, John J. **"John"** **"Ad"** 97BroN												
Unknown	Trenton, N.J.	Unknown	?	?	?	?	1	5	0	0	1	.000
Brown, Joseph E. **"Joe"** 84ChiN 85BalA												
4/4/59	Warren, Pa.	6/28/88	?	?	5'10	162	11	88	36	4	6	.400
Brown, Lewis J. **"Lew"** **"Blower"** 78ProN 84BosU (See C)												
2/1/58	Leominster, Mass.	1/16/89	R	R	5'10½	185	2	2	0	0	0	—
Brown, Richard P. **"Stub"** 93–94BalN 97CinN												
8/3/70	Baltimore, Md.	3/11/48	?	L	6'2	220	13	71.2	10	4	1	.800
Brown, Thomas Tarlton **"Tom"** 82BalA 83–84ColA 85–86PitA (See OF)												
9/21/60	Liverpool, England	10/25/27	L	R	5'10	168	12	49.1	16	2	2	.500
Browning, Lewis Rogers **"Pete"** **"The Gladiator"** 84LouA (See OF)												
6/17/61	Louisville, Ky.	9/10/05	R	R	6'	180	1	0.1	0	0	1	.000
Brynan, Charles Ruley **"Tod"** 88ChiN 91BosN												
7/?/63	Philadelphia, Pa.	5/10/25	R	R	?	?	4	26	11	2	2	.500
Buckingham, Edward Taylor **"Ed"** 95WasN												
5/12/74	Metuchen, N.J.	7/30/42	?	?	?	?	1	3	1	0	0	—

BIRTH DATE	BIRTHPLACE	DEATH DATE	B	T	HGT	WGT	G	INN	K	W	L	PCT
Buckley, John Edward "John" 90BufP												
3/20/69	Marlborough, Mass.	5/3/42	L	R	6'1	200	4	34	4	1	3	.250
Buffinton, Charles G. "Charlie" 82–86BosN 87–89PhiN 90PhiP 91BosA 92BalN (See P)												
6/14/61	Fall River, Mass.	9/23/07	R	R	6'1	180	414	3404	1700	232	152	.604
Burdick, William Byron "Bill" 88–89IndN												
10/11/59	Austin, Minn.	10/23/49	R	R	?	?	30	221.2	71	12	14	.462
Burke, James "James" 82–83BufN 84BosU												
Unknown	Attleboro, Mass.	Unknown	?	?	?	?	40	334	256	19	16	.543
Burke, William R. "Bill" 87DetN												
11/?/65	Cincinnati, Ohio	3/17/39	?	?	6'	200	2	15	3	0	1	.000
Burkett, Jesse Cail "Jesse" "Crab" 90NYN 94CleN (See OF)												
12/4/68	Wheeling, W. Va.	5/27/53	L	L	5'8	155	22	122	82	3	10	.231
Burns, Richard Simon "Dick" 83DetN 84CinA 85StLN (See OF)												
12/26/63	Holyoke, Mass.	11/16/37	L	L	5'7	140	58	460.1	199	25	27	.481
Burns, Thomas Everett "Tom" 80ChiN (See 2B)												
3/30/57	Honesdale, Pa.	3/19/02	R	R	5'7	152	1	1.1	1	0	0	—
Burns, Thomas P. "Oyster" 84–85BalA 87–88BalA (See OF)												
9/6/64	Philadelphia, Pa.	11/11/28	R	R	5'8	183	25	138.2	40	8	5	.615
Burrell, Harry J. "Harry" 91StLA												
5/26/69	Bethel, Vt.	12/11/14	R	R	?	?	7	43	19	4	2	.667
Burris, Alva Burton "Al" 94PhiN												
1/20/74	Warwick, Md.	3/24/38	R	R	?	?	1	5	0	0	0	—
Buttery, Frank "Frank" 72ManNA (See 3B)												
5/13/51	Silvermine, Conn.	12/16/02	?	?	?	?	7	54	0	3	2	.600
Cady, Charles B. "Charlie" 83CleN 84Chi–PitU (84KCU)												
12/?/65	Chicago, Ill.	6/7/09	?	?	5'11	180	5	43	20	3	2	.600
Cahill, John Patrick Parnell "Patsy" 84ColA 86StLN 87IndN (See OF)												
4/30/65	San Francisco, Cal.	10/31/01	R	R	5'7½	168	10	50	8	2	2	.500
Callahan, William T. "Will" (aka Calihan) 90RocA 91PhiA												
?/?/69	Oswego, N.Y.	12/20/17	?	?	5'8	150	50	408.1	155	24	21	.533
Callahan, James Joseph "Nixey" 94PhiN 97–00ChiN (See P)												
3/18/74	Fitchburg, Mass.	10/4/34	R	R	5'10½	180	130	792	288	67	49	.578
Callahan, James W. "Jim" 98StLN												
Unknown	Moberly, Mo.	Unknown	?	?	?	?	2	8.1	2	0	2	.000
*Camp, Winfield Scott "Kid" 92PitN 94ChiN												
?/?/70	Columbus, Ohio	3/2/95	?	R	6'	160	7	45	12	0	2	.000
*Campbell, Hugh F. "Hugh" 73ResNA												
?/?/50	?, Ireland	3/1/81	?	?	?	?	19	165	5	2	16	.111
Campfield, William Holton "Sal" 96NYN												
2/19/68	Meadville, Pa.	5/16/52	R	R	6'½	?	6	27	6	1	1	.500
Carrick, William Martin "Bill" "Doughnut Bill" 98–00NYN												
9/5/73	Erie, Pa.	3/7/32	?	R	?	?	94	443	133	38	50	.432
Carsey, Wilfred "Kid" 91WasA 92–97PhiN 97–98StLN 99CleN 99WasN (99NYN)												
10/22/70	New York, N.Y.	3/29/60	L	R	5'7	168	292	2215	480	115	138	.455
Caruthers, Robert Lee "Bob" 84–87StLA 88–89BroA 90–91BroN 92StLN (See OF)												
1/5/64	Memphis, Tenn.	8/5/11	L	R	5'7	138	340	2828.2	900	218	99	.688
*Casey, Daniel Maurice "Dan" 84WilU 85DetN 86–89PhiN 90SyrA												
11/20/62	Binghampton, N.Y.	2/8/43	R	L	6'	180	201	1680.1	743	96	90	.516

BIRTH DATE	BIRTHPLACE	DEATH DATE	B	T	HGT	WGT	G	INN	K	W	L	PCT
Casey, William B. "Bill" 87PhiA												
Unknown	St. Louis, Mo.	Unknown	?	?	?	?	1	1	0	0	0	—
Cassian, Edwin "Ed" 91PhiN 91WasA												
Unknown	?, Connecticut	Unknown	?	R	5'8½	160	13	91	24	3	7	.300
Cassidy, John P. "John" 75AtlNA 77HarN (See OF)												
?/?/57	Brooklyn, N.Y.	7/2/91	R	L	5'8	168	32	231.2	11	2	22	.083
Cattanach, John Leckie "John" 84ProN 84StLU												
5/10/63	Providence, R.I.	11/10/26	?	?	5'10	190	3	22	15	1	1	.500
Chamberlain, Elton P. "Elton" "Icebox" 86–88LouA 88–90StLA 90ColA 91PhiA 92–94CinN 96CleN												
11/5/67	Buffalo, N.Y.	9/22/29	R	B	5'9	168	321	2521.2	1133	157	120	.567
Chambers, Richard Jerome "Rome" 00BosN												
8/31/75	Weaverville, N.C.	8/30/02	L	L	6'2	173	1	4	2	0	0	—
Chapman, Frederick Joseph "Fred" 87PhiA												
11/14/72	Little Cooley, Pa.	12/14/57	R	R	5'8	165	1	5	4	0	0	—
Chatterton, James M "Jim" 84KCU (See OF)												
10/14/64	Brooklyn, N.Y.	12/15/44	?	?	?	?	1	5	2	0	0	—
Chesbro, John Dwight "Jack" "Happy Jack" 99–00PitN												
6/5/74	N. Adams, Mass.	11/6/31	R	R	5'9	180	51	264.2	84	21	22	.488
Childers, William "Bill" 95LouN												
Unknown	St. Louis, Mo.	Unknown	?	?	?	?	1	0	0	0	0	—
Clack, Robert S. "Bobby" b. Clark 76CinA (See OF)												
6/?/50	?, England	10/22/33	R	R	5'9	153	1	2	0	0	0	—
Clark, Edward C. "Ed" 86PhiA 91ColA												
Unknown	Cincinnati, Ohio	Unknown	?	?	?	?	2	10	3	0	1	.000
Clark, Owen F. "Spider" 90CleN (See OF)												
9/16/67	Brooklyn, N.Y.	2/8/92	?	R	5'10	150	1	4	2	0	0	—
Clarke, Henry Tefft "Henry" 97CleN 98ChiN												
8/28/75	Bellevue, Neb.	3/28/50	R	R	?	?	6	39.2	4	1	4	.200
Clarke, William H. "Dad" 88ChiN 91ColA 94–97NYN 97–98LouN												
1/7/65	Oswego, N.Y.	6/3/11	B	R	?	?	120	848.1	174	44	51	.463
***Clarkson, Arthur Hamilton "Dad" 91NYN 92BosN 93–95StLN 95–96BalN**												
8/31/66	Cambridge, Mass.	2/5/11	R	R	5'10	165	96	704.2	133	39	39	.500
***Clarkson, John Gibson "John" 82WorN 84–87ChiN 88–92BosN 92–94CleN (See P)**												
7/1/61	Cambridge, Mass.	2/4/09	R	R	5'10	155	531	4536.1	1978	328	178	.648
Clausen, Frederick William "Fritz" 92–93LouN 93–94ChiN 96LouN												
4/26/69	New York, N.Y.	2/11/60	R	L	5'11	190	42	324.1	134	16	22	.421
Clinton, James Lawrence "Jim" "Big Jim" 75AtlNA 76LouN (See OF)												
8/10/50	New York, N.Y.	9/3/21	R	R	5'8½	174	18	133	8	1	14	.067
Cobb, George Woodworth "George" 92BalN												
9/25/65	Independence, La.	8/19/26	?	?	6'	168	53	394.1	159	10	37	.213
Cogan, Richard Henry "Dick" 97BalN 99ChiN 00NYN												
12/5/71	Paterson, N.J.	5/2/48	R	R	5'7	150	8	54	10	2	3	.400
Colcolough, Thomas Bernard "Tom" 93–95PitN 99NYN												
10/8/70	Charleston, S.C.	12/10/19	R	R	5'10½	180	47	309.1	65	14	11	.560
Coleman, John "John" 90PhiN												
Unknown	Bristol, Pa.	Unknown	?	R	?	?	1	1.2	2	0	1	.000
Coleman, John "John" 95StLN												
?/?/74	Lee's Summit, Mo.	Unknown	?	L	5'10	174	1	8	5	0	1	.000

BIRTH DATE	BIRTHPLACE	DEATH DATE	B	T	HGT	WGT	G	INN	K	W	L	PCT
Coleman, John Francis "John"		83–84PhiN	84–86PhiA	89PhiA	90PitN	(See OF)						
3/6/63	Saratoga Springs, N.Y.	5/31/22	L	R	5'9½	170	107	842.2	224	23	72	.242
Coleman, Pierce D. "Percy"		97StLN	98CinN									
10/15/76	Mason, Ohio	2/16/48	?	R	?	?	13	66.1	12	1	3	.250
Colliflower, James Harry "Harry" "Collie"		99CleN										
3/11/69	Petersville, Md.	8/12/61	L	L	5'11½	175	14	98	8	1	11	.083
Collins, Daniel Thomas "Dan"		74ChiNA	(See OF)									
7/12/54	St. Louis, Mo.	9/21/83	?	?	?	?	2	11	0	1	1	.500
Comiskey, Charles Albert "Charlie" "Commie"		82StLA	84StLA	89StLA	(See 1B)							
8/15/59	Chicago, Ill.	10/26/31	R	R	6'	180	4	12.1	6	0	1	.000
Conley, Edward J. "Ed"		84ProN										
7/10/64	Sandwich, Mass.	10/16/94	?	?	5'8	142	8	71	33	4	4	.500
Conn, Albert Thomas "Bert"		98PhiN	00PhiN									
9/22/79	Philadelphia, Pa.	11/2/44	?	R	?	?	5	24.1	5	0	3	.000
Connor, John "John"		84BosN	85BufN	85LouA								
8/?/54	?, Scotland	10/13/32	?	?	?	?	12	104	48	2	8	.200
Connors, Joseph P. "Joe"		84AltU	84KCU									
Unknown	Paterson, N.J.	Unknown	?	?	?	?	3	21	1	0	2	.000
Conovar, Theodore "Ted" "Huck"		89CinA										
3/10/68	Lexington, Ky.	7/27/10	R	R	5'10½	165	1	2	1	0	0	—
*Conway, James P. "Jim"		84BroA	85PhiA	89KCA								
10/8/58	Clifton, Pa.	Unknown	?	R	?	?	56	452.2	140	22	29	.431
*Conway, Peter J. "Pete"		85BufN	86KCN	86–88DetN	89PitN							
10/30/66	Burmont, Pa.	1/13/03	R	R	5'10½	162	126	1040	428	61	61	.500
*Conway, Richard Butler "Dick"		86BalA	87–88BosN									
4/25/65	Lowell, Mass.	9/9/26	L	R	5'7½	140	41	352	121	15	24	.385
Coon, William K. "William"		76PhiN	(See OF)									
3/21/55	?, Pennsylvania	8/30/15	?	?	?	?	2	7	0	0	0	—
Corbett, Joseph A. "Joe"		95WasN	96–97BalN									
12/4/75	San Francisco, Cal.	5/2/45	R	R	5'10	?	48	373.2	180	27	10	.730
Corcoran, John H. "Jack"		84BroA	(See C)									
?/?/60	Lowell, Mass.	Unknown	?	?	?	?	1	1	0	0	0	—
*Corcoran, Lawrence J. "Larry"		80–85ChiN	85NYN	(86NYN)	86WasN	87IndN						
8/10/59	Brooklyn, N.Y.	10/14/91	L	B	?	120	277	2392.1	1103	177	89	.665
*Corcoran, Michael "Mike"		84ChiN										
Unknown	Brooklyn, N.Y.	Unknown	?	?	?	?	1	9	2	0	1	.000
Corey, Frederick Harrison "Fred"		78ProN	80–82WorN	83PhiA	85PhiA	(See 3B)						
?/?/57	S. Kingston, R.I.	11/27/12	R	R	?	?	93	656.1	168	27	46	.370
Corkhill, John Stewart "Pop"		84–88CinA	(See OF)									
4/11/58	Parkersburg, Pa.	4/4/21	L	R	5'10	180	17	62.1	21	3	4	.429
Cotter, Daniel Joseph "Dan"		90BufP										
4/14/67	Boston, Mass.	9/4/35	R	R	?	?	1	9	0	0	1	.000
Coughlin, Edward E. "Ed"		84 BufN										
8/5/61	Hartford, Conn.	12/25/52	?	?	?	?	1	0	0	0	0	—
Coughlin, William Edward "Roscoe"		90ChiN	91NYN									
3/15/68	Walpole, Mass.	3/20/51	?	R	5'10	160	19	156	51	7	10	.412
Coyle, William Claude "Bill"		93BosN										
Unknown	Pittsburgh, Pa.	Unknown	?	R	?	?	2	8	2	0	1	.000

BIRTH DATE	BIRTHPLACE	DEATH DATE	B	T	HGT	WGT	G	INN	K	W	L	PCT
Crane, Edward Nicholas "Cannonball" "Ed" 84BosU 86WasN 88–89NYN 90NYP 91CinA 91CinN 92–93NYN 93BroN (See OF)												
5/27/62	Boston, Mass.	9/19/96	R	R	5'10½	204	204	1550.1	720	72	96	.429
Critchley, Morris Arthur "Morrie" 82PitA 82StLA												
3/26/50	New London, Conn.	3/6/10	?	?	6'1	190	5	43	5	1	4	.200
Cronin, John J. "Jack" 95BroN 98PitN 99CinN												
5/26/74	W.New Brighton, S.I., N.Y.	7/12/29	R	R	6'	200	11	74	19	4	4	.500
Crosby, George W. "George" 84ChiN												
?/?/60	Chicago, Ill.	1/9/13	?	?	?	?	3	28	11	1	2	.333
Cross, George Lewis "Lem" 93–94CinN												
1/9/72	Sanbornton, N.H.	10/9/30	?	R	5'9	155	11	74	18	3	6	.333
Crothers, Douglas "Doug" 84KCU 85NYA												
11/16/59	Natchez, Miss.	3/29/07	R	R	?	?	21	179	51	8	13	.381
Crowell, William Theodore "Billy" 87–88CleA 88LouA												
11/6/65	Cincinnati, Ohio	7/24/35	R	R	5'8½	160	64	549	138	19	45	.297
Cudworth, James Alaric "Jim" "Cud" 84KCU (See 1B)												
8/22/58	Fairhaven, Mass.	12/21/43	R	R	6'	165	2	17	6	0	0	—
Cummings, William Arthur "Candy" 72MutNA 73BalNA 74PhiNA 75HarNA 76HarN 77CinN												
10/18/48	Ware, Mass.	5/16/24	R	R	5'9	120	242	2149.2	254	145	94	.607
Cunningham, Ellsworth Elmer "Bert" 87BroA 88–89BalA 90PhiP 90BufP 91BalA 95–99LouN 00ChiN												
11/25/65	Wilmington, Del.	5/14/52	R	R	?	187	340	2717.2	716	142	166	.461
Cuppy, George Joseph "Nig" b. Koppe 92–98CleN 99StLN 00BosN												
7/3/69	Logansport, Ind.	7/27/22	R	R	5'7	160	289	2173.1	482	158	92	.637
Curry, Wesley "Wes" 84VirA												
4/1/60	Wilmington, Del.	5/19/33	?	?	?	?	2	16	1	0	2	.000
Cushman, Edgar Leander "Ed" 83BufN 84MilU 85PhiA 85–87NYA 90TolA												
3/27/52	Eagleville, Ohio	9/26/15	R	L	6'	?	177	1225.2	607	62	81	.434
Dailey, Vincent Perry "Vince" 90CleN (See OF)												
12/25/64	Osceola, Pa.	11/14/19	?	?	6'	200	2	7	0	0	1	.000
***Daily, Edward M. "Ed"** 85–87PhiN 87–88WasN 89ColA 90BroA 90NYN 90–91LouA (See OF)												
9/7/62	Providence, R.I.	10/21/91	R	R	5'10½	174	151	1237.2	407	66	70	.485
Daily, Hugh Ignatius "Hugh" "One Arm" b. Harry Criss 82BufN 83CleN 84Chi–PitU 84WasU 85StLN 86WasN 87CleA												
?/?/57	Baltimore, Md.	Unknown	R	R	6'2	180	165	1415	846	73	87	.456
Daley, William "Bill" 89BosN 90BosP 91BosA												
6/27/68	Poughkeepsie, N.Y.	5/4/22	?	L	?	?	62	409.2	218	29	16	.644
Damman, William Henry "Bill" "Wee Willie" 97–99CinN												
8/9/72	Chicago, Ill.	12/6/48	L	L	5'7	155	60	367.2	74	24	15	.615
Daniels, Charles L. "Charlie" 84BosU												
7/1/61	Roxbury, Mass.	2/9/38	?	?	?	?	2	16.2	12	0	2	.000
Daniels, Peter J. "Pete" "Smiling Pete" 90PitN 98StLN												
4/8/64	County Cavan, Ireland	2/13/28	L	L	?	?	14	82.2	21	2	8	.200
Darby, George William "George" "Deacon" 93CinN												
2/6/69	Kansas City, Mo.	2/25/37	R	R	5'10½	160	4	29	6	1	1	.500
Daub, Daniel William "Dan" "Mickey" 92CinN 93–97BroN												
1/12/68	Middletown, Ohio	3/25/51	R	R	5'10	160	126	899.1	185	45	52	.464
Davies, George Washington "George" 91MilA 92–93CleN 93NYN												
2/22/68	Portage, Wis.	9/22/06	?	?	?	180	46	369	166	18	24	.429

BIRTH DATE	BIRTHPLACE	DEATH DATE	B	T	HGT	WGT	G	INN	K	W	L	PCT
Davis, George Stacey "George" 91CleN (See SS)												
8/23/70	Cohoes, N.Y.	10/17/40	B	R	5'9	180	3	4	4	0	1	.000
Davis, John Henry Albert "Daisy" 84StLA 84–85BosN												
11/28/58	Boston, Mass.	11/5/02	?	R	?	?	40	323.2	186	16	21	.432
Davis, Wiley Anderson "Wiley" 96CinN												
8/1/75	Seymour, Tenn.	9/22/42	R	R	5'10	165	2	4.1	1	1	1	.500
Day, William M. "Bill" 89–90PhiN 90PitN												
7/28/67	Wilmington, Del.	8/16/23	?	R	?	?	14	92.2	39	1	10	.091
Deagle, Lorenzo Burroughs "Ren" 83–84CinA 84LouA												
6/26/58	New York, N.Y.	12/24/36	R	R	5'9	190	34	269.1	83	17	15	.531
Dean, Charles Wilson "Dory" 76CinN												
11/6/52	Cincinnati, Ohio	5/4/35	R	R	?	?	30	262.2	22	4	26	.133
Demarais, Frederick "Fred" 90ChiN												
11/1/66	?, Canada	3/6/19	?	R	5'9	168	1	2	1	0	0	—
DeMiller, Harry "Harry" 92ChiN												
11/12/67	Wooster, Ohio	10/19/28	R	L	?	?	4	24	15	1	1	.500
Denny, Jeremiah Dennis "Jerry" b. Eldridge 88IndN (See 3B)												
3/16/59	New York, N.Y.	8/16/27	R	R	5'11½	180	1	4	1	0	0	—
Denzer, Roger "Roger" "Peaceful Valley" 97ChiN												
10/5/71	LeSueur, Minn.	9/18/49	L	R	6'	180	12	94.2	17	2	8	.200
Derby, George H. "George" "Jonah" 81–82DetN 83BufN												
7/6/57	Webster, Mass.	7/4/25	L	R	6'	175	110	964.1	428	48	56	.462
Devine, Walter James "Jim" 83BalA (86NYN)												
10/5/58	Brooklyn, N.Y.	1/11/05	?	L	?	?	2	11	3	1	1	.500
Devlin, James Alexander "Jim" 75ChiNA 76–77LouN (See 1B)												
?/?/49	Philadelphia, Pa.	10/10/83	R	R	5'11	175	157	1415	286	72	76	.486
Devlin, James H. "Jim" 86NYN 87PhiN 88–89StLA												
4/16/66	Troy, N.Y.	12/14/00	?	L	5'7	135	23	170.1	90	11	10	.524
Dewald, Charles H. "Charlie" 90CleP												
9/?/67	Newark, N.J.	8/22/04	?	L	?	?	2	14	6	2	0	1.000
Dinneen, William Henry "Bill" "Big Bill" 98–99WasN 00BosN												
4/5/76	Syracuse, N.Y.	1/13/55	R	R	6'1	190	106	830	281	43	50	.462
Doe, Alfred George "Fred" "Count" "Mary Ann" 90BufP 90PitP												
4/18/64	Rockport, Mass.	10/4/38	R	R	5'10	165	2	10	4	0	1	.000
Doheny, Edwin Richard "Ed" 95–00NYN												
11/24/73	Northfield, Vt.	12/29/16	L	L	5'10½	165	113	831	340	35	64	.354
Dolan, John "John" 90CinN 91ColA 92WasN 93StLN 95ChiN												
9/12/67	Newport, Ky.	5/8/48	?	R	5'10	170	39	286.2	87	15	16	.484
Dolan, Patrick Henry "Cozy" 95–96BosN (00ChiN)												
12/3/72	Cambridge, Mass.	3/29/07	L	L	5'10	160	31	239.1	61	12	11	.522
Dolan, Thomas J. "Tom" 83StLA (See C)												
1/10/59	New York, N.Y.	1/16/13	R	R	?	?	1	4	0	0	0	—
Donahue, Francis Rostell "Red" 93NYN 95–97StLN 98–00PhiN												
1/23/73	Waterbury, Conn.	8/25/13	R	R	6'	187	183	1431.1	286	69	95	.421
Donlin, Michael Joseph "Mike" "Turkey Mike" 99StLN (See OF)												
5/30/78	Peoria, Ill.	9/24/33	L	L	5'9	170	3	15.1	6	0	1	.000

BIRTH DATE	BIRTHPLACE	DEATH DATE	B	T	HGT	WGT	G	INN	K	W	L	PCT
Donnelly, Franklin Marion "Frank" 93ChiN												
10/7/69	Tamaroa, Ill.	2/3/53	?	?	5'6	180	7	42	6	3	1	.750
Donovan, William Edward "Bill" "Wild Bill" 98WasN 99–00BroN												
10/13/76	Lawrence, Mass.	12/9/23	R	R	5'11	190	27	144	60	3	10	.231
Doran, John F. "John" 91LouA												
?/?/67	Chicago, Ill.	Unknown	?	L	5'4	160	15	126	55	5	10	.333
***Dorgan, Michael Cornelius "Mike" 79SyrN 80ProN 83–84NYN (See OF)**												
10/2/53	Middletown, Conn.	4/26/09	R	R	5'9	180	18	140	103	8	7	.533
Dorr, Charles Albert "Bert" 82StLA												
2/2/62	New York, N.Y.	6/16/14	?	?	?	?	8	66	34	2	6	.250
Dorsey, Michael Jeremiah "Jerry" 84BalU												
?/?/54	?, Canada	11/3/38	?	?	?	?	1	4	3	0	1	.000
Doty, Elmer L. "Babe" 90TolA												
12/17/67	Genoa, Ohio	11/20/29	L	R	6'	160	1	9	4	1	0	1.000
Dowling, Henry Peter "Pete" 97–99LouN												
Unknown	St. Louis, Mo.	6/30/05	?	L	5'11	?	74	601.1	175	27	39	.409
Dowse, Thomas Joseph "Tom" 90CleN (See C)												
8/12/66	?, Ireland	12/14/46	R	R	5'11	175	1	5	0	0	0	—
Doyle, John Aloysius "John" 82StLA												
?/?/58	Nova Scotia, Canada	12/24/15	?	?	?	?	3	24	5	0	3	.000
Drew, David "Dave" 84PhiU (See SS)												
Unknown	Unknown	Unknown	?	?	?	?	1	7	2	0	1	.000
Driscoll, John F. "Denny" 80BufN 82–83PitA 84LouA (85BufN)												
11/19/55	Lowell, Mass.	7/11/86	L	L	5'10½	160	83	681	171	38	39	.494
***Dugan, Edward John "Ed" 84VirA**												
?/?/64	Brooklyn, N.Y.	Unknown	?	?	?	?	20	166.1	60	5	14	.263
Duggleby, William James "Bill" "Frosty Bill" 98PhiN												
3/16/74	Utica, N.Y.	8/30/44	?	R	?	?	9	54	12	3	3	.500
Duke, Martin F. "Martin" "Duck" b. Duck 91WasA												
?/?/67	Zanesville, Ohio	12/31/98	?	L	?	?	4	23	5	0	3	.000
Dundon, Edward Joseph "Ed" "Dummy" 83–84ColA												
7/10/59	Columbus, Ohio	8/18/93	?	R	?	?	31	247.2	68	9	20	.310
Dunkle, Edward Perks "Davey" 97–98PhiN 99WasN												
8/30/72	Philipsburg, Pa.	11/19/41	B	R	6'2	220	233	156.1	39	6	8	.429
Dunlap, Frederick C. "Fred" "Sure Shot" 84StLU 87DetN (See 2B)												
5/21/59	Philadelphia, Pa.	12/1/02	R	R	5'8	165	2	2.2	2	0	0	—
Dunn, John Joseph "Jack" 97–00BroN 00PhiN (See P)												
10/6/72	Meadville, Pa.	10/22/28	R	R	5'9	?	127	981.2	158	61	52	.540
Dunning, Andrew Jackson "Andy" 89PitN 91NYN												
8/12/71	New York, N.Y.	6/21/52	R	R	6'	175	3	20	6	0	3	.000
Duryea, James Newton "Jesse" "Cyclone Jim" 89CinA 90–91CinN 91StLA 92CinN 92–93WasN												
9/7/59	Osage, Iowa	8/19/42	R	R	5'10	175	143	1088	416	59	67	.468
Duzen, William George "Bill" 90BufP												
2/21/70	Buffalo, N.Y.	3/11/44	R	R	5'11	185	2	13	5	0	2	.000
Dwyer, John Francis "Frank" 88–89ChiN 90ChiP 91CinA 91MilA 92StLN 92–99CinN (See P)												
3/25/68	Lee, Mass.	2/4/43	R	R	5'8	145	365	2810	563	176	152	.537
Eason, Malcolm Wayne "Mal" "Kid" 00ChiN												
3/13/79	Brookville, Pa.	4/16/70	R	R	6'	175	1	9	2	1	0	1.000

BIRTH DATE	BIRTHPLACE	DEATH DATE	B	T	HGT	WGT	G	INN	K	W	L	PCT
Easton, John S. "Jack" 89–91ColA 91StLA 92StLN 94PitN												
2/28/67	Bridgeport, Ohio	11/28/03	?	?	?	?	76	522.1	246	26	29	.473
Eden, Charles M. "Charlie" 84–85PitA (See OF)												
1/18/55	Lexington, Ky.	9/17/20	L	L	?	168	6	27.2	8	1	3	.250
Edwards, ? 75AtlNA												
Unknown	Unknown	Unknown	?	?	?	?	1	2	0	0	1	.000
Egan, James K. "Jim" "The Toy Terrier" 82TroN (See OF)												
?/?/58	Derby, Conn.	9/26/84	?	L	?	?	12	100	20	4	6	.400
Egan, John Joseph "Rip" 94WasN												
7/9/71	Philadelphia, Pa.	12/22/50	?	R	5'11	168	1	5	2	0	0	—
Ehret, Philip Sydney "Red" 88KCA 89–91LouA 92–94PitN 95StLN 96–97CinN 98LouN												
8/31/68	Louisville, Ky.	7/28/40	R	R	6'	175	362	2754.1	848	139	167	.454
Eiteljorge, Edward Henry "Ed" 90ChiN 91WasA												
10/14/71	Berlin, Germany	12/5/42	R	R	6'2	190	9	63.1	24	1	6	.143
Ellick, Joseph J. "Joe" 78MilN (See OF)												
4/3/54	Cincinnati, Ohio	4/21/23	?	?	5'10	162	1	3	0	0	1	.000
Ely, William Frederick "Bones" 84BufN 86LouA 90SyrA 94NYN												
6/7/63	N. Girard, Pa.	1/10/52	R	R	6'1	155	9	52	32	0	5	.000
Ely, Harry "Harry" 92BalN												
Unknown	Unknown	Unknown	?	?	?	?	1	7	0	0	1	.000
Emig, Charles Henry "Charlie" 96LouN												
4/5/75	Cincinnati, Ohio	10/2/75	?	L	?	?	1	8	1	0	1	.000
Emslie, Robert Daniel "Bob" 83–85BalA 85PhiA												
1/27/59	Guelph, Ont., Can.	4/26/43	R	R	5'11	?	91	792.1	362	44	44	.500
Esper, Charles H. "Duke" 90PhiA 90PitN 90–92PhiN 92PitN 93–94WasN 94–96BalN 97–98StLN												
7/28/68	Salem, N.J.	8/31/10	?	L	5'11½	185	236	1727.2	453	101	100	.502
Evans, Roy "Roy" 97StLN 97LouN 98–99WasN												
3/19/74	Knoxville, Tenn.	8/15/15	R	R	6'	180	26	144.2	48	11	11	.500
Evans, Uriah L.P. "Jake" "Bloody Jake" 80TroN 82WorN 83CleN (See OF)												
9/?/56	Baltimore, Md.	1/16/07	?	R	5'8	154	3	15	3	0	1	.000
***Ewing, John "John" "Long John" "Camencita" (83StLA) (84CinU) (84WasU) 88–89LouA 90NYP 91NYN**												
6/1/63	Cincinnati, Ohio	4/23/95	?	R	?	?	129	1058.2	525	53	63	.457
***Ewing, William "Buck" 82TroN 84–85NYN 88–89NYN 90NYP (See C)**												
10/17/59	Hoagland, Ohio	10/20/06	R	R	5'10	188	9	47	23	2	3	.400
Fagan, William A. "Bill" "Clinkers" 87NYA 88KCA												
2/15/69	Troy, N.Y.	3/21/30	?	L	5'11	165	23	187.1	61	6	15	.286
Fanning, John Jacob "Jack" 89IndN 94PhiN												
?/?/63	S. Orange, N.J.	6/10/17	?	R	5'9	163	6	33.1	7	1	4	.200
Fast, ? 87IndN												
Unknown	Milwaukee, Wis.	Unknown	?	?	?	?	4	15.2	0	0	1	.000
Fauver, Clayton King "Clay" 99LouN												
8/1/72	N. Eaton, Ohio	3/3/42	B	R	5'10	?	1	9	1	1	0	1.000
Fee, John "Jack" 89IndN												
12/23/67	Carbondale, Pa.	3/3/13	?	?	?	?	7	40	10	2	2	.500
Ferguson, Charles J. "Charlie" 84–87PhiN (See P)												
4/17/63	Charlottesville, Va.	4/29/88	B	R	6'	165	183	1514.2	728	99	64	.607
Ferguson, Robert Vavasour "Bob" 71MutNA 73–74AtlNA 75HarNA 77HarN 83PhiN (See 3B)												
1/31/45	Brooklyn, N.Y.	5/3/94	B	R	5'9½	149	11	57.1	1	1	3	.250

BIRTH DATE	BIRTHPLACE	DEATH DATE	B	T	HGT	WGT	G	INN	K	W	L	PCT
Ferson, Alexander "Alex" "Colonel" 89WasN 90BufP 92BalP												
7/14/66	Philadelphia, Pa.	12/5/57	R	R	5'9	165	48	368.1	106	18	25	.419
Field, James C. "Jim" 90RocA (See 1B)												
4/24/63	Philadelphia, Pa.	5/13/53	?	?	6'1	170	2	9.2	2	1	0	1.000
Fields, John Joseph "Jocko" 87PitN (See OF)												
10/20/64	Cork, Ireland	10/14/50	R	R	5'10	160	1	1	0	0	0	—
Fifield, John Proctor "Jack" 97–99PhiN 99WasN												
10/5/71	Enfield, N.H.	11/27/39	R	R	5'11	160	68	521.2	89	21	39	.350
Figgemeier, Frank Y. "Frank" 94PhiN												
4/22/74	St. Louis, Mo.	4/15/15	?	?	?	?	1	8	2	0	1	.000
Firth, John E. "Ted" 84VirA												
?/?/56	Philadelphia, Pa.	4/18/85	?	?	?	?	1	9	0	0	1	.000
Fishel, Leo "Leo" 99NYN												
12/13/77	Babylon, N.Y.	5/19/60	R	R	6'	175	1	9	6	0	1	.000
Fisher, ? 84PhiU												
Unknown	Johnstown, Pa.	Unknown	?	?	?	?	8	70.2	42	1	7	.125
Fisher, ? 85BufN												
Unknown	Philadelphia, Pa.	Unknown	?	?	?	?	1	9	4	0	1	.000
Fisher, Chauncey Burr "Chauncey" "Peach" 93–94CleN 94CinN 96CinN 97BroN												
1/8/72	Anderson, Ind.	4/27/39	R	R	5'11	175	63	428.2	79	21	26	.447
Fisher, William Charles "Cherokee" 71RokNA 72BalNA 73AthNA 74HarNA 75PhiNA 76CinN (77ChiN) 78ProN												
(See P)												
12/?/45	Philadelphia, Pa.	9/26/12	R	R	5'9	164	165	1326.1	118	57	84	.402
Fitzgerald, John H. "John" 91BosA												
5/30/70	Natick, Mass.	3/21/21	?	?	?	?	6	32	16	1	1	.500
Fitzgerald, John J. "John" 90RocA												
Unknown	Unknown	Unknown	?	?	?	?	11	78	35	3	8	.273
Fitzgerald, John T. "John" 91–92LouA												
Unknown	Leadville, Col.	Unknown	?	?	?	?	36	301	113	15	20	.429
Flaherty, Patrick Joseph "Patsy" 99LouN 00PitN												
6/29/76	Mansfield, Pa.	1/23/68	L	L	5'8	165	9	61	10	2	3	.400
Fleet, Frank H. "Frank" 71MutNA 73ResNA 75StlNA 75AtlNA (See 2B)												
?/?/48	New York, N.Y.	6/13/00	?	?	?	?	9	75.1	1	2	6	.250
Flowers, Charles Richard "Dickie" 71TroNA (See SS)												
?/?/50	Philadelphia, Pa.	10/5/92	?	?	?	?	1	1	0	0	0	—
Flynn, Cornelius Francis Xavier "Carney" 94CinN 96NYN 96WasN												
1/23/75	Cincinnati, Ohio	2/10/47	L	L	5'11	165	9	38.1	11	0	5	.000
Flynn, John A. "Jocko" "Jackie" 86ChiN (87ChiN) (See P)												
6/30/64	Lawrence, Mass.	12/30/07	?	R	5'6½	143	32	257	146	23	6	.793
***Fogarty, James G. "Jim" 84PhiN 86–87PhiN 89PhiN (See OF)**												
2/12/64	San Francisco, Cal.	5/20/91	R	R	5'10½	180	7	14	5	0	1	.000
Foley, Charles Joseph "Curry" 79–80BosN 81–83BufN (See OF)												
1/14/56	Milltown, Ireland	10/20/98	?	L	5'10	160	69	442.2	127	27	27	.500
Foley, John J. "John" 85ProN												
3/?/60	Hannibal, Mo.	Unknown	?	L	?	?	1	8	2	0	1	.000
Force, David W. "Davy" "Wee Davy" 73BalNA 74ChiNA (See SS)												
7/27/49	New York, N.Y.	6/21/18	R	R	5'4	130	4	25	0	1	1	.500

BIRTH DATE	BIRTHPLACE	DEATH DATE	B	T	HGT	WGT	G	INN	K	W	L	PCT
Ford, Thomas Walter "Tom" 90ColA 90BroA												
?/?/66	Chattanooga, Tenn.	5/27/17	?	?	5'10½	155	8	51	12	0	6	.000
*Foreman, Francis Isiah "Frank" "Monkey" 84Chi–PitU 84KCU 85BalA 89BalA 90CinN (91CinN) 91WasA												
92WasN 92BalN 93NYN 95–96CinN (See P)												
5/1/63	Baltimore, Md.	11/19/57	L	L	6'	160	202	1506	542	84	84	.500
*Foreman, John Davis "Brownie" 95–96PitN 96CinN												
8/6/75	Baltimore, Md.	10/10/26	L	L	5'8	150	32	224.1	81	12	12	.500
Fournier, Julius Henry "Henry" "Frenchy" 94CinN												
8/8/65	Syracuse, N.Y.	12/8/45	?	L	?	?	6	45	5	1	3	.250
Foutz, David Luther "Dave" "Scissors" 84–87StLN 88–89BroA 90–94BroN (See 1B)												
9/7/56	Carroll Co., Md.	3/5/97	R	R	6'2	161	251	1997.1	790	147	66	.690
Fox, John Joseph "John" 81BosA 83BalA 84PitA 86WasN												
2/7/59	Roxbury, Mass.	4/18/93	?	?	?	?	45	356.2	104	13	28	.317
France, Osman Beverly "Ossie" "O.B." 90ChiN												
10/4/58	Greensburg, Ohio	5/2/47	L	L	5'8	155	1	2	0	0	0	—
Frank, Charles "Charlie" 94StLN (See OF)												
5/30/70	Mobile, Ala.	5/24/22	?	?	5'10	170	2	3	1	0	0	—
Fraser, Charles Carrolton "Chick" 96–98LouN 98CleN 99–00PhiN												
3/17/71	Chicago, Ill.	5/8/40	R	R	5'10½	188	174	1619.2	364	72	87	.453
Freeman, John Frank "Buck" 91WasA 99WasN (See OF)												
10/30/71	Catasauqua, Pa.	6/25/49	L	L	5'9	169	7	51	28	3	2	.600
Freeman, Julius Benjamin "Julie" 88StLA												
11/7/68	?, Missouri	6/10/21	R	?	?	?	1	6.1	1	0	1	.000
French, William "Bill" 73MarNA (See OF)												
Unknown	Baltimore, Md.	Unknown	?	?	?	?	1	9	0	0	1	.000
Friend, Daniel Sebastian "Danny" 95–98ChiN (See P)												
4/18/73	Cincinnati, Ohio	6/1/42	?	L	5'9	175	67	551.2	158	32	29	.525
Fries, Peter Martin "Pete" 83ColA (84IndA)												
10/30/57	Scranton, Pa.	7/30/37	L	L	5'8	160	3	25	7	0	3	.000
Frisk, John Emil "Emil" 99CinN												
10/15/74	Kalkaska, Mich.	1/27/22	L	R	6'1	190	9	68.1	17	3	6	.333
Fuller, Edward Ashton "Ed" 86WasN												
3/22/68	Washington, D.C.	3/16/35	R	R	6'	158	2	13	3	0	1	.000
*Fulmer, Charles John "Chick" 73PhiNA (See SS)												
2/12/51	Philadelphia, Pa.	2/15/40	R	R	6'	158	2	5	0	0	0	—
Fulmer, Christopher "Chris" 86BalA (See C)												
7/4/58	Tamaqua, Pa.	11/9/31	R	R	5'8	165	1	2	0	0	0	—
Fusselbach, Edward L. "Eddie" 82StLA (See C)												
7/17/56	Philadelphia, Pa.	4/14/26	?	?	5'6	156	4	23	3	1	2	.333
Gallagher, William John "Bill" 83BalA 84PhiU												
Unknown	Philadelphia, Pa.	Unknown	?	L	?	?	10	76.2	31	1	7	.125
Galvin, James Francis "Pud" "Jim" "Gentle Jeems" "The Little Steam Engine" 75StLNA 79–85BufN 85–86PitA												
87–89PitN 90PitP 91–92PitN 92StLN												
12/25/56	St. Louis, Mo.	3/7/02	R	R	5'8	190	705	6003.1	1815	364	310	.540
Galvin, Louis J. "Lou" 84StPU												
4/?/62	St. Paul, Minn.	6/17/95	?	?	?	?	3	25	17	0	2	.000
Gamble, Robert J. "Bob" 88PhiA												
2/?/67	Hazleton, Pa.	Unknown	?	R	5'10	155	1	9	2	0	1	.000

	BIRTH DATE	BIRTHPLACE	DEATH DATE	B	T	HGT	WGT	G	INN	K	W	L	PCT
Gannon, James Edward "Gussie"		95PitN											
	11/26/73	Erie, Pa.	4/12/66	L	L	5'11	154	1	5	0	0	0	—
Gannon, Joseph "Joe"		98StLN											
	Unknown	St. Louis, Mo.	Unknown	?	?	?	?	1	9	2	0	1	.000
Gardner, Frank Washington "Gid"		79TroN	80CleN	83BalA	84Chi–PitU	85BalA	(See OF)						
	6/9/59	Attleboro, Mass.	8/1/14	?	?	?	165	15	113	33	2	12	.143
Gardner, James Anderson "Jim"		95PitN	97–99PitN										
	10/4/74	Pittsburgh, Pa.	4/24/05	?	R	?	?	56	398.1	109	24	20	.545
Gardner, William A. "Bill"		87BalA											
	9/?/68	Baltimore, Md.	Unknown	?	?	?	?	3	13	3	0	1	.000
Garfield, William Milton "Will" "Bill"		89PitN	90CleN										
	10/26/67	Sheffield, Ohio	12/16/41	R	R	5'11½	160	13	99	20	1	9	.100
Garoni, William "Willie"		99NYN											
	7/28/77	Ft. Lee, N.J.	9/9/14	R	R	6'1	165	3	10	2	0	1	.000
Garry, James Thomas "Jim"		93BosN											
	9/21/69	Great Barrington, Mass.	1/15/17	?	L	?	?	1	1	2	0	1	.000
Garvin, Virgil Lee "Ned"		96PhiN	99–00ChiN										
	1/1/74	Navasota, Tex.	6/16/08	?	R	6'3½	160	56	458.1	180	19	32	.373
Gaston, Welcome Thornburg "Welcome"		98–99BroN											
	12/19/72	Guernsey Co., Ohio	12/13/44	?	L	?	?	3	19	0	1	1	.500
Gastright, Henry Carl "Hank" b. Gastreich		89–91ColA	92WasN	93PitN	93BosN	94BroN	96CinN						
	3/29/65	Covington, Ky.	10/9/37	R	R	6'2	190	171	1301.1	514	72	63	.533
Gear, Dale Dudley "Dale"		96CleN	(See OF)										
	2/2/72	Lone Elm, Kan.	9/23/51	R	R	5'11	165	37	23	6	0	2	.000
Gedney, Alfred W. "Count"		75MutNA	(See OF)										
	5/10/49	Brooklyn, N.Y.	3/26/22	?	?	5'9	140	2	11	2	1	0	1.000
Geer, William Henry Harrison "Billy" b. George Harrison Geer		84BroA	(See SS)										
	8/13/49	Syracuse, N.Y.	1/5/22	?	R	5'8	160	2	5	1	0	0	—
Geggus, Charles Fredrick "Charlie" (aka Gagus)		84WasU											
	3/25/62	San Francisco, Cal.	1/16/17	?	?	?	?	23	177.1	156	10	9	.526
Geis, Emil Michael "Emil"		82BalA											
	3/?/61	Villmar, Germany	Unknown	R	R	5'11	170	13	95.2	10	4	9	.308
***Geis, William J. "Bill"** b. Geiss		84DetN	(See 2B)										
	7/15/58	Chicago, Ill.	9/18/24	?	?	5'10	164	1	5	1	0	0	—
Geiss, Emil August "Emil"		87ChiN											
	3/20/67	Chicago, Ill.	10/4/11	R	R	5'11	170	1	9	4	0	1	.000
George, William M. "Bill"		87–88NYN	89ColA	(See OF)									
	1/27/65	Bellaire, Ohio	8/23/16	R	L	5'8	165	19	149.2	78	5	10	.333
German, Lester Stanley "Les"		90BalA	93–96NYN	96–97WasN									
	6/1/69	Baltimore, Md.	6/10/34	R	R	5'8	165	129	849.2	147	34	63	.351
Gessner, Charles J. "Charlie"		86PhiA											
	Unknown	Philadelphia, Pa.	Unknown	?	?	?	?	1	8	0	0	1	.000
Gettig, Charles Henry "Charlie"		96–99NYN	(See OF)										
	12/?/70	Baltimore, Md.	4/11/35	R	?	5'10	172	42	276	51	15	12	.556
Gettinger, Lewis Thomas Leyton "Tom" b. Gittinger		95LouN	(See OF)										
	12/11/68	Frederick, Md.	7/26/43	L	L	5'10	180	2	6.1	0	0	0	—
Getzein, Charles H. "Charlie" "Pretzels"		84–88DetN	89IndN	90–91BosN	91CleN	92StLN							
	2/14/64	?, Germany	6/19/32	R	R	5'10	172	296	2539.2	1070	145	139	.511

BIRTH DATE	BIRTHPLACE	DEATH DATE	B	T	HGT	WGT	G	INN	K	W	L	PCT
Gibson, Robert Murray "Robert" 90ChiN 90PitN												
8/2/69	Duncansville, Pa.	12/19/49	R	R	6'3	185	4	21	4	1	3	.250
Gilbert, Alfred Gideon "Bill" 92BalN												
3/13/68	Havre de Grace, Md.	Unknown	?	?	6'	180	2	14	5	0	1	.000
Gilks, Robert James "Bob" 87–88CleA 90CleN (See OF)												
7/2/64	Cincinnati, Ohio	8/21/44	R	R	5'8	178	21	160.2	36	9	9	.500
Gillpatrick, George F. "George" 98StLN												
2/28/75	Holden, Mo.	12/15/41	?	?	?	?	7	35	12	0	2	.000
Gilmore, Frank T. "Frank" "Shadow" 86–88WasN												
4/27/64	Webster, Mass.	7/21/29	R	?	?	?	49	405.1	212	12	33	.267
Gilroy, John M. "John" 95–96WasN												
10/26/69	Washington, D.C.	8/4/97	?	?	?	?	9	43.1	2	1	4	.200
Ging, William Joseph "Billy" 99BosN												
11/7/72	Elmira, N.Y.	9/14/50	R	R	5'10	170	1	8	2	1	0	1.000
Glasscock, John Wesley "Jack" "Pebbly Jack" 84CleN 87–89IndN (See SS)												
7/22/59	Wheeling, W.Va.	2/24/47	R	R	5'8	160	5	7	3	0	0	—
Gleason, William "Bill" 90CleP												
?/?/68	Cleveland, Ohio	12/2/93	?	?	?	?	1	4	0	0	1	.000
*Gleason, William J. "Kid" 88–91PhiN 92–94StLN 94–95BalN (See 2B)												
10/26/66	Camden, N.J.	1/2/33	B	R	5'7	158	299	2389.1	744	138	131	.513
Goar, Joshua Mercer "Jot" 96PitN 98CinN												
1/31/70	New Lisbon, Ind.	4/4/47	R	R	5'9	160	4	15.1	3	0	1	.000
Goetz, George Burt "George" 89BalA												
?/?/65	Greencastle, Pa.	Unknown	?	?	6'2	180	1	9	2	1	0	1.000
Golden, Michael Henry "Mike" 75WasNA 75ChiNA 78MilN (See OF)												
9/11/51	Shirley, Mass.	1/11/29	R	R	5'8	168	59	392	86	10	32	.188
Goldsmith, Fred Ernest "Fred" 79TroN 80–84ChiN 84BalA												
5/15/56	New Haven, Conn.	3/28/39	R	R	6'1	195	189	1609.2	433	112	68	.622
Goodall, Herbert Frank "Herb" 90LouA												
3/10/70	Mansfield, Pa.	1/20/38	R	R	5'9	180	18	109	46	8	5	.615
Gorman, John F. "Jack" "Stooping Jack" 84PitA (See 1B)												
?/?/59	St. Louis, Mo.	9/9/89	?	?	?	?	3	25	10	1	2	.333
Gormley, Joseph "Joe" 91PhiN												
12/20/66	Summit Hill, Pa.	7/2/50	L	L	?	?	1	8	2	0	1	.000
Gould, Charles Harvey "Charlie" 76CinN (See 1B)												
8/21/47	Cincinnati, Ohio	4/10/17	R	R	6'	172	2	4.1	0	0	0	—
Graff, John F. "John" 93WasN												
Unknown	Philadelphia, Pa.	Unknown	?	?	?	?	2	12	4	0	1	.000
Graves, Frank M. "Frank" 86StLN (See C)												
11/2/60	Cincinnati, Ohio	Unknown	?	?	6'	163	1	7	2	0	0	—
Gray, Charles "Charlie" 90PitN												
?/?/67	Indianapolis, Ind.	5/31/10	?	?	?	?	5	31	10	1	4	.200
Gray, George Edward "Chummy" 99PitN												
7/17/73	Rockland, Me.	8/14/13	?	R	5'11½	163	9	70.2	9	3	3	.500
Green, Edward M. "Ed" 90PhiA												
?/?/50	Philadelphia, Pa.	Unknown	?	?	?	?	25	191	56	7	15	.318
Greening, John A. "John" b. Greenig 88WasN												
Unknown	Philadelphia, Pa.	Unknown	?	?	?	?	1	9	2	0	1	.000

BIRTH DATE	BIRTHPLACE	DEATH DATE	B	T	HGT	WGT	G	INN	K	W	L	PCT
Greason, ? 73WasNA			?	L	?	?	7	63	3	1	6	.167
Unknown	Unknown	Unknown										
Griffith, Clark Calvin "Clark" 91StLA 91BosA 93–00ChiN (See P)			R	R	5'6½	156	299	2415	651	166	105	.613
11/20/69	Clear Creek, Mo.	10/27/55										
Griffith, Frank Wesley "Frank" 92ChiN 94CleN			L	L	?	?	8	46.1	18	1	3	.250
11/18/72	Gilman, Ill.	12/13/08										
Grim, John Helm "John" 90Roc (See C)			R	R	6'2	175	1	3.1	3	0	0	—
8/9/67	Lebanon, Ky.	7/28/61										
Grimes, John Thomas "John" 97StLN			R	R	5'11	160	3	19.2	4	0	2	.000
4/17/69	Woodstock, Md.	1/17/64										
Gruber, Henry John "Henry" 87–88DetN 89CleN 90CleP 91CleN			R	R	5'9	155	151	1239.1	346	61	78	.439
12/14/63	Hamden, Conn.	9/26/32										
***Gumbert, Addison Courtney** "Ad" 88–89ChiN 90BosP 91–92ChiN 93–94PitN 95–96BroN 96PhiN (See P)			R	R	5'10	200	262	1985.1	546	123	102	.547
10/10/68	Pittsburgh, Pa.	4/23/25										
***Gumbert, William Skeen** "Billy" 90PitN 92PitN 93LouN			R	R	6'1½	200	17	119.2	21	7	8	.467
8/8/65	Pittsburgh, Pa.	4/13/46										
Guth, Charles J. "Charlie" 80ChiN			?	?	?	?	1	9	7	1	0	1.000
?/?/56	Chicago, Ill.	7/5/83										
Haddock, George Silas "George" 88–89WasN 90BufP 91BosA 92–93BroN 94PhiN 94WasN			R	R	5'11	155	204	1580	599	95	87	.522
12/25/66	Portsmouth, N.H.	4/18/26										
Hafner, Francis R. "Frank" 88KCA			?	R	?	?	2	18	5	0	2	.000
8/14/67	Hannibal, Mo.	3/2/57										
Hagan, Arthur Charles "Art" 83PhiN 83–84BufN			?	R	?	?	22	178	50	2	18	.100
3/17/63	Providence, R.I.	3/25/36										
Hahn, Frank George "Noodles" 99–00Cin			L	L	5'9	160	77	621.1	277	39	28	.582
4/29/79	Nashville, Tenn.	2/6/60										
Halbriter, Edward L. "Ed" 82PhiA			?	?	?	?	1	8	4	0	1	.000
2/2/60	Auburn, N.Y.	8/9/36										
Hallman, William Wilson "Bill" 96PhiN (See 2B)			R	R	5'8	160	1	2	0	0	0	—
3/31/67	Pittsburgh, Pa.	9/11/20										
Hallstrom, Charles E. "Charlie" "Swedish Wonder" 85ProN			?	?	?	?	1	9	0	0	1	.000
1/22/64	Jönköping, Sweden	5/6/49										
Hamill, John Alexander Charles "John" 84WasA			R	R	5'8	158	19	156.2	50	2	17	.105
12/18/60	New York, N.Y.	12/6/11										
Handiboe, James Edward "Jim" "Nick" 86PitA			R	R	5'11	160	14	114	83	7	7	.500
7/17/66	Columbus, Ohio	11/8/42										
Hankinson, Frank Edward "Frank" 78–79ChiN 80CleN 85NYA			R	R	5'11	168	32	266.2	81	16	12	.571
4/29/56	New York, N.Y.	4/5/11										
Hansford, F.C. "F.C." 98BroN			?	L	6'	180	1	7	0	0	0	—
Unknown	Unknown	Unknown										
Harkins, John Joseph "John" "Pa" 84CleN 85–87BroA 88BalA			R	R	6'1	205	139	1183.1	489	51	83	.381
4/12/59	New Brunswick, N.J.	11/18/40										
Harper, Charles William "Jack" 99CleN 00StLN			R	R	6'	178	6	40	14	1	5	.167
4/2/78	Galloway, Pa.	9/30/50										
Harper, George B. "George" 94PhiN 96BroN			R	R	5'10	165	28	172.1	46	10	14	.417
8/17/66	Milwaukee, Wis.	12/11/31										
Hart, Robert Lee "Billy" 90StLA			?	?	5'8	?	26	201.1	95	12	8	.600
5/16/66	Palmyra, Mo.	5/14/44										

BIRTH DATE	BIRTHPLACE	DEATH DATE	B	T	HGT	WGT	G	INN	K	W	L	PCT
Hart, William Franklin "Bill" "Bond Hill Billy" 86–87PhiA 92BroN 95PitN 96–97StLN 98PitN												
7/19/65	Louisville, Ky.	9/19/36	?	R	5'10	163	186	1424.1	383	59	109	.352
Harvey, Ervin King "Ervin" "Zaza" 00ChiN												
1/5/79	Saratoga, Cal.	6/3/54	L	L	6'	190	1	4	0	0	0	—
Hastings, Charles Morton "Charlie" 93CleN 96–98PitN												
11/11/70	Ironton, Ohio	8/3/34	?	?	5'11	179	67	451.1	115	18	29	.383
***Hatfield, Gilbert "Gil" "Colonel" (See SS)** 89NYN 90NYP 91WasA												
1/27/55	Hoboken, N.J.	5/27/21	?	R	5'9½	168	13	77.2	34	3	5	.375
***Hatfield, John Van Buskirk "John"** 74MutNA (See OF)												
7/20/47	?, New Jersey	2/20/09	?	?	5'10	165	3	8	1	0	1	.000
Hawke, William Victor "Bill" "Dick" 92–93StLN 93–94BalN												
4/28/70	Elsmere, Del.	12/11/02	R	R	5'8½	169	76	533.2	193	32	31	.508
Hawley, Emerson P. "Pink" 92–94StLN 95–97PitN 98–99CinN 00NYN (See P)												
12/5/72	Beaver Dam, Wis.	9/19/38	L	R	5'10	185	367	2830.1	818	160	165	.492
Hawley, Marvin Hiram "Scott" 94BosN												
Unknown	Painesville, Ohio	4/28/04	?	?	?	?	1	7	1	0	1	.000
Healey, Thomas F. "Tom" 78ProN 78IndN												
?/?/53	Cranston, R.I.	2/6/91	?	R	?	?	14	113	20	6	7	.462
Healy, John J. "Egyptian" "John" 85–86StLN 87–88IndN 89WasN 89ChiN 90TolA 91BalA 92BalN 92LouN												
10/27/66	Cairo, Ill.	3/16/99	R	R	6'2	158	227	1875	822	78	136	.364
Heard, Charles "Charlie" 90PitN												
1/30/72	Philadelphia, Pa.	2/20/45	R	R	6'2	190	6	44	13	0	6	.000
Hecker, Guy Jackson "Guy" 82–89LouA 90PitN (See 1B)												
4/3/56	Youngsville, Pa.	12/3/38	R	R	6'	190	334	2906	1099	173	146	.542
Heifer, Franklin "Frank" "Heck" 75BosNA (See 1B)												
1/18/54	Reading, Pa.	8/29/93	?	?	5'10½	175	2	2.1	0	0	0	—
Helmbold, Horace "Horace" 90PhiA												
8/27/67	Philadelphia, Pa.	Unknown	?	?	?	?	1	7	3	0	1	.000
Hemming, George Earl "George" "Old Wax Figger" 90CleP 90BroP 91BroN 92CinN 92–94LouN 94–96BalN 97LouN												
12/15/68	Carrolton, Ohio	6/3/30	R	R	5'11	170	204	1587.2	362	91	82	.526
Henderson, James Harding "Hardie" 83PhiN 83–86BalA 86–87BroA 88PitN												
10/31/62	Philadelphia, Pa.	2/6/03	R	R	?	?	210	1788.1	930	81	121	.401
Henry, John Michael "John" 84CleN 85BalA 86WasN (See OF)												
9/2/63	Springfield, Mass.	6/11/39	?	L	?	?	18	140.2	73	4	14	.222
Herman, Arthur "Art" 96–97LouN												
5/11/71	Louisville, Ky.	9/20/55	?	?	?	?	17	112.1	17	4	7	.364
Herring, Silas Clarke "Lefty" 99WasN												
3/4/80	Philadelphia, Pa.	2/11/65	L	L	5'11	160	2	2	0	0	0	—
Hewitt, Charles Jacob "Jake" 95PitN												
6/6/70	Maidsville, W.Va.	5/18/59	L	L	5'7	150	4	13	4	1	0	1.000
Heyner, John "John" 90PitN												
Unknown	Hyde Park, Ill.	Unknown	?	?	?	?	1	4	1	0	0	—
Hibbard, John Denison "John" 84ChiN												
12/2/64	Chicago, Ill.	11/17/37	?	L	?	?	2	17	4	1	1	.500

	BIRTH DATE	BIRTHPLACE	DEATH DATE	B	T	HGT	WGT	G	INN	K	W	L	PCT
Hickman, Charles Taylor "Charlie" "Piano Legs" 97–99BosN (See 3B)													
	3/4/76	Taylortown, Pa.	4/19/34	R	R	5'11½	215	19	107	23	7	2	.778
Hickman, Ernest P. "Ernie" 84KCU													
	?/?/56	E. St. Louis, Ill.	11/19/91	?	?	?	?	17	137.1	68	4	13	.235
***Hill, William Cicero "Bill" "Still Bill" 96–97LouN 98CinN 99CleN 99BalN 99BroN**													
	8/2/74	Chattanooga, Tenn.	1/28/38	L	L	6'1	201	124	925	280	36	69	.343
Hilsey, Charles T. "Charlie" 83PhiN 84PhiA													
	3/23/64	Philadelphia, Pa.	10/31/18	?	?	5'7	180	6	53	18	2	4	.333
Hines, Paul A. "Paul" 84ProN (See OF)													
	3/1/52	Washington, D.C.	7/10/35	R	R	5'9½	173	1	1	0	0	0	—
Hodnett, Charles "Charlie" 83StLA 84StLU													
	?/?/61	?, Iowa	Unknown	?	?	?	?	18	153	47	14	4	.778
Hodson, George S. "George" 94BosN 95PhiN													
	6/?/70	?, Pennsylvania	Unknown	?	R	?	?	16	91	18	5	6	.455
Hoffer, William Leopold "Bill" "Chick" "Wizard" 95–98BalN 98–99PitN													
	11/8/70	Cedar Rapids, Iowa	7/21/59	R	R	5'9	155	145	1155.1	295	89	38	.701
Hoffman, Frank J. "Frank" "The Texas Wonder" 88KCA													
	Unknown	Houston, Tex.	Unknown	?	R	?	?	12	104	38	3	9	.250
Hofford, John William "John" 85PitA 86PhiA													
	5/25/63	Philadelphia, Pa.	12/16/15	?	?	?	?	12	106	46	3	9	.250
Hogan, Robert Edward "Eddie" 82StLA (See OF)													
	4/?/60	St. Louis, Mo.	Unknown	R	?	5'7	153	1	8	4	0	1	.000
Holliday, James Wear "Bug" 92CinN 96CinN (See OF)													
	2/8/67	St. Louis, Mo.	2/15/10	R	R	5'11	151	2	5	0	0	0	—
Hollison, John Henry "John" "Swede" 92ChiN													
	5/3/70	Chicago, Ill.	8/19/69	R	L	5'8	162	1	4	2	0	0	—
Holmes, James William "Ducky" 95–96LouN (See OF)													
	1/28/69	Des Moines, Iowa	8/6/32	L	R	5'6	170	4	26	3	1	1	.500
Hopper, Clarence F. "Lefty" 98BroN													
	5/27/74	Jersey City, N.J.	Unknown	?	L	?	?	2	11	5	0	2	.000
Horan, Patrick J. "John" 84Chi–PitU													
	?/?/63	?, Ireland	Unknown	?	?	5'10½	160	13	98	55	3	6	.333
Horner, William Frank "Jack" 94BalN													
	9/21/63	Baltimore, Md.	7/14/10	R	?	?	?	2	11	2	0	1	.000
Hornung, Michael Joseph "Joe" "Ubbo Ubbo" 1880BufN (See OF)													
	6/12/57	Carthage, N.Y.	10/30/31	R	R	5'8½	164	1	3	0	0	0	—
Horton, Elmer E. "Elmer" "Herky Jerky" 96PitN 98BroN													
	9/4/69	Hamilton, Ohio	8/12/20	?	?	?	?	3	24	3	0	3	.000
Householder, Charles F. "Charlie" 84Chi–PitU (See 3B)													
	?/?/56	Harrisburg, Pa.	Unknown	R	R	5'7	150	2	3	3	0	0	—
Houseman, Frank "Frank" 86BalA													
	Unknown	Baltimore, Md.	Unknown	?	?	?	?	1	8	5	0	1	.000
Howell, Henry Harry "Harry" "Handsome Harry" 98BroN 99BalN 00BroN													
	11/14/76	?, New Jersey	5/22/56	R	R	5'9	?	51	337.2	86	21	13	.618
Hudson, Nathaniel P. "Nat" 86–89StLA (See P)													
	1/12/59	Chicago, Ill.	3/14/28	R	R	?	?	86	694.1	258	48	26	.649
***Hughes, James Jay "Jim" "Jay" 98BalN 99BroN (See P)**													
	1/22/74	Sacramento, Cal.	6/2/24	R	R	?	185	73	592.1	180	51	18	.739

BIRTH DATE	BIRTHPLACE	DEATH DATE	B	T	HGT	WGT	G	INN	K	W	L	PCT
*Hughes, Michael J. "Mickey" 88–89BroA 90BroN 90PhiA												
10/25/66	New York, N.Y.	4/10/31	?	R	5'6	165	75	623.2	250	39	28	.582
Hughes, Thomas James "Tom" "Long Tom" 00ChiN												
11/29/78	Chicago, Ill.	2/8/56	R	R	6'1	175	3	21	12	1	1	.500
Hughes, William R. "Bill" 85PhiA												
11/25/66	Blandinsville, Ill.	8/25/43	L	L	?	?	2	16.2	4	0	2	.000
Hughey, James Ulysses "Jim" "Coldwater Jim" 91MilA 93ChiN 96–97PitN 98StLN 99CleN 00StLN												
3/8/69	Wakashma, Mich.	3/29/45	?	R	6'	?	145	1007.2	250	29	80	.266
Hunter, Robert Lemuel "Lem" 83CleN												
1/16/63	Warren, Ohio	11/9/56	?	?	?	?	1	6'1	4	0	0	—
Husted, William J. "Bill" 90PhiP												
10/11/66	Gloucester, N.J.	5/17/41	?	?	?	?	18	129	33	5	10	.333
Hutchison, William Forrest "Bill" "Wild Bill" 84KCU 89–95ChiN 97StLN												
12/17/59	New Haven, Conn.	3/19/26	R	R	5'9	175	375	3083	1236	184	163	.530
Hyndman, James William "Jim" 86PhiA												
7/?/65	Ontario, Canada	Unknown	?	?	?	?	1	2	1	0	1	.000
Inks, Albert John "Bert" 91–92Bro 92WasN 94BalN 94–95LouN 96CinN 96PhiN (See P)												
1/27/71	Ligonier, Ind.	10/3/41	L	L	6'3	175	89	603.2	167	27	46	.370
*Irwin, Arthur Albert "Arthur" "Doc" 84ProN 89WasN (See SS)												
2/14/58	Toronto, Ont., Can.	7/16/21	L	R	5'8 1/2	158	2	4	0	0	0	—
Irwin, William Franklin "Bill" "Phil" 86CinA												
9/16/59	Neville, Ohio	8/7/33	R	R	6'	195	2	17	6	0	2	.000
Isbell, William Frank "Frank" "Bald Eagle" 98ChiN												
8/21/75	Delevan, N.Y.	7/15/41	L	R	5'11	190	13	81	16	4	7	.364
Johnson, Abraham "Abe" 93ChiN												
Unknown	Chicago, Ill.	Unknown	?	?	?	?	1	1	0	0	0	—
Johnson, John Godfred "Youngy" 97PhiN 99NYN												
7/22/77	San Francisco, Cal.	8/28/36	?	R	?	?	6	31	8	1	2	.333
Johnson, John Louis "John" b. Mercer 94PhiN												
11/18/69	Pekin, Ill.	1/28/41	?	L	5'10	165	4	32.2	10	1	1	.500
Jones, Albert Edward "Cowboy" "Bronco" 98CleN 99–00StLN												
8/23/74	Golden, Colo.	2/9/58	L	L	5'11	160	60	450	122	23	28	.451
Jones, Alexander "Alex" 89PitN 92LouN 92WasN 94PhiN												
12/25/69	Pittsburgh, Pa.	4/4/41	L	L	5'6	135	24	192.1	63	7	14	.333
Jones, Charles Leander "Bumpus" 92–93CinN 93NYN												
1/1/70	Cedarville, Ohio	6/25/38	R	R	?	?	8	41.2	10	2	4	.333
Jones, Charles Wesley "Charley" "Baby" b. Benjamin Wesley Rippay 87NYA (See OF)												
4/30/50	Alamance Co., N.C.	Unknown	R	R	5'11 1/2	202	2	3	0	0	0	—
Jones, Daniel Albion "Jack" "Jumping Jack" 83DetN 83PhiA												
10/23/60	Litchfield, Conn.	10/19/36	?	R	?	?	19	157.2	61	11	7	.611
Jones, Henry "Henry" 90PitN												
Unknown	Pittsburgh, Pa.	Unknown	?	?	?	?	5	31	13	2	1	.667
Jones, James Tilford "Jim" "Sheriff" 97LouN												
12/25/76	London, Ky.	5/6/53	R	R	5'10	162	1	6.2	0	0	0	—
Jones, Michael "Mickey" 90LouA												
7/6/65	Hamilton, Ont., Can.	3/24/94	L	L	5'11 1/2	168	3	22	6	0	2	.000
Jordan, Charles T. "Charlie" "Kid" 96PhiN												
10/4/71	Baltimore, Md.	6/1/28	?	?	?	?	2	4.2	3	0	0	—

BIRTH DATE	BIRTHPLACE	DEATH DATE	B	T	HGT	WGT	G	INN	K	W	L	PCT
Jordan, Harry J. "Harry" 94–95PitN												
2/14/73	Pittsburgh, Pa.	3/1/20	?	?	?	?	3	26	5	1	2	.333
Katoll, John "Jack" "Big Jack" 98–99ChiN												
6/24/72	?, Germany	6/18/55	R	R	5'11	195	4	29	4	1	2	.333
Keas, Edward James "Ed" 88CleA												
2/2/63	Dubuque, Iowa	1/12/40	?	?	?	?	6	51	18	3	3	.500
Keating, Robert Edward "Ed" 87BalA												
9/22/62	Springfield, Mass.	1/19/22	L	L	6'4	190	1	9	0	0	1	.000
Keefe, George W. "George" 86–89WasN 90BufP 91WasA												
1/7/67	Washington, D.C.	8/24/35	L	L	5'9	168	78	616.1	213	20	48	.294
Keefe, John Thomas "John" 90SyrA												
5/5/67	Fitchburg, Mass.	8/9/37	?	L	?	?	43	352.1	120	17	24	.415
Keefe, Timothy John "Tim" "Sir Timothy" 80–82TroN 83–84NYA 85–89NYN 90NYP 91NYN 91–93PhiN (See P)												
1/1/57	Cambridge, Mass.	4/23/33	R	R	5'10½	185	599	5047.1	2543	342	225	.603
Keenan, Harry Leon "Kid" 91CinA												
?/?/75	Louisville, Ky.	6/11/03	?	R	?	?	1	8	5	0	1	.000
Keenan, James William "Jim" 84IndA 85–86CinA (See C)												
2/10/58	New Haven, Conn.	9/21/26	R	R	5'10	186	4	19	2	0	1	.000
Keener, Joshua Harry "Harry" "Beans" 96PhiN												
9/?/69	Easton, Pa.	3/5/12	?	R	?	?	16	113.1	28	3	11	.214
Keffer, Frank "Frank" 90SyrA												
Unknown	Harrisburg, Pa.	Unknown	?	?	?	?	2	16	4	1	1	.500
Kelb, George Francis "George" "Pugger" 98CleN												
7/17/70	Toledo, Ohio	10/20/36	L	L	?	?	3	16.1	8	0	1	.000
Kelly, Michael Joseph "King" 80ChiN 83–84ChiN 87BosN 90BosP 91CinA 92BosN (See OF)												
12/31/57	Troy, N.Y.	11/8/94	R	R	5'10	170	12	45.2	4	2	2	.500
Kennedy, Theodore A. "Ted" 85ChiN 86PhiA 86LouA												
2/?/65	Henry, Ill.	10/31/07	L	?	?	?	33	283.1	118	12	21	.364
Kennedy, William P. "Brickyard" 92–00BroN (See P)												
10/7/67	Bellaire, Ohio	9/23/15	R	R	5'11	160	367	2771.2	721	174	144	.547
Kent, Edward C. "Ed" 84TolA												
?/?/59	?, New York	Unknown	R	R	5'6½	152	1	9	4	0	1	.000
Kiley, John Frederick "John" 91BosN												
7/1/59	Dedham, Mass.	12/18/40	L	L	5'7	147	1	8	1	0	1	.000
Killeen, Henry "Henry" 91CleN												
?/?/71	Troy, N.Y.	Unknown	?	?	5'9	150	1	8.2	3	0	1	.000
Killen, Frank Bissell "Frank" "Lefty" 91MilA 92WasN 93–98PitN 98–99WasN 99BosN 00ChiN												
11/30/70	Pittsburgh, Pa.	12/3/39	L	L	6'1	200	321	2511.1	725	164	131	.556
*Kilroy, Matthew Aloysius "Matt" "Matches" 86–89BalA 90BosP 91CinA 92WasN 93–94LouN 98ChiP												
6/21/66	Philadelphia, Pa.	3/2/40	L	L	5'9	175	303	2435.2	1170	141	133	.515
*Kilroy, Michael Joseph "Mike" 88BalA 91PhiN												
11/4/72	Philadelphia, Pa.	10/2/60	R	R	5'11	188	4	19	4	0	3	.000
Kimber, Samuel Jackson "Sam" 84BroA 85ProN												
10/29/52	Philadelphia, Pa.	11/7/25	R	R	5'10½	165	42	369.1	126	18	21	.462
King, Charles Frederick "Silver" b. Koenig 86KCN 87–89StLA 90ChiP 91PitN 92–93NYN 93CinN 96–97WasN												
1/11/68	St. Louis, Mo.	5/21/38	R	R	6'	170	398	3190.2	1229	204	153	.571

	BIRTH DATE	BIRTHPLACE	DEATH DATE	B	T	HGT	WGT	G	INN	K	W	L	PCT
Kirby, John F. "John" 84KCU 85–86StLN 87IndN 87CleA 88KCA													
	1/13/65	St. Louis, Mo.	10/6/31	?	R	5'8	172	75	611.1	200	18	50	.265
Kissinger, William Francis "Bill" "Shang" 95BalN 95–97StLN (See P)													
	8/15/71	Dayton, Ky.	4/20/29	R	R	?	185	53	319.1	61	7	25	.219
Kitson, Frank R. "Frank" "Kitty" 98–99BalN 00BroN (See P)													
	9/11/69	Hopkins, Mich.	4/14/30	L	R	5'11	165	97	700.1	162	45	34	.570
Kittridge, Malachi Jeddidiah "Mal" "Jed" 96ChiN (See C)													
	10/12/69	Clinton, Mass.	6/23/28	R	R	5'7	170	1	1.2	0	0	0	—
***Kling, William** "Bill" 91PhiN 92BalN 95LouN													
	1/14/67	Kansas City, Mo.	8/26/34	L	R	6'	190	15	87	33	4	4	.500
Klobedanz, Frederick Augustus "Fred" "Duke" 96–99BosN (See P)													
	6/13/71	Waterbury, Conn.	4/12/40	L	L	5'11	190	88	694	177	52	25	.675
Knauss, Frank H. "Frank" 90ColA 91CleN 92CinN 94CleN 95NYN													
	?/?/68	Cleveland, Ohio	Unknown	L	L	5'10	170	44	313.1	159	17	16	.515
Knell, Philip Louis "Phil" 88PitN 90PhiP 91ColA 92WasN 92PhiN 94PitN 94–95LouN 95CleN													
	3/12/65	Mill Valley, Cal.	6/5/44	R	L	5'7½	154	192	1452.1	575	79	90	.467
Knepper, Charles "Charlie" 99CleN													
	2/18/71	Anderson, Ind.	2/6/46	R	R	6'4	190	27	219.2	43	4	22	.154
Knight, Alonzo P. "Lon" 75AthNA 76PhiN 84–85PhiA 85ProN (See OF)													
	6/16/53	Philadelphia, Pa.	4/23/32	R	R	5'11½	165	51	412	31	16	28	.364
Knight, George Henry "George" 75NHNA													
	11/24/55	Lakeville, Conn.	10/4/12	?	?	?	?	1	9	0	1	0	1.000
Knight, Joseph William "Joe" "Quiet Joe" 84PhiN (See OF)													
	9/28/59	Port Stanley, Ont., Can.	10/16/38	L	L	5'11	185	6	51	8	2	4	.333
Knouff, Edward "Ed" "Fred" 85PhiA 86–87BalA 87–88StLA 88CleA 89PhiA													
	6/?/68	Philadelphia, Pa.	9/14/00	R	R	?	210	44	343	128	20	20	.500
Kolb, Edward William "Eddie" 99CleN													
	7/20/80	Cincinnati, Ohio	Unknown	R	R	?	?	1	8	1	0	1	.000
Korwan, James "Jim" "Long Jim" 94BroN 97ChiN													
	3/4/74	Brooklyn, N.Y.	7/24/99	R	R	6'1	181	6	39	14	1	2	.333
Kostal, Joseph William "Joe" "Cudgey" 96LouN													
	3/17/76	Chicago, Ill.	10/17/33	R	R	5'6	130	2	2	0	0	0	—
Krieger, ? 84KCU													
	Unknown	Unknown	Unknown	?	?	?	?	1	7	3	0	1	.000
Krock, August H. "Gus" 88–89ChiN 89IndN 89WasN 90BufP													
	5/9/66	Milwaukee, Wis.	3/22/05	?	L	6'	196	60	505.1	209	32	26	.552
Krumm, Albert "Al" 89PitN													
	1/?/65	?, Pennsylvania	Unknown	?	R	?	?	1	9	4	0	1	.000
Lackey, ? 90PhiA													
	Unknown	Columbus, Ohio	Unknown	?	?	?	?	1	2	1	0	0	—
Ladew, Stephen "Steve" 89KCA													
	Unknown	St. Louis, Mo.	Unknown	?	?	?	?	1	2	0	0	0	—
Lafferty, Frank Bernard "Flip" 76PhiN (See OF)													
	5/4/54	Scranton, Pa.	2/8/10	?	R	?	?	1	9	0	0	1	.000
Lampe, Henry Joseph "Henry" 94BosN 95PhiN													
	9/19/72	Boston, Mass.	9/16/36	R	L	5'11½	175	9	49.1	19	0	3	.000
Landis, Samuel H. "Doc" 82PhiA 82BalA													
	8/16/54	Philadelphia, Pa.	Unknown	R	?	5'11	172	44	358	75	12	28	.300

	BIRTH DATE	BIRTHPLACE	DEATH DATE	B	T	HGT	WGT	G	INN	K	W	L	PCT
Larkin, Frank S. "Terry" 76NYN 77HarN 78–79ChiN 80TroN (84WasU) (84VirA) (See P)													
	?/?/56	Brooklyn, N.Y.	9/16/94	R	R	?	?	176	1567.1	406	89	80	.527
Lauer, John Charles "Chuck" 84PitA (See OF)													
	?/?/65	Pittsburgh, Pa.	Unknown	?	R	?	?	3	19	8	0	2	.000
Lawson, Alfred William "Al" 90BosN 90PitN													
	3/24/69	London, England	11/29/54	R	R	5'11	161	3	19	3	0	3	.000
Leary, John J. "Jack" 80BosN 81DetN 82PitA 82BalA 84AltU 84Chi–PitU (See SS)													
	?/?/58	New Haven, Conn.	Unknown	?	L	5'11	186	14	94.2	23	3	9	.250
Lee, Thomas Frank "Tom" 84ChiN 84BalU													
	6/8/62	Philadelphia, Pa.	3/4/86	?	?	?	?	20	167.1	95	6	12	.333
Leever, Samuel "Sam" "Deacon" "The Goshen Schoolmaster" 98–00PitN													
	12/23/71	Goshen, Ohio	5/19/53	R	R	5'10½	175	86	644.2	220	37	36	.507
Leiper, John Henry Thomas "Jack" 91ColA													
	12/23/67	Chester, Pa.	8/23/60	L	L	5'11	?	6	45	19	2	2	.500
Leith, William "Bill" "Shady Bill" 99WasN													
	5/31/73	Matteawan, N.Y.	7/16/40	?	L	?	?	1	2	1	0	0	—
Leitner, George Aloysius "Doc" 87IndN													
	9/14/65	Piermont, N.Y.	5/18/37	R	R	5'11½	185	8	65	27	2	6	.250
Lewis, ? 90BufP													
	Unknown	Brooklyn, N.Y.	Unknown	?	?	?	?	1	3	1	0	1	.000
Lewis, Edward Morgan "Ted" "Parson" 96–00BosN													
	12/25/72	Machynlleth, Wales	5/24/36	R	R	5'10	158	154	1088.2	275	78	47	.624
Lillie, James J. "Jim" "Grasshopper" b. Lilly 83–84BufN 86KCN (See OF)													
	7/27/61	New Haven, Conn.	11/9/90	?	?	?	?	6	31	8	0	2	.000
Lincoln, Ezra Perry "Ezra" 90CleN 90SyrA													
	11/17/68	Raynham, Mass.	5/7/51	L	L	5'11	160	18	138	28	3	14	.176
Lipp, Thomas Charles "Tom" b. Lieb 97PhiN													
	6/4/70	Baltimore, Md.	5/30/32	?	?	5'11½	170	1	3	1	0	1	.000
Lochhead, Robert Henry "Harry" 99CleN (See SS)													
	3/29/76	Stockton, Cal.	8/22/09	R	R	5'11½	172	1	3.2	0	0	0	—
Lockwood, Milo Hathaway "Milo" 84WasU													
	4/7/58	Solon, Ohio	10/9/97	?	?	5'10	160	11	67.2	48	1	9	.100
Lovett, Leonard Walker "Len" 73ResNA (See OF)													
	7/17/52	Lancaster Co., Pa.	11/18/22	R	R	?	?	1	9	1	0	1	.000
Lovett, Thomas Joseph "Tom" 85PhiA 89BroA 90–91BroN 93BroN 94BosN													
	12/7/63	Providence, R.I.	3/19/28	R	?	5'8	162	162	1305.1	439	88	59	.599
Lowe, Robert Lincoln "Link" 91BosN (See 2B)													
	7/10/68	Pittsburgh, Pa.	12/8/51	R	R	5'10	150	1	1	0	0	0	—
Luby, John Perkins "Pat" 90–92ChiN 95LouN (See P)													
	6/?/69	Charleston, S.C.	4/24/99	?	R	6'	185	106	792.1	213	39	41	.488
Lucid, Cornelius Cecil "Con" 93LouN 94–95BroN 95–96PhiN 97StLN													
	2/24/74	Dublin, Ireland	6/25/31	?	?	5'7	170	54	375	65	23	23	.500
Luff, Henry T. "Henry" 75NHNA													
	9/14/56	Philadelphia, Pa.	10/11/16	?	?	5'11	175	10	68.2	5	1	6	.167
Lukens, Albert P. "Al" 94PhiN													
	11/?/68	?, Pennsylvania	Unknown	?	?	5'9	168	3	15	0	0	1	.000
Lynch, John H. "Jack" 81BufN 83–87NYA 90BroA													
	2/5/57	New York, N.Y.	4/20/23	R	R	5'8	185	221	1924.1	859	110	105	.512

BIRTH DATE	BIRTHPLACE	DEATH DATE	B	T	HGT	WGT	G	INN	K	W	L	PCT
Lynch, Thomas S. "Tom" 84ChiN												
?/?/63	Peru, Ill.	5/13/03	L	?	5'11	175	1	7	2	0	0	—
Lyons, Harry P. "Harry" 90RocA (See OF)												
3/25/66	Chester, Pa.	6/30/12	R	R	5'10½	157	1	3.2	2	0	0	—
Lyons, Thomas A. "Toby" 90SyrA												
3/27/69	Cambridge, Mass.	8/27/20	?	?	?	?	3	22.1	6	0	2	.000
Lyston, William Edward "Bill" 91ColA 94CleN												
?/?/63	Baltimore, Md.	8/4/44	?	R	?	?	2	9.2	1	0	0	—
MacArthur, Malcolm "Mac" 84IndA												
1/19/62	Glasgow, Scotland	10/18/32	?	R	5'9½	164	6	52	19	1	5	.167
Mace, Harry L. "Jimmy" 91WasA												
Unknown	Washington, D.C.	Unknown	?	?	5'11	185	3	16	3	0	1	.000
Mack, Dennis Joseph "Denny" b. McGee 71RokNA (See SS)												
?/?/51	Easton, Pa.	4/10/88	R	R	5'7	164	3	13	1	0	1	.000
Macullar, James F. "Jimmy" "Little Mac" 85–86BalA (See SS)												
1/16/55	Boston, Mass.	4/8/24	R	L	5'6	155	2	3	1	0	0	—
Madden, Michael Joseph "Kid" 87–89BosN 90BosP 91BosA 91BalA (See P)												
10/22/66	Portland, Me.	3/16/96	?	L	5'7½	130	122	958	284	54	50	.519
Madigan, William J. "Tony" "Tice" 86WasN												
7/?/68	Washington, D.C.	12/4/54	?	R	5'5½	126	14	114.2	29	1	13	.071
Magee, William J. "Bill" 97–99LouN 99PhiN 99WasN												
?/?/75	?, Canada	Unknown	?	?	5'10	154	89	633.2	127	27	43	.386
Mahaffey, Louis Wood "Lou" 98LouN												
1/3/74	Madison, Wis.	10/26/49	R	?	5'9	170	1	9	1	0	1	.000
Mahoney, George W. "Mike" "Big Mike" 97BosN												
12/5/73	Boston, Mass.	1/3/40	R	?	6'4	200	1	1	1	0	0	—
Mains, Willard Eben "Willard" "Grasshopper" 88ChiN 91CinA 91MilA 96BosN												
7/7/68	N. Windham, Me.	5/23/23	?	R	6'2	190	42	267.2	96	16	17	.485
Malarkey, John S. "John" "Liz" 94–96WasN 99ChiN												
5/4/72	Springfield, Ohio	10/29/49	?	R	5'11	155	27	142.2	42	2	11	.154
Malone, Martin "Martin" 72EckNA												
Unknown	Unknown	Unknown	?	?	?	?	3	27	0	0	3	.000
Manning, John E. "Jack" 74BalNA 75BosNA 76BosN 77CinN 78BosN (See OF)												
12/20/53	Braintree, Mass.	8/15/29	R	R	5'8½	158	96	569	77	39	27	.591
*Mansell, Thomas E. "Brick" 83DetN (See OF)												
1/1/55	Auburn, N.Y.	10/6/34	L	L	5'8	160	1	6.2	3	0	0	—
Mars, Edward M. "Ed" 90SyrA												
12/4/66	Chicago, Ill.	12/9/41	?	?	5'9	166	16	121.1	59	9	5	.643
Martin, Alphonse Case "Phoney" 72TroNA 72EckNA 73MutNA (See 2B)												
8/4/45	New York, N.Y.	5/24/33	?	?	5'7	148	24	156.1	4	3	10	.231
Mason, Charles E. "Charlie" 75WasNA (See OF)												
6/25/53	New Orleans, La.	10/21/36	R	R	?	175	1	2	0	0	0	—
Mason, Ernest "Ernie" 94StLN												
Unknown	New Orleans, La.	7/30/04	?	?	?	?	4	22.2	3	0	3	.000
Mathews, Robert T. "Bobby" 71KekNA 72BalNA 73–75MutNA 76NYN 77CinN 79ProN 81ProN 81–82BosN 83–87PhiA (See P)												
11/21/51	Baltimore, Md.	4/17/98	R	R	5'5½	140	578	4955.1	1521	297	248	.545

BIRTH DATE	BIRTHPLACE	DEATH DATE	B	T	HGT	WGT	G	INN	K	W	L	PCT
*Mathewson, Christopher "Christy" "Matty" 00NYN												
8/12/80	Factoryville, Pa.	10/7/25	R	R	6'1½	195	6	33.2	15	0	3	.000
Matterson, C.V. "C.V." 84StLU												
Unknown	?, Ohio	Unknown	?	?	?	?	1	6	3	1	0	1.000
Mattimore, Michael Joseph "Mike" 87NYN 88–89PhiA 89KCA 90BroA (See OF)												
?/?/59	Renovo, Pa.	4/28/31	L	L	5'8½	160	58	490.2	132	26	27	.491
Mauck, Alfred Maris "Hal" 93ChiN												
3/6/69	Princeton, Ind.	4/27/21	R	R	5'11	185	23	143	23	8	10	.444
Maul, Albert Joseph "Al" "Smiling Al" 84PhiU 87PhiN 88–89PitN 90PitP 91PitN 93–97WasN 97–98BalN 99BroN 00PhiN (See P)												
10/9/65	Philadelphia, Pa.	5/3/58	R	R	6'	175	185	1415.2	341	84	77	.522
Maupin, Harry Carr "Harry" 98StL 99CleN												
7/11/72	Wellsville, Mo.	8/25/52	?	?	5'7	150	7	43	6	0	5	.000
Mays, Albert C. "Al" 85LouA 86–87NYA 88BroA 89–90ColA												
5/17/65	Canal Dover, Ohio	5/7/05	R	?	?	?	150	1251	469	53	89	.373
McAllister, Lewis William "Sport" 96–99CleN (See OF)												
7/23/74	Austin, Miss.	7/17/62	B	R	5'11	180	17	113.1	21	4	7	.364
McBride, James Dickson "Dick" 71–75AthNA 76BosN												
?/?/45	Philadelphia, Pa.	10/10/16	?	R	5'9	150	237	2081.2	149	149	78	.656
McBride, Peter William "Pete" 98CleN 99StLN												
7/9/75	Adams, Mass.	7/3/44	R	R	5'10	170	12	71	32	2	5	.286
McCaffrey, Harry Charles "Harry" 85CinA (See OF)												
11/25/58	St. Louis, Mo.	4/19/28	R	R	5'10½	185	1	9	2	1	0	1.000
McCarthy, Thomas Francis Michael "Tommy" 84BosU 86PhiN 88–89StLA 91StLA 94BosN (See OF)												
7/24/63	Boston, Mass.	8/5/22	R	R	5'7	170	13	69.1	21	0	7	.000
McCarty, John A. "John" 89KCA												
Unknown	St. Louis, Mo.	Unknown	?	R	?	?	15	119.2	36	8	6	.571
McCauley, Allen A. "Al" 84IndA (See 1B)												
3/4/63	Indianapolis, Ind.	8/24/17	L	L	6'	180	10	76	34	2	7	.222
McCormick, James "Jim" 78IndN 79–84CleN 84CinU 85ProN 85–86ChiN 87PitN												
11/3/56	Glasgow, Scotland	3/10/18	R	R	5'10½	215	492	4275.2	1704	265	214	.553
McCormick, John "Jerry" 84PhiU (See 3B)												
Unknown	Philadelphia, Pa.	9/19/05	?	?	?	?	1	2	3	0	0	—
McCormick, Patrick Henry "Harry" 79SyrN 81WorN 82–83CinA												
10/25/55	Syracuse, N.Y.	8/8/89	R	R	5'9	155	103	884	157	41	58	.414
McCreery, Thomas Livingston "Tom" 95–96LouN 00PitN (See OF)												
10/19/74	Beaver, Pa.	7/3/41	B	R	5'11	180	10	52.2	14	3	2	.600
McCullough, Charles F. "Charlie" 90BroA 90SyrA												
?/?/67	Dublin, Ireland	Unknown	?	?	?	?	29	241.2	69	5	23	.179
McDermott, Joseph "Joe" (71KekNA) 72EckNA												
Unknown	Unknown	Unknown	?	?	?	?	7	63	1	0	7	.000
McDermott, Michael H. "Mike" 89LouN												
5/6/64	Fall River, Mass.	5/7/47	?	?	?	?	9	84.1	22	1	8	.111
McDermott, Michael Joseph "Mike" 95–96LouN 97CleN 97StLN												
9/7/62	St. Louis, Mo.	6/30/43	?	R	5'10	152	58	353.2	69	11	33	.250
McDoolan, ? 73MarNA												
Unknown	Unknown	Unknown	?	?	?	?	1	9	0	0	1	.000

BIRTH DATE	BIRTHPLACE	DEATH DATE	B	T	HGT	WGT	G	INN	K	W	L	PCT
McDougal, John Auchanbolt "Sandy" 95BroN												
5/21/74	Buffalo, N.Y.	10/2/10	R	R	5'10	155	1	3	2	0	0	—
McDougal, John H. "Dewey" 95–96StLN												
9/19/71	Aledo, Ill.	4/28/36	?	R	5'10	170	21	124.2	23	3	11	.214
McElroy, James D. "Jim" 84PhiN 84WilU												
?/?/63	San Francisco, Cal.	7/24/89	?	?	5'10	170	14	116	48	1	13	.071
***McFarlan, Anderson Daniel "Dan" 95LouN 99BroN 99WasN**												
11/1/73	Gainesville, Tex.	9/23/24	?	?	?	?	40	263.2	51	8	25	.242
McFarland, Christopher "Chris" 84BalU (See OF)												
8/17/61	Fall River, Mass.	5/24/18	?	?	5'9	170	1	3	3	0	1	.000
***McFarland, La Mont Amos "Monte" 95–96ChiN**												
11/7/72	White Hill, Ill.	11/15/13	?	?	?	?	6	39	8	2	4	.333
McFetridge, John Reed "Jack" 90PhiN												
8/25/69	Philadelphia, Pa.	1/10/17	?	?	6'	175	1	9	4	1	0	1.000
McGeachy, John Charles "Jack" 87–89IndN (See OF)												
5/23/64	Clinton, Mass.	4/5/30	R	R	5'8	165	5	16	6	0	1	.000
McGill, William Vaness "Willie" "Kid" 90CleP 91CinA 91StLA 92CinN 93–94ChiN 95–96PhiN												
11/10/73	Atlanta, Ga.	8/29/44	?	L	5'6½	170	166	1234.2	503	71	73	.493
McGinnis, August "Gus" 93ChiN 93PhiN												
?/?/70	Painesville, Ohio	Unknown	?	L	5'11	168	18	104.2	25	3	8	.273
McGinnis, George Washington "Jumbo" 82–86StLA 86BalA 87CinA												
2/22/64	Alton, Ill.	5/18/34	?	?	5'10	197	187	1603.2	562	102	79	.564
McGinnity, Joseph Jerome "Joe" "Iron Man" b. McGinty 99BalN 00BroN												
3/19/71	Rock Island, Ill.	11/14/29	R	R	5'11	206	92	709.1	167	56	24	.700
McGuire, ? 94CinN												
Unknown	Unknown	Unknown	?	?	?	?	1	6	1	0	0	—
McGuire, James Thomas "Deacon" 90RocA (See C)												
11/18/63	Youngstown, Ohio	10/31/36	R	R	6'1	185	1	4	1	0	0	—
McGunnigle, William Henry "Bill" "Gunner" 79–80BufN (See OF)												
1/1/55	Boston, Mass.	3/9/99	R	R	5'9	155	19	157	65	11	8	.579
McIntyre, Frank W. "Frank" 83DetN 83ColA												
7/12/59	Walled Lake, Mich.	7/8/87	?	?	?	?	3	30	6	2	1	.667
McJames, James McCutchen "Doc" b. James McCutchen James 95–97WasN 98BalN 99BroN												
8/27/73	Williamsburg, S.C.	9/23/01	?	R	?	?	165	1271.1	551	74	74	.500
McKelvy, Russell Errett "Russ" 78IndN (See OF)												
9/8/54	Swissvale, Pa.	10/19/15	R	R	?	?	4	25	3	0	2	.000
McKenna, James William "Kit" 98BroN 99BalN												
2/10/73	Lynchburg, Va.	3/31/41	?	?	?	?	22	145.2	34	4	9	.308
McKeon, Lawrence G. "Larry" 84IndA 85–86CinA 86KCN												
3/25/66	New York, N.Y.	7/18/15	?	?	5'10	168	116	979	474	46	64	.418
***McLaughlin, Bernard "Barney" 84KCU (See SS)**												
?/?/57	?, Ireland	2/13/21	R	R	?	?	7	48.2	14	1	3	.250
***McLaughlin, Francis Edward "Frank" 83PitA 84KCU (See SS)**												
6/19/56	Lowell, Mass.	4/5/17	R	R	5'9	160	4	19	4	0	0	—
McLaughlin, James Thomas "Jim" 84BalA												
11/18/60	Cleveland, Ohio	11/16/95	L	L	?	157	3	22	8	1	2	.333
McLaughlin, Warren A. "Warren" 00PhiN												
1/22/76	N. Plainfield, N.J.	10/22/23	?	L	?	?	1	6	1	0	0	—

	BIRTH DATE	BIRTHPLACE	DEATH DATE	B	T	HGT	WGT	G	INN	K	W	L	PCT
McMahon, John Joseph "Sadie" 89–90PhiA 90–91BalA 92–96BalN 97BroN													
	9/19/67	Wilmington, Del.	2/20/54	R	R	5'9	165	321	2634	967	174	127	.578
McManus, Patrick "Pat" 79TroN													
	Unknown	?, Ireland	10/6/17	?	?	?	?	2	21	6	0	2	.000
McMullen, George "George" 87NYA													
	Unknown	?, California	Unknown	?	?	?	?	3	21	2	2	1	.667
McMullin, John F. "John" "Lefty" 71TroNA 72MutNA 73AthNA 75PhiNA (See OF)													
	?/?/48	Philadelphia, Pa.	4/11/81	R	L	5'9	160	37	283.1	15	14	15	.483
McNabb, Edgar J. "Edgar" "Texas" 93BalN													
	10/25/65	Coshocton, Ohio	2/28/94	R	R	5'11½	170	21	142	18	8	7	.533
McPartlin, Frank "Frank" 99NYN													
	2/16/72	Hoosick Falls, N.Y.	11/13/43	?	R	6'	180	1	4	2	0	0	—
McSorley, John Bernard "Trick" 84TolA (See 1B)													
	12/16/52	St. Louis, Mo.	2/9/36	?	R	5'4	142	1	2	1	0	0	—
McVey, Calvin Alexander "Cal" 75BosN 76–77ChiN 79CinN (See 1B)													
	8/30/50	Montrose, Iowa	8/20/26	R	R	5'9	170	34	176.1	37	10	12	.455
Meakim, George Clinton "George" 90LouA 91PhiA 92CinN 92ChiN 95LouN													
	7/11/65	Brooklyn, N.Y.	2/17/23	R	R	5'7½	154	39	256.2	142	15	13	.536
Meegan, Peter J. "Pete" "Steady Pete" 84VirA 85PitA													
	11/13/63	San Francisco, Cal.	3/15/05	?	?	?	?	40	325	164	14	20	.412
Meekin, Jouett "Jouett" 91LouA 92LouN 92–93WasN 94–99NYN 99BosN 99NYN 00PitN (See P)													
	2/21/67	New Albany, Ind.	12/14/44	R	R	6'1	180	323	2596.1	897	152	133	.533
#Meinke, Frank Louis "Frank" 84–85DetN (See SS)													
	10/18/63	Chicago, Ill.	11/8/31	R	?	5'10½	172	36	294	124	8	24	.250
Menefee, John "Jock" 92PitN 93–94LouN 94–95PitN 98NYN 00ChiN (See P)													
	1/15/68	Rowlesburg, W.Va.	3/11/53	R	R	6'	165	76	584.2	149	30	38	.441
Mercer, George Barclay "Win" 94–99WasN 00NYN (See P)													
	6/20/74	Chester, W.Va.	1/12/03	R	R	5'7	140	275	2018.2	460	108	133	.448
Meyerle, Levi Samuel "Levi" "Long Levi" 71AthNA 76PhiN (See OF)													
	7/?/45	Philadelphia, Pa.	11/4/21	R	R	6'1	177	3	19	0	0	2	.000
Miller, Herbert A. "Burt" 97LouN													
	10/28/75	Riley, Mich.	Unknown	?	?	?	?	4	17	3	0	1	.000
Miller, Joseph H. "Cyclone" 84Chi–PitU 84ProN 84PhiN 86PhiA													
	9/24/59	Springfield, Mass.	10/13/16	?	L	5'9½	165	27	222.1	125	13	11	.542
Miller, Ralph Darwin "Ralph" 98BroN 99BalN													
	3/15/73	Cincinnati, Ohio	5/8/73	R	R	5'11	170	29	187.2	46	5	17	.227
Miller, Robert W. "Bob" 90RocA 91WasA													
	?/?/62	Unknown	Unknown	?	?	?	?	20	134.1	33	5	12	.294
Mitchell, Robert McKasha "Bobby" 77–78CinN 79CleN 82StLA													
	2/6/56	Cincinnati, Ohio	5/1/33	L	L	5'5	135	45	381.2	184	20	23	.465
Moffett, Samuel R. "Sam" 84CleN 87–88IndN													
	3/14/57	Wheeling, W.Va.	5/5/07	R	R	6'	175	37	303.2	94	6	29	.171
Molesworth, Carlton "Carlton" 95WasN													
	2/15/76	Frederick, Md.	7/25/61	L	L	5'6	200	4	16	7	0	2	.000
Moran, Samuel "Sam" 95PitN													
	9/16/70	Rochester, N.Y.	8/29/97	?	L	?	160	10	62.2	19	2	4	.333
Morgan, Henry William "Bill" 75RedsNA (See OF)													
	10/?/57	Washington, D.C.	Unknown	?	?	?	?	7	42	7	1	3	.250

BIRTH DATE	BIRTHPLACE	DEATH DATE	B	T	HGT	WGT	G	INN	K	W	L	PCT
Moriarty, Eugene John "Gene" 84IndN 85DetN (See OF)												
1/5/65	Holyoke, Mass.	Unknown	L	L	5'8	130	3	15.2	5	0	2	.000
Morrill, John Francis "John" "Honest John" 80–84BosN 86BosN 89WasN (See 1B)												
2/19/55	Boston, Mass.	4/2/32	R	R	5'10½	155	18	58.2	22	1	2	.333
Morris, E. 84BalU												
Unknown	Trenton, N.J.	Unknown	?	?	?	?	1	1	0	0	0	—
Morris, Edward "Ed" "Cannonball" 84ColA 85–86PitA 87–89PitN 90PitP												
9/29/62	Brooklyn, N.Y.	4/12/37	R	L	5'7	165	311	2678	1217	171	123	.582
Morrison, Michael "Mike" 87–88CleA 90SyrA 90BalA												
2/6/67	Erie, Pa.	6/16/55	R	R	5'8½	156	65	504.2	254	20	39	.339
Morrison, Stephen Henry "Hank" 87IndN												
5/22/66	Olneyville, R.I.	9/30/27	R	R	5'10	180	7	57	13	3	4	.429
Morton, Charles Hazen "Charlie" 84TolA (See OF)												
10/12/54	Kingsville, Ohio	12/9/21	R	R	?	150	3	23.1	7	0	1	.000
Morton, William P. "Sparrow" 84PhiN												
Unknown	Unknown	Unknown	?	L	?	?	2	17	5	0	2	.000
Mountain, Frank Henry "Frank" 80TroN 81DetN 82WorN 82PhiA 82WorN 83–84ColA 85–86PitA (See P)												
5/17/60	Ft. Edward, N.Y.	11/19/39	R	R	5'11	185	143	1215.2	383	58	83	.411
Mountjoy, William Henry "Billy" "Bill" "Medicine Bill" 84–85CinA 85BalA												
12/11/58	London, Ont., Can.	5/19/94	L	R	5'6	150	57	503.2	164	31	24	.564
Mullane, Anthony John "Tony" "Count" "The Apollo Of The Box" 81DetN 82LouA 83StLA 84TolA 86–89CinA												
90–93CinN 93–94BalN 94CleN (See P)												
1/20/59	Cork, Ireland	4/25/44	B	B	5'10½	165	555	4531.1	1803	284	220	.563
Murphy, Cornelius B. "Con" "Monk" "Razzle Dazzle" 84PhiN 90BroA												
10/15/63	Worcester, Mass.	8/1/14	?	R	5'9	130	23	165	39	4	13	.235
Murphy, Edward J. "Ed" 98PhiN												
1/22/77	Auburn, N.Y.	1/29/35	?	R	6'1	186	7	30	8	1	2	.333
Murphy, John Henry "John" 84AltU 84WilU												
3/8/67	Fitchberg, Mass.	9/12/30	?	?	?	?	21	159.2	73	5	12	.294
Murphy, Joseph Akin "Joe" 86CinA 86StLN 86–87StLA												
9/7/66	St. Louis, Mo.	3/28/51	?	?	5'11	160	11	95	30	4	7	.364
Murphy, Robert J. "Bob" 90NYN 90BroA												
12/26/66	Duchess Co., N.Y.	Unknown	?	?	?	?	15	114	34	4	9	.308
Myers, Henry C. "Henry" 82BalA (See SS)												
5/?/58	Philadelphia, Pa.	4/18/95	R	R	5'9	159	6	26	7	0	2	.000
Nash, William Mitchell "Billy" 89BosN 90BosP (See 3B)												
6/24/65	Richmond, Va.	11/15/29	R	R	5'8½	167	2	1.1	0	0	0	—
Neagle, John Henry "Jack" 79CinN 83PhiN 83BalA 83–84PitA												
1/2/58	Syracuse, N.Y.	9/20/04	R	R	5'6	155	70	560.1	152	16	50	.242
Neale, Joseph Hunt "Joe" 86–87LouA 90–91StLA												
5/7/66	Wadsworth, Ohio	12/30/13	R	R	5'8	153	31	227.2	58	12	12	.500
Nelson, William F. "Bill" 84PitA												
9/28/63	Terre Haute, Ind.	6/23/41	?	R	?	?	3	26	6	1	2	.333
Newton, Eustace James "Doc" 00CinN												
10/26/77	Indianapolis, Ind.	5/14/31	L	L	6'	185	35	234.2	88	9	15	.375
Nichols, Charles Augustus "Kid" 90–00BosN												
9/14/69	Madison, Wis.	4/11/53	B	R	5'10½	175	518	4217	1524	310	167	.650

BIRTH DATE	BIRTHPLACE	DEATH DATE	B	T	HGT	WGT	G	INN	K	W	L	PCT
Nichols, Frederick C. "Tricky" 75NHNA 76BosN 77StLN 78ProN 80WorN 82BalA												
7/26/50	Bridgeport, Conn.	8/22/97	R	R	5'7½	150	106	881	174	28	73	.277
Nicol, George Edward "George" 90StLA 91ChiN 94PitN 94LouN (See OF)												
10/17/70	Barry, Ill.	8/10/24	?	L	5'7	155	15	81.1	42	5	7	.417
Nolan, Edward Sylvester "The Only Nolan" 78IndN 81CleN 83PitA 84WilU 85PhiN												
11/7/57	Paterson, N.J.	5/18/13	L	R	5'8	171	79	676	274	23	52	.307
Nops, Jeremiah H. "Jerry" 96PhiN 96–99BalN 00BroN												
6/23/75	Toledo, Ohio	3/26/37	L	L	5'8½	168	109	811.2	251	60	31	.659
Norton, Elisha Strong "Effie" "Leiter" 96–97WasN												
8/17/73	Conneaut, Ohio	3/5/50	R	R	?	?	12	61	16	5	2	.714
Oberbeck, Henry A. "Henry" 84BalU 84KCU (See OF)												
5/17/58	?, Missouri	8/26/21	?	?	?	?	8	35.2	7	0	5	.000
Oberlander, Hartman Louis "Doc" 88CleA												
5/12/64	Waukegan, Ill.	11/14/22	?	L	?	?	3	25.2	23	1	2	.333
O'Brien, John F. "Darby" 88CleA 89CleN 90CleP 91BosA												
4/15/67	Troy, N.Y.	3/11/92	R	R	5'10	165	136	1080.2	398	59	65	.476
O'Brien, Thomas H. "Tom" 87NYA (See 2B)												
6/22/60	Salem, Mass.	4/21/21	R	R	6'1	185	1	3.2	0	0	0	—
O'Brien, William D. "Darby" 87NYA (See OF)												
9/1/63	Peoria, Ill.	6/15/93	R	R	6'1	186	1	1	0	0	0	—
O'Brien, William Smith "Billy" 84StPU (See 1B)												
3/14/60	Albany, N.Y.	5/26/11	R	?	6'	185	2	10	7	1	0	1.000
O'Connell, Patrick H. "Pat" 86BalA (See OF)												
6/10/61	Bangor, Me.	1/24/43	R	R	5'10	175	1	3	1	0	0	—
O'Connor, Frank Henry "Frank" 93PhiN												
9/15/70	Keeseville, N.Y.	12/26/13	L	L	6'	185	3	4	0	0	0	—
O'Day, Henry Francis "Hank" 84TolA 85PitA 86–89WasN 89NYN 90NYP												
7/8/62	Chicago, Ill.	7/2/35	?	R	6'	180	201	1651.1	663	73	110	.399
O'Neil, Edward J. "Ed" 90TolA 90PhiA												
3/11/59	Fall River, Mass.	9/30/92	?	R	5'11	180	8	68	19	0	8	.000
O'Neill, J. 75AtlNA												
Unknown	Brooklyn, N.Y.	Unknown	?	?	?	?	5	34	0	0	4	.000
O'Neill, James Edward "Tip" 83NYN 84StLA (See OF)												
5/25/58	Woodstock, Ont., Can.	12/31/15	R	R	6'1½	167	36	289	91	16	16	.500
O'Rourke, ? 72EckNA												
Unknown	Unknown	Unknown	?	?	?	?	1	9	0	0	1	.000
***#O'Rourke, James Henry "Jim" "Orator Jim"** 83–84BufN (See OF)												
9/1/50	Bridgeport, Conn.	1/8/19	R	R	5'8	185	6	19.2	4	0	1	.000
O'Rourke, Michael J. "Mike" 90BalA												
Unknown	Unknown	Unknown	?	?	?	?	5	41	8	1	2	.333
Orr, David L. "Dave" 85NYA (See 1B)												
9/29/59	New York, N.Y.	6/3/15	R	R	5'11	250	3	10	1	0	0	—
Orth, Albert Lewis "Al" "The Curveless Wonder" 95–00PhiN (See P)												
9/5/72	Tipton, Ind.	10/8/48	L	R	6'	200	158	1223	267	80	60	.571
Osborne, Frederick W. "Fred" 90PitN (See OF)												
5/?/65	Hampton, Iowa	Unknown	?	L	?	?	8	58	14	0	5	.000
Pabor, Charles Henry "Charlie" 71–72CleNA 75AtlNA (See OF)												
9/24/46	New York, N.Y.	4/22/13	L	L	5'8	155	10	51.1	0	1	4	.200

BIRTH DATE	BIRTHPLACE	DEATH DATE	B	T	HGT	WGT	G	INN	K	W	L	PCT
Palmer, ? 85StLN												
Unknown	Unknown	Unknown	?	?	?	?	4	34	9	0	4	.000
Pappalau, John Joseph "John" 97CleN												
4/3/75	Albany, N.Y.	5/12/44	R	R	6'	175	2	12	3	0	1	.000
***Parker, Harley William "Doc" 93ChiN 95–96ChiN**												
6/14/72	Theresa, N.Y.	3/3/41	R	R	6'2	200	17	126.1	24	5	7	.417
***Parker, Jay "Jay" 99PitN**												
7/8/74	Theresa, N.Y.	6/8/35	R	R	5'11	185	1	0	0	0	0	—
Parks, William Robert "Bill" 75WasNA 75PhiNA (See OF)												
6/4/49	Easton, Pa.	10/10/11	R	R	5'8	150	16	112	3	4	8	.333
***Parrott, Thomas William "Tom" "Tacky Tom" 93ChiN 93–95CinN 96StLN (See OF)**												
4/10/68	Portland, Ore.	1/1/32	R	R	5'10½	170	115	795	166	39	48	.448
Parsons, Charles James "Charlie" 86BosN 87NYA 90CleN												
7/18/63	Cherry Flats, Pa.	3/24/36	L	L	5'10	160	8	59	12	1	4	.200
Payne, Harley Fenwick "Harley" "Lady" 96–98BroN 99PitN												
1/9/68	Windsor, Ont., Can.	12/29/35	B	L	6'	160	80	557	148	30	36	.455
Pearce, Franklin Joseph "Frank" 76LouNA												
3/30/60	Jefferson Co., Ky.	11/13/26	?	?	?	?	1	4	1	0	0	—
Pearce, Richard J. "Dickey" 75StLN (See SS)												
2/29/36	Brooklyn, N.Y.	10/12/08	R	R	5'3½	161	2	5.1	0	0	0	—
Pears, Frank H. "Frank" 89KCA 93StLN												
8/30/66	?, Kentucky	11/29/23	?	R	5'9	145	4	26	5	0	2	.000
Pechiney, George Adolphe "George" "Pisch" 85–86CinA 87CleA												
9/2/61	Cincinnati, Ohio	7/14/43	R	R	5'9	184	61	514.1	183	23	34	.404
***Peitz, Henry Clement "Heinie" 94StLN 97CinN 99CinN (See C)**												
11/28/70	St. Louis, Mo.	10/23/43	R	R	5'11	165	4	16	3	0	1	.000
Peoples, James Elsworth "Jimmy" 85CinA (See C)												
10/8/63	Big Beaver, Mich.	8/29/20	?	R	5'8	200	2	15	4	0	2	.000
Peppers, Harrison "Bill" b. William Harrison Pepper 94LouN												
9/?/66	?, Kentucky	11/5/03	L	?	?	?	2	8	0	0	1	.000
Peters, John Paul "John" 76ChiN (See SS)												
4/8/50	Louisiana, Mo.	1/4/24	R	R	5'7	180	1	1	0	0	0	—
Pettit, Robert Henry "Bob" 87ChiN (See OF)												
7/19/61	Williamstown, Mass.	11/1/10	L	R	5'9	160	1	1	0	0	0	—
Petty, Charles E. "Charlie" 89ChiN 93NYN 94WasN 94CleN												
6/28/66	Nashville, Tenn.	Unknown	?	R	?	?	34	228	40	10	15	.400
Pfann, William F. "Bill" 94CinN												
6/?/63	Hamilton, Ont., Can.	6/3/04	?	?	6'	205	1	3	0	0	1	.000
Pfeffer, Nathaniel Frederick "Fred" "Fritz" "Dandelion" 84–85ChiN 92LouN 94LouN (See 2B)												
3/17/60	Louisville, Ky.	4/10/32	R	R	5'10½	184	8	44.2	13	2	1	.667
Phillippe, Charles Louis "Deacon" 99LouN 00PitN												
5/23/72	Rural Retreat, Va.	3/30/52	R	R	6'½	180	80	600	143	41	30	.577
Phillips, William Corcoran "Bill" "Whoa Bill" 90PitN 95CinN 99–00CinN												
11/9/68	Allenport, Pa.	10/25/41	R	R	5'11	180	90	627	134	33	36	.478
Phyle, William Joseph "Bill" 98–99ChiN												
6/25/75	Duluth, Minn.	8/6/53	?	R	?	?	13	106.2	14	3	9	.250
Piatt, Wiley Harold "Wiley" 98–00PhiN												
7/13/74	Blue Creek, Ohio	9/20/46	L	L	5'10	175	100	771.2	257	56	39	.589

BIRTH DATE	BIRTHPLACE	DEATH DATE	B	T	HGT	WGT	G	INN	K	W	L	PCT
*Pierson, David P. "Dave" 76CinN (See C)												
8/20/55	Wilkes–Barre, Pa.	11/11/22	R	R	5'7	142	1	0	0	0	1	.000
Pinkham, Edward "Ed" 71ChiNA (See 3B)												
?/?/49	Brooklyn, N.Y.	Unknown	?	L	5'7	142	3	10.1	0	1	0	1.000
Pinkney, George Burton "George" 86BroA (See 3B)												
1/1/62	Orange Prairie, Ill.	11/10/26	R	R	5'7	160	1	2	0	0	0	—
Pittinger, Charles Reno "Togie" 00BosN												
1/12/72	Greencastle, Pa.	1/14/09	L	R	6'2	175	18	114	27	2	9	.182
Pond, Erasmus Arlington "Arlie" 95–98BalN												
1/19/72	Rutland, Vt.	9/19/30	R	R	5'10	160	69	496	156	35	19	.648
Poole, Edward I. "Ed" 00PitN												
9/7/74	Canton, Ohio	3/11/19	R	R	5'10	175	1	7	3	1	0	1.000
Poorman, Thomas Iverson "Tom" 80BufN 80ChiN 84TolA 87PhiA (See OF)												
10/14/57	Lock Haven, Pa.	2/18/05	L	R	5'7	135	15	109.2	14	3	9	.250
Porter, Henry "Henry" 84KCU 84MilU 85–87BroA 88–89KCA (See P)												
6/?/58	Vergennes, Vt.	12/30/06	R	R	?	?	207	1793.1	659	96	107	.473
Powell, Charles Abner "Abner" 84WasU 86BalA 86CinA (See OF)												
12/15/60	Shenandoah, Pa.	8/7/53	L	R	5'7	160	29	209.1	97	8	18	.308
Powell, John Joseph "Jack" "Red" 97–98CleN 99–00StLN												
7/9/74	Bloomington, Ill.	10/17/44	R	R	5'11	195	155	1227.2	318	78	60	.565
Powers, James T. "Jim" 90BroA												
?/?/68	New York, N.Y.	Unknown	?	?	5'10	150	4	30	3	1	2	.333
Pratt, Albert George "Al" "Uncle Al" 71–72CleNA												
11/19/48	Allegheny, Pa.	11/21/37	?	R	5'7	140	43	330.1	41	12	26	.316
Price, William "Bill" 90PhiA												
Unknown	Philadelphia, Pa.	Unknown	?	?	?	?	1	9	1	1	0	1.000
Proeser, George "George" "Yatz" 88CleA (See OF)												
5/30/64	Cincinnati, Ohio	10/13/41	L	L	5'10	190	7	59	20	3	4	.429
Purcell, William Aloysius "Blondie" 79SyrN 79-80CinN 81–82BufN 83–84PhiN 85PhiA 86–87BalA (See OF)												
3/16/54	Paterson, N.J.	2/20/12	R	R	5'9½	159	79	581.1	138	15	43	.259
Purner, Oscar E. "Oscar" 95WasN												
?/?/73	Washington, D.C.	Unknown	?	?	?	?	1	2	0	0	0	—
Pyle, Harry Thomas "Shadow" 84PhiN 87ChiN												
11/29/61	Reading, Pa.	12/26/08	?	L	5'8	136	5	35.2	9	1	4	.200
Quarles, William H. "Bill" 91WasA 93BosN												
?/?/69	Petersburg, Va.	3/25/97	?	?	6'3	?	6	49	16	3	2	.600
*Radbourn, Charles Gardner "Hoss" "Old Hoss" "Charley" 81–85ProN 86–89BosN 90BosP 91CinN (See OF)												
12/11/54	Rochester, N.Y.	2/5/97	R	R	5'9	168	528	4535.1	1830	311	195	.615
*Radbourn, George B. "George" "Dordy" 83DetN												
4/8/56	Bloomington, Ill.	1/1/04	?	?	?	160	3	22	2	1	2	.333
Radford, Paul Revere "Paul" "Shorty" 84–85ProN 87NYA 90CleP 91BosA 93WasN (See OF)												
10/14/61	Roxbury, Mass.	2/21/45	R	R	5'6	148	10	43.1	13	0	4	.000
Ramsey, Thomas A. "Toad" 85–89LouA 89–90StLA												
8/8/64	Indianapolis, Ind.	3/27/06	R	L	?	?	248	2100.2	1515	113	124	.477
Raymond, Harry H. "Harry" "Jack" 89LouA (See 3B)												
2/20/62	Utica, N.Y.	3/21/25	?	?	5'9	179	1	9	1	1	0	1.000
Reardon, James Matthew "Jim" 86StLN 86CinA												
?/?/66	Hoosick Falls, N.Y.	2/25/91	?	?	?	?	2	10	0	0	2	.000

BIRTH DATE	BIRTHPLACE	DEATH DATE	B	T	HGT	WGT	G	INN	K	W	L	PCT
*Reccius, John "John" 82–83LouA (See OF)												
10/29/59	Louisville, Ky.	9/1/30	?	?	5'6½	?	14	99	31	4	6	.400
*Reccius, Phillip "Phil" 84–86LouA 87CleA (See 3B)												
6/7/62	Louisville, Ky.	2/15/03	?	?	5'9	163	27	179.1	56	6	12	.333
Reidy, William Joseph "Bill" 96NYN 99BroN												
10/9/73	Cleveland, Ohio	10/14/15	R	R	5'10	175	4	20	3	1	1	.500
Reis, Lawrence P. "Laurie" 77–78ChiN												
11/20/58	Chicago, Ill.	1/24/21	R	R	?	160	8	72	19	4	4	.500
Rettger, George Edward "George" 91StLA 92CleN 92CinN												
7/29/68	Cleveland, Ohio	6/5/21	R	R	5'11	175	21	139.2	62	9	6	.600
Reynolds, Charles E. "Charlie" 82PhiA												
7/31/57	Allegany, N.Y.	5/1/13	?	?	?	?	2	12	4	1	1	.500
Rhines, William Pearl "Billy" "Bunker" 90–92CinN 93LouN 95–97CinN 98–99PitN												
3/14/69	Ridgway, Pa.	1/30/22	R	R	5'11	168	249	1900	555	114	103	.525
Rhodes, William Clarence "Bill" 93LouN												
Unknown	Pottstown, Pa.	Unknown	?	?	?	?	20	151.2	22	5	12	.294
Richardson, Abram Harding "Hardy" "Old True Blue" 85BufN 86DetN (See 2B)												
4/21/55	Clarksboro, N.J.	1/14/31	R	R	5'9½	170	5	16	6	3	0	1.000
Richardson, Daniel "Danny" 85–87NYN (See 2B)												
1/25/63	Elmira, N.Y.	9/12/26	R	R	5'8	165	15	100	38	7	3	.700
Richmond, J. Lee "Lee" 79BosN 80–82WorN 83ProN 86CinA (See P)												
5/5/57	Sheffield, Ohio	10/1/29	?	L	5'10	155	191	1583	552	75	100	.429
Riddlemoser, Dorsey Lee "Dorsey" 99WasN												
3/25/75	Frederick, Md.	5/11/54	R	R	?	?	1	2	0	0	0	—
Roach, John F. "John" 87NYN												
Unknown	Farrandsdale, Pa.	Unknown	R	L	5'9	175	1	8	3	0	1	.000
Roach, Rudolph Charles "Skel" b. Weichbrodt 99ChiN												
10/20/71	Danzig, Germany	3/9/58	R	R	6'2	?	1	9	0	1	0	1.000
Robinson, William "Bill" b. Anderson 89LouA												
Unknown	Taylorsville, Ky	Unknown	?	?	?	?	1	8	2	0	1	.000
Robinson, William H. "Yank" 82DetN 84BalU 86–87StLA (See 2B)												
9/19/59	Philadelphia, Pa.	8/25/94	R	R	5'6½	170	14	89	62	3	4	.429
Rosebraugh, Eli Ethelbert "Zeke" 98–99PitN												
9/8/70	Charleston, Ill.	7/16/30	?	L	?	?	6	27.2	8	0	3	.000
Roseman, James John "Chief" 85–87NYA (See OF)												
7/4/56	New York, N.Y.	7/4/38	R	R	5'7	167	4	16	1	0	1	.000
*Rowe, David Elwood "Dave" 77ChiN 82CleN 83BalA 84StLU (See OF)												
10/9/54	Harrisburg, Pa.	12/9/30	R	R	5'9	180	4	23	3	1	2	.333
Rusie, Amos Wilson "Amos" "The Hoosier Thunderbolt" 89IndN 90–95NYN 97–98NYN (See P)												
5/30/71	Mooresville, Ind.	12/6/42	R	R	6'1	200	459	3747.2	1928	245	173	.586
Russ, John "John" 82BalA												
4/1/58	Cannelton, Ind.	1/18/12	?	?	?	?	1	5	0	0	1	.000
Ryan, Daniel R. "Cyclone" 87NYA 91BosN (See 1B)												
?/?/66	Cappagh White, Ireland	1/30/17	?	R	6'	?	3	5.1	0	0	1	.000
Ryan, James Edward "Jimmy" "Pony" 86–88ChiN 91ChiN 93ChiN (See OF)												
2/11/63	Clinton, Mass.	10/26/23	R	L	5'9	162	24	117	43	6	1	.857

BIRTH DATE	BIRTHPLACE	DEATH DATE	B	T	HGT	WGT	G	INN	K	W	L	PCT
Ryan, John A. "John" (aka Daniel Sheehan) 84BalU												
Unknown	Birmingham, Mich.	Unknown	L	R	?	?	6	51	33	3	2	.600
Ryan, John Joseph "Johnny" 74BalNA 75NHNA 76LouN (See OF)												
10/?/53	Philadelphia, Pa.	3/22/02	?	?	5'7½	150	12	68.2	2	1	5	.167
Salisbury, Henry H. "Harry" 79TroN 82PitA												
5/15/55	Providence, R.I.	3/29/33	L	?	5'8½	162	48	424	166	24	24	.500
Sanders, Alexander Bennett "Ben" 88–89PhiN 90PhiP 91PhiA 92LouN (See P)												
2/26/65	Catharpin, Va.	8/29/30	R	R	6'	210	168	1385	468	80	70	.533
Sawyer, Willard Newton "Will" 84CleN												
7/29/64	Brimfield, Ohio	1/5/36	L	L	?	?	17	141	76	4	10	.286
Saylor, Philip Andrew "Phil" "Lefty" 91PhiN												
1/2/71	Van Wert Co., Ohio	7/23/37	?	L	?	?	1	3	0	0	0	—
Schappert, John "John" 82StLA												
Unknown	Brooklyn, N.Y.	7/29/16	R	R	5'10	170	15	128	38	8	7	.533
Scheibeck, Frank S. "Frank" 87CleA (See SS)												
6/28/65	Detroit, Mich.	10/22/56	R	R	5'7	145	1	9	3	0	0	—
Scheible, John G. "Jack" 93CleN 94PhiN												
2/16/66	Youngstown, Ohio	8/9/97	?	L	?	?	3	18.1	1	1	2	.333
Schenck, William G. "Bill" 82LouA (See 3B)												
Unknown	Brooklyn, N.Y.	Unknown	?	?	5'7	171	2	10	4	1	0	1.000
Schmit, Frederick M. "Crazy" "Germany" 90PitN 92–93BalN 93NYN 99CleN												
2/13/66	Chicago, Ill.	10/5/40	L	L	5'10½	165	50	338.2	91	7	34	.171
Schoeneck, Louis N. "Jumbo" 88IndN (See 1B)												
3/3/62	Chicago, Ill.	1/20/30	R	R	6'3	223	2	4.1	1	0	0	—
Schultze, John F. "John" 91PhiN												
Unknown	Burlington, N.J.	Unknown	?	?	6'1½	165	6	15	4	0	1	.000
Scott, Edward "Ed" 00CinN												
8/12/70	Walbridge, Ohio	11/1/33	R	R	6'3	?	42	315	87	17	20	.459
Scott, Milton Parker "Milt" "Mikado Milt" 86BalA (See 1B)												
1/17/66	Chicago, Ill.	11/3/38	R	?	5'9	160	1	3	0	0	0	—
Sechrist, Theodore O'Hara "Doc" 99NYN												
2/10/76	Williamstown, Ky.	4/2/50	R	R	5'9	160	1	0	0	0	0	—
Seery, John Emmett "Emmett" 86StLN (See OF)												
2/13/61	Priceville, Ill.	8/7/30	L	R	?	?	2	7	2	0	0	—
Selman, Frank C. "Frank" (aka Frank C. Williams) 73MarNA (See 3B)												
Unknown	Baltimore, Md.	Unknown	?	?	?	?	1	9	0	0	1	.000
Serad, William I. "Billy" 84–85BufN 87–88CinA												
?/?/63	Philadelphia, Pa.	11/1/25	R	R	5'7	156	95	787.1	278	35	55	.389
Seward, Edward William "Ed" b. Sourhardt 85ProN 87–90PhiA 91CleN												
6/19/67	Cleveland, Ohio	7/30/47	?	R	5'7	175	176	1485.2	589	89	72	.553
Sexton, Frank Joseph "Frank" 95BosN												
7/8/72	Brockton, Mass.	1/4/38	?	?	?	160	7	49	14	1	5	.167
Seymour, Jacob "Jake" b. Semer 82PitA												
?/?/54	Pittsburgh, Pa.	8/1/97	?	?	?	?	1	8	2	0	1	.000
Seymour, James Bentley "Cy" 96–00NYN (See P)												
12/9/72	Albany, N.Y.	9/20/19	L	L	6'	200	139	1026	582	61	56	.521
Shaffer, John W. "John" "Cannonball" 86–87NYA												
2/18/64	Lock Haven, Pa.	11/21/26	?	?	?	?	21	181	58	7	14	.333

BIRTH DATE	BIRTHPLACE	DEATH DATE	B	T	HGT	WGT	G	INN	K	W	L	PCT
Shallix, August "Gus" b. Shallick 84–85CinA												
3/29/58	Paderborn, Westphalia, Ger.	10/28/37	R	R	5'11	165	36	291	93	17	14	.548
Sharrott, George Oscar "George" 93–94BroN												
11/2/69	W. New Brighton, S.I., N.Y.	1/6/32	L	L	5'8	164	15	104	26	4	7	.364
Sharrott, John Henry "John" "Jack" 90–92NYN 93PhiN (See P)												
8/13/69	Bangor, Me.	12/31/27	R	R	5'9	165	48	311.1	137	20	17	.541
Shaw, Frederick Lander "Dupee" 83–84DetN 84BosU 85ProN 86–88WasN												
5/31/59	Charlestown, Mass.	6/11/38	L	L	5'8	165	211	1762	950	83	121	.407
Shaw, Samuel E. "Sam" 88BalA 93ChiN												
5/?/64	Baltimore, Md.	Unknown	R	R	5'5	140	8	69	23	3	4	.429
Shea, Michael J. "Mike" 87CinA												
3/10/67	New Orleans, La.	8/22/27	?	R	5'10	170	2	16.2	0	1	1	.500
Shearon, John M. "John" 91CleN												
?/?/70	Pittsburgh, Pa.	2/1/23	?	?	?	?	6	46	19	1	3	.250
Shoch, George Quintus "George" 88WasN (See OF)												
1/6/59	Philadelphia, Pa.	9/30/37	R	R	5'6	158	1	3	0	0	0	—
Shreve, Leven Lawrence "Lev" 87BalA 87–89IndN												
1/14/69	Louisville, Ky.	10/18/42	R	R	5'11	150	57	473.1	141	19	37	.339
Sigsby, Seth De Witt "Seth" b. Seth De Witt 93NYN												
4/30/74	Cobleskill, N.Y.	9/15/53	?	?	6'	175	1	3	2	0	0	—
Slagle, John A "John" 91CinA												
Unknown	Lawrence, Ind.	Unknown	L	R	?	?	1	1.1	1	0	0	—
Smith, ? 84BalU												
Unknown	Unknown	Unknown	?	?	?	?	1	6	2	0	0	—
Smith, ? 86CinA												
Unknown	Unknown	Unknown	?	?	?	?	1	9	1	0	1	.000
Smith, Charles Marvin "Pop" 83ColA (See 2B)												
10/12/56	Digby, N.S., Can.	4/18/27	R	R	5'11	170	3	5.2	0	0	0	—
Smith, Edgar Eugene "Edgar" 83PhiN 84WasA 85ProN 90CleN (See OF)												
6/12/62	Providence, R.I.	11/3/92	R	R	5'10	160	11	82	18	2	7	.222
Smith, Elmer Ellsworth "Elmer" 86–89CinA 92PitN 94PitN 98CinN (See OF)												
3/23/68	Pittsburgh, Pa.	11/3/45	L	L	5'11	178	149	1210.1	525	75	57	.568
Smith, F. William "Bill" 86DetN												
?/?/63	New Orleans, La.	Unknown	?	R	5'8	162	9	77	36	5	4	.556
Smith, Frederick C. "Fred" 90TolA												
3/25/63	Greene, N.Y.	1/9/41	L	R	5'11	156	35	286	116	19	13	.594
Smith, George J. "Germany" 84AltU (See SS)												
4/21/63	Pittsburgh, Pa.	12/1/27	R	R	6'	175	1	1	1	0	0	—
Smith, John Francis "Phenomenal" b. Gammon 84BalU 84PhiA 84PitA 85BroA 85PhiA 86DetN 87–88BalA												
88–89PhiA 90PhiN 90PitN 91PhiN												
12/12/64	Philadelphia, Pa.	4/3/52	L	L	5'6½	161	149	1231.1	532	57	78	.422
Smith, Rex "Rex" b. Henry W. Schmidt 86PhiA												
?/?/64	Louisville, Ky.	6/21/95	?	?	?	?	1	9	4	0	1	.000
Smith, Thomas Edward "Tom" 94BosN 95PhiN 96LouN 98StLN												
12/5/71	Boston, Mass.	3/2/29	R	R	5'7½	165	25	138	38	4	7	.364
Snyder, George T. "George" 82PhiA												
8/?/48	Philadelphia, Pa.	8/2/05	?	?	?	?	1	9	0	1	0	1.000

BIRTH DATE	BIRTHPLACE	DEATH DATE	B	T	HGT	WGT	G	INN	K	W	L	PCT
Sommer, Joseph John "Joe" 83CinA 85–87BalA 90CleN												
11/20/58	Covington, Ky.	1/16/38	R	R	?	?	6	14	3	0	0	—
Sommerville, Andrew Henry "Andy" b. Henry Travers Summersgill 94BroN												
2/6/76	Brooklyn, N.Y.	6/16/31	?	?	?	?	1	0.1	0	0	1	.000
***Sowders, John "John" 87IndN 89KCA 90BroP**												
12/10/66	Louisville, Ky.	7/29/39	R	L	6′	?	65	497	195	25	32	.439
***Sowders, William Jefferson "Bill" "Little Bill" 88–89BosN 89–90PitN**												
11/29/64	Louisville, Ky.	2/2/51	R	R	6′	155	71	517.2	205	29	30	.492
Spalding, Albert Goodwill "Al" 71–75BosNA 76–77ChiN (See P)												
9/2/50	Byron, Ill.	9/9/15	R	R	6′1	170	347	2887.1	227	252	65	.795
Sparks, Thomas Frank "Tully" 97PhiN 99PitN												
12/12/74	Etna, Ga.	7/15/37	R	R	?	?	29	178	53	8	7	.533
Sprague, Charles Wellington "Charlie" 87ChiN 89CleN 90TolA (See OF)												
10/10/64	Cleveland, Ohio	12/31/12	L	L	5′11	150	24	161.2	76	10	7	.588
Springer, Edward H. "Ed" 89LouA												
2/9/61	?, California	4/24/26	?	?	6′2	187	1	5	1	0	1	.000
***Stafford, James Joseph "General" "Jamsey" 90BufP (See OF)**												
7/9/68	Webster, Mass.	9/18/23	R	R	5′8	165	12	98	21	3	9	.250
***Stafford, John Henry "John" "Doc" 93CleN**												
4/8/70	Dudley, Mass.	7/3/40	R	R	5′10	170	2	7	4	0	1	.000
Stahl, Charles Sylvester "Chick" 99BosN (See OF)												
1/10/73	Avila, Ind.	3/28/07	L	L	5′10	160	1	2	0	0	0	—
Staley, Henry E. "Harry" 88–89PitN 90PitP 91PitN 91–94BosN 95StLN												
11/3/66	Jacksonville, Ill.	1/12/10	L	R	5′10	175	283	2269	746	136	119	.533
***Stanley, Joseph Bernard "Joe" 97WasN**												
4/2/81	Washington, D.C.	9/13/67	B	R	5′9¹⁄₂	150	1	0.2	0	0	0	—
Stearns, William E. "Bill" 71OlyNA 72NatNA 73WasNA 74HarNA 75WasNA												
3/20/53	Washington, D.C.	12/30/98	?	R	?	?	84	705	23	13	64	.169
Stecher, Charles "Charlie" 90PhiA												
Unknown	Bordentown, N.J.	Unknown	?	?	?	?	10	68	18	0	10	.000
Stein, Edward F. "Ed" 90–91ChiN 92–96BroN 98BroN												
9/5/69	Detroit, Mich.	5/10/28	R	R	5′11	170	215	1656	535	109	78	.583
Stellberger, William F. "Bill" 85ProN												
4/22/65	Detroit, Mich.	11/9/36	L	L	?	?	1	8	0	0	1	.000
Stemmeyer, William "Bill" "Cannonball" 85–87BosN 88CleA												
5/6/65	Cleveland, Ohio	5/3/45	R	R	6′2	190	60	495	295	29	29	.500
Stephens, Clarence Wright "Clarence" 86CinA 91–92CinN												
8/19/63	Cincinnati, Ohio	2/28/45	?	R	?	?	3	23	10	1	2	.333
Stephens, George Benjamin "Ben" 92BalN 93–94WasN												
9/28/67	Romeo, Mich.	8/5/96	?	?	5′10¹⁄₂	170	17	103.2	22	1	7	.125
Sterling, John A. "John" 90PhiA												
Unknown	Philadelphia, Pa.	Unknown	?	?	?	?	1	5	1	0	1	.000
Stimmel, Archibald May "Archie" "Lumbago" 00CinN												
5/30/73	Woodsboro, Md.	8/18/58	R	R	6′	175	2	13	2	1	1	.500
Stine, Harry C. "Harry" 90PhiA												
2/20/64	Shenandoah, Pa.	6/5/24	?	L	5′6	150	1	8	1	0	1	.000
Stivetts, John Elmer "Jack" "Happy Jack" 89–91StLA 92–98BosN 99CleN (See P)												
3/31/68	Ashland, Pa.	4/18/30	R	R	6′2	185	388	2887.2	1223	203	132	.606

	BIRTH DATE	BIRTHPLACE	DEATH DATE	B	T	HGT	WGT	G	INN	K	W	L	PCT
Stocksdale, Otis Hinkley "Otis"		"Old Gray Fox"	93–95WasN	95BosN		96BalN	(See P)						
	8/7/71	Arcadia, Md.	3/15/33	L	R	5'10½	180	54	347	48	15	31	.326
Stovey, Harry Duffield "Harry"		b. Stowe	80WorN	83PhiA	86PhiA	(See OF)							
	12/20/56	Philadelphia, Pa.	9/20/37	R	R	5'11½	175	4	9.1	7	0	0	—
Stratton, C. Scott "Scott"		88–90LouA	91PitN	91LouA	92–94LouN	94ChiN	95ChiN	(See P)					
	10/2/69	Campbellsburg, Ky.	3/8/39	L	R	6'	180	230	1883.1	569	97	114	.460
Stratton, William Edward "Ed"		73MarNA											
	Unknown	Baltimore, Md.	Unknown	?	?	?	?	3	27	0	0	3	.000
Strauss, Joseph "Joe" "Dutch"		"The Socker"	b. Strasser	86LouA	(See OF)								
	11/16/58	Cincinnati, Ohio	6/24/06	R	R	?	?	2	4	0	0	0	—
Streit, Oscar William "Oscar"		99BosN											
	7/7/73	Florence, Ala.	10/10/35	L	L	6'5	190	2	14.2	0	1	0	1.000
Stricker, John A. "Cub"		b. Streaker	82PhiA	84PhiA	87–88CleA	(See 2B)							
	6/5/59	Philadelphia, Pa.	11/19/37	R	R	5'3	138	8	27.2	10	2	0	1.000
Strike, John "John"		86PhiN											
	?/?/65	?, Pennsylvania	Unknown	?	?	?	?	2	15	11	1	1	.500
Stultz, George Irvin "George"		94BosN											
	6/30/73	Louisville, Ky.	3/19/55	?	?	5'10	150	1	9	1	1	0	1.000
Sudhoff, John William "Willie"		"Wee Willie"	97–98StLN	99CleN	99–00StLN								
	9/17/74	St. Louis, Mo.	5/25/17	R	R	5'7	165	104	799.1	152	34	60	.362
Sullivan, Florence P. "Fleury"		84PitA											
	?/?/62	E. St. Louis, Ill.	2/15/97	?	?	?	?	51	441	189	16	35	.314
Sullivan, James E. "Jim"		91BosN	91ColA	95–97BosN									
	4/25/69	Charlestown, Mass.	11/30/01	R	R	5'10	155	67	503	97	26	27	.491
Sullivan, Martin C. "Marty"		87ChiN	(See OF)										
	10/20/62	Lowell, Mass.	1/6/94	R	R	?	?	1	2.1	1	0	0	—
Sullivan, Michael Joseph "Mike"		"Big Mike"	89WasN	90ChiN	91PhiA	91NYN	92–93CinN	94WasN	94–95CleN				
96–97NYN	98–99BosN												
	10/23/66	Boston, Mass.	6/14/06	L	L	6'1	210	163	1123.1	286	54	66	.450
Sullivan, Patrick J. "Pat"		84KCU	(See 3B)										
	12/22/62	Milwaukee, Wis.	Unknown	?	R	5'11	165	1	7	1	0	1	.000
Sullivan, Suter G. "Suter"		98StLN	(See 3B)										
	10/14/72	Baltimore, Md.	4/19/25	?	?	6'	170	1	6	3	0	0	—
Sullivan, Thomas "Tom"		84ColA	86LouA	88–89KCA									
	3/1/60	New York, N.Y.	4/12/47	?	?	?	?	47	408	147	14	33	.298
Sullivan, Thomas Jefferson "Sleeper"		"Old Iron Hands"	84StLU	(See C)									
	Unknown	St. Louis, Mo.	9/25/99	R	R	?	175	1	6	3	1	0	1.000
Sullivan, William F. "Bill"		90SyrA											
	12/?/68	Providence, R.I.	10/8/05	?	?	?	?	6	42	13	1	4	.200
Sunday, William Ashley "Billy"		"Parson"	90PitN	(See OF)									
	11/19/62	Ames, Iowa	11/6/35	L	R	5'10	160	1	0	0	0	0	—
Sutthoff, John Gerhard "Jack"		"Sunny Jack"	98WasN	99StLN									
	6/29/73	Cincinnati, Ohio	8/3/42	L	R	5'9	175	5	32.1	11	1	2	.333
Sutton, Ezra Ballou "Ezra"		75AthNA	(See 3B)										
	9/17/50	Palmyra, N.Y.	6/20/07	R	R	5'8½	153	2	6	0	0	0	—
Swabach, William "Bill"		87NYN											
	Unknown	Unknown	Unknown	?	?	?	?	2	16	6	0	2	.000

BIRTH DATE	BIRTHPLACE	DEATH DATE	B	T	HGT	WGT	G	INN	K	W	L	PCT
Swaim, John Hillary "Cy" 97–98WasN												
3/11/74	Cadwallader, Ohio	12/27/45	?	?	6'6	180	41	284.1	82	12	22	.353
Swartwood, Cyrus Edward "Ed" 84PitA 90TolA (See OF)												
1/12/59	Rockford, Ill.	5/15/24	L	R	?	198	2	5.1	1	0	0	.000
Swartzel, Park B. "Park" 89KCA												
11/21/65	Knightstown, Ind.	1/3/40	R	R	5'10	?	48	410.1	147	19	27	.413
Sweeney, Charles J. "Charlie" 82–84ProN 84StLU 85–86StLN 87CleA (See P)												
4/13/63	San Francisco, Cal.	4/4/02	R	R	5'10½	181	129	1030.2	505	64	52	.552
Sweeney, William J. "Bill" 82PhiA 84BalU												
?/?/58	Philadelphia, Pa.	8/2/03	?	R	?	?	82	708	422	49	31	.613
Sylvester, Louis J. "Lou" 84CinU (See OF)												
2/14/55	Springfield, Ill.	Unknown	R	R	5'3	165	6	32.2	7	0	1	.000
Taber, John Pardon "John" 90BosN												
6/28/68	Acushnet, Mass.	2/21/40	R	R	5'8	?	2	13	3	0	1	.000
*Tannehill, Jesse Niles "Jesse" "Powder" 94CinN 97–00PitN (See P)												
7/14/74	Dayton, Ky.	9/22/56	B	L	5'8	150	134	1044.2	251	79	42	.653
Taylor, John Budd "Jack" "Brewery Jack" 91NYN 92–97PhiN 98StLN 99CinN (See P)												
5/23/73	Staten Island, N.Y.	2/7/00	R	R	6'1	190	270	2079	528	120	117	.506
Taylor, John W. "Jack" 98–00ChiN												
1/14/74	New Straitsville, Ohio	3/4/38	R	R	5'10	170	74	618	145	33	38	.465
Taylor, Luther Haden "Dummy" 00NYN												
2/21/75	Oskaloosa, Kan.	8/22/58	R	R	6'1	160	11	62.1	16	4	3	.571
Taylor, William Henry "Billy" "Bollicky Billy" 81WorN (81DetN) 81CleN 82–83PitA 84StLU 84–85PhiA 86BalA 87PhiA (See P)												
?/?/55	Washington, D.C.	5/14/00	R	R	5'11½	204	100	799.2	376	50	36	.581
*Tebeau, George E. "George" "White Wings" 87CinA 90TolA (See OF)												
12/26/61	St. Louis, Mo.	2/4/23	R	R	5'9	175	2	13	1	0	1	.000
*Tebeau, Oliver Wendell "Patsy" 96CleN (See 1B)												
12/5/64	St. Louis, Mo.	5/15/18	R	R	5'8	163	1	0	0	0	0	—
Tener, John Kinley "John" (85 BalA) 88–89ChiN 90PitP												
7/25/63	County Tyrone, Ireland	5/19/46	R	R	6'4	180	61	506	174	25	31	.446
Tenney, Fred Clay "Fred" 84BosU 84WilU (See OF)												
7/9/59	Marlborough, N.H.	6/15/19	?	?	?	?	5	43	28	3	2	.600
Terry, William H. "Adonis" 84–89BroA 90–91BroN 92BalN 92–94PitN 94–97ChiN (See P)												
8/7/64	Westfield, Mass.	2/24/15	R	R	5'11½	168	440	3514	1552	197	196	.501
*Thomas, Roy Allen "Roy" 00PhiN (See OF)												
3/24/74	Norristown, Pa.	11/20/59	L	L	5'11	150	1	2.2	0	0	0	—
Thomas, Thomas R. "Tom" "Savage Tom" 94CleN 99–00StLN												
12/27/73	Shawnee, Ohio	9/23/42	R	R	6'4	195	10	51.2	15	3	3	.500
Thompson, Arthur J. "Art" 84WasU												
Unknown	Unknown	Unknown	?	?	?	?	1	8	8	0	1	.000
Thompson, Will McLain "Will" 92PitN												
8/30/70	Pittsburgh, Pa.	6/9/62	R	R	5'11	190	1	3	0	0	1	.000
Thornton, John "John" 89WasN 91–92PhiN												
?/?/70	Washington, D.C.	Unknown	?	?	5'10½	175	41	290	57	15	19	.441
Thornton, Walter Miller "Walter" 95–98ChiN (See OF)												
2/18/75	Lewiston, Me.	7/14/60	L	L	6'1	180	56	409.1	134	23	18	.561

BIRTH DATE	BIRTHPLACE	DEATH DATE	B	T	HGT	WGT	G	INN	K	W	L	PCT
Tiernan, Michael Joseph "Mike" "Silent Mike" 87NYN (See OF)												
1/21/67	Trenton, N.J.	11/9/18	L	L	5'11	165	5	19.2	3	1	2	.333
Titcomb, Ledell "Cannonball" 86PhiN 87PhiA 87–89NYN 90RocA												
8/21/66	W. Baldwin, Me.	6/8/50	L	L	5'6	157	63	528.2	283	30	29	.508
Todd, George Franklin "Frank" 98LouN												
10/18/69	Aberdeen, Md.	8/11/19	?	L	?	?	4	11	5	0	2	.000
Toole, Stephen John "Steve" 86–87BroA 88KCA 90BroA (See P)												
4/9/59	New Orleans, La.	3/28/19	R	L	6'	170	55	443	141	27	26	.509
Trumbull, Edward J. "Ed" b. Trembly 84WasA												
11/3/60	Chicopee, Mass.	1/14/37	?	?	?	?	10	84	43	1	9	.100
Tucker, Thomas Joseph "Tommy" "Foghorn" 88BalA 91BosN (See 1B)												
10/28/63	Holyoke, Mass.	10/22/35	B	R	5'11	165	2	3.1	2	0	0	—
Turner, George A. "Tuck" 94PhiN (See OF)												
2/13/73	W. New Brighton, N.Y.	7/16/45	B	L	5'6½	155	1	6	3	0	0	—
Twitchell, Lawrence Grant "Larry" 86–88DetN 89CleN 90BufP 91ColA 94LouN (See OF)												
2/18/64	Cleveland, Ohio	8/23/30	R	R	6'	185	42	280.2	70	17	11	.607
Tyng, James Alexander "Jim" 79BosN 88PhiN												
3/27/56	Philadelphia, Pa.	10/30/31	?	?	5'9	155	4	31	9	1	2	.333
Underwood, Frederick Theodore "Fred" 94BroN												
10/14/68	St. Louis Co., Mo.	1/26/06	?	?	?	170	7	47	10	2	4	.333
Valentine, John Gill "John" 83ColA												
11/21/55	Brooklyn, N.Y.	10/10/03	?	?	?	?	13	102	13	2	10	.167
Van Haltren, George Edward Martin "George" "Rip" 87–88ChiN 90PitP 91BalA 92BalN 95–96NYN 00NYN												
(See OF)												
3/30/66	St. Louis, Mo.	9/29/45	L	L	5'11	170	92	683.1	279	40	31	.563
Vaughn, Harry France "Farmer" 91CinA (See C)												
3/1/64	Ruraldale, Ohio	2/21/14	R	R	6'3	177	1	7	0	0	0	—
Veach, William Walter "Peekaboo" 84KCU 87LouA (See 1B)												
6/15/62	Indianapolis, Ind.	11/12/37	?	?	?	?	13	113	64	3	10	.231
Viau, Leon A. "Leon" "Lee" 88–89CinA 90CinN 90–92CleN 92LouN 92BosN												
7/5/66	Corinth, Vt.	12/17/47	R	R	5'4	160	178	1442	554	83	11	.519
Vickery, Thomas Gill "Tom" "Vinegar Tom" 90PhiN 91ChiN 92BalN 93PhiN												
5/5/67	Milford, N.J.	3/21/21	?	R	6'	170	97	717.2	265	42	42	.500
Vinton, William Miller "Bill" 84–85PhiN 85PhiA												
4/27/65	Winthrop, Mass.	9/3/93	R	R	6'1	160	37	314	160	17	19	.472
Virtue, Jacob Kitchline "Jake" "Guesses" 93–94CleN (See 1B)												
3/2/65	Philadelphia, Pa.	2/3/43	B	L	5'9½	165	2	5	2	0	0	—
Von Fricken, Anthony "Tony" 90BosN												
5/30/70	Brooklyn, N.Y.	3/22/47	B	R	5'11½	160	1	8	2	0	1	.000
Voss, Alexander "Alex" 84WasU 84KCU												
5/16/58	Roswell, Ga.	8/31/06	R	R	6'1	180	34	239.1	129	5	20	.200
Waddell, George Edward "Rube" 97LouN 99LouN 00PitN												
10/13/76	Bradford, Pa.	4/1/14	R	L	6'1½	196	41	301.2	179	15	16	.484
Wadsworth, John L. "Jack" 90CleN 93BalN 94–95LouN												
12/17/67	Wellington, Ohio	7/8/41	L	R	?	180	47	367.2	87	6	38	.136
Wagner, John Peter "Honus" "The Flying Dutchman" 00PitN (See OF)												
2/24/74	Chartiers, Pa.	12/6/55	R	R	5'11	200	1	3	1	0	0	—

BIRTH DATE	BIRTHPLACE	DEATH DATE	B	T	HGT	WGT	G	INN	K	W	L	PCT
Walker, George A. "George" 88BalA												
?/?/63	Hamilton, Ont., Can.	Unknown	?	R	5'9	184	4	35	18	1	3	.250
Wallace, Rhoderick John "Bobby" 94–96CleN (See 3B)												
11/4/73	Pittsburgh, Pa.	11/3/60	R	R	5'8	170	56	400	119	24	22	.522
Ward, John "Johnny" 85ProN												
Unknown	E. St. Louis, Ill.	Unknown	?	?	?	?	1	8	3	0	1	.000
Ward, John Montgomery "Monte" "John" 78–82ProN 83–84NYN (See SS)												
3/3/60	Bellefonte, Pa.	3/4/25	L	R	5'9	165	292	2461.2	920	164	102	.617
Watson, Walter L. "Mother" 87CinA												
1/27/65	Middleport, Ohio	11/23/98	?	?	5'9	145	2	14	1	0	1	.000
Weaver, Samuel H. "Sam" 75PhiNA 78MilN 82PhiA 83LouA 84PhiU 86PhiA												
7/10/55	Philadelphia, Pa.	2/1/14	R	R	5'10	175	155	1325.2	359	70	80	.467
Weber, Charles P. "Charlie" "Count" 98WasN												
10/22/68	Cincinnati, Ohio	6/13/14	?	?	?	?	1	4	0	0	1	.000
Weidman, George E. "Stump" b. Wiedman 80BufN 81–85DetN 86KCN 87DetN 87NYA 87–88NYN (See P)												
2/17/61	Rochester, N.Y.	3/2/05	R	R	5'7½	165	279	2318.1	910	101	156	.393
Welch, Curtis Benton "Curt" 90PhiA (See OF)												
2/11/62	E. Liverpool, Ohio	8/29/96	R	R	5'10	175	1	1	1	0	0	—
Welch, Michael Francis "Mickey" "Smiling Mickey" 80–82TroN 83–92NYN												
7/4/59	Brooklyn, N.Y.	7/30/41	R	R	5'8	160	564	4802	1850	307	210	.594
Werden, Percival Wheritt "Perry" 84StLU (See 1B)												
7/21/65	St. Louis, Mo.	1/9/34	R	R	6'2	220	16	141.1	51	12	1	.923
West, J. Franklin "Frank" 94BosN												
1/?/74	Johnstown, Pa.	9/6/32	?	?	?	180	1	3	1	0	0	—
Westervelt, Huyler "Huyler" 94NYN												
10/1/70	Piermont, N.Y.	Unknown	?	?	5'9	170	23	141	35	7	10	.412
Wetzel, George William "Shorty" 85BalA												
?/?/68	Philadelphia, Pa.	2/25/99	?	?	?	?	2	17	6	0	2	.000
*Weyhing, August "Gus" "Cannonball" 87–89PhiA 90BroP 91PhiA 92–95PhiN 95PitN 95–96LouN 98–99WasN 00StLN 00BroN												
9/29/66	Louisville, Ky.	9/4/55	R	R	5'10	145	535	4304	1662	264	231	.533
*Weyhing, John "John" 88CinA 89ColA												
6/24/69	Louisville, Ky.	6/20/90	L	L	6'2	185	9	66.2	30	3	4	.429
Wheeler, George L. "George" b. Heroux 96–99PhiN												
8/3/69	Methuen, Mass.	3/23/46	B	B	?	?	50	358.2	60	21	20	.512
Wheeler, Harry Eugene "Harry" 78ProN 79CinN 82CinA 83ColA 84KCU (See OF)												
3/3/58	Versailles, Ind.	10/9/00	R	R	5'11	165	14	97.2	41	7	6	.538
Whitaker, William H. "Pat" 88–89BalA												
11/?/64	St. Louis, Mo.	7/15/02	?	R	?	?	3	23	6	2	1	.667
White, George Frederick "Deke" 95PhiN												
9/8/72	Albany, N.Y.	11/5/57	B	L	?	?	3	17.1	6	1	0	1.000
*White, James Laurie "Deacon" 76ChiN 90BufP (See 3B)												
12/7/47	Caton, N.Y.	7/7/39	L	R	5'11	175	2	10	3	0	0	—
White, William Dighton "Bill" 86LouA (See SS)												
5/1/60	Bridgeport, Ohio	12/29/24	?	R	?	?	1	1	1	0	0	—
*White, William Henry "Will" "Whoop–La" 77BosN 78–80CinN 81DetN 82–86CinA												
10/11/54	Caton, N.Y.	8/31/11	B	R	5'9½	175	403	3542.2	1041	229	166	.580

	BIRTH DATE	BIRTHPLACE	DEATH DATE	B	T	HGT	WGT	G	INN	K	W	L	PCT

Whitehead, Milton P. "Milt" 84StLU (See SS)
| | ?/?/62 | ?, Canada | 8/15/01 | B | ? | ? | ? | 1 | 8 | 2 | 0 | 1 | .000 |

*Whitney, Arthur Wilson "Art" 82DetN 86PitA 89NYN (See 3B)
| | 1/16/58 | Brockton, Mass. | 8/15/43 | R | R | 5'8 | 155 | 5 | 30 | 16 | 0 | 2 | .000 |

Whitney, James Evans "Jim" "Grasshopper" 81–85BosN 86KCN 87–88WasN 89IndN 90PhiA (See P)
| | 11/10/57 | Conklin, N.Y. | 5/21/91 | L | R | 6'2 | 172 | 413 | 3496.1 | 1571 | 191 | 204 | .484 |

Whitrock, William Franklin "Bill" 90StLA 93–94LouN 94CinN 96PhiN
| | 3/4/70 | Cincinnati, Ohio | 7/26/35 | ? | R | 5'7 1/2 | 170 | 37 | 235 | 57 | 9 | 19 | .321 |

Widner, William Waterfield "Bill" "Wild Bill" 87CinA 88WasN 89–90ColA 91CinA
| | 6/3/67 | Cincinnati, Ohio | 12/10/08 | R | R | 6' | 180 | 69 | 522 | 110 | 22 | 36 | .379 |

Wilhelm, Harry Lester "Harry" 99LouN
| | 4/7/74 | Uniontown, Pa. | 2/20/44 | R | R | 5'7 | 155 | 5 | 25 | 6 | 1 | 1 | .500 |

Williams, Augustine H. "Gus" 90BroA
| | ?/?/70 | New York, N.Y. | 10/14/90 | ? | ? | 5'11 | 170 | 2 | 12 | 2 | 0 | 1 | .000 |

Williams, Elisha Alphonso "Dale" 76CinN
| | 10/6/55 | Ludlow, Ky. | 10/22/39 | R | R | 5'9 | 175 | 9 | 83 | 9 | 1 | 8 | .111 |

Williams, Thomas C. "Tom" 92–93CleN
| | 8/19/70 | Minersville, Ohio | 7/27/40 | ? | ? | ? | ? | 7 | 33 | 9 | 2 | 1 | .667 |

Williams, Walter Merrill "Pop" 98WasN
| | 5/19/74 | Bowdoinham, Me. | 8/4/59 | L | R | 5'11 | 190 | 2 | 17 | 3 | 0 | 2 | .000 |

Willliams, Washington J. "Wash" 85ChiN (See OF)
| | Unknown | Philadelphia, Pa. | 8/9/92 | ? | ? | 5'11 | 180 | 1 | 2 | 0 | 0 | 0 | |

Williamson, Edward Nagle "Ned" 81–87ChiN (See 3B)
| | 10/24/57 | Philadelphia, Pa. | 3/3/94 | R | R | 5'11 | 210 | 12 | 35 | 7 | 1 | 1 | .500 |

Willis, Victor Gazaway "Vic" 98–00BosN
| | 4/12/76 | Cecil Co., Md. | 8/3/47 | R | R | 6'2 | 185 | 114 | 889.2 | 333 | 62 | 38 | .620 |

Wilson, Frank Ealton "Zeke" 95BosN 95–98CleN 99StLN
| | 12/24/69 | Benton, Ala. | 4/26/28 | R | R | 5'10 | 165 | 119 | 874 | 194 | 52 | 44 | .542 |

Wilson, Howard Paul "Highball" 99CleN
| | 8/9/78 | Philadelphia, Pa. | 10/16/34 | ? | R | ? | ? | 1 | 8 | 1 | 0 | 1 | .000 |

Winkelman, George Edward "George" 86WasN (See OF)
| | 6/14/61 | Philadelphia, Pa. | 5/19/60 | L | L | ? | ? | 1 | 6 | 4 | 0 | 1 | .000 |

Wise, William E. "Bill" 82BalA 84WasU 86WasN
| | 3/15/61 | Washington, D.C. | 5/5/40 | ? | ? | ? | ? | 54 | 393.1 | 277 | 24 | 21 | .533 |

Witherow, ? 75WasNA
| | Unknown | Unknown | Unknown | ? | ? | ? | ? | 1 | 1 | 0 | 0 | 1 | .000 |

Wolf, William Van Winkle "Jimmy" "Chicken" 82LouA 85–86LouA
| | 5/12/62 | Louisville, Ky. | 5/16/03 | R | R | 5'9 | 190 | 3 | 10 | 2 | 0 | 0 | — |

Wolters, Reinder Albertus "Rynie" 71MutNA 72CleNA 73ResNA
| | 3/17/42 | Schantz, Netherlands | 1/3/17 | ? | R | 6' | 165 | 45 | 367.1 | 27 | 19 | 23 | .452 |

Wood, George A. "George" "Dandy" 83DetN 85DetN 88–89PhiN (See OF)
| | 11/9/58 | Boston, Mass. | 4/4/24 | L | R | 5'10 1/2 | 175 | 5 | 12 | 3 | 0 | 0 | — |

Wood, John B. "John" 96StLN
| | ?/?/71 | Unknown | Unknown | ? | ? | 5'7 | 142 | 1 | 0 | 0 | 0 | 0 | — |

*Wood, Peter Burke "Pete" 85BufN 89PhiN
| | 2/1/57 | Hamilton, Ont., Can. | 3/15/23 | ? | R | 5'7 | 185 | 27 | 217.2 | 46 | 9 | 16 | .360 |

Woodcock, Fred Weyland "Fred" 92PitN
| | 5/17/68 | Winchendon, Mass. | 8/11/43 | L | L | 6'2 | 190 | 5 | 33 | 8 | 1 | 2 | .333 |

BIRTH DATE	BIRTHPLACE	DEATH DATE	B	T	HGT	WGT	G	INN	K	W	L	PCT
Woods, Walter Sydney "Walt"	98ChiN	99LouN	00PitN									
4/28/75	Rye, N.H.	10/30/51	R	R	5'9½	165	54	404.1	48	18	26	.409
Wright, David William "Dave"	95PitN	97ChiN										
8/27/75	Dennison, Ohio	1/18/46	R	R	6'	185	2	9	4	1	0	1.000
***Wright, George "George"**	75BosNA	76BosN	(See SS)									
1/28/47	Yonkers, N.Y.	8/21/37	R	R	5'9½	150	3	5	1	0	1	.000
***Wright, William Henry "Harry"**	71–74BosNA	(See OF)										
1/10/35	Sheffield, England	10/3/95	R	R	5'9½	157	34	99.1	1	4	4	.500
Wyman, Frank H. "Frank"	84KCU	(See OF)										
5/10/62	Haverhill, Mass.	2/4/16	?	?	?	?	3	21	9	0	1	.000
Wynne, William Andrew "Bill"	94WasN											
3/27/69	Neuse, N.C.	8/7/51	R	R	5'11½	161	1	8	2	0	1	.000
Yeager, Joseph F. "Joe" "Little Joe"	98–00BroN	(See P)										
8/28/75	Philadelphia, Pa.	7/2/37	R	R	5'10	160	48	356	78	15	25	.375
Yingling, Joseph Granville "Joe"	86WasN											
7/23/66	Westminster, Md.	10/24/46	R	L	5'7½	145	1	3	1	0	0	—
Yost, August "Gus"	93ChiN											
Unknown	Unknown	Unknown	?	?	6'5	?	1	2.2	1	0	1	.000
Young, Denton True "Cy"	90–98CleN	99–00StLN										
3/29/67	Gilmore, Ohio	11/4/55	R	R	6'2	210	505	4043.2	1240	286	170	.627
Young, Joe "Joe"	92StLN											
6/?/57	Mt. Carmel, Pa.	Unknown	?	?	?	?	1	2	1	0	0	—
Zay, ?	86BalA											
Unknown	Pittsburgh, Pa.	Unknown	?	?	?	?	1	2	2	0	1	.000
Zettlein, George "Charmer" "George"	71ChiNA	72TroNA	72EckNA	73PhiNA	74–75ChiNA	75PhiNA	76PhiN					
7/18/44	Brooklyn, N.Y.	5/23/05	R	R	5'9	162	250	2176.1	142	129	112	.535
Ziegler, George J. "George"	90PitN											
?/?/72	Chicago, Ill.	7/22/16	?	?	?	?	1	6	1	0	1	.000

Bob Caruthers's career winning percentage is second only to Whitey Ford among pitchers who racked up 200 or more career victories. His .282 career BA is third among 200-game winners only to Jack Stivetts and George Uhle. As an outfielder in 1892, his final full season, Caruthers hit 32 points above the league average.

Ed Morris's 12 shutouts in 1886 are still the season southpaw record. His productivity dropped in 1887 when new pitching restrictions forced him to quit taking a couple of skipping steps before he started his delivery. Morris rebounded to prominence in 1888 but then swiftly declined.

Joe McGinnity ranks just ahead of Amos Rusie in career wins— 246 to 245. The two were born just two months apart but were never teammates even though both spent most of their careers with the New York Giants. Nor did they ever pitch against each other for the simple reason that McGinnity, the older of the two, did not win his first major league game until the season after Rusie won his last one.

Rube Waddell, seen here with Pittsburgh in 1900, was one of many outstanding Deadball Era hurlers who debuted in the late 1890s. The 1900 Pirates were a dynasty in the making with a strong Louisville hue. Among the new arrivals from the defunct Colonels were Waddell (seated, far right), Claude Ritchey (beside Waddell), Tommy Leach (top, far left), Honus Wagner (beside Leach), Chief Zimmer (middle, far left) and player-manager Fred Clarke (middle, second from right). But the Pirates had plenty of home-grown budding stars too, including Jack Chesbro (front, third from left) and Ginger Beaumont (top, fourth from left).

MAJOR LEAGUE MANAGERS ROSTER (1871-1900)

A complete roster of men who served as managers in each of the five majors leagues between 1871 and 1900. Birth and death dates are provided only for men who are not also found in a player register.

Note:
(Ow)   Acted as both owner and manager of his team.
(Ex)   Also was a former, concurrent or future major league president.

	G	W	L	PCT	PENNANTS
Addy, Robert Edward "Bob" 75 PhiNA 77 CinN	31	8	23	.258	0
Allen, Robert Gilman "Bob" 99 PhiN 00 CinN	179	87	87	.500	0
Allison, Andrew K. "Andy" 72 EckNA	11	0	11	.000	0
Allison, Douglas L. "Doug" 73ResNA	23	2	21	.087	0
Anson, Adrian Constantine "Cap" "Pop" 75 PhiNA 79–97 ChiN 98 NYN	2288	1296	947	.578	5
Bancroft, Frank Carter "Frank" b. May 9, 1846, Lancaster, Mass d. May 30, 1921, Cincinnati, Ohio 80 WorN 81–82 DetN 83 CleN 84–85 ProN 87 PhiA 89 IndN	702	366	326	.529	1
Barkley, Samuel E. "Sam" 88 KCA	58	21	36	.368	0
Barnie, William Harrison "Billy" "Bald Billy" 83–91 BalA 92 WasN 93–94 LouN 97–98 BroN	1480	632	810	.438	0
Battin, Joseph V. "Joe" 83–84 PitA 84 Chi-PitU	32	9	23	.281	0
Benjamin, John W. b. 1835, Elizabeth, N.J. d. Nov. 14, 1895, Elizabeth, N.J. 73 ResNA	23	2	21	.087	0

	G	W	L	PCT	PENNANTS
Bickerson, ? b. unknown d. unknown					
84 WasA	1	0	1	.000	0
Bond, Thomas Henry "Tommy"					
82 WorN	6	2	4	.333	0
Boyd, William J. "Bill"					
75 AtlNA	2	0	2	.000	0
Brown, Freeman "Freeman" b. Jan. 31, 1845, Hubbardston, Mass. d. Dec. 27, 1916, Worcester, Mass.					
82 WorN	41	9	32	.220	0
Brown, Thomas Tarlton "Tom"					
97–98 WasN	137	64	72	.471	0
Buckenberger, Albert C. "Al" b. Jan. 31, 1861, Detroit, Mich. d. July 1, 1917, Syracuse, N.Y.					
88–90 ColA 92–94 PitN 95 StLN	606	302	297	.504	0
Buffinton, Charles G. "Charlie"					
90 PhiP	116	61	54	.530	0
Burdock, John Joseph "Jack"					
83 BosN	54	30	24	.556	0
Burnham, George Walter "Watch" b. May 20, 1860, Albion, Mich. d. Nov. 18, 1902, Detroit, Mich.					
87 IndN	28	6	22	.214	0
Burns, Thomas Everett "Tom"					
92 PitN 98–99 ChiN	364	187	170	.524	0
Butler, Ormond Hook b. Nov. 18, 1854, West Virginia d. Sept. 12, 1915, Mount Hope, Md.					
83 PitA	53	17	36	.321	0
Byrne, Charles H. "Charlie" (Ow) b. Sept. 1843, New York, N.Y. d. Jan. 4, 1898, New York, N.Y.					
85–87 BroA	354	174	172	.503	0
Campau, Charles Columbus "Count"					
90 StLA	41	26	14	.650	0
Carey, Thomas John "Tom"					
73 BalNA 74 NYNA	49	27	21	.563	0
Caruthers, Robert Lee "Bob"					
92 StLN	50	16	32	.333	0
Caylor, Oliver Perry "Opie" b. Dec. 14, 1849, Dayton, Ohio d. Oct. 19, 1897, Winona, Minn.					
85–86 CinA 87 NYA	353	163	182	.472	0
Chapman, John Curtis "Jack"					
76–77 LouN 78 MilN 82 WorN 83–84 DetN 85 BufN 89–91 LouA 92 LouN	867	350	501	.411	1
Clapp, John Edgar "John"					
72 ManNA 78 IndN 79 BufN 80 CinN 81 CleN 83 NYN	420	174	237	.423	0
Clarke, Fred Clifford "Fred"					
97–99 LouN 00 PitN	542	259	272	.478	0
Clements, John J. "Jack"					
90 PhiN	19	13	6	.684	0
Comiskey, Charles Albert "Charlie"					
83 StLA 84–89 StLA 90 ChiP 91 StLA 92–94 CinN	1408	838	541	.608	4
Connor, Roger "Roger"					
96 StLN	46	8	37	.178	0
Crane, Samuel Newhall "Sam"					
80 BufN 84 CinU	111	56	52	.519	0

	G	W	L	PCT	PENNANTS
Craver, William H. "Bill" 71 TroNA 72 BalNA 75 CenNA	80	41	37	.526	0
Creamer, George W. "George" 84 PitA	8	0	8	.000	0
Crooks, John Charles "Jack" 92 StLN	62	27	33	.450	0
Cross, Lafayette Napoleon "Lave" 99 CleN	38	8	30	.211	0
Curtis, Edwin R. "Ed" (Ow) b. unknown d. unknown 84 AltU	25	6	19	.240	0
Cushman, Charles H. "Charlie" b. May 25, 1850, New York, N.Y. d. June 29, 1909, Milwaukee, Wis. 91 MilA	36	21	15	.583	0
Cuthbert, Edgar Edward "Ned" 82 StLA	79	36	43	.456	0
Davidson, Mordecai H. "Mordecai" (Ow) b. Nov. 30, 1846, Port Washington, Ohio d. Sept. 6, 1940, Louisville, Ky. 88 LouA	93	35	54	.393	0
Davis, George Stacey 95 NYN ? NYN	111	55	54	.505	0
Day, John B. "John" b. Sept. 23, 1847, Colchester, Mass. d. Jan. 25, 1925, Cliffside, N.J. 99 NYN	66	29	35	.453	0
Deane, John Henry "Harry" 71 KekNA	5	2	3	.400	0
Diddlebock, Henry H. "Harry" b. June 27, 1854, Philadelphia, Pa. d. Feb. 5, 1900, Philadelphia, Pa. 96 StLN	17	7	10	.412	0
Donovan, Patrick Joseph "Patsy" 97 PitN 99 PitN	266	129	129	.500	0
Dorgan, Michael Cornelius "Mike" 79 SyrN 80 ProN 81 WorN	138	67	70	.489	0
Dowd, Thomas Jefferson "Tommy" 96–97 StLN	92	31	60	.341	0
Doyle, John Joseph "Jack" 95 NYN 98 WasN	81	40	40	.500	0
Dunlap, Frederick C. "Fred" 82 CleN 84 StLU 85 StLN 89 PitN	252	145	102	.587	1
Ebbets, Charles Hercules "Charlie" (Ow) b. Oct. 29, 1859, New York, N.Y. d. April 18, 1925, New York, N.Y. 98 BroN	110	38	68	.358	0
Ellick, Joseph J. "Joe" 84 Chi-PitU	13	6	6	.500	0
Esterbrook, Thomas Jefferson "Dude" 89 LouA	10	2	8	.200	0
Ewing, William "Buck" 90 NYP 95–99 CinNL 00 NYNL	903	489	395	.553	0
Faatz, Jayson S. "Jay" 90 BufP	34	9	24	.273	0
Farrell, John A. "Jack" 81 ProN	51	24	27	.471	0

	G	W	L	PCT	PENNANTS
Ferguson, Robert Vavasour "Bob" (Ex)					
71 NYNA 72–74 AtlNA 75 HarNA 76–77 HarN 78 ChiN 79–82 TroN 83 PhiN 84 PitA 86–87 NYA					
	949	417	516	.447	0
Fessenden, Wallace Clifton "Wallace" b. Oct. 5, 1860, Windham, N.H. d. 1933					
90 SyrA	11	4	7	.364	0
Flint, Frank Syvester "Silver"					
79 ChiN	19	5	12	.294	0
Fogarty, James G. "Jim"					
90 PhiP	16	7	9	.438	0
Fogel, Horace S. "Horace" b. March 2, 1861, Macungie, Pa. d. Nov. 15, 1928, Philadelphia, Pa.					
87 IndN	70	20	49	.290	0
Foutz, David Luther "Dave" "Scissors"					
93–96 BroN	532	264	257	.507	0
Frazer, George Kasson "George" (Ow) b. Jan 7, 1861, Syracuse, N.Y. d. Feb. 5, 1913, Philadelphia, Pa.					
90 SyrA	117	51	65	.440	0
Gaffney, John H. "Honest John" b. June 19, 1855, Roxbury, Mass. d. August 8, 1913, New York, N.Y.					
86–87 WasN	169	61	101	.377	0
Galvin, James Francis "Pud" "Jim" "Gentle Jeems"					
85 BufN	24	7	17	.290	0
Gerhardt, John Joseph "Joe" "Move Up Joe"					
83–84 LouA 90 StLA	191	111	79	.584	0
Gifford, James H. "Jim" "Gift Show" b. Oct. 18, 1845, Warren, N.Y. d. Dec. 19, 1901, Columbus, Ohio					
84 IndA 85–86 NYA	212	74	136	.352	0
Glasscock, John Wesley "Jack"					
89 IndN 92 StLN	71	35	35	.500	0
Gore, George F. "George" "Piano Legs"					
92 StLN	16	6	9	.400	0
Gould, Charles Harvey "Charlie"					
75 NHNA 76 CinN	88	11	77	.125	0
Graffen, Samuel Mason "Mase" b. 1845, Philadelphia, Pa. d. Nov. 18, 1883, Silver City, N. Mex.					
76 StLN	56	39	17	.696	0
Griffin, Michael Joseph "Mike"					
98 BroN	4	1	3	.250	0
Griffin, Tobias Charles "Sandy"					
91 WasA	6	2	4	.333	0
Hackett, Charles M. "Charlie" b. 1855, Lee, Mass. d. August 1, 1898, Holyoke, Mass.					
84 CleN 85 BroA	150	50	99	.336	0
Hallman, William Wilson "Bill"					
97 StLN	50	13	36	.265	0
Hanlon, Edward Hugh "Ned"					
89 PitN 90 PitP 91 PitN 92–98 BaltN 99–00 BroN					
	1493	855	603	.586	5
Hart, James Aristotle "Jim" b. July 10, 1855, Fairview, Pa. d. July 18, 1919, Chicago, Ill.					
85–86 LouA 89 BosN	383	202	174	.537	0
Hastings, Winfield Scott "Scott"					
71 RokNA 72 CleNA	45	10	35	.222	0

	G	W	L	PCT	PENNANTS
Hatfield, John Van Buren "John" 72–73 NYNA	68	35	31	.530	0
Hecker, Guy Jackson "Guy" 90 PitN	138	23	113	.169	0
Heilbroner, Louis Wilbur "Louie" b. July 4, 1861, Fort Wayne, Ind. d. Dec. 21, 1933, Fort Wayne, Ind. 00 StLN	50	23	25	.479	0
Henderson, William C. "Bill" b. Unknown d. Unknown 84 BalU	17	5	12	.294	0
Hengle, Edward S. "Ed" b. Chicago, Ill. d. Nov. 4, 1927, Norwich, Eng. 84 Chi-PitU	74	34	39	.466	0
Hewett, Walter F. "Walter" b. 1861, Washington, D.C. d. Oct. 7, 1944, Washington, D.C. 88 WasN	40	10	29	.256	0
Hicks, Nathaniel Woodall "Nat" 74 PhiNA 75 NYNA 76 NYN	186	80	102	.440	0
Higham, Richard "Dick" 74 NYNA	40	29	11	.725	0
Hoey, Frederick C. "Fred" b. 1866, New York, N.Y. d. Dec. 7, 1933, Paris, France 99 NYN	87	31	55	.360	0
Holbert, William H. "Bill" 79 SyrN	1	0	1	.000	0
Hollingshead, John Samuel "Holly" 75 WasNA 84 WasA	82	16	66	.195	0
Hurst, Timothy Carroll "Tim" b. June 30, 1865, Ashland, Pa. d. June 4, 1915, Pottsville, Pa. 98 StLN	154	39	111	.260	0
Irwin, Arthur Albert "Arthur" 89 WasN 91 BosA 92 WasN 94–95 PhiN 96 NYN 98–99 WasN	863	416	427	.493	1
Joyce, William Michael "Bill" "Scrappy" 96–98 NYN	316	179	122	.595	0
Kelly, John O. "Honest John" 87–88 LouA	178	86	89	.491	0
Kelly, Michael Joseph "King" 87 BosN 90 BosP 91 CinA	330	173	148	.539	1
Kennedy, James C. "Jim" b. 1867, New York, N.Y. d. Apr. 20, 1904, Brighton Beach, N.Y. 90 BroA	100	26	73	.263	0
Kerins, John Nelson "John" 88 LouA	7	3	4	.429	0
Knight, Alonzo P. "Lon" 83–84 PhiA	207	127	78	.620	1
Larkin, Henry E. "Henry" "Ted" 90 CleP	79	34	45	.430	0
Latham, George Warren "Juice" 75 NHNA 82 PhiA	93	45	48	.484	0
Latham, Walter Arlington "Arlie" "Jimmy Fresh" "The Freshest Man on Earth" 96 StLN	3	0	3	.000	0
Leadley, Robert H. "Bob" b. 1858, Brooklyn, N.Y. d. Unknown 88 DetN 90–91 CleN	166	76	86	.469	0

	G	W	L	PCT	PENNANTS
Lennon, William F. "Bill" 71 KekNA	14	5	9	.357	0
Loftus, Thomas Joseph "Tom" 84 MilU 88 CleA 89 CleN 90–91 CinN 00 ChiN	637	297	325	.477	0
Mack, Cornelius Alexander "Connie" 94–96 PitN	289	149	134	.527	0
Mack, Dennis Joseph "Denny" 82 LouA	80	42	37	.532	0
Macullar, James F. "Jimmy" "Little Mac" 79 SyrN	27	5	21	.192	0
Malone, Ferguson G. "Fergy" 73 PhiNA 74 ChiNA 84 PhiU	156	75	81	.481	0
Manning, John E. "Jack" 77 CinN	20	7	12	.368	0
Martin, Alphonse Case "Phoney" 72 EckNA	9	1	8	.111	0
Mason, Charles E. "Charlie" (Ow) 87 PhiA	82	38	40	.487	0
McBride, James Dickson "Dick" 71–75 AthNA	252	161	85	.654	1
McCarthy, Thomas Francis Michael "Tommy" 90 StLA	24	14	10	.583	0
McCloskey, John James "John" b. Apr. 4, 1862, Louisville, Ky. d. Nov. 17, 1940, Louisville, Ky. 95–96 LouN	152	37	113	.247	0
McCormick, James "Jim" 79–80 CleN 82 CleN	171	74	96	.435	0
McGeary, Michael Henry "Mike" 75 PhiNA 80 ProN 81 CleN	90	46	41	.529	0
McGraw, John Joseph "Mugsy" 99 BalN	152	86	62	.581	0
McGuire, James Thomas "Deacon" 98 WasN	70	21	47	.309	0
McGunnigle, William Henry "Bill" 88–89 BroA 90 BroN 91 PitN 96 LouN	586	328	247	.570	2
McKinnon, Alexander J. "Alex" 85 StLN	39	6	32	.158	0
McKnight, Dennis Hamar "Denny" (Ow) (Ex) b. 1847 Pittsburgh, Pa. d. May 5, 1900, Pittsburgh, Pa. 84 PitA	12	4	8	.333	0
McManus, George "George" b. Oct. 1846, Ireland d. Oct. 2, 1918, New York, N.Y. 76–77 StLN	68	34	34	.500	0
McVey, Calvin Alexander "Cal" 73 BalNA 78–79 CinN	156	90	64	.584	0
Miller, George Frederick "Doggie" "Foghorn" "Calliope" 94 StLN	133	56	76	.424	0
Mills, Everett "Everett" "Ev" 72 BalNA	17	8	6	.571	0

	G	W	L	PCT	PENNANTS
Morrill, John Francis "John" 82–88 BosN 89 WasN	696	348	334	.510	1
Morton, Charles Hazen "Charlie" 84 TolA 85 DetN 90 TolA	282	121	153	.442	0
Moses, Felix I. "Felix" (Ow) b. Richmond, Va. d. Unknown 84 VirA	46	12	30	.286	0
Murnane, Timothy Hayes "Tim" 84 BosU	111	58	51	.532	0
Mutrie, James J. "Jim" b. June 13, 1851, Chelsea, Mass. d. Jan. 24, 1938, New York, N.Y. 83–84 NYA 85–91 NYN	1114	658	419	.611	3
Myers, Henry C. "Henry" 82 BalA	74	19	54	.260	0
Nash, William Mitchell "Billy" 96 PhiN	130	62	68	.477	0
Nicol, Hugh N. "Wee Hugh" 97 StLN	40	8	32	.200	0
O'Leary, Daniel "Dan" "Hustling Dan" 84 CinA	62	33	29	.532	0
O'Rourke, James Henry "Jim" "Orator Jim" 81–84 BufN 93 WasN	510	246	258	.488	0
Orr, David L. "Dave" 87 NYA	8	3	5	.375	0
Pabor, Charles Henry "Charlie" 71 CleNA 75 AtlNA 75 NHNA	77	13	64	.169	0
Parks, William Robert "Bill" 75 WasNA	8	1	7	.125	0
Pearce, Richard J. "Dickey" 72 NYNA 75 StLNA	88	49	35	.583	0
Pfeffer, Nathaniel Frederick "Fred" "Fritz" "Dandelion" 92 LouN	100	42	56	.429	0
Phelan, Lewis G. "Lew" b. Unknown d. Unknown 95 StLN	45	11	30	.268	0
Phillips, Horace B. "Hustling Horace" b. May 14, 1853, Salem, Ohio d. Unknown 79 TroN 83 ColA 84–86 PitA 87–89 PitN	765	338	415	.449	0
Pike, Lipman Emanuel "Lip" 71 TroNA 74 HarNA 77 CinN	72	21	51	.292	0
Porter, Matthew Sheldon "Matt" 84 KCU	16	3	13	.188	0
Powers, Patrick Thomas "Pat" b. June 27, 1860, Trenton, N.J. d. August 29, 1925, Belmar, N.J. 90 RocA 92 NYN	286	134	143	.484	0
Pratt, Albert J. "Al" 82–83 PitA	111	51	59	.464	0
Price, James Lyman "Jim" b. 1847, New York, N.Y. d. Oct. 6, 1931, Chicago, Ill. 84 NYN	100	56	42	.571	0
Purcell, William Aloysius "Blondie" 83 PhiN	82	13	68	.160	0

	G	W	L	PCT	PENNANTS
Quinn, Joseph J. "Joe" 95 StLN 99 CleN	156	23	132	.148	0
Reach, Alfred James "Al" (Ow) 90 PhiN	11	4	7	.364	0
Richardson, Daniel "Danny" 92 WasN	43	12	31	.279	0
Rogers, James F. "Jim" 97 LouN	44	17	24	.415	0
Roseman, James John "Chief" 90 StLA	35	17	18	.486	0
Rowe, David E. "Dave" 86 KCN 88 KCA	176	44	127	.257	0
Rowe, John Charles "Jack" 90 BufP	100	27	72	.273	0
Scanlon, Michael B. "Mike" (Ow) b. Nov. 1847, Cork, Ireland d. Jan. 18, 1929, Washington, D.C. 84 WasU 86 WasN	196	60	132	.313	0
Schmelz, Gustav Heinrich "Gus" b. Sept. 26, 1850, Columbus, Ohio d. Oct. 14, 1925, Columbus, Ohio 84 ColA 86 StLN 87–89 CinA 90 CleN 90–91 ColA 94–97 WasN	1357	624	703	.470	0
Selee, Frank Gibson "Frank" b. Oct. 26, 1859, Amherst, Mass. d. July 5, 1909, Denver, Colo. 90–00 BosN	1537	935	580	.617	5
Shannon, Daniel W. "Dan" 89 LouA 91 WasA	109	25	80	.238	0
Sharsig, William A. "Bill" (Ow) b. 1855, Philadelphia, Pa. d. Feb. 1, 1902, Philadelphia, Pa. 86 PhiA 88–91 PhiA	466	238	216	.524	0
Shettsline, William Joseph "Bill" b. Oct. 25, 1863, Philadelphia, Pa. d.Feb. 22, 1933, Philadelphia, Pa. 98–00 PhiN	399	228	165	.580	0
Simmons, Joseph S. "Joe" 75 WesNA 84 WilU	31	3	28	.097	0
Simmons, Lewis "Lew" (Ow) b. Aug. 27, 1838, New Castle, Pa. d. Sept. 2, 1911, Jamestown, Pa. 86 PhiA	98	41	55	.427	0
Smith, William J. "Bill" 73 MarNA	5	0	5	.000	0
Snyder, Charles N. "Pop" 82 CinA 83–84 CinA 91 WasA	288	163	122	.572	1
Spalding, Albert Goodwill "Al" 76–77 ChiN	126	78	47	.624	1
Spence, Harrison L. "Harry" b. Feb. 22, 1856, New York, N.Y. d. May 17, 1908, Chicago, Ill. 88 IndN	136	50	85	.370	0
Stallings, George Tweedy "George" 97–98 PhiN	180	74	104	.416	0
Start, Joseph "Joe" 73 NYNA	25	18	7	.720	0
Stovey, Harry Duffield "Harry" 81 WorN 85 PhiA	140	63	75	.457	0
Stricker, John A. "Cub" 92 StLN	23	6	17	.261	0

George Davis, the only manager ever to sit at the helm of a big league team for more than half a season, pilot it to a winning record (39-37), yet finish in the cellar. Davis's performance with the 1900 New York Giants is but one of his many enormously underappreciated achievements. He set tons of season and career batting and fielding records, several of which still stand.

Jim Hart (1), later president and part owner of Chicago, launched his major league career as Louisville's manager in 1885. A solid contender in 1884, the Colonels dropped to sixth place under their new skipper. Hart's top players were: John Kerins (2), Amos Cross (3), Leech Maskrey (4), Guy Hecker (5), Pete Browning (6), Phil Reccius (7), Joe Miller (8), Tommy McLaughlin (9), Norm Baker (10), Dan Sullivan (12), Chicken Wolf (13) and Monk Cline (15).

Bill Joyce is remembered as one of the game's elite sluggers in the 1890s, but he also has the highest career winning percentage (.595) of any manager who held the reins of a big league team for at least 300 games— roughly the equivalent of two full seasons—without ever winning a pennant.

For over a century this picture moldered away in an attic, wrongly identified as the 1884 St. Louis Browns before Jimmy Williams (civvies) quit as manager. It's Williams, all right, but with his 1888 Cleveland Blues. Surrounding Williams—a brilliant organizer but no master at handling players— are his lieutenants, the men who really ran the show on the field: Jay Faatz to Williams's left, Pop Snyder to Williams's right and Chief Zimmer to Snyder's right. Left of Faatz is George Proeser, and Ed McKean stands at the far left end of the back row. Cub Stricker sits front center, his left shoulder pressed to Deacon McGuire's knee.

Sullivan, James Patrick "Pat" b. Unknown d. May 22, 1898					
90 ColA	3	2	1	.667	0
Sullivan, Timothy Paul "Ted"					
83 StLA 84 StLU 84 KCU 88 WasN	268	132	132	.500	0
Sweasy, Charles James "Charlie"					
75 RedsNA	19	4	15	.211	0
Taylor, George J. "George" b. Nov. 22, 1853, New York, N.Y. d. Unknown					
84 BroA	109	40	64	.385	0
Tebeau, Oliver Wendell "Patsy"					
90 CleP 91–98 CleN 99–00 StLN	1339	726	583	.555	0
Thomas, Frederick L. "Fred" b. Indiana d. Unknown					
87 IndN	29	11	18	.379	0
Thompson, Andrew M. "Andy" "A.M." (Ow)					
84 StPU	9	2	6	.250	0
Trott, Samuel W. "Sam"					
91 WasA	12	4	7	.364	0

	G	W	L	PCT	PENNANTS
Van Haltren, George Edward "George"					
92 BalN	11	1	10	.091	0
Von Der Ahe, Christian Frederick Wilhelm "Chris" (Ow) b. Oct. 7, 1851, Hille, Germany d. June 7, 1913, St. Louis, Mo.					
95, 96, 97 StLN	17	3	14	.176	0
Walsh, Michael John "Mike" b. Apr. 29, 1850, Ireland d. Feb. 2, 1929, Louisville, Ky.					
84 LouA	52	29	22	.569	0
Waltz, John "John" b. Unknown d. Unknown					
92 BalN	8	2	6	.250	0
Ward, John Montgomery "Monte" "John"					
80 ProN 84 NYN 90 BroP 91–92 BroN 93–94 NYN	751	412	320	.563	0
Waterman, Fredrick A. "Fred"					
72 OlyNA	9	2	7	.222	0
Watkins, Harvey L. "Harvey" b. unknown d. unknown					
95 NYN	35	18	17	.514	0
Watkins, William Henry "Bill"					
84 IndA 85–88 DetN 88–89 KCA 93 StLN 98–99 PitN	914	452	444	.504	1
Wheeler, Harry Eugene "Harry"					
84 KCU	4	0	4	.000	0
White, James Laurie "Deacon"					
72 CleNA 79 CinN	20	9	11	.450	0
White, William Henry "Will"					
84 CinA	72	44	27	.620	0
White, William Warren "Warren"					
72 NatNA 74 BalNA	58	9	49	.155	0
Williams, James A. "Jimmy" b. Jan. 3, 1848, Columbus, Ohio d. Oct. 24, 1918, N. Hempstead, N.Y.					
84 StLA 87–88 CleA	282	110	169	.394	0
Wolf, Willian Van Winkle "Jimmy" "Chicken"					
89 LouA	65	14	51	.215	0
Wood, George A. "George"					
91 PhiA	125	67	55	.549	0
Wood, James Leon "Jimmy"					
71 ChiNA 72 TroNA 72 EckNA 74–75 ChiNA	154	76	76	.500	0
Wright, Alfred Hector "Al" b. Mar. 30, 1842, Cedar Grove, N.J. d. Apr. 20, 1905, New York, N.Y.					
76 PhiN	60	14	45	.237	0
Wright, George "George"					
79 ProN	85	59	25	.702	1
Wright, William Henry "Harry"					
71–75 BosNA 76–81 BosN 82–83 ProN 84–93 PhiN	2145	1225	885	.581	6
York, Thomas J. "Tom"					
78 ProN 81 ProN	96	56	37	.602	0
Young, Nicholas Ephraim "Nick" (Ow) (Ex) b. Sept. 12, 1840, Fort Johnson, N.Y. d. Oct. 31, 1916, Washington, D.C.					
71 OlyNA 73 WasNA	71	23	46	.404	0

UMPIRE ROSTER

A complete roster of men who served as regular umpires in each of the five majors leagues between 1871 and 1900 with years of service in parentheses.

P   Also was a former, concurrent or future major league player
M   Also was a former, concurrent or future major league manager
O   Also was a former, concurrent or future major league official

NATIONAL ASSOCIATION (1871–75)

Avery, C. Hamilton (1875)
Beardslee, John J. (1871)
Blodgett, C. W. (1875)
Boardman, Frederick (1875)
Bomeisler, Theodore (1871–73)
Boyd, William J (1875) **P/M**
Burdock, John Joseph (1872–74) **P/M**
Carey, Thomas John (1874) **P/M**
Clapp, John Edgar (1874–75) **P/M**
Cone, Joseph Frederick (1875) **P**
Daniels, Charles F. (1874–75)
Dehlman, Herman J. (1874) **P**
Dole, Lester Carrington (1875) **P**
Ferguson, Robert Vavasour (1872–73, 1875) **P/M/O**
Fulmer, Charles John (1873) **P**
Heubel, George A. (1875) **P**

Hodges, Amory G. (1874–75)
Holly, Samuel J. (1871)
Lennon, William F. (1871–72, 1873–74) **P/M**
Mack, Dennis Joseph (1875) **P/M**
Martin, Alphonse Case (1875) **P/M**
Mathews, Robert T. (1873–75) **P**
McLean, William H. (1874–75)
Mills, Charles (1872–73) **P**
Patterson, Daniel Thomas (1874) **P**
Rogers, M. Mortimer (1871) **P**
Sensenderfer, John Phillips Jenkins (1874) **P**
Swandell, John Martin (1872–73) **P**
Tate, William (1874)
Walsh, Michael F. (1875) **M**
Young, Nicholas E. (1871–75) **M/O**

NATIONAL LEAGUE (1876–1900)

Andrews, George Edward (1895, 1898–99) **P**
Barnie, William Harrison (1892) **P/M**
Battin, Joseph V. (1891) **P/M**
Betts, William G. (1894–96, 1898–99)

Boles, Charles (1877)
Bond, Thomas Henry (1883, 1885) **P/M**
Bradley, George H. (1879–83) **P**
Brady, Jackson (1887)

Bredburg, George W. (1877)
Brennan, John E. (1899)
Brown, Thomas Tarton (1898–99) **P/M**
Bunce, Joshua (1877) **P**
Burnham, George Walter (1883, 1889, 1895) **M**
Burns, John S. (1884)
Burns, Thomas Everett (1892) **P/M**
Burns, Thomas P. (1899) **P**
Burtis, L. W. (1876–77)
Callahan, Edward Joseph (1881) **P**
Campbell, Daniel (1894–96)
Carpenter, William B. (1897)
Chapman, John Curtis (1880) **P/M**
Chipman, Harry F. (1883–85)
Conahan, ? (1896)
Cone, Joseph Frederick (1877) **P**
Connolly, John M. (1886)
Connolly, Thomas Henry (1898–1900)
Crandall, Robert (1877)
Cross, John A. (1878)
Curry, Wesley (1885–86, 1889, 1898) **P**
Cushman, Charles H. (1885, 1898) **M**
Dailey, John J. (1882)
Daniels, Charles F. (1876, 1878–80, 1887–88)
Decker, Stewart M. (1883–85, 1888)
Devinney, P.H. (1877)
Doscher, John Henry Sr. (1880–81, 1887) **P/M**
Ducharme, ? (1876–77)
Dunnigan, Joseph (1881–82)
Dwyer, John Francis (1899) **P**
Eagan, John J. (1878, 1886)
Ellick, Joseph J. (1886) **P/M**
Emslie, Robert Daniel (1891–1900) **P**
Ferguson, Robert V. (1879, 1884–85) **P/M/O**
Fessenden, Wallace Clifton (1889–90) **M**
Fountain, Edward G. (1879)
Fulmer, Charles John (1886) **P/M**
Furlong, William E. (1878–79, 1883–84)
Gaffney, John H. (1884–86, 1891–94, 1899–1900) **M**
Galvin, James Francis (1895) **P/M**
Gillean, Thomas (1879–80)
Gunning, Thomas Francis (1887) **P**
Hautz, Charles A. (1876, 1879) **P**
Henderson, James Harding (1895–96) **P**
Hengle, Edward S. (1887) **M**
Heubel, George A. (1876) **P**
Heydler, John A. (1898) **O**
Higham, Richard (1881–82) **P/M**
Hoagland, Willard A. (1894)
Hodges, A.D. (1876)
Holland, John A. (1887)
Hornung, Michael Joseph (1893, 1896) **P**
Hunt, John T. 1895, 1898–99)
Hurst, Timothy C. (1891–97, 1900) **M**
Jeffers, W. W. (1881)
Jevne, Frederick (1895)
Julian, Joseph O. (1878)

Keefe, Timothy John (1894–96) **P**
Kelly, John O. (1882, 1888, 1897) **P/M**
Kenney, John (1877)
Knight, Alonzo P. (1889) **P/M**
Lane, Frank H. (1883)
Latham, Walter Arlington (1899) **P/M**
Libby, Stephen A. (1880) **P**
Long, William H. (1895)
Lynch, Thomas James (1888–99) **P/O**
Macullar, James F. (1892) **P/M**
Mahoney, Michael J. (1892)
Malone, Ferguson G. (1884) **P/M**
Manassau, Alfred S. (1899)
Mathews, Robert T. (1880) **P**
McDermott, Michael Joseph (1890, 1897) **P**
McDonald, James F. (1895, 1897–99)
McElwee, Harvey (1877)
McFarland, Horace (1896–97)
McGarr, James B. (1899) **P**
McLaughlin, Michael (1893)
McLean, William H. (1876, 1878–80, 1882–84)
McQuaid, John H. (1889–94)
Miller, George E. (1879)
Mitchell, Charles (1892)
O'Day, Henry Francis (1895, 1897–1900) **P/M**
Odlin, Albert F. (1883)
O'Rourke, James Henry (1894) **P/M**
Pearce, Richard J. (1878, 1882) **P/M**
Pears, Frank H. (1897) **P**
Pierce, Grayson S. (1886–87) **P**
Powers, Philip B. (1879, 1881, 1886–91) **P**
Pratt, Albert George (1879) **P/M**
Pratt, Thomas J. (1886) **P**
Quest, Joseph L. (1886–87) **P**
Quinn, Joseph C. (1882) **P**
Riley, William James (1880) **P**
Seward, Edward William (1893) **P**
Seward, George E. (1876, 1878) **P**
Sheridan, John F. (1892, 1896–97)
Smith, Charles Melvin (1881) **P**
Smith, William W. (1898–99)
Snyder, Charles N. (1892–93, 1898–1900) **P/M**
Stage, Charles W. (1894)
Stambaugh, Calvin G. (1877–78)
Strief, George Andrew (1890) **P**
Sullivan, David F. (1882, 1885)
Sullivan, Jeremiah (1887)
Sullivan, Timothy Paul (1880) **P/M**
Summer, James G. (1877)
Swartwood, Cyrus Edward (1894, 1898–1900) **P**
Terry, William H. (1900) **P**
Tilden, Otis (1880)
Valentine, John G. (1887–88)
Van Court, Eugene (1884)
Walker, William E. (1876–77)
Walsh, Michael F. (1876, 1878, 1880) **M**
Warner, Albert (1898–1900)

Weidman, George E. (1896) **P**
White, Gideon F. (1878)
Wilbur, Charles E. (1879)
Wilson, John A. (1887)
Wise, Samuel Washington (1889, 1893) **P**

Wood, George A. (1898) **P/M**
York, Thomas Jefferson (1886) **P/M**
Young, Joseph (1879)
Zacharias, Thomas (1890)

AMERICAN ASSOCIATION (1882–91)

Barnum, George W. (1890)
Bauers, Albert J. (1887) **P**
Becannon, William H. (1883)
Bradley, George H. (1886) **P**
Brennan, John E. (1884)
Butler, Ormond H. (1883) **M**
Carey, Thomas John (1882) **P/M**
Clinton, James Lawrence (1886) **P**
Connell, Terence G. (1884, 1890) **P**
Connelly, John M. (1885, 1887)
Connelly, William (1884)
Curry, Wesley (1887, 1890) **P**
Cuthbert, Edgar Edward (1887) **P/M**
Dailey, John J. (1884)
Daniels, Charles F. (1883–85, 1889)
Davis, James J. (1891) **P**
Devinney, P. H. (1884)
Doscher, John Herman Sr. (1888, 1890) **P/M**
Dyler, John F. (1884)
Emslie, Robert Daniel (1890) **P**
Ferguson, Robert Vavasour (1886–89, 1891) **P/M/O**
Gaffney, John H. (1888–89) **M**
Gleason, William G. (1891) **P**
Goldsmith, Fred Ernest (1888–89) **P**
Griffith, E.A. (1884)
Hautz, Charles A. (1882) **P**
Hecker, Guy Jackson (1889) **P/M**
Holland, John A. (1884)
Holland, Willard A. (1889) **P**
Hurley, Daniel (1887)
Jennings, Alfred Gorden (1887) **P**
Jones, Charles Wesley (1891) **P**
Kelly, John O. (1883–86) **P/M**
Kerins, John Nelson (1889–91) **P/M**

Knight, Alonzo P. (1887) **P/M**
Lawler, John F. (1884)
Macullar, James F. (1891) **P**
Mack, Dennis Joseph (1886) **P/M**
Magner, John T. (1883) **P**
Mahoney, Michael J. (1891)
Mathews, Robert T. (1891) **P**
McLaughlin, Thomas (1891) **P**
McLean, William H. (1885)
McNichol, Robert (1883)
McQuaid, John H. (1886–88)
Morton, Charles Hazen (1886) **P/M**
O'Brien, Frank (1890)
Peoples, James Elsworth (1890) **P**
Pike, Lipman Emanuel (1889) **P/M**
Pratt, Albert George (1883) **P/M**
Quinn, A.J. (1886)
Riley, William James (1882) **P**
Ross, Robert T. (1882)
Seward, George E. (1884) **P**
Simmons, Joseph S. (1882) **P/M**
Smith, Charles Melvin (1882) **P**
Snyder, Charles N. (1891) **P/M**
Sommer, Benjamin F. (1883)
Sullivan, Jeremiah (1887)
Sullivan, Timothy Paul (1887) **P/M**
Taylor, Walter (1890)
Toole, Stephen John (1890) **P**
Tunnison, William (1885–86)
Valentine, John G. (1884–87)
Walsh, Michael F. (1882–83, 1885–86) **M**
York, Thomas Jefferson (1886) **P/M**
Young, Benjamin F. (1886)

UNION ASSOCIATION (1884)

Crawford, Alexander
Devinney, P.H.
Dutton, Patrick
Hengle, Emory J. **M**
Holland, John A.
Hooper, Michael H.
Jennings, Alfred Gorden **P**

Jordan, William H.
Mapledoram, Blake A.
McCaffrey, Harry Charles **P**
Seward, George E. **P**
Stearns, Daniel Eckford **P**
Sullivan, David F.

THE ONLY MAJOR LEAGUE UMPIRE EVER TO BE BANNED

Dick Higham in 1877 with the Syracuse Stars of the International Association. The future crooked umpire liked to go his own route. Higham abandoned the NL after the 1876 season to join the player-controlled IA, then returned to the NL for a last fling in 1878. Top: Tom Mansell, Hick Carpenter and Pete Hotaling. Middle: Harry McCormick, Alex McKinnon, Jim Clinton, unknown and Higham. Bottom: Billy Geer and Jack Farrell. McCormick was the Stars "star" in 1878 when the team nearly won the IA flag, collecting all but one of Syracuse's 27 victories. Geer, like Higham, was something of a bad egg. He and New Haven teammate Harry Luff were charged with a string of hotel burglaries in 1875.

Dick Higham was already a shadowy figure long before he was cut loose by Providence after he paced the National League in both runs and doubles in 1878. Only 26 at the time, Higham played just one more game in the majors. But perhaps choosing to believe that his lineage—Higham was born in England, the son of a well-respected cricket player—would eventually prevail over his reputation, National League president William Hulbert hired him as a regular umpire in 1881. The following season, while umpiring a string of games involving Detroit, Higham came under attack when he kept giving the Wolverines' opponents the benefit in every close call. Wolverines president W.G. Thompson, who was also the mayor of Detroit, was finally led to inspect his mail, much of which was in code and not particularly hard to decipher. It was simple to deduce that Higham was in collusion with gamblers who were betting against Detroit on his assurance that their money was safe.

After being booted from baseball, Higham parlayed the connections he'd made as a crooked umpire and became a bookmaker in Chicago. Thompson also left the game soon thereafter. In the late 1890s he told former Wolverines manager Frank Bancroft that he now loathed baseball and added, "Baseball is like the measles. I had it once, and that's enough."

PLAYERS LEAGUE (1890)

Barnes, Roscoe Charles **P**
Ferguson, Robert Vavasour **P/M/O**
Gaffney, John H. **M**
Gunning, Thomas Francis **P**
Holbert, William Henry **P/M**
Jones, Charles Wesley **P**

Knight, Alonzo P. **P/M**
Leach, Henry
Matthews, John
Pierce, Grayson S. **P**
Sheridan, John F.
Snyder, Charles N. **P/M**

ONE-GAME UMPIRE

Bill Gleason was the St. Louis Browns regular shortstop from 1882 to 1887 and concluded his major league playing career in 1889. Prior to the 1891 season the American Association appointed him to its regular umpiring staff. Gleason's first assignment was to officiate the Opening Day game at St. Louis on April 8 between the Browns and Cincinnati Kelly's Killers.

When the game went into overtime, knotted 7–7, Cincinnati began to stall on orders from manager King Kelly, who claimed it was too dark to continue. Gleason disagreed. Kelly went into a deeper stall and stepped up his accusations that everything Gleason did favored his old team. Finally, in exasperation, Gleason forfeited the game to St. Louis. He then stormed off the field and cabled his resignation to Association headquarters. Gleason's forfeiture was later overturned and the game had to be replayed, only confirming his judgment that the job was not for him. He never umpired another game in the majors.

Safe or out? This moment of action from a game at Washington's Swampoodle Grounds, blurred though it may be, is priceless. Captured here are the pitcher's box and both a batter's box and a base coach's box as they looked in the late 1880s. Note also that both teams are wearing light-colored uniforms and the pitcher wears a different shirt than the rest of his team. There were no rules then requiring the home team to wear white unis and the visitors dark, nor was every player on a team required to wear an identical uniform. Note, finally, the plight of the poor umpire. Although arbiters generally worked a game alone, most preferred to station themselves back of the plate even with men on base. The umpire here has scrambled from behind the catcher to a spot about 20 feet up the first-base line, where he will have to make a long-range call at second base on this steal attempt. Since it's going to be a close play, he's surely in for a hot argument.

NINETEENTH-CENTURY
SINGLE SEASON LEADERS

BATTING
(1871–92)

Batting Average (300 ABs)	.435	Tip O'Neill	ST. Louis (AA)	1887
	.429	Ross Barnes	Chicago (NL)	1876
	.425	Ross Barnes	Boston (NA)	1873
	.412	Fred Dunlap	St. Louis (UA)	1884
	.402	Pete Browning	Louisville (AA)	1887
Slugging Average (300 ABs)	.691	Tip O'Neill	St. Louis (AA)	1887
	.621	Fred Dunlap	St. Louis (UA)	1884
	.590	Ross Barnes	Chicago (NL)	1876
	.584	Ross Barnes	Boston (NA)	1873
	.581	Dan Brouthers	Detroit (NL)	1886
Total Bases	357	Tip O'Neill	St. Louis (AA)	1887
	311	Sam Thompson	Detroit (NL)	1887
	301	Dave Orr	New York (AA)	1886
	299	Pete Browning	Louisville (AA)	1887
	298	Denny Lyons	Philadelphia (AA)	1887
Hits	225	Tip O'Neill	St. Louis (AA)	1887
	220	Pete Browning	Louisville (AA)	1887
	209	Denny Lyons	Philadelphia (AA)	1887
	205	Jack Glasscock	Indianapolis (NL)	1889
	203	Sam Thompson	Detroit (NL)	1887
Runs	177	Tom Brown	Boston (AA)	1891
	167	Tip O'Neill	St. Louis (AA)	1887
	163	Arlie Latham	St. Louis (AA)	1887
	161	Hugh Duffy	Chicago (PL)	1890
	160	Fred Dunlap	St. Louis (UA)	1884

Doubles	52	Tip O'Neill	St. Louis (AA)	1887
	49	Ned Williamson	Chicago (NL)	1883
	43	Denny Lyons	Philadelphia (AA)	1887
	41	Dan Brouthers	Buffalo (NL)	1883
	41	King Kelly	Boston (NL)	1889
	41	Sam Thompson	Philadelphia (NL)	1890
Triples	31	Dave Orr	New York (AA)	1886
	26	Long John Reilly	Cincinnati (NL)	1890
	23	Harry Stovey	Philadelphia (AA)	1884
	23	Sam Thompson	Detroit (NL)	1887
	22	Roger Connor	New York (NL)	1887
	22	Bid McPhee	Cincinnati (NL)	1890
	22	Joe Visner	Pittsburgh (PL)	1890
	22	Jake Beckley	Pittsburgh (PL)	1890
Home Runs	27	Ned Williamson	Chicago (NL)	1884
	25	Fred Pfeffer	Chicago (NL)	1884
	22	Abner Dalrymple	Chicago (NL)	1884
	21	Cap Anson	Chicago (NL)	1884
	20	Sam Thompson	Philadelphia (NL)	1889
Walks	136	Jack Crooks	St. Louis (LA)	1892
	123	Bill Joyce	Brooklyn (PL)	1890
	118	Yank Robinson	St. Louis (AA)	1889
	117	Dummy Hoy	St. Louis (AA)	1891
	117	Cupid Childs	Cleveland (LA)	1892
Stolen Bases	138	Hugh Nicol	Cincinnati (AA)	1887
	129	Arlie Latham	St. Louis (AA)	1887
	117	Charlie Comiskey	St. Louis (AA)	1887
	111	Monte Ward	New York (NL)	1887
	111	Billy Hamilton	Kansas City (AA)	1889
	111	Billy Hamilton	Philadelphia (NL)	1891

Dan Brouthers holds many nineteenth-century career and single season batting records, but probably his most cherished is his mark for the most hitting titles—five— prior to the emergence of Honus Wagner and Ty Cobb.

(1893–1900)

Batting Average	.440	Hugh Duffy	Boston (LA)	1894
(350 ABs)	.424	Willy Keeler	Baltimore (LA)	1897
	.410	Ed Delahanty	Philadelphia (LA)	1899
	.410	Jesse Burkett	Cleveland (LA)	1896
	.409	Jesse Burkett	Cleveland (LA)	1895
Slugging Average	.694	Hugh Duffy	Boston (LA)	1894
(350 ABs)	.686	Sam Thompson	Philadelphia (LA)	1894
	.654	Sam Thompson	Philadelphia (LA)	1895
	.648	Bill Joyce	Washington (LA)	1894
	.631	Ed Delahanty	Philadelphia (LA)	1896
Total Bases	374	Hugh Duffy	Boston (LA)	1894
	352	Sam Thompson	Philadelphia (LA)	1895
	347	Ed Delahanty	Philadelphia (LA)	1893
	338	Ed Delahanty	Philadelphia (LA)	1899
	331	Buck Freeman	Washington (LA)	1899
Hits	240	Jesse Burkett	Cleveland (LA)	1896
	239	Willie Keeler	Baltimore (LA)	1897
	238	Ed Delahanty	Philadelphia (LA)	1899
	237	Hugh Duffy	Boston (LA)	1894
	225	Jesse Burkett	Cleveland (LA)	1895
Runs	192	Billy Hamilton	Philadelphia (LA)	1894
	166	Billy Hamilton	Philadelphia (LA)	1895
	165	Joe Kelley	Baltimore (LA)	1894
	165	Willie Keeler	Baltimore (LA)	1894
	162	Willie Keeler	Baltimore (LA)	1895
Doubles	55	Ed Delahanty	Philadelphia (LA)	1899
	51	Hugh Duffy	Boston (LA)	1894
	49	Ed Delahanty	Philadelphia (LA)	1895
	48	Joe Kelley	Baltimore (LA)	1894
	45	Honus Wagner	Pittsburgh (NL)	1900
	45	Sam Thompson	Philadelphia (LA)	1895
	45	Walt Wilmot	Chicago (LA)	1894
Triples	31	Heinie Reitz	Baltimore (LA)	1894
	29	Perry Werden	St. Louis (LA)	1893
	28	Harry Davis	Pittsburgh (LA)	1897
	27	George Davis	New York (LA)	1893
	27	Jimmy Williams	Pittsburgh (LA)	1899
	27	Sam Thompson	Philadelphia (LA)	1894
Home Runs	25	Buck Freeman	Washington (LA)	1899
	19	Ed Delahanty	Philadelphia (LA)	1893
	18	Sam Thompson	Philadelphia (LA)	1895
	18	Hugh Duffy	Boston (LA)	1894
	17	Bill Joyce	Washington (LA)	1895
	17	Jack Clements	Philadelphia (LA)	1893
	17	Bill Joyce	Washington (LA)	1894
	17	Bobby Lowe	Boston (LA)	1894

Walks	126	Billy Hamilton	Philadelphia (LA)	1894
	124	John McGraw	Baltimore (LA)	1899
	121	Jack Crooks	St. Louis (LA)	1893
	120	Cupid Childs	Cleveland (LA)	1893
	115	Roy Thomas	Philadelphia (LA)	1899
	115	Roy Thomas	Philadelphia (NL)	1900
Stolen Bases	98	Billy Hamilton	Philadelphia (LA)	1894
	97	Billy Hamilton	Philadelphia (LA)	1895
	87	Joe Kelley	Baltimore (LA)	1896
	84	Bill Lange	Chicago (LA)	1896
	83	Billy Hamilton	Boston (LA)	1896

PITCHING (1871-92)

Wins	60	Hoss Radbourn	Providence (NL)	1884
	55	Al Spalding	Boston (NA)	1875
	53	John Clarkson	Chicago (NL)	1885
	52	Guy Hecker	Louisville (AA)	1884
	52	Al Spalding	Boston (NA)	1874
Losses	48	John Coleman	Philadelphia (NL)	1884
	42	Will White	Cincinnati (NL)	1880
	41	Larry McKeon	Indianapolis (AA)	1884
	40	George Bradley	Troy (NL)	1879
	40	Jim McCormick	Cleveland (NL)	1879
Innings	680	Will White	Cincinnati (NL)	1879
	678.2	Hoss Radbourn	Providence (NL)	1884
	670.2	Guy Hecker	Louisville (AA)	1884
	657.2	Jim McCormick	Cleveland (NL)	1880
	656.1	Pud Galvin	Buffalo (NL)	1883
Complete Games	75	Will White	Cincinnati (NL)	1879
	73	Hoss Radbourn	Providence (NL)	1884
	72	Jim McCormick	Cleveland (NL)	1880
	72	Pud Galvin	Buffalo (NL)	1883
	72	Guy Hecker	Louisville (AA)	1884
Strikeouts	513	Matt Kilroy	Baltimore (AA)	1886
	499	Toad Ramsey	Louisville (AA)	1886
	483	Hugh Daily	CP-Washington (UA)	1884
	451	Dupee Shaw	Detroit (NL)-Boston (UA)	1884
	441	Hoss Radbourn	Providence (NL)	1884
Walks	289	Amos Rusie	New York (NL)	1890
	274	Mark Baldwin	Columbus (AA)	1889
	267	Amos Rusie	New York (NL)	1892
	262	Amos Rusie	New York (NL)	1891
	249	Mark Baldwin	Chicago (PL)	1890
*Lefthander's record	226	Phil Knell	Columbus (AA)	1891

Winning Percentage	.917	Al Spalding	Boston (NA)	1875
(Minimum 20 wins)	.850	Fred Goldsmith	Chicago (NL)	1880
	.833	Hoss Radbourn	Providence (NL)	1884
	.826	Al Spalding	Boston (NA)	1872
	.800	Mickey Welch	New York (NL)	1885
ERA (100 Inn.)	0.86	Tim Keefe	Troy (NL)	1880
	1.21	Denny Driscoll	Pittsburgh (AA)	1882
	1.23	George Bradley	St. Louis (NL)	1876
	1.30	Guy Hecker	Louisville (AA)	1882
	1.38	George Bradley	Providence (NL)	1880
	1.38	Hoss Radbourn	Providence (NL)	1884

(1893–1900)

Wins	36	Frank Killen	Pittsburgh (LA)	1893
	36	Amos Rusie	New York (LA)	1894
	35	Cy Young	Cleveland (LA)	1895
	34	Cy Young	Cleveland (LA)	1893
	34	Kid Nichols	Boston (LA)	1893
Losses	35	Red Donahue	St. Louis (LA)	1897
	30	Ted Breitenstein	St. Louis (LA)	1895
	30	Jim Hughey	Cleveland (LA)	1899
	29	Bill Hart	St. Louis (LA)	1896
	29	Jack Taylor	St. Louis (LA)	1898
Innings	482	Amos Rusie	New York (LA)	1893
	447.1	Ted Breitenstein	St. Louis (LA)	1894
	444.1	Pink Hawley	Pittsburgh (LA)	1895
	444	Amos Rusie	New York (LA)	1894
	431.1	Frank Killen	Pittsburgh (LA)	1896
Complete Games	50	Amos Rusie	New York (LA)	1893
	46	Ted Breitenstein	St. Louis (LA)	1894
	46	Ted Breitenstein	St. Louis (LA)	1895
	45	Amos Rusie	New York (LA)	1894
	44	Cy Young	Cleveland (LA)	1894
	44	Pink Hawley	Pittsburgh (LA)	1895
	44	Frank Killen	Pittsburgh (LA)	1896
Strikeouts	239	Cy Seymour	New York (LA)	1898
	208	Amos Rusie	New York (LA)	1893
	201	Amos Rusie	New York (LA)	1895
	195	Amos Rusie	New York (LA)	1894
	178	Doc McJames	Baltimore (LA)	1898
Walks	218	Amos Rusie	New York (LA)	1893
	213	Cy Seymour	New York (LA)	1898
	200	Amos Rusie	New York (LA)	1894
	191	Ted Breitenstein	St. Louis (LA)	1894
	189	Tony Mullane	Baltimore (LA)	1893

Winning Percentage	.835	Bill Hoffer	Baltimore (LA)	1895
(Minimum 20 wins)	.824	Jim Hughes	Brooklyn (LA)	1899
	.788	Fred Klobedanz	Boston (LA)	1897
	.786	Jouett Meekin	New York (LA)	1894
	.781	Bill Hoffer	Baltimore (LA)	1896
ERA (140 Inn.)	1.88	Clark Griffith	Chicago (LA)	1898
	2.10	Al Maul	Baltimore (LA)	1898
	2.13	Kid Nichols	Boston (LA)	1898
	2.36	Doc McJames	Baltimore (LA)	1898
	2.37	Rube Waddell	Pittsburgh (NL)	1900

FIELDING (1871-92)

First Basemen

Fielding Average	.993	Roger Connor	New York (NL)	1887
Total Chances	1693	Jake Beckley	Pittsburgh (IA)	1892
Putouts	1523	Jake Beckley	Pittsburgh (LA)	1892
Assists	132	Jake Beckley	Pittsburgh (LA)	1892

Second Basemen

Fielding Average	.957	Jack Crooks	Columbus (AA)	1891
Total Chances	1058	Bid McPhee	Cincinnati (AA)	1886
Putouts	529	Bid McPhee	Cincinnati (AA)	1886
Assists	555	Lou Bierbauer	Pittsburgh (LA)	1892

Third Basemen

Fielding Average	.933	Chippy McGarr	Boston (NL)	1890
Total Chances	660	Billy Shindle	Baltimore (LA)	1892
Putouts	256	Denny Lyons	Philadelphia (AA)	1887
Assists	382	Billy Shindle	Baltimore (LA)	1892

Shortstops

Fielding Average	.947	George Wright	Boston (NL)	1878
Total Chances	970	Hughie Jennings	Louisville (LA)	1892
Putouts	343	Hughie Jennings	Louisville (LA)	1892
Assists	561	Germany Smith	Cincinnati (LA)	1892

Outfielders

Fielding Average	.986	Mike Griffin	Brooklyn (LA)	1892
Total Chances	422	Tom Brown	Louisville (LA)	1892
Putouts	351	Tom Brown	Louisville (LA)	1892
Assists	50	Orator Shaffer	Chicago (NL)	1879

Catchers

Fielding Average	.962	Charlie Bennett	Detroit (NL)	1881
Total Chances	829	Doc Bushong	St. Louis (AA)	1886
Putouts	647	Doc Bushong	St. Louis (AA)	1886
Assists	188	Chief Zimmer	Cleveland (NL)	1890

Pitchers

Fielding Average	1.000	Jim McCormick	Cleveland (NL)	1884
Total Chances	257	Will White	Cincinnati (AA)	1882
Putouts	57	Dave Foutz	St. Louis (AA)	1886
Assists	223	Will White	Cincinnati (AA)	1882

(1893-00)

First Basemen

Fielding Average	.994	Patsy Tebeau	Cleveland (LA)	1897
Total Chances	1633	Bill Everett	Chicago (LA)	1899
Putouts	1519	Bill Everett	Chicago (LA)	1898
Assists	116	Perry Werden	Louisville (LA)	1897

Second Basemen

Fielding Average	.978	Bid McPhee	Cincinnati (LA)	1896
Total Chances	918	Kid Gleason	New York (LA)	1899
Putouts	442	Nap Lajoie	Philadelphia (LA)	1898
Assists	487	Cupid Childs	Cleveland (LA)	1896

Third Basemen

Fielding Average	.959	Lave Cross	Cle-StL (LA)	1899
Total Chances	671	Jimmy Williams	Pittsburgh (LA)	1899
Putouts	251	Jimmy Williams	Pittsburgh (LA)	1899
	251	Jimmy Collins	Boston (NL)	1900
Assists	376	Jimmy Collins	Boston (LA)	1899

Shortstops

Fielding Average	.945	George Davis	New York (LA)	1899
Total Chances	1003	Monte Cross	Philadelphia (LA)	1898
Putouts	404	Monte Cross	Philadelphia (LA)	1898
Assists	561	Tommy Corcoran	Cincinnati (LA)	1898

Outfielders

Fielding Average	.979	Steve Brodie	Baltimore (LA)	1899
Total Chances	448	Jimmy Slagle	Washington (LA)	1899
Putouts	407	Jimmy Slagle	Washington (LA)	1899
Assists	43	Jimmy Bannon	Boston (LA)	1894

Catchers

Fielding Average	.972	Chief Zimmer	Cleveland (LA)	1896
Total Chances	697	Jack Warner	New York (LA)	1898
Putouts	536	Jack Warner	New York (LA)	1898
Assists	179	Deacon McGuire	Washington (LA)	1895

Pitchers

Fielding Average	1.000	Ad Gumbert	Pittsburgh (LA)	1893
	1.000	Kid Nichols	Boston (LA)	1896
Total Chances	184	Jack Taylor	St. Louis (LA)	1898
Putouts	45	Ted Breitenstein	St. Louis (LA)	1895
Assists	144	Jack Taylor	St. Louis (LA)	1898

NINETEENTH-CENTURY CAREER LEADERS

BATTING

Top 20 Batting Averages

1.	Willie Keeler	.381
2.	Ross Barnes	.359
3.	Jesse Burkett	.357
4.	Billy Hamilton	.348
5.	Cal McVey	.346
6.	Nap Lajoie	.345
7.	Ed Delahanty	.343
8.	Dan Brouthers	.342
	Dave Orr	.342
10.	Pete Browning	.341
11.	Jake Stenzel	.339
12.	Joe Kelley	.338
13.	John McGraw	.337
14.	Cap Anson	.332
15.	Sam Thompson	.331
16.	Bill Lange	.330
17.	Fred Clarke	.327
	Chick Stahl	.327
19.	Tip O'Neill	.326
20.	Hugh Duffy	.325

Top 20 Slugging Averages

1.	Nap Lajoie	.520
2.	Dan Brouthers	.519
3.	Sam Thompson	.507
4.	Chick Stahl	.503
5.	Dave Orr	.502
6.	Joe Kelley	.492
7.	Roger Connor	.486
8.	Ed Delahanty	.483
9.	Jake Stenzel	.480
10.	Willie Keeler	.477
11.	Jesse Burkett	.470
12.	Bill Joyce	.467
	Pete Browning	.467
14.	Ross Barnes	.464
15.	Mike Tiernan	.463
16.	Harry Stovey	.461
17.	Bill Lange	.459
18.	Tip O'Neill	.458
19.	Buck Ewing	.456
20.	Jake Beckley	.452

740 Bases on Balls

1.	Billy Hamilton	1123
2.	Roger Connor	1002
3.	Bid McPhee	981
4.	Cupid Childs	961
5.	Cap Anson	952
6.	Dummy Hoy	876
7.	Dan Brouthers	840
8.	Mike Griffin	809
9.	Billy Nash	803
10.	Paul Radford	791
11.	George Van Haltren	772
12.	Tom Brown	748
13.	Mike Tiernan	747
14.	Jimmy Ryan	743

2800 Total Bases

1.	Cap Anson	4572
2.	Roger Connor	3788
3.	Jim O'Rourke	3600
4.	Dan Brouthers	3484
5.	Jimmy Ryan	3241
6.	Bid McPhee	3088
7.	Ed Delahanty	3061
8.	George Van Haltren	3018
9.	Sam Thompson	3011
10.	Hugh Duffy	3006
11.	Jake Beckley	2918
12.	Paul Hines	2884
13.	Ed McKean	2869
14.	Harry Stovey	2831

74 Home Runs

1.	Roger Connor	138
2.	Sam Thompson	127
3.	Harry Stovey	122
4.	Dan Brouthers	106
	Mike Tiernan	106
6.	Jimmy Ryan	105
7.	Hugh Duffy	104
8.	Cap Anson	98

1400 Runs

1.	Cap Anson	1996
2.	Bid McPhee	1678
3.	Jim O'Rourke	1730
4.	Roger Connor	1620
5.	Billy Hamilton	1619
6.	Dan Brouthers	1523
7.	Tom Brown	1521
8.	Jimmy Ryan	1508

*Minimum 2000 at bats for batting and slugging average leaders. Career RBI, stolen base and strikeout leaders are not included because too much of the needed data is unavailable.

74 Home Runs

9.	Fred Pfeffer	94
10.	Herman Long	86
11.	Ed Delahanty	82
12.	Jack Clements	77
13.	Jake Beckley	74
	Jerry Denny	74

2000 Hits

1.	Cap Anson	3416
2.	Roger Connor	2467
3.	Jim O'Rourke	2643
4.	Dan Brouthers	2296
5.	George Van Haltren	2255
6.	Bid McPhee	2250
7.	Jimmy Ryan	2238
8.	Ed Delahanty	2175
9.	Hugh Duffy	2171
10.	Paul Hines	2135
11.	Monte Ward	2105
12.	Ed McKean	2083
13.	Deacon White	2066
14.	Billy Hamilton	2058
15.	Jack Glasscock	2040
16.	Jesse Burkett	2001

300 Doubles

1.	Cap Anson	581
2.	Jim O'Rourke	465
3.	Dan Brouthers	460
4.	Roger Connor	441
5.	Ed Delahanty	430
6.	Paul Hines	404
7.	Jimmy Ryan	394
8.	Mike Kelly	359
9.	Sam Thompson	340
10.	Jake Beckley	322
11.	Jack Glasscock	313
	Mike Griffin	313
13.	Bid McPhee	303
	Hardy Richardson	303

1400 Runs

9.	Hugh Duffy	1505
10.	George Van Haltren	1501
11.	Harry Stovey	1492
12.	Arlie Latham	1478
13.	Monte Ward	1408
14.	Mike Griffin	1405

135 Triples

1.	Roger Connor	233
2.	Dan Brouthers	205
3.	Bid McPhee	188
	Jake Beckley	188
5.	Buck Ewing	178
6.	Harry Stovey	174
7.	Mike Tiernan	162
8.	Sam Thompson	159
9.	Ed McKean	158
10.	Ed Delahanty	154
11.	George Van Haltren	152
12.	Jim O'Rourke	151
13.	Jimmy Ryan	147
14.	Cap Anson	142
15.	John Reilly	139
16.	Tom Brown	138
17.	Joe Kelley	137
18.	Elmer Smith	135

At the close of his major league career in 1897, Roger Connor (above) stood first in both homers and triples. Most of the nine-teenth-century career slugging marks Connor doesn't hold belong either to Cap Anson or Dan Brouthers. The three first sackers all exited within a year of one another, leaving the game suddenly without any front-rank gateway guardians.

Hardy Richardson (left) is among the career leaders in doubles and ranks just a notch below the upper echelon in several other departments. Primarily a second baseman, he had a .299 career BA to top all pre-1893 middle infielders who compiled over 1,000 career hits.

PITCHING

Top 20 Wins

1.	Pud Galvin	364
2.	Tim Keefe	342
3.	John Clarkson	328
4.	Hoss Radbourn	311
5.	Kid Nichols	310
6.	Mickey Welch	307
7.	Bobby Mathews	297
8.	Cy Young	286
9.	Tony Mullane	284
10.	Jim McCormick	265
11.	Gus Weyhing	264
12.	Al Spalding	252
13.	Amos Rusie	245
14.	Tommy Bond	234
15.	Charlie Buffinton	232
16.	Will White	229
17.	Bob Caruthers	218
18.	Silver King	204
19.	Jack Stivetts	203
20.	Adonis Terry	197

Top 20 Losses

1.	Pud Galvin	310
2.	Bobby Mathews	248
3.	Gus Weyhing	231
4.	Tim Keefe	225
5.	Tommy Mullane	220
6.	Jim McCormick	214
7.	Mickey Welch	210
8.	Jim Whitney	204
9.	Adonis Terry	196
10.	Hoss Radbourn	195
11.	John Clarkson	178
12.	Amos Rusie	173
13.	Cy Young	170
14.	Ted Breitenstein	167
	Kid Nichols	167
16.	Bert Cunningham	166
17.	Pink Hawley	165
	Mark Baldwin	165
19.	Bill Hutchison	163
	Tommy Bond	163

4000 Innings

1.	Pud Galvin	6003.1
2.	Tim Keefe	5047.1
3.	Bobby Mathews	4955.1
4.	Mickey Welch	4802
5.	John Clarkson	4536.1
6.	Hoss Radbourn	4535.1
7.	Tony Mullane	4531.1
8.	Gus Weyhing	4304
9.	Jim McCormick	4275.2
10.	Kid Nichols	4217
11.	Cy Young	4043.2

400 Complete Games

1.	Pud Galvin	646
2.	Tim Keefe	554
3.	Mickey Welsh	525
	Bobby Mathews	525
5.	Hoss Radbourn	489
6.	John Clarkson	485
7.	Tony Mullane	468
8.	Jim McCormick	466
9.	Gus Weyhing	447
10.	Kid Nichols	444
11.	Cy Young	418

Pud Galvin, the first hurler to win 300 games, was also the first to lose 300. Galvin led the loop in strikeouts in four of his first five seasons in the NL—but as a batter. He was never a pacesetter in pitching strikeouts.

1500 Strikeouts

1.	Tim Keefe	2543
2.	John Clarkson	1978
3.	Amos Rusie	1928
4.	Mickey Welch	1850
5.	Hoss Radbourn	1830
6.	Pud Galvin	1815
7.	Tony Mullane	1803
8.	Jim McCormick	1704
9.	Charlie Buffinton	1700
10.	Gus Weyhing	1662
11.	Jim Whitney	1571
12.	Adonis Terry	1552
13.	Kid Nichols	1524
14.	Bobby Mathews	1521
15.	Toad Ramsey	1515

.600 Winning Pct. (150 decisions)

1.	Al Spalding	.795
2.	Dave Foutz	.690
3.	Bob Caruthers	.688
4.	Larry Corcoran	.665
5.	Dick McBride	.656
6.	Kid Nichols	.650
7.	John Clarkson	.648
8.	Nig Cuppy	.632
9.	Cy Young	.627
	Tommy Bond	.627
11.	Fred Goldsmith	.622
12.	Monte Ward	.617
13.	Hess Radbourn	.614
14.	Clark Griffith	.613
15.	Charlie Ferguson	.607
	Candy Cummings	.607
17.	Jack Stivetts	.606
18.	Charlie Buffinton	.604

ERA Below 2.76 (1000 Innings)

1.	Jim Devlin	2.06
2.	Monte Ward	2.10
3.	Al Spalding	2.14
4.	Will White	2.28
5.	Tommy Bond	2.32
6.	Larry Corcoran	2.36
7.	Terry Larkin	2.43
	Jim McCormick	2.43
9.	Candy Cummings	2.49
10.	George Bradley	2.53
11.	Tim Keefe	2.62
12.	Charlie Ferguson	2.67
	Hoss Radbourn	2.67
14.	Mickey Welch	2.71
15.	Fred Goldsmith	2.73

On-Base Pct. below .276

1.	Monte Ward	.254
2.	Jim Devlin	.259
3.	George Bradley	.262
4.	Terry Larkin	.263
	Tommy Bond	.263
6.	Larry Corcoran	.264
7.	Will White	.268
8.	Al Spalding	.269
9.	Charlie Ferguson	.270
10.	Ed Morris	.273
	Candy Cummings	.273
12.	Jim McCormick	.274
13.	Fred Goldsmith	.275
	Jim Whitney	.275
	Dick McBride	.275

Cy Young was 33 and had 286 wins when the gong tolled to end the last century. Since no pitcher as yet had continued to star much past the age of 33, Young seemed good for maybe 50 more wins. Instead he earned nearly another 230.

FIELDING

Games			Fielding Average*	
1B	Cap Anson	2151	Patsy Tebeau	.984
	Roger Connor	1758	Candy LaChance	.983
	Tommy Tucker	1669	Fred Tenney	.982
2B	Bid McPhee	2126	Heinie Reitz	.955
	Fred Pfeffer	1537	Bobby Lowe	.948
	Cupid Childs	1391	Jack Crooks	.946
3B	Arlie Latham	1571	Lave Cross	.937
	Billy Nash	1464	Jimmy Collins	.929
	Billy Shindle	1272	Charlie Irwin	.920
SS	Germany Smith	1665	George Davis	.935
	Jack Glasscock	1628	Hughie Jennings	.922
	Ed McKean	1564	Tommy Corcoran	.917
OF	Tom Brown	1783	Steve Brodie	.960
	Jimmy Ryan	1709	Chick Stahl	.960
	George Van Haltren	1593	Mike Griffin	.956
	Dummy Hoy	1591	Fielder Jones	.956
	Hugh Duffy	1582	Willie Keeler	.955
	Billy Hamilton	1485	Harry Blake	.948
	Mike Griffin	1478	Joe Kelley	.947
	Mike Tiernan	1474	Jimmy McAleer	.944
	Jim O'Rourke	1444	Hugh Duffy	.943
C	Deacon McGuire	1171	Heinie Peitz	.957
	Wilbert Robinson	1162	Chief Zimmer	.949
	Chief Zimmer	1095	Mal Kittridge	.948
P	Pud Galvin	705	Kid Nichols	.951
	Tim Keefe	599	Nig Cuppy	.949
	Tony Mullane	555	Zeke Wilson	.948

*Minimum 500 Games at each position

PHOTO CREDITS

Transcendental Graphics (Mark Rucker):
  X, 9, 11 (2), 13, 25, 26, 27, 28, 40, 41, 42, 43, 54, 55, 56, 57, 67, 69, 70, 84, 86, 87, 99, 100, 101, 102, 110, 111, 113, 114, 122, 123, 125, 135 (2), 137, 138, 149 (2), 169, 171, 173, 174, 193, 195, 196, 215, 217, 218, 264, 287, 289, 290, 291, 314, 315, 317, 318, 319, 341, 342, 343, 344, 399 (2), 402, 404, 406, 439 (2), 441 (2), 468, 471, 474, 493, 497—Nichols, 515, 516, 517, 519, 520, 537, 539, 540, 541, 560 (2), 563 (2), 564, 581, 582, 583, 607, 608, 610, 613, 630, 631, 632, 634, 653, 654 (2), 656, 658 (2), 690—McGann, 715—Long, 706 (2), 698—Lowe, 741—Delahanty, 741—Wagner, 757—Bushong, 757 Clements, 760—Mercer, 761—Stivetts, 804, 805—McGinnity, 805—Waddell, 814—Davis and Joyce, 820

Phillip Von Borries:
  88, 470

Joseph Santry:
  155, 192, 220—Toledo, 260, 819

Tom Hill:
  265, 374, 376, 401, 472, 690, 715 (2—Ely and Fennelly), 741—Ryan, 805—Morris

National Baseball Hall of Fame Library:
  126, 495, 690, 814—Hart, 825

Carnegie Library (Pittsburgh):
  497—Pittsburgh

New York State Museum:
  66

Kenneth Felder:
  377

Michael Olenick:
  371

David Nemec:
  561

BIBLIOGRAPHY

BOOKS

Adelman, Melvin. *A Sporting Time.* Chicago: University of Illinois Press, 1986.

Alexander, Charles. *John McGraw.* New York: Viking, 1988.

—. *Our Game.* New York: Henry Holt and Company, 1991.

Allen, Lee. *The Cincinnati Reds.* New York: G.P. Putnam's Sons, 1948.

—. *The Hot Stove League.* New York: A.S. Barnes and Company, 1955.

—. *The World Series: The Story of Baseball's Annual Championship.* New York: G.P. Putnam's Sons, 1969.

Anson, Adrian C. *A Ball Player's Career.* Chicago: Era Publishing Company, 1900.

Appel, Martin & Goldblatt, Burt. *Baseball's Best.* New York: McGraw-Hill, 1980.

Axelson, G.W., *"COMMY": The Life Story of Charles A. Comiskey.* Chicago: Reilly & Lee, 1919.

Benson, Michael. *Ballparks of North America.* Jefferson, North Carolina: McFarland & Company, Inc., 1989.

Bready, James. *The Home Team.* Baltimore: privately published, 1958.

Brown, Warren. *The Chicago Cubs.* New York: G.P. Putnam's Sons, 1952.

Coombs, Samm & Bob West, eds. *Baseball: America's National Game 1839–1915* by Albert G. Spalding. San Francisco: Halo Books, 1991.

Dewey, Donald & Acocella, Nicholas. *Encyclopedia of Major League Baseball Teams.* New York: Harper Collins, 1993.

Goldstein, Warren. *Playing for Keeps: A History of Early Baseball.* Ithaca: Cornell University Press, 1989.

Graham, Frank. *The Brooklyn Dodgers.* New York: G.P. Putnam's Sons, 1945.

—. *The New York Giants.* New York, G.P. Putnam's Sons, 1952.

James, Bill. *The Bill James Historical Baseball Abstract.* New York: Villard Books, 1988.

Kaese, Harold. *The Boston Braves.* New York: G.P. Putnam's Sons, 1948.

Kirsch, George. *The Creation of American Team Sports: Baseball and Cricket, 1838–72.* Urbana and Chicago: University of Illinois Press, 1989.

Lanigan, Ernest J., ed. *The Baseball Cyclopedia.* New York: The Baseball Magazine Company, 1922.

Lansche, Jerry. *Glory Fades Away.* Dallas: Taylor Publishing Company, 1991.

Levine, Peter. *A.G. Spalding and the Rise of Baseball: The Promise of an American Sport.* New York: Oxford University, 1985.

Lewis, Franklin. *The Cleveland Indians.* New York: G.P. Putnam's Sons, 1949.

Lieb, Frederick G. *The Baseball Story.* New York: G.P. Putnam's Sons, 1950.

—. *The St. Louis Cardinals: The Story of a Great Baseball Club.* New York, G.P. Putnam's Sons, 1947.

Lowry, Phillip J. *Green Cathedrals.* Cooperstown, New York: Society for American Baseball Research, 1986.

Mack, Connie. *My 66 Years in Baseball.* Philadelphia: Winston, 1950.

Neft, David S. and Cohen, Richard M. *The Sports Encyclopedia: Baseball.* New York, St. Martin's/Marek, 1985.

Nemec, David. *Great Baseball Feats, Facts & Firsts.* New York: New American Library, 1987.

—. *The Ultimate Baseball Book,* edited by Daniel Okrent and Harris Lewine. Boston: Houghton Mifflin, 1991.

—. *The Great American Baseball Team Book.* New York: New American Library, 1992.

—. *The Rules of Baseball.* New York: Lyons & Burford, 1994.

—. *The Beer and Whisky League.* New York: Lyons & Burford, 1995.

Palmer, Harry. *Stories of the Base Ball Field.* Chicago: Rand McNally & Company, 1890.

Povich, Shirley. *The Washington Senators.* New York: G.P. Putnam's Sons, 1954.

Rankin, June. *The New York and Brooklyn Base Ball Clubs.* New York: Richard Fox Printer, 1888.

Reichler, Joseph L. *The Great All-Time Baseball Record Book.* New York: Macmillan, 1993.

Richter, Francis. *A Brief History of Base Ball.* Philadelphia: Sporting Life Publishing Company, 1909.

Ritter, Lawrence. *The Glory of Their Times.* New York: Random House, 1985.

Ryczek, William J. *Blackguards and Red Stockings: A History of Baseball's National Association, 1871–75.* Jefferson, North Carolina: McFarland & Company, Inc., 1992.

Seymour, Harold. *Baseball: The Early Years.* New York: Oxford University Press, 1960.

Shannon, Bill and Kalinsky, George. *The Ballparks.* New York: Hawthorne Books, Inc., 1975.

Spalding, John. *Always on Sunday: The California Baseball League, 1886–1915.* Manhattan, Kansas: Ag Press, 1992.

Sullivan, Ted. *Humorous Stories of the Ball Field.* Chicago: M.A. Donohue and Company, 1903.

The Baseball Encyclopedia. New York: Macmillan Publishing Company, 1968, 1976, 1982, 1993 and 1996 editions.

Thompson S.C. *All-Time Rosters of Major League Baseball Clubs.* New York: A.S. Barnes and Company, 1973.

Thorn, John and Pete Palmer, eds., with Michael Gershman. *Total Baseball.* New York: Viking, 1995.

Tiemann, Robert L. and Mark Rucker, eds. *Nineteenth Century Stars.* Cleveland: The Society for American Baseball Research, 1989.

Tiemann, Robert L. *Dodger Classics.* St. Louis: Baseball Histories, Inc., 1983.

Turkin, Hy and Thompson, S.C. *The Official Encyclopedia of Baseball.* New York: A.S. Barnes and Company, 1951.

Vincent, Ted. *Mudville's Revenge.* New York: Seaview Books, 1981.

Voigt, David Quentin. *American Baseball,* Vol. 1. University Park, Pennsylvania: The Pennsylvania State University Press, 1983.

Von Borries, Phillip. *Legends of Louisville.* West Bloomfield, Michigan: Altwerger and Mandel Publishing Company, Inc., 1993.

Westlake, Charles. *Columbus Baseball History.* Columbus: Pfeiffer Printing Company, 1981.

PERIODICALS

1. NEWSPAPERS

Brooklyn *Eagle*, 1889–1900

Cincinnati *Commercial*, 1882–83

Cincinnati *Enquirer*, 1882, 1884–86

Cleveland *Leader*, 1882

Louisville *Courier-Journal*, 1882–99

New York *Clipper*, 1871–91

New York *Times*, 1871–1901

Providence *Journal*, 1884–85

St. Louis *Post-Dispatch*, 1884–91

Missouri *Republican*, 1882–83

2. SPORTING JOURNALS

Sporting Life, 1883–1901

Sporting News, 1886–1901

3. BASEBALL GUIDES

Beadles Dime Base-Ball

Reach's Official Base Ball Guide. Philadelphia: A.J. Reach & Bros., 1884–92.

Spalding's Official Base Ball Guide. Chicago. A.G. Spalding and Bros., 1876–1901.

INDEX